# DAŚAKUMĀRACARITA
of Daṇḍin

# DAŚAKUMĀRACARITA
## of Daṇḍin

*Text with Sanskrit Commentary, Various Readings,*
*A Literal English Translation, Explanatory*
*and Critical Notes*
*and*
*an Exhaustive Introduction*
*by*

M. R. KĀLE

MOTILAL BANARSIDASS PUBLISHERS
PRIVATE LIMITED • DELHI

*Reprint: Delhi, 1979, 1986, 1993, 1997, 2003, 2009*
*Fourth Edition: Delhi, 1966*



ISBN: 978-81-208-0171-4 (Cloth)
ISBN: 978-81-208-0172-1 (Paper)

MOTILAL BANARSIDASS
41 U.A. Bungalow Road, Jawahar Nagar, Delhi 110 007
8 Mahalaxmi Chamber, 22 Bhulabhai Desai Road, Mumbai 400 026
236, 9th Main III Block, Jayanagar, Bangalore 560 011
203 Royapettah High Road, Mylapore, Chennai 600 004
Sanas Plaza, 1302 Baji Rao Road, Pune 411 002
8 Camac Street, Kolkata 700 017
Ashok Rajpath, Patna 800 004
Chowk, Varanasi 221 001

Printed in India

BY JAINENDRA PRAKASH JAIN AT SHRI JAINENDRA PRESS,
A-45 NARAINA, PHASE-I, NEW DELHI 110 028
AND PUBLISHED BY NARENDRA PRAKASH JAIN FOR
MOTILAL BANARSIDASS PUBLISHERS PRIVATE LIMITED,
BUNGALOW ROAD, DELHI 110 007

# PREFACE.

The second edition of the present work had become unobtainable for the last two years, but having other works on hand, I was not able to take up the work of revising it for a fresh edition till February last, although my publishers were pressingly after me, there being a demand for copies of the book from the different parts of India; and in issuing this new edition I have tried to revise it as thoroughly as the short time at my disposal allowed me to to do it. Several better readings have been adopted in the text and improvements made in the commentary; copious additions have also been made in the notes; a new Index of important words in the text has been added; while the Introduction has been entirely recast, so as to increase its usefulness to the reader, by making it accord with new information about the work brought to light in recent times. The somewhat extensive summary of the stories has been replaced by a very brief one, as the former was unnecessary, now that a full translation has been added at the end. The translation appended to the last edition, which was originally prepared by one of my friends, was found to be much free, but was printed then with some alterations here and there; it has now been carefully revised, in some parts almost rewritten, so as to make it quite literal and better suited to the requirements of the University student. In all this work of revision I derived considerable assistance from the editions of Messrs. Agashe and Gajendragadkar, to whom my best thanks are due. Any suggestions &c. as regards further improvements will be cordially welcomed.

BOMBAY,
*November 1925.*

M. R. KALE,

## *Preface to the Fourth Edition*

The present edition is a reprint of the Third edition which was unobtainable for last several years. My thanks are due to Shri Sundarlal Jain of M/s. Motilal Banarsidass who gladly undertook publication of this work of my father late Shri M. R. Kale, in a short time, to meet the needs of needy students.

V. M. Kale

25, Goodwill Building
Bombay-16 (DD).
September 1966.

# CONTENTS

# INTRODUCTION.

## I. THE SANSKRIT PROSE ROMANCE.

### Is the Das'akuma'racharita an A'khya'yika'?

Poetry in Sanskrit, from its inherent nature, as apart from its intrinsic merit, is divided into two kinds, दृश्य (what is capable of being seen or exhibited on the stage), and श्रव्य (what can only be heard or read); the drama falls under the first division, while all other literary works would be grouped under the second. There is, however, another principle of division, which takes into account the *form*, and not the subject-matter, of a work; according to that, poetry is divided into three principal classes, गद्य (prose), पद्य (verse) and मिश्र[1] (mixed). पद्य is all-predominant in Sanskrit literature, while गद्य and मिश्र compositions form but a small portion of it. गद्य is found employed chiefly in the writing of commentaries and similar works, and is rarely utilized for the creation of imaginative literature, whence arises the extreme paucity of prose romances in Sanskrit. Indeed, excepting four, *viz.*, *Vâsavadattâ*, *Harshacharita*, *Kâdambarî*, and *Das'akumâracharita*, none of them are well-known, and the total number of those which are extant would barely exceed a dozen. According to Sanskrit rhetoricians, they fall into two[2] classes, the कथा and the आख्यायिका. As regards the exact demarcation between the two, however, there does not appear to be any unanimity. The Agnipurāṇa defines these as follows :—

कर्तृवंशप्रशंसा स्याद्यत्र गद्येन विस्तरात् ।<br>
कन्याहरणसंग्रामविप्रलम्भविपत्तयः ॥<br>
भवन्ति यत्र दीप्ताश्च रीतिवृत्तिप्रवृत्तयः ।<br>
उच्छ्वासैश्च परिच्छेदो यत्र सा चूर्णिकोत्तरा ॥<br>
वक्त्रं चापरवक्त्रं वा यत्र साऽऽख्यायिका मता ॥

---

1 Under this head come the *Champûs*, and also the dramas ( in which the dialogue is carried on in prose interspersed with metrical stanzas ).

2 The Agnipurāṇa gives five classes, *viz.* आख्यायिका, कथा, खण्डकथा, परिकथा and कथानिका; but it will be seen that the last three are merely minor varieties of the broader division कथा.

श्लोकैः स्ववंशं संक्षेपात्कविर्यत्र प्रशंसति
मुख्यार्थस्यावताराय भवेद्यत्र कथान्तरम् ॥
परिच्छेदो न यत्र स्याद्भवेद्वा लम्बकैः क्वचित् ।
सा **कथा...** ॥ (Adh. 337, Śl. 13–17).

While the rhetorician Bhâmaha practically lays stress on the same points :—

प्रकृतानाकुलश्रव्यशब्दार्थपदवृत्तिना ।
गद्येन युक्तोदात्तार्था सोच्छ्वासाऽऽख्यायिका मता ॥
वृत्तमाख्यायते तस्यां नायकेन स्वचेष्टितम् ।
वक्त्रं चापरवक्त्रं च काले भाव्यर्थशंसि च ॥.........
कन्याहरणसंग्रामविप्रलम्भोदयान्विता ।
न वक्त्रापरवक्त्राभ्यां युक्ता नोच्छ्वासवत्यपि ॥
संस्कृतं संस्कृता चेष्टा **कथा**ऽपभ्रंशभाक्तथा ।
अन्यैः स्वचरितं तस्यां नायकेन तु नोच्यते ॥ (I. 25–29).

From these old definitions it appears that (i) The आख्यायिका contains a detailed account of the poet's family in *prose,* while in the कथा the same is briefly narrated in *verse.* (ii) The आख्यायिका is devoted to the description of topics like the kidnapping of girl-brides, battles, the hero's separation from his beloved and other calamities that befall him ; the कथा is silent about such things. (iii) In the आख्यायिका the story is put in the mouth of the hero himself ; in the कथा it is narrated by persons other than the hero. (iv) The chapters into which an आख्यायिका is divided are called उच्छ्वासs. A कथा is generally not divided into chapters ; if so divided at all, they are there called लम्बकs. (v) In an आख्यायिका there are embedded stanzas in the वक्त्र and the अपरवक्त्र metres, suggestive of future events ; in a कथा they are conspicuous by their absence.

Daṇḍin, who in his *Kávyâdars'a* discusses these details, considers the distinctions to be arbitrary, unsatisfactory and unsound, and holds that कथा and आख्यायिका, being indistinguishable, *are but two names for the same species of composition.*[3] " Prose (गद्य) is a series of words not written in

---

3 अपादः पदसंतानो गद्यमाख्यायिका कथा । इति तस्य प्रभेदौ द्वौ तयोराख्यायिका किल ॥ नायकेनैव वाच्याऽन्या नायकेनेतरेण वा । स्वगुणाविष्क्रियादोषो नात्र भूतार्थशंसिनः ॥ अपि त्वनियमो दृष्टस्तत्राप्यन्यैरुदीरणात् । अन्यो वक्ता स्वयं वेति कीदृग्वा भेदलक्षणम् ॥ वक्त्रं चापरवक्त्रं च सोच्छ्वासत्वं

measured lines ; its two classes are said to be the आख्यायिका and the कथा. Now (it has been laid down that) the आख्यायिका should be spoken (narrated) by the hero, and the कथा either by the hero or some one else...... But we find that this rule is not rigidly observed, since even in an आख्यायिका the story is found to be told by another. In sooth, whether another is the speaker, or one's own self, seems to be a very strange basis for discrimination.........Therefore the कथा and the आख्यायिका are one category marked with a double name, and herein are comprised all the other categories of tales " This opinion of Daṇḍin is valuable, for as the author of prose romances himself he must have known well what he was writing about. Moreover, a far larger number of works of the कथा and the आख्यायिका type must have been accessible to him than are to be found now ; but even among those he must have been unable to discover entire consonance with the definitions. The student will note that the *Das'akumára-charita* itself agrees strictly with neither of the definitions ( of the Agnipurāṇa or Bhāmaha). Thus, taking in order the five points of distinction recorded above, (i) one finds no mention of the poet's family anywhere in the work ; (ii) from the nature of the topics included in it, the Das'ak. would appear to be an आख्यायिका; (iii) but, since the story is not narrated exclusively by the hero, it would come to be classed as a कथा ; (iv) from its division into उच्छ्वासs, it is entitled to be designated as an आख्यायिका; (v) but then again, the absence of the stanzas in the वक्त्र and the अपरवक्त्र metres would seem to point to its being a कथा. One is, therefore, inclined to agree with Daṇḍin, that these distinctions, not being supported by sufficient evidence, must be abandoned as untenable ; the Das'ak. would thus be simply called a गद्य काव्य (a prose romance ), as neither of the titles आख्यायिका and कथा would properly apply to it.

In spite of the scathing criticism passed on it by Daṇḍin, the traditional division into आख्यायिका and कथा, made by the older writers, continued to be accepted by their

---

च भेदकम् । चिह्नमाख्यायिकायाश्चेत्प्रसङ्गेन कथास्वपि ॥ आर्यादिवत्प्रवेशः किं न वक्त्रापरवक्त्रयोः । भेदश्च दृष्टो लम्भादिरुच्छ्वासो वाऽस्तु किं ततः ॥ तत्कथाऽऽख्यायिकेत्येका जातिः संज्ञाद्वयाङ्किता । अत्रैवान्तर्भविष्यन्ति शेषाश्चाख्यानजातयः ॥ कन्याहरणसंग्रामविप्रलम्भोदयादयः । सर्गबन्धसमा एव नैते वैशेषिका गुणाः ॥ कविभावकृतं चिह्नमन्यत्रापि न दुष्यति । मुखमिष्टार्थसंसिद्धौ किं हि न स्यात्कृतात्मनाम् ॥ Kávyâ. I. 23-30.

successors, among whom may be reckoned Rudraṭa, A'nandavardhana, Abhinavagupta, Vidyānātha and others. But even they do not agree as regards the details. Thus the author of the *Alaṃkārasaṃgraha* states[4] that an A'khyāyikâ is based on historical facts, while a Kathâ has a purely fictitious plot. This particular distinction, which is not to be found in the Agnipurāṇa or Bhāmaha, appears to have been deduced from a study of Bâṇa's Harshacharita and Kâdambarî, the two standard models of prose romances available to later writers. Similarly, A'nandavardhana, the the author of the Dhvanyâloka, has introduced a new matter of detail. Daṇḍin had already laid down that an abundance of compounds constituted *the very life* of prose ( ओजः समासभूयस्त्वमेतद्गद्यस्य जीवितम् । Kâvyâ. I. 80 ). He recognized varieties of compounds, as consisting of short vowels and long vowels in ratios of greater and less inequality ( *cf.* तद्—*i. e.* समासभूयस्त्वं—गुरूणां लघूनां च बाहुल्याल्पत्वमिश्रणैः । उच्चावचप्रकारं तद्द् दृश्यमाख्यायिकादिषु ॥ Kâvyâ I. 81 ). A'nandavardhana laid down certain restrictions[5] in the use of long compounds ; but in doing so he seems to be giving his own opinion and not to be following any older authority. The last important writer on poetics is Vis'vanâtha, who composed the *Sáhityadarpaṇa* in the fifteenth century; herein we find the following:—

> कथायां सरसं वस्तु गद्यैरेव विनिर्मितम् ।
> क्वचिदत्र भवेदार्या क्वचिद्वक्त्रापवक्त्रके ॥
> आदौ पद्यैर्नमस्कारः खलादेर्वृत्तकीर्तनम् ।
> आख्यायिका कथावत्स्यात्कवेर्वंशानुकीर्तनम् ॥
> अस्यामन्यकवीनां च वृत्तं पद्यं क्वचित्क्वचित् ।
> कथांशानां व्यवच्छेद आश्वास इति बध्यते ॥
> आर्यावक्त्रापवक्त्राणां छन्दसा येन केनचित् ।
> अन्यापदेशेनाश्वासमुखे भाव्यर्थसूचनम् ॥ (Pari. VI.)

"In a Kathá a charming plot is composed in prose, which is interspersed with stanzas in the A'rya', Vaktra, and Aparavaktra metres; in the beginning there should be a salutation to a deity, a description of the nature of villains, &c.

---

4 कथा कल्पितवृत्तान्ता सत्यार्थाऽऽख्यायिका मता । According to this, the Das'akumâracharita would be a Kathâ.

5 आख्यायिकायां तु भूम्ना मध्यमसमासादीर्घसमासे एव संघटने।......अतिदीर्घसमासा रचना न विप्रलम्भशृङ्गारकरुणयोः आख्यायिकायामपि शोभते। &c. *Dhvanyáloka*, pp. 143–144 ( Nirṇay. Ed. ).

An A'khyâyikâ is like a Kathâ. [In addition] it should include a genealogical account of the poet's family and also of other poets ; verses may occur in it at intervals. Its chapters are called A'śvâsas, and these should contain introductory verses suggestive of the future incidents of the story." These definitions read like echoes of older ones, but they do not help to clear the confusion ; their reliability is further vitiated by the introduction of the term *âs'vása*,[6] which we do not meet with anywhere else. Scholars who are disposed to describe the *Das'akumáracharita* as an A'khyāyikâ might also note that *not in a single particular* does it strictly conform to the definition of the Sáhityadarpaṇa. We are thus finally brought to adhere still more closely to the view of Daṇḍin, that the terms A'khyāyiká and Kathâ lack fixity of discrimination. They should really be treated as synonyms for what is known as गद्य kâvya, any further distinction being otiose.[7]

## II. THE POET.

### (1) THE IDENTITY OF DAṆḌIN.

All students of Sanskrit literature are familiar with the difficulties which beset the path of the earnest inquirer after truth in the matter of the chronology and the personal history of Sanskrit writers, not excluding such famous names as Bhása and Kálidása. There is little to be found by way of data from contemporary records, and many of our conclusions are at best surmises based on scraps of information collected from various sources, such as inscriptions, or quotations, or casual references in other works. The case of Daṇḍin is no exception to the general rule. By tradition he is credited with the authorship of the *Das'akuma'racharita* and the *Kâvya'dars'a*, and in the very beginning of our further search after information concerning him, we are confronted with the possibility of there being more writers than one who

---

6 This may, however, be a mislection for उच्छ्वास.

7 *Cf.* Keith, *Classical Sanskrit Literature* (p. 72)—" The distinction between A'khyāyikâ and Kathâ...is presented to us in a puzzling confusion in the writers on poetics, explaining and *justifying in large measure* the refusal of Daṇḍin in his Kávyádars'a to have anything to do with the distinction." (The Italics are ours).

bore the name Daṇḍin; and when we bear in mind that there have been really more than one Ka'lida'sa, and as many as five Śrî-Harshas, the existence of different authors who were all known as Daṇḍin does not seem to be so very improbable. And so we find Mr. Agashe, the learned editor of the Das'ak. in the Bombay Sanskrit Series, propounding a theory that there must have existed at least *three* different writers named Daṇḍin:—(i) the poet Daṇḍin whose works are no longer extant; ( ii ) the critic Daṇḍin, better known as A'chárya–Daṇḍin, the author of the *Ka'vya'dars'a,* a manual of rhetorics and poetics; and ( iii ) Daṇḍin the creator of the prose romance *Das'akumâracharita.* We might state at the outset that we are unable to agree with Mr. Agashe, nor has his theory yet found acceptance among Indian or Western scholars of note. We shall briefly discuss below, in order, the chief points raised by him.

(i) Mr. Agashe refers to a tradition about Daṇḍin having been a contemporary of Ka'lida'sa (for which see our next Section), and their rivalry as *poets*; this, coupled with the fact that there are stanzas attributed to a *poet* Daṇḍin in the various Sanskrit anthologies, and *Subháshitas*[8] eulogistic of Daṇḍin the poet, leads him to assume the existence of a *poet* Daṇḍin, since in his opinion the authors of the Ka'vya'. and the Das'ak., whoever they were, could hardly be designated as poets in the highest sense, and they do not merit such high-flown encomiums as we meet with in references to Daṇḍin. [ Mr. Agashe has of course to assume that the works of this Daṇḍin have been lost ]. The argument does not seem to us to be convincing. It is true enough that the Kávya'. and the Das'ak. do not stand as the highest patterns of poetical excellence. But then, every author is known to have written works of various degrees of excellence and perfection; and secondly, it is equally plausible to urge that the *same* Daṇḍin, whom we know as the author of the Kávyà. and the Daśak., also wrote other works, which are now no longer extant and on which those eulogies could have been based. There is not sufficien

8 *E. G.,* (*a*) जाते जगति वाल्मीकौ कविरित्यभिधाऽभवत्। कवी इति ततो व्यासे कवयस्त्वयि दण्डिनि ॥ (*b*) कविर्दण्डी कविर्दण्डी कविर्दण्डी न संशयः ॥ (*c*) त्रयोऽग्नयस्त्रयो देवास्त्रयो वेदास्त्रयो गुणाः। त्रयो दण्डिप्रबन्धाश्च त्रिषु लोकेषु विश्रुताः ॥ (*d*) उपमा कालिदासस्य भारवेरर्थगौरवम्। दण्डिनः पदलालित्यम्......॥.

ground, in our opinion, to make out the existence of a separate Daṇḍin by following the trail of the single word *Kavi*. (ii) The *Kávyádars'a* promulgates and expounds many canons of poetic composition which show that its author had refined notions about style and its functions, and was a literary purist to whom impropriety of diction or of matter was an abhorrence. Now it is an admitted fact that the style[9] of the Das'ak. offends against some of the rules[10] of the Kávya'., and that its stories, as the student will find later, are not all of them in the best taste, nor is their moral tone very high. (iii) So Mr. Agashe tries to distinguish the two authors, calling one A'cha'rya-Daṇḍin, as he is found styled in the colophon of the Ka'vya'., and the other simply Daṇḍin. The distinction is in our opinion unsound and futile, for the apparent disparity in the standard displayed by the two works can be very easily explained by supposing that the Das'ak. is the work of Daṇḍin as a young man, naturally taking a spectator's interest in the follies of youth, and also not perfect in the art of immaculate composition; riper studies in the realm of literary criticism must have led him, at a later date, to compose the Ka'vya'. Mr. Agashe appears to have assumed that the Das'ak. must have been written *after* the Ka'vya'. and therefore he finds it difficult to believe that it proceeded from the pen of the accomplished critic who wrote that manual as a Mirror of Poetic Composition. Such an assumption, however,

---

9 Instances of Daṇḍin's laxness in grammar and idiom will be found in a later Section. Mr. Agashe specifically notes only one rule of the Kávyâ. which is violated in the Das'ak., *viz.* ओजः समासभूयस्त्वमेतद् गद्यस्य जीवितम् (I. 80). It is true that the Das'ak. does not abound in compounds to the same extent as, for instance, Ba'ṇa's *Kâdambarî* does; indeed, its use of compounds seems to be quite normal, and certainly not भूयान्, if we are to interpret the canon literally.

10 Thus the verse त्वामयमाबद्धाञ्जलि दासजनस्तमिममर्थमर्थयते । स्वपिहि मया सह सुरतव्यतिकरखिन्नेव मा मैवम् ॥ (see p. 99)—is clearly against the principle enunciated in the Ka'vy'. in the words कामं सर्वोऽप्यलंकारो रसमर्थे निषिञ्चति । तथाऽप्यग्राम्यतैवैनं भारं वहति भूयसा ॥ कन्ये कामयमानं मां न त्वं कामयसे कथम् । इति ग्राम्योऽयमर्थात्मा वैरस्याय प्रकल्पते ॥ ( I. 62–63 ). The Ka'vya . is down upon all vulgarity and indelicacy ( *cf.* शब्देऽपि ग्राम्यताऽस्त्येव सा सभ्येतरकीर्तनात् । I. 65), while the Das'ak. is a frequent offender in this respect (see pp. 115, 167 &c.)

is entirely unwarranted, and need not be accepted in the absence of any definite evidence. Moreover, even if the Ka'vya'. were the earlier production of the two, we know how difficult it is to practise what one believes in and preaches; and Daṇḍin the theorist might be excused for his comparative failure as an author when he assumed the rôle of the romancist. So the three different names merge into one personality; and in this connexion it is interesting to note, as has been pointed out by Mr. Agashe himself, that the poetess Gaṅgādevî, in her Madhurāvijaya (I. 10), describes A'charya-Daṇḍin as a *poet* of a very high order (आचार्यदण्डिनो वाचामाचान्तामृतसंपदाम् । विकासो वेधसः पत्न्या विलासमणिदर्पणम् ॥); thus even Indian tradition is against the separation of the poet Daṇḍin from A cha'rya-Daṇḍin. Indeed, the case for the plurality of Daṇḍins is so weak, and the evidence adduced so slight and so controversial, that Mr. Agashe himself felt compelled to regard his theory as not quite well established; to quote his own words, he left it to "await further research." But no additional facts have been brought to light in support of his hypothesis, which still remains unproved.

---

## ( 2 ) THE PERSONAL HISTORY OF DAṆḌIN.

Like most Sanskrit writers, Daṇḍin has observed a complete silence about himself in his works, nor are any reliable biographical details of him available, contemporary or otherwise. Indian scholars do not appear to have attached much importance to the historial side of literature, and consequently there is usually an entire lack of information about the life of any poet whom one may wish to study. The only sources of direct information open to us are certain traditions, current among Pandits, which are interesting in themselves but are of no historical value whatever. Thus it is related in the *Kavi-charitra*, about our poet, that on one occasion Sarasvatî, the goddess of learning, manifested herself in the form of a beautiful damsel playing with a ball ( *Kanduka* ), when looking at her Daṇḍin said:—

एकोऽपि त्रय इव भाति कन्दुकोऽयं कान्तायाः करतलरागरक्तरक्तः ।
भूमौ तच्चरणनखांशुगौरगौरः खस्थः सन्नयनमरीचिनीलनीलः ॥

"It appears as if there are three balls, though there is really one; ( when just in contact with her palm ) it appears bright-red, being tinged with the redness of the palm of that beautiful lady; when fallen on the ground, the same appears white by the lustre of the rays of her nails; and when in air it looks charmingly blue by the rays darting from her dark-blue eyes."

Bhavabhúti described the incident in these lines—

विदितं ननु कन्दुक ते हृदयं दयिताधरसंगमलुब्ध इव ।
वनिताकरतामरसाभिहतः पतितः पतितः पुनरुत्पतसि ॥

"Indeed, O ball, I know thy heart. Though repeatedly beaten by the lotus-like hand of the lady and falling to the ground, thou, as if covetous of the contact of ( =wishing to kiss ) the lower lip of the damsel, reboundest again and again."

While Kálidása composed the following—

पयोधराकारधरो हि कन्दुकः करेण रोषादभिहन्यते मुहुः ।
इतीव नेत्राकृतिभीतमुत्पलं स्त्रियाः प्रसादाय पपात पादयोः ॥

"The lotus ( from the braid of the hair ) fell at the feet of the lady to implore her favour, being as it were terrified at its resemblance to her eyes, when it saw that the ball was again and again beaten with the hand, through anger caused by its assuming the form of her breasts."

This tradition represents the three poets as contemporaries, which of course is not possible. Its only value seems to us to lie in those three s'lokas, in which the three peculiar characteristics of the style of each poet are clearly indicated, *viz.* the jingling consonance of alliterative syllables ( of Daṇḍin ), the ability to make the sound an echo to the sense ( of Bhavabhúti ), and the cleverness in the handling of the *Utprekshâ* Figure ( of Kālidāsa ).

Another tradition is found in the *Bhoja-prabandha*, which is a comparatively modern work of one Balla'la in which almost all the well-known Sanskrit poets are described as being contemporaries at the court of one king Bhoja of Ma'lva'. It is a production which contains many curious stories and interesting stanzas, but it has no historical value whatever, since some of the poets whom it quotes (*e. g.* Ba'ṇa, Bhavabhu'ti and Ka'lidāsa) have been shown, on independent grounds, to have lived at different periods Even the commentator Mallinātha, who lived so late after Ka lidāsa, is described therein as a court-poet of king Bhoja! The work is thus utterly unreliable in fixing the date of Daṇḍin, though in the early days of Sanskrit scholarship

Prof. Wilson tried to prove, on its authority, that Daṇḍin lived at the court of Bhoja in the tenth century A. D. It records an interesting case of what is known as *Samasyá-púraṇa,* in which the three poets Bhavabhúti, Daṇḍin and Ka'lidāsa composed respectively the first three lines of a s'loka descriptive of early dawn, king Bhoja himself having first supplied the fourth—(भव०) अरुणकिरणजालैरन्तरिक्षे गतर्क्षे, (दण्डी) चलति शिशिरवाते मन्दमन्दं प्रभाते। (कालि०) युवतिजनकदम्बे नाथमुक्तौष्ठबिम्बे, (भोज०) चरमगिरिनितम्बे चन्द्रबिम्बं ललम्बे ॥. But, beyond giving us a charming verse, this account adds nothing to our knowledge of the poet.

A third tradition narrates that on one occasion, when the rivalry between Daṇḍin and Ka'lidāsa rose to a high pitch, Sarasvatî appeared on the scene in person and gave her opinion in the words—" कविर्दण्डी, कविर्दण्डी, कविर्दण्डी न संशयः. " On this, Kálidāsa, who fancied himself as her special protégé, grew wrathful and asked her who *he* was, when the goddess pacified him by declaring that he was her own self in another form—" कोऽहं ब्रूहि तदा मूढे"—" त्वमेवाहं न संशयः. " As we have noted above, such traditions cannot be relied upon in fixing the chronology of Sanskrit authors. On the contrary, they serve to deepen the mist, caused by the absence of history, that hangs over Sanskrit literature, and to make confusion worse confounded. The only purpose they may be said to serve is that they show in what great esteem our poet was held by ancient Pandits, who thought him a worthy rival of the illustrious Kálidāsa.

Efforts have been made to deduce some imaginary facts concerning the poet's life from his name 'Daṇḍin,' which signifies a *Saṃnyâsin*; thus it is suggested that the poet, whose real name has been lost to us, was endowed with this *sobriquet,* when, after having tasted the bitter-sweet cup of youthful pleasures, he turned a recluse and put on the garb of an ascetic.[11] Prof. Wilson also hazards a similar, though not exactly the same, conjecture. He

---

11 Such fanciful explanations of proper names are not uncommon. Thus the commentator Vîrarâghrava narrates how the poet Bhavabhúti got his name as a result of his having composed a verse in which the word भवभूति occurred. *Vide* p. 15 of our Introduction to the Uttara.

says—" The very name of the author suggests an uncertainty. Daṇḍin properly designates a 'staff-bearer,' but is commonly applied to a sect of religious mendicants...who are so termed because they carry a slender *daṇḍa* or wand. Many of the order have been literary characters; and it is not impossible that one of them may have amused his leisure with inventing the stories in question, however inconsistent with his religious meditations. The work would thus be of *a* Daṇḍî, not of Daṇḍî; but it is not generally so considered, Daṇḍî being ordinarily regarded, in this instance at least, as a proper name, and associated with the usual honorary prefix, as Śrî-Daṇḍin." Such suggestions, however, lack corroborative evidence, and are obviously attempts to twist the name of the poet so as to make it yield some meaning and then to invent a network of plausible circumstances around that meaning. Under these conditions we are finally left to gather what information we can from a study of the poet's own works; they contain no autobiographical matter, but still we may glean here and there a few facts, and draw some legitimate inferences therefrom, which are after all more reliable than a host of fanciful *danta kathâs.*

Reading the Das'ak. and the Kávyá. in this light, we can guess with some certainty that Daṇḍin was a Dákshiṇâtya, probably a native of the Vidarbha country, as he speaks proudly of the Mahârâshṭrî language and praises the Vaidarbhî style of writing ( *see* Kávyá. I. 34, 41-42 ). Cockfights, as has been pointed out by Mr. Agashe, were a common diversion in South India; the very vivid description of one in the Das'ak. ( pp. 143-144 ) seems to lend certainty to his being a southerner, a conclusion which is also supported by such definite expressions as कावेरीतीरपतन (p. 159), and by his references to Kaliṅga and A'ndhra. Further, the story of Gominî in the sixth Uchchh. is so realistic in all its details and gives such a minute description of economic housekeeping in Southern India—which is found unchanged even in our own times—that it could only have been written by one thoroughly at home with the habits of the people of South India. It appears that our author must have lived in affluent circumstances and had drunk deep at the fountain of worldly pleasures, as is evident from his life-like and intimate descriptions of royal palaces[12] and wealthy courtesans. His descriptions of gambling bouts and cockfights, of journeys through forests, and of adventures among thieves and marauders, show that he had seen life in all its shades of grave and gay. We do not know anything of his religious beliefs, as he never discusses such topics; the introductory stanza to the Das'ak. is in praise of Vishṇu; but this alone cannot prove him to have been a worshipper of that deity, since there is reason to believe that the stanza is not from the pen of Daṇḍin (as the student will find later on). From the clear vein of erotism that runs throughout the Das'ak., it seems that our author was well-read in the *Káma-Sûtra* of Vátsyāyana; while his detailed references to the science of politics in Uchchh. VIII. show that he had closely studied the *Artha-S'âstra* of Kauṭilya, the standerd text-book on ancient Hindu Polity.

Quite recently (in 1924) there has been published in South India a fragment of a Sanskrit prose romance entitled the *Avantisundarî-kathâ*, which is ascribed to Daṇḍin. Its learned editor, Mr. M. R. Kavi, M. A., to whom credit is due for having brought to light such an important work, accepts its authorship of Daṇḍin, whom he considers identical with the author of the Das'ak. The romance *Avantisundarîkathá* has been discovered in fragmentary and worm-eaten MSS.; it is full of lacunæ, and the fragment extends to only about 25 printed pages. We shall refer to it again later on, but we may say here that there appears to be no objection to accept Mr. Kavi's identification tentatively, although corroborative evidence on this topic is certainly needed. The *Kathá* is accompanied by a metrical *Kaṭhá-sâra*, probably by Daṇḍin himself; here we find several entirely new items of information about our poet and his genealogy, and also about a number of other poets who were his predecessors. According to this account, a family of Bra'hmaṇas of the Kaus'ika *gotra*, originally residing at Ânandapura (in Gujarat), migrated later to Achalapura

12 There is a tradition current that Daṇḍin composed the Kâvyâ. as a manual for the use of a prince to whom he was a tutor. There is nothing improbable in such a tradition, but we are afraid we must class it among those which are not supported by any direct evidence. The only argument advanced is the use of the word पद्य twice in the Kâvyâ. ( I..5, II. 172 ); but not much can be made out of such a casual reference.

(modern Ellichpur in the Berars). There one Nárâyaṇa-Svâmî had a son called Dámodara *alias* Bhàravi (the author of the *Kirátárjunîya*). Bháravi was a friend of king Durvinîta, a Western Gaṅga prince in exile whose date is given as about 570 A. D.; he was later a court-poet of the Pallava King Siṃhavishṇu of Kâñchî (Conjeeveram). Bháravi's son was Manoratha, who had a son named Vîradatta; the last married Gaurî, and to them was born Daṇḍin, who is thus the great-grandson of Bhâravi. Daṇḍin lost both his parents when he was quite young; afterwards, when the Châlukyas invaded Kâñchî, he had to flee from home and become an exile. He travelled extensively over the whole of India, and after the Pallavas had re-established themselves at Kāñchî he came back, after a period of twelve years, and maintained the "literary prestige of his ancestors" at the court of the Pallavas. Here he composed the *Avantisundarî* Kathâ, which was revealed to him, as is related, by divine favour. This account, if true, opens up for the first time several new avenues of inquiry which strictly lie within the province of the antiquary. At present it stands alone; probably there may be fresh discoveries of hitherto lost works, which may strengthen these facts. Until such come to light, however, we may note down the above details as tentatively true, especially as they do not contradict any known particulars about Daṇḍin; on the contrary, they lend support to the inference about Daṇḍin being a native of South India and a person in affluent circumstames, while the date they ascribe to Dandin ( about 650 A. D. ) is not far removed from that arrived at by other means.

## (3) The Date of Daṇḍin.

The determination of Daṇḍin's date is a problem which is still enveloped in the mist of controversy. The late Prof. Wilson, who was the first scholar who gave attention to this subject, was of opinion that the author of the Das'ak. flourished in the latter part of the eleventh century, or the first part of the twelfth. He based his conclusion on two points of internal evidence. He laid great stress first on the allusions to the *Yavanas* in the body of the work, and secondly on the mention of the race of Bhoja in the beginning of the eighth Uchchhvāsa. As the Yavanas are mentioned only as merchants or navigators or pirates, in which capacity the

Arabs were likely to have been known to the Hindus before the Mahomedan conquest, Prof. Wilson considered the fact as suggesting that the work was composed before the advent of the Mahomedans. Further, since in the last Uchchhvāsa a king of the race of Bhoja is introduced wherein his grandfather Puṇyavarman is spoken of in terms of high praise, it implied, in Prof. Wilson's opinion, the previous existence of king Bhoja; and as the special mention of the race is intended to be complimentary to the scions of the same, he inferred that Daṇḍin flourished at the court of one of the immediate descendants of king Bhoja who, as he held, ruled in the latter part of the tenth century. Now, these arguments have become antiquated, as they have been shown to be thoroughly unsound. The evidence afforded by the term *Yavana* is purely negative, and only shows that the work was composed *some time before* the Mahomedan conquest; how long, one cannot say. The meaning attached to the word *Yavana* may also be disputed, since in ancient Sanskrit works it is found applied to may different tribes of non-Hindu foreigners or Mlechchhas, and to the Ionians or Greeks. Regarding the inference drawn from the mention of king Bhoja, it may be pointed out that Bhoja is a family name; kings of the race of Bhoja are referred to by Kâlidāsa and also in the Mahābhārata, and it is impossible to say with certainty which particular king the author of the Daśak. had in his mind. Prof. Wilson seems to have been misled by the tradition that made king Bhoja the patron of Daṇḍin; the tradition is taken from the *Bhoja-prabandha*, which, as we have shown above, has no historial value, the work being a hotch-potch of miscellaneous literary anecdotes quite unreliable in character. It is evident, therefore, that we must seek elsewhere for the data concerning Daṇḍin's date.

It is generally admitted that of the two older writers on *Alaṃkāra*, Daṇḍin and Vāmana, Vâmana came later and Daṇḍin was his predecessor.[13] Vāmana has been placed in the latter

13 We need not go here into the question of examining in detail the arguments by which this conclusion has been arrived at, as it more strictly falls within the province of the historian of Alaṃkāra literature. Similarly, we need not discuss the relationship of the writings of the rhetorician Bhâmaba with our author's Kâvyâ., since the date of Bhâmaha himself is yet unsettled, and nothing can be profitably adduced in support of Daṇḍin's time, even if we succeeded in showing that Bhâmaha preceded him.

half of the eighth century; Dandin, therefore, must be placed earlier than that. This fixes the *latest date* that can be assigned to our author, and finally disposes of the attempt of Wilson to place him two centuries later. The *earliest limit* is established by the fact that his Kāvyā. refers by name (महाराष्ट्राश्रयां भाषां प्रकृष्टं प्राकृतं विदुः। सागरः सूक्तिरत्नानां सेतुबन्धादि यन्मयम् ॥ I. 34) to the Prâkrit poem *Setubandha* of king Pravarasena, who lived in the fifth century. But between these two limits of 500 A. D. and 800 A. D., it has not yet been possible to fix an *absolutely definite* date for our author, for lack of sufficient evidence Attempts have been made to draw some tangible conclusions from the state of Hindu society depicted in the Das'ak., but they fail to prove anything definite. The social manners, customs and conditions depicted by Daṇḍin, in which gamesters and courtesans play such an important part, seem to resemble those we find portrayed in the Mrich. They do not, therefore, assist us in placing the composition of the Daśak in any particular century, since it is a patent fact that Hindu society remained unchanged in its outward aspects, both grave and gay, during the first thousand years or so of the Christian era. Similarly, nothing can be argued from the political and geographical divisions of India referred to by Daṇḍin, since all that can be said of them is that they belong to a period prior to the Mahomedan conquest; but how much prior, we cannot say.

If, however, we judge from the internal evidence of style, we think there will be found good grounds for placing him towards the end of the sixth century, before the time of Bāṇa, or at the most in the first half of the seventh century, as a contemporary of Báṇa. The comparative ease and simplicity of the diction of the Das'ak. precludes the possibility of its belonging to the school of Bāṇa, as it shows no traces of the influence of the extravagant puns, immoderate conceits, and interminable compounds of that author. In its absence of artificiality, and directness of expression, the Das'ak. resembles the works of Kálidāsa or Bhāravi much more than those of Bāṇa or the later writers, to whom *s'lesha, vakrokti* and such-like figures were the very life and soul of ornate prose. To Daṇḍin the life and soul of good prose was a profusion of compounds, and nothing more (*cf.* ओजः समासभूय-

स्त्वमेतद्द्वयस्य जीवितम् । Kávyā. I. 80). He appears to have been one of the pioneers who introduced the new style of writing. Of the three romantic prose compositions, the Das'ak., the Kádambarî and the Vāsavadattâ, the Daśak. seems to be the earliest production. The style of Subandhu and Báṇa is more artificial and elaborate; that of Daṇḍin is not often of a high poetical elevation, as he does not aim to produce a work purely poetical but to offer an example of classical prose composition written in a language simple, elegant and intelligible. Our author belonged to that period of Sanskrit literature when style was in a transitional state, being developed from the simple to the complex and the elaborate. Had Daṇḍin lived after Bāṇa, his work could not but have received some tinge from the writings of his predecessor. His description of Rājahaṃsa, of the Hero and Heroine, of the education of Prince Rājavāhana &c., could not have been so tame, terse and unornamental as it is. Hence we consider that there are reasonable grounds for placing our author before Bāṇa and Subandhu. It is not possible to judge, however, as to exactly what period separated Daṇḍin from Bāṇa; perhaps they might even have been contemporaries, one writing in the south and the other in the north. Thus approximately Daṇḍin's date may be held to lie somewhere between 550 A. D. and 650 A. D.

Recently Mr. Agashe, the editor of the Das'ak., who tries to distinguish the author of the Kāvyā. from the author of the Das'ak., has endeavoured to show that the latter wrote in the eleventh or the twelfth century of the Christian era. His principal argument is that the Das'ak. is not quoted or referred to by any Sanskrit writer earlier than the tenth century. To quote his own words[14]: "What is more pertinent to our present inquiry is the question whether any trace of the Das'ak. is found in Nṛipatuṅga's work. Prof. Pathak refers to Nṛipatuṅga's extolling Bāṇa's two works, Harshacharita and Kādambarî, as masterpieces of Sanskrit prose. But there is absolutely no mention of the prose work of a Sanskrit author [*viz.* Daṇḍin] from whom he has borrowed so much in his own work... Is it possible that Nṛipatuṅga knew not the Das'ak., or if he did, did he deliberately ignore it ? Neither of the two

14 See his Introduction, p. xxxvi. Nṛipatuṅga was a Kanarese writer who composed the *Kavi-rája-márga*, which is a work on Alaṃkâra, and to which Mr. Agashe refers.

inferences is, we think, justified. To us it appears more likely that the Das'ak. was [ then ] simply non-existent. This absence of any mention in Nṛipatuṅga's work should also suffice to dispose of the argument that this work was perhaps an earlier production." But Mr. Agashe is here arguing by relying on merely negative evidence, which is an unsound principle in the conduct of controversies, unless it is supported by collateral circumstances. Writers on rhetorics or other critics are not bound to quote each and every book they are acquainted with, but only a selection of such as they find particularly helpful or suggestive, or otherwise deserving of mention. If anything is to be insisted upon, we can at the most say that the absence of any mention of the Das'ak. before the tenth century shows that the Das'ak. may not have become so very popular till then, and not that it "did not exist." Scholars are well aware of the fallacy underlying such an *argumentum ex silentio*; who will venture to urge, for instance, that because Bāṇa in the introductory verses of his Harsha-charita has not mentioned the Rámáyaṇa, *therefore* the latter did not exist in his time? Mr. Agashe has placed the *Kávyádars'a* in the latter half of the seventh century, and we have shown previously that there are no reasons for rejecting the the common authorship of the Kávyā. and the Das'ak. Mr. Agashe's date is based on two assumptions:—(i) that Daṇḍin in Kávyā. III. 114 ( नासिक्यमध्या परितश्चतुर्वर्णविभूषिता । अस्ति काचित्पुरी यस्यामष्टवर्णाह्वया नृपाः ॥ ) is referring to the town of Kāñchî or Conjeeveram and its kings of the Pallava Dynasty; (ii) and that the King Rājavarman (or Rátavarman) mentioned in Kāvyā. II. 279 (इति साक्षात्कृते देवे राज्ञो यद्राजवर्मण: । &c.) is identical with a certain Pallava prince who ruled over Kāñchî in South India in the latter half of the seventh century. Unfortunately, however, the existence of a king of that name has not at all been proved; it is the result of mere conjecture. Another attempt of Mr. Agashe to support this date (*viz.* 650 A. D.) is also equally based on mere conjectural speculation and guess-work. Thus, the *S'âr̊ngadharapaddhati* quotes the verse "नीलोत्पलदलश्यामां विज्जकां मामजानता । वृथैव दण्डिना प्रोक्तं सर्वशुक्ला सरस्वती ॥" as composed by the poetess Vijjakā, with reference to the introductory s'loka of the Kāvyādars'a. Mr. Agashe has tried to identify this Vijjakā with a certain queen Vijayā of the Karnáṭaka, whose date is given at about 650 A. D.; but it is an attempt based on conjecture. As it is, both the lines of inquiry pursued by Mr. Agashe converge to the same date (650 A. D.), which is not far removed from the date we ourselves have tentatively offered above. Very recently new light has been shed on this discussion by the discovery of the *Avantisundarīkathā* (see *supra*, p. xvi), which seems to strengthen the conclusions of Mr. Agashe. According to that work, Bhāravi flourished at about 570 A. D.; so Daṇḍin, who was Bhāravi's great-grandson, and was a court-poet of the Pallava kings of Kāñchī, will have to be placed at about 650 A. D. This date, if established by further incontestable testimony, will remove once for all the veil of uncertainty hanging over the time when our author lived and composed his works; but for that we must await further research.

## (4) The Works of Daṇḍin.

There is abundant evidence to show that in the case of many ancient Sanskrit writers known to literary fame, only a few of their productions have survived the lapse of time; the rest have disappeared for ever, except in those rare instances where the ceaseless efforts of scholars have brought to light MSS. of works supposed to have been no longer extant. Something similar has happened in the case of our author, too. Daṇḍin has long been recognized as the author of two works, the Kávyá. and the Daśak.; but to the question whether he wrote any more, no answer could definitely be made. The question is one of particular importance, for in the *S'ārṅgdhara-paddhati* we have a verse ascribed to Rājaśekhara which declares that Daṇḍin wrote *three* works, all of them of surpassing literary merit (त्रयोऽग्नयस्त्रयो देवास्त्रयो वेदास्त्रयो गुणाः। त्रयो दण्डिप्रबन्धाश्च त्रिषु लोकेषु विश्रुताः ॥ Ś.-P. 174). Rājas'ekhara's explicit statement is not one to be easily set aside, and it has called forth a display of considerable ingenuity on the part of scholars who have sought to attribute this or that work to Daṇḍin, as a complement of the triad of which the Kāvyā. and the Das'ak. are two. Thus, it was pointed out by some that perhaps the third work was either छन्दोविचिति or कलापरिच्छेद, since in the Kàvyà. Daṇḍin apparently refers,[15] by

15 Cf. छन्दोविचित्यां सकलस्तत्प्रपञ्चो निदर्शितः। सा विद्या नौस्तितीर्षूणां गम्भीरं काव्यसागरम् ॥ I. 12 ; and इत्थं कलाचतुःषष्टिविरोधः साधु नीयताम्। तस्याः कलापरिच्छेदे रूपमाविर्भविष्यति ॥ III. 171.

these titles, to some other compositions. These references, however, read somewhat ambiguous, and do not convince us as to whether Daṇḍin has referred to them as *his own works*, or as some treatises well known to his readers by those names. *Chhandovichiti*, for instance, is a common name for the subject of prosody or any text-book thereon, and might as well apply to the Chhandaḥsútra of Piṅgala or some similar work. The title Kalâparichchheda is still more obscure; perhaps Daṇḍin might have intended to write a *fourth* chapter of his Kávyā, bearing that title, in which case it could not count as an independent work, being a part of the Kāvyā. itself. Then the late Prof. Pischel had advanced the somewhat bold theory that the Mṛichchhakaṭika was to be regarded as the missing work of Daṇḍin. His main reasons were two:—(i) that the verse लिम्पतीव तमोऽङ्गानि etc., which occurs in the Kâvyā. (II. 226), occurs also in the Mṛich. (I. 34), pointing to the probability of both the works being by the same author; and (ii) that the state of society depicted in the Mṛich. closely resembles that described in the Das'ak. But the discovery of the works of Bhāsa, in which the verse लिम्पतीव etc. occurs twice, nullified the former argument; and as regards the latter, it is easy to see how very preposterous it would be to ascribe any two different works to the same writer simply because of the similarity of the society portrayed therein. Prof. Pischel's theory received in fact very little support from scholars, and is now happily consigued to oblivion.[16] Some Pandits have tried to ascribe the drama *Mallikā-māruta*[17] to our poet; but the drama has been shown to be the work of one Uddaṇḍa Raṅganâtha, who wrote in Malabar in the fifteenth century A. D. This Raṅganátha must have been an admirer of our author, as is seen from his having copied several incidents of the Das'ak. in his play; but his date, which has been proved beyond any doubt, shows the utter impossibility of Daṇḍin having been its author.

Which, then, are we to consider as the third work of Daṇḍin? We have already referred to the recent discovery in south India of a fragmentary prose romance, styled the अवन्तिसुन्दरीकथा, which is ascribed to our author by its editor.

---

16 See pp. xvi.—xvii of our Introduction to the Mṛich. for a further discussion of this point.

17 Edited and published by Pandit Jibanand Vidyasagar of Calcutta in 1878.

The fragment is really too short to enable us to give any decided opinion; but from the portion that is now avaible, its claim to be treated as the third work of Daṇḍin does not appear to be quite groundless. The *Avantisundarīkathâ* is in fact the same story that we find in the Das'ak., with this difference that the Avanti. is written in a distinctly elaborate and highly polished style, by the side of which the Das'ak. pales into comparative mediocrity. It may be that the Das'ak. was the earliest production of our author, who in his riper and maturer years re-wrote and elaborated the same into the *Âvantisundarīkathâ*. The style of the latter work bears the impress of a master-hand and presents a picture not unworthy of a great poet. We cull here a few passages from which the student may judge for himself:—

(*a*) शरदिव सरसा कान्तिमुद्वहन्ती हेमन्तवृत्तिरिव प्रालम्बिनी हारमालिनी शिशिरश्रीरिव नवनवमालिका वसन्तवेलेव चारुभुजवासभूषिततनुलता घर्मसंपदिव कोमलपाटलाधरा सर्वर्तुसमवृत्तितयैव नन्दनस्वभावा सर्वावरोधप्रधानभू रतिरिव दर्पकस्य शचीव शतमखस्य शैलसुतेव विश्वेश्वरस्य लक्ष्मीरिव पुष्करेक्षणस्य बुद्धिरिव धनाधिपस्य देवसेनेव सेनापतेः रोहिणीव बुधभावनस्य असुम्योऽपि वल्लभा देवी वसुमती नाम । p. 13

(*b*) प्रतिमुखस्थितकुवलयक्रोडादिवातिवामानि भामिनीनामरज्यन्त लोचनानि । चकोरलोचनाकुचारोहचक्रः संमर्देऽपि कलुषीभवद्भिरम्बुभिरोत्पत्तिकत्वं जलत्वमनक्षरमाचचक्षे । गुरूनपि निरपेक्षो जघान वारिवेगो वरोरूणामुरोरुहभरान् । न हि विवेकः क्षुभितस्य । जलमध्ये मौनमाचरन्तो मेखलाकलापाः स्थान एव गुणत्वं समर्थयांबभूवुः etc. । p. 16

(*c*) तासु च ग्रीष्मातपातुरत्रिलोकलक्ष्मीविश्रान्तिधारागृहेषु वर्षावासरेषु कुटजकुड्मलहारमालिनीभिः लम्बकदम्बकाञ्चीदामभिः केतकबर्हदन्तपत्रभूषितश्रवणपाशाभिः मदमयललामलाञ्छितललाटिकाभिः आर्द्रगैरिकरागरञ्जितचरणपल्लवाभिः कुन्तलवलबिनीभिः सुन्दरीभिः कृतकिरातनितम्बिनीवेषविभ्रमाभिः रटन्मयूरेषु नटच्छिखण्डिषु स्फुटन्नीपेषु रटन्निर्झरेषु वर्षजलधाराधौतरत्नोपलतलेषु क्रीडापर्वतेषु विजहार । pp. 18–19.

(*d*) कुसुमशरशरावलीष्विव विरहिजनहृदयदारिणीषु समन्ततः पतन्तीषु हंसमालासु वसुधाविभ्रमहेमचूर्णैरसनरेणुभिरभिनवमनसिजातुरास्विन्नसुभगासु वनस्थलीषु बाणमालिनीरिषुधीरिव मनोभवो भुवः परिहरत्सु समाधिच्छेदशंसिषु स्वमुखानेकवारोदीरितमधुरशात्कृतग्राहिणीनां शुकश्रेणीनामचकितमुक्तमञ्जुलप्रतिशारशासितास्वनुमन्यमानकलमकणिशभङ्गासु कलमगोपिकासु सकलकामुकानीकोत्कम्पकारिणीं खड्गधारामिव श्यामामवलम्बमाने द्विगुणतेजसि ज्योतिषामधीशे शान्तगर्जितानि शशाङ्कपादच्छायश्रीयीणि शाल्मलीतूलपरिलघूनि मेघकुलानि विलोक्य दर्पादिव मत्तमधुकरीमधुरध्वानगर्भं हसन्तीषु कुमुदिनीषु विशदायां शरदि etc. etc. । p. 20.

All thanks are due to Mr. M. R. Kavi, M. A., the learned editor of the Avanti., for bringing to light this hitherto unknown work, which is obviously the production of a higly gifted writer. There appears to be no reason for denying Mr. Kavi's ascription of it to Daṇḍin, and we may, therefore, tentatively accept that romance as the missing third work of the author of the Das'akumâracharita.

---

## III. THE DAŚAKUMÂRACHARITA.

### (1) The Plot.

The student, who has to study this book for examination purposes, will be required to keep in mind the bare thread of the narrative of the Das'ak. in order to understand the sequence of the whole. We, therefore, give below, for ready reference, a very brief summary of the entire plot as presented in the various Uchchhvāsas:—

( The Pu'rvapi'thika' )

Uch. I. Rājahaṃsa, a benevolent and accomplished monarch, ruled in Pashpapurî, the capital of the kingdom of Magadha. His queen, a peerless beauty, was named Vasumatî. He had three ministers, Dharmapâla, Padmodbhava and Sitavarman by name, who held their offices by hereditary succession. Of these Dharmapâla had three sons, Sumantra, Sumitra and Kámapála; Padmodbhava had two, Sus'ruta and Ratnodbhava; and Sitavarman two, Sumati and Satyavarman. Kâmapàla turned out a vagabond and led a life of dissolute profligacy. Ratnodbhava, engaged in foreign trade, constantly performed distant voyages; while Satyavarman, disgusted with the world, went on a pilgrimage to foreign parts. The remaining four brothers succeeded to the ministerial offices held by their fathers.

War once broke out between Rājahamsa and Mānasāra, king of Málwá. Rājahaṃsa was, in the first instance, victorious, but was finally defeated and obliged to take shelter in a forest of the Vindhya mountains. There he approached a sage, Vâmadeva by name, for the recovery of his lost kingdom The sage advised him to live there for a few years, which he did accordingly. His four ministers followed him in his retreat, and here his wife gave birth to a son, Rājavāhana. About the same time the four ministers also got sons—that of Sumati was named Pramti, of Sumantra Mitragupta, of Sumitra Mantragupta, and of Sus'ruta Viśruta. While Rājahaṃsa was residing in the forest, there were brought to him, on different occasions, five other young boys, making, with the sons of the ministers and Rājavāhana, the "*Ten Kumáras*" of the story. Thus:—(1) Prahāravarman, the king of Mithilâ, was a friend and ally of Rājahaṃsa. On the defeat of the latter, Prahâra. beat a hasty retreat towards his own country. But on his way he was attacked by the foresters (Śabaras) and lost his baggage and attendants. His two sons were separated from him in this skirmish. One of them was rescued from the Śabaras by a Brāhmaṇa, who took him to Rājahaṃsa. The latter called him Upahāravarman, and brought him up along with the other princes. (2) On another occasion the King came across the second son of Prahára., whom he took under his protection, naming him Apahāravarman. (3) Ratnodbhava was shipwrecked when voyaging with his wife. The latter was delivered of a son, but owing to an accident the boy was separated from his mother. A Brahmaṇa saved him and brought him to the King, who bestowed on him the name of Pushpodbhava. (4) Kàmapála had married Tārāvalí, the daughter of a Yaksha-chief. Tárávalî brought her son to the queen of Rājahaṃsa; this boy was called Arthapāla. (5) The son of Satyavarman was rescued from a river into which he had been thrown by his step-mother in jealousy. This boy was brought to Rājahaṃsa who had him named Somadatta. These ten boys, thus assembled, were educated together, and became adepts in all the necessary arts and sciences.

UCH. II. As the princes had now all grown up, the King, in accordance with the advice of the sage Vàmadeva, sent them on a campaign 'to conquer the world' (*digvijaya*). They departed accordingly, and for a time journeyed together; but when in the Vindhya forest, Prince Rājavāhana was induced by a stranger Bráhmaṇa to leave his companions secretly and to assist him in obtaining the sovereignty of the Pátâla, which was foretold for him by god Śiva in a vision. Accordingly the two left secretly for Pâtâla through a chasm in the earth. The enterprise succeeded; but when the prince returned to the spot where he had left his companions, he found them all gone. Alarmed by his inexplicable disappearance they had left in various directions in quest of him. [The adventures they met with before their re-union with Rājavâhana are narrated subsequently, and lend its title to our romance.] Roaming in search of his friends, Rājavāhana came to Ujjayinî where in a garden he encountered Somadatta, accompanied by a splendid retinue and a beautiful damsel. Upon being asked by Rājavāhaṇa, Somadatta began to narrate his adventures.

UCH. III. King Mattakâla of the Lâṭā country had invaded the territory of king Vîraketu of Ujjayinî with a view to compel the latter to give his daughter, Vāmalochanā, in marriage to him (Matta.). Somadatta ranged himself on the side of Vîraketu, defeated the forces of Mattakāla, and succeeded in killing him in single combat. Overwhelmed by gratitude, Vîraketu gave his daughter to Somadatta, and also adopted him as his Yuvarāja (heir-apparent.) While Soma. with his bride was going to the temple of Mahākāla, in accordance with the instructions of an astrologer, he was met by Rājavâhana.—When Somadatta had finished his narrative, there arrived on the scene Pushpodbhava, who, being requested, next proceeded to unfold his tale.

UCH. IV. After wandering for several days, Pushpodbhava once saw a man falling from a precipice in front of him; this proved to be Ratnodbhava, who had been shipwrecked sixteen years ago and was separated from his wife on that occasion. Being unable to bear his grief any longer, he tried to commit suicide, when his son found him. Shortly after that, as good luck would have it, Pushpodbhava prevented a woman from immolating herself in fire; she proved to be his mother. After being thus re-united with his parents, Pushpodbhava journeyed on to Ujjayinî, where he made friends with a rich merchant called Bandhupâla. There he fell in love with his daughter Bālachandrikā, who returned his affection. She was, however, sought in marriage by Prince Dāruvarman, whom she detested for his violence. So, under Pushpodbhava's advice, she gave out that her person was possessed by a Yaksha and that she would marry that brave man who would free her from the evil spirit. Dáruvarman tried to defy the Yaksha and to win Bālachandrikā, when Pushp., disguised as her female attendant, killed him, and rushed out of the chamber exclaiming that the Yaksha had killed Dâruvarman. In the tumult which followed, he slipped out with Bâla., and they were married a few days later. The arrival of Rājavāhana was made known to Pushp. by Bandhupāla who was an expert in foretelling events by the observation of omens.—At the end of his narrative, Râjaváhana along with Somadatta and Pushp. repaired to Ujiayinî, where he disguised himself as the son of a Brâhmaṇa, and soon earned distinction by his high attainments.

UCH. V. Dwelling in Ujjayinî, Rājavābana once beheld Avantisundarî, the lovely daughter of king Mānasāra, the foe of his father Rājahaṃsa. The prince and the princess were equally smitten with love at the sight of each other. Now, Mānasára had abdicated the kingdom in favour of his son Darpasāra, who too had retired to practise penance after appointing his cousins Dāruvarman and Chaṇḍavarman as joint regents; of these the former was killed by Pushpodbhava, so that Chaṇḍavarman was left the sole ruler. Rājavāhana and Avantisundarî were legally married in the presence of the fire through the contrivance of a friendly conjuror, who made Chaṇḍ. believe at that time that the marriage was a delusion, being part of a magic show. Thereafter Rāja. and Avan. retired into the inner apartments for sport.

( THE DAS'AKUMA'RACHARITA )

UCH. I. The two lovers were discovered by the attendants and reported to Chaṇḍavarmâ, who got furious when he recognized Rāja. as the friend of Pushpodbhava, the husband of the wicked Bálachandriká on whose account his brother was killed. Chaṇḍavarmā wanted to execute Rāja. immediately; but the old king Mānasāra intervened, and so Rāja. was temporarily kept imprisoned in a wooden cage, pending the final orders of king Darpasāra. In the meanwhile, Chaṇḍavarmā marched against Siṃhavarmā, the king of the Aṅgas, whose daughter he wanted to wed; Rājavâhana had to accompany the invading army in his wooden cage. Champā, the capital city of the Aṅgas, was besieged, and Siṃhavarmà was vanquished and taken captive along with his daughter. Just then the orders of Darpasāra were received, sanctioning the execution of Rájavāhana. Accordingly, the prince was taken out for being trampled to death under the feet of an elephant but just at the moment the chain tied round his feet fell off and assumed the form of a nymph who had been cursed into that form by a sage. While Rājā. thus became free, a cry arose that Chaṇḍavarmā was killed in a mêlée by a thief; this thief turned out to be Râja.'s friend and companion Apahāravarmá. In the meanwhile, several allies of king Siṃhavarmâ, that were invited by him for help, arrived on the scene with their forces, so that the safety of him and his daughter was assured. Among these allies, Rájavāhana found all the rest of his missing companions, and by his desire they severally narrated to him their adventures; of these Apahāravarmā was the first to recount his tale, with which the next chapter begins.

UCH. II. In the course of his wanderings Apahāra. came across the sage Marîchi, from whom he sought to obtain the tidings of his master Râjavāhana. The sage promised him help and asked him to abide in the city of Champā; at the same time he related to Apahāra. his own adventures: how he was beguiled into her love by a courtesan named Kāmamañjarî who won a wager by succeeding in enticing him into the meshes of her charms and thereafter repudiated him and made him a laughing-stock of the people. After spending a night at Marîchi's hermitage, Apahāra. proceeded to Champā; on his way there he made friends with Vimardaka, a gentleman who was one of the victims of Kāmamañjarî who had stripped him of all his possessions and made him a beggar. Apahára. promised help to Vimardaka in redeeming his lost fortune, and himself took to the profession of a gamester and a burglar. On one of his nightly sallies he met a beautiful maiden, Kulapālikā by name, the daughter of one Kuberadatta. Her father had first promised her in marriage to Dhanamitra, who, however, became poor afterwards through his princely charities. Kulapâlikâ loved Dhanamitra, but her father cancelled the old arrangement and wanted to bestow her upon one Arthapati; and she was then going to Dhanamitra's house from her home to avoid that marriage. Apahâravarmâ met her in the dark of the night. He promised to help her, and took her to her lover; the two then went back with her to her father's house, which they plundered; they left her at home, but on their way burgled Arthapati's house. In consequence of these troubles the marriage was postponed for one month. Apahára. enriched Dhanamitra with the proceeds of his robberies; a story was then got up and circulated to the effect that Dhanamitra was in possession of a magic purse or leather-bag which daily produced immense gold. On hearing of this Kuberadatta gave his daughter to Dhanamitra.

Apaharavarmâ fell in love with Rágamañjarî, the younger sister of Kámamañjarî, whose consent for the union he obtained by promising to procure for her that magic purse, provided she fulfilled one condition necessary for its being fruitful, *viz.* that she restored their wealth to all those persons whom she had reduced to poverty. She agreed, and thus Vimardaka got back what he had lost. The purse came to Kámamañjarî; but Dhanamitra having reported its theft to the king, she had to return it to him; and, to save herself from punishment, she gave out, under Apahâra.'s instuctions, that the purse was given to her by Arthapati. Arthapati was in consequence expelled the country and his property confiscated.

On one night, in a fit of foolhardiness, Apahâra. attacked the patrolling police and was made a prisoner; his jailer Kántaka, who was enamoured of the princess Ambálikâ, utilized the services of this expert burglar to dig a subterranean passage from the prison to the palace. Apahára. excavated the passage, but managed to kill Kântaka, and himself visited the apartment of the princess Ambâlikâ, with whom he fell in love; but, as she was asleep, he returned without awakening her. Afterwards, when Chaṇḍavarmá besieged Champâ and took her captive along with her father, Apahâra. came to the rescue and killed Chaṇḍavarmâ in a fight. Later on he was met by Rājavāhana, as was foretold to him by the sage Marîchi.

Uch. III. Upahāravarmâ next began his story. He had gone to his own country Videha in search of Rájavâhana He there met his old nurse, who related to him how his father's kingdom had been seized by Vikaṭavarman and other sons of his elder brother and how his parents had been imprisoned by them. Upahâravarmá resolved to effect their release, and through the medium of his nurse's daughter managed to win the affection of Vikaṭavarman's queen, who was offended by the dissolute habits of her husband. At the instance of Upahára. she persuaded Vikaṭavarman to undertake to perform a magical rite whereby he might exchange his body, which was ugly and deformed, for a most beautiful one. He readily fell into the trap, and was killed by Upahâra., who then boldly usurped the throne, pretending to be the old king metamorphosed. He succeeded in deceiving all, including even his ministers, and reversed all the iniquitous deeds of the former occupant of the throne. He then released his parents, and made his father the king; and himself becoming the Yuvarāja, he led an army to the assistance of his ally Siṃhavarmá, when he met Rája. in Champâ.

UCH. IV. Arthapâla next narrated his account. He had gone to Kâśî, where he met a certain man in great distress who related to him the story of Kâmapâla who was the minister of the King of Káśî and whom Arthapâla knew to be his father and the husband of that Târâvalî ( the Yaksha damsel) who had made him over to queen Vasumatî. Kâmapâla was appointed minister by the old king Chandasimha of Káśî; but the new king Siṃhaghosha, who was an evil-minded youth without judgement, had dismissed Kāmapāla and sentenced him to death. On hearing this, Arthapála determined to effect the release of his father. He secured a poisonous snake, and when his father was being led to be put to death, he dropped it on his head, so that it bit him and he fell down senseless. Arthapâla knew anti-poison charms by means of which he counteracted the effect of the poison; and having removed the apparently dead body with the permission of the king, he restored Kámapâla to life. They then concerted a plan for the overthrow of Siṃhaghosha. Arthapâla excavated a subterranean passage to the royal palace; this passage opened in an underground chamber where dwelt princess Maṇikarṇiká, whose attendants requested Arthapâla to wed her. Arthapâla promised to do so, and entered the royal apartments, where he found the king asleep. He took him captive and carried him to Kámapâla, who then administered the kingdom. Arthapála married Maṇikarṇiká, became installed Yuvarâja, and led an army to the assistance of the king of the Aṅgas, when he met Rāja. in Champâ.

UCH. V. Thereafter Pramati proceeded to describe his adventures. While on his journey he was benighted in a forest of the Vindhya mountains, where, commending himself to the guardian-deity of the place for protection, he lay down for repose under a true. While asleep, he fancied himself transported to a palace where he beheld a lovely maiden with whom he immediately fell in love. On awakening he was wondering whether it was a dream or a delusion, when a nymph appeared and told him how it was all real, snd how she had carried him asleep to the chamber of princess Navamālikā of Śrâvastî, who was the damsel seen by him. The nymph, who was none other than Târāvalî, the wife of Kâmapâla, prophesied success for him in his suit and then took her departure. Pramati then proceeded to Śrâvastî. On his way he met a Brâhmaṇa at a cock-fight, and made friends with him. These two hatched a plan; the Bràhmaṇa took Pramati, dressed in female garb as his daughter, to the king, and left her under his protection, while he went off to find out the youth to whom he professed to have betrothed her. In the palace Pramati won the affection of Navamâlikâ; afterwards one day he disappeared and joined the Bra'hmaṇa. The latter then went to the king with Pramati as his intended son-in-law, and demanded to see his daughter. The King was not of course able to produce her, whereupon the Brâhmaṇa threatened to immolate himself in the fire. The king was then forced to offer his own daughter to Pramati, in order to pacify the Bráhmaṇa. Pramati thus became the son-in-law of the king and soon won his confidence. While he was leading his troops to succour Siṃhavarmâ, he met his friend Ràjavâhana.

UCH. VI. Next it was the turn of Mitragupta to narrate his adventures. He had journeyed to the Suhma country and arrived at its capital Dámalipta. The King of the Suhmas, by the favour of the goddess Durgā, had obtained two children, one son (Bhîmadhanvâ) and one daughter (Kandukâvatî), on condition that the former should be subordinate to the husband of the latter, and that the husband should be chosen by her at an annual festival where she was to play in public with a ball (*kanduka*). That being the time of the festival, Mitragupta went to behold it, and the princess happened to choose him; but this roused the ire of Bhímadhanvā, who did not like to see himself subordinated to a stranger. So Mitragupta was seized by his orders, and cast into the sea. He was luckily picked up by a passing Yavana vessel; the Yavanas wanted to hold him as a slave, but their ship was attacked by another, and Mitragupta fought valiantly on their behalf and routed the assailants; so he was treated by them with great respect and given his freedom. Bhîmadhanvâ turned out to be the captain of the attacking ship and was taken prisoner. The ship was driven by a contrary gale to an island, where they cast anchor and Mitragupta landed ashore. He there met a Rákshasa who threatened to devour him unless he answered his four questions. They were—What is naturally cruel? What contributes best to the happiness of a house-holder? What is love? And, What is the best means of achieving difficult things? His answers were, in order:—The heart of a woman; The virtues of the wife; The determination to possess; and Talent. He illustrated his answers by four stories, each having a woman for the heroine, *viz.* Dhûminî, Gominî, Nimbavatî and Nitambavatî (see pp. 157–170). The Rákshasa was pleased with the replies. Just then another Ràkshasa was found carrying along a struggling maiden by the aerial path; she was rescued, and proved to be Kandukāvatî, Mitragupta's destined bride. Mitragupta then set sail and arrived at Dāmalipta, where he was welcomed as his son-in-law by the old king. The latter was an ally of Siṃhavarmá; so Mitragupta was dispatched to his aid with an army, when he met Rājavāhana in Champā.

UCH. VII. It was the turn of Mantragupta next to relate his story. He had gone to the country of Kaliṅga where in a cemetery he rescued the princess of Kaliṅga, Kanakalekhā by name, from the hands of a *Siddha* ( a sorcerer) who had procured her presence through a goblin, and who was about to kill and sacrifice her for obtaining miraculous powers. Mantragupta fell in love with the princess, and accompanied her to the palace, where he lived in her apartment without being discovered. Now Kardana, the king of Kaliṅga, once went with his family to spend a few days by the sea-side. There he was attacked and taken captive by Jayaiṃha, the king of A'ndhra. Mantragupta wanted to rescue him, and soon found the necessary means. It happened that Jayasiṃha wished to wed Kanakalekhá, but a report had got abroad that she was possessed by an evil spirit (Yaksha) who had to be exorcized first. Mantragupta disguised himself as a great asectic and offered his help to the King in driving away the Yaksha. It was planned that the king should bathe in a lake, when, by virtue of Mantragupta's magical rites, he would emerge with his body metamorphosed, and would then be enabled to combat the Yaksha. Accordingly, Jayasiṃha entered the lake, when Mantragupta contrived to kill him, and himself issued forth as the metamorphosed King. Thereupon he found no difficulty in releasing Kardana and the princess; the former became the king of both the A'ndhras and the Kaliṅgas, and the latter was married to Mantragupta. Coming to the assistance of Siṃhavarmā, he met Rájavâhana. [The whole story is narrated without the use of any labial latters, which is a literary *tour de force*; a poetical reason for Mantragupta's avoidance of labials will be found given on p. 172, l. 2].

Uch. VIII. Vis'ruta now narrated his adventures, being the last of the series. While wandering through the Vindhya forest he came upon a young boy attended by an old man. The boy was the young prince of Vidarbha. His father Anantavarma' kept vicious company, and owing to his dissolute habits neglected the affairs of the state; he was thereupon attacked by Vasantabhānu, a neighbouring prince, who killed him and usurped his throne. On the death of Anantavarmā, his queen Vasuṃdhará with her daughter Mañjuvâdinî and son Bhāskarávarmá went to stay with Mitravarmá, king of Māhishmatî, who was the half-brother of her husband. Mitravarmā, however, was discovered to be a treacherous ally, and the queen sent her son away with an attendant, with instructions to the latter to take the prince to a place of safety. Vis'ruta listened to their account, and discovering that the prince was distantly related to himself, promised him help in recovering his lost kingdom. Learning from a forester that a marriage was being arranged in Mâhishmatî by Mitravarmā between Mañjuvādinî and Prachaṇḍavarmā, Vis'ruta sent the old servant back to queen Vasuṃdharā, asking her to spread a false report about her son's death; he also sent her a poisoned necklace with which she was to kill Mitravarmá and then to await his (Vis'ruta's) arrival. Vis'ruta himself shortly afterwards arrived in the city, accompanied by the prince, and for a while took up the diguise of a mendicant. He soon found an opportunity to kill Prachaṇḍavarmā; he thereafter repaired to the temple of Durgā; entering, he hid himself underneath the pedestal of the idol. The queen arrived there according to a preconcerted plan; she had already given out that owing to the favour of the goddess—as revealed in a vision—her dead son would return to her alive on that day in the temple. Vis'ruta issued forth with the prince from the interior of the temple, and announced to the assembled people that the prince was under the special protection of the goddess, who was pleased to send him back to them as their lawful ruler. Thus Bhāskaravarman was recognized as the king of Mâhishmatî; and Viśruta, marrying Mañjuvâdinî, became the king's chief adviser, and conducted the affairs of the kingdom for him.

(THE UTTARAPI'THIKA')

Vis'ruta next directed his attention to the task of restoring Bhāskaravarman to his paternal throne of Vidarbha, which had been seized by Vasantabhānu. He led an expedition against the latter, and killed him in single combat; thus the road was clear for Bhāskaravarman's succession, and Vis'ruta' efforts were crowned with fruition. When coming to the help of Siṃhavarmà, he met Rājavâhana in Champá.

On the termination of these narratives, there arrived a messenger from the old King Rájahaṃsa, the father of Rájavàhana, with a letter. Rájahamsa was struck with grief when he had heard of the sudden disapparance of his son and the consequent dispersal of the band of the princes; but he had been comforted by the sage Vámadeva prophesying that they would all return safe and sound after sixteen years. That period had now elapsed, and the sage having told him how they had all assembled at Champā, he desired them to start at once to see him. In obedience to this mandate the princes set out for Pushpapura. Coming to Ujjayinî they defeated and killed Mánasāra and took possession of the kingdom of Málwâ. After that they repaired to Pushpapura. The old king was highly pleased to see them, and having distributed among them the various kingdoms they had won, he retired from public life. Then Ra'java hana became the king of the united kingdoms of Pushpapura and Ujjayinî; the princes governed their respective principalities with justice, and all lived happily ever afterwards.

## (2) The Three Parts of The Present Text.

The complete available text of the Daśak., a summary of which has been given above, presents one curious feature in that it consists of three separate fragments, known respectively as the *Pûrvapîṭhikâ* (in 5 Uchchhvâsas), the *Das'akumâra-charita* proper (in 8 Uch.), and the *Uttarapîṭhikâ* (in 1 Uch., or rather, not divided into any Uch.). Of these three, only the middle portion is believed to have been from the pen of Daṇḍin himself. As the student will have noticed, it begins abruptly in the middle of the story of Ra'javáhana, and also ends abruptly, leaving Vis'ruta's narrative unfinished; the word *das'a* in the title of the work is proof enough to show that two more tales are lacking in the middle portion as it is extant at present. It is impossible to give any satisfactory explanation of how the original work of Daṇḍin came to be in such a fragmentary state. In the case of Bâṇa's Ka'dambarî, which originally ended abruptly, we know that it was the author's death which left it incomplete, as we have been told by his son who composed its supplement or the Uttarabhâga. But concerning the Das'ak., the writers who have provided the Supplements have offered no explanations, and we are left to surmise the probable cause best as we may. It is patent on the face of it, that the Das'ak. once existed in a complete state; for, though an author may sometimes leave his work incomplete towards the end, he would scarcely begin it abruptly in the middle. Later, owing to some accident or other, a considerable portion in the beginning and in the end came to be lost; and either the disciples of Daṇḍin, or some other admirers of his work, who must have remembered how the missing portion read,[18] supplied the deficiency to the best of their abilities. That the Pûrvapîṭhiká and the Uttarapîṭhika', as printed here, are not by the same hand that wrote the Das'ak., will be clear when we carefully examine them. The Pûrva., from its length, appears to be

---

18 Mr. M. R. Kavi, the editor of the Avantisundarîkathâ, has offered another explanation which is also possible. According to him, the original work of Daṇḍin was translated in Telugu by about 1250 A. D.; and, when the original could not be found complete, some skilful scholar must have re-translated the Pûrvabhâga backwards into Sanskrit from that translation.

an ambitious work, and its author has done his best to imitate the style of Daṇḍin; nevertheless it lacks the grace and felicity of the original part. The author seems to have acquired greater skill in composition as he proceeded with his narrative, for its earlier Uchchhvâsas are cruder and less polished than the later ones. There are, moreover, discrepancies between the Púrva. and the Das'ak. proper, that stamp the former as being the work of a different writer. The following are the more important among these discrepancies:—(i) In the Pûrva. Arthapa'la is stated to be the son of Ka'mapa'la from his wife Ta'ra'valî; the Das'ak. (Uch. IV.) makes him the son of Ka'mapa'la from his wife Ka'ntimatî. (ii) The Pûrva. makes Pramati the son of Sumati; the Daśak. shows him as the son of Ka'mapâla. (iii) The account given of the nurse of Upaha'ravarman in the Pûrv. differs in several details from that found in Uch. III. of the Daśak. Similarly, there are variations between the *Uttarapîṭhikâ* and the preceding portion of the work, as for example the reference to Ma'nasâra on p. 215 is not in agreement with what has been stated before. Such details confirm us in our suspicion that the beginning and the end of the Daśak. have been supplied by later writers; even their names have remained unknown, and it is therefore natural that in MSS. the entire work should be frequently found ascribed to Daṇḍin.

Before concluding, it is necessary to draw attention to the fact that there have been many writers who have tried to compose similar supplements. Thus, Mr. Agashe has printed in his edition a small Pûrvapîṭhikâ, by one Bhaṭṭa-Nára'yaṇa; he claims that it is a better piece of work than the current Pûrvapîṭhikâ. It seems to us, however, to be quite an inferior production, reading almost like a school-boy's summary; and it is far less fitted to stand as part of the well-finished, easy-flowing work of Daṇḍin. As regards the Uttarapîṭhikâ, the first ed. of the Das'ak. issued by the Nirṇ. press contained a version (called therein Daśakumāra-chaitas'esha) by Chakrapa'ṇi; this was the same version which was accessible to Prof. Wilson, and on which he commented adversely. It is of considerable length, and its style does not accord with Daṇḍin's in purity and vigour; it was therefore omitted in subsequent editions, and the current Uttarapîṭhika', which is a more suitable and concise production, substituted in its place; the author of this Uttara. is, however, unknown. There is a third Uttarapîṭhikā by one Padmanābha, which is printed at Madras, and a fourth one, ascribed to Pandit Gopînâtha, exists in MS. It will thus be seen that criticism on Daṇḍin's work will only be pertinent when it is made with reference to the main body of the text as it is available in its eight Uchchhvāsas.

---

### (3) General and Critical Remarks.

The Daśak. has long enjoyed a well-deserved popularity in India both on account of its easy style and its attractive subject-matter. Daṇḍin is a writer of great merit and considerable literary attainments; the high esteem in which he is held by Indian scholars is shown by the number of current Subha'shitas (*cf.* some quoted by us *supra* p. x) eulogizing him for his pre-eminent position among Sanskrit poets. Like the great masters Kālidāsa, Bāṇa and Bhavabhûti, he has a perfect command over language. As a lover of nature and a descriptive poet, he is inferior to the three great authors just named,. but inferior to them only. His descriptions of the first meeting between Rājavâhana and Avantisundarî, Pramati's account of the unknown princess, Kandukâvatî's play at the ball, &c., are very fair specimens of descriptive composition. Of the whole collection the story of Apahāra-varman is the best, being richer in varied incidents, and that of Mitragupta would rank next. Daṇḍin's mastery over the art of writing short stories is illustrated by the vividly picturesque group of four stories narrated in response to the demand of the Rákshasa in Uch. VI.

The plot of the Daśak. seems on the whole to be of the poet's own invention, and does not appear to have been borrowed from or based on any older accounts. It is, however, probable that in some minor particulars Daṇḍin might have received hints from other sources, legendary or historical. The Bṛihatkathâ of Guṇâdhya has long been recognized in India as a veritable mine of fable-literature on which later authors have drawn repeatedly and copiously for the material of their works. If we examine the Bṛihatkathâ (as summarized in the Kathásaritsâgara or the Bṛihatkathâmañjarî), we do not find any wholesale borrowing on the part of Daṇḍin anywhere. There are, however, certain similar incidents in both the Daśak. and the Bṛihatkathá, from which it may be argued that Daṇḍin's writing is occasionally reminiscent of Guṇâdhya. Mr. Agashe has collected together several of these similarities, among which we may mention the prostitute's mother remonstrating with her daughter (pp. 66–68), the snatching of an anklet off the foot of a woman (p. 169), and the visit of the prince to the nether regions (p. 64). But these are mere hints, not complete stories, and they do not detract from the originality of Daṇḍin's plot. The accounts of Rájahaṃsa's kingdom being usurped by Mânasára and the overthrow of Vasantabhānu (in Uch. VIII.) are understood by some to be based on certain contemporary historical events, though it is impossible to establish that Daṇḍin was referring to any particular historical personages. If there are any historical allusions in the Daśak., they are too slight, and made casually in passing; the groundwork of the Daśak. is not historical, but fictitious; and in the evolution of his narratives Daṇḍin cannot be held to be indebted to any previous author or authors, though he may have here and there unconsciously borrowed a phrase or an incident from the Bṛihatkathâ. He is fully entitled to the credit of having created an original romance of great interest and charm in which the life of the middle class as well as of the ruling caste is portrayed with discrimination and a due sense of proportion.

Viewing the Daśak. as a masterpiece of constructive art, it reveals to us, as aptly remarked by Prof, Keith, "the graces of the Kávya style applied to the folk-tale, vivified by the genius of the writer." High praise it undoubtedly deserves; but, as no human work is perfect, it suffers from defects which are indeeed noticeable even on a cursory perusal of the whole. Fistly, as the work stands, it is faulty to a certain extent as regards its general dénouement; the events described seem to hang loosely together instead of leading to a definite end. (But we should hesitate to hold Daṇḍin responsible for this, for it is most likely due to the fragmentary condition of the available text, and not to any constructive defect in the orignial). And secondly, the work does not teach a moral. Indeed, when one remembers how all Hindu fable-literature is distinctly didactic in tone, it is not a little surprising that Daṇḍin should have contented himself with a realistic portrait only, without endeavouring to point to any distinct moral derived therefrom. He observes, but does not diagnose; he describes, but does not instruct. The evils he sees around him he knows to be evils, but he does not tell us how to steer clear of them or how to cure them; at any rate, if any moral is to be drawn, he leaves it to the reader, and does not concern himself with it. It would seem that *rañjana*, and not *bodha*, was what he was chiefly aiming at; and in that no doubt he has succeeded to a very high degree.

One serious charge that has been brought against this highly popular romance of Daṇḍin is its lack of good taste in the descriptions of the princes' adventures, and its occasional indelicacy of expression. Now, it is quite true that the poet has interspersed thieving, adultery and murders somewhat too freely in his narratives, and heinous crimes such as these have evoked from him expressions which are more palliative than condemnatory. But in this he appears to have yielded to the taste of certain sections of the society of the times when he wrote; it was his business to portray the occurrences in the royal harems and the intrigues at court, along with the irresponsible daily life of vagabonds, tramps and soldiers of fortune, as occasion arose. He pictured what he observed, and we know that he did not picture with any exaggeration; for history tells us but too frequently how succession in a royal family in India was shrouded in an atmosphere of crime and fraud. The charge of indelicacy of expression is one that cannot be seriously maintained against an established classic of repute, such as the Daśak. undoubtedly is; moreover, the standards of delicacy vary among different peoples and different civilizations; and what sounds indelicate to our modern ears might have been a common mode of expression in those less sophisticated days. We have here, as Prof. Keith remarks, a confusion of morality and literature, and the ignoring of the diverse standards of taste of the west and pre-Mahomedan India.

Prof. Wilson has attached great importance to the geography of the Daśak.; and lately Mr. Mark Collins has tried to discuss its geographical data in a separate pamphlet. We have already remarked above that the geographical references of Daṇḍin do not help us in fixing his age; and though he mentions a large number of countries and places in his narratives, very little definite can be inferred therefrom; nor does he make any new additions to our knowledge. Either the names are quite well known on the map of ancient India, or, when it is not so, the reference is so vague (*e. g.* सुरलेश on p. 201) as to be of little use in enabling us to fix its location properly. Similarly, the picture of Hindu society drawn by Daṇḍin does not present any extraordinary features calling for any special comment. We read therein of the prevalence of polygamy, idol-worship, belief in dreams, omens, ghosts and sorcery, gambling houses, courtesans, the doctrine of former birth and Karma. In these particulars Hindu society has remained almost stationary for many centuries past, although certain barbarous practices like human sacrifice have been put a stop to by law. Too much stress should not be laid on the profligacy and superstition that we find in the Daśak.; these two features characterize more or less certain sections of every society even now, but nobody imagines thereby that the entire structure of that society is raised on them. The mercantile community of ancient India was enterprising; one reads of vast caravans journeying through the forests, and the account of Mitragupta shows that Indian merchants even traded by sea with far-off countries like Arabia; this maritime trade of India is now a thing of the past.

## STYLE.

The style of the Daśak. is in general simple, easy-flowing, polished and idiomatic. There are in it occasional lapses from good grammar, solecisms and inaccuracies; we have noticed most of these in our Notes, such as the irregular use of the Perfect in अहं चकमे ( p. 126 ) and अहं सस्वजे ( p. 202 ), or the defective syntax as in मरीचिं वेशकृच्छ्रादुत्थाय......तेनास्मि त्वद्दर्शनमवगमितः ( p. 101 ), or such unfamiliar use of words as in परिवव्राज उज्जयिनीम् ( p. 167 ); but too much should not be made of such errors and irregularities, many of which occur in the Púrvapîṭhikâ, and not in the Daśak., and we know that Daṇḍin was not responsible for the Púrva. Further, it is quite probable that not a few of them may have been introduced owing to the ignorance and negligence of scribes. On the whole, the style of the Das'ak. resembles more the easier narrative style of works like the Pañchatantra and the Hitopadeśa; it stands on a different plane from the gorgeous splendour of Báṇa's Kádambarî, for instance. Bàṇa utilizes every kind of literary embellishment known to him, including innumerable puns, high-flown conceits, and extra-ordinarily long compounds, so that the thread of his narrative is often lost in these; he appears to be more concerned with displaying his skill in the use of words, rather than with the progress of his narrative. Daṇḍin avoids such temptations, and makes the narration of the story his principal aim; that he could have written like Báṇa had he so chosen, it would be apparent on an examination of his Avantisundarîkathâ ( for extracts from which work the student may turn to p. xxiv *supra* ). The literary *tour de force* in the 7th Uch., the whole of which is composed without the use of labial letters, finds no parallel in the works of Báṇa. That he could accomplish this feat in writing चित्र काव्य without importing any obscurity of expression in his style, is a very high testimony to his command over language; it is done so cleverly and unostentatiously, and the narrative reads so very normal as usual, that had it not been for the author's own statement in the beginning, the reader would hardly have discovered the absence of labial letters even on reaching the end of the chapter. Daṇḍin is generally happy in his choice of words, and has a special facility in embodying common truths in homely and forceful language ( *Cf.* स्वदेशो देशान्तरमिति नेयं गणना विदग्धस्य पुरुषस्य p. 80 ; आत्मानमात्मनाऽनवसाद्यैवोद्धरन्ति सन्तः p. 82 ; न ह्यलमतिनिपुणोऽपि पुरुषो नियतिलिखितां लेखामतिक्रमितुम् p. 89; इह जगति हि न निरीहं देहिनं श्रियः संश्रयन्ते p. 181; जीवितं हि नाम जन्मवतां चतुःपञ्चाण्यहानि p. 194; &c. ). There is one feature of style for which Daṇḍin was especially famed, according to an old Subháshita already quoted above ( p. x ), *viz* his selection of beautiful and alliterative words. Instances of this are strewn all over the work, from which we cull a few at random :—आरब्धकामिजनवृत्तं निवृत्तस्ववृत्ताभिलाषं p. 71 ; अयुग्मशरः शरशयने शाययिष्यति p. 84; असत्येनास्य नास्यं संसृज्यते p. 179 ; अनेकस्यानेक आतङ्कश्चिरं चिकित्सकैरसंहार्यः संहृतः p. 179 ; स पुण्यैः कर्मभिः प्राण्य पुरुषायुषं पुनरपुण्येन प्रजानामगण्यतामरेषु p. 188 ; etc. ). The student can add many more.

## Characterization

The student will find at the end of this Section a list of the ten Kumáras, from which he can see at a glance their relationships. In describing their adventures, Daṇḍin seems to have made narration of the incidents his chief concern, characterization being only secondary. This was necessitated by the framework of the romance, which was a series of tales in which no great scope could be found for the consistent development of any particular character; so our author has contented himself with delineating their personalities with a few deft and bold strokes, as there was no room for any very deep analysis of character. The hero is Rājavāhana, who is young, well-educated, and handsome in form. His readiness in going to the help of a Bráhmaṇa ( Pûrva. II. ) shows the innate nobility of his heart. His union with Avantisundarî leads to his arrest by Chaṇḍavarmā; although brave and not lacking in courage, he accepts it without resistance, as it had been pre-ordained by destiny (p. 57). The various remarks he makes at the conclusion of the narrative of each of the Kumáras show his courtesy and his generosity: he would only comment on the good points in the tale, ignoring any objectionable features of it, so as not to wound the feelings of his friend. His prompt departure to visit his father on receiving his letter (p. 215) shows him as a loving son conscious of his filial obligations. The student will remember how Bâṇa has made Chandrâpîḍa obey promptly a similar order of his father.

Among the remaining Kumâras, Somadatta is portrayed as a very brave warrior; Pushpodbhava is a dutiful son; Apahâravarmā is a loyal and faithful friend, and withal a shrewd and successful plotter, a characteristic which evokes a compliment from Rájavāhana himself (p. 102). Upahâravarmà appears as a scheming gallant, though the author has taken pains to explain away his immoral intrigues (see pp. 111, 122). Arthapâla is a brave young man and a clever schemer. Pramati is depicted as a man of gentle temperament who gains his object by gentle means alone. Mitragupta meets with rather strange adventures; his encounter with the Yavanas shows his intrepid bravery, and that with the

Ra'kshasa his ready wit. Mantragupta is a resourcefu adventurer; and Viśruta appears to be a clever administrator' especially learned in the principles of practical politics. On the whole it may be said that Dandin has presented to us a gallery of portraits of varied and interesting types.

---

## The ten Kumâras and their Relationships.

(A) राजहंस ( King of Magadha )
- **राजवाहन (१)**

(B) प्रहारवर्मन् ( King of Videha )
- **अपहारवर्मन् (२)**
- **उपहारवर्मन् (३)**

(C) धर्मपाल ( Minister of Râjahaṃsa )
- सुमन्त्र
  - **मित्रगुप्त (४)**
- सुमित्र
  - **मन्त्रगुप्त (५)**
- कामपाल
  - **अर्थपाल (६)**

(D) पद्मोद्भव ( Minister of Râjahaṃsa )
- सुश्रुत
  - **विश्रुत (७)**
- रत्नोद्भव
  - **पुष्पोद्भव (८)**

(E) सितवर्मन् ( Minister of Râjahaṃsa )
- सुमति
- सत्यवर्मन्
  - **सोमदत्त (१०)**

## Important Abbreviations.

———:o:———

A. G.- Apte's Guide to Sanskrit Composition.

A.-K.—Amarakośa.

BG.—Bhagavadgîtâ

BH.—Bhartṛihari's Śatakas.*

BHATTI.—Bhaṭṭi-Kāvya.*

BHU'.—Bhúshaṇâ (Com.).

BṚIH.- UP.—Bṛihadâraṇyakopanishad.

BR.-SÛ.—Brahmasûtras.

CHHA'N.-UP.—Chhândogyopanishad.

COM.—Commentary; commentator.

D.-K.—Daśakumâracharita.*

D.-R.—Daśarūpaka.

GI'T.—Gîtagovinda.

HITOP.—Hitopadeśa.*

KA'D.—Kâdambarî.*

KA'M.-N.—Kâmandakîya-Nîtisâra.

KATHA'S.—Kathásaritsá gara.

KAUT.—Kauṭilya's Arthaśâstra.

KIR.—Kirâtârjunîya.*

K.-P.—Kāvya-Prakâśa.

KUM.—Kumârasambhava.*

LAGHU.—Laghudîpikâ (Com.).

MAH.-BH.—Mahá-Bhárata.

MA'LAV.—Mâlavikâgnimitra.*

MALLI.—Mallinâtha.

MA'L.-MA'DH.—Mâlatî-Mâdhava.*

MEGH.—Meghadûta.*

MṚICH.—Mṛichchhakaṭika *

M.-S.—Manusmṛiti.

MUD.—Mudrârâkshasa.*

NA'G.—Nâgânanda.*

PAD. –Padachandrikâ (Com.).

PA'N.—Pâṇini's Ashṭâdhyâyî

PT.—Pañchatantra.*

RAGH.—Raghuvaṃśa.*

RA'M.—Râmâyaṇa.

RATN.—Ratnâvalî.*

ṚITUS.—Ṛitusaṃhâra.*

Ṛ.-V.—Ṛig-Veda.

ŚA'K.—Śâkuntala.*

S.-D.—Sâhitya-darpaṇa.

SID.-K.—Siddhānta-kaumudî.

ŚIS'.—Śiśupâlavadha.

UP.—Upanishad.

UTTAR.—Uttararâmacharita.*

VA'RT.—Vârttika.

VENI'.—Veṇîsaṃhâra.*

VIK.—Vikramorvas'îya.*

V.-P.—Vishṇu-Purâṇa.

* Annotated by the Editor.



अथ

# दशकुमारचरितम् ।

## पूर्वपीठिका ।

### प्रथमोच्छ्वासः ।

ब्रह्माण्डच्छत्रदण्डः शतधृतिभवनाम्भोरुहो नालदण्डः
क्षोणीनौकूपदण्डः क्षरदमरसरित्पट्टिकाकेतुदण्डः ।
ज्योतिश्चक्राक्षदण्डस्त्रिभुवनविजयस्तम्भदण्डोऽङ्घ्रिदण्डः
श्रेयस्त्रैविक्रमस्ते[1] वितरतु विबुधद्वेषिणां कालदण्डः ॥

अस्ति समस्तनगरीनिकषायमाणा शश्वदगण्यपण्यविस्तारितमणिगणादिवस्तुजातव्याख्यातरत्नाकरमाहात्म्या मगधदेशशेखरीभूता पुष्पपुरी नाम नगरी । तत्र वीरभटपटलोत्तरङ्गतुरङ्गकुञ्जरमकरभीषणसकल-

---

**ब्रह्माण्डेति** । ब्रह्माण्डमेव छत्रं तस्य दण्डः आधारयष्टिः । ब्रह्माण्डं भुवनम् । शतं धृतयो यस्य स शतधृतिर्ब्रह्मा । तस्य भवनमुत्पत्तिस्थानं वासस्थानं वा तद्भूतस्याम्भोरुहोऽम्भसि रोहतीति व्युत्पत्त्या कमलस्य । हान्तोऽयं शब्दः । क्षोणी पृथ्वी तद्रूपा या नौस्तरिस्तस्याः कूपदण्डो गुणवृक्षकः । 'डोलकाठी' इति भाषायाम् । क्षरन्ती प्रस्रवन्ती या अमरसरिद्दियद्गङ्गा सैव पट्टिका तस्याः केतुदण्डः । ज्योतिश्चक्रं ज्योतिःसमूहस्तस्याक्षदण्डो नाभिक्षेपं काष्ठम् । त्रयाणां भुवनानां समाहारस्त्रिभुवनं तस्य विजयस्तद्दर्शकः स्तम्भदण्डः । अङ्घ्रिश्चरणो दण्ड इवेत्युपमितसमासः । श्रेयो निःश्रेयसं सुकृतं पुण्यं वा । अतिशयेन प्रशस्यम् । त्रैविक्रमस्त्रिविक्रमस्यायम् । वितरतु ददातु । विबुधद्वेषिणां दनुजानाम् । कालदण्डः कृतान्तः । मृत्युरिति यावत् । **अस्तीति** । निकषः कषपाषाणः तद्वदाचरति निकषायते । निकषायतेऽसौ निकषायमाणा । पण्यानि विक्रेयवस्तूनि । रत्नाकर उदधिः । शेखरीभुता भूषणभूता । **वीरेति** । वीराश्च ते भटाश्च तेषां पटलानि तैः उद्गताः तरङ्गा वीचयो यस्यासौ उत्तरङ्गः । तुरङ्गाश्च कुञ्जराश्च त एव मकरास्तैर्भीषणश्च ।

---

१ मो वो.

रिपुगणकटकजलनिधिमथनमन्दरायमाणसमुद्दण्डभुजदण्डः, पुरंदरपुराङ्गणवनविहरणपरायणगीर्वाणतरुणगणिकागणजेगीयमानयाऽतिमानया शरदिन्दुकुन्दघनसारनीहारहारमृणालमरालसुरगजनीरक्षीरगिरिशाट्टहासकैलासकाशनीकाशमूर्त्या रचितदिगन्तरालपूर्त्या कीर्त्याऽभितः सुरभितः, स्वर्लोकशिखरोरुरुचिररत्नरत्नाकरवेलामेखलावलयितधरणीरमणीसौभाग्यभोगभाग्यवान्, अनवरतयागदक्षिणारक्षितशिष्टविशिष्टविद्यासंभारभासुरभूसुरनिकरः, विरचितारातिसंतापेन प्रतापेन सततनुलितवियन्मध्यहंसः, राजहंसो नाम घनदर्पकंदर्पसौन्दर्यसोदर्यहृद्यनिरवद्यरूपो भूपो बभूव। तस्य वसुमती नाम सुमती लीलावतीकुलशेखरमणी रमणी बभूव। रोषरूक्षणेन निटिलेक्षणेन

एतादृशः यः सकलाश्च ते रिपवश्च तेषां गणस्तस्य कटकं तदेव जलनिधिस्तस्य मथने मन्दर इवाचरन्समुद्दण्डो भुजदण्डो यस्य सः। भटा योद्धारः। पटलं समूहः। कटकं सेना। **पुरंदरेति**। पुरंदर इन्द्रः तस्य पुरस्य अङ्गणानि चत्वराणि तत्संबन्धीनि वनानि तेषु विहरणपरायणः यो गीर्वाणतरुणगणिकानां वेश्यानामप्सरसामित्यर्थः गणस्तेन जेगीयमानया भृशं पुनः पुनर्वा कीर्त्यमानया। अतिमानयाऽतिप्रमाणया। विस्तृतयेति यावत्। **शरदिन्द्विति**। कुन्दं पुष्पविशेषः। 'कर्पूरो हिमवालुका। घनसारः' इति हैमः। नीहारो हिमम्। मृणालं बिसम्। मरालो हंसः। सुरगज ऐरावतः। गिरिशस्य शिवस्याट्टहासो महान्हासः। काशस्तृणपुष्पभेदः। शरदिन्दुश्च कुन्दं चेत्यादिः काशान्तो द्वन्द्वः। तैः सदृशी तन्नीकाशा। नित्यसमासः। मूर्तिर्यस्यास्तया। रचिता कृता दिशामन्तरालं दिगन्तरालं तस्य पूर्तिः दिगन्तरालपूर्तिर्यया। सुरभितो मनोज्ञः। **स्वर्लोकेति**। स्वर्लोकः सुरालयो मेरुस्तस्य शिखरं तद्वत्तत्संबन्धीनि वा उरूणि स्थूलानि रुचिराणि सुन्दराणि च यानि रत्नानि तेषां तद्युक्तो वा यो रत्नाकरस्तस्य वेला जलवृद्धेर्मर्यादा सैव मेखला काञ्ची तया वलयिता या धरणी सैव रमणी। अनवरता नित्याः। यागा यज्ञाः। तेषु या दक्षिणा तया रक्षितः शिष्टाश्च ते विशिष्टविद्यासंभारेण भासुरा देदीप्यमानाः भुवो भुवि वा सुरा इव भूसुराः ब्राह्मणाः। तेषां निकरो वृन्दं येन। विरचितोऽरातिसंतापो येन। रिपुदत्तसंताप इत्यर्थः। वियत आकाशस्य मध्ये हंसः सूर्यः। घनः दर्पोऽवलेपः यस्य तादृशो कंदर्पो मन्मथः तस्य सौन्दर्यस्य सोदर्यं (सोदर्यो बन्धुः समानोदर्यः। अत्र.) सदृशम्। हृद्यं मनोहरं निरवद्यं निर्दोषं च रूपं यस्य। लीलावत्यो योषितस्तासां कुलं तस्य शेखरमणिर्भूषणमवतंसः। **रोषणेति**। रोषणमीक्षणं नेत्रं यस्य तेन। क्रोधताम्रदृशेत्यर्थः। निटिले भालस्थले ईक्षणं नयनं यस्येति निटिलेक्षणः शिवः तेन। मकरकेतनो

१ भुजदण्डमण्डनः. २ गणिकाजनगीयमानया. ३ परिचित. ४ मेखलायित. ५ वसुमतीव. ६ रोषरूक्षेण निटिलाक्षेण.

भस्मीकृतचेतने मकरकेतने तदा भयेनानवद्या वनितेति मत्वा, [1]तस्या रोलम्बावली केशजालम्, प्रेमाकरो रजनीकरो विजितारविन्दं वदनम्, जयध्वजायमानो मीनो जायायुतोऽक्षियुगलम्, सकलसैनिकाङ्गवीरो मलयसमीरो निःश्वासः, [2]पथिकहृद्दलनकरवालः प्रवालश्चाधरबिम्बम्, जयशङ्खो बन्धुरा लावण्यधरा कंधरा, पूर्णकुम्भौ चक्रवाकानुकारौ पयोधरौ, [3]ज्यायमाने मार्दवासमाने बिसलते च बाहू, ईषत्फुल्ललीलावतंसकह्लारकोरको गङ्गावर्तसनाभिर्नाभिः, दूरीकृतयोगिमनोरथो जैत्ररथोऽतिघनं जघनम्, जयस्तम्भभूते सौन्दर्यभूते विघ्नितयतिजनारम्भे रम्भे चोरुयुगम्, आतपत्रसहस्रपत्रं पादद्वयम्, अस्त्रभूतानि प्रसूनानि तानीतराण्यङ्गानि च समभूवन्निव । विजितामरपुरे पुष्पपुरे निवसता साऽनन्तभोगलालिता वसुमती वसुमतीव मगधराजेन यथासुखमन्वभावि ।

तस्य राज्ञः परमविधेया धर्मपालपद्मोद्भवसितवर्मनामधेया धीरधिषणावधीरितविबुधाचार्यविचार्यकार्यसाहित्याः कुलामात्यास्त्रयोऽभूवन् ।

---

मन्मथः । अनवद्या निर्दोषा । **रोलम्बेति** । रोलम्बावली भ्रमरपङ्क्तिः । अर्थात्कामस्य मौर्वीस्थिता । तस्याः केशजालं समभूत् । एवं सर्वत्र । प्रेम्ण आकरः खनिः । विजितारविन्दं विजितं कान्त्या तिरस्कृतमरविन्दं कमलं येन तत् । जयध्वज इवाचरति जयध्वजे तिष्ठति वा जयध्वजायते । जायायुतः पत्नीसहितः । अक्षियुगलमक्ष्णोर्द्वयम् । अङ्गवीरः प्रधानयोधः । मलयसमीरो दक्षिणानिलः । पथिकाः प्रोषिताः पान्थाः तेषां हृदयस्य यद्दलनं पाटनं तस्मिन्करवालः कृपाणः । प्रवालः किसलयः । बन्धुरोन्नतानता । कंधरा ग्रीवा । ज्यायमाने ज्येवाचरन्त्यौ । मार्दवे मृदुत्वेऽसमाने । कह्लारं कमलं तस्य कोरकः कुड्मलः । गङ्गाया आवर्तोऽम्भसां भ्रमः । तस्य सनाभिः सदृशा । दूरीकृता अपनीता योगिजनानां मनोरथा येनेति । जैत्रो जयनशीलः । रथो लक्षणया रथचक्रम् । **जयस्तम्भेति** । आरम्भाः कर्माणि । आरभ्यन्त इत्यारम्भाः । रम्भे कदली । ऊर्वोर्युगमूरुयुगम् । **आतपत्रेति** । आतपात्त्रायते तदातपत्रं छत्रं तद्रूपं यत्सहस्रपत्रं कमलं तत् । प्रसूनानि पुष्पाणि । तदुक्तम्—'अरविन्दमशोकं च चूतं च नवमल्लिका। नीलोत्पलं च पञ्चैते पञ्चबाणस्य सायकाः' इति । **विजितेति** । विजितं स्ववैभवेन तिरस्कृतममरपुरमिन्द्रनगरी येन तस्मिन् । अनन्ताश्च ते भोगाश्च तैः लालिता । पक्षे अनन्तस्य शेषस्य भोगः शरीरं तेन लालिता उपरिधारणेन । अन्वभावि अनुपूर्वकात् 'भू सत्तायाम्' इति धातोः कर्मणि लुङ् । **तस्येति** । परमं विधेया विनयग्राहिणः । धीरा प्रगल्भा या धिषणा बुद्धिस्तया अवधीरितं विबुधाचार्यः सुरगुरुर्गुरुस्तस्यापि विचार्यं विचारार्हं कार्यसाहित्यं यैस्ते । अतीव पटु-

---

१ तस्य. २ पथिकहृद्दलनः करवालप्रवालः. ३ अतः परं 'भ्रुकुटी' इत्य० क्वचित्.

तेषां सितवर्मणः सुमतिसत्यवर्माणौ, धर्मपालस्य सुमन्त्रसुमित्रकामपालाः, पद्मोद्भवस्य सुश्रुतरत्नोद्भवाविति तनयाः [1]समभूवन्। तेषु धर्मशीलः सत्यवर्मा संसारासारतां बुद्ध्वा तीर्थयात्राभिलाषी देशान्तरमगमत्। विटनटवारनारीपरायणो दुर्विनीतः कामपालो जनकाग्रजन्मनोः शासनमतिक्रम्य भुवं बभ्राम। रत्नोद्भवोऽपि वाणिज्यनिपुणतया पारावारतरणमकरोत्। इतरे मन्त्रिसूनवः पुरंदरपुरातिथिषु पितृषु यथापूर्वमन्वतिष्ठन्।

ततः कदाचिन्नानाविधमहदायुधनैपुण्यरचितागण्यजन्यराजन्यमौलिपालिनिहितनिशितसायको मगधनायको मालवेश्वरं प्रत्यग्रसंग्रामघस्मरं समुत्कटमानसारं मानसारं प्रति [2]सहेलंन्यक्कृतजलधिनिर्घोषाहंकारेण भेरीझांकारेण हठिकाकर्णनाक्रान्तभयचण्डिमानं दिग्दन्तावलवलयं विघूर्णयन्निजभरनमन्मेदिनी[3]भरेणायस्तभुजगराजमस्तकबलेन

बुद्ध्य इति भावः। कुलामात्या वंशक्रमागताः। धर्मशीलो धार्मिकः। असारतां फल्गुताम्। अध्रुवत्वमित्यर्थः। अन्यो देशो देशान्तरम्। वारस्य वृन्दस्य नार्याः साधारणत्वात् वारनार्यो गणिकाः। परायणस्तत्परः। दुर्विनीतोऽविनीतः। जनकश्चाग्रजन्मा च तयोः। पितुर्ज्येष्ठभ्रातुश्चेत्यर्थः। शासनं निदेशम्। वाणिज्यं वणिक्कर्म भाण्डस्य द्वीपान्तरे नयनं द्वीपान्तरादानयनमित्यादि। पारावारः समुद्रः। पुरंदर इन्द्रस्तस्य पुरं नगरं तदतिथयो गृहागताः। 'दूराच्चोपनतं श्रान्तं वैश्वदेव उपस्थितम्। अतिथिं तं विजानीयात्' इति व्यासः। प्रेत्य महेन्द्रनगरं गतेषु। मृतेष्विति तात्पर्यार्थः। पूर्वमनतिक्रम्य वर्तत इति यथापूर्वम्। अतिष्ठन्कार्याण्यकुर्वन्नित्यर्थः। **तत इति।** नानाविधान्यनेकप्रकाराणि महान्त्यायुधानि तेषु निपुणता तया रचितानि कृतानि यान्यगण्यान्यसंख्यानि जन्यानि युद्धानि तेषु राजन्यानां क्षत्रियाणां मौलीनां किरीटानां पालिषु प्रान्तप्रदेशेषु निहिता अध्यारोपिताः स्थापिता वा निशितास्तीक्ष्णाः सायका बाणा येनैतादृशः। प्रत्यग्रो नवीनः यः संग्रामो युद्धं तत्र घस्मरो भक्षकः। शत्रुनाशक इत्यर्थः। 'सृघस्यदः क्मरच्' इति क्मरच्। समुत्कटोऽतिरिक्तो मान एव सारो यस्य तम्। यद्वा समुत्कटौ मानो दर्पः सारो बलं च यस्य तम्। मानसार इति नृपनाम। सहेलं लीलया न्यक्कृतोऽवधूतस्तिरस्कृतो जलधेः सागरस्य निर्घोषविषयेऽहंकारोऽभिमानो येन। भेरीझांकारेणेत्यस्य विशेषणम्। भेर्या दुन्दुभेर्झांकारो महाशब्दः। हठिकाकर्णनान्महतो ध्वनेर्बलाच्छ्रवणादाक्रान्तो भयस्य चण्डिमा महाभयमित्यर्थः यं तम्। दिशां दन्तावला हस्तिनस्तेषां वलयश्चक्रं समूहः तम्। विघूर्णयंश्चालयन्। निजभरेण स्वभारेण नमन्त्यधोगच्छन्ती या मेदिनी पृथ्वी तस्या भरेण भारेणायस्तं पीडितं भुजगानां राजा शेषस्तस्य मस्तकबलं येन। तस्य मेदिन्या आधारभूतत्वात्।

१ समभ्रमभू०. २ सहेलम्. ३ भरणायस्त.

चतुरङ्गबलेन संयुतः संग्रामाभिलाषेण रोषेण महताऽऽविष्टो निर्ययौ । मालवनाथोऽप्यनेकानेकपयूथसनाथो विग्रहः सविग्रह इव साग्रहोऽभिमुखीभूय भूयो निर्जगाम । तयोरथ रथतुरगखुरक्षुण्णक्षोणीसमुद्भूते करिघटाकटस्रवन्मदधाराधौतमूले नव्यवल्लभवरणागतदिव्यकन्याजनजवनिकापट[1]मण्डप इव वियत्तलव्याकुले धूलीपटले दिविषदध्वनि धिक्कृतान्यध्वनिपटहध्वान[2]बधिरिताशेषदिगन्तरालं शस्त्राशस्त्रि हस्ताहस्ति परस्पराभिहतसैन्यं जन्यमजनि । तत्र मगधराजः प्रक्षीणसकलसैन्यमण्डलं मालवराजं जीवग्राहमभिगृह्य कृपालुतया पुनरपि स्वराज्ये प्रतिष्ठापयामास ।

ततः स रत्नाकरमेखलामिलामनन्यशासनां शासदनपत्यतया नारायणं सकललोकैककारणं निरन्तरमर्चयामास । अथ कदाचित्तदग्रमहिषी देवी 'देवेन कल्पवल्लीफलमा[3]प्नुहि' इति प्रभातसमये

---

चतुरङ्गबलेन हस्त्यश्वरथपादातेन । महता रोषेणाभिनिवेशेनेत्यर्थः आविष्टो व्याप्ताकारः । अनेके येऽनेकपा द्विपाः । हस्तिन इति यावत् । तेषां यूथं वृन्दं तेन सनाथो युक्तः । विग्रहः संग्रामः । सविग्रहो मूर्तिमान् । साग्रह आग्रहेण सहितः । 'तयोः अथ' इति छेदः । रथैरथाद्रथचक्रनेमिभिः । तुरगाणामश्वानां खुरैः शफैः क्षुण्णायाश्चूर्णितायाः क्षोण्याः पृथ्व्याः समुद्भूते उत्पन्ने । करिणां हस्तिनां घटाः । 'बहूनां घटना घटा' इति हलायुधः । तासां कटा गण्डाः । तेभ्यः स्रवन्त्यो या मदधारा दानसलिलासारास्ताभिर्धौतं निर्मलीकृतं मूलं यस्य । नव्या नवीना ये वल्लभा रमणास्तेषां वरणं पतित्वेन स्वीकरणं तदर्थमागतो यो दिव्यकन्याजनोऽप्सरःसमुदायस्तस्य जवनिका तिरस्करिणी तदर्थं पटमण्डपो इव । वियत आकाशस्य तले व्याकुलं संभृतं तस्मिन् । धूल्याः पांसोः पटलं चयस्तस्मिन् । दिवि सीदन्ति ते दिविषदः देवाः तेषामध्वनि मार्गे । धिक्कृता अन्यध्वनयो येनैतादृशो यः पटहध्वानो ढक्काध्वनिस्तेन बधिरितमशेषदिगन्तरालं यस्मिन् । शस्त्राशस्त्रि । शस्त्रैः शस्त्रैश्च प्रहृत्येदं युद्धं प्रवृत्तमिति । 'तत्र तेनेदम्–' इति बहुव्रीहिः । 'इच्कर्मव्यतिहारे' इतीच्समासान्तः । परस्परस्याभिहतं सैन्यं यस्मिन् । जन्यं युद्धम् । प्रक्षीणं हतविध्वस्तम् । जीवग्राहं जीवन्तमित्यर्थः । **तत इति** । रत्नाकरः सागरो मेखला कटिसूत्रं यस्याः । इलां पृथ्वीम् । नास्त्यन्यशासनं यस्याम् । शासत् । अभ्यस्तत्वान्नुमभावः । सकल-

---

१ मण्डले. २ अवधीरित. ३ आदेहि; आधेहि.

सुस्वप्नमवलोकितवती । सा तदा दयितमनोरथपुष्पभूतं गर्भमधत्त[1] । राजाऽपि संपन्न्यक्कृताखण्डलः सुहृन्नृपमण्डलं समाहूय निजसंपन्मनोरथानुरूपं देव्याः सीमन्तोत्सवं व्यधत्त ।

एकदा हितैः सुहृन्मन्त्रिपुरोहितैः सभायां सिंहासनासीनो गुणैरहीनो ललाटतटन्यस्ताञ्जलिना द्वारपालेन व्यज्ञापि—'देव, देवसंदर्शनलालसमानसः कोऽपि देवेन विरच्यार्चनार्हो यतिर्द्वारदेशमध्यास्ते' इति । तदनुज्ञातेन तेन स संयमी नृपसमीपमनायि । भूपतिरायान्तं तं विलोक्य सम्यग्ज्ञाततदीयगूढचारभावो निखिलमनुचरनिकरं विसृज्य मन्त्रिजनसमेतः प्रणतमेनं[2] मन्दहासमभाषत—'ननु तापस, देशं सापदेशं भ्रमन्भवांस्तत्र तत्र भवदभिज्ञातं कथयतु' इति । तेनाभाषि भूभ्रमणबलिना प्राञ्जलिना—'देव, शिरसि देवस्याज्ञामादायैनं निर्दोषं वेषं स्वीकृत्य मालवेन्द्रनगरं प्रविश्य तत्र गूढतरं वर्तमानस्तस्य राज्ञः समस्तमुदन्तजातं विदित्वा

---

लोकस्यैककारणमादिहेतुः । दयितमनोरथफलस्य पुष्पमिव भूतम् । संपदा न्यक्कृत आखण्डल इन्द्रो येन । सुहृदश्च ये नृपाश्च स्तेषां मण्डलम् । सुहृदश्च नृपाश्चेति वा । **निजेति** । निजसंपन्मनोरथयोरनुरूपं सदृशम् । रूपस्य योग्यमनुरूपम् । सीमन्तोत्सवं सीमन्तोन्नयनसंज्ञः संस्कारस्तदनुषङ्गिकमुत्सवम् । तथा चाश्वलायनः— 'चतुर्थे गर्भमासे सीमन्तोन्नयनम्' इति । सीमन्तः केशवेशो यस्मिन्कर्मण्युन्नीयत तत्सीमन्तोन्नयनम् । **एकदेति** । हितैः पथ्यैः । सिंहासनं भद्रासनं तत्रासीनः । अहीनोऽन्यूनः । ललाटतटे न्यस्तः अञ्जलिर्येन तेन । लालसमभिलाषयुक्तम् । विरच्या कर्तव्या यार्चना तामर्हतीति । यतिर्भिक्षुः । **द्वारदेशमिति** । 'अधिशीङ्स्थासाम्-' इति कर्मत्वम् । द्वारि तिष्ठतीत्यर्थः । तेनानुज्ञातस्तदनुज्ञातः । संयमी यतिः । आयान्तमागच्छन्तम् । सम्यक्सुष्ठु ज्ञातोऽवगतः । तदीयः तत्संबन्धी गूढः प्रच्छन्नश्चारभावो यस्य सः । निखिलं सर्वम् । अनुचरनिकरमनुयायिवर्गम् । विसृज्य दूरमपसार्य । प्रणतं प्रह्वम् । मन्दहासमिति क्रियाविशेषणम् । तत्र तत्र तेषु तेषु स्थानेषु । भवताऽभिज्ञातं भवदभिज्ञातम् । कथयत्वित्यत्र भवच्छब्दस्य कर्तृत्वेन प्रयोगात्प्रथमपुरुषः । भूभ्रमणे भ्रमणविषये बली समर्थस्तेन । प्रबद्धोऽञ्जलिर्येन । **शिरसीति** । अङ्गीकृत्येत्यर्थः । निर्दोषं दोषविवर्जितम् । मालवेन्द्रो मानसारः । गूढतरम् । अतिशयेन गूढमित्यर्थः । उदन्तो वार्ता उदन्तजात

---

१ आधत्त. २ प्रणमन्तम्.

प्रत्यागमम् । मानी मानसारः स्वसैनिकायुष्मत्तान्तराये संपराये भवतः पराजयमनुभूय वैलक्ष्यलक्ष्यहृदयो वीतदयो महाकालनिवासिनं कालीविलासिनमनश्वरं महेश्वरं समाराध्य तपःप्रभावसंतुष्टादस्मादेकवीरारातिघ्नीं[1] भयदां गदां लब्ध्वाऽऽत्मानमप्रतिभटं मन्यमानो महाभिमानो भवन्तमभियोक्तुमुद्युङ्क्ते । ततः परं देव एव प्रमाणम्' इति। तदालोच्य निश्चितैस्तत्कृत्यैरमात्यै[2] राजा विज्ञापितोऽभूत्–'देव, निरुपायेन देवसहायेन[3] योद्धुमरातिरायाति । तस्मादस्माकं युद्धं सांप्रतमसांप्रतम् । सहसा दुर्गसंश्रयः कार्यः' इति । तैर्बहुधा विज्ञापितोऽप्यखर्वेण गर्वेण विराजमानो राजा तद्वाक्यमकृत्यमित्यनादृत्य प्रतियोद्धुमना बभूव । शितिकण्ठदत्तशक्तिसारो मानसारो[4] योद्धुमनसामग्रीभूय सामग्रीसमेतोऽक्लेशं मगधदेशं प्रविवेश । तदा तदाकर्ण्य मन्त्रिणो भूमहेन्द्रं मगधेन्द्रं कथंचिदनुनीय रिपुभिरसाध्ये[5] विन्ध्याटवीमध्येऽवरोधान्मूलबल-

मखिलां प्रवृत्तिम् । विदित्वा ज्ञात्वा । **मानीति** । ताच्छील्ये णिनिः । स्वसैनिका निजभटास्तेषामायुष्मत्ता जीवितमर्यादा तस्या अन्तरायो विघ्नस्तस्मिन् । संपराये युद्धे । भवतो देवात् । वैलक्ष्येण दैन्येन लक्ष्यमाक्रान्तं हृदयं यस्य सः । वीता नष्टा दया यस्य सः । महाकाले निवासोऽस्त्यस्य तस्य । कालीविलासिनं कालीपतिम् । अनश्वरं नाशरहितम् । महांश्चासावीश्वरश्च महेश्वरस्तम् । समाराध्य सम्यगाराध्य । तपसस्तदाचरितस्य प्रभावः सामर्थ्यं तेन संतुष्टात्प्रीतात् । अस्मान्महेश्वरात् । एकवीरश्चासावरातिश्च तं हन्तीति । भयदां भयदात्रीम् । गदामायुधविशेषम् । अप्रतिभटं न विद्यते प्रतिभटो यस्य तम् । महानभिमानोऽहंकारो यस्य सः । अभियोक्तुमभिषेणयितुम् । उद्युङ्क्ते उद्युक्तो भवति । देव एव प्रमाणम् । किंकर्तव्यतानिर्णेतेत्यर्थः । निश्चितं निर्णीतं तत्कृत्यं तत्कालोचितं कृत्यं राजकृत्यं वा यैस्तैः । अमात्यैर्मन्त्रिभिः । निरुपायेन नास्त्युपायः प्रतीकारो यस्य तेन । देवसहायेन दैवसामग्र्येति यावत् । अरातिः शत्रुः । सांप्रतमधुना । असांप्रतमयुक्तम् । न खर्वोऽखर्वः । महानित्यर्थः । विराजमानः शोभमानः । अकृत्यं कर्तुमनुचितम् । अनादृत्य अनादरं कृत्वा । शितिकण्ठः शिवस्तेन दत्ता या शक्तिः प्रहरणविशेषः स एव सारो बलं यस्य सः । योद्धुमनसां युद्धकामानाम् । 'तुं काममनसोरपि' इत्यनुस्वारलोपः । अग्रीभूय पुरो भूत्वा । सामग्र्या समेतो युक्तः । अक्लेशमिति क्रियाविशेषणम् । 'तत आकर्ण्य' इति छेदः । भुवि पृथिव्यां महेन्द्रस्तम् । कथंचिद्यत्नेन । अनुनीय प्रार्थ्य । असाध्ये दुर्ग्राहनीये । अवरोधान्राजस्त्रियः । मूलबलेन प्रधानसैन्येन

१ एव वीरारातिघ्नीं. २ निश्चितकृ०. ३ दैवसहायेन. ४ अस्मात्पूर्वं मानसार इत्यधि०. ५ अबाध्ये.

रक्षितान्निवेशयामासुः । राजहंसस्तु प्रशस्तवीतदैन्यसैन्यसमेतस्तीव्रगत्या निर्गत्याधिकरुषं द्विषं रुरोध । परस्परबद्धवैरयोरेतयोः शूरयोस्तदा तदालोकनकुतूहलागतगगनचराश्चर्यकारणे रणे वर्तमाने जयाकाङ्क्षी मालवदेशरक्षी विविधायुधस्थैर्यचर्याञ्चितसमरतुलितामरेश्वरस्य मगधेश्वरस्य तस्योपरि पुरा पुरारातिदत्तां गदां प्राहिणोत्[1] । निशितशरनिकरशकलीकृताऽपि[2] सा पशुपतिशासनस्यावन्ध्यतया सूतं निहत्य रथस्थं राजानं मूर्छितमकार्षीत् । ततो वीतप्रग्रहा अक्षतविग्रहा वाहा रथमादाय दैवगत्याऽन्तःपुरशरण्यं महारण्यं प्राविशन् । मालवनाथो जयलक्ष्मीसनाथो मगधराज्यं प्राज्यं समाक्रम्य पुष्पपुरमध्यतिष्ठत् ।

तत्र हेतिततिहतिश्रान्ता अमात्या दैवगत्याऽनुत्क्रान्तजीविता[3] निशान्तवातलब्धसंज्ञाः कथंचिदाश्वस्य राजानं समन्तादन्वीक्ष्या-

---

रक्षितान् । निवेशयामासुः स्थापितवन्तः । **प्रशस्तेति** । वीतं गतं दैन्यं यस्मात्तद्वीतदैन्यम् । प्रशस्तं च तद्वीतदैन्यं च तादृशं सैन्यं तेन समेतः । तीव्रा चासौ गतिश्च तया । **निर्गत्येति** । अधिका रुट् यस्य तम् । द्विषमरिं रुरोध । **परस्परेति** । परस्परेण बद्धं वैरं याभ्यां तयोः । **तदालोकनेति** । तस्यालोकने दर्शने यत्कुतूहलं कौतुकं तदर्थमागता ये गगनचरा देवाः तेषामाश्चर्यस्य कारणं तस्मिन् । वर्तमाने प्रवृत्ते । जयमाकाङ्क्षते सः । मालवदेशस्य रक्षी रक्षिता नृपः । **विविधेति** । विविधानि नैकप्रकाराणि यान्यायुधानि प्रहरणानि तेषां स्थैर्येण चर्या चालनमुपयोगः प्रयोगो वा । तयाऽञ्चितं युक्तं यत्समरं युद्धं तस्मिंस्तुलितोऽमरेश्वर इन्द्रो येन तस्य । **पुरारातीति** । पुरारातिः शंकरस्तेन दत्ताम् । निशितास्तीक्ष्णाश्च ते शराश्च तेषां निकरः समुदायस्तेन शकलीकृता खण्डशः कृताऽपि । सा गदा । पशूनां जीवानां पतिः पशुपतिः शिवस्तस्य शासनस्याज्ञाया अवन्ध्यतया सफलभावित्वात् । **रथस्थं** रथे तिष्ठतीति । वीताः प्रग्रहा येषां ते वीतप्रग्रहा मुक्तरश्मयः । अक्षतो विग्रहः शरीरं येषाम् । वाहा अश्वाः । दैवगत्या यदृच्छया । अन्तःपुरस्य राजस्त्रीणां शरणे साधु शरण्यम् । **जयलक्ष्मीति** । जयलक्ष्म्या सनाथो युक्तः । प्राज्यं पुष्कलम् । पुष्पपुरमिति । 'अधिशीङ्स्थासां–' इति कर्मत्वम् । **तत्रेति** । हेतीनामायुधानां ततयः समुदायास्तैर्हतिस्ताडनं प्रहारस्तेन श्रान्ताः । **अनुत्क्रान्तेति** । न उत्क्रान्तं जीवितं प्राणा येषां ते । निशाया अन्तोऽवसानं तत्संबन्धिवातेनार्थाच्छीतलेन लब्धा प्राप्ता संज्ञा यैस्ते । कथंचिन्महता आयासेन । आश्वस्य

---

१ श्वरस्योपरि पुराराति०. २ शरशतेन शकलीकृता. ३ अप्रत्युत्क्रान्त; प्रत्यु०.

नवलोकितवन्तो दैन्यवन्तो देवीमवापुः । वसुमती तु तेभ्यो निखिलसैन्यक्षतिं राज्ञोऽदृश्यत्वं चाकर्ण्योद्विग्ना शोकसागरमग्ना रमणानुगमने[1] मतिं व्यधत्त । 'कल्याणि, भूरमणमरणमनिश्चितम् । किं च दैवज्ञकथितो मथितोद्धताराति: सार्वभौमोऽभिरामो भविता सुकुमारः कुमारस्त्वदुदरे वसति । तस्मादद्य तव मरणमनुचितम्' इति भूषितभाषितैरमात्यपुरोहितैरनुनीयमानया तया क्षणं क्षणहीनया तूष्णीमस्थायि । अथार्धरात्रे निद्रानिलीढनेत्रे परिजने विजने शोकपारावारमपारमुत्तर्तुमशक्नुवती सेनानिवेशदेश निःशब्दलेशं शनैरतिक्रम्य यस्मिन्रथस्य संसक्ततया तदानयनपलायनश्रान्ता गन्तुमक्षमाः क्षमापतिरथ्याः पथ्याकुलाः पूर्वमातिष्ठंस्तस्य निकटवटतरोः शाखायां मृतिरेखायामिव क्वचिदुत्तरीयार्धेन बन्धनं मृतिसाधनं विरच्य मर्तुकामाऽभिरामा[2]

---

धैर्यावष्टम्भं कृत्वा । समन्तादितस्ततः । दैन्यवन्तो दैन्यं खेदस्तद्वन्तः । **निखिलेति** । निखिलस्य सर्वस्य सैन्यस्य क्षतिर्नाशस्तम् । **शोकेति** । शोक एव सागरस्तस्मिन्मग्ना । रमणानुगमने पतिमनु मरणे । मतिं व्यधत्त निश्चयं चकार । **कल्याणीति** । कल्याणि कल्याणलक्ष गोपते इति संबुद्धिः । भुवो रमणो वल्लभः । पतिरित्यर्थः । देवस्येति तात्पर्यम् । अनिश्चितं न निर्णीतम् । किं चापि चान्यच्च । दैवज्ञेन कार्तान्तिकेन । ज्यौतिषिकेणेत्यर्थः । कथितः । मथिता मथिष्यमाणा उद्धता धृष्टा अरातयो येन सः । सार्वभौमश्चक्रवर्ती । अभिरामो मनोज्ञः । अनुचितमयुक्तम् । भूषितं भूषणैराढ्यं भाषितं भाषणं येषां तैः । भाषितमिति भावे क्तः । **अमात्येति** । अमात्याश्च पुरोहिताश्च तैः । पुरोहिताः पुरोधसः । अनुनीयत इत्यनुनीयमाना तया । क्षणं क्षणपर्यन्तम् । 'कालाध्वनोः-' इति द्वितीया । तूष्णीं जोषम् । अथानन्तरम् । अर्धरात्रे निशीथे । निद्रया निलीढे नेत्रे यस्य स तस्मिन् । परिजनेऽनुचरवर्गे । विजने विविक्ते । शोकपारावारं शोकसमुद्रम् । अपारं पारयितुमशक्यम् । सेनाया निवेशः शिबिरम् । वासस्थानमिति यावत् । तस्य देशः प्रदेशः । निर्गतः शब्दलेशो यस्मात्तम् । संसक्तस्य भावस्तया । तस्यानयनं तदानयनं तस्मिन्यत्पलायनं तेन श्रान्ताः । अक्षमा असमर्थाः । क्षमायाः पृथ्व्याः पतिः स्वामी भर्ता वा तस्य रथ्या वाहाः । 'तद्वहति रथयुग-' इति यः । 'पथि आकुलाः' इति च्छेदः । मृतेर्मरणस्य रेखा तस्याम् । उत्तरीयस्य संव्यानस्य । विरच्य कृत्वा । मर्तुं कामो यस्याः सा । 'तुं काममनसोरपि' इत्यनुस्वारलोपः ।

---

१ नुमरणे. २ अभिरामेति नास्ति क्वचित्.

वाङ्माधुरीविरसी[1]कृतकलकण्ठा साश्रुकण्ठा व्यलपत्—‘ लावण्योपमितपुष्पसायक भूनायक, [2]भवानेव भाविन्यपि जन्मनि वल्लभो भवतु ’ इति । तदाकर्ण्य नीहारकरकिरणनिकरसंपर्कलब्धावबोधो मागधोऽगाधरुधिरवि[3]क्षरणनष्टचेष्टो देवीवाक्य[4]मेव निश्चिन्वानस्तन्वानः प्रियवचनानि शनैस्तामाह्वयत् । सा ससंभ्रममागत्यामन्दहृदयानन्दसंफुल्लवदनारविन्दा तमुपोषिताभ्यामिवानिमिषिताभ्यां लोचनाभ्यां पिब[5]न्ती विकस्वरेण स्वरेण पुरोहितामात्यजनमुच्चैराहूय तेभ्यस्तमदर्शयत् । राजा निटिलत[6]टचुम्बितनिजचरणाम्बुजैः प्रशंसितदैवमाहात्म्यैरमात्यैरभाणि—‘ देव, रथ्यचयः सारथ्यपगमे रथं रभसादरण्यमनयत् ’ इति । ‘ तत्र निहतसैनिकग्रामे संग्रामे मालवपतिनाऽऽराधितपुरारातिना प्रहितया गदया दयाहीनेन ताडितो मूर्छामागत्यात्र वने निशा[7]न्तपवनेन बोधितोऽभवम् ’ इति महीपतिरकथयत् ।

---

वाचो माधुरी माधुर्यं तया विरसीकृतोऽधरीकृतः कलकण्ठः कोकिलो यया सा । व्यलपत् । रुरोदेत्यर्थः । लावण्येनोपमितः पुष्पसायको मदनो येन तत्संबुद्धौ । भूनायक पृथ्वीपते । भाविन्यागामिनि । वल्लभो रमणः । नीहारकरश्चन्द्रस्तस्य किरणानां मयूखानां निकरस्य समुदायस्य संपर्केण लब्धः प्राप्तोऽवबोधः संज्ञा येन सः । प्रकृतिमापन्न इत्यर्थः । मागधो मगधाधिपो राजहंसः । अगाधं बहुलम् । निश्चिन्वानो निश्चयं कुर्वन् । ससंभ्रमं सत्वरम् । न मन्दोऽमन्दः । हृदयस्यानन्दो हृदयानन्दः । अमन्दश्चासौ हृदयानन्दश्चामन्दहृदयानन्दः । तेन संफुल्लं सम्यग्विकासितं प्रसन्नं वदनारविन्दं मुखकमलं यस्याः सा । उपोषिताभ्यां जातोत्कण्ठाभ्यामित्यर्थः । अनिमिषिताभ्यां निमेषरहिताभ्याम् । विकस्वरेण समुन्मीलितेन । उच्चैरिति क्रियाविशेषणम् । निटिलतटेन भालस्थलेन चुम्बितं निजचरणाम्बुजं यैस्तैः । प्रशंसितं दैवस्य माहात्म्यं महिमा यैस्तैः । रथ्यचयोऽश्वसमुदायः । सारथेरपगमो नाशस्तस्मिन् । रभसाद्वेगेन । निहतो निःशेषं हतः सैनिकग्रामो योधसमूहो यस्मिंस्तथाभूते । आराधितः संतोषितः पुरारातिः शिवो येन तेन । प्रहितया प्रेरितया । निशान्तः प्रभातं तत्संबन्धिना पवनेन वायुना । ‘ निशीत– ’ इति पाठे नितरां शीत इति पवनविशेषणम् । ‘ निशीथ– ’ इति पाठे निशीथोऽ-

---

१ दूरीकृतकलकण्ठकण्ठा. २ भवानेकः. ३ चिरक्षरण. ४ देवीवाक्यमिव. ५ संपीय. ६ तल. ७ निशीत; निशीथ.

ततो विरचितमहेन मन्त्रिनिवहेन विरचितदैवानुकूल्येन कालेन शिबिरमानीयापनीताशेषशल्यो विकसितनिजाननारविन्दो राजा सहसा विरोपितव्रणोऽकारि । विरोधिदैवधिक्कृतपुरुषकारो दैन्यव्याप्ताकारो मगधाधिपतिरधिकाधिरमात्यसंमत्या मृदुभाषितया तया वसुमत्या मत्या कलितया च समबोधि—'देव, सकलस्य भूपालकुलस्य मध्ये तेजोवरिष्ठो गरिष्ठो भवानद्य विन्ध्यवनमध्यं निवसतीति जलबुद्बुदसमाना विराजमाना संपत्तडिल्लतेव सहसैवोदेति नश्यति च । तन्निखिलं दैवायत्तमेवावधार्य कार्यम् । किं च पुरा हरिश्चन्द्ररामचन्द्रमुख्या असंख्या महीन्द्रा ऐश्वर्योपमितमहेन्द्रा दैवतन्त्रं दुःखयन्त्रं सम्यगनुभूय पश्चादनेककालं निजराज्यमकुर्वन् । तद्वदेव भवान्भविष्यति । कंचन कालं विरचितदैवसमाधिर्गताधिस्तिष्ठतु तावत्' इति ।

ततः सकलसैन्यसमन्वितो राजहंसस्तपोविभ्राजमानं वामदेवनामानं तपोधनं निजाभिलाषावाप्तिसाधनं जगाम । तं प्रणम्य

---

धराश्रस्तत्संबन्धिनेति । विरचितो महः पूजासत्कारो येन तेन । मन्त्रिणां निवहो वृन्दं तेन । विरचितं कृतं दैवानुकूल्यं येन तेन । शिबिरं सेनाया वासस्थानम् । अपनीतान्युद्धृतान्यशेषाणि सर्वाणि शल्यानि बाणाग्राणि शङ्कवो वा यस्य सः । शलति गच्छतीति शल्यम् । विरोपिताश्चिकित्सिता व्रणा यस्य सः । विरोधिनाऽननुकूलेन दैवेन भागधेयेन धिक्कृतः पुरुषकारो विक्रमः पौरुषमिति यावद्यस्य सः । दैन्येन खेदेन व्याप्त आकारो यस्य सः । अतिशयेनाधिका आधिर्मनोव्यथा यस्य सः । अमात्यानां संमतिस्तया । मृदु भाषितं यस्यास्तया । मत्या बुद्ध्या कलितया युक्तया । तेजसा वरिष्ठः । अतिशयेन गुरुर्गरिष्ठः । 'प्रियस्थिर—' इत्यादिना 'वर्' 'गर्' इत्यादेशाः । जलस्य बुद्बुदो विकारस्तत्समाना तत्सदृशी । तडिल्लता विद्युत् । सहसाऽकस्मात् । उदेत्युद्गच्छति दृक्पथमायाति । अवधार्य निर्णेतव्यम् । ऐश्वर्येण विभवेनोपमितस्तुल्यीकृतो महेन्द्रो देवराजो यैस्ते । दैवतन्त्रं दैवचालितम् । दुःखयन्त्रं दुःखमेव यन्त्रं तत् । विरचिता दैवसमाधिर्येन सः । गत आधिर्यस्य सः । **तत इति** । समन्वितो युक्तः । तपसा विशेषेण भ्राजते दीप्यतेऽसौ तम् । तप एव धनं यस्य तम् । निजोऽभिलाषस्तस्यावाप्तिः

---

१ अधिकाधिकार्तिः. २ निजकार्यम्.

तेन कृतातिथ्यस्तस्मै कथितकथ्यस्तदाश्रमे दूरीकृतश्रमे कंचन कालमुषित्वा निजराज्याभिलाषी मितभाषी सोमकुलावतंसो राजहंसो मुनिमभाषत—'भगवन्, मानसारः प्रबलेन दैवबलेन मां निर्जित्य मद्भोग्यं राज्यमनुभवति। तद्वदहमप्युग्रं तपो विरच्य तमरातिमुन्मूलयिष्यामि लोकशरण्येन भवत्कारुण्येनेति नियमवन्तं भवन्तं प्राप्नवम्' इति। ततस्त्रिकालज्ञस्तपोधनो राजानमवोचत्—'सखे, शरीरकार्श्यकारिणा तपसाऽलम्। वसुमतीगर्भस्थः सकलरिपुकुलमर्दनो राजनन्दनो नूनं संभविष्यति। कंचन कालं तूष्णीमास्स्व' इति। गगनचारिण्याऽपि वाण्या 'सत्यमेतत्' इति तदैवावाचि[1]। राजाऽपि मुनिवाक्यमङ्गीकृत्यातिष्ठत्।

ततः संपूर्णगर्भदिवसा वसुमती सुमुहूर्ते सकललक्षणलक्षितं सुतमसूत। ब्रह्मवर्चसेन तुलितवेधसं पुरोधसं पुरस्कृत्य कृत्यविन्महीपतिः कुमारं सुकुमारं जातसंस्कारेण बालालंकारेण च विराजमानं राजवाहननामानं व्यधत्त। तस्मिन्नेव काले सुमतिसुमन्त्रसुमित्रसुश्रुतानां मन्त्रिणां प्रमतिमित्रगुप्तमन्त्रगुप्तविश्रुताख्या महाभिख्याः[2]

---

प्राप्तिस्तस्य साधनं साधनभूतम्। कृतमातिथ्यं यस्य सः। कथितं निवेदितं कथ्यं कथयितुं योग्यं सर्वं येनैतादृशः। **तदाश्रम इति**। दूरीकृतः श्रमो यत्रैतादृशे। सोमकुलस्य चन्द्रवंशस्यावतंसो भूषणं ललामभूतः। मानसार इति राजनाम। मया भोग्यं भोक्तव्यम्। अरातिं शत्रुम्। उन्मूलयिष्याम्युन्मूलयितुमुद्यतोऽस्मि। लोकानां शरणे रक्षणे साधु तेन। नियमवन्तं व्रतिनम्। त्रिकालज्ञो भूतभविष्यद्वर्तमानकालगतं जानातीति तथा। सखे इति कोमलामन्त्रणम्। शरीरस्य देहस्य कार्श्यं कृशस्य भावस्तत्करोतीति तेन। तपसाऽलं तपो माऽनुतिष्ठेति भावः। नूनं निश्चितम्। तूष्णीं जोषम्। **तत इति**। संपूर्णा गर्भदिवसा नव मासा नव दिवसाश्च यस्याः सा। सकललक्षणैर्लक्षितं युक्तम्। ब्रह्मणो वर्चो ब्रह्मवर्चसम्। 'ब्रह्महस्तिभ्यां वर्चसः' इत्यच्। तुलितो वेधा ब्रह्मा येन तम्। पुरोधसमुपाध्यायम्। कृत्यं वेत्तीति तथा। जातसंस्कारेण जननकालेऽनुष्ठितसंस्कारेण बालार्हैरलंकारैश्च विराजमानं विशेषेण शोभमानम्। व्यधत्त कृतवान्। सुमत्यादीनि मन्त्रिनामानि। प्रमत्यादीनि सुतनामानि। महत्यभिख्या शोभा येषां ते महाभिख्याः। 'महदभिख्याः' इति प्रयोगश्चिन्त्यः।

---

१ ०वावोचि. २ महदभिख्याः.

सूनवो नवोद्यदिन्दुरुचश्चिरायुषः समजायन्त। राजवाहनो मन्त्रिपुत्रै-रात्ममित्रैः सह बालकेलीरनुभवन्नवर्धत।

अथ कदाचिदेकेन तापसेन रसेन राजलक्षणविराजितं कंचिन्नयनानन्दकरं सुकुमारं कुमारं राज्ञे समर्प्यावाचि—'भूवल्लभ कुशसमिदानयनाय वनं गतेन मया काचिदशरण्या व्यक्तकार्पण्याऽश्रु मुञ्चन्ती वनिता विलोकिता। 'निर्जने वने किंनिमित्तं रुद्यते त्वया' इति पृष्टा सा करुरुहैरश्रु[1] प्रमृज्य सगद्गदं मामवोचत्—'मुने लावण्याजितपुष्पसायके मिथिलानायके कीर्तिव्यापृत[2]सुधर्मणि निजसुहृदो मगधराजस्य सीमन्तिनीसीमन्तमहोत्सवाय पुत्रदारसमन्विते पुष्पपुरमुपेत्य कंचन कालमधिवसति समाराधितगिरीशो मालवाधीशो मगधराजं योद्धुमभ्यगात्। तत्र प्रख्यातयोरेतयोरसंख्ये संख्ये वर्तमाने सुहृत्साहाय्यकं कुर्वाणो निजबले सति[3] विदेहे विदेहेश्वरः प्रहारवर्मा जयवता रिपुणाऽभिगृह्य कारुण्येन पुण्येन विसृष्टो हतावशेषेण शून्येन सैन्येन

नवः प्रातिपदिकः। उद्यन्नुद्गच्छन्। इन्दुश्चन्द्रमाः। तस्य रुक्कान्तिरिव कान्तिर्येषां ते। चिरायुषश्चिरजीविनः। अथेति। तापसेन मुनिना। रसेन रागेण। कुशाश्च समिधश्च तेषामानयनं तस्मै। नास्ति शरण्यं रक्षिता यस्याः सा। व्यक्तं कार्पण्यं दैन्यं यस्याः सा। मुञ्चन्तीत्यत्र तुदादित्वाद्वैकल्पिको नुम्। निर्जने जनसंचाररहिते। कररुहैः अङ्गुलिभिः। करे रोहन्तीति तैः। यद्यपि कररुहशब्दो नखपरस्तथाऽप्यत्राङ्गुलिवाचकः। करसरोरुहैरिति पाठे करावेव सरोरुहाणि तैः। करसरोरुहाभ्यामिति समीचीनः पाठः। प्रमृज्य। 'मृजू शुद्धौ' इति धातुः। ल्यबन्तम्। सगद्गदं गद्गदस्वरेण। लावण्येन सौन्दर्येण जितः पुष्पसायको मदनो येन तस्मिन्। कीर्त्या व्यापृता सुधर्मा देवसभा येन तस्मिन्। 'धर्मादनिच्केवलात्' इति धर्मशब्दस्य धर्मन्नादेशः। निजसुहृदः स्वमित्रस्य। सीमन्तिनी वधूस्तस्याः सीमन्तमहोत्सवो गर्भिण्यवस्थायामनुष्ठातव्यस्य सीमन्तोन्नयनाख्यसंस्कारस्योत्सवस्तदर्थम्। पुत्रश्च दाराश्च पुत्रदारास्तैः समन्विते युक्ते। 'उपान्वध्याङ्वसः' इत्यनेन कालस्य कर्मत्वम्। समाराधितः सम्यक्पूजितः संतोषितो वा गिरीशः शिवो येन सः। संख्ये युद्धे। सुहृदः साहाय्यकम्। साहाय्यमेव साहाय्यकम्। स्वार्थे कप्। निजबले आत्मसैन्ये। विदेहे मृत इत्यर्थः। 'असति विधेये' इति पाठे 'विधेयो विनयग्राही' इति कोशाद्विनयातिक्रमणशील इति भावः। विदेहानामीश्वरः प्रभुः। शून्येन रिक्तेन।

१ करसरोरुहैः. २ व्याप्त. ३ असति विधेये.

सह स्वपुरगमनमकरोत् । ततो वनमार्गेण दुर्गेण गच्छन्नधिकबलेन शबरबलेन रभसादभिहन्यमानो मूलबलाभिरक्षितावरोधः स महानिरोधः पलायिष्ट । तदीयार्भकयोर्यमयोर्धात्रीभावेन परिकल्पिताऽहं मद्दुहिताऽपि तीव्रगतिं भूपतिमनुगन्तुमक्षमे अभूव । तत्र विवृतवदनः कोऽपि रूपी कोप इव व्याघ्रः शीघ्रं मामाघ्रातुमागतवान् । भीताऽहमुदग्रग्राविण स्खलन्ती पर्यपतम् । मदीयपाणिभ्रष्टो बालकः कस्यापि कपिलाशवस्य क्रोडमभ्यलीयत । तच्छवाकर्षिणोऽमर्षिणो व्याघ्रस्य प्राणान्बाणो बाणासनयन्त्रमुक्तोऽपाहरत् । विलोलालको बालकोऽपि शबरैरादाय कुत्रचिदुपानीयत । कुमारमपरमुद्वहन्ती मद्दुहिता कुत्र गता न जाने । साऽहं मोहं गता केनापि कृपालुना वृष्णिपालेन स्वकुटीरमावेश्य विरोपितव्रणाऽभवम् । ततः स्वस्थीभूय भूयः क्ष्माभर्तुरन्तिकमुपतिष्ठासुरसहायतया दुहितुरनभिज्ञाततया च व्याकुलीभवामि ' इत्यभिदधाना ' एकाकिन्यपि स्वामिनं गमिष्यामि ' इति सा तदैव

---

दुःखेन गन्तुं शक्यो दुर्गस्तेन । अधिकं बलं यस्य तेन । शबराणां भिल्लानां बलेन सेनया । रभसाद्वेगेन । अभिहन्यमानः । कर्मणि शानच् । मूलबलं प्रधानसैन्यं तेनाभिरक्षितोऽवरोधः शुद्धान्तो यस्य सः । महान्निरोधो यस्य स तथा । पलायिष्ट । ' अय गतौ ' इति धातुः । परेत्युपसर्गस्थरस्य स्थाने ' उपसर्गस्यायतौ ' इति लादेशः । लुङ् । तस्येमौ तदीयौ च तावर्भकौ तयोः । यमयोः सहजातयोः । धात्र्या उपमातुर्भावस्तेन । तीव्रा गतिर्यस्य तम् । अक्षमे अभूवेत्यत्र प्रगृह्यत्वान्न संधिः । रूपी मूर्तिमान् । आघ्रातुं नाशयितुम् । उद्गतान्यग्राणि यस्यैतादृशो यो ग्रावा तस्मिन् । ' उदग्रपाणिः ' इति पाठे उदग्रः पाणिर्यस्याः सेत्यहमित्यस्य विशेषणं द्रष्टव्यम् । भ्रष्टश्च्युतः । कपिलाया गोः शवः कुणपस्तस्य । क्रोडमङ्कदेशम् । अभ्यलीयत प्रच्छन्नः अभूत् । बाणासनं धनुस्तदेव यन्त्रं तस्मान्मुक्तः । अपाहरज्जहार । विलोलाश्चञ्चला अलकाश्चूर्णकुन्तला यस्य सः । आदाय गृहीत्वा । कुत्रचिदनिर्दिष्टे । अज्ञातप्रदेशे इति यावत् । अपरं यमजं द्वितियम् । उद्वहन्ती धारयन्ती । सेति पूर्वनिर्दिष्टा । मोहं गता विगतसंज्ञा । वृष्णिपालेन मेषपालेन । स्वकुटीरं स्ववासगृहम् । आवेश्य । णिजन्ताल्ल्यप् । विरोपिता व्रणा यस्याः सा । भूयः पुनः । क्ष्माभर्तुर्नरेन्द्रस्य । उपतिष्ठासुरुपस्थातुमिच्छुः । अभिदधानाऽभिधत्तेऽसौ । एका एवैकाकिन्यसहाया । तदैव तस्मिन्नेव क्षणे ।

---

१ उदग्रपाणिः. २ उपा०.

निरगात् । अहमपि भवन्मित्रस्य विदेहनाथस्य विपन्निमित्तं विषादमनुभवंस्तदन्वयाङ्कुरं कुमारमन्विष्यंस्तदैकं चण्डिकामन्दिरं सुन्दरं प्रागाम् । तत्र संततमेवंविधविजयसिद्धये कुमारं देवतोपहारं करिष्यन्तः किराताः 'महीरुहशाखावलम्बितमेनमसिलतया वा, सैकततले खनननिक्षिप्तचरणं लक्ष्यीकृत्य शितशरनिकरेण वा, अनेकचरणैः पलायमानं कुक्कुरबालकैर्वा दंशयित्वा संहनिष्यामः' इति भाषमाणा मया समभ्यभाष्यन्त—'ननु किरातोत्तमाः घोरप्रचारे कान्तारे स्खलितपथः स्थविरभूसुरोऽहं मम पुत्रकं क्वचिच्छायायां निक्षिप्य मार्गान्वेषणाय किंचिदन्तरमगच्छम् । स कुत्र गतः केन वा गृहीतः परीक्ष्यापि न वीक्ष्यते । तन्मुखावलोकनेन विनाऽनेकान्यहान्यतीतानि । किं करोमि क्व यामि भवद्भिर्न किमदर्शि' इति । 'द्विजोत्तम कश्चिदत्र तिष्ठति । किमेष तव नन्दनः सत्यमेव । तदेनं गृहाण' इत्युक्त्वा दैवानुकूल्येन मह्यं तं व्यतरन् । तेभ्यो दत्ताशीरहं बालकमङ्गीकृत्य शिशिरोदकादिनोपचारे-

---

विषादं खेदम् । तस्यान्वयो वंशस्तस्याङ्कुरः प्ररोहः । चण्डिकाया मन्दिरमायतनम् । एवं विधा प्रकारो यस्य तादृशो यो विजयस्तस्य सिद्धिस्तस्यै । देवतायै उपहारस्तम् । महीरुहो वृक्षस्तस्य शाखायामवलम्बितम् । असिलता खड्गः । इदं केचित्किराता आहुः । सिकताः सन्त्यस्मिन्निति सैकतम् । सैकतं च तत्तलं च । खनने निक्षिप्तौ भूमौ कीलितौ चरणौ यस्य तम् । शितास्तीक्ष्णाश्च ते शराश्च तेषां निकरेण । इत्यन्ये । अनेकचरणैरिति कुक्कुरबालकैरित्यस्य विशेषणम् । पलायमानमेनं बालकम् । दंशयित्वा दंशं कारयित्वा । 'दंदशयित्वा' इति पाठे यङन्तप्रयोगः । इदमप्यपरे । किरातोत्तमाः । प्रार्थनानुकूलमेतत्संबोधनम् । घोरः प्रचारः संचारो यस्मिंस्तथा । कान्तारे वने । स्खलितः पन्था यस्य सः । 'ऋक्पूरब्धूःपथामानक्षे' इत्यनेन पथिन् इत्यस्य पथः । स्थविरो वृद्धः । भूसुरो भुवि पृथ्व्यां सुरो द्विजः । निक्षिप्य संस्थाप्य । मार्गस्यान्वेषणं गवेषणम् । मुखावलोकनेन विना । 'पृथग्विनानाना—' इति तृतीया । अतीतानि गतानि । अदर्शि । 'दृशिर् प्रेक्षणे' । कर्मणि लुङ् । गृहाण । 'ग्रह उपादाने' । लोटो रूपम् । दैवस्यानुकूल्यं तेन । व्यतरन्दत्तवन्तः । दत्ता आशीः आशीर्वादो येन सः ।

---

१ विलम्बि°. २ दंदश°. ३ किराताः; तमोघोरप्रचारे, सुघोरप्र°. ४ °वलोकनसुखेन. ५ सत्यमेतदेवं तदेनं गृहाण.

णाश्वास्य निःशङ्कं भवदङ्कं समानीतवानस्मि । एनमायुष्मन्तं पितृरूपो भवानभिरक्षतात्' इति । राजा सुहृदापन्निमित्तं शोकं तन्नन्दनविलोकनसुखेन किंचिदधरीकृत्य तमुपहारवर्मनाम्नाऽऽहूय राजवाहनमिव पुपोष ।

जनपतिरेकस्मिन्पुण्यदिवसे तीर्थस्नानाय पक्कणनिकटमार्गेण गच्छन्नबलया कयाचिदुपलालितमनुपमशरीरं कुमारं कंचिदवलोक्य कुतूहलाकुलस्तामपृच्छत—' भामिनि रुचिरमूर्तिः सराजगुणसंपूर्तिरसावर्भको भवदन्वयसंभवो न भवति । कस्य नयनानन्दनः, निमित्तेन केन भवदधीनो जातः, कथ्यतां याथातथ्येन त्वया ' इति । प्रणतया तया शबर्या सलीलमलापि—' राजन् आत्मपल्लीसमीपे पदव्यां वर्तमानस्य शक्रसमानस्य मिथिलेश्वरस्य सर्वस्वमपहरति शबरसैन्ये मद्दयितेनापहृत्य कुमार एष मह्यमर्पितो व्यवर्धत । ' तदवधार्य कार्यज्ञो राजा मुनिकथितं द्वितीयं राजकुमारमेव निश्चित्य सामदानाभ्यां तामनुनीयापहारवर्मेत्याख्याय देव्यै ' वर्धय ' इति समर्पितवान् ।

कदाचिद्वामदेवशिष्यः सोमदेवशर्मा नाम कंचिदेकं बालकं राज्ञः पुरो निक्षिप्याभाषत—' देव रामतीर्थे स्नात्वा प्रत्यागच्छता

शिशिरं शीतं च तदुदकं च तदादिर्यस्मिंस्तेन । निःशङ्कमिति क्रियाविशेषणम् । भवदङ्कं भवन्निकटम् । अभिरक्षतात् ' तुह्योस्तातङ्ङाशिष्यन्यतरस्याम् ' इति तातङ् । सुहृदः आपन्निमित्तं यस्य तम् । तस्य सुहृदो नन्दनस्तन्नन्दनः । अधरीकृत्य लघूकृत्य । पुपोष वृद्धिं निनाय । **जनपतिरिति** । पुण्यदिवसे पर्वणि । पक्कणः शबरालयः । उपलालितं प्रेमविधृतम् । अनुपमं शरीरं यस्य तम् । कुतूहलेन कौतुकेनाकुलो व्याप्तः । भामिनि कोपने । 'कोपना सैव भामिनी' इत्यमरः । अत्र तु केवलस्त्रीवाचकोऽयं शब्दः कोपकारणाभावात् । रुचिरा सुन्दरा । राज्ञो गुणास्तेषां संपूर्तिस्तत्सहितः । अन्वयो वंशः । नयने आनन्दयति तथा । कस्य सूनुरित्यर्थः । निमित्तेन कारणेन । भवदधीनस्त्वदायत्तः । याथातथ्येन तत्त्वतः । प्रकर्षेण नता तया । पल्ली घोषः । पदव्यां मार्गे । शक्र इन्द्रः । मिथिलेश्वरस्य मिथिलाधिपस्य प्रहारवर्मणः । दयितेन वल्लभेन । भर्त्रेत्यर्थः । व्यवर्धत वृद्धिं प्राप्तः । अवधार्य विमृश्येत्यर्थः । कार्यं जानातीति तथा । साम च दानं च ताभ्याम् । अनुनीय संतोष्य । आख्यायं नाम कृत्वा । **कदाचिदिति** । रामतीर्थे एतन्नाम्नि क्षेत्रे । प्रत्यागच्छता प्रतिनिवर्तमानेन ।

१ भवदन्तिकमानीत०. २ संकुचीकृत्य. ३ सुराज०. ४ व्यवर्ध्यत.

मया काननावनौ वनितया कयाऽपि धार्यमाणमेनमुज्ज्वलाकारं कुमारं विलोक्य सादरमभाणि—'स्थविरे का त्वम् । एतस्मिन्नटवीमध्ये बालकमुद्वहन्ती किमर्थमायासेन भ्रमसि' इति । वृद्धयाऽप्यभाषि—'मुनिवर, कालयवननाम्नि द्वीपे कालगुप्तो नाम धनाढ्यो वैश्यवरः कश्चिदस्ति । तन्नन्दिनीं नयनानन्दकारिणीं सुवृत्तां नामैतस्माद् द्वीपादागतो मगधनाथमन्त्रिसंभवो रत्नोद्भवो नाम रमणीयगुणालयो भ्रान्तभूवलयो मनोहारी व्यवहार्युपयम्य सुवस्तुसंपदा श्वशुरेण संमानितोऽभूत् । कालक्रमेण नताङ्गी गर्भिणी जाता । ततः सोदरविलोकनकुतूहलेन रत्नोद्भवः कथंचिच्छ्वशुरमनुनीय चपललोचनयाऽनया सह प्रवहणमारुह्य पुष्पपुरमभिप्रतस्थे । कल्लोलमालिकाभिहतः पोतः समुद्राम्भस्यमज्जत् । गर्भभरालसां तां ललनां धात्रीभावेन कल्पिताऽहं कराभ्यामुद्वहन्ती फलकमेकमधिरुह्य दैवगत्या तीरभूमिमगमम् । सुहृज्जनपरिवृतो रत्नोद्भवस्तत्र निमग्नो वा केनाप्युपायेन तीरमगमद्वा न जानामि । क्लेशस्य परा काष्ठामधिगता सुवृत्ताऽस्मिन्नटवीमध्येऽद्य सुतमसूत । प्रसववेदनया विचेतना सा प्रच्छायशीतले तरुतले निवसति । विजने वने

---

काननावनौ अरण्यभुवि । उज्ज्वलो दीप्तिमान् आकारो यस्य तम् । स्थविरे वृद्धे इति संबुद्धिः । अटवी अरण्यम् । आयासेन कष्टेन । मुनिवर ऋषिश्रेष्ठ । धनाढ्यो धनसमृद्धः । वैश्यवरो वणिक्श्रेष्ठः । नन्दिनीं कन्याम् । नयनयोरानन्दं करोति तथा । मन्त्रिसंभवो मन्त्रिणः पुत्रः । रमणीयगुणानामालयो वसतिस्थानम् । भ्रान्तं भुवो वलयं चक्रं येनेति तथा । मनोहारी अभिराम इत्यर्थः । व्यवहारी वाणिज्यकर्ता । उपयम्य विवाह्य । सुवस्तुसंपदा सुवस्तूनां शोभनवस्तूनां संपदा समृद्ध्या । संमानितः पूजितः । सत्कृत इति यावत् । नतान्यवनम्राण्यङ्गानि यस्यास्तथा । सोदरः समानोदर्यः । चपले लोचने यस्यास्तथा । प्रवहणं नावम् । अभिप्रतस्थे इत्यत्र 'समवप्रविभ्यः स्थः' इत्यात्मनेपदम् । कल्लोलाः महातरङ्गाः तेषां मालिकाः परंपरास्ताभिरभिहतस्ताडितः । पोतो नौः । ललना स्त्री । धात्रीभावेनोपमातृत्वेन । परां काष्ठामतिशयम् । प्रसवकाले या वेदना तया । विचेतना निःसंज्ञा । नष्टचेष्टेत्यर्थः । प्रच्छायेन शीतले । 'गोस्त्रियोरुपसर्जनस्य'

---

१ वनितया तया. २ गर्भभरान्ताम्, गर्भविलासालसाम्.

स्थातुमशक्यतया जनपदगामिनं मार्गमन्वेष्टुमुद्युक्तया मया विवशायास्तस्याः समीपे बालकं निक्षिप्य गन्तुमनुचितमिति कुमारोऽप्यानायि' इति। तस्मिन्नेव क्षणे वन्यो वारणः कश्चिददृश्यत। तं विलोक्य भीता सा बालकं निपात्य प्राद्रवत्। अहं समीपलतागुल्मके प्रविश्य परीक्षमाणोऽतिष्ठम्। निपतितं बालकं पल्लवकवलमिवाददति गजपतौ कण्ठीरवो भीमरवो महाग्रहेण न्यपतत्। भयाकुलेन दन्तावलेन झटिति वियति समुत्पात्यमानो बालको न्यपतत्। चिरायुष्मत्तया[1] स चोन्नततरुशाखासमासीनेन वानरेण केनचित्पक्वफलबुद्ध्या[2] परिगृह्य फलेतरतया विततस्कन्धमूले निक्षिप्तोऽभूत्। सोऽपि मर्कटः क्वचिदगात्। बालकेन सत्त्वसंपन्नतया सकलक्लेशसहेनाभावि। केसरिणा करिणं निहत्य कुत्रचिदगामि। लतागृहान्निर्गतोऽहमपि तेजःपुञ्जं बालकं शनैरवनिरुहादवतार्य वनान्तरे वनितामन्विष्याविलोक्यैनमानीय गुरवे निवेद्य तन्निदेशेन भवन्निकटमानीतवानस्मि' इति। सर्वेषां सुहृदामेकदैवानुकूलदैवाभावेन महदाश्चर्यं बिभ्राणो राजा रत्नोद्भवः कथमभवदिति चिन्तयंस्तन्नन्दनं[3] पुष्पोद्भवनामधेयं विधाय तदुदन्तं

---

इति ह्रस्वः। विजने निर्जने। जनपदं देशं गच्छतीति तथाभूतम्। विवशा विह्वला। विकलेत्यर्थः। वने भवो वन्यः। वारणो गजः। निपात्य अधः पातयित्वा। प्राद्रवदधावत्। द्रुतगत्याऽपासरदित्यर्थः। गुल्मके स्तम्बे। स्वार्थेऽल्पार्थे वा कः। परीक्षमाणः परित ईक्षमाणः। कवलं ग्रासम्। कण्ठीरवः सिंहः। भीमो भयंकरो रवो यस्य तथा। महाग्रहेण महताऽऽवेशेन। चिरायुष्मत्तया दीर्घायुषो भावस्तया। उन्नतस्योच्छ्रितस्य। 'आसन्नोन्नत-' इति पाठे आसन्नः समीपवर्ती। पक्वफलबुद्ध्या पक्वं फलं किमप्येतदिति भ्रान्त्या। फलादितरदिति दृष्ट्वा। वितते विस्तृते स्कन्धस्य प्रकाण्डस्य मूले। सत्त्वेन संपन्नस्तस्य भावस्तया। सकलक्लेशसहेनाखिलक्लेशसहिष्णुना। कुत्रचिदनिर्दिष्टे स्थले। लतागृहात्कुञ्जात्। अवन्यां रोहतीत्यवनिरुहो वृक्षस्तस्मात्। अन्यद्वनं वनान्तरं तस्मिन्। एनम्। अन्वादेश इदं रूपम्। निदेशेनाज्ञया। **अनुकूलेति**। दैवस्य प्रातिकूल्येनेत्यर्थः। महत् आश्चर्यम् इति भिन्ने पदे। **रत्नोद्भव इति**। रत्नोद्भवस्य का गतिः। किमभवदित्यर्थः। नामधेयं नाम। 'भागरूपनामभ्यो धेयः' इति धेयप्रत्ययः। विधाय कृत्वा। उदन्तं वार्ताम्।

---

१ चिरायुष्यतयाऽऽसन्नोन्नत. २ मनीषया. ३ तं नन्दनम्.

व्याख्याय सुश्रुताय विषादसंतोषावनुभवंस्तदनुजतनयं समर्पितवान् ।

अन्येद्युः कंचन बालकमुरसि दधती वसुमती वल्लभमभिगता । तेन 'कुत्रत्योऽयम्' इति पृष्टा समभाषत—'राजन् अतीतायां रात्रौ काचन दिव्यवनिता मत्पुरतः कुमारमेकं संस्थाप्य निद्रामुद्रितां मां विबोध्य विनीताऽब्रवीत्—'देवि त्वन्मन्त्रिणो धर्मपालनन्दनस्य कामपालस्य वल्लभा [1]यक्षकन्याऽहं तारावली नाम नन्दिनी मणिभद्रस्य । यक्षेश्वरानुमत्या मदात्मजमेतं भवत्तनूजस्याम्भोनिधिवलयवेष्टितक्षोणीमण्डलेश्वरस्य भाविनो विशुद्धयशोनिधे राजवाहनस्य परिचर्याकरणायानीतवत्यस्मि । त्वमेनं मनोजसंनिभमभिवर्धय' इति । विस्मयविकसितनयनया मया [2]सविनयं सत्कृता स्वक्षी यक्षी साऽप्यदृश्यतामयासीत्' इति । कामपालस्य यक्षकन्यासंगमे विस्मयमानमानसो राजहंसो रञ्जितमित्रं सुमित्रं मन्त्रिणमाहूय तदीयभ्रातृपुत्रमर्थपालं विधाय तस्मै सर्वं वार्त्तादिकं व्याख्यायादात् ।

ततः परस्मिन्दिवसे वामदेवान्तेवासी तदाश्रमवासी समाराधितदेव-

---

व्याख्याय कथयित्वा । रत्नोद्भवस्य नाशाद्विषादः तन्नन्दनस्य च लाभात्संतोषः । अनु पश्चाज्जातोऽनुजः । **अन्येद्युरिति** । अन्येद्युः अपरेद्युः । 'सद्यः-परुत्परार्यैषमः-' इति निपातः । उरसि दधती वक्षसि धारयन्ती । अभ्यस्तत्वान्नुमभावः । कुत्र भवः कुत्रत्यः । 'अव्ययात्त्यप्' इति त्यप् । अतीतायां गतायाम् । दिवि भवा दिव्या सा चासौ वनिता । निद्रया मुद्रितां निमीलितनेत्राम् । विनीता नम्रा । यक्षेश्वरः कुबेरः । अम्भोनिधिः समुद्रः । स एव वलयः कटकस्तेन वेष्टितं क्षोणीमण्डलं धरामण्डलं तस्येश्वर ईशिता तस्य । भाविनो नाद्यापि भूतस्य । विशेषेण शुद्धो यशसो निधिर्यस्य तस्य । परिचर्या शुश्रूषा । मनोजः कामः । संनिभः सदृशः । विस्मयेनाश्चर्येण विकसिते नयने नेत्रे यस्यास्तया । सविनयमिति क्रियाविशेषणम् । 'सविनया' इति पाठे यक्षीविशेषणम् । सत्कृता संमानिता । स्वक्षी शोभननयना । यक्षकन्यया संगमस्तस्मिन् । विस्मयमानं मानसं यस्य सः । रञ्जितानि मित्राणि येन तम् । आहूय आकार्य । आनाय्येत्यर्थः । **तत इति** । अन्तेवासी शिष्यः । 'छात्रान्तेवासिनौ शिष्ये' इत्यमरः । अन्ते वसतीति तथा । 'शयवास-' इत्यलुक् । समारा-

---

१ यक्षकान्ता. २ सविनया.

कीर्तिं निर्भर्त्सितमारमूर्तिं कुसुमसुकुमारं कुमारमेकमवगमय्य नरपतिमवादीत्—'देव तीर्थयात्राप्रसङ्गेन कावेरीतीरमागतोऽहं विलोलालकं बालकं निजोत्सङ्गतले निधाय रुदतीं स्थविरामेकां विलोक्यावोचम्—'स्थविरे का त्वम्, अयमर्भकः कस्य नयनानन्दकरः, कान्तारं किमर्थमागता, शोककारणं किम्' इति। सा करयुगेन बाष्पजलमुन्मृज्य[1] निजशोकशङ्कूत्पाटनक्षममिव मामवलोक्य शोकहेतुमवोचत्—'द्विजात्मज राजहंसमन्त्रिणः सितवर्मणः कनीयानात्मजः सत्यवर्मा तीर्थयात्राभिलाषेण देशमेनमागच्छत्। स कस्मिंश्चिदग्रहारे कालीं नाम कस्यचिद्भूसुरस्य नन्दिनीं विवाह्य तस्या अनपत्यतया गौरीं नाम तद्भगिनीं काञ्चनकान्तिं परिणीय तस्यामेकं तनयमलभत। काली सासूयमेकदा धात्र्या मया सह बालमेनमेकेन मिषेणानीय तटिन्यामेतस्यामक्षिपत्। करेणैकेन बालमुद्धृत्यापरेण प्लवमाना[2] नदीवेगागतस्य कस्यचित्तरोः शाखामवलम्ब्य तत्र शिशुं निधाय नदीवेगेनोह्यमाना केनचित्तरुलग्नेन कालभोगिनाऽहमदंशि। मदवलम्बीभूतो भूरुहोऽयमस्मिन्देशे तीरमगमत्। गरलस्योद्दीपनतया मयि मृतायामरण्ये कश्चन शरण्यो नास्तीति मया शोच्यते' इति। ततो विषमविष[3]ज्वालावलीढावयवा सा धरणीतले न्यपतत्। दयाविष्टहृदयोऽहं

---

धिता लब्धेति यावत् देवकीर्तिर्येन तम्। निर्भर्त्सिता स्वरूपेण मारस्य कंदर्पस्य मूर्तिर्येन तम्। कुसुममिव कुसुमारं पेलवम्। अवगमय्य प्रापय्य। यात्रा गमनम्। प्रसङ्गेन क्रमेण। कावेरी दक्षिणदेशस्था काचिन्नदी। विलोलाश्चञ्चला अलका यस्य तम्। उत्सङ्गोऽङ्कः। कान्तारं महारण्यम्। करयोः युगेन द्वन्द्वेन। बाष्पजलमश्रूणि। निजशोक एव शङ्कुः शल्यं तस्योत्पाटनं तत्र क्षमं समर्थम्। कनीयान्। 'युवाल्पयोः कनन्यतरस्याम्' इति कनादेशः। अग्रहारे नृपात्प्रतिग्रहेण लब्धभूमिप्रदेशे ग्रामादौ वा। भूसुरस्य द्विजस्य। धात्र्युपमाता। मिषेण व्याजेन। तटिन्यां नद्याम्। प्लवमाना तरन्ती। भोगी सर्पः। अदंशि। कर्मणि लुङ्। भूरुहो वृक्षः। गरलस्य विषस्य। उद्दीपनतया प्रबलतरतया। शरण्यो रक्षिता। विषमं दुर्धरम्। अविषह्यमित्यर्थः। विषमविषस्य ज्वालाभिरवलीढा व्याप्ता अवयवा यस्याः सा।

---

१ उत्सृज्य. २ अम्भसि प्लवमाना. ३ विषोल्बणज्वाला.

मन्त्रबलेन विषव्यवस्थामपनेतुमक्षमः समीपकुञ्जेष्वोषधिविशेषमान्विष्य प्रत्यागतो[1] व्युत्क्रान्तजीवितां तां व्यलोकयम् । तदनु तस्याः पावकसंस्कारं विरच्य शोकाकुलचेता बालमेनमगतिमादाय सत्यवर्मवृत्तान्तश्रवणवेलायां तन्निवासाग्रहारनामधेयस्याश्रुततया तदन्वेषणमशक्यमित्यालोच्य भवदमात्यतनयस्य भवानेवाभिरक्षितेति भवन्तमेनमनयम्' इति । तन्निशम्य सत्यवर्मस्थितेः सम्यगनिश्चिततया खिन्नमानसो नरपतिः सुमतये मन्त्रिणे सोमदत्तं नाम तदनुजतनयमर्पितवान् । सोऽपि सोदरमागतमिव मन्यमानो विशेषेण पुपोष ।

एवं मिलितेन कुमारमण्डलेन बालकेलीरनुभवन्नधिरूढानेकवाहनो राजवाहनोऽनुक्रमेण चौलोपनयनादिसंस्कारजामतलभत । ततः सकललिपिज्ञानं निखिलदेशीयभाषापाण्डित्यं षडङ्गसहितवेदसमुदायकोविदत्वं काव्यनाटकाख्यानकाख्यायिकेतिहासचित्रकथासहितपुराणगणनैपुण्यं धर्मशब्दज्योतिस्तर्कमीमांसादिसमस्तशास्त्रनिकरचातुर्यं कौटिल्यकामन्दकीयादिनीतिपटलकौशलं वीणाद्यशेषवाद्यदाक्ष्यं संगीत-

---

दयया आविष्टं हृदयं यस्य । मन्त्रबलेन मन्त्रसामर्थ्येन । अपनेतुं दूरीकर्तुम् । कुञ्जेषु निकुञ्जेषु । व्युत्क्रान्तजीवितां मृताम् । तदनु ततः । पावकसंस्कारं विरच्याग्निसंस्कारं कृत्वा । चिताधिरोपणेन तस्याः शरीरमग्निसात्कृत्वेत्यर्थः । अगतिमशरण्यम् । अनाथमित्यर्थः । **एवमिति** । कुमारमण्डलेन कुमारसमुदायेन । केलीः क्रीडाः । अधिरूढान्यनेकवाहनानि येन सः । चौलं चोपनयनं च चौलोपनयने । एते आदी यस्य तत्संस्कारजातम् । तत्र चौलं चूडाकर्म । 'तृतीये वर्षे चौलं यथाकुलधर्मं वा' इति सूत्रम् । जन्मप्रभृति तृतीये वर्षे कुलधर्ममादत्यान्यस्मिन्वा केशसंनिवेशानां करणम् । उपनयनं प्रसिद्धम् । लिपिरक्षरसंस्थानं तस्य ज्ञानम् । षडङ्गसहितस्य वेदसमुदायस्य कोविदत्वं ज्ञातृत्वम् । 'शिक्षा कल्पो व्याकरणं निरुक्तं ज्योतिषां गणः । छन्दसां विचितिश्चैव षडङ्गो वेद उच्यते ॥' इति । आख्यानकानि चूर्णकानि । आख्यायिकाः बृहत्कथाद्याः । इतिहासः पुरावृत्तकथनम् । चित्रकथा रम्यकथा । एतैः सर्वैः सहिते पुराणगणे ब्राह्माग्न्यादिपुराणसमुदाये नैपुण्यम् । धर्मशास्त्रं स्मृतयः । शब्दशास्त्रं व्याकरणम् । ज्योतिःशास्त्रं प्रसिद्धम् । तर्कशास्त्रं न्यायः । मीमांसा पूर्वोत्तरभेदेन प्रसिद्धं शास्त्रम् । निकरः समूहः । कौटिल्यश्चाणक्यस्तत्प्रणीतम् ।

---

१ प्रत्यागच्छन्व्युत्क्रान्त.

साहित्यहारित्वं मणिमन्त्रौषधादिमायाप्रपञ्चचञ्चुत्वं मातङ्गतुरङ्गादिवाहनारोहणपाटवं विविधायुधप्रयोगचणत्वं चौर्यदुरोदरादिकपटकलाप्रौढत्वं च तत्तदाचार्येभ्यः सम्यग्लब्ध्वा यौवनेन विलसन्तं कृत्येष्वनलसं तं कुमारनिकरं निरीक्ष्य महीवल्लभः सः 'अहं शत्रुजनदुर्लभः' इति परमानन्दममन्दमविन्दत ।

इति श्रीदण्डिनः कृतौ दशकुमारचरिते कुमारोत्पत्तिर्नाम प्रथम उच्छ्वासः ।

## द्वितीयोच्छ्वासः ।

अथैकदा वामदेवः सकलकलाकुशलेन कुसुमसायकसंशयितसौन्दर्येण कल्पितसोदर्येण साहसोपहसितकुमारेण सुकुमारेण जयध्वजातपवारणकुलिशा[3]ङ्कितकरेण कुमारनिकरेण परिवेष्टितं राजानमानतशिरसं समभिगम्य तेन तां कृतां परिचर्यामङ्गीकृत्य निजचरणकमलयुगलमि[4]लन्मधुकरायमाणकाकपक्षं विदलिष्यमाण-

कामन्दकीयमिति प्रसिद्धम् । दाक्ष्यं दक्षता । साहित्यं शिल्पं नृत्यादिकलाः । हारित्वं मनोहारित्वम् । मायाप्रपञ्चः कपटप्रबन्धः । चञ्चुत्वं कुशलत्वम् । ' 'तेन वित्तश्चञ्चुप्चणपौ' इति चञ्चुप् । चणत्वं कौशलम् । 'तेन वित्त–' इति चणप् । दुरोदरं द्यूतम् । तत्तदाचार्येभ्यस्तेषु तेषु शास्त्रेषु निष्णातेभ्य आचार्येभ्य इत्यर्थः । विलसन्तं शोभमानम् । अनलसमुद्यमशीलम् । महीवल्लभो राजा राजहंसः ।

**इति श्रीदशकुमारचरितपूर्वपीठिकाटीकायां पददीपिकाभिधायां प्रथम उच्छ्वासः ।**

**अथेति** । सकलकलासु कुशलस्तेन । कुसुमसायकः कामः । संशयितं संशयं प्रापितम् । कल्पितं सोदर्यं बन्धुता येन तथा । साहसेनोपहसितो धिकृतः कुमारो गुहो येन सः । जयध्वजः पताका । आतपवारणं छत्रम् । कुलिशं वज्रम् । एतैः रेखामात्रैरङ्कितौ करौ यस्य तेन । परिवेष्टितं परिवृतम् । निजौ वामदेवस्येत्यर्थः चरणौ तावेव कमले तयोर्युगलं तस्मिन्मिलन्तः संयुक्ता ये मधुकरा इवाचरन्तः काकपक्षाः शिखण्डकाः यस्य तम् । विदलिष्यमाणा उद्धरिष्यमाणा विपक्षाः शत्रवो

१ चाटवम्; चुञ्चुत्वम्. २ चतुरत्वम्; चरणत्वम्. ३ कलशाङ्कित. ४ गलन्म०.

विपक्षं कुमारचयं गाढमालिङ्ग्य मितसत्यवाक्येन विहिताशीरभ्यभाषत—'भूवल्लभ भवदीयमनोरथफलमिव समृद्धलावण्यं तारुण्यं नुतमित्रो भवत्पुत्रोऽनुभवति। सहचरसमेतस्य नूनमेतस्य दिग्विजयारम्भसमय एषः। तदस्य सकलक्लेशसहस्य राजवाहनस्य दिग्विजयप्रयाणं क्रियताम्' इति। कुमारा माराभिरामा रामाद्यपौरुषा रुषा भस्मीकृतारयो रयोपहसितसमीरणा रणाभियानेन यानेनाभ्युदयाशंसं राजानमकार्षुः। तत्साचिव्यमितरेषां विधाय समुचितां बुद्धिमुपदिश्य शुभे मुहूर्ते सपरीवारं कुमारं विजयाय विससर्ज।

राजवाहनो मङ्गलसूचकं शुभशकुनं विलोकयन्देशं कंचिदतिक्रम्य विन्ध्याटवीमध्यमविशत्। तत्र हेतिहतिकिणाङ्कं कालायसकर्कशकायं यज्ञोपवीतेनानुमेयविप्रभावं व्यक्तकिरातप्रभावं लोचनपरुषं कमपि पुरुषं ददर्श। तेन विहितपूजनो राजवाहनो-

---

येन तम्। चयं समुदायम्। गाढं निर्भरम्। मितं च सत्यं च यद्वाक्यं तेन। 'सत्यं मृदु प्रियम्' इति सत्यशब्दप्रयोगः। विहिता आशीराशीर्वादो येन सः। भवदीयानां मनोरथानामिच्छानां फलम्। समृद्धं परिपूर्णं लावण्यं यस्मिन्। नुतानि स्तुतानि स्तुत्यानि वा मित्राणि येन यस्य वा सः। दिशां विजयस्तस्यारम्भस्तस्य समयः कालः। सकलक्लेशसहस्य। सत्त्वशीलसंपन्नत्वात्। **दिग्विजयेति।** दिग्विजयं कर्तुमयं प्रहीयतामित्यर्थः। मारः कंदर्प इवाभिरामाः सुन्दराः। रामो दाशरथिः स आद्यो येषां ते रामाद्यास्तेषां पौरुषं पराक्रम इव पौरुषं येषां ते। रयेण वेगेन। आवेशेनेति यावत्। उपहसितो न्यक्कृतः समीरणो वायुर्यैः। रणमभियातीत्येतादृशेन। यानेन गमनेन। अभ्युदयस्य वृद्धेराशंसा विद्यते यस्य तम्। इतरेषां कुमाराणाम्। विजयाय। विजयं कर्तुमित्यर्थः। 'तुमर्थाच्च भाववचनात्' इति चतुर्थी। **राजवाहन इति।** मङ्गलं शुभोदर्कं सूचयति तथा। शुभं शकुनं निमित्तम्। हेतिभिः शस्त्रैर्या हतिः प्रहारस्तस्य किणा व्रणजचिह्नानि तेषामङ्का यस्मिन्। कालायसं लोहं तदिव कर्कशः कठिनः कायो यस्य। यज्ञस्य यज्ञार्थं वा उपवीतं यज्ञोपवीतम्। अनुमातुं योग्यो विप्रभावो विप्रत्वं यस्येति तथा। व्यक्तः स्पष्टः किरातस्य वनचरस्येव प्रभावो यस्य। लोचनयोः परुषं कर्कशम्। दुर्दर्शनमिति यावत्।

---

१ अमित. २ सहनस्य. ३ रामास्त्र, रामाढ्य.

ऽभाषत—'ननु मानव जनसङ्गरहिते मृगहिते घोरप्रचारे कान्तारे विन्ध्याटवीमध्ये भवानेकाकी किमिति निवसति। भवदंसोपनीतं यज्ञोपवीतं भूसुरभावं द्योतयति। हेतिहैतिभिः[1] किरातरीतिरनुमीयते। कथयं किमेतत्' इति। 'तेजोमयोऽयं मानुषमात्रपौरुषो नूनं न भवति' इति मत्वा स पुरुषस्तद्वयस्यमुखान्नामजनने विज्ञाय तस्मै निजवृत्तान्तमकथयत्—'राजनन्दन केचिदस्यामटव्यां वेदादिविद्याभ्यासमपहाय निजकुलाचारं दूरीकृत्य सत्यशौचादिधर्मव्रातं परिहृत्य किल्बिषमन्विष्यन्तः पुलिन्दपुरोगमास्तदन्नमुपभुञ्जाना बहवो ब्राह्मणब्रुवा निवसन्ति। तेषु कस्यचित्पुत्रो निन्दापात्रचारित्रो[2] मातङ्गो नामाहं सह किरातबलेन जनपदं प्रविश्य ग्रामेषु धनिनः स्त्रीबालसहितानानीयाटव्यां बन्धने निधाय तेषां सकलधनमपहरन्नुद्धृत्य[3] वीतदयो व्यचरम्। कदाचिदेकस्मिन्कान्तारे मदीयसहचरगणेन जिघांस्यमानं भूसुरमेकमवलोक्य दयायत्तचित्तोऽब्रवम्—'ननु पापाः न हन्तव्यो ब्राह्मणः' इति। ते रोषारुणनयना मां बहुधा निरभर्त्सयन्। तेषां

विहितं कृतं पूजनं सत्कारो यस्य सः। जनसङ्गेन रहिते विवर्जिते। मृगेभ्यो हितमनुकूलं तस्मिन्। घोरः प्रचारः संचारो यस्मिन्निति तथा। एकाक्यसहायः। 'एकादाकिनिच्चासहाये' इत्याकिनिच्प्रत्ययः। अंसो भुजशिरः। उपनीतं गतं प्राप्तम्। भूसुरभावं विप्रत्वम्। हेतिहतिभिः शस्त्रप्रहारचिह्नैः। किरातरीतिर्वनचरवृत्तिः। अनुमीयते उह्यते तर्क्यते। तेजोमयस्तेजःप्रचुरः। 'तत्प्रकृतवचने मयट्' इति मयट्। मानुषमात्रं मानुषप्रमाणं पौरुषं पराक्रमो यस्येति तथा। 'प्रमाणे द्वयसज्दघ्न–' इति प्रमाणार्थे मात्रच्। वेदादि। आदिशब्देन स्मृतिपुराणादीनि गृह्यन्ते। निजकुलाचारं विप्रविहितधर्मान्। सत्यमवितथभाषित्वम्। शौचं शुचित्वम्। आदिशब्देन दयादमक्षान्तिशान्त्यादि गृह्यते। धर्मव्रातं कुलधर्मसमुदायम्। किल्बिषं पापम्। पुलिन्दा म्लेच्छजातिष्वेका जातिः। ते पुरोगमा नेतारो येषां ते। उपभुञ्जाना भक्षयन्तः। ब्राह्मणब्रुवा ब्राह्मणाधमाः। कुत्सनार्थेऽत्र ब्रुवपदम्। निन्दापात्रं गर्ह्यं चारित्रं यस्यैतादृशः। वीता दया यस्य सः। जिघांस्यमानं हन्तुमिष्यमाणम्। निरभर्त्सयंस्तर्जितवन्तः।

१ हेतिततिभिः. २ निन्दामात्रचरित्रः. ३ उद्धृत्य.

भाषणपारुष्यमसहिष्णुरहमवनिसुररक्षणाय चिरं प्रयुध्य तैरभिहतो गतजीवितोऽभवम् । ततः प्रेतपुरीमुपेत्य तत्र देहधारिभिः पुरुषैः परिवेष्टितं सभामध्ये रत्नखचितसिंहासनासीनं शमनं विलोक्य तस्मै दण्डप्रणाममकरवम् । सोऽपि मामवेक्ष्य चित्रगुप्तं नाम निजामात्यमाहूय तमवोचत्—'सचिव नैषोऽमुष्य मृत्युसमयः । निन्दितचरितोऽप्ययं महीसुरनिमित्तं गतजीवितोऽभूत् । इतः प्रभृति विगलितकल्मषस्यास्य पुण्यकर्मकरणे रुचिरुदेष्यति । पापिष्ठैरनुभूयमानमत्र यातनाविशेषं विलोक्य पुनरपि पूर्वशरीरमनेन गम्यताम्' इति । चित्रगुप्तोऽपि तत्र तत्र संतप्तेष्वायसस्तम्भेषु बध्यमानान्, अत्युष्णीकृते वितत[1]शरावे तैले निक्षिप्यमाणान्, लगुडैर्जर्जरीकृतावयवान्, निशितटङ्कैः परितक्ष्यमाणानपि दर्शयित्वा पुण्यबुद्धिमुपदिश्य माममुञ्चत् । तदेव पूर्वशरीरमहं प्राप्तो महाटवीमध्ये शीतलोपचारं [2]रचयता महीसुरेण परीक्ष्यमाणः शिलायां शयितः क्षणमतिष्ठम् । तदनु विदितोदन्तो मदीयवंश[3]बन्धुगणः सहसाऽऽगत्य मन्दिरमानीय मामपक्रान्तव्रणमकरोत् । द्विजन्मा कृतज्ञो मह्यमक्षरशिक्षां विधाय विविधागमतन्त्रमाख्याय कल्मषक्षयकारणं सदाचारमुपदिश्य ज्ञानेक्षणगम्यमानस्य शशिखण्डशेखरस्य

---

भाषणपारुष्यं कठोरवचांसि । असहिष्णुः सोढुमसमर्थः । 'अलंकृञ्निराकृञ्–' इतीष्णुच् । प्रेतपुरीं यमनगरीम् । रत्नैः खचितं प्रत्युप्तं यत्सिंहासनं तत्रासीनम् । शमनं यमम् । दण्डप्रणामं दण्डवद्भूमौ शयित्वा प्रणाममित्यर्थः । विगलितं नष्टं कल्मषं पापं यस्य तस्य । रुचिः प्रीतिः । उदेष्यत्युत्पत्स्यते । अतिशयेन पापाः पापिष्ठाः । 'अतिशायने तमबिष्ठनौ' इतीष्ठन् । अयस इमे आयसाश्च ते स्तम्भास्तेषु । विततो विस्तीर्णो यः शरावः पात्रविशेषः । 'कढई' इति भाषायाम् । जर्जरीकृताः । अर्थात्प्रहारैः । निशितास्तीक्ष्णास्तेजिताष्टङ्काः पाषाणदारणास्तैः परितक्ष्यमाणान्परितस्तक्षणेन तनूक्रियमाणान् । रचयता कुर्वता । विदित उदन्तो वार्ता येन तथा । अपक्रान्ताश्चिकित्सिता व्रणाः प्रहारस्थानानि यस्य तादृशः । अक्षराणां शिक्षोपदेशः । विविधागमानां शास्त्राणां तन्त्रं सिद्धान्तम् । कल्मषस्य पापस्य यः क्षयस्तस्य कारणं निमित्तम् । सदाचारं सद्भिरुपदर्शितं मार्गम् । ज्ञानेक्षणेन न तु चर्मचक्षुषा गम्यमान आसाद्यः प्राप्यस्तस्य । शशिनः खण्डः कला सा शेखरो-

---

१ शरावतैले. २ रचयित्वा. ३ वंशेति नास्ति क्वचित्.

पूजाविधानमभिधाय पूजां मत्कृतामङ्गीकृत्य निरगात् । तदारभ्याहं किरातकृतसंसर्गं बन्धुकुलवर्गमुत्सृज्य सकललोकैकगुरुमिन्दुकलावतंसं चेतसि स्मरन्नस्मिन्कानने दूरीकृतकलङ्को वसामि । देव भवते विज्ञापनीयं रहस्यं किंचिदस्ति । आगम्यताम् ' इति । स वयस्यगणादपनीय रहसि पुनरेनमभाषत—' राजन्, अतीते निशान्ते गौरीपतिः स्वप्नसंनिहितो निद्रामुद्रितलोचनं विबोध्य प्रसन्नवदनकान्तिः प्रश्रयानतं मामवोचत्—'मातङ्ग, दण्डकारण्यान्तरालगामिन्यास्तटिन्यास्तीरभूमौ सिद्धसाध्याराध्यमानस्य स्फटिकलिङ्गस्य पश्चाददद्रिपतिकन्यापदपङ्क्तिचिह्नितस्याश्मनः सविधे विधेराननमिव किमपि बिलं विद्यते । तत्प्रविश्य तत्र निक्षिप्तं ताम्रशासनं शासनं विधातुरिव समादाय विधिं तदुपदिष्टं दिष्टविजयमिव विधाय पातालोकाधीश्वरेण भवता भवितव्यम् । भवत्साहाय्यकरो राजकुमारोऽद्य श्वो वा समागमिष्यति ' इति । तदादेशानुगुणमेव भवदागमनमभूत् । साधनाभिलाषिणो मम तोषिणो रचय साहाय्यम् ' इति । ' तथा ' इति राज-

---

ऽवतंसो यस्य तस्य । धूर्जटेरित्यर्थः । विधानं विधिम् । अभिधाय कथयित्वा । तदारभ्य ततः प्रभृति । किरातैः कृतः संसर्गो येन तथा । सकललोकानामेकं मुख्यं गुरुम् । इन्दुकला अवतंसः शिरोभूषणं यस्य तम् । दूरीकृतकलङ्को निष्पापः । रहस्यं गुह्यम् । रहस्येकान्ते । निशाया अन्ते प्रत्यूषे । संनिहितः समीपमागतः । निद्रया मुद्रिते निमीलिते लोचने यस्य तम् । प्रश्रयेण विनयेनानतं प्रह्वम् । अन्तरालं मध्यम् । तटिन्या नद्याः । सिद्धाः साध्याश्च तैराराध्यमानस्य पूज्यमानस्य । 'पिशाचो गुह्यकः सिद्धः,' 'महाराजिकसाध्याश्च' इत्युभयत्राप्यमरः । तत्र सिद्धा देवयोनिविशेषाः, साध्या गणदेवताः । स्फटिकलिङ्गस्य स्फटिकनिर्मितलिङ्गस्य विशिष्टाकृतेः शंकरशरीरस्य । अद्रिपतिर्हिमालयस्तत्कन्या पार्वती तस्याः पदपङ्क्त्या चिह्नितस्य अश्मनो ग्राव्णः । सविधे समीपे । निक्षिप्तं स्थापितम् । ताम्रशासनं ताम्रपट्टम् । शासनमाज्ञा । विधिं कल्पम् । तदुपदिष्टं तेन ताम्रशासनेनोपदिष्टम् । ' तदुपरिष्ठम् ' इति पाठे तदुपरि तिष्ठतीत्यसौ तम् । दिष्टमदृष्टं तस्य विजयः । अधीश्वरः । ' राजा तु प्रणताशेषसामन्तः स्यादधीश्वरः ' इत्यमरः । अनुगुणमनुरूपम् । साधनमुपायस्तमभिलषतीति तथा । तोषिण आनन्दयुक्तस्य । रचय कुर्वित्यर्थः ।

---

१ एवं. २ तदुपरिष्ठम्.

वाहनः साकं मातङ्गेन नमितोत्तमाङ्गेन विहायार्धरात्रे निद्रापरतन्त्रं मित्रगणं वनान्तरमवाप। तदनु तदनुचराः कल्ये साकल्येन राजकुमारमनवलोकयन्तो विषण्णहृदयास्तेषु तेषु वनेषु सम्यगन्विष्यानवेक्षमाणा[1] एतदन्वेषणमनीषया देशान्तरं चरिष्णवोऽतिसाहिष्णवो निश्चितपुनःसंगमसंकेतस्थानाः परस्परं वियुज्य ययुः।

लोकैकवीरेण कुमारेण रक्ष्यमाणः संतुष्टान्तरङ्गो मातङ्गोऽपि बिलं शशिशेखरकथिताभिज्ञानपरिज्ञातं निःशङ्कं प्रविश्य गृहीतताम्रशासनो रसातलं पथा तेनैवोपेत्य तत्र कस्यचित्पत्तनस्य निकटे केलीकाननकासारस्य वितत[2]सारसस्य समीपे नानाविधेनेश[3]शासनविधानोपपादितेन हविषा होमं विरच्य प्रत्यूहपरिहारिणि सविस्मयं विलोकयति राजवाहने समिदाज्यसमुज्ज्वलिते ज्वलने पुण्यगेहं देहं मन्त्रपूर्वकमाहुतीकृत्य तडित्समानकान्तिं दिव्यां तनुमलभत। तदनु मणिमयमण्डनमण्डलमण्डिता सकललोकललनाकुलललामभूता

---

साकमित्यव्ययं सहेत्यर्थे। नमितमुत्तमाङ्गं शीर्षं येन तेन। निद्रापरतन्त्रं निद्राधीनम्। अनुचराः सचिवा अनुगामिनः। कल्ये प्रातःकाले। 'प्रत्यूषोऽहर्मुखं कल्यमुषःप्रत्युषसी अपि' इत्यमरः। साकल्येन समग्रतः। विषण्णं खिन्नं हृदयं येषां ते। तेषु तेष्वखिलेषु। मनीषया बुद्ध्या। चरिष्णवो गन्तुमनसः। 'अलंकृञ्–' इतीष्णुच्प्रत्ययः। पुनः संगमः पुनःसंगमस्तस्य संकेतस्थानम्। निश्चितं निर्णीतं पुनःसंगमसंकेतस्थानं यैस्ते। वियुज्य वियुक्ता भूत्वा। **लोकैकेति**। लोकेष्वेकवीरः प्रधानयोधः। रक्ष्यमाणः इति कर्मणि शानच्। संतुष्टान्तरङ्गो हृष्टमनाः। अभिज्ञानं चिह्नम्। रसातलं पातालम्। केलीकाननं क्रीडावनम्। कासारः सरः। वितता बहवः सारसाः पक्षिविशेषा यत्र। 'विगत–' इति पाठे नष्टा इत्यर्थः। नानाविधेनानेकप्रकारेण। उपपादितेन संपादितेन। हविषा हूयते तद्धविस्तेन। आज्यादियाज्यद्रव्येणेत्यर्थः। प्रत्यूहो विघ्नः। विलोकयति सति। समिधश्चाज्यं च तैः समुज्ज्वलिते दीपिते। ज्वलनेऽग्नौ। पुण्यस्य गेहं वसतिस्थानम्। देहविशेषणमेतत्। आहुतीकृत्याग्नौ क्षिप्त्वा। तडिद्विद्युत्। दिव्यां देवतार्हाम्। तनुं शरीरम्। मणिमयानि मणिप्रचुराणि। 'तत्प्रकृतवचने [ प्राचुर्येण प्रकृतं प्रस्तुतं तस्य वचने ] मयट्' इति मयट्। मण्डनानि भूषणानि। मण्डितोपशोभिता। ललामभूता भूषणभूता। विनीता

---

१ अन्वेक्षमाणाः. २ विगत. ३ ईशेति नास्ति क्वचित्.

कन्यका काचन विनीतानेकसखीजनानुगम्यमाना कलहंसगत्या शनैरागत्यावनिसुरोत्तमाय मणिमेकमुज्ज्वलाकारमुपायनीकृत्य तेन 'का त्वम्' इति पृष्टा सोत्कण्ठा कलकण्ठस्वनेन मन्दं मन्दमुदञ्जलिरभाषत—'भूसुरोत्तम, अहमसुरोत्तमनन्दिनी कालिन्दी नाम । मम पिताऽस्य लोकस्य शासिता महानुभावो निजपराक्रमासहिष्णुना विष्णुना दूरीकृतामरे समरे यमनगरातिथिरकारि । तद्वियोगशोकसागरमग्नां मामवेक्ष्य कोऽपि कारुणिकः सिद्धतापसोऽभाषत—'बाले, कश्चिद्दिव्यदेहधारी मानवो नवो वल्लभस्तव भूत्वा सकलं रसातलं पालयिष्यति' इति । तदादेशं निशम्य घनशब्दोन्मुखी चातकी वर्षागमनमिव तवालोकनकाङ्क्षिणी चिरमतिष्ठम् । मन्मनोरथफलायमानं भवदागमनमवगम्य मद्राज्यावलम्बभूतामात्यानुमत्या मदनकृतसारथ्येन मनसा भवन्तमागच्छम् । लोकस्यास्य राज्यलक्ष्मीमङ्गीकृत्य मां तत्सपत्नीं करोतु भवान्' इति । मातङ्गोऽपि राजवाहनानुमत्या तां तरुणीं परिणीय दिव्याङ्गनालाभेन हृष्टतरो रसातलराज्यमुररीकृत्य परमानन्दमाससाद ।

वञ्चयित्वा वयस्यगणं समागतो राजवाहनस्तदवलोकनकौतूहलेन भुवं गमिष्णुः कालिन्दीदत्तं क्षुत्पिपासादिक्लेशनाशनं मणिं साहाय्यकरणसंतुष्टान्मातङ्गाल्लब्ध्वा कंचनाध्वानमनुवर्तमानं तं विसृज्य बिलपथेन तेन निर्ययौ । तत्र च मित्रगणमनवलोक्य भुवं बभ्राम ।

---

नम्रा । कलहंसस्य गत्या । मन्थरगत्येत्यर्थः । अवनिसुरोत्तमाय द्विजश्रेष्ठाय । उज्ज्वलाकारं दीप्तम् । उपायनीकृत्य । उपायनं दत्त्वेत्यर्थः । सोत्कण्ठा उत्कण्ठया सहिता । कलकण्ठः कोकिलः । उदञ्जलिः प्रबद्धाञ्जलिः । शासिता पालकः । महाननुभावः प्रभावो यस्यैतादृशः । असहिष्णुना सहनासमर्थेन । दूरीकृताः । पराजिता इति यावत् । अमरा देवा यस्मात् । यमनगरस्यातिथिरकारि हत इत्यर्थः । तेन वियोगस्तस्मादुद्भूतो यः शोकः स एव सागरस्तस्मिन्मग्नाम् । कारुणिकोऽनुकम्पावान् । सिद्धतापसो हस्तधृतसिद्धिस्तपस्वी । वल्लभो रमणः । घनशब्दो मेघशब्दः । तस्योन्मुखी उन्नतं मुखं यस्या इति तथा । फलायमानं फलवदाचरति तथा । मम राज्यस्यावलम्बभूतानाममात्यानामनुमत्या । मदनेन कृतं सारथ्यं यस्यैतादृशेन । समानः पतिर्यस्याः सा सपत्नी । तस्या राजलक्ष्म्याः सपत्नीम् । उररीकृत्य स्वीकृत्य । **वञ्चयित्वेति** । वञ्चयित्वा प्रतार्य । कौतूहलेन कौतुकेन । कालिन्दी रसातलगतमातङ्गपत्नी । नाशयतीति नाशनस्तम् । उपशल्ये ग्रामान्ते ।

भ्रमंश्च विशालोपशल्ये कमप्याक्रीडमासाद्य तत्र विशिश्रमिषुरान्दोलिकारूढं रमणीसहितमाप्तजनपरिवृतमुद्याने समागतमेकं पुरुषमपश्यत् । सोऽपि परमानन्देन पल्लवितचेता विकासितवदनारविन्दः 'मम स्वामी सोमकुलावतंसो विशुद्धयशोनिधी राजवाहन एषः । महाभाग्यतयाऽकाण्ड एवास्य पादमूलं गतवानस्मि । संप्रति महान्नयनोत्सवो जातः' इति ससंभ्रममान्दोलिकाया अवतीर्य सरभसपदविन्यासविलासिहर्षोत्कर्षचरितास्त्रिचतुरपदान्युद्गतस्य चरणकमलयुगलं गलदुल्लसन्मल्लिकावलयेन मौलिना पस्पर्श । प्रमोदाश्रुपूर्णो राजा पुलकिताङ्गं तं गाढमालिङ्ग्य 'अये सौम्य सोमदत्त' इति व्याजहार । ततः कस्यापि पुंनागभूरुहस्य प्रच्छायशीतले तले संविष्टेन मनुजनाथेन सप्रणयमभाणि—'सखे कालमेतावन्तं देशे कस्मिन् प्रकारेण केनास्थायि भवता, संप्रति कुत्र गम्यते, तरुणी केयम्, एष परिजनः संपादितः कथम्, कथय' इति । सोऽपि मित्रसंदर्शनव्यतिकरापगतचिन्ताज्वरातिशयो मुकुलितकरकमलः सविनयमात्मीयप्रचारप्रकारमवोचत्—

इति श्रीदण्डिनः कृतौ दशकुमारचरिते द्विजोपकृतिर्नाम द्वितीय उच्छ्वासः ।

---

आक्रीड उद्यानम् । विशिश्रमिषुर्विश्रमितुमिच्छुः । आन्दोलिका दोला । पल्लवितं विकसितं प्रसन्नमिति यावत् चेतोऽन्तःकरणं यस्य स तथा । वदनं अरविन्दं कमलमिव । सोमकुलस्य चन्द्रवंशस्य । अवतंसो भूषणम् । विशुद्धोऽतिशुद्धो यशोनिधिर्यस्य । 'निधिः राजवाहनः' इति च्छेदः । अकाण्डे सहसा । ससंभ्रमं सत्वरं सादरं च । रभसेन सहेति सरभसः । सरभसो यः पदविन्यासस्तस्य यो विलासस्तद्वान् । हर्षोत्कर्षो हर्षातिरेकश्चरिते यस्य सः । पश्चात्कर्मधारयः । त्रिचतुरपदानि त्रीणि वा चत्वारि वा । उद्गतस्य प्रत्युद्यातस्य । मल्लिका पुष्पविशेषः । गलत्स्खलदुल्लसदुद्धतं च मल्लिकावलयं यस्य तेन । मौलिना शीर्षेण । प्रमोदाश्रुभिः पूर्णः । पुलका अस्य संजातास्तत् पुलकितं हृषितरोमाञ्चमङ्गं यस्य तम् । गाढं दृढम् । पुनागः केसरः । भूरुहो वृक्षः । संविष्टेनोपविष्टेन । मित्रसंदर्शनमेव व्यतिकरस्तेनापगतश्चिन्ता एव ज्वरस्तस्यातिशयो यस्य । व्यतिकरो व्यापारः । 'व्यतिकरः समाख्यातो व्यसनव्यतिषङ्गयोः' इति विश्वः । मुकुलिते करकमले यस्य । मुकुलितकरकमलः संयोजितकरयुगलः । बद्धाञ्जलिरिति यावत् । प्रचारो यात्रा भूभ्रमणम् ।

इति श्रीदशकुमारचरितपूर्वपीठिकाटीकायां पददीपिकाभिधायां द्वितीय उच्छ्वासः ।

## तृतीयोच्छ्वासः ।

'देव, भवच्चरणकमलसेवाभिलाषीभूतोऽहं भ्रमन्नेकस्यां वनावनौ पिपासाकुलो लतापरिवृतं शीतलं नदसलिलं पिबन्नुज्ज्वलाकारं रत्नं तत्रैकमद्राक्षम् । तदादाय गत्वा कंचनाध्वानमम्बरमणेरत्युष्णतया गन्तुमक्षमो वनेऽस्मिन्नेव किमपि देवतायतनं प्रविष्टो दीनाननं बहुतनयसमेतं स्थविरमहीसुरमेकमवलोक्य कुशलमुदितदयोऽहमपृच्छम् । कार्पण्यविवर्णवदनो महदाशापूर्णमानसोऽवोचदग्रजन्मा—'महाभाग, सुतानेतान्मातृहीनाननेकैरुपायै रक्षन्निदानीमस्मिन्कुदेशे भैक्ष्यं[1] संपाद्य ददद्देतेभ्यो वसामि शिवालयेऽस्मिन्' इति । 'भूदेव, एतत्कटकाधिपती राजा कस्य देशस्य, किंनामधेयः, किमत्रागमनकारणमस्य' इति पृष्टोऽभाषत महीसुरः—'सौम्य, मत्तकालो नाम लाटेश्वरो देशस्यास्य पालयितुर्वीरकेतोस्तनयां वामलोचनां नाम तरुणीरत्नमसमानलावण्यं श्रावंश्रावमवधूतदुहितृप्रार्थनस्य तस्य नगरीम[2]रौत्सीत् । वीरकेतुरपि भीतो महदुपायनमिव तनयां मत्तकालायादात् । तरुणीलाभहृष्टचेता लाटपतिः 'परिणेया निजपुर एव' इति निश्चित्य गच्छन्निजदेशं प्रति संप्रति मृगयादरेणात्र वने सैन्यवासमकारयत् । [3]कन्यासारणे

देवेति । वनावनौ काननभूमौ । पातुमिच्छा पिपासा तयाऽऽकुलः । अम्बरमणिः सूर्यः । देवतायतनं मन्दिरम् । दीनं दैन्यव्याप्तमाननं यस्य । उदिता उत्पन्ना दया यस्य सः । कार्पण्यं कृपणस्य भावः । दैन्यमित्यर्थः । विवर्णं विगतवर्णं पाण्डु । महदाशेति प्रयोगश्चिन्त्यः । महति कार्ये आशा इति वा व्याख्येयम् । अग्रजन्मा ब्राह्मणः । भैक्ष्यं भिक्षावृत्त्या संपादितमन्नादि । कटकस्य निवेशितसैन्यस्य । किं नामधेयं यस्येति बहुव्रीहिः । लाट इति देशनाम । तरुणीषु रत्नम् । 'जातौ जातौ यदुत्कृष्टं तद्रत्नमभिधीयते' इति । असमानमनुपमं लावण्यं सौन्दर्यं यस्य तत् । श्रावं श्रावमिति णमुलन्तमेतत् । असकृच्छ्रुत्वेत्यर्थः । आभीक्ष्ण्ये णमुल् । अवधूता तिरस्कृता दुहितुः प्रार्थना तत्कृताऽभ्यर्थना येन । अरौत्सीदभियुयोज । मृगयादरेण मृगयानुरोधेन । कन्यायाः सारणे प्रापणे । कन्यासारेणेति पाठे कन्यैव सारो धनं तेन । 'सारो बले स्थिरांशे च मज्जि पुंसि

१ भैक्षम्. २ पाटलीं नाम्ना नगरीम्. ३ कन्यासारेण.

नियुक्तो मानपालो नाम वीरकेतुमन्त्री मानधनश्चतुरङ्गबलसमन्वितोऽन्यत्र रचितशिबिरस्तं निजनाथावमानखिन्नमानसोऽन्तर्बिभेद ' इति । ' विप्रोऽसौ बहुतनयो विद्वान्निर्धनः स्थविरश्च दानयोग्यः ' इति तस्मै करुणापूर्णमना रत्नमदाम् । परमाह्लादविकसिताननोऽभिहिताने काशीः कुत्रचिदग्रजन्मा जगाम । अध्वश्रमखिन्नेन मया तत्र निरवेशि निद्रासुखम् । तदनु पश्चान्निगडितबाहुयुगलः स भूसुरः कशाघातचिह्नितगात्रोऽनेकनैस्त्रिंशिकानुयातोऽभ्येत्य माम् ' असौ दस्युः ' इत्यदर्शयत् । परित्यक्तभूसुरा राजभटा रत्नावाप्तिप्रकारं मदुक्तमनाकर्ण्य भयरहितं मां गाढं नियम्य रज्जुभिरानीय कारागारम् ' एते तव सखायः ' इति निगडितान्कांश्चिन्निर्दिष्टवन्तो मामपि निगडितचरणयुगलमकार्षुः । किंकर्तव्यतामूढेन निराशक्लेशानुभवेनावाँचि मया—' ननु पुरुषा वीर्यपरुषाः, निमित्तेन केन निर्विशथ कारावासदुःखं दुस्तरम् । यूयं वयस्या इति निर्दिष्टमेतैः, किमिदम् ' इति । तथाविधं मामवेक्ष्य भूसुरान्मया श्रुतं लाटपतिवृत्तान्तं व्याख्याय चौरवीराः पुनरवोचन्—' महाभाग, वीरकेतुमन्त्रिणो मानपालस्य किंकरा वयम् । तदाज्ञया लाटेश्वरमारणाय रात्रौ सुरँङ्गाद्वारेण तदगारं प्रविश्य तत्र राजाभावेन विषण्णा बहु धनमपहृत्य महाटवीं प्राविशाम । अपरेद्युश्च पदा-

जले धने ' इति मेदिनी । मान एव धनं यस्येति तथा । शिबिरं सैन्यवासस्थानम् । ' तळ ' इति ख्यातम् । नाथः स्वामी राजा । बिभेद भेदं चकार । अभिहिता उच्चारिताः । दत्ता इति यावत् । अनेकाशिषो येन सः । निद्रासुखं निरवेश्युपभुक्तम् । अहं निद्रावशोऽभवमित्यर्थः । पश्चात्पृष्ठदेशे निगडितं शृङ्खलादिना बद्धं बाहुयुगलं यस्येति तथा । दत्तपश्चाद्बन्ध इत्यर्थः । कशायाः कशया वा घात आघातो वा ताडनम् । नैस्त्रिंशिकाः खड्गधारिणः । दस्युश्चौरः । परित्यक्तो बन्धनान्मुक्तो भूसुरो यैस्ते । रत्नस्यावाप्तेः प्रकारम् । रज्जुभिर्दोरकैः । कारागारं बन्धनगृहम् । निगडितान्बद्धान् । किंकर्तव्यतायां तद्विषये मूढः । किं कर्तव्यमित्यजानतेत्यर्थः । वीर्येण पराक्रमेण परुषाः कठिनाः । निमित्तेन कारणेन । निर्विशथानुभवथ । व्याख्याय कथयित्वा । चौराश्च ते वीराश्च । सुरङ्गा बिलपथः । अगारं गृहम् । विषण्णाः खिन्नाः । पदानि पादप्रतिमास्ता

१ रस्तन्निजनाथा०. २ अवोचि. ३ सुरुङ्गा.

न्वेषिणो राजानुचरा बहवोऽभ्येत्य धृतधनचयानस्मान्परितः परिवृत्य दृढतरं बद्ध्वा निकटमानीय समस्तवस्तुशोधनवेलायामेकस्यानर्घ्यरत्नस्याभावेनास्मद्वधाय माणिक्यादानायास्मान्किलाशृङ्खलयन्' इति। श्रुतरत्नरत्नावलोकनस्थानोऽहम् 'इदं तदेव माणिक्यम्' इति निश्चित्य भूदेवदाननिमित्तां दुरवस्थामात्मनो जन्म नामधेयं युष्मदन्वेषणपर्यटनप्रकारं चाभाष्य समयोचितैः संलापैर्मैत्रीमकार्षम्। ततोऽर्धरात्रे तेषां मम च शृङ्खलाबन्धनं निर्भिद्य तैरनुगम्यमानो निद्रितस्य द्वाःस्थगणस्यायुधजाल[1]मादाय पुररक्षान्पुरतोऽभिमुखागतान्पटुपराक्रमलीलयाऽभिद्राव्य मानपालशिबिरं प्राविशम्। मानपालो निजकिंकरेभ्यो मम कुलाभिमानवृत्तान्तं तत्कालीनं विक्रमं च निशम्य मामार्चयत्। परेद्युर्मत्तकालेन प्रेषिताः केचन पुरुषा मानपालमुपेत्य 'मन्त्रिन् मदीयराजमन्दिरे सुरङ्गया बहु धनमपहृत्य चौरवीरा भवदीयं कटकं प्राविशन्। तानर्पय। नो चेन्महाननर्थः संभविष्यति' इति क्रूरतरं वाक्यमब्रुवन्। तदाकर्ण्य रोषारुणितनेत्रो मन्त्री 'लाटपतिः कः, तेन मैत्री का, पुनरस्य वराकस्य सेवया किं लभ्यम्' इति तान्निरभर्त्सयत्। ते च मानपालेनोक्तं विप्रलापं मत्तकालाय तथैवाकथयन्। कुपितोऽपि लाटपतिर्दोर्वीर्यगर्वेणाल्पसैनिकसमेतो योद्धुमभ्यगात्। पूर्वमेव कृतरणनिश्चयो मानी मानपालः संनद्धयोधो युद्धकामो[2] भूत्वा निःशङ्कं निरगात्।

---

अन्विष्यन्तीति पदान्वेषिणः। शोधनमन्वेषणम्। अनर्घ्यममूल्यम्। महामूल्यमित्यर्थः। माणिक्यस्य आदानाय ग्रहणाय। अशृङ्खलयन् शृङ्खलाभिर्निगडितानकुर्वन्। श्रुतं रत्नस्य रत्नावलोकनस्य च स्थानं येन सः। भूदेवेति। विप्रदानात् संजाताम्। दुरवस्थां संकटम्। नामधेयं नाम। युष्मच्छब्देन राजवाहनग्रहणम्। द्वारि तिष्ठन्ति ते द्वाःस्थास्तेषां गणस्तस्य। आयुधानां जालं समूहम्। पुररक्षान्पुररक्षणनियुक्तपुरुषान्। अभिद्राव्य प्रपलाय्य। तत्काले भवं तत्कालीनम्। भवदीयं युष्माकम्। रोषेणारुणिते नेत्रे यस्य तथा। वराकस्य नीचस्य। निरभर्त्सयद्धिक्चकार। विप्रलापं विरोधोक्तिम्। दोर्वीर्यं भुजबलम्। सैनिका योद्धारः। कृतरणनिश्चयः कृतयुद्धव्यवसायः। संनद्धाः सज्जाः। वर्मिता इति

---

१ आयुधजातम्. २ योद्धुकामः.

अहमपि सबहुमानं मन्त्रिदत्तानि बहुलतुरङ्गमोपेतं चतुरसारथिं रथं च दृढतरं कवचं मदनुरूपं चापं च विविधबाणपूर्णं तूणीरद्वयं रणसमुचितान्यायुधानि गृहीत्वा युद्धसंनद्धो मदीयबलविश्वासेन रिपूद्धरणोद्युक्तं मन्त्रिणमन्वगाम् । परस्परमत्सरेण तुमुलसंगरकरमुभयसैन्यमतिक्रम्य समुल्लसद्भुजाटोपेन बाणवर्षं तदङ्गे विमुञ्चन्नराति[1] प्राहरम् । ततोऽतिरयतुरङ्गमं मद्रथं तन्निकटं नीत्वा शीघ्रलङ्घनोपेततदीयरथोऽहमरातेः शिरःकर्तनमकार्षम् । तस्मिन्निपतिते तदवशिष्टसैनिकेषु[2] पलायितेषु नानाविधहयगजादिवस्तुजातमादाय परमानन्दसंनतो[3] मन्त्री ममानेकविधां संभावनामकार्षीत् । मानपालप्रेषितात्तदनुचरादेतदखिलमुदन्तजातमाकर्ण्य संतुष्टमना राजाऽभ्युद्गतो मदीयपराक्रमे विस्मयमानः समहोत्सवममात्यबान्धवानुमत्या शुभदिने निजतनयां मह्यमदात् । ततो यौवराज्याभिषिक्तोऽहमनुदिनमाराधितमहीपालचित्तो वामलोचनयाऽनया सह नानाविधं सौख्यमनुभवन्भवद्विरहवेदनाशल्यसुलभवैकल्यहृदयः सिद्धादेशेन सुहृज्जनावलोकनफलं प्रदेशं महाकालनिवासिनः परमेश्वरस्याराधनायाद्य पत्नीसमेतः समागतोऽस्मि । भक्तवत्सलस्य गौरीपतेः कारुण्येन त्वत्पदारविन्दसंदर्शनानन्दसंदोहो मया लब्धः ' इति ।

तन्निशम्याभिनन्दितपराक्रमो राजवाहनस्तन्निरपराधदण्डे दैवमुपा-

---

यावत् । योधा यस्य सः । बहुलैः महाकायैः तुरङ्गमैरुपेतम् । चतुरसारथिमिति बहुव्रीहिः । कवचं वर्म । ' चिलखत ' इति भाषायाम् । तूणीर इषुधिः । ' भाता ' इति ख्यातः । उद्धरणमुच्छेदः । तुमुलः संकुलः संगरो युद्धम् । समुल्लसन्तौ भ्राजमाने भुजे बाहू तयोः आटोपो गर्वः । बाणानां वर्षो वृष्टिः । अरातिं शत्रुम् । अतिरया वेगवन्तस्तुरङ्गमा यस्य तम् । शीघ्रं लङ्घनमाक्रमणं तेन उपेतः प्राप्तः तस्येयं तदीयो रथो येन । तद्रथं गत्वेत्यर्थः । संनतो युक्तः । संभावनां सत्कारम् । अभ्युद्गतः संमानार्थं प्रत्युद्यातः । युवा चासौ राजा चेति युवराजः । तस्य भावः यौवराज्यम् । आराधितं संतोषितम् । शल्यं शङ्कुम् । विकलस्य भावो वैकल्यं विह्वलत्वम् । भवतो विरहस्तस्य वेदना एव शल्यानि तेभ्यः सुलभं वैकल्यं यस्य तादृक् हृदयं यस्य । महाकालेत्याख्यस्थले निवसतीति तम् । संदोहोऽतिशयः । तदिति । निशम्य श्रुत्वा । अभिनन्दितः स्तुतः पराक्रमो येन । दण्डः कारावासादिरूपः ।

---

१ अरातीन्. २ तदाऽवशिष्ट. ३ संभृतः.

लभ्य तस्मै क्रमेणात्मचरितं कथयामास। तस्मिन्नवसरे पुरतः पुष्पोद्भवं विलोक्य ससंभ्रमं निजानिटिलतटस्पृष्टचरणाङ्गुलिमुदञ्जलिममुं गाढमालिङ्ग्यानन्दबाष्पसंकुलसंफुल्ललोचनः 'सौम्य सोमदत्त, अयं स पुष्पोद्भवः' इति तस्मै तं दर्शयामास। तौ च चिरविरहदुःखं विसृज्यान्योन्यालिङ्गनसुखमन्वभूताम् । ततस्तस्यैव महीरुहस्य च्छायायामुपविश्य राजा सादरहासमभाषत—'वयस्य, भूसुरकार्यं करिष्णुरहं मित्रगणो विदितार्थः सर्वथाऽन्तरायं करिष्यतीति निद्रितान्भवतः परित्यज्य निरगाम्। तदनु प्रबुद्धो वयस्यवर्गः किमिति निश्चित्य मदन्वेषणाय कुत्र गतवान् । भवानेकाकी कुत्र गतः' इति। सोऽपि ललाटतटचुम्बदञ्जलिपुटः सविनयमलपत्—

इति श्रीदण्डिनः कृतौ दशकुमारचरिते सोमदत्तचरितं नाम तृतीय उच्छ्वासः।

---

## चतुर्थोच्छ्वासः।

'देव, महीसुरोपकारायैव देवो गतवानिति निश्चित्यापि देवेन गन्तव्यं[1] देशं निर्णेतुमशक्नुवानो मित्रगणः परस्परं वियुज्य दिक्षु देवमन्वेष्टुमगच्छत् । अहमपि देवस्यान्वेषणाय महीमटन्कदाचिदम्बरमध्यगतस्याम्बरमणेः किरणमसहिष्णुरेकस्य गिरितटमहीरुहस्य प्रच्छायशीतले तले क्षणमुपाविशम् । मम पुरोभागे दिनमध्यसंकुचितसर्वावयवां[2] कूर्माकृतिं[3] मानुषच्छायां निरीक्ष्योन्मुखो गगनतलान्महारयेण पतन्तं पुरुषं कंचिदन्तराल एव दयोपनतहृदयोऽहमवलम्ब्य शनैरवनितले

---

उपालभ्य गर्हित्वा । निजं निटिलं ललाटं तस्य तटेन स्पृष्टः चरणयोरङ्गुल्यो येन तम्। आनन्दस्य बाष्पाणि तैः संकुले पूर्णे संफुल्ले च लोचने यस्य। अन्तरायं विघ्नम्। ललाटतटं चुम्बद् अञ्जलिपुटं यस्य। अलपद्बभाषे।

**इति श्रीदशकुमारचरितपूर्वपीठिकाटीकायां पददीपिकाभिधायां तृतीय उच्छ्वासः।**

---

**देवेति** । अशक्नुवानः। अत्र आत्मनेपदं चिन्त्यम्। यद्वा 'ताच्छील्यवयोवचनशक्तिषु चानश्' इति चानश्। अम्बरमणेः सूर्यस्य । दिनमध्येन संकुचिताः सर्वेऽवयवा यस्याः सा । कूर्मस्येवाकृतिर्यस्याः सा ताम्। वीतसंज्ञं नष्टचेष्टम्।

---

१ गन्ता. २ दिनमध्यसमये संकु०. ३ अस्मात्प्राक् 'शूर्पाकृतिम्' इत्यधि० ए० पुस्तके.

निक्षिप्य दूरापातवीतसंज्ञं तं शिशिरोपचारेण विबोध्य शोकातिरेकेणोद्गतबाष्पलोचनं तं भृगुपतनकारणमपृच्छम् । सोऽपि कररुहैरश्रुकणानपनयन्नभाषत—'सौम्य, मगधाधिनाथामात्यस्य पद्मोद्भवस्यात्मसंभवो रत्नोद्भवो नामाहम् । वाणिज्यरूपेण कालयवनद्वीपमुपेत्य कामपि वणिक्कन्यकां परिणीय तया सह प्रत्यागच्छन्नम्बुधौ[1] तीरस्यानतिदूर एव प्रवहणस्य भग्नतया सर्वेषु निमग्नेषु कथं कथमपि दैवानुकूल्येन तीरभूमिमभिगम्य निजाङ्गनावियोगदुःखार्णवे प्लवमानः कस्यापि सिद्धतापसस्यादेशादरेण षोडश हायनानि कथंचिन्नीत्वा दुःखस्य पारमनवेक्षमाणो गिरिपतनमकार्षम्' इति । तस्मिन्नेवावसरे किमपि नारीकूजितमश्रावि—'न खलु समुचितमिदं यत्सिद्धादिष्टे पतितनयमिलने विरहमसहिष्णुर्वैश्वानरं विशसि' इति । तन्निशम्य मनोविदितजनकभावं तमवादिषम्—'तात, भवते विज्ञापनीयानि बहूनि सन्ति । भवतु । पश्चादखिलमाख्यातव्यम् । अधुना नारीकूजितमनुपेक्षणीयं मया । क्षणमात्रमत्र भवता स्थीयताम्' इति । तदनु सोऽहं त्वरया किंचिदन्तरमगमम् । तत्र पुरतो भयंकरज्वालाकुलहुतभुगवगाहनसाहसिकां मुकुलिताञ्जलिपुटां वनितां कांचिदवलोक्य ससंभ्रममनलादपनीय कूजन्त्या वृद्धया सह मत्पितुरभ्यर्णमभिगमय्य स्थविरामवोचम्—'वृद्धे, भवत्यौ कुत्रत्ये । कान्तारे निमित्तेन केन दुरवस्थाऽनुभूयते । कथ्यताम्' इति । सा सगद्गदमवादीत—'पुत्र, कालयवनद्वीपे कालगुप्तनाम्नो

विबोध्य प्रकृतिमापाद्य । अतिरेकोऽतिशयः । भृगोः पतनस्य कारणं हेतुम् । कररुहैर्नखैः । प्रवहणस्य पोतस्य । कथं कथमपि महताऽऽयासेन । अङ्गना भार्या । तस्या वियोगदुःखमेवार्णवस्तास्मिन् । हायनानि वत्सरान् । कूजितं शब्दः । सिद्धेनादिष्टे कथिते । वैश्वानरं वह्निम् । मनसा विदितो जनकभावो यस्य तम् । विज्ञापनीयानि विज्ञापयितुं योग्यानि । ज्वालाभिराकुलो व्याप्तो यो हुतभुगग्निस्तत्रावगाहनं प्रवेशः तदेव साहसं तत्रोद्यतामित्यर्थः । कूजन्त्या विलपन्त्या । अभ्यर्णं समीपम् । अभिगमय्य प्रापय्य । णिजन्ताल्ल्यप् । कुत्रत्ये कुत आगते । दुरवस्था सव्यसनिता । सगद्गदं गद्गदस्वरेण ।

१ अम्बुतीरस्य.

वणिजः कस्यचिदेषा सुता सुवृत्ता नाम रत्नोद्भवेन निजकान्ते-नागच्छन्ती जलधौ मग्ने प्रवहणे निजधात्र्या मया सह फलकमेक-मवलम्ब्य दैवयोगेन कूलमुपेताऽऽसन्नप्रसवसमया कस्यांचिदटव्यामात्मज-मसूत। मम तु मन्दभाग्यतया बाले वनमातङ्गेन गृहीते मद्द्वितीया परिभ्रमन्ती 'षोडशवर्षानन्तरं भर्तृपुत्रसंगमो भविष्यति' इति सिद्ध-वाक्यविश्वासादेकस्मिन्पुण्याश्रमे तावन्तं समयं नीत्वा शोकमपारं सोढुमक्षमा समुज्ज्वलिते वैश्वानरे शरीरमाहुतीकर्तुमुद्युक्ताऽऽसीत्' इति। तदाकर्ण्य निजजननीं ज्ञात्वा तामहं दण्डवत्प्रणम्य तस्यै मदुदन्त-मखिलमाख्याय धात्रीभाषणफुल्लवदनं विस्मयविकसिताक्षं जनकमदर्शयम्। पितरौ तौ साभिज्ञानमन्योन्यं ज्ञात्वा मुदितान्तरात्मानौ विनीतं मामान-न्दाश्रुवर्षेणाभिषिच्य गाढमाश्लिष्य शिरस्युपाघ्राय कस्यांचिन्महीरुह-च्छायायामुपाविशताम्। 'कथं निवसति महीवल्लभो राजहंसः' इति जनकेन पृष्टोऽहं तस्य राज्यच्युतिं त्वदीयजननं सकलकुमारावाप्तिं तव दिग्विजयारम्भं भवतो मातङ्गानुयानमस्माकं युष्मदन्वेषणकारणं सकल-मभ्यधाम्। ततस्तौ कस्यचिदाश्रमे मुनेरस्थापयम्। ततो देवस्यान्वेषण-परायणोऽहमखिलकार्यनिमित्तं वित्तं निश्चित्य भवदनुग्रहाल्लब्धस्य साधकत्वस्य साहाय्यकरणदक्षं शिष्यगणं निष्पाद्य विन्ध्यवनमध्ये पुरातनपत्तनस्थानान्युपेत्य विविधनिधिसूचकानां महीरुहाणामधोनिक्षिप्ता-न्वसुपूर्णान्कलशान्सिद्धाञ्जनेन ज्ञात्वा रक्षिषु परितः स्थितेषु खनन-

---

आसन्नः प्राप्तः प्रसवस्य समयो यस्याः सा। वनमातङ्गेन वन्यकरिणा। अहं द्वितीया सहायभूता यस्याः सा। तावन्तं तत्परिमाणकं समयं षोडशाब्दानित्यर्थः। अक्षमाऽसमर्था। दण्डः काष्ठदण्डस्तेन तुल्यं दण्डवत्। धात्र्या यद्भाषणं तेन फुल्लानन्द-विकसितं वदनं यस्य तम्। साभिज्ञानमन्योन्यप्रत्यभिज्ञादर्शकचिह्नानि दृष्ट्वा पृष्ट्वा च। मुदितो हृष्टोऽन्तरात्मा ययोस्तौ। विनीतं प्रश्रयावनतम्। च्युतिर्भ्रंशः। परायणस्त-त्परः। दक्षश्चतुरः। सिद्धाञ्जनेन सिद्धादिष्टेन दत्तेन वाऽञ्जनेन। खननसाधनैः

---

१ अमन्दा. २ पुरतः.

साधनैरुत्पाद्य दीनारानसंख्यान्राशीकृत्य तत्कालगतमनतिदूरे निवेशितं वणिक्कटकं कंचिदभ्येत्य तत्र बलिनो बलीवर्दान्गोणीश्च क्रीत्वाऽन्यद्रव्यमिषेण वसु तद्गोणीसंचितं तैरुह्यमानं शनैः कटकमनयम् । तदधिकारिणा चन्द्रपालेन केनचिद्वणिक्पुत्रेण विरचितसौहृदोऽहममुनैव साकमुज्जयिनीमुपाविशम् । मत्पितरावपि तां पुरीमभिगमय्य सकलगुणनिलयेन बन्धुपालनाम्ना चन्द्रपालजनकेन नीयमानो मालवनाथदर्शनं विधाय तदनुमत्या गूढवसतिमकरवम् । ततः काननभूमिषु भवन्तमन्वेष्टुमुद्युक्तं मां परममित्रं बन्धुपालो निशम्यावदत्—'सकलं धरणीतलमपारमन्वेष्टुमक्षमो भवान्मनोग्लानिं विहाय तूष्णीं तिष्ठतु । भवन्नायकालोकनकारणं शुभशकुनं निरीक्ष्य कथयिष्यामि' इति । तल्लपितामृताश्वासितहृदयोऽहमनुदिनं तदुपकण्ठवर्ती कदाचिदिन्दुमुखीं नवयौवनावलीढावयवा नयनचन्द्रिकां बालचन्द्रिकां नाम तरुणीरत्नं वणिङ्मन्दिरलक्ष्मीं मूर्तामिवावलोक्य तदीयलावण्यावधूतधीरभावो लतान्तबाणबाणलक्ष्यतामयासिषम् । चकितबालकुरङ्गलोचना साऽपि कुसुमसायकसायकायमानेन कटाक्षवीक्षणेन मामसकृन्निरीक्ष्य मन्दमारुतान्दोलिता लतेवाकम्पत । मनसाऽभिमुखैश्च समाकुञ्चितै

खनित्रादिभिः । दीनारानेतत्संज्ञकनाणकान् । वणिक्कटकं वणिक्समाजम् । बलीवर्दान्वृषभान् । गोणीर्धान्यावपनानि । 'जानपदकुण्डगोण—' इति ङीष् आवपनार्थे । अन्यद्रव्यमिषेणान्यद्रव्यमिति कथयित्वा । अभिगमय्य प्रापय्य । निलयो गृहं वासस्थानम् । न विद्यते पारोऽन्तो यस्य तदपारम् । ग्लानिं हर्षक्षयं निर्वेदम् । तस्या लपितं भाषितमेवामृतं तेनाश्वासितं हृदयं यस्य । उपकण्ठवर्ती समीपवर्ती । नवयौवनेन अवलीढा व्याप्ता अवयवा यस्यास्ताम् । मूर्तां मूर्तिमतीम् । तदीयेति । तस्या लावण्येन सौन्दर्येणावधूतश्चालितो धीरभावो धैर्यं यस्यैतादृशः । लतान्ता बाणा यस्य स लतान्तबाणः कामस्तस्य बाणास्तेषां लक्ष्यतां शरव्यत्वम् । लावण्यवतीं तां दृष्ट्वा कामबाणैर्बिद्धोऽभवमिति तात्पर्यार्थः । चकितो भीतो यः बालकुरङ्गस्तस्येव लोचने यस्याः । बालशब्देनातिकातरत्वमतिलोलत्वं च नयनयोर्दर्शितम् । कुसुमानि सायका यस्य स कामस्तस्य सायक इवाचरतीति तथा तेन । कटाक्षवीक्षणेन चेष्टाविशेषेणापाङ्गदर्शनेन । असकृद्वारंवारम् । आन्दोलिता कम्पिता । मनसा अकथयदिति संबन्धः । रागश्च लज्जा च तयोरन्तराले मध्ये वर्तन्ते इति तैः ।

१ उत्पाद्य. २ तत्कालगतम्. ३ संमितम्.

रागलज्जान्तरालवर्तिभिरपाङ्ग[1]वर्तिभिरीक्षणविशेषैर्निजमनोवृत्तिमकथयत् । चतुरगूढचेष्टाभिरस्या मनोनुरागं सम्यग्ज्ञात्वा सुखसंगमोपायमचिन्तयम् । अन्यदा बन्धुपालः शकुनैर्भवद्गतिं प्रेक्षिष्यमाणः पुरोपान्तविहारवनं मया सहोपेत्य कस्मिंश्चिन्महीरुहे शकुन्तवचनानि शृण्वन्नतिष्ठत् । अहमुत्कलिकाविनोदपरायणो वनान्तरे[2] परिभ्रमन्सरोवरतीरे चिन्ताक्रान्तचित्तां दीनवदनां मन्मनोरथैकभूमिं बालचन्द्रिकां व्यलोकयम् । तस्याः ससंभ्रमप्रेमलज्जाकौतुकमनोरमं लीलाविलोकनसुखमनुभवन्सुदत्या वदनारविन्दे विषण्णभावं मदनकदनखेदानुभूतं ज्ञात्वा तन्निमित्तं ज्ञास्यँल्लीलया तदुपकण्ठमुपेत्यावोचम्[3]—' सुमुखि तव मुखारविन्दस्य दैन्यकारणं कथय ' इति । सा रहस्यसंजातविश्रम्भतया विहाय लज्जाभये शनैरभाषत—' सौम्य मानसारो मालवाधीश्वरो वार्द्धकस्य प्रबलतया निजनन्दनं दर्पसारमुज्जयिन्यामभ्यषिञ्चत् । स कुमारः सप्तसागरपर्यन्तं महीमण्डलं पालयिष्यन्निजपैतृष्वस्रीयावुद्दण्डकर्माणौ चण्डवर्मदारुवर्माणौ धरणीभरणे नियुज्य तपश्चरणाय राजराजगिरिम्[4]अभ्यगात् । राज्यं सर्वमसपत्नं शासति चण्डवर्मणि दारुवर्मा मातुलाग्रजन्मनोः शासनमतिक्रम्य

---

अपाङ्गयोर्नयनप्रान्तयोर्वर्तन्ते तैः । ' साङ्गभाङ्गिभिः ' इति पाठेऽङ्गभङ्गिभिः विकृतिभिः सहितैः । ' व्याजच्छलनिभे भङ्गिः ' इति रभसः । विशेषावस्थानशोभिभिरित्यर्थः । मनोवृत्तिं मनोव्यापारम् । अभिलाषमिति यावत् । अनुरागं प्रीतिम् । अन्यदैकस्मिन्काले । भवतो गतिं दशां स्थितिमिति यावत् । ' गतिर्मार्गे दशायां च ' इति विश्वः । उपान्ते समीपे । विहारवनं क्रीडोद्यानम् । शकुन्ताः पक्षिणः । उत्कलिकोत्कण्ठा । चिन्तयाऽऽक्रान्तं पर्याकुलं चित्तं यस्याः । दीनवदनां विषण्णमुखीम् । एकभूमिं मुख्यस्थानम् । संभ्रमेण सहितं ससंभ्रमं यत् प्रेम च लज्जा च कौतुकं च तैर्मनोरमम् । लीलया लीलानां वा विलोकनं तस्य सुखम् । मदनकदनं उन्माथस्तस्मात्खेदः तस्मादनुभूतम् । उपकण्ठं समीपम् । रहस्याविषये संजात उत्पन्नो विश्रम्भः तत्तया । वार्द्धकस्य जरायाः । पैतृष्वस्रीयौ पितुः स्वसायास्तनयौ । 'पितृष्वसुश्छण्' इति छण् । ' मातृपितृभ्यां स्वसा ' इति स्वसुः सस्य षत्वं च । उद्दण्डं घोरं कर्म ययोः । धरणीभरणे पृथ्वीपोषणे । राज्यपालन इत्यर्थः । राजराजः कुबेरस्तस्य गिरिः कैलासः । असपत्नं निर्जितशत्रुम् । निष्कण्टकमिति यावत् । शासति सति । मातुलो मातुर्भ्राता अग्रजन्मा ज्यायान्भ्राता च तयोः । ' मातुर्डुलच् ' । ' पितृव्यमातुल-' इति

---

१ साऽङ्गवर्तिभिः; साङ्गभङ्गिभिः. २ वनान्ते. ३ अवोचिषम. ४ राजगिरिम्.

पारदार्यपरद्रव्यापहरणादि दुष्कर्म कुर्वाणो मन्मथसमानस्य भवतो लावण्यायत्तचित्तां मामेकदा विलोक्य कन्यादूषणदोषं दूरीकृत्य बलात्कारेण रन्तुमुद्युङ्क्ते । तच्चिन्तया दैन्यमगच्छम् ' इति । तस्या मनोगतं मयि रागोद्रेकं मन्मनोरथसिद्ध्यन्तरायं च निशम्य बाष्पपर्णलोचनां तामाश्वास्य दारुवर्मणो मारणोपायं च विचार्य वल्लभामवोचम्—'तरुणि भवदभिलाषिणं दुष्टहृदयमेनं निहन्तुं मृदुरुपायः कश्चिन्मया चिन्त्यते । यक्षः कश्चिदधिष्ठाय बालचन्द्रिकां निवसति । तदाकारसंपदाशाशृङ्खलितहृदयो यः संबन्धयोग्यः साहसिको रतिमन्दिरे तं यक्षं निर्जित्य तयैकसखीसमेतया मृगाक्ष्या संलापामृतसुखमनुभूय कुशली निर्गमिष्यति तेन चक्रवाकसंशयाकारपयोधरा विवाहनीयेति सिद्धेनैकेनावादीति पुरजनस्य पुरतो भवदीयैः सत्यवाक्यैर्जनैरसकृत्कथनीयम् । तदनु दारुवर्मा वाक्यानीत्थंविधानि श्रावंश्रावं तूष्णीं यदि भिया स्थास्यति तर्हि वरम् । यदि वा दौर्जन्येन त्वया संगमङ्गीकरिष्यति तदा स भवदीयैरित्थं वाच्यः— ' सौम्य दर्पसारवसुधाधिपामात्यस्य भवतोऽस्मन्निवासे साहसकरणमनुचितम् । पौरजनसाक्षिकं भवन्मदिरमानीतया तया तोयजाक्ष्या सह क्रीडन्नायुष्मान्यदि भविष्यसि तदा परिणीय तरुणीं मनोरथान्निर्विश ' इति । सोऽप्येतदङ्गीकरिष्यति । त्वं सखीवेषधारिणा मया सह तस्य मन्दिरं गच्छ । अहमेकान्तनिकेतने मुष्टिजानुपादाघातैस्तं रभसान्निहत्य पुनरपि वयस्यामिषेण भवतीमनु निःशङ्कं निर्ग-

---

निपातः । शासनमतिक्रम्य तन्निदेशमतिवृत्य । उल्लङ्घ्येत्यर्थः । पारदार्यं परदाराभिमर्शः । मन्मथः कामः । मनो मथ्नातीति मन्मथः । आयत्तमधीनम् । रागोद्रेकं प्रीत्यतिशयम् । मृदुः कोमलः । बालचन्द्रिकामिति 'अधिशीङ्स्थासां कर्म' इति कर्मत्वम् । तस्या आकारसंपदः शोभनाकृतेराशा तया शृङ्खलितं हृदयं यस्य सः । साहसिकः साहसं कर्तुमुद्यतः । सत्यवाक्यैः आप्तैरित्यर्थः । श्रावंश्रावं श्रुत्वा श्रुत्वा । णमुल् । तोयजं कमलम् । निर्विशोपभुङ्क्ष्व । निकेतने गृहे । रभसाद्वेगेन ।

मिष्यामि । तदेनमुपायमङ्गीकृत्य विगतसाध्वसलज्जा भवज्जनकजननीसहोदराणां पुरत आवयोः प्रेमातिशयमाख्याय सर्वथाऽस्मत्परिणयकरणेताननुनयेः । तेऽपि वंशसंपल्लावण्याढ्याय यूने मह्यं त्वां दास्यन्त्येव । दारुवर्मणो मारणोपायं तेभ्यः कथयित्वा तेषामुत्तरमाख्येयं मह्यम्' इति । साऽपि किंचिदुत्फुल्लसरसिजानना मामब्रवीत्—'सुभग क्रूरकर्माणं दारुवर्माणं भवानेव हन्तुमर्हति । तस्मिन्हते सर्वथा युष्मन्मनोरथः फलिष्यति । एवं क्रियताम् । भवदुक्तं सर्वमहमपि तथा करिष्ये' इति मामसकृद्विवृत्तवदना विलोकयन्ती मन्दं मन्दमगारमगात् । अहमपि बन्धुपालमुपेत्य शकुनज्ञात्तस्मात् 'त्रिंशद्दिवसानन्तरमेव भवत्स : संभविष्यति' इत्यशृणवम् । तदनु मदनुगम्यमानो बन्धुपालो निजावासं प्रविश्य मामपि निलयाय विससर्ज । मन्मायोपायवागुरापाशलम्भेन दारुवर्मणा रतिमन्दिरे रन्तुं समाहूता बालचन्द्रिका तं गमिष्यन्ती दूतिकां मन्निकटमभिप्रेषितवती । अहमपि मणिनूपुरमेखलाकङ्कणकटकताटङ्कहारक्षौमकज्जलं वनितायोग्यं मण्डनजातं निपुणतया तत्तत्स्थानेषु निक्षिप्य सम्यगङ्गीकृतमनोज्ञवेषो वल्लभया तया सह तदागारद्वारोपान्तमगच्छम् । द्वाःस्थकथितास्मदागमनेन सादरं विहिताभ्युद्गतिना तेन द्वारोपान्तनिवारिताशेषपरिवारेण मदन्विता बालचन्द्रिका संकेतागारमनीयत । नगरव्याकुलां यक्षकथां परीक्षन्नागरिकजनोऽपि कुतूहलेन दारुवर्मणः प्रतीहारभूमिमगमत् । विवेकशून्य-

---

अनुनयेस्तोषयेः । लिङ् । वंशसंपच्च लावण्यं च ताभ्यामाढ्याय युक्ताय संपन्नाय वा । किंचिदुत्फुल्लं यत्सरसिजं कमलं तद्वदाननं यस्याः । अलुक्समासः । विवृत्तं परावृत्तं वदनं मुखं यस्याः सा । अगारं गृहम् । निलयाय । गृहं गन्तुमित्यर्थः । 'तुमर्थाच्च भाववचनात्' इति चतुर्थी । मम मायोपायः कपटयुक्तिः स एव वागुरा बन्धनं तस्याः पाशलम्भेन । नूपुरो मञ्जीरः पादभूषणम् । मेखला काञ्चीदाम कटिभूषणम् । कङ्कणं कटकं च हस्तभूषणे । ताटङ्कं कर्णभूषणम् । क्षौमं दुकूलम् । तत्तत्स्थानेषु योग्यस्थानेषु । विहिताऽभ्युद्गतिर्येन । नगरव्याकुलां पुरप्रसृताम् । परीक्षन्निति प्रयोगः प्रामादिकः । परीक्षमाण इति वक्तव्यम् । कुतूहलेन कौतुकेन । प्रतीहारभूमिं द्वार-

मतिरसौ रागातिरेकेण रत्नखचितहेमपर्यङ्के हंसतूलगर्भशयन-मानीय तरुणीं तस्यै मह्यं तामिस्रासम्यगनवलोकितपुंभावाय मनोरम-स्त्रीवेषाय च चामीकरमणिमयमण्डनानि सूक्ष्माणि चित्रवस्त्राणि कस्तूरिकामिलितं हरिचन्दनं कर्पूरसहितं ताम्बूलं सुरभीणि कुसुमानीत्यादिवस्तुजातं समर्प्य मुहूर्तद्वयमात्रं हासवचनैः संलपन्नतिष्ठत् । ततो रागान्धतया सुमुख्यालिङ्गने मतिं व्यधत्त । रोषारुणितोऽहमेनं पर्यङ्कतलान्निःशङ्को निपात्य मुष्टिजानुपादा-घातैः प्राहरम् । नियुद्धरभसविकलमलंकारं पूर्ववन्मेलयित्वा भयकम्पितां नताङ्गीमुपलालयन्मन्दिराङ्गणमुपेतः साध्वस-कम्पित इवोच्चैरकूजमहम्[३]—'हा बालचन्द्रिकाधिष्ठितेन घोरा-कारेण यक्षेण दारुवर्मा निहन्यते । सहसा समागच्छत । पश्यतेमम्' इति । तदाकर्ण्य मिलिता जनाः समुद्यद्बाष्पा हाहानिनादेन दिशो बधिरयन्तः 'बालचन्द्रिकामधिष्ठितं यक्षं बलवन्तं शृण्वन्नपि दारुवर्मा मदान्धस्तामेवायाचत । तदसौ स्वकीयेन कर्मणा निहतः । किं तस्य विलापेन' इति मिथो लपन्तः प्राविशन् । कोलाहले तस्मिंश्चटुल-लोचनया सह नैपुण्येन सहसा निर्गतो निजावासमगाम् । ततो गतेषु कतिपयदिनेषु पौरजनसमक्षं सिद्धादेशप्रकारेण विवाह्य तामिन्दुमुखीं पूर्वसंकल्पितान्सुरतविशेषान्यथेष्टमन्वभूवम् । बन्धुपालशकुननिर्दिष्टे दिवसे-ऽस्मिन्निर्गत्य पुराद्बहिर्वर्तमानो नेत्रोत्सवकारि भवदवलोकनसुखमप्य-नुभवामि' इति ।

---

प्रदेशम् । विवेकेन शून्या रहिता मतिर्यस्य । हंसतूलो गर्भे यस्य तत् । तमिस्रा रात्रिस्तस्यां सम्यगनवलोकितो न दृष्टः पुंभावः पुंस्त्वं यस्य तस्मै । चामीकरं सुवर्णं मणयश्च तेषां विकाराः चामीकरमणिमयानि । 'चामीकरं जातरूपम्' इत्यमरः । मण्डनान्यलंकारान् । चित्राणि रमणीयानि । मुहूर्तो द्वादशक्षणा-वधिः कालः । नियुद्धस्य बाहुयुद्धस्य रभसेन वेगेन विकलं स्वस्थानच्युतम् । 'नियुद्धं बाहुयुद्धेऽथ' इत्यमरः । मेलयित्वा स्थाने स्थाने पर्यवस्थाप्य । उपलाल-यन्सान्त्वयन् । अङ्गणमजिरम् । साध्वसं भयम् । अकूजमाक्रोशं कृतवान् । घोर आकारो यस्य । समुद्यन्ति बाष्पाणि येषां ते । हाहानिनादेन हा हा इति शब्देन ।

---

१ कुसुमानि ललितं वस्तुजातम्. २ ०स्त्रीकुच-कच-ग्रहणे. ३ अहह.

एवं मित्रवृत्तान्तं निशम्याम्लानमानसो राजवाहनः स्वस्य च सोमदत्तस्य च वृत्तान्तमस्मै निवेद्य सोमदत्तम् 'महाकालेश्वराराधनानन्तरं भवद्वल्लभां सपरिवारां निजकटकं प्रापय्यागच्छ' इति नियुज्य पुष्पोद्भवेन सेव्यमानो भूस्वर्गायमानमवन्तिकापुरं विवेश। तत्र 'अयं मम स्वामिकुमारः' इति बन्धुपालादये बन्धुजनाय कथयित्वा तेन राजवाहनाय बहुविधां सपर्यां कारयन्सकलकलाकुशलो महीसुरवर इति पुरि प्रकटयन्पुष्पोद्भवोऽमुष्य राज्ञो मज्जनभोजनादिकमनुदिनं स्वमन्दिरे कारयामास।

इति श्रीदण्डिनः कृतौ दशकुमारचरिते पुष्पोद्भवचरितं नाम चतुर्थ उच्छ्वासः।

---

## पञ्चमोच्छ्वासः।

अथ मीनकेतनसेनानायकेन मलयगिरिमहीरुहनिरन्तरावासिभुजंगमभुक्तावशिष्टेनेव सूक्ष्मतरेण धृतहरिचन्दनपरिमलभरेणेव मन्दगतिना दक्षिणानिलेन वियोगिहृदयस्थं मन्मथानलमुज्ज्वलयन्, सहकारकिसलयमकरन्दास्वादनरक्तकण्ठानां मधुकरकल-

---

दिशो बधिरयन्त उच्चैराक्रोशन्तः। चटुले चञ्चले। **एवमिति**। निजकटकं स्ववासस्थानम्। भुवि स्वर्ग इव आचरति तम्। सपर्यां पूजां सत्कारं वा। प्रकटयन्प्रथयन्। मज्जनं स्नानम्।

**इति श्रीदशकुमारचरितपूर्वपीठिकाटीकायां पददीपिकाभिधायां चतुर्थ उच्छ्वासः।**

---

**अथेति**। मीनो मत्स्यः केतनो ध्वजो यस्य। काम इत्यर्थः। तस्य सेनाया नायकोऽङ्गवीरः। सेनापतिरित्यर्थः। दक्षिणानिलस्यात्युद्दीपकत्वान्नायक इत्युक्तिः। मलय एतत्संज्ञको दक्षिणदेशवर्ती कोऽपि गिरिः। निरन्तरं निबिडमित्यर्थः। सर्पा वाताशिन इत्यनिलस्य भुक्तत्वम्। अनिलः सूक्ष्मतरोऽल्पोऽतीव मन्दः। मन्दत्वे पूर्वपदं हेतुः। एवमुत्तरत्रापि धृतहरीत्यादि मन्दगतित्वे हेतुभूतम्। परिमल आमोदः। यो भाराक्रान्तः स मन्दं यातीति स्वभावोक्तिः। अनिलो वायुः। मन्मथानलं कामाग्निम्। उज्ज्वलयन्दीप्तं कुर्वन्। मकरन्दो मधु। रक्तो रागयुक्तः।

---

१ अञ्जन. २ धूत.

कण्ठानां काकलीकलकलेन दिक्चक्रं वाचालयन्, मानिनीमानसोत्कलिकामुपनयन्, माकन्दसिन्दुवाररक्ताशोककिंशुकातिलकेषु कलिकामुपपादयन्, मदनमहोत्सवाय रसिकमनांसि समुल्लासयन्, वसन्तसमयः समाजगाम । तस्मिन्नतिरमणीये कालेऽवन्तिसुन्दरी नाम मानसारनन्दिनी प्रियवयस्यया बालचन्द्रिकया सह नगरोपान्तरम्योद्याने विहारोत्कण्ठया पौरसुन्दरीसमवायसमन्विता कस्यचिच्चूतपोतकस्य च्छायाशीतले सैकततले गन्धकुसुमहरिद्राक्षतचीनाम्बरादिनानाविधेन परिमलद्रव्यनिकरेण मनोभवमर्चयन्ती रेमे । तत्र रतिप्रातिकृतिमवन्तिसुन्दरीं द्रष्टुकामः काम इव वसन्तसहायः पुष्पोद्भवसमन्वितो राजवाहनस्तदुपवनं प्रविश्य तत्र तत्र मलयमारुतान्दोलितशाखानिरन्तरसमुद्भिन्नकिसलयकुसुमफलसमुल्लसितेषु रसालतरुषु कोकिल[1]कुलकीरालिमधुकराणामालापाञ्श्रावंश्रावं किंचिद्विकसदिन्दीवरकह्लारकैरवराजीवराजिकेलिलोलकलहंससारसकारण्डवचक्रवाकचक्रवालकलरवव्याकुलविमलशीतलसलिलललितानि सरांसि दर्शंदर्शम्, अमन्दलीलया ललनासमीपमवाप । बालचन्द्रिकया 'निःशङ्कमित आगम्यताम्' इति

---

कलकण्ठाः कोकिलाः । कलकलः कोलाहलः । वाचालयन्मुखरं कुर्वन् । मानिन्यो मानवत्यः स्त्रियः । उत्कलिकोत्कण्ठा । उपनयन्प्रापयन् । माकन्दः सहकारः । सिन्दुवारो निर्गुण्डी । किंशुकः पलाशः । तिलकस्तत्संज्ञको वृक्षः । कलिका कोरकः । उपपादयन् जनयन् । रसिकशब्देनात्र कामिजना गृह्यन्ते । समुल्लासयन्नुत्साहयन् । मानसार इति मालवेश्वरनाम । वयस्या सखी । चूतपोतको बालाम्रः । सैकतः सिकतामयः प्रदेशः । चीनाम्बरं सूक्ष्मवस्त्रम् । एतान्यादौ येषां तानि गन्धादीनि तैर्नानाविधस्तेन । प्रतिकृतिं प्रतिमाम् । वसन्तः सहायो यस्येति तथा । मलयमारुतो दक्षिणानिलस्तेन आन्दोलिताश्चालिताः याः शाखाः तत्र निरन्तरं समुद्भिन्नानि यानि किस०फलानि तैः समुल्लसितेषु । रसालतरुराम्रवृक्षः । कीराः शुकाः । आलयः पङ्क्तयः । आलापान्रवान् । किंचिद्विकसन्ति यानि इन्दीवरकह्लारकैरवराजीवानि तेषां राजिषु याः केलयः क्रीडास्तत्र लोला आसक्ता ये कलहंससारसकारण्डवचक्रवाकास्तेषां चक्रवालस्य मण्डलस्य यः कलरवः कलोऽव्यक्तमधुरः स्वरः तेन व्याकुलानि व्याप्तानि यानि विमल०सलिलानि तैः ललितानि । इन्दीवरं नीलम् । कह्लारं शुक्लम् । कैरवमपि सितम् । राजीवमिति कमलसामान्यनाम । कलहंसो हंसजातिः पक्षिविशेषः । सारसः पुष्कराह्वः । कारण्डवो मद्गुः । 'पाणकोंबडा' इति ख्यातः । विमलान्यकलुषाणि । दर्शंदर्शम् ।

---

१ कोकिलकीरालिकुलमधु०

हस्तसंज्ञया समाहूतो निजतेजोनिर्जितपुरुहूतो राजवाहनः कृशोदर्या अवन्तिसुन्दर्या अन्तिकं समाजगाम। या वसन्तसहायेन समुत्सुकतया रतेः केलीशालभञ्जिकाविधित्सया कंचन नारीविशेषं विरच्यात्मनः क्रीडाकासारशारदारविन्दसौन्दर्येण पादद्वयम्, उद्यानवनदीर्घिकामत्तमरालिकागमनरीत्या लीलालसगतिविलासम्, तूणीरलावण्येन जङ्घे, लीलामन्दिरद्वारकदलीलालित्येन मनोज्ञमूरुयुगम्, जैत्ररथचक्रचातुर्येण घनं जघनम्, किंचिद्विकसल्लीलावतंसकह्लारकोरककोटरानुवृत्त्या गङ्गावर्तसनाभिं नाभिम्, सौधारोहणपरिपाट्या वलित्रयम्, मौर्वीमधुकरपङ्क्तिनीलिमलीलया रोमावलिम्, पूर्णसुवर्णकलशशोभया कुचद्वन्द्वम्, लतामण्डपसौकुमार्येण बाहू, जयशङ्खाभिख्यया कण्ठम्, कमनीयकर्णपूरसहकारपल्लवरागेण प्रतिबिम्बीकृतबिम्बं रदनच्छदम्, बाणायमानपुष्पलावण्येन शुचिस्मितम्, अग्रदूतिकाकलकण्ठिकाकलालापमाधुर्येण वचनजातम्, सकलसैनिकनायकमलयमारुतसौरभ्येण निःश्वासपवनम्, जयध्वजमीनदर्पेण लोचनयुगलम्, चापयष्टिश्रिया भ्रूलते, प्रथमसुहृदः सुधा-

वारंवारं दृष्ट्वेत्यर्थः। णमुल्। निजतेजसा स्वानुभावेन निःशेषं जितः पुरुहूत इन्द्रो येन। कृशमुदरं यस्याः। येति। वसन्तसहायेन कामेन। रतेः कामपत्न्याः केलीशालभञ्जिका क्रीडार्थं निर्मिता पुत्रिका। विधातुं कर्तुमिच्छा विधित्सा तया। 'सनि मीमाघुरभलभ–' इत्यच इसभ्यासलोपश्च। शारदं शरत्संबन्धि। दीर्घिका वापी। मरालिका हंसी। लीलया अलसा जडा गतिः। तूणीरो निषङ्गः। लालित्येन सौन्दर्येण। किंचिद्विकसन् यः लीलावतंसभूतः कह्लारकोरकस्तस्य कोटरं मध्यभागः तस्य अनुवृत्तिः साहश्यं तया। सौधः सुधानिर्मितं शिरोगृहं प्रासादतलं वा। परिपाट्यनुक्रमः। सोपानपङ्क्तिरित्यर्थः। वलीनामुदरस्थानां त्रयम्। मौर्वी ज्या। नीलिमा नीलत्वम्। रोमावलिं रोमपङ्क्तिम्। पूर्णाः जलेनेति शेषः। सुवर्णकलशा अनङ्गद्वारमङ्गलसूचकाः। अभिख्या शोभा। कमनीयः सुन्दरः कर्णपूरः कर्णभूषणभूतः यः सहकारपल्लवस्तस्य रागेण। प्रतिबिम्बीकृतं बिम्बं येनैतादृशः। बिम्बफलमधरनिर्माणात्प्राक् बिम्बमासीत्। अधुना तु प्रतिबिम्बं जातम्। बिम्बफलादप्यस्या अधरोष्ठेऽधिको राग इति तात्पर्यम्। रदनच्छदमोष्ठम्। बाणवदाचरति तत्। अग्रदूतिका या कलकण्ठिका कोकिला तस्या यः कल आलापस्तस्य माधुर्येण। जातं समूहः। सुरभेर्भावः सौरभ्यम्। सुधाकरश्चन्द्रः। अपनीतः कलङ्कोऽङ्को यस्यास्तया।

१ शारारविन्द. २ कामि कर्ण०.

करस्यापनीतकलङ्कया कान्त्या वदनम्, लीलामयूरबर्हभङ्ग्या केशपाशं च विधाय समस्तमकरन्दकस्तूरिकासंमितेन मलयजरसेन प्रक्षाल्य कर्पूरपरागेण संमृज्य निर्मितेव रराज । सा मूर्तिमतीव लक्ष्मीर्मालवेशकन्यका स्वेनैवाराध्यमानं संकल्पितवरप्रदानायाविर्भूतं मूर्तिमन्तं मन्मथमिव तमालोक्य मन्दमारुतान्दोलिता लतेव मदनावेशवती चकम्पे । तदनु क्रीडाविश्रम्भान्निवृत्ता लज्जया कानि कान्यपि भावान्तराणि व्यधत्त । 'ललनाजनं सृजता विधात्रा नूनमेषा घुणाक्षरन्यायेन निर्मिता । नो चेदब्जभूरेवंविधनिर्माणनिपुणो यदि स्यात्तर्हि तत्समानलावण्यामन्यां तरुणीं किं न करोति' इति सविस्मयानुरागं विलोकयतस्तस्य समक्षं स्थातुं लज्जिता सती किंचित्सखीजनान्तरितगात्रा तन्नयनाभिमुखैः किंचिदाकुञ्चितै रेचितभ्रूलतैरपाङ्गवीक्षितैरात्मनः कुरङ्गस्यानायमानलावण्यं राजवाहनं विलोकयन्त्यतिष्ठत् । सोऽपि तस्यास्तदोत्पादितभावरसानां सामग्र्या लब्धबलस्येव विषमशरस्य शरव्यायमाणमानसो बभूव । सा मनसीत्थमचिन्तयत्—'अनन्यसाधारणसौन्दर्येणानेन कस्यां पुरि भाग्यवतीनां तरुणीनां लोचनोत्सवः क्रियते । पुत्ररत्नेनामुना पुरंध्रीणां पुत्रवतीनां सीमन्तिनीनां का नाम सीमन्तमौक्तिकीक्रियते । काऽस्य देवी । किमत्रागमनकारण-

---

बर्हं पिच्छम् । भङ्गी रचना । पाशं कलापम् । 'पाशः पक्षश्च हस्तश्च कलापार्थाः कचात्परे' इत्यमरः । समस्तः सर्वः एकीकृतो वा । संमितेन युक्तेन । मलये जातं मलयजं चन्दनम् । परागो धूलिः । मूर्तिमती साक्षात् । संकल्पितस्य मनसि चिन्तितस्य वरस्य प्रदानाय । आविर्भूतमागतम् । मन्मथः कामः । विश्रम्भो विश्वासः । यथा घुणसंज्ञः कीटः काष्ठं विध्यन्नक्षराकृतिं निर्मातुं यदृच्छया कदाऽपि प्रभवति तथा । काकतालीयन्यायेनेत्यर्थः । नोचेद्यद्येवं न स्यात्तर्हि । अब्जभूर्ब्रह्मा । अन्तरितान्यावृतानि । रेचिता तिर्यग्विवर्तिता । कुरङ्गो मृगः । आनायो जालं स इवाचरत् लावण्यं यस्य । विषमाः पञ्च कठिनास्तीव्रा वा शरा यस्य । कामस्येत्यर्थः । शरव्यं लक्ष्यम् । पुरंध्रीणां पतिपुत्रवतीनाम् । सीमन्तिनी नारी । सीमन्तः केशवेशः तत्र मौक्तिकं तत्क्रियते । का पुत्रवतीनां धुरि तिष्ठतीति तात्पर्यार्थः ।

---

१ अञ्चित.

मस्य । मन्मथो मामपहसितनिजलावण्यमेनं विलोकयन्तीमसूययेवातिमात्रं मथ्नन्निजनाम सान्वयं करोति । किं करोमि । कथमयं ज्ञातव्यः' इति । ततो बालचन्द्रिका तयोरन्तरङ्गवृत्तिं[1] भावविवेकैर्ज्ञात्वा कान्तासमाजसंनिधौ राजनन्दनोदन्तस्य सम्यगाख्यानमनुचितमिति लोकसाधारणैर्वाक्यैरभाषत—'भर्तृदारिके अयं सकलकलाप्रवीणो देवतासांनिध्यकरण आहवनिपुणो भूसुरकुमारो मणिमन्त्रौषधिज्ञः परिचर्यार्हो भवत्या पूज्यताम्' इति। तदाकर्ण्य निजमनोरथमनुवदन्त्या बालचन्द्रिकया संतुष्टान्तरङ्गा तरङ्गावली मन्दानिलेनेव संकल्पजेनाकुलीकृता राजकन्या जितमारं कुमारं समुचितासनासीनं विधाय सखीहस्तेन शस्तेन गन्धकुसुमाक्षतघनसारताम्बूलादिनानाजातिवस्तुनिचयेन पूजां तस्मै कारयामास । राजवाहनोऽप्येवमचिन्तयत्—'नूनमेषा पूर्वजन्मनि मे जाया यज्ञवती । नो चेदेतस्यामेवंविधोऽनुरागो मन्मनसि न जायेत । शापावसानसमये तपोनिधिदत्तं जातिस्मरत्वमावयोः समानमेव । तथाऽपि कालजनितविशेषसूचकवाक्यैरस्या ज्ञानमुत्पादयिष्यामि ।' तस्मिन्नेव समये कोऽपि मनोरमो राजहंसः केलीविधित्सया तदुपकण्ठमगमत् । समुत्सुकया राजकन्यया मरालग्रहणे नियुक्तां बालचन्द्रिकामवलोक्य 'समुचितो वाक्यावसर एषः' इति संभाषणनिपुणो राजवाहनः सलीलमलपत्—'सखि पुरा शाम्बो नाम कश्चिन्महीवल्लभो मनोवल्लभया सह विहारवाञ्छया कमलाकरमवाप्य तत्र कोकनदकदम्बसमीपे निद्राधीनमानसं राजहंसं शनैर्गृहीत्वा बिसगुणेन तस्य चरणयुगलं निगडयित्वा कान्तामुखं सानुरागं विलोकयन्मन्दस्मितविकसितैककपोलमण्डलस्तामभाषत—'इन्दुमुखि मया बद्धो मरालः

---

असूययाऽक्षमया । सान्वयमन्वर्थम् । मननं मत् संज्ञा । मथतीति मथः । मतो मथः मन्मथः इति व्युत्पत्त्येति भावः । अन्तरङ्गवृत्तिं मनोवृत्तिम् । भावो मानसो विकारः । सांनिध्यकरणो देवतासाक्षात्कारवान् । आहवो युद्धम् । अनुवदन्त्या सदृशं वदन्त्या । संकल्पजः कामः । नाना जातयो येषां तानि नानाजातीनि ताम्बूलादीनि वस्तूनि तेषां निचयेन समूहेन । जातिस्मरत्वं पूर्वजातिस्मरणम् । विधित्सा कर्तुमिच्छा । मरालो हंसः । महीवल्लभो राजा । कमलाकरः सरः । कोकनदं रक्तोत्पलम् । बिसानां मृणाल-

---

१ इतरेतररागवृत्तिम्.

शान्तो मुनिवदास्ते । स्वेच्छयाऽनेन गम्यताम्' इति । सोऽपि राजहंसः शाम्बमशपत्—'महीपाल यदस्मिन्नम्बुजखण्डेऽनुष्ठानपरायणतया परमानन्देन तिष्ठन्तं नैष्ठिकं मामकारणं राज्यगर्वेणावमानितवानासि तदेतत्पाप्मना रमणीविरहसंतापमनुभव' इति । विषण्णवदनः शाम्बो जीवितेश्वरीविरहमसहिष्णुर्भूमौ दण्डवत्प्रणम्य सविनयमभाषत—'महाभाग यदज्ञानेनाकरवं तत्क्षमस्व' इति । स तापसः करुणाकृष्टचेतास्तमवदत्—'राजन् इह जन्मनि भवतः शापफलाभावो भवतु । मद्वचनस्यामोघतया भाविनि जनने शरीरान्तरं गताया अस्याः सरसिजाक्ष्या रसेन रमणो भूत्वा मुहूर्तद्वयं मच्चरणयुगलबन्धनकारितया मासद्वयं शृङ्खलानिगडितचरणो रमणीवियोगविषादमनुभूय पश्चादनेककालं वल्लभया सह राज्यसुखं लभस्व' इति । तदनु जातिस्मरत्वमपि तयोरन्वगृह्णात् । तस्मान्मरालबन्धनं न करणीयं त्वया' इति । साऽपि भर्तृदारिका तद्वचनाकर्णनाभिज्ञातस्वपुरातनजननवृत्तान्ता 'नूनमयं मत्प्राणवल्लभः' इति मनसि जानती रागपल्लवितमानसा [1]समन्दहासमवोचत्—'सौम्य पुरा शाम्बो यज्ञवतीसंदेशपरिपालनाय तथाविधं हंसबन्धनमकार्षीत् । तथा हि लोके पण्डिता अपि दाक्षिण्येनाकार्यं कुर्वन्ति' इति । कन्याकुमारावेवमन्योन्यपुरातनजननना[2]मधेये परिचिते परस्परज्ञानाय साभिज्ञमुक्त्वा मनोजरागपूर्णमानसौ बभूवतुः ।

तस्मिन्नवसरे मालवेन्द्रमहिषी परिजनपरिवृता दुहितृकेलीविलोकनाय तं देशमवाप । बालचन्द्रिका तु तां दूरतो विलोक्य ससंभ्रमं रहस्यनिर्भेदभिया हस्तसंज्ञया पुष्पोद्भवसेव्यमानं राजवाहनं वृक्षवाटिकान्तरितगात्रमकरोत् । सा मानसारमहिषी सखीसमेताया

---

तन्तूनां गुणो रज्जुः । तन्निर्मित इत्यर्थः । खण्डे समुदाये । नैष्ठिकं ब्रह्मचारिणम् । पाप्मना पापेन । **इहेति** । मम शापो न त्वां बाधेतेत्यर्थः । अमोघतया अनिष्फलतया । जनने जन्मनि । रसेनानुरागेण । निगडितौ बद्धौ । रागपल्लवितमुद्भूतप्रेमपूर्णमित्यर्थः । दाक्षिण्यं 'दाक्षिण्यं चेष्टया वाचा परच्छन्दानुवर्तनम्' इति । साभिज्ञं सप्रत्यभिज्ञम् । परस्परप्रत्ययो यथा स्यात्तथेत्यर्थः । **तस्मिन्निति** । महिषी पट्टाभिषिक्ता । रहस्यं भिद्येदिति भिया । वाटिका गृहोद्यानम् । 'वाटी वास्तौ गृहोद्यानकट्योः'

---

१ मन्दहासपूर्वम्. २ नामधेयपरिचितेः.

दुहितुर्नानाविधां विहारलीलामनुभवन्ती क्षणं स्थित्वा दुहित्रा समेता निजागारगमनायोद्युक्ता बभूव । मातरमनुगच्छन्त्यवन्तिसुन्दरी ‘ राजहंसकुलतिलक विहारवाञ्छया केलीवने मदन्तिकमागतं भवन्तमकाण्ड एव विसृज्य मया समुचितमिति जनन्यनुगमनं क्रियते । तदनेन भवन्मनो[1]रागोऽन्यथा मा भूत् ’ इति मरालमित्र कुमारमुद्दिश्य समुचितालापकलापं वदन्ती पुनः पुनः परि[2]वृत्तदीननयना वदनं विलोकयन्ती निजमन्दिरमगात् । तत्र हृदयवल्लभकथाप्रसङ्गे बालचन्द्रिकाकथिततदन्वयनामधेया मन्मथबाणपतनव्याकुलमानसा विरहवेदनया दिने दिने बहुलपक्षशशिकलेव क्षामक्षामाऽऽहारादिसकलव्यापारं परिहृत्य रहस्यमन्दिरे मलयजरसक्षालितपल्लवकुसुमकल्पिततल्प[3]तलावर्तितनुलता बभूव । तत्र तथाविधावस्थामनुभवन्तीं मन्मथानलसंतप्तां सुकुमारीं कुमारीं निरीक्ष्य खिन्नो वयस्यागणः काञ्चनकलशसंचितानि हरिचन्दनोशीरघनसारमिलितानि तदभिषेककल्पितानि सलिलानि बिसतन्तुमयानि वासांसि च नलिनीदलमयानि तालवृन्तानि च संतापहरणानि बहूनि संपाद्य तस्याः शरीरमशिशिरयत् । तदपि शीतलोपचरणं सलिलमिव तप्ततैले तदङ्गे दहनमेव समन्तादाविश्चकार । किंकर्तव्यतामूढां विषण्णां बालचन्द्रिकामीषदुन्मीलितेन कटाक्षवीक्षितेन बाष्पकणाकुलेन विलोक्य विरहानलोष्णनिःश्वासग्लपिताधरया नताङ्ग्या शनैः सगद्गदं व्यलापि—‘ प्रियसखि कामः कुसुमायुधः पञ्चबाण इति नूनमसत्यमुच्यते । इयमहमयोमयैरसंख्यैरिषुभिरनेन हन्ये । सखि चन्द्रमसं [4]वाडवानलादतितापकरं मन्ये ।

---

इति हैमः । राजहंसस्य पक्षिविशेषस्य कुले तिलक इव भूषणभूतः । पक्षे राजहंसस्यैतन्नाम्नो राज्ञः कुले तिलकः । अकाण्डे सहसा । आलापकलापं वचनजातम् । बहुलपक्षः कृष्णपक्षः । क्षामक्षामाऽतिकृशा । मलयजं चन्दनं तस्य रसेन क्षालिताः पल्लवाः ते च कुसुमानि च तैः कल्पितं तल्पं शय्या तस्य तले आवर्तिनी तनुलता यस्याः । उशीरो नलदः । ‘वाळा’ इति ख्यातः । घनसारः कर्पूरः । अभिषेकः स्नानम् । तालवृन्तानि व्यजनानि । वयस्यागणोऽशिशिरयदिति संबन्धः । शीतलोपचरणं शिशिरोपचारकल्पना । दहनमग्निम् । अयोमयैर्लोहनिर्मितैः । वाडवानलात्सागरान्तर्गताद्वह्नेः । पारावारः समुद्रः । तदैव तस्मिन्नेव

---

१ अनुरागः. २ परिवृत्य. ३ तलायत्त. ४ वडवा०.

यदस्मिन्नन्तः प्रविशति शुष्यति पारावारः । सति निर्गते तदैव वर्धते । दोषाकरस्य दुष्कर्म किं वर्ण्यते मया । यदनेन निजसहोदर्याः पद्मालयाया गेहभूतमपि कमलं विहन्यते । विरहानलसंतप्तहृदयस्पर्शेन नूनमुष्णीकृतः स्वल्पीभवति मलयानिलः । नवपल्लवकल्पितं तल्पमिदमनङ्गाग्निशिखापटलमिव संतापं तनोस्तनोति । हरिचन्दनमपि पुरा निजयष्टिसंश्लेषवदुरगरदनलिप्तोल्बणगरलसंकलितमिव तापयति शरीरम् । तस्मादलमलमायासेन शीतलोपचारे । लावण्यजितमारो राजकुमार एवागदंकारो मन्मथज्वरापहरणे । सोऽपि लब्धुमशक्यो मया । किं करोमि' इति । बालचन्द्रिका मनोजज्वरावस्थापरमकाष्ठां गतां कोमलाङ्गीं तां राजवाहनलावण्याधीनमानसामनन्यशरणामवेक्ष्यात्मन्यचिन्तयत्—'कुमारः सत्वरमानेतव्यो मया । नो चेदेनां स्मरणीयां गतिं नेष्यति मीनकेतनः । तत्रोद्याने कुमारयोरन्योन्यावलोकनवेलायामसमसायकः समं मुक्तसायकोऽभूत् । तस्मात्कुमारानयनं सुकरम्' । ततोऽवन्तिसुन्दरीरक्षणाय समयोचितकरणीयचतुरं सखीगणं नियुज्य राजकुमारमन्दिरमवाप । पुष्पबाणबाणतूणीरायमानमानसोऽनङ्गतप्तावयवसंपर्कपरिम्लानपल्लवशयनमधिष्ठितो राजवाहनः प्राणेश्वरीमुद्दिश्य सह पुष्पोद्भवेन संलपन्नागतां प्रियवयस्यामालोक्य पादमूलम्[1], अन्वेषणीया लतेव बालचन्द्रिकाऽऽगतेति संतुष्टमना निटिलतटमण्डनीभवदम्बुजकोरकाकृतिलसदञ्जलिपुटाम् 'इतो निषीद' इति

---

काले । दोषा रात्रिस्तां करोतीति तथा । दोषाणामाकरश्च । सहोदरी भागिनी । पद्मालया लक्ष्मीः । गेहं गृहम् । विरहानलेन संतप्तं च तद्धृदयं च तस्य स्पर्शेन । निजयष्टेः निजकाण्डस्य संश्लेषवन्त आश्लेषिणो ये उरगाः पन्नगास्तेषां रदनेषु दन्तेषु लिप्तं यदुल्बणं तीव्रं गरलं तेन संकलितं व्याप्तम् । न विद्यते गदः अस्य असौ अगदः । अगदमरोगं जन्तुं करोतीति अगदंकारो भिषक् । 'कारे सत्यागदस्य' इति मुम् । स्मरणीयां गतिं नेष्यति कथीकृतवपुषं करिष्यति । कुमारः कुमारी च कुमारौ तयोः । असमसायको मदनः । सममेककाले । मुक्तसायकोऽभूद्वेधमकरोत् । समयस्योचितानि समयोचितानि च तानि करणीयानि च तत्र चतुरम् । **अनङ्गेति** । अनङ्गेन कामेन तप्ता ये अवयवास्तैः संपर्कस्तेन परिम्लानाः पल्लवा यस्य तादृक् शयनम् । पादमूलमागतामित्यन्वयः । अन्वेषणीया महौषधत्वादन्वेषणार्हा । **निटिलेति** । निटिलतटे ललाटदेशे मण्डनीभवन् अम्बुजकोरकस्य इव आकृतिर्यस्य सः अम्बुजकोरकाकृतिः लसन् यद्वा ०कृतिरिव लसन् शोभमानः अञ्जलिपुटो यस्यास्ताम् ।

---

१ पादपद्ममूलम्.

निर्दिष्टसमुचितासनासीनामवन्तिसुन्दरीप्रेषितं सकर्पूरं ताम्बूलं विनयेन ददतीं तां कान्तावृत्तान्तमपृच्छत्[1] । तया सविनयमभाणि—'देव क्रीडावने भवदवलोकनकालमारभ्य मन्मथमथ्यमाना पुष्पतल्पादिषु तापशमनमलभमाना वामनेनेवोन्नततरुफलमलभ्यं त्वदुरःस्थलालिङ्गन-सौख्यं स्मरान्धतया लिप्सुः सा स्वयमेव पत्रिकामालिख्य 'वल्लभायै-नामर्पय' इति मां नियुक्तवती'। राजकुमारः पत्रिकां तामादाय पपाठ—

'सुभग कुसुमसुकुमारं जगदनवद्यं विलोक्य ते रूपम् ।
मम मानसमभिलषति त्वं चित्तं कुरु तथा मृदुलम्' ॥

इति पठित्वा सादरमभाषत—'सखि छायावन्मामनुवर्तमानस्य पुष्पोद्भवस्य वल्लभा त्वमेव तस्या मृगीदृशो बहिश्चराः प्राणा इव वर्तसे । त्वच्चातुर्यमस्यां[2] क्रियालतायामालवालमभूत् । तदखिलं[3] करिष्यामि । नताङ्ग्या मन्मनःकाठिन्यमाख्यातम् । यदा केलीवने कुरङ्गलोचना[4] लोचनपथमवर्तत[5] तदैवापहृतमदीयमानसा सा स्वमन्दिर-मगात् । सा चेतसो माधुर्यकाठिन्ये स्वयमेव जानाति । दुष्करः कन्यान्तःपुरप्रवेशः । तदनुरूपमुपायमुपपाद्य श्वः परश्वो वा नताङ्गीं संगमिष्यामि । मदुदन्तमेवमाख्याय शिरीषकुसुमसुकुमाराया यथा शरीरबाधा न जायेत तथाविधमुपायमाचर' इति । बाल-चन्द्रिकाऽपि तस्य प्रेमगर्भितं वचनमाकर्ण्य संतुष्टा कन्यापुरमगच्छत् । राजवाहनोऽपि यत्र हृदयवल्लभावलोकनसुखमलभत तदुद्यानं विरहविनोदाय पुष्पोद्भवसमन्वितो जगाम । तत्र चकोर-

---

वामनो ह्रस्वाकृतिर्नरः । उन्नत उच्चः । लिप्सुर्लब्धुमिच्छति तथा । **सुभगेति** । सुभग सुन्दरेति कोमलामन्त्रणे । कुसुममिव सुकुमारं पेलवम् । जगति अनवद्यं निर्दोषम् । यथा तव वपुः कोमलं न तथा तव चित्तमिति तद्विषया प्रार्थना । अत एवाग्र उक्तम्-'नताङ्ग्या मन्मनःकाठिन्यमाख्यातम्' इति । बहिश्चरन्ति ते । त्वं तस्याः प्राणतुल्या । ते प्राणा अन्तर्निवसन्ति त्वद्रूपा बहिश्चरन्तीत्येव भेदः । क्रियैव लता तस्याम् । आलवालमावालम् । 'अळें'. इति भाषायाम् । तस्या अनुरागवर्धनमिति भावः । लोचनपथमवर्तत दृष्टेत्यर्थः । अनुरूपं योग्यम् । उपपाद्य संपाद्य । श्व आगामिनि दिवसे । परश्वस्ततः परस्मिन्दिवसे । प्रेमगर्भितं प्रेमयुक्तम् । चकोरस्येव लोचने यस्याः सा चकोरलोचना । तया

---

१ कान्तवृत्तान्तम्. २ त्वच्चित्तं. ३ यत्तवाभीष्टं येन क्रियामनोरथः फलिष्यति तदखिलम्. ४ रन्तु-गन्तु-ममाः कुरङ्ग०; ०नयना. ५ अभ्यवर्तत.

लोचनावचितपल्लवकुसुमनिकुरम्बं महीरुहसमूहं शरदिन्दुमुख्या मन्मथसमाराधनस्थानं च नताङ्गीपदपङ्क्तिचिह्नितं शीतलसैकततलं च सुदतीभुक्तमुक्तं माधवीलतामण्डपान्तरपल्लवतल्पं च विलोकयँल्ललनातिलकविलोकनवेलाजनितशेषाणि स्मारंस्मारं मन्दमारुतकम्पितानि नवचूतपल्लवानि मदनाग्निशिखा इव चकितो दर्शंदर्शं मनोजकर्णेजपानामिव कोकिलकीरमधुकराणां क्वणितानि श्रावंश्रावं मारविकारेण क्वचिदप्यवस्थातुमसहिष्णुः परिबभ्राम ।

तस्मिन्नवसरे धरणीसुर एकः सूक्ष्मचित्रनिवसनः स्फुरन्मणिकुण्डलमण्डितो मुण्डितमस्तकमानवसमेतश्चतुरवेषमनोरमो यदृच्छया समागतः समन्ततोऽभ्युल्लसत्तेजोमण्डलं राजवाहनमाशीर्वादपूर्वकं ददर्श । राजा सादरम् 'को भवान् कस्यां विद्यायां निपुणः' इति तं पप्रच्छ । स च 'विद्येश्वरनामधेयोऽहमैन्द्रजालिकविद्याकोविदो विविधदेशेषु राजमनोरञ्जनाय भ्रमन्नुज्जयिनीमद्यागतोऽस्मि' इति शशंस । पुनरपि राजवाहनं सम्यगालोक्य 'अस्यां लीलावनौ पाण्डुरतानिमित्तं किम्' इति साभिप्रायं विहस्यापृच्छत् । पुष्पोद्भवश्च[1] निजकार्यकरणं तर्कयन्नेनमादरेण[2] बभाषे—"ननु सतां सख्यस्याभाषणपूर्वतयाऽचिरं रुचिरभाषणो भवानस्माकं प्रियवयस्यो जातः । सुहृदामकथ्यं च किमस्ति । केलीवनेऽस्मिन्वसन्तमहोत्सवायागताया मालवेन्द्रसुताया राजनन्दन-

---

अवचितं पल्लवकुसुमानां निकुरम्बं समूहः यस्य । शरद इन्दुः शरदिन्दुस्तद्वन्मुखं यस्यास्तस्याः । शोभना दन्ता यस्याः सा सुदती तया आदौ भुक्तं पश्चान्मुक्तम् । ललनातिलकशब्देन सैव गृह्यते । ०जनितानि यानि शेषाणि स्मरणीयानि । स्मारंस्मारं स्मृत्वा । दर्शंदर्शं दृष्ट्वा दृष्ट्वा । कर्णेजपः सूचकः । 'तत्पुरुषे कृति बहुलम्' इत्यनेन सप्तम्या अलुक् । **तस्मिन्निति** । सूक्ष्मं चित्रं च निवसनं वासो यस्य । स्फुरद्भ्यां मणिनिर्मिताभ्यां कुण्डलाभ्यां कर्णभूषणाभ्यां मण्डितः शोभितः । मुण्डितं मस्तकं येषामेतादृशैर्मानवैः समेतो युक्तः । यदृच्छया अकस्मात् । अभ्युल्लसत्तेजसो मण्डलं यस्य तम् । ऐन्द्रजालिकविद्या गारुडम् । लीलायाः क्रीडाया अवनिर्भूमिः । आभाषणं पूर्वं यस्मिंस्तत्तस्य भावस्तया । अकथ्यं कथनायोग्यम् ।

---

१ पुष्पोद्भवश्चैन्द्रजालिके, ०श्चैन्द्रजालिकचातुर्यम्. २ एवम्.

स्यास्य चाकस्मिकदर्शनेऽन्योन्यानुरागातिरेकः समजायत। सततसंभोगसिद्ध्युपायाभावेनासावीदृशीमवस्थामनुभवति' इति। विद्येश्वरो लज्जाभिरामं राजकुमारमुखमभिवीक्ष्य विरचितमन्दहासो व्याजहार—'देव भवदनुचरे मयि तिष्ठति तव कार्यमसाध्यं किमस्ति। अहमिन्द्रजालविद्यया मालवेन्द्रं मोहयन्पौरजनसमक्षमेव तत्तनयापरिणयं रचयित्वा कन्यान्तःपुरप्रवेशं कारयिष्यामीति वृत्तान्त एष राजकन्यकायै सखीमुखेन पूर्वमेव कथयितव्यः' इति। संतुष्टमना महीपतिरनिमित्तं मित्रं प्रकटीकृतकृत्रिमक्रियापाटवं विप्रलम्भकृत्रिमप्रेमसहजसौहार्दवेदिनं तं विद्येश्वरं सबहुमानं विससर्ज।

अथ राजवाहनो विद्येश्वरस्य क्रियापाटवेन फलितमिव मनोरथं मन्यमानः पुष्पोद्भवेन सह स्वमन्दिरमुपेत्य सादरं बालचन्द्रिकामुखेन निजवल्लभायै महीसुरक्रियमाणं संगमोपायं वेदयित्वा कौतुकाकृष्टहृदयः 'कथमिमां क्षपां क्षपयामि' इत्यतिष्ठत्। परेद्युः प्रभाते विद्येश्वरो रसभावरीतिगतिचतुरस्तादृशेन[1] महता निजपरिजनेन सह राजभवनद्वारान्तिकमुपेत्य दौवारिकनिवेदितनिजवृत्तान्तः सहसोपगम्य सप्रणामम्[2] 'ऐन्द्रजालिकः समागतः' इति द्वाःस्थैर्विज्ञापितेन तद्दर्शनकुतूहलाविष्टेन समुत्सुकावरोधसहितेन मालवेन्द्रेण समाहूयमानो विद्येश्वरः कक्षान्तरं प्रविश्य सविनयमाशिषं दत्त्वा तदनुज्ञातः परिजनताड्यमानेषु वाद्येषु नदत्सु, गायकीषु मदकलकोकिलामञ्जुलध्वनिषु

सततो नित्यः। नित्यसंभोगसिद्धिर्यथा भवेत्तथोपायं न लभत इत्यर्थः। लज्जयाऽभिरामं सुन्दरम्। अनिमित्तं निष्कारणम्। प्रकटीकृतं दर्शितं कृत्रिमक्रियायामिन्द्रजालविद्यायां पाटवं कुशलत्वं येन तम्। विप्रलम्भं च कृत्रिमप्रेम च सहजसौहार्दं च वेत्तीति तथा। अथेति। क्षपां रात्रिम्। क्षपयामि नयामि। 'क्षै क्षये' इति धातुः। णिजन्तम्। 'आदेच उपदेशे–' इत्यात्वम्। 'अर्तिह्री–' इत्यादिना पुगागमः। मित्त्वाद्ध्रस्वः। परेद्युरन्येद्युः। रसाः शृङ्गारादयः। भावोऽभिप्रायसूचनम्। रीतिगतयः इन्द्रजालविद्यान्तर्गताः। दौवारिको द्वाःस्थः। अवरोधः शुद्धान्तः। राजस्त्रिय इत्यर्थः। कक्षान्तरमन्यां कक्षाम्। गायक्यो गानकर्त्र्यः स्त्रियः। मदेन कलोऽव्यक्तमधुरस्वनो यः कोकिलस्तद्वन्मञ्जुलो ध्वनिर्यासां तासु। सामा-

१ रसभावगीतिरीतिगति०. २ इदं नास्ति क्वचित्.

समधिकरागरञ्जितसामाजिकमनोवृत्तिषु, पिच्छिकाभ्रमणेषु स परिवारं परिवृतं भ्रामयन्मुकुलितनयनः क्षणमतिष्ठत् । तदनु विषमं विषमुल्बणं वमन्तः फणालंकरणा रत्नराजिनीराजितराजमन्दिराभोगा भोगिनो भयं जनयन्तो निश्चेरुः । गृध्राश्च बहवस्तुण्डैरहिपतीनादाय दिवि समचरन् । ततोऽग्रजन्मा नरसिंहस्य हिरण्यकशिपोर्दैत्येश्वरस्य विदारणमभिनीय महदाश्चर्यान्वितं राजानमभाषत—'राजन् अवसानसमये भवता शुभसूचकं द्रष्टुमुचितम् । ततः कल्याणपरंपरावाप्तये भवदात्मजाकारायास्तरुण्या निखिललक्षणोपेतस्य राजनन्दनस्य [च] विवाहः कार्यः' इति । तदवलोकनकुतूहलेन महीपालेनानुज्ञातः स संकल्पितार्थसिद्धिसंभावनसंफुल्लवदनः सकलमोहजनकमञ्जनं लोचनयोर्निक्षिप्य परितो व्यलोकयत् । सर्वेषु 'तदैन्द्रजालिकमेव कर्म' इति साद्भुतं पश्यत्सु रागपल्लवितहृदयेन राजवाहनेन पूर्वसंकेतसमागतामनेकभूषणभूषिताङ्गीमवन्तिसुन्दरीं वैवाहिकमन्त्रतन्त्रनैपुण्येनाग्निं साक्षीकृत्य संयोजयामास । क्रियावसाने सति 'इन्द्रजालपुरुषाः, सर्वे गच्छन्तु भवन्तः' इति द्विजन्मनोच्चैरुच्यमाने सर्वे मायामानवा यथायथमन्तर्भावं गताः । राजवाहनोऽपि पूर्वसंकल्पितेन गूढोपायचातुर्येणैन्द्रजालिकपुरुषवत्कन्यान्तःपुरं विवेश । मालवेन्द्रोऽपि तदद्भुतं मन्यमानस्तस्मै वाडवाय

---

जिकाः सभ्याः प्रेक्षकजनाः । पिच्छिकाः पिच्छगुच्छाः । ऐन्द्रजालिकानामुपकरणभूता एताः । परिवृतं मण्डलाकारम् । 'परिवृढम्' इति पाठे बहुनेकविधं वेत्यर्थः । मुकुलिते पिहिते ईषदुन्मीलिते वा । उल्बणं तीव्रम् । रत्नानां शिरःस्थितानामित्यर्थः । राजयः पङ्क्तयस्ताभिर्नीराजितो राजमन्दिरप्रदेशो यैस्ते । भोगिनः सर्पाः । तुण्डैर्मुखैः । अहिपतीन्भोगश्रेष्ठान् । विदारणं नखैः पाटनम् । अभिनीय दर्शयित्वा । भूमिकादिग्रहणेनेत्यर्थः । महदाश्चर्यान्वितमिति प्रामादिकम् । कल्याणानां परंपरा तस्या अवाप्तिस्तस्यै । निखिलानि सर्वाणि । संकल्पितस्यार्थस्य सिद्धेः संभावनं संभवस्तेन संफुल्लं वदनं यस्य सः । इन्द्रजालस्येदमैन्द्रजालिकम् । साद्भुतमिति क्रियाविशेषणम् । वैवाहिका विवाहसंबन्धिनः । तन्त्राणि नानाविधदेवतोपासनामार्गप्रतिपादका ग्रन्थविशेषाः । अवसानमन्तः । इन्द्रजालपुरुषा मायापुरुषाः । अन्तर्भावमदर्शनम् ।

---

१ सपरिवारः परिवृढम्.

प्रचुरतरं धनं दत्त्वा विद्येश्वरम् 'इदानीं साधय' इति विसृज्य स्वयमन्तर्मन्दिरं जगाम। ततोऽवन्तिसुन्दरी प्रियसहचरीवरपरिवारा वल्लभोपेता सुन्दरं मन्दिरं ययौ। एवं दैवमानुषबलेन मनोरथसाफल्यमुपेतो राजवाहनः सरसमधुरचेष्टाभिः शनैः शनैर्हरिणलोचनाया लज्जामपनयन्सुरतरागमुपनयन्रहो विश्रम्भमुपजनयन्संलापे तदनुलापपीयूषपानलोलश्चित्रचित्रं चित्तहारिणं चतुर्दशभुवनवृत्तान्तं श्रावयामास।

इति श्रीदण्डिनः कृतौ दशकुमारचरितेऽवन्तिसुन्दरीपरिणयो नाम पञ्चम उच्छ्वासः।

समाप्तेयं दशकुमारचरितपूर्वपीठिका।

---

# दशकुमारचरितम्।

## प्रथमोच्छ्वासः।

श्रुत्वा तु भुवनवृत्तान्तमुत्तमाङ्गना विस्मयविकासिताक्षी सस्मितमिदमभाषत—'दयित त्वत्प्रसादादद्य मे चरितार्था श्रोत्र-

---

वाडवाय ब्राह्मणाय। साधय गच्छ। दैवं च तन्मानुषं च। अनुलापः पुनः पुनर्भाषणं स एव पीयूषममृतं तस्य पाने लोलः सतृष्णः। चित्रचित्रमतिशयेन चित्रम्। श्रावयामास श्रावयति स्म।

इति श्रीदशकुमारचरितपूर्वपीठिकाटीकायां पददीपिकाभिधायां पञ्चम उच्छ्वासः।

---

**श्रुत्वेति**। भुवनवृत्तान्तं चतुर्दशभुवनवृत्तान्तम्। 'भुवनस्य जगतो वृत्तान्तं रुक्मिण्यादिभिः कृष्णस्येन्द्रस्य गुरोः पितामहस्य शकुन्तलादुष्यन्तादीनां च गान्धर्वविवाहकरणविषयां प्रवृत्तिम्। अनेन गान्धर्वविवाहेन परिणीतानां पुण्यवत्त्वज्ञानाद्राजवाहनेन सह गान्धर्वविवाहो मम पुण्यवत्त्वं संपादयेदिति मतिरुत्पन्ना। तेन च तस्मिन्राजवाहनेऽतिरागः। अत एव 'त्रिभुवनसर्गयात्रासंहारसंश्रिताभिः प्रत्यानीयमानरागपूराम्' इति वक्ष्यति' इति भूषणा। उत्तमाङ्गना नायिका मालवेन्द्रतनया। विस्मयेन विकसिते अक्षिणी लोचने यस्याः। 'विस्मयोऽद्भुतमाश्चर्यम्' इत्यमरः। सस्मितमिति क्रियाविशेषणम्। सहासमित्यर्थः। 'स्यादाच्छुरितकं हासः सोत्प्रासः स मनाक् स्मितम्' इत्यमरः। **दयितेति**।

---

१ विद्येश्वर त्वमिदानीं साधयेति तं विसृज्य. २ सुन्दरीमन्दिरम्.

वृत्तिः । अद्य मे मनसि तमोपहस्त्वया दत्तो ज्ञानप्रदीपः । पक्कमिदानीं त्वत्पादपद्मपरिचर्याफलम् । अस्य च त्वत्प्रसादस्य किमुपकृत्य प्रत्युपकृतवती भवेयम् । अभवदीयं हि नैव किंचिन्मत्संबद्धम् । अथ वाऽस्त्येवास्यापि जनस्य कचित्प्रभुत्वम् । अशक्यं हि मदिच्छया विना सरस्वतीमुखग्रहणोच्छेषणीकृतो दशनच्छद[1] एष चुम्बयितुम् । अम्बुजासनास्तनतटोपभुक्तमुरःस्थलं चेदमालिङ्गयितुम् ' इति प्रियोरसि प्रावृडिव नभस्युपास्तीर्णगुरुपयोधरमण्डला प्रौढकन्दलीकुड्मलमिव रूढरागरूषितं चक्षुरुल्लासयन्ती बर्हिबर्हावली[2]विडम्बिना कुसुमचन्द्रकशारेण मधुकरकुलव्याकुलेन केशकलापेन स्फुरदरुणकिरणकेसरकरालं कदम्बमुकुलमिव[3] कान्तस्याधरमणिमधीरमाचुचुम्ब । तदारम्भस्फुरितया च रागवृत्त्या भूयोऽप्यावर्तता[4]तिमात्रचित्रोपचारशीकरो रतिप्रबन्धः । सुरत-

---

चरितार्था सफलेत्यर्थः । तमोपहोऽज्ञानहन्ता । ' अभिमतवरलाभेऽपि कन्यानामात्मदाने न प्रभुत्वमित्येवंरूपाज्ञानापहः । ज्ञानप्रदीपः । गान्धर्वादिभिः परिणीतानां पुण्यश्लोकता । पुण्यकृतां न जातु पातकं पीडयतीत्येवंरूपं यज्ज्ञानं तदेव प्रदीप इत्यर्थः ' इति भूषणा । पक्कं परिणतम् । परिचर्योपासना । किमुपकृत्य कमुपकारं कृत्वेत्यर्थः । प्रत्युपकृतवती कृतप्रत्युपकारेत्यर्थः । अभवदीयम् । न भवदीयमित्यर्थः । ममैव भवदीयत्वादिति भावः । अथ वेति पूर्वापरितोषे । **अशक्यमिति** । मदिच्छया विना । ' पृथग्विना—' इति तृतीया । सरस्वत्या मुखग्रहणेनोच्छेषणीकृत उच्छिष्टीकृतः । एषः । भवदीय इत्यर्थः । दशनच्छद ओष्ठः । अम्बुजासना लक्ष्मीस्तस्याः स्तनतटोपभुक्तमिदमुरःस्थलम् । त्वदीयमित्यर्थः । ' एतेन विशेषणद्वयेन विष्णुरूपवर्णनाद्भावि सार्वभौमत्वं सूचितं ' इति भूषणा । **इतीति** । उक्त्वेति शेषः । प्रियोरसि प्रावृडिव नभसि । पयोधरमण्डलं स्तनमण्डलम् । पक्षे मेघमण्डलम् । 'स्त्रीस्तनाब्दौ पयोधरौ' इत्यमरः । प्रौढा या कन्दली द्रोणपर्णी तस्याः कुड्मला मुकुलाः । रूषितम् । युक्तमित्यर्थः । बर्ही मयूरः तस्य बर्हाणि पिच्छानि । विडम्बिना निर्भर्त्सयता । कुसुमान्येव चन्द्रका मेचकास्तैः शारेण विचित्रेण । केशकलापेनोपलक्षितेति उपलक्षणे तृतीया । स्फुरन्तोऽरुणा ये किरणास्त एव केसराणि किञ्जल्कानि तैः करालमुन्नतम् । तदारम्भेण । चुम्बनारम्भेणेत्यर्थः । अतिमात्रम् । ' अतिवेलभृशात्यर्थातिमात्रोद्गाढनिर्भरम् ' इत्यमरः । शीकरो रम्यः । ' शीकरः स्फीतरम्ययोः ' इत्यजयः । **सुरतेति** । बिसगुणेन मृणालतन्तुना

---

१ रदन. २ ०वलीं विडम्बयता. ३ बन्धूकमुकुल–कुसुम–मिव. ४ भूयोभूयः प्रावर्तत.

खेदसुप्तयोस्तु तयोः स्वप्ने बिसगुणनिगडितपादो जरठः कश्चिज्जालपादोऽदृश्यत। प्रत्यबुध्येतां चोभौ। अथ तस्य राजकुमारस्य कमलमूढशशिकिरणरज्जुदामनिगृहीतमिव रजतशृङ्खलोपगूढं चरणयुगलमासीत्। उपलभ्यैव च 'किमेतत्' इत्यतिपरित्रासविह्वला मुक्तकण्ठमाचक्रन्द राजकन्या। येन च तत्सकलमेव कन्यान्तःपुरमग्निपरीतमिव पिशाचोपहतमिव वेपमानमनिरूप्यमाणतदात्वायतिविभागम्, अगण्यमानरहस्यरक्षासमयम्, अवनितलविप्रविध्यमानगात्रम्, आक्रन्दविदीर्यमाणकण्ठम्, अश्रुस्त्रोतोवगुण्ठितकपोलतलमाकुलीबभूव। तुमुले चास्मिन्समयेऽनियन्त्रितप्रवेशाः 'किं किम्' इति सहसोपसृत्य विविशुरन्तर्वंशिकाः पुरुषा ददृशुश्च तदवस्थं राजकुमारम्। तदनुभावनिरुद्धनिग्रहेच्छास्तु सद्य एव ते तमर्थं चण्डवर्मणे निवेदयांचक्रुः। सोऽपि कोपादागत्य निर्दहन्निव दहनगर्भया दृशा निशाम्योत्पन्नप्रत्यभिज्ञः 'कथं स एवैष मदनुजमरणनिमित्तभूतायाः पापाया बालचन्द्रिकायाः पत्युरत्यभिनिविष्टवित्तदर्पस्य वैदेशिकवणिक्पुत्रस्य पुष्पोद्भवस्य मित्रं रूपमत्तः कलाभिमानी नैकविधविप्रलम्भोपाय-

---

निगडितः। 'तदस्य संजातं–' इतीतच्। जालपादो हंसः। जरठग्रहणमशुभसूचकम्। **अदृश्यतेति**। ताभ्यामित्यर्थादध्याहार्यम्। **अथेति**। कमलमूढः कमलत्वेन भ्रान्तो यः शशी तस्य किरणानां रज्जुदाम समुदायस्तेन निगृहीतमिव। मुक्तकण्ठमुच्चैःस्वरम्। **येन चेति**। 'तत्कालस्तु तदात्वं स्यादुत्तरः काल आयतिः' इत्यमरः। विभागः कृत्यम्। अनिरूप्यमाणस्तदात्वायत्योर्विभागो यस्मिन्कर्मणि तथा। तत्काले उत्तरकाले वा किं कर्तव्यमित्यत्र मूढमित्यर्थः। रहस्यमेकान्तोद्भूतं राजकन्यायाः कान्तसंगमादिकम्। आक्रन्दो रोदनम्। अवगुण्ठितं वेष्टितम्। तुमुले संकुले। अनियन्त्रितप्रवेशा अनिवारितप्रवेशाः। अन्तर्वंशिकाः अन्तःपुरे अधिकृताः पुरुषाः। तदवस्थम्। निगडितपादमित्यर्थः। तस्य राजकुमारस्यानुभावेन सामर्थ्येन। 'अनुभावः प्रभावे च निश्चये भावसूचके' इति वैजयन्ती। निरुद्धा निग्रहेच्छा येषां ते। अन्तर्वंशिका इत्यर्थः। **सोऽपीति**। सोऽपि चण्डवर्मेत्यर्थः। दहनगर्भयाऽग्निगर्भया। निशाम्यालोक्य। 'शम आलोचने' इत्यस्मात्स्वार्थणिजन्तात्क्त्वाप्रत्यये समासे ल्यप्। अत्यभिनिविष्टोऽत्यारूढः। नैकविधा अनेकप्रकारा ये विप्रलम्भोपायाः प्रतारणयुक्तयस्तेषु यत्पाटवं कौशलं

---

१ जरठजालपादः. २ कपोलम्. ३ राजपुत्रम्.

पाटवावर्जितमूढपौरजनमिथ्यारोपितवितथदेवतानुभावः कपटधर्मकञ्चुको निगूढपापशीलश्चपलो ब्राह्मणब्रुवः । कथमिवैनमनुरक्ता माद्दशेष्वपि पुरुषसिंहेषु सावमाना पापेयमवन्तिसुन्दरी । पश्यतु पतिमद्यैव शूलावतंसितमियमनार्यशीला कुलपांसनी' इति निर्भर्त्सयन्भीषणभ्रुकुटिदूषितललाटः काल इव काललोहदण्डकर्कशेन बाहुदण्डेनावलम्ब्य हस्ताम्बुजे रेखाम्बुजरथाङ्गलाञ्छने राजपुत्रं सरभसमाचकर्ष । स तु स्वभावधीरः सर्वपौरुषातिभूमिः सहिष्णुतैकप्रतिक्रियां दैवीमेव तामापदमवधार्य 'स्मर तस्या हंसगामिनि हंसकथायाः। सहस्व वासु मासद्वयम्' इति प्राणपरित्यागरागिणीं प्राणसमां समाश्वास्यारिवश्यतामयासीत् ।

अथ विदितवार्तावार्तौ महादेवीमालवेन्द्रौ जामातरमाकारपक्षपातिनावात्मपरित्यागोपन्यासेनारिणा जिघांस्यमानं ररक्षतुः । न शेकतुस्तु तमप्रभुत्वादुत्तारयितुमापदः । स किल चण्डशीलश्चण्डवर्मा सर्वमिदमुदन्तजातं राजराजगिरौ तपस्यते दर्पसाराय संदिश्य सर्वमेव पुष्पोद्भवकुटुम्बकं सर्वस्वहरणपूर्वकं सद्य एव बन्धने क्षिप्त्वा कृत्वा च राजवाहनं राजकेसरिकिशोरकमिव दारुपञ्जरनिबद्धं मूर्धजजाल-

---

तेनावर्जितो वशीकृतो मूढो यः पौरजनस्तेन मिथ्यारोपितो वितथो निष्फलो देवतानुभावो यस्मिन्निति । कपटमेव धर्मकञ्चुकं यस्येति । निगूढं गुप्तम् । ब्राह्मणब्रुवः आत्मानं ब्राह्मणं ब्रूतेऽसौ तथा । पुरुषसिंहेषु पुरुषश्रेष्ठेषु । सावमाना हेलनापरा । 'अनेन तस्यां साभिलाषध्वनिः' इति भूषणा । शूलावतंसितं शूलारोपितम् । कुलपांसनी कुलदूषिका । कालो यमः । काललोहः श्यामायसम् । रेखारूपाण्यम्बुजानि रथाङ्गानि चक्राणि लाञ्छनानि यस्मिन्निति । सरभसं सवेगम् । **स त्विति** । सर्वपौरुषाणां पुरुषार्थानामतिभूमिरधिष्ठानम् । सहिष्णुतैव सहनशीलतैवैका प्रतिक्रिया प्रतीकारो यस्या इति । दैवीमदृष्टकृतामेव । तस्या हंसकथाया इति 'अधीगर्थदयेशां—' इति कर्मणि षष्ठी । वासु बाले । **अथेति** । विदितवार्तौ ज्ञातवृत्तान्तौ । आर्तौ पीडितौ । आकारेण सौन्दर्येण पक्षपातिनाविति महादेवीमालवेन्द्रयोर्विशेषणम् । आत्मपरित्यागस्य देहपरित्यागस्योपन्यासेन । वचनेनेत्यर्थः । **स किलेति** । राजराजगिरौ कैलासपर्वते । बन्धने कारागृहे । किशोरकमिव बालकमिव । दारुपञ्जरे

---

१ जनाध्यारोपित. २ किशोरम्.

विलीनचूडामणिप्रभावविक्षिप्तक्षुत्पिपासादिखेदं च तमवधूतदुहितृप्रार्थनस्याङ्गराजस्योद्धरणायाङ्गानभियास्यन्ननन्यविश्वासान्निनाय। रुरोध च बलभरदत्तकम्पश्चम्पाम्। चम्पेश्वरोऽपि सिंहवर्मा सिंह इवासह्यविक्रमः प्राकारं भेदयित्वा महता बलसमुदायेन निर्गत्य स्वप्रहितदूतव्राताहूतानां साहाय्यदानायातिसत्वरमापततां धरापतीनामचिरकालभाविन्यपि संनिधावदत्तापेक्षः साक्षादिवावलेपो वपुष्मानक्षमापरीतः प्रतिबलं प्रतिजग्राह। जगृहे च महति संपराये क्षीणसकलसैन्यमण्डलः प्रचण्डप्रहरणशतभिन्नवर्मा[1] सिंहवर्मा करिणः करिणमवप्लुत्यातिमानुषप्राणबलेन चण्डवर्मणा। स च तद्दुहितर्यम्बालिकायामबलारत्नसमाख्यातायामतिमात्राभिलाषः प्राणैरेनं न व्ययूयुजत्। अपि त्वनीनयदपनीताशेषशल्यमकल्यसंधो[2] बन्धनम्[3]। अजीगणच्च गणकसंघैः—'अद्यैव क्षपावसाने विवाहनीया राजदुहिता' इति। कृतकौतुकमङ्गले च तस्मिन्नेकपिङ्गाचलात्प्रतिनिवृत्यैणजङ्घो नाम जङ्घाकरिकः प्रभवतो दर्पसारस्य प्रतिसंदेशमावेदयत्—'अयि मूढ किमस्ति कन्यान्तःपुरदूषकेऽपि

---

काष्ठपञ्जरे। मूर्धजजाले केशसमूहे विलीनो यश्चूडामणिर्मुनिकन्यया दत्तस्तस्य प्रभावेन विक्षिप्तो दूरीकृतः क्षुत्पिपासादिखेदो यस्येति तम्। अवधूता तिरस्कृता दुहितुः कन्यायाः प्रार्थना येनेति तस्याङ्गराजस्योद्धरणायोन्मूलनायाङ्गान्देशानभियास्यन्गच्छन्ननन्यविश्वासादन्यविश्वासाभावान्निनायेत्यन्वयः। **चम्पेश्वर इति।** प्राकारो वप्रः। दूतव्रातो दूतसमूहः। अचिरकालभाविनि अचिराद्भविष्यति। न दत्ताऽपेक्षा येनेति। अवलेपो गर्वः। संपराये युद्धे। 'संपरायस्तु संयुगे' इति हैमः। वर्म कवचम्। मानुषमतिक्रम्य वर्तत इत्यतिमानुषं प्राणबलं यस्येति। स चेति चण्डवर्मा। तद्दुहितरि सिंहवर्मकन्यायाम्। अम्बालिकेति नाम्ना प्रसिद्धायाम्। रत्नत्वेनोत्कृष्टत्वेन। अतिमात्रत्यन्तमभिलाषो यस्येति तथा। **अपि त्विति।** अकल्या अचिन्त्या संधा प्रतिज्ञा यस्येति स तथा। गणकसंघैः। ज्यौतिषिकसमूहैः। क्षपावसाने प्रातःकाले। कृतकौतुकमङ्गले बद्धवैवाहिककङ्कणे तस्मिंश्चण्डवर्मणि। एकपिङ्गस्य कुबेरस्य। एणजङ्घो नाम जङ्घाकरिकः। जङ्घैव करी गमनवाहनं हस्ती यस्य सः। शीघ्रगामीत्यर्थः। 'जङ्घालोऽतिजवो जङ्घाकरिको जाङ्घिको जवी' इति हैमः। दर्पसारस्य प्रतिसंदेशं प्रत्युत्तरम्। अयीति कोमलामन्त्रणे। मूढेत्यात्मीयतया संबोधनम्। कन्यान्तःपुरदूषके दूषणोद्भाविके। स्थविरो

---

१ भिन्नमर्मा. २ अकल्प्यसंधः. ३ बन्धनगृहम.

कश्चित्कृपावसरः । स्थविरः स राजा जराविलुप्तमानावमानचित्तो दुश्चरितदुहितृपक्षपाती यदेव किंचित्प्रलपति त्वयाऽपि किं तदनुमत्या स्थातव्यम् । अविलम्बितमेव तस्य कामोन्मत्तस्य चित्रवधवार्ताप्रेषणेन श्रवणोत्सवोऽस्माकं विधेयः । सा च दुष्टकन्या सहानुजेन कीर्तिसारेण निगडितचरणा चारके निरोद्धव्या' इति । तच्चाकर्ण्य 'प्रातरेव राजभवनद्वारे स दुरात्मा कन्यान्तःपुरदूषकः संनिधापयितव्यः । चण्डपोतश्च मातङ्गपतिरु[1]चितकल्पनोपपन्नस्तत्रैव समुपस्थापनीयः । कृतविवाहकृत्यश्चोत्थायाहमेव तमर्नो[2]यशीलं तस्य हस्तिनः कृत्वा क्रीडनकं[3] तदधिरूढ एव गत्वा शत्रुसाहाय्यकाय[4] प्रत्यासीदतो राजन्यकस्य सकोशवाहनस्यावग्रहणं करिष्यामि' इति पार्श्वचरानवेक्षांचक्रे । निन्ये चासावहन्यन्यस्मिन्नुन्मिषत्येवोषोरागे राजपुत्रो राजाङ्गणं रक्षिभिः । उपतस्थे च क्षरितगण्डश्चण्डपोतः । क्षणे च तस्मिन्मुमुचे तदङ्घ्रियुगलं रजतशृङ्खलया । सा चैनं चन्द्रलेखाच्छविः काचिदप्सरो[5]रूपिणी भूत्वा प्रदक्षिणीकृत्य प्राञ्जलिर्व्यजिज्ञपत्— 'देव दीयतामनुग्रहार्द्रं चित्तम् । अहमस्मि सोमरश्मिसंभवा सुरतमञ्जरी

---

वृद्धः । जरया विलुप्तौ मानावमानौ यस्यैवंविधं चित्तं यस्येति । दुश्चरिता दुराचारा । 'प्रलापोऽनर्थकं वचः' इत्यमरः । किमित्याक्षेपे । **सा चेति** । सा दुष्टकन्या । अनुजेन कीर्तिसारेण सह । चारके बन्धनागारे । 'चारकं बन्धनालयः' इति वैजयन्ती । **तच्चेति** । संनिधौ स्थापनीय इत्यर्थः । चण्डपोतनामा मातङ्गपतिः करिवरः । उचिताः याः कल्पनाः अलंकारादिरचनाः तैरुपपन्नो युक्तः । तमनार्यशीलं दुष्टस्वभावं तस्य हस्तिनः क्रीडनकं खेलनं कृत्वेति । प्रत्यासीदतः समीपमागच्छतः । राजन्यकस्य क्षत्रियसमूहस्य । वाहनानि हस्त्यश्वादीनि । अवग्रहणं बन्धनम् । **निन्ये चेति** । द्विकर्मकोऽयं धातुः । असौ राजपुत्रो राजवाहन इति । उषोरागे प्रातःकालसंबन्धिनि लौहित्ये । राजाङ्गणम् । 'अङ्गणं चत्वराजिरे' इत्यमरः । उपतस्थे । 'ष्ठा गतिनिवृत्तौ' । प्राप्तेत्यर्थः । 'अकर्मकाच्च' इत्यात्मनेपदम् । क्षरितः स्रवन्गण्डः कटो यस्येति । **सा चेति** । सा च रजतशृङ्खला । नभ-

---

१ उपचित. २ अनार्यम्. ३ क्रीडनम्. ४ साहाय्याय. ५ अप्सराः.

नाम सुरसुन्दरी। तस्या मे नभसि [1]नलिनलुब्धमुग्धकलहंसानुबद्धवक्त्रागास्तन्निवारणक्षोभविच्छिन्नविगलिता हारयष्टिर्यदृच्छया जातु हैमवते सरसि मन्दोदके मग्नोन्मग्नस्य महर्षेर्मार्कण्डेयस्य मस्तके मणिकिरणद्विगुणितपलितमपतत्। पातितश्च कोपितेन कोऽपि तेन मयि शापः—'पापे भजस्व लोहजातिमजातचैतन्या सती' इति। स पुनः प्रसाद्यमानस्त्वत्पादपद्मद्वयस्य मासद्वयमात्रं संदानतामेत्य निस्तरणीयामिमामापदमपरिक्षीणशक्तित्वं [2]चेन्द्रियाणामकल्पयत्। अनल्पेन च पाप्मना रजतशृङ्खलीभूतां मामैक्ष्वाकस्य राज्ञो वेगवतः पौत्रः पुत्रो मानसवेगस्य वीरशेखरो नाम विद्याधरः शंकरगिरौ समध्यगमत्। आत्मसात्कृता च तेनाहमासम्। अथासौ पितृप्रयुक्तवैरे [3]प्रवर्तमाने विद्याधरचक्रवर्तिनि वत्सराजवंशवर्धने नरवाहनदत्ते विरसाशयस्तदपकारक्षमोऽयमिति तपस्यता दर्पसारेण सह समसृज्यत। प्रतिश्रुतं च तेन तस्मै [4]स्वसुरवन्तिसुन्दर्याः प्रदानम्। अन्यदा तु वियति व्यवदायमानचन्द्रिके मनोरथप्रियतमामवन्तिसुन्दरीं दिदृक्षुरवशेन्द्रियस्तदिन्द्रमन्दिरद्युति कुमारीपुरमुपासरत्। अन्तारितश्च तिरस्करिण्या विद्यया स च

---

स्याकाशे। मुग्धो मूढः यः कलहंसस्तेनानुबद्धं वक्त्रं यस्याः। तन्निवारणं कलहंसनिवारणम्। तत्र विच्छिन्ना त्रुटिताऽत एव विगलिता। हारयष्टिर्हारलता। जातु कदाचित्। मग्नोन्मग्नस्य स्नानं कृत्वोत्थितस्य। पलितं जराजातशौक्ल्यम्। मणीत्यादि क्रियाविशेषणम्। कोपितेन कोपः संजातो यस्येति तथा। 'तदस्य संजातं–' इतीतच्। लोहजातिं लोहत्वम्। 'जातिर्जातं च सामान्यम्' इत्यमरः। मासद्वयमात्रं मासद्वयप्रमाणम्। 'प्रमाणे द्वयसच्–' इति मात्रच्। संदानतां पादबन्धनताम्। निस्तरणीयां समापनीयामित्यर्थः। अनल्पेन बहुना। पाप्मना पापेन। रजतशृङ्खलीभूतामिति 'अभूत–' इति च्विः। इक्ष्वाकोरयमैक्ष्वाकः। वेगवतस्तन्नाम्नो राज्ञः। शंकरगिरौ कैलासपर्वते। मां समध्यगमत् प्रापेत्यर्थः। आत्मसादात्माधीना। तदधीने सातिः। **अथेति**। असौ वीरशेखरो विद्याधरः। पित्रा प्रयुक्तं यद्वैरं तस्मिन्। प्रवर्तमाने कुर्वाण इत्यर्थः। नरवाहनदत्ते विरसाशयः परुषान्तःकरणः। तस्य नरवाहनदत्तस्यापकारे निग्रहे क्षमः समर्थ इति। दर्पसारेण समसृज्यत। संगतोऽभूदित्यर्थः। तेन दर्पसारेण। **अन्यदेति**। व्यवदायमानचन्द्रिके निर्मलज्योत्स्ने। 'दैप् शोधने'। मनोरथैः प्रियतमाम्। तिरस्करिण्याऽन्तर्धानकारिण्या विद्यया। स चेति वीरशेखरः।

---

१ परिपतन्नालिन०. २ च पञ्चेन्द्रियाणाम्. ३ वर्तमाने. ४ स्वस्वसु०.

तां तदा त्वदङ्कापाश्रयां सुरतखेदसुप्तगात्रीं त्रिभुवनसर्गयात्रासंहार-संबद्धाभिः कथाभिरमृतस्यन्दिनीभिः प्रत्यानीयमानरागपूरा न्यरूपयत्। स तु प्रकुपितोऽपि त्वदनुभावप्रतिबद्धनिग्रहान्तराध्यवसायः समाश्लिङ्गचेतरेतरमत्यन्तसुखसुप्तयोर्युवयोर्दैवदत्तोत्साहः पाण्डुलोहशृङ्खलात्मना मया पादपद्मयोर्युगलं तव निगडयित्वा सरोषरभसमपासरत्। अवसितश्च ममाद्य शापः। तच्च मासद्वयं तव पारतन्त्र्यम्। प्रसीदेदानीम्। किं तव करणीयम्' इति प्रणिपतन्तीं 'वार्तयाऽनया मत्प्राणसमां समाश्वासय' इति व्यादिश्य विससर्ज।

तस्मिन्नेव क्षणान्तरे 'हतो हतश्चण्डवर्मा सिंहवर्मदुहितुरम्बालिकायाः पाणिस्पर्शरागप्रसारिते बाहुदण्ड एव बलवदवलम्ब्य सरभसमाकृष्य केनापि दुष्करकर्मणा तस्करेण नखप्रहारेण। राजमन्दिरोद्देशं च शवशतमयमापादयन्नचकितगतिरसौ विहरति' इति वाचः समभवन्। श्रुत्वा चैतत्तमेव मत्तहस्तिनमुदस्ताधोरणो राजपुत्रोऽधिरुह्य रंहसोत्तमेन राजभवनमभ्यवर्तत। स्तम्बेरमरयावधूतपत्तिदत्तवर्त्मा च प्रविश्य वेश्माभ्यन्तरमदभ्राभ्रनिर्घोषगम्भीरेण स्वरेणाभ्यधात्—

---

तामवन्तिसुन्दरीम्। त्वदङ्कोऽपाश्रयो यस्या इति। 'अपाश्रयः शिरोभागः' इति वैजयन्ती। सर्ग उत्पत्तिः। यात्रा व्यवहारस्थितिरिति यावत्। अमृतस्यन्दिनीभिरमृतस्राविणीभिः। प्रत्यानीयमानः परावृत्त्या साध्यमानो रागपूरो यस्यास्ताम्। न्यरूपयत्। दृष्टवानित्यर्थः। त्वदनुभावेन त्वत्सामर्थ्येन प्रतिबद्धो निवारितो निग्रहान्तराध्यवसायो निग्रहे मारणादावन्तरोऽन्तर्गतोऽध्यवसायो निश्चयात्मिका बुद्धिर्यस्य। दैवेन दत्त उत्साहो यस्येति स विद्याधरः। पाण्डुलोहं रजतम्। 'सर्वं च तैजसं लोहम्' इत्यमरः। सरोषरभसं सक्रोधवेगम्। अवसितः समाप्तिं प्राप्तः। व्यादिश्य कथयित्वा। सरभसं सवेगम्। दुष्करकर्मणाऽसुकरकर्मणा। नखं व्याघ्रनखाख्यमायुधम्। 'एकेनैव नखरप्रहारेण' इति पाठे नखरश्छुरिका। 'नखरस्त्वसिपुत्रिका' इति वैजयन्ती। राजमन्दिरोद्देशं राजगृहप्रदेशम्। आपादयन्कुर्वन्। अचकितगतिरत्रस्तगमनः। श्रुत्वेति। तमेव चण्डवर्माधिष्ठितमेव। उदस्तोऽधःक्षिप्तः आधोरणो हस्तिपको येनेति। उत्तमेन रंहसा वेगेन। स्तम्बेरमो हस्ती। स्तम्बे रमते असौ। 'स्तम्बकर्णयो रमिजपोः' इत्यच्। 'हलदन्तात्—' इत्यलुक्। तस्य रयो वेगस्तेनावधूता दूरीकृता ये पत्तयः पदातयस्तैर्दत्तं वर्त्म यस्येति। अदभ्रं बहुलम्। अभ्रनिर्घोषगम्भीरेण मेघरसितगम्भीरेण। 'निर्घोषे रसितादि च' इत्यमरः।

---

१ त्वदङ्कोपा०. २ संश्रिताभिः. ३ दुष्करकर्मकारिणा. ४ नखर. ५ पदाति

'कः स महापुरुषो येनैतन्मानुषमात्रदुष्करं महत्कर्मानुष्ठितम् । आगच्छतु । मया सहेमं मत्तहस्तिनमारोहतु । अभयं मदुपकण्ठवर्तिनो देवदानवैरपि विगृह्णानस्य' इति । निशम्यैवं स पुमानुपोढहर्षो निर्गत्य कृताञ्जलिराक्रम्य संज्ञासंकुचितं कुञ्जरगात्रमसक्तमध्यरुक्षत् । आरोहन्तमेवैनं निर्वर्ण्य हर्षोत्फुल्लदृष्टिः ' अये प्रियसखोऽयमपहारवर्मैव ' इति पश्चान्निषीदतोऽस्य बाहुदण्डयुगलमुभयभुजमूलप्रवेशितमग्रेऽवलम्ब्य स्वमङ्गमालिङ्गयामास । स्वयं च पृष्ठतो वलिताभ्यां भुजाभ्यां पर्यवेष्टयत् । तत्क्षणोपसंहृतालिङ्गनव्यतिकरश्चापहारवर्मा चापचक्रकणप[1]कर्पणप्रासपट्टिशमुसलतोमरादिप्रहरण[2]जातमु[3]पयुञ्जानान्बलावलिप्तान्प्रतिबलवीरान्बहुप्रकारायोधिनः परिक्षिपतः क्षितौ विचिक्षेप । क्षणेन चाद्राक्षीत्तदपि सैन्यमन्येन समन्ततोऽभिमुखमभिधावता बलनिकायेन परिक्षिप्तम् ।

[4]अनन्तरं च कश्चित्कर्णिकारगौरः कुरुविन्दसवर्णकुन्तलः कमलकोमलपाणिपादः कर्णचुम्बिदुग्धधवलस्निग्धनीललोचनः कटि-

---

विगृह्णानस्य विरोधं कुर्वतः । उपोढहर्षो वर्धमानहर्षः । संज्ञया संकेतेन संकुचितम् । कुञ्जरगात्रं पूर्वपदजाङ्घप्रदेशम् । ' द्वौ पूर्वपश्चाज्जङ्घादिदेशौ गात्रावरे क्रमात् ' इत्यमरः । असक्तं त्वरितमित्यर्थः । अध्यरुक्षदारुरोह । **अये इति** । ' अतर्कोपतिते त्वये ' इति केशवः । प्रियसखोऽयमिति ' राजाहःसखिभ्यष्टच् ' इत्यदन्तता । वलिताभ्यां चालिताभ्याम् । ' वल चलने ' । वक्रिताभ्यामित्यर्थः । उपसंहृत आलिङ्गनव्यतिकर आश्लेषसंपर्को येनेति तथा । कणपो लोहस्तम्भः । ' लोहस्तम्भस्तु कणपः ' इति वैजयन्ती । कर्पणः सरावः । ' कुटिलाग्रस्तु कर्पणः' इति च । प्रासः कुन्तः । ' प्रासस्तु कुन्तः ' इत्यमरः । पट्टिशः शस्त्रविशेषः । भाषया 'पट्टा' इति प्रसिद्धः । ' पट्टिशः स्याद्द्विशालाग्रः ' इति वैजयन्ती । मुसलं कण्डनसाधनकाष्ठतुल्यमायसायुधम् । मुशलमिति वा । तोमरो लोहगुच्छः । भाषया ' गुर्ज ' इति ख्यातः । ' तोमरो वेगदण्डवान् ' इति वैजयन्ती । प्रहरणजातं शस्त्रसमूहम् । उपयुञ्जानान्प्रेरयतः । बहुप्रकारमायोधिनो युद्धं कुर्वतः । परिक्षिपतः । लोकानिति शेषः । विचिक्षेप । पातितवानित्यर्थः । बलनिकायेन सेनासमूहेन । ' निकायो निवहो व्यूहः समूहो विसरो व्रजः ' इति कोशः । **अनन्तरमिति** । कर्णिकारो द्रुमोत्पलस्तद्वद्गौरः । कुरुविन्देन सवर्णाः समानाः कुन्तलाः केशा यस्येति । कुरुविन्दो नीलगुच्छः नीलमणिरिति यावत् । कटि-

---

१ कर्णप. २ जालं. ३ उपयुञ्जानः. ४ अन्तरे.

तटनिविष्टरत्ननखः पट्टनिवसनः कृशाकृशोदरोरःस्थलः कृतहस्ततया रिपुकुलमिषुवर्षेणा[1]भिवर्षन् पादाङ्गुष्ठनिष्ठुरावघृष्टकर्णमूलेन जविना गजेन संनिकृष्य पूर्वोपदेशप्रत्ययात् 'अयमेव स देवो राजवाहनः' इति प्राञ्जलिः प्रणम्यापहारवर्माणि निविष्टदृष्टिराचष्ट—'त्वदादिष्टेन मार्गेण संनिपातितमेतदङ्गराजसाहाय्यदानायोपस्थितं रा[2]जकम् । [3]अरिबलं च विहतविध्वस्तं स्त्रीबालहार्यशस्त्रं वर्तते । किमन्यत्कृत्यम्' इति । हृष्टस्तु व्याजहारापहारवर्मा—'देव दृष्टिदानेनानुगृह्यतामयमाज्ञाकरः । सोऽ[4]यमहमेवामुना रूपेण धनमित्राख्यया चान्तरितो मन्तव्यः । स एवायं निर्गमय्य बन्धनादङ्गराजमपवार्जितं च कोशवाहनमेकीकृत्यास्मद्गृह्येणामुना सह राजन्यकेनैकान्ते सुखोपविष्टमिह देवमुपातिष्ठतु यदि न दोषः' इति । देवोऽपि 'यथा ते रोचते' इति तमाभाष्य गत्वा च तन्निर्दिष्टेन मार्गेण नगराद्बहिरतिमहतो रोहिणद्रुमस्य क[5]स्यचित्क्षौमावदातसैकते गङ्गातरङ्गपवनपातशीतले तले द्विरदादवततार । प्रथमसमवतीर्णेनापहारवर्मणा च स्वहस्तसत्वर-

---

तटे निविष्टो रत्नयुक्तो नखः नखरः छुरिका इति वा यस्येति । पट्टं दुकूलं निवसनं यस्येति तथा । कृशाकृशे उदरोरःस्थले यस्येति स तथा । कृशोदरः स्थूलोरःस्थलश्चेति योज्यम् । कृतहस्ततया शिक्षितहस्ततया । 'शिक्षितं कृतमर्थवत्' इति भागुरिः । इषुवर्षेण बाणवृष्ट्या । अङ्गुष्ठाभ्यां निष्ठुरं यथा तथाऽवघृष्टं घर्षितं कर्णमूलं यस्येति तेन । निविष्टदृष्टिर्दत्तदृष्टिः । **त्वदादिष्टेनेति** । राजकं राजसमूहः । स्त्रीबालैर्हार्याणि शस्त्राणि यस्य । आज्ञाकरः सेवकः । **सोऽयमहमेवेति** । अन्तरितः भिन्न इत्यर्थः । स एव धनमित्रोऽङ्गराजं सिंहवर्माणं बन्धनान्निर्गमय्य निष्क्रामय्य । अपवार्जितम् । इतस्ततो गतमित्यर्थः । अस्मद्गृह्येणास्मत्पक्षस्थेन । 'गृह्यः पक्षस्थ उच्यते' इति वैजयन्ती । राजन्यकेन क्षत्रियसमूहेन । देवम् । त्वामिति यावत् । **देव इति** । देवो राजवाहनः । तमपहारवर्माणम् । तन्निर्दिष्टेनापहारवर्मकथितेन मार्गेण । रोहिणद्रुमस्य वटवृक्षस्य । 'वटवृक्षस्तु रोहिणः' इति वैजयन्ती । क्षौममिवावदातं शुद्धं यत्सैकतं तस्मिन् । **प्रथमेति** । स्वहस्तेनात्मकरेण सत्वरं सवेगं समीकृते समतां प्रापिते ।

---

१ अभिपात्य. २ राजन्यकम्. ३ अखिलारि०, अखिलं चा०. ४ सोऽयमप्यह०; सोऽयमेवाद्य. ५ कस्यचिन्मूले.

समीकृते मातङ्ग इव भागीरथीपुलिनमण्डले सुखं निषसाद। तथा निषण्णं च तमुपहारवमार्थपालप्रमतिमित्रगुप्तमन्त्रगुप्तविश्रुतैर्मैथिलेन च प्रहारवर्मणा, काशीभर्त्रा च कामपालेन, चम्पेश्वरेण सिंहवर्मणा सहोपागत्य धनमित्रः प्राणिपपात। देवोऽपि हर्षाविद्धमभ्युत्थितः 'कथं समस्त एषं मित्रगणः समागतः, को नामायमभ्युदयः' इति कृतयथोचितोपचारान्निर्भरतरं परिरेभे। काशीपतिमैथिलाङ्गराजांश्च सुहृन्निवेदितान्पितृवदपश्यत्। तैश्च हर्षकम्पितपलितं संरभसोपगूढः परमभिननन्द। ततः प्रवृत्तासु प्रीतिसंकथासु प्रियवयस्यगणानुयुक्तः स्वस्य च सोमदत्तपुष्पोद्भवयोश्चरितमनुवर्ण्य सुहृदामपि वृत्तान्तं क्रमेण श्रोतुं कृतप्रस्तावस्तांश्च तदुक्तावन्वयुङ्क्त। तेषु प्रथमं प्राह स्म किलापहारवर्मा—

इति श्रीदण्डिनः कृतौ दशकुमारचरिते राजवाहनचरितं नाम प्रथम उच्छ्वासः।

---

## द्वितीयोच्छ्वासः।

'देव त्वयि तदाऽवतीर्णे द्विजोपकारायासुरविवरं त्वदन्वेषणप्रसृते च मित्रगणेऽहमपि महीमटन्नङ्गेषु गङ्गातटे बहिश्चम्पायाः 'कश्चिदस्ति तपःप्रभावोत्पन्नदिव्यचक्षुर्मरीचिर्नाम महर्षिः' इति

---

**तथेति**। तं राजवाहनम्। उपहारवर्मादिविश्रुतान्तैः षड्भिर्दशकुमारान्तर्गतैः। मैथिलेन मिथिलाधिपेन। निर्भरतरं दृढतरम्। **हर्षेति**—हर्षेण कम्पितं पलितं जरया शुक्लाः केशा यथा स्यात्तथा। **तत इति**। सोमदत्तपुष्पोद्भवयोश्चरितमाचरणं पूर्वपीठिकायामुक्तमनुवर्ण्य। सुहृदां सर्वेषाम्। कृतप्रस्तावः कृतोपक्रमः। तदुक्तौ सुहृद्वृत्तान्तोक्तौ। अन्वयुङ्क्त। योजितवानित्यर्थः। तेषु सुहृत्सु मध्ये प्रथममपहारवर्मा प्राह स्मेत्यन्वयः।

इति श्रीदशकुमारचरितटीकायां प्रथम उच्छ्वासः।

---

किमाहापहारवर्मा—**देवेति**। प्रसृते परितश्चरिते। दिव्यचक्षुरतीन्द्रियद्रष्टा। 'संलापो भाषणं मिथः' इत्यमरः। उपलभ्य ज्ञात्वा। अमुतः मुनेरित्यर्थः।

---

१ मातङ्ग इव स्फटिकमय इव. २ एव. ३ उत्पीडिततरम्. ४ हर्षनिर्भरतरम्; ०निर्भररभसो०. ५ सहसोपगूढः. ६ प्रस्थिते.

कुतश्चित्संलपतो जनसमाजादुपलभ्यामुतो बुभुत्सुस्त्वद्गतिं तमुद्देशमगमम्। न्यशामयं च तस्मिन्नाश्रमे कस्याचिच्चूतपोतकस्य च्छायायां कमप्युद्विग्नवर्णं तापसम्। अमुना चातिथिवदुपचरितः क्षणं विश्रान्तः 'क्वासौ भगवान्मरीचिः, तस्मादहमुपलिप्सुः प्रसङ्गप्रोषितस्य सुहृदो गतिम्, आश्चर्यज्ञानविभवो हि स महर्षिर्मह्या विश्रुतः' इत्यवादिषम्। अथासावुष्णमायतं च निःश्वस्याशंसत्[1]—'आसीत्तादृशो मुनिरस्मिन्नाश्रमे। तमेकदा काममञ्जरी नामाङ्गपुरीवतंस[2]स्थानीया वारयुवतिरश्रुबिन्दुतारकितपयोधरा सनिर्वेदमभ्येत्य कीर्णशिखण्डास्तीर्णभूमिरभ्यवन्दिष्ट। तस्मिन्नेव च क्षणे मातृप्रमुखस्तदाप्तवर्गः[3] सानुक्रोशमनुप्रधावितस्तत्रैवावनिविच्छिन्नपातमपतत्[4]। स किल कृपालुस्तं जनमार्द्रया गिराऽऽश्वास्या[5]र्तिकारणं तां गणिकामपृच्छत्। सा तु सव्रीडेव सविषादेव सगौरवेव चाब्रवीत्—'भगवन् ऐहिकस्य सुखस्याभाजनं[6] जनोऽयमामुष्मिकाय श्रोवसीयायार्ताभ्युपपत्तिवित्तयोर्भगवत्पादयोर्मूलं शरणमभिप्रपन्नः' इति। तस्यास्तु जनन्युदञ्जलिः पलितशार-

बुभुत्सुर्बोद्धुमिच्छुः। त्वद्गतिं त्वन्मार्गमित्यर्थः। तमुद्देशं महर्ष्यधिष्ठितप्रदेशम्। न्यशामयमपश्यम्। उद्विग्नवर्णमुद्विग्नस्य वर्ण इव वर्णः कान्तिर्यस्येति स तम्। उपचरितः सत्कृतः। तस्मान्मरीचेः। उपलिप्सुरुपलब्धुमिच्छुः। प्रसङ्गप्रोषितस्य केनापि कारणेन गतस्य। आश्चर्यैश्चमत्कारकारी ज्ञानविभवो ज्ञानसामर्थ्यं यस्य तथा। अवादिषं उक्तवानित्यर्थः। **अथेति**। असौ तापसः। तं महर्षिम्। अङ्गपुरीवतंसस्थानीया तन्नगरीशेखरभूता। 'वष्टि भागुरिरल्लोपमवाप्योरुपसर्गयोः' इत्यकारलोपः। वारयुवतिर्वेश्या। अश्रुबिन्दुतारकितपयोधरा अश्रुबिन्दुभिस्तारकितौ पयोधरौ यस्या इति। तारकाः संजाता अस्येति व्युत्पत्तिः। सनिर्वेदं सर्वत्रोपेक्षासहितम्। कीर्णभूमिः कीर्णः प्रसृतो यः शिखण्डः केशपाशस्तेनास्तीर्णा कृतास्तरणा भूमिर्ययेति। **तस्मिन्निति**। तस्या वाराङ्गनायाः आप्तवर्गः। सानुक्रोशं सकृपम्। आर्तिकारणं पीडानिदानम्। **सेति**। ऐहिकस्येह भवं तथा तस्य। अभाजनमपात्रम्। अमुत्र जातमामुष्मिकम्। पारलौकिकायेत्यर्थः। श्रोवसीयाय कल्याणाय। 'श्रोवसीयं शिवं शुभम्' इति हलायुधः। आर्ताभ्युपपत्तिवित्तयोरार्तानां पीडितानामभ्युपपत्तिरनुग्रहस्तद्वित्तयोः ख्यातयोः। चरणविशेषणम्। जननी माता। उद्गतोऽञ्जलिर्यस्याः सा उदञ्जलिरूर्ध्वीकृताञ्जलिः।

१ आशशंसे. २ पुर्यवतंस. ३ तद्दासीवर्गः. ४ अवनिपातम्. ५ गिराऽश्वाप्य. ६ भाजनम्.

शिखण्डबन्धस्पृष्टमुक्तभूमिरभाषत—‘भगवन्, अस्य[1] मे दोषमेषा वो दासी विज्ञापयति। दोषश्च मम स्वाधिकारानुष्ठापनम्। एष हि गणिकामातुरधिकारो यद्दुहितुर्जन्मनः प्रभृत्येवाङ्गक्रिया, तेजोबलवर्णमेधासंवर्धनेन दोषाग्निधातुसाम्यकृता मितेनाहारेण शरीरपोषणम्, आ पञ्चमाद्वर्षात्पितुरप्यनतिदर्शनम्, जन्मदिने पुण्यदिने चोत्सवोत्तरो मङ्गलविधिः, अध्यापनमनङ्गविद्यानां साङ्गानाम्, नृत्यगीतवाद्यनाट्यचित्रास्वाद्यगन्धपुष्पकलासु लिपिज्ञानवचनकौशला[2]दिषु च सम्यग्विनयनम्, शब्दहेतुसमयविद्यासु वार्तामात्रा[3]वबोधनम्, आजीवज्ञाने क्रीडाकौशले सजीवनिर्जीवासु च द्यूतकलास्वभ्यन्तरीकरणम्, अभ्यन्तरकलासु वैश्वासिकजनात्प्रयत्नेन प्रयोगग्रहणम्, यात्रोत्सवादिष्वादरप्रसाधितायाः स्फीतपरिबर्हायाः प्रकाशनम्, प्रसङ्गवत्यां संगीतादिक्रियाया पूर्वसंगृहीतैर्ग्राह्यवाग्भिः

---

पलितेन रजसा शौक्ल्येन शारश्चित्रो यः शिखण्डबन्धस्तेनादौ स्पृष्टा पश्चान्मुक्ता भूमिर्यया। ‘पूर्वकालैक–’ इति समासः। **भगवन्निति**। मे दोषं मद्दूषणम्। वो युष्माकं दासी। मत्कन्येत्यर्थः। स्वाधिकारानुष्ठापनं स्वोचितकर्माचरणप्रेरणम्। अङ्गक्रियोद्वर्तनादिः। ‘अङ्गक्रिया यदङ्गेषु हरिद्रातैलमर्दनम्’ इति वात्स्यायने। तेजः शरीरकान्तिः। बलं सामर्थ्यम्। मेधा धारणावती बुद्धिः। एतेषां सम्यग्वर्धनेन पोषणेन। दोषा वातपित्तश्लेष्माणः। अग्निर्जाठरः। धातवः सप्त। एतेषां साम्यकृताऽवैषम्यकृता। आ पञ्चमात् पञ्चमवर्षादुत्तरमित्यर्थः। ‘आङ् मर्यादाभिविध्योः’ इति पञ्चमी। अनतिदर्शनमत्यन्तदर्शनाभावः। जन्मदिन उत्पत्तिदिवसे। पुण्यदिने संक्रमणादौ। अनङ्गविद्यानां कामप्रतिपादकविद्यानाम्। विनयनं शिक्षणम्। शब्दो व्याकरणम्। हेतुस्तर्कः। ‘समयः ज्यौतिषः सिद्धान्तः’ इति भूषणा। अवबोधनं ज्ञानम्। आजीवो जीविका। क्रीडाकौशले नर्मभाषणनैपुण्ये। सजीवाः कुक्कुटादियोधनानि, निर्जीवाश्चतुरङ्गाद्याः। अभ्यन्तरीकरणं स्वायत्तीकरणम्। अभ्यन्तरकलासु रतकलासु। ‘साऽभ्यन्तरकला यत्तु स्पर्श्याङ्गस्पर्शनं रतौ’ इति वात्स्यायनः। वैश्वासिकजनादाप्तजनात्। प्रयोगः कर्तव्यता। प्रसाधिताया अलंकृतायाः। ‘प्रसाधितोऽलंकृतश्च भूषितश्च परिष्कृतः’ इति वैजयन्ती। परिबर्हः परिच्छदः। ‘परिबर्हस्तु राजार्हे वस्तुन्यपि परिच्छदे’ इत्यपि। सेवकजन इति यावत्।

---

१ अस्यां मे दोष एषा. २ कौशलेषु. ३ वार्तावार्तावबोधनम्.

सिद्धिलम्भनम्, दिङ्मुखेषु तत्तच्छिल्पवित्तकैर्यशःप्रख्यापनम् , कार्तान्तिकादिभिः कल्याणलक्षणोद्घोषणम्, पीठमर्दविटविदूषकैर्भिक्षुक्यादिभिश्च नागरिकपुरुषसमवायेषु रूपशीलशिल्पसौन्दर्यमाधुर्यप्रस्तावना, युवजनमनोरथलक्ष्यभूतायाः प्रभूततमेन शुल्केनावस्थापनम्, स्वतो रागान्धाय तद्भावदर्शनोन्मादिताय वा जातिरूपवयोर्थशक्तिशौचत्यागदाक्ष्यदाक्षिण्यशिल्पशीलमाधुर्योपपन्नाय स्वतन्त्राय प्रदानम्, अधिकगुणायास्वतन्त्राय प्राज्ञतमायाल्पेनापि बहुव्यपदेशेनार्पणम्, अस्वतन्त्रेण वा गान्धर्वसमागमेन तद्गुरुभ्यः शुल्कापहरणम्, अलाभेऽर्थस्य कामस्वीकृते स्वामिन्यधिकरणे च साधनम्, रक्तस्य दुहित्रैकचारिणीव्रतानुष्ठापनम्, नित्यनैमित्तिकप्रीतिदायकतया हृतशिष्टानां गम्यधनाना चित्रैरुपायैरपहरणम्, अददता लुब्धप्रायेण च विगृह्यासनम्, प्रतिहस्तिप्रोत्साहनेन लुब्धस्य रागिणस्त्यागशक्तिसंधुक्षणम्, असारस्य वाक्संतक्षणैर्लोकोपक्रोशनैर्दुहितृनिरोधनैर्व्रीडोत्पादनैरन्य(-

ग्राह्यवाग्भिः शिक्षकैः । ' ग्राह्यवागुपलालकः ' इति वैजयन्ती । सिद्धिलम्भनं सिद्धिप्रापणम् । शिल्पवित्तकैः कलाप्रसिद्धैर्मार्दङ्गिकमौराजिकादिभिः । कार्तान्तिका लक्षणज्ञाः । उद्घोषणं ख्यापनम् । पीठमर्दो नटविशेषः । ' पीठमर्दो विटश्चेति तथा चेटविदूषकौ ' इत्युक्तेष्वतिधृष्टो नायकप्रियः पीठमर्द इति। 'पीठमर्दोऽतिधृष्टे स्यान्नाट्योक्तया नायकप्रिये ' इति विश्वः । कुपितस्त्रीप्रसादकः इति भू० । विट एकविद्यः । विदूषकः । 'विकृताङ्गवचोवेषैर्हास्यकारी विदूषकः' इति । भिक्षुकी श्रमणा । 'श्रमणा भिक्षुकी मुण्डा' इति हैमः । नागरिका निपुणाः । समवायेषु समुदायेषु । प्रभूततमेन प्रचुरतरेण । शुल्को मौल्यम् । उन्मादित उन्मादं प्रापितस्तस्मै । शौचं शुद्धता । 'शौचमर्थेष्ववञ्चनम्' इति वैजयन्ती । दाक्ष्यं कुशलत्वम् । दाक्षिण्यं सरलता । गान्धर्वसमागमेन । गान्धर्वविवाहेनेत्यर्थः । कामस्वीकृते स्वायत्तीकृते । स्वामिन्यधिकारिणि। अधिकरणे चोत्तरादौ । ' अलाभे अर्थस्य धूर्तात्स्वशुल्कालाभे। कामस्वीकृते मैत्र्यादङ्गीकृते। स्वामिनि प्रभौ ग्रामाध्यक्षे । अधिकरणे नागरिकसंसदि । साधनमुच्चावचवागादिभिः स्वोपयुक्तविधानम् । ' इति भूषणा । रक्तस्य । अनुरक्तस्येत्यर्थः । एकचारिणीव्रतं पातिव्रत्यम् । हृतशिष्टानां गृहीतावशिष्टानाम् । गम्यधनानाम् । गम्या भुजङ्गाः । ' गम्यो विटः पाल्लविको भुजङ्गः' इति भागुरिः । असनं क्षेपणम् । प्रतिहस्त्यासन्नगृहवेश्यापतिः । 'प्रतिहस्ती प्रातिवेश्यः' इति वैजयन्ती । त्यागशक्तेः संधुक्षणमुद्दीपीकरणम् । असारस्य निर्धनस्य । वाक्संतक्षणैर्वचनतिरस्कारैः । लोकोपक्रोशनैर्लोकेषु

१ प्रभौ. २ अधिकगुणे. ३ आहृत.

भियोगैरवमानैश्चापवाहनम्, अर्थदैरनर्थप्रतिघातिभिश्चानिन्द्यैरिभ्यैर[1]नुबद्धार्थानर्थसंशयान्विचार्य भूयोभूयः संयोजनमिति । गणिकायाश्च गम्यं प्रति सज्जतैव न सङ्गः । सत्यामपि प्रीतौ न मातुर्मातृकाया वा शासनातिवृत्तिः । एवं स्थितेऽनया प्रजापतिविहितं स्वधर्ममुल्लङ्घ्य क्वचिदागन्तुके रूपमात्रधने विप्रयूनि स्वेनैव धनव्ययेन रममाणया मासमात्रमत्यवाहि । गम्यजनश्च भूयानर्थयोग्यः प्रत्याचक्षाणयाऽनया प्रकोपितः । स्वकुटुम्बकं चावसादितम् । 'एषा कुमतिर्न कल्याणी' इति निवारयन्त्यां मयि वनवासाय कोपात्प्रस्थिता । सा चेदियमहार्यनिश्चया सर्व एष जनोऽत्रैवानन्यगतिरनशनेन संस्थास्यते' इत्यरोदीत्[2] ।

अथ सा वारयुवतिस्तेन 'भद्रे ननु दुःखाकरोऽयं वनवासः । तस्य फलमपवर्गः स्वर्गो वा । प्रथमस्तु तयोः प्रकृष्टज्ञानसाध्यः प्रायो दुःसंपाद एव, द्वितीयस्तु सर्वस्यैव सुलभः कुलधर्मानुष्ठायिनः । तदशक्यारम्भादुपरम्य मातुर्मते वर्तस्व' इति सानुकम्पमभिहिता[3] 'यदीह भगवत्पादमूलमशरणम्, शरणमस्तु मम कृपणाया हिरण्यरेता देव एव' इत्युदमनायत । स तु मुनिरनुविमृश्य गणिकामातरमवदत्—'संप्रति गच्छ गृहान् । प्रतीक्षस्व कानिचिद्दिनानि यावादियं सुकुमारा सुखोपभोगसमुचिता सत्यरण्यवा[4]सव्यसनेनोद्वेजिता भूयोभूय-

निन्दनैः । अपवाहनं दूरीकरणम् । अनर्थप्रतिघातिभिरुपद्रवनिवारकैः । इभ्यैर्धनिकैः । सज्जता तत्परता । मातृकाया मातामह्याः । 'मातुर्माता तु मातृका' इति वैजयन्ती । अतिवृत्तिस्त्यागः । गम्यजनो विटजनः । 'गम्यो विटः पाल्लविको भुजङ्गः' इति भागुरिः । प्रत्याचक्षाणया प्रत्याख्यानं कुर्वत्या । अवसादितं नाशितम् । अहार्यनिश्चया दृढनिश्चया । संस्थास्यते मरिष्यतीत्यर्थः । 'संस्थानं मरणं मतम्' इति वैजयन्ती । **अथेति** । दुःखाकरो दुःखजनकः । 'दुःखात्प्रातिलोम्ये' इति डाच्प्रत्ययः । प्रथमोऽपवर्गः दुःसंपादो दुःसाध्यः । कुलधर्मानुष्ठायिनः स्वकुलोचितकर्मकारिणः । अशक्यारम्भात्तपस इत्यर्थः । अशरणमरक्षितृ । हिरण्यरेता दहन । उदमनायत उन्मना अभवत् । 'दुर्मना विमना अन्तर्मनाः स्यादुत्क उन्मनाः' इत्यमरः । गृहान् । 'गृहाः पुंसि च भूम्न्येव' इत्यमरः । प्रकृतौ स्वभावे । अलघुभक्तिर्दृढभक्तिः ।

१ अन्यैः. २ अवादीत्. ३ अस्मात्परं 'सा तु प्रत्यवादीत्' इत्य० एक० पुस्तके. ४ वासोद्वेजिता.

श्चास्माभिर्विबोध्यमाना प्रकृतावेव स्थास्यति' इति। 'तथा' इति तस्याः प्रतियाते स्वजने सा गणिका तमृषिमलघुभक्तिर्धौतोद्गमनीयवासिनी नात्यादृतशरीरसंस्कारा वनतरुपोतालवालपूरणैर्देवतार्चन[1]कुसुमोच्चयावचयप्रयासैर्नैकै[2]विकल्पोपहारकर्मभिः कामशासनार्थे च गन्धमाल्यधूपदीपनृत्यगीतवाद्याभिः क्रियाभिरेकान्ते च त्रिवर्गसंबन्धिनीभिः कथाभिरध्यात्मवादैश्चा[3]नुरूपैरल्पीयसैव कालेनान्वरञ्जयत्।

एकदा च रहसि रक्तं तमुपलक्ष्य 'मूढः खलु लोको यत्सह धर्मेणार्थकामावपि गणयति' इति किंचिदस्मयत। 'कथय वासु केनांशेनार्थकामातिशायी धर्मस्तवाभिप्रेतः' इति प्रेरिता मरीचिना लज्जामन्थरमारभताभिधातुम्—'इतः किल जनाद्भगवतस्त्रिवर्गबलाबलज्ञानम्। अथ वैतदपि प्रकारान्तरं दासजनानुग्रहस्य। भवतु। श्रूयताम्। ननु धर्मादृतेऽर्थकामयोरनुत्पत्तिरेव। तदनपेक्ष एव धर्मो[4] निवृत्तिसुखप्रसूतिहेतुरा[5]त्मसमाधानमात्रसाध्यश्च। सोऽर्थकामवद्बाह्यसाधनेषु नात्यायतते। तत्त्वदर्शनोपबृंहित[6]श्च यथाकथंचिदप्यनुष्ठीय-

---

**धौतोद्गमनीयेति**। धौतं यदुद्गमनीयं वस्त्रयुगलं तद्वस्ते सा तद्वासिनी। 'तत्स्यादुद्गमनीयं यद्धौतयोर्वस्त्रयोर्युगम्' इत्यमरः। धौतोद्गमनीयमित्यत्र 'विशिष्टवाचकानाम्' इति वचनाद्विशेष्यपरतया व्याख्येयम्। **नात्यादृतेति**। नात्यादृत आदरितः शरीरस्य संस्कारः परिकर्मादिर्यया सा। वनतरूणां पोता बालवृक्षास्तेषामालवालानि। देवतार्चनार्थे कुसुमानि पुष्पाणि तेषामुच्चयः समूहस्तस्यावचयो ग्रहणं तत्प्रयासैः श्रमैः। 'उच्चयस्तरोरादानमवचयो भूमेः' इति भूषणा। नैका अनेका ये विकल्पा भेदाः। 'विकल्पः संशये भेदे' इति वररुचिः। उपहारकर्मभिर्बलिकर्मभिः। कामशासनो महादेवस्तदर्थे तन्निमित्तम्। 'कामशासनार्थे कामोद्दीपनार्थे च' इति भूषणा। त्रिवर्गो धर्मार्थकामाः। अध्यात्मवादैरात्मानमधिकृत्य ये वादास्तत्त्वबुभुत्सुकथाः तैः। **एकदेति**। रक्तमनुरक्तम्। किंचिदल्पम्। **कथयेति**। वासु बाले। 'अथ बाला स्याद्वासूः' इत्यमरः। 'अम्बार्थनद्योर्ह्रस्वः' इति संबुद्धौ ह्रस्वता। अर्थकामावतिशेते अतिक्रम्य वर्तत इति तथा। अभिप्रेतः संमतः। इतो जनान्मल्लक्षणात्। 'धर्मादृते इति। तथा च व्यासः—धर्मादर्थश्च कामश्चेति इ०' इति भू०। तदनपेक्षोऽर्थकामनिरपेक्ष एव। स्वतन्त्र एवेत्यर्थः। निवृत्तिसुखं मोक्षसुखं तदुद्भवहेतुः। आत्मसमाधानं बुद्धेरेकाग्रतामात्रम्। 'आत्मा यत्नो धृतिर्बुद्धिः स्वभावो ब्रह्म वर्ष्म च' इत्यमरादयः। स धर्मः। नात्यायतते नात्यन्तमधीनो भवती-

---

१ कुसुमसमुच्चय. २ अनेक. ३ अनुकूलैः. ४ स धर्मः. ५ आत्मनः समा०. ६ ०तस्तु.

मानाभ्यां नार्थकामाभ्यां बाध्यते। बाधितोऽपि चाल्पायासप्रतिसमाहितस्तमपि दोषं निर्हृत्य श्रेयसेऽनल्पाय कल्पते। तथा हि। पितामहस्य तिलोत्तमाभिलाषः, भवानीपतेर्मुनिपत्नीसहस्रसंदूषणम्, पद्मनाभस्य षोडशसहस्रान्तःपुरविहारः, प्रजापतेः स्वदुहितर्यपि प्रणयप्रवृत्तिः, शचीपतेरहल्याजारता, शशाङ्कस्य गुरुतल्पगमनम्, अंशुमालिनो वडवालङ्घनम्, अनिलस्य केसरिकलत्रसमागमः, बृहस्पतेरुतथ्यभार्याभिसरणम्, पराशरस्य दाशकन्यादूषणम्, पाराशर्यस्य भ्रातृदारसंगतिः, अत्रेर्मृगीसमागम इति। अमराणां च तेषु तेषु कार्येष्वासुरविप्रलम्भनानि ज्ञानबलान्न धर्मपीडामावहन्ति। धर्मपूते च मनसि नभसीव न जातु रजोऽनुषज्यते। तन्मन्ये नार्थकामौ धर्मस्य शततमीमपि कलां स्पृशतः' इति।

श्रुत्वैतद्दषिरुदीर्णरागवृत्तिरभ्यधात्—'अयि विलासिनि साधु पश्यसि। न धर्मस्तत्त्वदर्शिनां विषयोपभोगेनोपरुध्यत इति। किं तु जन्मनः प्रभृत्यर्थकामवार्तानभिज्ञा वयम्। ज्ञेयौ चेमौ किंरूपौ किंपरिवारौ किंफलौ च' इति। सा त्वाबादीत्—'अर्थस्तावदर्जनवर्धनरक्षणात्मकः, कृषि-

---

त्यर्थः। 'यती प्रयत्ने'। उपसर्गादर्थान्तरम्। तत्त्वदर्शनेनोपबृंहितो वर्धितो धर्मोऽर्थकामाभ्यां न बाध्यते। बाधितोऽपि धर्मोऽल्पायासेनाल्पयत्नेन प्रतिसमाहितः समाधानं प्रापितः। अनल्पाय श्रेयसे मोक्षाय। **तथा हीति**। तिलोत्तमाऽप्सरोविशेषः। संदूषणं गमनम्। पद्मनाभस्य कृष्णस्य प्रणयेन प्रीत्या प्रवृत्तिः प्रवर्तनम्। अहल्या गौतमपत्नी। गुरुतल्पं बृहस्पतिभार्या। 'तल्पं शय्याट्टदारेषु' इत्यमरः। अंशुमाली सूर्यः। वडवाऽश्विनी। अनिलस्य वायोः। केसरी वानरभेदः। उतथ्यो बृहस्पतेर्ज्येष्ठभ्राता। अभिसरणं गमनम्। पराशरस्य व्यासपितुः। दाशः कैवर्तः तत्कन्या सत्यवती तद्दूषणं तद्गमनम्। पाराशर्यस्य भ्राता विचित्रवीर्यः। आसुरविप्रलम्भनान्यकृत्याचरणानि। 'अकृत्याचरणं यत्तदासुरं विप्रलम्भनम्' इत्यजयः। ज्ञानबलात्तत्प्राबल्यात्। धर्मपूते धर्मपवित्रे। जातु कदाचित्। यथा नभसि रजो नानुषक्तं भवति तथेत्यर्थः। **श्रुत्वेति**। उदीर्णा वृद्धिं गता रागवृत्तिरिच्छावृत्तिः यस्येति। अयि विलासिनीति सानुरागोक्तिः। तत्त्वदर्शिनां तत्त्वसाक्षात्कारिणाम्। धर्मो विषयोपभोगेन स्त्र्याद्युपभोगेन नोपरुध्यते नोपक्षीयते। ज्ञेयौ चेमावर्थकामौ ज्ञातव्याविति। रूपं स्वरूपम्। परिवारः परिकरः। अर्जनं संपादनम्। वर्धनं वृद्धिः

पाशुपाल्यवाणिज्यसंधिविग्रहादिपरिवारः तीर्थप्रतिपादनफलश्च । कामस्तु विषयातिसक्तचेतसोः स्त्रीपुंसयोर्निरतिशयसुखस्पर्शविशेषः । परिवारस्त्वस्य यावदिह रम्यमुज्ज्वलं[2] च । फलं पुनः परमाह्लादनम्, परस्परविमर्दजन्म, स्मर्यमाणमधुरम्, उदीरिताभिमानमनुत्तमम्[3], सुखमपरोक्षं स्वसंवेद्यमेव । तस्यैव कृते विशिष्टस्थानवर्तिनः कष्टानि तपांसि महान्ति दानानि दारुणानि युद्धानि भीमानि समुद्रलङ्घनादीनि च नराः समाचरन्ति ' इति ।

निशम्यैतन्नियतिबलान्नु[4] तत्पाटवान्नु स्वबुद्धिमान्द्यान्नु स्वनियममनादृत्य तस्यामसौ प्रासजत् । सा सुदूरं मूढात्मानं च तं प्रवहणेन नीत्वा पुरमुदारशोभया राजवीथ्या स्वभवनमनैषीत् । अभूच्च घोषणा ' श्वः कामोत्सवः ' इति । उत्तरेद्युः स्नातानुलिप्तमाचितमञ्जु[5]मालमारब्धकामिजनवृत्तं निवृत्तस्ववृत्ताभिलाषं क्षणमात्रगतेऽपि तया विना दूय[6]मानं तमृषिमृद्धिमता राजमार्गेणोत्सवसमाजं नीत्वा क्वचिदुपवनोद्देशे युवतिजनशतपरिवृतस्य राज्ञः

---

कलादिभिः । रक्षणं पालनम् । कृषिः कर्षणकर्म । पाशुपाल्यं पशुपालनम् । तीर्थेषु सत्पात्रेषु प्रतिपादनं दानम् । स्त्रीपुंसयोरिति ' अचतुर–' इत्यादिना निपातनाददन्तता । निरतिशयः । श्रेष्ठ इत्यर्थः । यावदिति साकल्ये । परस्परविमर्दजन्मान्योन्यालिङ्गनचुम्बनादिजन्म । ' उदीरित इत्यत्राभिमानः सार्थक्यबुद्धिर्यत इत्यर्थः ' इति भूषणा । अपरोक्षं प्रत्यक्षम् । तस्यैव सुखस्यैव निमित्तम् । कृते इत्यव्ययं तादर्थ्ये । ' अर्थे कृतेऽव्ययं तावत्तादर्थ्ये वर्तते द्वयम् ' इति कोशः । विशिष्टस्थानवर्तिनः सत्तीर्थवासिनः । निशम्य श्रुत्वा । नियतिर्दैवम् । तस्याः काममञ्जर्याः पाटवं पटुत्वम् । मान्द्यं मन्दत्वम् । नुः सर्वत्र वितर्के । स्वनियमं मुनिसमयम् । असौ मरीचिस्तस्यां काममञ्जर्यां प्रासजत् प्रसक्तोऽभूदित्यर्थः । **सेति** । सा काममञ्जरी । मूढात्मानं मूर्खबुद्धिम् । तं मुनिम् । प्रवहणेन कर्णीरथसंज्ञकेन वाहनविशेषेण । उदारशोभयोत्कृष्टशोभया । राजवीथ्या राजमार्गेण । स्वभवनं स्वगृहमनैषीदनयत् । **अभूच्चेति** । घोषणा डिण्डिमः । ' दांडोरा ' इति प्रसिद्धः । श्व आगामिनि दिवसे । उत्तरेद्युरुत्तरदिवसे । पूर्वं स्नातः पश्चादनुलिप्तस्तथा तम् । आचरिता धृता मञ्जुर्मनोहरा माला येनेति तम् । वृत्तं वर्तनम् । निवृत्तो दूरापास्तः स्ववृत्ते स्वाचरणेऽभिलाषो यस्य तम् ।

---

१ अभिषक्त, अभिव्यक्त. २ उज्ज्वलं च वस्तु. ३ अनुत्तमसुखम्. ४ निमित्तबलान्नु. ५ मुण्ड. ६ दूयमानचित्तम्.

संनिधौ स्मितमुखेन तेन 'भद्रे भगवता सह निषीद' इत्यादिष्टा सविभ्रमं कृतप्रणामा सस्मितं न्यषीदत्[1]। तत्र काचिदुत्थाय बद्धाञ्जलिरुत्तमाङ्गना 'देव जिताऽनयाऽहम्। अस्यै दास्यमद्यप्रभृत्यभ्युपेतं मया' इति प्रभुं प्राणंसीत्। विस्मयहर्षमूलश्च कोलाहलो लोकस्योदजिहीत। हृष्टेन च राज्ञा महार्हैं रत्नालंकारैर्महता च परिबर्हेणानुगृह्य विसृष्टा वारमुख्याभिः पौरमुख्यैश्च गणशः प्रशस्यमाना स्वभवनमगत्वैव तमृषिमभाषत—'भगवन् अयमञ्जलिः। चिरमनुगृहीतोऽयं दासजनः। स्वार्थ इदानीमनुष्ठेयः' इति। स तु रागादशनिहत इवोद्भ्राम्याब्रवीत्—'प्रिये किमेतत्। कुत इदमौदासीन्यम्। क गतस्तव मय्यसाधारणोऽनुरागः' इति। अथ सा सस्मितमिदमवादीत्—'भगवन् ययाऽद्य राजकुले मत्तः पराजयोऽभ्युपेतस्तस्याश्च मम च कस्मिंश्चित्संघर्षे 'मरीचिमावर्जितवतीव[2] श्लाघसे' इति तयाऽस्म्यहमाधिक्षिप्ता[3]। दास्यपणबन्धेन चास्मिन्नर्थे प्रावर्तिषि। सिद्धार्था चास्मि त्वत्प्रसादात्' इति। स तया तथाऽवधूतो दुर्मतिः कृतानुशयः शून्यवन्न्यवर्तिष्ट। यस्तयैवं कृतस्तपस्वी तमेव मा महाभाग मन्यस्व। स्वशक्तिनिषिक्तं[4] रागमुद्धृत्य तयैव बन्धक्या महद्वैराग्य-

दूयमानं खिद्यमानम्। ऋद्धिमता समृद्धेन। उत्सवसमाजं क्रीडासभाम्। भगवता मुनिना सह। निषीद उपविश। **तत्रेति**। तत्र सभायाम्। अनया काममञ्जर्या। अभ्युपेतमङ्गीकृतम्। कोलाहलः कलकलः। उदजिहीत। 'ओहाङ् गतौ' इति धातुः। उद्गतोऽभूदित्यर्थः। अर्हो मूल्यम्। परिबर्हः परिकरः। सेवकजन इति यावत्। अयं दासजनो मल्लक्षणः। स्वार्थस्तपश्चरणादिः। **स त्विति**। उदासीनस्य भाव औदासीन्यम्। **अथेति**। संघर्षः स्पर्धा। आवर्जितवतीव। वशीकृतवतीवेत्यर्थः। पणबन्धः प्रतिज्ञा। अस्मिन्नर्थे भवद्वशीकरणरूपेऽर्थे। प्रावर्तिषि प्रवृत्ता अभूवम्। सिद्धार्था कृतार्था। अवधूतो दूरीकृतः। कृतानुशयः कृतपश्चात्तापः। शून्यवच्छून्यहृदय इव। **य इति**। तपस्व्यनुकम्प्यः। 'तपस्वी चानुकम्पार्हः' इत्यमरः। महाभागेत्यपहारवर्मसंबोधनम्। तमेव मरीचिमेव मां मन्यस्व। जानीहीत्यर्थः। स्वशक्तिनिषिक्तं स्वशक्त्या स्वसामर्थ्येन। 'स्वशक्तिः प्रलोभनशक्तिः' इति भूषणा। निषिक्तं निक्षिप्तम्। रागमनुरागम्। उद्धृत्य दूरीकृत्य। बन्धक्या पुंश्चल्या। 'पुंश्चली धर्षणी

1 समासदत्। तत्र तेन. 2 महर्षिं मरीचिम्. 3 तयाऽहमधिक्षिप्ता. 4 स्वनिषिक्तम्.

मर्पितम्। अचिरादेव शक्य आत्मा त्वदर्थ[1]साधनक्षमः कर्तुम्। अस्यामेव तावद्वसाङ्गपुर्यां चम्पायाम्' इति।

अथ तन्मनश्च्युततमःस्पर्शभियेवास्तं रविरगात्। ऋषिमुक्तश्च रागः संध्यात्वेनास्फुरत्। तत्कथादत्तवैराग्याणीव कमलवनानि समकुचन्। अनुमतमुनिशासनस्त्वहममुनैव सहोपास्य संध्यामनुरूपाभिः कथाभिस्तमनुशय्य नीतरात्रिः प्रत्युन्मिषत्युदयप्रस्थदावकल्पे कल्पद्रुमकिसलयावधीरिण्यरुणार्चिषि तं नमस्कृत्य नगरायोदचलम्। अदर्शं च मार्गा[2]भ्यासवर्तिनः कस्यापि क्षपणकविहारस्य बहिर्विविक्ते रक्ताशोकखण्डे निषण्णमस्पृष्टसमाधिमाधिक्षीणमग्रगण्यमनभिरूपाणां कृपणवर्णं कमपि क्षपणकम्। उरसि चास्य शिथिलितमलनिचयान्मुखान्निप[3]ततोऽश्रुबिन्दूनलक्षयम्। अप्राक्षं चान्तिकोपविष्टः—'क तपः क च रुदितम्। न चेद्रहस्यमिच्छामि

---

बन्धक्यसती कुलटेत्वरी' इत्यमरः। त्वदर्थसाधनक्षमस्त्वत्प्रयोजनसंपादनसमर्थः। **अथेति**। तस्य मुनेर्यन्मनस्तस्मात् च्युतं गलितं यत्तमोऽज्ञानं तत्स्पर्शभियेव। सूर्यतमसोर्वैरादिति भियेवेत्यर्थः। ऋषिमुक्तः स रागः काममञ्जरीविषयकः। संध्यात्वेनास्फुरदिति प्रकटीबभूवेत्यर्थः। तत्कथाः मुनिवार्तास्ताभिर्दत्तवैराग्याणीव कमलवनानि समकुचन्संकुचितानि बभूवुः। इवशब्दोऽत्रोत्प्रेक्षायाम्। अनुमतमङ्गीकृतं मुनिशासनं येनेति सः। अमुना सह मुनिना सह। सहयोगे तृतीया। अनुरूपाभिरनुकूलाभिः। तमनुशय्य। तेन सह शयित्वेत्यर्थः। 'तृतीयार्थे—' इत्यनोः कर्मप्रवचनीयत्वम्। 'कर्मप्रवचनीययुक्ते द्वितीया'। प्रत्युन्मिषत्युदयति सतीति सप्तम्यन्तम्। उदयः पूर्वपर्वतः। तस्य प्रस्थः सानुः। 'स्नुः प्रस्थः सानुरस्त्रियाम्' इत्यमरः। तत्र दावकल्पे वह्निसदृशे। कल्पद्रुमस्य किसलयानि पल्लवानि। अवधीरिणि तिरस्कारकारिणि। अरुणमर्चिर्यस्य तस्मिन् अरुणार्चिषि सूर्ये। तं मुनिम्। नगराय नगरं प्रतीत्यर्थः। उदचलम्। चलित इत्यर्थः। अदर्शमिति दृष्टवान्। मार्गस्याभ्यासं समीपम्। 'समीपे निकटासन्नसंनिकृष्टसनीडवत्। सदेशाभ्याससविधसमर्यादसवेशवत्' इत्यमरः। क्षपणकविहारस्य सौगतावासस्य बहिः विविक्ते विजने। रक्ताशोकखण्डे रक्ताशोककदम्बे। 'कदम्बे खण्डमस्त्रियाम्' इत्यमरः। अस्पृष्टसमाधिं नियमरहितम्। 'समाधिर्नियमे ध्याने' इति विश्वः। आधिक्षीणं मानसपीडादुर्बलम्। अनभिरूपाणां कुरूपाणाम्। कृपणवर्णं दीनवर्णम्। क्षपणकं बौद्धम्। शिथिलितो मलनिचयो यत्रेति तथा तस्मात्। अन्तिकोपविष्टः समीपस्थितः। न चेद्रहस्यं न

---

१ संपादन. २ अभ्यास. ३ निपतितान्.

श्रोतुं शोकहेतुम्' इति। सोऽब्रूत—'सौम्य, श्रूयताम्। अहमस्यामेव चम्पायां निधिपालितनाम्नः श्रेष्ठिनो ज्येष्ठसूनुर्वसुपालितो नाम। वैरूप्यात्तु मम विरूपक इति प्रसिद्धिरासीत्। अन्यश्चात्र सुन्दरक इति यथार्थनामा कलागुणैः समृद्धो वसुना नातिपुष्टोऽभवत्। तस्य च मम च वपुर्वसुनी निमित्तीकृत्य वैरं वैरोपजीविभिः पौरधूर्तैरुदपाद्यत। त एव कदाचिदावयोरुत्सवसमाजे स्वयमुत्पादितमन्योन्यावमानमूलमधिक्षेपवचनव्यतिकरमुपशमय्य 'न वपुर्वसु वा पुंस्त्वमूलम्, अपि तु प्रकृष्टगणिकाप्रार्थ्ययौवनो हि यः स पुमान्। अतो युवतिललामभूता काममञ्जरी यं वा कामयते स हरतु सुभगपताकाम्' इति व्यवास्थापयन्। अभ्युपेत्यावां प्राहिणुव तस्यै दूतान्। अहमेव किलामुष्याः स्मरोन्मादहेतुरासम्। आसीनयोश्चावयोर्मामेवोपगम्य सा नीलोत्पलमयमिवापाङ्गदामाङ्के मम मुञ्चन्ती तं जनमपत्रपयाऽधोमुखं व्यधत्त। सुभगंमन्येन च मया स्वधनस्य स्वगृहस्य स्वगणस्य स्वदेहस्य स्वजीवितस्य च सैवेश्वरीकृता। कृतश्चाहमनया मलमल्लकशेषः।

चेद्गोप्यम्। **सोऽब्रूतेति**। श्रेष्ठिनो वणिग्वरस्य। अन्यः कश्चन। वसुना नातिपुष्टः। दरिद्र इति यावत्। तस्य सुन्दरकस्य मम च वपुर्वसुनी शरीरद्रव्ये। वैरोपजीविभिर्वैरेणोपजीवन्तीति तथोक्तैः। **त इति**। स्वयं तैः पौरधूर्तैः। अन्योन्यावमानमूलं परस्परावज्ञानिदानम्। अधिक्षेपस्य वचनानां व्यतिकरस्तं अधिक्षेपवचनव्यतिकरं तिरस्कारवाक्यप्रसरम्। उपशमय्य शान्तिं नीत्वा। प्रकृष्टगणिकयोत्तमवेश्यया प्रार्थ्यमानं यौवनं यस्येति स तथा। युवतिललामभूता युवतिभूषणभूता। सुभग इति पताकाम्। चिह्नमिति यावत्। व्यवास्थापयन्निति मर्यादां चक्रुरित्यर्थः। अभ्युपेत्याङ्गीकृत्य। तस्यै तामानेतुम्। 'क्रियार्थोपपदस्य—' इति कर्मणि चतुर्थी। **अहमिति**। 'अर्थवद्ग्रहणे यस्मान्नानर्थकपरिग्रहः। सुरूपधनिनोर्वेश्या गृह्णाति धनिनं ततः॥' इति नक्षत्रमाला। 'अपाङ्गदाम शृङ्गारानुभावः' इति भूषणा। अपाङ्गं नेत्रप्रान्तम्। तं जनं मत्प्रतिद्वन्द्विनं सुन्दरकम्। अपत्रपया लज्जया। 'लज्जा साऽपत्रपाऽन्यतः' इत्यमरः। **सुभगमिति**। आत्मानं सुभगं मनुते स सुभगंमन्यः। ईश्वरीकृता स्वामिनीकृता। च्व्यन्तमेतत्। मलमल्लकं कौपीनम्। 'आच्छादनं संपिधानं कौपीनं मलमल्लकम्' इति वैजयन्ती।

१ कल्याणगुणैः. २ वचनशत. ३ अस्यै. ४ अपाङ्गमङ्के. ५ सुभगेन.

हृतसर्वस्वैस्तया चापवाहितः प्रपद्य लोकोपहासलक्ष्यतामक्षमश्च सोढुं धिक्कृतानि पौरवृद्धानामिहैं जैनायतने मुनिनैकेनोपदिष्टमोक्षवर्त्मा सुकर एष वेषो वेशनिर्गतानामित्युदीर्णवैराग्यस्तदपि कौपीनमजहाम् । अथ पुनः प्रकीर्णमलपङ्कः प्रबलकेशलुञ्चनव्यथः प्रकृष्टतमक्षुत्पिपासादिदुःखः स्थानासनशयनभोजनेष्वपि द्विप इव नवग्रहो बलवतीभिर्यन्त्रणाभिरुद्वेजितः प्रत्यवामृशम् । 'अहमस्मि द्विजातिः । अस्वधर्मो ममैष पाँखण्डपथावतारः । श्रुतिस्मृतिविहितेनैव वर्त्मना मम पूर्वजाः प्रावर्तन्त । मम तु मन्दभाग्यस्य निन्द्यवेषममन्ददुःखायतनं हरिहरहिरण्यगर्भादिदेवतापवादश्रवणनैरन्तर्यात्प्रेत्यापि निरयफलमफलं विप्रलम्भप्रायमीदृशमिदमधर्मवर्त्म धर्मवत्समाचरणीयमासीत् ।' इति प्रत्याकलितस्वदुर्नयः पिण्डीखण्डं विविक्तमेतदासाद्य पर्याप्तमश्रु मुञ्चामि ' इति । श्रुत्वा चैतदनुकम्पमानोऽब्रवम्—'भद्र, क्षमस्व । कंचित्कालमत्रैव निवस । निजेन द्युम्नेनासावेव वेश्या यथा त्वां योजयिष्यति तथा यतिष्ये । सन्त्युपायास्तादृशाः' इत्याश्वास्य

अपवाहितो बहिष्कृतः । प्रपद्य प्राप्य । लोकानामुपहासास्तेषां लक्ष्यतां स्थानताम् । धिक्कृतानि तिरस्कारवचनानि । पौरवृद्धानां नागरिकश्रेष्ठानाम् । जैनायतने क्षपणकदेवतागारे । वेशो वेश्यागृहम् । उदीर्णवैराग्योऽधिकवैराग्यः । कौपीनमजहामत्यजम् । **अथेति** । प्रकीर्णः प्रसृतः मलपङ्कः यस्य । प्रबला केशानां लुञ्चनमुत्पाटनं तस्य व्यथा यस्य सः । प्रकृष्टतमेत्यत्र 'अतिशायने तमबिष्ठनौ' इति तमप् । क्षुत्क्षुधा पिपासा तृषा । नवग्रहो नूतनं ग्रहणमुपादानं यस्येति । प्रत्यवामृशं व्यचारयम् । द्विजातिर्वैश्यः । पाखण्डानां पन्थाः पाखण्डपथः । 'ऋक्पूर्–' इत्यबन्तता । पाखण्डपथावतारः बौद्धमार्गावतरणम् । अमन्ददुःखायतनं महद्दुःखस्थानम् । अपवादो निन्दा । श्रवणस्य नैरन्तर्यान्निरन्तरस्य भावस्तेन । अविच्छेदादित्यर्थः । प्रेत्य जन्मान्तरे । 'प्रेत्यामुत्र भवान्तरे ' इत्यमरः । निरयो नरकः । विप्रलम्भप्रायं वञ्चनाप्रायम् । अधर्मवर्त्माधर्ममार्गः । प्रत्याकलितो विचारितः । पिण्ड्यशोकः । खण्डं समूहः । 'अशोकः पिण्डिका पिण्डी' इति वैजयन्ती । विविक्तमेकान्तम् । पर्याप्तं यथेष्टम् । भद्रेति संबोधनम् । द्युम्नेन धनेन । 'हिरण्यं द्रविणं द्युम्नम्' इत्यमरः । अनु पश्चात् । आविशन्नेव प्रविशन्नेव ।

१ ०सर्वस्वतया. २ इहैवायतने. ३ पाखण्डि.

तमनूत्थितोऽहम् । नगरमाविशन्नेव चोपलभ्य लोकवादाल्लुब्धेसमृद्ध-पूर्णं पुरमित्यर्थानां नश्वरत्वं च प्रदर्श्य प्रकृतिस्थानमूर्न्विधास्यन्कर्णीसुतप्रहिते पथि मतिमकरवम् । अनुप्रविश्य च द्यूतसभामक्षधूर्तैः समगंसि । तेषां च पञ्चविंशतिप्रकारासु सर्वासु द्यूताश्रयासु कलासु कौशलमक्षभूमिहस्तादिषु चात्यन्तदुरुपलक्ष्याणि कूटकर्माणि तन्मूलानि सावलेपान्यधिक्षेपवचनानि जीवितनिरपेक्षाणि संरम्भविचेष्टितानि सभिकप्रत्ययव्यवहारान् न्यायबलप्रतापप्रायोनङ्गीकृतार्थसाधनक्षमान्बलिषु सान्त्वनानि दुर्बलेषु भर्त्सितानि पक्षरचनानैपुणमुच्चावचानि प्रलोभनानि ग्लहप्रभेदवर्णनानि द्रव्यसंविभागौदार्यमन्तरान्तराऽश्लील-प्रायान्कलकलानित्येतानि चान्यानि चानुभवन्न तृप्तिमध्यगच्छम् । अहसं च किंचित्प्रमाददत्तशारे क्वचित्कितवे । प्रतिकितवस्तु निर्दहन्निव क्रोधताम्रया दृशा मामभिवीक्ष्य 'शिक्षयसि रे द्यूतवर्त्म हासव्याजेन । आस्तामयमशिक्षितो वराकः । त्वयैव तावद्विचक्षणेन देविष्यामि' इति द्यूताध्यक्षानुमत्या व्यत्यषजत् । मया जितश्चासौ

---

लोकवादाज्जनवाक्यात् । लुब्धाः कृपणाः । समृद्धाः श्रीमन्तः । 'अधिकर्द्धिः समृद्धः स्यात्' इत्यमरः । कर्णीसुतप्रहिते कर्णीसुतः स्तेयशास्त्रकर्ता तेन प्रहिते प्रवर्तिते । अक्षधूर्तैः पाशनिपुणैः । समगंसि संगतोऽभवम् । **तेषां चेति** । तेषामक्षधूर्तानाम् । अक्षभूमिः शारीस्थापनगृहम् । कूटकर्माणि कपटकर्माणि तन्मूलानि कूटकर्ममूलानि । 'सभिका द्यूतकारकाः' इत्यमरः । **'० व्यवहारन्यायबलेति** । व्यवहारो लोकानां व्यवहारः न्यायो युक्तिः तयोर्बलमुपन्यासः प्रतापः प्रागल्भ्यं तैः प्रयोजितार्थसाधने क्षमस्तस्मादिति प्रत्ययस्य विशेषणम् । क्वचित्प्रत्ययव्यवहारादिति पाठः । 'प्रत्ययजनको व्यवहारः इत्यर्थः ।' इति भूषणा । अङ्गीकृतार्थः स्वीकृतार्थस्तत्साधने क्षमान्समर्थान् । पक्षरचनानैपुणं स्वपक्षीकरणे नैपुण्यम् । सर्वलोकानां स्वायत्तीकरणे कुशलत्वमित्यर्थः । उच्चावचान्यनेकप्रकाराणि । प्रलोभनानि मोहनानि । ग्लहः पणः । 'पणोऽक्षेषु ग्लहो मतः' इत्यमरः । 'ग्लहप्रभेदवर्णनानि पणस्यान्यथाभाववर्णनानि' इति भूषणा । अन्तरान्तरा मध्येमध्ये इत्यर्थः । अश्लीलप्रायानसभ्यबहुलान् । 'अश्लीलं ग्राम्यभाषणम्' इति वैजयन्ती । कलकलान्कोलाहलान् । प्रमाददत्तशारे प्रमादेनानवधानतया दत्तः शारः क्षेपकरणं येन तस्मिन् । प्रतिकितवः प्रतिकूलकितवः । द्यूतवर्त्म द्यूतमार्गम् । हासव्याजेन हासमिषेण । व्यत्यषजद्व्यतिषक्तोऽभूत् । दीनाराणां

---

१ लुब्धेभ्यपूर्णं; लुब्धसभिकमिभ्यपू०. २ अनुप्रपद्य. ३ अक्षभ्रामि. ४ व्यवहारन्याय. ५ प्रयोजितार्थ; जितार्थ. ६ परपक्षरचनानैपुण्यम्. ७ उपप्रलोभनानि.

षोडशसहस्राणि दीनाराणाम्। तदर्धं सभिकाय सभ्येभ्यश्च दत्त्वाऽर्धं स्वीकृत्योदतिष्ठम्। उदतिष्ठंश्च तत्रगतानां हर्षगर्भाः प्रशंसालापाः। प्रार्थ्यमानस्सभिकानुरोधाच्च तदगारेऽत्युदारमभ्यवहारविधिमकरवम्। यन्मूलश्च मे दुरोदरावतारः स मे विमर्दको नाम विश्वास्यतरं द्वितीयं हृदयमासीत्।

तन्मुखेन च सारतः कर्मतः शीलतश्च सकलमेव नगरमवधार्य धूर्जटिकण्ठकल्माषकालतमे तमसि नीलनिवसनार्धोरुकपरिहितो बद्धतीक्ष्णकौक्षेयकः फणिमुखकाकलीसंदंशकपुरुषशीर्षकयोगचूर्णयोगवर्तिकामानसूत्रकर्कटकरज्जुदीपभाजनभ्रमरकरण्डकप्रभृत्यनेकोपकरणयुक्तो गत्वा कस्यचिल्लुब्धेश्वरस्य गृहे संधिं छित्त्वा पटभाससूक्ष्मच्छिद्रालक्षितान्तर्गृहप्रवृत्तिरव्यथो निजगृहमिवानुप्रविश्य नीवीं सारमहतीमादाय निरगाम्। नीलनीरदनिकरपीवरतिमिरनिबिडितायां राजवीथ्यां झटिति शतह्रदासंपातमिव क्षणमालोकमलक्षयम्। अथासौ नगरदेवतेव नगरमोषरोषिता निःसंबाधवेलायां निःसृता संनिकृष्टा काचिदुन्मिषद्भूषणा युवतिराविरासीत्। 'कासि वासु, क्व यासि' इति सदयमुक्ता

---

निष्काणाम्। सुवर्णानामिति यावत्। तत्रगतानां सभिकसभ्यानाम्। अभ्यवहारविधिं भोजनविधिम्। दुरोदरं द्यूतम्। **धूर्जटीति**। धूर्जटिर्महादेवः तत्कण्ठे यत्कल्माषं कालिमा तद्वत्कालतमेऽतिश्यामले। नीलनिवसनं नीलवस्त्रं तस्य यदर्धोरुकमवगुण्ठनवस्त्रं तेन परिहित आच्छादितः। कौक्षेयकः करवालः। 'कुलकुक्षिग्रीवाभ्यः—' इति ढकञ्। फणिमुखं सुरङ्गासाधनम्। काकली कर्तरी। "निद्राति जागर्ति वेति बोधनार्थं कलमधुरध्वनिवाद्यविशेषः" इति केचित्। 'काकली तु कले सूक्ष्मे ध्वनौ तु मधुरास्फुटे' इत्यमरः। संदंशकः भाषायां 'सांडशी' इति ख्यातः। पुरुषशीर्षकं पुरुषशीर्षप्रतिकृति काष्ठमयं शिरः। योगचूर्णं निधिप्रदर्शकमौषधम्। योगवर्तिकोपायाञ्जनम्। 'यस्याः प्रज्वालनात्सर्वत्र स[illegible] एव लोचनगोचरा भवन्ति। यत्प्रभया मोहमुपयान्ति जनाः' इति भूष[illegible]। मा[illegible]सूत्रं प्रमाणरज्जुः। कर्कटको यन्त्रसाधनम्। भाषया 'कर्काटक' इत्युच्यते। रज्जुरारोहणसाधनम्। भ्रमरकरण्डकं दीपनिर्वापणशलभभाण्डम्। संधिमिष्टकासंधिम्। पटभासो जालान्तरम्। तस्य इव सूक्ष्मं छिद्रं तेन आलक्षिता इ०। पटभाक्षेति पाठे पटभाक्षः प्रेक्षणसाधनं इति भूषणा। नीवीं मूलधनम्। **नीलेति**। नीला ये नीरदा मेघास्तेषां निकरः समूहस्तेन पीवरं पुष्टं यत्तिमिरमन्धकारस्तन्निबिडितायाम्। शतह्रदा विद्युत्। संपातः स्फुरणम्। आलोकं प्रकाशम्। **अथेति**। असौ विद्युत्प्रकाशः। नगरस्य मोषश्चौर्यं तेन रोषिता रुष्टा नगरदेवतेव। निःसंबाधं निःसंकटम्। उन्मिषद्भूषणा प्र[illegible] रद्भूषणा। त्रासगद्गदं

---

१ बाणमान०. २ पटभाक्ष. ३ तमो०; ०निबिडपीडितायाम्.

त्रासगद्गदमगादीत्—' आर्य, पुर्यस्यामर्यवर्यः कुबेरदत्तनामा वसति। अस्म्यहं तस्य कन्या। मां जातमात्रां धनमित्रनाम्नेऽत्रत्यायैव कस्मैचिदिभ्यकुमारायान्वजानाद्भार्यां मे पिता। स पुनरस्मिन्नत्युदारतया पित्रोरन्ते वित्तैर्निजैः क्रीत्वेवार्थिवर्गाद्दारिद्र्यं दरिद्रति सत्यथोदारक इति च प्रीतलोकाधिरोपितापरश्लाघ्यनामनि वरयत्येव तस्मिन्मां तरुणीभूतामधन इत्यदत्त्वाऽर्थपतिनाम्ने कस्मैचिदितरस्मै यथार्थनाम्ने सार्थवाहाय दित्सति मे पिता। तदमङ्गलमद्य किल प्रभाते भावीति ज्ञात्वा प्रागेव प्रियतमदत्तसंकेता वञ्चितस्वजना निर्गत्य बाल्याभ्यस्तेन वर्त्मना मन्मथाभिसरा तदगारमभिसरामि। तन्मां मुञ्च। गृहाणैतद्भाण्डं' इत्युन्मुच्य मह्यमर्पितवती। दयमानश्चाहमब्रवम्—' एहि साध्वि, त्वां नयेयं त्वत्प्रियावसथम्' इति त्रिचतुराणि पदान्युदचलम्। आपतच्च दीपिकालोकपरिलुप्यमानतिमिरभारं यष्टिकृपाणपाणि नागरिकबलमनल्पम्। दृष्ट्वैव प्रवेपमानां कन्यकामवदम्—'भद्रे मा भैषीः। अस्त्ययमसिद्वितीयो मे बाहुः। अपि तु मृदुरयमुपायस्त्वदपेक्षया चिन्तितः। शयेऽहं भावितविषवेगविक्रियः। त्वयाऽप्यमी वाच्याः— 'निशि वयमिमां पुरीं प्रविष्टाः। दष्टश्च ममैष नायको दर्वीकरे-

---

भयविह्वलम्। अगादीत्। 'गद व्यक्तायां वाचि'। अर्यवर्यो वैश्यवर्यः। 'अर्यः स्वामिवैश्ययोः' इति सूत्रेण निपातः। अत्रत्यायैतद्देशभवाय। 'अव्ययात्त्यप्'। 'अमेहक्वतसित्रेभ्य एव' इति वार्त्तिकम्। धनमित्रनाम्ने इभ्यकुमाराय धनिककुमाराय। अन्वजानात्प्रतिज्ञातवान्। **स इति**। स पिता। अस्मिन्धनमित्रे। प्रीतेन लोकेनाधिरोपितं दत्तमुदारक इत्यपरं श्लाघ्यं नाम यस्य तस्मिन्। सार्थवाहाय वणिजे। दित्सति दातुमिच्छति। तदमङ्गलमर्थपतिदानरूपम्। प्रियतमो धनमित्रनामा तेन दत्तः संकेतो यस्यै सेति। मन्मथो मदनोऽभिसरः सहायो यस्याः सा। अगारं गृहम्। अभिसरामि गच्छामि। एतद्भाण्डमेतद्भूषणम्। उन्मुच्योत्तार्य। आवसथं गृहम्। **आपतच्चेति**। दीपिका 'दिवटी' इति लोकप्रसिद्धा। 'दीपशब्दात्संज्ञायां कन्' इति भूषणा। 'दीपिका हस्तदीपः स्यात्' इति वैजयन्ती। 'नागरिकस्य नगररक्षाकर्तुः भाषया 'कोतवाल' इत्याख्यस्य' इति भूषणा। त्वदपेक्षया। त्वदनुरोधेनेत्यर्थः। वयमिति द्वयोरपि बहुवचनम्। 'अस्मदो द्वयोश्च' इति। दर्वीकरेण सर्पेण। (१३२ पृष्ठे द्रष्टव्यम्।)

---

१ वल्लभ. २ क्रीत्वैव. ३ ०सारा, मन्मथैकाभि०. ४ शयीय.

णामुष्मिन्सभागृहकोणे । यदि वः कश्चिन्मन्त्रवित्कृपालुः स एनमुज्जीवयन्मम प्राणानाहरेदनाथायाः ' इति । साऽपि बाला गत्यन्तराभावाद्भयगद्गदस्वरा बाष्पदुर्दिनाक्षी बद्धवेपथुः कथंकथमपि गत्व मदुक्तमन्वतिष्ठत् । अशयिषि चाहं भावितविषविक्रियः । तेषु कश्चिन्नरेन्द्राभिमानी[1] मां निर्वर्ण्य मुद्रातन्त्रमन्त्रध्यानादिभिश्चोपक्रम्याकृतार्थः ' गत एवायं कालदष्टः । तथा हि स्तब्धश्यावमङ्गम्[2], रुद्धा दृष्टिः, शान्त एवोष्मा । शुचाऽलं वासु, श्वोऽग्निसात्करिष्यामः । कोऽतिवर्तते दैवम् ' इति सहेतरैः प्रायात् ।

उत्थितश्चाहमुदारकाय तां नत्वाऽब्रवम्—'अहमस्मि कोऽपि तस्करः । त्वद्गतेनैव चेतसा सहायभूतेन त्वामिमामभिसरन्तीमन्तरोपलभ्य कृपया त्वत्समीपमनैषम् । भूषणमिदमस्याः' इत्यंशुपटलपाटितध्वान्तजालं तदप्यार्पितवान् । उदारकस्तु तदादाय सलज्जं च सहर्षं च ससंभ्रमं च माममाषत—' आर्य, त्वयैवेयमस्यां निशि प्रिया मे दत्ता । वाक्पुनर्ममापहृता । तथा हि न जाने वक्तुम् । त्वत्कर्मैतदद्भुतमिति । इदं ननु[3] ते स्वशीलमद्भुतवत्प्रतिभाति । नैवमन्येनापि कृत पूर्वमिति प्रतिनियतैव वस्तुशक्तिः । न हि त्वय्यन्यदीया लोभादयः ।

---

सभागृहं बहुतरजनावस्थानगृहं तस्य कोणे । मन्त्रविन्मान्त्रिकः । गत्यन्तराभावादुपायान्तराभावात् । बाष्पदुर्दिनाक्षी बाष्पव्याप्तनेत्रा । बद्धवेपथुः प्राप्तकम्पा । अशयिषि शयितवान् । भाविता प्रकाशिता विषविक्रिया विषविकारो येनेति । नरेन्द्रो विषवैद्यः । ' नरेन्द्रो वार्तिके राज्ञि विषवैद्येऽपि कथ्यते ' इति विश्वः । निर्वर्ण्य निरीक्ष्य । उपक्रम्य चिकित्सित्वा । ' उपक्रमश्चिकित्सा स्यात् ' इति वैजयन्ती । **तथा हीति**। स्तब्धं निश्चेष्टं श्यावं श्यामलम् । "श्याववर्णः कपिशवर्णः । ' श्यावास्यता विषकृता ' इति माधवाचार्यः " इति भूषणा । अग्निसादग्न्यधीनम् । उदारकाय धनमित्रनाम्ने । तस्करश्चौरः । अन्तरा मार्गमध्ये । अंशुपटलेन किरणजालेन पाटितं नाशितं ध्वान्तजालमन्धकारसमूहो येनेति तथा । प्रिया दत्ता वागपहृतेत्यत्र परिवृत्तिरलंकारः । ' परिवृत्तिर्विनिमयो न्यूनाभ्यधिकयोर्मिथः ' इति लक्षणात् । तथा हीत्यादिना काव्यलिङ्गमपि । **न जाने इति** । " यदिदमद्भुतं त्वत्कर्म वक्तुं न जाने न शक्नोमि । स्वप्रतिभाया अभावात् । एवं च वाणी हृतैवेति स्पष्टम्." इति भूषणा । **न ते स्वशीलमिति** । ' इदं द्रव्यस्य प्रियायाश्च समर्पणं ते चौरत्वेन व्यवहृतस्य स्वशीलं स्वभावो न भवतीत्यतोऽद्भुतवत्प्रतिभाति ' इति भूषणा ।

---

1 नरेन्द्रमानी. 2 श्यावर्णमङ्गम्. 3 नु.

त्वयाऽद्य साधुतोन्मीलितेति तत्प्रायस्त्वत्पूर्वावदानेभ्यो न रोचते। दृष्टमिदानीमौदार्यस्य स्वरूपमिति त्वदाशयमननुमान्य न युक्तो निश्चयः। त्वयाऽमुना सुकृतेन क्रीतोऽयं दासजन इत्यसारमतिगरीयसा क्रीणासीति स ते प्रज्ञाधिक्षेपः। प्रियादानस्य प्रतिदानमिदं शरीरमिति तदलाभे निधनोन्मुखमिदमपि त्वयैव दत्तम्। अथ वैतावदत्र प्राप्तरूपम्। अद्यप्रभृति भर्तव्योऽयं दासजनः' इति मम पादयोरपतत्। उत्थाप्य चैनमुरसोपश्लिष्याभाषिषि—'भद्र, काऽद्य ते प्रतिपत्तिः' इति। सोऽभ्यधत्त—'न शक्नोमि चैनामत्र पित्रोरनभ्यनुज्ञयोपयम्य जीवितुम्। अतोऽस्यामेव यामिन्यां देशमिमं जिहासामि। को वाऽहम्, यथा त्वमाज्ञापयसि' इति। अथ मयोक्तम्—'अस्त्येतत्। स्वदेशो देशान्तरमिति नेयं गणना विदग्धस्य पुरुषस्य। किं तु बालेयमनल्पसौकुमार्या, कष्टाः प्रत्यवायभूयिष्ठाश्च कान्तारपथाः। शैथिल्यमिव किंचित्प्रज्ञासत्त्वयोरनर्थेनेदृशेन देशत्यागेन संभाव्यते। तत्सहानया सुखमिहैव वस्तव्यम्। एहि। नयावैनां स्वमेवावासम्' इति। अविचारानुमतेन[1] तेन सद्य एवैनां तद्गृहमुपनीय तयैवापसर्पभूतया तत्र मृद्भाण्डावशेषमचोरयाव। ततो निष्पत्य क्वचिन्मुषितकं[2] निधाय समुच्चलन्तौ नागरिकसंपाते[3] मार्गपार्श्व-

प्रतिनियता विषयविशेषनिष्ठा। तत्तद्व्यक्तिविश्रान्तेत्यर्थः। **तत्प्राय इति**। इदं द्रव्यस्य प्रियायाश्च समर्पणं पूर्वावदानेभ्यः पूर्वजातकर्मभ्यो न रोचते। 'रुच्यर्थानां–' इति चतुर्थी। 'कर्मणां न शोभते इत्यत्र तात्पर्यम्' इति भूषणा। अवदानं महत्कर्म। त्वदाशयं त्वदभिप्रायम्। अननुमान्यानुमतिमकारयित्वा। अतिगरीयसा बहुतरेण। क्रीणासि गृह्णासि। प्रज्ञाधिक्षेपो बुद्धिनिन्दा। निधनं मरणम्। इदं मच्छरीरम्। प्राप्तरूपं प्रशस्तं प्राप्तम्। प्रशंसायां रूपप्। उपश्लिष्यालिङ्गय। प्रतिपत्तिः कर्तव्यम्। जिहासामि त्यक्तुमिच्छामि। **अथेति**। विदग्धस्य चतुरस्य। "बालेयमित्यादि विषमालंकारः। 'विषमं वर्ण्यते यत्र घटनाऽननुरूपयोः' इति लक्षणात्" इति भूषणा। अनल्पसौकुमार्या अत्यन्तसुकुमारेत्यर्थः। प्रत्यवायो बाधकम्। कान्तारपथा वनमार्गाः। 'ऋक्पूरब्धूः–' इत्यदन्तता। शैथिल्यं शिथिलता। 'इव एवार्थे' इति भूषणा। सत्त्वं बलम्। आवासं गृहम्। अपसर्पभूतया चरभूतया। 'अपसर्पश्चरः स्पशः' इत्यमरः। तत्र नगरे। **तत इति**। क्वचित्प्रदेशे। मुषितकं चोरितं वस्तुजातम्। नागरिकसंपाते नगरस्य लोकसंमर्दे। 'नगर-

१ अविचार्यानुमते. २ मुषितम्. ३ नागरिकपुरुष०.

शायिनं क्वचिन्मत्तवारणमुपरिपुरुषमाकृष्याध्यारोहाव। ग्रैवेयप्रोतपादयुगलेन च मयोत्थाप्यमान एव पातिताधोरणपृथुलोरःस्थलपरिणतः पुरीतल्लतापरीतदन्तकाण्डः स रक्षिकबलमक्षिणोत्। अध्वंसयाव चामुनैवार्थपतिभवनम्। अपवाह्य च क्वचन जीर्णोद्याने शाखाग्राहिकयाऽवातराव। स्वगृहगतौ च स्नातौ शयनमध्यशिश्रियाव।

तावदेवोदगादुदधेरुदयाचलेन्द्रपद्मरागशृङ्गकल्पं कल्पद्रुमहेमपल्लवापीडपाटलं पतङ्गमण्डलम्। उत्थाय च धौतवक्त्रौ प्रगेतनानि मङ्गलान्यनुष्ठायास्मत्कर्मतुमुलं पुरमनुविचरन्तावश्रृणुव वरवधूगृहेषु कोलाहलम्। अथार्थैरर्थपतिः कुबेरदत्तमाश्वास्य कुलपालिकाविवाहं मासावधिकमकल्पयत्। उपह्वरे पुनरित्याशिक्षयं धनमित्रम्—'उपतिष्ठ सखे एकान्त एव चर्मरत्नभस्त्रिकामिमां पुरस्कृत्याङ्गराजम्। आचक्ष्व च—' जानात्येव देवो नैककोटिसारस्य वसुमित्रस्य मां धनमित्रं नामैकपुत्रम्। सोऽहं मूलहरत्वमेत्यार्थिवर्गादस्म्यवज्ञातः। मदर्थमेव संवर्धितायां कुलपालिकायां महादारिद्र्यदोषात्पुनः कुबेरदत्तेन दुहितरर्थपतये दित्सितायामुद्वेगा-

रक्षकपुरुषसंपाते' इति भू०। उपरिपुरुषमाधोरणम्। "उपरिपुरुषं पुरुषोन्मानादधिकम्। आकृष्य गजपृष्ठस्थां रज्जुम्। मत्तगजे सर्वकाले रज्ज्वा नियन्त्रितत्वात्" इति तु भूषणा। ग्रैवेयं कण्ठरज्जुः। 'कुलकुक्षि-' इति ढकञ्। भाषया 'किलावा' इति प्रसिद्धम्। प्रोतं प्रवेशितम्। पातितो य आधोरणो हस्तिपकस्तस्य पृथुलं विशालं यदुरःस्थलं तत्र परिणतो दन्तेन तिर्यक्प्रहारी। 'तिर्यग्दन्तप्रहारस्तु गजः परिणतो मतः' इति हलायुधः। पुरीतल्लताऽन्त्रवल्ली। 'अन्त्रं पुरीतत्' इत्यमरः। ताभिः परीतं व्याप्तं दन्तकाण्डं यस्येति तथा। अक्षिणोत्क्षपितवान्। शाखाग्राहिकया शाखां गृहीत्वेत्यर्थः। अध्यशिश्रियावाधिष्ठितवन्तौ। **तावदिति**। पद्मरागो रक्तमणिस्तस्य शृङ्गं शिखरं तत्कल्पं तदीषन्न्यूनम्। कल्पद्रुमस्य हेमपल्लवाः सुवर्णपल्लवास्तेषामापीडः समूहः तद्वत् पाटलमनेकवर्णम्। 'श्वेतरक्तस्तु पाटलः' इत्यमरः। पतङ्गमण्डलं सूर्यबिम्बम्। प्रगेतनानि प्रातःकालोचितानि। तुमुलं व्याकुलरवम्। **अर्थेति**। अर्थपतिर्वैश्यः। कुबेरदत्तं कन्यापितरम्। मासावधिकम्। मासोत्तरमित्यर्थः। उपह्वरे। 'रहोऽन्तिकमुपह्वरे' इत्यमरः। चर्मरत्नमुत्तमचर्म तस्य भस्त्रिका प्रसेविका 'भाता' इति भाषया प्रसिद्धा। नैककोटिसारस्य। अनेककोटिद्रव्यस्येत्यर्थः। वसुमित्रस्यैकपुत्रम्। 'मूलहरत्वं मूलद्रव्यनाशकत्वं काष्ठवाहिकत्वं वा' इति भूषणा। कुलपालिकायां कन्यायाम्। 'कन्या तु कुलपालिका' इत्यमरः। दित्सितायां दातुमिष्टायाम्। उद्वेगाच्छोकात्। 'उद्वेगौ शोकसंभ्रमौ' इति

१ उपरिपुच्छम. २ पतिताधोरण. ३ तावनोद०. ४ चर्मभस्त्रिकाम.

दुज्झितुमसूनुपनगरभवं जरद्वनमवगाह्य कण्ठन्यस्तशस्त्रिकः केनापि जटाधरेण निवार्यैवमुक्तः—'किं ते साहसस्य मूलम्' इति। मयोक्तम्—'अवज्ञासोदर्यं दारिद्र्यम्' इति। स पुनरेवं कृपालुरन्वग्रहीत्—'तात, मूढोऽसि। नान्यत्पापिष्ठतममात्मत्यागात्। आत्मानमात्मनाऽनवसाद्यैवोद्धरन्ति सन्तः। सन्त्युपाया धनार्जनस्य बहवः, नैकोऽपि च्छिन्नकण्ठप्रतिसंधानपूर्वस्य प्राणलाभस्य। किमनेन। सोऽस्म्यहं मन्त्रसिद्धः। साधितेयं लक्षग्राहिणी चर्मरत्नभस्त्रिका। चिरमहमस्याः प्रसादात्कामरूपेषु कामप्रदः प्रजानामवात्सम्। मत्सरिण्यां जरसि भूमिस्वर्गमत्रोद्देशे प्रवेक्ष्यन्नागतः। तामिमां प्रतिगृहाण। मदन्यत्र चेयं वणिग्भ्यो वार[1]मुख्याभ्यो वा दुग्धे इति हि तद्गता प्रतीतिः। किं तु यत्सकाशादन्यायापहृतं त[2]त्तस्मै प्रत्यर्पणीयम्। न्यायार्जितं तु देवब्राह्मणेभ्यस्त्याज्यम्। अथेयं देवतेव शुचौ देशे निवेश्याच्यर्माना प्रातःप्रातः सुवर्णपूर्णैव दृश्यते। स एष कल्पः' इति बद्धाञ्जलये मह्यमेना दत्त्वा किमपि ग्रावच्छिद्रं प्राविशत्। इयं च रत्नभूता चर्मभस्त्रिका देवायानिवेद्य नोपजीव्येत्यानीता। परं तु देवः प्रमाणम्' इति। राजा च नियतमेव वक्ष्यति—

---

वैजयन्ती। जरद्वनं प्रचाररहितं वनम्। साहसस्योद्योगस्य। अवज्ञा हेलना तस्याः सोदर्यं बन्धुरिव स्थितमित्यर्थः। **स इति**। स जटाधरः। तात अर्भकेत्यर्थः। 'तातस्तु जनकेऽर्भके' इति कोशः। अनवसाद्याविनाश्य। एकोऽप्युपायः। छिन्नो यः कण्ठस्तस्य यत्प्रतिसंधानं पुनःसंबन्धस्तत्पूर्वस्य प्राणलाभस्य प्राणप्राप्तेः। नेति नास्तीत्यर्थः। किमनेन प्राणत्यागेन। लक्षग्राहिणी लक्षं ग्राहयतीति तथा। कामरूपेषु एतदाख्यदेशेषु। अवात्सं वसतिमकरवम्। मत्सरिण्यां मत्सरकारिण्याम्। जरसि वार्द्धके। भूमिस्वर्गे भूम्यां स्वर्ग इव भूमिस्वर्गस्तम्। अत्रोद्देशेऽस्मिन्प्रदेशे। इमां चर्मरत्नभस्त्रिकाम्। मदन्यत्र मां विहायान्यत्रेत्यर्थः। दुग्धे 'दुह प्रपूरणे'। पूरयतीत्यर्थः। इत्येवम्। तद्गता चर्मभस्त्रिकागता। प्रतीतिः ख्यातिः। **अथेयमिति**। अर्च्यमाना पूज्यमाना। प्रातःप्रातरिति वीप्सायां द्विर्वचनम्। प्रतिप्रातःकाले इत्यर्थः। कल्पः प्रकारः। ग्रावच्छिद्रं पर्वतच्छिद्रम्। 'अद्रिगोत्रगिरिग्रावाचलशैलशिलोच्चयाः' इत्यमरः। अनिवेद्याकथयित्वा। नोपजीव्योपजीवितुमशक्या। प्रमाणं निर्णयकर्ता। अभ्युपेत्य-

---

१ वारयोषिन्मुख्याभ्यः. २ वित्तं तत.

'भद्र, प्रीतोऽस्मि। गच्छ। यथेष्टमिमामुपभुङ्क्ष्व' इति। भूयश्च ब्रूहि—'यथा न कश्चिदेनां मुष्णाति तथाऽनुगृह्यताम्' इति। तदप्यवश्यमसावभ्युपेष्यति। ततः स्वगृहमेत्य यथोक्तमर्थत्यागं कृत्वा दिने दिने वरिवस्यमानां स्तेयलब्धैरर्थैर्नक्तमापूर्य प्राह्णे लोकाय दर्शयिष्यसि। ततः कुबेरदत्तस्तृणाय मत्वाऽर्थपतिमर्थलुब्धः कन्यकया स्वयमेव त्वामुपस्थास्यति। अथ कुपितोऽर्थपतिर्व्यवहर्तुमर्थगर्वादभियोक्ष्यते। तं च भूयश्चित्रैरुपायैः कौपीनावशेषं करिष्यावः। स्वकं चौर्यमनेनैवाभ्युपायेन सुप्रच्छन्नं भविष्यति' इति। हृष्टश्च धनमित्रो यथोक्तमन्वतिष्ठत्। तदहरेव मन्नियोगाद्विमर्दकोऽर्थपतिसेवाभियुक्तस्तस्योदारके वैरमभ्यवर्धयत्। अर्थलुब्धश्च कुबेरदत्तो निवृत्यार्थपतेर्धनमित्रायैव तनयां सानुनयं प्रादित्सत। प्रत्यबध्नाच्चार्थपतिः।

एष्वेव दिवसेषु काममञ्जर्याः स्वसा यवीयसी रागमञ्जरी नाम पञ्चवीरगोष्ठे संगीतकम[1]नुष्ठास्यतीति सान्द्रादरः समागमन्नागरजनः। स चाहं सह सख्या धनमित्रेण तत्र संन्यधिषि। प्रवृत्तनृत्या[2]यां च तस्यां द्वितीयं रङ्गपीठं ममाभून्मनः। तद्दृष्टिविभ्रमोत्पलवनसच्चापा[3]श्रयश्च पञ्च-

---

त्यङ्गीकरिष्यति। **तत इति**। अर्थत्यागं द्रव्यदानम्। वरिवस्यमानां सेव्यमानाम्। 'वरिवस्या तु शुश्रूषा' इत्यमरः। स्तेयलब्धैश्चौर्यप्राप्तैः। कुबेरदत्तः कन्यापिता। तृणाय मत्वा तृणप्रायं मत्वा ज्ञात्वा। 'मन्यकर्मण्यनादरे विभाषाऽप्राणिषु' इति चतुर्थी। उपस्थास्यत्याराधयिष्यति। **अथेति**। अर्थगर्वाद्द्रव्योन्मादात्। अभियोक्ष्यते द्वेषं करिष्यति। 'अभियोगः स्मृतो द्वेषः' इति। तमर्थपतिम्। चित्रैरनेकैः। **तदिति**। तदहरेव तस्मिन्नेव दिवसे। विमर्दक एतन्नाम्ना ख्यातः। अर्थपतिसेवायामभियुक्तः संनद्धः। तस्यार्थपतेः। उदारके धनमित्रे। वैरं द्वेषम्। अभ्यवर्धयदभिवर्धितवान्। प्रादित्सत दत्तवान्। प्रत्यबध्नात् प्रतिबन्धं चकारेत्यर्थः। **एष्विति**। पञ्चवीरगोष्ठे जानपदे सदसि। 'तत्पञ्चवीरगोष्ठं तु यत्तु जानपदं सदः' इति कोशसारः। संगीतकं गीतादि। 'गीतं वाद्यं च नृत्यं च त्रिभिः संगीतमुच्यते' इति संगीतसर्वस्वे। अहमपहारवर्मा। तत्र सभायाम्। रङ्गपीठं नृत्यस्थानम्। तस्या दृष्टिस्तद्दृष्टिस्तस्या विभ्रमा एव उत्पलवनं तद्दृष्टिविभ्रमोत्पलवनं तदेव सच्चापं समीचीनं धनुः तस्याश्रयो यस्य सः। अत्र सन्नापाश्रयेति

---

1 संगीतम्. 2 नृत्तायाम्. 3 सन्नापा°.

शरो भावरसाना सामग्र्यात्समुदितबल इव मामतिमात्रमन्यथयत्। अथासौ नगरदेवतेव नगरमोषरोषिता लीलाकटाक्षमालाशृङ्खलाभिर्नीलोत्पल-पलाशश्यामलाभिर्मामबध्नात्। नृत्योत्थिता च सा सिद्धिलाभशोभिनी—किं विलासात्, किमभिलाषात्, किमकस्मादेव वा, न जाने—असकृन्मां सखीभिरप्यनुपलक्षितेनापाङ्गप्रेक्षितेन सविभ्रमैरारेचितभ्रूलतमभिवीक्ष्य, सापदेशं च किंचिदाविष्कृतदशनचन्द्रिकं स्मित्वा, लोकलोचनमानसानुयाता प्रातिष्ठत।

सोऽहं स्वगृहमेत्य दुर्निवारयोत्कण्ठया दूरीकृताहारस्पृहः शिरःशूलस्पर्शनमपादिशन्विविक्ते तल्पे मुक्तैरवयवैरशायिषि। अतिनिष्णातश्च मदनतन्त्रे मामभ्युपेत्य धनमित्रो रहस्यकथयत्—'सखे, सैव धन्या गणिकादारिका, यामेवं भवन्मनोऽभिनिविशते। तस्याश्च मया सुलक्षिता भाववृत्तिः। तामप्यचिरादयुग्मशरः शरशयने शाययिष्यति। स्थानाभिनिवेशिनोश्च वामयत्नसाध्यः समागमः। किं तु

पाठः प्रामादिको दुर्व्याख्यतया हेयश्च। भावरसानाम्। भावा विभावादयः। रसाः शृङ्गारादयः। 'बाह्यार्थालम्बनो यस्तु विकारो मानसो भवेत्। स भावः कथ्यते सद्भिरस्योत्कर्षो रसः स्मृतः॥' इति हलायुधः। सामग्र्यात् संपूर्णतया। समुदितबल इव मिलितबल इव। अतिमात्रं निर्भरम्। 'अतिमात्रोद्गाढनिर्भरम्' इत्यमरः। **अथेति**। असौ रागमञ्जरी। नगरमोषो नगरचौर्यं तेन रोषितेव रुष्टेव। लीलाकटाक्षमाला एव शृङ्खलास्ताभिः। नीलोत्पलपलाशानि नीलोत्पलपत्राणि। 'पत्रं पलाशं छदनं दलं पर्णं छदः पुमान्' इत्यमरः। तद्वच्छ्यामलाः कृष्णवर्णाः। 'कालश्यामलमेचकाः' इत्यमरः। सिद्धिलाभशोभिनी समृद्धिफलप्राप्तिशोभिनी। अनुपलक्षितेनाज्ञातेन। आरेचितभ्रूलतं वक्रीकृतभ्रूलतमिति क्रियाविशेषणम्। सापदेशं सव्याजम्। लोकानां लोचनानि नेत्राणि मानसानि चित्तानि तैरनुयातानुगता। **सोऽहमिति**। दूरीकृता त्यक्ता आहारस्पृहा भक्षणेच्छा येनेति तथा। शिरःशूलस्पर्शनं शिरोवेदनाप्राप्तिम्। विविक्ते विजने। अतिनिष्णातोऽतिनिपुणः। 'निष्णातो निपुणोऽभिज्ञः' इति वैजयन्ती। 'निनदीभ्यां स्नातेः कौशले' इति षत्वम्। मदनतन्त्रे मदनशास्त्रे। भाववृत्तिश्चित्तवृत्तिः। अयुग्मशरो विषमबाणः मदन इत्यर्थः। शाययिष्यति स्वापयिष्यति। णिजन्तम्। स्थानाभिनिवेशिनोर्युक्ताभिनिवेशिनोः। 'युक्ते द्वे सांप्रतं स्थाने' इत्यमरः। गणिकानां वेश्यानां यः स्वधर्मः शुल्कादिग्रहणरूपस्तेन

१ पलाशदाम. २ सविभ्रममारे०.

सा किल वारकन्यका गणिकास्वधर्मप्रतीपगामिना भद्रोदारेणाशयेन समगिरत—'गुणशुल्काऽहम्, न धनशुल्का। न च पाणिग्रहणादृते-ऽन्यभोग्यं यौवनम्' इति। तच्च मुहुः प्रतिषिध्याकृतार्था तद्भगिनी काममञ्जरी माता च माधवसेना राजानमश्रुकण्ठ्यौ व्यजिज्ञपताम्—'देव युष्मद्दासी रागमञ्जरी रूपानुरूपशीलशिल्पकौशला पूरयिष्यति मनोरथानित्यासीदस्माकमतिमहत्याशा। साऽद्य मूलच्छिन्ना। यदियमति-क्रम्य स्वकुलधर्ममर्थनिरपेक्षा गुणेभ्य एव स्वं यौवनं विचिक्रीषते। कुलस्त्रीवृत्तमेवाच्युतमनुतिष्ठासति। सा[1] चेदियं देवपादाज्ञयाऽपि ताव-त्प्रकृतिमापद्येत तदा पेशलं भवेत्' इति। राज्ञा च तदनुरोधात्तथाऽनु-शिष्टा सत्यप्यनाश्रवैव सा यदाऽऽसीत्तदाऽस्याः स्वसा माता च रुदित-निर्बन्धेन राज्ञे स[2]मगिरेताम्—'यदि कश्चिद्भुजङ्गोऽस्मदिच्छया विनैनां बालां विप्रलभ्य नाशयिष्यति स तस्करवद्वध्यः' इति। तदेवं स्थिते धनादृते न तत्स्वजनोऽनुमन्यते। न तु धनदायासावभ्युपगच्छतीति विचिन्त्योऽत्राभ्युपायः' इति। अथ मयोक्तम्—'किमत्र चिन्त्यम्। गुणैस्तामावर्ज्य गूढं धनै[3]स्तत्स्वजनं तो[4]षयावः' इति।

ततश्च कांचित्काममञ्जर्याः प्रधानदूतीं धर्मरक्षितां नाम शाक्य-भिक्षुकीं चीवरपिण्डदानादिनोपसंगृह्य तन्मुखेन तया बन्धक्या पण-बन्धमकरवम्—'अजिनरत्नमुदारकान्मुषित्वा मया तुभ्यं देयं, यदि

प्रतीपगामिना विरुद्धवर्तिना। भद्रोदारेण कल्याणोदारेण। आशयेनाभिप्रायेण। समगिरत अवददित्यर्थः। गुणशुल्का गुणमूल्या। ऋत इत्यव्ययं विनेत्यर्थे। अकृतार्थाऽसिद्धार्था। व्यजिज्ञपतां विज्ञापयामासतुः। स्वकुलधर्मं धनग्रहणादिम्। विचिक्रीषते विक्रेतुमिच्छति। वृत्तमाचरणम्। अच्युतं बद्धमूलम्। अनुतिष्ठासत्यनुष्ठातुमिच्छति। प्रकृतिः स्वभावः। पेशलं सुकुमारम्। 'कुशलम्' इति भूषणा। अनाश्रवा। 'वचनेस्थित आश्रवः' इत्यमरः। तथा न भवतीत्यर्थः। **यदीति**। भुजङ्गो विटः। "विलासी। 'भुजङ्गो-ऽहिविलासिनोः' इति विश्वः।" इति भूषणा। विप्रलभ्य प्रतार्य। तत्स्वजनस्तन्मा-त्रादिः। धनदाय वित्तदायिने। तां कन्यकां गुणैरावर्ज्य वशीकृत्य। तत्स्वजनं तन्मात्रादिकम्। **ततश्चेति**। प्रधानदूतीं मुख्यदूतीम्। शाक्यभिक्षुकीं बौद्ध-सिद्धान्ततपस्विनीम्। 'शाक्यस्तु बौद्धेष्वन्यतमः' इति। चीवरपिण्डदाना-दिना वस्त्रखण्डान्नदानादिना। उपसंगृह्य वशीकृत्य। तया बन्धक्या कुलटया।

१ एवं सति सा. २ समगिरताम् ३ अर्थैः. ४ तोषयिष्यामि.

प्रतिदानं रागमञ्जरी ' इति । सोऽहं सं[1]प्रतिपन्नायां च तस्या तथा तमर्थं संपाद्य मद्गुणोन्मादिताया रागमञ्जर्याः करकिसलयमग्रहीषम् । यस्यां च निशि चर्मरत्नस्तेयवादस्तस्याः प्रारम्भे कार्यान्तरापदेशेनाहूतेषु शृण्वत्स्वेव नागरमुख्येषु मत्प्रणिधिर्विमर्दकोऽर्थपतिगृह्यो नाम भूत्वा धनमित्रमुल्लङ्घ्य बह्वतर्जयत् । उक्तं च धनमित्रेण—' भद्र कस्तवार्थो यत्परस्य हेतोर्मामाक्रोशसि । न स्मरामि स्वल्पमपि तवापकारं मत्कृतम् ' इति । स भूयोऽपि तर्जयन्निवाब्रवीत्—' स एष धनगर्वो नाम यत्परस्य भार्यां शुल्कक्रीतां पुनस्तत्पितरौ द्रव्येण विलोभ्य स्वीचिकीर्षसि । ब्रवीषि च—' कस्तवापकारो मत्कृतः ' इति । ननु प्रतीतमेवैतत् ' सार्थवाहस्यार्थपतेर्विमर्दको बहिश्चराः प्राणाः ' इति । सोऽहं तत्कृते प्राणानपि परित्यजामि । ब्रह्महत्यामपि न परिहरामि । ममैकरात्रजागरप्रतीकारस्तवैष चर्मरत्नाहंकारदाहज्वरः ' इति । तथा ब्रुवाणश्च पौरमुख्यैः सामर्षं निषि[3]ध्यापवाहितोऽभूत् । इयं च वार्ता कृत्रिमार्तिना धनमित्रेण चर्मरत्ननाशमादावेवोपक्षिप्य पार्थिवाय निवेदिता । स चार्थपतिमाहूयोपह्वरे पृष्टवान्—' अङ्ग किमस्ति कश्चिद्विमर्दको नामात्रभवतः ' इति । तेन च मूढात्मना ' अस्ति देव परं मित्रम् । कश्च तेनार्थः ' इति कथिते राज्ञोक्तम्—' अपि शक्नोषि तमाह्वातुम् ' इति । ' बाढमस्मि शक्तः ' इति निर्गत्य स्वगृ[2]हे वेशवाटे द्यूतसभायामापणे च निपुणमन्विष्यन्नोपलब्धवान् । कथं वो[4]-

---

प्रतिदानं प्रत्याम्नायप्रदानम् । संप्रतिपन्नायां सम्यगङ्गीकृतायाम् । तमर्थं चर्मभस्त्रिकादानरूपम् । मद्गुणैरुन्मादितायाः । करकिसलयं पाणिपल्लवम् । **यस्यां चेति** । कार्यान्तरापदेशेन कार्यान्तरव्याजेन । मत्प्रणिधिर्गूढपुरुषो विमर्दको नाम । अर्थपतिगृह्यो तत्पक्षस्थो भूत्वा । धनमित्रमुदारकनामानम् । उल्लङ्घ्यातिक्रम्य । परस्य हेतोः । परार्थमित्यर्थः । ' षष्ठी हेतुप्रयोगे ' इति षष्ठी । आक्रोशसि निन्दसि । प्रतीतं प्रसिद्धम् । न परिहरामि । अङ्गीकरोमीति भावः । **एकरात्रेति** । एकरात्रं जागरः जागरणमेव प्रतीकारो यस्य । एकेनैव जागरेण चर्मरत्नापहाराद्दाहज्वरं दूरीकरोमीति भावः । अपवाहितो निराकृतः । " उपक्षिप्य प्रस्तावं कृत्वा । ' प्रस्तावः स्यादुपक्षेपे ' इति वैजयन्ती " इ० भू० । कृत्रिमा आर्तिः पीडा यस्येति तेन । चर्मरत्ननाशं चर्मरत्नचोरणरूपम् । उपक्षिप्य प्रस्ताव्य । स चेति राजा । उपह्वरे एकान्ते । अङ्गेत्यामन्त्रणेऽव्ययम् । बाढमित्यङ्गीकारे । वेशवाटे वेश्यागृहमार्गे ।

---

१ तथेति प्रतिप०. २ स्वां. ३ आक्रुश्य ४ चोपलभेत.

पलभ्येत स वराकः । स खलु विमर्दको मद्ग्राहितत्वदभिज्ञानचिह्नो मन्नियोगात्त्वदन्वेषणायोज्जयिनीं तदहरेव प्रातिष्ठत । अर्थपतिस्तु तमदृष्ट्वा तत्कृतमपराधमात्मसंबद्धं मत्वा मोहाद्भयाद्वा प्रत्याख्याय पुनर्धनमित्रेण विभाविते कुपितेन राज्ञा निगृह्य निगडबन्धनमनीयत ।

तेष्वेव दिवसेषु विधिनां कल्पोक्तेन चर्मरत्नं दोग्धुकामा काममञ्जरी पूर्वदुग्धं क्षपणीभूतं विरूपकं रहस्युपसृत्य ततोऽपहृतं सर्वमर्थजातं तस्मै प्रत्यर्प्य सप्रश्रयं च बह्वनुनीय प्रत्यागमत् । सोऽपि कथंचिन्निर्ग्रन्थिकग्रहान्मोचितात्मा मदनुशिष्टो हृष्टतमः स्वधर्ममेव प्रत्यपद्यत । काममञ्जर्यपि कतिपयैरेवाहोभिरश्मन्तकशेषमजिनरत्नदोहाशया स्वमभ्युदयमकरोत् । अथ मत्प्रयुक्तो धनमित्रः पार्थिवं मिथो व्यज्ञापयत्—'देव येयं गणिका काममञ्जरी लोभोत्कर्षाल्लोभमञ्जरीति लोकोपक्रोशपात्रमासीत्साऽद्य मुशलोलूखलान्यपि निरपेक्षं त्यजति । तन्मन्ये मच्चर्मरत्नलाभहेतुः । तस्य खलु कल्पस्तादृशः । वणिग्भ्यो वारमुख्याभ्यश्च दुग्धे नान्येभ्य इति हि तद्गता प्रतीतिः । अतोऽमुष्यामस्ति मे शङ्का' इति । सा सद्य एव राज्ञा सह जनन्या समाहूयत । व्यथितवर्णेनेव मयोपह्वरे कथितम्—

स वराकस्तुच्छोऽर्थपतिः । **मद्ग्राहितेति** । मयाऽपहारवर्मणा ग्राहितमङ्गीकारितं त्वदभिज्ञानचिह्नं तव राजवाहनस्याभिज्ञानचिह्नं यस्येति स तथा । मन्नियोगान्ममाज्ञावशात् । प्रातिष्ठत प्रस्थितवान् । अर्थपतिस्तं विमर्दकम् । तत्कृतं विमर्दककृतम् । आत्मसंबद्धमात्मीयमेव । प्रत्याख्याय विपरीतमुक्त्वा । विभाविते आविष्कृते । प्रकटीकृत इत्यर्थः । सप्रश्रयं साविनयम् । 'सप्रत्ययम्' इति पाठे सशपथम् । सोऽपि क्षपणकवेषधारी विरूपकनामा । निर्ग्रन्थिकग्रहात्क्षपणकसिद्धान्तात् । 'निर्ग्रन्थोऽर्हः क्षपणकः श्रमणो जिन इत्यपि ।' इति वैजयन्ती । मदनुशिष्टो मया बोधितः । अश्मन्तकं चुल्लिः । 'अश्मन्तमुद्धानमधिश्रयणी चुल्लिरन्तिका' इत्यमरः । दोहः सुवर्णेन पूरणम् । मत्प्रयुक्तः मदुपदिष्टः । लोकोपक्रोशपात्रम् । लोकनिन्दापात्रमित्यर्थः । तस्य मच्चर्मरत्नस्य । कल्पः प्रकारः । प्रतीतिः ख्यातिः । उपह्वरे एकान्ते । व्यथितवर्णेनेवेतीवकारेण कृत्रिमव्यथात्वं सूचितम् ।

१ ०ज्ञानवित्तो. २ तु भ्रमन्. ३ विभावितेन. ४ विधिकल्पेन. ५ निर्ग्रन्थाग्र०; निर्ग्रन्थिकाग्रहात्. ६ लाभहेतुस्तस्याः; ०लाभं हेतुम्; ०लाभहेतु.

' नूनमार्ये सर्वस्वैत्यागादतिप्रकाशादाशङ्कनीयचर्मरत्नलाभा तदनुयोगायाङ्गराजेन समाहूयसे । भूयोभूयश्च निर्बद्धया त्वया नियतमस्मि तदागतित्वेनाहमपदेश्यः । ततश्च मे भावी चित्रवधः । मृते च मयि न जीविष्यत्येव ते भगिनी । त्वं च निःस्वीभूता । चर्मरत्नं च धनमित्रमेव प्रतिभजिष्यति । तदियमापत्समन्ततोऽनर्थानुबन्धिनी । तत्किमत्र प्रतिविधेयम् ' इति । तया तज्जनन्या चाश्रूणि विसृज्योक्तम्—' अस्त्येवैतदस्मद्बालिश्यान्निर्भिन्नप्रायं रहस्यम् । राज्ञश्च निर्बन्धाद्द्वित्रिश्चतुर्निह्नुत्यापि नियतमागतिरपदेश्यैव चोरितस्य त्वयि । त्वयि त्वपदिष्टे सर्वमस्मत्कुटुम्बमवसीदेत् । अर्थपतौ च तदपयशो रूढम् । अङ्गपुरप्रासिद्धं च तस्य कीनाशस्यास्माभिः संगतम् । अमुनैव तदस्मभ्यं दत्तमित्यपदिश्य वरमात्मा गोपायितुम् ' इति मामभ्युपगमय्य राजकुलमगमताम् । राज्ञाऽनुयुक्ते च ' नैष न्यायो वेशकुलस्य यद्दातुरपदेशः । न ह्यर्थैर्न्यायार्जितैरेव पुरुषा वेशमुपतिष्ठन्ति ' इत्यसकृदतिप्रणुद्य कर्णनासाच्छेदोपक्षेपभीषिताभ्यां दग्धबन्धकीभ्यां स एव तपस्वी तस्करत्वेनार्थपतिरग्राह्यत । कुपितेन च राज्ञा तस्य प्राणे-

---

**नूनमिति** । अतिप्रकाशादतिप्रसिद्धात् । आशङ्कनीयश्चर्मरत्नलाभो यस्याः सा । तदनुयोगाय तत्प्रश्नाय । निर्बद्धया आग्रहपृष्टया । तदागतित्वेन चर्मरत्नप्राप्तिहेतुत्वेन । अपदेश्यः कथनीयः । **तत इति** । निःस्वीभूता दरिद्रीभूता । अनर्थानुबन्धिन्यनर्थकारिणी । अत्रास्मिन्नर्थे । प्रतिविधेयं प्रतिकर्तव्यम् । बालिशस्य भावो बालिश्यं मूर्खत्वम् । ' द्वित्रिश्चतुः इति सुजन्तः पाठः । द्वित्रिश्चतुर्वारमित्यर्थः । ' इति भूषणा । निह्नुत्य निगूह्य । आगतिरागमनहेतुत्वम् । अपदेश्या कथनीयेत्यर्थः । चोरितस्य पदार्थस्य । त्वयि भवद्विषये । अवसीदेन्नश्येत् । तदपयशस्तच्चर्मरत्नचौर्यापयशः । कीनाशस्य क्षुद्रस्य धूर्तस्य वा । अमुनैवार्थपतिनैव । अभ्युपगमय्य बोधयित्वा । अनुयुक्ते । पृष्टे सतीत्यर्थः । वेशकुलस्य वेश्याजनस्य । दातुरपदेशो नामग्रहणम् । न्यायार्जितैर्न्यायप्राप्तैः । असकृद्वारंवारम् । अतिप्रणुद्य निह्नुत्य । कर्णनासस्य च्छेदस्तस्योपक्षेपः प्रस्तावस्तेन भीषिताभ्याम् । **कुपितेनेति** । प्रत्यषिध्यत प्रत्यवार्यत । मौर्यो राजनीतिकर्ता ।

---

१ सर्वस्य. २ बन्धिनी महत्यापातिता. ३ द्वित्रिचतुरम्. ४ च व्यपदिष्टे. ५ अपदेश्य. ६ माम्भुपगमय्य. ७ प्ररुध्य.

षूद्यतो दण्डः । प्राञ्जलिना धनमित्रेणैव प्रत्यषिध्यत—' आर्य, मौर्यदत्त एष वरो वणिजाम् । ईदृशेष्वपराधेष्वसुभिरवियोगः । यदि कुपितोऽसि हृतसर्वस्वो निर्वासनीयः पाप एषः ' इति । तन्मूला च धनमित्रस्य कीर्तिरप्रथत । अप्रीयत च भर्ता । पटच्चरच्छेदशेषोऽर्थपतिरर्थमत्तः सर्वपौरजनसमक्षं निरवास्यत । तस्यैव द्रव्याणां तु केनचिदवयवेन सा वराकी काममञ्जरी चर्मरत्नमृगतृष्णिकापविद्धसर्वस्वा सानुकम्पं धनमित्राभिनोदितेन भूपेनान्वगृह्यत । धनमित्रश्चाहनि गुणिनि कुलपालिकामुपायंस्त । तदेवं सिद्धसंकल्पो रागमञ्जरीगृहं हेमरत्नपूर्णमकरवम् ।

अस्मिंश्च पुरे लुब्धसमृद्धवर्गस्तथा मुषितो यथा कपालपाणिः स्वैरेव धनैर्मद्विश्राणितैः समृद्धीकृतस्यार्थिवर्गस्य गृहेषु भिक्षार्थमभ्रमत् । न ह्यलमतिनिपुणोऽपि पुरुषो नियतिलिखितां लेखामतिक्रमितुम् । यतोऽहमेकदा रागमञ्जर्याः प्रणयकोपप्रशमनाय सानुनयं पायिताया[3]ः पुनः पुनः प्रणयसमर्पितमुखमधुगण्डूषमास्वादमास्वादं मदेनास्पृश्ये । शीलं हि मदोन्मादयोरमार्गेणाप्यु[4]चितकर्मस्वेव प्रवर्तनम् । यदहमुपोढमदः ' नगरमिदमेकयै[5]व शर्वर्या निर्धनीकृत्य त्वद्भवनं पूर-

निर्वासनीयो बहिःकार्यः । तन्मूला तत्प्राणरक्षणमूला । अप्रथत ख्याता बभूवेत्यर्थः । अप्रीयत प्रीतोऽभूदित्यर्थः । पटच्चरच्छेदशेषो जीर्णवस्त्रखण्डावशेषः । **तस्यैवेति** । तस्यार्थपतेः । अवयवेनांशेन । मृगतृष्णिका मरीचिका तयाऽपविद्धं हारितं सर्वस्वं ययेति तथा । अभिनोदितेन प्रेरितेन । गुणिन्यहनि गुणवद्दिवस इत्यर्थः । ' मुहूर्तादिगुणयुक्ते ' इति भूषणा । उपायंस्त परिणीतवान् । सिद्धसंकल्पोऽहमपहारवर्मा । **अस्मिन्निति** । लुब्धसमृद्धवर्गो लुब्धाश्च ते समृद्धाश्च तेषां वर्गः समूहः । कपालं खर्परं पाणौ यस्येति तथा । स्वैरात्मीयैः । मद्विश्राणितैर्मद्दत्तैः । नियतिरदृष्टम् । प्रणयकोपः प्रीतिकलहस्तत्प्रशमनाय तन्नाशाय । पायितायाः पानं कारितायाः । मुखमधु मुखमद्यं तद्गण्डूषं पीतोज्झितम् । ' पीतशेषं तु गण्डूषम् ' इति हलायुधः । आस्वादमास्वादं आस्वाद्यास्वाद्येत्यर्थः । णमुल् । अस्पृश्ये स्पृष्टवानस्मि । उचितकर्मस्वभ्यस्तकर्मसु । 'अभ्यस्तेऽप्युचिते न्याय्यम् ' इति वैजयन्ती । प्रवर्तनमनुष्ठानम् । **यदहमिति** । उपोढमदोऽधिकमदः । शर्वर्या रात्र्या । ' अथ शर्वरी । निशा

१ ०धेषु नास्त्यसुभिरभियोगः. २ अभिचोदितेन. ३ यापितायाः; पाययितायाः. ४ अनुचित; उपाचित. ५ इदमनयैकया.

येयम्' इति प्रव्यथितप्रियतमाप्रणामाञ्जलिशपथशतातिवर्ती मत्तवारण इव रभसच्छिन्नशृङ्खलः कयाऽपि धा[1]त्र्या शृगालिकाख्ययाऽनुगम्यमानो नातिपरिकरोऽसिद्वितीयो रंहसा परेणोदचलम् । अभिपततोऽपि नागरिकपुरुषानशङ्कमेव विगृह्य तस्कर इति तैरभिहन्यमानोऽपि नातिप्रकुपितः क्रीडन्निव मदावसन्नहस्तपतितेन निस्त्रिंशेन द्वित्रानेव हत्वाऽवघूर्णमानताम्रदृष्टिरपतम् । अनन्तरमार्तरवान्विसृजन्ती शृगालिका ममा[2]भ्यासमगमत् । अबध्ये चाहमरिभिः । आपदा तु मदापहारिण्या सद्य एव बोधितस्तत्क्षणोपजातया प्रतिभया व्यचीचरम्—' अहो ममेयं मोहमूला महत्यापदापतिता । प्र[3]सृततरं च सख्यं मया सह धनमित्रस्य मत्परिग्रहत्वं च रागमञ्जर्याः । मदेनसा च तौ प्रो[4]र्णुतौ श्वो नियतं निग्र[5]हीष्येते । तदियमिह प्रतिपत्तिर्यथाऽनुष्ठीयमानया मन्नियोगतस्तौ परित्रास्येते । मां च कदाचिदनर्थादितस्तारयि[6]ष्यतः' इति कमप्युपायमात्मनैव निर्णीय शृगालिकामगादिषम्—' अपेहि जरतिके । या ता[7]मर्थलुब्धां दग्धगणिकां रागमञ्जरिकाम

निशीथिनी रात्रिः' इत्यमरः । शपथशतमतिक्रम्य वर्तत इति तथा । ' अनेन मधुपानं कृतमतोऽयमुन्मत्त इत्येतदर्थं तया शपथादिकं कृतमिति भावः' इति भूषणा । मत्तवारण इव मत्तगज इव । रभसेन वेगेन छिन्ना त्रोटिता शृङ्खला येनेति तथा । धात्र्युपमाता । परिकरः परिवारः । रंहसा वेगेन । अभिपततः संमुखमागच्छतः । विगृह्य युद्धं कृत्वा । अभिहन्यमानस्ताड्यमानः । मदेनावसन्नः शिथिलो यो हस्तस्तस्मात्पतितेन । निस्त्रिंशेन खड्गेन । ' नृशंसखड्गौ निस्त्रिंशौ ' इत्यमरः । अवघूर्णमाना विह्वला । **अनन्तरमिति** । अभ्यासं समीपम् । मदापहारिण्या मदनाशकर्त्र्या । प्रतिभया प्रज्ञया । ' प्रज्ञा नवनवोल्लासशालिनी प्रतिभा मता ' इति भरतः । व्यचीचरं विचारितवान् । मोहमूलाऽज्ञानमूला । महत्यतिशयिता । आपतिता आगता । प्रसृततरं ख्याततरम् । मत्परिग्रहत्वं मत्पत्नीत्वम् । ' परिग्रहस्तु स्वीकारे शापे पत्न्यां परिच्छदे ' इति महीपः । मदेनसा मत्पापेन । ' कलुषं वृजिनैनोघम् ' इत्यमरः । तौ रागमञ्जरीधनमित्रौ । प्रोर्णुतावभिभूतौ । निग्रहीष्येते । निगृहीतौ भविष्यत इत्यर्थः । प्रतिपत्तिः कर्तव्यम् । यया प्रतिपत्त्या । नियोगतो नियमात् । परित्रास्येते परिरक्षितौ भविष्यतः । अगादिषमवदम् । अपेहि गच्छेत्यर्थः । जरतिका वृद्धा ।

१ धूर्तया धात्र्या. २ अभ्याशम्. ३ प्रथिततरं. ४ संप्रोर्णुतौ. ५ निग्राहयिष्येते. ६ ०ष्यति. ७ त्वम्.

जिनरत्नमत्तेन शत्रुणा मे मित्रच्छद्मना धनमित्रेण संगमितवती सा हताऽसि । तस्य पापस्य चर्मरत्नमोषाद्दुहितुश्च ते साराभरणापहारादहमद्य निःशल्यमुत्सृजेयं जीवितम् ' इति । सा पुनरुद्धटितज्ञा[1] परमधूर्ता साश्रुगद्गदमुदञ्जलिस्तान्पुरुषान्सप्रणाममासादितवती सामपूर्वं मम पुरस्तादयाचत—' भद्रकाः प्रतीक्षध्वं[2] कंचित्कालं यावदस्मादस्मदीयं सर्वं मुषितमर्थजातमवगच्छेयम् ' इति । तथेति तैः प्रतिपन्ने पुनर्मत्समीपमासाद्य ' सौम्य क्षमस्वास्य दासीजनस्यैकमपराधम् । अस्तु स कामं त्वत्कलत्राभिमर्शी वैरास्पदं धनमित्रः । स्मरंस्तु चिरकृतां ते परिचर्यामनुग्रहीतुमर्हसि दासीं रागमञ्जरीम् । आकल्पसारो हि रूपाजीवा[3]जनः । तद्ब्रूहि क्व निहितं तस्या भूषणम् ।' इति पादयोरपतत् । ततो दयमान इवाहमब्रवम्—' भवतु, मृत्युहस्तवर्तिनः किं ममामुष्याँ[4] वैरानुबन्धेन ' इति । तद्ब्रुवन्निव कर्णे एवैनामशिक्षयम्—' एवमेवं प्रतिपत्तव्यम् ' इति । सा तु प्रतिपन्नार्थेव ' जीव चिरम्, प्रसीदन्तु ते देवताः, देवोऽप्यङ्गराजः पौरुषप्रीतो मोचयतु त्वाम्, एतेऽपि भद्रमुखास्तव दयन्ताम् ' इति क्षणादपासरत् । आनीये चाहमार[5]क्षिकनायकस्य शासनाच्चारकम् ।

---

**या तामिति** । मित्रच्छद्मना कपटमित्रेण । संगमितवती संबन्धं कारितवती । तस्य पापस्य धनमित्रस्य । साराभरणानामपहारात्स्तेयात् । सा शृगालिका । उद्धटितज्ञा सूचितज्ञा । ' सूचनमुद्धटनं बोधिः ' इत्यजयः । उदञ्जलिर्बद्धाञ्जलिः । भद्रकाः कल्याणरूपाः । मुषितं चोरितम् । प्रतिपन्नेऽङ्गीकृते । सः धनमित्रः । त्वत्कलत्राभिमर्शी त्वत्स्त्रीगामी । वैरास्पदं वैरस्थानम् । **स्मरन्निति** । आकल्पसारो भूषणसारः । ' आकल्पवेषौ नेपथ्यम् ' इत्यमरः । रूपाजीवा वेश्या । ' वारस्त्री गणिका वेश्या रूपाजीवा ' इत्यमरः । भवतु किं तेनेत्यर्थः । अमुष्या रागमञ्जर्याः । वैरानुबन्धेन वैरसंबन्धेन । ' अनुबन्धोऽनुवृत्तिः ' इति भूषणा । प्रतिपत्तव्यं कर्तव्यम् । प्रतिपन्नार्थेव प्राप्तार्थेव । पौरुषप्रीतः पुरुषार्थसंतुष्टः । तवेति त्वामित्यर्थः । तव दयन्तामित्यत्र ' अधीगर्थदयेशां– ' इति कर्मणि षष्ठी । अपासरदपसृता । आरक्षिका रक्षणकारकास्तेषां नायकस्य कोष्टपालस्य । शासनान्नियोगात् ।

---

१ °ज्ञाना. २ प्रतीक्ष्यताम्. ३ °जीवी; °जीवः. ४ अमुष्यां. ५ आरक्षक.

अथोत्तरेद्युरागत्य दृप्ततरः सुभगमानी सुन्दरंमन्यः पितुरत्ययादचिराधिष्ठिताधिकारस्तारुण्यमदादनतिपक्कः कान्तको नाम नागरिकः किंचिदिव भर्त्सयित्वा मां समभ्यधत्त—'न चेद्धनमित्रस्याजिनरत्नं प्रतिप्रयच्छसि न चेद्वा नागरिकेभ्यश्चोरितकानि प्रत्यपर्यसि द्रक्ष्यसि पारमष्टादशानां कारणानाम्, अन्ते च मृत्युमुखम्' इति। मया तु स्मयमानेनाभिहितम्—'सौम्य, यद्यपि दद्यामा जन्मनो मुषितं धनं न त्वर्थपतिदारापहारिणः शत्रोर्मे मित्रमुखस्य धनमित्रस्य चर्मरत्नप्रत्याशां पूरयेयम्। अदत्त्वैव तदयुतमपि यातनानामनुभवेयम्। इयं मे साधीयसी संधा' इति। तेनैव क्रमेण वर्तमाने सान्त्वनतर्जनप्राये प्रतिदिनमनुयोगव्यतिकरेऽनुगुणान्नपानलाभात्कतिपयैरेवाहोभिर्विरोपितव्रणः प्रकृतिस्थोऽहमासम्।

अथ कदाचिदच्युताम्बरपीतातपत्विषि क्षयिणि वासरे हृष्टवर्णा श्रृगालिकोज्ज्वलेन वेषेणोपसृत्य दूरस्थानुचरा मामुपश्लिष्याब्रवीत्—'आर्य दिष्ट्या वर्धसे। फलिता तव सुनीतिः। यथा

---

चारकं बन्धनालयम्। **अथेति**। उत्तरेद्युः परदिवसे। 'सद्यःपरुत्-' इति निपातः। सुभगमानी सुभगमात्मानं मन्यमानः। 'सर्वोन्नतत्वं सौभाग्यं तद्वान्सुभग उच्यते' इति दिवाकरः। सुन्दरंमन्यः सौन्दर्याभिमानी। पितुरत्ययात्पितृनाशात्। अचिराधिष्ठिताधिकारोऽल्पकालप्राप्ताधिकारः। अनतिपक्कोऽनतिपरिणतः। नागरिकः कारापतिः। 'कारापतिर्नागरिकः' इति वैजयन्ती। **न चेदिति**। कारणानां यातनानाम्। 'कारणा तु यातना तीव्रवेदना' इत्यमरः। स्मयमानेन स्मितमुखेन। मित्रमुखस्य मित्रच्छद्मनः। 'मुखं तु वदने मुख्ये तान्त्रे छद्मनि वा पुमान्' इति भागुरिः। प्रत्याशां पुनःप्राप्तीच्छाम। 'प्रत्याशा पुनराप्तीच्छा' इति वैजयन्ती। साधीयसी दृढतरा। संधा प्रतिज्ञा। 'संधा स्थितौ प्रतिज्ञायाम्' इति विश्वः। अनुयोगव्यतिकरे प्रश्नप्रकारे। 'संपर्के च व्यतिकरः प्रकारेऽपि' इत्यजयः। अनुगुणान्नपानालाभादनुकूलाशनपानप्राप्तेः। विरोपितव्रण उपशान्तक्षतः। 'विरोपित उपशान्तश्चिकित्सितः' इति बोपालितः। **अथेति**। अच्युतो विष्णुस्तस्याम्बरं वस्त्रं तद्वत्पीता पिशङ्गा आतपत्विट् उद्द्योतप्रभा यस्येति। क्षयिणि क्षीणे। वासरे दिवसे। हृष्टस्य इव वर्ण आकृतिर्यस्याः सा हृष्टवर्णा। उपश्लिष्य संनिकृष्य।

---

१ कारापतिः.

त्वयाऽऽदिश्ये तथा धनमित्रमेत्याब्रवम्—‘ आर्य तवैवमापन्नः सुहृ[1]दित्युवाच—‘ अहमद्य वेशसंसर्गसुलभात्पानदोषाद्बद्धः । त्वया पुनरविशङ्कमद्यैव राजा विज्ञापनीयः—‘ देव, देवप्रसादादेव पुराऽपि तदर्जितरत्नमर्थपतिमुषितमासादितम् । अथ तु भर्ता रागमञ्जर्याः कश्चिदक्षधूर्तः कलासु कवित्वेषु लोकवार्तासु चातिवैचक्षण्यान्मया समसृज्यत । तत्संबन्धाच्च वस्त्राभरणप्रेषणादिना तद्भार्यां प्रतिदिनमन्ववर्ते । तदसावशङ्किष्ट नि[2]कृष्टाशयः कितवः । तेन च कुपितेन हृतं तच्चर्मरत्नमाभरणसमुद्गकश्च तस्याः। स तु भूयः स्तेयाय भ्रमन्नगृह्यत नागरिकपुरुषैः । आपन्नेन चामुनाऽनुसृत्य रुदत्यै रागमञ्जरीप[3]रिचारिकायै पूर्वप्रणयानुवर्तिना तद्भाण्डनिधानोद्देशः कथितः । ममापि चर्मरत्नमुपायोपक्रान्तो यदि प्रयच्छेदिह देवपादैः प्रसादः कार्यः ’ इति । तथा निवेदितश्च नरपतिरसुभिर्मामवियोज्योपच्छन्दनैरेव स्वं ते दापयितुं प्रयतिष्यते । तन्नः पथ्यम् ’ इति । श्रुत्वैव च त्वदनुभावप्रत्ययादनतित्रस्नुना तेन तत्तथैव संपादितम् । अथाहं [4]त्वदभिज्ञानप्रत्यायिताया रागमञ्जर्याः सकाशाद्यथेप्सितानि व[5]स्तूनि लभमाना राजदुहितुरम्बालिकाया धात्रीं माङ्गलिकां त्वदादिष्टेन मार्गेणान्वरञ्जयम् । तामेव च संक्रमीकृत्य रागमञ्जर्याश्चाम्बालिकायाः सख्यं परमवीवृधम् ।

आदिश्ये आदिष्टम् । आपन्न आपत्तिं प्राप्तः । ‘ आपन्न आपत्प्राप्तः स्यात् ’ इत्यमरः । **अथ त्विति** । अक्षधूर्तोऽक्षनिपुणः । समसृज्यत । संगतोऽभवदित्यर्थः । ‘ अन्ववर्ते स्वसंबन्धिवर्गवत्सादरमाचरामीति फलितार्थः ’ इति भूषणा । असावक्षधूर्तः । निकृष्टाशयः क्षुद्रान्तःकरणः । समुद्गकः संपुटकः । स्तेयाय चौर्याय । नागरिकपुरुषैः कारापतिपुरुषैरित्यर्थः । तस्या यद्भाण्डं भूषणम् । ‘ भाण्डं भूषणमात्रेऽपि भाण्डं मूलवणिग्धने ’ इति विश्वः । तस्य निधानोद्देशः स्थापनप्रदेशः । उपायैरुपक्रान्तो वशीकृतः । ‘ उपक्रमो वशीकारे समारम्भे चिकित्सने । ’ इति वैजयन्ती । उपच्छन्दनैः सान्त्वनैः । ‘ सान्त्वनोपच्छन्दने च समावनुनये ’ इति केशवः । स्वं चर्मरत्नम् । पथ्यमनुगुणम् । त्वदनुभावप्रत्ययात्त्वत्प्रभावज्ञानात् । अनतित्रस्नुनाऽतिशयितत्रासरहितेन । ‘त्रसिगृधि-’ इति क्नुप्रत्ययः । तेन धनमित्रेण । **अथेति** । त्वदभिज्ञानप्रत्यायितायास्त्वत्प्रत्यायकवस्तुविश्वासितायाः । संक्रमीकृत्योपायीकृत्य । ‘प्रत्युपाये संक्रमे च

१ सुहृदमुना चैवमादिष्टोऽसि. २ निकृष्टाशयतया. ३ परिचारिकायै शृगालिकायै. ४ त्वदनुभाव. ५ वस्तूनि.

अहरहश्च नवनवानि प्राभृतान्युपहरन्ती कथाश्चित्राश्चित्तहारिणीः कथयन्ती तस्याः परं प्रसादपात्रमासम् । एकदा च हर्म्य[1]गतायास्तस्याः स्थानस्थितमपि कर्णकुवलयं स्रस्तमिति समादधती प्रमत्तेव प्रच्याव्य पुनरुत्क्षिप्य भूमेस्तेनोपकन्यापुरं कारणेन केनापि भवनाङ्गणं प्रविष्टस्य कान्तकस्योपरि [2]प्रवृत्तकुहरपारावतत्रासनापदेशात्प्रहसन्ती प्राहार्षम् । सोऽपि तेन धन्यंमन्यैः[3] किंचिदुन्मुखः स्मयमानो मत्कर्मप्रहासिताया राजदुहितुर्विलासप्रायमाकारमात्माभिलाषमूलमिव यथा संक[4]ल्पयेत्तथा मयाऽपि संज्ञयैव किमपि चतुरमाचेष्टितम् । आकृष्टधन्वना च मनसिजेन विद्धः स दिग्धफलेन पत्त्रिणाऽतिमुग्धः कथंकथमप्यपासरत् । सायं च राजकन्याङ्गुलीयकमुद्रितां वासताम्बूलपट्टांशुकयुगलभूषणावयवगर्भां च [5]वङ्गेरिका कयाचिद्बालिकया ग्राहयित्वा रागमञ्जर्या इति नीत्वा कान्तकस्यागारमगाम् । अगाधे च रागसागरे मग्नो नावमिव मामुपलभ्य परमहृष्यत् । अवस्थान्तराणि च राजदुहितुः सुदारुणानि व्यावर्णयन्त्या मया स दुर्मतिः

---

निःश्रेण्यां संक्रमो मतः' इत्युत्पलिनी । अवीवृधम् । अवर्धयमित्यर्थः । प्राभृतान्युपायनानि । ' प्राभृतं तु प्रदेशनम् । उपायनमुपग्राह्यम् ' इत्यमरः । चित्तहारिणीर्मनोहराः । **एकदेति** । स्थानस्थितमपि यथास्थितमपि । स्रस्तं गलितमिति समादधती सज्जयन्ती । प्रमत्तेवानवहितेव । प्रच्याव्य पातयित्वा । तेन कर्णकुवलयेन । उपकन्यापुरं कन्यान्तःपुरसमीपे । कान्तकस्य कारापतेः । प्रवृत्तकुहर आरब्धसुरतः । ' कुहरं सुषिरे दम्भे नागलोके रतेऽपि च । ' इत्यजयः । पारावतः कपोतः तस्य त्रासनापदेशाद्भयोत्पादनमिषात् । तेन कर्णकुवलयप्रहारेण आत्मनि योऽभिलाषः स मूलं कारणं यत्रेति तथा । संकल्पयेच्चिन्तयेत् । आकृष्टधन्वना सज्जीकृतचापेन । विद्धो भिन्नः । दिग्धं विषलिप्तम् । ' दिग्धलिप्तौ विषाक्ते च ' इति वैजयन्ती । फलं शल्यम् । **सायं चेति** । राजकन्याया अङ्गुलीयकं मुद्रिका तया मुद्रितां कृतमुद्राम् । वासताम्बूलं एलालवङ्गकर्पूरादिभिः सुगन्धीकृतं ताम्बूलम् । ' घनसारादिभिर्यत्तु वासितं वासमुच्यते । ' इति वैजयन्ती । पट्टांशुकयुगलं पट्टवस्त्रयुगलम् । भूषणावयवाः कतिपयभूषणानि तद्गर्भाम् । वङ्गेरिकां वेत्रपुटिकाम् । ' वङ्गेरी वेत्रपुटिका ' इति वैजयन्ती । **अगाधे चेति** । अगाधेऽतलस्पर्शे । अहृष्यत् हर्षं प्राप । सुदारुणान्यसह्यानि । स दुर्मतिः कान्तकः । सुदूरमत्यन्तम् । उदमाद्यत उन्ममादेत्यर्थः ।

---

१ हर्म्याङ्गणगतायाः. २ प्रसक्तकुहर. ३ ०मन्यः पुरा. ४ संकल्पयेत. ५ वङ्गेलिकां; चङ्कोलिकां; पेटिकाम्.

सुदूरमुदमाद्यत। तत्प्रार्थिता चाहं त्वत्प्रियाप्रहितमिति ममैव मुखताम्बूलोच्छिष्टानुलेपनं निर्माल्यं मलिनांशुकं चान्येद्युरुपाहरम्। तदीयानि च राजकन्यार्थमित्युपादाय च्छन्नमेवा[1]पोढानि।

इत्थं च संधुक्षितमन्मथाग्निः स एवैकान्ते मयोपमन्त्रितोऽभूत्—'आर्य, लक्षणान्येव तवाविसंवादीनि। तथा हि मत्प्रातिवेश्यः कश्चित्कार्तान्तिकः 'कान्तकस्य हस्ते राज्यमिदं पतिष्यति। तादृशानि तस्य लक्षणानि' इत्यादिक्षत्। तदनुरूपमेव च त्वामियं राजकन्यका कामयते। तदेकापत्यश्च राजा तया त्वां समागतमुपलभ्य कुपितोऽपि दुहितुर्मरणभयान्नोच्छे[2]त्स्यति। प्रत्युत प्रापयिष्यत्येव यौवराज्यम्। इत्थं चायमर्थोऽर्थानुबन्धी। किमिति तात नाराध्यते। यदि कुमारीपुरप्रवेशाभ्युपायं नावबुध्यसे ननु बन्धनागारभित्तेर्व्यामत्रयमन्तरालमारामप्राकारस्य। केनचित्तु हस्तवतैकागारिकेण तावतीं सुर[3]ङ्गां कारयित्वा प्रविष्टस्योपवनं तवोपरिष्टादस्मदायत्तैव रक्षा। रक्ततरो हि तस्याः परिजनो न रहस्यं भेत्स्यति' इति। सोऽब्रवीत्—'साधु भद्रे दर्शितम्। अस्ति कश्चित्तस्करः खननकर्मणि सगरसुतानामिवान्यतमः। स चेल्लब्धः क्षणेनैतत्कर्म साधयिष्यति' इति। 'कतमोऽसौ, किमिति न लभ्यते' इति मयोक्ते येन तद्धनमित्रस्य चर्मरत्नं मुषितमिति त्वामेव स निर-

त्वत्प्रियाप्रहितमिति प्रेषितमिति। उच्छिष्टानुलेपनं स्वभुक्तावशिष्टाङ्गरागम्। तदीयानि कान्तकसंबन्धीनि। उपादाय गृहीत्वा। छन्नमेव गुप्तमेव। अपोढानि त्यक्तानि। **इत्थमिति**। संधुक्षितो वृद्धिं प्रापितः। उपमन्त्रित उपदिष्टः। अविसंवादीनि विसंवादरहितानि। 'प्रतिवेशे चरति यः प्रातिवेश्यः स उच्यते' इति, 'कार्तान्तिको लक्षणज्ञः' इति च वैजयन्ती। आदिक्षदवोचत्। तदेकापत्यः सैवैकमपत्यं यस्येति स तथा। समागतं संगतम्। अर्थानुबन्धी राजरूपार्थसंबन्धी। तातेत्यात्मीयतासूचकं संबोधनम्। व्यामत्रयम्। व्यामः परिमाणविशेषः। भाषया 'वांव' इति प्रसिद्धः। 'व्यामो बाह्वोः सकरयोस्ततयोस्तिर्यगन्तरम्' इत्यमरः। आराम उपवनम्। हस्तवता शिक्षितहस्तेन। ऐकागारिकेण चौरेण। 'चौरैकागारिकस्तेनदस्युतस्करमोषकाः।' इत्यमरः। तावतीं तत्प्रमाणाम्। सुरङ्गा भूम्यन्तर्गतखनितमार्गविशेषः। अस्मदायत्ताऽस्मदधीना। 'अधीनो निघ्न आयत्तः' इत्यमरः। भेत्स्यति प्रकटं करिष्यति। **अस्तीति**। निरदिक्षन्निर्दिष्टवान्। तेन चौरेण सह।

१ अपाविध्यम्; प्राक्षिपम्; अपविद्धानि. २ उत्सेत्स्यति. ३ सुरुङ्गाम्.

दिक्षत् । 'यद्येवमेहि, त्वयाऽस्मिन्कर्मणि साधिते चित्रैरुपायै-स्त्वामहं मोचयिष्यामीति शपथपूर्वं तेना[1]भिसंधाय सिद्धेऽर्थे भूयोऽपि निगडयित्वा 'योऽसौ चौरः स सर्वथोपक्रान्तः, न तु धाष्टर्च-भूमिः प्रकृष्टवैरस्तदाजिनरत्नं दर्शयिष्यति' इति राज्ञे विज्ञाप्य चित्र-मेनं ह[2]निष्यसि । तथा च सत्यर्थः सिध्यति, रहस्यं च न स्रवति' इति मयोक्ते सोऽतिहृष्टः प्रतिपद्य मामेव त्वदुपप्रलोभने नियुज्य बहिरवस्थितः । [3]प्राप्तमितः परं चिन्त्यताम्' इति । प्रीतेन च मयो-क्तम्—'मदुक्तमल्पम्, त्वन्नय एवात्र भूयान् । आनयैनम्' इति । अथानीतेनामुना मन्मोचनाय शपथः कृतः, मया च रहस्यानिर्भेदाय । विनिगडीकृतश्च स्नानभोजनविलेपनान्यनुभूय नित्यान्धका[4]रात्कारा-भित्तिकोणादारभ्योरगास्येन सुरङ्गामकरवम् । अचिन्तयं चैवम्—'हन्तुमनसैवामुना मन्मोचनाय शपथः कृतः । त[5]देनं हत्वाऽपि नासत्य-वाद्दोषेण स्पृश्ये' इति । निष्पततश्च मे निगडनाय प्रसार्यमाणपाणे-स्तस्य पादेनोरसि निहत्य पतितस्य तस्यैवासिधेन्वा शिरो न्यकृन्तम् । अकथयं च शृगालिकाम्—'भण भद्रे कथंभूत[6]ः कन्यापुरसंनिवेशो महानयं प्रयासो वृथैव मा भूत् । अमुत्र किंचिच्चोरायित्वा निवर्तिष्ये' इति । तदुपदर्शितविभाँ[7]गं चावगाह्य कन्यान्तःपुरं प्रज्वलत्सु मणिप्रदीपेषु नैकक्रीडाखेदसुप्तस्य परिजनस्य मध्ये महितमहा[8]र्घरत्नप्रत्युप्त[9]सिंहाकार-

---

अभिसंधाय । प्रतिज्ञायेत्यर्थः । निगडयित्वा बद्ध्वा । उपक्रान्तश्चिकित्सितः । धाष्टर्यभूमिरचलधैर्य इत्यर्थः । चित्रमनेकप्रकारम् । प्रतिपद्याभ्युपगम्य । त्वदुप-प्रलोभने त्वद्वशीकरणे । प्राप्तं कर्तव्यम् । त्वन्नय एव त्वन्नीतिरेव । **अथानीतेनेति ।** रहस्यानिर्भेदाय गोप्यस्याप्रकटीकरणाय । विनिगडीकृतः । मुक्त इत्यर्थः । नित्यान्ध-कारादखण्डतमसः । उरगास्येन फणिमुखाकारखननसाधनेन । हन्तुमनसा मन्मारण-निश्चितचेतसा । निष्पततो निर्गच्छतः । तस्यैव । असिधेन्वा छुरिकया । 'छुरिका चासिधेनुका' इत्यमरः । न्यकृन्तं कृत्तवानस्मि । संनिवेशः संस्थानम् । 'संस्थानं संनिवेशे च स्वरूपे च निगद्यते' इति वररुचिः । अयं प्रयासः सुरङ्गाकरणक्लेशः । अमुत्र कन्यापुरे । तदुपदर्शितविभागं शृगालिकाकथितप्रदेशम् । महितानि उत्कृष्टानि महार्घाणि बहुमूल्यानि रत्नानि तैः प्रत्युप्ताः खचिताः सिंहाकारा दन्तपादा

---

१ संधाय. २ घातयिष्यसि. ३ प्राप्तरूपम्. ४ ०अन्धकाराद्भित्ति. ५ तदमुं. ६ ०भूतं कन्यापुरसंस्थानम्. ७ विभागे; विभागः. ८ महार्हरत्न; महति महार्हरत्न. ९ प्रसुप्त.

दन्तपादे हंसतूलगर्भशय्योपधानशालिनि कुसुमलवच्छुरितपर्यन्ते पर्यङ्क-तले दक्षिणपादपार्ष्ण्यधोभागा[1]नुवलितेतरचरणाग्रपृष्ठम्, ईषद्विवृत्त[2]-मधुरगुल्फसंधि, परस्पराश्लिष्टजङ्घाकाण्डम्, आकुञ्चितकोमलोभयजानु, किंचिद्वेल्लितोरुदण्डयुगलम्, अधिनितम्बस्रस्तमुक्तैकभुजलताग्रपेशलम्, अपाश्रयान्तनिर्मि[3]ताकुञ्चितेतरभुजलतोत्तानतलकरकिसलयम्, आभुग्न-श्रोणिमण्डलम्, अतिश्लिष्टचीनांशुकान्तरी[4]यम्, अनतिवलित[5]तनुतरोद-रम्, [6]अतनुतरनिःश्वा[7]सारम्भकम्पमानकठोरकुचकुड्मलम्, आतिरश्चीन-बन्धुरशिरोधरोद्देशदृश्यमाननिष्टप्ततपनीयसूत्रपर्यस्तपद्मरागरुचकम्, अर्ध-लक्ष्याधरकर्णपाशनिभृतकुण्डलम्, उपरिपरावृत्तश्रवणपाशरत्नकर्णिका-

---

यस्येति तस्मिन् । हंसतूलः पक्षिपक्ष्माणि गर्भे यस्या एवंविधा । उपधानमुपबर्हः । कुसुम-लवैश्छुरितो मिश्रितः । शोभित इति यावत् । पर्यन्तो यस्येति । पर्यङ्कः मञ्चः । 'शयनं मञ्चपर्यङ्कपल्यङ्काः खट्वया समाः' इत्यमरः । पार्ष्णिः पादमूलम् । अनुवलितः संवृतः । 'संवृतः स्यात्संवलितो भिन्नोऽनुवालितोऽपि च ।' इति बोपालितः । इतरचरणो वामचरणः । गुल्फं घुटिका । काण्डं स्तम्भः । वेल्लितं वक्रितम् । अधिनितम्बमिति विभक्त्यर्थे अव्ययीभावः । पेशलं चारु यथा तथा । अपाश्रयः शिरोभागः । निमितं निक्षिप्तम् । 'डुमिञ् प्रक्षेपणे ।' अपाश्रयान्ते निमितः आकुञ्चिता या इतरभुजलता तस्याः उत्तानतलः करः किसलय इव उत्तानतलकरकिसलयो यथा स्यात्तथा । आभु-ग्नमीषत्कुटिलम् । चीनांशुकस्य चीनदेशीयवस्त्रस्य । अन्तरीयमधोवस्त्रम् । अनति-वलितं नातिप्रह्वम् । आ ईषत्तिरश्चीनो वक्रः । बन्धुरः सुन्दरः । निष्टप्तं तापितम् । तपनीयं सुवर्णम् । 'तपनीयं शातकुम्भं गाङ्गेयं भर्म कर्बुरम् ।' इत्यमरः । रुचको-ऽङ्गुलिकामणिः । आतिरश्चीना बन्धुरा च या शिरोधरा तस्या उद्देशे दृश्यमानः निष्टप्त-तपनीयसूत्रपर्यन्स्तः पद्मरागरुचको यत्र तद्यथा तथा । 'रुचको मङ्गलद्रव्ये ग्रीवाभ-रणदन्तयोः ।' इति विश्वप्रकाशः । अधरोऽधः । 'अधस्तादपि चाधरः' इत्यमरः । अधरकर्णपाशः अधस्ताद्भूतः कर्णपाशः शय्यालग्नः चारुकर्णः । 'इदानीं द्वितीयकर्ण-विषयकमाह—उपरीति ।' इति भूषणा । परावृत्तः समुत्तानः । कर्णिका कर्णभूषणम् । विषममयथार्थकम् । व्याविद्धो बद्धः । 'सम्यक्तया न बद्धः' इति भूषणा । शिखण्डः केशकलापः । उपरि परावृत्तः य श्रवणपाशस्तत्र या रत्नकर्णिका तस्याः

---

१ अनुवेल्लिते०. २ विवृत. ३ निहित; निमित्त. ४ उत्तरीयम्. ५ नातिवलित. ६ अणुतर. ७ श्वासारम्भ.

किरणमञ्जरीपिञ्जरितविषमव्याविद्धा[1]शिथिलशिखण्डबन्धनम्, आत्मप्रभापटलदुर्लक्ष्यपाटलोत्तराधरविवरम्, गण्डस्थलीसंक्रान्तहस्तपल्लवदर्शितकर्णावतंसकृत्यम्, उपरिकपोलादर्शतलनिषिक्त[2]चित्रवितानपत्र[3]जातिजनितविशेषकक्रियम्, आमीलितलोचनेन्दीवरम्, अविभ्रान्तभ्रूपताकम्, उद्भिद्यमानश्रमजलपुलकभिन्नशिथिलचन्दनतिलकम्, आननेन्दुसंमुखा[4]लकलतं च विश्रब्धप्रसुप्तामतिधवलोत्तरच्छदनिमग्नप्रायैकपार्श्वतया चिरविलसनखेदनिश्चलां शरदम्भोधरोत्सङ्गशायिनीमिव सौदामनीं राजकन्यामपश्यम् । दृष्ट्वैव स्फुरदनङ्गरागश्चकितश्चोरयितव्यनिःस्पृहस्तयैव तावच्चोर्यमाणहृदयः किंकर्तव्यतामूढः क्षणमतिष्ठम् । अतर्कयं च—'न चेदिमां वामलोचनामाप्नुयां न मृष्यति मां जीवितुं वसन्तबन्धुः । असंकेतितपरामृष्टा चेयमतिबाला[5] व्यक्तमार्तस्वरेण[6] निहन्यान्मे मनोरथम् । ततोऽहमेवाघ्नीय[7] । तादियमत्र प्रतिपात्तिः ।' इति नाग-

---

किरणमञ्जरीभिः पिञ्जरितः विषमव्याविद्धः आशिथिलः शिखण्डबन्धः यस्मिन्कर्मणि तथा । पाटलः श्वेतरक्तः । उत्तराधर उत्तरोष्ठः । गण्डस्थली गल्लप्रदेशस्तत्र संक्रान्तो मिलितो यः हस्तपल्लवः करपल्लवः तेन दर्शितं कर्णावतंसस्य कृत्यं यथा स्यात्तथा । कपोल एवादर्शतलं तस्योपरि निषिक्तं प्रतिबिम्बितं यच्चित्रं वितानमुल्लोचः । 'अस्त्री वितानमुल्लोचः' इत्यमरः । तदेव पत्रजातिः पत्रक्रिया तया जनितोत्पादिता विशेषक्रिया तिलकादिक्रिया । अविभ्रान्ता निश्चला । उद्भिद्यमानं जायमानम् । श्रमजलं घर्मस्तस्य पुलका बिन्दवः । अलकलता केशवल्लिः । इत्येतानि क्रियाविशेषणानि । विश्रब्धप्रसुप्तां विश्वासकृतनिद्राम् । उत्तरच्छद आस्तरणपटः । निमग्नप्रायः निमग्न इवेत्यर्थः । 'मन्ये शङ्के ध्रुवं प्राय इति वेवार्थवाचकाः' इत्यभिधानात् । विलसनं स्फुरणम् । उत्सङ्गो मध्यम् । 'मध्योन्नतिः समुत्सङ्गः' इति वैजयन्ती । सौदामनी विद्युत् । **दृष्ट्वैवेति** । स्फुरन् द्विगुणीभूतोऽनङ्गरागो यस्येति । किंकर्तव्यतामूढोऽग्रे किं कर्तव्यमिति ज्ञानरहितः । **अतर्कयमिति** । मृष्यति सहते । 'वर्तमानसामीप्ये वर्तमानवद्वा' इति लट् । वसन्तबन्धुर्मदनः । असंकेतितपरामृष्टा अकृतसंकेता सती परामृष्टा स्पृष्टा । आर्तस्वरेण पीडितस्वरेण । आङ्पूर्वकस्य हन्तेः 'आङो यमहनः' इत्यनेन तङि विधिलिङि उत्तमपुरुषैकवचनम् । हतो भवेयमित्यर्थः । प्रतिपत्तिः कर्तव्यम् । नागदन्तोऽवलम्बनकाष्ठम् । 'खुंटी' इति भाषया प्रसिद्धम् ।

---

१ व्याविद्धाशिथिल. २ निषक्त. ३ पत्रक्रिया. ४ •खागतालकलतम्. ५ अतिवेलम्. ६ रवेण. ७ आघ्नीये.

दन्तलग्ननिर्यासकल्कवर्णितं फलकमादाय मणिसमुद्गकाद्वर्णवर्तिका-मुद्धृत्य ता तथा शयानां तस्याश्च मामाबद्धाञ्जलिं चरणलग्नमालिखमार्यां चैताम्—

'त्वामयमाबद्धाञ्जलि दासजनस्तमिममर्थमर्थयते ।
स्वपिहि मया सह सुरतव्यतिकरखिन्नैवं मा मैवम् ॥ '

हेमकरण्डकाच्च वासताम्बूलवीटिकां कर्पूरस्फुटिकां पारिजातकं चोप-युज्यालक्तकपाटलेन तद्रसेन सुधाभित्तौ चक्रवाकमिथुनं निरष्ठीवम् । अङ्गुलीयकविनिमयं च कृत्वा कथंकथमपि निरगाम् । सुरङ्गया च प्रत्येत्य बन्धनागारं तत्र बद्धस्य नागरिकवरस्य सिंहघोषनाम्नस्तेष्वेव दिनेषु मित्र-त्वेनोपचरितस्य 'एवं मया हतस्तपस्वी कान्तकः, तत्त्वया प्रतिभिद्य रहस्यं लब्धव्यो मोक्षः' इत्युपदिश्य सह श्रृगालिकया निरक्रामिषम् । नृपतिपथे च समागत्य रक्षिकपुरुषैरगृह्ये । अचिन्तयं च—'अलमस्मि जवेनापसर्तुमनामृष्ट एवैभिः । एषा पुनर्वराकी गृह्येत । तदिदमत्र प्राप्तरूपम्'

---

तत्र लग्नं संस्थापितम् । निर्यासकल्केन चिक्कणद्रव्यक्वाथेन वर्णितम् । वर्णो रक्तादिः स संजातो यस्मिन्निति तम् । फलकं काष्ठपट्टिकाम् । हिङ्गुलरक्तपट्टिकामिति यावत् । मणिसमुद्गकाद्रत्नसंपुटकात् । 'समुद्गकः संपुटकः' इत्यमरः । वर्तिकां तूलिकाम् । 'तूलिका वर्णवर्तिका' इति वैजयन्ती । चरणलग्नं पादलग्नम् । **आर्यामिति** । आर्या-लक्षणं वृत्तरत्नाकरोक्तम्—'लक्ष्मैतत्सप्तगणा गोपेता भवति नेह विषमे जः ।' इति । **त्वामयमिति** । अयं दासजनो मद्रूपः सेवकजनः आबद्धाञ्जलि कृताञ्जलीति क्रियाविशेषणम् । त्वामिमर्थं अर्थयते प्रार्थयते । द्विकर्मकोऽयम् । सुरतस्य व्यति-करः ससर्गस्तेन खिन्नैव मया सह स्वपिहि निद्रां कुरु । एवं सुरतखेदं विना मा मेति । 'अमानोनाः प्रतिषेधे' । वीप्सायां द्विर्वचनम् । हेमकरण्डकात्सुवर्णपेटकात् । वास-ताम्बूलवीटिकां सुवासितनागवल्लीपत्रवीटिकाम् । कर्पूरस्फुटिकां कर्पूरखण्डम् । पारि-जातकं सुगन्धखदिरसारम् । उपयुज्य भुक्त्वा । अलक्तकपाटलेन यावकवद्रक्तेन । तद्रसेन ताम्बूलवीटिकारसेन । सुधया लिप्ता संस्कृता वा भित्तिः सुधाभित्तिः तस्यां सुधाभित्तौ । चूर्णकुड्ये इत्यर्थः । चक्रवाकमिथुनं निरष्ठीवमम्बूकृतवान् । विनिमयो व्यत्ययः । बन्धनागारं प्रत्येत्यागत्य । उपचरितस्य सेवितस्य । तपस्वी शोच्यः । मोक्षो मोचनम् । अलं समर्थः । अपसर्तुं पलाय्य गन्तुम् । अनामृष्टोऽस्पृष्टः । एषा वराकी दीना श्रृगालिका । तदिदमत्र प्राप्तरूपं तस्मादिदं प्रशस्तं प्राप्तं वक्ष्यमाणं

---

१ निर्यासवालुका. २ तूलिकावर्तिकाम्. ३ मदन. ४ खिन्नेव. ५ व्यतिकरम. ६ समापत्य.

इति तानेव चपलमभिपत्य स्वपृष्ठसमार्पितकूर्परः पराङ्मुखः स्थित्वा 'यद्यहमस्मि तस्करः, भद्रा बध्नीत माम्। युष्माकमयमधिकारः, न पुनरस्या वर्षीयस्याः' इत्यवादिषम्। सा तु तावतैवोन्नीतमदभिप्राया तान्सप्रणाममभ्येत्य 'भद्रमुखाः ममैष पुत्रो वायुग्रस्तश्चिरं चिकित्सितः। पूर्वेद्युः प्रसन्नकल्पः प्रकृतिस्थ एव जातः। जातास्थया मया बन्धनान्निष्क्रमय्य स्नापितोऽनुलेपितश्च परिधाप्य निष्प्रवाणियुगलम्[1] अभ्यवहार्य परमान्नमौशीरेऽद्य कामचारः कृतोऽभूत्। अथ निशीथे भूय एव वायुनिघ्नः 'निहत्य कान्तकं नृपतिदुहित्रा रमेयम्' इति रंहसा परेण राजपथमभ्यपतत्। निरूप्य चाहं पुत्रमेवंगतमस्यां वेलायामनुधावामि। तत्प्रसीदत। बद्ध्वैनं मह्यमर्पयत' इति यावदसौ क्रन्दति तावदहं 'स्थविरे, केन देवो मातरिश्वा बद्धपूर्वः। किमेते काकाः शौङ्गेयस्य मे निग्रहीतारः। शान्तं पापम्' इत्यधावम्। असावप्यमीभिः 'त्वमेवोन्मत्तयाऽनुन्मत्त इत्युन्मत्तं मुक्तवती। कस्तमिदानीं बध्नाति' इति कदर्थिता रुदत्येव मामन्वधावत्। गत्वा च रागमञ्जरीगृहं चिरं[2] विरहखेदविह्वलाम्[3] इमां बहुविधं समाश्वास्य तं निशाशेषमनयम्। प्रत्यूषे [4]चोदारकेण समगच्छे।

अथ भगवन्तं मरीचिं वेशकृच्छ्रादुत्थाय पुनः [5]प्रतितप्ततपः-

---

प्रशस्तं कर्तव्यम्। चपलं शीघ्रम्। स्वपृष्ठे समर्पितौ निहितौ कूर्परौ येनेति सः। अयमधिकारस्तस्करबन्धनरूपः। वर्षीयस्या वृद्धायाः। **सा त्विति**। तावतैव तावन्मात्रेणैव। उन्नीतस्तर्कितः। वायुग्रस्तो वातुलः। प्रकृतिस्थः स्वभावस्थः। जातास्थया जातादरया। निष्प्रवाणियुगलमनाहतवस्त्रयुगलम्। 'अनाहतं निष्प्रवाणि तन्त्रकं च नवाम्बरे।' इत्यमरः। अभ्यवहार्य भोजयित्वा। परमान्नं पायसम्। औशीरे शयनासने। 'औशीरं शयनासनम्' इति हलायुधः। कामचारः स्वेच्छाचारित्वम्। **अथेति**। निशीथेऽर्धरात्रे। वायुनिघ्नो वाताधीनः। रंहसा वेगेन। मातरिश्वा वायुः। 'मातरिश्वा सदागतिः' इत्यमरः। शौङ्गेयस्य। 'तिलच्छदस्तु शौङ्गेयो विहङ्गारातिरित्यपि।' इति वैजयन्ती। 'ससाणा' इति प्रसिद्धः। तद्बन्धने काकानामसामर्थ्यमिति भावः। **असाविति**। असौ शृगालिका। कदर्थिता निन्दिता। 'निन्दितः क्लेशने चैव वर्णने च कदर्थने' इति सज्जनः। **गत्वा चेति**। चिरं बहुकालं यो विरहखेदो वियोगदुःखं तेन विह्वलाम्। प्रातःकाले। उदारकेण मित्रेण। **अथेति**। वेशकृच्छ्राद्वेश्याकष्टात्।

---

१ अनाहतयुगलम्. २ चिरवियोग. ३ विक्लवाम्. ४ पुनरुदा०. ५ प्रतिपन्न.

प्रभावप्रत्यापन्नदिव्यचक्षुषमुपसंगम्य तेनास्म्येवंभूतं त्वद्दर्शनमवगमितः। सिंहघोषश्च कान्तकापचारं निर्भिद्य तत्पदे प्रसन्नेन राज्ञा प्रतिष्ठापितस्तेनैव चारकसुरङ्गापथेन कन्यापुरप्रवेशं भूयोऽपि मे समपादयत्। समगंसि चाहं शृगालिकामुखविसृतवार्तानुरक्तया राजदुहित्रा। तेष्वेव दिवसेषु चण्डवर्मा सिंहवर्मावधूतदुहितृप्रार्थनः कुपितोऽभियुज्य पुरमवारुणत्। अमर्षणश्चाङ्गराजो यावदरिः पौरि[1]ग्रामिकं विधिमाचिकीर्षति तावत्स्वयमेव प्राकारं[2] निर्भिद्य प्रत्यासन्नानपि सहायानप्रतीक्षमाणो निर्गत्याभ्यधिकबलेन विद्विषा महति संपराये भिन्नवर्मा[3] सिंहवर्मा बलाद्गृह्यत। अम्बालिका[4] च बलवदभिगृह्य चण्डवर्मणा हठात्परिणेतुमात्मभवनमनीयत। कौतुकं च स किल क्षपावसाने विवाह इत्यबध्नात्। अहं च धनमित्रगृहे तद्विवाहार्यैव पिनद्धमङ्गलप्रतिसरस्तमेवमवोचम्— 'सखे समापतितमेवाङ्गराजाभिसरं[5] राजमण्डलम्। सुगूढमेव संभूय पौरवृद्धैस्तदुपावर्तय। उपावृत्तश्च कृत्त[6]शिरसमेव शत्रुं द्रक्ष्यसि' इति। 'तथा' इति तेनाभ्युपगते गतायुषोऽमुष्य भवनमुत्सवाकुलमुपसमाधीय-

---

प्रतितप्तं यत्तपस्तस्य प्रभावात्सामर्थ्यात्प्रत्यापन्नं प्राप्तं दिव्यं चक्षुर्येनेति तथा तम्। एवंभूतममुना प्रकारेण जातम्। त्वद्दर्शनम्। त्वच्छब्दे राजवाहनस्योपस्थितिः। 'उपसंगम्य इत्यस्यावगमित इत्यवगमेऽन्वयः। अतः समानकर्तृत्वम्।' इति भूषणा। अवगमितो बोधितः। सिंहघोषः कारागृहमित्रम्। कान्तकापचारं कारापत्यपकारम्। निर्भिद्य प्रकटीकृत्य। तेनैव मत्कृतमार्गेण। विसृतवार्तया निर्गतगोष्ठ्या। अनुरक्तयाऽऽसक्तया। तेष्वेवेति। चण्डवर्मा राजवाहनबन्धनकर्ता। सिंहवर्मणाऽङ्गदेशस्थचम्पानगरराज्ञा। अभियुज्याभिभूय। 'अभियोगस्त्वभिभवः' इति कोशः। अमर्षणः सकोपः। अङ्गराजः सिंहवर्मा। पारिग्रामिकं ग्रामस्य परितः क्रियमाणम्। 'ग्रामात्पर्यनुपूर्वात्' इति ठञ्। प्राकारमावरणभित्तिम्। प्रत्यासन्नान्समीपवर्तिनः। संपराये संग्रामे। भिन्नवर्मा भिन्नतनुत्रः। अम्बालिका सिंहवर्मदुहिता। कौतुकं मङ्गलसूत्रम्। स किल चण्डवर्मा अहमपहारवर्मा। तद्विवाहायाम्बालिकाविवाहाय। पिनद्धः मङ्गलप्रतिसरो येन स तथा। बद्धमङ्गलहस्तसूत्रः इत्यर्थः। 'हस्तसूत्रं प्रतिसरः' इति वैजयन्ती। समापतितं समागतम्। अङ्गराजाभिसरमङ्गराजसहायीभूतम्। सुगूढं सुगुप्तम्। तद्राजमण्डलमुपावर्तय समीपमानय। उपावृत्तश्च पुनरागतः सन्। शत्रुं चण्डवर्माणम्। अभ्युपगतेऽङ्गीकृते। गतायुषोऽल्पायुषः। अमुष्य चण्डवर्मणः। उपसमाधीयमान-

---

१ पारग्रा०, २ सालम्, ३ ०र्मर्मा, ४ अम्बालिकाम्, ५ अनभिसरम्, ६ कृतकृत्यः कृत्त०.

मानपरिणयोपकरणमितस्ततःप्रवेशनिर्गमप्रवृत्तलोकसंबाधमलक्ष्यशस्त्रिकः सह प्रविश्य मङ्गलपाठकैरम्बालिकापाणिपल्लवमग्नौ साक्षिण्याथर्वणेन विधिनाऽर्प्यमाणमादित्समानस्यायामिनं बाहुदण्डमाकृष्य च्छुरिकयोरासि प्राहार्षम् । स्फुरतश्च कतिपयानन्यानपि यमविषयमगमयम् । हतविध्वस्तं च तद्गृहमनुविचरन्वेपमानमधुरगात्रीं विशाललोचनामभिनिशाम्य तदालिङ्गनसुखमनुबुभूषुस्तामादाय गर्भगृहमविक्षम् । अस्मिन्नेव क्षणे तवास्मि नवाम्बुवाहस्तनितगम्भीरेण स्वरेणानुगृहीतः ' इति ।

श्रुत्वा च स्मित्वा च देवोऽपि राजवाहनः ' कथमसि कार्कश्येन कर्णीसुतमप्यतिक्रान्तः ' इत्यभिधाय पुनरवेक्ष्योपहारवर्माणम् 'आचक्ष्व । तवेदानीमवसरः' इत्यभाषत । सोऽपि सस्मितं प्रणम्यारभताभिधातुम् ।

इति श्रीदण्डिनः कृतौ दशकुमारचरितेऽपहारवर्मचरितं नाम द्वितीय उच्छ्वासः ।

## तृतीयोच्छ्वासः ।

एषोऽस्मि पर्यटन्नेकदा गतो विदेहेषु । मिथिलामप्रविश्यैव बहिः क्वचिन्मठिकाया विश्रमितुमेत्य कयाऽपि वृद्धतापस्या दत्तपाद्यः क्षणम-

परिणयोपकरणं संपाद्यमानविवाहोपयुक्तवस्तुजातम् । इतस्ततः प्रवेशनिर्गमाः गतागतानि तत्र प्रवृत्त उपक्रान्तो यो लोकस्तेन संबाधं संकटम् । अलक्ष्याऽदृश्या शस्त्रिका च्छुरिका यस्येति स तथा । मङ्गलपाठकैर्ब्राह्मणैः सह । अग्नौ साक्षिणी सत्यग्निसाक्षिकमित्यर्थः । आथर्वणेन पुरोधसा । 'आथर्वणः पुरोधाः स्याच्छान्तिपुष्टिकरो द्विजः । ' इति कामन्दकः । विधिना विध्युक्तप्रकारेण । अर्प्यमाणं दीयमानम् । आदित्समानस्य ग्रहीतुकामस्य । आयामिनं दैर्घ्यवन्तम् । प्राहार्षं हृतवान् । यमविषयं यमदेशम् । मधुरं सुन्दरम् । अभिनिशाम्य संमुखं दृष्ट्वा । अनुबुभूषुरनुभवितुमिच्छुः । गर्भगृहम् । **अस्मिन्निति** । नवाम्बुवाहो नूतनमेघस्तस्य स्तनितं गर्जितम् । कार्कश्येन कर्कशस्य भावस्तेन । काठिन्येनेत्यर्थः । कर्णीसुतः स्तेयशास्त्रकर्ता ।

**इति श्रीदशकुमारचरितटीकायां द्वितीय उच्छ्वासः ।**

इदानीमुपहारवर्मचरितमभिधातुमुपक्रमते–**एषोऽस्मीति** । मठिका अल्पमठः । दत्तपाद्यो दत्तपादोदकः । 'पाद्यं पादाय वारिणि ' इत्यमरः । अलिन्दभूमौ ।

१ संपातम्. २ पुनर्निरीक्ष्य. ३ एषोऽप्यहमस्मि.

लिन्दभूमाववास्थिषि । तस्यास्तु मद्दर्शनादेव किमप्याबद्धधारमश्रु प्रावर्तत । 'किमेतदम्ब, कथय कारणम्' इति पृष्टा सकरुणमाचष्ट— 'जैवातृक ननु श्रूयते पतिरस्या मिथिलायाः प्रहारवर्मा नामासीत् । तस्य खलु मगधराजो राजहंसः परं मित्रमासीत् । तयोश्च वल्लभे बलशम्[1]बलयोरिव वसुमतीप्रियंवदे सख्यमप्रतिममधत्ताम् । अथ प्रथमगर्भाभिनन्दितां तां च प्रियसखीं दिदृक्षुः प्रियंवदा वसुमतीं सह भर्त्रा पुष्पपुरमगमत् । तस्मिन्नेव च समये मालवेन मगधराजस्य महज्जन्यमजनि । तत्र लेशतोऽपि दुर्लक्षां[2] गतिमगमन्मगधराजः । मैथिलेन्द्रस्तु[3] मालवेन्द्रप्रयत्नप्राणितः स्वविषयं प्रतिनिवृत्तो ज्येष्ठस्य संहारवर्मणः सुतैर्विकटवर्मप्रभृतिभिर्व्याप्तं राज्यम्[4]आकर्ण्य स्वस्रीयात्सुह्मपतेर्दण्डावयवमादित्सुरटवीपथमवगाह्य लुब्धकलुप्तसर्वस्वोऽभूत् । तत्सुतेन च कनीयसा हस्तवर्तिना सहैकाकिनी वनचरशरवर्षभयपलायिता वनमगाहिषि । तत्र च मे शार्दूलनखावलीढनिपतितायाः पाणिभ्रष्टः स बालकः कस्यापि कपिलाशवस्य क्रोडमभ्यलीयत । तच्छवाकर्षिणश्च व्याघ्रस्यासूनिषुरिष्वसनयन्त्रमुक्तः क्षणादलिक्षत् । भिल्ल-

---

अलिन्दभूमिर्बहिर्द्वाराग्रवर्तिचतुष्कम् । 'ओटा' इति भाषया प्रसिद्धम् । 'प्रघाणप्रघणालिन्दा बहिर्द्वारप्रकोष्ठके ।' इत्यमरः । अवास्थिषीत्यत्र 'समवप्रविभ्यः स्थः' इत्यात्मनेपदम् । आबद्धधारमविच्छिन्नधारम् । जैवातृक आयुष्मन् । जीवतीति जैवातृकः । जीवेः आतृकन् वृद्धिश्च । तयोः राजहंसप्रहारवर्मणोः । बलश्च शम्बलश्च द्वावप्यसुरौ तयोरिव । अप्रतिममसदृशम् । अधत्तां दधतुः । **अथेति** । प्रियंवदा प्रहारवर्मस्त्री । भर्त्रा प्रहारवर्मणा सह । पुष्पपुरं वसुमतीभर्तृ राजहंसस्य नगरम् । **तस्मिन्निति** । मालवेनान्यराज्ञा । मगधराजस्य राजहंसस्य । जन्यं युद्धम् । लेशतः किंचित् । सार्वविभक्तिकस्तसिः । मगधराजो राजहंसः । मालवेन्द्रप्रयत्नेन प्राणितो जीवितः । स्वविषयमात्मदेशम् । ज्येष्ठस्य भ्रातुः । स्वस्रीयाद्भगिनीपुत्रात् । 'स्वसुश्छः' इति छः । दण्डावयवं सैन्यैकदेशम् । लुब्धका व्याधाः । तत्सुतेन प्रहारवर्मपुत्रेण । वनचराणां भिल्लानां शरवर्षाद्भयं तेन पलायिता । अगाहिव्यालोडितवती । शार्दूलो व्याघ्रः । कपिलाशवस्य मृतगोशरीरस्य । क्रोडो वक्षःस्थलम् । इष्वसनं धनुः । अलिक्षदपाहरत् । वृष्णिपालेन गोपालेन ।

---

१ शम्बर. २ दुर्लक्षताम्. ३ मैथिलस्तु. ४ राष्ट्रम्

दारकैः स बालोऽपाहारि । सा त्वहं मोहसुप्ता केनापि वृष्णिपालेनोपनीय स्वं कुटीरमावेश्य कृपयोपक्रान्तव्रणा स्वस्थीभूय स्वभर्तुरन्तिकमुपतिष्ठासुरसहायतया यावद्‌व्याकुलीभवामि तावन्ममैव दुहिता सह यूना केनापि तमेवोद्देशमागमत् । सा भृशं रुरोद । रुदितान्ते च सा सार्थघाते स्वहस्तगतस्य राजपुत्रस्य किरातभर्तृहस्तगमनम्, आत्मनश्च केनापि वनचरेण व्रणविरोपणम्, स्वस्थायाश्च पुनस्तेनोपयन्तुं चिन्तितताया निकृष्टजातिसंसर्गवैक्लव्यात्प्रत्याख्यानपारुष्यम्, तदक्षमेण चामुना विविक्ते विपिने स्वशिरःकर्तनोद्यमम्, अनेन यूना यदृच्छया दृष्टेन तस्य दुरात्मनो हननम्, आत्मनश्चोपयमनम्, इत्यकथयत् । स तु पृष्टो मैथिलेन्द्रस्यैव कोऽपि सेवकः कारणविलम्बी तन्मार्गानुसारी जातः । सह तेन भर्तुरन्तिकमुपसृत्य पुत्रवृत्तान्तेन श्रोत्रमस्य देव्याः प्रियंवदायाश्चादहाव ।

स च राजा दिष्टदोषाज्ज्येष्ठ[2]पुत्रैश्चिरं विगृह्य पुनरहसाहिष्णुतयाऽतिमात्रं चिरं प्रयुध्य बद्धः । देवी च बन्धनं गमिता । दग्धा पुनरहमस्मिन्नपि वार्द्धके हतजीवितमपारयन्ती हातुं प्रव्रज्यां किलाग्रहीषम् । दुहिता तु मम हत[3]जीविताकृष्टा विकटवर्ममहा[4]देवीं कल्पसुन्दरीं किलाशिश्रियत् । तौ चेद्राजपुत्रौ निरुपद्रवावेवावर्धिष्येताम्, इयता

अविपालेनेति वा । कुटीरमल्पगृहम् । 'कुटीशमीशुण्डाभ्यो रः' इति रः । उपक्रान्तव्रणा चिकित्सितक्षता । उपतिष्ठासुर्गन्तुमिच्छुः । तमेवोद्देशं कुटीरप्रदेशम् । सा मत्कन्या । सार्थघाते संघभ्रंशे । किरातभर्तुर्भिल्लप्रभोः । व्रणविरोपणं क्षतचिकित्सनम् । उपयन्तुं परिणेतुम् । निकृष्टा हीना । प्रत्याख्याने दूरीकरणे पारुष्यं काठिन्यम् । तदक्षमेण पारुष्यासहेन । विविक्ते विजने । स तु परिणेता । मैथिलेन्द्रस्य प्रहारवर्मणः । कारणविलम्बी प्रयोजनविलम्बितः । भर्तुर्मिथिलेन्द्रस्य । स राजा प्रहारवर्मा । दिष्टं दैवम् । अतिमात्रमत्यन्तम् । देवी प्रियंवदा । हातुं त्यक्तुम् । प्रव्रज्यां संन्यासम् । विकटवर्मा प्रहारवर्मज्येष्ठभ्रातृपुत्रः । महादेवीं पट्टमहिषीम् ।

१ मिथिलेन्द्रस्य. २ ज्येष्ठभ्रातृपुत्रैः. ३ हतजीविकाकृष्टा; हतजीवना०. ४ महिषीम्.

कालेन तवेमां वयोवस्थामस्प्रक्ष्येताम् । तयोश्च सतोर्न दायादा नरेन्द्रस्य प्रसह्यकारिणो भवेयुः' इति प्र[1]मन्युरभिरुरोद । श्रुत्वा च तापसीगिरमहमपि प्रवृद्धबाष्पो निगूढमभ्यधाम्—'यद्येवमम्ब समाश्वसिहि । नन्वस्ति कश्चिन्मुनिस्त्वया तदवस्थया पुत्राभ्युपपादनार्थं याचितस्तेन स लब्धो वर्धितश्च । वार्तेयमतिमहती । किमनया । सोऽहमस्मि । शक्यश्च मयाऽसौ विकटवर्मा यथाकथंचिदुपश्लिष्य व्यापादयितुम् । अनुजाः पुनरतिबहवः, तैरपि घटन्ते पौरजानपदाः । मां तु न कश्चिदिहत्य ईदृक्तया जनो जानाति । पितरावपि तां[2]वन्मां न संविदाते किमुतेतरे । [3]तदेनमर्थमुपायेन साधयिष्यामि' इत्यगादिषम् । सा तु वृद्धा सरुदितं परिष्वज्य मुहुः शिरस्युपाघ्राय प्रस्नु[4]तस्तनी सगद्गदमगदत्—'वत्स चिरं जीव । भ[5]द्रं तव । प्रसन्नोऽद्य भगवान्विधिः । अद्यैव प्रहारवर्मण्यधि विदेहा जाताः, यतः प्रलम्बमानपीनबाहुर्भवानपारमेतच्छोकसागरमद्यो[6]त्तारयितुं स्थितः । अहो महद्भागधेयं देव्याः प्रियंवदायाः'. इति हर्षनिर्भरा स्नानभोजनादिना मामुपाचरत् । अशिश्रियं चास्मिन्मठैकदेशे निशि कटशय्याम् । अचिन्तयं च–'विनोपधिनाऽयमर्थो न साध्यः । स्त्रियश्चोपधीनामुद्भव-

---

अस्प्रक्ष्येतां स्प्रष्टौ भविष्यतः । दायादा बान्धवाः । प्रसह्यकारिणो बलात्कारकारिणः । प्रमन्युः प्रकृष्टशोका । निगूढं गुप्तम् । सोऽहमस्मीत्यात्मनिरूपणम् । उपश्लिष्य संनिधानं प्राप्य । व्यापादयितुं हन्तुम् । अनुजाः विकटवर्मणः कनिष्ठा भ्रातरः । तैरपि घटन्ते मिलन्ति पौरजनाः । 'एवं तस्मिन्हतेऽपि तस्यानुजा राज्यं करिष्यन्ति । तथा च मत्कृतं व्यापादनं व्यर्थमेव भवेत् इति भावः ।' इति भूषणा । इहत्योऽत्रत्यो जनः । 'अव्ययात्त्यप्' इति त्यप् । ईदृक्तया ईदृशस्य भावस्तथा तया । उपाघ्रायाघ्राणं कृत्वा । प्रस्नुतस्तनी क्षरद्दुग्धस्तनी । भद्रं कल्याणम् । प्रहारवर्मण्यधि प्रहारवर्माधीनाः । 'अधिरीश्वरे' इति कर्मप्रवचनीयसंज्ञा । 'यस्मादधिकं यस्य चेश्वरवचनं तत्र सप्तमी' । प्रलम्बमानौ दीर्घौ पीनौ पुष्टौ बाहु यस्येति स तथा । एतच्छोकसागरं प्रहारवर्मशोकसमुद्रम् । उपाचरदुपचारमकरोत् । अशिश्रियमाश्रितवान् । कटशय्यां तृणास्तरणम् । उपधिना कपटेन । 'कपटोऽस्त्री व्याजदम्भोपधयश्छद्मकैतवे' इत्यमरः । उद्भवक्षेत्रमुत्पत्तिस्थानम् ।

---

१ प्रवृद्धमन्युः. २ यावन्मामू; तावदित्थम्. ३ तमेनम्. ४ प्रस्नुत. ५ भद्र. ६ उत्तारयिता.

क्षेत्रम् । अतोऽन्तःपुरवृत्तान्तमस्या अवगम्य तद्द्वारेण किंचिज्जालमाचरेयम्' इति चिन्तयत्येव[1] मयि महार्णवोन्मग्नमार्तण्डतुरङ्गमश्वासरयावधूतेव व्यावर्तत त्रियामा । समुद्रगर्भवासजडीकृत इव मन्दप्रतापो दिवसंकरः[2] प्रादुरासीत् ।

उत्थायावसायितदिनमुखनियमविधिस्तां मे मातरमवादिषम्—'अम्ब जाल्मस्य विकटवर्मणः कच्चिदन्तःपुरवृत्तान्तमभिजानासि' इत्यनवसितवचन एव मयि काचिदङ्गना प्रत्यदृश्यत । तां चावेक्ष्य सा मे धात्री हर्षाश्रुकुण्ठित[3]कण्ठमाचष्ट—'पुत्रि पुष्करिके पश्य भर्तृदारकम् । अयमसावकृपया मया वने परित्यक्तः पुनरप्येवमागतः' इति । सा तु हर्षनिर्भरनिपीडिता चिरं प्ररुद्य बहु विलप्य शान्ता पुनः स्वमात्रा राजान्तःपुरवृत्तान्ताख्याने न्ययुज्यत । उक्तं च तया—'कुमार कामरूपेश्वरस्य कलिन्दवर्मनाम्नः कन्या कल्पसुन्दरी कलासु रूपे चाप्सरसोऽप्यतिक्रान्ता पतिमभिभूय वर्तते । तदेकवल्लभः स तु बह्ववरोधोऽपि विकटवर्मा' इति । तामवोचम्—'उपसर्पैनां मत्प्रयुक्तैर्गन्धमाल्यैः । उपजनय चासमानदोषनिन्दादिना स्वभर्तरि द्वेषम् । अनुरूपभर्तृगामिनीनां च वासवदत्तादीनां वर्णनेन ग्राह-

---

अस्या वृद्धायाः सकाशात् । जालं कपटम् । 'जालं समूह आनाये गवाक्षे कपटेऽपि च' इति वैजयन्ती । **चिन्तयत्येवेति** । महार्णवोन्मग्नः समुद्रमध्यान्निःसृतो यो मार्तण्डः सूर्यः तस्य तुरङ्गमा अश्वाः तेषां श्वासरयो मुखमारुतवेगस्तेनावधूतेव कम्पितेव । त्रियामा रात्रिः । समुद्रगर्भवासः समुद्रमध्यवसतिः । जडीकृतः शीतलीकृतः । मन्दप्रतापः स्वल्पतापः । अवसायितः समापितः । दिनमुखनियमविधिः प्रातःकालनियमकृत्यम् । जाल्मस्य मूढस्य । 'जडो जाल्मश्च निर्बुद्धौ स्तब्धेऽनालोच्यकारिणि ।' इति वैजयन्ती । कच्चिदिति प्रश्ने । 'कच्चित्कामप्रवेदने' इत्यमरः । अनवसितवचनेऽसमापितवचने । धात्र्युपमाता । हर्षाश्रु आनन्दाश्रु तेन कुण्ठितोऽवरुद्धः कण्ठो यथा तथेति क्रियाविशेषणम् । अकृपया निर्दयया । राजान्तःपुरं विकटवर्मान्तःपुरं तस्य वृत्तान्तो वार्ता तदाख्याने तत्कथने । न्ययुज्यत नियोजिता । अप्सरसोऽप्यतिक्रान्तोत्कृष्टेत्यर्थः । अभिभूय पराभूय । बह्ववरोधोऽपि बहुपत्नीकोऽपि । एनां कल्पसुन्दरीम् । मत्प्रयुक्तैर्मत्प्रेषितैः । उपजनयोत्पादय । असमानोऽतुल्यः ।

---

१ चिन्तापन्ने. २ दिवाकरः. ३ कुञ्चित; कुण्ठ.

यानुशयम्। अवरोधान्तरेषु च राज्ञो विलसितानि सुगूढान्यपि प्रयत्नेनान्विष्य प्रकाशयन्ती मानमस्या वर्धय' इति। पुनरिदमम्बामवोचम्—'इत्थमेव त्वयाऽप्यनन्यव्यापारया नृपाङ्गनाऽसावुपस्थातव्या। प्रत्यहं च यद्यत्तत्र वृत्तं तदस्मि त्वयैव[1] बोध्यः। मदुक्त्या पुनरियमुदर्कस्वादुनोऽस्मत्कर्मणः प्रसाधनाय च्छायेवानपायिनी कल्पसुन्दरीमनुवर्तताम्' इति। ते च तमर्थं तथैवान्वतिष्ठताम्।

केषुचिद्दिनेषु गतेष्वाचष्ट मां मदम्बा—'वत्स माधवीव पिचुमन्दा[2]श्लेषिणी यथाऽसौ शोच्यमात्मानं मन्येत[3] तथोपपाद्य स्थापिता। किं भूयः कृत्यम्' इति। पुनरहमभिलिख्यात्मनः प्रतिकृतिम् 'इत्थम[4]मुष्यै नेया। नीतां चैनां निर्वर्ण्य सा नियतमेवं वक्ष्यति—'नन्वस्ति कश्चिदीदृशाकारः पुमान्' इति। प्रतिब्रूह्येनाम्—'यदि स्यात्ततः किम्' इति। तस्य यदुत्तरं सा दास्यति तदहमस्मि प्रतिबोधनीयः' इति। सा 'तथा' इति राजकुलमुपसंक्रम्य प्रतिनिवृत्ता मामेकान्ते[5] न्यवेदयत्—'वत्स, दर्शितोऽसौ चित्रपटस्तस्यै मत्तकाशिन्यै। चित्रीयमाणा चासौ 'भुवनमिदं सनाथीकृतं यद्देवेऽपि कुसुमधन्वनि नेदृशी

वासवदत्तादीनामित्यत्र आदिशब्देन शकुन्तलादमयन्त्यादयो ग्राह्याः। अनुशयं पश्चात्तापम्। अवरोधान्तरेष्वपरस्त्रीषु। राज्ञो विकटवर्मणः। विलसितानि विलासान्। मानमीर्ष्याकृतं कोपम्। अनन्यव्यापारा त्यक्तसर्वान्यकार्या। असौ नृपाङ्गना। उपस्थातव्या सेवनीया। अस्मीत्यहमर्थेऽव्ययम्। त्वयैव बुद्ध्यैव। मदुक्त्येयं पुष्करिका। उदर्के उत्तरं फलम्। स्वादु मधुरम्। प्रसाधनाय करणाय। अनपायिनी नाशरहिता। कल्पसुन्दरी राजपत्नी। माधवी वासन्ती। 'वासन्ती माधवी लता' इत्यमरः। पिचुमन्दो निम्बवृक्षः। 'पिचुमन्दश्च निम्बे' इत्यमरः। उपपाद्य सयुक्तिकं संबोध्य। प्रतिकृतिं स्वरूपम्। नियतं असंशयम्। ईदृश आकारो यस्येति स तथा। मत्तकाशिनी उत्तमाङ्गना। चित्रीयमाणा विस्मयमाना। 'नमोवरिवश्चित्रङः क्यच्' इति क्यजन्तादात्मनेपदम्। सनाथीकृतं नाथवत्कृतमित्यर्थः। यद्यस्मात्। कुसुमधन्वनि मदने। ईदृश्येतत्सदृशा। वपुःश्रीः शरीरशोभा। न संनिधत्ते। नास्तीत्यर्थः

१ त्वयाऽवबोध्यः. २ पिचुमन्दा. ३ मन्यते. ४ अस्मत्प्रतिकृतिरियम्. ५ मह्यम्.

वपुःश्रीः संनिधत्ते। चित्रमेतच्चित्रतरम्। न च तमवैमि य ईदृशामिहत्यो निर्मिमीते। केनेदमालिखितम्' इत्यादृतवती व्याहृतवती च। मया च स्मेरयोदीरितम्—'देवि सदृशमाज्ञापयसि। भगवान्मकरकेतुरप्येवं सुन्दर इति न शक्यमेव संभावयितुम्। अथ च विस्तीर्णेयमर्णवनेमिः। क्वचिदीदृशमपि रूपं दैवशक्त्या संभवेत्। अथ तु यद्येवंरूपो रूपानुरूपशिल्पशीलविद्याज्ञानकौशलो युवा महाकुलीनश्च कश्चित्संनिहितः स्यात्स किं लप्स्यते' इति। तयोक्तम्—'अम्ब किं ब्रवीमि। शरीरं हृदयं जीवितमिति सर्वमिदमल्पमनर्हं च। ततो न किंचिल्लप्स्यते। न चेदयं विप्रलम्भस्तस्यामुष्य दर्शनानुभवेन यथेदं चक्षुश्चरितार्थं भवेत्तथाऽनुग्रहः कार्यः' इति। भूयोऽपि मया दृढतरीकर्तुमुपन्यस्तम्—'अस्ति कोऽपि राजसूनुर्निगूढं चरन्। अमुष्य वसन्तोत्सवे सह सखीभिर्नगरोपवनविहारिणी रतिरिव विग्रहिणी यदृच्छया दर्शनपथं गताऽसि। गतश्चासौ कामशरैकलक्ष्यतां मामन्ववर्तिष्ट। मया च वामन्योन्यानुरूपैरन्यदुर्लभैराकारादिभिर्गुणातिशयैश्च प्रेर्यमाणया तद्रचितैरेव कुसुमशेखरस्रगनुलेपनादिभिश्चिरमुपासिताऽसि। सादृश्यं च स्वमनेन स्वयमेवाभिलिख्य त्वत्समाधिगाढत्वद्दर्शनाय

---

चित्रतरमतितरामाश्चर्यकरम्। स्मेरया सहासया। उदीरितमुक्तम्। सदृशं युक्तम्। एवं संभावयितुं सुन्दरत्वेन निदर्शयितुम्। अथ चेति तथाऽपि। विस्तीर्णा विशाला। अर्णवनेमिः पृथिवीत्यर्थः। अथ त्विति। तिष्ठत्वित्यर्थः। 'अथ त्वित्यभिधेयेऽस्मिन्नास्तामथ तु चाव्ययम्।' इत्यजयः। रूपस्यानुरूपं अनुकूलम्। शिल्पं चातुर्यम्। विद्याश्चतुर्दशाष्टादश वा। ज्ञानं लिप्यादि। अनर्हमयोग्यम्। न किंचिल्लप्स्यते प्राप्यते। अमुष्य पुरुषस्य। चरितार्थं कृतकृत्यम्। उपन्यस्तम्। उक्तमित्यर्थः। **अस्तीति**। विग्रहिणी शरीरधारिणी। यदृच्छया स्वेच्छया। **गतश्चेति**। असौ राजपुरुषः। लक्ष्यतां वेध्यताम्। **मया चेति**। वामिति युवयोः। अन्योन्यानुरूपैः परस्परानुरक्तैः। प्रेर्यमाणयोद्योजितया। तद्रचितैस्तन्निर्मितैः। शेखर आपीडः। स्रङ् माला। अनुलेपनमुद्वर्तनम्। उपासिताऽसि। सेविताऽसीत्यर्थः। सादृश्यं स्वस्य प्रतिकृतिः। त्वत्समाधिगाढं त्वद्ध्यानदृढम्।

---

१ स्यादमु०; स्यात्तस्या अमुष्य. २ अवरुद्धः. ३ त्वत्समधिगमाय गाढं त्वद्दर्शनाय.

प्रेषितम् । एष चेदर्थो निश्चितस्तस्यामुष्यातिमानुषप्राणसत्त्वप्रज्ञाप्रकर्षस्य न किंचिद्दुष्करं नाम। तमद्यैव दर्शयेयम्। संकेतो देयः' इति। तया तु किंचिदिव ध्यात्वा पुनरभिहितम्—'अम्ब तव नैतदिदानीं गोप्यतमम्। अतः कथयामि। मम तातस्य राज्ञा प्रहारवर्मणा सह महती प्रीतिरासीत्। मातुश्च मे मानवत्याः प्रियवयस्या देवी प्रियंवदाऽऽसीत्। ताभ्यां पुनरजातापत्याभ्यामेव कृतः समयोऽभूत्—'आवयोः पुत्रवत्याः पुत्राय दुहितृमत्या दुहिता देया' इति। तातस्तु मां जातां प्रनष्टापत्या प्रियंवदेति प्रार्थयमानाय विकटवर्मणे दैवाद्दत्तवान्। अयं च निष्ठुरः पितृद्रोही नात्युपपन्नसंस्थानः कामोपचारेष्वलब्धवैचक्षण्यः कलासु काव्यनाटकादिषु मन्दाभिनिवेशः शौर्योन्मादी दुर्विकत्थनोऽनृतवादी चास्थानवर्षी। नातिरोचते म एष भर्ता विशेषतश्चैषु वासरेषु। यदयमुद्याने मदन्तरङ्गभूतां पुष्करिकामप्युपान्तवर्तिनीमनादृत्य मयि [1]बद्धसापत्न्यमत्सरामनात्मज्ञामात्मनाटकीयां रमयन्तिकां [2]नामापत्यनिर्विशेषं मत्संव-

'गाढत्वदर्शनाय दृढत्वज्ञानाय' इति भूषणा। एष चेदिति पूर्वोक्तोऽयमर्थः। अतिमानुषो मनुष्यमतिक्रान्तः। प्राणो बलम्। सत्त्वं पराक्रमः। प्रकर्ष आधिक्यं यस्येति स तथा तस्य। नामेति निश्चयार्थे। **अद्यैवेति**। स्वस्यैतत्कार्यघटनापटुत्वद्योतनार्थमेवकारः। ध्यात्वा विचार्य। गोप्यतममतिशयेन गोप्यमिति तथा। प्रियवयस्या प्रियसखी। अजातापत्याभ्यामनुत्पन्नापत्याभ्याम्। समयः शपथः। प्रनष्टापत्या हृतापत्या। निष्ठुरः कठिनः। 'नात्युपपन्नसंस्थानोऽननुगुणावयवः' इति भूषणा। 'उपपन्नं समृद्धे च संपन्नेऽनुगुणेऽपि च।' इति केशवः। 'संस्थानं मरणे गात्रे संनिवेशे च वर्तते' इति भागुरिः। कामोपचारेषु मदनतन्त्रेषु। अलब्धमप्राप्तं वैचक्षण्यं विचक्षणस्य भावः कौशलं येनेति स तथा। कलासु चतुःषष्टयाम्। काव्येषु श्रव्यरूपेषु नाटकादिषु दृश्यरूपेषु च। आदिशब्देन रूपकाख्यायिकाचम्पूरूपेषु। मन्दो निश्चलोऽभिनिवेश आग्रहो यस्येति। शौर्योन्मादी शौर्योन्मत्तः। दुर्विकत्थनो दुष्टश्चासौ विकत्थनश्चेति तथा। आत्मश्लाघात्यर्थः। अस्थानवर्ष्यपात्रदाता। म इति 'रुच्यर्थानां प्रीयमाणः' इति चतुर्थी। मदन्तरङ्गभूतामाप्तभूताम्। बद्धः सपत्नस्य भावः सापत्न्यं तस्य मत्सरोऽसह्यता ययेति तथा। नाटकीयां नर्तकीम्। 'नाटकीयो नृत्तकरः' इत्यजयः। अपत्यनिर्विशेषमपत्यतुल्यमिति क्रियाविशेषणम्। मत्संवर्धितायाः

१ आबद्ध. २ नामेति क्वचिन्नास्ति.

धितायाश्चम्पकलतायाः स्वयमवचिताभिः सुमनोभिरलमकार्षीत् । मदुपभुक्तमुक्ते चित्रकूटगर्भवेदिकागते रत्नतल्पे तया सह व्यहार्षीत् । अयोग्यश्च पुमानवज्ञातुं च प्रवृत्तः । तत्किमित्यपेक्ष्यते । परलोकभयं चैहिकेन दुःखेनान्तरितम् । अविषह्यं हि योषितामनङ्गशरनिषङ्गीभूतचेतसामनिष्टजनसंवासयन्त्रणादुःखम् । अतोऽमुना पुरुषेण मामद्योद्यानमाधवीगृहे समागमय । तद्वार्ताश्रवणमात्रेणैव हि ममातिमात्रं मनोऽनुरक्तम् । अस्ति चायमर्थराशिः । अनेनामुष्य पदे प्रतिष्ठाप्य तमेवात्यन्तमुपचर्य जीविष्यामि' इति । मयाऽपि तदभ्युपेत्य प्रत्यागतम् । अतः परं भर्तृदारकः प्रमाणम्' इति ।

ततस्तस्या एव सकाशादन्तःपुरनिवेशमन्तर्वंशिकपुरुषस्थानानि प्रमदवनप्रदेशानपि विभागेनावगम्य, अस्तगिरिकूटपातक्षुभितशोणित इव शोणीभवति भानुबिम्बे, पाश्चिमाम्बुधिपयःपातनिर्वापितपत-

मत्पालितायाः । चम्पकलतायाः अल्पचम्पकस्येत्यर्थः । अवचिताभिर्लूनाभिः सुमनोभिः पुष्पैः । 'स्त्रियः सुमनसः पुष्पम्' इत्यमरः । अलमकार्षीत्पूर्णमकरोत् । अलंकृतवानिति वा । 'अलं भूषणपर्याप्तिशक्तिवारणवाचकम्' इत्यमरः । मदुपभुक्तमुक्ते मयाऽऽदौ उपभुक्ते पश्चान्मुक्ते । चित्रकूटः क्रीडापर्वतः । तद्गर्भवेदिकागते । रत्नतल्पे रत्नमञ्चके । तया रमयन्तिकया । व्यहार्षीद्विहारं कृतवान् । अयोग्यो मूर्खः । अवज्ञातुमवमन्तुम् । ऐहिकेनेह भवं तथा तेन । अन्तरितं व्यवधानीकृतम् । अनङ्गस्य मदनस्य शराणां निषङ्गीभूतं तूणीभूतम् । स्थानतां प्राप्तमिति भावः । चेतश्चित्तं यासामिति तथा तासाम् । अनिष्टजनः शत्रुलोकस्तत्संवासस्तत्समागमः स एव यन्त्रणा निर्बन्धस्तद्दुःखमिति । अतिमात्रमत्यन्तम् । **अस्तीति** । अर्थराशिर्द्रव्यराशिः । अमुष्य विकटवर्मणः । उपचर्याराध्य । मयाऽपि वृद्धतापस्या । **तत इति** । अन्तःपुरनिवेशमन्तःपुरप्रदेशम् । अन्तर्वंशिकपुरुषाः । 'अन्तःपुरे त्वधिकृतः स्यादन्तर्वंशिको जनः ।' इत्यमरः । प्रमदवनम्–'विज्ञेयं प्रमदवनं पुरोपकण्ठे शुद्धान्तैः सह रमते नृपस्तु यस्मिन् ।' इति हलायुधः । विभागेन विवेकेन । अस्तगिरेः कूटं शिखरं तस्माद्यः पातः पतनं तेन क्षुभितं निःसृतं शोणितं रक्तं यस्येति तथा तस्मिन् । शोणीभवति सति । पतङ्ग एव सूर्य एवाङ्गारः प्रदीप्तकाष्ठावयवस्तस्य

१ अद्य भा वा. २ अमुं स्वे पदे. ३ संनिवेशम्. ४ शिखर.

झाङ्कारधूमसंभार इव भरितनभसि तमसि विजृम्भिते, परदारपरामर्शोन्मुखस्य ममाचार्यकमिव कर्तुमुत्थिते गुरुपरिग्रहश्लाघिनि ग्रहाग्रेसरे क्षपाकरे, कल्पसुन्दरीवदनपुण्डरीकेणेव मद्दर्शनातिरागप्रथमोपनतेन स्मयमानेन चन्द्रमण्डलेन संधुक्षमाणतेजसि भुवनविजिगीषोद्यते देवे कुसुमधन्वनि, यथोचितं शयनीयमभजे। व्यचीचरं च—'सिद्धप्राय एवायमर्थः। किं तु परकलत्रलङ्घनाद्धर्मपीडा भवेत्। साऽप्यर्थकामयोर्द्वयोरुपलम्भे शास्त्रकारैरनुमतैवेति। गुरुजनबन्धमोक्षोपायसंधिना मया चैष व्यतिक्रमः कृतस्तदपि पापं निर्हृत्य कियत्याऽपि धर्मकलया मां समग्रयेदिति। अपि त्वेतदाकर्ण्य देवो राजवाहनः सुहृदो वा किं नु वक्ष्यन्ति' इति चिन्तापराधीन एव निद्रया परामृश्ये। अदृश्यत च स्वप्ने हस्तिवक्त्रो भगवान्। आह स्म च—'सौम्य उपहारवर्मन्, मा स्म ते दुर्विकल्पो भूत्। यतस्त्वमसि मदंशः। शंकरजटाभारलालनोचिता सुरसरिदसौ वरवार्णिनी। सा च कदाचिन्मद्विलोडनासहिष्णुर्मामशपत्—'एहि

---

धूमस्तस्य संभारो यस्मिन्निति तथा तस्मिन्। भरितं व्याप्तं नभो येनेति तथा तस्मिन्। विजृम्भिते प्रसृते। परामर्शो गमनम्। तत्रोन्मुखस्योत्काण्ठितस्य। आचार्यकमिवोपदेशमिव। इवशब्दोऽत्रोत्प्रेक्षायाम्। गुरुपरिग्रहो गुरुपत्न्यभिलाषस्तच्छ्लाघिनि श्लाघतेऽसौ तथा तस्मिन्। ग्रहाग्रेसरे ग्रहमुख्ये। क्षपाकरे चन्द्रे। 'नक्षत्रेशः क्षपाकरः' इत्यमरः। मद्दर्शनातिरागो मद्दर्शनेच्छा तेन प्रथमोपनतेन प्रागेव प्राप्तेन। संधुक्षमाणतेजसि प्रवृद्धतेजसि। भुवनविजिगीषा जगद्विजेतुमिच्छा तत्रोद्यते उद्युक्ते। अभजेऽधिष्ठितवान्। क्रियाबलादहमिति पदमध्याहार्यम्। **व्यचीचरं चेति**। अचिन्तयं च। परकलत्रलङ्घनं परस्त्रीगमनम्। धर्मपीडा धर्मनाशः। उपलम्भे प्राप्तौ। शास्त्रकारैर्मन्वादिभिः अनुमतैवानिषिद्धैव। संधिः साधकता। अभिसंधिनेति पाठे 'अभिसंधिरुद्योगः' इति भूषणा। व्यतिक्रमो धर्मनाशरूपः। तदपि पापम्। समग्रयेत्संपूर्णं करिष्यति। **अदृश्यतेति**। हस्तिवक्त्रो गजाननः। दुर्विकल्पो दुर्विचारः। सुरसरिद्गङ्गा। सैवासौ कल्पसुन्दरी। वरवर्णिनी। 'उत्तमा वरवर्णिनी' इत्यमरः। मद्विलोडनं मज्जलेलनं तदसहिष्णुः

---

१ भरिततमसि नभसि. २ उपस्थिते. ३ परिग्रहग्रहण. ४ त्रिभुवन. ५ अभिसंधिना. ६ धर्मः कलया. ७ समाश्रयेत् ८ अदृश्यत स्वप्ने भगवान्भर्गः. ९ मज्जटा. १० तां च कदाचिद्गजाननो जलक्रीडां कुर्वन्नतिव्यगाहत। सा च सपत्नीनयविहितां विलोडनामसहमाना तमशपत।

मर्त्यत्वम्' इति । अशप्यत[1] मया च—'यथेह बहुभोग्या तथा प्राप्यापि मानुष्यकमनेकसाधारणी भव' इति । अभ्यर्थितश्चानया[2] 'एकपूर्वा पुनस्त्वामेवोपचर्य यावज्जीवं रमेयम्' इति । तदयमर्थो भव्य एव भवता निराशङ्क्यः' इति । प्रतिबुध्य च प्रीतियुक्तस्तदहरपि प्रियासंकेतव्यतिकरादिस्मरणेनाहमनैषम् ।

अन्येद्युरनन्यथावृत्तिरनङ्गो मय्येवेषुवर्षमवर्षत् । अशुष्यच्च ज्योतिष्मतः प्रभामयं सरः । प्रासरच्च तिमिरमयः कर्दमः । कार्दमिकनिव[3]सनश्च दृढतरपरिकरः खड्गपाणिरुपहृत[4]प्रकृतोपस्करः स्मरन्मातृदत्तान्यभिज्ञानानि राजमन्दिरपरिखामुदम्भसमुपातिष्ठम् । अथोपखातं मातृगृहद्वारे पुष्करिकया प्रथमसंनिधापितां वेणुयष्टिमादाय तया शायितया च परिखाम्, स्थापितया च प्राकारभित्तिमलङ्घयम्[5] । अधिरुह्य

---

तदसहनशीला । इह बहुभोग्या गङ्गात्वेन । अनेकसाधारणी बहुभोग्या भवेति । अभ्यर्थितः प्रार्थितः । एकः पूर्वं यस्या इति तथा । त्वां द्वितीयम् । उपचर्य संसेव्य । **तदयमिति** । अयमर्थः कल्पसुन्दरीभोगरूपः । भव्य एव कुशल एव । प्रतिबुध्य ज्ञात्वा । तदहस्तद्दिनम् । अनन्यथावृत्तिर्मदेकवृत्तिः । इषुवर्षमिषून्वर्षयित्वेति तथा । णमुल् । अवर्षत ववर्षेत्यर्थः । ज्योतिष्मतः सूर्यस्य । प्रभामयं दीप्तिरूपं सरः । ताद्रूप्ये मयट् । प्रासरत् प्रसरति स्मेत्यर्थः । तिमिरमयोऽन्धकारमयः । कर्दमः पङ्कः । कार्दमिकनिवसनः कर्दमेनाक्तं कार्दमिकम् । 'तेन रक्तं रागात्' इत्यधिकारे 'लाक्षारोचनाट्ठक्' इति सूत्रे 'शकलकर्दमाभ्यामुपसंख्यानम्' इति ठक् । नीलवस्त्रः । दृढतरः परिकरः संनाहो यस्येति सः । उपहृतोऽङ्गीकृतः प्रकृतोपस्करो योग्यसामग्री येनेति स तथा । मातृदत्तानि धात्रीदत्तानि । परिखां प्राचीरसंनिकृष्टखनिम् । उदम्भसमुत्कटजलाम् । उपातिष्ठं समीपमगच्छम् । **अथेति** । उपखातं खातस्य समीपे । सामीप्यार्थेऽव्ययीभावः । प्रथमसंनिधापितां प्रागेव स्थापिताम् । शायितया प्रसारितया । स्थापितयोर्ध्वीकृतया च । पक्वेष्टका भर्जितेष्टकास्ताभिश्चितेन

---

१ सोऽप्यहेतुकशापप्रदानात्क्रुद्धस्तामशपत्. २ ततस्तेन प्रतिशप्ता सा विलक्षेव मामुपसृत्य सगद्गदमगदत्—'स्वामिन्, अहमनवरतभवच्चरणवरिवस्याविधायिनी न शापार्हा ।' इत्याकर्ण्य कृपाक्रान्तमनसा मयोक्तम्—'प्रिये नास्य शापोऽन्यथा भवितुमर्हति । परं त्वदनुग्रहार्थमहमात्मनोंऽशं द्विधा विभज्य विकटवर्मनृपरूपेण मिथिलापतिप्रहारवर्मात्मजोपहारवर्मात्मना च मर्त्यलोकेऽवतरिष्यामि । त्वं च कामरूपाधिपतेः कलिङ्गवर्मनाम्नः कन्या कल्पसुन्दरी नाम भूत्वा ज्यायसा मदंशेन विकटवर्मणा प्रथममल्पीयांसमनेहसं संगता तस्मिन्विकटवर्मणि मन्मूर्ताविव लयमुपगते पुनरुपहारवर्मात्मकं कनीयांसं मदंशमुपलभ्य तेन साकं विविधसुखोपभोगमनुभविष्यसि । तदयमर्थः...इत्यादि. ३ अहं च कार्द०. ४ उपसंहृतप्रस्तुत. ५ अत्यलङ्घयम्.

पक्केष्टकचितेन गोपुरोपरितलाधिरोहिणा[1] सोपानपथेन भुवमवातरम्। अवतीर्णश्च बकुलवीथीमतिक्रम्य चम्पकावलिवर्त्मना मनागिवोपसृत्योत्तराहि करुणं चक्रवाकमिथुनरवमशृणवम्। पुनरुदीचा पाटलिपथेन स्पर्शलभ्यविशाल[2]सौधकुड्योदरेण शरक्षेपमिव गत्वा पुनः प्राचा पिण्डीभाण्डीरखण्डमण्डितोभयपार्श्वेन सैकतपथेन किंचिदुत्तरम्[3]अतिक्रम्य पुनरवाचीं चूतवीथीमगाहिषि। ततश्च गहनतरमुदरोपरचितरत्नवेदिकं माधवीलतामण्डपमीषद्विवृतसमुद्गको[4]न्मिषितभासा दीपवर्त्या न्यरूपयम्। प्रविश्य चैकपार्श्वे फुल्लपुष्पनिरन्तरकुरण्टपोतपङ्क्तिभित्तिपरिगतं गर्भगृहम्, अवनिपतितारुणाशोकलता[5]मयमभिनवकुसुमकोरकपुलकलाञ्छितं प्रत्यग्रप्रवालपटलपाटलं कपाटमुद्घाट्य प्राविक्षम्। तत्र चासीत्स्वास्तीर्णं[6] कुसुमशयनम्, सुरतो[7]पकरणवस्तुगर्भाश्च कमलिनीपलाशसंपुटाः, दन्तमयस्तालवृन्तः, सुरभिसलिलभरितश्च भृङ्गारकः[8]। समुपविश्य मुहूर्तं

---

कृतेन। 'इष्टकेषीकामालानां चिततूलभारिषु' इति ह्रस्वता। गोपुरस्य पुरद्वारस्योपरितलं तत्राधिरोहो यस्येति। सोपानपथेन सोपानमार्गेणावातरम्। चम्पकावलिवर्त्मना चम्पकश्रेणिमार्गेण। मनागिवोपसृत्याल्पमिव गत्वा। उत्तराहीत्यव्ययमुत्तरस्यां दिशि दूरे इत्यर्थे। 'आहि च दूरे' इत्याहिप्रत्ययः। उदीचा उत्तरेणेत्यर्थः। पाटलिपथेन कृष्णवृन्तामार्गेण। सौधं राजसदनम्। कुड्यं भित्तिः। शरक्षेपमिव बाणक्षेपभूमिपर्यन्तमिव। प्राचा पूर्वेण। पिण्डी तगरः। 'पिण्डी स्यात्तगरेऽलाबूखर्जूरीभेदयोरपि।' इति विश्वः। अथ वा 'रक्ताशोके तु पिण्डी स्यात्' इति वैजयन्ती। भाण्डीरो मल्लिका। खण्डं समूहः। तेन मण्डिताबुभौ पार्श्वौ यस्येति तेन। उत्तरमुत्तरप्रदेशम्। अवाचीं दक्षिणाम्। ततश्चेति। ईषदल्पम्। विवृत उद्घाटितः। समुद्गकः संपुटकः। उन्मिषितभासा निःसृतदीप्त्या। एकपार्श्वे एकस्मिन्भागे। फुल्लानि पुष्पाणि येषां ते फुल्लपुष्पाश्च ते निरन्तराश्च कुरण्टपोता अल्पपीतकुरबकाः। 'कुरण्टस्तु सुपीतकः' इत्यमरः। तेषां पङ्क्तिः सैव भित्तिस्तत्परिगतं तद्युक्तम्। गर्भगृहं गर्भागारम्। अवनिपतिताः पृथिव्यां लग्ना अरुणा आरक्ता अशोकलता अशोकशाखास्तन्मयम्। अभिनवा नूतनाः कुसुमकोरकाः पुष्पमुकुलास्त एव पुलकास्तैर्लाञ्छितं चिह्नितम्। प्रत्यग्रं नूतनं प्रवालपटलं पल्लवसमूहस्तेन पाटलं श्वेतरक्तम्। तत्र चेति। स्वास्तीर्णं सुष्ठ्वास्तरणं यस्मिंस्तत्। कुसुमशयनं पुष्पयुक्तं पर्यङ्कम्। सुरतार्थमुपकरणवस्तूनि गर्भे येषामिति। कमलिनीपलाशानां कमलिनीपत्राणाम्। संपुटा द्रोणाः। सुरभिसलिलं सुगन्धोदकं तेन भरितः पूरितः। भृङ्गारकः पात्रविशेषः।

---

१ रोहेण. २ विमलसौधकुट्टिमोदरेण. ३ अन्तरम्. ४ समुद्गकसंपुटको°. ५ शाखा. ६ विस्तीर्णम्. ७ मदनो°. ८ भृङ्गारः.

विश्रान्तः परिमलमतिशयवन्तमाघ्रासिषम् । अश्रौषं च मन्दमन्दं पदशब्दम् । श्रुत्वैव संकेतगृहान्निर्गत्य रक्ताशोकस्कन्धपार्श्वव्यवहिताङ्गयष्टिः स्थितोऽस्मि । सा च सुभ्रूः[1]सुषीमकामा शनैरुपेत्य तत्र मामदृष्ट्वा बलवदव्यथिष्ट । व्यसृजच्च मत्तराजहंसीव कण्ठरागवल्गुगद्गदां गिरम्—'व्यक्तमस्मि विप्रलब्धा । नास्त्युपायः प्राणितुम् । अयि हृदय किमिदमकार्यं कार्यवद[2]ध्यवस्य तदसंभवेन[3] किमेवमुत्ताम्यसि । भगवन्पञ्चबाण कस्तवापराधः कृतो मया यदेवं दहसि न च भस्मीकरोषि' इति । अथाहमाविर्भूय विवृतदीपभाजनः 'भामिनि ननु बह्वपराद्धं भवत्या चित्तजन्मनो यदमुष्य जीवितभूता[4] रतिराकृत्या कदर्थिता, धनुर्यष्टि[5]र्भ्रूलताभ्याम्, भ्रमरमाला[6]मयी ज्या नीलालकद्युतिभिः, अस्त्राण्यपाङ्गवीक्षित[7]वृष्टिभिः, महारजनध्वजपटांशुकं दन्तच्छदमयूखजालैः, प्रथमसुहृ[8]न्मलयमारुतः परिमल-

'भृङ्गारः कनकालुका' इत्यमरः । रक्ताशोकस्कन्धस्य पार्श्वे व्यवहिताऽङ्गयष्टिर्यस्येति सुषीमः शिशिरः कामो यस्याः सा । 'सुषीमः शिशिरो जडः' इत्यमरः । 'असुषीमकामा तीव्रमन्मथा' इति भूषणा । बलवदत्यर्थम् । अव्यथिष्ट । व्यथां प्रापेत्यर्थः । वल्गुः सुन्दरो गद्गदो यस्यां तथा ताम् । विप्रलब्धा प्रतारिता । 'विप्रलब्धा प्रियं तत्रादृष्ट्वा संतापसंकुला' इति रसरत्नहारः—इति भूषणा । अयीति खेदोक्त्या कोमलामन्त्रणे । अध्यवस्य निश्चित्य । तदसंभवेन कार्यासंभवेन । उत्ताम्यस्युत्तप्तं भवसि । दहसि दाहमात्रं करोषि । परं तु न भस्मीकरोषीति । भस्मीकरणे दुःखानुभवव्यथा न स्यादिति भावः । **अथाहमिति** । आविर्भूय प्रकटीभूय । विवृतदीपभाजन उद्घाटितदीपपात्रः । भामिनीति सकोपकामिनीसंबोधनम् । 'कोपना सैव भामिनी' इत्यमरः । चित्तजन्मनो मदनस्य । यद्यस्मात् । अमुष्य चित्तजन्मनः । आकृत्या आकारेण कदर्थिताऽधिक्षिप्ता । ज्या मौर्वी । नीला श्यामा येऽलकाः कुन्तलास्तेषां द्युतिभिः कान्तिभिः । अपाङ्गवीक्षितं नेत्रप्रान्तदर्शनम् । तद्वृष्टिभिः । महारजनं कुसुम्भम् । 'स्यात्कुसुम्भं वह्निशिखं महारजनमित्यपि ।' इत्यमरः । तद्युक्तो यो ध्वजपटः पताकावस्त्रं तस्यांशुरेवांशुकम् । दन्तच्छद ओष्ठः । जालैः समूहैः । प्रथमसुहृन्मुख्यमित्रम् । परिमलपटीयसा सौगन्ध्यसमर्थेन । परभृतरुतं

१ सुषी (शी) मकामा. २ अध्यवसाय. ३ ०संभवे. ४ ०भूतां रतिमाकृत्या कदर्थितवती. ५ धनुर्यष्टिम्. ६ ०मयीं ज्याम्. ७ वीक्षितैः. ८ सुहृदं...मारुतम्.

पटीयसा निःश्वासपवनेन, परभृतरुतैमतिमञ्जुलैः प्रलापैः, पुष्पमयी[2] पताका भुजयष्टिभ्याम्, दिग्विजयारम्भपूर्णकुम्भमिथुनमुरोजकुम्भयुगलेन, क्रीडासरो नाभिमण्डलेन, संनाह्यरथैः[3] श्रोणिमण्डलेन, भवरत्नतोरणस्तम्भयुगलमूरुयुगलेन, लीलाकर्णकिसलयं चरणतलप्रभाभिः । अतः स्थान एव त्वां दुनोति मीनकेतुः । मां पुनरनपराधमधिकमायासयतीत्येष एव तस्य दोषः । तत्प्रसीद सुन्दरि, जीवय मां जीवनौषधिभिरिवापाङ्गैरनङ्गभुजङ्गदष्टम् ।' इत्याश्लिष्टवान् । अरीरमं चानङ्गरागपेशलविशाललोचनाम् । अवसितार्थां चारक्तवलितेक्षणाम्, ईषत्स्वेदरेखोद्भेदजर्जरितकपोलमूलाम्, अनर्गलकलप्रलापिनीम्, अरुणदशनकररुहार्पणव्यतिकराम्, अत्यर्थपरिश्लथाङ्गीमार्तामिव लक्षयित्वा मानसीं शारीरीं च धारणां शिथिलयन्नात्मानमपि तया समानाथमापादयम् । तत्क्षणविमुक्तसंगतौ रतावसानिकं विधिमनुभवन्तौ चिरपरिचिताविवातिगूढविश्रम्भौ क्षणमवातिष्ठावहि । पुनरहमुष्णमायतं च निःश्वस्य किंचिद्दीनदृष्टिः

कोकिलरवः । अतिमञ्जुलैरतिमनोज्ञैः । 'मनोज्ञं मञ्जु मञ्जुलम्' इत्यमरः । दिग्विजयारम्भे पूर्णकुम्भमिथुनं पूर्णघटद्वन्द्वम् । उरोजकुम्भौ स्तनकलशौ । संनाह्यरथः संग्रामार्थं सज्जीकृतो रथः । रत्नयुक्तौ तोरणस्तम्भौ तयोर्युगलम् । कर्णकिसलयं कर्णावतंसपल्लवम् । स्थाने युक्तमित्यर्थः । 'युक्ते द्वे सांप्रतं स्थाने' इत्यमरः । जीवनौषधिभिरिवापाङ्गैरित्यत्रोपमेयोपमानभावश्चन्द्रमुखवज्ज्ञेयः । **अरीरममिति** । अनङ्गरागेण मदनरागेण पेशले रम्ये विशाले लोचने यस्यास्ताम् । अवसितार्थां कृतार्थाम् । वलितं वक्रितमीक्षणमवलोकनं यस्याः । स्वेदरेखा घर्मराजिस्तस्या उद्भेदः प्रारम्भस्तेन जर्जरितं क्लिष्टं कपोलमूलं यस्यास्ताम् । अनर्गलोऽप्रतिहतः कलकलः कोलाहलस्तं प्रलपतीति ताम् । अरुणं यद्दशनकररुहं दन्तनखं तस्यार्पणं करणं तद्व्यतिकरो यस्याः । श्लथाङ्गीं निःसहावयवाम् । मानसीं शारीरीं च धारणाम् । 'शरीरधारणा यत्तु भौतिकं तु निरीक्षणम् । मानसं तु मुनीनां स्यादाश्रमेषु विसर्पणम् । अभ्यासं धारयेद्रेतो यावत्स्यात्कृतिनिर्वृतिः ॥' इति वात्स्यायनीये कामशास्त्रे । तया नायिकया । समानाथमापादयं समापादयम् । **तदिति** । विमुक्तौ च तौ संगतौ चेति । अनाश्लिष्टस्थिताविति भावः । रतावसानिकं सुरतान्तसमयोचितम् । विधिं व्यापारम् । अतिगूढविश्रम्भावतिगुप्तविश्वासौ । क्षणं किंचित्कालम् । आयतं दीर्घम् । प्रयातमेव गतमेव । गणय जानीही-

१ कुलम्. २ ० मयी पताकाम्. ३ रथमण्डलम्. ४ अनङ्गरागावेशपेशलो विशाल०. ५ चिकुरितेक्षणाम्. ६ कलकलप्रलापिनीम्. ७ अकरुण. ८ अतिरूढ. ९ तदा ऽस्त्वयोर्वियोगकाले समुपायान्ति पुनरहमुष्णम्.

सचकितप्रसारिताभ्यां भुजाभ्यामेनामनतिपीडं परिष्वज्य नातिविशदमचुम्बिषम्। अश्रुमुखी तु सा 'यदि प्रयासि नाथ प्रयातमेव मे जीवितं गणय। नय मामपि। न चेदसौ दासजनो निष्प्रयोजनः' इत्यञ्जलिमवतंसतामनैषीत्। अवादिषं च ताम्—'अयि मुग्धे कः सचेतनः स्त्रियमभिकामयमानां नाभिनन्दति। यदि मदनुग्रहनिश्चलस्तवाभिसंधिराचराविचारं मदुपदिष्टम्। आदर्शय रहसि राज्ञे मत्सादृश्यगर्भं चित्रपटम्। आचक्ष्व च—'किमियमाकृतिः पुरुषसौन्दर्यस्य पारमारूढा न वा' इति। 'बाढमारूढा' इति नूनमसौ वक्ष्यति। ब्रूहि भूयः—'यद्येवम्, अस्ति काऽपि तापसी देशान्तरभ्रमणलब्धप्रागल्भ्या मम च मातृभूता। तयेदमालेख्यरूपं पुरस्कृत्याहमुक्ता—'सोऽस्ति तादृशो मन्त्रो येन त्वमुपोषिता पर्वणि विविक्तायां भूमौ पुरोहितैर्हुतमुक्ते सप्तार्चिषि नक्तमेकाकिनी शतं चन्दनसमिधः, शतमगुरुसमिधः, कर्पूरमुष्टीः, पट्टवस्त्राणि च प्रभूतानि हुत्वा भविष्यस्येवमाकृतिः। अथ चालयिष्यसि घण्टाम्। घण्टापुटक्वणिताहूतश्च भर्ता भवत्यै सर्वरहस्यमाख्याय निमीलिताक्षो यदि त्वामालिङ्गेत्, इयमाकृतिरमुमुपसंक्रामेत्। त्वं तु भविष्यसि यथा पुराकारैव। यदि भवत्यै भवत्प्रियाय चैवं

त्यर्थः। असौ मद्रूपः। निष्प्रयोजनोऽकिंचित्कर इति यावत्। अवतंसतां शिरोभूषणताम्। अभिकामयमानामभिकामयतेऽसौ तथा। स्वयमनुरक्तामित्यर्थः। यदीति। अभिसंधिरभिप्रायः। रहस्येकान्ते। मत्सादृश्यगर्भं मत्सदृशरूपयुक्तम्। इयमाकृतिश्चित्रपटस्था। काऽप्यपरिमितशक्तिः। देशान्तरभ्रमणेनानेकदेशगमनेन लब्धं प्रागल्भ्यं प्रगल्भता ययेति सा। तादृशः प्रभाववानित्यर्थः। उपोषिताऽऽहारवर्जिता। 'उपवासः स विज्ञेयः सर्वाहारविवर्जितः।' इति स्मृतेः। पर्वण्यमावास्यादौ। विविक्तायां पूतायां विजनायां वा। 'विविक्तौ पूतविजनौ' इति कोशः। पूर्वं हुतः पश्चान्मुक्तस्तस्मिन्। सप्तार्चिष्यग्नौ। नक्तं रात्रौ। एकाकिनीत्यत्र 'एकादाकिनिच्चासहाये' इत्याकिनिच्प्रत्ययः। अद्वितीयेत्यर्थः। समिध इति द्वितीयाबहुवचनम्। कर्पुरमुष्टीः बद्धकरपरिमितकर्पूरानित्यर्थः। 'मुष्टिर्बद्धकरे' इति विश्वः। एवमाकृतिश्चित्रफलकलिखिताकृतिः। क्वणितं प्रतिशब्दः। 'क्वणितं प्रतिशब्दः स्याद्वीणानादः' इति। उपसंक्रामेत्। संक्रान्ता भविष्यतीत्यर्थः। पुराकारा पूर्वा-

१ परमा०. २ सर्वं रहस्यजातम्.

रोचेत[1], न चास्मिन्विधौ विसंवादः कार्यः[2]' इति । वपुश्चेदिदं तवाभिमतं सह सुहृन्मन्त्रिभिरनुजैः पौरजानपदैश्च संप्रधार्य[3] तेषामप्यनुमते कर्मण्य[4]भिमुखेन स्थेयम्' इति । स नियतमभ्युपैष्यति । पुनरस्यामेव प्रमदवनवाटी[5]शृङ्गाटिकायामाथर्वणिकेन विधिना संज्ञपितपशुनाऽभिहुत्य मुक्ते हिरण्यरेतसि तद्धूम[6]शमनेन संप्रविष्टेन मयाऽस्मिन्नेव लतामण्डपे स्थातव्यम् । त्व पुनः प्रगाढाया प्रदोषवेलायामालपिष्यसि कर्णे कृतनर्मस्मिता विकटवर्माणम्—'धूर्तोऽसि त्वमकृतज्ञश्च । मदनुग्रहलब्धेनापि रूपेण लोकलोचनोत्सवायमानेन मत्सपत्नीरभिरमयिष्यसि । नाहमात्मविनाशाय वेतालोत्थापनमाचरेयम्' इति । श्रुत्वेदं त्वद्वचः स यद्वदिष्यति[7] तन्मह्यमेकाकिन्युपागत्य निवेदयिष्यसि । ततः परमहमेव ज्ञास्यामि । मत्पदचिह्नानि चोपवने पुष्करिकया प्रमार्जय' इति । सा 'तथा' इति शास्त्रोपदेशमिव मदुक्तमादृत्यातृप्तसुरतरागैव कथंकथमप्यगादन्तःपुरम् । अहमपि यथाप्रवेशं निर्गत्य स्वमेवावासमयासिषम् ।

अथ सा मत्तकाशिनी तथा तमर्थमन्वतिष्ठत् । अतिष्ठच्च तन्मते स दुर्मतिः । अभ्रमच्च पौरजानपदेष्वियमद्भुतायमाना वार्ता—'राजा

कृतिः । अस्मिन्विधौ अस्मिन्प्रयोजने । विसंवादः । 'विसंवादोऽन्यथाभावः' इति वैजयन्ती । अन्यथाभावो न कार्यः । अभिमतं संमतम् । संप्रधार्य निश्चित्य । 'निर्णयः संप्रधारणम्' इति । शृङ्गाटिकायामल्पचतुष्पथे । 'शृङ्गाटकचतुष्पथे' इत्यमरः । आथर्वणिकेन पुरोहितेन । संज्ञपितो मारितो यः पशुस्तेन । 'संज्ञपितं विशसितं समालब्धम्' इति वररुचिः । अभिहुत्य हुत्वा । हिरण्यरेतस्यग्नौ । **त्वं पुनरिति** । प्रगाढायामतिदृढायाम् । प्रदोषवेलायां रजनीमुखसमये । आलपिष्यसि वदिष्यसि । कृतं नर्मस्मितं परिहासहसितं ययेति सा । धूर्तो वञ्चकः । मदनुग्रहलब्धेन मत्प्रसादप्राप्तेन । लोकलोचनानां लोकनेत्राणामुत्सववदाचरतीति तथा तेन । वेतालोत्थापनं भूतविशेषोत्पादनम् । प्रमार्जय प्रोञ्छय । अतृप्तसुरतरागैवासंपूर्णसुरतेच्छैव । कथंकथमपि महता प्रबन्धेन । आवासं वसतिस्थानम् । **अथेति** । मत्तकाशिन्युत्तमाङ्गना । 'वरारोहा मत्तकाशिन्युत्तमा वरवर्णिनी' इत्यमरः । तमर्थं मदुपदिष्टं प्रयोजनम् । अन्वतिष्ठत् अकरोदित्यर्थः । स दुर्मतिर्विकटवर्मा । पौरजानपदेषु नागरिकलोकसंघेषु । अद्भुतायमाना आश्चर्यायमाणा ।

१ रोचते. २ शङ्क्यः. ३ संमन्त्र्य. ४ कर्मण्यस्मिन्. ५ वीथी. ६ धूमपटलेन सह ७ वक्ष्यति.

किल विकटवर्मा देवीमन्त्रबलेन देवयोग्यं वपुरासादयिष्यति । नूनमेषै विप्रलम्भो नातिकल्याणः । कैव कथा प्रमादस्य । स्वस्मिंन्नेवान्तःपुरोपवने स्वाग्रमहिष्यैव संपाद्यः किलायमर्थः । तथा हि बृहस्पतिप्रतिमबुद्धिभिर्मन्त्रिभिरप्यैभ्यूह्यानुमतः । यद्येवं भावि नान्यदतः परमस्ति किंचिदद्भुतम् । अचिन्त्यो हि मणिमन्त्रौषधीनां प्रभावः । ' इति प्रसृतेषु लोकप्रवादेषु प्राप्ते पर्वदिवसे प्रगाढाया प्रौढतमसि प्रदोषवेलायामन्तःपुरोद्यानादुदैरैयद्धूर्जटिकण्ठधूम्रो धूमोद्गमः । क्षीराज्यदधितिलगौरसर्षपवसामांसरुधिराहुतीनां च परिमलः पवनानुसारी दिशि दिशि प्रावात्सीत् । प्रशान्ते च सहसा धूमोद्गमे तस्मिन्नहमविशम् । निशान्तोद्यानमागमच्च गजगामिनी । आलिङ्ग्य च मां सस्मितं समभ्यधत्त—' धूर्त सिद्धं ते समीहितम् । अवसितश्च पशुरसौ । अमुष्य प्रलोभनाय त्वदादिष्टया दिशा मयोक्तम्—' कितव न साधयामि ते सौन्दर्यम् । एवं सुन्दरो हि त्वमप्सरसामपि स्पृहणीयो भविष्यसि किमुत मानुषीणाम् । मधुकर

---

नूनं ध्रुवमेष विप्रलम्भो वञ्चना न किं त्वतिकल्याणः अतिशुभः । कैव कथा प्रमादस्य प्रमादः कथमपि न स्यादित्यर्थः । स्वाग्रमहिषी । ' कृताभिषेका महिषी ' इत्यमरः । **तथा हीति** । बृहस्पतिप्रतिमा गुरुसमाना बुद्धिर्येषामिति तैः । अभ्यूह्य वितर्क्य । भावि भविष्यत् । प्रसृतेष्वितस्ततो गतेषु । लोकप्रवादेषु जनवार्तासु । प्राप्ते पर्वदिवसेऽमावास्यायाम् । प्रौढतमसि गाढतमसि । अन्तःपुरस्योद्यानमुपवनम् । उदैरयदुदगच्छत् । धूर्जटिकण्ठवद् धूम्रः कृष्णलोहितः । धूमोद्गमो धूमप्रारम्भः । **क्षीरेति** । आज्यं घृतम् । तिलाश्च गौरसर्षपाः सिद्धार्थाश्च । ' सिद्धार्थस्त्वेष धवलः ' इत्यमरः । वसा वपा । रुधिरं चैतेषामाहुतीनाम् । परिमलो गन्धः । पवनानुसारी यथावायुगामी । दिशि दिशि प्रतिदिशम् । प्रावात्सीत् । आगच्छदित्यर्थः । प्रशान्ते विनष्टे । निशान्तोद्यानं गृहोपवनम् । ' निशान्तवस्त्यसदनम् ' इत्यमरः । समभ्यधत्त । उवाचेत्यर्थः । समीहितमीप्सितम् । अवसितोऽवसानं प्राप्तः । पक्षे कृतनिश्चयः । अमुष्येति । त्वदादिष्टया दिशा । त्वदादिष्टेन मार्गेणेत्यर्थः । स्पृहणीयः

---

१ एष न विप्रलम्भोऽतिक०. २ अभूदनुमतः. ३ उदैरत. ४ चोपप्रलोभनाय.

इव निसर्गचपलो[1] यत्र क्वचिदासज्जति भवादृशो नृशंसः' इति। तेन तु मे पादयोर्निपत्याभिहितम्—'रम्भोरु सहस्व मत्कृतानि दुश्चरितानि[2]। मनसाऽपि न चिन्तयेयमितः परमितरनारीम्। त्वरस्व प्रस्तुते[3] कर्मणि' इति। तदहमीदृशेन वैवाहिकेन नेपथ्येन त्वामभिसृतवती। प्रागपि रागाग्निसाक्षिकमनङ्गेन गुरुणा दत्तैव तुभ्यमेषा जाया। पुनरपीमं जातवेदसं साक्षीकृत्य स्वहृदयेन दत्ता' इति प्रपदेन[4] चरणपृष्ठे निष्पीड्योत्क्षिप्तपादपार्ष्णिरितरेतरव्यतिषक्तकोमलाङ्गुलिदलेन[5] भुजलताद्वयेन कंधरां ममावेष्ट्य सलीलमाननमानमय्य स्वयमुन्नामितमुखकमला विभ्रान्तविशालदृष्टिरसकृदभ्यचुम्बत्।

अथैनाम् 'इहैव कुरण्टकगुल्मगर्भे तिष्ठ यावदहं निर्गत्य साधयेयं साध्यं सम्यक्' इति विसृज्य तामुपसृत्य होमानलप्रदेशमशोकशाखावलम्बिनीं घण्टामचालयम्। अकूजच्च सा तं जनं कृतान्तदूतीवाह्वयन्ती। प्रावर्तिषि चाहमगुरु[6]चन्दनप्रमुखानि होतुम्। आयासीच्च राजा यथोक्तं देशम्। शङ्का-

---

अभिलषणीयः। यत्र क्वचिद्यत्र कुत्रापि। आसज्जत्यासक्तो भवति। नृशंसः क्रूरः। प्रस्तुत उपक्रान्ते। वैवाहिकेन विवाहसंबन्धिना। नेपथ्येन वेषेण। राग एवाग्निः रागाग्निरिच्छाग्निः। गुरुणा पितृभूतेनेत्यर्थः। जातं वेदो धनं यस्मात् जातं वेत्ति वेदयते वा इति जातवेदाः तं जातवेदसमग्निम्। प्रपदं पादाग्रम्। 'पादाग्रं प्रपदम्' इत्यमरः। **उत्क्षिप्तेति**। 'पादोत्क्षेपणादेव पार्ष्ण्युत्क्षेपेऽपि गोबलीवर्दन्यायात्पृथगुक्तिः' इति भूषणा। इतरेतरं परस्परम्। व्यतिषक्तं मिलितम्। इतरेतरं व्यतिषिक्तानि कोमलाङ्गुलिदलानि यस्य तेन। कंधरां ग्रीवाम्। **अथेति**। कुरण्टकाः पीतकुरबकाः। 'तत्र शोणे कुरबकस्तत्र पीते कुरण्टकः' इत्यमरः। तेषां गुल्मः स्तम्बः। 'अप्रकाण्डे स्तम्बगुल्मौ' इत्यमरः। साध्यं कार्यम्। अचालयं चालितवानस्मि। तं जनं विकटवर्मरूपम्। कृतान्तदूतीव यमदूतीव। प्रावर्तिषि प्रवृत्तोऽभवम्। **आयासीदिति**। अत्र कामन्दकः—'न हि देवीगृहं गच्छेदात्मीयात्संनिवेशनात्। अत्यन्तवल्लभोऽपीह विश्वासं स्त्रीषु न व्रजेत्॥ देवीगृह-

---

१ निसर्गचापलात्. २ दुश्चरित्राणि. ३ प्रकृते. ४ पादाग्रेण. ५ तलेन. ६ अगरु.

पन्नमिव किंचित्सविस्मयं [1]विचार्य तिष्ठन्तमब्रवम्—'ब्रूहि सत्यं भूयोऽपि मे भगवन्त चित्रभानुमेव साक्षीकृत्य। न चेदनेन रूपेण मत्सपत्नीरभिरमयिष्यसि ततस्त्वयीदं रूपं [2]संक्रामयेयम्' इति। स तदैव देव्येवेयम्, नोपधिः, इति स्फुटोपजातसंप्रत्ययः प्रावर्तत शपथाय। स्मित्वा पुनर्मयोक्तम्—'किं वा शपथेन। कैव हि मानुषी मां परिभविष्यति। यद्यप्सरोभिः संगच्छसे, संगच्छस्व कामम्। कथय कानि ते रहस्यानि। तत्कथनान्ते हि त्वत्स्वरूपभ्रंशः' इति। सोऽब्रवीत्—'अस्ति बद्धो मत्पितुः [3]कनीयान्भ्राता प्रहारवर्मा। तं विषान्नेन व्यापाद्याजीर्णदोषं ख्यापयेयमिति मन्त्रिभिः सहाध्यवसितम्। अनुज्ञाय विशालवर्मणे दण्डचक्रं [4]पुण्ड्रदेशाभिक्रमणाय दित्सितम्। पौरवृद्धश्च पाञ्चालिकः परित्रातश्च सार्थवाहः [5]खनतिनाम्नो यवनाद्वज्रमेकं वसुंधरामूल्यं लघीयसाऽर्घेण लभ्यमिति ममैकान्तेऽमन्त्रयेताम्। गृहपतिश्च ममान्तरङ्गभूतो जनपदमहत्तरः शतहलिरलीकवादशीलमवलेपवन्तं दुष्टग्रामण्यमनन्तसीरं जनपद-

---

गतं भ्राता भद्रसेनमारयत्। मातुः शय्यान्तरे लीनः कारूषं चौरसः सुतः॥ लाजान्विषेण संयोज्य मधुनेति विलोभितम्। देवी तु काशिराजेन्द्रं निजघान रहोगतम्॥ विषाक्तेन च सौवीरं मेखलामणिना नृपम्। नूपुरेण च वैरन्त्यं जारूषं दर्पणेन च॥ वेण्यां शस्त्रं समाधाय तथैव च विदूरथम्। अहिवृत्तं परिहरेच्छत्रौ चापि प्रयोजयेत॥' इति। शङ्कापन्नमिव प्राप्तसंशयमिव। चित्रभानुमग्निम्। संक्रामयेयं योजयेयम्। उपधिः कपटम्। उपजातसंप्रत्ययः प्राप्तविश्वासः। कामं यथेष्टम्। विषान्नेन विषमिश्रणान्नेन। अजीर्णदोषं विषूचिकाम्। अध्यवसितं निश्चितम्। दण्डचक्रं सेनाचक्रम्। 'दण्डो यमे मानभेदे लगुडे दमसैन्ययोः' इति विश्वः। पुण्ड्रदेशाभिक्रमणाय तद्देशग्रहणाय। दित्सितं दातुमभिलषितम्। पाञ्चालिकस्तन्नामा। सार्थवाहस्तन्नामा। वज्रं हीरकम्। गृहपतिर्ग्रामाध्यक्षः। 'ग्रामाध्यक्षो गृहपतिः' इति कोशः। अन्तरङ्गभूतः आत्मभूतः। जनपदमहत्तरो देशश्रेष्ठः। 'नीवृज्जनपदो देशविषयौ तूपवर्तनम्' इत्यमरः। शतहलिः शतं हला यस्येति तथा। अलीकवादशीलं मिथ्याभाषणस्वभावम्। अवलेपवन्तं सगर्वम्। दुष्टश्चासौ ग्रामणीश्च तम्। अनन्तसीरमेतन्नामकम्। जनपदकोपेन लोकक्रोधेन। दण्डधरः

---

१ निचाय्य. २ संक्रम०. ३ कनिष्ठः प्रहार०. ४ पुण्ड्राभियोगाय. ५ असभीति.

कोपेन घातयेयमिति दण्डधरानुद्धारकर्माणि मत्प्रयोगान्नियोक्तुमभ्युपागमत्। इत्थमिदमाचिरप्रस्तुतं[1] रहस्यम्' इत्याकर्ण्य तम् 'दुरात्मन्। उपपद्यस्व स्वकर्मोचितां गतिम्' इति च्छुरिकया द्विधाकृत्य कृत्त[2]मात्रं तास्मिन्नेव प्रवृत्तस्फीतसर्पिषि हिरण्यरेतस्यजुहवम्। अभूच्चासौ भस्मसात्। अथ स्त्रीस्वभावादीषद्विह्वलां हृदयवल्लभां समाश्वास्य हस्तकिसलयेऽवलम्ब्य गत्वा तद्गृहमनुज्ञयाऽस्याः सर्वाण्यन्तःपुराण्याहूय सद्य एव सेवां दत्तवान्। सविस्मितविलासिनीसार्थमध्ये कंचिद्विहृत्य कालं विसृष्टावरोधमण्डलस्तामेव संहतोरूमूरूपपीडं[3] भुजोपपीडं चोपगूह्य तल्पेऽभिरमयन्नल्पामिव तां निशामत्यनैषम्। अलभे च तन्मुखात्तद्राजकुलस्य शीलम्। उषसि स्नात्वा कृतमङ्गलो मन्त्रिभिः सह समगच्छे। तांश्चाब्रवम्—'आर्याः, रूपेणैव सह परिवृत्तो मम स्वभावः। य एष विषान्नेन हन्तुं चिन्तितः पिता मे स मुक्त्वा स्वमेतद्राज्यं[4] भूय एव ग्राहयितव्यः। पितृवदमुष्मिन्वयं शुश्रूषयैव वर्तामहे। न ह्यस्ति पितृवधात्परं पातकम्' इति। भ्रातरं च विशालवर्माणमाहूयोक्तवान्—'वत्स न सुभिक्षाः सांप्रतं पुण्ड्राः। ते दुःखमोहोपहतास्त्यक्तात्मानो राष्ट्रं नः संमृद्धमभिद्रवेयुः[5]। अतो मुष्टिवधः[6]

सेनापतिः। उद्धारकर्माणि निर्याणकर्माणि। नियोक्तुं नियोजयितुम्। उपपद्यस्व प्राप्नुहि। भस्मसाद्रक्षावशेषः। 'विभाषा सातिः कार्त्स्न्यें' इति सातिप्रत्ययः। हस्तकिसलये पाणिपल्लवे। सविस्मितः साश्चर्यः। विलासिनीसार्थः स्त्रीसमूहः। विसृष्टावरोधमण्डलो विसर्जितान्तःपुरस्त्रीसमूहः। तामेव कल्पसुन्दरीमेव। ऊर्वोरुपपीडा यत्रेति क्रियाविशेषणम्। 'सप्तम्यां चोपपीडरुधकर्षः' इति णमुल् इति तु भूषणा। भुजोपपीडं च गाढालिङ्गनपूर्वकमिति भावः। तान्मन्त्रिणः। परिवृत्तः परावृत्तिं प्राप्तः। "पितृवत् पितरीव। 'तत्र तस्येव' इति वतिः" इति भूषणा। अमुष्मिन्प्रहारवर्मणि। शुश्रूषया सेवया। सुभिक्षाः समृद्धान्नाः। नोऽस्माकम्। समृद्धं सस्यादिसंपन्नम्। मुष्टिवधो बीजप्रक्षेपघातः। सस्यवधः परिणत-

१ प्रसृतम्. २ कृत्तगात्रम्. ३ ऊरुपीडमुरःपीडं च. ४ स्वयमेव तद्राज्यम्. ५ सुभिक्षम्. ६ वधः.

स्थवधो वा यदोत्पद्यते तदाऽभियास्यसि। नाद्य यात्रा युक्ता' इति। नगरवृद्धावप्यलापिषम—'अल्पीयसा मूल्येन महार्हं वज्रवस्तु माऽस्तु मे लभ्यं धर्मरक्षायै, तदनुगुणेनैव मूल्येनादः क्रीयताम्' इति। शतहलिं च राष्ट्रमुख्यमाहूयाख्यातवान्—'योऽसावनन्तसीरः प्रहारवर्मणः पक्ष इति निनाशयिषितः, सोऽपि पितरि मे प्रकृतिस्थे किमिति नाश्येत, तत्त्वयाऽपि तस्मिन्संरम्भो न कार्यः' इति। त इमे सर्वमाभिज्ञानिकमुपलभ्य 'स एवायम्' इति निश्चित्वाना विस्मयमानाश्च मां महादेवीं च प्रशंसन्तो मन्त्रबलानि चोद्घोषयन्तो बन्धनात्पितरौ निष्क्राम्य्य स्वं राज्यं प्रत्यपादयन्। अहं च तया मे धात्र्या सर्वमिदं मम चेष्टितं रहसि पित्रोरवगमय्य प्रहर्षकाष्ठाधिरूढयोस्तयोः पादमूलमभजे। अभज्ये च यौवराज्यलक्ष्म्या तदनुज्ञातया। प्रसाधितात्मा देवपादविरहदुःखदुर्भगान्भोगान्निर्विशन्भूयोऽस्य पितृसखस्य सिंहवर्मणो लेख्याच्चण्डवर्मणश्चम्पाभियोगमवगम्य 'शत्रुवधो मित्ररक्षा चोभयमपि करणीयमेव' इत्यलघुना लघुसमुत्थानेन सैन्यचक्रेणाभ्यसरम्। अभूवं च भूमिस्त्वत्पादलक्ष्मीसाक्षात्क्रियामहोत्सवानन्दराशेः' इति।

श्रुत्वैतद्देवो राजवाहनः सस्मितमवादीत्—'पश्यत पारतल्पिकमुपधियुक्तमपि गुरुजनबन्धव्यसनमुक्तिहेतुतया दुष्टामित्रप्रमापणाभ्युपायतया राज्योपलब्धिमूलतया च पुष्कलावर्थधर्मावप्यरीरधत्।

---

धान्यच्छेदः। "यानकालमाह याज्ञवल्क्यः—'यदा सस्यगुणोपेतं परराष्ट्रं तदा व्रजेत्' इति।" इति भूषणा। नगरवृद्धौ पाञ्चालिकसार्थवाहौ। महार्हं बहुमूल्यम्। तदनुगुणेन वज्रमण्यनुकूलेन। पक्षः सहायः। निनाशयिषितो नाशयितुमिष्टः। प्रकृतिस्थे स्वराज्यस्थिते। तस्मिन्ननन्तसीरनाशे। संरम्भ आदरः। आभिज्ञानिकमभिज्ञानम्। स्वार्थे ठक्। महादेवीं राजपत्नीम्। उद्घोषयन्तः प्रकटयन्तः। प्रत्यपादयन्ददुः। प्रहर्षकाष्ठा संतोषमर्यादा। प्रसाधितात्मोपयुक्तबुद्धिः। देवस्त्वं राजवाहनः। दुर्भगान् विरसान्। निर्विशन्नुपभुञ्जन्। चम्पाभियोगं चम्पोपद्रावणम्। लघुसमुत्थानेन शीघ्रगामिना। अभ्यसरं गतवान्। भूमिः स्थानम्। त्वत्पादलक्ष्मीस्त्वच्चरणशोभा तस्याः साक्षात्क्रिया प्रत्यक्षीकरणं स एव महोत्सवः। पारतल्पिकं परस्त्रीगमनम्। कर्तृ। उपधियुक्तं कपटयुक्तम्। गुरुजनः पितृजनः। व्यसनं दुःखम्। प्रमापणं मरणम्। राज्योपलब्धिः राज्यप्राप्तिः। पुष्कलौ

---

१ वज्रम्; वस्तु. २ मूल्येनादानं क्रियताम्. ३ निष्क्रमय्य.

किं हि बुद्धिमत्प्रयुक्तं नाभ्युपैति शोभाम्' इति । अर्थपालमुखे निधाय स्निग्धदीर्घां दृष्टिम् 'आचष्टां भवानात्मीयचरितम्' इत्यादिदेश । सोऽपि बद्धाञ्जलिरभिदधे—

इति श्रीदण्डिनः कृतौ दशकुमारचरित उपहारवर्मचरितं नाम तृतीय उच्छ्वासः ।

---

## चतुर्थोच्छ्वासः ।

देव सोऽहमप्येभिरेव सुहृद्भिरेककर्मोर्मिमालिनेमिभूमिवलयं परिभ्रमन्नुपासरं कदाचित्काशीपुरीं वाराणसीम् । उपस्पृश्य मणिभङ्गनिर्मलाम्भसि मणिकर्णिकायामविमुक्तेश्वरं भगवन्तमन्धकमथनमभिप्रणम्य प्रदक्षिणं परिभ्रमन्पुरुषमेकमायामवन्तमायसपरिघपीवराभ्यां भुजाभ्यामाबध्यमानपरिकरमविरतरुदितोच्छूनताम्रदृष्टिमद्राक्षम् । अतर्कयं च—'कर्कशोऽयं पुरुषः, कार्पण्यमिव वर्षति क्षीणतारं चक्षुः, आरम्भश्च साहसानुवादी । नूनमसौ प्राणनिःस्पृहः किमपि कृच्छ्रं प्रियजनव्यसनमूलं प्रेपित्सते । तत्पृच्छेयमेनमस्ति चेन्ममापि कोऽपि साहाय्यदानावकाशः' तमेनमभ्युपेत्येत्यपृच्छम्—'भद्र संनाहोऽयं साहसमवगमयति । न चेद्गोप्यमिच्छामि श्रोतुं शोकहेतुम्' इति । स मां सबहुमानं

---

बहुतरौ । अरीरधदसाधयत् । 'राध साध संसिद्धौ' । अर्थपालो दशकुमारेष्वन्यतमः तस्य मुखे । अभिदधे वक्तुमुपचक्रमे ।

इति श्रीदशकुमारचरितटीकायां तृतीय उच्छ्वासः ।

---

**देवेति** । एककर्मा अनन्यकार्यः । कर्म च भवदन्वेषणम् । ऊर्मिमालिनेमिः समुद्रावधिका भूमिः । 'नेमिस्तु चक्रधारायां सीमधर्मव्यवस्थयोः' इत्यजयः । उपासरं गतवान् । उपस्पृश्य स्नात्वा । मणिभङ्गो रत्नशकलं तद्वन्निर्मलं शुद्धमम्भो जलं यस्यास्तथा ताम् । अन्धकमथनमन्धकासुरसंहारकं शिवम् । तदुक्तं—'स व्रजत्यन्धवद्यस्मादनन्धोऽपि हि भारत । तमन्धकोऽयं नाम्नेति प्रोचुस्तत्र निवासिनः ॥' इति । आयामो दैर्घ्यं तद्वन्तम् । आयसः अयोनिर्मितः परिघोऽर्गलः तद्वत्पीवराभ्यां मांसलाभ्याम् । 'कक्षाबन्धः परिकरः' इति वैजयन्ती । उच्छूना उन्नता । कर्कशः कठिनः । क्षीणा म्लाना तारका कनीनिका यस्येति । आरम्भ उद्योगः । साहसं महत्कर्म । तदनुवादी तद्बोधकः । "साहसानुवादी साहसस्य सदृशः । 'सदृक्सदृशसंवादी सजातीयानुवादिनः ।' इति दण्डी ।" इति भूषणा । कृच्छ्रं कष्टम् । प्रतिपत्स्यते प्राप्स्यति । **तदिति** । सहायस्य कर्म भावो वा साहाय्यम् । संनाहः परिकरः ।

---

१ बुद्धिमद्भिः प्र०. २ एतन्नास्ति क्वचित्. ३ म्लाननारम्. ४ प्रतिपत्स्यते. ५ साहाय्यावकाशः. ६ अभ्युपयेे इति.

निर्वर्ण्य 'को दोषः श्रूयताम्' इति क्वचित्करवीरतले मया सह निषण्णः कथामकार्षीत्—'महाभाग सोऽहमस्मि पूर्वेषु[1] कामचरः पूर्णभद्रो नाम गृहपतिपुत्रः। प्रयत्नसंवर्धितोऽपि पित्रा दैवच्छन्दानुवर्ती चौर्यवृत्तिरासम्। अथास्यां काशीपुर्यामर्यवर्यस्य कस्यचिद्गृहे चोरयित्वा रूपाभिग्राहितो बद्धः[2]। वध्ये[3] च मयि मत्तहस्ती मृत्युविजयो नाम हिंसाविहारी राजगोपुरो[4]परितलाधिरूढस्य पश्यतः कामपालनाम्न उत्तमामात्यस्य शासनाज्जनकण्ठरवद्विगुणितघण्टारवो मण्डलितहस्तकाण्डं[5] समभ्यधावत्। अभिपत्य च मया निर्भयेन निर्भर्त्सितः परिणमन्दारुखण्डसुषिरानुप्रविष्टोभयभुजदण्डचण्डघट्टित[6]प्रतिमानो भीतवन्न्यवर्तिष्ट[7]। भूयश्च नेत्रा जातसंरम्भेण निकामदारुणैर्वागङ्कुशपादघातै[8]रभिमुखीकृतः। मयाऽपि द्विगुणाबद्धमन्युना निर्भर्त्स्याभिहतो निवृत्या[9]पाद्रवत्। अथ मयोपेत्य[10] सरभसमाकुष्टो रुष्टश्च[11] यन्ता 'हन्त

---

प्राणनिरपेक्षं कर्म साहसमुच्यते। गोप्यमप्रकाश्यम्। निर्वर्ण्य दृष्ट्वा। करवीरो वृक्षविशेषः। पूर्वेषु पूर्वदेशेषु। कामचरः स्वेच्छागमनकर्ता। 'इषुकामेति देशस्य संज्ञा' इति भूषणा। गृहपतिर्ग्रामाध्यक्षः। दैवच्छन्दो दैववशः। अर्यवर्यस्य वैश्यश्रेष्ठस्य। 'स्यादर्यः स्वामिवैश्ययोः' इत्यमरः। रूपाभिग्राहितश्चौर्यवस्तुनाणकेन ग्राहितो धारितः। 'रूपं श्लोके यशोनाटकादौ सौन्दर्यशब्दयोः। ग्रन्थावृत्तौ तथाकारे स्वभावे नाणके मृगे॥' इति महीपः। 'लोप्त्रेण गृहीतः' इति भूषणा। राजद्वारस्य गोपुरं प्रतोली। 'गोपुरं हि प्रतोल्यां च नगरद्वारयोरपि' इति महीपः। उपरितलमूर्ध्वप्रदेशस्तत्राधिरूढस्य। जनकण्ठरवो लोकसांनिध्यशब्दः। 'कण्ठो गले संनिधाने ध्वनौ मदनपादपे' इति विश्वः। मण्डलितं मण्डलाकारं कृतं हस्तकाण्डं शुण्डादण्डः यस्यां क्रियायां इति क्रियाविशेषणम्। निर्भर्त्सितस्तर्जितः। परिणमंस्तिर्यग्दन्तप्रहारं कुर्वन्। 'तिर्यग्दन्तप्रहारस्तु गजः परिणतो मतः' इति हलायुधः। दारुखण्डं काष्ठखण्डं तस्य सुषिरं बिलं तत्रानुप्रविष्टावुभयभुजदण्डौ ताभ्यां चण्डं यथा तथा घट्टितं संघर्षितं प्रतिमानं यस्य। 'दन्तयोरुभयोर्मध्यं प्रतिमानं प्रचक्षते।' इति वैजयन्ती। नेत्रा आधोरणेन। जातसंरम्भेण जातक्रोधेन। निकामदारुणैरतिकठोरैः। अभिमुखीकृतः संमुखीकृतः। **मयाऽपीति**। द्विगुणाबद्धमन्युना द्विगुणितक्रोधेन। 'मन्युर्दैन्ये क्रतौ क्रुधि' इत्यमरः। अभिहतस्ताडितः। निवृत्य परावृत्य। अपाद्रवत्पलायनपरोऽभूदित्यर्थः। **अथेति**। उपेत्य गत्वा। सरभसं सवेगम्। आकुष्ट आक्रोशं प्रापितः। निन्दित इत्यर्थः। यन्ता हस्तिपकः। अपसद

---

१ पूर्वेषुकाम॰. २ अबध्ये. ३ बद्धे. ४ राजद्वारगोपु॰. ५ ॰काण्डः; मण्डलितकरः. ६ दण्डघटित. ७ भीत इव. ८ पादैः. ९ विवृत्य. १० अनुपत्य. ११ रुष्टः स.

मृतोऽसि कुञ्जरापसद' इति निशितेन वारणेन वारणं मुहुर्मुहुरभिघ्नन्निर्याणभागे कथमपि मदभिमुखमकरोत् । अथावोचम्—'अपसरतु द्विर[1]कीट एषः । अन्यः कश्चिन्मातङ्गपतिरानीयताम्, येनाहं मुहूर्तं विहृत्य गच्छामि गन्तव्यां गतिम्' इति । दृष्ट्वैव स मां रुष्टमुद्गर्जन्तमुत्क्रा[2]न्तयन्तृनिष्ठुराज्ञः पलायिष्ट । मन्त्रिणा पुनरहमाहूयाभ्यधायिषि—'भद्र मृ[3]त्युरेवैष मृत्युविजयो नाम हिंसाविहारी । सोऽयमपि तावत्त्वयैवंभूतः कृतः । तद्विरम्य कर्मणोऽस्मान्मलीमसात् । किमलमसि प्रतिपद्यास्मानार्यवृत्त्या वर्तितुम्' इति । '[4]यथाऽऽज्ञापितोऽस्मि' इति विज्ञापितोऽयं मया मित्रवन्मय्यवर्तिष्ट ।

पृष्टश्च मयैकदा रहसि जातविश्रम्भेणाभाषत स्वचरितम्—'आसीत्कुसुमपुरे राज्ञो रिपुंजयस्य मन्त्री धर्मपालो नाम विश्रुतधीः [5]श्रुतर्षिः । अमुष्य पुत्रः सुमित्रो नाम पित्रैव समः प्रज्ञागुणेषु । तस्यास्मि द्वैमातुरः कनीयान्भ्राताऽहम् । वेशेषु विलसन्तं मामसौ विनयरुचिरवारयत् । अवार्यदुर्नयश्चाहमपसृत्य दिङ्मुखेषु भ्रमन्यदृच्छयाऽस्यां वाराणस्यां प्रमदवने मदनदमनाराधनाय निर्गत्य सह सखीभिः कन्दुकेनानु[6]क्रीडमानां काशीभर्तुश्चण्डसिंहस्य क[7]न्यां

अधम । 'निहीनोऽपसदो जाल्मः' इति वैजयन्ती । निशितेन तीक्ष्णेन । वारणेनाङ्कुशेन । वारणं गजम् । 'वारणस्तु गजे प्रोक्तो वारणं तन्निवारणे' इत्यजयः । निर्याणभागेऽपाङ्गदेशे । 'अपाङ्गदेशो निर्याणम्' इत्यमरः । द्विपकीटो हस्तिकीटः । गन्तव्यां प्राप्तव्यां गतिम् । मरणमित्यर्थः । स गजः । उद्गर्जन्तं दीर्घस्वरं वदन्तम् । उत्क्रान्ताऽतिक्रान्ता यन्तुराधोरणस्य निष्ठुरा क्रूरा आज्ञा येनेति । अभ्यधायिष्यभिहितः । मृत्युविजय एतन्नामा गजः । अस्मात्कर्मणश्चौर्यरूपात् । मलीमसान्मलिनात् । अलमसि शक्तोऽसि । आर्यवृत्त्या श्रेष्ठवृत्त्या । अयममात्यः । **मयेति** । रहसि एकान्ते । विश्रम्भो विश्वासः । **आसीदिति** । रिपुंजयस्यैतन्नाम्नः । श्रुतर्षिरधीतवेदः । "श्रुतऋषिः । 'ऋत्यकः' इति प्रकृतिभावः" इति भूषणा । प्रज्ञागुणेषु धीगुणेषु । ते गुणाः षट्—'शुश्रूषा ग्रहणं चैव श्रवणं चावधारणम् । ऊहापोहोऽर्थविज्ञानं तत्त्वज्ञानं च धीगुणाः ॥' इति कामन्दके । द्वैमातुरो द्वयोर्मात्रोरपत्यम् । द्विमातृज इत्यर्थः । 'मातुरुत्संख्या—' इत्युदादेशः । वेशेषु वेश्यासु । असौ सुमित्रनामा ज्येष्ठभ्राता । अवार्यदुर्नयोऽवार्यो दूरीकर्तुमशक्यो दुर्नयो दुर्नीतिर्यस्येति सः । दिङ्मुखेषु दिगन्तेषु । प्रमदवनेऽन्तःपुरोचितवने । 'स्यादेतदेव प्रमदवनमन्तःपुरोचितम् ।' इत्यमरः । मदनदमनः मदनशत्रुर्महादेवः । तदा-

१ द्विरदवराकः. २ उत्क्रामन्तम्. ३ मृत्युरिवैष. ४ यथाऽऽज्ञापयसि ५ नाम श्रुतऋषिः वेदश्रुतऋषिः. ६ परिक्रीडमानाम्. ७ क्रीडमाना कन्या कान्तिमती नाम चकमे.

कान्तिमतीं नाम चकमे । कथमपि समगच्छे च । अथ च्छन्नं विहरता कुमारीपुरे सा मयाऽऽसीदापन्नसत्त्वा । कंचित्सुतं च प्रसूतवती । मृतजात[१] इति सोऽपविद्धो रहस्यनिर्भेदभयात्परिजनेन क्रीडाशैले । शबर्या च श्मशानाभ्यासं नीतः । तयैव निवर्तमानया निशीथे राजवीथ्यामारक्षिकपुरुषैरभिगृह्य तर्जितया दण्डपारुष्यभीतया निर्भिन्नप्रायं रहस्यम् । राजाज्ञया निशीथेऽहमा[२]क्रीडनगिरिदरीगृहे विश्रब्धप्रसुप्तस्तयोपदर्शितो यथोपपन्नरज्जुबद्धः श्मशानमुपनीय मातङ्गेनोद्यतेन कृपाणेन प्राजिहीर्ष्ये । नियतिबलाल्लूनबन्ध[३]स्तमसिमाच्छिद्यान्त्यजं तमन्यांश्च कांश्चित्प्रहृत्यापासरम् । अशरणश्च भ्रमन्नटव्यामेकदाऽश्रुमुख्या[४] कयाऽपि दिव्याकारया सपरिचारया[५] कन्ययोपास्थायिषि । सा मामञ्जलिकिसलयोत्तंसितेन मुखविलोलकुन्तलेन मूर्ध्ना प्रणम्य[६] मया सह वनवटद्रुमस्य कस्यापि महतः प्रच्छायशीतले तले निषण्णा 'काऽसि वासु, कुतोऽस्यागता, कस्य हेतोरस्य मे प्रसीदसि' इति साभिलाषमाभाषिता मया वाङ्मयं मधुवर्षमवर्षत्—'आर्य, नाथस्य[७] यक्षाणां मणिभद्रस्यास्मि दुहिता तारावली नाम । साऽहं कदाचिदगस्त्यपत्नीं लोपामुद्रां नमस्कृत्यापावर्तमाना मलयगिरेः परेतावासे वाराणस्याः[८] कमपि दारकं रुदन्तमद्राक्षम् । आदाय चैनं तीव्रस्नेहा[९]न्मम

---

राधनाय तत्पूजनाय । चकमे अभिलषितवान् । **अथेति** । छन्नं गुप्तम् । आपन्नसत्त्वा जातगर्भा । 'आपन्नसत्त्वा स्याद्गुर्विण्यन्तर्वत्नी च गर्भिणी ।' इत्यमरः । अपविद्धस्त्यक्तः । रहस्यं गोप्यं तस्य निर्भेदः प्रकटीभावस्तस्माद्भयं भीतिस्तस्मात् । शबर्या भिल्लया । अभ्यासं समीपम् । आरक्षिकपुरुषैः संरक्षणकारकपुरुषैः । तर्जितया भीषितया । दण्डपारुष्यं मारणादि । निर्भिन्नप्रायं प्रकाशितप्रायम् । निशीथेऽर्धरात्रे । आक्रीडनगिरिदरीगृहे क्रीडापर्वतकन्दरायामित्यर्थः । यथोपपन्नरज्जुबद्धो यथाप्राप्तदोरकबद्धः । मातङ्गश्चण्डालः । कृपाणेन खड्गेन । प्राजिहीर्ष्ये प्रहर्तुमिष्टः । नियतिबलाददृष्टप्रभावात् । तमसिं मातङ्गकरकृपाणम् । आच्छिद्यापहृत्य । अशरणो गृहरक्षकहीनः । दिव्यः स्वर्ग्य आकारो यस्यास्तया । परिचारः सेवा लक्षणया तदुपकरणानि तत्समेतया । उपास्थायिषि समीपवर्त्यासम् । अञ्जलिकिसलयोत्तंसितेनाञ्जलिपल्लवशिखरितेन । मुखे विलोलाः कुन्तलाः केशा यस्येति तथा तेन । वाङ्मयं वाक्प्रचुरम् । मधुवर्षं मधुवृष्टिम् । परेतावासे महाश्मशान इत्यर्थः । दारकं

---

१ मृतजातः. २ आक्रीड. ३ बन्धनः. ४ उदश्रुमुख्या. ५ सपरिवारया. ६ प्रणिपत्य.
७ नाथ. ८ वाराणस्याम्. ९ तीव्रस्नेहा.

पित्रोः संनिधिमनैषम्। अनैषीच्च मे पिता देवस्यालकेश्वरस्यास्थानीम्। अथाहमाहूयाज्ञप्ता हरसखेन—'बाले, बालेऽस्मिन्कीदृशस्ते भावः' इति। 'औरस इवास्मिन्वत्से वत्सलता' इति मया विज्ञापितः 'सत्यमाह वराकी' इति तन्मूलामतिमहतीं कथामकरोत्। तत्रैतावन्मयाऽवगतम्। त्वं किल शौनकः शूद्रकः कामपालश्चाभिन्नः। बन्धुमती विनयवती कान्तिमती चाभिन्ना। वेदिमत्यार्यदासी[1] सोमदेवी चैकैव। हंसावली[2] शूरसेना[3] सुलोचना चानन्या। नन्दिनी रङ्गपताकेन्द्रसेना चापृथग्भूता। या किल शौनकावस्थायामग्निसाक्षिकमात्मसात्कृता गोपकन्या सैव किलार्यदासी पुनश्चाद्य तारावलीत्यभूवम्। बालश्च किल शूद्रकावस्थे त्वय्यार्यदास्यवस्थायां मय्युदभूत्। अवर्ध्यत च विनयवत्या स्नेहवासनया। स तु तस्यां कान्तिमत्यवस्थायामद्योदभूत्। एवमनेकमृत्युमुखपरिभ्रष्टं[4] दैवान्मयोपलब्धं तमेकपिङ्गादेशाद्वने तपस्यतो राजहंसस्य देव्यै वसुमत्यै तत्सुतस्य भाविचक्रवर्तिनो राजवाहनस्य परिचर्यार्थं समर्प्य गुरुभिरभ्यनुज्ञाता कृतान्तयोगात्कृतान्तमुखभ्रष्टस्य ते पादपद्मशुश्रूषार्थमागताऽस्मि' इति।

तच्छ्रुत्वा तामनेकजन्मरमणीमसकृदाश्लिष्य हर्षाश्रुमुखो मुहुर्मुहुः सान्त्वयित्वा तत्प्रभावदर्शिते महति मन्दिरेऽहर्निशं भूमिदुर्लभान्भो-

---

बालकम्। अलकेश्वरस्य कुबेरस्य। आस्थानीं सभाम्। 'आस्थानी क्लीबमास्थानम्' इत्यमरः। हरसखेन कुबेरेण। बाले कन्ये इति संबोधनं प्रथमम्। बालेऽस्मिन्निति अस्मिन्बालक इत्यर्थः। भावः स्नेहः। औरस उरसि भवस्तस्मिन्। पुत्र इति यावत्। वत्सलता स्नेहः। वराकी कृपार्हा। तन्मूलां बालकमूलाम्। तत्रेति। त्वं कामपालः। त्रिष्वपि जन्मसु नाम्नैव भिन्नः न तु स्वरूपेणेति। शौनकावस्थायां बन्धुमती वेदिमती हंसावली नन्दिन्यश्चतस्रः। शूद्रकावस्थायां विनयवत्यार्यदासी शूरसेना रङ्गपताका। कामपालावस्थायां कान्तिमती सोमदेवी सुलोचनेन्द्रसेना। एतास्तिस्रोऽभिन्नाः। एकरूपा इत्यर्थः। वेदिमतीप्रभृतयस्तिस्रोऽप्यभिन्नाः। हंसावलीप्रभृतयस्तिस्रोऽप्यभिन्नाः। नन्दिनीमुखाः तिस्रोऽप्यभिन्नाः। शौनकावस्थायाम्। आत्मसात्कृता परिणीतेत्यर्थः। अनेकमृत्युमुखेत्यत्र 'कान्तिमतीसखीभिः क्रीडागिरौ त्यक्तं शबर्या च श्मशाने' इति भूषणा। एकपिङ्गादेशात्कुबेरादेशात्। कृतान्तयोगाद्दैवयोगात्। कृतान्तमुखभ्रष्टस्य यममुखनिर्गतस्य। 'कृतान्तो यमसिद्धान्तदैवाकुशलकर्मसु।' इत्यमरः। तत्प्रभावदर्शिते तारावलीसामर्थ्यप्रकटीकृते। अहर्निशं दिवारात्रम्।

---

१ अर्यदासी; यक्षदासी; यज्ञदासी. २ हंसावती. ३ सुरसेना. ४ परिभ्रष्टस्य. ५ इन्द्रद्व०.

गमन्नभूवम् । द्वित्राणि दिनान्यतिक्रम्य[1] मत्तकाशिनीं तामवादिषम्—'प्रिये प्रत्यपकृत्य मत्प्राणद्रोहिणश्चण्डसिंहस्य वैरनिर्यातनसुखमनुबुभूषामि' इति । तया सास्मितमभिहितम्—'एहि कान्त, कान्तिमतीदर्शनाय नयामि त्वाम्' इति । स्थितेऽर्धरात्रे राज्ञो वासगृहमनीये । ततस्तच्छिरोभागवर्तिनीमादायासियष्टिं प्रबोध्यैनं प्रस्फुरन्तमब्रवम्—'अहमस्मि भवज्जामाता भवदनुमत्या विना तव कन्याभिमर्शी । तमपराधमनुवृत्त्या प्रमार्ष्टुमागतः' इति । सोऽतिभीतो[2] मामभिप्रणम्याह—'अहमेव मूढोऽपराद्धः, यस्तव दुहितृसंसर्गानुग्राहिणो ग्रहग्रस्त इवोत्क्रान्तसीमा समादिष्टवान्वधम् । तदास्ता कान्तिमती, राज्यमिदं मम च जीवितमप्यद्यप्रभृति भवदधीनम्[3]' इत्यवादीत् । अथापरेद्युः प्रकृतिमण्डलं संनिपात्य[4] विधिवदात्मजायाः पाणिमग्राहयत् । अश्रावयच्च तनयवार्तां तारावली कान्तिमत्यै, सोमदेवीसुलोचनेन्द्रसेनाभ्यश्च पूर्वजातिवृत्तान्तम् । इत्थमहं मन्त्रिपदापदेशं यौवराज्यमनुभवन्विहरामि विलासिनीभिः' इति ।

स एवं मादृशेऽपि जन्तौ परिचर्यानुबन्धी बन्धुरेकः सर्वभूतानामलसकेन स्वर्गते श्वशुरे, ज्यायसि च श्याले चण्डघोषनाम्नि स्त्रीष्वतिप्रसङ्गात्प्रागेव क्षयक्षीणायुषि, पञ्चवर्षदेशीयं सिंहघोषनामानं कुमार-

---

मत्तकाशिनीमुत्तमां स्त्रियम् । अवादिषमवोचम् । प्रत्यपकृत्य प्रत्यपकारं कृत्वेत्यर्थः । वैरनिर्यातनं वैरशुद्धिः । अनुबुभूषाम्यनुभवितुमिच्छामि । तया तारावल्या । वासगृहं गर्भागारम् । **तत इति** । एनं चण्डसिंहम् । प्रस्फुरन्तं कम्पमानम् । अनुवृत्त्या सेवया । प्रमार्ष्टुं दूरीकर्तुम् । अपराद्धः कृतापराधः । दुहितृसंसर्गानुग्राहिणः कन्यासंसर्गकृपाकर्तुः । उत्क्रान्तसीमोज्झितमर्यादः । कान्तिमती कन्या । **अथेति** । प्रकृतिमण्डलं प्रजासमूहम् । मन्त्रिपदस्यापदेशो मिषम् । स एवमिति पूर्णभद्रोक्तिः । परिचर्यानुबन्धी सेवानुबन्धी । अलसकेन क्षयेण । 'क्षयस्त्वलसको मतः' इति वैजयन्ती । ज्यायसि ज्येष्ठे । श्याले पत्नीभ्रातरि । 'श्यालाः स्युर्भ्रातरः पत्न्याः' इत्यमरः । अतिप्रसङ्गादतियोगादत्यन्तासक्तेरित्यर्थः । 'अतियोगवियोगाद्वा क्षयो भवति जन्मिनः' इति निदानम् । पञ्चवर्षदेशीयमीषदसमाप्तपञ्चवर्षदशम् । 'ईषदसमाप्तौ कल्पब्देश्यदेशीयरः' इति देशीयप्रत्ययः । यौवनोन्मादिनस्तारुण्योन्मादवतः ।

---

१ अतीत्य. २ सोऽथ भीतः. ३ त्वदधीनम्. ४ संनिधाप्य.

मभ्यषेचयत् । अवर्धयच्च विधिनैनं स साधुः । तस्याद्य यौवनोन्मादिनः पैशुन्यवादिनो दुर्मन्त्रिणः कतिचिदासन्नन्तरङ्गभूताः । तैः किलासावितथमग्राह्यत—'प्रसह्यैव स्वसा तवामुना भुजङ्गेन संगृहीता । पुनः प्रसुप्ते राजनि प्रहर्तुमुद्यतासिरासीत् । तेनास्मै तत्क्षणप्रबुद्धेन[1] भीत्याऽनुनीय दत्ता कन्या । तं च देवज्येष्ठं चण्डघोषं विषेण हत्वा बालोऽयमसमर्थ इति त्वमद्यापि प्रकृतिविश्रम्भणायोपेक्षितः । क्षिणोति च पुरा स कृतघ्नो भवन्तम् । तमेवान्तकपुरमभिगमयितुं यतस्व' इति । स तथा दूषितोऽपि यक्षिणीभयान्[2]नामुष्मिन्पापमाचरितुमशक्नत् । एषु किल दिवसेष्वयथापूर्वमाकृतौ[3] कान्तिमत्याः समुपलक्ष्य राजमहिषी सुलक्षणा नाम सप्रणयमपृच्छत्—'देवि नाहमयथातथ्येन[4] विप्रलम्भनीया । कथय तथ्यं केनेदमयथापूर्वमाननारविन्दे[5] तवैषु वासरेषु' इति । सा त्ववादीत्—'भद्रे स्मरसि किमद्याप्ययथातथ्येन किंचिन्मयोक्तपूर्वम् । सखी मे तारावली सपत्नी च किमपि कलुषिताशया रहसि भर्त्रा मद्गोत्रापदिष्टा प्रणयमप्युपेक्ष्य[6] प्रणम्यमानाऽप्यस्माभिरुपोढमत्सरा प्रावसत् । अवसीदति च नः पतिः । अतो मे दौर्मनस्यम्' इति । तत्प्रायेणैकान्ते सुलक्षणया कान्ताय कथितम् ।

---

पैशुन्यं दौर्जन्यम् । दुष्टजनोचितमित्यर्थः । तद्वदन्तीति तथा । दुर्मन्त्रिणो दुष्टप्रधानाः । अन्तरङ्गभूता आप्ततराः । अग्राह्यत अबोध्यतेत्यर्थः । अमुनेति मामुद्दिश्योक्तिः । भुजङ्गेन विटेन । उद्यतासिरूर्ध्वीकृतखड्गः । अनुनीय सान्त्वयित्वा । विश्रम्भणं विश्वासः । क्षिणोति च पुरा । क्षयिष्यतीत्यर्थः । 'यावत्पुरानिपातयोर्लट्' । भवन्तं सिंहघोषम् । अभिगमयितुं प्रापयितुम् । दूषितो भेदितः । अमुष्मिन्कन्यादूषके । पापं हननरूपम् । अयथापूर्वमयथाभावम् । नवीनमित्यर्थः । आकृतौ शरीरे । यथातथं वास्तवं तस्याभावः तेन अयथातथ्येन । असत्येनेत्यर्थः । विप्रलम्भनीया प्रतारणीयेत्यर्थः । तथ्यं सत्यम् । सा कान्तिमती । भद्रे इति सुलक्षणासंबोधनम् । कलुषिताशया मलिनितबुद्धिः । मद्गोत्रापदिष्टा मन्नाम्नाऽऽहूता । 'गोत्रं नाम्नि कुलेऽचले' इति वैजयन्ती । प्रणयं प्रीतिम् । उपोढमत्सरा प्ररूढद्वेषा । दौर्मनस्यं दौश्चित्त्यम् । प्रायेण बाहुल्येन ।

---

१ दैवात्तत्क्षण. २ प्रभावात्; प्रभावभयात्. ३ अयथापूर्व्यम्. ४ अयाथातथ्येन. ५ आननारबिन्दम्. ६ अभ्युपेक्ष्य.

अथासौ निर्भयोऽद्य प्रियतमाविरहपाण्डुभिरवयवैर्धैर्यस्तम्भिताश्रुपर्याकुलेन चक्षुषोष्मश्वासशोषिताभिरिवानतिपेशलाभिर्वाग्भिर्वियोगं दर्शयन्तं कथमपि राजकुले कार्याणि कारयन्तं, पूर्वसंकेतितैः पुरुषैरभिग्राह्याबन्धयत्। तस्य किल स्थाने स्थाने दोषानुद्घोष्य तथोद्धरणीये चक्षुषी यथा तन्मूलमेवास्य मरणं भवेत्' इति। अतोऽत्रैकान्ते यथेष्टमश्रु मुक्त्वा तस्य साधोः पुरः प्राणान्मोक्तुकामो बध्नामि परिकरम्' इति।

मयाऽपि तत्पितृव्यसनमाकर्ण्य पर्यश्रुणा सोऽभिहितः—'सौम्य, किं तव गोपायित्वा। यस्तस्य सुतो यक्षकन्यया देवस्य राजवाहनस्य पादशुश्रूषार्थं देव्या वसुमत्या हस्तन्यासः कृतः सोऽहमस्मि। शक्ष्यामि सहस्रमपि सुभटानामुदायुधानां हत्वा पितरं मोचयितुम्। अपि तु संकुले यदि कश्चित्पातयेत्तदङ्गे शस्त्रिकां सर्व एव मे यत्नो भस्मनि हुतमिव भवेत्' इति। अनवसितवचन एव मयि महानाशीविषः प्राकाररन्ध्रेणोदैरयच्छिरः। तमहं मन्त्रौषधिबलेनाभिगृह्य पूर्णभद्रमब्रवम्—'भद्र सिद्धं नः समीहितम्। अनेन तातमलक्ष्यमाणः संकुले यदृच्छया पतितेन नाम दंशयित्वा तथा विषं स्तम्भयेयं यथा मृत इत्युदास्येत। त्वया तु मुक्तसाध्वसेन माता मे बोधयितव्या—'यो यक्ष्या वने देव्या वसुमत्या हस्तार्पितो युष्मत्सूनुः सोऽनुप्राप्तः पितुरवस्थां मदुपलभ्य बुद्धिबलादित्थमाचरिष्यति। त्वया तु मुक्तत्रासया राज्ञे प्रेषणीयम्—'एष खलु

---

अथेति। 'अथ स्वस्त्रीमुखात्तारावलीकामपालयोर्वियोगश्रवणोत्तरम्' इति भूषणा। असौ राजा। धैर्येण स्तम्भितान्यश्रूणि तैः पर्याकुलेन। अनतिपेशलाभिरनतिकोमलाभिः। पूर्वसंकेतितैः प्रागेव मन्त्रितैः। अभिग्राह्य ग्राहयित्वा। उद्घोष्योद्घाष्य। उद्धरणीये निष्कासनीये। मोक्तुकामस्त्यक्तुकामः। 'लुम्पेदवश्यमः कृत्ये तुम्काममनसोरपि। समो वा हिततयोर्मांसस्य पचियुज्घञोः॥' इति मकारलोपः। पर्यश्रुणा कृतरोदनेन। हस्तन्यासो हस्तनिक्षेपः। उदायुधानामुद्यतशस्त्राणाम्। संकुले संबाधे। तदङ्गे पितुरङ्गे। अनवसितवचनेऽसमाप्तवचने। आशीविषः सर्पः। आशिषि विषमस्य। पृषोदरादित्वाद्दीर्घसलोपौ। उदैरयत्। ऊर्ध्वमकरोदित्यर्थः। समीहितं वाञ्छितम्। यदृच्छया दैवेन। स्तम्भयेयं स्तम्भितं करिष्ये। त्वया पूर्णभद्रेण। मुक्तसाध्वसेन त्यक्तभयेन। मदुपलभ्य मत्तो ज्ञात्वा। निग्राह्यो निग्रहीतव्यः।

---

१ निर्भरोद्यात्प्रिय०. २ स्थानस्थानेषु. ३ दोषम्. ४ हस्ते न्यासः. ५ अपदिश्येत; उत्सृज्येत. ६ मुक्तसाध्वसया.

क्षत्रधर्मो यद्बन्धुरबन्धुर्वा दुष्टः स निरपेक्षं निग्राह्य इति। स्त्रीधर्मश्चैष यद्दुष्टस्य दुष्टस्य वा भर्तुर्गतिर्गन्तव्येति। तदहममुनैव सह चिताग्निमारोक्ष्यामि। युवतिजनानुकूलः[1] पश्चिमो विधिरनुज्ञातव्यः' इति। स एवं निवेदितो नियतमनुज्ञास्यति। ततः स्वमेवागारमानीय काण्डपटी[2]परिक्षिप्ते विविक्तोद्देशे दर्भसंस्तरणमधिशाय्य स्वयं कृतानुमरणमण्डनया त्वया च तत्र संनिधेयम्। अहं च बाह्यकक्षागतस्त्वया प्रवेशयिष्ये। ततः पितरमुज्जीव्य तदभिरुचितेनाभ्युपायेन चेष्टिष्यामहे' इति। स 'तथा' इति हृष्टतरस्तूर्णमगमत्।

अहं तु घोषणास्थाने चिञ्चावृक्षं घनतर[3]विपुलशाखमारुह्य गूढतनुरतिष्ठम्। आरूढश्च लोको यथायथमुच्चैः[4]स्थानानि। उच्चावचप्रलापाः[5] प्रस्तुताः। तावन्मे पितरं तस्करमिव पश्चाद्बद्धभुजमुद्धुरध्वनिमहाजनानुयातमानीय मदभ्यास[6] एव स्थापयित्वा मातङ्गस्त्रिरघोषयत्—'एष मन्त्री कामपालो राज्यलोभाद्भर्तारं चण्डसिंहं, युवराजं चण्डघोषं च विषान्नेन[7]ोपांशु हत्वा पुनर्देवोऽपि सिंहघोषः पूर्णयौवन इत्यमुष्मिन्पापमाचरिष्यन्विश्वासाद्रहस्यभूमौ पुनरमात्यं शिवनागमाहूय स्थूणमङ्गारवर्षं च राजवधायोपजप्य तैः स्वामिभक्त्या विवृतगुह्यो राज्यकामुकस्य ब्राह्मणस्यान्धतमसप्रवेशो न्याय्य इति प्राड्विवाकवाक्यादक्ष्युद्धरणाय नीयते। पुनरन्योऽपि यदि स्यादन्याय-

---

युवतिजनानुकूलः स्त्रीलोकानुगुणः। 'अभिजनानुरूपः' इति पाठे वंशानुरूप इत्यर्थः। 'संततिर्गोत्रजननकुलान्यभिजनान्वयौ' इत्यमरः। पश्चिमश्चरमः। काण्डपटीपरिक्षिप्ते तिरस्करिणीपरिवृते। 'अपटी काण्डपटः स्यात्प्रतिसीरा जवन्यपि। तिरस्करिणी' इति हैमः। दर्भसंस्तरणं दर्भास्तरणम्। बाह्यकक्षा बहिःप्रकोष्ठः। तदभिरुचितेन पितुरभिमतेन। स पूर्णभद्रः। तूर्णं सत्वरम्। **अहमिति।** घोषणास्थाने डिण्डिमस्थले। गूढतनुर्गुप्तशरीरः। उच्चावचप्रलापा उच्चनीचवचनानि। उद्धुरध्वनीति क्रियाविशेषणं महाजनविशेषणं वा। मदभ्यासे मत्समीपे। मातङ्गश्चण्डालः। उपांशु रहसि। अमुष्मिन्सिंहघोषे। शिवनागं तन्नामानम्। स्थूणमङ्गारवर्षं चेति द्वावप्यमात्यौ। उपजप्य भेदं कृत्वा। तैर्मन्त्रिभिः। विवृतगुह्यः प्रकटीकृतमन्त्रः। अन्धं च तत्तमश्चान्धतमसम्। 'अवसमन्धेभ्यस्तमसः' इत्यच्। प्राड्विवाको व्यवहारनिर्णायकः। 'द्रष्टरि व्यवहाराणां प्राड्विवाकाक्षदर्शकौ' इत्यमरः। अक्ष्युद्धरणाय

---

१ अभिजनानुरूपः. २ पट. ३ लम्बघनतर. ४ उच्चस्था०. ५ प्रलापः प्रस्थितः ६ अभ्याशे. ७ विषेण.

वृत्तिस्तमप्येवमेव यथार्हेण दण्डेन योजयिष्यति देवः ' इति । श्रुत्वैतद्बद्धकलकले महाजने पितुरङ्के प्रदीप्तशिरस[1]माशीविषं न्यक्षिपम्[2] । अहं च भीतो नामावप्लुत्य तत्रैव जनानुलीनः[3] क्रुद्धव्यालदष्टस्य तातस्य विहितजीवरक्षो विषं क्षणादस्तम्भयम् । अपतच्च स[4] भूमौ मृतकल्पः । प्रालपं च—' सत्यमिदं राजावमानिनं दैवो दण्ड एव स्पृशतीति । यदयमक्षिभ्यामवनिपेन विनाचिकीर्षितः प्राणैरेव वियोजितो विधिना ' इति । मदुक्तं च केचिदन्वमन्यन्त, अपरे पुनर्निनिन्दुः । दर्वीकरस्तु तमपि चण्डालं दष्ट्वाऽऽरूढत्रासद्रुतलोकदत्तमार्गः प्राद्रवत् ।

अथ मदम्बा पूर्णभद्रबोधितार्था तादृशेऽपि व्यसने नातिविह्वला कुल[5]परिजनानुयाता पद्भ्यामेव धीर[6]मागत्य मत्पितुरुत्तमाङ्गमुत्सङ्गे धारयन्त्यासित्वा राज्ञे समादिशत्[7]—' एष मे पतिस्तवापकर्ता न वेति दैवमेव[8] जानाति । न मेऽनयाऽस्ति चिन्तया फलम् । अस्य तु पाणिग्राहकस्य गतिमननुप्रपद्यमाना भवत्कुलं कलङ्कयेयम् । अतोऽनुमन्तुमर्हसि भर्त्रा सह चिताधिरोहणाय माम् ' इति । श्रुत्वा चैतत्प्रीतियुक्तः समादिक्षत्[9]क्षितीश्वरः—' क्रियतां कुलोचितः संस्कारः । उत्संवोत्तरं[10] च पश्चिमं विधिसंस्कारमनुभवतु मे भगिनीपतिः ' इति । चण्डाले तु मत्प्रतिषिद्धसकलमन्त्रवादिप्रयासे संस्थिते ' कामपालोऽपि कालदष्ट एव ' इति स्वभवनोपनयनममुष्य स्वमाहात्म्यप्रकाशनाय महीपतिरन्वमंस्त । आनीतश्च[11]

नेत्रोत्पाटनाय । अन्यायवृत्तिरन्यायकर्ता । आशीविष सर्पम् । भीतो नाम मिथ्यैव भयं प्राप्त इति । अवप्लुत्योड्डीय । जनादनुलीनो लोकाद्गुप्तः । ' अन्तर्धौ येनादर्शनमिच्छति ' इत्यपादानम् । अस्तम्भयं स्तम्भितवान् । देवानामयं दैवः । अवनिपेन राज्ञा । अक्षिभ्यां विना हृतनयन इत्यर्थः चिकीर्षितः कर्तुमिष्टः । दर्व्याकारः फणा एव करो यस्य । प्रहारसाधनत्वात् । दर्वीं फणां करोतीति वा दर्वीकरः सर्पः । रूढो जातस्त्रासो भयं तेन द्रुतः पलायितो यो लोकस्तेन दत्तो मार्गो यस्येति स तथा । **अथेति** । व्यसने दुःखे । नातिविह्वला न तिव्याकुला । उत्तमाङ्गं शिरः । अननुप्रपद्यमानाऽप्राप्तवती । कलङ्कयेयं कलङ्कितं करिष्यामि । समादिक्षत् । आज्ञापयामासेत्यर्थः । मन्त्रवादिनां गारुडिकानाम् । संस्थिते मरणं प्राप्ते । कालदष्टो मृत इति यावत् । अमुष्य कामपालस्य । स्वमाहात्म्यप्रकाशनाय स्वधार्मिकत्वकीर्तिप्राकट्यार्थम् ।

१ शिखम्. २ व्यक्षि०. ३ जनादनुलीनः, जनादुपलीनः. ४ एष. ५ अल्पपरिजना०. ६ सधीरम्. ७ समदिशत्. ८ देवो जानाति. ९ प्रतिसमादिक्षत्. १० उत्सवान्तरम्. ११ नीतश्च.

पिता मे विविक्तायां भूमौ दर्भशय्यामधिशय्य[1] स्थितोऽभूत्। अथ मदम्बा मरणमण्डनमनुष्ठाय सकरुणं सखीरामन्त्र्य मुहुरभिप्रणम्य भवनदेवतां यत्ननिवारितपरिजनाक्रन्दिता[2] पितुर्मे शयनस्थानमेकाकिनी प्राविक्षत्। तत्र च पूर्वमेव पूर्णभद्रोपस्थापितेन च मया वैनतेयतां गतेन निर्विषीकृतं भर्तारमैक्षत। हृष्टतमा पत्युः पादयोः पर्यश्रुमुखी प्रणिपत्य मां च मुहुर्मुहुः प्रस्नुतस्तनी परिष्वज्य सहर्षबाष्पगद्गदमगदत्—'पुत्र योऽसि जातमात्रः पापया मया परित्यक्तः स किमर्थमेवं मामातिनिर्घृणामनुगृह्णासि। अथ वैष निरपराध एव ते जनयिता। युक्तमस्य प्रत्यानयनमन्तकाननात्। क्रूरा खलु तारावली या त्वामुपलभ्यापि तत्त्वतः कुबेराद् असमर्प्य मह्यमर्पितवती देव्यै वसुमत्यै। सैव वा सदृशकारिणी। न हि तादृशाद्भाग्यराशेर्विना मादृशो[3] जनोऽल्पपुण्यस्तवार्हति कलप्रलापामृतानि कर्णाभ्यां पातुम्। एहि परिष्वजस्व' इति भूयो भूयः शिरसि जिघ्रन्त्यङ्कमारोपयन्ती तारावलीं गर्हयन्ती आलिङ्गयन्त्यश्रुभिरभिषिञ्चन्ती चोत्कम्पिताङ्गयष्टिरन्यादृश्येव[4] क्षणमजनिष्ट। जनयिताऽपि मे नरकादिव स्वर्गम्, तादृशाद्व्यसनात्तथाभूतमभ्युदयमारूढः पूर्णभद्रेण त्रिस्तरेण यथावृत्तान्तमावेदितो भगवतो मघवतोऽपि भाग्यवन्तमात्मानमजीगणत्। मनागिव[5] च मत्संबन्धमाख्याय हर्षविस्मितात्मनोः पित्रोरकथयम्—'आज्ञापयतं काऽद्य नः प्रतिपत्तिः।' पिता मे प्राब्रवीत्—'वत्स

अन्वमंस्तानुमोदितवान्। विविक्तायां विजनायाम्। अथेति। मरणमण्डनं मरणकालोचितभूषणम्। वैनतेयतां गरुडताम्। प्रस्नुतस्तनी स्रवत्पयःस्तनी। जात उत्पन्न एव जातमात्रः। निर्घृणां निष्कृपाम्। प्रत्यानयनं परावृत्यानयनम्। अन्तकाननाद्यममुखात्। क्रूरा कठिना। सदृशकारिणी युक्तकारिणी। कलो मञ्जुलो यः प्रलापः शिशुशब्दः स एवामृतम्। गर्हयन्ती निन्दन्ती। उत्कम्पिताङ्गयष्टिर्जातोत्कम्पशरीरा। अन्यादृश्येवान्यसमा। 'त्यदादिषु दृशोऽनालोचने कञ्च' इति सूत्रे 'सामान्ययोश्च' इति वक्तव्यात् दृशेः कञ्। 'आ सर्वनाम्नः' इत्यात्वम्। तादृशाद्व्यसनान्नेत्रोत्पाटनादिरूपाद् दुःखात्। तथाभूतं पुनर्जीवनपुत्रमिलनरूपम्। मघवत इन्द्रादपि भाग्यवन्तम्। मनागल्पम्। हर्षेण विस्मित आत्मा ययोः। प्रतिपत्तिः कर्तव्यता।

१ संस्तरमधिशयानः. २ यत्नेन निवार्य परिजनाक्रन्दितानि. ३ अस्मादृशः. ४ अन्यादृशीव. ५ एव.

गृहमेवेदमस्मदीयमतिविशाल[1]प्राकारवलयमक्षय्या[2]युधस्थानम् । अलङ्घ्यतमा च गुप्तिः । उपकृताश्च मयाऽतिबहवः सन्ति सामन्ताः । प्रकृतयश्च भूयस्यो न मे व्यसनमनुरुध्यन्ते । सुभटानां चानेकसहस्रमस्त्येव ससुहृत्पुत्रदारम् । अतोऽत्रैव कतिपयान्यहानि स्थित्वा बाह्याभ्यन्तरङ्गान्कोपानुत्पादयिष्यामः । कुपितांश्च संगृह्य प्रोत्साह्यास्य प्रकृ[3]त्यमित्रानुत्थाप्य सहजांश्च द्विषः दुर्दान्तमेनमुच्छेत्स्यामः ' इति । ' को दोषः । तथाऽस्तु ' इति तातस्य मतमन्वमंसि ।

तथाऽस्मासु प्रतिविधाय तिष्ठत्सु राजाऽपि विज्ञापितोदन्तो जातानुतापः पारग्रामिकान्प्रयोगान्प्रायः प्रायुङ्क्त । ते चास्माभिः प्रत्यहमहन्यन्त । अस्मिन्नेवावकाशे पूर्णभद्रमुखाच्च राज्ञः शय्यास्थानमवगम्य तदैव स्वोदवसितभित्तिकोणादारभ्योरगास्येन सुरङ्गामकार्षम् । गता च सा भूमिस्वर्गकल्पमनल्पकन्यकाजनं कमप्युद्देशम् । अव्यथिष्ट च दृष्ट्वैव स मां नारीजनः । तत्र काचिदिन्दुकलेव स्व[4]लावण्येन रसातलान्धकारं निर्धु[5]नाना विग्रहिणीव देवी विश्वं[6]भरा हरगृहिणीवासुरविजयायावतीर्णा पातालमागता गृहिणीव भगवतः कुसुमधन्वनः राजलक्ष्मीरिवानेकदुर्नृपदर्शनपरिहाराय महीविवरं प्रविष्टा निष्टप्तकनकपुत्रिकेवावदातकान्तिः कन्यका चन्दनलतेव मलयमारुतेन मद्दर्शनेनोदकम्पत । तथाभूते च तस्मिन्नङ्गना-

---

अतिविशालप्राकारवलयमतिविस्तीर्णवरणभित्तिमण्डलम् । अक्षय्यायुधस्थानमपरिमितायुधगृहम् । गुप्तिर्गोपनम् । प्रकृतयः प्रजाः । सुभटानां वीराणाम् । सुहृदः संबन्धिनः दाराः स्त्रियस्तैः सह वर्तमानम् । बाह्याभ्यन्तरङ्गान्बहिरङ्गानन्तरङ्गांश्च । प्रोत्साह्य प्रोत्साहवतो विधाय । दुर्दान्तं दुःखेन दमनीयम् । **तथेति** । प्रतिविधाय प्रतिविधानं कृत्वा । उदन्तो वार्ता । पारग्रामिकान्परग्रामे भवान् । प्रयोगान् कटकप्रेषणादिरूपान् । अत्र मिताक्षरायां विज्ञानेश्वरः–' उपरुध्यारिमासीत राष्ट्रं चास्योपपीडयेत् । दूषयेच्चास्य सततं यवसान्नोदकेन्धनम् ॥ ' इति । प्रायो बहुलान् । ' बहुलं प्रयुक्तवानित्यर्थः ' इति भूषणा । अवकाशेऽवसरे । स्वोदवसितं स्वगृहम् । भूम्यां स्वर्गः भूमिस्वर्गः तस्मादीषन्न्यूनः भूमिस्वर्गकल्पः तम् । अनल्पः कन्यकाजनः यस्मिन् तम् । उद्देशं प्रदेशम् । रसातलान्धकारं पातालान्धकारम् । ' निर्धुनाना अतितरां निरस्यन्ती ' इति भूषणा । विग्रहिणी शरीरधारिणी । विश्वंभरा पृथ्वी । हरगृहिणीव दुर्गेव । दुर्नृपदर्शनपरिहाराय दुष्टराजावलोकनपरिहाराय । निष्टप्ता संतापिता । कनकपुत्रिका सुवर्णपुत्तलिका । अङ्गनासमाजे स्त्रीसमूहे । ' पशूनां समजोऽन्येषु

---

१ शाल. २ आयुधग्रामम्. ३ प्राक्तनानमि०. ४ आत्मका०. ५ निह्नुवाना. ६ वसुंधरा.

समाजे कुसुमितेव काशयष्टिः पाण्डुशिरसिजा स्थविरा काचिच्चरणयोर्मे निपत्य त्रासदीनमब्रूत—'दीयतामभयदानमस्मा अनन्यशरणाय स्त्रीजनाय। किमसि देवकुमारो दनुजयुद्धतृष्णया रसातलं विविक्षुः। आज्ञापय कोऽसि कस्य हेतोरागतोऽसि' इति। सा तु मया प्रत्यवादि—'सुदत्यः मा स्म भवत्यो भैषुः[1]। अहमस्मि द्विजातिवृषात्[2]काम-पालाद्देव्यां कान्तिमत्यामुत्पन्नोऽर्थपालो नाम। सत्यर्थे निजगृहान्नृपगृहं सुरङ्गयोपसरन्निहान्तरे वो दृष्टवान्। कथयत काः स्थ यूयं, कथमिह निवसथ' इति[3]। सोदञ्जलिरुदीरितवती—'भर्तृदारक[4] भाग्यवत्यो वयं यास्त्वामेभिरेव चक्षुर्भिरनघमद्राक्ष्म। श्रूयताम्। यस्तव मातामहश्चण्डसिंहः तेनास्यां देव्यां लीलावत्यां चण्डघोषः कान्तिमतीत्यपत्यद्वयमुदपादि। चण्डघोषस्तु युवराजोऽत्यासङ्गादङ्गनासु राजयक्ष्मणा सुरक्षय[5]मगादन्तर्वत्न्यां देव्यामाचारवत्याम्। अमुया चेयं मणिकर्णिका नाम कन्या प्रसूता। अथ प्रसववेदनया मुक्तजीविताऽऽचारवती पत्युरन्तिकमगमत्। अथ देवश्चण्डसिंहो मामाहूयोपह्वरे समाज्ञापयत्—'ऋद्धिमति कन्यकेयं कल्याणलक्षणा। तामिमां मालवेन्द्रनन्दनाय दर्पसाराय विधिवद्वर्धयित्वा दित्सामि। बिभेमि च कान्तिमतीवृत्तान्तादारभ्य कन्यकानां प्रकाशावस्थापनात्। अत इयमरातिव्यसनाय कारिते महति भूमिगृहे कृत्रिमशैलगर्भोत्कीर्णनानामण्डपप्रेक्षागृहे प्रचुरपारिबर्हया भवत्या

---

समाजोऽथ सधर्मिणाम्।' इत्यमरः। कुसुमिता संजातकुसुमा। काशयष्टिः 'सरस' इति प्रसिद्धा। पाण्डुशिरसिजा श्वेतकेशा। अनन्यशरणाय त्वदेकशरणायेत्यर्थः। दनुजा दैत्याः। विविक्षुः प्रवेष्टुमिच्छुः। कस्य हेतोः किमर्थमित्यर्थः। सुदत्य इति सर्वाभिप्रायेण संबोधनम्। शोभना दन्ता यस्याः सा सुदती। 'वयसि दन्तस्य दतृ' इति दत्रादेशः समासान्तः। द्विजातिवृषात् ब्राह्मणश्रेष्ठात्। सत्यर्थे कार्यवस्तुनि सतीत्यर्थः। सुरङ्गया भूम्यन्तर्मार्गेण। सा वृद्धा। उदञ्जलिः बद्धाञ्जलिः। उदीरितवत्युक्तवती। अनघं निष्पापम्। अद्राक्ष्म दृष्टवत्यः। उदपाद्युत्पादितवान्। 'चिण् ते पदः' इति कर्तरि चिण्। राजयक्ष्मा क्षयरोगः। सुरक्षयं देवगृहम्। स्वर्गमित्यर्थः। अन्तर्वत्न्यां गर्भिण्याम्। अन्तरस्त्यस्यां गर्भः। 'अन्तर्वत्पतिवतोर्नुक्' इति साधुः। अथेति। उपह्वरे रहसि। विधिवद्विध्युक्तमार्गेण। दित्सामि दातुमिच्छामि। अरातिव्यसनाय। वैरिकृतदुःखायेत्यर्थः। कृत्रिमः शैलः पर्वतः तस्य गर्भो मध्यं तत्रोत्कीर्णा नाना मण्डपा यत्र तादृक् प्रेक्षागृहं नृत्येक्षणगृहम्। प्रचुरपरिबर्हया प्रचुरपरिवारया।

---

१ बिभयुः. २ वृषभात्. ३ इति प्राब्रवम्. ४ भट्टारक. ५ असुक्षयम्.

संवर्ध्यताम् । अस्त्यत्र भोग्यवस्तु वर्षशतोपभोगेनाप्यक्षय्यम्' इति । स तथोक्त्वा निजवासगृहस्य द्व्यङ्गुलभित्तावर्धपादं किष्कुविष्कम्भमुद्धृत्य तेनैव द्वारेण स्थानमिदमस्मानवीविशत् । इह च नो वसन्तीना द्वादश समाः समत्ययुः । इयं च वत्सा तरुणीभूता । न चाद्यापि स्मरति राजा । काममियं पितामहेन दर्पसाराय संकल्पिता । त्वदन्वया कान्तिमत्या चेयं गर्भस्थैव द्यूतजिता स्वमात्रा तवैव जायात्वेन समकल्प्यत । तदत्र प्राप्तरूपं चिन्त्यतां कुमारेणैव' इति । तां पुनरवोचम्—'अद्यैव राजगृहे किमपि कार्यं साधयित्वा प्रतिनिवृत्तो युष्मासु यथार्हं प्रतिपत्स्ये' इति । तेनैव दीपदर्शितबिलपथेन गत्वा स्थितेऽर्धरात्रे तदर्धपादं प्रत्युद्धृत्य वासगृहं प्रविष्टो विश्रब्धसुप्तं सिंहघोषं जीवग्राहमग्रहीषम् । आकृष्य च तमहिमिवाहिशत्रुः स्फुरन्तममुनैव भित्तिरन्ध्रपथेन स्त्रैणसंनिधिमनैषम् । आनीय च स्वभवनमायसनिगडसंदितचरणयुगलम्, अवनमितमलिनवदनम्, अश्रुबहलरक्तचक्षुषमेकान्ते जनयित्रोर्ममादर्शयम् । अकथयं च बिलकथाम् । अथ पितरौ प्रहृष्टतरौ तं निकृष्टाशयं निशाम्य बन्धने नियम्य तस्या दारिकाया यथार्हेण कर्मणा मां पाणिमग्राहयेताम् । अनाथकं च तद्राज्यमस्मदायत्तमेव जातम् । प्रकृतिकोपभयात्तु मन्मात्रा मुमुक्षितोऽपि न मुक्त एव सिंहघोषः । तथास्थिताश्च वयमङ्गराजः

---

**अस्तीति** । भोग्यं वस्तु । भोगार्हमित्यर्थः । अक्षय्यमशक्यक्षयम् । 'क्षय्यजय्यौ शक्यार्थे' इति निपातः । द्व्यङ्गुलभित्तावङ्गुलद्वयपरिमाणायां भित्तौ । अर्धपादं प्रस्तरपिधानम् । किष्कुविष्कम्भं हस्तपरिणाहम् । वितास्तिपरिणाहं वा । 'किष्कुर्हस्ते वितस्तौ च' इत्यमरः । 'परिणाहस्तु विष्कम्भः' इति वैजयन्ती । अवीविशत् प्रवेशं कारयति स्मेत्यर्थः । समत्ययुरतिक्रान्ताः । प्राप्तरूपं प्रशस्तं प्राप्तं कर्तव्यम् । 'प्रशंसायां रूपप्' । यथार्हं यथायोग्यम् । प्रतिपत्स्ये वर्तिष्ये । जीवग्राहं जीवं गृहीत्वेत्यि तथा । 'समूलाकृतजीवेषु हन्कृञ्ग्रहः' इति णमुल् । अहिशत्रुर्गरुडः । स्त्रैणं स्त्रीणां समूहः । 'स्त्रीपुंसाभ्यां नञ्स्नञौ भवनात्' इति समूहार्थे नञ् । अयः लोहं तस्येदमायसम् । निगडं शृङ्खला । संदितं बद्धम् । 'बद्धं निगडितं दितम्' इति वैजयन्ती । निकृष्टाशयं नीचचित्तम् । आयत्तमधीनम् । प्रकृतयः प्रजाः । मुमुक्षितोऽपि मोक्तुमिष्टोऽपि ।

---

१ वर्षशतेन. २ तथोक्तम्. ३ अङ्गनभित्ता०. ४ ०प्रसुप्तम्. ५ संदानित. ६ नितरां हृष्टौ. ७ अनायकम्.

सिंहवर्मा देवपादानां भक्तिमान्कृतकर्मा चेत्यमित्राभियुक्तमेनमभ्यसराम । अभूवं च भवत्पादपङ्कजरजोनुग्राह्यः । स चेदानीं भवच्चरणप्रणाम-प्रायश्चित्तमनुतिष्ठतु सर्वदुश्चरितक्षालनमनार्यः सिंहघोषः ' इत्यर्थपालः प्राञ्जलिः प्रणनाम । देवोऽपि राजवाहनः ' बहु पराक्रान्तम्, बहूपयुक्ता च बुद्धिः मुक्तबन्धस्ते श्वशुरः पश्यतु माम् ' इत्यभिधाय भूयः प्रमतिमेव पश्यन्प्रीतिस्मेरः ' प्रस्तूयतां तावदात्मीयं चरितम् ' इत्याज्ञापयत् ।

इति श्रीदण्डिनः कृतौ दशकुमारचरितेऽर्थपालचरितं नाम चतुर्थ उच्छ्वासः ।

---

## पञ्चमोच्छ्वासः ।

सोऽपि प्रणम्य विज्ञापयामास—' देव देवस्यान्वेषणाथ दिक्षु भ्रमन्नभ्रंकषस्यापि विन्ध्यपार्श्वरूढस्य[1] वनस्पतेरधः, परिणतपतङ्ग-बालपल्लवावतंसिते पश्चिमदिगङ्गनामुखे पल्वलाम्भस्युपस्पृश्योपास्य संध्यां तमःसमीकृतेषु निम्नोन्नतेषु गन्तुमक्षमः क्षमातले किसलयै-रुपरचय्य शय्यां शिशयिषमाणः शिरसि कुर्वन्नञ्जलिम् ' याऽस्मि-न्वनस्पतौ वसति देवता सैव मे शरणमस्तु शरारुचक्रचारभीषणायां शर्वगलश्यामशार्वरान्धकारपूराध्मातगभीरगह्वरायामस्यां महाटव्या-

---

भक्तिमान् भक्तियुक्तः । राजवाहनसंतोषार्थेयमुक्तिः । श्वशुरः पितृव्यश्वशुरः । ' कान्तिमतीसंबन्धान्मातुलः ' इति भूषणा । प्रस्तूयतामुपक्रम्यताम् ।

### इति श्रीदशकुमारचरितटीकायां चतुर्थ उच्छ्वासः ।

---

इदानीं प्रमतिः स्वचरितं वक्तुमुपक्रमते—सोऽपीति । अभ्रंकषस्याभ्रंलिहस्य । ' व्योमस्पृशो मेघस्पृशो वा ' इति भूषणा । ' अभ्रं मेघो वारिवाहः ' इति, ' द्योदिवौ द्वे स्त्रियामभ्रम् ' इति चामरः । ' सर्वकूलाभ्रकरीरेषु कषः ' इति खच् । ' अरुर्द्विषद-जन्तस्य मुम् ' इति मुमागमश्च । वनस्पतेरपुष्पवृक्षस्य । ' तैरपुष्पाद्वनस्पतिः ' इत्यमरः । परिणतः अस्ताभिमुख इत्यर्थः । पतङ्गः सूर्यः । स एव बालपल्लवः सोऽवतंसो यस्येति स तस्मिन् । पल्वलमल्पसरः । ' वेशन्तः पल्वलं चाल्पसरः ' इत्यमरः । उपस्पृश्य आचम्येत्यर्थः । ' उपस्पर्शस्त्वाचमनम् ' इत्यमरः । तमःसमीकृतेषु अन्धकारपूर्णीकृते-ष्वित्यर्थः । किसलयैः पल्लवैः । शिशयिषमाणः शयितुकामः । शरारुर्घातुकः । हिंसकः प्राणीति यावत् । शरारूणां चक्रं समूहस्तस्य चारस्तेन भीषणायाम् । शर्वगलो महादेवकण्ठः । शर्वर्या इदं शार्वरम् । आध्मातं पूरितम् । शर्वगलवत्

---

१ विन्ध्यपादपार्श्वरूढवन०.

मेकैकस्य मे प्रसुप्तस्य' इत्युपधाय वामभुजमशायिषि। ततः क्षणादेवावनिदुर्लभेन स्पर्शेनासुखायिषत किमपि गात्राणि अह्लादयिषतेन्द्रियाणि अभ्यमनायिष्ट चान्तरात्मा विशेषतश्च हृषितास्तनूरुहाः पर्यस्फुरन्मे दक्षिणभुजः। 'कथं न्विदम्' इति मन्दमन्दमुन्मिषन्नुपर्यच्छचन्द्रातपच्छेदकल्पं शुक्लांशुकवितानमैक्षिषि। वामतो वैलितदृष्टिः समया सौधभित्तिं चित्रास्तरणशायिनमतिविश्रब्धप्रसुप्तमङ्गनाजनमलक्षयम्। दक्षिणतो दत्तचक्षुरागलितस्तनांशुकाम्, अमृतफेनपटलपाण्डुरशयनशायिनीम्, आदिवराहदंष्ट्रांशुजाललग्नामंसस्रस्तदुग्धसागरदुकूलोत्तरीयां भयसाध्वसमूर्छितामिव धरणीम्, अरुणाधरकिरणबालकिसलयलास्यहेतुभिराननारविन्दपरिमलोद्वाहिभिर्निःश्वासमातरिश्वभिरीश्वरेक्षणदहनदग्धं स्फुलिङ्गशेषमनङ्गमिव संधुक्षयन्तीम्, अन्तःसुप्तषट्पदमम्बुजमिव जातनिद्रं सरसमामीलितलोचनेन्दीवरमाननं दधानाम्, ऐरावतमदावलेपलूनापविद्धामिव नन्दनवनकल्पवृक्षरत्नवल्लरीं,

---

श्यामो यः शार्वरः अन्धकारस्तस्य पूरेणाध्मातानि गभीराणि गह्वराणि यस्याम्। एककस्यैकाकिनः। उपधाय उपधानीकृत्वेत्यर्थः। असुखायिषत। सुखानि जातानीत्यर्थः। 'सुखादिभ्यः कर्तृवेदनायाम्' इति क्यङ्। लुङि सिच इट्। आह्लादयिषत। आह्लादं प्रापुरित्यर्थः। हृषिता उदञ्चिताः। हृषेरुदञ्चनेऽर्थे 'हृषेर्लोमसु' इतीडागमः। तनूरुहा लोमानि। दक्षिणभुजस्पन्द इष्टसमागमसूचकः। वर्णितं च कालिदासेन–'तस्यां रघोः सूनुरुपस्थितायां वृणीत मां नेति समाकुलोऽभूत्। वामेतरः संशयमस्य बाहुः केयूरबन्धोच्छ्वसितैर्नुनोद॥' इति। अच्छो निर्मलः' चन्द्रातपश्चन्द्रालोकः। छेदकल्पं भङ्गादीषन्न्यूनम्। तत्सदृशमित्यर्थः। वितानमुल्लोचम्। ऐक्षिषि दृष्टवान्। समया सौधभित्तिं सौधभित्तेः समीपे। 'समयेत्यन्तिकमध्ययोः। इति सामीप्यार्थेऽव्ययम्। 'अभितःपरितःसमयानिकषा–' इति द्वितीया। विश्रब्धो विश्वस्तः। **दक्षिणत इति**। पाण्डुरं श्वेतम्। अंसः स्कन्धः तस्मात्स्रस्तं दुग्धसागर एव दुकूलोत्तरीयं यस्यास्ताम्। भयमनुरागस्तेन साध्वसमूर्छितामिव। 'घोरसाध्वसमूर्छिताम्' इति भूषणा। अरुणस्ताम्रो यः अधरस्तस्य किरणास्त एव बालकिसलयानि तेषां लास्यं नृत्यं तद्धेतुभिः कारणभूतैः। परिमलमुद्वहन्ति ते परिमलोद्वाहिनस्तैः। मातरिश्वभिर्वायुभिः। ईश्वरेक्षणं महादेवतृतीयनेत्रम्। संधुक्षयन्तीं वर्धयन्तीम्। अन्तः सुप्ताः षट्पदा भ्रमरा यस्मिंस्तत्। ऐरावतस्य यो मदजनितोऽवलेपस्तेनादौ लूनां पश्चाद् अपविद्धां त्यक्ताम्। कल्पवृक्षस्य

---

१ एकाकिनः. २ आह्लादिषत. ३ चलित. ४ क्षीरसागर.

कामपि तरुणीमालोकयम् । अतर्कयं च—'क्व गता सा महाटवी कुत इदमूर्ध्वाण्डकपालसंपुटोदरोल्लेखि शक्तिध्वजशिखरशूलोत्सेधं सौधमागतं, क्व च तदरण्यस्थलीसमास्तीर्णं पल्लवशयनम्, कुतस्त्यं चेदमिन्दुगभस्तिसंभारभासुरं हंसतूलदुकूलशयनम्। एष च को नु शीतरश्मिकिरणरज्जुदोलापरिभ्रष्टमूर्छित इवाप्सरोगणः स्वैरसुप्तः सुन्दरीजनः का चेयं देवीवारविन्दहस्ता शारदशशाङ्कमण्डलामलदुकूलोत्तरच्छदमाधिशेते शयनतलम् । न तावदेषा देवयोषा यतो मन्दमन्दमिन्दुकिरणैः संवाह्यमाना कमलिनीव संकुचति । भग्नवृन्तच्युतरसबिन्दुशबलितं पाकपाण्डुचूतफलमिवोद्भिन्नस्वेदरेखमालक्ष्यते गण्डस्थलम् । अभिनवयौवनविदाहनिर्भरोष्मणि कुचतटे वैवर्ण्यमुपैति वर्णकम् । वाससी च परिभोगानुरूपं धूसरिमाणमादर्शयतः । तदेषा मानुष्येव । दिष्ट्या चानुच्छिष्टयौवना यतः सौकुमार्यमागताः संहता इवावयवाः प्रस्निग्धतमाऽपि पाण्डुतानुविद्धेव देहच्छविः दन्तपीडानभिज्ञतया नातिविशदरागो मुखे, विद्रुमद्युतिरधरमणिः अनत्यापूर्णमारक्तमूलं चम्पककुड्मलदलमिव कठोरं कपोल-

---

रत्नमयी वल्लरी मञ्जरी । 'वल्लरी मञ्जरी स्त्रियौ' इत्यमरः । ऊर्ध्वाण्डकपालम् । आकाशमित्यर्थः । 'अप एव ससर्जादौ तासु वीर्यमथासृजत् । तदण्डमभवद्धैमं सहस्रांशुसमप्रभम् ॥ तस्मिञ्जज्ञे स्वयं ब्रह्मा सर्वलोकपितामहः । नखैर्हिरण्यगर्भः स तदण्डं बिभिदे समम् ॥ ताभ्यां स शकलाभ्यां च दिवं भूमिं च निर्ममे ।' इति मनुः । शक्तिध्वजः सेनानीः । 'शक्तिध्वजः कुमारस्तस्य शिखरं तदालयाग्रं तत्र शूलं तद्वदुत्सेध उच्छ्रायो यस्य सः ।' इति भूषणा । 'सेनानीः कौञ्चशत्रुश्च कुमारः शक्तिकेतनः' इत्यजयः । 'शिखरं मण्डपतलमग्रिमं वृक्षशैलयोः' इत्युत्पलः । उत्सेध उन्नतिः । शक्तिध्वजो मण्डपतले शूलमग्रे च यस्य । 'अन्त्राण्यारोपयेदग्रे कुमारं स्थापयेत्तले । नन्द्यावर्त इति ख्यातः प्रासादो देवभूभुजाम् ॥'—इति लघुदीपिका । कुतस्त्यं कुत आगतम् । इन्दुगभस्तयश्चन्द्रकिरणाः । दोला हिन्दोलिका । शरदि भवं शारदं शशाङ्कमण्डलमिवामलं दुकूलमुत्तरच्छदो यस्य तत् । देवयोषा देवस्त्री । संवाह्यमानाऽऽचर्यमाणा । 'संवाहनं मर्दनं स्यात्' इति कोशः । 'यतो निद्राति न देवयोषा । देवानामस्वप्नत्वात्' इति भूषणा । कमलिनीवेन्दुकिरणैः संकुचति । भग्नवृन्तं नष्टप्रसवबन्धनम् । शबलितं नानावर्णम् । अभिनवं यद्यौवनं तस्य विशिष्टो यो दाहस्तेन निर्भरोऽतिशयितः ऊष्मा यस्मिन् । वर्णकमङ्गरागः । धूसरिमाणं मलिनत्वम् । संहता मिलिताः । पाण्डुतायामनुविद्धेव स्यूतेव । विद्रुमं प्रवालं तद्द्युतिस्तत्कान्तिः । अनत्यापूर्णमीषत्पूर्णम् । कुड्मलदलं मुकुलपत्रम् ।

---

१ ०ण्डसंपुटो०; ०कपालोल्लेखि. २ किरणरजतरज्जु. ३ ०ण्डलं पर्यङ्कतलमेतदमल...च्छदमधिशेते. ४ निद्राति. ५ दुर्लभोष्मणि. ६ वर्णकः. ७ परीभोग.

तलम्, अनङ्गबाणपातमुक्ताशङ्कं च विश्रब्धमधुरं सुप्यते न चैतद्वक्षःस्थलं निर्दयविमर्दविस्तारितमुखस्तनयुगलम् अस्ति चानतिक्रान्तशिष्टमर्यादचेतसो ममास्यामासक्तिः। आसक्त्यनुरूपं पुनराश्लिष्टा यदि स्पष्टमार्तरवेणैव सह निद्रां मोक्ष्यति। अथाहं न शक्ष्यामि चानुपश्लिष्य शयितुम्। अतो यद्भावि तद्भवतु। भाग्यमत्र परीक्षिष्ये।' इति स्पृष्टास्पृष्टमेव किमप्याविद्धरागसाध्वसं लक्ष्यसुप्तः स्थितोऽस्मि। साऽपि किमप्युत्कम्पिना रोमोद्भेदवता वामपार्श्वेन सुखायमानेन मन्दमन्दजृम्भिकारम्भमन्थराङ्गी त्वङ्गदग्रपक्ष्मणोश्चक्षुषोरलसतान्ततारकेणानतिपक्वनिद्राकषायितापाङ्गपरभागेण युगलेनेषदुन्मिषन्ती त्रासविस्मयहर्षरागशङ्काविलासविभ्रमव्यवहितानि व्रीडान्तराणि कानि कान्यपि कामेनाद्भुतानुभावेनावस्थान्तराणि कार्यमाणा परिजनप्रबोधनोद्यता गिरं कामावेगपरवशं हृदयमङ्गानि च साध्वसायाससंबध्यमानस्वेदपुलकानि

अनङ्गः कामस्तस्य बाणपातानां मुक्ता आशङ्का यस्मिन् कर्मणि तद्यथा तथा। विश्रब्धमधुरं विश्वाससुन्दरम्। निर्दयं यः विमर्दस्तेन विस्तारितं मुखं यस्य तादृक् स्तनयुगलं यत्र तत्। अनतिक्रान्ता अदूरीकृता शिष्टमर्यादा येनैवंविधं चेतो यस्येति तस्य। 'अनतिक्रान्तशिष्टमर्यादचेतसो धर्मात्मनोऽस्यामासक्तिरत इयं मदुपभोगयोग्येति व्यङ्ग्यम्। तथा च कालिदासः—'असंशयं क्षत्रपरिग्रहक्षमा यदार्यमस्यामभिलाषि मे मनः' इत्या —इति भूषणा। **अथेति**। अनुपश्लिष्यानालिङ्ग्य। स्पृष्टास्पृष्टम्। अल्पस्पर्शमित्यर्थः। राग आसक्तिः। 'आविद्धे रागसाध्वसे यस्यां क्रियायाम्। अनुपमस्त्रीलाभाद्रागः। यथेष्टं स्पृष्टं चैतदार्तरवं भविष्यतीति साध्वसम्।' इति भूषणा। लक्ष्यसुप्तः सुप्त इवेत्यर्थः। उत्कम्पिनोत्कम्पनशीलेन। मन्थराङ्गी सुन्दराङ्गी। 'मन्थरौ नम्रसुन्दरौ' इति वैजयन्ती। 'सालसाङ्गी' इति तु भूषणा। त्वङ्गच्चलत्। 'त्वगि कम्पने' इति धातुः। त्वङ्गदग्रपक्ष्म ययोरिति त्वङ्गदग्रपक्ष्मणोः। अनतिपक्वा नातिपूर्णा मध्ये विच्छेदाद्या निद्रा तया कषायितः आरक्तीकृतः अपाङ्गयोः परभागो गुणोत्कर्षः यस्य तेन। "अपूर्वपुरुषदर्शनात् त्रासः। आगमप्रकारानवबोधाद्विस्मयः। तदङ्गसङ्गसुखानुभवाद्धर्षः। तत एव रागः। ततो यथर्थं मां बलात्कारेण करिष्यति स्वाङ्के ततः किं भवेदिति शङ्का। ततो भूषणादीनामस्थाने विन्यासः। अस्रस्तमपि वस्त्रं भूषणं वा स्रस्तमिति पुनस्तद्देशे स्थाप्यते यथास्थितमपि तद्देशाच्चाल्यते शङ्कापराधीनचित्तेन जनेन। 'अस्थाने भूषणादीनां विन्यासो विभ्रमो मतः।' इति रसरत्नहारः। व्रीडा अन्तरा मध्ये येषां तानि।" इति भूषणा। कामावेगपरवशं मदनवेगपराधीनम्। "साध्वसेनापरिचितपुरुषदर्शनेनायासेन तदङ्गसङ्गानङ्गपीडया संबध्यमानस्वेदपुलकानि। सात्त्विकभावाविर्भावादिति भावः।" इति भूषणा। साध्वसं भयम्। आयासः खेदः। अथ वा

१ शङ्कामुक्ततया. २ युगमुकुलम्. ३ उत्कम्पिता. ४ कषायदर्शितरागोपाङ्गपरभागेण. ५ विन्यास. ६ संवर्धमान.

कथं कथमपि निगृह्य सस्पृहेण मधुरकूणितात्रिभागेण मन्दमन्दप्रचारितेन चक्षुषा मदङ्गानि निर्वर्ण्य दूरोत्सर्पितपूर्वकायाऽपि तस्मिन्नेव शयने सचकितमशयिष्ट। अजनिष्ट मे रागाविष्टचेतसोऽपि किमपि निद्रा। पुनरननुकूलस्पर्शदुःखाँयत्तगात्रः प्राबुध्ये। प्रबुद्धस्य च मे सैव महाटवी तदेव तरुतलं स एव पत्रास्तरोऽभूत्। विभावरी च व्यभासीत्। अभूच्च मे मनसि—'किमयं स्वप्नः किं विप्रलम्भो वा किमियमासुरी दैवी वा काऽपि माया। यद्भावि तद्भवतु। नाहमिदं तत्त्वतो नाँवबुध्य मोक्ष्यामि भूमिशय्याम्। यावदायुरत्रत्यायै देवतायै प्रतिशयितो भवामि' इति निश्चितमतिरतिष्ठम्।

अथाविर्भूय काऽपि रविकराभितप्तकुवलयदामतान्ताङ्गयष्टिः क्लिष्टनिवसनोत्तरीया निरलक्तकरूक्षपाटलेन निःश्वासोष्मजर्जरितत्विषा दन्तच्छदेन वमन्तीव कपिलधूमधूम्रं विरहानलम्, अनवरतसलिलधाराविसर्जनाद्रुधिरावशेषमिव लोहिततरं द्वितयमक्ष्णोरुद्वहन्ती कुलचारित्रबन्धनपाशविभ्रमेणैकवेणीभूतेन केशपाशेन नीलांशुकचीरचूडिकापरिवृता पतिव्रतापताकेव संचरन्ती क्षामक्षामाऽपि देवतानुभावादनतिक्षीणवर्णावकाशा सीमन्तिनी प्रणिपतन्तं मां प्रहर्षोत्कम्पितेन भुजलताद्वयेनोत्थाप्य पुत्रवत्परिष्वज्य शिरस्युपाघ्राय वात्सल्यमिव स्तनयुगलेन स्तन्यच्छलात्प्रक्षरन्ती शिशिरेणाश्रुणा निरुद्धकण्ठी स्नेह-

---

साध्वसमेवायासः। संबध्यमानाः स्वेदपुलका येषु तानि। कूणितः संकुचितः। त्रिभागः। नेत्रप्रान्त इत्यर्थः। 'संकोचितास्त्रयो भागाः अपाङ्गो मध्यो नासिकासमीपश्च यस्येत्यर्थः' इति भूषणा। उत्सर्पित ऊर्ध्वीकृतः। विभावरी रात्रिः। व्यभासीद्विभाताऽभूत्। असुरस्येयमासुरी। देवस्येयं दैवी। तत्त्वतः सत्यत्वेन। यावदायुर्यावदायुष्यम्। प्रतिशयितः कृतशय्यः। **अथेति**। रविकरैः सूर्यकिरणैः अभितप्तं यत्कुवलयदाम तद्वत्तान्ता क्लान्ता अङ्गयष्टिः शरीरयष्टिः यस्याः। क्लिष्टं जीर्णं निवसनोत्तरीयं यस्याः सा। दन्तच्छदेनौष्ठेन। कपिलः पिङ्गलः। धूम्रं किंचिदारक्तश्यामम्। अनवरतं निरन्तरम्। लोहिततरमत्यारक्तम्। एकवेणीभूतेनाद्वितीयेन। केशपाशः केशकलापः। चूडिका कूर्पासः। 'चीरचूडिका सुवासिनीभिर्हस्तेषु ध्रियमाणः खड्गशृङ्गनिर्मितो वलयाकृतिः भूषणविशेषः' इति भूषणा। क्षामक्षामाऽतिक्षीणा। देवतानुभावाद्देवतासामर्थ्यात्। अनतिक्षीणवर्णा नातिक्षीणो वर्णो यस्याः सा तथा। प्रणिपतन्तं नमस्कारं कुर्वन्तम्। वात्सल्यं पुत्रस्नेहम्। स्तने भवं स्तन्यं तस्य छलान्मिषात्। प्रक्षरन्ती स्रवन्ती।

---

१ दुःखायमान. २ व्ययासीत्. ३ अनवबुध्य. ४ प्रतिशयितोऽस्मि. ५ क्लिन्न. ६ कलापेन. ७ अंशुकरचितचीरचूलिका. ८ मुखेन.

गद्गदं[1] व्याहार्षीत्—'वत्स यदि[2] वः कथितवती मगधराजमहिषी वसुमती मम हस्ते बालमर्थपालं निधाय[3] कथां च काचिदात्मभर्तृपुत्रसखीजनानुबद्धां[4] राजराजप्रवर्तितां कृत्वाऽन्तर्धानमगादात्मजा मणिभद्रस्येति साऽहमस्मि वो जननी। पितुर्वो धर्मपालसूनोः सुमित्रानुजस्य कामपालस्य पादमूलान्निष्कारणकोपकलुषिताशया प्रोष्यानुशयविधुरा स्वप्ने केनापि रक्षोरूपेणोपेत्य शप्ताऽस्मि—'चण्डिकायां त्वयि वर्षमात्रं वसामि प्रवासदुःखाय' इति ब्रुवतैवाहमाविष्टा प्राबुध्ये। गतं च तद्वर्षं वर्षसहस्रदीर्घम्। अतीतायां तु यामिन्यां देवदेवस्य त्र्यम्बकस्य श्रावस्त्यामुत्सवसमाजमनुभूय बन्धुजनं च स्थानस्थानेभ्यः संनिपतितमभि[5]समीक्ष्य मुक्तशापा पत्युः पार्श्वमभिसरामीति प्रस्थितायामेव मयि त्वमत्राभ्युपेत्य 'प्रपन्नोऽस्मि[6] शरणमिहत्यां देवताम्' इति प्रसुप्तोऽसि। एवं शापदुःखाविष्टया तु मया तदा न तत्त्वतः परिच्छिन्नो भवान्। अपि तु शरणागतमविरल[7]प्रमादायामस्यां महाटव्यामयुक्तं परित्यज्य गन्तुमिति मया त्वमपि स्वपन्नेवासि नीतः। प्रत्यासन्ने च तस्मिन्देवगृहे पुनरचिन्तयम्—'कथमिह तरुणेनानेन सह समाजं गमिष्यामि' इति। अथ राज्ञः श्रावस्तीश्वरस्य यथार्थनाम्नो धर्मवर्धनस्य कन्यां नवमालिकां घर्मकालसुभगे कन्यापुरविमानहर्म्यतले विशालकोमलं शय्यातलमधिशयानां यदृच्छयोपलभ्य 'दिष्ट्येयं सुप्ता परिजनश्च गाढनिद्रः[8]। शेतामयमत्र मुहूर्तमात्रं ब्राह्मणकुमारो यावत्कृतकृत्या निवर्तेय' इति त्वां तत्र[9] शाययित्वा तमुद्देशमगमम्। दृष्ट्वा चोत्सवश्रियम् निर्विश्य च स्वजनदर्शनसुखम् अभिवाद्य च त्रिभुवनेश्वरमा-

---

व्याहार्षीत्। अवोचदित्यर्थः। 'वो जननी भर्तृपित्रपेक्षया कनिष्ठस्य पितृव्यस्य पत्नी' इति भूषणा। 'कृताभिषेका महिषी' इत्यमरः। कलुषिताशया मलिनचित्ता। प्रोष्य प्रवासं कृत्वा। आविष्टा आवेशं प्राप्ता। दीर्घमतिमहत्। यामिन्यां रात्रौ। श्रावस्त्यामेतन्नामनगर्याम्। संनिपतितमागतम्। तत्त्वतः सत्यतः। अविरलप्रमादायां बहुतरप्रमादायाम्। प्रत्यासन्ने समीपवर्तिनि। समाजं सधर्मिणां समूहम्। अथेति। यदृच्छया दैवयोगेन। दिष्ट्याऽदृष्टेन। उद्देशं

---

१ गर्भम्. २ यद्.३ परिदाय. ४ अनुविद्धाम्. ५ समापतितम्. ६ प्रतिपन्नः. ७ अविरत. ८ गाढसुप्तः. ९ अमुत्र.

तमालीकप्रत्याकलनोपारूढसाध्वसं च नमस्कृत्य भक्तिप्रणतहृदया भगवतीमम्बिकाम् तया गिरिदुहित्रा देव्या सस्मितम् 'अयि भद्रे मा भैषीः । भवेदानीं भर्तृपार्श्वगामिनी । गतस्ते शापः' इत्यनुगृहीता सद्य एव प्रत्यापन्नमहिमा प्रतिनिवृत्य दृष्ट्वैव त्वां यथावदभ्यजानाम्—'कथं मत्सुत एवायं वत्सस्यार्थपालस्य प्राणभूतः सखा प्रमतिरिति । पापया मयाऽस्मिन्नज्ञानादौदासीन्यमाचरितम् । अपि चायमस्यामासक्तभावः । कन्या चैनं कामयते युवानम् । उभौ चेमौ लक्ष्यसुप्तौ त्रपया साध्वसेन वाऽन्योन्यमात्मानं न विवृण्वाते । गन्तव्यं च मया । कामाघ्रातयाऽप्यनया कन्यया रहस्य[1]रक्षणाय न समाभाषितः सखीजनः परिजनो वा । नयामि तावत्कुमारम् । पुनरपीममर्थं लब्धलक्षो[2] यथोपपन्नैरुपायैः साधयिष्यति' इति मत्प्रभावप्रस्वापितं भवन्तमेतदेव पत्रशयनं प्रत्यनैषम् । एवमिदं वृत्तम् । एषा चाहं पितुस्ते पादमूलं प्रत्युपसर्पेयम्' इति प्राञ्जलिं मां भूयो भूयः परिष्वज्य शिरस्युपाघ्राय कपोलयोश्चुम्बित्वा स्नेहविह्वला गताऽऽसीत् ।

अहं च पञ्चबाणवश्यः श्रावस्तीमभ्यवर्तिषि । मार्गे च महति निगमे नैगमानां ताम्रचूडयुद्धकोलाहलो महानासीत् । अहं च तत्र संनिहितः किंचिदस्मेषि । संनिधिनिषण्णस्तु मे वृद्धविटः कोऽपि ब्राह्मणः शनैः स्मितहेतुमपृच्छत् । अब्रवं च—'कथमिव नारिकेलजातेः प्राच्यवाटकुक्कुटस्य प्रतीच्यवाट[3]ः पुरुषैरसमीक्ष्य बलाकाजातिस्ताम्रचूडो बलप्रमाणाधिकस्यैवं प्रतिविसृष्टः' इति । सोऽपि तज्ज्ञः

---

प्रदेशम् । अलीकमपराधः । 'अलीकमपराधः स्यादसत्याप्रिययोरपि ।' इति सज्जनः । प्रत्याकलनं साक्षात्करणम् । उपारूढं जातं साध्वसं यथेति क्रियाविशेषणम् । गिरिदुहित्रा पार्वत्या । प्रत्यापन्नमहिमा प्राप्तमहिमा । उदासीनस्य भाव औदासीन्यम् । कामाघ्रातया । मदनस्पृष्टयेत्यर्थः । लब्धलक्षो लब्धावसरः । अहमिति । निगमो वणिग्ग्रामः 'निगमः सुरे । वेदे वणिक्पथे मार्गे ।' इति महीपः । तत्र भवा नैगमास्तेषां नैगमानां वणिजाम् । ताम्रचूडः कुक्कुटः । 'कृकवाकुस्ताम्रचूडः कुक्कुटश्चरणायुधः ।' इत्यमरः । अस्मेषि हास्यमकरवम् । संनिधिनिषण्णः समीपस्थितः । नारिकेलजातिरेकः कुक्कुटः । द्वितीयः कुक्कुटो बलाकाजातीयः । 'दीर्घग्रीवः सितवपुर्महाप्राणः स्रवन्मदः । बलाकाजातिरित्युक्तस्तदन्यो नारिकेलजः ॥' इति वैजयन्ती ।

---

१ गुह्य०. २ लब्धक्षणः; लब्धलक्षणः. ३ वाटपुरुषैः.

'किमङ्गैरेभिर्व्युत्पादितैः। तूष्णीमास्स्व' इत्युपहस्तिकायास्ताम्बूलं कर्पूरसहितमुद्धृत्य मह्यं दत्त्वा चित्राः कथाः कथयन्क्षणमतिष्ठत्। प्रायुध्यत चातिसंरब्धमनुप्रहारप्रवृत्तस्वपक्षमुक्तकण्ठीरवरवं विहंगमद्वयम्। जितश्चासौ प्रतीच्यवाटकुक्कुटः। सोऽपि विटब्राह्मणः स्ववाटकुक्कुटविजयहृष्टो मयि वयोविरुद्धं सख्यमुपेत्य तदहः स्वगृह एव स्नानभोजनादि कारयित्वोत्तरेद्युः श्रावस्तीं प्रति यान्तं मामनुगम्य 'स्मर्तव्योऽस्मि सत्यर्थे' इति मित्रवद्विसृज्य प्रत्ययासीत्।

अहं च गत्वा श्रावस्तीमध्वश्रान्तो बाह्योद्याने लतामण्डपे शायितोऽस्मि। हंसकेरवप्रबोधितश्चोत्थाय कामपि क्वणितनूपुरमुखराभ्यां चरणाभ्यां मदन्तिकमुपसरन्तीं युवतीमद्राक्षम्। सा त्वागत्य स्वहस्तवर्तिनि चित्रपटे लिखितं मत्सदृशं किमपि पुंरूपं मां च पर्यायेण निर्वर्णयन्ती सविस्मयं सवितर्कं सहर्षं च क्षणमवातिष्ठत। मयाऽपि तत्र चित्रपटे मत्सादृश्यं पश्यता तद्दृष्टिचेष्टितमनाकस्मिकं मन्यमानेन 'ननु सर्वसाधारणोऽयं रमणीयः पुण्यारामभूमिभागः। किमिति चिरस्थितिक्लेशोऽनुभूयते। ननूपवेष्टव्यम्' इत्यभिहिता सा सस्मितम् 'अनुगृहीताऽस्मि' इति न्यषीदत्। संकथा च देशवार्तानुबद्धा काचनावयोरभूत्। कथासंश्रिता च सा 'देशातिथिरसि। दृश्यन्ते च तेऽध्वश्रान्तानीव गात्राणि। यदि न दोषो मद्गृहेऽद्य विश्रमितुमनुग्रहः क्रियताम्' इत्यशंसत्। अहं च 'अयि मुग्धे नैष दोषो गुण एव' इति तदनुमार्गगामी तद्गृहगतो राजार्हेण स्नानभोजनादिनोपचरितः सुखं निषण्णो रहसि पर्यपृच्छ्ये—'महाभाग दिगन्तराणि भ्रमता कच्चिदस्ति किंचिदद्भुतं

---

उपहस्तिका ताम्बूलस्थापनाय चर्म (वस्त्र) पेशी। 'पूगाद्यावपनी चर्म (वस्त्र) भस्त्रिका चोपहस्तिका' इति वैजयन्ती। भाषया 'चंची' इति प्रसिद्धा। 'उपदस्तिका' इति पाठे स एवार्थः। अनुप्रहारे प्रवृत्तः यः स्वपक्षः कुक्कुटान्यतरपक्षस्तेन मुक्तः कण्ठीरवरवः सिंहनादः यस्य। वाटः श्रेणिः। 'वाटः पुमान्पथि श्रेणौ' इति वररुचिः। वयोविरुद्धं 'समवयसोर्मैत्री' इति वचनात्तद्विरुद्धम्। नूपुरं पादभूषणम्। मुखरं वाचालम्। मदन्तिकं मत्समीपम्। पुंरूपं पुरुषरूपम्। संकथा मिथोभाषणम्। देशवार्ता लौकिकगोष्ठी। काचन वचनातीता। सा चाहं चावां तयोः। अनुग्रहः कृपा। राजार्हेण राजयोग्येन। कच्चिदिति प्रश्ने। आशास्पदमाशास्थानम्। संबाधः संघः।

---

१ स्वकुक्कुट. २ मण्डले. ३ हंसरव. ४ कमपि पुरुषम्. ५ अनुविद्धा.

भवतोपलब्धम्' इति । ममाभवन्मनसि—' महदिदमाशास्पदम् । एषा खलु निखिलपरिजनसंबाधसंलक्षितायाः सखी राजदारिकायाः चित्रपटे चास्मिन्नपि तदुपरिविरचितसितवितानं हर्म्यतलम्, तद्गतं च प्रकामविस्तीर्णं शरदभ्रपटलपाण्डुरं शयनम्, तदधिशायिनी च निद्रालीढलोचना ममैवेयं प्रतिकृतिः । अतो नूनमनङ्गेन साऽपि राजकन्या तावतीं भूमिमारोपिता यस्यामसह्यमदनज्वरे[1]व्यथितोन्मादिता सती सखीनिर्बन्धपृष्टविक्रियानिमित्ता चातुर्येणैतद्रूपनिर्माणेनैव समर्थमुत्तरं दत्तवती । रूपसंवादाच्च संशयानया[2]ऽनया पृष्टो[3] भिन्द्यामस्याः[4] संशयं यथानुभवकथनेन' इति जातनिश्चयोऽब्रवम्—'भद्रे देहि चित्रपटम्' इति । सा त्वर्पितवती मद्धस्ते । पुनस्तमादाय तामपि व्याजसुप्तामुल्लसन्मदनरागविह्वलां वल्लभामेकत्रै[5]वाभिलिख्य ' काचिदेवंभूता युवतिरीदृशस्य पुंसः पार्श्वशायिन्यरण्यानीप्रसुप्तेन मयोपलब्धा । किमेष स्वप्नः ' इत्यालपं च । हृष्टया तु तया विस्तरतः पृष्टः सर्वमेव वृत्तान्तमकथयम् । असौ च सख्या मन्निमित्तान्यवस्थान्तराण्यवर्णयत् । तदाकर्ण्य च ' यदि तव सख्या मदनुग्रहोन्मुखं मानसम्, गमय कानिचिदहानि । कमपि कन्यापुरे निराशङ्कनिवासकर[6]णमुपायमारचय्यागमिष्यामि ' इति कथंचिदेनामभ्युपगमय्य गत्वा तदेव खर्वटं वृद्धविटेन समगंसि ।

सोऽपि ससंभ्रमं विश्रमय्य तथैव स्नानभोजनादि कारयित्वा रहस्यपृच्छत्—' आर्य, कस्य हेतोरचिरेणैव प्रत्यागतोऽसि । ' प्रत्यवादिषमेनम्—'स्थान एवाहमार्येणास्मि पृष्टः । श्रूयताम् । अस्ति

उपरि विरचितं सितवितानं सितोल्लोचो यस्य । शरदभ्रं शरत्कालमेघस्तस्य पटलं तद्वत्पाण्डुरं शुभ्रम् । आलीढे व्याप्ते लोचने यस्याः सा । प्रतिकृतिरालेख्यम् । तावतीं भूमिं मदनपरवशतारूपां मर्यादाम् । असह्यश्चासौ मदनज्वरश्च तेन व्यथिता चासौ उन्मादिता च । सखीभिर्निर्बन्धेन आग्रहेण पृष्टं विक्रियाया निमित्तं यस्याः । रूपस्य लिखितपुरुषस्यास्य च संवादात्सादृश्यात् । ' रूपसंवादाद्रूपदर्शनात् ' इति भूषणा । व्याजेन मिषेण । उल्लसन्स्फुरन् यो मदनरागस्तेन विह्वलाम् । एकत्रैकस्मिन्प्रदेशे । अरण्यानी । ' महारण्यमरण्यानी ' इत्यमरः । उपलब्धा प्राप्ता । मदनुग्रहोन्मुखं मयि योऽनुग्रहस्तत्रोन्मुखमुत्कण्ठितम् । खर्वटो ग्रामः । स्थाने युक्तमित्यर्थः ।

१ कामज्वरोन्माथिता. २ संशयादनया. ३ आपृच्छ्ये. ४ भिन्द्यानि. ५ तत्रैव. ६ कारणम्

हि श्रावस्ती नाम नगरी। तस्याः पतिरपर इव धर्मपुत्रो धर्मवर्धनो नाम राजा। तस्य दुहिता प्रत्यादेश इव श्रियः प्राणा इव कुसुमधन्वनः सौकुमार्यविडम्बितनवमालिका नवमालिका नाम कन्यका। सा मया समापत्तिदृष्टा कामनाराचपङ्क्तिमिव कटाक्षमालां मम मर्मणि व्यकिरत्। तच्छल्योद्धरणक्षमश्च धन्वन्तरिसदृशस्त्वदृते नेतरोऽस्ति वैद्य इति प्रत्यागतोऽस्मि। तत्प्रसीद कंचिदुपायमाचरितुम्[1]। अयमहं परिवर्तितस्त्रीवेषस्ते कन्या नाम भवेयम्। अनुगतश्च मया त्वमुपगम्य धर्मासनगतं धर्मवर्धनं वक्ष्यसि—'ममेयमेकैव दुहिता। जातमात्रायां त्वस्यां जनन्यस्याः संस्थिता। माता च पिता च भूत्वाऽहमेव व्यवर्धयम्। एतदर्थमेव विद्यामयं शुल्कमर्जितुं गतोऽभूदवन्तिनगरीमुज्जयिनीमस्मद्वैवाह्यकुलजः कोऽपि विप्रदारकः। तस्मै चेयमनुमता दातुमितरस्मै न योग्या। तरुणीभूता चेयम्। स च विलम्बितः। तेन तमानीय पाणिमस्या ग्राहयित्वा तस्मिन्न्यस्तभारः संन्यसिष्ये। दुरभिरक्षतया तु दुहितॄणां मुक्तशैशवानां विशेषतश्चामातृकाणाम्, इह देवं मातृपितृस्थानीयं प्रजानामापन्नशरणमागतोऽस्मि। यदि वृद्धं ब्राह्मणमधीतिनमगतिमतिथिं[2] च मामनुग्राह्यपक्षे गणयत्यादिराजचरितधुर्यो देवः,

---

प्रत्यादेशो निरसनम्। 'प्रत्याख्यानं निरसनं प्रत्यादेशो निराकृतिः।' इत्यमरः। सौकुमार्येण विडम्बिता कदर्थिता नवमालिका ययेति तथा। समापत्तिर्यदृच्छासंगतिः। नाराचा बाणाः। मर्मणि जीवस्थाने। 'जीवस्थानं भवेन्मर्म' इति हलायुधः। तच्छल्योद्धरणं तच्छल्यदूरीकरणं तत्र क्षमः समर्थः। धन्वतरिर्देववैद्यः। संस्थिता मरणं प्राप्ता। व्यवर्धयं वर्धितवान्। शुल्कं जामात्रा देयं वस्तु। विवाहाय योग्यं वैवाह्यं यत्कुलं वंशस्तत्र जातः। संन्यसिष्ये संन्यासमाश्रयिष्ये। दुरभिरक्षतया दुःखेन रक्षणयोग्यतया। मुक्तशैशवानाम्। प्राप्ततारुण्यानामित्यर्थः। आपन्नशरणमापन्नानामापत्प्राप्तानां शरणं रक्षकम्। 'शरणं गृहरक्षित्रोः' इत्यमरः। अधीतिनम्। 'योऽधीतकृत्स्नवेदः स्यात्सोऽधीतीत्युच्यते बुधैः' इति कोशः। 'इष्टादिभ्यश्च' इति कर्तरि इनिः। अगतिं निराश्रयम्। अनुग्राह्यपक्षे कृपास्थानीये। आदिराजो मनुस्तस्येव चरितं येषां ते आदिराजचरितास्तेषां धुर्यः श्रेष्ठः। 'धुरो यड्ढकौ' इति यत्।

---

1 आरचयितुमर्हसि. 2 अतिथिमिति नास्ति क्वचित्.

सैषा भवद्भुजच्छायामखण्डितचारित्रा तावदध्यास्तां यावदस्याः पाणिग्राहकमानयेयम्' इति । स एवमुक्तो नियतमभिमनायमानः स्वदुहितृसंनिधौ मां वासयिष्यति । गतस्तु भवानागामिनि मासि फाल्गुने फल्गुनीषूत्तरासु भाविनि राजान्तःपुरजनस्य तीर्थयात्रोत्सवे तीर्थस्थानात्प्राच्यां दिशि गोरुतान्तरमतिक्रम्य वानीरवलयमध्यवर्तिनि कार्त्तिकेयगृहे करतलगतेन शुक्लाम्बरयुगलेन स्थास्यसि । स खल्वहमनभिशङ्क एवैतावन्तं कालं सहाभिविहृत्य राजकन्यया भूयस्तस्मिन्नुत्सवे गङ्गाम्भसि विहरन्विहारव्याकुले कन्यकासमाजे मग्नोपसृतस्त्वदभ्यास एवोन्मङ्क्ष्यामि । पुनस्त्वदुपहृते वाससी परिधायापनीतदारिकावेषो जामाता नाम भूत्वा त्वामेवानुगच्छेयम् । नृपात्मजा तु मामितस्ततोऽन्विष्यानासादयन्ती 'तया विना न भोक्ष्ये' इति रुदत्येवावरोधने स्थास्यति । तन्मूले च महति कोलाहले, क्रन्दत्सु परिजनेषु, रुदत्सु सखीजनेषु, शोचत्सु पौरजनेषु, किंकर्तव्यतामूढे सामात्ये पार्थिवे, त्वमास्थानीमेत्य मां स्थापयित्वा वक्ष्यसि—'देव स एष मे जामाता तवार्हति श्रीभुजाराधनम् । अधीती चतुर्ष्वाम्नायेषु, गृहीती षट्स्वङ्गेषु, आन्वीक्षिकीविचक्षणः, चतुःषष्टिकलागमप्रयोगचतुरः, विशेषेण गजरथतुरङ्गतन्त्रवित्, इष्वसनास्त्रकर्मणि गदायुद्धे च निरुपमः, पुराणेतिहासकुशल, कर्ता काव्यनाटकाख्यायिकानाम्, वेत्ता सोपनिषदोऽर्थशास्त्रस्य, निर्मत्सरो गुणेषु, विश्रम्भी

---

अखण्डितं चारित्रं यस्याः सा अखण्डितचारित्रा अदूषितकन्यावस्था । पाणिग्राहकं पाणिग्रहणकर्तारम् । फल्गुनीषूत्तरासु । उत्तराफल्गुनीष्वित्यर्थः । अनभिशङ्को निःशङ्कः । मग्नोपसृतो मग्नः सन्नुपसृतः । त्वदभ्यासे त्वत्समीपे । उन्मङ्क्ष्यामि प्रादुर्भविष्यामि । अवरोधनं राजान्तःपुरम् । 'अधीती चतुर्ष्वाम्नायेषु' इत्यत्र 'क्तस्येन्विषयस्य कर्मण्युपसंख्यानम्' इति सप्तमी । आन्वीक्षिकी तर्कविद्या तस्यां विचक्षणः कुशलः । 'इतिहासः पुरावृत्तम्' इत्यमरः । आख्यायिका प्रबन्धविशेषः कादम्बरीहर्षचरित्रादिः । 'प्रसृतानाकुलश्रव्यशब्दार्थपदवृत्तिना । गद्येन युक्तोदात्तार्था सोच्छ्वासाऽऽख्यायिका मता ॥' इति भामः । "वृत्तं व्याख्यायते तस्या नायकेनाथ चेष्टितम् । वक्त्रं चापरवक्त्रं च काले भाव्यर्थशंसि च ॥ कवेरभिप्रायकृतैरङ्कनैः कैश्चिदाननैः ॥" इत्यधिकं भूषणायाम् । सोपनिषदोऽर्थशास्त्रस्य कर्मज्ञानमीमांसयोः । निर्मत्सरो मात्सर्यरहितः ।

---

१ भुजतरु. २ आवास°. ३ °रासु राजा°...त्सवो भविष्यति. ४ रुदत्यवस्थास्यते. ५ अवरोध.

सुहृत्सु, [1]शंक्यः संविभागशीलः श्रुतधरो गतस्मयश्च । नास्य दोषमणीयांसमप्युपलभे । न च गुणेष्वविद्यमानम् । तन्मादृशस्य ब्राह्मणमात्रस्य न लभ्य एष संबन्धी । दुहितरमस्मै समर्प्य वार्द्धकोचितमन्त्यमाश्रमं संक्रमेयं यदि देवः साधु मन्यते ' इति । स इदमाकर्ण्य वैवर्ण्याक्रान्तवक्त्रः परमुपेतो वैलक्ष्यमारप्स्यते[2]ऽनुनेतुमानित्यतादिसंकीर्तनेनात्रभवन्तं मन्त्रिभिः सह । त्वं तु तेषामदत्तश्रोत्रो मुक्तकण्ठं [3]रुदित्वा चिरस्य बाष्पकुण्ठकण्ठः काष्ठान्याहृत्याग्निं संधुक्ष्य रा[4]जमन्दिरद्वारे चिताधिरोहणायोपक्रमिष्यसे । स तावदेव त्वत्पादयोर्निपत्य सामात्यो नरपति[5]रनूनैरर्थैस्त्वामुपच्छन्द्य दुहितरं मह्यं दत्त्वा मद्योग्यतासमाराधितः समस्तमेव राज्यभारं मयि समर्पयिष्यति । सोऽयमभ्युपायोऽनुष्ठेयः, यदि तुभ्यं रोचते ' इति । सो[6]ऽपि पटुविटानामग्रणीरसकृदभ्यस्तकपटप्रपञ्चः पाञ्चालशर्मा यथोक्तमभ्यधिकं च निपुणमुपक्रान्तवान् । आसीच्च मम समीहितानाम[7]हीनकालसिद्धिः । अन्वभवं च मधुकर इव नवमालिकामार्द्रसुमनसम् । अस्य राज्ञः सिंहवर्मणः साहाय्यदानं सुहृत्संकेतभूमिगमनमित्युभयमपेक्ष्य सर्वबलसंदोहेन चम्पामिमामुपगतो दैवाद्देवदर्शनसुखमनुभवामि ' इति ।

श्रुत्वैतत्प्रमातिचरितं स्मित[8]मुकुलितमुखनलिनः ' विलासप्रायमूर्जितम्, मृदुप्रायं चेष्टितम्, इष्ट एष मार्गः प्रज्ञावताम् । अथेदानीमत्रभवान्प्रविशतु ' इति मित्रगुप्तमैक्षत क्षितीशपुत्रः ।

इति श्रीदण्डिनः कृतौ दशकुमारचरिते प्रमतिचरितं नाम पञ्चम उच्छ्वासः ।

---

विश्रम्भी विश्वासवान् । ' शक्यः प्रियंवदः प्रोक्तः' इति हलायुधः । गतस्मयो गर्वरहितः । अविद्यमानम् । उपलभे इति शेषः । अन्त्यमाश्रमं संन्यासम् । विवर्णस्य भावो वैवर्ण्यम् । वैलक्ष्यं परं वैक्लव्यमुपेत इत्यन्वयः । ' समनुनेतुं खेदं दूरीकर्तुम् ' इति भूषणा । संधुक्ष्य प्रज्वाल्येत्यर्थः । अनूनैः महामूल्यैरित्यर्थः । कपटप्रपञ्चश्छलरचना । उपक्रान्तवान्संपादितवान् । अहीनकालसिद्धिरत्युच्चकालसिद्धिः । नवमालिकाम् । मालतीमित्यर्थः । आर्द्रसुमनसं सरसपुष्पम् । मधुकर आर्द्रसुमनसमिव नवमालिकां राजकन्यामन्वभवमित्यन्वयः । संदोहेन समूहेन । मुकुलितं हास्यसंकुचितम् । मुखनलिनं मुखकमलम् । विलासप्रायं विलासबहुलम् । प्रज्ञावतां बुद्धिमताम् ।

इति श्रीदशकुमारचरितटीकायां पञ्चम उच्छ्वासः ।

---

१ शक्तः. २ समनुनेतुम्. ३ विरुद्य बाष्प०. ४ राजद्वारे. ५ रभिमतैः. ६ सोऽतिपटुर्विटग्रामणीः. ७ अचिरकाल; काल-फल. ८ मुकुलितनयनः.

## षष्ठ उच्छ्वासः ।

सोऽप्याचचक्षे—' देव सोऽहमपि सुहृत्साधारणभ्रमणकारणः सुह्मेषु दामलिप्ताह्वयस्य नगरस्य बाह्योद्याने महान्तमुत्सवसमाजमालोकयम् । तत्र कचिदतिमुक्तलतामण्डपे कमपि वीणावादेनात्मानं विनोदयन्तमुत्कण्ठितं युवानमद्राक्षम् । अप्राक्षं च—' भद्र को नामायमुत्सवः किमर्थं वा समारब्धः केन वा निमित्तेनोत्सवमनादृत्यैकान्ते भवानुत्कण्ठित इव परिवादिनीद्वितीयस्तिष्ठति ' इति । सोऽभ्यधत्त—' सौम्य, सुह्मपतिस्तुङ्गधन्वा नामानपत्यः प्रार्थितवानमुष्मिन्नायतने विस्मृतविन्ध्यवासरागं वसन्त्या विन्ध्यवासिन्याः पादमूलादपत्यद्वयम् । अनया च किलास्मै प्रतिशयिताय स्वप्ने समादिष्टम्—' समुत्पत्स्यते तवैकः पुत्रः, जनिष्यते चैका दुहिता । स तु तस्याः पाणिग्राहकमनुजीविष्यति । सा तु सप्तमाद्वर्षादारभ्या परिणयनात्प्रतिमासं कृत्तिकासु कन्दुकनृत्येन गुणवद्भर्तृलाभाय मां समाराधयतु । यं चाभिलषेत्साऽमुष्मै देया । स चोत्सवः कन्दुकोत्सवनामाऽस्तु ' इति । ततोऽल्पीयसा कालेन राज्ञः प्रियमहिषी मेदिनी नामैकं पुत्रमसूत । समुत्पन्ना चैका दुहिता । साऽद्य कन्या कन्दुकावती नाम सोमापीडां देवीं कन्दुकविहारेणाराधयितुमागमिष्यति । तस्यास्तु सखी चन्द्रसेना नाम धात्रेयिका मम प्रियाऽऽसीत् । सा चैषु दिवसेषु राजपुत्रेण

सोऽपि मित्रगुप्तोऽपि । सुह्मेषु देशविशेषेषु । ' अग्निकोणादिक्स्थेषु ' इति भूषणा । दामलिप्ताह्वयस्य दामलिप्तनाम्ना ख्यातस्य । ' अतिमुक्तः पुण्ड्रकः स्यात् ' इत्यमरः । उत्कण्ठितं जातोकण्ठम् । भद्रेति कल्याणवत्संबोधनम् । अनादृत्य उपेक्ष्येत्यर्थः । परिवादिनीद्वितीयः वीणासहायः । ' विपञ्ची सा तु तन्त्रीभिः सप्तभिः परिवादिनी ' इत्यमरः । अभ्यधत्त प्रत्युत्तरं दत्तवान् । सौम्येत्यासतया संबोधनम् । आयतनं देवस्थानम् । विन्ध्यवासिन्याः दुर्गायाः । प्रतिशयिताय निद्रिताय । प्रायोपवेशनार्थितायेत्यर्थः । आ परिणयनाद्विवाहकालं यावत् । कृत्तिकासु तन्नामनक्षत्रेषु । कन्दुकनृत्येन कन्दुकवन्नृत्यं तेन । कन्दुकावतीत्यत्र ' मतौ बह्वचोऽनजिरादीनाम् ' इति दीर्घः संज्ञायाम्–इति भूषणा । सोमापीडां देवीं चन्द्रशेखराम् । ' आपीडः शेखरः समौ ' इति वैजयन्ती । धात्र्युपमाता

१ दामलिप्ताह्वस्य. २ अतिमुक्तक. ३ साऽभिलषेत्. ४ कन्दुकनामा. ५ आराधयिष्यति.

भीमधन्वना बलवदनुरुद्धा। तदहमुत्कण्ठितो मन्मथशरशल्यदुःखोद्विग्नचेताः कलेन वीणारवेणात्मानं किंचिदाश्वासयन्विविक्तमध्यासे' इति।

अस्मिन्नेव च क्षणे किमपि नूपुरक्वणितमुपातिष्ठत्। आगता च काचिदङ्गना। दृष्ट्वैव स एनामुत्फुल्लदृष्टिरुत्थायोप[1]गूह्य गाढमुपगूढकण्ठश्च तया तत्रैवोपाविशत्। अशंसच्च—'सैषा मे प्राणसमा यद्विरहो दहन इव दहति माम्। इदं च मे जीवितमपहरता राजपुत्रेण मृत्युनेव निरुष्मतां नीतः। न च शक्ष्यामि राजसूनुरित्यमुष्मिन्पापमाचरितुम्। अतोऽनयाऽऽत्मानं सुदृष्टं कारयित्वा त्यक्ष्यामि निष्प्रतिक्रियान्प्राणान्' इति। सा तु पर्यश्रुमुखी समभ्यधात्—'मा स्म नाथ मत्कृतेऽध्यवस्यः साहसम्। यस्त्वमुत्तमात्सार्थवाहादर्थदासादुत्पद्य कोशदास इति गुरुभिरभिहितनामधेयः पुनर्मदत्यासङ्गाद्वेशदास इति द्विषद्भिः प्रख्यापितोऽसि तस्मिंस्त्वय्युपरते यद्यहं जीवेयं नृशंसो वेश[2] इति समर्थयेयं लोकवादम्। अतोऽद्यैव नय मामीप्सितं देशम्' इति। स तु मामभ्यधत्त—'भद्र भवद्दृष्टेषु राष्ट्रेषु कतमत्समृद्धं संपन्नसस्यं सत्पुरुषभूयिष्ठं च' इति। तमहमीषद्विहस्याब्रवम्—'भद्र विस्तीर्णेयमर्णवाम्बरा। न पर्यन्तोऽस्ति स्थानस्थानेषु रम्याणां जनपदानाम्। अपि तु न चेदिह युवयोः सुखनिवासकारणं कमप्युपायमुत्पादयितुं शक्नुयां ततोऽहमेव भवेयमध्वदर्शी' इति। तावतोदैरत रणितानि मणिनूपुराणाम्। अथासौ जातसंभ्रमा 'प्राप्तैवेयं भर्तृदारिका कन्दुकावती कन्दुकक्रीडितेन देवीं विन्ध्यवासिनीमाराधयितुम्। अनिषिद्धदर्शना चेयमस्मिन्कन्दुकोत्सवे। सफलमस्तु युष्मच्चक्षुः।

---

तस्याः कन्या धात्रेयिका। 'स्त्रीभ्यो ढक्'। शरशल्यं बाणाग्रम्। शल्येभ्यो दुःखं तेनोद्विग्नं चेतो यस्य। कलेन गम्भीरेण। 'कलो मन्द्रस्तु गम्भीरे' इत्यमरः। विविक्तं विजनम्। उपगूह्यालिङ्ग्य। उपगूढकण्ठ आश्लिष्टकण्ठः। निरुष्मतां निस्तेजस्त्वम्। निष्प्रतिक्रियान्निष्प्रतीकारान्। **सा त्विति**। पर्यश्रुमुखी परिगतान्यश्रूणि यस्मिन्निति। उपरते मृते। नृशंसो घातुकः। ईप्सितमिष्टम्। संपन्नसस्यं प्रचुरधान्यम्। अर्णवाम्बरा समुद्रवसना पृथ्वी। पर्यन्तः समाप्तिः। जनपदानां देशानाम्। 'नीवृज्जनपदो देशः' इत्यमरः। अध्वदर्शी मार्गोपदेष्टा। तावता तत्कालेनेत्यर्थः। उदैरत उत्पन्नानीत्यर्थः। रणितानि शब्दितानि। **अथेति**। अनिषिद्ध-

---

१ उपगूह्य गाढमिति नास्ति क्वचित्. २ वेशजनः.

आगच्छतं द्रष्टुम् । अहमस्याः सकाशवर्तिनी भवेयम्' इत्ययासीत् । तामन्वयाव चावाम् । महति रत्नरङ्गपीठे स्थितां प्रथमं ताम्रोष्ठीमपश्यम् । अतिष्ठच्च सा सद्य एव मम हृदये । न मयाऽन्येन वाऽन्तराले दृष्टा । चित्रीयाविष्टचित्तश्चाचिन्तयम्—'किमियं लक्ष्मीः । न हि न हि । तस्याः किल हस्ते विन्यस्तं कमलम्, अस्यास्तु हस्त एव कमलम् । भुक्तपूर्वा[1] च सा पुरातनेन पुंसा पूर्वराजैश्च, अस्याः पुनरनवद्यमयातयामं च यौवनम्' इति चिन्तयत्येव मयि साऽनर्घ[2]सर्वगात्री व्यत्यस्तहस्तपल्लवाग्रस्पृष्टभूमिरालोलनीलकुटिलालका सविभ्रमं[3] भगवतीमभिवन्द्य[4] कन्दुकममन्दरागरूषिताक्षमनङ्गमिवालम्बत । लीलाशिथिलं च भूमौ मुक्तवती । मन्दोत्थितं च किंचित्कुञ्चिताङ्गुष्ठेन प्रसृतकोमलाङ्गुलिना पाणिपल्लवेन समाहत्य हस्तपृष्ठेन चोन्नीय, चटुलदृष्टिलाञ्छितं स्तबकमिव भ्रमरमालानुविद्धमवपतन्तमाकाश एवाग्रहीत् । अमुञ्चच्च । मध्ये[5]विलम्बितलये द्रुतलये मृद्वमृदु[6] च प्रहरन्ती तत्क्षणं चूर्णपदमदर्शयत् । प्रशान्तं च तं निर्दयप्रहारैरुदपातयत् । विपर्ययेण च प्राशमयत् । पक्षमृज्वागतं च वामदक्षिणाभ्यां कराभ्यां पर्यायेणाभिघ्नती शकुन्तमिवोदस्थापयत् । दूरोत्थितं च प्रपतन्तमाहत्य गीतमार्गमारच[7]यत् ।

---

दर्शना अप्रतिहतदर्शना । चित्रीयाविष्टचित्तः विस्मयाविष्टचित्तः । 'चित्रीया विस्मयोऽद्भुतम्' इति कोशः । 'चित्रीया । नमोवरिवश्चित्रङः क्यच्—इति क्यजन्तादप्रत्ययः स्त्रियाम् । किमियमित्याद्याक्षेपालंकारः । आक्षेपः स्वयमुक्तस्य प्रतिषेधो विचारणात्—इति लक्षणात्' इति भूषणा । अयातयाममपरिभुक्तमिति यावत् । 'जीर्णे च परिभुक्तं च यातयाममिदं द्वयम् ।' इति कोशः । अनघं निर्दोषम् । व्यत्यस्तौ परावर्तितौ हस्तपल्लवौ तयोरग्राभ्यां स्पृष्टा भूमिर्यया । कुटिला वक्राः । अलक श्चूर्णकुन्तलाः । अमन्देन बहलेन रागेण रूषितानि रञ्जितानि अक्षीणि यस्य । पक्षे अमन्देन रागेणानुरागेण रूषिते अक्षिणी येन तम् । शिथिलं श्लथम् । मन्दं निश्चलम् । कुञ्चितो वक्रितः । चटुलश्चञ्चलः । स्तबको गुच्छः । आकाश एव मध्य एव । मध्यविलम्बितं मध्ये विलम्बितम् । द्रुतं लयः पतनं यत्रेति तस्मिन्सतीति सतिसप्तमी । 'विलम्बितं द्रुतं मध्यं तत्त्वमोघो घनं क्रमात् । तालः कालक्रियामानम्' इत्यमरः । चूर्णपदम् । 'गत्यागत्योरानुलोम्येन न्यूनाधिक्यक्षेपणं तच्चूर्णपदम्' इति कन्दुकतन्त्रे । उदपातयदुत्थितमकरोत् । पक्षं पार्श्वतः । शकुन्तः पक्षी । गीतमार्गम् । 'दशपदचंक्रमणं गीतमार्गं विदुः'

---

१ अभुक्तपूर्वा चासौ. २ अनवद्य. ३ ससंभ्रमम्. ४ भगवतीं भवानीम्. ५ विलम्बितद्रुतमध्यलये. ६ च मृदुमृदु. ७ आचरत्.

प्रतिदिशं च गमयित्वा [1]प्रत्यागमयत्। एवमनेककरणमधुरं विहरन्ती रङ्गगतस्य रक्तचेतसो जनस्य प्रतिक्षणमु[2]च्चावचाः प्रशंसावाचः प्रतिगृह्णती, तत्क्ष[3]णारूढविश्रम्भं कोशदासमंसेऽवलम्ब्य कण्टकितगण्डमुत्फुल्लेक्षणं च मय्यभिमुखीभूय तिष्ठति तत्प्रथमावतीर्णकन्दर्पकारितकटाक्षदृष्टिस्तदनुमार्गविलसितलीलाञ्चितभ्रूलता, श्वासानिलवेगान्दोलितैर्दन्तच्छदरश्मिजालैर्लीलापल्लवैरिव मुखकमलपरिमलग्रहणलोलानालिनस्ताडयन्ती, मण्डलभ्रमणेषु कन्दुकस्यातिशीघ्रप्रचारितया विशन्तीव मद्दर्शनलज्जया पुष्पमयं पञ्जरम्, पञ्चबिन्दुप्रसृतेषु पञ्चापि पञ्चबाणबाणान्युगपदिवाभिपतत्त्रासेनावघट्टयन्ती, गोमूत्रिकाप्रचारेषु घनदर्शितरागविभ्रमां विद्युल्लतामिव विडम्बयन्ती, भूषणमणिरणितदत्तलयसंवादिपादचारम्, अपदेशस्मितप्रभानिषिक्तबिम्बाधरम्, असत्स्रंसितप्रतिसमाहितशिखण्डभारम्, [4]समाघट्टितक्वणितरत्नमेखलागुणम्, अञ्चितोत्थितपृथुनितम्बल[5]म्बिविचलदंशुकोज्ज्व[6]लम्, आकुञ्चितप्रसृतवेल्लितभुजलताभिहतललितकन्दुकम्, [7]आवर्जितबाहुपाशम्, [9]परिवर्तितत्रिकाविलग्नलोलकुन्तलम्, अवगलितकर्णपूरकनकपत्रप्रतिसमाधानशीघ्रतानतिक्रमितप्रकृतक्रीडम्, असकृदु-

---

इति कन्दुकतन्त्रे। अनेककरणमधुरमनेकव्यापाररम्यम्। उच्चावचाः स्थूलसूक्ष्माः। तत्क्षणे आरूढो विश्रम्भो विश्वासो यस्मिंस्तत्म्। प्रतिक्षणारूढविभ्रममिति पाठे प्रतिक्षणमारूढ उत्पन्नो विभ्रमो विलासो यस्येति तथा। कण्टकितौ रोमाञ्चितौ गण्डौ यस्मिन्कर्मणि तद्यथा स्यात्तथा। तिष्ठति सतीति सतिसप्तमी। तत्प्रथमं तदेव प्रथममवतीर्ण आगतो यः कन्दर्पः कामस्तेन कारिता कटाक्षदृष्टिर्यस्याः सेति तथा। तदनुमार्गे कन्दुकानुमार्गे विलसितस्य खेलनस्य लीला तयाऽञ्चिते भ्रूलते यस्याः। अनिलवेगो वायुवगः। पञ्चबिन्दुप्रसृतेषु। 'पञ्चावर्तप्रहारस्तु पञ्चबिन्दुरुदाहृतः' इति। अवघट्टयन्त्यालोडयन्ती। गोमूत्रिकाप्रचारेषु। 'गोमूत्रिकेति विद्भिश्चारः शातहृदो मतः' इति च। घनं दर्शितोऽतिमात्रदर्शितः। मेघ दर्शितश्च। विभ्रमः स्फुरणम्। विडम्बयन्त्यनुकुर्वती। रणितं शब्दितम्। लयसंवादि लयानुरोधि। समाघट्टितः समीकृतः क्वणितः शब्दवान्मेखलागुणो यत्र। अञ्चितं सम्यग्यथा तथोत्थित उन्नतः पृथुर्महान् नितम्बस्तत्र लम्बि विचलच्च यदंशुकं तेनोज्ज्वलं यथा तथा। वेल्लिता भ्रामिता। परिवर्तितं यत् त्रिकम्। 'त्रिकं त्रिकाटिकायां च पृष्ठवंशाधरेऽपि च' इति वैजयन्ती। तत्र विलग्ना लोला कुन्तला यथा स्युस्तथा। अवगलितं स्रस्तं कर्णपूरभूतं कनकपत्रं तस्य प्रतिसमाधानं स्वस्थाने पुनर्निवेशनं तत्र या शीघ्रता तयाऽनतिक्रमिता प्रकृता क्रीडा

---

१ प्रत्यागमत्. २ उच्चावचम्. ३ प्रतिक्षणारूढविभ्रमम्. ४ आद्याहृतक्वणितमेखलागुणम्. ५ लम्बितचेलम्; नितम्बविलम्बित. ६ अंशुकाञ्चलम्. ७ आवर्तित. ८ पाशानुविद्धपरि०. ९ उपरि परि०.

त्क्षिप्यमाणहस्तपादबाह्याभ्यन्तरभ्रान्तकन्दुकम्, अवनमनोन्नमननैरन्तर्य-नष्टदृष्टमध्ययष्टिकम्, अवपतनोत्पतनविपर्यस्तमुक्ताहारम्, अङ्कुरित-घर्मसलिलदूषितकपोलपत्रभङ्गशोषणाधिकृतश्रवणपल्लवानिलम्, आगलित-स्तनतटांशुकनियमनव्यापृतैकपाणिपल्लवं च निषद्योत्थाय निमी-ल्योन्मील्य स्थित्वा गत्वा चैवातिचित्रं पर्यक्रीडत राजकन्या। अभिहत्य भूतलाकाशयोरपि क्रीडान्तराणि दर्शनीयान्येकेनैवानेकेनेव कन्दुकेनादर्शयत् । चन्द्रसेनादिभिश्च प्रियसखीभिः सह विहृत्य विहृतान्ते चाभिवन्द्य देवीं मनसा मे सानुरागेणेव परिजनेन चानु-गम्यमाना, कुवलयशरमिव कुसुमशरस्य मय्यपाङ्गं समर्पयन्ती, साप-देशमसकृदावर्त्यमानवदनचन्द्रमण्डलतया स्वहृदयमिव मत्समीपे प्रेरितं प्रतिनिवृत्तं न वेत्यालोकयन्ती, सह सखीभिः कुमारीपुरमगमत् ।

अहं चानङ्गविह्वलः स्ववेश्म गत्वा कोशदासेन यत्नवदत्युदारं स्नानभोजनादिकमनुभावितोऽस्मि । सायं चोपसृत्य चन्द्रसेना रहसि मां प्रणिपत्य पत्युरंसमंसेन प्रणयपेशलमाघट्टयन्त्युपाविशत् । आचष्ट च हृष्टः कोशदासः—'भूयासमेवं यावदायुरायताक्षि त्वत्प्रसादस्य पात्रम्' इति । मया तु सस्मितमभिहितम्—'सखे किमेतदाशा-स्यम् । अस्ति किंचिदञ्जनम् । अनया तदक्तनेत्रया राजसूनुरुप-स्थितो वानरीमिवैनां द्रक्ष्यति विरक्तश्चैनां पुनस्त्यक्ष्यति' इति ।

---

तया युक्तं यथा तथा । **असकृदिति** । हस्तौ पादौ च तेषां बाह्याभ्यन्तरे भ्रान्तः कन्दुकः यस्मिन्कर्मणि तद्यथा तथा । 'बनेटी' इति लोकप्रसिद्धं क्रीडनकम्-इति भूषणा । अवनमनोन्नमनयोर्नैरन्तर्यान्नष्टा च दृष्टा च मध्ययष्टिः शरीरमध्यभागो यथा तथा । अङ्कुरितमीषत्प्रादुर्भूतं यद् घर्मसलिलं स्वेदजलं तेन दूषितो यः कपोलयोः पत्रभङ्गः तस्य शोषणे अधिकृतोऽधिकारी कृतः श्रवणपल्लवः कर्णावतंसपल्लवस्तस्या-निलो यत्र । स्तनतटांशुकनियमनं कुचतटोपरिगतवस्त्रसमीकरणं तत्र व्यापृतो व्यासक्तः । अतिचित्रमनेकप्रकारम् । विहृतान्ते खेलनान्ते । अपाङ्गं नेत्रप्रान्तम् । सापदेशं सव्याजम् । 'अपदेशः स्मृतो लक्ष्ये निमित्तव्याजयोरपि' इति विश्वः । **अहमिति** । अनङ्गविह्वलो मदनव्याकुलः । अनुभावितोऽस्मि । अनुभवविषयीकृत इत्यर्थः । प्रणयपेशलं प्रीतिसुन्दरम् । भूयासं भविष्य इत्यर्थः । तदक्तनेत्रयाऽञ्जनाक्तनेत्रया ।

---

१ निर्व्यवस्थ. २ एकेनैव वाऽनेकेनैव. ३ मन्मनसा सानु०. ४ विद्धः. ५ यदक्त.

तया तु स्मेरयाऽस्मि कथितः—‘सोऽयमार्येणाज्ञाकरो जनोऽत्यर्थमनुगृहीतः यदस्मिन्नेव जन्मनि मानुषं वपुरपनीय वानरीकरिष्यते। तद्वास्तामिदम्। अन्यथाऽपि सिद्धं नः समीहितम्। अद्य खलु कन्दुकोत्सवे भवन्तं[1]मवहसितमनोभवाकारमभिलषन्ती रोषादिव [2]शम्बरद्विषाऽतिमात्रमायास्यते राजपुत्री। सोऽयमर्थो विदितभावया मया स्वमात्रे तया च तन्मात्रे महिष्या च मनुजेन्द्राय निवेदयिष्यते। विदितार्थस्तु पार्थिवस्त्वया दुहितुः पाणिं ग्राहयिष्यति। ततश्च त्वदनुजीविना राजपुत्रेण भवितव्यम्। एष हि देवतासमादिष्टो विधिः। त्वदायत्ते च राज्ये नालमेवं[3] त्वामतिक्रम्य मामवरोद्धुं भीमधन्वा। तत्सह्यतामयं त्रिचतुराणि दिनानि।’ इति मामामन्त्र्य प्रियं चोपगूह्य प्रत्ययासीत्। मम कोशदासस्य च तदुक्तानुसारेण बहु विकल्पयतोः कथंचिदक्षीयत क्षपा। क्षपान्ते च कृतयथोचितनियमस्तमेव प्रियादर्शनसुभगमुद्यानोद्देशमुपगतोऽस्मि। तत्रैव चोपसृत्य राजपुत्रो निरभिमानमनुकूलाभिः कथाभिर्मामनुवर्तमानो मुहूर्तमास्त। नीत्वा चोपकार्यामात्मसमेन स्नानभोजनशयनादिव्यतिकरेणोपाचरत्। तल्पगतं च स्वप्नेनानुभूयमानप्रियादर्शनालिङ्गनसुखमायसेन निगडेनाति[4]बलवद्बहुपुरुषैः पीवरभुजदण्डोपरुद्धमबन्धयन्माम्। प्रतिबुद्धं च सहसा समभ्यधात्—‘अयि दुर्मते श्रुतमालपितं हतायाश्चन्द्रसेनाया जालरन्ध्रनिःसृतं तच्चेष्टावबोधप्रयुक्तयाऽनया कुब्जया। त्वं किलाभिलषितो वराक्या कन्दुकावत्या, तव किलानुजीविना मया स्थेयं, त्वद्वचः किलानतिक्रमता मया चन्द्र-

आज्ञाकरः सेवकजनः। अन्यथाऽपि मनुष्यस्य वानरीकरणं विनाऽपि। **अद्येति**। अवहसित उपहासं प्रापितो मनोभवाकारो मदनशरीरं येनेति। शम्बरद्विषा कामेन। अतिमात्रं निर्भरम्। ‘अतिमात्रोद्गाढनिर्भरम्’ इत्यमरः। आयास्यते आयासं प्राप्यते। त्वामनुजीवतीति तथा। विधिरदृष्टम्। सह्यतामयं कोशदासः। कथंचिन्महता प्रयासेन। क्षपा रात्रिः। अनुकूलाभिः स्वेष्टाभिः। उपकार्या राजगृहम्। आयसन लोहमयेन। पीवरौ मांसलौ भुजदण्डौ बाहुदण्डौ ताभ्यामुपरुद्धं यथा तथा। जालरन्ध्रं गवाक्षच्छिद्रम्। किलेति असंभाव्यार्थे। ‘वार्तासंभाव्ययोः किल’ इत्यमरः।

१ अपहसित. २ हरद्विषा. ३ एष. ४ अतिबलपुरुषैः.

सेना कोशदासाय दास्यते' इत्युक्त्वा पार्श्वचरं पुरुषमेकमालोक्याकथयत्—'प्रक्षिपैनं सागरे' इति। स तु लब्धराज्य इवातिहृष्टः 'देव यदाज्ञापयसि' इति यथादिष्टमकरोत्। अहं तु निरालम्बनो भुजाभ्यामितस्ततः स्पन्दमानः किमपि काष्ठं दैवदत्तमुरसोपाश्लिष्य तावदप्लोषि यावदपासरद्वासरः शर्वरी च सर्वा। प्रत्युषस्यदृश्यत किमपि वहित्रम्। अमुत्रासन्यवनाः। ते मामुद्धृत्य रामेषुनाम्ने नाविकनायकाय कथितवन्तः—'कोऽप्ययमायसनिगडबद्ध एव जले लब्धः पुरुषः। सोऽयमपि सिञ्चेत्सहस्रं द्राक्षाणां क्षणेनैकेन' इति। अस्मिन्नेव क्षणे नैकनौकापरिवृतः कोऽपि मद्गुरभ्यधावत्। अबिभयुर्यवनाः। तावदतिजवा नौकाः श्वान इव वराहमस्मत्पोतं पर्यरुत्सत। प्रावर्तत च संप्रहारः। पराजायिषत[1] यवनाः। तानहमगतीनवसीदतः समाश्वास्यालपिषम्—'अपनयत मे निगडबन्धनम्। अयमहमवसादयामि वः सपत्नान्' इति। अमी तथाऽकुर्वन्। सर्वांश्च तान्प्रतिभटान्भल्लवर्षिणा भीमटंकृतेन शार्ङ्गेण लवलवीकृताङ्गानकार्षम्। अवप्लुत्य हतविध्वस्तयोधमस्मत्पोतसंसक्तपोतममुत्र नाविकनायकमनभिसरमभिपत्य जीवग्राहमग्रहीषम्। असौ चासीत्स एव भीमधन्वा। तं चाहमवबुध्य जातव्रीडमब्रवम्—'तात किं दृष्टानि कृतान्तविलसितानि' इति। ते तु सांयात्रिका मदीयेनैव शृङ्खलेन तमतिगाढं बद्ध्वा हर्षकिलकिलारवमकुर्वन्मां चापूजयन्।

---

स्पन्दमानः चेष्टमानः। उपश्लिष्यालिङ्ग्य। अपासरदतिक्रान्तः। शर्वरी रात्रिः। वहित्रं वहनम्। अपि सिञ्चेत्। अपिशब्दः संभावनायाम्। 'गर्हासमुच्चयप्रश्नशङ्कासंभावनास्वपि।' इत्यमरः। मद्गुः पोतविशेषः। अतिजवा अतिवेगवत्यः। पर्यरुत्सत परितो रुरुधुरित्यर्थः। पराजायिषत पराजयं प्राप्ता इत्यर्थः। आलपिषमवदम्। अवसादयामि। नाशयिष्यामीत्यर्थः। सपत्नान्वैरिणः। भल्लवर्षिणा बाणवर्षिणेत्यर्थः। टंकृतेन टंकारेण। 'नपुंसके भावे क्तः'। शार्ङ्गेण चापेन। लवलवीकृताङ्गान् लेशलेशीकृताङ्गान्। "लवो भागस्तस्य लवस्तथाकृतान्। चूर्णितानित्यर्थः।" इति भूषणा। अनभिसरमसहायम्। 'अनुप्लवः सहायश्चानुचरोऽभिसरः समाः।' इत्यमरः। जीवग्राहं जीवं गृहीत्वेति णमुल्। जातव्रीडं जातलज्जम्। कृतान्तो यमः। सांयात्रिकाः पोतवणिजः। 'सांयात्रिकः पोतवणिक्' इत्यमरः। किलकिलारवमित्यनुकरणम्।

---

१ पराजयिषत; पराजेषत.

दुर्वारा तु सा नौरननुकूलवातनुन्ना दूरमभिपत्य कमपि द्वीपं निबिडमाश्लिष्टवती। तत्र च स्वादु पानीयमेधांसि कन्दमूलफलानि च संजिघृक्षवो गाढपातिताशिलावलयमवातराम। तत्र चासीन्महाशैलः। सोऽहम्—'अहो रमणीयोऽयं पर्वतनितम्बभागः, कान्ततरेयं गन्धपाषाणवत्युपत्यका, शिशिरमिदमिन्दीवरारविन्दमकरन्दबिन्दुचन्द्रकोत्तरं गोत्रवारि, रम्योऽयमनेकवर्णकुसुममञ्जरीमञ्जुलतरस्तरुवनाभोगः' इत्यतृप्ततरया दृशा बहुबहु पश्यन्नलक्षिताध्यारूढक्षोणीधराशिखरः शोणीभूतमुत्प्रभाभिः पद्मरागसोपानशिलाभिः किमपि नालीकपरागधूसरं सरः समध्यगमम्। तत्र स्नातश्च कांश्चिदमृतस्वादून्बिसभङ्गानास्वाद्य, अंसलग्नकह्लारस्तीरवर्तिना केनापि भीमरूपेण ब्रह्मराक्षसेनाभिपत्य 'कोऽसि, कुतस्त्योऽसि' इति निर्भर्त्सयताऽभ्यधीये। निर्भयेन च मया सोऽभ्यधीयत—'सौम्य सोऽहमस्मि द्विजन्मा। शत्रुहस्तादर्णवम्, अर्णवाद्यवननावम्, यवननावश्चित्रग्रावाणमेनं पर्वतप्रवरं गतो यदृच्छयाऽस्मिन्सरसि विश्रान्तः। भद्रं तव' इति। सोऽब्रूत—'न चेद्ब्रवीषि प्रश्नानश्नामि त्वाम्' इति। मयोक्तम्—'पृच्छा तावत् भवतु' इति। अथावयोरेकयाऽऽर्ययाऽऽसीत्संलापः—

**किं क्रूरं स्त्रीहृदयं किं गृहिणः प्रियहिताय दारगुणाः।**
**कः कामः संकल्पः किं दुष्करसाधनं प्रज्ञा॥**

---

अननुकूलेन प्रतिकूलवातेन नुन्ना प्रेरिता। एधांसि काष्ठानि। 'काष्ठं दार्विन्धनं त्वेधः' इत्यमरः। संजिघृक्षवो ग्रहीतुकामाः। गाढं पातितं शिलावलयं शिलामण्डलं यत्र तथा। नितम्बभागः तटप्रदेशः। गन्धपाषाणवती मनःशिलादिधातुपाषणमयीत्यर्थः। अथ वा गन्धपाषाणः शैलेयम्। 'शैलेयं गन्धपाषाणः शिलापुष्पं च कथ्यते' इति कोशः। उपत्यका पर्वतासन्नभूमिः। 'उपत्यकाऽद्रेरासन्ना भूमिः' इत्यमरः। इन्दीवरारविन्दानां मकरन्दबिन्दवः। गोत्रवारि पर्वतनिर्झरजलम्। अनेकवर्णानि नानावर्णानि यानि कुसुमानि तेषां मञ्जरीभिः मञ्जुलतरोऽतिरम्यः। तरुवनाभोगस्तरुवनपूर्णता। अतृप्ततरया दर्शनेच्छावत्येत्यर्थः। अलक्षितमध्यारूढं क्षोणीधरस्य पर्वतस्य शिखरं येन सः। अतिदूरं गत इति यावत्। शोणीभूतमारक्तीभूतम्। नालीकं पद्मम्। 'नालीकं पद्मबाणयोः' इति वैजयन्ती। अर्णवं समुद्रम्। यवननावः। पञ्चम्यन्तमिदम्। पर्वतप्रवरं पर्वतश्रेष्ठम्। गत इति प्रत्येकं द्वितीयान्तमन्वेति। संलापो मिथोभाषणम्। **किं क्रूरमिति**। प्रियहिताय प्रियं च हितं च तस्मै। दारगुणा भार्याया गुणाः। संकल्पो निश्चयः।

---

१ दुर्वहा. २ पतित. ३ शैलेयवती. ४ मञ्जरीभरः. ५ स्नात्वा ततश्च.

'तत्र[1] धूमिनीगोमिनीनिम्बवतीनितम्बवत्यः प्रमाणम् ।' इत्युपदिष्टो मया सोऽब्रूत—'कथय कीदृश्यस्ताः' इति । अत्रो[2]दाहरम्—

'अस्ति त्रिगर्तो नाम जनपदः । तत्रासन्गृहिणस्त्रयः स्फीतसारधनाः सोदर्या धनकधान्यकधन्यकाख्याः । तेषु जीवत्सु न ववर्ष वर्षाणि द्वादश दशशताक्षः । क्षीणसारं सस्यम्, ओषध्यो वन्ध्याः, न फलवन्तो वनस्पतयः, क्लीबा मेघाः, क्षीणस्रोतसः स्रवन्त्यः, पङ्कशेषाणि पल्वलानि, निर्निस्यन्दान्युत्समण्डलानि, विरलीभूतं कन्दमूलफलम्, अवहीनाः कथाः, गलिताः कल्याणोत्सवक्रियाः, बहुलीभूतानि तस्करकुलानि, अन्योन्यमभक्षयन्प्रजाः, पर्यलुठन्नितस्ततो बलाकापाण्डुराणि नरशिरःकपालानि, पर्यहिण्डन्त शुष्काः काकमण्डल्यः, शून्यीभूतानि नगरग्रामखर्वटपुटभेदनादीनि । त एते गृहपतयः सर्वधान्यनिचयमुपयुज्या[3]जाविकं गवलगणं गवां यूथं दासीदासजनमपत्यानि ज्येष्ठमध्यमभार्ये च क्रमेण भक्षयित्वा 'कनिष्ठभार्या धूमिनी श्वो भक्षणीया' इति समकल्पयन् । अथ कनिष्ठो धन्यकः प्रियां स्वामत्तुमक्षमस्तया सह तस्यामेव निश्यपासरत् । मार्गक्लान्तां चोद्वहन्वनं जगाहे । स्वमांसासृगपनीतक्षुत्पिपासां तां नयन्न[4]न्तरे कमपि निकृ[5]त्तपाणिपादकर्णनासिकमवनिपृष्ठे विचेष्टमानं पुरुषमद्राक्षीत् । तमप्यार्द्राशयः स्कन्धेनोद्वहन्कन्दमूलमृगबहुले गहनोद्देशे यत्नरचितपर्णशालश्चिरमवसत् । अमुं च रोपितव्रणमिङ्गुदी-

---

अस्तीति । स्फीतो महान्सारः स्थिरांशो धनं च येषाम् । न ववर्ष वृष्टिं न चकारेत्यर्थः । दशशताक्ष इन्द्रः । ओषध्यः फलपाकान्ताः । स्रवन्त्यो नद्यः । पल्वलान्यल्पसरांसि । उत्समण्डलानि प्रस्रवणमण्डलानि । 'उत्सः प्रस्रवणं वारिप्रवाहो निर्झरो झरः ।' इत्यमरः । बलाकाः बिसकण्ठिकाः । पर्यहिण्डन्त पर्यभ्रमन् । 'हिडि भ्रमणे' । अजाश्च अवयश्च तत्समूहोऽजाविकम् । 'अजाविकटम्' इति पाठः । 'घ्यन्तादजाद्यदन्तं विप्रतिषेधेन' इत्यजशब्दस्य पूर्वनिपातः । 'संघाते कटच्' इति सामूहिकापवादः कटच् ।—इति भूषणा । गवला महिषाः । यूथं समूहः । अक्षमोऽसमर्थः । असृग्रक्तम् । क्षुत्क्षुधा । पिपासा तृट् । निकृत्तं पाणिपादकर्णनासिकं यस्य तम् । गहनोद्देशे वनप्रदेशे । इङ्गुदी । भाषया 'हिंगणबेट' इति

---

१ इतीयदुक्त्वा. २ अथो०. ३ अजाविकटम्. ४ अन्तरा. ५ अरिनिकृत्त.

तैलादिभिरामिषेण शाकेनात्मनिर्विशेषं पुपोष । पुष्टं च तमुद्रिक्तधातुमेकदा मृगान्वेषणाय च प्रयाते धन्यके सा धूमिनी रिरंसयोपातिष्ठत् । भर्त्सिताऽपि तेन बलात्कारमरीरमत् । निवृत्तं च पतिमुदकाभ्यर्थिनम् ' उद्धृत्य कूपात्पिब[1], रुजति मे शिरः शिरोरोगः ' इत्युदञ्चनं सरज्जुं पुरश्चिक्षेप । उदञ्चन्तं[2] च तं कूपादपः क्षणात्पृष्ठतो गत्वा प्रणुनोद । तं च विकलं स्कन्धेनोदुह्य देशाद्देशान्तरं परिभ्रमन्ती पतिव्रताप्रतीतिं लेभे बहुविधाश्च पूजाः । पुनरवन्तिराजानुग्रहादातिमहत्या भूत्या न्यवसत् । अथ पानीयार्थिसार्थजनसमापत्तिदृष्टोद्धृतमवन्तिषु भ्रमन्तमाहारार्थिनं भर्तारमुपलभ्य सा धूमिनी ' येन मे पतिर्विकलीकृतः स दुरात्माऽयम् ' इति तस्य साधोश्चित्रवधमज्ञेन राज्ञा समादेशयांचकार । धन्यकस्तु दत्तपश्चाद्बन्धो वध्यभूमिं नीयमानः सशेषत्वादायुषः ' यो मया विकलीकृतोऽभिमतो भिक्षुः स चेन्मे पापमाचक्षीत युक्तो मे दण्डः ' इत्यदीनमधिकृतं जगाद । ' को दोषः ' इत्युपनीय दर्शितेऽमुष्मिन्स विकलः पर्यश्रुः पादपतितस्तस्य साधोस्तत्सुकृतमसत्याश्च तस्यास्तथाभूतं दुश्चरितमार्यबुद्धिराचचक्षे । कुपितेन राज्ञा विरूपितमुखी सा दुष्कृतकारिणी कृता श्वभ्यः पाचिका । कृतश्च धन्यकः प्रसादभूमिः । तद्ब्रवीमि—' स्त्रीहृदयं क्रूरम् ' इति ।

---

प्रसिद्धः । ' इङ्गुदी तापसतरुः ' इत्यमरः । आमिषं मांसम् । आत्मनिर्विशेषमात्मतुल्यम् । रिरंसया रन्तुमिच्छया । बलात्कारमिति क्रियाविशेषणम् । अरीरमत्क्रीडां चक्रे । निवृत्तं परावृत्यागतम् । उदकाभ्यर्थिनं जलाकाङ्क्षिणम् । रुजति । ' रुज व्यथने ' । व्यथां प्राप्नोतीत्यर्थः । उदञ्चनं जलनिष्कासनपात्रम् । ' उत्सेचनं सेकपात्रं तथोदञ्चनमित्यपि । ' इति वैजयन्ती । भाषया ' डोल ' इति । सरज्जुं सदोरकम् । पुरोऽग्रे । चिक्षेप त्यक्तवतीत्यर्थः । विकलं विह्वलम् । प्रतीतिं ख्यातिम् । भूत्या ऐश्वर्येण । **अथेति** । पानीयं जलं तदर्थी तत्प्रार्थकः । ०सार्थजनेन समापत्त्या यदृच्छया दृष्टश्चासौ उद्धृतश्च तम् । वध्यभूमिं मारणभुवम् । श्वभ्यः पाचिका पुटपाककर्त्री ।

---

१ पिब जलम्. २ उदञ्चयन्तम्.

पुनरनुयुक्तो गोमिनीवृत्तान्तमाख्यातवान्—'अस्ति द्रविडेषु काञ्ची नाम नगरी । तस्यामनेककोटिसारः श्रेष्ठिपुत्रः शक्तिकुमारो नामासीत् । सोऽष्टादशवर्षदेशीयश्चिन्तामापेदे—' नास्त्यदाराणामननुगुणदाराणां वा सुखं नाम । तत्कथं नु गुणवद्वि[1]न्देयं कलत्रम् ' इति । अथ परप्रत्ययाहृतेषु दारेषु यादृच्छिकीं संपत्तिमनभिसमीक्ष्य कार्तान्तिको नाम भूत्वा वस्त्रान्तपिनद्धशालिप्रस्थो भुवं बभ्राम । ' लक्षणज्ञोऽयम् ' इत्यमुष्मै कन्याः कन्यावन्तः प्रदर्शयांबभूवुः । यां कांचिल्लक्षणवतीं सवर्णां कन्यां दृष्ट्वा स किल स्म ब्रवीति—' भद्रे शक्नोषि किमनेन शालिप्रस्थेन गुणवदन्नमस्मानभ्यवहारयितुम् ' इति । स हसितावधूतो गृहाद्गृहं प्रविश्याभ्रमत् । एकदा तु शिबिषु कावेरीतीरे[2]पत्तने सह पितृभ्यामवसितमहर्द्धिमवशीर्णभवनसारां धात्र्या प्रदर्श्यमानां कांचन विरलभूषणां कुमारीं ददर्श । अस्यां संसक्तचक्षुश्चातर्कयत्—' अस्याः खलु कन्यकायाः सर्व एवावयवा नातिस्थूला नातिकृशा नातिह्रस्वा नातिदीर्घा न विकटा मृजावन्तश्च । रक्ततलाङ्गुली यवमत्स्यकमलकलशाद्यनेकपुण्यलेखालाञ्छितौ करौ, स[3]मगुल्फसंधी मांसलावशिरालौ चाङ्घ्री, जङ्घे चानुपूर्ववृत्ते, पीवरोरुग्रस्ते इव दुरुपलक्ष्ये जानुनी, सकृद्विभक्तश्चतु-

---

प्रसादभूमिः प्रसादास्पदम् । अष्टादशवर्षदेशीयः किंचिन्न्यूनाष्टादशवर्षः । 'ईषदसमाप्तौ कल्पब्देश्यदेशीयरः' । यादृच्छिकीमभीष्टाम् । संपत्तिमर्थाद्गुणानाम् । ' कार्तान्तिको लक्षणज्ञः ' इति वैजयन्ती । शालिस्तण्डुलविशेषः । ' कण्डनेन विना श्वेतं हैमन्तं शालि संस्मृतम् ' इति भावमिश्रः । प्रस्थं मानाविशेषः । ' माषटङ्काक्षबिल्वानि कुडवः प्रस्थमाढकम् । राशिर्गोणी खारिकेति यथोत्तरचतुर्गुणम् ॥ ' इति शार्ङ्गधरोक्तेः । शेरचतुष्कपरिमाणमिति यावत् । कन्यावन्तः कन्यापितरः । शिबिषु कावेरीदक्षिणतीरेषु । ' शिबिर्मरुद्रथायास्तु दक्षिणं तीर ( वर्ष ) मिष्यते । ' इति वैजयन्ती । अवसिता नष्टा महती ऋद्धिर्भूतिर्यस्यास्ताम् । मृजा शुद्धिः तद्वन्तः । यवोऽङ्गुष्ठविरहं चिह्नम् । आदिशब्देनान्यानि शुभविरह्माणि सूच्यन्ते । गुल्फं घुटिका । ' तद्ग्रन्थी घुटिके गुल्फौ ' इत्यमरः । मांसलौ पुष्टौ । अत एव मग्नगुल्फसंधी अत एवादृश्यमानाशिरावेष्टितौ—इति भूषणा । अशिरालौ शिरारहितौ । अङ्घ्री चरणौ । पीवरौ मांसलावूरू ताभ्यां ग्रस्ते । सकृद्विभक्तः समं विभक्तः । 'एकवारे समे सकृत्'

---

१ विधेयम्. २ कावेरीदक्षिणतीरेषु. ३ मग्नगुल्फसंधी.

स्तः ककुन्दरविभागशोभी रथाङ्गाकारसंस्थितश्च नितम्बभागः, तनुतरमीषन्निम्नं गम्भीरं नाभिमण्डलम्, वलित्रयेण चालंकृतमुदरम्, उरोभागव्यापिनावुन्मग्नचूचुकौ विशालारम्भशोभिनौ पयोधरौ, धनधान्यपुत्रभूयस्त्वचिह्नलेखालाञ्छिततले स्निग्धोदग्रकोमलनखमणी ऋज्वनुपूर्ववृत्तताम्राङ्गुली संनतांसदेशे सौकुमार्यवत्यौ निमग्नपर्वसंधी च बाहुलते, तन्वी कम्बुवृत्तबन्धुरा च कन्धरा, वृत्तमध्यविभक्तरागाधरम् असंक्षिप्तचारुचिबुकम् आपूर्णकठिनगण्डमण्डलम् असंगतानुवक्रनीलस्निग्धभ्रूलतम् अनतिप्रौढतिलकुसुमसदृशनासिकम् असितधवलरक्तत्रिभागभासुरमधुराधीरसंचारमन्थरायतेक्षणम् इन्दुशकलसुन्दरललाटम् इन्द्रनीलशिलाकाररम्यालकपङ्क्ति द्विगुणकुण्डलितम्लाननालीकनालललितलम्बश्रवणपाशयुगलमाननकमलम्, अनतिभङ्गुरो बहुलः पर्यन्तेऽप्यकपिलरुचिरायामवानेकैकनिसर्गसमस्निग्धनीलो गन्धग्राही च मूर्धजकलापः । सेयमाकृतिर्न व्यभिचरति शीलम् ।

---

इत्यजयः । ककुन्दरं नितम्बास्थितकूपकद्वयम् । 'कूपकौ तु नितम्बस्थौ द्वयहीने ककुन्दरे ।' इत्यमरः । रथाङ्गं चक्रम् । संस्थितिर्मर्यादा । तनुतरमतिसूक्ष्मम् । चूचुकं कुचाग्रम् । 'चूचुकं तु कुचाग्रं स्यात्' इत्यमरः । पयोधरौ स्तनौ । पुत्रभूयस्त्वं पुत्रबाहुल्यम् । स्निग्धा उदग्राः कोमलाश्च नखमणयो ययोस्ते । अंसः स्कन्धः । कम्बुः शङ्खः । 'शङ्खः स्यात्कम्बुरस्त्रियौ' इत्यमरः । कन्धरा ग्रीवा । चिबुकं हनुः । त्रिभागे च भासुरे च मधुराधीरसंचारे च मन्थरे च आयते च ईक्षणे नेत्रे यस्य । इन्दुशकलमर्धचन्द्रः । नालीकं कमलम् । 'नालीकः शरशल्याङ्गेष्वब्जखण्डे नपुंसकम्' इति मेदिनी । श्रवणः कर्णः । द्वौ गुणौ यस्य तद् द्विगुणं कुण्डलितं च यन्म्लानं नालीकनालं तद्वल्ललितौ लम्बौ च यौ प्रशस्तौ कर्णौ कर्णपाशौ तयोर्युगलं यत्र । कपिलरुचिः पिङ्गलरुचिः । न कपिलरुचिरकपिलरुचिः । 'कडारः कपिलः पिङ्गः' इत्यमरः । आयामो दैर्घ्यं तद्वान् । मूर्धजकलापः केशकलापः । "स्निग्धोन्नताग्रतनुताम्रनखौ कुमार्याः पादौ समोपचितचारुनिगूढगुल्फौ । श्लिष्टाङ्गुली कमलकान्तितलौ च यस्यास्तामुद्वहेद्यदि भुवोऽधिपतित्वमिच्छेत् ॥ मत्स्याङ्कुशाब्जयववज्रहलासिचिह्नावस्वेदनौ मृदुतलौ चरणौ प्रशस्तौ । जङ्घे च रोमरहिते विपुले सुवृत्ते जानुद्वयं सममतुल्यमसंधिदेशम् ॥ ऊरू घनौ करिकरप्रतिमावरोमावश्वत्थपत्रसदृशं विपुलं च गुह्यम् ॥ विस्तीर्णमांसोपचितो नितम्बो गुरुश्च धत्ते रशनाकलापम् । नाभिर्गभीरा विपुलाऽङ्गनानां प्रदक्षिणावर्तगता च शस्ता ॥ मध्यं स्त्रियास्त्रिवलनान्तमरोमशं च वृत्तौ घनावविषमौ कठिनावुरःस्थौ । रोमप्रवर्जितमुरो मृदु चाङ्गनानां ग्रीवा च कम्बुनिचिता-

---

१ उन्मग्नवाननचूचुकौ. २ स्निग्धोदर. ३ मृदु. ४ संगता०. ५ मधुरधीर.

आसज्जति च मे हृदयमस्यामेव। तत्परीक्ष्यैनामुद्वहेयम्। अविमृश्यकारिणा हि नियतमनेकाः पतन्त्यनुशयपरंपराः' इति स्निग्धदृष्टिराचष्ट—'भद्रे, कच्चिदस्ति कौशलं शालिप्रस्थेनानेन संपन्नमाहारमस्मानभ्यवहारयितुम्' इति। ततस्तया वृद्धदासी साकूतमालोकिता। तस्य हस्तात्प्रस्थमात्रं धान्यमादाय कचिदलिन्दोद्देशे सुसिक्तसंमृष्टे दत्तपादशौचमुपावेशयत्। सा कन्या तान्गन्धशालीन्संक्षुद्य मात्रया विशोष्यातपे मुहुर्मुहुः परिवर्त्य स्थिरसमायां भूमौ नालीपृष्ठेन मृदुमृदु घट्टयन्ती तुषैरखण्डैस्तण्डुलान्पृथक्चकार। जगाद च धात्रीम्—'मातः, एभिस्तुषैरर्थिनो भूषणमृजाक्रियाक्षमैः स्वर्णकाराः। तेभ्य इमान्दत्त्वा लब्धाभिः काकिणीभिः स्थिरतराण्यनत्यार्द्राणि नातिशुष्काणि काष्ठानि मितंपचां स्थालीमुभे शरावे चाहर' इति। तथाकृते तया तांस्तण्डुलाननतिनिम्नोत्तानविस्तीर्णकुक्षौ ककुभोलूखले लोहपत्रवेष्टितमुखेन समशरीरेण विभाव्यमानमध्यतानवेन

ऽर्थसुखानि धत्ते॥ बन्धुजीवकुसुमोपमोऽधरो मांसलो रुचिरबिम्बरूपधृक्। कुन्दकुड्मलनिभाः समा द्विजा योषितां पतिसुखामितार्थदाः॥ दाक्षिण्ययुक्तमशठं परपुष्टहंसवल्गुप्रभाषणमदीनमसौख्यं च। नासा समा समपुटा रुचिरप्रशस्ता दृङ्नीलनीरजदले द्युतिहारिणी च॥ नो संगते नातिपृथू न लम्बे शस्ते भ्रुवौ बालशशाङ्कवक्रे। अर्धेन्दुसंस्थानमलोमशं च शस्तं ललाटं न तलं न तुङ्गम्॥ कर्णयुग्ममपि युक्तमांसलं शस्यते मृदु समं समाहितम्। स्निग्धनीलमृदुकुञ्चितलम्बाः मूर्धजाः शुभकराः शिरःस्थिताः॥ इति वराहमिहिरः।" इति भूषणा। आसज्जति। सक्तं भवतीत्यर्थः। उद्वहेयम्। उद्वहामीत्यर्थः। अनुशयः पश्चात्तापः। 'भवेदनुशयो द्वेषे पश्चात्तापानुबन्धयोः' इति विश्वः। अभ्यवहारयितुं भोजयितुम्। साकूतं साभिप्रायम्। 'आकूतं स्यादभिप्रायः' इति हलायुधः। अलिन्दं देहली। सेति। मात्रयाऽल्पपरिमाणेन। 'मात्रा परिच्छदे वर्णे मानेऽल्पे' इति रत्नमाला। आतपे उष्णे। मृदुमृदु शनैःशनैरित्यर्थः। तुषैरिति 'पृथग्विनानाना—' इति तृतीया। मृजा शुद्धिः। काकिणीभिः कपर्दिकाभिः। 'वराटकानां दशकद्वयं स्यात्सा काकिणी' इति भास्कराचार्यः। स्थिरतराणि सारवन्ति। मितंपचाम्। 'मितनखे च' इति खश्। शरावे मृत्पात्रे। 'शरावो वर्धमानकः' इत्यमरः। विस्तीर्णकुक्षौ बृहदुदरे। 'नातिनम्रोत्तानविस्तीर्णः कुक्षिर्यस्येत्यर्थः।' इति भूषणा। ककुभो वृक्षविशेषः। 'ककुभो भूरुहे वीणाप्रसेवे' इति महीपः। काष्ठोलूखले इति भावः। विभाव्यमानं संभाव्यमानम्। मध्यतानवं मध्ये कृशत्वम्। तनो-

१ अथ च. २ नातिनिम्न.

व्यायतेन गुरुणा खादिरेण मुसलेन चतुर[1]ललितोत्क्षेपणावक्षेपणायासितभुजमसकृदङ्गुलीभिरुद्धृत्योद्धृत्यावहत्य शूर्पशोधितकणकिंशारुकांस्तण्डुलानसकृदद्भिः प्रक्षाल्य क्वथितपञ्चगुणे जले दत्तचुल्लीपूजा प्राक्षिपत्। प्रश्लथावयवेषु प्रस्फुरत्सु तण्डुलेषु मुकुलावस्थामतिवर्तमानेषु संक्षिप्यानलमुपहितमुखपिधानया स्थाल्याऽन्नमण्डमगालयत्। दर्व्या चा[2]वघट्ट्य मात्रया [3]परिवर्त्य समपक्वेषु सिक्थेषु तां स्थालीमधोमुखीमवातिष्ठिपत्। इन्धनान्यन्तःसाराण्यम्भसा समभ्युक्ष्य प्रशमिताग्नीनि [4]कृष्णाङ्गारीकृत्य तदर्थिभ्यः प्राहिणोत्—'एभिर्लब्धाः काकिणीर्दत्त्वा शाकं घृतं दधि तैलमामलकं चिञ्चाफलं च यथालाभमानय' इति। तथाऽनुष्ठिते च तया द्वित्रानुपदंशानुपपाद्य तदन्नमण्डमार्द्रवालुकोपाहितनवशरावगतमतिमृदुना तालवृन्तानिलेन शीतलीकृत्य सलवणसंभारं दत्ताङ्गारधूपवासं च संपाद्य, तदप्यामलकं श्लक्ष्णपिष्टमुत्पलगन्धि कृत्वा धात्रीमुखेन स्नानाय तमचोदयत्। तया च स्नानशुद्धया दत्ततैलामलकः क्रमेण सस्नौ। [5]स्नातः सिक्तमृष्टे कुट्टिमे फलकमारुह्य पाण्डुहरित[6]स्य त्रिभागशेषलूनस्याङ्गणकदलीपलाशस्योपरि शरावद्वयं दत्त[7]मार्द्रमभिमृशन्नतिष्ठत्। सा तु तां पेयामेवाग्रे समुपाहरत्। पीत्वा चापनीताध्वक्लमः प्रहृष्टः प्रक्लिन्नसकलगात्रः स्थितोऽभूत्। ततस्तस्य शाल्योदनस्य दर्वीद्वयं दत्त्वा सर्पिर्मात्रां सूपमुपदंशं चोपजहार। इमं च

---

भावस्तानवम्। व्यायतेन दीर्घेण। गुरुणा स्थूलेन। उत्क्षेपणमूर्ध्वीकरणम्। अवक्षेपणमधः पातनम्। किंशारुम्। 'किंशारुः सस्यशूकं स्यात्' इत्यमरः। असकृद्वारंवारम्। क्वथितेति। 'क्वथितं च तत्पञ्चगुणं चेत्यर्थः' इति भूषणा। मुकुलावस्थां कलिकावस्थाम्। अन्नमण्डं भक्तपानीयम्। अवघट्ट्य अवगाह्येत्यर्थः। अन्तःसाराण्युपर्येव दग्धानि। द्वित्रान्कतिपयान्। उपदंशाञ्शाकादीन्। अचोदयत् प्रेरयामासेत्यर्थः। सिक्तमृष्ट आदौ सिक्तः पश्चान्मृष्टः। कुट्टिमं बद्धभूमिकम्। 'त्रिषु भागेषु यः शेषोऽग्रिमस्तत्र लूनस्य छिन्नस्येत्यर्थः।' इति भूषणा। अङ्गणे या कदली रम्भा तस्याः पलाशं पत्रं तस्योपरि। अभिमृशन्स्पृशन्। सा त्विति। पेया ससिक्था। 'मण्डोऽसिक्थः, ससिक्था पेया, परिसिक्था यवागूश्च, घनसिक्था विलेपी, परिस्रुतस्त्वोदनो भक्तः' इति वाग्भटोक्तेः। ओदनस्य दर्वीद्वयं दत्त्वा। दर्वीद्वयमात्रमोदनं दत्त्वेत्यर्थः। सर्पिर्मात्राम्। अल्पघृतमिति यावत्। सूपं वरान्नम्।

---

१ ललितक्षेपणोत्क्षेपणायासित. २ चावगाह्य. ३ परावृत्य. ४ निरुष्णाङ्गारीकृत्य ५ स्नापितः. ६ हरितात्रि०. ७ अद्भिः.

दध्ना च त्रिजातकावचूर्णितेन सुरभिशीतलाभ्यां च कालशेयकाञ्जिकाभ्या शेषमन्नमभोजयत्। सशेष एवान्धस्यसावतृप्यत्। अयाचत च पानीयम्। अथ नवभृङ्गारसंभृतमगुरुधूपधूपितमभिनवपाटलाकुसुमवासितमुत्फुल्लो-त्पलग्रथितसौरभं वारि नालीधारात्मना पातयांबभूव। सोऽपि मुखोपहित-शरावेण हिमशिशिरकणकरालितारुणायमानाक्षिपक्ष्मा धारारवाभिनन्दित-श्रवणः स्पर्शसुखोद्भिन्नरोमाञ्चकर्कशकपोलः परिमलप्रवालोत्पीडफुल्ल-घ्राणरन्ध्रो माधुर्यप्रकर्षावर्जितरसनेन्द्रियस्तदच्छं पानीयमाकण्ठं पपौ। शिरःकम्पसंज्ञावारिता च पुनरपरकरकेणाचमनमदत्त कन्या। वृद्धया तु तदुच्छिष्टमपोह्य हरितगोमयोपलिप्ते कुट्टिमे स्वमेवोत्तरीयकर्पटं व्यवधाय क्षणमशेत। परितुष्टश्च विधिवदुपयम्य कन्यां निन्ये। नीत्वै-तदनपेक्षः कामपि गणिकामवरोधमकरोत्। तामप्यसौ प्रियसखीमिवो-पाचरत्। पतिं च दैवतमिव मुक्ततन्द्रा पर्यचरत्। गृहकार्याणि चाहीन-मन्वतिष्ठत्। परिजनं च दाक्षिण्यनिधिरात्माधीनमकरोत्। तद्गुणवशी-कृतश्च भर्ता सर्वमेव कुटुम्बं तदायत्तमेव कृत्वा तदेकाधीनजीवितशरीर-स्त्रिवर्गं निर्विवेश। तद्ब्रवीमि—'गृहिणः प्रियहिताय दारगुणाः' इति।

---

उपदंशं च शाकादि। त्रिजातकं त्वक्तैलं त्रिकटुं वा। अवचूर्णितेन विलोडितेन। कालशेयं तक्रम्। 'दण्डाहतं कालशेयमरिष्टमपि गोरसः।' इत्यमरः। 'कलशिर्घटस्तत्र भवम्।' 'दृतिकुक्षिकलशि–' इति ढञ्।'–इति भूषणा। काञ्जिकम्। 'आरनालकसौवीरकुल्माषाभिषुतानि च। अवन्तिसोमधान्याम्लकुञ्जलानि च काञ्जिके॥' इत्यमरः। अन्धस्योदने। 'भिस्सा स्त्री भक्तमन्धोऽन्नमोदनोऽस्त्री सदीदिविः' इत्यमरः। **अथेति**। धारात्मना अविरलधारयेत्यर्थः। हिमशिशिर कणैः करालितानि अरुणायमानानि च अक्षिपक्ष्माणि यस्य। 'हिमशिशिरेतीन्द्रिय तृप्तिरुक्ता। उक्तं च माघेऽपि–'क्रान्तकान्तवदनप्रतिबिम्बे भग्नबालसहकारसुगन्धौ। स्वादुनि प्रणदितालिनि शीते निर्ववार मधुनीन्द्रियवर्गः॥'–इति भूषणा। माधुर्यस्य प्रकर्षेण आवर्जितं तर्पितं रसनेन्द्रियं घ्राणेन्द्रियं यस्य। **आचमनमदत्तेति**। अत्र याज्ञवल्क्यः–'स्नात्वा पीत्वा क्षुते सुप्ते भुक्त्वा रथ्योपसर्पणे। आचान्तः पुनराचामे-द्वासो विपरिधाय च॥' इति। हरितगोमयम्। 'गोश्च पुरीषे' इति मयट्। कर्पटं जीर्णवस्त्रम्। मुक्ततन्द्रा त्यक्तालस्या। अहीनमत्यर्थम्। दक्षिणस्य भावः दाक्षिण्यं तस्य निधिः। तदायत्तं तदधीनम्। त्रिवर्गं धर्मार्थकामान्।

---

१ नालीति नास्ति क्वचित्. २ प्रवाहो०. ३ आवर्तित.

ततस्तेनानुयुक्तो निम्बवतीवृत्तमाख्यातवान्—'अस्ति सौराष्ट्रेषु वलभी नाम नगरी। तस्यां गृहगुप्तनाम्नो गुह्यकेन्द्रतुल्यविभवस्य नाविकपतेर्दुहिता रत्नवती नाम। तां किल मधुमत्याः समुपागम्य बलभद्रो नाम सार्थवाहपुत्रः पर्यणैषीत्। तयाऽपि नववध्वा रहसि रभसविघ्नितसुरतसुखो झटिति द्वेषमल्पेतरं बबन्ध। न तां पुनर्द्रष्टुमिष्टवान्। तद्गृहागमनमपि सुहृद्वाक्यशतातिवर्ती लज्जया परिजहार। तां च दुर्भगां तदाप्रभृत्येव 'नेयं रत्नवती निम्बवती चेयम्' इति स्वजनः पैरजनश्च परिबभूव। गते च कस्मिंश्चित्काले सा त्वनुतप्यमाना 'का मे गतिः' इति विमृशन्ती कामपि वृद्धप्रव्राजिकां मातृस्थानीयां देवशेषकुसुमैरुपस्थितामपश्यत्। तस्याः पुरो रहसि सकरुणं रुरोद। तयाऽप्युदश्रुमुख्या बहुप्रकारमनुनीय रुदितकारणं पृष्टा त्रपमाणाऽपि कार्यगौरवात्कथंचिदब्रवीत्—'अम्ब किं ब्रवीमि। दौर्भाग्यं नाम जीवन्मरणमेवाङ्गनानां, विशेषतश्च कुलवधूनाम्। तस्याहमस्म्युदाहरणभूता। मातृप्रमुखोऽपि ज्ञातिवर्गो मामवज्ञयैव पश्यति। तेन सुदृष्टां मां कुरु। न चेत्त्यजेयमद्यैव निष्प्रयोजनान्प्राणान्। आ विरामाच्च मे रहस्यं नाश्राव्यम्' इति पादयोः पपात। सैनामुत्थाप्योद्बाष्पोवाच—'वत्से मा अध्यवस्यः साहसम्। इयमस्मि त्वन्निदेशवर्तिनी। यावति ममोपयोगस्तव तावति भवाम्यनन्याधीना। यद्येवासि निर्विण्णा तपश्चर त्वं मदधिष्ठिता पारलौकिकाय कल्याणाय। नन्वयमुदर्कः प्राक्तनस्य दुष्कृतस्य यदनेनाकारणेद्दशेन

---

**अस्तीति**। गुह्यकेन्द्रः कुबेरः। नाविका नौभिर्जीवन्तीति तथा। मधुमत्या नगर्याः। पर्यणैषीत्परिणयनमकरोत्। अल्पेतरं बह्वित्यर्थः। दुर्भगां दुरदृष्टाम्। सा निम्बवती। अनुतप्यमानाऽनुतापं प्राप्तवती। प्रव्राजिका संन्यासिनी। देवशेषकुसुमैर्निर्माल्यपुष्पैः। तयाऽपि वृद्धप्रव्राजिकया। रुदितं रोदनम्। त्रपमाणा लज्जावती। गौरवात् महत्त्वात्। दौर्भाग्यं भर्तृवैमुख्यम्। निष्प्रयोजनानकिंचित्करान्। रहस्यं गोप्यम्। उद्बाष्पोद्गतबाष्पा। **यावति तावतीति**। प्रयोजने इत्यर्थः। परलोके भवं पारलौकिकं तस्मै पारलौकिकाय। उदर्कः भावि कर्मफलम्। 'उदर्कः फलमुत्तरम्' इत्यमरः।

---

१ परिजनश्च. २ कालान्तरे. ३ पारव्राजिकाम्. ४ यावत्...तावत्. ५ यद्येवम्.

शीलेन जात्या चैवंभूतया समनुगता सत्यकस्मादेव[1] भर्तृद्वेष्यतां गताऽसि। यदि कश्चिदस्त्युपायः पतिद्रोहप्रतिक्रियायै, दर्शयामुम्। मतिर्हि ते पटीयसी ' इति। अथासौ कथंचित्क्षणमधोमुखी ध्यात्वा दीर्घोष्णश्वासपूर्वमवोचत्—' भगवति पतिरेव दैवतं वनितानाम्, विशेषतश्च कुलजानाम्। अतस्तच्छुश्रूषणाभ्युपायहेतुभूतं किंचिदाचरणीयम्। अस्त्यस्मत्प्रातिवेश्यो वणिक्। अभिजनेन विभवेन राजान्तरङ्गभावेन च सर्वपौरानतीत्य वर्तते। तस्य कन्या कनकवती नाम मत्समानरूपावयवा ममातिस्निग्धा सखी। तया सह तद्विमानहर्म्यतले ततोऽपि द्विगुणमण्डिता विहरिष्यामि। त्वया तु तन्मातृप्रार्थनं सकरुणमभिधाय मत्पतिरेतद्गृहं कथंचनानेयः। समीपगतेषु च युष्मासु क्रीडामत्ता नाम कन्दुकं भ्रंशयेयम्। अथ तमादाय तस्य हस्ते दत्त्वा वक्ष्यसि—' पुत्र, तवेयं भार्यासखी निधिपतिदत्तस्य सर्वश्रेष्ठिमुख्यस्य कन्या कनकवती नाम। त्वामियमनवस्थो निष्करुणश्चेति रत्नवतीनिमित्तमत्यर्थं निन्दति। तदेष कन्दुको विपक्षधनं प्रत्यर्पणीयम् ' इति। स तथोक्तो नियतमुन्मुखीभूय तामेव प्रियसखीं मन्यमानो मां, बद्धाञ्जलि याचमानायै मह्यं भूयस्त्वत्प्रार्थितः साभिलाषमर्पयिष्यति। तेन रन्ध्रेणोपश्लिष्य रागमुज्ज्वलीकृत्य यथाऽसौ कृतसंकेतो देशान्तरमादाय मां गमिष्यति तथोपपादनीयम् ' इति। हर्षाभ्युपेतया[2] चानया तथैव संपादितम्। अथैतां कनकवतीति वृद्धतापसीविप्रलब्धो बलभद्रः सरत्न[3]साराभरणामादाय निशि नीरन्ध्रे तमसि प्रावसत्। सा तु तापसी

---

आकारेण शरीराकृत्या। सौन्दर्येणेत्यर्थः। जात्या विशिष्टकुलेन। एवंभूतया स्पृहणीययेत्यर्थः। **यदीति**। पत्युर्द्रोहः पराङ्मुखता। पटीयस्यतिशयेन पटुः। असौ निम्बवती। शुश्रूषणं सेवा। प्रातिवेश्यः प्रतिवेशे समीपगृहे भवः। वणिग्वाणिज्यकर्ता। अभिजनेन कुलीनतया। विभवेन सामर्थ्येन। राजान्तरङ्गभावेन राज्ञो विश्वासभूमित्वेनेत्यर्थः। अतीत्यातिक्रम्य। मण्डिताऽलंकृता। **विमानहर्म्येति**। ' विमानो व्योमयाने च सप्तभूमिगृहेऽपि च। ' इति कोशः। तन्मातृप्रार्थनं कनकवतीमातृप्रार्थनमिति। मां तामेव प्रियसखीं मन्यमानः। बद्धाञ्जलि बद्धः अञ्जलिर्यस्मिन्कर्मणि तद् यथा स्यात्तथा। क्रियाविशेषणमिदम्। रन्ध्रेण मिषेण। उपाश्लिष्यालिङ्ग्य। उपेत्येत्यर्थः। रागमिच्छाम्। उज्ज्वलीकृत्य। प्रकटीकृत्येत्यर्थः। **अथेति**। नीरन्ध्रे तमसि गाढान्धकारे।

---

१ एकदैव. २ सहर्षा०. ३ सरत्नाभरणाम्.

वार्तामापादयत्—'मन्देन मया निर्निमित्तमुपेक्षिता रत्नवती श्वशुरौ च परिभूतौ सुहृदश्चातिवर्तिताः। तदत्रैव संसृष्टो जीवितुं जिहेमीति बलभद्रः पूर्वेद्युर्मामकथयत्। नूनमसौ तेन नीता व्यक्तिश्चाचिराद्भविष्यति' इति। तच्छ्रुत्वा तद्बान्धवास्तदन्वेषणं प्रति शिथिलयत्नास्तस्थुः। रत्नवती तु मार्गे कांचित्पण्यदासीं संगृह्य तयोह्यमानपाथेयाद्युपस्करा खेटकपुरमगमत्। अमुत्र च व्यवहारकुशलो बलभद्रः स्वल्पेनैव मूलेन महद्धनमुपार्जयत्। पौराग्रगण्यश्चासीत्। परिजनश्च भूयानर्थवशात्समाजगाम। ततस्तां प्रथमदासीं 'न कर्म करोषि, दृष्टं मुष्णासि, अप्रियं ब्रवीषि' इति परुषमुक्त्वा बह्वताडयत्। चेटी तु प्रसादकालोपाख्यातरहस्यस्य[1] वृत्तान्तैकदेशमात्तरोषा निर्बिभेद। तच्छ्रुत्वा तु लुब्धेन दण्डवाहिना पौरवृद्धसंनिधौ 'निधिपतिदत्तस्य कन्यां कनकवतीं मोषेणापहृत्यास्मत्पुरे निवसत्येष दुर्मतिर्बलभद्रः। तस्य सर्वस्वहरणं न भवद्भिः प्रतिबन्धनीयम्' इति नितरामभर्त्सयत[2]। भीतं च बलभद्रमभिजगाद रत्नवती—'न भेतव्यम्। ब्रूहि—नेयं निधिपतिर्दत्तकन्या[3] कनकवती। वलभ्यामेव गृहगुप्तदुहिता रत्नवती नामेयं दत्ता पितृभ्यां मया च न्यायोढा। न चेत्प्रतीथं[4] प्राणिधिं प्रहिणुतास्या बन्धुपार्श्वम्' इति। बलभद्रस्तु तथोक्त्वा श्रेणीप्रातिभाव्येन तावदेवातिष्ठद्यावत्तत्पुरलेख्यलब्धवृत्तान्तो गृहगुप्तः खेटकपुरमागत्य सह जामात्रा दुहितरमतिप्रीतः[5] प्रत्यनैषीत्। तथा दृष्ट्वा रत्नवती कनकवतीति भावयतस्तस्यैव बलभद्रस्यातिवल्लभा जाता। तद्ब्रवीमि—'कामो नाम संकल्पः' इति।

---

अतिवर्तिताः क्रान्ताः। संसृष्टः तया संगतः। दासीं चेटीम्। 'चेटी चिरण्टी दासी च' इति वैजयन्ती। पाथेयं मार्गे भक्षणसामग्री। खेटकपुरमल्पनगरम्। मूलेन मूलधनेन। उपाख्यातरहस्यस्य कथितकनकवत्यपहारवृत्तान्तस्य। लुब्धेन। 'लुब्धोऽभिलाषुकस्तृष्णक्' इत्यमरः। दण्डवाहिना दण्डाधिकारिणा। न्यायोढा न्यायमार्गेणोढा। परिणीतेत्यर्थः। प्रणिधिः सेवकः। श्रेणीप्रातिभाव्येन वणिजां श्रेणीं प्रतिभूस्थाने कृत्वेत्यर्थः।

---

१ पाख्यातमस्या वृ॰. २ अतर्जयत. ३ दत्तस्य. ४ प्रतीतिरस्मिन्नर्थे. ५ अतिप्रीतिः.

तदनन्तरमसौ नितम्बवतीवृत्तान्तमप्राक्षीत्। सोऽहमब्रवम्—'अस्ति शूरसेनेषु मथुरा नाम नगरी। तत्र कश्चित्कुलपुत्रः कलासु गणिकासु चातिरक्तः मित्रार्थे स्वभुजमात्रनिर्व्यूढानेककलहः कलहकण्टक इति कर्कशैरभिख्यापिताख्यः [1]प्रत्यवात्सीत्। स चैकदा कस्यचिदागन्तोश्चित्रकरस्य हस्ते चित्रपटं ददर्श। तत्र काचिदालेख्यगता युवतिरालोकमात्रेणैव कलहकण्टकस्य कामातुरं चेतश्चकार। स च तमब्रवीत्—'भद्र विरुद्धमिवैतत्प्रतिभाति। यतः कुलजादुर्लभं वपुः, आभिजात्यशंसिनी च नम्रता, पाण्डुरा च मुखच्छविः, [2]अनतिपरिभुक्तसुभगा च तनुः, प्रौढतानुविद्धा च दृष्टिः। न चैषा प्रोषितभर्तृका प्रवासचिह्नस्यै[3]कवेण्यादेरदर्शनात्। लक्ष्म चैतद्दक्षिणपार्श्ववर्ति। तदियं वृद्धस्य कस्यचिद्वणिजो नातिपुंस्त्वस्य यथार्हसंभोगालाभपीडिता गृहिणी त्वयाऽतिकौशलाद्यथादृष्टमालिखिता भवितुमर्हति' इति। स तमभिप्रशस्याशंसत्—'सत्यमिदम्। अवन्तिपुर्यामुज्जायिन्यामनन्तकीर्तिनाम्नः सार्थवाहस्य भार्या यथार्थन[4]मा नितम्बवती नामैषा सौन्दर्यविस्मितेन मयैवमालिखिता' इति। स तदैवोन्मनायमानस्तद्दर्शनाय परिवव्राजोज्जयिनीम्। भार्गवो नाम भूत्वा भिक्षानिभेन तद्गृहं प्रविश्य तां ददर्श। दृष्ट्वा चात्यारूढमन्मथो निर्गत्य पौरमुख्येभ्यः श्मशानरक्षामयाचत। अलभत च।

---

**अस्तीति**। शूरसेनेषु देशेषु। कुलपुत्रः शूद्रः। 'कुलपुत्रः कुलीने च शूद्रे च' इति वैजयन्ती। कलासु चतुःषष्टिमितासु। गणिकासु वेश्यासु। स्वभुज एव स्वभुजमात्रं तेन निर्व्यूढा दृढीकृताः समाप्तिं नीताः अनेके कलहा येन। कर्कशैः परुषवादिभिः। स च कलहकण्टकः। तं चित्रकारम्। **भद्रेति**। अभिजातस्य भाव आभिजात्यं कुलीनता। पाण्डुरा शुभ्रा। अनतिपरिभुक्ताऽलब्धातिभोगा। प्रौढतानुविद्धा प्रौढतासक्ता। वेणी कचबन्धः। 'वेणी कचस्य बन्धे स्यान्नदीनां संगमेऽपि च' इति विश्वः। 'लक्ष्म नखक्षतरूपं चिह्नम्' इति भूषणा। संभोगस्यालाभोऽप्राप्तिस्तेन पीडिता। उन्मनायमान उन्मनायतेऽसौ तथा। परिवव्राज अगच्छादित्यर्थः। भार्गवो ज्यौतिषिकः। 'भार्गवौ शुक्रदैवज्ञौ' इति वैजयन्ती। निभं मिषम्। 'निभो व्याजसदृक्षयोः' इति विश्वः। **दृष्ट्वा चेति**। अत्यारूढमन्मथोऽतिप्रवृद्धकामः।

---

१ परिबव्राज. २ नातिपरिभोगसुलभा. ३ एकेति नास्ति क्वचित्. ४ नामधेया. ५ मिषेण.

तत्र लब्धैश्च शवावगुण्ठनपटादिभिः कामप्यर्हन्तिकां नाम श्रमणिकामुपासांचक्रे। तन्मुखेन च नितम्बवतीमुपांशु मन्त्रयामास[1]। सा चैनां निर्भर्त्सयन्ती प्रत्याचचक्षे। श्रमणिकामुखाच्च दुष्करशीलभ्रंशां कुलस्त्रियमुपलभ्य रहसि दूतिकामशिक्षयत्—'भूयोऽप्युपतिष्ठ सार्थवाहभार्याम्। ब्रूहि चोपह्वरे, संसारदोषदर्शनात्समाधिमास्थाय मुमुक्षमाणो मादृशो जनः कुलवधूनां शीलपातने घटत इति क्व घटते। एतदपि त्वमत्युदारया[2] समृद्ध्या रूपेणातिमानुषेण प्रथमेन वयसोपपन्नां किमितरनारीसुलभं चापलं स्पृष्टं न वेति परीक्षा कृता। तुष्टाऽस्मि तवैवमदुष्टभावतया। त्वामिदानीमुत्पन्नापत्यां द्रष्टुमिच्छामि। भर्ता तु भवत्याः केनचिद्ग्रहेणाधिष्ठितः पाण्डुरोगदुर्बलो भोगे चासमर्थः स्थितोऽभूत्। न च शक्यं तस्य विघ्नमप्रतिकृत्यापत्यमस्माल्लब्धुम्। अतः प्रसीद। वृक्षवाटिकामेकाकिनी प्रविश्य मदुपनीतस्य कस्यचिन्मन्त्रवादिनश्छन्न[3]मेव हस्ते चरणमर्पयित्वा तदभिमन्त्रितेन प्रणयकुपिता नाम भूत्वा भर्तारमुरसि प्रहर्तुमर्हसि। उपर्यसावुत्तमधातुपुष्टिमूर्जितापत्योत्पादनक्षमामासादयिष्यति। अनुवर्तिष्यते देवीमिवात्रभवतीम्। नात्र शङ्का कार्या' इति। सा तथोक्ता व्यक्तमभ्युपैष्यति। नक्तं मां वृक्षवाटिकां प्रवेश्य तामपि प्रवेशयिष्यसि। तावतैव त्वयाऽहमनुगृहीतो भवेयम्' इति। सा तथैवो[4]पपादितवती। सोऽतिप्रीतस्तस्यामेव क्षपायां वृक्षवाटिकां गतो नितम्बवतीं निर्ग्रन्थिका-

पौरमुख्येभ्यः पौरश्रेष्ठेभ्यः। तत्र श्मशाने। शवावगुण्ठनपटः शववेष्टितवस्त्रम्। अर्हन्तिकां बौद्धपरिव्राजिकाम्। तन्मुखेन श्रमणिकामुखेन। उपांशु रहसि। मन्त्रयामास। भेदयामासेत्यर्थः। भ्रंशो नाशः। घटत ईहते। 'घट चेष्टायाम्'। क्व घटते क्व संगच्छते। 'घट योजने'। अतिमानुषेण मानुषमतिक्रम्य वर्तत इति तथा तेन। प्रथमेन वयसा यौवनेन। अदुष्टभावः सुभावः। पातिव्रत्यादभ्रंश इत्यर्थः। उत्पन्नापत्यां जातापत्याम्। भोगे विषयसङ्गे। अप्रतिकृत्य। प्रतीकारमकृत्वेत्यर्थः। वृक्षवाटिकां गृहोपवनम्। ऊर्जितं च तदपत्यमूर्जितापत्यं समीचीनापत्यं तस्योत्पादने क्षमां समर्थाम्। न पतन्ति पितरोऽनेनेत्यपत्यम्। नक्तं रात्रौ। उपग्राहितवत्यङ्गीकृतवती।

१ उपनिमन्त्रयामास. २ अत्युदारतया. ३ स्वच्छन्दमेव. ४ उपग्राहितवती.

प्रयत्नेनोपनीतां पादे परामृशन्निव हेमनूपुरमेकमाक्षिप्य[1] च्छुरिकयोरुमूले किंचिदालिख्य[2] द्रुततरमपासरत् । सा तु सान्द्रत्रासा स्वमेव दुर्नयं गर्हमाणा जिघांसन्तीव श्रमणिकां तद्व्रणं भवनदीर्घिकायां प्रक्षाल्य दत्त्वा[3] पटबन्धनं सामयापदेशादपरं चापनीय नूपुरं शयनपरा त्रिचतुराणि दिनान्येकान्ते निन्ये । स धूर्तः 'विक्रेष्ये' इति तेन नूपुरेण तमनन्तकीर्तिमुपाससाद । स दृष्ट्वा 'मम गृहिण्या एवैष नूपुरः कथमयमुपलब्धस्त्वया' इति तमब्रुवाणं निर्बन्धेन पप्रच्छ । स तु 'वणिग्ग्रामस्याग्रे वक्ष्यामि' इति स्थितोऽभूत् । पुनरसौ गृहिण्यै 'स्वनूपुरयुगलं प्रेषय' इति संदिदेश । सा च सलज्जं ससाध्वसं च 'अद्य रात्रौ विश्रामप्रविष्टायां वृक्षवाटिकायां प्रभ्रष्टो ममैकः प्रशिथिलबन्धो नूपुरः । सोऽद्याप्यन्विष्टो न दृष्टः । स पुनरयं द्वितीयः' इत्यपरं प्राहिणोत् । अनया च वार्तयाऽमुं पुरस्कृत्य स वणिग्वणिग्जनसमाजमाजगाम । स चानुयुक्तो धूर्तः सविनयमावेदयत—'विदितमेव खलु वो यथाऽहं युष्मदाज्ञया पितृवनमभिरक्ष्य तदुपजीवी प्रतिवसामि । लुब्धाश्च कदाचिन्मद्दर्शनभीरवो निशि दहेयुरपि शवानीति निशास्वपि श्मशानमधिशये । अपरेद्युर्दग्धादग्धं मृतकं चितायाः प्रसभमाकर्षन्तीं श्यामाकारां नारीमपश्यम् । अर्थलोभात्तु निगृह्य भयं[4] सा संगृहीता[5] । शस्त्रिकयोरुमूले यदृच्छया किंचिदुल्लिखितम् । एष च नूपुरश्चरणादाक्षिप्तः । तावत्येव द्रुतगतिः सा पलायिष्ट । सोऽयमस्यागमः । परं भवन्तः प्रमाणम्' इति । विमर्शे[6] च तस्याः

---

निर्ग्रन्थिका भिक्षुकी श्रमणिका । सान्द्रत्रासा निबिडभया । पटबन्धनं वस्त्रबन्धनम् । सामयापदेशाद् रुग्णतामपदिश्य । गृहिणी स्त्री । नूपुरः पादभूषणम् । 'मञ्जीरो नूपुरोऽस्त्रियाम्' इत्यमरः । वणिग्ग्रामस्य वणिजां समूहस्य । प्रशिथिलबन्धः श्लथबन्धः । न दृष्टो न लब्ध इत्यर्थः । पितृवनं श्मशानम् । तदुपजीवी श्मशानजीवी । मद्दर्शनभीरवो मद्दर्शनभयशीलाः । दहेयुरपीत्यत्र अपिः संभावनायाम् । दग्धं ज्वलितम् । मृतकं शवम् । चितायाः । चितामध्यादित्यर्थः । प्रसभं बलात् । विमर्शे

---

१ आकृष्य. २ उल्लिख्य. ३ पटेन च बद्ध्वा. ४ साध्वसं. ५ संनिगृ. ६ विमर्शेन.

शाकिनीत्वमैकमत्येन पौराणामभिमतमासीत् । भर्त्रा च परित्यक्ता तस्मिन्नेव श्मशाने बहु विलप्य पाशेनोद्बध्य मर्तुकामा तेन धूर्तेन नक्तमगृह्यत । अनुनीता च—'सुन्दरि त्वदाकारोन्मादितेन मया त्वदावर्जने बहूनुपायान्भिक्षुकीमुखेनोपन्यस्य तेष्वसिद्धेषु पुनरयमुपायो यावज्जीवमसाधारणीकृत्य रन्तुमाचरितः । तत्प्रसीदानन्यशरणायास्मै दासजनाय' इति मुहुर्मुहुश्चरणयोर्निपत्य प्रयुज्य सान्त्वशतानि तामगत्यन्तरामात्मवश्यामकरोत् । तदिदमुक्तम्—'दुष्करसाधनं प्रज्ञा' इति ।

स चेदमाकर्ण्य ब्रह्मराक्षसो मामपूपुजत् । अस्मिन्नेव क्षणे नातिप्रौढपुंनागमुकुलस्थूलानि मुक्ताफलानि सह सलिलबिन्दुभिरम्बरतलादपतन् । अहं तु 'किं न्विदम्' इत्युच्चक्षुरालोकयन्कमपि राक्षसं कांचिदङ्गनां विचेष्टमानगात्रीमाकर्षन्तमपश्यम् । कथमपहरत्यकामामपि स्त्रियमनाचारो नैर्ऋतः इति गगनगमनमन्दशक्तिरशस्त्रश्चातप्ये । स तु मत्संबन्धी ब्रह्मराक्षसः 'तिष्ठ तिष्ठ पाप, क्वापहरसि' इति भर्त्सयन्नुत्थाय राक्षसेन समसृज्यत । तां तु रोषादनपेक्षापविद्धाममरवृक्षमञ्जरीमिवान्तरिक्षादापतन्तीमुन्मुखप्रसारितोभयकरः कराभ्यामग्रहीषम् । उपगृह्य च वेपमानां संमीलिताक्षीं मदङ्गस्पर्शसुखेनोद्भिन्नरोमाञ्चां तादृशीमेव तामनवतारयन्नतिष्ठम् । तावत्तावुभावपि शैलशृङ्गभङ्गैः पादपैश्च रमसोन्मूलितैर्मुष्टिपादप्रहारैश्च परस्परमक्षपयेताम् । पुनरहमतिमृदुनि पुलिनवति कुसुमलवलाञ्छिते सरस्तीरेऽवरोप्य सस्पृह

मिथो विचारे । शाकिनीत्वं पिशाचदैवतत्वम् । ऐयकत्येन विसंवादाभावेन । पौराणां नागरिकाणाम् । त्वदावर्जने त्वत्संमुखीकरणे । यावज्जीवं रन्तुमिति संबन्धः । अगत्यन्तरां न विद्यते गत्यन्तरं यस्यास्ताम् । आत्मवश्यामात्माधीनाम् । **स चेदमिति** । पुंनागो बकुलः । उच्चक्षुरूर्ध्वीकृतनेत्रः । विचेष्टमानगात्रीमात्ममोचनार्थं स्वाङ्गैश्चेष्टमानाम् । नैर्ऋतो राक्षसः । अतप्ये तापमापम् । अनपेक्षापविद्धामेवं त्यक्ता चेन्नश्येदित्यपेक्षाया अभावेन त्यक्ताम् । अमरवृक्षः कल्पद्रुमः । अन्तरिक्षादाकाशात् । वेपमानां कम्पमानाम् । उद्भिन्ना रोमाञ्चा यस्याः सा उद्भिन्नरोमाञ्चा उद्गतसात्त्विकभावा ताम् । तावुभौ राक्षसब्रह्मराक्षसौ । पुलिनं तोयोत्थितो देशः । कुसमलवलाञ्छिते पुष्पलेशचिह्निते ।

१ तम्. २ अनपेक्षया. ३ स्पर्शसुखेनेव. ४ अस्मात्परं 'जानुभिश्च' इत्य० ए० पु०.

निर्वर्णयंस्तां मत्प्राणैकवल्लभां राजकन्यां कन्दुकावतीमलक्षयम् । सा हि मया समाश्वास्यमाना तिर्यङ् मामभिनिरूप्य जातप्रत्यभिज्ञा सकरुणमरोदीत् । अवादीच्च—' नाथ त्वद्दर्शनादुपोढरागा तस्मिन्कन्दुकोत्सवे पुनः सख्या चन्द्रसेनया त्वत्कथाभिरेव समाश्वासिताऽस्मि। त्वं किल समुद्रमध्ये मज्जितः पापेन मद्भ्रात्रा भीमधन्वना इति श्रुत्वा सखीजनं परिजनं च वञ्चयित्वा जीवितं जिहासुरेकाकिनी क्रीडावनमुपागमम् । तत्र च मामचकमत कामरूप एष राक्षसाधमः। सोऽयं मया भीतयाऽवधूतप्रार्थनः स्फुरन्तीं मां निगृह्याभ्यधावत् । अत्रैवमवसितोऽभूत् । अहं च दैवात्तवैव जीवितेशस्य हस्ते पतिता। भद्रं तव ' इति । श्रुत्वा च तया सहावरुह्य नावमध्यारोहम् । मुक्ता च नौः प्रतिवातप्रेरिता तामेव दामलिप्तां प्रत्युपातिष्ठत् । अवरूढाश्च वयमश्रमेण । ' तनयस्य च तनयायाश्च नाशादनन्यापत्यस्तुङ्गधन्वा सुह्मपतिर्निष्कल[1]ः स्वयं सकलत्र एव निष्कलङ्कगङ्गारोधस्यनशनेनोपरन्तुं प्रतिष्ठते। सह तेन मर्तुमिच्छत्यनन्यनाथोऽनुरक्तः पौरवृद्धलोकः।' इत्यश्रुमुखीनां प्रजानामाक्रन्दमशृणुम । अथाहमस्मै राज्ञे यथावृत्तमाख्याय तदपत्यद्वयं प्रत्यर्पितवान् । प्रीतेन तेन जामाता कृतोऽस्मि दामलिप्तेश्वरेण । तत्पुत्रो मदनुजीवी जातः । मदाज्ञप्तेन चामुना प्रा[2]णवदुज्झिता चन्द्रसेना कोशदासमभजत् । ततश्च सिंहवर्मसाहाय्यार्थमत्रागत्य भर्तुस्तव दर्शनोत्सवसुखमनुभवामि ' इति ।

श्रुत्वा ' चित्रेयं दैवगतिः । अवसरेषु पुष्कलः पुरुषकारः।' इत्यभिधाय भूयः स्मिताभिषिक्तदन्तच्छ[3]दो मन्त्रगुप्ते हर्षोत्फुल्लं चक्षुः

---

प्रत्यभिज्ञा पूर्वदृष्टत्वम्। उपोढरागा प्ररूढमन्मथा । मामचकमत मय्यभिलाषं बबन्ध। अवसितो मृत्युं प्राप्तः । जीवितेशः प्रियः। ' जीवितेशः प्रिये यमे ' इति कोशः। भद्रं कल्याणम् । निष्कलो वृद्धः । ' निष्कलः स्थविरः समौ ' इति वैजयन्ती। निष्कलङ्कं पुण्यम्। उपरन्तुं मरणं संपादयितुम् । पुष्कलो महान् । पुरुषकारः पुरुषार्थः। स्मितेन हास्येन अभिषिक्तः सिञ्चितो व्याप्त इति यावत् दन्तच्छद ओष्ठो यस्य सः।

---

१ विकलः २ प्रणिहिता; त्यक्ता प्राणाद्दूर्जिता. ३ ०च्छदे.

पातयामास देवो राजवाहनः । स किल करकमलेन किंचित्संवृताननो ललितवल्लभारभसदत्तदन्तक्षतव्यसनविह्वलाधरमणिर्निरोष्ठ्यवर्णमात्मचरितमाचचक्षे—

इति श्रीदण्डिनः कृतौ दशकुमारचरिते मित्रगुप्तचरितं नाम षष्ठ उच्छ्वासः ।

## सप्तमोच्छ्वासः ।

राजाधिराजनन्दन नगरन्ध्रगतस्य ते गतिं ज्ञास्यन्नहं च गतः कैदाचित्कलिङ्गान् । कलिङ्गनगरस्य नात्यासन्नसंस्थितजनदाहस्थानसंसक्तस्य कस्यचित्कान्तारधरणिजस्यास्तीर्णसरसकिसलयसंस्तरे तले निषद्य निद्रालीढदृष्टिरशयिषि । गलति च कालरात्रिशिखण्डजालकान्धकारे चलि[2]तरक्षसि क्षरितनीहारे निजनिलयनिलीननिःशेषजने नि[3]तान्तशीते निशीथे घनतरसालशाखान्तरालनिर्ह्रादि[4] नेत्रनिंसिनीं निद्रां निगृह्णं[5]त् कर्णदेशं गतं 'कथं खलेनानेन दग्धसिद्धेन रिरंसाकाले निदेशं दित्सता जन एष रागेणानर्गलेनार्दित इत्थं खिलीकृतः[7] । क्रियेतास्याणकनरेन्द्रस्य[6] केनचिदनन्तशक्तिना सिद्ध्यन्तरायः'

ललिता या वल्लभा तया रभसेन दत्तानि दन्तक्षतानि एव व्यसनं यद्वा तेभ्यो व्यसनं तेन विह्वलः अधरमणिर्यस्य । निरोष्ठ्यवर्णमोष्ठ्यचरितवर्णरहितम् ॥

इति श्रीदशकुमारचरितटीकायां षष्ठ उच्छ्वासः ।

इदानीं मन्त्रगुप्तः स्वचरितं वक्तुमुपक्रमते—राजेति । अत्रौष्ठ्यवर्णाभावरूपं चित्रं कविना साधितम् । अत्यासन्नमतिसमीपम् । संस्थितो मृतः । 'परेतप्रेतसंस्थिताः' इत्यमरः । 'कान्तारं वर्त्म दुर्गमम्' इत्यमरः । धरणिजो वृक्षः । सरसमार्द्रम् । आलीढा व्याप्ता । शिखण्डजालकं केशसमूहः । कालरात्र्याः शिखण्डजालकमिव अन्धकारस्तस्मिन् । चलितरक्षसीत्यनेन रात्रिंचरत्वद्योतनम् । क्षरितनीहारे निःसृतहिमे । निलयं गृहम् । निलीनाः स्थिताः । साला एतदाख्या वृक्षाः । घनतराणां निबिडानां सालशाखानामन्तरालानि तेषु निर्ह्रादि इति रटितमित्यस्य विशेषणम् । 'निर्ह्रादिनि' इति पाठे निशीथे इत्यस्य विशेषणम् । नेत्रनिंसिनीं नेत्रस्पर्शिनीम् । 'णिसि चुम्बने' । दग्धसिद्धेन सिद्धाधमेन । रिरंसा रन्तुमिच्छा । अनर्गलेनाप्रतिबन्धेन । खिलीकृतः प्रतिहतः । क्रियेत कर्मणि संभावनायां लिङ् । अणकः कुत्सितः । 'पापाणके कुत्सितैः' इति । नरेन्द्रो मन्त्रज्ञः । दिदृक्षा द्रष्टुमिच्छा ।

१ तदा. २ चरित. ३ निशान्त. ४ निर्ह्रादिनि. ५ निगृह्णन्. ६ नरेन्द्रेण. ७ खलीकृतः

इति किंकरस्य किंकर्याश्चातिकातरं रटितं । तदाकर्ण्य 'क एषः सिद्धः का च सिद्धिः किं चानेन किंकरेण करिष्यते' इति दिदृक्षाक्रान्तहृदयः किंकरगतया दिशा किंचिदन्तरं गतस्तरलतरनरास्थिशकलरचितालंकाराक्रान्तकायं दहनदग्धकाष्ठनिष्ठाङ्गाररजःकृताङ्गरागं तडिल्लताकारजटाधरं हिरण्यरेतस्यरण्यचक्रान्धकारराक्षसे क्षणक्षणगृहीतनानेन्धनग्रासचञ्चदर्चिषि दक्षिणेतरेण करेण तिलसिद्धार्थकादीन्निरन्तरचटचटायितानाकिरन्तं कंचिदद्राक्षं । तस्याग्रे स कृताञ्जलिः किंकरः 'किं करणीयं, दीयतां निदेशः' इत्यतिष्ठत् । आदिष्टश्चाथं तेनातिनिकृष्टाशयेन—'गच्छ कलिङ्गराजस्य कर्दनस्य कन्यां कनकलेखां कन्यागृहादिहानय' इति । स च तथाऽकार्षीत् । ततश्च तां त्रासेनालघीयसाऽस्रजर्जरेण च कण्ठेन रणरणिकागृहीतेन च हृदयेन 'हा तात हा जननि' इति क्रन्दन्तीं कीर्णम्लानशेखरस्रजि शीर्णनहने शिरसिजानां संचये निगृह्यासिना शिलाशितेन शिरश्छिकर्तिषयाऽचेष्टत । झटिति चाच्छिद्य तस्य हस्तात्तां शस्त्रिकां तया निकृत्य तच्छिरः सजटाजालं निकटस्थस्य

---

तरलतराण्यत्युज्ज्वलानि । 'तरलो हाररत्ने च चञ्चले चोज्ज्वलेऽपि च ।' इति केशवः । नरास्थि मनुष्यास्थि । शकलं खण्डम् । अलंकार आभरणम् । निष्ठाङ्गाररजः । भस्मेत्यर्थः । 'निष्ठा निष्पत्तिनाशान्ताः' इति कोशः । तडिल्लता विद्युल्लता । हिरण्यरेतसि वह्नौ । 'हिरण्यरेता हुतभुक्' इत्यमरः । अरण्यचक्रे योऽन्धकारस्तस्य राक्षसे विनाशके इत्यर्थः । क्षणक्षणगृहीतानि यानि नानाविध नीन्धनानि काष्ठानि तेषां ग्रासेन चञ्चन्त्यः अर्चिषो ज्वाला यस्य तस्मिन् । दक्षिणेतरेण । वामेनेत्यर्थः । आकिरन्तं क्षिपन्तम् । अद्राक्षम् । दृष्टवानित्यर्थः । तस्येति होमकर्तुः । निदेश आज्ञा । अतिनिकृष्टो अतिनीचः आशयो मनो यस्येति तेन । कर्दन इति कलिङ्गराजनाम । अस्रजर्जरेणाश्रुक्लिन्नेन । 'अस्रः कोणे शिरसिजे चास्रमश्रुणि शोणिते ।' इति विश्वः । रणरणिकौत्सुक्यम् । 'औत्सुक्यं रणरणिका' इति महीपः । हृदयेनेत्युपलक्षणे तृतीया । शीर्णनहने श्लथबन्धने । संचयः समूहः । असिना खड्गेन । शिलाशितेन शाणतेजितेन । शिलासितेनेति पाठे शिलावदसितः श्यामस्तेन । शिरश्छिकर्तिषया शिरःकर्तनेच्छया । झटिति शीघ्रम् । आच्छिद्यापकृष्य । 'आच्छेदनं स्यादाक्षेपः' इति वररुचिः । तया शस्त्रिकया । तच्छिरः । होमकर्तुर्मस्तकमित्यर्थः । निकटस्थस्य समीपवर्तिनः ।

---

१ °कारकान्तकायम्. २ शिलासितेन. ३ हस्तादसिलतां ताम्.

कस्यचिज्जीर्णसालस्य स्कन्धरन्ध्रे न्यधिषि[1] । तन्निध्याय हृष्टतरः स राक्षसः क्षीणाधिरकथयत्—'आर्य कदर्यस्यास्य कदर्थनान्न कदाचिन्निद्राऽऽयाति नेत्रे । तर्जयति त्रासयति च अकृत्ये चाज्ञां ददाति । तदत्र कल्याणराशिना साधीयः कृतं यदेष नरकाकः कारणानां नारकीणां रसज्ञानाय नीतः[2] शीतेतरदीधितिदेहजस्य नगरं । तदत्र दयानिधेरनन्ततेजसस्तेऽयं जनः कांचिदाज्ञां चिकीर्षति । आदिश अलं कालहरणेन' इत्यनंसीत् । आदिशं च तं—'सखे सैषा सज्जनाचरिता सरणिर्यदणीयसि कारणेऽनणीयानादरः संदृश्यते । न चेदिदं नेच्छसि सेयं संनताङ्गयष्टिरक्लेशार्हा सत्यनेनाकृत्यकारिणाऽत्यर्थं क्लेशिता तन्नयैनां निजनिलयं नान्यदितः किंचिदस्ति चित्ताराधनं नः' इति । अथ तदाकर्ण्य कर्णशेखरनीलै[3]र्नीरजायितां धीरतर[4]तारकां दृशं तिर्यक्किंचिदञ्चितां संचारयन्ती सलिलचरकेतनशरासनानतां चिल्लिकालतां ललाटरङ्गस्थलीनर्तकीं लीलालसं लासयन्ती[5] कण्टकितरक्तगण्डलेखा रागलज्जान्तराल-

---

जीर्णसालस्य जीर्णवृक्षस्य । न्यदधां निवेशितवान् । निध्याय आलोक्य । क्षीणाधिर्गतमानसव्यथः । कदर्यस्य कृपणस्य । 'कदर्ये कृपणक्षुद्रकिंपचानमितंपचाः ।' इत्यमरः । कदर्थनात्क्लेशनात् । 'क्लेशनं तु कदर्थनम्' इति कोशः । अकृत्येऽपकारे । [कुत्सितकृत्ये ।] साधीयोऽतिशयेन साध्विति तथा । नरकाको मनुष्यनिन्द्यः । कारणानां यातनानाम् । नारकीणां नरकसंबन्धिनीनाम् । शीतेतरदीधितिः सूर्यस्तद्देहजस्य । यमस्येत्यर्थः । अयं जनो मद्रूपः । कालहरणेन कालातिपातेन । अनंसीत् ननाम । 'णम प्रह्वत्वे' । आदिशमिति । सरणिः पद्धतिः । 'सरणिः पद्धतिः पद्या वर्तन्येकपदीति च' इत्यमरः । अणीयस्यल्पे । इदं मदुक्तम् । 'अणीयसि कारणेऽनणीयानादर इति नेच्छसीत्यर्थः' इति भूषणा । संनता नम्रा । अकृत्यकारिणाऽसमीचीनकारकेण । नय प्रापय । निजनिलयं स्वगृहम् । कर्णशेखरे कर्णोच्चप्रदेशे । निलीनं लग्नम् । नीलनीरजं नीलोत्पलम् । धीरा निश्चला । तिर्यग्वक्रम् । सलिलचरो जलचरो मत्स्यः केतनमस्येति । मदनस्येत्यर्थः । शरासनं धनुस्तद्वदानतां वक्राम् । चिल्लिकालतां भ्रूलतावल्लीम् । ललाटमेव रङ्गस्थली तत्र नर्तकीम् । लीलालसं लीलासौम्यम् । 'अलसं मन्दसौम्ययोः' इत्यजयः । लासयन्ती नर्तयन्ती । कण्टका रोमाञ्चा अस्याः संजाता इति कण्ट-

---

१ न्यदधाम्. २ नीतः शेते शीतेतर...नगरे. ३ ०निलीननील. ४ धीरतरल. ५ लालयन्ती.

चारिणी चरणाग्रेण तिरश्चीननखार्चिश्चन्द्रिकेण धरणीतलं साचीकृताननसरसिजं लिखन्ती दन्तच्छदकिसलयलङ्घिना हर्षास्रसलिलधाराशीकरकणजालक्लेदितस्य स्तनतटचन्दनस्यार्द्रतां निरस्यताऽऽस्यान्तरालेनिःसृतेन[1] तनीयसाऽनिलेन[2] हृदयलक्ष्यदलनदक्ष[3]रतिसहचरशरस्यदायितेन[4] तरङ्गितदशनचन्द्रिकाणि कानिचिदेतान्यक्षराणि कलकण्ठीकलान्यसृजत्—'आर्य केन कारणेनैनं दासजनं कालहस्तादाच्छिद्यानन्तरं रागानिलचा[5]लितरणरणिकातरङ्गिण्यनङ्गसागरे क्षिपसि। यथा ते चरणसरसिजरजःकणिका तथाऽहं चिन्तनीया। यद्यस्ति दया तेऽत्र जने अनन्यसाधारणः करणीयः स एष चरणाराधनक्रियायां। यदि च कन्यागाराध्यासने रहस्यक्षरणादनर्थं आश[6]ङ्क्येत नैतदस्ति। रक्ततरा हि नस्तत्र सख्यश्चेट्यश्च। यथा न कश्चिदेतज्ज्ञास्यति तथा यति[7]ष्यन्ते' इति। स चाहं देहजेनाकर्णाकृष्टसायकासनेन चेतस्यतिनिर्दयं ताडितस्तत्कटाक्षकालायसनिगडगाढसंयतः किंकराननिहितदृष्टिरगादिषं—'यथेयं रथचरणजघना कथयति तथा चेन्नाचरेयं

---

क्विता। गण्डलेखा गण्डपाली। राग इच्छा। लज्जा व्रीडा। तयोरन्तरालं मध्यस्तत्र चारिणी वर्तमाना। तिरश्चीनो वक्रो नखरतस्यार्चिरेव चन्द्रिका यस्येति स तथा तेन। साचीकृतं वक्रीकृतमाननसरसिजं वक्रकमलं यस्मिन्कर्मणि तथा। दन्तच्छदकिसलयमोष्ठपल्लवं लङ्घयतीति लङ्घी तेन। क्लेदितं विकलीकृतम्। आस्यान्तरालं मुखमध्यः। तनीयसा मन्देन। अनिलेन वायुना। हृदयमेव लक्ष्यं वेध्यम्। दलनं भेदनम्। दक्षिणः सरलः। 'दक्षिणे सरलोदारौ' इत्यमरः। रतिसहचरो मदनस्तस्य शरो बाणः। स्यदायितेन जवायितेन। 'स्यदो जवे' इति निपातः। तद्वदाचरति स तथा तेन। तरङ्गिता तरङ्गं प्राप्ता। एतानि वक्ष्यमाणानि। कलकण्ठी कोकिला। कलानि मधुराणि। **आर्येति**। एनं दासजनम्। मद्रूपमित्यर्थः। कालहस्ताद्यमहस्तात्। रागानिल इच्छावायुः। रणरणिका व्याकुलता सैव तरङ्गा यस्मिन्निति। अनङ्गसागरे मदनसमुद्रे। चरणसरसिजं पादपद्मम्। अत्र जने मत्स्वरूपे। नान्यसाधारणोऽनन्यसाधारणः। अत्युच्चैरित्यर्थः। रहस्यं गोप्यम्। क्षरणमन्यत्र प्रकटीभावः। स चाहमिति। मन्त्रगुप्त इत्यर्थः। देहजेन मदनेन। सायकासनं धनुः। कालायसं लोहम्। निगडं शृङ्खलादि। रथचरणं

---

१ ०लनासान्तरनिःसृतेन. २ अतनीयसा. ३ दक्षिण. ४ सहचरसायकस्य दयितेन. ५ चलित. ६ आशङ्क्यते. ७ यतिष्ये.

नयेत नक्रकेतनः क्षणेनैकेनां[1]कीर्तनीयां दशां। जनं चैनं सह नयानया कन्यया कन्यागृहं हरिणनयनया' इति। नीतश्चाहं निशाचरेण शारदजलधरजालकान्ति कन्यकानिकेतनं। तत्र च कांचित्कालकला चन्द्राननानिदेशाचन्द्रशालैकदेशे तद्दर्शनचलितधृतिरतिष्ठं। सा च स्वच्छन्दं[2] शयानाः करतलालससंघट्टनापनीतनिद्राः काश्चिदधिगतार्थाः सखीरकार्षीत्। अथागत्य ताश्चरणनिहितशिरसः क्षरदस्रकरालितेक्षणा निजशेखरकेसराग्रसंलग्नषट्चरणगणरणितसंशयितकलगिरः शनैरकथयन्—'आर्य[3] यदत्यादित्यतेजसस्त एषा नयनलक्ष्यतां गता ततः कृतान्तेन न गृहीता। दत्ता चेयं चित्तजेन गरीयसा साक्षीकृत्य रागानलं। तदनेनाश्चर्यरत्नेन नलिनाक्षस्य ते रत्नशैलशिलातलस्थिरं रागतरलेनालंक्रियतां हृदयं। तदस्याश्चरितार्थं स्तनतटं गाढालिङ्गनैः सदृशतरस्य सहचरस्य' इति। ततः सखीजनेनातिदक्षिणेन दृढतरीकृतस्नेहनिगलस्तया संनताङ्ग्या संगत्यारंसि।

अथ कदाचिदायासितजायारहितचेतसि लालसालिलङ्घनग्लानघन-

---

चक्रम्। नक्रकेतनः कामः। अकीर्तनीयामवचनीयाम्। दशामवस्थाम्। एनं जनं मद्रूपम्। हरिणनयनया मृगलोचनया। **नीतश्चेति**। शारदजलधरः शरन्मेघः। निकेतनं गृहम्। कालकलां कालस्य समयस्य कलां लेशम्। चन्द्रशालोर्ध्वगृहम्। 'चन्द्रशाला शिरोगृहम्' इत्यमरः। करतलेनालसं यत्संघट्टनं तेनापनीता निद्रा यासाम्। **अथेति**। क्षरता निःसरताऽस्रेणाश्रुणा करालितानि विकृतानीक्षणानि यासां ताः। षट्चरणा भ्रमराः। रणितं शब्दितम्। अत्यादित्यतेजसोऽतिक्रान्तमादित्यस्य तेजो येनेति। नयनलक्ष्यतां नेत्रग्राह्यताम्। ततस्तस्मात्कारणात्। कृतान्तेन यमेन। चित्तजेन कामेन। रागानल इच्छाग्निः। आश्चर्यरत्नेनाश्चर्यश्रेष्ठेन। नलिनाक्षस्य कमलनेत्रस्य। रत्नशैलो मेरुः। रागेन रक्तप्रभया तरलं विद्योतमानम्। पक्षे रागेणानुरागेण चञ्चलम्। चरितार्थं कृतार्थम्। दक्षिणेन सरलेन। संनताङ्ग्या। कुचभारादित्यर्थः। अरंसि क्रीडां कृतवान्। **अथेति**। कलिङ्गराजः कर्दननामा सागरतीरकानने क्रीडारसजातसत्क्रियानीदित्यन्वयः। किंविधे कानने। आयासितानि जायारहितानाम्। विरहिणामित्यर्थः। चेतांसि यत्र। लालसा लुब्धाः अलयो भ्रमरास्तेषां लङ्घनं घट्टनं तेन ग्लानानि घनकेसराणि निबिडपुंनागकुसुमानि यस्मिन्। 'पुंनागे पुरुषस्तुङ्गः केसरो देववल्लभः।' इत्यमरः। अथ वा

---

१ कीर्तनीयाम्. २ ०च्छन्दतः. ३ नाथ.

केसरे राजदरण्यस्थलीललाटलीलायिततिलके ललितानङ्गराजाङ्गीकृत-निर्निद्र[1]कर्णिकारकाञ्चनच्छत्रे दक्षिणदहनसारथिरयो[2]हृतसहकारचञ्च[3]-रीककलिके कालाण्डजकण्ठरागरक्तरक्ताधरारातिरणाग्रसंनाहशालिनि शालिनिकन्यकान्तःकरणसंक्रान्तरा[4]गलङ्घितलज्जे दर्दुरगिरितटचन्दना-श्लेषशीतलानिलाचार्यदत्तनानालतानृत्तलीले काले कलिङ्गराजः सहा-ङ्गनाजनेन सह च तनयया सकलेन च नगरजनेन दश त्रीणि च दिनानि दिनकरकिरणजालालङ्घनीये रणदलिसंघलङ्घितनतलताग्रकिस-लयालीढसैकततटे तरलतरङ्गशीकरासारसङ्गशीतले सागरतीरकानने क्रीडारसजातासक्तिरासीत्। अथ संततगीतसंगीतसंगताङ्गनासहस्र-शृङ्गारहेलानिरर्गलानङ्गसंघर्षहर्षितश्च रागतृष्णैकतन्त्रस्तत्र रन्ध्रे आन्ध्र[5]नाथेन जयसिंहेन सलिलतरणसाधनानीतेनानेकसंख्येनानीकेन द्रागागत्यागृह्यत सकलत्रः। सा चानीयत त्रासतरलाक्षी दयिता

---

घनकेसरे निबिडबकुले। 'अथ केसरे बकुलः' इत्यमरः। लीलायिततिलके शोभायितक्षुरके। 'तिलकः क्षुरकः श्रीमान्' इत्यमरः। ललितोऽनङ्गराजो मदनराजः। निर्निद्राः विकसिताः। दक्षिणो दहनसारथिर्मलयानिलः। रयो वेगः। सहकारा आम्रवृक्षाः। चञ्चरीका भ्रमराः। कलिकाः कोरकाः। कालाण्डजः कोकिलः। 'वनप्रियः परभृतः पिकः कालाण्डजः स्मृतः।' इति वैजयन्ती। रक्तरक्ताधराः स्निग्धाः स्त्रियः। 'किंनरस्त्रियः' इति भूषणा। शालीनः अधृष्टः। 'शालीनकौपीने अधृष्टाकार्ययोः' इति निपातः। दर्दुरं ग्रामजालम्। 'दर्दुरा चण्डिकायां च ग्रामजाले तु दर्दुरम्।' इति विश्वः। अथ वा दर्दुरवद्वाद्यभाण्डवद्य-द्गिरितटम्। 'दर्दुरस्तोयदे भेके वाद्यभाण्डाद्रिभेदयोः।' इति मेदिनी। अलङ्घनीये दुर्लङ्घ्ये। रणन्तः शब्दं कुर्वन्तः। अलयो भ्रमराः। संघः समूहः। लताग्रकिसलयानि वल्ल्यग्रपल्लवानि। सैकतं सिकतामयम्। रणन्तो ये अलिसंघा भ्रमरसमूहास्तैर्लङ्घिता अत एव नता या लतास्तासामग्रकिसलयैः आलीढं स्पृष्टं सैकततटं यत्र। सागरतीरकानने समुद्रतटवने। अथेति। शृङ्गारहेला क्रियानादरः। 'हेला लीलेत्यमी हावाः क्रियाः शृङ्गारभावजाः।' इति भूषणा। निरर्गलोऽप्रतिहतः। अनङ्गो मदनः। तत्र रन्ध्रे तत्रावकाशे। आन्ध्रनाथेन आन्ध्रराजेन। सलिलतरणं जलतरणं तस्य यत्साधनं नौकादि। अनीकं सैन्यम्। द्राक् शीघ्रम्।

---

१ गलितनिद्र॰ २ रयाहत. ३ चञ्चलकलिके: सहकाराङ्कलग्नचञ्चलचञ्च॰. ४ कान्तराग. ५ अन्ध॰.

नः सह सखीजनेन कनकलेखा। तदाऽहं दाहेनानङ्गदहनजनितेनान्तरिताहाराचिन्ताश्चिन्तयन्दयितां गलितगात्रकान्तिरित्यतर्कयं—'गता सा कलिङ्गराजतनया जनित्रा जनयित्र्या च सहारिहस्तं। निरस्तधैर्यश्च तां स राजा नियतं संजिघृक्षेत्। तदसहा च सा सती गररसादिना सद्यः संतिष्ठेत। तस्यां च तादृशीं दशां गतायां जनस्यास्यानन्यजेन हन्येत शरीरधारणा[1]। सा का स्याद्गतिः' इति।

अत्रान्तर आन्ध्र[3]नगरादागच्छन्नग्रजः कश्चिदैक्ष्यत। तेन चेयं कथा कथिता—'यथा किल जयसिंहेनानेक[4]निकारदत्तसंघर्षेण[5] जिघांसितः स कर्दनः कनकलेखादर्शनैधितेन रागेणारक्ष्यत। सा च दारिका यक्षेण केनचिदधिष्ठिता न तिष्ठत्यग्रे नरान्तरस्य नरेन्द्रस्य च। आयस्यति च नरेन्द्रसार्थसंग्रहणेन तन्निराकरिष्यन्नरेन्द्रो न चास्ति सिद्धिः' इति। तेन चाहं दर्शिताशः शंकरनृत्त[6]देशजातस्य जरत्सालस्य स्कन्धरन्ध्रान्तर्जटाजालं निष्कृष्य तेन जटिलतां गतः कन्थाचीरसंचयान्तरितसकलगात्रः कांश्चिच्छिष्यानग्रहीषं। तांश्च नानाश्चर्यक्रियाति[7]संहिताञ्जनादाकृष्टान्नचेलादित्यागान्नित्यहृष्टानकार्षं। अयासिषं च दिनैः कैश्चिदान्ध्रनगरम्। तस्य नात्यासन्ने सलिलराशिसदृशस्य कलहंसगणदलितनलिनदलसंहतिगलितकिञ्जल्कशकलशारस्य सारसश्रेणिशेखरस्य सरसस्तीरकानने कृतनिकेतनः स्थितः। शिष्यजनकथित-

---

अनङ्ग एव दहनः। अन्तरिता दूरं गता। आहारो भक्षणम्। तदसहा तन्न सहते इति सा तथा। गरं विषम्। **अत्रान्तर इति**। अग्रजो ब्राह्मणः। निकारो यातना। अपकारो वा। 'अपराधोऽपकारश्च निकारोऽपि समाः।' इति वैजयन्ती। संघर्षणमभिभवेच्छा। एधितो वर्धितः। दारिका कन्यका। नरान्तरस्य राज्ञोऽन्यस्येत्यर्थः। नरेन्द्रा मन्त्रवादिनः। आयस्यति यतते। 'यसु प्रयत्ने' इति धातोः। नरेन्द्रसार्थो मान्त्रिकसमाजः। जरत्सालस्य जीर्णवृक्षस्य। नाना विविधा आश्चर्यक्रियास्ताभिः अतिसंहिताद्वञ्चितात्। आकृष्टानामन्नचेलादीनां त्यागाद्दानात्। तस्यान्ध्रनगरस्य। नात्यासन्ने किंचिद्दूरे। सलिलराशिः समुद्रः। कलहंसगणेन दलितानि भग्नानि यानि नलिनानि कमलानि तेषां दलानां संहतिर्वृन्दम्। 'स्त्रियां तु संहतिर्वृन्दम्' इत्यमरः। तस्याः गलिताः किंजल्काः केसराः तेषां शकलैः शारस्य चित्रवर्णस्य। कृतनिकेतनः कृतगृहः।

---

१ गत. २ धारणाशा। का स्यात्. ३ अन्ध्र० ४ नैक० ५ दत्तसंघर्षण०. ६ नृत्यरङ्ग. ७ अतिसंहितान्.

चित्रचेष्टाकृष्टसकलनागरजनाभिसंधानदक्षः सन् दिशि दिशीत्यकीर्त्यै जनेन—'य एष जरदरण्यस्थलीसरस्तीरे स्थण्डिलशायी यतिस्तस्य किल सकलानि सरहस्यानि सषडङ्गानि च च्छन्दांसि रसनाग्रे संनिहितानि, अन्यानि च शास्त्राणि । येन यानि न ज्ञायन्ते स तेषां तत्सकाशादर्थनिर्णयं करिष्यति । असत्येनास्य नास्यं संसृज्यते । सशरीरश्चैष दयाराशिः । एतत्संग्रहेणाद्य चिरं चरितार्था दीक्षा । तच्चरणरजःकणैः कैश्चन शिरसि कीर्णैरनेकस्यानेक आतङ्कश्चिरं चिकित्सकैरसंहार्यः संहृतः । तदङ्घ्रिक्षालनसलिलसेकैर्निष्कलङ्कशिरसां नश्यन्ति क्षणेनैकेनाखिलनरेन्द्रयन्त्रैर्लङ्घिनश्चण्डतारा ग्रहाः । न तस्य शक्यं शक्तेरियत्ताज्ञानं । न चास्याहंकारकणिका' इति । सा चेयं कथाऽनेकजनास्यसंचारिणी तस्य कनकलेखाधिष्ठानधनदाज्ञाकरनिराक्रियासक्तचेतसः क्षत्रियस्याकर्षणायाशकत् । स चाहरहरागत्यादरेणातिगरीयसाऽर्चयन्नर्थैश्च शिष्यान्संगृह्णन्नधिगतक्षणः कदाचित्काङ्क्षितार्थसाधनाय शनैरयाचिष्ट । ध्यानधीरः स्थानदर्शितज्ञानसंनिधिश्चैनं निरीक्ष्य निचाय्याकथयं—'तात स्थान एष हि यत्नः ।

---

अभिसंधानं प्रतारणं तत्र दक्षः । दिशि दिशि प्रतिदिशम् । अकीर्त्यै ख्यापित इत्यर्थः । जरदरण्यं जीर्णारण्यम् । स्थण्डिलशायी । 'स्थण्डिलाच्छयितरि व्रते' इति णिनिः । षडङ्गानि शिक्षादीनि । 'निरुक्तं ज्योतिषं कल्पसूत्रं व्याकरणं तथा । छन्दोविचितिशिक्षे च वेदाङ्गानि वदन्ति षट् ॥' इति भूषणा । छन्दांसि वेदाः । रसनाग्रं जिह्वाग्रम् । आस्यं मुखम् । सशरीरः शरीरवान् । दयाराशिः कृपासमुद्रः । संग्रहेण स्वीकारेण । आतङ्को भयम् । चिकित्सकैर्मन्त्रवादिभिः । अखिलनरेन्द्रा मन्त्रवादिनः । यन्त्राणि मन्त्रविन्यासरेखाक्रमाः । इयत्ता परिमाणम् । कणिका लेशः । तस्य जयसिंहस्येत्यर्थः । धनदः कुबेरस्तस्याज्ञाकरो यक्षः । निराक्रिया दूरीकरणम् । स चेति । स जयसिंहः । अहरहः प्रतिदिनम् । क्षण उत्सवः । अथ वा अधिगतः प्राप्तः क्षण एकान्तकालो येन । 'स्थाने योग्ये काले दर्शितो ज्ञानस्य तदधिष्ठितपिशाचादिज्ञानस्य संनिधिः सांनिध्यं येन सः' इति भूषणा । निचाय्य दृष्ट्वेत्यर्थः । अधिगतिः प्राप्तिः ।

---

१ अतिसंधान. २ सलिलशायी. ३ एतत्सकाशादर्थग्रहेण. ४ चिकित्सकैः, ५ यत्न. ६ चण्डतरग्रहाः. ७ धिष्ठित.

तस्य हि कन्यारत्नस्य सकलकल्याणलक्षणैकराशेरधिगतिः क्षीरसागररशनालंकृतायाः गङ्गादिनदीसहस्रहारयष्टिराजिताया धराङ्गनाया एवासादनाय साधनं । न च स यक्षस्तदधिष्ठायी केनचिन्नरेन्द्रेण तस्या लीलाञ्चितनीलनीरजदर्शनाया दर्शनं सहते । तदत्र सह्यतां त्रीण्यहानि यैरहं यतिष्येऽर्थस्यास्य साधनाय ' इति । तथादिष्टे च हृष्टे क्षितीशे गते निशि[1] निर्निशाकरार्चिषि नीरन्ध्रान्धकारकणनिकरनिगीर्णदशदिशि निद्रानिगडितनिखिलजनदृशि निर्गत्य जलतल[2]निलीनगाहनीयं नीरन्ध्रं कृच्छ्राच्छिद्रीकृता[3]न्तरालं तदेकतः सरस्तटं तीर्थसंनिकृष्टं केनचित्खननसाधनेनाकार्षं । घनशिलेष्टिकाच्छन्नच्छिद्राननं तत्सरस्तीरदेशं जनैरशङ्कनीयं निश्चित्य दिनादिस्नाननिर्णिक्तगात्रश्च नक्षत्रसंतानहा[4]रयष्ट्यग्रग्रथितरत्नं क्षणदान्धकारगन्धहस्तिदारणैककेसरिणं कनकशैलशृङ्ग-

---

रशना मेखला । ' स्त्रीकट्या मेखला काञ्ची सप्तकी रशना तथा ' इत्यमरः । नदीसहस्रमेव हारयष्टिस्तया राजितायाः शोभितायाः । नीरजं कमलं तद्वद्दर्शनं नेत्रम् । ' दर्शनं नयनस्वप्नबुद्धिधर्मोपलब्धिषु ' इति मेदिनी । निर्निशाकरार्चिषि निर्गतं निशाकरस्य चन्द्रस्यार्चिस्तेजो यस्यामिति । निशीत्यस्य विशेषणम् । नीरन्ध्रान्धकारो गाढान्धकारः । नीगीर्णदशदिशि । ' निगीर्णं खादितं ग्रस्तं क्षतमन्तःकृतं च तत् । ' इति कोशः । निगडितं बद्धम् । जलतलेति । ' जलतललीनेनान्तःप्रविष्टेनैव गम्यं कृच्छ्रमज्ञेयमन्तरालमवकाशो यस्य तथा सरस्तटं तदेकत एकत्र कृतम् । तत्तटे गुप्तं स्थानं जले कृतमिति यावत् ' इति भूषणा । सरस्तटमेकतः सरस्तटस्यान्तिके । ' एकतः क्वचिदन्तिके ' इति वैजयन्ती । ' एकतःसर्वतोयोगे शेषार्थे कर्म वेष्यते ' इति द्वितीया । घना निबिडाः शिलाः पाषाणाः इष्टिकाश्च ताभिश्छन्नमाच्छादितम् । दिनादिः प्रातःकालः । निर्णिक्तं शोधितम् । ' निर्णिक्तं शोधितं मृष्टम् ' इत्यमरः । संतानं विस्तारः । ०हारिहार० इति पाठे संतानं हरति लोपयतीति हारिणी हारयष्टिः प्रातस्तनप्रभासंतानरूपा तस्याः इत्यादि । क्षणदा रात्रिः । गन्धहस्ती मत्तद्विपः । " यस्य गन्धं समाघ्राय न तिष्ठन्ति प्रतिद्विपाः । तं गन्धहस्तिनं प्राहुर्नृपतेर्विजयावहम् ॥ " इति पालकाप्ये । दारणं विदारणम् । कनकशैलः मेरुः ।

---

[1] निशि निशि. [2] तललीन. [3] कृतान्तरम्. [4] हारिहार.

रङ्गलास्यलीलानटं गगनसागरघनतरङ्गराजिलङ्घनैकनक्रं कार्याकार्यसाक्षिणं सहस्रार्चिषं सहस्राक्षदिगङ्गनाङ्गरागरागायितकिरणजालं रक्तनीरजाञ्जलिनाऽऽराध्य निजनिकेतनं न्यशिश्रियम्[1]।

याते च दिनत्रये, अस्तगिरिशिखरगैरिकतटसाधारणच्छायतेजसि अचलराजकन्यकाकदर्थनयाऽन्तरिक्षाख्येन शंकरशरीरेण संसृष्टायाः संध्याङ्गनाया रक्तचन्दनचर्चितैकस्तनकलशदर्शनीये दिनाधिनाथे जनाधिनाथः स आगत्य जनस्यास्य धरणिन्यस्तचरणनखकिरणच्छादितकिरीटः कृताञ्जलिरतिष्ठत्। आदिष्टश्च—'दिष्ट्या दृष्टेष्टसिद्धिः। इह जगति हि न निरीहं देहिनं श्रियः संश्रयन्ते। श्रेयांसि च सकलान्यनलसानां हस्ते नित्यसांनिध्यानि। यतस्ते साधीयसा सच्चरितेनानाकलितकलङ्केनार्चितेनात्यादरनिचितेनाकृष्टचेतसा जनेनानेन सर इदं तथा संस्कृतं यथेह तेऽद्य सिद्धिः स्यात्। तदेतस्यां निशि गलदर्धायां गाहनीयं। गाहनानन्तरं च सलिलतले सततगतीनन्तःसंचारिणः संनिगृह्य यथाशक्ति शय्या कार्या। ततश्च तटस्खलितजलस्थगितजलजखण्डचलितदण्डकण्टकाग्रदलितदेहराजहंसत्रासजर्जररसितसंदत्तकर्णस्य जनस्य

---

लास्यलीला विलासक्रिया। गगनसागरः गगनसमुद्रः। घना एव तरङ्गाः। राजिः परंपरा। लङ्घनमतिक्रम्य गमनम्। सहस्राक्ष इन्द्रस्तद्दिगङ्गना। प्राचीत्यर्थः। रागायितं रागवदाचरितम्। रक्तनीरजं रक्तोत्पलम्। निजनिकेतनं स्वगृहम्। अशिश्रियमाश्रितवान्। 'अस्तगिरिशिखरगैरिकतटसाधारणच्छायतेजसि' इत्यग्रिमस्य 'दिनाधिनाथे' इति पदस्य विशेषणम्। अचलराजकन्यका पार्वती। कदर्थनया कुत्सितप्रार्थनया। अन्तरिक्षाख्येन। अष्टमूर्तिमध्य आकाशाभिधेयेनेत्यर्थः। संसृष्टाया मिलितायाः। संध्यैवाङ्गना। चर्चितः आलिप्तः। 'चर्चा चर्चिक्यमालेपे' इति वैजयन्ती। दिष्ट्याऽदृष्टेन। इष्टसिद्धिर्दृष्टेत्यन्वयः। निरीहं निर्गतेहा यस्येति तम्। निःस्पृहमित्यर्थः। सस्पृहमेव श्रिय आश्रयन्त इति भावः। श्रेयांसि सुकृतानि। 'स्याद्धर्ममस्त्रियां पुण्यश्रेयसी सुकृतं वृषः' इत्यमरः। अनलसानामुद्योगिनाम्। साधीयसा अतिशयेन साध्विति साधीयस्तेन। अनाकलितं दूरीकृतम्। कलङ्को दूषणम्। तत्सरः। गाहनीयमालोडनीयम्। संनिगृह्य निग्रहं कृत्वा। स्थगितं मन्दीभूतम्। जलजखण्डं कमलसमूहः। दलितं घर्षितम्। जर्जरमतिश्लथम्। रसितं शब्दितम्। 'रस शब्दने'। "तटात्स्खलिताः पतिताश्च ते जले स्थगिताः स्थिता ये जलजसमूहस्य चञ्चलदण्डस्य कण्टकाः

---

1 चाध्यशिश्रियम्.

क्षणादाकर्णनीयं जनिष्यते जलसंघातस्य किंचिदारटितं। शान्ते च तत्र सलिलरटिते क्लिन्नगात्रः किंचिदारक्तदृष्टिर्येनाकारेण निर्यास्यसि निचाय्य तं[1] निखिलजननेत्रानन्दकारिणं न स यक्षः शक्ष्यत्यग्रतः स्थितये। स्थिरतरनिहितस्नेहशृङ्खलानिगडितं च कन्यकाहृदयं[2] क्षणेनैकेनासहनीयदर्शनान्तरायं स्यात्। अस्याश्च धराङ्गनाया नात्यादरनिराकृतारिचक्रं[3] चक्रं करतलगतं चिन्तनीयं। न तत्र संशयः। तच्चेदिच्छस्यनेकशास्त्र-[4] ज्ञानधीरधिषणैरधिकृतैरितरैश्च हितैषिगणैराकलय्य जालिकशतं चानाय्य, अन्तरङ्गनरशतैर्यथेष्टदृष्टान्तरालं सरः क्रियेत। रक्षा च तीरात्त्रिंशद्दण्डान्तराले सैनिकजनेन सादरं रचनीया। कस्तत्र तज्जानाति यच्छिद्रेणारयश्चिकीर्षन्ति' इति। तत्तस्य हृदयहारि जातं। तदधिकृतैश्च तत्र कृत्ये रन्ध्रदर्शनासहैरिच्छां च राज्ञः कन्यकातिरागजनितां नितान्तनिश्चलां निश्चित्यार्थ[5] एष न निषिद्धः। तथास्थितश्च तदासादनदृढतराशयश्च स आख्यायत—'राजन्, अत्र त[6] जनान्ते चिरं स्थितं न चैकत्र चिरस्थानं नः शस्तं। कृतकृत्यश्च न इह द्रष्टासि[7]। यस्य ते राष्ट्रे ग्रासाद्यासादितं तस्य ते किंचिदनाचर्य[8] कार्यं गतिरार्यगर्ह्या' इति। अत्रैतच्चिरस्थानस्य कारणं। तच्चाद्य सिद्धं। गच्छ गृहान्। यथाहं जलेन हृद्यगन्धेन स्नातः सितस्रगङ्गरागः

---

तैर्दलितो देहो येषां ते तेषां राजहंसानां त्रासजर्जरं त्रासेन कठोरं रसितं शब्दस्तत्र दत्तः कर्णो येन तस्य" इति भूषणा। आरटितं पीडाशब्दितम्। क्लिन्नगात्र आर्द्रशरीरः। निचाय्य निश्चित्य। अग्रतः स्थितये पुरो वर्तितुमित्यर्थः। नात्यादरेण। 'विलासेनैवेत्यर्थः' इति भूषणा। निराकृतमरिचक्रं यस्मात्तत्। शास्त्रज्ञानेन धीरा धीषणा बुद्धिः येषां तैः। 'बुद्धिर्मनीषा धिषणा' इत्यमरः। जालिका जालवर्तिनः। दृष्टान्तरालं ज्ञातमध्यम्। दण्डः प्रकाण्डः। 'दण्डोऽस्त्री लगुडे पुमान्। व्यूहभेदे प्रकाण्डे च' इति मेदिनी। षोडशहस्त इति यावत्। 'काण्डान्तात्क्षेत्रे' इति सूत्रे काण्डशब्दस्य षोडशहस्तप्रमाणमिति व्याख्यातं वृत्तिकृता। हृदयहारि चित्तहारि। अतिरागः रागातिशयः। तदासादनं तच्छब्देन सरसस्तस्यासादनमधिष्ठानम्। अतिशयेन दृढ आशयः यस्य। एकत्रैकस्मिन्स्थाने। शस्तं प्रशस्तम्। गृहान्। 'गृहाः पुंसि च भूम्न्येव' इत्यमरः। स्रङ्माला। अङ्गरागश्चर्चा। धरणि-

---

१ तस्य...कारिणः. २ कन्यकारत्नम्. ३ नात्यादृत. ४ नैक. ५ विचार्य. ६ अनन्तरं. ७ निष्ठामि. ८ अतिथेयादि.

शक्तिसदृशेन दानेनाराधितधरणितैलतैतिलगणस्तिलस्नेहसिक्तयष्टयग्रग्रथितवर्तिकाग्निशिखासहस्रग्रस्तनैशान्धकारराशिरागत्यार्थसिद्धये यतेथाः' इति। स किल कृतज्ञतां दर्शयन्—'असिद्धिरेषा सिद्धिः, यदसंनिधिरिहार्याणां। कष्टा चेयं निःसंगता या निरागसं दासजनं त्याजयति। न च निषेधनीया गरीयसां गिरः' इति स्नानाय गृहःनयासीत्। अहं च निर्गत्य निर्जने निशीथे सरस्तीररन्ध्रनिलीनः सन्नीषच्छिद्रदत्तकर्णः स्थितः। स्थिते चार्धरात्रे कृतयथादिष्टक्रियः स्थानस्थानरचितरक्षः स राजा जालिकजनानानीय निराकृतान्तःशल्यं शङ्काहीनः सरःसलिलं सलीलगतिरगाहत। गतं च कीर्णकेशं संहतकर्णनासं सरसस्तलं हास्तिनं नक्रलीलया नीरातिनिलीनयायी तं तथाशयानं कंधरायां कन्थया न्यग्रहीषं। खरतरकालदण्डघट्टनातिचण्डैश्च करचरणतलाघातैर्निर्दयदत्तनिग्रहः क्षणे-

---

तलं पृथ्वीतलं तत्र तैतिलगणा देवगणाः। 'तैतिलौ देवकालिङ्गौ' इति कोशः। तिलस्नेहसिक्ताश्च ता यष्ट्यग्रग्रथितवर्तिकाश्च तासामाग्निशिखासहस्रेण ग्रस्तः निशायां भवो नैशः अन्धकारराशिर्यस्य। तिलस्नेहं तिलतैलम्। वर्तिका वस्त्रकृतनालिका। भाषया 'पलीता' इति ख्यातः। अस्यामाग्निशिखा अग्निज्वाला। ग्रस्तो गिलितः। नैशान्धकारराशी रात्रितिमिरसमूहः। अर्थसिद्धयेऽर्थप्राप्त्यर्थम्। यतेथाः। 'यती प्रयत्ने' इत्यस्माल्लिङि मध्यमपुरुषैकवचनम्। असंनिधिरसंनिधानम्। आर्याणां श्रेष्ठानाम्। निरागसं निरपराधम्। गरीयसां गुरूणाम्। निराकृतं दूरीकृतम्। सरःसलिलं सरोजलम्। अगाहत आलोडयामासेत्यर्थः। कीर्णकेशं प्रसृतकेशम्। संहतकर्णनासं कर्णौ च नासा च कर्णनासम्। प्राण्यङ्गत्वादेकवद्भावः। पश्चात्संहतपदेन समासः। नासा नासिका। हास्तिनं हस्तिप्रमाणम्। 'पुरुषहस्तिभ्यामण् च'। 'हास्तिनलीलया 'पुरुषहस्तिभ्यामण् च' इति पक्षे अणि 'संयोगादिश्च' इति प्रकृतिभावः। हस्तिप्रमाणस्य या लीला तया। न तु ह्रस्वप्रमाणस्य लीलया। तथा सति प्रतीकारसंभवापत्तेः' इति भूषणा। अतिनिलीनतया यातीति अतिनिलीनयायी। कन्थया प्रावरणेन। 'कन्था प्रावरणान्तरे' इति विश्वः। खरतरस्तीक्ष्णः। कालदण्डो यमदण्डः। तस्य घट्टनादतिचण्डैः सुतरां कठिनैः। निग्रहो निकारः। अजहात् तत्याजेत्यर्थः। 'ओहाक् त्यागे'। आकारान्तरग्रहणमन्याकार-

---

१ तलेति नास्ति क्वचित्. २ चेलाञ्चलखण्डकाग्निशिखासहस्रास्त. ३ गतः. ४ हस्तिनक्र.

नैकेनाजहात्स चेष्टां। ततश्चाकृष्य तच्छरीरं छिद्रे निधाय नीराग्निरयासिषं।

सद्यः संगतानां च सैनिकानां तदत्यचित्रीयताकारान्तरग्रहणं। गजस्कन्धगतः सितच्छत्रादिसकलराजचिह्नराजितश्चण्डतरदण्डिदण्डताडनत्रस्तजनदत्तान्तरालया राजवीथ्या[1] यातस्तां निशां रसनयना[2]निरस्तनिद्रारातिरनैषं। नीते च जनाक्षिलक्ष्यतां लाक्षारसदिग्धदिग्गजशिरःसदृक्षे शक्रदिगङ्गनारत्नादर्शेऽर्कचक्रे कृतकरणीयः किरणजालकरालरत्नराजिराजितराजार्हासनाध्यासी यथासदृशाचारदर्शिनः शङ्कायन्त्रिताङ्गान्संनिधिनिषादिनः सहायानगादिषं—'दृश्यतां शक्तिरार्षी यत्तस्य यतेरजेयस्येन्द्रियाणां संस्कारेण नीरजसा नीरजसांनिध्यशालिनि सहर्षालिनि सरसि सरसिजदलसंनिकाशच्छायस्याधिकतरदर्शनीयस्याकारान्तरस्य सिद्धिरासीत्। अद्य सकलनास्तिकानां जायेत लज्जानतं शिरः। तदिदानीं चन्द्रशेखरनरकशासनसरसिजासनादीनां त्रिदशेशानां स्थानान्यत्यादररचितनृत्यगीताद्या[3]राधनानि क्रियन्तां। ह्रियन्तां च गृहादितः क्लेशनिरसनसहान्यर्थिसार्थैर्धनानि' इति। आश्चर्यरसातिरेकहृष्टदृष्टयस्ते 'जय जगदीश, जयेन सातिशयं दश दिशः स्थगयन्निजेन यशसाऽऽदिराजयशांसि'[4]

प्राप्तिः। गजस्कन्धगतो हस्तिमस्तकगतः। चण्डतरा अतिप्रचण्डाः दण्डिनो दण्डधराः तेषां दण्डास्तैस्ताडनं तस्मात् त्रस्तेन जनेन दत्तमन्तरालं यस्यां तया। अन्तरालमभ्यन्तरम्। रसः क्रीडारसः। निरस्ता त्यक्ता। निद्रारातिर्निद्रासुखम्। जनाक्षीणि लोकनेत्राणि तेषां लक्ष्यतां ग्राह्यकत्वम्। दिग्धं लिप्तम्। शक्रदिगङ्गना प्राची दिक्। किरणजालेन करालं च तद्रत्नराज्या राजितं च यत् राजार्हमासनं तदध्यास्तेऽसौ तथा। राजार्हं राजयोग्यम्। संनिधौ निषीदन्ति ते संनिधिनिषादिनः। आर्षी ऋषेरियं तथा। अजेयस्य जेतुमशक्यस्य। 'इन्द्रियाणामजेयस्य जितेन्द्रियस्येत्यर्थः' इति भूषणा। नीरजसा निवृत्तरजोगुणेन। नीरजानि कमलानि। अद्येति। नरकशासनो विष्णुः। सरसिजासनः ब्रह्मा। अर्थिसार्थैर्याचकसमाजैः। क्लेशानां निरसनं दूरीकरणं तत्सहानि समर्थानि। आश्चर्यरसातिरेक आश्चर्यरसाधिक्यम्। जयेन सातिशयमतिशयेन सह वर्तमानं तथा यथा। स्थगयन् व्याप्नुवन्। निजेन यशसा स्वकीर्त्या आदिराजस्य मनोः यशांसि जयेति पूर्वेणान्वयः। यद्वा आदिराजास्तात्पितृ-

१ राजरथ्यया. २ नयनरस. ३ गीतार्चनाश्चितानि. ४ जय जय जगदीश दश दिशः स्थगयन्निजतेजसाऽऽदिराज०. ५ स्वतेजसाऽतिशय्य.

इत्यसकृदाशास्यारचयन्यथादिष्टाः क्रियाः। स चाहं दयितायाः सखीं हृदयस्थानीयां शशाङ्कसेनां कन्यकां कदाचित्कार्यान्तरागतां रहस्याचक्षिषि—'कच्चिदयं जनः कदाचिदासीद्दृष्टः' इति। अथ सा हर्षकाष्ठा गतेन हृदयेनेषदालक्ष्य दशनदीधितिलतां लीलालसं लासयन्ती ललिताञ्चितकरशाखान्तरितदन्तच्छदकिसलया हर्षजलक्लेदजर्जरनिरञ्जनेक्षणा रचिताञ्जलिः 'नितरां जाने यदि न स्यादैन्द्रजालिकस्य जालं किंचिदेतादृशं। कथं चैतत्। कथय' इति स्नेहनिर्यन्त्रणं शनैरगादीत्। अहं चास्यै कार्त्स्न्येनाख्याय तदाननसंक्रान्तेन संदेशेन संजनय्य सहचर्या निरतिशयं हृदयाह्लादं ततश्चैतया दयितया निरर्गलीकृतातिसत्कृतकलिङ्गनाथन्यायदत्तया संगत्यान्ध्रकलिङ्गराज्यशासी तस्यास्यारिणा लिलङ्घयिषितस्याङ्गराजस्य साहाय्यकायालघीयसा साधनेनागत्यात्र ते सखिजनसंगतस्य यादृच्छिकदर्शनानन्दराशिलङ्घितचेता जातः' इति।

तस्य तत्कौशलं स्मितज्योत्स्नाभिषिक्तदन्तच्छदः सह सुहृद्भि-

---

पितामहादयः। असकृद्वारंवारम्। आशास्य प्रशस्य। आरचयन् चकुरित्यर्थः। क्रियाः कार्याणि। हृदयस्थानीयां प्राणभूताम्। **अथेति**। हर्षकाष्ठां हर्षमर्यादाम्। ईषदल्पम्। दशनदीधितयो दन्तमयूखाः त एव लता तां लीलयाऽलसं मन्थरं यथा तथा लासयन्ती नर्तयन्ती। कर एव शाखा। दन्तच्छद ओष्ठः। हर्षजलमानन्दाश्रु। क्लेद आर्द्रभावः तेन जर्जरं विशीर्णम्। 'इन्द्रध्वजे विशीर्णे च जर्जरं परिचक्षते' इति शाश्वतः। निरञ्जनं कज्जलरहितमीक्षणं नेत्रं यस्याः सा। स्नेहनिर्यन्त्रणं स्नेहबद्धम्। स्नेहेन निर्गता यन्त्रणा यथा स्यात्तथा। कार्त्स्न्येन कृत्स्नस्य भावस्तथा। समग्रेणेत्यर्थः। तदाननसंक्रान्तेन तन्मुखोद्गतेन। संदेशेन वाचिकेन। संजनय्योत्पाद्य। सहचर्याः कनकलेखायाः। निरर्गलीकृतो मुक्तबन्धनः अतिसत्कृतश्च यः कलिङ्गनाथस्तेन न्यायेन दत्ता तया। न्यायेन विधिपूर्वकम्। आन्ध्रश्चासौ कलिङ्गराजश्चेति। तस्य राज्यं तच्छास्तीति शासी। यादृच्छिकं प्रसङ्गजातम्। आनन्दराशिः सुखसमूहः। **तस्येति**। स्मितज्योत्स्ना हास्यदीप्तिः तया अभिषिक्तः दन्तच्छदः यस्य। सुहृद्भिः सखिभिः। नर्म परिहासः। 'द्रवकेलिपरीहासाः क्रीडा लीला च नर्म च

---

१ अस्मात्परं 'हसन्ती' इत्य० ए० पु०. २ लीलाञ्चित. ३ अवादीत्.

रभिनन्द्य 'चित्रमिदं महामुनेर्वृत्तम्। अत्रैव खलु फलितमतिकष्टं तपः। तिष्ठतु तावन्नर्म। हर्षप्रकर्षस्पृशोः प्रज्ञासत्त्वयोर्दृष्टमिह स्वरूपम्' इत्यभिधाय पुनः 'अवतरतु भवान्' इति बहुश्रुते विश्रुते विकचराजीवसदृशं दृशं चिक्षेप देवो राजवाहनः।

इति श्रीदण्डिनः कृतौ दशकुमारचरिते मन्त्रगुप्तचरितं नाम सप्तम उच्छ्वासः।

## अष्टम उच्छ्वासः।

अथ सोऽप्याचचक्षे—'देव मयाऽपि परिभ्रमता विन्ध्याटव्या कोऽपि कुमारः क्षुधा तृषा च क्लिश्यन्नक्लेशार्हः क्वचित्कूपाभ्याशेऽष्टवर्षदेशीयो दृष्टः। स च त्रासगद्गदमगदत—'महाभाग, क्लिष्टस्य मे क्रियतामार्य साहाय्यकम्। अस्य मे प्राणापहारिणीं पिपासां प्रतिकर्तुमुदकमुदञ्चन्निह कूपे कोऽपि निष्कलो ममैकशरणभूतः पतितः। तमलमस्मि नाहमुद्धर्तुम्' इति। अथाहमभ्येत्य व्रतत्या कयाऽपि वृद्धमुत्तार्य तं च बालं वंशनालीमुखोद्धृताभिरद्भिः फलैश्च पञ्चषैः शरक्षेपोच्छ्रितस्य लकुचवृक्षस्य[3] शिखरात्पाषाणपातितैः

इत्यमरः। प्रकर्ष आधिक्यम्। प्रज्ञा बुद्धिः। सत्त्वं बलम्। बहुश्रुते बहुनेकं श्रुतं शास्त्रादिश्रवणं यस्येति। विश्रुत एतन्नाम्नि।

इति श्रीदशकुमारचरितटीकायां सप्तम उच्छ्वासः।

इदानीं विश्रुतनामा कुमारः स्वचरितं वक्तुमुपक्रमते—**अथेति**। अथानन्तर्यार्थे। स विश्रुतनामा। अक्लेशार्हः। क्लेशं नार्हतीति स तथोक्तः। कूपो जलाशयः तस्य अभ्याशे समीपे। अष्टवर्षदेशीयः असमाप्ताष्टवर्षः। 'ईषदसमाप्तौ कल्पब्देश्यदेशीयरः' इति शब्दान्न्यूनार्थे देशीयप्रत्ययः। साहाय्यकं सहायस्य भावस्तत्। पिपासा पातुमिच्छा। प्रतिकर्तुं दूरीकर्तुम्। उदञ्चन्निष्कासयन्। कोऽप्यविदितकुलनामा। निष्कलः स्थविरः। वृद्ध इति यावत्। 'निष्कलः स्थविरः समौ' इति वैजयन्ती। **अथेति**। व्रतत्या वल्ल्या। 'वल्ली तु व्रततिर्लता' इत्यमरः। रज्जुस्थानीकृतयेति भावः। वंशनाली वंशदण्डः। पञ्चषैः पञ्च षड् वा। 'संख्ययाव्यय—' इत्यादिना बहुव्रीहिः। 'बहुव्रीहौ संख्येये डजबहुगणात्' इति समासान्तो डच्। शरक्षेपो बाणगमनम्। ततोऽप्युच्छ्रितस्य। उच्चस्येत्यर्थः। लकुच इति भाषया 'बडहर' इति प्रसिद्धः वृक्षः।

१ भवन्नर्म. २ चतुःप०. ३ लिकुच.

प्रत्यानीतप्राणवृत्तिमापाद्य, तरुतलनिषण्णस्तं जरन्तमब्रवम्—'तात, क एष बालः, को वा भवान्, कथं चेयमापदापन्ना' इति । सोऽश्रुगद्गदमगदत्—'श्रूयतां महाभाग । विदर्भो नाम जनपदः । तस्मिन्भोजवंशभूषणम्, अंशावतार इव धर्मस्य, अतिसत्त्वः, सत्यवादी, वदान्यः, विनीतः, विनेता प्रजानाम्, रञ्जितभृत्यः, कीर्तिमान्, उदग्रो बुद्धिमूर्तिभ्याम्[1], उत्थानशीलः, शास्त्रप्रमाणः, शक्यभव्यकल्पारम्भी, संभावयिता बुधान्, प्रभावयिता सेवकान्, उद्भावयिता बन्धून्, न्यग्भावयिता शत्रून्, असंबद्धप्रलापेष्वदत्तकर्णः, कदाचिदप्यवितृष्णो गुणेषु, अतिनदीष्णः कलासु, नेदिष्ठो धर्मार्थसंहितासु, स्वल्पेऽपि सुकृते सुतरां प्रत्युपकर्ता, प्रत्यवेक्षिता[2] कोशवाहनयोः, यत्नेन परीक्षिता सर्वाध्यक्षणाम्, उत्साहयिता कृतकर्मणामनुरूपैर्दानमानैः, सद्यः

---

प्रत्यानीता परावर्तिता प्राणानां वृत्तिः स्थितिर्यस्य । जरन्तं वृद्धम् । अश्रुभिर्गद्गदं यथा तथा । श्रूयतामिति । जनपदो देशः । अंशेनैकदेशेन । अत्यन्तं सत्त्वं बलं यस्येति अतिसत्त्वो महाबलः । सत्त्वं सत्त्वगुणो वा । वदान्यो बहुप्रदः । 'स्युर्वदान्यस्थूललक्ष्यदानशौण्डा बहुप्रदे ।' इत्यमरः । विनीतो नम्रः । विनेता शिक्षाकर्ता । रञ्जिता अनुरागं प्रापिता भृत्याः सेवका येनेति । उदग्र उन्नतः । बुद्धिर्मतिः मूर्तिः कायः । उत्थानशीलः पौरुषस्वभावः । 'उत्थानं पौरुषे तन्त्रे' इत्यमरः । शास्त्रमेव प्रमाणं यस्येति स तथा । शक्यभव्यकल्पारम्भी । 'शक्यं तु सुकरं कर्म भव्यं तु जनलालितम् । कल्पं युक्तं न भङ्गेन सदैवैष समाचरेत् ॥' इति दिवाकरः । शक्यं स्वसाध्यम् । भव्यं कुशलम् । 'भावुकं भविकं भव्यं कुशलं क्षेमम्' इत्यमरः । कल्पो विधिः । 'कल्पो न्याय्ये विधौ शास्त्रे संवर्ते ब्रह्मवासरे । कल्पद्रुमे विकल्पे च' इति महीपः । तेषामारम्भस्तच्छीलः । संभावयिता संभावना मानधनादिनेति । एवं सर्वत्र । प्रभावयिता अभ्युदयं प्रापयिता । 'प्रभुत्वं कारयिता' इति भूषणा । असंबद्धाः परस्परामिलिताः । प्रलापा निरर्थकवचनानि । 'प्रलापोऽनर्थकं वचः' इत्यमरः । अवितृष्णो न विगता तृष्णा यस्येति स तथा । सर्वदा सतृष्ण एवेत्यर्थः । नदीष्णो निपुणः । 'नदीष्णाभिज्ञनिष्णात-प्रवीणनिपुणा अपि' इति कोशः । नदीपूर्वात्स्नातेरातोऽनुपसर्गे कप्रत्ययः । 'निनदीभ्यां स्नातेः कौशले' इति सूर्धन्यः । नेदिष्ठो निकटवर्ती । 'अन्तिकबाढयोर्नेदसाधौ' इति साधुः । प्रत्यवेक्षा गवेषणम् । कोशो भाण्डागारम् । वाहनान्यश्वादीनि ।

---

1 मूर्तिबुद्धिभ्याम्. 2 प्रत्यवसिता.

प्रतिकर्ता दैवमानुषीणामापदाम्, षाड्गुण्योपयोगनिपुणः, मनुमार्गेण प्रणेता चातुर्वर्ण्यस्य, पुण्यश्लोकः, पुण्यवर्मा नामासीत्। स पुण्यैः कर्मभिः प्राप्य[1] पुरुषायुषम्, पुनरपुण्येन प्रजानामगण्यतामरेषु। तदनन्तरमनन्तवर्मा नाम तदायतिरवनिमध्यतिष्ठत्। स सर्वगुणैः समृद्धोऽपि दैवाद्दण्डनीत्यां नात्यादृतोऽभूत्। तमेकदा रहसि वसुरक्षितो नाम मन्त्रिवृद्धः, पितुरस्य बहुमतः, प्रगल्भवागभाषत—'तात, सर्वैवात्मसंपदभिजनात्प्रभृत्यन्यूनैवात्रभवति लक्ष्यते। बुद्धिश्च निसर्गपट्वी कलासु नृत्यगीतादिषु चित्रेषु च काव्यविस्तरेषु प्राप्तविस्तारा तवेतरेभ्यः प्रतिविशिष्यते। तथाऽप्यसावप्रतिपद्यात्मसंस्कारमर्थशास्त्रेषु, अनग्निसंशोधितेव हेमजातिर्नातिभाति बुद्धिः। बुद्धि-

प्रतिकर्ता प्रतीकारकर्ता। षाड्गुण्यं षड्गुणाः। चातुर्वर्ण्यादिपाठात्स्वार्थे ष्यञ्प्रत्ययः। 'संधिर्ना विग्रहो यानमासनं द्वैधमाश्रयः। षड्गुणाः शक्तयस्तिस्रः प्रभावोत्साहमन्त्रजाः' इत्यमरः। चतुर्वर्णा एव चातुवर्ण्यम्। पुण्यश्लोकः पवित्रकीर्तिः। 'पद्ये यशसि च श्लोकः' इत्यमरः। अतिसत्त्व इत्यादिनयवर्णने कामन्दकः—'न्यायेनार्जनमर्थस्य वर्धनं रक्षणं तथा। सत्पात्रप्रतिपत्तिश्च राजवृत्तं चतुर्विधम्। नयविक्रमसंपन्नः सूत्थानश्चिन्तयेच्छ्रियम्। नयस्य विनयो मूलं विनयः शास्त्रनिश्चयः॥ शास्त्रं प्रज्ञा धृतिर्दाक्ष्यं प्रागल्भ्यं धारयिष्णुता। उत्साहो वाग्मिता दार्ढ्यमापत्क्लेशसहिष्णुता॥ प्रभावः शुचिता मैत्री त्यागः सत्यं कृतज्ञता। कुलं शीलं दमश्चेति गुणाः संपत्तिहेतवः॥' इति। याज्ञवल्क्योऽपि—'ब्राह्मणेषु क्षमी स्निग्धेष्वजिह्मः क्रोधनो रिपौ। स्याद्राजा भृत्यवर्गे च प्रजासु च यथा पिता॥' इति। पुण्यवर्मेति नाम राजा। **स इति**। प्राप्य जीवित्वेत्यर्थः। पुरुषायुषं पूर्णमायुः वर्षशतमितम्। 'अचतुर–' इति सूत्रेण निपातः। अपुण्येन पापेनेत्यर्थः। अगण्यत। 'गण संख्याने'। अमरेषु देवेषु। तदनन्तरं पुण्यवर्मोत्तरमित्यर्थः। **अनन्तवर्मेति**। तदायतिस्तस्मात्पुण्यवर्मण आयतिः प्रभावो यस्येति स तथा। 'स्यात्प्रभावेऽपि चायतिः' इत्यमरः। दण्डनीत्यां राजनीत्याम्। प्रगल्भा प्रौढा वाग्यस्येति स तथा। 'आत्मसंपत् पुरुषगुणाः। ते च समनन्तरमेव 'शास्त्रं प्रज्ञा–' इति श्लोकद्वयेन दर्शिताः' इति भूषणा। अभिजनात् कुलात्। अन्यूना संपूर्णेत्यर्थः। अतिशयेन पटुः पट्वी। विस्तरो विस्तृतत्वम्। इतरेभ्योऽन्येभ्यः प्रतिविशिष्यते विशिष्टा भवतीत्यर्थः। अर्थशास्त्रेष्वान्वीक्षिक्यादिषु। हेमजातिः

[1] प्राप्य.

शून्यो हि भूभृदत्युच्छ्रितोऽपि परैरध्यारुह्यमाणमात्मानं न चेतयते। न च शक्तः साध्यं साधनं वा विभज्य वर्तितुम्। अयथावृत्तश्च कर्मसु प्रतिहन्यमानः स्वैः परैश्च परिभूयते। न चावज्ञातस्याज्ञा प्रभवति प्रजानां योगक्षेमाराधनाय। अतिक्रान्तशासनाश्च प्रजा यत्किंचनवादिन्यो यथाकथंचिद्वर्तिन्यः सर्वाः स्थितीः संकिरेयुः। निर्मर्यादश्च लोको लोकादितोऽमुतश्च स्वामिनमात्मानं च भ्रंशयते। आगमदीपदृष्टेन खल्वध्वना सुखेन वर्तते लोकयात्रा। दिव्यं हि चक्षुर्भूतभवद्भविष्यत्सु व्यवहितविप्रकृष्टादिषु च विषयेषु शास्त्रं नामाप्रतिहतवृत्ति। तेन हीनः सतोरप्यायतविशालयोर्लोचनयोरन्ध एव जन्तुरर्थदर्शनेष्वसामर्थ्यात्। अतो विहाय बाह्यविद्यास्वभिषङ्गमागमय दण्डनीतिं कुलविद्याम्। तदर्थानुष्ठानेन चावर्जितशक्तिसिद्धिरस्खलितशासनः शाधि चिरमुदधिमेखलामुर्वीम्' इति।

---

सुवर्णजातिः। अत्युच्छ्रितोऽपि महानपि। परैः शत्रुभिः। अध्यारुह्यमाणमासाद्यमानम्। न चेतयते विना संज्ञानेन स्मारयत इत्यर्थः। साध्यं कार्यम्। साधनं कारणम्। साध्यं विपक्षभूतम्। साधनं सहायभूतम्। कर्मसु कार्येषु। स्वैरात्मीयैः। परिभूयते पराभवं प्राप्यते। अवज्ञातस्यावगणितस्य। योगोऽलब्धलाभः। क्षेमं लब्धसंरक्षणम्। 'अप्राप्तप्रापणं योगः क्षेमं प्राप्तस्य रक्षणम्। द्वयं च साधयेद्भूपः प्रजानां विधिवत्प्रदः॥' इत्युक्तेः। स्थितीर्मर्यादाः। संकिरेयुः संकीर्णाः कुर्युः। इतो लोकादिहलोकात्। अमुतः परलोकात्। भ्रंशयते पातयति। तथा च याज्ञवल्क्यः—"अरक्ष्यमाणाः कुर्वन्ति यत्किंचित्किल्बिषं प्रजाः। तस्मात्तु नृपतेरर्धं यस्माद् गृह्णात्यसौ करान्॥" इति। कामन्दकोऽपि—"अहिंसा सूनृता वाणी सत्यं शौचं दया क्षमा। वर्णिनां लिङ्गिनां चैव सामान्यो धर्म उच्यते॥ स्वर्गानन्त्याय धर्मोऽयं सर्वेषां वर्णिलिङ्गिनाम्॥ तस्याभावे च लोकोऽयं संकरान्नाशमाप्नुयात्॥ सर्वस्यास्य यथान्यायं भूपतिः संप्रवर्तकः। तस्याभावे धर्मनाशस्तदभावे जगच्च्युतिः॥' इति। चाणक्योऽपि—'राज्ञि धर्मिणि धर्मिष्ठा पापे पापाः समे समाः। लोकास्तमनुवर्तन्ते यथा राजा तथा प्रजाः॥' इति। आगम एव दीपस्तेन दृष्टेन। अध्वना मार्गेण। लोकयात्रा लोकस्थितिः। अप्रतिहतवृत्ति न प्रतिहता कुण्ठिता वृत्तिर्यस्येति। तेन शास्त्रचक्षुषेत्यर्थः। सतोर्विद्यमानयोः। बाह्यविद्यास्वितरविद्यासु। अभिषङ्गं सङ्गम्। आगमय प्रापयेत्यर्थः। तदर्थानुष्ठानेन। कुलविद्यानुष्ठानेनेत्यर्थः। आवर्जिता प्राप्ता शक्तीनां प्रभावोत्साहमन्त्रजानां सिद्धिर्येन। अस्खलितशासनो-

---

१ क्षेमसाधनाय; ०क्षेमयोराराधनाय.

एतदाकर्ण्य 'स्थान एव गुरुभिरनुशिष्टम्। तथा क्रियते' इत्यन्तःपुरमविशत्। तां च वार्तां पार्थिवेन प्रमदासंनिधौ प्रसङ्गेनोदीरितामुपनिशम्य समीपोपविष्टश्चित्तानुवृत्तिकुशलः प्रसादवित्तो गीतनृत्यवाद्यादिष्वबाह्यो बाह्यनारीपरायणः पटुरयन्त्रितमुखो बहुभाङ्गिविशारदः परमर्मान्वेषणपरः परिहासयिता परिवादरुचिः पैशुन्यपण्डितः सचिवमण्डलादप्युत्कोचहारी सकलदुर्नयोपाध्यायः कामतन्त्रकर्णधारः कुमारसेवको विहारभद्रो नाम स्मितपूर्वं व्यज्ञापयत्—'देव, दैवानुग्रहेण यदि कश्चिद्राजनं भवति विभूतेस्तमकस्मादुच्चावचैरुपप्रलोभनैः कदर्थयन्तः स्वार्थं साधयन्ति धूर्ताः। तथा हि। केचित्प्रेत्य किल लभ्यैरभ्युदयातिशयैराशामुत्पाद्य मुण्डयित्वा शिरो बद्ध्वा दर्भरज्जुभिरजिनेनाच्छाद्य नवनीतेनोपलिप्यानशनं च शाययित्वा सर्वस्वं स्वीकरिष्यन्ति। तेभ्योऽपि घोरतराः पाषाण्डिनः[1] पुत्रदारशरीरजीवितान्यपि मोचयन्ति। यदि कश्चित्पटुजातीयो नास्यै मृगतृष्णिकायै हस्तगतं त्यक्तुमिच्छेत्, तमन्ये परिवार्याहुः—'एकामपि काकिणीं कार्षापणलक्षमापादयेम, शस्त्राद्दते सर्वशत्रून्घातयेम, एक

ऽप्रतिहताज्ञः। शाधि शिक्षय। 'शासु अनुशिष्टौ'। **एतदिति**। स्थाने। युक्तमित्यर्थः। अनुशिष्टमुपदिष्टम्। चित्तानुवृत्तिर्मनोगतं तत्र कुशलः। प्रसादवित्तो राजप्रसादेन ख्यातः। 'वित्तविज्ञातविश्रुताः' इत्यमरः। विशेषेण राजप्रसादभूमिरित्यर्थः। यद्वा प्रसादेन वित्तं धनं यस्य। अबाह्योऽभिन्नः। तन्मय इति भावः। अयन्त्रितमुखोऽनियतमुखः। बहुभाषीत्यर्थः। 'भङ्गी स्याद्वक्रभाषितम्' इति वैजयन्ती। परमर्म परगोप्यम्। परिवादो निन्दा। उत्कोचो गुप्तद्रव्यादिग्रहणम्। दुर्नयानामुपाध्यायोऽध्यापकः। कामतन्त्रे कामशास्त्रे। कर्णधारो नाविकः। कुमारसेवकः कुमारावस्थायाः प्रभृति सेवकः। कदर्थयन्तो निन्दयन्तः। **तथा हीति**। प्रेत्य जन्मान्तरे। 'प्रेत्यामुत्र भवान्तरे' इत्यमरः। किलेत्यलीके। अजिनेन चर्मणा। अनशनं निराहारम्। पाषण्डिनो शास्त्रविरुद्धाचाराः। पटुजातीयः। 'प्रकारवचने जातीयर्'। काकिणी विंशद्वराटकाः। 'वराटकानां दशकद्वयं यत्सा काकिणी' इति भास्कराचार्यः। 'कार्षापणस्तु विज्ञेयस्ताम्रिकः कार्षिकः पणः।' इति मनुः—इति भूषणा। कार्षापणम्। 'कार्षापणः कार्षिके स्यात्पणषोडशकेऽपि च' इति विश्वः।

१ पाखण्डिनः.

शरीर[1]मात्रमपि मर्त्यं चक्रवर्तिनं विदधीमहि, यद्यस्मदुद्दिष्टेन मार्गेणाचर्येत' इति । स पुनरिमान्प्रत्याह—'कोऽसौ मार्गः' इति । पुनरिमे ब्रुवते—'ननु चतस्रो राजविद्याः, त्रयी वार्ताऽऽन्वीक्षिकी दण्डनीतिरिति । तासु तिस्रस्त्रयीवार्तान्वीक्षिक्यो महत्यो मन्दफलाश्च । तास्तावदासताम् । अधीष्व तावद्दण्डनीतिम् । इयमिदानीमाचार्यविष्णुगुप्तेन मौर्यार्थे षड्भिः श्लोकसहस्रैः संक्षिप्ता । सैवेयमधीत्य सम्यगनुष्ठीयमाना यथोक्तकर्मक्षमा' इति । स 'तथा' इत्यधीते शृणोति च । तत्रैव जरां गच्छति । तत्तु किल शास्त्रं शास्त्रान्तरानुबन्धि[2] । सर्वमेव वाङ्मयमविदित्वा न तत्त्वतोऽधिगम्यते । भवतु कालेन बहुनाऽल्पेन वा तदर्थाधिगतिः । अधिगतशास्त्रेण चादावेव पुत्रदारमपि न विश्वास्यम् । आत्मकुक्षेरपि कृते तण्डुलैरियद्भिरियानोदनः संपद्यते । इयत ओदनस्य पाकायैतावदिन्धनं पर्याप्तमिति मानोन्मानपूर्वकं देयम् ।

उत्थितेन च राज्ञा क्षालिताक्षालिते मुखे मुष्टिमर्धमुष्टिं वाऽभ्यन्तरीकृत्य कृत्स्नमायव्ययजातमह्नः प्रथमेऽष्टमे भागे श्रोतव्यम् । शृण्वत एवास्य द्विगुणमपहरन्ति तेऽध्यक्षधूर्ताः । चत्वारिंशतं चाणक्योपदिष्टानाहरणोपायान्सहस्रधाऽऽत्मबुद्ध्या चैव ते विकल्पयितारः । द्वितीयेऽन्योन्यं विवदमानानां प्रजानामाक्रोशादह्यमानकर्णः कष्टं जीवति । तत्रापि प्राड्विवाकादयः स्वेच्छया जयपराजयौ विदधानाः[3] पापेनाकीर्त्या च भर्तारमात्मानं चार्थैर्योजयन्ति । तृतीये स्नातुं भोक्तुं च लभते । भुक्तस्य यावदन्धःपरिणामस्तावदस्य विषमयं न शाम्यत्येव । चतुर्थे

---

एकशरीरिणं एकाकिनमित्यर्थः । मर्त्यचक्रवर्तिनं मनुष्यसमूहवर्तिनम् । आचर्येत आचरतीत्यर्थः । तदुक्तं कामन्दके—'आन्वीक्षिक्यात्मविज्ञानं धर्माधर्मौ त्रयीस्थितौ । अर्थानर्थौ तु वार्तायां दण्डनीतौ नयानयौ ॥' इति । अधीष्व अङ्गीकुर्वित्यर्थः । मौर्यः चन्द्रगुप्तो नृपः । वाङ्मयं वाग्जालम् । समूहार्थे मयट् । 'तुलावच्छेद उन्मानो मानः प्रस्थादिभिः कृतः' इति वैजयन्ती । मुष्ट्यर्धमुष्टी परिमाणविशेषौ । 'शुक्तिभ्यां च पलं ज्ञेयं मुष्टिरष्टमिका तथा ॥' 'जनपदाव्ययशोधको मुष्टिः । ग्रामस्य शोधकोऽर्धमुष्टिः' इति भूषणा । अथ वा कृत्स्नानामायव्ययप्रदेशोऽवशिष्टमात्रगणनायुक्तोऽर्धमुष्टिः । कृत्स्नावान्तरस्थलविषय आयादिचतुर्विधगणनायुक्तो मुष्टिः ।—इति लघुदीपिका । शृण्वत एवेत्यनादरे षष्ठी । आक्रोशात् । 'यः सनिन्द उपालम्भस्तत्र स्यात्परिभाषणम् । तत्र त्वाक्षारणा यः स्यादाक्रोशो मैथुनं प्रति' इत्यमरः । प्राड्विवाकाः सभ्याः । अन्धःपरिणाम ओदनपरिपाकः । महान्तमायासं क्लेशम् ।

---

१ शरीरिणमपि. २ सर्वशास्त्रानुबन्धि. ३ विवादधनाः.

हिरण्यप्रतिग्रहाय हस्तं प्रसारयन्नेवोत्तिष्ठति । पञ्चमे मन्त्रचिन्तया महान्तमायासमनुभवति । तत्रापि मन्त्रिणो मध्यस्था[1] इवान्योन्यं मिथः संभूय, दोषगुणौ दूतचारवाक्यानि शक्याशक्यतां देशकालकार्यावस्थाश्च स्वेच्छया विपरिवर्तयन्तः स्वपरमित्रमण्डलान्युपजीवन्ति । बाह्याभ्यन्तरांश्च कोपान्गूढमुत्पाद्य प्रकाशं प्रशमयन्त इव स्वामिनमवशमवगृह्णन्ति । षष्ठे स्वैरविहारो मन्त्रो वा सेव्यः । सोऽस्यैतावान्स्वैरविहारकालो यस्य तिस्रस्त्रिपादोत्तरा नाडिकाः । सप्तमे चतुरङ्गबलप्रत्यवेक्षणप्रयासः । अष्टमेऽस्य सेनापतिसखस्य विक्रमचिन्ताक्लेशः । पुनरुपास्यैव संध्यां प्रथमे रात्रिभागे गूढपुरुषा द्रष्टव्याः । तन्मुखेन चातिनृशंसाः शस्त्राग्निरस[3]प्रणिधयोऽनुष्ठेयाः । द्वितीये भोजनानन्तरं श्रोत्रिय इव स्वाध्यायमारभते । तृतीये तूर्यघोषेण संविष्टश्चतुर्थपञ्चमौ शयीत किल । कथमिवास्याजस्रचिन्[4]तायासविह्वलमनसो वराकस्य निद्रासुखमुपनमेत् । पुनः षष्ठे शास्त्रचिन्ताकार्यचिन्तारम्भः । सप्तमे तु मन्त्रग्रहो दूताभिप्रेषणानि च । दूताश्च नामोभयत्र प्रियाख्यानलब्धानर्थान्वीतशु[5]ल्कबाधवर्त्मनि वणिज्यया वर्धयन्तः कार्यमविद्यमानमपि ले[6]शेनोत्पाद्यानवरतं भ्रमन्ति ।

मध्यस्थाः मध्यस्थायिनः । 'भाषया 'वकील' पदवाच्याः'—इति भूषणा । संभूय मिलित्वा । चारा गूढदूताः । स्वपरमित्राणां मण्डलम् । 'द्वन्द्वान्ते श्रूयमाणं पदं प्रत्येकं संबध्यते' इति परिभाषया स्वमण्डलं परमण्डलं मित्रमण्डलं वेत्यर्थः । प्रशमयन्तः शान्तिं प्रापयन्तः । नृशंसा घातुकाः । शस्त्रप्रणिधिः शस्त्रमारकः । अग्निप्रणिधिरग्निदायकः । रसप्रणिधिर्विषदायकः । 'शृङ्गारादौ विषे वीर्ये गुणे रागे द्रवे रसः' इत्यमरः । संविष्टः कृतशयनः । 'संवेशः शयने स्थाने' इत्यजयः । अजस्रं निरन्तरम् । 'नित्यानवरताजस्रम्' इत्यमरः । विह्वलमनसो व्याकुलचित्तस्य । शास्त्रचिन्ता कार्यचिन्ता चेति । वीता शुल्कबाधा यत्रेति क्रियाविशेषणम् । शुल्कं वाणिज्यकर्मणि राजदेयः करविशेषः । 'घट्टादिदेयं शुल्कोऽस्त्री' इत्यमरः । 'राजकीयमित्युक्त्वा बाधामपहरन्ति' इति भूषणा । वणिज्यया वणिक्कर्मणा । अनवरतं निरन्तरम् ।

१ मध्यस्थायिनः. २ स ह्यतां स्वैर०. ३ रसेति नास्ति क्वचित्. ४ चिन्तायासैर्विह्वलमनसो वा कस्य. ५ वीतशुल्कं निराबाधम्. ६ क्लेशेन.

अष्टमे पुरोहितादयोऽभ्येत्यैनमाहुः—'अद्य दृष्टो दुःस्वप्नः । दुःस्था ग्रहाः । शकुनानि चाशुभानि । शान्तयः क्रियन्ताम् । सर्वमस्तु सौवर्णमेव होमसाधनम् । एवं सति कर्म गुणवद्भवति । ब्रह्मकल्पा इमे ब्राह्मणाः । कृतमेभिः स्वस्त्ययनं कल्याणतरं भवति । ते चामी कष्टदारिद्र्या बह्वपत्या यज्वानो वीर्यवन्तश्चाद्याप्यप्राप्तप्रतिग्रहाः । दत्तं चैभ्यः स्वर्ग्यमायुष्यमरिष्टनाशनं च भवति' इति बहु बहु दापयित्वा तन्मुखेन स्वयमुपांशु भक्षयन्ति । तदेवमहर्निशम[1]विहितसुखलेशमायासबहुलमविरलकदर्थनं च नयतो नयज्ञस्यास्तां चक्रवर्तिता स्वमण्डलमात्रमपि दुरारक्ष्यं[2] भवेत् । शास्त्रज्ञसमाज्ञातो हि यद्ददाति, यन्मानयति, यत्प्रियं ब्रवीति, तत्सर्वमतिसंधातुमित्यविश्वासः । अविश्वास्यता हि जन्मभूमिरलक्ष्म्याः । यावता च नयेन विना यांति[3] लोकयात्रा स लोकंत[4] एव सिद्धः । नात्र शास्त्रेणार्थः । स्तनंधयो[5]ऽपि हि तैस्तैरुपायैः स्तनपानं जनन्या लिप्सते । तदपास्यातियन्त्रणामनुभूयन्तां यथेष्टमिन्द्रियसुखानि । येऽप्युपदिशन्ति—'एवमिन्द्रियाणि जेतव्यानि, एवमरिषड्वर्गस्त्याज्यः, सामादिरुपायवर्गः स्वेषु परेषु चाजस्रं प्रयोज्यः, संधिविग्रहचिन्तयैव नेयः कालः, स्वल्पोऽपि सुखस्यावकाशो न देयः' इति, तैरप्येभिर्मन्त्रिबकैर्युष्मत्तश्चौर्यार्जितं धनं दासीगृहेष्वेव भुज्यते । के चैते वराकाः । येऽपि मन्त्र[6]कर्कशाः शास्त्रतन्त्रकाराः शुक्राङ्गिरसविशालाक्ष[7]बाहुदन्तिपुत्रपराशरप्रभृतयस्तैः किमरिषड्वर्गो जितः

गुणवत्सार्थकम् । ब्रह्मकल्पा ब्रह्मण ईषन्न्यूनाः । स्वस्त्ययनं क्षेमप्रापणम् । कष्टं दारिद्र्यं येषाम् । स्वर्ग्यं स्वर्गसाधनमायुष्यमायुर्वृद्धिकरमरिष्टनाशनमशुभशान्तिकरम् । उपांशु एकान्ते । अविरला कदर्थना यस्मिन् । चक्रवर्तिता राष्ट्रव्यापकता । अरिषड्वर्गः कामक्रोधलोभमदमोहमात्सर्याणि । सामादिरुपायवर्गः । 'सामदाने भेददण्डावित्युपायचतुष्टयम्' इत्यमरः । मन्त्रिबकैर्मन्त्रिकुत्सितैः । 'कुत्सितानि कुत्सनैः' इति समासः । 'अधोदृष्टिर्नैष्कृतिकः स्वार्थसाधनतत्परः । शठो मिथ्याविनीतश्च बकवृत्तिचरो द्विजः ॥' इति मनुः । मन्त्रकर्कशा मन्त्रकठिनाः । तन्त्रकाराः कर्मकर्तारः । प्रारब्धेषु कृता-

१ अविदित. २ दुरारक्षम्. ३ न याति लोक०; समयेन विना लोक०. ४ लोके. ५ नन चालिशोऽपि. ६ मन्त्रिक० ७ विशालचयवनपुत्र.

कृतं वा तैः शास्त्रानुष्ठानम् । तैरपि हि प्रारब्धेषु कार्येषु दृष्टे सिद्ध्यसिद्धी । पठन्तश्चापठद्भिरतिसंधीयमाना बहवः । नन्विदमुपपन्नं देवस्य यदुत सर्वलोकस्य वन्द्या जातिरयातयामं वयो दर्शनीयं वपुरपरिमाणा विभूतिः । तत्सर्वं सर्वाविश्वासहेतुना सुखोपभोगप्रतिबन्धिना बहुमार्गविकल्पनात्सर्वकार्येष्वमुक्तसंशयेन तन्त्रावापेनैव मा कृथा वृथा । सन्ति हि ते दन्तिना दश सहस्राणि हयाना लक्षत्रयमनन्तं च पादातम् । अपि च पर्णान्येव हेमरत्नैः कोशगृहाणि । सर्वश्चैष जीवलोकः समग्रमपि युगसहस्रं भुञ्जानो न ते कोष्ठागाराणि रेचयिष्यति । किमिदमपर्याप्तं यदन्यार्जितायायासः क्रियते । जीवितं हि नाम जन्मवतां चतुःपञ्चाप्यहानि । तत्रापि भोगयोग्यमल्पाल्पं वयःखण्डम् । अपण्डिताः पुनरर्जयन्त एव ध्वंसन्ते । नार्जितस्य वस्तुनो लवमप्यास्वादयितुमीहन्ते । किं बहुना । राज्यभारं भारक्षमेष्वन्तरङ्गेषु[1] भक्तिमत्सु समर्प्य, अप्सरःप्रतिरूपाभिरन्तःपुरिकाभी रममाणो गीतसंगीतपानगोष्ठीश्च यथर्तु बध्नन्यथार्हं[2] कुरु शरीरलाभम् ' इति पञ्चाङ्ग[3]स्पृष्ट[4]भूमिरञ्जलिचुम्बितचूडश्चिरमशेत । प्राहसीच्च प्रीतिफुल्ललोचनोऽन्तःपुरप्रमदाजनः । जननाथश्च सास्मितम्—' उत्तिष्ठ[5] । ननु हितोपदेशाद्गुरवो भवन्तः । किमिति गुरुत्वविपरीतमनुष्ठितम् ' इति तमुत्थाप्य क्रीडा[6]निर्भरमतिष्ठत् ।

रम्भेषु । यातः यामः उपभोगकालो यस्य तद्यातयामं न यातयामं अयातयाममजीर्णमित्यर्थः । अपरिमाणेयत्तारहिता । विभूतिरैश्वर्यम् । तन्त्रावापेन । 'तन्त्रं स्वराष्ट्रचिन्ता स्यादावापस्त्वरिचिन्तनम् ' इति कोशः । ' तन्त्रावापो नीतिविचारः ' इति भूषणा । हीति निश्चये । पदातीनां समूहः पादातं पत्तिसंहतिः । ' भिक्षादिभ्योऽण् ' इति अण् । कोशगृहाणि भाण्डागाराणि । कोष्ठागाराणि धान्यचयगृहाणि । ' पुंसि कोष्ठोऽन्तर्जठरं कुसूलोऽन्तर्गृहं तथा ' इति कोशः । अन्यार्जितं परकीयम् । वयःखण्डमायुर्लेशम् । अपण्डिता नीचजनाः । अन्तःपुरिकाभिः स्त्रीभिः । यथार्हम् । वीप्सायां यथाशब्दः । पञ्चाङ्गी पञ्चानामङ्गानां समाहारस्तथा । ' द्विगोः ' इति ङीप् । ' जानू बाहुद्वयं मूर्धा पञ्चाङ्गम् ' इत्युत्पलिनी । अञ्जलिना चुम्बितः स्पृष्टश्चूडो मौलिर्येनेति तथा ।

१ अन्तरङ्गभूतेषु. २ यथार्थम्. ३ पञ्चाङ्गी. ४ मृष्ट. ५ उत्तिष्ठत. ६ क्रीडारसनिर्भरमतिः.

अथैषु दिनेषु भूयोभूयः प्रस्तुतेऽर्थे प्रेर्यमाणो मन्त्रिवृद्धेन वचसाऽभ्युपेत्य मनसैवाचित्तज्ञ इत्यवज्ञातवान्। अथैवं मन्त्रिणो मनस्यभूत्—'अहो मे मोहाद्बालिश्यम्। [1]अरुचितेऽर्थे चोदयन्नर्थीवाक्षिगतोऽहमस्य हास्यो जातः। स्पष्टमस्य चेष्टानामायथापूर्व्यम्। तथा हि। न मां स्निग्धं पश्यति, न स्मितपूर्वं भाषते, न रहस्यानि विवृणोति, न हस्ते स्पृशति, न व्यसनेष्वनुकम्पते, नोत्सवेष्वनुगृह्णाति, न विलोभनवस्तूनि प्रेषयति, न मत्सुकृतानि प्रगणयति, न मे गृहवार्तां पृच्छति, न मत्पक्ष्यान्प्रत्यवेक्षते, न मामासन्नकार्येष्वभ्यन्तरीकरोति, न मामन्तःपुरं प्रवेशयति। अपि च। मामनर्हेषु कर्मसु नियुङ्क्ते, मदासनमन्यैरवष्टभ्यमानमनुजानाति, मद्वैरिषु विश्रम्भं दर्शयति, मदुक्तस्योत्तरं न ददाति, मत्समानदोषान्विगर्हयति, मर्मणि मामुपहसति, स्वमतमपि मया वर्ण्यमानं प्रतिक्षिपति, महार्हाणि वस्तूनि मत्प्रहितानि नाभिनन्दति, नयज्ञानां स्खलितानि मत्समक्षं मूर्खैरुद्घोषयति। सत्यमाह चाणक्यः—'चित्तज्ञानानुवर्तिनो[2]ऽनर्थ्या अपि प्रियाः स्युः। दक्षिणा अपि तद्भावबहिष्कृता द्वेष्या भवेयुः' इति। तथाऽपि का गतिः। अविनीतोऽपि न परित्याज्यः [3]पितृपैतामहैर[4]स्मादृशैरयमधिपतिः। अपरित्यजन्तोऽपि कमुपकारमश्रूयमाणवाचः कुर्मः। सर्वथा नयज्ञस्य वसन्तभानोरश्मकेन्द्रस्य हस्ते राज्यमिदं पतितम्। अपि नामापदो माविन्यः प्रकृतिस्थमेनमापादयेयुः। अनर्थेषु [5]सुलभव्यलीकेषु क्वचिदुत्पन्नोऽपि द्वेषः सद्वृत्तमस्मै न रोचयेत्। भवतु। भविता तावदनर्थः। स्तम्भितपिशुनजिह्वो यथाकथंचिदभ्रष्टपदास्तिष्ठेयम्' इति।

---

प्रस्तुतेऽर्थे प्रवृत्ते कार्ये। अक्षिगतो द्वेष्यः। 'द्वेष्योऽक्षिगत उच्यते' इति हलायुधः। विलोभनवस्तूनि दानवस्तूनि। 'आदरणीयवस्तूनि' इति लघुदीपिका। मत्पक्ष्यान्मदीयपक्षवर्तिनः। अवष्टभ्यमानमाक्रम्यमाणम्। प्रतिक्षिपति अवगणयति। नयज्ञानां नीतिविदाम्। चाणक्यो नीतिशास्त्रकर्ता। चित्तज्ञानमनुवर्तन्ते ते तथा। दक्षिणाः सरला अपि। तस्य चित्तस्य भावस्तद्भावबहिष्कृताः। द्वेष्या वैरिणः। अविनीतोऽप्यत्युद्धतोऽपि। अपरित्यजन्त आश्रयन्तः। कमुपकारं प्रयोजनादिकम्। कर्मचयमित्यध्याहारः। किंविधाः। अश्रूयमाणवाचः। सुलभं व्यलीकं पीडा येषु। 'पीडार्थेऽपि व्यलीकं स्यात्' इत्यमरः। स्तम्भिता स्तम्भं प्रापिता। पिशुनाः खलाः। अभ्रष्टपदोऽगताधिकारः।

---

१ अनुचिते. २ अनर्थाः. ३ पितृपितामहानुयातैः. ४ अस्माकमुपसेवितमिदं राजकुलमीदृशश्चायमधिपतिः. ५ सुलभालीकेषु.

एवंगते मन्त्रिणि राजनि च कामवृत्ते चन्द्रपालितो नामाश्मकेन्द्रामात्यस्येन्द्रपालितस्य सूनुरसद्वृत्तः पितृनिर्वासितो माम भूत्वा बहुभिश्चारणगणैर्बह्वीभिरनल्पकौशलाभिः शिल्पकारिणीभिरनेकच्छन्नकिंकरैश्च गूढपुरुषैः परिवृतोऽभ्येत्य विविधाभिः क्रीडाभिर्विहारभद्रमात्मसादकरोत् । अमुना चैव संक्रमेण राजन्यास्पदमलभत । लब्धरन्ध्रश्च स यद्यद्व्यसनमारमते तत्तथेत्यवर्णयत्—'देव, यथा मृगया ह्यौपकारिकी न तथाऽन्यत् । अत्र हि व्यायामोत्कर्षादापत्सूपकर्ता दीर्घाध्वलङ्घनक्षमो जङ्घाजवः, कफापचयादारोग्यैकमूलमाशयाग्निदीप्तिः, मेदोपकर्षादङ्गानां स्थैर्यकार्कश्यातिलाघवादीनि, शीतोष्णवातवर्षक्षुत्पिपासासहत्वं, सत्त्वानामवस्थान्तरेषु चित्तचेष्टितज्ञानं, हरिणगवलगवयादिवधेन सस्यलोपप्रतिक्रिया, वृकव्याघ्रादिघातेन स्थलपथशल्यशोधनं, शैलाटवीप्रदेशानां विविधकर्मक्षमाणामालोचनम्, आटविकवर्गविश्रम्भणम्, उत्साहशक्तिसंधुक्षणेन प्रत्यनीकवित्रासनमिति बहुतमा गुणाः । द्यूतेऽपि द्रव्यराशेस्तृणवत्त्यागादनुपमानमाशयौदार्यं, जयपराजयानवस्थानाद्धर्षविषादयोरविधेयत्वं, पौरुषैकनिमित्तस्यामर्षस्य

---

चारणगणैर्गायकसमूहैः । 'चारणो गायकः समौ' इति वैजयन्ती । शिल्पकारिणीभिश्चित्रकारिणीभिः । आस्पदं प्रतिष्ठाप्रयोजकं स्थानम् । व्यसनम् । 'यस्माद्धि व्यस्यति श्रेयस्ततो व्यसनमुच्यते' इति कामन्दकः । 'स्त्रियोऽक्षा मृगया पानं वाक्पारुष्यार्थदूषणे । दण्डपारुष्यमित्येतन्महाव्यसनसप्तकम् ॥' इति वैजयन्ती । मृगया पापर्द्धिः । औपकारिक्युपकारायाही सा तथा । व्यायामो हिण्डनम् । कफः श्लेष्मा । मेदोपकर्षात् । मेदो धातुः । 'मेदोवृद्ध्यभावादङ्गानि लघूनि भवन्ति' इति वैद्यकम् । स्थैर्यं कर्मसहत्वम् । वर्षो वृष्टिः । सत्त्वानां प्राणिनाम् । चित्तस्य मनसः । चेष्टितस्य तत्क्रियायाश्च । गवलोऽरण्यमहिषः । गवयो गोसदृशः पशुः । 'गवयः स्याद्वनगवो गोसदृक्षोऽश्ववारणः' इत्यभिधानचिन्तामणिः । वृक ईहामृगः । 'कोक ईहामृगो वृकः' इत्यमरः । भाषया 'विक' इति प्रसिद्धः । अटव्यां चरन्ति ते आटविकाः । विश्रम्भणं विश्वासोत्पादनम् । अत्र शाकुन्तलम्—'मेदश्छेदकृशोदरं लघु भवत्युत्थानयोग्यं वपुः सत्त्वानामपि लक्ष्यते विकृतिमच्चित्तं भयक्रोधयोः । उत्कर्षः स च धन्विनां यदिषवः सिध्यन्ति लक्ष्ये चले मिथ्यैव व्यसनं वदन्ति मृगयामीदृग्विनोदः कुतः ॥' इति । द्यूतेऽपीति । आशयौदार्यं

वृद्धिः, अक्षहस्तभूम्यादिगोचराणामत्यन्तदुरुपलक्ष्याणां कूटकर्मणामुपलक्षणादनन्तबुद्धिनैपुण्यम्, एकविषयोपसंहाराच्चित्तस्यातिचित्रमैकाग्र्यम्, अध्यवसायसहचरेषु साहसेष्वतिरतिः[1], अतिकर्कशपुरुषप्रतिसंसर्गादनन्यधर्षणीयता, मानावधारणम्[2], अकृपणं च शरीरयापनमिति। उत्तमाङ्गनोपभोगेऽप्यर्थधर्मयोः सफलीकरणं, पुष्कलः पुरुषाभिमानः, भावज्ञानकौशलम्, अलोभक्लिष्टमाचेष्टितम्, अखिलासु कलासु वैचक्षण्यम्, अलब्धोपलब्धिलब्धानुरक्षणरक्षितोपभोगभुक्तानुसंधानरुष्टानुनयादिष्वजस्रमभ्युपायरचनया बुद्धिवाचोः पाटवम्, उत्कृष्टशरीरसंस्कारात्सुभगवेषतया लोकसंभावनीयता[3], परं सुहृत्प्रियत्वम्, गरीयसी परिजनव्यपेक्षा, स्मितपूर्वाभिभाषित्वम्, उद्रिक्तसत्त्वता, दाक्षिण्यानुवर्तनम्, अपत्योत्पादनेनोभयलोकश्रेयस्करत्वमिति। पानेऽपि नानाविधरोगभङ्गपटीयसामासवानामासेवनात्स्पृहणीयवयोऽवस्थापनम्[4], अहंकारप्रकर्षादशेषदुःखतिरस्करणम्, अङ्गजरागदीपनादङ्गनोपभोगशक्तिसंधुक्षणम्, अपराधप्रमार्जनान्मनःशल्योन्मार्जनम्[5][6], अशाठ्यशंसिभिरनर्गलप्रलापैर्विश्वासोपबृंहणं[7], मत्सराननुबन्धादानन्दैकतानता, शब्दादीनामिन्द्रियार्थानां सातत्येनानुभवः, संविभाग-

---

चित्तौदार्यम्। कूटकर्मणाम् कपटकर्मणाम्। उपलक्षणात् ज्ञानात्। अनन्तमगाधम्। एकविषयोपसंहारात्तदेकवृत्तित्वात्। ऐकाग्र्यमेकाग्रस्य भावस्तथा। अध्यवसाय उद्योगः तस्य सहचरेषु तन्निष्ठेषु। साहसमद्भुतं कर्म। अतिरतिः प्रीतिः। प्रतिसंसर्गः प्रत्यवस्थानम्। धर्षणीयताऽभिभवनीयत्वम्। 'मानावधारणमभिमाननिश्चयः' इति भूषणा। पुष्कलः श्रेयान्। 'श्रेयान्श्रेष्ठः पुष्कलः स्यात्' इत्यमरः। भावश्चित्ताभिप्रायः। तस्य ज्ञानम्। ज्ञानं ग्रन्थादिविषयम्। अलब्धोपलब्धिरप्राप्तप्राप्तिः। लब्धानुरक्षणं प्राप्तस्य पालनम्। भुक्तानुसंधानं भुक्तस्मृतेः। रुष्टस्यानुनयः क्रुद्धस्य समाधानम्। बुद्धिवाचोर्मतिवचनयोः। पाटवं पटुत्वम्। उत्कृष्टो यः शरीरसंस्कारः। पानेऽपीति। आसवानां मद्यानाम्। अङ्गजो मदनः। रागः इच्छा। दीपनं वृद्धिः। संधुक्षणमुद्द्योतनम्। उन्मार्जनमुद्धरणम्। अनर्गला यथेष्टा ये प्रलापा अनर्थकवचनानि तैः। मत्सरस्याननुबन्धादधारणात्। एकतानता। तत्परतेत्यर्थः। 'एकतानोऽनन्यवृत्तिः' इत्यमरः। सततस्य भावः सातत्यम्। 'पानसमये आगतेभ्यो दीयन्त आसवाः'

---

१ अभिरतिः. २ धीरणम्. ३ नीयतया. ४ वयोव्यवस्था०. ५ मानशल्य. ६ उन्मूलनम्. ७ अश्राव्य.

शीलतया सुहृद्वर्गसंवर्गणम्, अनुपमानमङ्गलावण्यम्, अनुत्तराणि विलसितानि, भयार्तिहरणाच्च सांग्रामिकत्वमिति । वाक्पारुष्यं दण्डो दारुणो दूषणानि चार्थानामेव यथावकाशमौपकारिकाणि । न हि मुनिरिव नरपतिरुपशमरतिरभिभवितुमरिकुलमलम्, अवलम्बितुं च लोकतन्त्रम्' इति । असावपि गुरूपदेशमिवात्यादरेण तस्य मतमन्ववर्तत । तच्छीलानुसारिण्यश्च प्रकृतयो विशृङ्खलमसेवन्त व्यसनानि । सर्वश्च समानदोषतया न कस्यचिच्छिद्रान्वेषणायायतिष्ट । समानभर्तृप्रकृतयस्तन्त्राध्यक्षाः स्वानि कर्मफलान्यभक्षयन् । ततः क्रमादायद्वाराणि व्यशीर्यन्त । व्ययमुखानि विटविधेयैतया विभोरहरहर्व्यवर्धन्त । सामन्तपौरजानपदमुख्याश्च समानशीलतयोपारूढविश्रम्भेण राज्ञा सैजानयः पानगोष्ठीष्वभ्यन्तरीकृताः स्वं स्वमाचारमत्यचारिषुः । तदङ्गनासु चानेकापदेशपूर्वमपाचरन्नरेन्द्रः । तदन्तःपुरेषु चामी भिन्नवृत्तेषु मन्दत्रासा बहुसुखैरवर्तन्त । सर्वश्च कुलाङ्गनाजनः पांसुलजनभङ्गिभाषणरतो भग्नचारित्रयन्त्रणस्तृणायापि न गणयित्वा भर्तॄन्धातृगणमन्त्रणान्यश्रृणोत् । तन्मूलाश्च कलहाः सामर्षाणामुदभवन् । अहन्यन्त दुर्बला बलिभिः । अपहृतानि धनवतां धनानि तस्करादिभिः । अपहृतपरिभूतयः प्रहताश्च पातकपथाः । हतबान्धवा हृतवित्ता वध-

---

इति संप्रदायवशादत्र विभागशीलता' इति भूषणा । संवर्गणं संयोजनं एकीकरणमित्यर्थः । अनुपमानमसदृशम् । संग्रामे साधु सांग्रामिकम् । औपकारिकाण्युपकारक्षमाणि । उपशमः शान्तिः । लोकतन्त्रं प्रजाशासनाधिकारम् । प्रकृतयः प्रजाः । विशृङ्खलं बन्धशून्यम् । छिद्रान्वेषणाय । दोषगवेषणायेत्यर्थः । तन्त्राध्यक्षाः सेनापतयः । कर्मफलानि तत्तत्कर्मणि लब्धानि राजधनानि । आयद्वाराण्यागमनोपायाः । व्यशीर्यन्त भग्नानि । व्ययमुखानि व्ययद्वाराणि । विटस्य षिङ्गस्य । विधेयतया विनयग्राहितया । 'विधेयो विनयग्राही' इत्यमरः । 'वैधेयतया' इति पाठे बालिशतया । 'मूर्खवैधेयबालिशाः' इत्यमरः । अहरहः प्रतिदिवसम् । सजानयः सस्त्रीकाः । 'जायाया निङ्' इति समासान्तः । पानगोष्ठी मद्यशाला । अत्यचारिषुरतिक्रमयामासुः । मन्दत्रासाः । निर्भया इत्यर्थः । भङ्गिभाषणं वक्रोक्तयः । धातॄणां गणाः जारसमूहाः । 'धाता जारे विधातरि' इत्यजयः । सामर्षाणां तच्चेष्टितान्यसहमानानाम् ।

---

१ संवर्धनम्. २ वैधेय°. ३ सजानपदाः. ४ संलग्नसुलभभङ्गि°. ५ अपहतपरिहृतयः.

बन्धातुराश्च मुक्तकण्ठमाक्रोशन्नश्रुकण्ठ्यः प्रजाः। दण्डश्चायथाप्रणीतो मयक्रोधावजनयत्। कृशकुटुम्बेषु लोभः पदमधत्त। विमानिताश्च तेजस्विनो मानेनादह्यन्त। तेषु तेषु चाकृत्येषु प्रासरन्परोपजापाः। तदा च मृगयुवेषमृगबाहुल्यवर्णनेनाद्रिद्रोणीरनपसारमार्गाः शुष्कतृणवंशगुल्माः प्रवेश्य द्वारतोऽग्निविसर्गैः, व्याघ्रादिवधे प्रोत्साह्य तन्मुखपातनैः, इष्टकूपतृष्णोत्पादनेनातिदूरहारितानां प्राणहारिभिः क्षुत्पिपासाभिवर्धनैः, तृणगुल्मगूढच्छन्नतटप्रदरपातहेतुभिर्विषममार्गप्रधावनैः, विषमुखीभिः क्षुरिकाभिश्चरणकण्टकोद्धरणैः, विष्वग्विसरविच्छिन्नानुयातृतयैकाकीकृतानां यथेष्टघातनैः, मृगदेहापराद्धैर्नामेषुमोक्षणैः, सपणबन्धमधिरुह्याद्रिशृङ्गाणि दुरधिरोहाण्यनन्यलक्ष्यैः प्रभ्रंशनैः, आटविकच्छद्मना विपिनेषु विरलसैनिकानां प्रतिरोधनैः, अक्षद्यूतपक्षियुद्धयात्रोत्सवादिसंकुलेषु बलवदनुप्रवेशनैरितरेषां हिंसोत्पादनैः, गूढोत्पादितव्यलीकेभ्योऽप्रियाणि प्रकाशं लब्ध्वा साक्षिषु तद्विख्याप्याकीर्तिगुप्तिहेतुभिः पराक्रमैः, परकलत्रेषु सुहृत्त्वेनाभियोज्य जारान्भर्तृनुभयं वा प्रहृत्य तत्साहसोपन्यासैः, योगनारीहारितानां संकेतेषु प्रागुपनिलीय पश्चादभिद्रुत्याकीर्तनीयैः प्रमापणैः, उपप्रलोभ्य बिलप्रवेशेषु निधानखननेषु

---

परिभूतिः परिभ . :। अश्रुकण्ठ्यः गद्गदवाचः इत्यर्थः। परोपजापाः शत्रुप्रयुक्ता भेदाः। अद्रिद्रोणी गिरिमध्यपद्धतिः। अनपसारमार्गा अनिर्याणमार्गाः। वंशगुल्मा वेणुगहनानि अग्निविसर्गैराग्निदानैः। प्रोत्साह्य प्रेरयित्वा। तट उन्नतप्रदेशे। प्रदरो निम्नगो भागः। विषममार्गैः कठिनमार्गैः। क्षुरिकाः शस्त्रिकाः। विसरः समुदायः। 'समूहे निवहव्यूहसंदोहविसरव्रजाः' इत्यमरः। विष्वक् सर्वतो यो विसरः प्रचारस्तेन विच्छिन्ना अनुयातारो येषां तेषां भावस्तत्ता तया। अनुयाताऽनुगामी। अपराद्धो लक्ष्यच्युतः। इषुमोक्षणैर्बाणपातनैः। सपणबन्धं सनियमम्। अटवीमटान्ति त आटविकाः। तेषां छद्मना तन्मिषेण। तत्कृतानीति ग्राहयित्वेत्यर्थः। व्यलीकं दुःखम्। 'तत्साहसं नरसाहसम्' इति भूषणा। योगा नारी। 'योगो विस्रब्धघाती स्यात्' इति कोषः। 'योगा मध्येयनं स्थिता। शतात्परं सहस्राधिगावतत्पुरुषायिता' इति वैजयन्ती। मध्येयनमिति मार्गमध्ये इत्यर्थः इति लघुदी०। प्राक्प्रथमम्। उपनिलीय लीनतां प्रापय्येत्यर्थः। प्रमापणैः हिंसनैः।

---

१ मृगाटवीषु मृगबाहु०. २ गुल्मतृण. ३ प्रचार. ४ भर्तृभयमपहृत्य. ५ योग्य.

मन्त्रसाधनेषु च विघ्नव्याजसाध्यैर्व्यापादनैः, मत्तगजाधिरोहणाय प्रेर्य प्रत्य[1]पायनिवर्तनैः, व्यालहस्तिनं कोपयित्वा लक्ष्यीकृतमुख्यमण्डलेष्वप[2]क्रमणैः, दायाद्यर्थे विवदमानानुपांशु हत्वा प्रतिपक्षेष्वयशःपातनैः, सामन्तपुरजनपदेष्वयथावृत्तानप्रकाशमभिव्याहृत्य तद्वैरिनामघोषणैः, योगा[3]ङ्गनाभिरहर्निशमभिरमय्य राजयक्ष्मोत्पादनैः, वस्त्राभरणमाल्याङ्गरागादिषु रस[4]विधानकौशलैः, चिकित्सामुखेनामयोप[5]बृंहणैरन्यैश्चाभ्युपायैरश्मकेन्द्रप्रयुक्तास्तीक्ष्णरसदादयः प्रक्षपितप्रवीरमनन्तवर्मकटकं जर्जरमकुर्वन्।

अथ वसन्तभानुर्भानुवर्माणं नाम वानवास्यं प्रोत्साह्यानन्तवर्मणा व्यग्राहयत्। तत्परामृष्टराष्ट्रपर्यन्तश्चानन्तवर्मा तमभियोक्तुं बलसमुत्थानमकरोत्। सर्वसामन्तेभ्यश्चाश्मकेन्द्रः प्रागुपेत्यास्य प्रियतरोऽभूत्। अपरेऽपि सामन्ताः समगंसत। गत्वा चा[6]भ्यर्णे नर्मदारोधसि न्यविशन्। तस्मिंश्चावसरे महासामन्तस्य कुन्तलपतेरवन्तिदेवस्यात्मनाटकीयां क्षमातलोर्वशीं नाम चन्द्रपालितादिभिरतिप्रशस्तनृत्यकौशलामाहूयानन्तवर्मा नृत्यमद्राक्षीत्। अतिरक्तश्च भुक्तवानिमां मधु[7]मत्ताम्। अश्मकेन्द्रस्तु कुन्तलपतिमेकान्ते समभ्यधत्त—'प्रमत्त एष राजा कलत्राणि नः परामृशति। कियत्यवज्ञा सोढव्या। मम

प्रेर्य प्रोत्साह्य। प्रत्यपायानां नाशप्रतिबन्धकानामुपायानां निवर्तनैर्हिंसोत्पादनैरित्यर्थः। प्रत्यवायनिर्वर्तनैरिति पाठे प्रत्यवायो नाशस्तत्संपादनैः। व्यालहस्तिनं दुष्टदन्तिनम्। 'व्यालो दुष्टगजः प्रोक्तः' इति हलायुधः। लक्ष्यीकृतानि मुख्यानां प्रधानपुरुषाणां मण्डलानि तेष्वपक्रमणैर्मोचनैः। अक्रमपणैरितिपाठेऽक्रमग्लहैः। 'पणो वराटमाने स्यान्मूल्ये कार्षापणे ग्लहे' इति विश्वः। उपांशु रहसि। घोषणैर्डिण्डिमैः। अहर्निशं रात्रिंदिवम्। राजयक्ष्मा क्षयरोगः। रसविधानं विषाधानम्। आमयो रोगः। उपबृंहणं वर्धनम्। 'तीक्ष्णा मर्मणि घातकाः' इति वैजयन्ती। **अथेति**। वानवास्यम्। 'वानवास्यो वनप्रभुः' इति कोशः। प्रोत्साह्य रणोत्साहं वर्धयित्वा। तेन परामृष्टोऽभिद्रुतो राष्ट्रपर्यन्तो राष्ट्रप्रान्तभागो यस्य। अभियोक्तुं पराभावितुम्। समगंसत। 'गम्लृ गतौ'। समुपसर्गः। लुङ्। 'समो गम्यृच्छिभ्याम्' इत्यात्मनेपदम्। मिलिता इत्यर्थः। अभ्यर्णे समीपे। आत्मनाटकीयां स्वीयनृत्याङ्गनाम्। संभूय मिलित्वा।

१ प्रत्यवायनिर्वर्तनैः. २ अक्रमपणैः. ३ योग्या. ४ रसधान. ५ उपबर्हणैः. ६ चाभ्यराति. ७ वधूत्तमाम्.

शतमस्ति हस्तिनां पञ्चशतानि च ते। तदावां संभूय मुरलेशं वीरसेन-भृषीकेश[1]मेकवीरं कोङ्कणपतिं कुमारगुप्तं नासिक्यनाथं च नागपाल-मुञ्जपाव[2]। ते चावश्यमस्याविनयमसहमाना अस्मन्मतेनैवोपावर्तेरन्। अयं च वानवास्यः प्रिय[3] मे मित्रम्। अमुनैनं दुर्विनीतमग्रतो व्यतिषक्तं पृष्ठतः प्राहरेम। कोशवाहनं च विभज्य गृह्णीमः' इति। हृष्टेन चामुना-ऽभ्युपेते विंशतिं वरांशुकानां पञ्चविंशतिं काञ्चनकुङ्कुमकम्बलाना प्राभृतीकृत्याप्तमुखेन तैः सामन्तैः संमन्त्र्य तानपि स्वमतावस्थापयत्। उत्तरेद्युस्तेषां सामन्तानां वानवास्यस्य चानन्तवर्मा नयद्वेषादामिषत्व-मगमत्। वसन्तभानुश्च तत्कोशवाहनमवशीर्णमात्मधिष्ठितमेव कृत्वा यथाबलं[4] च विभज्य गृह्णीत। युष्मदनुज्ञया येन केनाचिदंशेनाहं तु-ष्यामि' इति शाठ्यात्सर्वानुवर्ती तेनैवामिषेण निमित्तीकृते[5]नोत्पादित-कलहः सर्वसामन्तानध्वंसयत्। तदीयं च सर्वस्वं स्वयमेवाग्रसत्। वान-वास्यं केनचिदंशेनानुगृह्य प्रत्यावृत्य सर्वमनन्तवर्मराज्यमात्मसादकरोत्।

अस्मिंश्चान्तरे[6] मन्त्रिवृद्धो वसुरक्षितः कैश्चिन्मौलैः संभूय बालमेनं भास्करवर्माणमस्यैव ज्यायसीं भगिनीं त्रयोदशवर्षां मञ्जुवादिनीमनयोश्च मातरं महादेवीं वसुंधरामादायापसर्पन्नापदोऽस्या भावितया दाहज्वरेण देहमजहात्। अस्मादृशैर्मित्रैस्तु[7] नीत्वा माहिष्मतीं भर्तृद्वैमातुराय भ्रात्रे मित्रवर्मणे सापत्या देवी दर्शिताऽभूत्। तां चायामनार्योऽसावन्यथा-ऽभ्यमन्यत। निर्भर्त्सितश्च तया 'सुतमियमखण्डचारित्रा राज्यार्हं चिकीर्षति' इति नैर्घृण्यात्तमेनं बालमजिघांसीत्[8]। इदं तु ज्ञात्वा देव्या-ऽहमाज्ञप्तः—'तात नालीजङ्घ जीवताऽनेनार्भकेण यत्र क्वचिदवधाय[9]

व्यतिषक्तं युद्धव्यापृतम्। वरांशुकानि बहुमूल्यवस्त्राणि। प्राभृतीकृत्योपायनीकृत्य। आप्ताः विश्वस्ताः। हितैषिण इत्यर्थः। नयद्वेषान्नीतिमार्गाननुसरणात्। अवशीर्णं विध्वस्तम्। यथाबलं स्वस्वबलानुरूपम्। आमिषेण प्रलोभनद्रव्येण। **अस्मिन्निति**। मौलैः कुलक्रमागतैः प्रधानपुरुषैः। अपसर्पन्निर्गच्छन्। द्वैमातुराय सापत्नभ्रात्र इत्यर्थः। द्वयोर्मात्रोरपत्यं द्वैमातुरः। 'मातुरुत्संख्यासंभद्रपूर्वायाः' इति अणि उत्वं रपरत्वं च। अखण्डचारित्राऽभ्रष्टचारित्रा सतीत्यर्थः। राज्यार्हं राज्याधिकारिणम्।

१ ऋचीके०. २ उपजपावः. ३ परम्. ४ यथाप्रयासं यथाबलम्. ५ निमित्तीकृत्य. ६ अवसरे. ७ अस्मन्मित्रैस्तु. ८ अजिघांसत्. ९ अवस्थाय.

जीवं । जीवेयं चेदहमप्येनमनुसरिष्यामि । ज्ञापय मां क्षेमप्रवृत्तः स्ववार्ताम्' इति । अहं तु संकुले राजकुले कथंचिदेनं निर्गमय्य विन्ध्याटवीं व्यगाहिषि । पादचारदुःखितं चैनमाश्वासयितुं घोषे क्वचिदहानि कानिचिद्विश्रमय्य तत्रापि राजपुरुषसंपातभीतो दूराध्वमपासरम् । तत्रास्य दारुणपिपासापीडितस्य वारि दातुकामः कूपेऽस्मिन्नपभ्रश्य पतितस्त्वयैवमनुगृहीतः । त्वमेवास्यातः शरणमेधि विशरणस्य राजसूनोः' इत्यञ्जलिमबध्नात् । 'किमीयो जात्याऽस्य माता' इत्यनुयुक्ते मयाऽमुनोक्तम्— 'पाटलिपुत्रस्य वणिजो वैश्रवणस्य दुहितरि सागरदत्तायां कोसलेन्द्रात्कुसुमधन्वनोऽस्य माता जाता' इति । 'यद्येवमेतन्मातुर्मत्पितुश्चैको मातामहः' इति सस्नेहं तमहं सस्वजे । वृद्धेनोक्तम्— 'सिन्धुदत्तापुत्राणां कतमस्ते पिता' इति । 'सुश्रुतः' इत्युक्ते सोऽत्यहृष्यत् । अहं तु 'तं नयावलिप्तमश्मकेन्द्रं नयेनैवोन्मूल्य बालमेनं पित्र्ये पदे प्रतिष्ठापयेयम्' इति प्रतिज्ञाय 'कथमस्यैनां क्षुधं क्षपयेयम्' इत्यचिन्तयम् । तावदापतितौ च कस्यापि व्याधस्य त्रीनिषूनतीत्य द्वौ मृगौ स च व्याधः । तस्य हस्तादवशिष्टमिषुद्वयं कोदण्डं चाक्षिप्याविध्यम् । एकः सपत्राकृतोऽन्यश्च निष्पत्राकृतोऽपतत् । तं चैकं मृगं दत्त्वा मृगयवे, अन्यस्यापलोमत्वचः क्लोमापोह्य निष्कुलाकृत्य विकृत्योर्वस्थिग्रीवादीनि शूलाकृत्य दावाङ्गारेषु तप्तेनामिषेण तयोरात्मनश्च

पादचारिणं चरणगामिनम् । घोषे आभीराल्पग्रामे । 'घोष आभीरपल्ली स्यात्' इत्यमरः । दूराध्वं दूरमार्गम् । पिपासा तृषा । विशरणस्य शरणरहितस्य । कस्येयं किमीया । पित्र्ये पदे पितुः स्थाने । सपत्राकृतः पत्रेण सह विद्धः । 'वाहने तु च्छदे पत्रम्' इति भागुरिः । 'सपत्रनिष्पत्रादतिव्यथने' इति डाच् । अन्यो द्वितीयो निष्पत्राकृतः । मृगयवे लुब्धकाय । अपलोम रोमशून्यम् । त्वचश्चर्मणः । क्लोम मस्तिष्कम् । 'तिलकं क्लोम मस्तिष्कम्' इत्यमरः । निष्कुलाकृत्य निष्कोष्य । 'निष्कुलान्निःकोषणे' इति डाच् । विकृत्य विच्छेद्य । शूलाकृत्य शूले कृत्वा । शूलेन पाचयित्वेत्यर्थः । 'शूलात्पाके' इति डाच् । दावाङ्गारेषु वनवह्निषु । तप्तेन भर्जितेन । आमिषेण मांसेन ।

१ जीवेः. २ ०दुःस्थितं; पादचारिणं. ३ दूराध्वमपसरन्नत्रास्य. ४ किमीयोऽयमित्यनुयुक्ते. ५ दत्त०. ६ दुर्नयाव०. ७ अवधिषम्. ८ एकश्च.

क्षुधमत्य[1]तार्षम् । एतस्मिन्कर्मणि मत्सौष्ठवेनातिहृष्टं किरातमास्मि पृष्टवान्—'अपि जानासि माहिष्मतीवृत्तान्तम्' इति । असावाचष्ट—'तत्र व्याघ्रत्वचो दृतीश्च विक्रीयाद्यैवागतः । किं न जानामि । प्रचण्डवर्मा नाम चण्डवर्मानुजो मित्रवर्मदुहितरं मञ्जुवादिनीं विलिप्सुरभ्येतीति तेनोत्स[2]वोत्तरा पुरी' इति । अथ कर्णे जीर्णमब्रवम्—'धूर्तो मित्रवर्मा दुहितरि सम्यक्प्रतिपत्त्या मातरं विश्वास्य तन्मुखेन प्रत्याकृष्य बालकं जिघांसति । तत्प्रतिगत्य कुशलमस्य मद्वार्तां च देव्यै रहो निवेद्य पुनः कुमारः शार्दूलभक्षित इति प्रकाशमाक्रोशनं कार्यम् । स दुर्मतिरन्तःप्रीतो बहिर्दुःखं दर्शयन्देवीमनुनेष्यति । पुनस्त्वया तन्मुखेन स वाच्यः—'यदपेक्षया त्व[3]न्मतमत्यक्रमिषं सोऽपि बालः पापेन मे परलोकमगात् । अद्य तु त्वदादेशकारिण्येवाहम्' इति । स तथोक्तः प्रीतिं प्रतिपद्याभिपत्स्यति । पुनरनेन वत्सनाभनाम्ना महाविषेण संनीय[4] तोयं तत्र मालां मज्जयित्वा तया स वक्षसि मुखे च हन्तव्यः । 'स एवायमसिप्रहारः पापीयसस्तव भवतु यद्यस्मि पतिव्रता' इति । पुनरनेनागदेन संगमितेऽम्भसि तां मालां मज्जयित्वा स्वदुहित्रे देया । मृते तु तस्मिंस्तस्यां च निर्विकारायां सत्यां सतीत्येवैनां प्रकृतयोऽनुवर्तिष्यन्ते । पुनः प्रचण्डवर्मणे संदेश्यम्—'अनायकमिदं राज्यम् । अनेनैव सह बालिकेयं स्वीकर्तव्या' इति । तावदावां कापालिकवेषच्छन्नौ देव्यैव दीयमानभिक्षौ पुरो

---

अत्यतार्षमतिक्रान्तवान् । व्याघ्रत्वचो व्याघ्रचर्माणि । दृतीश्चर्मपुटानि । 'दृतिभिस्त्रतनीयज्ञभस्त्री चापि स्त्रियः समाः' इति कोशः । उत्सवोत्तरोत्सवपूर्णा । जीर्णं वृद्धम् । सम्यक्प्रतिपत्त्योचिताचरणेन । आक्रोशनमाक्षारणा । अभिपत्स्यत्यङ्गीकरिष्यति । वत्सनाभः । 'बच्चनाग' इति ख्यातः । संनीय संमिश्र्य । तया मालया । अगदेनौषधेन । तस्यां स्वदुहितरि । निर्विकारायां विकारशून्यायाम् । प्रकृतयः प्रजाः । संदेश्यम् कथनीयमित्यर्थः । कापालिको व्रतधारी । पुरो बहिः । नगराद्बहिरित्यर्थः

---

१ अन्यताप्सम; अताक्षिषम्. २ सोत्सवा. ३ त्वदुक्तम्. ४ संमील्य.

बहिरुपश्मशानं वत्स्यावः। पुनरार्यप्रायान्पौरवृद्धानाप्तांश्च मन्त्रिवृद्धान्-कान्ते ब्रवीतु देवी—'स्वप्नेऽद्य मे देव्या विन्ध्यवासिन्या कृतः प्रसादः। अद्य चतुर्थेऽहनि प्रचण्डवर्मा मरिष्यति। पञ्चमेऽहनि रेवातटवर्तिनि मद्भवने परीक्ष्य वैजन्यं जनेषु निर्गतेषु कपाटमुद्घाट्य त्वत्सुतेन सह कोऽपि द्विजकुमारो निर्यास्यति। स राज्यमिदमनुपाल्य बालं ते प्रतिष्ठापयिष्यति। स खलु बालो मया व्याघ्रीरूपया तिरस्कृत्य स्थापितः। सा चेयं वत्सा मञ्जुवादिनी तस्य द्विजातिदारकस्य दारत्वेनैव कल्पिता' इति। तदेतदतिरहस्यं युष्मास्वेव गुप्तं तिष्ठतु यावदेतदुपपत्स्यते' इति। स सांप्रतमतिप्रीतः प्रयातोऽर्थश्चायं यथाचिन्तितमनुष्ठितोऽभूत्। प्रतिदिशं च लोकवादः प्रासर्पत्—'अहो माहात्म्यं पतिव्रतानाम्। असिप्रहार एव हि स मालाप्रहारस्तास्मिञ्जातः। न शक्यमुपधियुक्तमेतत्कर्मेति वक्तुं यतस्तदेव दत्तं दाम दुहित्रे स्तनमण्डनमेव तस्यै जातं, न मृत्युः। योऽस्याः पतिव्रतायाः शासनमतिवर्तते स भस्मैव भवेत्' इति।

अथ महाव्रतिवेषेण मां च पुत्रं च भिक्षायै प्रविष्टौ दृष्ट्वा प्रस्नुतस्तनी प्रत्युत्थाय हर्षाकुलमब्रवीत्—'भगवन्, अयमञ्जलिः। अनाथोऽयं जनोऽनुगृह्यताम्। अस्ति ममैकः स्वप्नः स किं सत्यो न वा' इति। मयोक्तम्—'फलमस्याद्यैव द्रक्ष्यसि' इति। 'यद्येवं बहु भागधेयमस्या वो दास्याः। स खल्वस्याः सानाथ्यशंसी स्वप्नः'

---

आर्यप्रायान्। श्रेष्ठीनित्यर्थः। वैजन्यं विजनस्य भावम्। 'विगतो जनता जनसमूहो यस्मात् तस्य भावम्' इति भूषणा। तिरस्कृत्य लोकलोचनत आच्छिद्य। द्विजातिदारकस्य वणिक्पुत्रस्य। दारत्वेन स्त्रीत्वेन। स जीर्णः नालीजङ्घः। सांप्रतं तदा। प्रासर्पत्प्रसृतोऽभूत्। उपधिः कपटम्। दाम माला। स्तनमण्डनं कुचभूषणम्। शासनमाज्ञाम्। अतिवर्ततेऽतिक्रामति। व्रतमस्यास्तीति व्रती। प्रस्नुतस्तनी प्रसरत्पयःस्तनी। हर्षाकुलं सहर्षम्। भागधेयं भाग्यम्। अस्या वो दास्याः। मञ्जुवादिन्याः इत्यर्थः। सानाथ्यशंसी सनाथस्य भावः सानाथ्यं तच्छंसत्यसौ तथा।

---

१ पुनरार्यकार्याग्रप्रायान्. २ सांप्रतमित्यतिप्रीतः प्रयातः। अर्थं०. ३ हर्षकलम्.

इति मद्दर्शनरागबद्धसाध्वसां मञ्जुवादिनीं प्रणमय्य, भूयोऽपि सा हर्षगर्भमब्रूत—'तच्चेन्मिथ्या सोऽयं युष्मदीयो बालकपाली श्वो मया निरोद्धव्यः' इति। मयाऽपि सस्मितं मञ्जुवादिनीरागलीनदृष्टिलीढधैर्येणाभिहितं 'एवमस्तु' इति। लब्धभैक्षो नालीजङ्घमाकार्य निर्गम्य ततश्च तं चानुयान्तं शनैरपृच्छम्—'क्वासावल्पायुः प्रथितः प्रचण्डवर्मा' इति। सोऽब्रूत—'राज्यमिदं ममेत्यपास्तशङ्को राजास्थानमण्डप एव तिष्ठत्युपास्यमानः कुशीलवैः' इति। 'यद्येवमुद्याने तिष्ठ' इति तं जरन्तमादिश्य तत्प्राकारैकपार्श्वे क्वचिच्छून्यमठिकायां मात्राः समवतार्य तद्रक्षणनियुक्तराजपुत्रः कृतकुशीलववेषलीलः प्रचण्डवर्माणमेत्यान्वरञ्जयम्। अनुरञ्जितातपे तु समये जनसमाज[3]ज्ञानोपयोगीनि संहृत्य नृत्यगीतनानारुदितानि[4] हस्तचङ्क्रमणमूर्ध्वपादालातपादापीडवृश्चिकमकरलङ्घनादीनि मत्स्योद्वर्तनादीनि च करणानि पुनरादायादाय आ-

मद्दर्शनरागेण बद्धं साध्वसं ययेति सा ताम्। मञ्जुवादिनीम्। 'मञ्जु मञ्जुलम्' इत्यमरः। वदति सा वादिनी ताम्। प्रणमय्य। नमस्कारं कारयित्वेत्यर्थः। सस्मितं सहासमभिहितम्। रागलीना या दृष्टिस्तया लीढमास्वादितं धैर्यं यस्य तेन। लब्धभैक्षो लब्धा प्राप्ता भिक्षा येनेति। 'भिक्षादिभ्योऽण्'। नालीजङ्घमेतन्नामानम्। आकार्याहूय। अनुयान्तं पश्चादनुवर्तमानम्। आस्थानमण्डपे सभामण्डपे। कुशीलवैर्गायकैः। 'गायकास्तु कुशीलवाः' इति वैजयन्ती। जरन्तं जीर्णम्। 'प्राकारो वरणः सालः' इत्यमरः। अल्पो मठो मठिका। मात्राः परिच्छदादीन्। 'मात्रा परिच्छदेऽल्पेंऽशे' इति वैजयन्ती। तद्रक्षणे मात्रारक्षणे। जनसमाजस्य लोकसमूहस्य ज्ञानोपयोगीनि। नृत्यं नर्तनम्। गीतं गानम्। नानारुदितानि रोदनशब्दानुकरणानि। हस्तयोश्चङ्क्रमणमितस्ततः प्रसारणम्। भ्रमणं वा। ऊर्ध्वपादमलातपादम्। 'कराभ्यामवनीं स्पृष्ट्वा मूर्धानं भ्रामयेन्मुहुः। उत्तानीकृत्य चरणावूर्ध्वपादं तदुच्यते॥' इति नृत्याध्याये भरतः। 'उद्धृत्यैकं तु चरणमन्यं कृत्वैव कुञ्चितम्। नृत्यत्यनुमतं तिर्यक्तदालातकमेव च॥' इत्यपि तत्रैव। वृश्चिकलङ्घनं मकरलङ्घनं चेति 'द्वन्द्वान्ते श्रूयमाणं पदं प्रत्येकं संबध्यते' इति न्यायात्। मत्स्योद्वर्तनानि मीनवद्विलसितानि। आदायादायेति

१ बद्धराग. २ बाल. ३ समाजोप०. ४ रुदितादि–नि.

सन्नवर्तिनां क्षुरिकास्ताभिरुपहितवर्ष्मा[1] चित्रदुष्कराणि करणानि श्येनपातोत्क्रोशपातादीनि दर्शयन् विंशतिचापान्तरालावस्थितस्य प्रचण्डवर्मणश्छुरिकयैकया प्रत्युरसं प्रहृत्य 'जीव्याद्वर्षसहस्रं[2] वसन्तभानुः' इत्यभिगर्जन् मद्गात्रमुत्कर्तुमुद्यतासेः[3] कस्यापि चारभटस्य पीवरांसबाहुशिखरमाक्रम्य तावतैव तं विचेतीकुर्वन्नाकुलं च लोकमुच्चक्षूकुर्वन् द्विपुरुषोच्छ्रितं प्राकारमत्यलङ्घयम् । अवप्लुत्य चोपवने 'मदनुपातिनामेष पन्था दृश्यते' इति ब्रुवाण एव नालीजङ्घसमीकृतसैकतास्पष्टपादन्यासया तमालवीथ्या चानुप्राकारं प्राचा प्रतिप्रधावितः पुनरवाचोच्चितेष्टकचितत्वादलक्ष्यपातेन[4] प्रद्रुत्य लङ्घितप्राकारवप्रखातवलयस्तस्यां शून्यमठिकायां तूर्णमेव प्रविश्य प्रतिमुक्तपूर्ववेषः सह कुमारेण मत्कर्मतुमुलराजद्वारि दुःखलब्धवर्त्मा श्मशानोद्देशमभ्यगाम् । प्रागेव तस्मिन्दुर्गागृहे प्रतिमाधिष्ठान एव मया कृतं मग्नपार्श्वस्थैर्यस्थूलप्रस्तरस्थगितबाह्यद्वारं बिलम् ।

---

विश्वासद्योतनार्थं द्विरुक्तिः । क्षुरिकाः शस्त्राणि । उपहितवर्ष्मा संयुक्तदेहः । 'आच्छिन्नशरीरः' इति भूषणा । 'वर्ष्म विग्रहः' इत्यमरः । श्येनपातः । 'परिक्रम्यान्तरिक्षेण संप्राप्योच्चैरदृश्यताम् । आकस्मिकाभिपातेन श्येनपात इतीरितः ॥' इति । उत्क्रोशपातः कुररपातः । 'उत्क्रोशकुररौ समौ' इत्यमरः । चापः । प्रसारितबाहुद्वयप्रमाणं चाप इत्युच्यते । भाषया 'वांव' इति प्रसिद्धिः । मद्गात्रं मच्छरीरम् । उत्कर्तुं त्रोटितुम् । उद्यतासेरूर्ध्वीकृतखड्गस्य । चारभटस्य चारश्चासौ भटश्चेति व्युत्पत्तिः । 'भटश्चारभटो मतः' इति हलायुधः । पीवरांसं मांसलस्कन्धम् । विचेतीकुर्वन्नित्यत्र 'अरुर्मनश्चक्षुः—' इति सलोपः । द्विपुरुषोच्छ्रितं पुरुषद्वयप्रमाणोच्चम् । अवप्लुत्योड्डीय । सैकतं सिकतामयम् । अस्पष्टपादन्यासया न स्पष्टः पादन्यासश्चरणपातो यस्यामिति । तमालवीथ्या तमालपङ्क्त्या । अवाचोच्चितेष्टका उच्चनीचबद्धेष्टकाः । प्रतिमुक्तः संबद्धः पूर्ववेषो येन । 'अमुक्तं प्रतिमुक्तं च पिनद्धं चापिनद्धवत्' इति लघुदी० । 'तुमुलो व्याकुलरवः' इति महीपः । प्रस्तरः पाषाणः । 'पाषाणप्रस्तरग्रावोपलाश्मानः शिला दृषत् ।' इत्यमरः । अथेति । गलति । गच्छतीत्यर्थः । वर्षवरः । 'षण्ढो वर्षवरः' इत्यमरः ।

---

१ उपाहित. २ जीयात्. ३ अलङ्कर्तुम्; प्रहर्तुम्. ४ पादेन.

अथ गलति मध्यरात्रे वर्षवरोपनीतमहार्हरत्नभूषणपट्टनिवसनौ तद्बिलमावां प्रविश्य तूष्णीमतिष्ठाव । देवी तु पूर्वेद्युरेव यथार्हमग्निसंस्कारं मालवाय दत्त्वा[1] प्रचण्डवर्मणे, चण्डवर्मणे च तामवस्थामश्मकेन्द्रोपधिकृतामेव संदिश्य उत्तरेद्युः प्रत्युषस्येव पूर्वसंकेतितपौरामात्यसामन्तवृद्धैः सहाभ्येत्य भगवतीमर्चयित्वा सर्वजनप्रत्यक्षं परीक्षितकुक्षिवैजन्यं तद्भवनं विधाय दत्तदृष्टिः[2] सह जनेन स्थित्वा पटीयांसं पटहशब्दमकारयत् । अणुतररन्ध्रप्रविष्टेन तेन नादेनाहं दत्तसंज्ञः शिरसैवोत्क्षिप्य सप्रतिमं लोहपादपीठमंसलपुरुषप्रयत्नदुश्चलमुभयकरविधृतैकपार्श्वमेकतो[3] निवेश्य निरगमम् । निरगमयं च कुमारम् । अथ यथापूर्वमर्पयित्वा[4] दुर्गामुद्घाटितकपाटः प्रत्यक्षीभूय प्रत्ययहृष्टदृष्टि स्पष्टरोमाञ्चमुद्यताञ्जलि रूढविस्मयं च प्रणिपतन्तीः[5] प्रकृतीरभ्यधाम्—'इत्थं देवी विन्ध्यवासिनी मन्मुखेन युष्मानाज्ञापयति—'स एष राजसूनुरापन्नो मया सकृपया शार्दूलरूपेण तिरस्कृत्याद्य वो दत्तः । तमेनमद्यप्रभृति मत्पुत्रतयाऽमन्दमातृपक्ष[6] इति परिगृह्णन्तु भवन्तः ।' अपि च दुर्घटकूटकोटिघटनापाटवप्रकटशाठ्यनिष्ठुराश्मकघटघट्टनात्मानं मां मन्यध्वमस्य रक्षितारम् । रक्षानिर्वेशश्चास्य स्वसेयं सुभ्रूरभ्यनुज्ञाता मह्यमार्यया' इति । श्रुत्वैतत् 'अहो भाग्यवान्भोजवंशो यस्य त्वमार्यादत्तो नाथः' इत्यप्रीयन्त प्रकृतयः । सा तु वाचामगोचरां

---

तेनोपनीतानि महार्हाणि महामूल्यानि रत्नभूषणानि पट्टनिवसनानि पट्टवस्त्राणि च ययोस्तौ । पूर्वेद्युः पूर्वदिवसे । प्रत्युषसि प्रातःकाले । वैजन्यं विजनस्य भावस्तथा । पटीयांसं श्रेष्ठम् । पटहशब्द दुन्दुभिध्वनिम् । अंसलपुरुषः मांसलपुरुषः । 'बलवान्मांसलोंऽसलः' इत्यमरः । 'वत्सांसाभ्यां कामबले' इति लच् । प्रत्ययः साक्षात्कारः । हृष्टा हर्षं प्राप्ता दृष्टिर्यैत्रेति । प्रकृतीः प्रजाः । तिरस्कृत्यान्तर्धाय । अमन्दो बलवान् । मन्दो दुर्भाग्यो मातृपक्षो यस्य । दुर्घटं घटनाशक्यं यत् कूटं कपटं तस्य कोटिरग्रं संख्या वा तस्याः घटना योजना तस्याः पाटवं कौशलं तेन प्रकटं सुव्यक्तं यच्छाठ्यं तेन निष्ठुरोऽश्मक एव घटस्तस्य घट्टनो चालयिता आत्मा यस्य । निर्वेशः वेतनम् । 'निर्वेशस्तु पुमान्भोगे वेतने' इति मेदिनी । अप्रीयन्त प्रीताः । अगोचरामविषयाम् ।

---

१ ज्ञापयित्वा. २ दृष्टिरेव. ३ विधृतपार्श्वम्. ४ यथापुरम्. ५ प्रति०. ६ मन्द.

हर्षावस्थामस्पृशन्मे श्वश्रूः। तदहरेव च यथावदग्राहयन्मञ्जुवादिनीपाणिपल्लवम्। प्रपन्नायां च यामिन्यां सम्यगेव बिलं प्रत्यपूरयम्। अलब्धरन्ध्रश्च लोको नष्टमुष्टिचिन्तादिकथनैरभ्युपायान्तरप्रयुक्तैर्दिव्यांशतामेव मम समर्थयमानो मदाज्ञां[1] नात्यवर्तत। राजपुत्रस्यार्यपुत्र इति प्रभावहेतुः प्रसिद्धिरासीत्[2]। तं च गुणवत्यहनि भद्राकृतमुपनाय्य पुरोहितेन पाठयन्नीतिं राजकार्याण्यन्वतिष्ठम्। अचिन्तयं च—'राज्यं नाम शक्तित्रयायत्तम्। शक्तयश्च मन्त्रप्रभावोत्साहाः परस्परानुगृहीताः कृत्येषु क्रमन्ते। मन्त्रेण हि विनिश्चयोऽर्थानां, प्रभावेण प्रारम्भः, उत्साहेन निर्वहणम्। अतः पञ्चाङ्गमन्त्रमूलो द्विरूपप्रभावस्कन्धश्चतुर्गुणोत्साहविटपो द्विसप्ततिप्रकृतिपत्रः षड्गुणकिसलयः शक्तिसिद्धिपुष्पफलश्च नयवनस्पतिर्नेतुरुपकरोति। स चायमनेकाधिकरणत्वादसहायेन दुरुपजीव्यः[3]। यस्त्वयमार्यकेतुर्नाम मित्रवर्ममन्त्री स कोसलाभिजनत्वात्कुमारमातृपक्षो मन्त्रिगुणैश्च युक्तः तन्मतिमवमत्यैव ध्वस्तो मित्रवर्मा, स चेल्लब्धः पेशलम्' इति। अथ नालीजङ्घं

दिव्यांशतां दिवि भवा दिव्यास्तेषामंशस्तस्य भावस्तत्ता ताम्। आर्यपुत्र इति भवानीपुत्र इति। भद्राकृतं कृतकल्याणश्मश्रुम्। उपनाय्योपनयनं कारयित्वा। **राज्यमिति**। शक्तित्रयायत्तं शक्ति याधीनम्। परस्परानुगृहीता अन्योन्यकृतसहायाः। पञ्चाङ्गमन्त्रमूलः। 'सहायाः साधनोपाया विभागो देशकालयोः। विपत्तेश्च प्रतीकारः सिद्धिः पञ्चाङ्गमुच्यते॥' इति कामन्दकः। द्विरूपप्रभावोऽर्थानां पुरुषाणां च समृद्धिः। 'स प्रभावः प्रतापश्च यत्तेजः कोषदण्डजम्' इत्यमरः। स स्कन्धः शाखा यस्य। चतुर्गुणो य उत्साहः स एव विटपाः शाखाः यस्य। द्विसप्ततिप्रकृतयः प्रजाः पत्राणि यस्येति सः। षड्गुणाः 'संधिर्ना विग्रहो यानमासनं द्वैधमाश्रयः इत्युक्ताः।' ते किसलयानि यस्येति सः। शक्तिसिद्धिपुष्पफलश्च। शक्तित्रयं पुष्पं सिद्धित्रयं च फलमिति। 'षड्गुणाः शक्तयस्तिस्रः सिद्धयश्चोदयास्त्रयः।' इति। नय एव वनस्पतिर्नीतितरुः। अनेकाधिकरणत्वादनेकप्रकारत्वात्। असहायेन सहायहीनेन। दुरुपजीव्यो दुःखेनोपजीवितुं शक्यः। कोसलाभिजनत्वात्कोसलवंशत्वात्। 'संततिर्गोत्रजननकुलान्यभिजनान्वयौ।' इत्यमरः। मन्त्रिगुणैः प्रधानगुणैः।

1 त्वदाज्ञाम्. 2 ०हेतुप्रसिद्धिः. 3 ०जीवः.

रहस्यशिक्षयम्—' तात आर्यमार्यकेतुमेकान्ते ब्रूहि—'को न्वेष मायापुरुषो य इमां राज्यलक्ष्मीमनुभवति। स चायमस्मद्बालो भुजङ्गेनामुना परिगृहीतः। किमुद्गीर्येत ग्रस्येत वा' इति। स यद्वदिष्यति तदस्मि बोध्यः' इति। सोऽन्यदैवं मामावेदयत्—' मुहुरुपास्य प्राभृतैः प्रवर्त्य चित्राः कथाः संवाह्य पाणिपादमतिविस्रम्भदत्तक्षणं तमप्राक्षं त्वदुपदिष्टेन नयेन। सोऽप्येवमकथयत्—' भद्र मैवं वादीः। अभिजनस्य शुद्धिर्दर्शनमसाधारणं बुद्धिनैपुणमतिमानुषं प्राणबलमपरिमाणमौदार्यमत्याश्चर्यमस्त्रकौशलमनल्पं शिल्पज्ञानमनुग्रहार्द्रं चेतस्तेजश्चाप्यविषह्यमभ्यमित्रीणमित्यस्मिन्नेव संनिपातिनो गुणाः, येऽन्यत्रैकैकशोऽपि दुर्लभाः। द्विषतामेष चिरंबिल्वद्रुमः प्रह्वानां तु चन्दनतरुस्तमुद्धृत्य नीतिज्ञंमन्यमश्मकामिमं च राजपुत्रमनेन पित्र्ये पदे प्रतिष्ठितमेव विद्धि। नात्र संशयः कार्यः' इति। तच्चापि श्रुत्वा भूयोभूयश्चोपधाभिर्विशोध्य तं मे मतिसहायमकरवम्। तत्सखश्च सत्यशौचयुक्तानमात्यान्विविधव्यञ्जनांश्च गूढपुरुषानुदपादयम्। तेभ्यश्चोपलभ्य लुब्धसमृद्धमत्युत्सिक्तमविधेयप्रायं च प्रकृतिमण्डलमलुब्धतामभिख्यापयन्

---

अवमत्यावगणय्य। पेशलं सुन्दरम्। तातेति। न्विति वितर्के। भुजङ्गेन सर्पेण। उद्गीर्येत त्यज्येतेत्यर्थः। ग्रस्येत वेति भक्षयिष्यति वा। उपास्य सेवित्वा। प्राभृतैरुपायनैः। संवाह्य। 'संवाहनं पुरस्कारः' इति। विस्रम्भो विश्वासः तेन दत्तः क्षणो यस्य येन वा। भद्र कल्याणेति संबोधनम्। अभिजनस्य कुलस्य। असाधारणम्। महदित्यर्थः। अतिमानुषं मानुषमतिक्रम्य वर्तत इति। अपरिमाणं परिमाणरहितम्। अस्त्रकौशलमस्त्रकुशलता। शिल्पज्ञानं रचनाज्ञानम्। अविषह्यं सोढुमशक्यम्। अभ्यमित्रीणममित्रान् शत्रूनभिमुखमलं गच्छतीति तथा। 'अभ्यमित्राच्छ च' इति चकारात्खः। संनिपातिन एकत्रावस्थिताः। चिरबिल्वद्रुमो विषद्रुमः। प्रह्वानां नम्राणाम्। अनुरागवतामित्यर्थः। पित्र्यं पितुरिदम्। भूयोभूयो वारंवारम्। उपधाभिः। 'उपधा धर्माद्यैर्यत्परीक्षणम्' इत्यमरः। तस्य सखा तत्सखः। 'राजाहःसखिभ्यष्टच्' इति टच्। सत्यं सत्यप्रतिज्ञानम्। शौचं शुद्धिः। गूढपुरुषान्गुप्तसेवकान्। अभिख्यापयन्प्रकटीकुर्वन्। नास्तिकान्नास्तिक्ययुक्तान्। कण्टकान्रिपून्।

---

१ चिलिबिलि.

धार्मिकत्वमुद्भावयन् नास्तिकान्कदर्थयन् कण्टकान्विशोधयन् अमित्रोपधीरै[1]पघ्नन् चातुर्वर्ण्यं च स्वधर्मकर्मसु स्थापयन् अभिसमाहरेयमर्थान् । अर्थमूला हि दण्डविशिष्टकर्मारम्भाः । न चान्यदस्ति पापिष्ठं तत्र दौर्बल्यात् । इत्याकलय्य योगानन्वतिष्ठम् ।

इति श्रीदाण्डिनः कृतौ दशकुमारचरिते विश्रुतचरितं नामाष्टम उच्छ्वासः ।

## उत्तरपीठिका ।

व्यचिन्तयं च—' सर्वोऽप्यतिशूरः सेवकवर्गो मयि तथाऽनुरक्तो यथाऽऽज्ञया जीवितमपि तृणाय मन्यते । राज्यद्वितयसैन्यसामग्र्या च नाहमश्मकेशाद्वसन्तभानोर्न्यूनो नीत्याविष्टश्च । अतो वसन्तभानुं पराजित्य विदर्भाधिपतेरनन्तवर्मणस्तनयं भास्करवर्माणं पित्र्ये पदे स्थापयितुमलमस्मि । ' अयं च राजसूनुर्भवान्या पुत्रत्वेन परिकल्पितः । अहं चास्य साहाय्ये नियुक्तः ' इति सर्वत्र किंवदन्ती संजाताऽस्ति । अद्यापि चैतन्मत्कपटकृत्यं न केनापि विदितम्, अत्रस्थाश्च अस्मिन् भास्करवर्माणि राजतनये ' अयमस्मत्स्वामिनोऽनन्तवर्मणः पुत्रो भवान्याः प्रसादादेतद्राज्यमवाप्स्यति ', इति बद्धाशा वर्तन्ते । अश्मकेशसैन्यं च राजसूनोर्भवानीसाहाय्यं वि-

---

उपधीः कूटप्रयोगान् । चातुर्वर्ण्यं चतुर्णां वर्णानां ब्राह्मणादीनां समाहारश्चातुर्वर्ण्यम् । अर्थमूला अर्थाधीनाः । दौर्बल्याद् दुर्बलस्य भावस्तेन । आकलय्य । मनसि कृत्वेत्यर्थः । योगान्विविधोपायान् । ' योगो युक्तौ च संगत्यां कार्मणालभ्यलाभयोः । देहदार्ढ्ये प्रयोगे च विष्कम्भादौ तथाऽऽत्मनि ॥ उपाये भेषजे विद्भिर्दृष्टिसंनहने धने । विश्रब्धघातिनि ध्याने युक्तिन्याये च योजने ॥ ' इति महीपः ।

इति श्रीमत्कवीन्द्राचार्यसरस्वतीकृतायां दशकुमारचरितव्याख्यायां पदचन्द्रिकाभिधायां विश्रुतचरितं नामाष्टम उच्छ्वासः ।

---

तृणाय मन्यते विगणयति । स्वासुभिरपि मत्प्रियं कर्तुमिच्छतीत्यर्थः । राज्यद्वितयस्य मित्रवर्मप्रचण्डवर्मराज्ययोः । नीत्याविष्टो नीत्यनुसंधानपरः । किंवदन्ती

---

१ उपघ्नन्.

दित्वा 'दैव्याः शक्तेः पुरो न बलवती मानवी शक्तिः' इत्यस्माभिर्विग्रहे चलचित्तमिवोपलक्ष्यते। अत्रत्याश्च मौलाः प्रकृतयः प्रथममेव राजसुताभ्युदयाभिलाषिण्य इदानीं च पुनर्मया दानमानाद्यावर्जनेन विश्वासिता विशेषेण राजपुत्रमेवाभिकाङ्क्षन्ति । अश्मकेन्द्रान्तरङ्गाश्च भृत्या मदीयैर्विश्वास्यतमैः पुरुषैः प्रभूतां प्रीतिमुत्पाद्य मदाज्ञया रहसीत्युपजप्ताः—'यूयमस्मान्मित्राणि, अतोऽस्माकं शुभोदर्कं वचो वाच्यमेव। अत्र भवान्या राजसूनोः साहाय्यकाय विश्रुतं विश्रुतं नियुज्य तद्धस्तेनाश्मकेन्द्रस्य वसन्तभानोस्तत्पक्षे स्थित्वा ये चानेन सह योत्स्यन्ते तेषामप्यन्तकातिथिभवनम् । यावदश्मकेन्द्रेण स जन्यवृत्तिर्न जातस्तावदेनमनन्तवर्मतनयं भास्करवर्माणमनुसरिष्यथ । स वीतभयो भूयसीं प्रवृत्तिमासाद्य सपरिजनः सुखेन निवत्स्यति न चेद्भवानीत्रिशूलवश्यो भविष्यति। भवान्या च ममेत्याज्ञप्तमस्ति यदेकवारं सर्वेषां कथय। अतोऽस्माकं युष्माभिः सह मैत्रीमवबुध्यास्मन्मुखेन सर्वेभ्यो वार्तम्[1] ।' इत्याकर्ण्य तेऽश्मकेन्द्रान्तरङ्गभृत्या राजसूनोर्भवानीवरं विदित्वा पूर्वमेव भिन्नमनस आसन् । विशेषतश्च मदीयमिति वचनं श्रुत्वा ते सर्वेऽपि मद्वशे समभवन् । एतं सर्वमपि वृत्तान्तमवबुध्याश्मकेशेन व्यचिन्ति—'यद्राजसूनोर्मौलाः प्रजास्ताः सर्वा अप्येनमेव प्रभुमभिलषान्ति । मदीयश्च बाह्य आभ्यन्तरो भृत्यवर्गो भिन्नमना इव लक्ष्यते । एवं यद्यहं क्षमामवलम्ब्य गृह एव स्थास्यामि तत उत्पन्नोपजापं स्वराज्यमपि परित्रातुं न शक्ष्यामि । अतो यावता भिन्नचित्तेन मदवबोधकं प्रकटयता

---

अनश्रुतिः । मौला मूलाद् विदर्भनगरादित्यर्थः आगताः । आवर्जनेन दानेनाभिमुखीकरणेन वा । अन्तरङ्गा विश्वासपात्राणि । उपजप्ताः कृतोपजापाः । शुभोदर्कं कल्याणोत्तरफलम् । विश्रुतं दत्तम् । विश्रुतं तदाख्यम् । जन्यवृत्तिः युद्धव्यापारोद्यतः । स इति—युष्माकं मध्ये इति शेषः । प्रवृत्तिं गौरवं संपत्प्रवाहं वा । क्षमा उपेक्षा । उत्पन्नोपजापं जातभेदम् । मदवबोधकं मद्युद्धनिश्चयावबोधकम् ।

---

1 गदितम्.

मद्बलेन सह मिथोवचनं न संजातं तावत्तैव तेन साकं विग्रहं रचयामि। इत्येवं विहिते सोऽवश्यं मदग्रे क्षणमवस्थास्यति' इति निश्चित्यान्यायेन परराज्यक्रमणपातकप्रेरितः ससैन्यो मृत्युमुखमिवासमत्सैन्यमभ्ययात्। तमभ्यायान्तं विदित्वा राजपुत्रः पुरोऽभवत्। अतोऽश्मकेन्द्रमेव तुरगाधिरूढो यान्तमभ्यसरम्। तावत्सर्वा एव तत्सेना 'यदयमेतावतोऽपरिमितस्यास्मत्सैन्यस्योपर्येक एवाभ्यागच्छति तत्र भवानीवर एवासाधारणं कारणं, नान्यत्' इति निश्चित्यालेख्यलिखितेवावस्थिता। ततो मयाऽभिगम्य संगराय समाहूतो वसन्तभानुः समेत्य मामसिप्रहारेण दृढमभ्यहन्। अहं च शिक्षाविशेषविफलिततदसिप्रहारः प्रतिप्रहारेण तं प्रहृत्यावकृत्तमश्मकेन्द्रशिरोऽवनौ विनिपात्य तत्सैनिकानवदम्—'अतः परमपि ये युयुत्सवो भवन्ति ते समेत्य मया युध्यन्ताम्। न चेद्राजतनयचरणप्रणामं विधाय तदीयाः सन्तः स्वस्ववृत्त्युपभोगपूर्वकं निजान्निजानधिकारान्निःशङ्कं परिपालयन्तः सुखेनावतिष्ठन्तु' इति। मद्वचनश्रवणानन्तरं सर्वेऽप्यश्मकेन्द्रसेवकाः स्वस्ववाहनात्सहसाऽवतीर्य राजसूनुमानम्य तद्वशवर्तिनः समभवन्। ततोऽहं तदश्मकेन्द्रराज्यं राजसूनुसाद्विधाय तद्रक्षणार्थं मौलान्स्वानधिकारिणो नियुज्यात्मीभूतेनाश्मकेन्द्रसैन्येन च साकं विदर्भानभ्येत्य राजधान्यां तं राजतनयं भास्करवर्माणमभिषिच्य पित्रे पदे न्यवेशयम्।

एकदा च मात्रा वसुमत्या सहावस्थितं तं राजानं व्यजिज्ञपम्—'मयैकस्य कार्यस्यारम्भश्चिकीर्षितोऽस्ति। स यावन्न सिध्यति तावन्मया न कुत्राप्येकत्रावस्थातुं शक्यम्। अत इयं मद्भार्या त्वद्भगिनी मञ्जुवादिनी कियन्त्यहानि युष्मदन्तिकमेव तिष्ठतु। अहं च यावदिष्टजनोपलम्भं कियन्तमप्यनेहसं भुवं

---

क्षणं न महान्तं कालम्। आलेख्यलिखिता चित्रन्यस्ता। शिक्षा अस्त्रकौशलम्। विफलितः प्रभ्रष्टलक्ष्यः कृतः। तदीयास्तदनुयायिनः। वृत्तिर्जीवनसाधनम्। तद्वशवर्तिनस्तदिच्छानुवर्तिनः। राजसूनुसात्सात्कल्येन तदधीनम्। चिकीर्षितः कर्तुमिष्टः। उपलम्भः प्राप्तिः। अनेहसं कालम्। 'कालो दिष्टोऽप्यनेहाऽपि' इत्यमरः।

विश्रम्य तमासाद्य पुनरत्र समेष्यामि।' इत्याकर्ण्य मात्राऽनुमतेन राज्ञाऽहमगादि—'यदेतदस्माकमेतद्राज्योपलम्भलक्षणस्यैतावतोऽभ्युदयस्यासाधारणो हेतुर्भवानेव। भवन्तं विना क्षणमप्यस्माभिरियं राज्यधूर्न निर्वाह्या। अतः किमेवं वक्ति भवान्।' इत्याकर्ण्य मया प्रत्यवादि—'युष्माभिरयं चिन्तालवोऽपि न चित्ते चिन्तनीयः। युष्मद्गृहे यः सचिवरत्नमार्यकेतुरस्ति स ईदृग्विधानामनेकेषां राज्यानां धुरमुद्वोढुं शक्तः। ततस्तं तत्र नियुज्याहं गमिष्यामि' इत्यादिवचनसंदोहैः प्रलोभितोऽपि सजननीको नृपोऽनेकैराग्रहैर्मां कियन्तमपि कालं प्रयाणोपक्रमान्न्यवर्तयत्। उत्कलाधिपतेः प्रचण्डवर्मणो राज्यं मह्यं प्रादात्। अहं च तद्राज्यमात्मसात्कृत्वा राजानमामन्त्र्य यावत्त्वदन्वेषणाय प्रयाणोपक्रमं करोमि तावदेवाङ्गनाथेन सिंहवर्मणा स्वसाहाय्यायाकारितोऽत्र समागतः पूर्वपुण्यविपाकात्स्वामिना समगंसि।'

ततस्ते तत्र संगता अपहारवर्मोपहारवर्मार्थपालप्रमतिमित्रगुप्तमन्त्रगुप्तविश्रुताः कुमाराः पाटलिपुरे यौवराज्यमुपभुञ्जानं समाकारणे पूर्वकृतसंकेतं वामलोचनया भार्यया सह कुमारं सोमदत्तं सेवकैरानाय्य सराजवाहनाः संभूयावस्थिता मिथः सप्रमोदसंवलिताः कथा यावद्विदधति तावत्पुष्पपुराद्राज्ञो राजहंसस्याज्ञापत्रमादाय समागता राजपुरुषाः प्रणम्य राजवाहनं व्यजिज्ञपन्—'स्वामिन् एतज्जनकस्य राजहंसस्याज्ञापत्रं गृह्यताम्' इत्याकर्ण्य समुत्थाय भूयोभूयः सादरं प्रणम्य सदसि तदाज्ञापत्रमग्रहीत्। शिरसि चाधाय तत उत्तार्योत्कील्य राजा राजवाहनः सर्वेषां शृण्वतामेवावाचयत्—'स्वस्ति श्रीः पुष्पपुरराजधान्याः श्रीराजहंसभूपतिश्चम्पानगरीमधिवसतो राजवाहनप्रमुखान्कुमारानाशास्याज्ञापत्रं प्रेषयति। यथा यूयमितो मामामन्त्र्य प्रणम्य प्रास्थिताः

---

राज्यस्य धूः राज्यधुरा। राज्यधूरिति प्रयोगश्चिन्त्यः। संदोहः समूहः। प्रयाणोपक्रमाद्यात्रारम्भात्। आकारित आहूतः। स्वामिना त्वया राजवाहनेन। समाकारणे आह्वाने। संवलिताः संमिलिताः। उत्कील्योद्घाट्य। आशास्याशीर्भिरभिनन्द्य।

---

१ परिपाकात्.

पथि कस्मिंश्चिद्वनोद्देश उपशिवालयं स्कन्धावारमवस्थाप्य स्थिताः। तत्र राजवाहनं शिवपूजार्थं निशि शिवालये स्थितं प्रातरनुपलभ्यावशिष्टाः सर्वेऽपि कुमाराः 'सहैव राजवाहनेन राजहंसं प्रणंस्यामो न चेत्प्राणांस्त्यक्ष्यामः' इति प्रतिज्ञाय सैन्यं परावर्त्य राजवाहनमन्वेष्टुं पृथक्प्रस्थिताः। एतं भवद्वृत्तान्तं ततः प्रत्यावृत्तानां सैनिकानां मुखादाकर्ण्यासह्यदुःखोदन्वति मग्नमनसावुभावहं युष्मज्जननी च 'वामदेवाश्रमं गत्वैतद्वृत्तान्तं तद्विदितं विधाय प्राणपरित्यागं कुर्वः' इति निश्चित्य तदाश्रममुपगतौ तं मुनिं प्रणम्य यावत्स्थितौ तावदेव तेन त्रिकालवेदिना मुनिना विदितमेवास्मन्मनीषितम्। निश्चयमवबुद्ध्य प्रावाचि—'राजन् प्रथममेवैतत्सर्वं युष्मन्मनीषितं विज्ञानबलादज्ञायि। यदेते त्वत्कुमारा राजवाहननिमित्ते कियन्तमनेहसमापदमासाद्य भाग्योदयादसाधारणेन विक्रमेण विहितदिग्विजयाः प्रभूतानि राज्यान्युपलभ्य षोडशाब्दान्ते विजयिनं राजवाहनं पुरस्कृत्य प्रत्येत्य तव वसुमत्याश्च पादानभिवाद्य भवदाज्ञाविधायिनो भविष्यन्ति। अतस्तन्निमित्तं किमपि साहसं न विधेयम्' इति। तदाकर्ण्य तत्प्रत्ययाद्धैर्यमवलम्ब्याद्यप्रभृत्यहं देवी च प्राणानधारयाव। इदानीमासन्नवर्तिन्यवधौ वामदेवाश्रमं गत्वा विज्ञप्तिः कृता—'स्वामिन् त्वदुक्तावधिः पूर्णप्रायो भवति। तत्प्रवृत्तिस्त्वयाऽद्यापि विज्ञायते' इति। श्रुत्वा मुनिरवदत्—'राजन् राजवाहनप्रमुखाः सर्वेऽपि कुमारा अनेकान्दुर्जयाञ्शत्रून्विजित्य दिग्विजयं विधाय भूवलयं वशीकृत्य चम्पायामेकत्र स्थिताः। तवाज्ञापत्रमादाय तदानयनाय प्रेष्यन्तां शीघ्रमेव सेवकाः।' इति मुनिवचनमाकर्ण्य भवदाकारणायाज्ञापत्रं

---

स्कन्धावारं सेनाम्। दुःखोदन्वति दुःखसागरे। त्रिकालवेदिना भूतभविष्यद्वर्तमानज्ञेन। विज्ञानं योगबलजन्यं ज्ञानम्। 'योगबलात्' इति पाठे योगश्चित्तैकाग्र्यरूपः समाधिः। प्रत्येत्य प्रत्यागत्य। साहसं प्राणपरित्यागादिरूपम्। प्रत्ययाद्विश्वासात्। अवधिः राजपुत्रनिवर्तनकालः। प्रवृत्तिर्वृत्तान्तः।

---

१ योगबलात्.

प्रेषितमस्ति। अतः परं चेत्क्षणमपि यूयं विलम्ब विधास्यथ ततो मां वसुमतीं च मातरं कथावशेषावेव श्रोष्यथेति ज्ञात्वा पानीयमपि पथि भूत्वा पेयम्।' इत्येवं पितुराज्ञापत्रं मूर्ध्नि विधृत्य गच्छेमेति निश्चयं चक्रुः। अथ वशीकृतराज्यरक्षापर्याप्तानि सैन्यानि समर्थतरान्पुरुषानाप्तान्स्थाने स्थाने नियुज्य कियता सैन्येन मार्गरक्षां विधाय पूर्ववैरिणं मालवेशं मानसारं पराजित्य तदपि राज्यं वशीकृत्य पुष्पपुरे राज्ञो राजहंसस्य देव्या वसुमत्याश्च पादान्नमस्यामः। एवं निश्चित्य स्वस्वभार्यासंयुताः परिमितेन सैन्येन मालवेशं प्रति प्रस्थिताः। प्राप्य चोज्जयिनीं तदैव सहायभूतैस्तैः कुमारैः परिवृतेन राजवाहनेनातिबलवानपि मालवेशो मानसारः क्षणेन पराजिग्ये निहतश्च। ततस्तद्दुहितरमवन्तिसुदरीं समादाय चण्डवर्मणा तन्मन्त्रिणा पूर्वं कारागृहे रक्षितं पुष्पोद्भवं कुमारं सकुटुम्बं तत उन्मोचितं सह नीत्वा मालवेन्द्रराज्यं वशीकृत्य तद्रक्षणाय कांश्चित्सैन्यसहितान्मन्त्रिणो नियुज्यावशिष्टपरिमितसैन्यसहितास्ते कुमाराः पुष्पपुरं समेत्य राजवाहनं पुरस्कृत्य तस्य राजहंसस्य मातुर्वसुमत्याश्च चरणानाभिवान्दितवन्तः। तौ च पुत्रसमागमं प्राप्य परमानन्दमधिगतौ। ततो राज्ञो वसुमत्याश्च देव्याः समक्षं वामदेवो राजवाहनप्रमुखानां दशानामपि कुमाराणामभिलाषं विज्ञाय तानाज्ञापयत्—' भवन्तः सर्वेऽप्येकवारं गत्वा स्वानि राज्यानि न्यायेन परिपालयन्तु। पुनर्यदेच्छा भवति तदा पित्रोश्चरणाभिवन्दनायागन्तव्यम्' इति। ततस्ते सर्वेऽपि कुमारास्तन्मुनिवचनं शिरस्याधाय तं प्रणम्य पितरौ च, गत्वा दिग्विजयं विधाय, प्रत्यागमनान्तं स्वस्ववृत्तं पृथक्पृथङ् मुनिसमक्षं न्यवेदयन्। पितरौ च कुमाराणां निजपराक्रमावबोधकान्यतिदुर्घटानि चरितान्याकर्ण्य परमानन्दमाप्नुताम्। ततो राजा मुनिं सविनयं व्यजिज्ञपत्—

---

कथावशेषौ मृतावित्यर्थः। पानीयमिति। आज्ञापत्रवाचनविरामे एव प्रयाणं कार्यमित्यर्थः। आप्तान् हितैषिणः। एकवारमेकदैव। गत्वेति स्वगमनादारभ्येत्यर्थः। प्रत्यागमनमन्तो यस्य तत्। प्रत्यागमनं यावदित्यर्थः। अवबोधकानि गमकानि।

'भगवन् तव प्रसादादस्माभिर्मनुजमनोरथाधिकमवाङ्मनसगोचर सुखमाधिगतम् । अतः परं मम स्वामिचरणसंनिधौ वानप्रस्थाश्रममधिगत्यात्मसाधनमेव विधातुमुचितम् । अतः पुष्पपुरराज्ये मानसारराज्ये च राजवाहनमाभिषिच्यावशिष्टानि राज्यानि नवभ्यः कुमारेभ्यो यथोदितं संप्रदाय ते कुमारा राजवाहनाज्ञाविधायिनस्तदेकमत्या वर्तमानाश्चतुरुदधिमेखलां वसुंधरां समुद्धृत्य कण्टकानुपभुञ्जन्ति तथा विधेयं स्वामिना' इति । तेषां तत्पितुर्वानप्रस्थाश्रमग्रहणोपक्रमनिषेधे भूयांसमाग्रहं विलोक्य मुनिस्तानवदत्—'भोः कुमारकाः अयं युष्मज्जनक एतद्वयःसमुचिते पथि वर्तमानः कायक्लेशं विनैव मदाश्रमस्थो वानप्रस्थाश्रमाश्रयणं सर्वथा भवद्भिर्न निवारणीयः । अत्र स्थितस्त्वयं भगवद्भक्तिमुपलप्स्यते । भवन्तश्च पितृसंनिधौ न सुखमवाप्स्यन्ति ।' इति महर्षेराज्ञामधिगम्य ते पितुर्वानप्रस्थाश्रमाधिगमप्रतिषेधाग्रहमत्यजन् । राजवाहनं पुष्पपुरेऽवस्थाप्य तदनुज्ञया सर्वेऽपि परिजनाः स्वानि स्वानि राज्यानि प्रतिपाल्य स्वेच्छया पित्रोः समीपे गतागतमकुर्वन् । एवमवस्थितास्ते राजवाहनप्रमुखाः सर्वेऽपि कुमारा राजवाहनाज्ञया सर्वमपि वसुधावलयं न्यायेन परिपालयन्तः परस्परमैकमत्येन वर्तमानाः पुरंदरप्रभृतिभिरप्यतिदुर्लभानि राज्यसुखान्यन्वभूवन् ।

इति श्रीदण्डिनः कृतौ दशकुमारचरित उत्तरपीठिका ।

---

**समाप्तं दशकुमारचरितम् ।**

---

अवाङ्मनसगोचरं वाङ्मनसयोर्व्यापारातिक्रान्तम् । वाङ्मनसे इति 'अचतुर–'इत्यादिना अजन्तो निपातः । वानप्रस्थेत्यत्र याज्ञवल्क्यः—'सुतविन्यस्तपत्नीकस्तया वाऽनुगतो वनम् । वानप्रस्थो ब्रह्मचारी साग्निः सोपासनो व्रजेत् ॥' इति । आत्मसाधनं परमात्मचिन्तनेन मोक्षसाधनम् । यथोदितं यथाभ्युदयं यथोक्तं वा । पुरंदरप्रभृतिभिरिन्द्रादिदेवैः ।

इति समाप्तोत्तरपीठिकाव्याख्या ।

# TRANSLATION
## OF THE
# DAS'AKUMA'RACHARITA.

## PÛRVAPÎṬHIKÂ.

### UCHCHHVA'SA I.

May the staff-like foot of Trivikrama (Vishṇu) grant you eternal bliss!—the foot which is the pole of the umbrella in the form of the Mundane egg, which is the long stalk of the lotus, the residence (*or*, birth-place) of Brahmâ, which is as it were the main-mast of the ship of the earth which serves as the flag-staff of the bannerlike heavenly river gliding along (the sky), which is the axle of the wheel in the form of the (revolving) firmament of stars, which is (as it were) the pillar that proclaims his (*i. e.*, Vishṇu's) victory over the three worlds, and which is the very rod of Death to the enemies of gods (*i.e.* the demons).

There was a city, Pushpapurî by name, which, serving as a touchstone to all other towns (*i.e.* being the best model of a city), proclaimed the greatness of the ocean by the various articles such as collections of gems and others spread out at all times among countless commodities for sale, and which (consequently) had become an ornament to the country of the Magadhas. It was ruled by a king named Râjahaṃsa, who possessed a beauty that was as attractive and faultless as that of the highly proud Cupid. His mighty, long arm served him like the Mandára mountain, in churning the ocean of the army of the host of all his enemies, terrific on account of its sharks in the form of the horses and elephants, and with heaving waves in the shape of the array of brave warriors. He was rendered fragrant (*i.e.* illustrious) all round by very great fame, which was repeatedly sung by the youthful courtesans of heaven diverting themselves in the groves adjoining the suburbs of the capital of Indra, and which filled all the spaces of the quarters, being white (spotless) like the autumnal moon, the *Kunda* flower, camphor, snow, a pearl-necklace, the stalk of a (white) lotus, the swan, the Airávata, water, milk, the loud and boisterous laughter of Śiva, the Kailása mountain and the *Kás'a* flower. Fortunate in the enjoyment of the beauty of the lovely damsel in the form of the earth with the girdle in the form of the border of the ocean which contains gems as large and beautiful as those on the peaks of the mountain Meru, he patronized, with rich gifts in sacrifices constantly going on, thousands of learned and eminent Bràhmaṇas refulgent with the fund of learning they possessed. He always equalled the sun, in the middle of the sky, by his valour that (constantly) caused torment to his foes. His queen was Vasumatî, gifted with talent, and the foremost (*lit.* crest-jewel) of the whole class of graceful women. Cupid (*lit.* the fish-bannered god), having been reduced to ashes by S'iva (*lit.* god with an eye in his forehead) by means of his angry look, his accompaniments, thinking that a lady of exquisite beauty was the proper resort for them (being unassailable), became through fear her various limbs. Thus, the row of bees (on his bow-string) assumed the form of her mass of hair (thick tresses); the moon, the source of the passion of love, became her face that surpassed a lotus in beauty; the fish with its mate, that acted like his banner of victory, became her two eyes; the Malaya-breeze, the chief of all his warriors (for the conquest of the whole of the human world), became her breath; the tender sprout, the saw that harrows the hearts of travellers, her red (lit. *bimba*-like) lower lip; his victorious conch, her tapering and beautiful neck; his two full jars became her breasts, looking like two Chakraváka birds; the two soft lotus-stalks of incomparable tenderness, that formed his bow-string, her two arms; the slightly-blown lotus-bud that served as his sportive ear-ornament became her navel that resembled an eddy of the Ganges; (the wheels of) his victorious chariot, that keeps off the attainment of desires of even the ascetics, became her exceedingly plump hips; the two plantain-trees which were like his pillars of victory, were the very essence of beauty, and had hindered the practice (of penance) of sages, became her two thighs; the lotus with thousand petals that formed his umbrella, became her two feet; and the flowers that served as his missiles, the other limbs. Like the earth, borne on his hoods by Śesha, that Vasumatî, fondled with endless enjoyments, was enjoyed so as to taste all sorts of pleasures by the king of the Magadhas, residing in Pushpapura. which surpassed (in grandeur) even the city of the immortals (*i.e.* Amaràvatî, the capital of Indra).

That king had three hereditary ministers, named Dharmapála, Padmodbhava and Sitavarman, who were ever at his service ( *lit.* very obedient ), and who, on account of their deep political insight, quite easily disposed of matters that would have demanded serious attention even on the part of Bṛihaspati. Of these, Sitavarman had two sons, Sumati and Satyavarman ; Dharmapála had three, Sumantra, Sumitra and Kámapála ; and Padmodbhava had two, Suśruta and Ratnodbhava. Of these, Satyavarman, who was pious, realizing the worthlessness of worldly life, went to foreign lands, desiring to visit holy places. Kámapâla, who was ill-trained and attached to parasites, actors and courtesans, wandered over the earth, disregarding the advice of his father and his elder brother. Ratnodbhava, too, being an expert merchant, crossed (carried on trade by) the sea. The other sons of the ministers when their fathers were dead (*lit.*, had become the guests of the city of Indra), succeeded to their offices (*lit.* remained doing the duties as before).

Once, the lord of the Magadhas, who had set his sharp arrows on the row of the heads (*or*, crowns) of princes in the countless battles he fought with them on account of his skill in the use of great weapons of various kinds, marched out in great rage, thirsting for fight, and accompanied by the fourfold army, that sorely taxed the might of the hoods of Śesha by the weight of the earth which sank under its burden, against the King of Málwâ, Mánasára, who was the worker of havoc in every fresh battle and whose pride and power were at their height ;—he (Râjahaṃsa), who, by the deep sound of his kettle-drums which easily quelled the ocean's pride of its loud roar, made the guardian-elephants of the quarters stagger, as they were seized by an overpowering terror, being forced to hear a loud noise. The king of Mâlwá also, who was the spirit of war incarnate, marched forth to meet him with a determined purpose, accompanied by many arrays of war-elephants. Then there was a close fight between them, wherein warriors struck one another with weapons and with hands, wherein the army was slaughtered on both the sides, and wherein all space in the quarters was deafened by the sound of drums that drowned all other sounds in the aerial region, beneath a cloud of dust thickly spread over the surface of the sky, which (dust) arose from the earth as it was struck up by the hoofs of the horses of the chariots ( *or*, of the horses and by the chariots ), the root of which was washed away by the streams of rut oozing from the temples of the arrays of elephants, and which looked as if it were a cloth-*Mandap*, screening the number of Apsarasas that had come ( in the sky ) for choosing new lovers for themselves ( from among the fallen warriors ). In it Râjahaṃsa captured alive the king of Mâlwâ, whose army was completely destroyed ; but he re-instated him on his throne, out of mercy.

Râjahaṃsa now ruled the earth engirdled by the oceans, without a rival. As he was not blessed with progeny, he devoted all his time to the worship of Nârâyaṇa, the one Creator of the universe. Now one day his chief queen saw at daybreak a happy dream, saying to her : "Get a fruit of the desire-fulfilling creeper through (*or*, along with) your lord." She then bore a fœtus which was like the flower (*i.e.* productive of the fruit) of the desires of her lord. Thereupon the King, too, who excelled even Indra in riches, having invited all his princely friends, celebrated with great splendour befitting his riches and desires, the *Sîmanta* festival of his queen.

Once, while seated on the throne in the audience-hall, with his well-wishing (*or*, trusty) friends, ministers and family-priest, the King, who lacked not merits, was humbly informed by the door-keeper with his folded hands touching his forehead, that an ascetic, worthy of being worshipped with special preparation by His Majesty, and desirous of being admitted to His Majesty's presence, had arrived at the door of the court. Permitted by him (the king), he conducted the ascetic into the royal presence. The King, looking at him as he was coming, recognized him well to be one of his spies in disguise, dismissed all his followers, and, accompanied by his ministers, asked him with a smile as he humbly bowed before him—"Well, ascetic, do you communicate to us the information gathered by you while wandering over the country in a disguise." The spy, who was able to wander over the world, replied with folded hands :—"Your Majesty, in profound obedience to Your royal command, putting on this blameless garb of a hermit (*i e.*, which leaves no room for suspicion) I entered the capital of the King of Mâlwá; and living there with the utmost secrecy, I collected all the information with regard to the King and returned here. Having suffered a defeat at the hands of Your Majesty in a battle in which all his warriors were killed (*lit.*, which proved an obstacle in the way of the long life of his warriors), proud Mánasára, with his heart touched by (*i.e.* filled with) shame and full of cruel thoughts (of vengeance), propitiated the imperishable Maheśvara, the lord of Kâlî, abiding in the shrine of Mahâkâla. Having obtained from the deity, pleased by the power (fervour) of his penance, a formidable mace having power to slay one mighty enemy, he, looking upon himself as a matchless warrior, is preparing in the height of his pride to march against Your Majesty. Now Your Majesty will decide what further to do." When the ministers heard this, they determined what was proper for the King to do, and said to him—"Lord, the enemy is coming with the God (Śiva) for his helper, against whom there is no remedy. It is not, therefore, advisable on our part to fight at this time; the fort should be at once rosorted to." Though thus repeatedly requested by them, the King, distinguished by not a little pride, disdained their counsel as unworthy of being acted upon, and determined to offer a counter-fight. Mânasára, powerful on account of the weapon given by God Śiva, took the lead of the warriors who were bent on fighting, and, equipped with all the necessaries (of war), easily advanced into Magadha. Informed of this, the ministers prevailed upon the King, the lord of Magadha, with great difficulty, and lodged the women of the palace, guarded by the hereditary force, in a place impregnable to the enemies, in the heart of the Vindhya forest. Râjahaṃsa marched out with great speed with a select and intrepid force, and opposed his enemy, exasperated (on that account). In the battle, which took place between these two warriors who had formed enmity towards each other, and which filled with wonder the heavenly beings that had come to observe the fight out of curiosity, the King of Málwâ, desirous of victory, hurled the mace previously given to him by Śiva, against the King of the Magadhas, who had equalled the lord of immortals (*viz.* Indra) in battles which were graced by his steady use of various weapons. Though splintered by a number of sharp arrows, the mace, through the infallibility of the decree of Śiva, killed the charioteer, and left the king senseless in the chariot; the horses, that were unwounded, being freed from the control of reins, ran off with the chariot, fortunately into the very thickets that had given shelter to that King's household. The King of Mâlwá, now crowned with success, overran the great kingdom of the Magadhas and took his own residence in Pushpapura.

The ministers of Râjahaṃsa exhausted with wounds (*or*, strokes) from numerous weapons, but fortunately not dead, having revived owing to the breezes at the close of the night, somehow took heart and sought for the King on all sides; but not finding him, they approached the Queen in a miserable plight. Having heard from them of the destruction of the whole army and the disappearance of the King, Vasumatî, dejected and plunged in the ocean of sorrow, determined to follow her lord (in death); but the ministers and the family-priest dissuaded her from her purpose, with soothing words, saying—"O blessed Queen, the King's death is uncertain; moreover, there resides in your womb a beautiful and delicate prince, who, as predicted by the astrologers, is to uproot the enemy who is puffed up with pride, and is to be the supreme lord of the whole earth. So it will be improper on your part to put an end to your life now." Then at this, though uneasy at heart, she stood silent for a while. At midnight, when the eyes of the attendants were sealed with sleep, the Queen, unable to bear the excessive grief (*lit.*, to get over the ocean of grief), being left alone, slowly and noiselessly crossed the place where the camp lay and came to the Vaṭa-tree hard by, where, the chariot being entangled, the horses of the King, completely exhausted on account of the journey and fatigued by running while drawing the chariot and unable to proceed further, had halted before. Having prepared a noose with the half of her upper-garment, as a means of death, tied to the branch of the tree, which was as it were the line of death, that beautiful lady, who was desirous of dying and who by the sweetness of her voice surpassed (*lit.* rendered unmelodious the note of) the cuckoo, exclaimed mournfully, with her throat choked with tears—"Lord of Earth, who by your beauty equalled Cupid, may you yourself be my husband in my next life also." The King of Magadha, who had fainted owing to the loss of profuse blood, but who had just gained consciousness by the touch of the flood of the rays of the moon, heard these words, and making quite sure that they were of his queen, gently called out to her with sweet words. She, with her lotus-like face blooming with the overwhelming joy of her heart, hastily came to him, and devouring him with her winkless eyes that had fasted as it were, loudly called out to her ministers and family-priest and showed him to them. The ministers praised the greatness of luck, touched the lotus-like feet of the King with their foreheads, and said—"Lord, the horses, when the charioter was killed, brought the chariot, with great speed, to the wood." The King related to them that in the battle wherein the bulk of his army was killed, he fainted, being struck with the mace which the relentless Mánasára, who had propitiated Śiva, had discharged at him, and that it was but just then that he was brought back to his senses in that forest by the cool breezes of the early morning. Then the ministers observed a festival, and in good time, when fate showed itself to be favourable, brought the king to the camp, took out all the tips of arrows (from his body), and quickly made him, whose lotus-like face (now) bloomed, free from his wounds. And now at the desire of the ministers, the wise queen Vasumatî consoled, in sweet words, the King, whose valour was set aside by adverse fate, who was looking extremely miserable and whose agony was excessive. She said—"Lord, since Your Majesty, the most illustrious and greatest of the whole host of kings, has now to reside in the midst of this Vindhya forest, prosperity that shines, being comparable with water-bubbles, rises and disappears suddenly like a flash of lightning; all affairs must, therefore, be regarded as depending on destiny. Moreover, formerly, Hariśchandra, Rámachandra and other innumerable kings, who with their riches equalled Indra, after fully experiencing adversity as a consequence of ill-luck, enjoyed their kingdoms afterwards for a long time. Similar will be the case of Your Majesty. Now, being free from mental affliction, you should pass some time being reconciled to fate (*or*, with the consolation that your misery is due to providence only)."

Then Ràjahaṃsa, accompanied by the whole of his army, went to see a holy sage, named Vámadeva, resplendent with penance and the means of gaining his object. He bowed to him, and being hospitably received by him, he told him everything. Having lived for some time in his hermitage, which removed all his fatigue, Rájahaṃsa, who was an ornament to the lunar race, and who was laconic in his speech, desirous of regaining his kingdom, said to the sage—"Revered Sir, Mánasára, having defeated me with the power of luck that was excessively great, has now been enjoying the kingdom which is rightfully my own. I have now approached your reverence devoted to asceticism, with the thought that I, too, like him, shall be able to uproot my enemy through your all-saving compassion, by practising severe religious austerities." Then the omniscient sage replied—"Friend, there is no necessity for practising penance which causes emaciation of the body. The prince, that lies in the womb of Vasumatî, will assuredly turn out to be the exterminator of all your foes; remain quiet for some time." These words were confirmed in their truth at that very time by a voice in the air. The King, too, waited (*i. e.*, remained inactive), fully relying upon the words of the sage.

Then after the completion of the period of pregnancy, Vasumatî, at an auspicious moment, gave birth to a son endowed with all the auspicious signs. Under the guidance of the family-priest, who equalled even Brahmá by his spiritual effulgence, the King who knew what was be done bestowed the name Rájavâhana on his delicate son who looked bright on occount of his birth-rites being performed, and with child's ornaments. At the same time there were born sons of great beauty, having the lustre of the rising moon, and endowed with long life, to the King's four ministers. The son of Sumati was named Pramati; of Sumantra, Mitragupta; of Sumitra, Mantragupta; and of Suśruta, Viśruta. Rájavâhana grew up, together with his friends, the sons of the ministers, enjoying the sports of childhood.

One day a hermit affectionately delivered a young boy, that gave delight to the eyes and was decked with the auspicious marks of a prince, to the King, and said,—"O King, being out in the forest one day to bring the *Kus'a* grass and holy sticks, I saw a young woman, who looked helpless and obviously miserable, and who was shedding tears. Being asked by me why she was weeping in that dreary forest, she wiped off her tears with her fingers and replied with sobs—" Revered sage, while Prahâravarman, the king of Mithila', who had conquered ( surpassed ) even Cupid by his beauty and who by his fame had occupied the assembly of gods, was staying for some time with his queen and sons in Pushpapura, for the celebrations of the *Sîmanta* festival of the queen of his friend, the King of Magadha, the King of Mâlwâ, who had propitiated Śiva with his devotion, marched upon the King of Magadha. In the great battle that ensued between these two great warriors, Prahâravarman, the king of Mithilâ, who was helping his friend, was captured, his army being destroyed, by the victorious enemy, but was released by him, owing to his own religious merit and out of mercy. He returned to his own capital with that portion of his army which had escaped being slaughtered and which was spiritless. Then, while passing by a perilous forest-path, he was impetuously attacked by a party of Śabaras superior in strength. Meeting with this formidable obstruction on the way, he effected his escape, the ladies of his harem being safely escorted by his hereditary troops. I and my daughter, who were engaged as nurses to the King's twin sons, were unable to keep pace with him in his rapid flight; while there (in the wood), a certain tiger, as if fury incarnate, and open-mouthed, hastily came up to devour me. I, who was terrified, stumbled over a projecting stone and fell down; the boy, who dropped from my hands, lay hidden beneath the carcass of a brown cow. An arrow let fly from a bow deprived the tiger of his life as he was furiously dragging that carcass. The Śabaras took away—I know not where—the boy (beautiful) with the moving locks of hair; nor do I know where my daughter, who had charge of the other prince, went. I, who lay in a trance, was found by a kind-hearted cowherd who took me to his hut and healed me of my wounds. Thus recovered, I now wish to go to the King again, but I am now perplexed (do not know what to do), on account of my helpless condition and of the ignorance of the whereabouts of my daughter." At this she departed, adding that she would go even alone to her master. I, too, experiencing the sorrow caused by the distress of your friend, the king of Mithilâ, and desiring to seek his son, the scion of his family, approached at the time a beautiful temple of Chaṇḍiká. There I addressed the Kirátas, who were desirous of making an oblation of a fair child to the goddess, to ensure continual success of the sort they had then achieved, and who were saying among themselves—"We shall kill him with a sword by suspending him by the branch of a tree, or by means of a number of sharp arrows aimed at him after fixing his feet by digging (a hole) in the surface of sand, or by causing young dogs to kill him as he will be running on all fours." I said—"Valiant foresters, I am an old Bráhmaṇa, who missed my way as I passed with my son through this wood where a journey is perilous. I left him somewhere in the shade, and went some distance to recover the track. [When I returned I had lost him]. I do not know, even after a careful search, where he went or by whom he was taken. Several days have passed without my seeing his face. What am I to do or where am I to go to? Was he not seen by you?" They said, "Revered Brâhmaṇa, we have here a boy; if he be really your son, then you may take him away." With these words they luckily handed him over to me. I gave them many blessings, took the child, and revived him by means of cool water and other remedies, and have brought him unhesitatingly to you; may you, who are in the place of a father to him, protect him, of long life!" The King, in his pleasure at the sight of that prince, forgot to some extent his grief at the distress of his friend, named him Upahávaravarman, and brought him up like his own son Râjaváhana.

One holy day, as Ra'jahaṃsa was going for bath at a holy place, along a path close by the habitation of the Śabaras, he, observing child of incomparable form (beauty), fondled by a woman, out of curiosity asked her—"Fair woman, this boy, of a charming form and endowed with princely qualities, does not seem to be one of your own race. Kindly tell me, in truth, (as to) whose eyes he used to delight and and for what reason he came to be in your charge." The Sa'bara woman bowed down and gracefully replied,—Sire, while the army of the Śabaras was making away with all the property of the king of Mithilá, Indra's peer, as he happened to be on the road near their residence, my husband took this child and gave him to me, and thus he grew up." The King who knew his duty, on hearing this concluded that he was the second prince as told by the sage, and having prevailed on the woman by persuasion and gifts ( to relinquish the child ), called him Apaha'ravarman and gave him over to his Queen to be taken care of.

Somadevas'arman, the pupil of the sage Va'madeva, one day placed a boy before the King and said—" King, as was returning, after having bathed at Ra'matîrtha, I saw on the forest-ground this child of a bright from who was held up (in her hands) by a certain woman ; and I respectfully asked her—" Old woman, who are you and why are you wandering with great difficulty in this forest bearing this child ?" The old lady replied—" Excellent ascetic, in the island called Kálayavana there lives an eminent merchant, of great opulence, Kálagupta by name. A handsome merchant called Ratnodbhava, the son of a minister of the King of Magadha, who had come from this island, who was the abode of (all) amiable qualities, and who had wandered over the circle of the earth, married his daughter, named Suvṛittâ, who gave joy to the eyes (of all), and was honoured with an abundance of rich presents by his father-in-law. In course of time his fair wife became pregnant ; then Ratnodbhava, with a desire to see his brother, somehow prevailed upon his father-in-law, and having got on board a ship with this (young lady) of tremulous eyes, set off for Pushpapura ; the boat, lashed by a series of angry breakers, sank in the ocean. I who was engaged as her nurse bore the lady, dull on account of the weight of her (developed) fœtus, on my hands; and getting upon a plank fortunately reached shore-land. I do not know whether Ratnodbhava with his friends was drowned there or reached the coast by some means. Suvṛittâ, having suffered the utmost pain, gave birth to a son to-day in this forest. She is lying under a tree with a thick shade, senseless on account of the throes of child-birth. As it was not possible to live in this lonely forest, I who set out in search of a way leading to some country, also took the infant with me, thinking that it would be improper to leave the baby beside her, as she was unconscious." Just at that moment a wild elephant appeared on the scene. Frightened at the sight she dropped the boy and ran away. I hid myself in a neighbouring thicket of creepers, and stood awaiting the issue of events. As the elephant picked up the fallen infant with his trunk, as if it were a mouthful of sprouts, a lion, with a terrific roar, fell upon the animal with a fierce grip. The boy, hurled at once into the sky by the elephant overpowered with fear, fell down. As he had a long lease of life, he was caught by a monkey that was seated on a lofty branch of a tree, taking him for some ripe fruit, but was thrown at the root of a stretching branch on finding that he was other than a fruit. The monkey too went somewhere; the infant, on account of its innate vitality, bore all that trouble. The lion, having killed the elephant, likewise disappeared somewhere. I, too, issuing forth from my creeper-house, gently took down the lustrous child from the tree and went in quest of the woman. Not finding her in the forest I brought the child with me, presented it to my preceptor, and by his direction have brought it to your presence." The King, who was filled with great wonder at the simultaneous misfortune of all his friends, feeling concerned as to what might have become of Ratnodbhava, named the infant Pushpodbhava, and having imparted all the particulars to Suśruta, consigned the son of his younger brother to his care, experiencing sorrow and pleasure at the same time.

Another day Vasumatî, holding a child to her breast, came to her lord. Asked by him as to where the child came from, she replied—"Lord, last night a certain celestial damsel, having placed an infant boy before me and awakened me who was under the seal of sleep, said respectfully—"O Queen, I am a Yaksha girl, Táravalî by name, the daughter of Maṇibhadra and the beloved of Kâmapâla, the son of your minister Dharmapála. With the consent of the King of the Yakshas, I have brought this my son (to you) that he might serve your son Râjavâhana, who is to be in future, the sovereign-lord of the whole earth begirt by the circle of the oceans, and the store of spotless fame. Kindly bring him up who looks like Cupid (the mind-born)." The Yaksha female of bewitching eyes who was respectfully received by me with my eyes dilated with astonishment, also vanished from view. Râjahaṃsa, whose mind was filled with wonder at Kámapála's union with a Yaksha damsel, having named his brother's son Arthapâla and informed him of all particulars, called his minister Sumitra, the delighter of his friends, and gave him in his charge.

On another day, a pupil of Vámadeva, living in his hermitage, brought (*lit.* announced) a boy who was delicate like a flower and who far surpassed even Cupid in form, to the King who had obtained the glory of the gods, and said—"O Monarch, in the course of my pilgrimage to the holy places, I went to the bank of the Kaverî, and there seeing an old woman weeping bitterly, having placed on her lap a child with flowing locks, I asked her who she was, whose eyes the child delighted (*i e.,* son it was), why she came into the forest and what was the cause of her grief. She wiped off her tears with her hands, and thinking that I was able to take out the dart of sorrow from her heart, (thus) narrated the cause of her grief—'O Bráhmaṇa youth, Satyavarmá, the younger son of Sitavarmá, the minister of Rájahaṃsa, came to this spot through the desire of visiting holy places. He married, in a certain village (that was a grant to a Bráhmaṇa), Kálî, the daughter of a Bráhmaṇa; she proving barren, he espoused her sister Gaurî, who had the lustre of gold, and by her he had a son. Kálî, out of jealousy, one day took the child with me, his nurse, to this river under some pretext, and pushed us into the stream. Holding up the boy with one hand and swimming (*or,* floating) with the other, I caught hold of the branch of a tree that was borne down by the current of the river and laid the child upon it. As I was thus being borne away by the current of the river, I was bitten by a deadly (*or,* black) serpent clinging to the tree; the tree to which I had clung reached the bank at this spot. I weep with the thought that there is no one to take care of this child in this forest, after I shall be dead on account of the virulence of the poison.' Just then she fell to the ground (senseless), owing to all her limbs being affected (enveloped) by the flames of the virulent poison spreading within. I, although my heart was touched with pity, was not able to undo the effect of the poison by means of spells; so I looked for a particular medicinal herb in the neighbouring bowers; but when I came back I found her dead (*lit.* with her life departed). Thereupon I consigned her body to flames, full of sorrow, took this helpless child, and seeing that it was impossible to look for Satyavarmá as I had not heard at the time of hearing his story the name of the village where he lived, I have brought it to Your Majesty, thinking that you alone are the sole protector of the son of your minister." The King, on hearing this, was sad at heart at the uncertainty of the life of Satyavarmá, named the boy Somadatta, and gave him in charge of his uncle Sumati ; and he too brought him up with particular care, considering him as his own brother come back.

Rájaváhana, who had practised riding different vehicles and enjoyed the sports of childhood in the company of the boys thus gathered together, had all his purificatory rites performed in due order beginning with the tonsure and the thread-ceremony. Seeing that the Kumáras had attained from their respective teachers the knowledge of all the scripts (*or*, alphabets), cleverness in the languages of all countries, proficiency in the knowledge of the group of the Vedas with their six auxiliaries, a deep insight in poetry, dramatic art, legends, narratives, history, and the multitude of the Puráṇas with diverse tales ; a clever acquaintance with Law, Grammar, Astrology, Logic, Mîmáṃsá and all other sciences, as well as with the intricacies of the political science as taught by Cháṇakya, Kámandaka and others ; skill in playing upon lutes and all other musical instruments ; attractive excellence in music and poetics ; deftness in the use of gems with medicinal virtue, spells, medicine and the province of magic ; skill in riding elephants, horses, and other vehicles ; adroitness in handling various weapons ; and perfection in thieving, gambling and such other crooked arts ; also that they were in blooming youth and active in all undertakings, the King at once obtained very great joy at the thought that he was beyond the reach of all his foes.

## UCHCHHVÂSA II.

On one occasion Vàmadeva approached the King who bent before him in reverence, and who was surrounded by the group of the young men who were expert in all the arts, who caused their loveliness to be confounded with the beauty of (*i.e.* who looked beautiful like) Cupid, who had formed a relation of fraternity with one another, who surpassed by their daring even Kàrttikeya, who were delicate, and whose palms were marked with signs, such as the victorious flag, (royal) umbrella, the thunderbolt and the sword. After accepting the worship offered by the King and closely embracing the band of young men whose dark side-locks of hair looked like bees settling upon the two lotuses of his feet and who were to root out their foes (in future), he uttered benedictions upon them and addressed the King in a few and earnest words—" Lord of the earth, your son with his noble (*lit.* praiseworthy) companions is enjoying youth which has enhanced his beauty and which is as it were the very fruit of your desires. This is, indeed, the time for him to set out with his companions for the conquest of the quarters; so let Ràjaváhana, who is now capable of enduring all hardships, start on his tour of the conquest of the quarters." The princes, lovely like Cupid, with valour like that of Ráma and others, capable of reducing their foes to ashes by their (mere) anger, and surpassing even wind in impetuosity, made the King hopeful of success, by marching on for battle. Appointing the other youths as his ministers (*or*, helpers) and having given him proper advice, Rájahaṃsa, on an auspicious occasion, sent the Prince with his attendants for the conquest (of the whole world).

Rájaváhana, noticing good omens (on the way), after having gone over some distance, entered the heart of the Vindhya forest. There he saw a man covered with scars of wounds inflicted by weapons, whose body was as hard as iron, whose Bráhmaṇahood was inferable from his sacred thread, (but) who clearly displayed the valour of a Kiráta and who was hideous to look at. Rájavâhana, on being hospitably received by him, said—" Well, man, why is it that you reside alone in this dreary wood in the midst of the Vindhya forest which is destitute of human habitation and is fit only for wild beasts, and which is haunted by fierce animals (*or*, wherein it is dangerous to move)? This sacred thread lying across your shoulder pronounces you to be a Bráhmaṇa; while these scars of weapons (*i.e.* wounds) indicate (*lit.* lead one to infer) the course of life of a Kiráta. Tell me what this can be." The stranger, considering that Rájaváhana, being so highly lustrous, could not indeed be an ordinary person possessing ordinary (human) prowess, and, coming to know his name and birth from his friends, related to him his story as follows—" Prince, in this wood reside many who are Bráhmaṇas (only) in name, who, led by barbarians, go in quest of sinful acts, and eat their food, foregoing the study of the lores such as the Vedas and others, ignoring the observances of their tribes, and setting aside their religious and social duties such as the observance of truth, purity and the like. Of one of these I am the son, of questionable (evil) habits, named Mátaṅga. With a party of the Kirátas I used to harry the neighbouring country, seize the wealthy villagers with their women and children, and, having brought them to this forest, I used to put them in custody, taking all their wealth; and thus I led a life of lawlessness (*or*, haughtiness) and cruelty. On one occasion, I observed a party of my associates in a dreary wood on the point of putting to death a Bráhmaṇa, and overcome with compassion I said to them—"Forbear, ye villains, kill not a Bráhmaṇa." They, with their eyes red with anger, reviled me in various ways. Unable to brook their harsh words I fought with them for a long time in order to save the Bráhmaṇa; but being struck by them I lost my life. Thereupon I went to the City of the Dead, and there beholding Yama seated upon a lofty throne studded with splendid jewels in the midst of the assembly and surrounded on all sides by men, in a restored form, I fell prostrate before him; he looked at me, and calling his minister named Chitragupta, said to him—"Minister, this man's last hour is not yet come; though living a censurable life, he has died in the defence of a Bráhmaṇa. Henceforth there will arise in him a strong desire to do holy deeds, now that all his former sins have been effaced. Let him behold the various tortures here undergone by the greatest sinners and then let him go back to his former body." Chitragupta, too, showed me the various spots where the sinners were being fastened to red-hot iron pillars, hurled into huge caldrons of scalding oil, had their limbs shattered with clubs or pealed with sharp chisels (*or*, hatchets) and then giving me holy counsel, dismissed me. Restored to that same former body, I found myself in the vast wilderness attended by the (same) Bráhmaṇa whom I had rescued and who was applying cool remedies to me; I lay there for a time sleeping on a stone. After that my agnatic relations, who had heard the story (of my encounter), quickly arrived, and carried me home and dressed my wounds. The grateful Bráhmaṇa taught me the alphabet, explained in detail various Śâstras and the Tantras, gave me full instructions as regards the rules of good conduct which annihilate sin, and told me the proper way to worship Śiva (*lit.* the moon-crested god) who can be perceived only by the eye of knowledge, and having accepted the worship I paid to him, left me. From that time, being free from the taint (of sin), I quitted the group of the families of my relatives who were associating with the Kirâtas, and have been living here in this forest, mentally meditating upon the One God of all the worlds, Śiva (*lit.* the god who bears on his head the crescent-moon as an ornament). Lord, I have some secret to communicate to you in private; please follow me." Having led him away from his friends, he thus continued in private—"Towards the close of last night Śiva approached me in a dream, and awakening me whose eyes were sealed with sleep, said with a beaming face to me as I bowed humbly before him—"Mátaṅga, in the region along the bank of the river that flows through the Daṇḍaka forest, and behind the Sphaṭikaliṅga that is worshipped by the Siddhas and the Sádhyas, and near the stone marked with the rows of the foot-prints of the daughter of the Himálaya mountain, is a chasm, which is as it were the door (*lit.* mouth) of a propitious fate Entering it, take the copper-plate that is placed there as though it were a command of Fate, and perform the rites prescribed thereon as though it were gaining victory over Fate, and you will be the sovereign of Pátála; the Prince who is to help you in this undertaking will come here to-day or to-morrow." And Your Honour's coming here happens quite in conformity with his injunctions. Now please give me, who am well pleased and desirous of securing means, your aid." Rájaváhana assented, and at mid-night, leaving his friends who were in the power of sleep, went, accompanied by Mátaṅga who bowed his head before him, to another wood. Thereafter, when his followers woke in the morning and missed him completely, they were sad at heart; they carefully searched for him in various parts of the forest; but, not finding him, they, who were very hardy, departed separating from one another for going to various places with a desire to find him out, after having appointed their place of meeting.

Mátaṅga, full of joy at heart at being protected by the Prince, the world's matchless warrior, fearlessly entered the chasm made out by means of the signs described to him by the moon crested Śiva, took the copper plate and with it penetrated the path to Pátála. There, in the vicinity of a city near a tank in a sportive garden with full-blown lotuses (*or*, with swans swimming about), Mátaṅga offered a sacrifice with oblations of various kinds prepared in accordance with the directions of Śiva, and whilst Rájavahana was looking on with astonishment and ready to remove obstacles, he (Mátaṅga), after reciting some *mantras*, cast his holy frame into fire well-kindled with the *samidhs* and ghee, and obtained a celestial form with the dazzling brightness of lightning. After this a damsel, an ornament to womankind in all the three worlds, decorated with a number of ornaments richly set with gems, and attended with a train of modest female friends, gently approached with the gait of a swan and presented to the excellent Bráhmaṇa a splendid jewel; and to his inquiry as to who she was, she, with the impassioned accents of a cuckoo, thus very gently replied with folded hands—" O worthy Bráhmaṇa, I am the daughter of the King of the Asuras. My name is Kálindî. My father of mighty prowess, who was the ruler of this world, was destroyed (*lit.* made a guest of the capital of Yama) by Vishṇu impatient of his (my father's) fame, in a fight in which the gods were routed. A Siddha ascetic, seeing that I was plunged in an ocean of grief at his loss, compassionately announced to me that a man, unknown to me and appearing in a heavenly form, would become my husband and be the protector of the whole Pátála. On hearing his prediction, I long awaited your sight, as the female Châtaka awaits the rainy season, looking up for the roaring of clouds. On learning of your arrival which is as it were the fruit of my desires, I have come here with the concurrence of my ministers, the very pillars of the state, and with the guidance of my mind impelled by love; so kindly accept the Royalty of this Nether World and make me her rival wife." Mátaṅga, too, with the assent of Rájavábana, married that youthful damsel, and being exceedingly pleased by his acquisition of the celestial lady, accepted the kingdom of Pátála and attained (thereby) the highest joy.

Râjavâhana, wishing to go to the earth with a desire to see his friends from whom he had stolen away, asked Mátaṅga, who had followed him to some distance, to go back, receiving, from him who was pleased with the help rendered to him, the jewel that was given to him by Kâlindî and that had the virtue of dispelling the pain caused by thirst, hunger and the like; and he came out by the path of the chasm. Not finding his friends there, he wandered over the earth (in search of them). In the course of his wanderings he came to a garden in a suburb of Ujjain, and as he was about to rest there he saw a man, who had come to the garden, who was mounted in a palanquin (*or*, on a swing) with his wife and attended by his relatives. He, too, with his mind swelling with ecstatic joy, and his lotus-like face beaming, exclaimed—"Oh, this is my master, Ràjaváhana, the ornament of the lunar race, and the store of spotless fame! Owing to extreme good luck I have come to be at his lotus-like feet all of a sudden! It now has been a great festival to my eyes!" With these words he quickly alighted from the swing, and, advancing gracefully with hasty steps indicative of excessive joy, touched with his head, from which the wreath of blooming Mállikâ flowers dropped down, the two lotus-like feet of Ràjavâhana who had advanced three or four steps to recieve him. The Prince, with eyes filled with the tears of great joy, closely embraced him whose body was thrilled (with emotion), and exclaimed—"Ah, here is our Somadatta!" Then, sitting under the cool shade of some Puṃnága tree, the Prince affectionately said to him—"Friend, in what place and in what manner were you staying so long? Where do you go to now, who is this damsel, and how did you come to have this retinue? Explain (all)." Somadatta, too, folding his lotus-like hands so as to resemble a bud, now free from the excessively burning (*lit.* violent) fever of anxiety on account of the meeting with his friend, modestly narrated (thus) the account of his own wanderings:—

---

## UCHCHHVÂSA III.

"Lord, whilst wandering (in quest of Your Highness) I, who had a strong desire to serve these lotus-like feet, was oppressed with thirst; while drinking the water of a river, cool and shaded by creepers, in a forest-region, I saw there a gem of a very brilliant appearance. I took it and walked some distance, when, being unable to proceed owing to the sun's growing excessively scorching, I entered a temple that was in that same forest; in it I saw an old Bráhmana with a sad face and surrounded by several sons. With my compassion roused, I asked him if he fared well. With a face turned pale on account of misery, and full of great hopes, the Bráhmaṇa replied—"Sir, I live here in this temple of Śiva, protecting these motherless sons of mine by various means, and feeding them on food obtained by begging in this barren spot." Asked as to the country over which the master of of the army lying encamped there ruled, his name, and the cause of his coming there, the Bráhmaṇa answered—"Gentle sir, Mattakála, King of the Láṭa country, having repeatedly heard of the daughter of Vîraketu, the King of this country, Vámalochaná by name and a jewel of matchless beauty among young women, asked for her; but his suit being rejected, he besieged his capital, when, being greatly terrified, Vîraketu also gave her up to him as a rich present. The Láṭa King (Mattakâla), delighted at heart by the acquisition of the young lady, determined to espouse her in his own capital and being on his way back to his country has encamped with his army in this forest out of an earnest desire to hunt. The minister of Vîraketu, Mánapála by name, who regards self-respect as his treasure, appointed to escort the Princess, encamped separately with his four-fold army, and being pained at heart by the humiliation of his master, secretly plotted treason against him." Finding that the Bráhmaṇa had many sons, was learned, poor, old, and so worthy of a gift, I, with my mind filled with pity, gave him the jewel. At that, with his face beaming with very great joy, he pronounced many blessings upon me and departed to some place. Exhausted with the fatigue of the journey, I enjoyed sound sleep in that place. Soon after, the Bráhmaṇa, with his arms pinioned behind him, and with his body marked with slashes of whips, came there under the guard of a number of swordsmen, and pointed at me with the words—"This is the thief." The king's officers quitted the Bráhmaṇa, and without listening to my explanation as to how I got the jewel, bound me, who was quite fearless, closely with ropes, and taking me to a prison pointed out to me a number of people in fetters, saying—'These are your comrades,' and put my feet also in chains. Being at a loss to know what to do next, and suffering from a distress which offered no hope of extrication, I addressed them—"Men of intrepid valour, for what reason are you suffering from the misery, difficult to be got over, of a prison life? I was pointed out by these as your associate; what does it mean?" Seeing me in that condition and having told me the story of the king of Láṭa that I had heard from the Bráhmaṇa, the valiant robbers further said—"We are the servants of Mánapála, Vîraketu's minister. At his command we broke by night through a subterranean passage into the apartment of the king of Láṭa with intention to kill him; but, being disappointed at not finding him there, we stole a large quantity of valuables and entered a dense forest. Next day many attendants of the King, following the track of our foot-steps, came upon us as we had the mass of wealth in our possession, and surrounding us from all sides, closely tied us and led us near (the King). At the time of recounting all the stolen things, they, missing a precious (*lit.* priceless) jewel, put us in chains in order to kill us for the recovery of the gem." From what I heard of the gem and the place where it was found, I concluded that it was the same gem, and told them how my bad plight was due to the gift of it to the Bràhmaṇa, also my birth, name, and how I wandered in quest of Your Honour; and by means of mutual conversations suited to the occasion, I contracted their friendship. Then at midnight, having broken my chains as well as theirs, and being followed by them, I took hold of the weapons of the guards who were asleep, and putting to flight, with an easy display of sharp valour, those of the city-guards who faced us, we entered the camp of Mànapála. When he heard from his servants the account of my family, and my self-respect and valour shown at that time, he treated me with respect. The following day, men sent by Mattakála came to Mànapála and uttered before him these exceedingly harsh words—"Minister, some daring thieves coming to my palace through a subterranean passage, and having stolen a good deal of wealth, have entered your camp. Hand them over to me, or else a great disaster will follow." On hearing these words, the minister with his eyes reddened with ire, sent them back with this reproof—"Who is this King of Láṭa? Of what avail is his friendship to us, and what are we to gain by serving that pauper?" They reproduced the very vaunting words of Mánapála before Mattakálá; though enraged, the Láṭa King, through the pride of power of his arms, marched for fight with a few soldiers. Proud Mánapála, who had eady determined to fight and was fully prepared with all his soldiers, fearlessly marched out, strongly desiring the contest. I also was respectfully provided by the minister with a chariot with good steeds and a skilful charioteer, a very strong breast-plate, a suitable bow with a pair of quivers full of various kinds of arrows, and various arms required for fighting; with these I equipped myself for fight, and followed the minister who had made ready to root out his enemy, relying on my prowess. Leaving the two armies that were fighting fiercely out of mutual spite, I struck the foe by showering arrows upon him with the quick and dexterous movement of my arms. Then I led near the foe my chariot with very fleet horses, and overtaking his chariot with a quick jump, I cut off his head. He having fallen dead on the battle-field, his remaining troops fled, and the minister filled with (*lit.* bent under) ecstatic joy took all kinds of war-prizes such as horses, elephants and others, and honoured me in many ways. The King, having fully heard this account from the attendant dispatched by Mánapàla, was highly pleased, and came to honour me; and being struck with my valour, with the full assent of his minister and relatives he gave his daughter to me in marriage on an auspicious day, celebrating the event with great festivities. Appointed as heir-apparent, I gratified the King's mind day by day, and though being in company of this beautiful lady I was enjoying various kinds of pleasures, still my heart experiencing the distress easily to be felt owing to the dart of the pain of your separation, I came to-day with my wife to this region, the fruit whereof is the sight of a friend, by the direction of a Siddha (seer) in order to propitiate Śiva who resides in this temple of Mahákâla. Through the mercy of Śiva (*lit.* the lord of Párvatî) who is kind to his devotees, I have now obtained the excess of joy at the sight of your lotus-like feet."

On hearing this, Rájaváhana praised him highly for his valour, and censuring Fate for the punishment he suffered without any fault of his, he related to him in due order his own account. Just then, seeing before him Pushpodbhava, Rájaváhana in great hurry embraced him very closely as he stood before him with folded hands after touching his feet with his own forehead, and with his large eyes filled with the tears of joy, said to Somadatta—"Friend Somadatta, here is our Pushpodbhava !" Forgetting their grief of long separation, they enjoyed the pleasure of embracing each other. Seated under the shade of the same tree, the Prince with a respectful smile said—"Friend, wishing to aid the Bráhamaṇa in his undertaking and knowing full well that my friends, if they came to know my object would surely come in my way, I went away, leaving all of you asleep. Where did my friends go to in quest of me after being awake, and what did they think was the reason of my disappearance? Where had you been alone?" At this he raised his folded hands to his forehead and humbly replied :—

## UCHCHHVÂSA IV.

"Lord, although we, your friends, made quite sure that Your Highness left us only for doing good to the Bráhmaṇa, yet being unable to come to a decision as to where you went, we separated from one another and went out in all the directions to seek for you. I, too, while wandering over the earth in search of Your Highness, rested for a moment, unable to bear the hot rays of the mid-day sun, under the cool shade of a tree at the foot of a mountain. Suddenly I saw before me the shadow of a human being, with all its limbs contracted owing to it being mid-day, and having the form of a tortoise; and looking up, I with my heart over-powered by compassion supported, while yet in midway, a person falling down from the sky with great velocity. Slowly placing him on the earth, I revived him with cool remedies, as he had become unconscious on account of his fall from a great height, and asked him, whose eyes were filled with tears owing to extreme grief, the reason of his falling from a precipice. He wiped off his tears with his hands (*lit.* fingers) and said—"I am the son of Padmodbhava, the minister of the king of Magadha; my name is Ratnodbhava. I went as a merchant to Kálayavana island, where I married a merchant's daughter. I waa returning with her, when our ship sank in the sea not far from the shore, and all were drowned except myself, who reached land with great difficulty, fate being favourable to me. Weltering in the ocean of grief consequent on the loss of my wife, I passed sixteen years, with great difficulty, out of respect to the counsel of a holy seer; but seeing no end of my misery even yet, I threw myself from a precipice." Just at this moment, the sonorous sound of a female's plaint was heard—"Indeed, it is not proper that you, being unable to bear separation any longer, are throwing yourself in fire, when according to the prediction of the holy seer, you are to be reunited with your husband and son." On hearing this, I said to him, knowing in my mind that he was my father—"Father, I have much to say to you; well, I will tell you everything afterwards. I must first attend to (*lit.* must not neglect) this female voice (of pain); kindly rest here for a moment." I ran off accordingly to some distance, when I beheld before me a woman with folded hands about to do the desperate deed of throwing herself into a fire filled with fierce flames; I hastily took her away from the fire, and with her old attendant who was crying aloud, brought her into my father's presence, and asked the old woman to tell us who they were and why they were in such a hard condition in the forest. She sobbingly replied—"Son, this is Suvṛittá, the daughter of a certain merchant named Kâlagupta of Kálayavana island. While returning with her husband, Ratnodbhava, the ship was wrecked and sank in the ocean. She supported herself getting on a plank along with me, her nurse, and fortunately reached the shore; and the time of her delivery being near, she was delivered of a son in the forest. The boy being carried off (from me) owing to my ill-luck by a wild elephant, she, while wandering with me, was told by a seer that sixteen years would restore her to her child and husband Fully relying upon the words of the sage, she passed that time in a holy hermitage; but, unable to endure the endless grief, she was ready to cast her body into the blazing fire." On hearing it I knew that she was my mother, and prostrating myself at her feet told her my full story and presented her to my father whose face had brightened at the words of the nurse and eyes dilated through wonder. My parents knew each other from the tokens of recognition, and, delighted at heart, bathed me, as I stood humbly before them, with a shower of the tears of joy, embraced me closely, and smelling me on the forehead sat down in the shade of a tree. Being asked by my father how His Majesty Rájahaṃsa was doing, I related to him everything, his loss of his kingdom, your birth, the way in which all other *Kumâras* came together, your commencement of the conquest of the quarters, how you went with Mátaṅga, and the reason why we were searching for you. Then, leaving them both in the hermitage of a sage, I prosecuted my search for you. Knowing full well that money was the chief means for all undertakings, I procured a group of disciples very skilful in aiding me in the magic-power that I had obtained through your favour, and came to the (ruined) sites of old cities in the Vindhya forest. Knowing, by means of the collyrium of magical virtue, that there lay vessels full of riches under trees which indicated various treasures underneath, I dug them out with spades, while the guards kept watch all round, and formed a heap of countless Dînâras. Thence, going to a caravan of traders that had just arrived and had encamped not far off, I bought stout oxen and bags. I loaded the bags with that gold, giving out that it was some other substance, and got them slowly conveyed to the camp by those (bullocks). I formed friendship with Chandrapála, a merchant's son, the leader of that caravan, and came to Ujjain in his company. I also brought my parents thither, and being introduced to the king of Málwá by Bandhupála, Chandrapâla's father and a very accomplished man, I lived under disguise with the assent of the king. Then, as I was ready to go in search of you in forest-lands, Bandhupála, my great friend, coming to know that, asked me to sit quiet with an easy mind, it being impossible for me to search you over the whole boundless earth, and said that he would impart to me favourable signs indicating a meeting with you, our leader. My heart being comforted by his nectar-like words, I waited upon him daily, and there I saw, one day, Bálachandriká, the loveliest of (*lit.* a jewel among) maidens, with a face (charming) like the moon, all her limbs in fresh (blooming) youth, and the very moon-light to the eyes, as if she were the Glory incarnate of her father's family; and the constancy of my mind being shaken by her beauty, I became an easy mark of the arrows of Cupid. She also, with her eyes unsteady like those of a startled young fawn, often looked at me with sidelong glances which served as the arrows of Cupid, and trembled like a creeper waved by a gentle breeze. She silently (*lit.* mentally) conveyed the desire of her mind by means of her meaning glances directed to me, which were contracted, in which the pupils were driven to the corners, and which stood midway between love and bashfulness. Having clearly perceived her love for me from her clever but covert gestures, I began to think of some remedy that would bring about an easy union with her. On one occasion, Bandhupála, wishing to know by means of omens what had become of you, went, accompanied by me, to a pleasure-garden in the suburbs of Ujjain and stood under a tree, listening to the language of the birds. While he was thus engaged, I, seeking to dispel the uneasiness of my mind, wandered through the woods, and, coming to the bank of a pool, beheld Bálachandriká, who had become the sole object of my desires, looking sad, and with her mind labouring under (some) anxiety. I enjoyed for a time the pleasure of observing her amorous actions, rendered charming by the sudden rise of love, bashfulness and curiosity; and noticing dejection, arising from the pain of love-torment, on the lotus-like face of that maid with beautiful teeth, I, out of a desire to know its cause, approached the fair-faced one amorously, and said—"Tell me, O sweet-faced one, the cause of the sad look on your lotus-like face." Encouraged by the privacy of the place, she banished her coyness and diffidence, and thus slowly addressed me—"Noble youth, Mánasâra, the lord of Mâlwâ, being far advanced in years, crowned his son, Darpasâra, as the sovereign of Ujjayinî. That prince, in the hope of ruling over the whole earth bounded by the seven seas, has gone to the mountain Kailása to practise religious austerities, having appointed the sons of his paternal aunt, Chaṇḍavarmâ and Dáruvarmá, of dreadful deeds, to govern the earth Chaṇḍavarmâ is managing the kingdom with a firm hand (*lit.* so as to leave no enemy), while Dàruvarmâ, disregarding the admonitions of his elder brother and uncle, commits all sorts of atrocious acts, such as seizing the wives and wealth of his people. He once saw me, who have fixed my mind on you having a beauty like that of Cupid; and, regardless of the crime of polluting a virgin, he is seeking to appropriate my person by violence. In (constant) alarm of his attempts I live wretched." I learnt her wishes as well as her intense love for me, and having heard what the obstacle was in the way of the accomplishment of my desires, I comforted her whose eyes were filled with tears; and having thought over a plan to bring about the death of Dáruvarmá, I said to my beloved—"Youthful damsel, I have just hit upon a clever plan to put to death this wicked man who has a wishful eye on you. Your relations, whose veracity is undoubted, should repeatedly circulate among the citizens a report that a Yaksha dwells in Bâlachandrikâ, having taken possession of her person, and that a Seer has pronounced that, that man of enterprise fit to be united with her, who, having his heart chained with the hope of ( enjoying ) her superb charms, will overcome the Yaksha in the sleeping apartment and come out safely after enjoying the pleasure of the sweet words of the fawn-eyed one, accompanied by one female friend, can alone take the hand of the beauteous maiden (*lit.* she whose breasts resemble in shape a pair of *chakraváka* birds). If Dâruvarmâ, hearing speeches of this sort often and often, would sit quiet through fear, it would be well and good; but if, out of his wicked nature, he would offer to have a union with you, your friends should say to him that it would not be proper for the minister of Darpasára, the king of the world, to embark upon an adventure in their mansion; and that if he should take you with lotus-like eyes to his own dwelling in the presence of the people, and sport with you without danger to his life, he should marry you and enjoy the fruit of his desires. He, too, will consent to this. You should go to his place, accompanied by me dressed in a woman's garb as your female attendant. In the privacy of the place, I shall forcibly kill him with the strokes of my fists, knees and feet; and then, still in the capacity of an attendant, I shall follow you fearlessly out. Thus, having recourse to ( *or*, accepting ) this plan, you being free from fear and bashfulness should apprise your parents and brothers of our very deep mutual love, and persuade them to bring about our marriage. They will surely give you in marriage to me, a young man of noble birth and richly endowed with beauty and wealth. Impart to them the means I have devised for killing Dáruvarmá, and let me know their answer." She, too, the lotus of her face blooming a little, said—"Noble one, it is you alone who can kill the wicked Dáruvarmá. After his death all your desires will be completely fulfilled. Let the plan be carried out. I shall do everything exactly as you have said." This said, she, repeatedly turning her face and looking at me, wended her way home with gentle steps. I, too, on returning to Bandhupála, learnt from him, who was an expert in interpreting omens, that I should see you after thirty days. After that he went home accompanied by me, and then dismissed me to my place. Bálachandriká, being invited for enjoyment in his pleasure-apartment by Dáruvarmá, who was caught in the nooses of the snares of my deceitful plan, prepared to go to his place, and dispatched a female messenger to me. I, too, skilfully put in their respective places the various articles of decoration proper for a young damsel, such as the jewelled anklets, the girdle, the bracelets, the armlets, the ear-ornaments, the pearl necklace, silk-garments and the collyrium, and thus putting on a charming disguise, went with my beloved to the door of his house. Our arrival being reported to him by the door-keeper, he received us with respect, dismissed all his attendants near the door, and took Bálachandriká with me to the house previously settled upon. The citizens, wishing to test the wide-spread report of a Yaksha being in possession of Bálachandriká, flocked to the courtyard of Dáruvarman's house with great curiosity. That indiscriminate fool, in the height of passion, took the young lady to a bed of the downy feathers of geese spread on a golden bedstead inlaid with jewels, gave her and to me—who had put on a charming woman's dress and whom he could not recognize as a male in the darkness of night—, gold ornaments set with jewels, very fine garments of diverse colours, sandal-paste mixed with musk, Támbúla (a roll of betel-leaves) with camphor, fragrant flowers, and similar other things, and remained talking with us with jocular words for a period of two *muhûrtas*. Then, blind with passion, he thought of embracing that beautiful girl. Inflamed with anger, I fearlessly hurled him from the bedstead and struck him with fists, knees and feet. I set right my ornaments that had snapped off in the heat of the scuffle, comforted Bàlachandriká who was trembling, and coming out into the courtyard, cried out, as if trembling from fear, in loud tones—" Ah ! Dâruvarman is being killed by the frightful Yaksha who had seized Bâlachandrikâ ! Come at once and see him !" The people gathered there on hearing it, had tears gushing forth, and deafened the quarters with the cries of 'Alas ! Alas !' and entered, saying to one another—" In spite of his hearing the report of a mighty Yaksha having possessed Bálachandriká, Dáruvaramâ courted her, being simply blind with passion. So he has been killed by his own deed; what is the use of mourning for him?" In that bustle I quickly withdrew with great dexterity with her of unsteady eyes, and returned to my place. When some days had passed, I, in the presence of the citizens, married the moon-faced maiden according to those instructions of the Seer, and enjoyed in her company many pleasures, previously wished for. On this day, as announced by Bandhupâla's omen, I came forth from the town and am fortunate enough to enjoy the pleasure of the sight of Your Highness."

Thus having heard the account of his friend, Rájavâhana with a joyful heart narrated to him his own adventures and those of Somadatta, and having directed Somadatta to follow him after his worship of Śiva was over, and after he had conveyed his wife with her retinue to his camp, he, attended by Pushpodbhava, entered the town of Avanti, which looked like a heaven on earth. Pushpodbhava introduced the prince, as the son of his lord, to Bandhupâla and his other relatives, and, causing great honour to be shown to him, arranged about his bath, meals, etc. every day at his own place, making it known in the whole town that he was an eminent Brâhmaṇa, proficient in all the arts.

---

## UCHCHHVASA V.

The season of Spring now arrived—kindling the fire of love, in the hearts of persons separated from their beloveds, by means of the southern breeze, the leader of Kama's forces, moving slowly as if under the burden of the fragrance of the sandal-trees, and grown very thin as if it were a remnant of itself after it was eaten up by the serpents, the perpetual residents of the trees on the Malaya Mountain; making the circle of the quarters resound with the sweet tunes of the bees and of the cuckoos with their throats rendered melodious by the feast of the honey of the mango-blossoms; creating longings in the hearts of proud women, causing buds to appear on the Mákandas, Sinduváras, the red Aśokas, the Kiṁśukas and the Tilas, and exhilarating the minds of amorous persons for Love's festival. In that exceedingly delightful season, Avantisundarî, the daughter of Mánasára, attended by her dear friend Bálachandriká and a train of town-ladies, went for enjoying herself to the delightful garden on the border of the city, and diverted herself by worshipping Kâma with a multitude of fragrant materials such as sandal-paste, flowers, turmeric, Akshatâs, and fine silk-garments, in a shady place full of sand at the foot of a young mango-tree. Desirous of beholding the Princess, who was the very image of Rati, Rájaváhana, accompanied by Pushpodbhava, as if Káma in company of Vasanta, entered the garden, listened again and again, in various spots, to the sweet cooings of flocks of cuckoos, the notes of rows of parrots, and the hummings of the bees on the mango-trees, bright with fruit, blossoms and tender foliage grown in thick clusters from the branches gently agitated by the Malaya breeze; and after repeatedly enjoying the sight of charming pools having pure and cool water and resounding with the sweet notes of the swarms of swans, cranes, ducks and Chakravákas, sporting in the beds of the *indîvara*, the *kahlára*, the *kairava* and the *rájîva* lotuses, a little opened, gently and gracefully came to where the princess stood. Beckoned by Bâlachandrikâ to come without any fear, Râjavâhana, who surpassed Indra in lustre, approached the beautiful Avantisundarî, who shone as if created by the God of love, who, wishing, on account of the eager desire of Rati, to make a sportive image for her, framed an excellent figure of a woman, and formed its feet out of the beauty of autumnal lotuses growing in his pleasure-lake, and its slow and sportive gait out of the mode of the movement of the intoxicated swans in the garden-ponds; he fashioned its shanks with the beauty of his quiver, and its pair of beautiful thighs with the softness and grace of the (two) plantain-trees, at the door of his pleasure-house; its massive hips he made with the beauty of the wheels of his victorious chariot; he formed her navel, deep like an eddy of the Ganges, in imitation of the hollow of the bud of a lotus just opening, and the three folds in the manner of a flight of steps leading to a terrace, and the thick line of hair out of the beauty of the dark row of bees which forms his bow-string. He fashioned the two breasts with the beauty of the two full golden pots, the arms with the tenderness of his bower of creepers, the neck with the beauty of the victorious conch, its lips, which caused the *bimba* fruit to be compared with them, with the lovely tinge of the sprouts of the mango-tree, placed on the ear as an ornament, the pure smile out of the beauty of the flowers which form his arrows, its tuneful words with the sweetness of the attractive warblings of the cuckoo, his first messenger, and the wind of its breath out of the fragrance of the Malaya breeze, the leader of all his hosts. He fashioned the two eyes with the grace of the proud fish, his triumphant banner; the eye-brows with the beauty of his bow; its face with the lustre—without its inherent spots—of the moon, his best friend; its thick tresses he formed with the graceful arrangement of the eyes in the peacock's feathers; and its complexion was formed by rubbing it with camphor after being washed with sandal-paste mixed with flower-juice of every kind and musk. That daughter of the king of Mâlwâ, who was like Lakshmî incarnate, thought him to be Kâma, the object of her worship, appearing in a visible form to grant the boon sought for, and trembled under the influence of love, like a creeper waving in the gentle breeze. And then desisting from her free sports, she, through modesty, manifested several indescribabls emotions. "Indeed, she must have been created quite accidentally by the Creator when creating women; or else, if he be clever at creating such extraordinary female forms, why is it that he creates no other damsel resembling her in beauty?"—thus obseved the Prince in wonder and great admiration, and stood looking at her; when, feeling abashed to stand before him, she hid herself among her friends and stood looking with sidelong glances, with eyebrows a little contracted and knit, cast in the direction of Ra'java hana, whose beauty captivated her as the net captivates the deer. The mind of the prince also became the target of the arrows of Cupid, who had as it were got power on account of the full help he received from the various amorous feelings produced in her at that time. She thought thus to herself—"To the eyes of the fortunate young damsels of what town is a feast provided (with his sight) by this prince of uncommon beauty? What among matronly ladies, having sons, is given the first rank by this most eminent of sons being born of her? Who is his queen? What brings him here? Cupid, by tormenting me beyond measure, as if in envy, as I am looking at him who laughs scornfully at his beauty, is really giving significance to his name (*viz.*, 'tormentor of mind'). What am I to do? How can I get information about him?" Then Bâlachandrika', knowing the state of their minds by the judicious observance of their feelings, but thinking it improper to relate the true history of the prince in the presence of an assembly of ladies, addressed her in words that had a common import—"Princess, this is a young Brâhmaṇa, well-versed in all the arts, who can make a goddess reveal herself before him (when necessary), who is skilled in warfare, who knows the use of jewels, spells and herbs, and is entitled to your reverence. Let him be honoured by you." Hearing this, the princess, much pleased at heart with Bâlachandriká who had recounted what passed in her own mind, and agitated by love like a line of waves ruffled by a gentle breeze, gave a proper seat to the prince who far surpassed Kâma, and offered him the customary worship through her friend, with the best materials such as sandal-paste, flowers, Akshatâs, camphor, a roll of betel-leaves and various other things. Ràjaváhana also thought to himself—"Certainly, this must be my wife Yajñavatî in my former birth; else such a love for her could not have arisen in my mind; and to both of us equally belongs the power, conferred upon us by the ascetic to remember (the incidents of) our previous life when the curse (pronounced by him) is to cease Still, I shall arouse knowledge in her by means of sentences suggestive of particular circumstances and given rise to by the occasion." Just then a charming swan arrived near her with a desire to sport. Seeing that Bálachandriká was deputed by the eager princess to catch the swan, and considering it a fit opportunity to speak, the prince, who was very clever at conversation, gracefully said—"Friend, formerly a certain king, named Śâmba, went with his beloved to a lake full of lotuses for diversion; there, beside a bed of red lotuses, he gently caught a swan whose mind was overpowered by sleep, bound its legs with lotus-fibres, and looking lovingly at the face of his beloved, with one of his round cheeks blooming with a gentle smile, addressed her—"Moon-faced lady, this swan, held captive by me, stands quiet like a sage; let him go as he wills." The swan, on its part, cursed Śámba, saying—"King, since you, proud of your kingship, have without any cause insulted me. while I, a lifelong religious student, being lost in contemplation, was in the enjoyment of supreme felicity in this lotus-bed, you shall suffer the pangs of separation from your beloved, as a penalty for this sinful act." Śâmba, with his face dejected, and unable to bear separation from the mistress of his life, bowed to him, falling on the ground stick-like, and humbly said—"Noble sage, kindly forgive me what I did through ignorance." The hermit, his heart touched with pity, said—"King, my curse will not operate upon you in this life; but, on account of the infallibility of my words, in your next life you will be, through affection, the lover of this lotus-eyed one, who will have another form; but being put in chains for two months, as a penalty for your crime of holding me a captive for two *muhûrtas*, you will suffer the anguish of separation from your beloved, and will afterwards enjoy the pleasures of a kingdom with your beloved for a long time." After this, he favoured them also with the power to remember the incidents of their previous lives. Hence you must not take this swan a captive." The princess, on hearing his words, recollected the incidents of her previous life, and decided in her mind that he was her lord. With her mind affected by love, she said with a gentle smile—"Gentle Sir, formerly Śâmba captured the swan in that manner only to please Yajñavatî by doing her bidding. For in this world, out of over-courtesy, even learned persons commit improper acts." The prince and the princess, having thus mentioned for mutual information their respective names in the previous birth, known to them, so as to carry conviction, had their minds replete with love.

Just at the time the queen of Mánasára, attended by her retinue, came to the place to see her daughter's sport. Bálachandrikà saw her from afar, and fearing that the secret might be disclosed, hastily gave a signal with her hand to Rájaváhana and his companion Pushpodbhava, her husband, who both hid themselves among the trees. The queen saw, for a short time, the various graceful sports of her daughter with her companions, and then became intent on going home with her daughter. Avantisundarî, starting to go with her mother, addressed the prince, apparently meaning a swan, saying—"O you, the ornament of the family of Rájahaṃsa (*also*, swans) here I leave you, all of a sudden, come to the pleasure-garden with the desire to sport (with me), and go with my mother, as is but proper for me to do. May the desire of your mind be not otherwise (*i.e.* be fulfilled) by this my act (*also,* may your love undergo no change)!" Uttering these words suited to the occasion, and again and again casting back a sad look and gazing upon his face, she returned home. There, in the course of conversation with regard to her lover, she, coming to know his family and name from Bálachandrikà, was overpowered with intense love (*lit.* with the fall of Cupid's arrows), and began to grow emaciated day by day, like the crescent of the moon in the dark half of the month, from the pangs of separation. She gave up taking food and her other daily pursuits, and in her secret chamber restlessly rolled her creeper-like (*i.e.* slender) frame on a bed formed of (tender) leaves and flowers wetted with sandal-juice. Her female friends, seeing the delicate princess in that state withering with the fire of love, and feeling very sad, tried to cool her body, with materials for relief from the torment, such as water prepared for her bath, mixed with sandal, *us'îra* and camphor and kept in gold vessels, garments made of lotus-fibres, and fans of lotus-leaves. Even that application of cooling remedies caused simply (flames of) fire to appear on all sides (*i. e.* spread through) in her body like water dropped in heated oil. Looking at Bálachandriká, who was sad at heart, and did not know what to do, with a glance from the corner of her eye bedimmed with drops of tears and a little opened, the beautiful princess, whose lower lip was parched by sighs that were hot with the fire of separation, spoke to her plaintively and slowly in a choked voice—"Dear friend, it is indeed falsely said that Káma is flower-weaponed and has only five arrows; for here I am struck by him with numberless arrows with points of steel. Friend, I think the moon is more distressing than the submarine fire, since the ocean is drained as soon as it enters it, while the selfsame ocean is augmented when it leaves it. How can I describe the evil actions of this moon (the mine of faults)?—for it is he who destroys the day-lotus, the very home of his sister Lakshmî. The Malaya breeze, being heated by coming in touch with my heart burning with the fire of separation, is surely rarefied; this bed, formed with tender shoots, adds to the heat of the body as if it were the concentrated flames of the fire of love: even the sandal (-paste) heats the body, as if it were infected with the virulent poison smeared to the parent trunk by the fangs of serpents formerly entwining it. So, enough, enough of troubling yourself with the application of cooling remedies : only the prince, who surpasses even Cupid in beauty, can successfully cure this heat of the fever of love. But he is beyond my reach ; what am I to do ?" Bálachandriká, seeing that she (the princess) of delicate limbs was affected by the highest stage of the feverish condition of love, had her mind subdued by the beauty of Ràjaváhana, and had no other protector, thought to herself—" I must quickly bring the prince (here), or else Cupid will surely reduce her to the state of being only remembered (*i.e.* she will die). Cupid discharged his arrows equally at both these in the garden when both the prince and the princess were looking at each other; hence it will be easy for me to bring the prince here." Then, leaving some female friends, who were skilled in the timely use of remedies, to guard the princess, she went to the house of the prince. Ràjaváhana, whose mind had become the quiver of the arrows of Cupid, and who lay on a bed of leaves withered on account of their contact with his body heated by love-torment, saw, as he was talking with Pushpodbhava with regard to his beloved, her dear friend come near him ; and being pleased at heart to find that Bálachandriká had arrived like a potent herb to be sought, he asked her, whose folded hands, graceful like the bud of a lotus, decked her spacious forehead, and who had sat on a proper seat pointed out to her with the words—" Sit there," the news about his beloved, as she respectfully offered the camphor-mixed Támbûla to him, given by Avantisundarî. She with modesty replied—" Lord, ever since the time she saw you in the pleasure-garden, she is being tortured by Cupid ; and finding no relief from beds of flowers and such other things, she, like a dwarf trying to get at the fruit of a tall tree, is desirous of obtaining, on account of being blinded by love, the inaccessible pleasure of a close embrace of your bosom ; and having herself written this epistle she has asked me to hand it over to you with the words—Give this to my lover." The prince took the letter and read as follows :—

" O blessed prince, having seen your form, delicate like a flower and perfect (*lit.* flawless) in beauty in the whole world, my mind desires that you should make your heart as tender (as your form is graceful) [*or*, my heart entertains love (for you); so please make your heart etc.]"

Having read it he said to her respectfully—"Friend, you, the wife of Pushpodbhava who follows me like my shadow, are yourself like the external life of that fawn-eyed lady. Your shrewdness has served as a basin to the creeper of this whole affair; so I will do everything. The beautiful princess refers in her letter (indirectly) to the hardness of my heart. The very moment when that fawn-eyed damsel came within the range of my sight in the pleasure-grove, she robbed me of my heart and (with it) went to her place; so she herself best knows whether it is tender or hard. It is very difficult to get access to the chamber of the princess. I shall devise some remedy favourable to our object, and shall approach that beautiful damsel to-morrow or the day after. Tell her everything about me as you have seen it, and make use of remedies in such a way that she, who is as tender as a Śirîsha flower, will not suffer any bodily torment." Bálachandrikà on her part was satisfied on hearing his words that implied love, and returned to the princess' chamber. Rájaváhana also went with Pushpodbhava, to dispel the pangs of separation, to the pleasure-park where he had (first) obtained the pleasure of the sight of his heart's beloved. There, unable to rest (*lit.* stop) in any place, being affected by love, he reviewed the many trees, the clusters of leaves and flowers of which had been collected by the *chakora*-eyed princess, the place where the damsel with a face like the autumnal moon had worshipped the image of the God of love, the cool sandy surface, marked by the rows of the foot-prints of the lovely lady, and the leafy bed under the bower of the Màdhavî creeper that she, having pearly teeth, had left after resting on it for a time. And he wandered about, remembering again and again the several events that occurred at the time he saw that ornament of the womankind; seeing again and again the fresh leaves of the mango-trees shaken by the gentle breezes, tremblingly, as if they were the flames of the fire of love, and repeatedly hearing the notes of cuckoos, parrots and the bees, which were as it were the spies of Love whispering in his ears.

Just then a Bráhmaṇa, clad in thin and variegated raiment, decked with bright ear-rings, and attractive with his sumptuous apparel, came there unexpectedly, accompanied by persons with their heads clean-shaved, and with a blessing duly pronounced, saw Rájaváhana glowing with a halo of light all round. The Prince respectfully asked him who he was and what art he was versed in. He replied that he was an expert in the art of magic, named Vidyeśvara, and that he came that day to Ujjain in the course of his visits to many countries for the amusement of the princes. Again he looked at Rájaváhana closely, and with a significant smile asked him what was the reason of his pallor in that land of pleasure. Pushpodbhava, on his part, thinking that he would be of use to them in the accomplishment of their object, respectfully addressed him—"Since the friendship of the good arises out of a conversation, you have become our dear friend in such a short time owing to your sweet talk with us just now; and what is there that can be withheld from a friend? There arose an intense mutual love, at an unexpected meeting in this pleasure-grove, between the daughter of the king of Mâlwá, when she came here for the celebration of the great Spring-festival, and this prince. It is on account of the absence of some means of attaining constant enjoyment that he is in this miserable plight." Vidyeśvara looked at the face of the prince, charmingly blushing, and said with a gentle smile—"What object of yours, my lord, can be beyond accomplishment, when I, your servant, am ready to serve you? By means of my art of magic I shall beguile the king of Málwá, and, bringing about the marriage of his daughter with you in the presence of the citizens, cause your entrance into the apartment of the princess; but let the princess be informed of this beforehand through her friend." The prince, highly pleased at this, greatly honoured and then took leave of that Vidyeśvara, his disinterested friend who had declared his skill in magic (*or*, in bringing about results by artificial means) and who knew deception, counterfeit love and natural affection.

Râjaváhana now looked upon his desires as almost fulfilled on account of Vidyeśvara's skill in magic, and, returning home with Pushpodbhava, took care to inform the princess, through Bàlachandriká, of the means of union that were going to be used by the Bráhmaṇa, and with his mind full of curiosity remained thinking as to how to pass the night. Next morning Vidyeśvara, well-versed in the mode and progress of the sentiments and feelings, went to the gate of the palace, accompanied by his numerous attendants, and declared his profession to the door-keeper, who thereupon hastened to announce the approach of the magician to the king. Called in by the king of Málwá, full of curiosity, in company with the equally curious ladies of the harem, Vidyeśvara entered the inner court, humbly uttered benedictions upon the king, and, permitted by the king, began his performance. Then, as the roll of drums beaten by the servants swelled and the songs of singing girls, sweet like the tune of intoxicated cuckoos, flowed in sweet succession, and the minds of all present there were overpowered with great curiosity, he stood for a moment with his eyes half-closed, making his attendants move round him, as he whirled his magic bundle of peacock's feathers. After this, serpents, decked with hoods copiously emitting virulent poison and illumining the expanse of the palace with the array of the gems in their hoods, moved about, causing fright; and many vultures taking up those big snakes in their beaks whisked about in the sky. Then the Bráhmaṇa, after having exhibited the tearing of Hiraṇyakaśipu, the monarch of the demons, by Nṛisiṃha, said to the greatly astonished king—"O king, now at the close of my performance it is but proper that you should see something auspicious; hence, to insure the attainment of a number of blessings, I shall perform the marriage of a prince endowed with all the auspicious signs, with a princess, having a form exactly like that of your daughter." The king, out of curiosity to see it, assented; and Vidyeśvara, with his face brightened at the prospect of his desired object being accomplished, put in his eyes a collyrium which had the virtue of stupefying all, and looked around. Then, as all were looking at the spectacle in astonishment as a feat of magic, he united, in the presence of the sacred fire, on account of his proficiency in the religious rites and other performances attendant on a marriage, Avantisundarî, who had come there decorated with numerous ornaments as previously arranged, with Rájaváhana, with his heart swelling with love. At the close of the performance, the magician loudly ordered all the magical persons to disappear, when all persons conjured up by magic disappeared one by one. Rájaváhana also, skilfully carrying out the secret plan as previously arranged, entered the chamber of the princess like a man conjured up by magic. The king of Málwá also thought it a miracle, rewarded that Bráhmaṇa with a large sum of money, and having asked Vidyeśyara to depart, himself went into the inner apartment. Then Avantisundarî, attended by her dear companions, went to her beautiful mansion with her husband. Then Ràjaváhana, who had his desires thus fulfilled with the help of fate and man, gently removed the feeling of bashfulness of that fawn-eyed damsel with his sweet and loving acts of endearment, infused in her a desire for amorous sport, engendered confidence in her on account of the privacy, and, eager to drink the nectar of her conversation, related to her the diversified and heart-ravishing tales (from the Mahábhárata &c.) of the fourteen worlds.

END OF THE PU'RVAPÎTHIKA'.

## DAŚAKUMÂRACHARITA.

### UCHCHHVÂSA I.

Having heard the description of the universe from the prince, that beautiful princess, with her eyes dilated through wonder, said with a smile—"Dearest, to-day my ears have been blessed (*lit.* the function of my ears has had its mission fulfilled) through your favour; to-day you have set in my mind the lamp of knowledge that dispels all darkness of ignorance; to-day is ripened the fruit of the service of your lotus-like feet. What service shall I do unto you so as to make a return for this your favour? There is nothing mine that is not yours. Or why, this person too does possess power in some matter; impossible it is to cause this lower lip of yours, that has already been used by Sarasvatî, when she seized your mouth, to be kissed by me without my desire;—or to cause this bosom of yours, that has been enjoyed by the plump breasts of Lakshmî, to be embraced by me without my permission." With these words, resting her rounded breasts on the bosom of her dear husband like the monsoon spreading in the sky the train of big clouds, expanding her eye sparkling with deep love, like a full-developed Kandalî-bud of deep red, and graceful (*lit.* marked) with her ample tresses that imitated the plumage of a peacock, being variegated with flowers that looked like eyes in a peacock's tail and hanging about disorderly like a row of bees, she impatiently kissed his ruby-like lower lip magnified by the stream of its spreading reddish lustre and hence resembling the bud of a Kadamba flower rugged with its filaments like the throbbing rays of the morning sun. At this the feeling of passion being excited, there proceeded an uninterrupted course of enjoyments highly pleasing on account of the various modes of enjoyment. As they were in sound sleep brought on by the fatigue of enjoyment, they saw in a dream an old swan with its legs bound with a string of lotus-fibres, and both awoke at the vision. On waking, the prince found his feet bound by a silver-chain, as if they were embraced by a series of the rays of the moon mistaking them (his feet) for lotuses. Perceiving it, and not knowing what to make of it, the princess, beside herself with great fright, screamed aloud. Thereupon the whole of the apartment of the princess was thrown into commotion, all the inmates trembling, as if it were set on fire, as though some evil spirit had taken possession of it, not knowing how to act then or after, quite regardless of the necessity to keep the secret intact, dashing their limbs against the floor, screaming at the top of their voice, and having their cheeks covered with the stream of tears. At this time of confusion, the guards of the female apartments, their entrance not being barred, rushed in all at once to see what the matter was, and they discovered the prince in that state; their desire to arrest him, however, being curbed by his majestic appearance, they at once communicated the incident to Chaṇḍavarmá. He came, foaming with fury, as if burning him with his eyes that contained fire; and looking at the prince, he recognized him and said—"How now! This, indeed, is the same mischievous fellow, bearing the designation of a Bráhmaṇa, the friend of Pushpodbhava—that foreign merchant, inflated with the pride of his riches and the husband of that wicked Bálachandriká who was the cause of my younger brother's death—who, intoxicated with the pride of beauty and vain of his knowledge of the arts, has, by means of skill in the various arts of deception, imposed upon the silly citizens, who falsely attribute impossible divine (superhuman) powers to him, and who, wearing the cloak of religious hypocricy, practises evil secretly. How possibly was this wicked Avantisundarî, treating valorous persons like us with disdain, attached to him? Let the wicked girl, the defiler of her family, to-day see her lord exalted to the dignity of the gibbet!" Thus he reviled Avantisundarî, and with his forehead fierce on account of the terrible knitting of the eye-brows and looking like Kála, he dragged the prince with his hand rigid like an iron rod, seizing him by his lotus-like hand marked with the linear marks of a lotus and a wheel. Rájavàhana, bold by nature, and possessing prowess of every kind to the highest degree, knew for certain that it was a calamity brought on by destiny, and that it could only be met with by means of submission; so he gave himself up to the enemy, comforting his dearly-loved wife, who was thinking of putting an end to her life, with the words—"Call to your mind, O you with a swan's gait, that incident about the swan! Bear yourself up for two months, O fair one!"

When the King and Queen of Málwá heard the story, they were distressed, and, being attracted by his handsome form, saved their son-in-law who was about to be put to death by his foe, threatening else to put an end to their own lives; but they could not, owing to their powerlessness (*lit.* they not being the sovereigns), deliver him from his calamity. That Chaṇḍavarmâ, known for his fierce disposition, sent a courier to inform Darpasára, who was practising religious austerities on the Kailása mountain, of the whole of this affair, and at once seized Pushpodbhava with all his family, threw him into prison and confiscated all his effects. He then secured Rájaváhana, like the cub of a lordly lion, in a wooden cage, and being distrustful of all, took him, who felt no pain due to hunger, thirst and the like by virtue of the magical jewel concealed in his hair, with him as he proceeded on an expedition against the Aṅga country in order to uproot the king of the Aṅgas who had contemptuously treated his request for the hand of his daughter. He besieged Champá, making it shake under the weight of his army. The king of Champá, Siṃhavarmá, whose prowess was as irresistible as that of a lion, having caused a passage to be made in the rampart, issued forth with a mighty force, appearing like pride incarnate, impatient of aggression and not caring to wait for the arrival, which was quite imminent, of the princes, who were called by the multitude of messengers sent by himself and who were coming very fast to help him, and opposed the rival army. In the great battle that ensued, however, Siṃhavarmá, with all his forces destroyed and having his own armour battered by hundreds of blows from mighty weapons, was captured by Chaṇḍavarmá who had superhuman vital strength, by jumping upon his elephant from his own elephant. Chaṇḍavarmá, through the great love he bore to his daughter Ambâliká, also named Abalá-Ratna (*lit.* 'a jewel among women') did not, however, put him to death. But he whose intentions were not to be divined, kept him in custody, after having taken out all the arrow-darts from his body. He resolved, in conformity with the calculations of the astrologers, to espouse the princess the next morning.

Just as the ceremony of fastening the auspicious marriage-string was performed, the courier named Aiṇajaṅgha arrived from the Kailása mountain with the reply of Darpasára who was the king in authority, which ran thus—"Fool! Is there room for showing pity to the defiler of the princess' apartment? Does it behove even you to abide by whatever nonsense the old king utters, whose mind is deprived of all sense of honour and dishonour owing to his age, and who is only partial to his ill-behaved daughter? You should create joy for (*i.e.* gladden) my ears by at once sending me the news about the love-crazed miscreant being put to death with tortures; the wicked girl also with her younger brother Kîrtisára should be thrown into prison with her feet in irons." On hearing this message Chaṇḍavarmá ordered his attendants, fixing on them a look of command, thus—"Let the villain, the violator of the chastity of the princess' apartment, be brought before the palace-gates tomorrow morning, and let also the lordly elephant, named Chaṇḍapota, decked with the usual decorations, be brought there. After completing the marriage-rites, I shall get up and myself make that the fellow of depraved character a plaything of the elepant (*i.e.* so as to be smashed to pieces), and then riding the same elephant I will march forth and capture the multitude of kings that are approaching to help the foe, together with their treasures and conveyances." The next day, as the dawn was just breaking, Rájaváhana was led forth by the guards to the palace-yard, and the elephant Chaṇḍapota, with ichor flowing from his temples, was also brought there. At that very instant the silver chain fell off from the prince's ankles, and, assuming the form of an Apsaras, beautiful like the digit of the moon, went round him keeping him to the right, and with folded hands addressed him—"Prince, please listen to me with a mind softened with kindliness. I am an Apsaras, named Suratamañjarî, born of the rays of the moon; in the sky a foolish swan mistook my face for a lotus and pursued it, when in the confusion of keeping it off, my necklace snapped, and dropping off happened to fall on the head of the great sage Márkaṇḍeya who had just emerged after having bathed in a lake of the Himàlayas, called Mandodaka, and made it doubly hoary by means of the rays of its jewels. Incensed by the affront, he denounced upon me an unjust curse (thus):—"O wicked girl, assume thou a metallic form, wherein your consciousness will be suspended." Then, being propitiated by me, he arranged that the calamity would end after I had served as fetters for your lotus-like feet for two months only, and further that my senses would not lose their powers (all the while). I, who was transformed into a silver-chain as a penalty for my great sin, was found in that state on the Kailása mountain by a demigod, named Víraśekhara, the son of Mánasavega, and the grandson of Vegavat, a prince of the family of Ikshváku; and I remained in his possession. Now when the hostilities commenced by his father (Mánasavega) were still proceeding, Vîraśekhara, hostilely disposed towards Naraváhanadatta, the extender of Vatsa's race and the reigning emperor of the Vidyádharas, entered into an alliance with Darpasâra, who was practising penance, and whom he thought capable of punishing his foe. Darpasára agreed to give him his sister Avantisundarî in marriage. Once, as the moon shone brightly in the sky, Vîraśekhara, desirous of seeing the beloved of his heart, Avantisundarî, and unable to curb his passion, descended into the princess' chamber, beautiful like the palace of Indra. Himself invisible by virtue of the charm of concealment, he beheld the princess, who, with her limbs drooping, through the fatigue of sexual sports, lay reclined on your lap, and in whom the tide of passion was caused to swell by means of tales, sweet like nectar, of the creation, maintenance and destruction of the three worlds. Though enraged at the sight, he was frustrated in his mental resolve to seize you by your prowess; but finding both of you sleeping soundly in each other's arms, he, urged by favourable fate, passed me in the form of a silver chain round your lotus-like feet and hastily departed in great anger. To-day my curse expires; and your imprisonment also extended over the same two months; be pleased to tell me what I can do for you." The prince, saying—"Go and cheer up my heart's beloved with the news of my liberation," dismissed the nymph as she was bowing before him.

Just at that time a sudden cry arose that Chaṇḍavarmâ was killed with the stroke of a scimitar by a single thief of extraordinary prowess, being violently pulled down by being forcibly seized by the arm stretched forth through ardent desire to seize the hand of Ambáliká, the daughter of Siṃhavarmâ, and that covering the precincts of the palace with hundreds of dead bodies he (the thief) was moving about freely, unimpeded in his course. On hearing this, Rájaváhana, having knocked off the driver, leaped upon the same furious elephant and drove it to the palace with utmost speed. The way was cleared for him by the foot-soldiers who fell off as the elephant advanced with speed, and he entered the palace-yard, and in a tone deep like the thunder of a train of clouds said—“ Where is that hero who performed this great feat impossible for a human being to achieve? Let him come and sit here beside me on this infuriated elephant, so that by my side he can be safe ( *lit.* will have no fear ) even when fighting with the gods and demons.” On hearing this, the valiant youth was greatly delighted, and came with folded hands and dexterously mounted the elephant that contracted its body at a signal. R'ajaváhana saw him closely just as he was mounting ( the elephant ), and exclaimed with his eyes dilated through joy—“ Oh, this is none but my dear friend Apaháravarmá !” And, catching the foreparts of both his arms that were thrust into his arm-pits as he was sitting behind, caused himself to be embraced by him, and himself also embraced him by throwing his arms backwards. Having disengaged himself from the embrace the very instant, Apaháravarmá hurled to the ground the opposing warriors who, puffed up with the pride of their strength, were fighting in various ways closing round him, making use of various weapons such as bows, the disc, iron clubs, harpoons, darts, double-edged swords, javelins and maces. In a moment he saw even that hostile army besieged by another army rapidly advancing in the front from an opposite direction.

Just after that, a man, of a complexion yellowish-white like the Karṇikára flower, with his curly hair blue like the sapphire, his hands and feet tender like the lotus, with his blue, glossy, milk-white and attractive eyes stretching as far as the ears, having a poniard, with its hilt set with jewels, deposited in his waist-band, wearing a silk-garment, of a slender waist but a broad chest, pouring a shower of arrows upon the hostile army as he was well-practised in the use of weapons, urging his swift elephant by rubbing hard the roots of its ears with the toes of his feet, advanced, and recognizing Râjavâhana from his knowledge of the description formerly given, bowed down to him with folded hands, and fixing his eyes on Apaháravarmâ said—“ Here has arrived the force of the allies for rendering assistance to the king of the Aṅgas and led by me hither by the way pointed out by you. The army of the enemy is now thoroughly routed and broken, and is reduced to such a helpless condition that its weapons can be easily snatched away even by women and children; what further am I to do for you?" Apáharavarmá was highly pleased and said—"Lord, favour this servant with a gracious look; Your Highness should consider him as my own self, only concealed under this form and under the designation of Dhanamitra. If Your Highness does not find fault with it, let him (go and) liberate the king of the Aṅgas, and get together (the spoil *i.e.*) the treasures and the conveyances, and then attend upon Your Highness sitting at ease in a quiet place, accompanied by these princes who are siding with us." The prince assented, and riding out of the town with him by the way he pointed out, alighted from the elephant on the ground under a large Rohiṇa tree, cool with the breezes from the waves of the Ganges that blew there, and having a bed of sand white like a silk-garment. Rájaváhana sat at ease, as on an elephant, on the sandy Gangetic plain, the surface whereof was quickly smoothed with his own hands by Apaháravarmá, having alighted first. While he was thus seated, Dhanamitra came with Upaháravarmâ, Arthapála, Pramati, Mitragupta, Mantragupta and Viśruta, and with Prahárvarmâ the king of Mithilá, Kámapála the king of Káśî, and Siṃhavarmâ the king of Champá, and bowed before Rájaváhana. The prince also, transported with joy, rose (to receive them), wondering at the singular turn of good fortune in that all his friends had come together at the same time, and after receiving them with proper civilities closely embraced them. He looked upon (*i.e.*, treated) the Kings of Kâśî, Mithilá and Aṅga, who were introduced to him by his friend, with the respect due to his father. They, with their white hair bristling through joy, embraced him in great haste and he also felt greatly delighted.

Then, as affectionate talks went on between them, he, being requested by his friends, narrated to them his own adventures and those of Somadatta and Pushpodbhava; and thus, having made a beginning, he asked his friends, with a desire to hear their narratives, to recount to him the incidents that severally befell them. Of these Apaháravarmá began (his own narrative) first:—

---

## UCHCHHVÂSA II.

"Lord, when the group of friends dispersed in search of Your Highness, who had then entered the nether regions for assisting that Bráhmaṇa in his object, I, too, wandered over the earth.

Having heard somewhere from a conclave of people talking among themselves that there resided on the bank of the Ganges, outside the city of Champâ, a great sage, named Marîchi, who was possessed of divine sight got by the power of his austerities, I. desirous of knowing your whereabouts from him, directed my steps to that region. And in that hermitage I beheld, under the shade of a young mango-tree, an ascetic who was looking like one dejected. Received as a guest by him I took rest for a short time, and asked him, saying—"Where is the great seer, Marîchi? I wish to know from him the fate of a dear friend gone away for some reason; for, the sage is known over the earth as possessed of a wonderful power of knowledge." He, thereupon, heaved a long sigh and said—"In this hermitage there was such a sage formerly. A courtesan named Kámamañjarî, who was the ornament of the Aṅga-capital, once approached him full of dejection and with breasts bespangled with large tear-drops, and bowed to him, sweeping the ground with her long dishevelled tresses. Just then the multitude of her relatives, led by her mother, who ran after her with piteous cries arrived there close upon her heels. The merciful sage, as the story goes, comforted them with sweet words and asked the harlot the cause of her distress. She, appearing to be full now of hashfulness, now of sorrow and now of respect, replied—"Revered Sir, this person, not destined to enjoy the pleasures of this world, has approached, for protection, the root of your feet, renowned for their being the asylum of the afflicted, for obtaining the felicity of the other world." But her mother, having raised her folded hands and after rising up from the ground having touched it (in the act of bowing) with the knot of her hair interspered with the grey of age, said—"Revered sage, here your slave begs to submit her offence with respect to her; my fault lies simply in making her perform the duties of her proper profession (*or*, duties as required by my office). This is the special office (duty) of the mother of a courtesan—*viz.* to cultivate the beauty of the person of her daughter from the very birth; to nurture the body of her daughter by means of congenial (*lit.* measured) diet, that will help the development of lustre, strength, complexion and intelligence and will keep the humours, the gastric fire and the vital fluids in harmony; from her fifth year (of age) not to expose her very much to the view even of her father; on her birth-day and on other auspicious days, to perform the auspicious rites marked with great festivities; to train her in the erotic science in all its branches, to carefully initiate her in the arts of dancing, singing, playing on musical instruments, acting, painting, as well as in the confectionary (culinary art), in the art of preparing perfumes, wreathing flowers and also in reading writing and expressing herself with elegance and wit; to teach her the simple outlines of grammar, logic and astrology. She (the mother) has to make her adept in the art of gaining a livelihood, in sportive graces, and in games of chance and strife; (the daughter) also receives practical instruction with great pains, at the hands of confidential persons, in the secrets of the sexual science; she has to appear, carefully decorated and attended with a large retinue, at public festivals; she has to attain perfection in the art of singing as would suit particular occasions, at the hands of experts previously engaged; she has to be advertised through experts in various arts in different places; she must be proclaimed through palmists and astrologers as being endowed with all the auspicious marks; with the help of parasites, gay companions, jesters and the Buddhistic nuns (female mendicants), she has to get her beauty, behaviour, accomplishments, charms and amiableness discussed in the circles of the townspeople. When she becomes the constant object of the desires of young men, then to set a very high price on her hand (*or*, to bestow her on a youth at a very great price); or to give her away to one who is independent (*i.e.* master of his own affairs) and of his own accord is either very powerfully affected by (*lit.* is blinded by) love for her or whose passion is furiously excited at the sight of her coquettish actions, and who is endowed with high birth, beauty, youth, power to give riches, honesty, munificence, skill, politeness, (knowledge of) the arts, good disposition and affability; or to deliver her over to one who is not independent but possesses superior qualities and is extremely intelligent, even for a small sum, giving out in public that much was received; and (sometimes) to extort money from the elders of such by bringing about a connexion with him by the Gândharva marriage,* and if no money comes in, to gain the object in the local court by winning over by friendship the king (*or*, the chief authority). When one is attached to her, to make the daughter observe the vow of chastity towards him. (It is also her duty) to appropriate by various artifices what remains of the wealth of

---

* Or, according to some, 'under the pretence that a Gândharva marriage was contracted.'

lovers after it has been expended by daily, occasional and love gifts; to reject one who, though almost seduced, does not give anything, by picking a quarrel with him; to stimulate the liberality of one, who, being attracted, is deep in love, by inciting him through a deputy (*or*, neighbour;—*or*, the lover of a neighbouring courtesan, *Com.*); to get rid of one who is without money by means of sarcastic remarks, by reviling him in public, by keeping her daughter off from him, and thus inspiring him with shame or by accepting another lover for her, and by insults; and often to unite her with rich persons, capable of giving much money, who are able to remove all difficulties, and who are unobjectionable, after duly considering all doubts about the advantages and disadvantages (from the connexion). A mere attendance upon a lover, and not real attachment to him, is the duty of a courtesan; and even when she really loves him, she must not disobey her mother or grandmother. Such being the settled practice, this damsel, having transgressed the duties prescribed by the god Brahmâ, passed exactly a month indulging her passion at her own expense in company of a Bràhmaṇa youth, who is altogether a stranger and whose only wealth is his handsome form. A large number of admirers, capable of giving much wealth, she offended by rejecting them, and thus ruined her family; and when I dissuaded her, saying—'This is foolish and not a wise thought,' she, in a rage, set out to take up her abode in the woods. Now if she, who has thus acted, proves unshaken in her resolve, all these persons, who have no other means of subsistence, will starve themselves to death, just here." With these words she burst into tears.

Upon this the sage, full of mercy, addressed the damsel—"Good girl, this forest-life is surely a life of suffering. Its object is either final beatitude or the attainment of paradise; the first of these, being attainable by the perfection of spiritual knowledge, is generally difficult to accomplish; the second is within the reach of every one who discharges the duties of his family. It were well, therefore, that you should desist from an impossible attempt and abide by the advice of your mother." Thus addressed she, saying—"If the root of the feet of Your Reverence be not my refuge, helpless that I am, let the God of fire be!" became agitated (uneasy) at heart. The sage then thought to himself, and said to her mother—"Go home for the present; wait for a few days till she, of a tender body and accustomed to the enjoyment of pleasures, grows weary of the hardships of a forest life, and being constantly awakened to her duties by me, comes to her senses." When the relatives of the young courtesan returned home, saying 'Very well,' the damsel, full of of deep devotion, wearing a couple of freshly-washed garments and not much attentive to personal decoration, won the sage's heart in a few days by such actions as filling the basins of the young plants with water, taking pains to pluck and collect the flowers for the worship of the deities, preparing offerings of various sorts, keeping ready the sandal-paste, flowers, frankincense, lamp-light, dancing, singing and playing on musical instruments, for (the propitiation of) S'iva, and by engaging herself in a secluded place in conversations with him touching the three objects of worldly existence and suitable discussions concerning the nature of the Self

Once, when in private, finding that he was affected by passion, she observed with some astonishment—"Foolish, indeed, are the worldly people that place Artha (wealth) and Káma (pleasure) on an equal footing with Dharma (virtue, religion). Urged by the Marîchi, saying—"Tell me, child, in what degree you would have Dharma transcend Artha and Káma," she began slowly to speak through modesty—"Your Reverence should, indeed, seek to learn of the superiority or inferiorty of the three objects of worldly existence from a person like myself! Or, even this may be a new way of showing favour to your slave! Very well; may Your Reverence attend:—To be sure, Artha and Káma cannot come into being without Dharma; but even without regard to them, Dharma alone is the creative cause of final beatitude, and is attainable only by the concentration of the mind. It does not (like Artha and Káma) much depend on external means. Supported (*i.e.* held up) by the knowledge of the reality, it is not affected by Artha and Káma, howsoever pursued; and, even if affected, it is set right by a little exertion; and, eradicating that defect also, it conduces to the highest (*lit.* not a little) bliss. Hence the passion of the Grandsire (Brahmá) for Tilottamâ; the pollution of thousands of the wives of the ascetics by Śiva; Kṛishṇa's amorous sporting with sixteen thousand wives in his harem; Brahmâ's passionate inclination towards his own daughter; the seduction of Ahalyá by Indra; the Moon's violation of the bed of his preceptor (Bṛihaspati); the Sun's unnatural connexion with a mare; the union of Váyu with Añjanà; Bṛihaspati's illicit intercourse with the wife of (his elder brother) Utathya; Paráśara's despoiling of the daughter of a fisherman; his son's (Vyása's) connexion with the wives of his brother (Vichitravîrya); and Atri's union with a doe. Also, the various artifices employed by gods towards the demons (*or*, deeds worthy of the demons alone) to gain their various objects do not affect Dharma, by the power of knowledge. And, when the mind is purified by piety, passion (Rajas) does not at all defile (*lit.* stick to) it, as dust does not the sky. I therefore hold that Artha and Kâma do not come up even to a hundredth part of Dharma."

On hearing this the sage with his passion enkindled (*or*, augmented) said—"Graceful damsel, you have taken a proper view (of matters), in that you say that the Dharma of him who has known the Truth is not obstructed (*or*, interfered with) by worldly enjoyment. But we, from our birth, are quite ignorant of matters relating to Artha and Káma. It is necessary to know what their natures are, their attendant circumstances and their results." She replied—"Artha is of the form of (*i.e.* consists in) its acquisition, increase and conservation; its concomitants are agriculture, rearing up of cattle, trade, peace, war and the like; and its fruit (*i.e.* final object) is its bestowal on deserving persons. Káma is a peculiar kind of touch (contact) yielding the highest pleasure to persons whose hearts are deeply attached to sensual objects; its concomitants are all that are lovely and bright in this world; its fruit is the highest gratification, which gives the highest delight, which springs up from mutual, close contact, which is sweet to remember, in which all self-conceit disappears, which is supreme, which is bliss directly enjoyed, and which is to be felt by one's own self only. It is for the sake of this pleasure only that men practise in particular (holy) places severe penance, give liberal gifts, fight terrible battles, and undertake dangerous enterprises, such as voyages.

Hearing this, the Ṛishi—it may be owing to the power of destiny, or to her eloquence, or to infirmity of his own mind—became attached to her, disregarding his devotions. She took him, who was too far gone in forgetting himself (*i.e.* his proper duty), in a car to the town, and led him to her own house by the magnificent high road. And (as they passed), the festival of Káma was proclaimed as taking place on the morrow. Next day, when the ascetic had bathed and applied perfumes to his body, and put on beautiful garlands, she led him, who had begun to act like a votary of the God of love, and who had no longer any desire to keep up his former character, and who felt uneasy if he was without her even for an instant, by the splendid royal road to where people were celebrating the festival, and approached the King who was sitting, surrounded by hundreds of damsels, in one part of the garden. The King, with a smiling face, said—"Fair damsel, sit down with the sage." Thereupon she made a graceful bow and smilingly sat down; which done, a certain beauteous woman with folded hands rose up, saying—"Sire, I am vanquished by her and own myself the damsel's slave," and bowed to the king. A general uproar due to wonder and joy rose up from the people. The damsel, dismissed by the delighted King after being rewarded with jewelled ornaments of great value and a large retinue, and also applauded by the different groups of courtesans and the principal citizens, said to the sage even without going home—"Revered Sir, here I fold my hands to you; this your servant has been long favoured; now return to your pious duties." But he, as if struck by the thunderbolt and greatly agitated by his passion, said to her—"Dear damsel, what d.es this mean? Whence is this indifference? Where has gone that uncommon affection you showed for me?" Thereupon she smiled and said—"Sir, the damsel, who in the assembly acknowledged herself defeated, formerly in some conflict with me rebuked me, saying—'You are boasting as if you have won over Marîchi;' so I proceeded in this affair, it being agreed (between us) that the vanquished one should become the slave of the other, and by your favour I have won the wager." The silly ascetic, thus repulsed by her, greatly repented, and like one vacant-minded, returned to his dwelling.—And know me, O noble youth, to be the same who was so gulled by that girl. And that same whore, having uprooted the passion instilled in me by her power of fascination, has now infused (*i. e.* created) in me a great disgust for worldly pleasures. Before long I shall render my soul capable of achieving your object. In the meanwhile do you abide in this very Champá, the capital of Aṅga."

At this time the sun set, as if in fear of the touch of the darkness (of ignorance) that fell off from the sage's mind; the *Rága* (passion, redness), cast off by him, glimmered in the shape of the twilight; and the beds of lotuses faded away, as if they had colourlessness imparted to them (—as if filled with disgust) by his narration. In conformity with the sage's directions I performed the evening devotions with him, sleeping after him, and passed the night talking on various topics suited to the occasion. At day-break, while the red-rayed (morning) sun, that looked almost like a wild conflagration on the peak of the rising mountain, and that despised (*i. e.* far surpassed the lustre of) the tender sprouts of the desire-fulfilling trees, was peeping up, I bowed to him and proceeded to the city. On my way, outside a convent of Jain mendicants, I saw, seated in a lonely clump of red Aśoka trees, a certain Jain mendicant, of a miserable look, who had not yet taken to asceticism (*or,* who had not begun to practise Samádhi--abstract meditation), who was reduced by mental anxiety, and who was the foremost among the ugly. I also noticed drops of tears falling on his chest from his face, the accumulation of dust whereon was loosened. I sat down by him, and asked him—"Penance and this shedding of tears, how to reconcile the two! If not a secret, please let me know the cause of your sorrow." He answered—"Gentle youth, listen. I am Vasupâlita by name, the eldest son of a merchant named Nidhipálita, an inhabitant of this very Champâ. On account of my ugliness I came to be distinguished by the name Virûpaka. There was here another (youth) called Sundaraka, a name quite significant in his case, who, rich in virtues and (skilled) in arts, was not much favoured (*lit.* fattened) by wealth. An ill-feeling was created between him and me, based on our form and wealth, by the designing town-sharpers who live by creating discord. Once, at a festival, they themselves put down an altercation in reproachful language between us, due to mutual insult and given rise to by themselves, and settled the matter, saying—"Neither form nor wealth is the test of manliness; but he alone is a man whose youth would be sought by the most eminent harlot. Let him, therefore, whom Kâmamañjarî, the ornament of young women, would love, have the banner of grace." We agreed to it and sent messengers to her. I alone (as it appeared) became the inflamer of her passion; for, as we were seated, she, approaching me alone, invested me with a string (*i.e.* succession) of side-glances as if of blue lotuses, and thus made my rival hang down his face through shame. I, who considered myself blessed, made her the mistress of my wealth, my house, my retinue, my body and even of my very life. And she reduced me to utter poverty (*lit.* made me one to whom a rag was left). I, who was deprived of everything and turned out by her, became an object of ridicule to the world; and being unable to bear the contempt (*lit.* the utterings of 'fie') of the aged citizens, I came here to this Jain convent, where the path to final beatitude being shown to me by a Muni, I, thinking that my present garb should be easy to those who had left the house of a harlot, and being filled with disgust, threw off that strip of cloth also. Then again, with my body covered with a thick layer of dirt, smarting under the great pain caused by the plucking off of the hair, tormented with severe thirst and hunger, and troubled by severe restraints, like a newly-caught elephant, in matters such as dwelling, sitting, sleeping and taking food, I thus thought over my state—"I am a Brâhmaṇa, and in following the path of the heretics I deviate from my proper faith. My ancestors followed the path (principles) laid down by the Vedas and the Smṛitis alone. But I, an unlucky creature, had to follow this unrighteous path of this nature as if it were that of righteousness, where the dress (to be worn) is condemnable, which is the abode of excessive suffering, the fruit whereof is hell even after death owing to one's having constantly to listen to the blasphemy against the gods Vishṇu, Śiva, Brahmá and others, which is rewarded with no (real) fruit, and which is almost a deception." Thus, with a full realization of my improper course of action, I freely give vent to my tears, having come to this solitary clump of Aśoka trees."

Moved to pity on hearing his account, I said to him—"Friend, be patient and wait for a time here. I shall so manage it that that harlot herself will restore your wealth to you; there are means of that sort." Having thus cheered him up, I rose after he had done so. Just as I entered the city I came to know from the general talk that that city abounded in rogues (*or*, covetous) and wealthy people; and wishing to restore them to their primitive natures by proving to them the transitoriness of wealth, I resolved to take to the path laid down by Karṇîsuta (*i.e.*, to thieving). I then entered the gambling house and joined the company of the gamesters. As I observed their skill in all the twenty-five sorts of arts connected with gambling; their tricks, execedingly difficult to notice, in cogging a die on the dice-board or shifting a piece, and the consequent abusive words uttered with vanity, and their desperate acts regardless of life; the transactions begun with the knowledge of their president, consisting chiefly in the employment of argument, force and valour, and capable of enforcing payment; their power to wheedle the resolute and bully the timid; their dexterity in making partisans; the various proffering of tempting advantages; the descriptions of different ways of betting; their generosity in the distribution of the money gained; their clamours at intervals, mostly consisting of indecent talk, and such other things;—I derived no satisfaction; and I happened to laugh at a gamester who made a blunder in moving a piece. His rival, burning as it were with his eyes inflamed with anger, looked at me and said—"Ah! Dare you teach us the way to play, under the pretext of laughter? Let the poor fellow alone; he is but a novice. With you, then, who are such an expert in the art, I will gamble." With these words he joined with me in play with the consent of the president, and I won from him 16,000 Dînâras; half of this I gave to the president and the assembly, and with the other half I rose to go. And there rose up expressions of my praise, full of joy, from the people assembled there. Acceding to the request of the president I went to his house and had a sumptuous meal there. He, Vimardaka by name, on whose account I descended into (the field of) gambling, became my most trustworthy second heart (as it were).

By his means I came to know everything about the townsmen as regards their wealth, dealings and their behaviour; and on a night extremely dark like the throat of Śiva, putting on a black veil (*or*, cloak), with a sharp sword fastened (to my person) and equipped with such implements as a scoop, a whistle, tongs, a sham head, magic powder, a magic wick, a measuring thread, a wrench, a rope, a lamp-case, and a beetle in a box, I went to the house of a celebrated usurer (*lit.* miser). Making a breach in his house after finding out the state of things inside through the small hole (*or*, a hole of the size) of a lattice-window, I entered it without any fear, as if it were my own house, took his purse, valuable on account of its costly contents, and departed. On (*i.e.* as I passed along) the main road, covered with dense darkness thick like a mass of dark clouds, I saw for a moment a flash of light like the fall of lightning; and just then there stood before me a young damsel, with glittering ornaments, as though she were the presiding goddess of the city coming to encounter me at a time when the streets were devoid of crowds, angered at the theft committed in the city. "Damsel, who are you and where are you going?"—thus compassionately asked by me, she replied in words faltering through fear—"Respected Sir, an eminent merchant lives in this city, named Kuberadatta. I am his daughter. My father betrothed me as soon as I was born to Dhanamitra, the son of a wealthy man of this very city; but now he has grown poor, having purchased, as it were, with his wealth, upon the death of his parents, owing to extreme liberality, the condition of a pauper from his supplicants. Now, although he has thus gained from the gratified world the laudable epithet of 'Udáraka' (munificient), and has offered to marry me now grown up, my father refuses to give me in marriage to him as being now destitute, and wishes to marry me to another merchant-leader, named Arthapati, who, true to his name, is a man of great opulence. Knowing that that inauspicious event (*i.e.* my marriage) is sure to come off to-day at dawn, I, agreeably to an appointment already made with my beloved, have started, having eluded my relations, and am going, under the guidance of Cupid, to my lover's abode by this path familiar to me from my childhood. So please let me pass; take this treasure of ornaments." So saying she took them off and made them over to me. But, pitying her, I said—"Come, O virtuous maiden! I will lead you to the dwelling of your lover," and proceeded a few steps, when there came a large force of the city-watch who dispelled the mass of darkness by means of the light of the torches, and who had sticks and swords in hand. I said to the maiden who trembled (with fear) at their very sight—"Fear not, gentle damsel; here is my arm armed with a sword (to protect you). But for your sake I have thought of this clever (*lit.* gentle) plan. I will lie down, affecting to be overcome by the pangs of poison; do you address these people thus:—We entered the city this night; this my husband was bitten by a snake in a corner of that public stall. If any one among you knows the charm (that removes poison) and feels compassion for me, he should kindly give life to a helpless woman by restoring him to life." That maiden, having no alternative, with her voice faltering through fear, and her eyes overflooded with tears, tremblingly somehow went up to them and did as I desired. I also lay down, showing as if I was affected by the virulence of the poison. One of them, who prided himself on his being a poison-doctor, carefully surveyed me, and after treating me with a talisman, mystical formularies, charms and mental efforts, without success, declared—"Gone indeed, is he, bitten by the Destroyer (the deadly serpent); for his body is stiff and dark-blue, his eye-sight is steadied, and his warm breath stopped. Enough of grieving, O maiden! We shall consign the body to fire to-morrow. Who can transgress fate?" So saying, he departed with his comrades.

I rose up, and having taken her to Udáraka addressed him—"I am a certain thief; encountering on my way this maiden coming to you with no other companion than her heart set on you, I have attended her through compassion hither; here are her ornaments." So saying, I also handed over to him those ornaments, which pierced the mass of darkness by their numerous rays. Udâraka, too, took them up, and with shame, joy and excitement said—"Honoured Sir, you have given me my beloved this night, but again have deprived me of speech. For I do not know what to say (how to thank you): If I were to say (इति) that this your act (*viz.* your escorting this damsel to me and restoring the ornaments) is wonderful, (it would be objected that) your character, indeed, appears to be something marvellous. If I were to say that this has never been done by any other (thief) before, (then it might be urged against me) that the power of things is fixed in each individually: for avarice and such other qualities which are found in others are absent in you. (If I were to say), that to-day you have clearly displayed what saintly character is, it would not agree with your previous virtuous acts mostly of such nature; also (if I were to say) that to-day is seen what the real nature of nobility of mind is, it will not be reasonable to arrive at such a decision without having consulted your opinion (your estimate of it). To say that you have bought this slave by this good act, would be an insult to your high mental faculties (*or*, judgement), as it would amount to saying that you bought a worthless thing for an extremely valuable one. If I were to say that I offer my body to you as a return-gift for your gift of my beloved to me, (it would not also be reasonable, for) my body is (virtually) a gift from you, as it would have perished had I not obtained my beloved. Or this much will be proper for me to say on this occasion—"From to-day, this your slave, should be supported by you." So saying he fell at my feet. I raised him, embraced him and asked him what course of conduct he meant to adopt. He replied—"I shall not be able to reside in the city with safety upon marrying the damsel without the consent of her parents. I, therefore, propose to leave the city this very night." "Or rather," he added, "who I am I to decide? I will follow *your* advice." Then I said—"It is as you say; (staying in) one's own country or change of country is no consideration with a man of talent. But this maiden is tender in no small degree; the paths through a wilderness are very difficult, and abound in obstacles; and (again), such an abandonment of the native place bespeaks something like want of talent and spirit on one's part. You should, therefore, just live here happily with her. Come, let us conduct her to her own house." He readily assenting (*lit.* without giving thought to it), we at once took her to her house; and with her serving as our guide, we stole everything (in the house) except the earthen pots. Going forth from that place we placed our booty somewhere, and then proceeding, as we encountered a party of city-guards we mounted a powerful (*lit.* intoxicated) elephant lying down by the road-side after having pulled down the rider. Just as he was being urged to rise by me with my feet thrust into the chain round his neck, he, striking a blow slantingly with his tusk on the broad chest of the driver that was thrown down, and with his tusk encircled by his entrails, destroyed the city-guards. And by means of that very beast we destroyed the house of Arthapati Driving him on we alighted in an old grove by catching hold of the branches of a tree (and holding fast to them till the animal passed on); then going to our house we took a bath and lay down on bed.

Just then rose up from the ocean the orb of the Sun, looking almost like a ruby peak of the rising mountain, and red like a wreath of the golden sprouts of the desire-fulfilling trees. We got up, washed our faces, and after performing the customary rites of the morning, walked about the town, astir on account of our deeds, when in the houses of the bride and the bridegroom, we heard a great clamour. Arthapati comforted Kuberadatta with a gift of riches, and arranged to have the marriage of Kulapáliká put off for a month. I then (thus) instructed Dhanamitra in secret—"Friend, wait upon the king of the Angas with special reference to this jewel of a leather-bag just in private, and say—"Your Majesty knows that I am Dhanamitra, the only son of Vasumitra, whose wealth consisted of many crores. Having lost all my paternal wealth on account of a number of supplicants, I came to be despised by men. Now, as owing to the fault of my poverty Kuberadatta wished to give to Arthapati his daughter Kulapáliká, who was brought up for my sake only, I, in grief (*or*, through despondency) entered an old grove situated near the city, wishing to give up my life; but when about to place the scimitar on my throat, I was prevented by an ascetic and thus asked—'What is the reason of this desperate act?' I replied—'Poverty, the sister of contempt.' Then he, the compassionate one, thus favoured me—"Young man, you are under a delusion; no sin is more heinous than suicide. The good raise themselves (*i.e.* improve their position) by personal efforts, without destroying themselves. There are many ways of recovering lost wealth, but none to regain life that would depend on the re-joining of a throat that is cut off. But why go on thus? I am perfect in the power of spells; this leather-bag is endowed with magical power so as to grant a lac of coins. I lived for a long time in Kámarûpa, fulfilling the desires of the people there through its favour. Being exposed to jealousy in my old age, I came to this place wishing to enter a heaven on earth (as it were). So take this bag of that virtue. Excepting me, it yields treasures only to merchants or the best of courtesans; such is the experience about it. But one must first restore to a person whatever one might have dishonestly got from him, and must also give away to Bráhmaṇas and gods whatever is gained by just means. After this, being worshipped daily after being placed like an idol in a pure place, it will be found to be filled with gold every morning. This is the prescribed mode for making it work (*i. e.* yield the treasure)." With this he gave it to me who had folded my hands before him, and himself entered a cave. Thinking that this leather-bag, which is a precious gem, should not be used without informing Your Majesty about it, I have brought it to you; so Your Majesty should decide what is proper in this case." The king will surely say—"Good man, I am pleased. Go; use it just as you like." Then say to him again—"May I be so favoured that none can steal it away from me." This also he will undoubtedly undertake to do. After this, go home and according to your statement give away everything you have. Afterwards fill the bag, which will be emptied by daily demands, at night with money obtained by theft, and show it in the morning to the people. Then Kuberadatta, who is ever covetous of money, will esteem Arthapati as insignificant as grass, and will himself wait upon you with his daughter. Then Arthapati, being enraged, will, through the pride of riches, try to seek redress by legal means Him, also, we will again reduce to a rag by various means. By this means our own theft also will be quite concealed." Dhanamitra, being delighted, did exactly as he was told. That very day Vimardaka, who had taken service under Arthapati, at my direction excited his enmity against Udáraka (Dhanamitra). The avaricious Kuberadatta, giving up Arthapati, earnestly wished to give his daughter in marriage to Dhanamitra alone. And Arthápati came in his way (*lit.* opposed him).

Just at this time (*lit.* in these days), as Rágamañjarî, the younger sister of Kâmamañjarî, was to give a musical concert at the public hall, the citizens, full of eager curiosity, were collected there. I, with such precedents, was present there with my friend Dhanamitra. When she had commenced dancing, my mind became (as it were) a second stage-ground (for her to dance, *i.e.* she made a deep impression on my mind). Cupid, taking refuge in the excellent bow in the form of the lotus-bed of her amorous glances, and gaining strength as it were on account of the display of feelings and sentiments in their entirety, tormented me exceedingly. Thereupon she bound me with the chains of a series of her sporting side-glances, dark-blue like the petals of blue lotuses, as if she were the presiding deity of the town, incensed at my thefts in the town. As she rose after dancing, appearing more graceful by the flush of success, she repeatedly looked at me, I know not whether through coquetry, or through desire for me, or merely by chance, with a glance from the corner of her eye, unnoticed even by her friends, and in a manner in which the creeper-like eyebrows were gracefully contracted; and smiling under some pretext, so as to display the moonlight of her teeth a little, she set out (for her house) followed by the eyes and minds of the people.

I, thus conditioned, went home; but on account of an irresistible longing, I had no desire, whatsoever, to take food; and under pretence of a headache I lay on my solitary bed, with drooping limbs. Dhanamitra, who was an adept in love-affairs, came to me and privately said to me—" Friend, blessed is that courtesan girl alone, since your mind is so deeply attached to her; I closely marked the affected state of her mind, too. Cupid will make her also lie on a bed of his arrows in no time. And the union of you two, who have each fixed your affection on the worthy person, can be brought about without any efforts. But that courtesan girl, as the report goes, with a noble and generous thought (mind) that goes contrary to the proper duties of courtesans, is said to have declared—" I am to be won by merit, and not by money; and my youth will not be enjoyed by another except by marriage." Her sister, Kámamañjarî, and her mother Mádhavasená, remonstrated with her against that; and not succeeding in their object, they, with tears choking their throats, applied to the King, saying—" Sire, we had a very great hope that your slave,

Rágamañjarî, as perfect in character and in accomplishments as in form, would fulfil our desires; but that (hope) to-day is nipped in the bud; for she, setting aside the duties of her family, and quite regardless of wealth, wishes to sell her youth for merits only, and desires to follow only the unfailing course of life of a woman-of-family. It will be a nice thing, if even at the words of Your Majesty she comes to her senses." When she refused to listen, even though advised accordingly by the King out of regard to them, her sister and mother with persistent tears said to the King earnestly—"If any lover would mislead and seduce her without our wish (consent), he should be put to death as a thief." Such being the case, her relations will not give their consent without wealth, while she will not approach (*i.e* accept) one who will give money. So here we have to think of a remedy." I said to him—"What is there to be thought over? We shall win her over by our virtues, while (at the same time) we shall secretly gratify her relatives with riches."

Then I won over Dharmarakshitá, a Buddhist female mendicant, the chief agent of Kàmamañjarî, with gifts of old garments, food and the like, and through her medium I made an agreement with that harlot that I should steal Dhanamitra's wonderful bag and give it to her if she would give me in return Rágamañjarî. I, then, when she accepted my proposal, accomplished the business in that way (*i.e.* stole the bag for her) and took the sprout-like (tender) hand of Rágamañjarî, who was fascinated (*lit.* intoxicated) with my qualities. In the beginning of the night on which the wonderful bag was to be given out as stolen, while the prominent townsmen, called under the pretext of some other business, were listening, Vimardaka, my secret agent, having insulted Dhanamitra, spoke many an angry word, showing himself as a partisan of Arthapati. Dhanamitra said—"What is your gain that you revile me for the sake of another? I do not remember to have done even a small injury to you." As if in a threatening tone, Vimardaka said again—"This is what is known as the pride of wealth, that you seek to make your own another's bride, bought off with the bride's-money, by alluring her parents again by means of wealth; and again you ask me, 'What wrong I have done to you' Why, it is well known that Vimardaka is the external life (*i.e.* second self) (as it were) of Arthapati, the leader of merchants. Such being the case, I will even give up my life for him, and will not shrink even from the murder of a Brâhmaṇa. It needs only one night's awakening on my part to chase away this your fever of pride of the wonderful bag." As he was saying so, the principal citizens angrily interrupted him and drove him away. First mentioning the loss of the wonderful bag, Dhanamitra, feigning uneasiness, communicated this news to the king, who sent for Arthapati and asked him in private—" Sir, have you some one connected with you, named Vimardaka ?" The silly-minded Arthapati said—" Yes, Sire; he is my great friend; what is to be done with him?" When this was said the King asked him if he could call him to his presence. Arthapati, saying that he could, by all means, went home and carefully looked for him in his own house, in the streets, through the residence of courtesans, in the gaming houses, and in the market-place, but did not find him. And how could the poor fellow find him out? For verily that Vimardaka, fully instructed by me as to the marks for reconizing Your Highness, had started for Ujjain, that very day, at my command. Arthapati, on his part, not seeing him (Vimardaka), thought that the crime committed by him would be connected with himself, and denied the charge, either through delusion or through fear; but again, when the matter was brought home to him by Dhanamitra, he was seized by the enraged King and put in chains.

Just in these days Kámamañjarî, desirous of making the wonderful bag yield treasures according to the prescribed procedure for its use, went in secret to Virûpaka whom she had previously milked (deprived) of everything and who had become a Jain mendicant, and having greatly pacified him restored to him with courtesy all the property appropriated from him, and returned home. He, too, somehow freeing himself from the clutches of the Jains and being advised by me with the greatest gladness, resumed his former religion. Within a few days, Kámamañjarî also reduced her large fortune to the residue of a hearth, with the hope of milking the wonderful bag. Dhanamitra, instructed by me, humbly requested the King in private, saying—" Sire, the courtesan Kámamañjarî, who by her inordinate greed had become the object of the censure of the people by being nicknamed Lobha-mañjarî, is to-day indifferently giving away, in charity, even the pestle and mortar in her house. So I think it must be due to her acquisition of my magical bag; for such is the prescribed mode for its use; and it has been known about it that it yields treasures only to merchants and the best among the courtesans, and not to anyone else. Hence it is that I suspect her." She was immediately summoned with her mother by the King. With apparent concern, I said to her in private—"Lady, surely you must have been suspected of having the wonderful bag, on account of your very widely-known abandonment of everything in charity. You are summoned by the King to be questioned about it. When pressed again and again, you will certainly point me out as the source of its acquisition; and then I shall be put to a torture-death; and when I am dead, your sister will not certainly live. As for you, you have not a pie with you, while the wonderful bag will again go into the possession of Dhanamitra. Thus this calamity will on all sides carry in its train a series of misfortunes. So, what should be done?" Her mother and she, both in tears, said—"It is surely on account of our folly that this secret has almost leaked out; though we may hide it for a day or two ( *lit.* two, three or four times ), still, being pressed hard by the King, we shall have to give out your name as the source of the thing stolen, *viz.* the wonderful bag, and you being thus pointed out, our family will certainly be ruined. That infamy has ( already ) settled itself on Arthapati; and that niggardly fellow's close connexion with us is quite well-known in the town of Aṅga. So we had better save ourselves by declaring that it was he who gave it to us." Having thus communicated their intention to me, they both went to the palace. Being questioned by the King, they first prevaricated by saying again and again that it would not be just for harlots to expose their patrons, adding that it was not always the case that people came to them with money honestly acquired; but being threatened with the punishment of having their noses and ears cut off, those wretched harlots saddled the theft on that poor fellow, Arthapati. The King, in a rage, sentenced him to death; when Dhanamitra with folded hands interposed, saying—"Sire, the merchants have a special privilege from Maurya, *viz.* immunity from death in such offences. If Your Majesty is angry, let this villain have his whole property confiscated and be banished." On account of this (noble act of saving Arthapati) the fame of Dhanamitra spread far and wide; the King also was highly pleased ( with him ). Arthapati, who was vain of his wealth ere now, was banished in rags before the very eyes of the citizens. The wretched Kámamañjarî, who had given away everything through the mirage of the wonderful bag, was, at the instance of Dhanamitra, compassionately favoured by the King with a portion of his (Arthapati's) treasures Dhanamitra married Kulapálikâ on an auspicious day. Thus, having succeeded in all my plans, I filled the house of Râgamañjarî with gold and jewels.

The wealthy misers of the city were so robbed of their wealth that, with broken platters in their hands, they wandered all over, begging for alms at the houses of the supplicants whom I had enriched with their wealth Man, though extremely ingenious, cannot transgress the line drawn by fate. For, one day, in order to pacify the love-anger of Râgamañjarî, I coaxed her to drink; and with the mouthfuls of wine that she affectionately passed into my mouth I became intoxicated. It is but the nature of drunkenness and over-excitement, to follow even by taking a wrong course their wonted practices; and so I, in the height of my intoxication, promised to her that I would fill her house, having despoiled the city of its wealth in a single night; and, disregarding hundreds of oaths (protestations) and bows with folded hands of my beloved who was very much (distressed at it), like a mad elephant that has forcibly snapped its chains, I, without properly equipping myself set off at the greatest speed, armed only with my sword and followed by a certain nurse, named S'ṛigálikâ. I fought with the city-guards fearlessly although advancing towards me; and without being much enraged though struck by them, being taken for a thief, I, as if in sport, slew two or three of them with the sword that fell from my hand enfeebled through intoxication, and fell down with my reddened eyes rolling. Then Śṛigàlikà, uttering cries of distress, came up to me and I was bound (at the same time). Roused to my senses at once by the misfortune that dissipated my drunkenness, I pondered with the help of the ready wit that came to me at that instant, (thus;—"Oh, this great calamity has befallen me on account of my drunken state; my friendship with Dhanamitra, as also my acceptance of Rágamañjarî in marriage, are but too well-known in this town; both of them, being involved in consequence of this my offence, will be arrested to-morrow; so this is the course to be adopted at this juncture, which being followed at my direction they will surely be saved, and will perchance save me from this distress." Thus reflecting and having definitely settled some plan within myself, I said to Śṛigâlikâ—"Away with you, old wench; undone (disappointed in your wishes) are you who brought about a union between that wretched harlot, Râgamañjarî, who is covetous of wealth, and Dhanamitra, who is drunk with (the pride) of the wonderful bag and who is my enemy wearing the garb of a friend; but having stolen that wonderful bag of that villain and carried off the precious ornaments of your daughter, I shall now relinquish life with an easy heart (*lit.* free from its dart)." She (Śṛigâlikâ), an exceedingly clever woman, took the hint, folded her hands, and approaching with tears and sobs, bowed low to the guards and said in a conciliatory tone—"Good sirs, please wait for some time so that I shall know from him about the whole of our property that has been stolen." They assenting with the words 'Very well,' she came up to me and said—"Gentle sir, kindly forgive this one offence of your slave; let that Dhanamitra be the object of your hatred if you like, since he violated your wife; but remembering the long and faithful service she did to you, it is proper for you to be kind to Râgamañjarî. Courtesans entirely depend (for their livelihood) upon decorations (dress and ornaments); so kindly tell me where you have deposited her ornaments." With these words she fell at my feet. I appearing to take pity on her said—"All right: what am I to gain by my persistence in my enmity with her, now that I am in the clutches of death?" And as if I were going to say that (*i.e.* everything about the ornaments) to her, I whispered into her ear what was to be done. She as if having understood me, blessed me, saying—"May you live long; may the gods be pleased with you; may the King of Aṅgas, pleased by your manliness, release you; may these good people also be kind to you!"—and withdrew in an instant. And I, too, was taken to the prison by the order of the chief constable.

The next day, Kântaka, the chief of the city-police who had lately succeeded to his father's post, who was exceedingly arrogant, who considered himself highly fortunate and beautiful, and who was inexperienced owing to the pride of youth, came to me, and threatening me a little, said—"If you will not return Dhanamitra's wonderful purse, and their stolen property to the citizens, you will see the end of the eighteen tortures and finally the jaws of death." I laughed at him and said—"Gentle sir, though I may give up all the wealth I have stolen from my birth, I will never gratify the desire for the wonderful purse of my enemy, Dhanamitra, the ravisher of the wife of Arthapati, who only outwardly passes for my friend. I will suffer even a myriad of tortures, but not give it back ; this is my firm resolve." While there went on in the same manner all kinds of questionings in which there were conciliations and threats held out, I, getting wholesome food and drink, had all my wounds healed within a few days and was restored to health.

After this once, as the day drew to its close with its light yellow like the garment of Vishṇu, Śṛigálikâ, with a smiling countenance and handsomely dressed, approached me, her follower standing at a distance, and said—"Sir, you are fortunate: your wisely devised plans have borne fruit (*i e.* become successful); I went to Dhanamitra as directed by you and said - "Your friend who is thus in distress has sent this message to you : "I am to-day made a prisoner on account of the vice of drinking so easy to contract by being in the company of courtesans. But you on your part should without any fear address the King just to-day saying—"Sire, through the favour of Your Majesty alone, the wonderful bag was recovered on a former occasion from Arthapati, who had stolen it. Thereafter the husband of Rágamañjarî, a certain expert gambler, came in contact with me (became my friend) owing to his extreme proficiency in arts, poesy and in popular parlance; on account of his friendship I used to please his wife every day by sending her garments and ornaments and by such other means. That base-hearted sharper grew suspicious about it; and he being enraged took away that wonderful bag and also her casket of ornaments. But he, roaming over the town again to steal, was arrested by the city-guards. Now being in distress, he, having regard for his former love (for Râgamañjarî), told the place where he had deposited the casket to the nurse of Rágamañjarî, who had followed him in tears; so if he, being won over by (proper) remedies, will give back my purse, I solicit Your Majesty to show me such a favour." Thus informed, the King will not deprive me of my life, but will try by conciliatory means alone to induce me to restore your property to you. And this will be advantageous to us." Just as he heard it, he, as he had confidence in your prowess, without being much alarmed did all that exactly in that manner. Now I also, getting whatever things I desired from Rágamañjarî whose confidence I gained by means of the token of recognition from you, pleased in the way pointed out by you Máṅgaliká, the nurse of the princess Ambâlikâ. Through her medium I developed a fast friendship between Rágamañjarî and Ambâlikâ. Bringing to her over-new presents every day and telling her wonderful tales, attractive to the mind, I became a great object of favour with her. One day, as she ( Ambáliká ) was sitting on the terrace of her mansion, I, while putting right the lotus, her ear-ornament, pretending that it had slipped down though it was in its proper place, let it fall as if through carelessness, and then picking it up again from the ground and laughing out under the pretext of frightening away the pair of pigeons that were engaged in amorous sport, I struck with it Kántaka who had entered for some reason the court-yard of the palace adjacent to the apartment of the princess. As he, too, owing to that, considered himself blessed and looked up with a smile, I also, with a gesture, acted in an indescribably clever way so as to make him think the almost amorous-looking features of the princess, who was induced to burst into laughter by my act, due to her strong partiality for him. Wounded by the Mind-born One ( Cupid ), who had fully drawn his bow, with a shaft the dart of which was venomed, he being quite beside himself thereby, went away with difficulty. In the evening, I made a certain girl take a cane-box sealed with the princess' signet-ring and containing in it perfumed *támbûla* (*or*, perfumes and támbûla) silk-garments and a few ornaments ; and taking it as meant for Râgamañjarî, went with her to the house of Kántaka. He who was plunged in the unfathomable passion's ocean, felt greatly rejoiced on getting me as a boat. The silly (*or*, wicked) man's passion was raised to a very high pitch by me by describing in detail the extremely tormenting states of the princess' love-affected condition. At his instance, I brought him, the next day, as presents from his beloved, a garland worn the previous day by me, a *tâmbûla* (betel-roll) from my own mouth, an unguent used by me, and an unclean garment. The things that he gave I took as for the princess, but they were carried away in secret elsewhere.

He himself, whose fire of love was thus kindled, was addressed by me in private—"Sir, the auspicious marks themselves (of elevation) that you bear are not to falsify themselves (i. e. will prove true). For a neighbour of mine, an astrologer, told me—"This kingdom shall fall into Kântaka's hands ; he bears such marks." And just in accordance with that the princess has fallen in love with you ; and the King, whose only child the princess is, though incensed on knowing about your union with her, will not, through fear of his daughter's death, execute you, but on the contrary will certainly crown you heir-apparent.

Thus this good fortune is to be followed by another one. Why don't you then, dear one, try to secure it? If you cannot think of some means to get an entrance into the princess' apartment, then, I say, the distance between the prison-wall and the rampart of the pleasure-garden is only three *Vyámas*. If by some skilful robber you get a subterranean passage made of that length, then, once in, your protection will rest with us; for her attendants are deeply attached to her and will never divulge the secret." He replied—"Well suggested, friend! There is a thief who is as it were one (equal to any) of the sons of Sagara in the act of digging; if he is secured, he will accomplish the work in a moment." When I said—"Who can he be, and why can he not be procured?" he pointed you out, saying—"It is the man who stole Dhanamitra's magic purse;" I said—"If it be so, come on. Make an agreement with him with an oath; that you will liberate him by various ways if he achieved the task; and that being done, fetter him again, and representing to the King that though prevailed upon in every way that thief, who is the very abode of intrepidity and whose enmity is inveterate, would not show the magic purse, you will put him to death by submitting him to peculiar tortures. This being accomplished you will gain your object and the secret will not leak out." When I said this he was highly pleased and having accepted (my counsel), appointed my own self to persuade you to it, and is himself standing outside. [So far the plans have been successfully carried out]. Now think of what is proper to do next." I was very much pleased and said—"What I said was but nothing; your own policy has greatly contributed to this. Very well, bring him in." When brought in he took an oath to set me free and I never to divulge his secret. My chains were removed, and I had a bath and food given to me along with unguents. Beginning in an ever-dark corner of the prison-wall, I excavated a subterranean passage with a snake-headed tool Then I thought to myself—"This man has taken an oath to liberate me simply with a mind (desire) to murder me; so I shall not incur (*lit*. be touched with) the sin of proving false to my promise, even if I kill him.' As I was going out, he extended his hand to fetter me, when I kicked him on the breast; and as he fell down I cut off his head with my knife. Then I said to Śṛigáliká—"Tell me, friend, how the apartment of the princess is situated; (let me know it) so that (all) this great labour would not go in vain; there I shall steal something and return."

I entered the princess' apartment whose different parts were shown to me by her (Śṛigáliká), and in the midst of her attendants that were asleep owing to the exhaustion caused by sports not of one kind, I beheld the princess gone to sleep in full confidence while jewel-lamps were burning brightly, and looking, on account of her one side being almost buried in the exceedingly white bed-sheet, (charmingly slender and bright) like lightning lying steady, as it were, on account of the exhaustion caused by its flashing for a long time on the lap of an autumnal cloud; (she lay), on the surface of a couch the ivory feet of which had the shape of a recumbent lion and were set with big and precious jewels, which appeared splendid with the bed and pillows stuffed with downy feathers, and had its borders decked (*or*, engraved) with petals of flowers; in a manner in which the upper fore-part of her left foot was entwined with the inner side of her right heel, her beautiful ankle-joints were a little turned to the side, the stout and long calves of her legs were in close contact with each other; her tender knees were a little bent and her thighs a little curled; (in which) she looked attractive on account of the extremity of one of her slender (*lit.* creeper-like) arms loosely thrown over the hips, while the sprout-like hand, with its palm outstretched, of the other creeper-like arm, was contracted and thrown under the crown of the head; (in which) her round hips were a little curved, the fine under-garment of China-silk lay closely adhering to her person, and her extremely slender belly was not much bent; her budlike and fully-developed breasts were heaving as she was breathing perceptibly, while the neck-ornament made of rubies and interwoven in (the middle of) her necklace of burnished gold, was to be seen lying near the region of her lovely neck resting slantingly; her ear-ornament lying motionless under her beautiful ear turned down was half-visible; and her somewhat loosened braid of hair lying unevenly was tinged red with the cluster of rays from the jewelled ornament of the ear that was turned up, while the space between the red upper and lower lips was difficult to be discovered owing to the mass of their own lustre; (in which) the purpose of the ear-pendant was served by her sprout-like hand passed under the broad cheek; while the act of drawing the ornamental painting on her cheek was done by the different leaves in the embroidered canopy mirrored into her transparent cheek that was turned upwards; (in which) her lotus-like eyes were closed and the banner-like eyebrows still; (in which) the sandal *tilaka* had been moistened and mixed with the drops of perspiration that were rising up and her long and curly hair hung about ( *lit.* faced ) the moon of her face. With my passion kindled at her very sight, awe struck, without the least desire to steal, but robbed, instead, of my heart, I stood for a moment quite at a loss to know what to do. I then thought to myself—" Love will not suffer me to live, if I do not secure this maiden with beauteous eyes. If I touch her without previous intimation ( *or*, appointment ), this extremely young girl ( quite inexperienced in love-matters ) will evidently destroy my desire by her cry of distress, and then I shall have struck at myself (*i.e.* destroyed my prospects); so this is the way to be followed in the present case."—Thus reflecting I took a board dyed with the paste of a kind of gum, which was hanging from a peg, picked up a painting brush from a jewelled drawing-box, and sketched her sleeping in that manner, and myself kneeling at her feet with hands folded, and wrote this Áryá ( verse ):—

" This your slave here, with folded hands, implores of you " this object that is so well known, *viz.*—sleep with me, exhausted " in sport alone, and not in this manner."

Then taking from the golden betel-box a spiced roll of betel-nut leaves, a bit of camphor, and scented catechu, and chewing these I spat (*i.e.* spat in such a way as to give rise to) a pair of Chakravákas on the white wall, with its juice reddish like the *alaktaka* dye. After this, exchanging rings ( hers and mine ) I somehow (with great reluctance ) departed. Returning to the prison-house through that subterranean passage, I counselled a leading citizen, Siṃhaghosha by name, who was imprisoned there and who was treated by me in those days as a friend, saying—" Thus I have killed the poor Kántaka ; you should disclose the secrets ( intrigue of Kántaka ) and procure your freedom thereby," and I then set off with Śṛigáliká. Come to the royal road, I encountered the men of the guard. I thought—" I am able to run away untouched by these ; but this poor old woman will be seized ( arrested ) ; so this is the best thing to be done at this time." So I quickly ran up to them, and placing my elbows on my back and standing with my face turned away from them, I said—" If I am a thief, do you seize me ; for it is your duty and not of this old hag." She, on her part, having guessed my intention from that much (those my words), came to them and bowing said—" My good friends, this is my son : being affected by hysteria ( *or*, lunacy ), he was under treatment for a long time. The other day he was almost cured and restored to the natural condition of his health. Filled with hope ( that he was cured ), I procured his release from the prison, made him take a bath, apply unguents to his body, wear a pair of unbleached ( new ) garments and take excellent food ; and he was allowed to-day freedom of action as regards sitting and sleeping. But at midnight, being seized by his malady again, he ran off with great speed to the public road, exclaiming that he would put Kántaka to death and sport with the princess. Finding my son in this condition, I am running after him at this hour of the night ; so please have mercy on me and catch hold of him, and give him over to me." As she thus cried out I exclaimed—"Away, you wench! Who has ever bound the god Wind? Can these crows ( presume to ) restrain (*or*, catch ) me, a hawk? Tush ! "—and away I ran. Reproved by them with the words—"You yourself were mad who set him free, thinking him to be sane when he was not so ; who can catch him now? "—she ran after me, just weeping. I went to the house of Rágamañjarî, and having in many ways cheered her up who was distressed with the sorrow of long separation, passed the remaining part of the night. In the morning I joined the campany of Udáraka.

I then went to the revered Marîchi, who had regained his divine ken by the power of the penance practised by him after having got out of the calamity of the harlot, and by him I was told that I should thus obtain your sight. Siṃhaghosha, who was installed in Kántaka's place by the King who was much pleased with him after publicly announcing his ( Kántaka's ) misconduct, again effected my entrance into the apartment of the princess by that very subterranean passage from the prison-house, and I was united with the princess, who grew attached to me on hearing the account coming from the lips of Śṛigáliká. Just about this time Chaṇḍavarmá, highly incensed at his request for the hand of his daughter being refused by Siṃhavarmâ, attacked and besieged the city. The king of Aṅga, Siṃhavarmâ, impatient ( of the outrage ), himself made a breach into the rampart just as the enemy was thinking of commencing operations (in connexion with the siege), and without waiting for his allies although arrived very near, came out of the city ; but having his armour shattered to pieces by his mighty foe with superior numbers in a great battle, was forcibly taken captive. The princess Ambâlikâ was also powerfully seized and carried to his own camp by Chaṇḍavarmá, for being married to himself forcibly; and it was said that he (even) tied the auspicious marriage-string, as the marriage was to take place at the close of the night. I also, having fastened the auspicious marriage-string to my wrist at Dhanamitra's house, in order to marry the very same princess, said to him—"Friend, the allies advancing for helping the king of the Aṅgas are close at hand; conspiring with the grown-up men of the city with the greatest secrecy, bring them near; when you return, you will surely find the enemy with his head cut off." When he agreed to it, saying 'Very well,' I, with my weapon concealed, entered, along with the Brâhmaṇas (having to repeat the auspicious verses), the palace of him (my foe), doomed to die, which was full of the bustle attendant on the festival, and wherein the materials for the ceremony were being collected and the people were busy going in and out. And as Chaṇḍavarmá was about to take the tender hand of Ambáliká that was offered by the domestic priest with the holy fire standing as witness, I dragged his long arm and stabbed him in the chest with my dagger. I also despatched to Yama's abode (killed) some others that strove to seize me. Moving from one room to another of the house wherein some were destroyed and others were routed, I saw the long-eyed one, with her lovely limbs trembling through fear, and taking her with me entered an inner apartment with the desire to enjoy the pleasure of her embrace. At that very moment I had the good fortune to hear your voice, deep like the sound of fresh clouds."

Rájaváhana, having heard this narrative, smiled, and remarking—"How now! You have surpassed by desperate deeds (*lit.* hardihood) even Karṇîsuta," turned his eyes to Upahára-varmâ and desired him to narrate his adventures as it was his turn. He, too, having bowed (to him) with a smile, began to narrate (thus):—

---

## UCHCHHVÂSA III.

I once went (started in search of you), in the course of my peregrinations, to Videha; even without entering Mithilâ, I repaired for rest to a certain convent outside the city. There having water-for-my feet, given me by a certain old female devotee, I sat at the threshold for a short time. At my very sight tears flowed forth (from her eyes) forming into a stream, for some reason or another. Asked by me—"Mother, what is this, tell me the reason," she replied in a pitiful tone—"O you of long life, surely it is well known that Prahâravarmá was the king of this city of Mithilá; Râjahaṃsa, the king of Magadha, was, indeed, his fast friend. Their queens, Vasumatî and Priyaṃvadá, like those of the demons Bala and Śambala, formed an uncommon friendship between themselves. Priyaṃvadá went with her lord to Pushapura to see her dear friend, Vasumatî, on the festive occasion of her first pregnancy. Just at that time a war broke out between the king of Magadha and the king of Málwá, in which the king of Magadha met with a fate that could not to be ascertained in the least. Prahâravarman, who was spared by the efforts of the king of Málwá, returned to his country; but hearing that his kingdom was occupied by the sons of his elder brother Saṃhârvarman, Vikaṭavarman and others, he, wishing to take for his assistance a portion of the army of his sister's son, the king of Suhma, entered a forest (on his way) and there was plundered of everything by forest bandits. I fled with the younger of his sons in my arms from fear of the shower of arrows of the foresters, and plunged into a wood. There as I fell, being struck by the paw of a tiger, the child, fallen from my hands, hid himself under the bosom of the dead body of a brown cow. An arrow discharged from a bow deprived in an instant the tiger, who was dragging that carcass, of his life; and the child was carried off by the boys of the foresters. A certain cowherd conveyed me who lay senseless in that manner to his hut and placed me in it. There through his kindness I had my wounds dressed and healed; and then as I, wishing to repair to my master's presence after recovery, felt distressed owing to my helplessness, my own daughter, accompanied by a youth, arrived at the very place. She wept very much. When she had done weeping, she related her account: How the caravan-troops being defeated, the prince that was in her hands fell into the hands of the leader of the mountaineers; how she had her wounds healed by a forester, and how after her recovery she had to do the harshness of a refusal, owing to her disgust for the connexion with a low tribe, on his proposing to marry her; how he, not brooking that, attempted to cut off her head in the lonely forest, and (lastly) how the youth (in her company), who was accidentally seen, put the ruffian to death and espoused her. He, being asked, turned out to be a servant of the king of Mithilá who had stayed behind on some business, and was now preceeding by the same way.

We, in his company, approached our master, and burnt with the news of (the loss of) their sons, his ears and also those of the queen Priyaṃvadá.

Prahâravarmá fought long with the sons of his elder brothers, and again finding his position unbearable fought desperately for a very long time, and through the adverseness of fate was made a prisoner; and the queen, too, was made a captive. Then I, an unfortunate wretch, unable to give up my wretched life even in this old age, turned out a recluse; while my daughter, out of love for her accursed life, took service with Kalpasundarî, the queen of Vikaṭavarman. Had the two princes grown up without injury (to their life), by this time they would have been of your age; and they being present, the relatives of the king could not have laid violent hands upon him." At this her grief being increased she wept violently. On hearing the words of the nun, I also burst into tears, and very secretly said to her—"If it be so, mother, be comforted. You remember there was a sage to whom under the circumstances you applied for finding out the boy? He was found and brought up by him; it is a very long tale; what is to be done with that? I am that boy. It is in my power to approach that Vikaṭavarman somehow and to kill him; but again, he has many brothers; and the people will make common cause even with them. Besides, no one here knows me as being such and such (*i.e.* my parentage and rank); even my parents do not know me, much less any other persons. So I shall achieve my object by means of some stratagem." Thus I spoke to her. That old woman embraced me weepingly, smelled me on my head and with her breasts dropping milk said to me—"Son, may you be long lived! May good luck attend you! Revered fate seems to be favourable now; even to-day the country of Videha has come to be under the rule of Prahâravarman, since here you, of long and massive arms, stand ready to ferry us all over the ocean of misery! Ah! very fortunate, indeed, is Queen Priyaṃvadá"—and then she, full of excessive joy, ministered to my comfort by giving me bath, food and everything else. I lay on a mat in a part of the convent, and thought to myself—"This object cannot be achieved without a stratagem, and women alone are the source of stratagems. So I should formulate a plan by procuring information about the harem through the old nurse." As I was thus meditating, the night passed off as if blown away by the force of the breath of the horses of the Sun emerged from the ocean. The sun rose shining with a faint light, as if rendered sluggish by his stay in the depth of the ocean.

I got up, finished all the rites proper for the morning, and then said to my foster-mother—"Mother, do you know anything of the harem of that rogue, Vikaṭavarman?" I had scarcely spoken, when a young female appeared. That my nurse, as soon as she saw her, exclaimed, her throat choked with tears of joy—"Daughter Pushkariká, see our master's son! I relentlessly left him in the forest and now he comes to us in this manner." She, too, overcome with excess of joy, wept (with joy) for a long time. When the excitement subsided, she was desired by her mother to tell the state of affairs in the harem. She said—"Prince, Kalpasundarî, the daughter of Kalindavarman, the Lord of Kâmarûpa, excels the Apsarasas in beauty as well as in the knowledge of arts, and has not much regard for her husband. Vikaṭavarmá is excessively attached to her alone, though he has many other ladies in his harem." On hearing this, I said to her—"Kindly approach the queen with perfumes and garlands prepared by me; create hatred in her for her lord, by such things as finding fault with the connexion of two unequal persons; make her repent by citing to her the example of Vásavadattá and other distinguished females, who obtained lords quite worthy of themselves; and heighten her jealous anger by bringing to her knowledge the diversions of the king with other females in the palace, after diligently finding them out though very secret." Then to my old nurse I said—"Similarly, you also, leaving every other business, should attend upon the queen and you yourself should every day report to me whatever should happen there; again, this your daughter should, as advised by me, always attend upon Kalpasundarî like her own shadow, with a view to accomplish this our object which will have an agreeable end." Both of them performed their missions exactly as I desired.

When a few days had elapsed, my nurse told me that the queen had been so worked up that she considered herself as ill-matched as the lovely Mádhavî creeper with the bitter Nimba tree, and then asked me what further was to be done. I then drew a likeness of myself, and said to her—"Take this to the queen; when presented, she would surely, on looking at it, ask if there was a man possessing a form like that. Then ask the queen, in return, "What, if there be one?"—and then communicate to me her answer to this question. She, saying that she would do so, repaired to the palace, and after returning said to me in private—"Son, I showed that picture-canvas to that lovely beauty, when, full of astonishment, she said—"Indeed, this earth is blessed since even in the divine Cupid such exquisite beauty of form is not present. The picture itself is still more wonderful; to my knowledge no resident of this place is able to delineate one like this. Who is it that painted it?"—thus she asked in great earnestness. I smiled and said—"Queen, what you say is but proper. It is impossible to think that even Cupid is so beautiful; but again, this sea-begirt earth is wide enough, and therefore such a form due to the power of fate can be found somewhere. Now, if a youth endowed with such a form and born in a high family were to be here with talents, graces, lores and knowledge to correspond (to his beauty), what may he expect?" Kalpasundarî replied—"Mother, what should I say? For, my body, heart, and life itself,—all these are insignificant and unworthy of him; so he would get nothing. If this be not a fiction, so favour me that these my eyes will have their purpose fulfilled by obtaining the sight of such a person." Again, in order to confirm her in her longing, I said—"There *is* such a youth, the son of a king, who is living *incognito*. You, like Rati incarnate, came within the range of his eyes by chance, at the Spring-festival, while diverting yourself in the gardens of the city with your friends; and being penetrated by (*lit.* being the one mark of) the arrows of Káma, he offered to be guided by me in the matter. I (thus approached), impelled by the excellent virtues and extraordinary forms, befitting each other, of you both, served you for a long time with bouquets and garlands of flowers, unguents and other things, all prepared by him. It was also he who painted his own likeness and sent it to you to show how deep his devotion was to you. If this matter be determined upon, nothing can come in his way who possesses extraordinary valour and talents. I shall even show him to you this very day; you have simply to make an appointment." The queen, too, reflected a little as it were, and then replied—"Mother, now I need not at all conceal this from you, and therefore I shall tell you. My father was a great friend of Prahâravarman, and my mother Mánavatî was equally devoted to the queen Priyaṃvadá. These two, before they had children, agreed between themselves that she who would have a son, should marry him to the daughter of the      r. As the sons of Priyaṃvadá were lost, my father, as luck would have it, gave me in marriage to Vikaṭavarman, who solicited me. This my husband is a cruel man, a treacherous son, of a mis-shapen body, wanting in skill in amorous sports, not much attached to arts, poetry or dramas, of reckless valour, a vain boaster, a liar and a man bestowing his favours on unworthy objects. I don't like him, and not especially in these days, since even disregarding Pushkariká, my confidential maid standing by his side, he, with flowers plucked by himself from the Champaka creeper that I had planted and reared as if it had been my child, decorated Ramayantikà, a dancing girl in his service who does not know her own interest, and has entertained against me the jealousy of a rival wife; and he even amused himself in her company on the jewelled couch lying on the dais in the cave of the pleasure-mountain, when it was left by me after being enjoyed. The man is unworthy of me and has now commenced insulting me. Then why should regard be shown to him? The fear of the next world is obscured by the sufferings in this, and the misery of being compelled to associate with a man they hate can ill be borne by women whose minds have become the quiver (*i.e.* the constant target) of the arrows of Cupid. Do you therefore unite me with this man to-day in the Mádhavî bower in the garden; for, my mind has been very deeply attached to him on my merely hearing the information about him. I have this treasure in my possession; by its means I will establish him in his (Vikaṭavarman's) place and pass my life entirely in his service (*lit.* in attending on him)." Having accepted her proposal I have returned; now what to do further rests with the Prince (yourself)."

Then having learnt just from her the situation of the inner apartments, the places of the men keeping guard over these, and even the sites of the pleasure-garden as regards their distinct position, when the orb of the Sun was reddened as if the blood was thrown up to its surface in consequence of its fall on the summit of the setting mountain, when the sky was filled with the darkness spreading about, as if it were the mass of smoke arising out of the burning charcoal in the form of the Sun extinguished by his fall in the waters of the western ocean; when the moon, the chief of the planets, the admirer (covetor) of the wife of Bṛihaspati, rose as if to instruct me, disposed to violate another's wife; and when Cupid was getting ready with a desire for the conquest of the world, his valour being accelerated by the smiling disc of the moon, as if it were the lotus-like face of Kalpasundarî, that first showed itself with an eager desire to see me, I reclined on my bed as usual and reflected—"This object of mine is almost achieved. But, on account of the violation of another's wife, Dharma (righteousness) may be obstructed. But it is quite allowed by the writers of sacred books, if thereby wealth and love can both be secured. Again, I am going to incur the sin having in view the liberation of my parents; this (my motive) will extenuate the sin and will endow me with some religious merit at least. But then, on hearing this, how would the prince and my friends judge of my conduct?" While lost in such thoughts I was overtaken by sleep. The god with an elephant's mouth (Gajánana) appeared in my dream and said—"Gentle Upahâravarman, don't you have any misgivings since you are a portion of me, and that beautiful lady (Kalpasundarî) is the heavenly river (Ganges), deemed worthy of being fondled (by being borne) on the mass of the matted hair by Śiva; once she, not liking my wading through her (stream), denounced a curse upon me that I should be born a mortal, when in return I also cursed her that she should also be a mortal and that, as here, she should be an object of common enjoyment. She then addressed a request to me, saying—"Being the wife of one man first, I should sport throughout my life with you, ministering to your comfort." So this is a matter destined to happen, and you should have no scruples about it at all." I awoke, and quite pleased at heart passed that day also in thinking about everything with reference to the appointment of my beloved.

Kàma, unoccupied the next day elsewhere, poured a shower of arrows upon me; the lake of the brilliant lustre of the Sun became dry, and there spread about the mud of darkness. Clothed in dusky raiment, with my loins tightly girdled, grasping my sword, and furnishing myself with all the implements necessary for my purpose, I repaired to the ditch round the palace, filled with water, all the while bearing in mind the directions given by my foster-mother. When I reached the ditch I took up the bamboo-pole that was previously placed there near the door of my foster-mother's house by Pushkarikâ, and by laying it first crosswise and then erect I first got over the ditch and then the rampart. Then I reached the ground by means of a flight of steps madeof baked bricks, that rose up to the tower attached to the gate of the palace. When got down I passed beyond the row of the Bakula trees, and going a little further by the Champaka avenue, I heard away in the north the piteous cries of the Chakraváka pairs. I then turned to the north, nearly a bow-shot distance, by the row of Páṭali trees, where the bulging wall of the spacious palace could be felt, then due east by the gravel path, both the sides of which were decked with thickets of red Aśokas and Jasmines, and then walking a little further north, I entered the mango-grove to the south. Then, with the help of the meagre light shooting from a covered lantern slightly open, in one place I observed a very dense Mádhavî bower having in its centre a raised floor formed of gems. Entering from one part of it, I entered an inner bower surrounded on all sides with walls of the thick rows of young *Kurabakas* with full-blown flowers, by opening a door formed of the branches of red Aśoka plants that touched the earth, marked with bristling hair in the form of fresh buds and looking red with the mass of tender foliage. In it there were a well-spread couch of flowers, caskets of lotus-leaves filled with materials for amorous enjoyment, an ivory fan, and a vase filled with fragrant water. There having rested after sitting awhile, I inhaled the extremely pleasant odours about me; and I heard the gentle sound of foot-steps (approaching). Just as I heard it, I left the chamber of assignation, and hid myself behind a part of the trunk of a red Aśoka tree. That beautiful-eyebrowed lady, full of intense passion, slowly arrived, and not finding me there, felt considerably uneasy, and then, like an intoxicated female swan, broke into faltering accents charming and impassioned. "It is quite plain that I am deceived; I see no means of bearing my life. O my heart, having undertaken as possible what was impossible, why do you pine now, having failed to gain your object? Revered God of Love, what offence did I give you that you, instead of reducing me to ashes, thus burn me (slowly by causing despair &c.)?" I then appeared before her, and uncovering the lantern (so that it might give full light), said—"Charming damsel, truly have you greatly offended Cupid, since you have put to shame Rati who is his very life with your form; his bow, with your creeper-like eye-brows; his bow-string, formed of a row of bees, with your beautiful dark-blue tresses; his missiles, with your unceasing (*lit.* showers of) side-long glances; the safflower-coloured cloth of his banner, by the net-work of rays from your beautiful lips; his chief friend the Malaya breeze, by the excessively fragrant air of your breath; the cooings of the cuckoos, by your sweet words; his flowery banner, by your long and slender arms; the two bulging pots filled with water as an auspicious mark at the beginning of his conquest of the quarters, by your stout breasts; his pleasure-pond, by your round and deep navel; his chariot fully equipped for battle, by your round hips; the two postal columns set with jewels before his mansion, by your thighs; and the tender sprout sportively hung on his ears, by the lustre of the soles of your feet. Hence it is but just that Cupid is tormenting you. But to me who am quite innocent, he is the more distressing; so *this* is his real fault. Be pleased, therefore, O fair one, and with your side-long glances, as with herbs tending to bring back life, receive me who am bitten by the serpent in the form of Cupid." So saying I closely embraced her and sported with her, whose large eyes looked beautiful on account of the passion of love. And I found that she being gratified her eyes were a little red and rolling, and her cheeks thickly covered with the rise of slight lines of perspiration; that she talked unrestrained but sweet murmurs, bore the reddish marks of nails and teeth, had her limbs extremety relaxed and looked as if exhausted. I, therefore, slackening the fixity of mind and body, put myself also in a like condition. Then at once separating and again sitting together, * * * we, for a short time, remained putting implicit confidence in each other, as if we had known each other long since. Again I heaved a long and heavy sigh, and with a somewhat sad look, I feebly embraced her, with arms tremblingly stretched out, and gave her a faint kiss. She, in tears, with folded hands, said—"Lord, if you go, be sure that my life too will depart; so take me also with you; if not, this thy slave will feel life to be without purpose." I replied to her—"Charming damsel, who that has feelings will not joyfully hail a woman herself loving him? If you are firm in your resolve to favour me, do what I tell you without giving thought to it (*i.e.* unhesitatingly). In private, show the canvas with my portrait to the king, and ask him if the figure has reached the highest perfection of male beauty or not. He will surely say—"Yes, indeed it has." Then do you say to him again—"If it be so, there is an old female ascetic who has acquired great skill by travelling through different countries, and who has been a mother to me. Placing this painting before me she said—"There is a charm possessing that virtue whereby, under fast, on the night of the new moon, if you, being alone, offer in a lonely place, to the holy fire after the priest has worshipped it with offerings and retired, a hundred *samidhs* of the sandal tree, a hundred of aloe-wood, a handful of camphor, and many rich garments, you will surely obtain this very form. Then you are to sound a bell, when, being summoned by the sound of the bell, if your husband will tell you all his secrets (*i.e.* purposes and plans) and with his eyes closed embrace you, this form will be transferred from you to him, while you will have your own form as before. If you and your husband approve of this, you should not fail to carry out my instructions." If you like this form very much, then you should take counsel with your friends, counsellors, younger brothers and the people of the city and the country, and with their approval proceed in this business (to achieve this object). He will undoubtedly agree to this. Again, in this part of the female garden where four roads meet, when the fire will be fed with the sacrifice of beasts killed (for the purpose) according to the rites prescribed by the Atharvaveda and left (by the priest), I shall enter and hide myself in this bower at the disappearance of the smoke. When the night will be far advanced, you with a humorous smile on your lips, shall whisper into Vikaṭavarman's ear—"Indeed, you are cunning and ungrateful; you will divert yourself with my rivals though only through my favour you will have gained a beautiful form, serving as a high festival to the eyes of the people. So I will not raise a goblin for my own destruction." You shall then come to me alone, and tell me what he will say on hearing these words of yours. I alone shall know what to do next. Have the marks of my foot-steps in the garden effaced by Pushkariká." She, saying—'So it shall be done,' respected my words as though they were the injunctions of the scriptures, and retired reluctantly, with her passion not fully gratified, to the inner apartments. I also departed by the same way that I had come in, and went to my own dwelling.

In a short time, the fair lady did everything as I desired and that silly fellow acted up to her advice; and a wonderful rumour ran through the city that the king Vikaṭavarman was to obtain, by the magic skill of the queen, a form worthy of gods, that it could not be a deception but a fortunate occurrence, that no mischief was possible since the object was to be achieved by the queen herself in the garden attached to the inner apartments, and further that it was allowed by the ministers, as talented as

Bṛihaspati himself, after full thought; and, if it turns out a fact, nothing could be more wonderful than that; for incomprehensible is the power of gems, charms and herbs. While such rumours were afloat, as the new-moon day came on, in the dense darkness of its night, when well advanced, there issued from the garden near the inner apartments a mass of smoke, dark like the throat of Śiva; and the smell of the offerings, such as milk, ghee, curds, sesamum, white mustard, fat, flesh and blood, following (wafted by) the wind, spread in all the quarters. When the smoke had suddenly disappeared, I entered the garden, and that beautiful woman (*lit.* she with an elephant's gait) also came into the garden attached to the palace. She embraced me and smilingly said—"Dear one, your desires have been accomplished; the beastly fellow is doomed. In order to deceive him, I said to him according to your instructions—" Cunning sir, I will not endow you with beauty; for, handsome to such an extent you will be sought even by the Apsarasas; much more by women: Like a bee, fickle by nature, a treacherous (*or*, cruel) person like you becomes attached to any one without discretion." He, however, fell at my feet, and said—"Fair damsel, excuse me for my evil actions; henceforth, I will not even so much as think of any other woman; so kindly hasten to accomplish the object in hand." So I have now come to you, clad in a bridal dress. I have been already given to you, in the presence of the fire of love, by Cupid, officiating as my father; and I am now once more given over to you by my heart before this holy fire standing as witness to our union." So saying, she placed her tip-toe on my feet, and raising the heels of her feet entwined her creeper-like arms, with the beautiful fingers intertwined, round my neck; and having gracefully bent down my face a little, she raised up her own lotus-like face and kissed me repeatedly, her broad eyes all the while turning about sportively.

Then I left her, saying to her—"Stay here in the thicket of the Kuraṇṭaka shrubs till I go out and successfully accomplish everything." Then I went to the place where the sacrificial fire was burning and shook the bell that was hanging from a branch of an *As'oka* tree, and, summoning the king to that place, it sounded as if like a messenger from Death. I began to throw into the fire sticks of aloe and sandal-wood, and the king also came to the place as was settled before. I said to him, as he stood there full of wonder pondering and hesitating as it were through fear—"Declare again, taking this holy fire to witness, that you will never, when you assume this form, divert yourself with my rivals; and then I shall transfer this figure to you." Then he became quite sure that it was the queen, and no imposition; his confidence returned to him and he proceeded to take an oath. I then smiled, and said—"What need is there of an oath? What woman on earth will dare offend (*or,* insult) me? If you will come to be united with the Apsarasas, do as you desire. Now, then, tell me your secrets, and those being related your natural form will disappear (*lit.* your body will fall)." He replied—"I have in confinement Praháravarman, the younger brother of my father. I have plotted with my ministers to put him to death by means of poisoned food, intending to give out that he died of indigestion. I have purposed to give over a portion of my army to my brother Viśálavarman that he should invade the country of Puṇḍra. Páñchálika, an aged citizen, and Paritráta, a merchant-chief, have told me that they would get from the Yavana, named Khanati, a jewel of inestimable value for a very small price. Śatahali, the sheriff, and governor of the town, who is my confidant, has already gone, at my instigation, to send away the generals (on some mission), that he might destroy Anantasîra, a wicked and proud landlord who is a habitual liar, by exciting the people of the district against him. These are the secret designs lately planned." Having heard this, I said—"The lease of your life expires here; now meet a fate merited by your actions." With these words I cut him in two with my sword; and as soon as he was cut I offered him as an oblation to the fire into which a great quantity of ghee was poured, and soon he was reduced to ashes. Then cheering my beloved, who with the timidity of her sex was agitated a little, I caught her by her tender hand and went with her to the palace, where summoning, with her permission, all the inmates of the harem, I received their homage. Amusing myself for a time in the midst of the bevy of the astonished damsels, I dismissed them, and embracing my beloved with stout thighs so as to press her firmly with my thighs and arms, passed in her company the night which appeared to be very short. From her lips I learnt the customary practices of the royal house.

Early in the morning I took my bath; and, having performed the usual auspicious rites, I joined my ministers and addressed them thus—"Respectable ministers, with my figure my nature, too, has undergone a change; my uncle, who is to me as my father, and whom I was thinking of putting to death by means of poisoned food, should be liberated and be reinstated on the throne. I will be devoted to his service as to that of my father; there is no other sin more atrocious than that of murdering one's father." I then sent for my brother Viśâlavarman and said to him—"Dear brother, the people of the Puṇḍras are not in a prosperous condition at present. So, being overpowered with distress and despair, they might desperately attack our prosperous kingdom. You should, therefore, march against them when there will be time to spoil their seed-corn or ripe harvest; your invasion at the present time, therefore, is not advisable." I also addressed the two old citizens—"I do not wish to get a highly precious jewel for a very small price, that there should be no transgression of righteousness or justice on my part. Let it be bought at the proper price." I sent for the sheriff Śatahali and said—"Why should that Anantasîra, who, as a partisan of Prahára-varman, was desired to be destroyed, be destroyed now, when my uncle has been restored to his dignity? So you, too, should not proceed actively against him." The ministers, (thus) getting from me all the secrets convincing them (of my identity), came to the conclusion (felt sure) that I was the same (Vikaṭavarman), and full of wonder highly praised me and the queen, loudly proclaimed the unfailing virtue of charms, and getting my parents out of the prison, restored to them their sovereignty. I, through that nurse, made known to them, in secret, all my doings, and then repaired to the feet of them who had reached the highest point of ecstatic joy. I was at once installed the crown prince at the command of my parents. With my mind gratified, I enjoyed pleasures, insipid on account of the grief due to separation from the feet of Your Highness. Coming to know from the letter of Simhavarman, a friend of my father, of the attack on Champá by Chaṇḍavarman, I marched with my large army, swift of foot, thinking that it was my duty to protect the friend as well as to kill the foe, and found myself an object of the treasure of joy of the festival of seeing with my own eyes the glorious feet of Your Highness."

Having heard this, Rájavâhana observed with a smile—"See how even adultery helped by fraud has secured to a considerable extent Dharma and Artha, inasmuch as it served as a means of liberating parents from the calamity of imprisonment, as it was a remedy to put to death an inveterate foe and as it was essential for regaining a kingdom. What is there that does not become commendable when (employed) by the talented ?" Then, fixing an affectionate and prolonged glance on Arthapála's face, he desired him to narrate his adventures. When, with folded hands, he began :—

---

## UCHCHHVÂSA IV.

"Lord, I too having, along with these friends, the same mission to perform, wandered ever this sea-girt earth and once arrived at Kâśîpurî, Vâráṇasî. Having bathed in the waters of the Maṇikarṇiká, pure like a cut gem, I bowed before Avimukteśvara, the destroyer of Andhaka, and in course of walking round the temple keeping it to the right, I saw a very tall man, girding up his loins with his arms massive like a long iron bar, and with his eyes reddish and swollen with incessant weeping. I reflected to myself—"This man is hard; (but) his eyes with their pupils faded (dull) seem to pour as it were misery, and the act he is about is indicative of rashness (*or,* desperation). Surely he, recklesss of life, means to do an act of daring (*e.g.* suicide), in consequence of a mishap to some dearly loved person. So I shall ask him if there be any way for me to give help." Then I approached and addressed him—"Brother, this your preparation (*lit.* equipment) betokens some desperate purpose; if it be not a secret, I should like to know the cause of your grief." He looked at me awhile with great respect (for me), and saying—"What harm is there? Hear it," sat down with me under a Karavîra tree and thus related his tale—"Sir, I am the son of the headman of a town, Púrṇabhadra by name, an inhabitant of the Eastern Ishukàma (name of a country ;–*or,* given to wandering at will among the eastern districts). Though brought up with care by my father, in obedience to the will of destiny I took to the profession of a thief. Now one day I was caught red-handed, when I had committed a theft in the house of some leading merchant in this city, and was confined in a prison. When I was to be put to death, a furious elephant, that delighted in killing, Mṛityuvijaya by name, let loose upon me by the order of Kámapâla, the chief minister, who was looking from the terrace of the principal gate of the town, rushed on amidst the clamour of the multitude that doubled the sound of the bells about his neck, curling his trunk (to seize me). I fearlessly encountered the animal, and as he was bending down to strike with the tusk, I violently struck him at the space between the tusks with my arms which were passed through the holes of a log of wood, when he retreated as if in fright. His driver, being exasperated, drove him once more to the encounter, with a profuse use of abuse, heels and goad. Being rebuked and struck by me with my fury doubled, he turned tail and fled. I then approached the driver and censured him violently, when he, full of rage, addressing the elephant in the words—"Woe to you, you are condemned, wretched elephant," struck the animal frequently in the outer corner of the eye with his sharp goad, and somehow pitched him against me. I said—"Let this vermin of an elephant move away, and let some other lordly elephant be brought in, so that I shall sport with him for a time and then meet my doom." As soon as the elephant saw me, shouting through rage, he ran off, disregarding the peremptory order of his driver. The minister then called for me and said, "This elephant, Mṛityuvijaya, that delights in killing, is but Death himself; he, too, has been thus discomfited by you. Can you, therefore, desist from this unworthy profession, and make up your mind to follow some honourable course of life by accepting service under me?" I respectfully replied that I would do as I was desired; and he behaved towards me as a friend.

Once, being requested by me, in private, he, feeling confidence in me, narrated to me his own story as follows—"In Kusumapura there was one, Dharmapála by name, the minister of the King (Rájahaṃsa) the subduer of his foes, who was well-known for his talent and adept in the Vedas. His son named Sumitra was equal to his father in all the qualities of mind. I am his youger brother born of his step-mother. He (Sumitra) who liked virtue tried to check me who was given to sporting in the company of harlots. As my dissoluteness was incapable of being checked, I left home, and while wandering in the regions of the quarter I chanced to come to this Vârâṇasî, where I fell in love with Kántimatî', the daughter of Chaṇḍasiṃha, the King of Káśî, as she way playing at ball with her companions in the pleasure-garden, where she had come to worship God Śiva, and somehow got united with her. My secret enjoyment of sport in her apartments resulted in her pregnancy, and she was delivered of a son. Her attendants, apprehensive of the secret being divulged, cast him on the pleasure-hill, giving out to her that he was still-born, whereafter a female mountaineer took him to the cemetery. As she returned along the king's road at night, she was seized by the city-watch, and being threatened, through fear of the severity of the punishment, she disclosed nearly the whole of our secret. She pointed me out as I was sleeping at ease in the grotto in the pleasure-mountain, and by the king's command I was bound fast at midnight with ropes that were available then and there, and was led to the cemetery where I was intended to be killed with the stroke of a sword by a Mátaṅga. But, owing to the force of good fortune, I had the cords that bound me cut off, and snatching the sword (raised to strike me) I dispatched the executioner and others, and made my escape. As I was wandering in the forest without shelter, I was waited upon by some damsel of celestial beauty, having her face suffused with tears, and with materials for worship in her hand. She bowed down before me with her head decked with her sprout-like hands, while her curly hair waved about her face ; and she sat with me under the cool shade of a large wild Vaṭa tree. Being longingly asked by me who she was, whence she came and why she was thus conferring favour upon one like me (a helpless man), she replied in (*lit.* showered upon me) a stream of honied words—"Respectable Sir, I am Táráválî, the daughter of Maṇibhadra, the lord of the Yakshas. As I was once returning from the Malaya mountain, after paying my respects to the venerable Lopàmudrá, the wife of Agastya, I saw an infant weeping in the charnel-ground at Benares. I felt a great affection for him. and taking him up conveyed him to my parents. My father carried him into the royal court of Kubera, the lord of Alakâ. He, the friend of Śiva, called me to him and asked me—"Daughter, what is the disposition of your mind towards this child ?" I replied,—"I feel affection for him as though he were born of me." Thus told, he said—"The poor girl speaks the truth," and related to us a long narrative in connexion with it. I gathered this much from it—That you were Śaunaka, Śûdraka and Kámapála (being) the same (in different lives); Bandhumatî, Vinayavatî, and Kântimatî are not different, so Vedimatî, A'ryadâsî, and Somadevî are but the same; Haṃsâvalî, Śúrasená and Sulochaná are but the same individuals. Nandinî, Raṅgapatâkâ and Indrasenà are not different from one another. I am born at present as Tára'valî, the same A'ryada'sî, whom, as a milkmaid, you, in your birth as Śaunaka, married in the presence of the sacred fire. We in our previous births as A'ryadási and Śûdraka respectively, had a son who was affectionately brought up by Vinayavatî, and who was again born of her now in her birth as Kântimatî. Fortunately I found him who was dropped many a time from the jaws of death, and at the command of Kubera delivered him over to Vasumatî, the queen of Ra'jahamsa who is practising penance in a forest, that he may serve her son, Rájava'hana, who is to be the Emperor in future; and by the permission of my elders, I have come to serve the feet of you, escaped from the mouth of Death by the interference of Destiny."

Having heard her account, I again and again embraced her who had been my beloved in several lives, and shedding tears of joy I repeatedly consoled her and enjoyed pleasures, difficult to be obtained on earth, in a grand mansion created by her superhuman power. After having passed two or three days, I said to that beauteous lady—"I wish to enjoy the pleasure of retaliation by doing injury in return to Chaṇḍasiṃha, who had aimed at my life." She smilingly replied—"Come on, my dear lord, I shall take you to see Kântimatî." Accordingly, I was transported at midnight to the palace of the King of Kâśî. Then I took up the sword lying near his head, and woke him from his sleep and addressed him, as he was trembling—"Behold your son-in-law, the espouser of your daughter without your consent! Now I have come to wipe away my fault by an act of service (*or*, by means of an equally desperate act)." Extremely frightened, he bowed down to me and said—"I myself, who did not know my duty, am the offender, since I, like one possessed by some evil star, transgressing the bounds of propriety (*or*, justice), pronounced capital punishment on you who did me the favour of accepting my daughter's hand. So, why talk of Kántimatî? My kingdom and my life are henceforth at your service." The next day he called together his ministers and had the ceremony of our marriage duly performed. Târâvalî communicated to Kántimatî the news about her son, and the account of their former lives to Somadevî, Sulochaná and Indrasená. Thus under the guise of the ministerial post I enjoy the dignity of a Yuvarája and sport in the company of amorous damsels."

Kámapála, the one friend of all, continued to show the same favour to me, an ordinary being as I was; and when his father-in-law had gone to heaven owing to consumption (*or*, dropsy) he installed on the throne the youngest son of the late king, Siṃhaghosha, a child five years of age, his elder brother Chaṇḍaghosha having been already reduced to premature decay by consumption brought on by his debaucheries; and the good man brought him up with due attention. The boy, now intoxicated with youth, has some evil counsellors, the insinuators of something wicked, who are his confidants. By them he was persuaded into this belief—"Your sister was obtained by this gallant by force alone; then again he raised a sword to strike the King, when he was asleep, owing to which he, who immediately woke up, won him over (through fear) by giving him his daughter. He put to death Chaṇḍaghosha, the elder brother of Your Majesty, by means of poison, and has as yet spared you as being young and therefore unable to do harm, to gain the confidence of his subjects. He, an ungrateful wretch, will before long destroy Your Majesty also. So try to dispatch him to the capital of Yama." The prince, though prejudiced, could do no harm to him (Kámapála) through fear of the Yakshiṇî. In these days, as the report goes, the chief queen Sulakshaṇá, observing a change in the form of Kántimatî, politely asked her—"Queen, I should not be imposed upon (by you) by telling a lie. Tell me the truth. On what account is there such a marked change now-a-days on this lotus-like face of yours?" She replied—"Friend, do you remember me ever to have told a lie? My friend and fellow-wife Tárávalî, who was offended for some reason or other, being addressed in private by my name by our lord, disregarded his entreaties, and being far advanced in jealousy, went away in spite of our supplications. Our lord is pining away on her account, and hence my mental affliction." Sulakshaṇá fully reported this to her husband when in private. He (the King), being now free from all fear, had him seized to-day by men already engaged for the purpose and thrown into prison, as he was (all the while) exhibiting his bereavement by means of words not very much pleasing, being parched up as it were by his warm sighs, by his eyes disturbed on account of the flow of tears being restrained with firmness of mind, and by his limbs pale owing to the separation from his beloved, and was somehow getting the affairs of state managed in the palace (by the respective officers). The charges against him are to be publicly promulgated and his eyes are to be put out in such a manner that death will surely ensue." For this reason, I gave full vent to my tears in this solitary place, and am now preparing (*lit.* girding up my loins) to give up my life before the good man (meets his doom)."

Having heard from him the peril in which my father stood, I, shedding tears, said to him—"Gentle sir, why should I hide it from you? I am that son of him whom the Yakshiṇî had entrusted to the care of Vasumatî for serving the feet of His Highness, Prince Rájaváhana. I can effect the release of my father even in the teeth of (*lit* by putting to death) thousands of warriors with uplifted weapons. But, if some one in the crowd were to let fall his weapon upon him (*i.e.* kill him), all my efforts would be as useless as offering an oblation into ashes." I had hardly finished, when a huge snake raised his head out of a hole in the rampart. I secured him by the power of charms and herbs, and said to Pûrṇabhadra—"Good man, now, indeed, our object is gained! I, unseen in the crowd, shall cause my father to be bitten by this (snake) as if it had fallen on him accidentally and will restrain the venom from acting in such away that he (my father) will be treated with indifference (*i.e.* neglected), being considered as dead. You, giving up all fear, should then tell my mother—"That son of yours, whom the Yakshiṇî had handed over to Vasumatî in the forest, has arrived; he, having known from me the situation in which his father is, will act thus by the power of his talent. You, dismissing all fear, should send word to the King in this way—'It is, indeed, the duty of a Kshatriya to suppress without any consideration one maliciously disposed, may he be his kindred or otherwise. But it is also a woman's duty to share the fate (*lit.* to follow the course) of her husband, may he be good or wicked. I will, therefore, mount the funeral pyre along with him (my husband); this last rite should be permitted (by you) so as to be worthy of a young woman." The King, thus informed, will surely assent. You should then take the body (of your husband) to your own house, and cause it to be placed on a bed of *darbhas* in a retired place enclosed with canvas-screens; and putting on the ornaments proper for (a woman) dying after her husband, you yourself should be present there. I who shall have come to the court-yard, should be given admittance by you; then I will revive my father; and thereafter we will all act in a way that will be approved of by him." He, very much pleased at heart, saying that he would act accordingly, immediately set off.

I, climbing a tamarind-tree having abundant thick-grown branches, at the place of proclamation, remained there with my body concealed. The people also mounted high places as they were available, and talks on diverse subjects began. Presently the excutioner brought on my father, with his hands bound behind him like a thief, followed by a tumultous mob, and having stationed him just below me, thrice proclaimed—"Here this minister Kâmapâla is now being taken to have his eyes put out according to the sentence of the judge who deemed it but just that a Bṛáhmaṇa, greedy of regal power, should be condemned to a perpetual loss of sight, inasmuch as his secret was exposed, out of loyalty, by Sthúṇa and Aṅgàravarsha whom he had secretly instructed for the murder of the King after calling the minister Śivanága in a retired place to take him into confidence, as he meant evil to the person of the king, Siṃhaghosha—now that he had attained majority (full youth)—, when he had already out of a wicked passion for power procured the death of his master Chaṇḍasiṃha as well as of the heir-apparent Chaṇḍaghosha, by means of poisoned food. Should any one be (thus) treacherously disposed (towards the king), he would meet with merited punishment at the hands of the King." Vociferous was the crowd on hearing this, when I let fall the serpent, with its glowing hood, on the body of my father; I also jumped down, pretending to be seized with terror, and mingling with the crowd just there, ensured the preservation of the life of my father bitten by the angry snake by immediately arresting the operation of the poison. My father dropped down dead to all appearances. I uttered loudly—

" Indeed, it is true that divine punishment is meted out to one, traitor to the king, since he has been deprived of his life by Fate, while he was but meant to be deprived of his eyes by the King." Some concurred with me, while others reproached me. The serpent bit the executioner, too, and ran off, the way being quickly cleared for him by the multitude of people that were seized with fright.

Now my mother, apprised of the matter (*i.e.*, the real state of things) by Pûrṇabhadra, not much distressed even under such a calamity, courageously hastened to the spot on foot, followed by her attendants, and taking my father's head on her lap, she sat there and sent word to the king—" Whether this my husband offended against you or not, heaven alone knows; I am to gain nothing by thinking about that. But if I do not take to the path (course) of him who had taken my hand (at the sacred marriage-rite), I shall be disgracing your family. You will, therefore, kindly give me permission to ascend the funeral pile along with my husband. " The king was pleased to hear this, and issued an order—"Let the rites proper for a (noble) family be performed; and let my brother-in-law have his obsequial rites performed, distinguished by festivities. " The King, in order to manifest (*or*, proclaim) the greatness of his mind, further permitted the body of Kámapála to be taken to his house, thinking that he too was dead, as the executioner had lost his life, the efforts of the snake-bite-curers bening rendered inoperative by me. My father, who was taken home, was placed on a bed of *darbhas* in a retired place. Thereafter my mother, having put on the decorations suited to death (by mounting the funeral pyre), took leave of her friends in piteous terms, bowed again and again before the family-gods, and having prevented with efforts her attendants from weeping, entered, all alone, the place where my father lay. There she saw her lord restored to animation ( *lit.* cured of the poison ) by me who had become for the nonce the very Garuḍa and who had been previously admitted by Pûrṇabhadra as agreed upon. Exceedingly delighted, she fell repeatedly at her husband's feet with tears of joy, embraced me again and again with oozing breasts, and addressed me, her throat being choked with tears of joy and sobs,—" Son why are you so kind to me who had been exceedingly cruel to you, since by me, a wicked woman, you were cast away the moment you were born? Or rather, this your father was in no way an offender, and hence well did he deserve to be snatched away from the jaws of death. Very wicked is

Táràvalî, indeed, since, after having learnt from Kubera who you really were, instead of giving you over to me she handed you over to queen Vasumatî. Or why, she did but what was quite proper; for, a person poor in merit like myself cannot be worthy of drinking in the nectar of your sweet words, except a treasure of good fortune like her ( Vasumatî ). Come on, my son, embrace me!" So saying, she again and again smelt me on the head, placed me on her lap, censured Táràvalî, embraced me shedding a shower of joyful tears on me, and with a trembling frame looked for a moment quite changed. My father, too, thus raised to prosperity (*or*, good fortune) of that kind, from that sort of (overwhelming) calamity, as if to heaven from hell, and fully informed of everything as it had happened by Pûrṇabhadra, considered himself more fortunate than even the divine Indra. Having slightly indicated my part in the matter to my parents who were overjoyed and astonished (at it,) I asked them to tell me what course we should have to adopt that day. My father then said—"My son, this our house itself is protected by a mighty rampart and has an inexahaustible armoury, while the defence is impregnable. There are many subordinate princes whom I have laid under obligation; and many of the subjects do not like to see the calamity I am in. Besides there are thousands of warriors who are devoted to me with their friends and relatives. We shall, therefore, pass some days here and foment disturbances ( *or*, disaffection ) outside and inside ( the kingdom ). We shall then secure ( take over to our side) the disaffected, encourage the King's neighbouring foes, incite his natural enemies, and then uproot this King who is difficult to subdue." "Let this plan be followed; what harm is there?"—with these words I approved of my father's opinion.

Whilst we, having taken defensive measures, were abiding our opportunity, the King, who was informed of the whole matter, was vexed, and employed hostile stratagems against us (as against people besieged); but they were every day counteracted by us. During this interval, having learnt from Pûrṇabhadra the place ( situation ) of the chamber where the King slept, I made a subterranean passage to it with a hood-shaped instrument, beginning at the angle of the wall of our house. The excavation (*or*, the passage) reached a certain spot which looked almost like a paradise on earth, wherein there were not a small number of beautiful damsels. At my very site the multitude got agitated. There a certain maiden, whose bodily complexion was as bright as an image of burnished gold :—who was entirely dispelling the darkness of the subterranean spot with her bodily lustre like the digit of the moon ; who looked as if she were the earth incarnate, or the goddess Durgá (*lit.* the wife of S'iva) descended into the nether regions for the conquest of the demons, or (Rati) the wife of Cupid (*lit.* the flower-armed god), come down to the Pátála, or the goddess of royalty that had entered the cavern in order to avoid the sight of iniquitous monarchs, trembled at the sight of me, like a branch of the sandal-tree shaken by the Malaya breeze. In that assembly of damsels thus disturbed, there was an old woman, looking with her white hair like a Káśa tree in blossom, who fell at my feet, and through fear humbly said to me—" Sir, give the gift of safety to these damsels who have none else to protect them ! May it be that you are a young god desirous of entering this nether world with a thirst for fighting with the demons ? Tell us who you are, and with what object you have come to this place. " I replied to her—" Fair maids, relinquish all your fears ; I am Arthapála, the son of Kántimatî and Kámapala, the best of Bráhmaṇas ; I saw you here on my way as I was going from my house to the King's palace through this subterranean passage, as I had an object to accomplish (there). Tell me who you are, and why you dwell here. " With folded hands raised to her forehead she replied—" Son of our lord, fortunate, indeed, are we that we see you all safe, with our own eyes. Be pleased to listen.—That Chaṇḍasiṃha, who was your grandfather (on your mother's side), had by his queen Lîlâvatî two children, Kántimatî and the prince Chaṇḍaghosha. Prince Chaṇḍaghosha, the heir-apparent, departed to heaven through consumption brought on by his excessive addiction to women, leaving his wife A'cháravatî pregnant. She gave birth to this daughter, Maṇikarṇiká, by name. Thereafter A'cháravatî died of the throes of labour. Upon this king Chaṇḍasiṃha called me and said to me in private—" Ṛiddhimatî, this girl possesses auspicious signs. I wish to rear her up properly and then give her in marriage to Darpasára, the son of the King of Málwá. But, since the occurrence of the events in connexion with Kántimatî, I fear to keep girls exposed to public sight. So let her be brought up, attended upon by a train of retinue, in the spacious underground mansion constructed as an asylum for protection against calamity from an enemy, which is furnished with a number of arbours and drawing-rooms carved out in the interior of an artificial hill. It is provided with stores which will not be exhausted even in a hundred years." Having said so, he raised a stone-covering, as large as a square hand (a trap-door), about two inches deep in the wall of his chamber, and by that door introduced us into this place. It is for the last twelve years that we have been dwelling here This princess has now become young, but the King does not yet remember us. Granted that she was meant to be given in marriage to Darpasâra by her grandfather, but by her mother she was meant as a wife for you, being won as a pledge ( by your mother Kántimatî ) in gambling (with her mother ), even when she was in the womb. So in this case the prince (*i.e.* you ) should decide what is best to be done. " I said to her—" I will do what is proper to be done for you when I come back from the palace, having accomplished some business there. " I went through that very subterranean passage shown to me by means of a lamp at midnight, opened the trap-door, and having entered the King's chamber, caught alive Siṃhaghosha who had slept in full confidence. Having pulled him who was struggling, as an eagle does a snake, I dragged him off to the multitude of damsels through the underground passage. I then took him to my house, and with his feet bound with iron fetters presented him, whose gloomy face was hung down and wherein the eyes were red owing to an excessive flow of tears, before my parents in private. I told them also the story about the subterranean passage. My parents, who were exceedingly pleased, saw that mean-hearted wretch, detained him in confinement, and married that beautiful damsel to me with due rites. The kingdom, now without a master, fell into our hands. Siṃhaghosha, though my mother wished it much, was not set at liberty for fear of a revolt. We, thus situated, hastened to the assistance of Siṃhavarmá the king of Aṅga, who was attacked by the enemy, as he was loyal and had rendered service to Your Majesty. And thus I became the object of favour of the pollen of the lotuses of your feet. Let the unworthy Siṃhaghosha perform the penance of falling at your feet that will wipe away ( the infamy of ) all of his wicked acts. " So said Arthapála, and bowed before the prince with folded hands. Prince Rájaváhana said that he (Arthapála) had performed great exploits, that he had used his intellect to the utmost, and desired that his father-in-law (Siṃhaghosha) should present himself before him ( the Prince Rájaváhana) being set free from confinement; and then, looking at Pramati himself, asked him with a loving smile to narrate his adventures.

---

## UCHCHHVASA V.

Bowing low before the Prince, he began—" Lord, after having wandered some time in search of Your Highness, I, being unable to proceed, formed my bed with tender leaves on the ground, under a tree, that grew on the slope of the Vindhya mountain, and that seemed to touch the sky ( *or*, pierce the clouds ), after having washed my face in the water of a pond and performed Saṃdhyâ-adorations, at the time when the face of the lady in the form of the western quarter was decked with the crimson sprouts of the setting rays of the sun, and the irregularities (*lit.* the ups and downs) of the road were levelled by the gloom; and when about to sleep, I raised my folded hands to my forehead, and praying—" May the very deity that resides in (*i.e.* is the presiding soul of) this tree be the protector of me, when gone to sleep all alone in this great forest, which is terrible on account of the number of ferocious animals stalking about and wherein the caverns are filled with the flood of noctural darkness which is pitchy dark like the throat of Śiva! "—I slept, using my left hand as a pillow. Then in an instant my limbs were inexpressibly gratified by a touch difficult to be obtained on the surface of the earth ; my senses thrilled with delight ; my soul felt quite cheered up ; and more particularly my hair bristled with joy, and my right arm throbbed. Wondering how this could be, I very slowly opened my eyes, and beheld a canopy of white cloth looking like a portion of moonlight cut off. As I turned my eyes to the left, I saw, near the wall of a mansion, a number of damsels lying asleep in great confidence on beds with variegated bed-sheets. Then I directed my gaze to the right, where I beheld a lovely maiden, as graceful as a jewelled branch of (*or*, a creeper clinging to ) a Kalpavṛiksha ( the wish-granting tree ) in Indra's garden rent from it by Airávata in the pride of youthful vigour, with her lovely face bowed in sleep wherein the lilies of her eyes were closed and which therefore looked like a lotus with a bee slept within it ; as she lay on a couch which was white like the mass of nectar-foam with her breast-garment a little displaced, she looked like the earth reclining, in faint, on the bright tusk of the Primeval Boar (A'divaráha), whilst the fine upper-garment in the form of the milky ocean receded from her shoulders ; by the breezes of her breath wafting the fragrance of the lotus of her face and causing to dance the tender sprouts in the form of the beaming off-shoots of her red lips, she seemed to kindle to life Cupid, remaining as a spark after he was burnt by the fire from the eye of S'iva. I then thought—"Where is that vast forest gone and what building is this with the image of Kárttikeya situated on the ground floor and a trident forming its spire which touches (*lit.* rubs against) the (inner surface of the) sky! Where is that leafy bed spread on the forest ground and whence comes this silken bed stuffed with downy feathers (instead), bright like a multitude of moon-beams? Who again can these maidens be who are lying asleep at ease, like a bevy of nymphs in faint, being tossed down from the swing formed of the ropes of moon-beams, and who is this damsel lying on a bed covered with a silk mantle pure (white) like the orb of the autumnal moon, like the Goddess Lakshmî, that has a lotus in her hand? Certainly, she cannot be a heavenly damsel; for she has closed her eyes in sleep like the lotus when acted upon by the rays of the moon; her expansive cheek, bearing lines of the drops of perspiration appearing upon it, appears like a mango-fruit yellowish-white by being ripe and spotted with drops of sap dropping from the broken stem; the unguent assumes a palish hue on her expansive breasts exceedingly hot on account of the fire of budding youth; and her raiments disclose a dustiness according as they have been used. So she is undoubtedly a mortal. Fortunately, she is unmarried (*lit.* her youth is unenjoyed by anyone else), since her limbs that have attained loveliness are well-turned and firm; her complexion, though exceedingly charming, is tinged with pallor; her face, being yet unused to the pleasing pain of teeth-bites, does not betray a glowing red; her ruby-like lower lip possesses the lustre of coral; her blooming cheeks are like the petals of a Champaka bud, a little reddish at the root and not yet fully developed;—since also she is lying asleep in sweetened ease free from the fear of being assailed by the arrows of Cupid, and her bosom has its twin breasts such as have not their nipples flattened by being hard pressed. My mind, which has never as yet entertained a thought unworthy of an honourable man (*or*, contrary to propriety), seems to be full of love for her. But, if I embrace her, acting in accordance with the inspiration of love, surely she will wake up with a loud cry of alarm; and yet I cannot sleep without embracing her. Never mind; let things have their due course. I shall put to test my luck." So saying, I slightly touched her and lay there as if asleep, in a manner in which love and fear were mingled. She, too, with her left side experiencing a peculiarly pleasing and thrilling sensation causing the hair to stand on end, in her pleasing dullness began gently to yawn, and slightly opened her pair of eyes, with the tips of their eyelids trembling, their pupils languid through dullness, and their highly beautiful corners reddened on account of broken sleep. Made to pass by Cupid, of wonderful power, through strange conditions intermixed with the feelings of alarm, wonder, joy, passion, fear and graceful and sportive gestures, and influenced by modesty, she with difficulty restrained her speech about to break out into a call to her attendants, her heart which was swayed by vehement love, and her limbs, too, full of perspiration due to alarm; and surveying carefully my limbs with eager eyes charmingly contracted at the corners (*or*, in the third part) and very slowly directed, she, although far removing the upper part of her body, lay startled, in the same bed. I, too, though my mind was upset by passion, was somehow mysteriously overpowered by sleep, and again awoke, disturbed by some disagreeable touch, and found myself again in the same forest under the same tree and on the same leafy bed. Night, too, drew to a close; and I thought in my mind—"Is this a dream, or some illusion, or some conjuration, divine or demoniacal? Come what may; I will not leave my earthy bed without knowing what this really is. I will lie down here as long as life exists, before the Goddess of this spot, without food, till death (to gain my object)."

Upon this (*i. e.* when I had formed this determination), a certain woman appeared (before me). Her frame was languid like a garland of lotuses scorched by the rays of the sun; her lower and upper garments were worn out; by her lip that was dry and pale-red owing to the want of red lac, and the lustre of which was destroyed by the heat of her breathings, she seemed to emit the fire of separation dusky with its tawny fumes; both her eyes were extremely red as if blood only was left in them on account of their having shed ceaseless streams of tears; with her beautiful tresses reduced to a single braid of hair, that had the grace of a noose holding her fast to the virtuous conduct of her family, she, wearing a blue garment and a bodice, looked like the moving banner of chaste ladies; and though she was greatly emaciated, her bright (*lit.* spreading) complexion had not much faded, owing to her superhuman power. She raised me up with her creeper-like arms trembling in the height of joy as I bowed before her, embraced me like a son, smelt me on my head, and with her affection for me appearing to ooze out in the form of milk from her breasts and her throat choked with cold tears, she said—" My dear child, if Vasumatî, the queen of the king of the Magadhas, (at all) informed you that the daughter of Maṇibhadra having entrusted the infant Arthapàla to her care disappeared after having communicated to her the tale as disclosed by Kubera regarding her lord, sons and friends, behold in me that person, your mother! My mind being clouded by causeless anger against your father, Kâmapâla, the son of Dharmapâla and the younger brother of Sumitra, I quitted him; and while I was afflicted by remorse I was cursed in a dream by some one coming to me in the form of a Rakshasa, saying—" I take up my abode in you, O violent woman, for a year, that you may experience the pangs of separation. " I awoke, possessed by the evil spirit just as he spoke this. That year, as long as a thousand years, has expired. Last night just as I started, purposing to attend, in the city of Śrâvastî, the assembly gathered at the festival of lord Tryambaka, after seeing my kinsmen thronged there from different places to repair to the side of my lord, now that I was free from the curse, you came here and saying—" I solicit the protection of the dryad of the place, " slept here. As my mind was entirely overpowered by the pain caused by the curse, I did not properly recognize you; but then, thinking that it was not proper to abandon you who had sought my protection in the great forest beset with many terrors, I transported you, too, while just in sleep, with me. As we neared the temple I thought it improper to attend the meeting with you; and, as I found by chance the princess Navamâliká, the daughter of Dharmavardhana, the King of Śrâvastî, bearing a name true to its syllables, lying fast asleep on a splendid couch on the lofty terrace of her mansion, so pleasant in summer, I said to myself—" Thank God! The princess is asleep; her servants also are buried in sleep. Let this young Bráhmaṇa sleep here for a time, till I return after gratifying myself with the sight of the festival. " Having thus reflected I placed you there and directed my steps to the place of the festival. Having witnessed the glorious festival and enjoyed the pleasure of the sight of my kinsmen, I bowed to the lord of the three worlds and was bent in reverence, with my mind rapt in devotion, dreading all the while lest she should divine my crime, before Ambikâ, when that goddess, the daughter of Himâlaya, said to me with a smile—" O dear girl, give up your fear; go to your husband's presence; your curse is over." Thus favoured, I at once regained my superhuman power; and, returning, at your very sight I knew you properly." "How now," I said, he is my son (so to speak) Pramati, the dear friend of my dear son Arthapála! I, wicked that I was, acted indifferently towards him through ignorance! Moreover, his mind it attached to the princess and she also loves this young man; but the two, who are feigning sleep, do not open their hearts (feelings) to each other owing to fear and modesty; and I have to go. The damsel, though overpowered by love, has not spoken about it to her friends or attendants in order to keep her secret. Let me take away the young man; he will accomplish his purpose by suitable means when he will come to know of it." Thinking thus, I brought you again to this leafy bed in a sleepy condition induced by my superhuman power. This is how all this happened. Here I go to the feet of your father." With these words she again and again embraced me who had folded my hands, smelt me on my head, kissed me on my cheeks, and departed, deeply moved with affection for me.

I, entirely subdued by love, directed my steps to Śrâvastî; on the road in a great market-place the merchants were in a very great uproar over a cock-fight. I approached the place and smiled a little. An old wily Bráhmaṇa seated near me gently asked me the reason of my smile. I said to him—"How comes this, that a cock of the Western country and of the Baláká breed is thus thoughtlessly matched by the people against one belonging to the eastern country and of the cocoanut tribe, its superior in strength and size!" He, too, an adept in the matter, said—"What is the use of enlightening these ignorant folks on this subject? So better be silent." And having offered me betel with camphor from his betel-case, he remained for a short while telling me diverse tales. The two birds fought, furiously excited, as the shouts of encouragement were uttered by their partisans after each stroke. The cock of the Western country was beaten, and the clever Bráhmaṇa, higly delighted at the victory of the cock belonging to his province, made friends with me, contrary to our ages, and made me take my bath and meals at his place that day. The next day, as I set out for Śrávastî, he followed me, and asking me not to foreget him if there was need, dismissed me like a friend and went back.

I reached Śrávastî, and being fatigued by the journey lay asleep in a bower of creepers in an outer garden. Roused by the tinklings of anklets, I rose up and beheld a young woman coming to me with feet resounding with the jinglings of anklets. She came, and alternately looking intently at me and at the form of a male resembling me painted on a canvas in her hand, stood there for a moment full of wonder, surmises and joy. I, seeing my own likeness on the canvas, thought that the motions of her eyes could not have been accidental (*i e.* were based on some motive), and said to her—"Oh, surely this charming site of the holy grove is common to all! Why do you suffer the trouble of standing for a long time? Please sit down." Thus addressed she smiled, and saying that it was a favour, sat down. Then we had some conversation regarding the affairs of the country. While engaged in conversation she remarked—"Ah! You are a guest coming from the country; and your limbs look as if wearied by the journey. If there be no objection, you should oblige me by resting at my house." I replied—"Charming lady, this is no cause for dissatisfaction, but a favour;" and I followed her home, where I was treated with such princely comforts as a bath, food and the like. While sitting at ease, she asked me—"Noble one, was there anything marvellous that you came across in your travels in the different lands?" I thought to myself—"Here is great scope for my hope. This is, indeed, the friend of the princess, who was well seen in the midst of the crowd of all her attendants. On this picture-board also there is the terrace overhung with a white canopy; also the spacious couch lying therein, yellowish-white like the multitude of autumnal clouds; and this likeness lying on it with eyes sealed in sleep, is also of me alone. Surely, then, the princess must have been brought by Cupid to that stage, wherein, being tormented and rendered delirious by the unbearable fever of love, she must have given an adequate reply, by skilfully drawing this form alone, to her friends when insistently asked by them the cause of her affliction. I am asked by her, being in suspicion on account of the agreement (resemblance) of forms; I will, therefore, dispel her doubts, stating my experience." Thus resolved I asked for the picture-board, and she handed it over to me. I took it; and having painted the beloved of my heart, overpowered by the passion of love rising in her and lying in a feigned sleep just in the same place, I said—"As I slept once in a large forest I saw a certain damsel of this form lying by the side of a youth like this (picture). May it be a dream?" She was extremely delighted, and begged me to explain the whole; and I did so. She then related to me the various sufferings of her friend on my account. On hearing that I persuaded her, saying—"If your friend's mind is really disposed to favour me, let some days pass. I will arrange some plan, which will enable me to remain freely in the palace of the princess, and approach you;" and then, going to the same village, I joined the company of the old Bráhmaṇa.

With a hasty (*i.e.* warm) reception he asked me to take rest, gave me food and drink as before, and then asked me in private,—"Noble one, what is the reason of your coming back so soon?" I said to him in reply—"It is but proper that I have been thus questioned by your honour. Listen: There is a town named Śrâvastî. Its ruler is a king named Dharmavardhana, who is like another son of Dharma (Dharmarája). He has a daughter, who is as if a repeller of even the Goddess of Beauty, and the very life of Cupid, Navamáliká by name, who by her tenderness resembles the *Navamáliká* creeper. I accidentally saw her, and she directed her glances like so many arrows of love at the vital parts of my body. And since there is no other physician than you, like Dhanvantari, able to take out those darts, I have come to you. Be kind, therefore, and find out some remedy. Here I shall put on female apparel and profess to be your daughter. I shall follow you, and you should go to Dharmavardhana, when sitting in the judgement-hall, and say to him—"This is my only daughter. Her mother died as soon as she was born, and I myself, acting as father and mother to her, have brought her up. A certain Brâhmaṇa youth, born in a family fit for marriage-connexion with us, has gone to Ujjayinî, the capital of Avanti, to acquire wealth in the form of learning for securing her hand. She being betrothed to him, it is not proper to give her away to anyone else. She has now attained youth, and he is delaying. I shall, therefore, bring him and marry her to him, and after having placed the burden (of family) on him, I will turn a recluse. Since it is difficult to guard daughters that have passed the stage of girlhood, and more particularly those that have no mother, I have come to Your Majesty here, standing in the place of mother and father to the subjects and the protector of the distressed. If Your Majesty, whose career is as noble and exalted as that of Manu, be pleased to favour me, a helpless Bráhmaṇa coming to you of his own will (*lit.* as a guest), may this (my daughter) here be allowed to repose, in the shadow of your arms, with her character unblemished, until I should return with the bridegroom" The king, thus addressed, will surely approve of it and will make me stay with his daughter ( as a companion ). Then you should depart, and in the ensuing month of Phâlgûna at the time of the festival of holy pilgrimage—on the day of the Uttaráphalgunî—of the inmates of the female apartment, await me, with a pair of white garments in your hand, in the temple of Kárttikeya, which you will find in the midst of a clump of cane-plants after going over a distance covered by the bellowing of a bull to the east of the bathing-place. I shall, indeed, on my part divert myself freely during that interval with the princess, and again sporting in the waters of the Ganges during the festival, will dive, while the multitude of the damsels will be engaged deeply in sport, and swim over up to you; and wearing the garments brought by you, I shall come with you as your intended son-in-law. The princess, on her part, will search for me here and there, and not finding me will remain in the palace, weeping, saying that she would not take food without me. In the midst of a scene of uproar consequent on this, the attendants crying out, her female friends lamenting my loss, and the citizens expressing their sorrow, and the king and his ministers at a loss to know what to do, you should take me to the royal assembly, and placing me before the king, should say—" Sire, here is my son-in-law, who is fit to serve your royal arms. He has studied the four

Vedas, has mastered the six Aṅgas, has a thorough knowledge of logic, and is an expert in the manipulation of the sixty-four arts; he is a specialist in the art of managing elephants, chariots and horses; he is a matchless expert in archery and mace-fight: he knows the Purāṇas and Itihāsas and is a composer of poems, dramas and tales. He knows both the Mîmâṃsâs, is an impartial appreciator of merits, a reliable friend, has a sweet address, is munificent, learned, and free from pride. I see not even the slightest fault in him; nor do I see an virtue which he does not possess. Such a relative is, in fact, inaccessible to me, merely a Bráhmaṇa in name. Having given over my daughter to him, I shall take to the last stage of life fit for old age, if it so pleases Your Majesty." Having heard this, the king, his face overcast by paleness, and entirely perplexed, will try, in the company of the ministers, to console you by dwelling upon the transitoriness of worldly things. You should turn a deaf ear to all that they will say, and after lamenting long with sobs till your throat is be parched, collect fagots, and kindling a fire before the palace-gate prepare for ascending the funeral pile. He will just then fall at your feet, and having gratified you with an unstinted gift of wealth, wlll give his daughter to me, and being fully satisfied with my abilities will place the whole administration into my hands. This plan is to be adopted, if you approve of it." That clever Páñchálásarmá, too, the prince of cunning accomplices, who had more than once practised all kinds of deceit, skilfully achieved everything according to my instructions, and yet more; and all my desires were fulfilled in a short time. I enjoyed the company of Navamáliká, as a bee does a juicy flower. At this time, thinking that I should be serving the double purpose of giving assistance to Siṃhavarmá and of reaching the place of meeting of my friends, I advanced with the whole mass of the army to Champâ, and now enjoy through good luck the pleasure of the sight of Your Majesty."

Having heard this account of Pramati, Rájaváhana, with the lotus of his face beaming with a smile, said—" Exploits full of graceful sports, and actions tempered down by gentleness —this, indeed, will appeal to the taste of the learned. *You* may now enter (the course of narration)" Saying so, the prince fixed his eyes on Mitragupta.

## UCHCHHVÂSA VI.

Mitragupta, on his part, said—“ Lord, whilst wandering with the same object as my companions, I came to a city in Suhma, called Dâmalipta, where in the suburban grove I observed a crowd collected in observance of some festival. There I also saw, in a bower of Atimukta creepers, a young man full of longing (*or*, anxious thoughts) diverting himself by playing on a lute. I asked him—“Good man, what festival is this, what is the occasion for it, and why are you sitting here in a solitary place like one affected by longing, with nothing but your lute with you, disregarding the festival ?” He replied—“Gentle sir, Tuṅgadhanvâ, the king of Suhma, who had no progeny, solicited, it is said, by prayers, from Vindhyavâsinî (the goddess Durgâ), living in this very temple having forgotton her passion for a residence on Vindhya, two children. The goddess said to him in a dream as he slept before her without food—“ You will get one son and one daughter ; the former will be dependent on the husband of the latter. Let the girl, from the age of seven until her marriage, worship me every month on the Kṛittiká day by playing at ball in public, that she might obtain a suitable husband ; also, let her be given over to whomsoever she chooses, and let the festival be called Kandukotsava.” Then, after a short time, Medinî, the beloved queen of the king, gave birth to a son ; and after him, a daughter, too, was born. That princess, named Kandukâvatî, will come out to-day to propitiate the goddess Somâpîḍá with her play at ball. Her foster-sister and friend, Chandrasená, was my beloved. But she has been wooed against her will (*or*, forcibly detained) in these days by the prince Bhîmadhanvâ. Being therefore uneasy and afflicted in mind owing to the pain caused by the points of Cupid's arrows, I resort to this solitude, comforting myself to some extent by means of the sweet tunes of this Vîṇâ.”

Just at that moment the tinkling of anklets was suddenly heard, and there entered a female. Just as the youth beheld her, he rose up with his eyes expanded in joy, embraced her, and lightly clasped by her (in return), he sat down just there. He then addressed me thus—“ Here is she whom I regard as my life, and whose separation burns me like fire In carrying away this very life of me, the prince has, like Death, deprived me of the warmth of life ; nor can I do him any harm, as he is the king's son. So, having made her take a full view of me, I will give up this helpless life (*or*, which cannot offer any resistance to the violence of the prince)." Here she, with her face suffused with tears, said—"Lord, do not take this rash step, for my sake; for, if I were to live after you are dead,—you who, born of Arthadása, the best of merchants, having been agreeably named Kośadása by your elders, are now described by your enemies as Veśadása (the slave of a harlot, owing to your excessive attachment to me),—I may be simply confirming the scandal that the courtesan class as a whole is very wicked. So please take me off this very day to the country you like." He then inquired of me which of the various countries that I had seen was prosperous, rich in corn, and mostly peopled by good men. With a smile I replied,—"Gentle sir, this earth (*lit.* that has the ocean for its waist-garment) is very extensive, and there is no end of (*or*, limit to) pleasant regions (to be found) in different places. However, if I can devise no remedy that might enable you to live here in happiness, then I shall myself show you the way." Just then, the tinklings of jewelled anklets were distinctly heard, and the damsel, being in a hurry, said to us—"Here has approached the princess Kandukávatî in order to propitiate the goddess Vindhyavâsinî (Durgà) with her ball-sport In this Kanduka-festival she can be freely seen by all. Come along to behold her; let your sight have its fruit; I must go and be by her side;" and then she departed. We two followed her; and I beheld first the red-lipped (damsel) seated on a jewelled seat. The moment I saw her she stood in (*i.e.* captivated) my heart, and neither any one else nor I could see her in the interval (of her leaving her seat and entering my heart). Overcome with wonder, I thought—"What, is she Lakshmî herself? No, no; for Lakshmî has a lotus placed in her hand, while the very hand of this damsel is a lotus; besides, Lakshmî was enjoyed by the Primeval Purusha (Vishṇu) as well as by former kings, while the youth of this (maiden) is fresh and untainted." While I was thinking thus, that princess of perfect limbs, touched the earth with the tips of her tender hand turned downwards, gracefully bowed before the goddess while her dark and curly hair waved, and then took the ball spotted deep-red all about, like Cupid with eyes glowing with intense passion. She let it fall to the ground in gentle grace, and as it slowly rose up beat it down with her tender hand having the thumb drawn in a little and the delicate fingers stretched out, and after having tossed it up with the back part of her hand, caught it aloft as it was falling, marked by her unsteady glances, like a bunch of flowers full of swarms of bees, and again let it fall down. Striking it with greater or less force as it slackened in its speed or otherwise, she showed her aptitude for the motion of the ball; and when it stopped, she tossed it up with blows struck without mercy and made it come to a standstill as well; (occasionally) she kept it fluttering in space like a bird, hitting it alternately with her right or left hand as it approached her obliquely or in a straight line; when it rose to a great height, she struck it in its rapid descent and took the musical leap (*i. e.* sprang forward ten steps to catch it); having sent the ball in all directions, she brought it back to its original point. Thus, sporting in a manner attractive on account of the various feats of dexterity, she won every now and then the loud and manifold applause of persons gathered in the pavilion, having their minds attracted by the play. As I stood facing her, with my cheeks thrilling, and eyes expanded through joy, leaning on the shoulder of Kośadâsa, in whom my confidence grew the very moment, she cast a side-glance at me under the influence of love that affected her for the first time then, with her eyebrows gracefully contracted in consequence of her eyes following the motion of the ball, and repelled the bees that were hovering about to inhale (*i. e.* enjoy) the sweet fragance of the lotus of her face with multitudes of rays offshooting from her lips and waved about by the force of her breathings as if with tender sprouts. As she moved about in circles on account of the ball being whirled round with extreme speed, she seemed to enter, as if abashed at the sight of me, a flowery cage; when giving five strokes to the ball (rapidly) so as to make it appear like five specks, she appeared to repel as it were, through fear, all the five arrows of Cupid all falling upon her at one and the same time, and in the course of her forked movements, strongly indicating the graces of love, she seemed to imitate the flashes of lightning that displays the play of its redness in the clouds. Thus the princess pursued the sport in various ways, now sitting, now rising, now contracting her form, now out-stretching it, now standing still, now darting forward, in a manner in which the jewels in her ornaments jingled in consonance with the movements of her feet; her *bimba*-like lower lip was invested with (*lit.* bathed in) the lustre of a smile under some pretext or another; her luxuriant tresses that hung loosely about her shoulders were set right again, and her jewelled waist-band jingled (as its bells struck against each other); in a manner bright (or beautiful) with the fluttering silken garment that hung on her broad posteriors that rose up in a beautiful elevation; in which the ball was gracefully struck by her tender arms now drawn in, now stretched out, and now tossed about; her long arms were converged; and her waving ringlets touched her shoulder-blade as it was turned round; in which the displaced gold sockets of her ear-ornaments were put back with a quickness that did not interrupt her ball-sport that was going on; in which the ball was whirled in circles round and within the space of the hands and feet lifted up; wherein the slender middle part of her body was seen and again lost to view owing to her bending down and rising up in quick succession, and her pearl-necklace was tossed about as she frisked up and down; in which the gentle breeze from the sprout used as ear-ornament was authorized (as it were) to dry up the leafy ornamental decorations on her cheeks soiled (by being wetted) by the rising drops of perspiration; and in which one of her tender hands was busy in holding up the garment that (now and then) slipped off from her protuberant breasts. Having struck the ball through the space between heaven and earth, she, though playing with one ball, displayed various attractive pastimes as it were with balls more than one. Then, having sported with her companions, Chandrasenâ and others, and having bowed to the Goddess at the close of her play, she repaired to her residence, followed by my mind full of love, and her attendants full of affection for her, darting at me as she passed a sidelong glance as though it were the blue lotus-shaft of the flower-arrowed God, and appearing to see, as she often reverted, under some pretext or other, the full orb of the moon of her face, if her heart that she had sent towards me had returned or not.

I, who was quite beside myself with love, was splendidly entertained by Kos'adása after going home, with special care, with bath, food &c. In the evening Chandrasená approached us in private, and having saluted me, sat down, touching closely her lover's shoulder with her own in a manner charming on account of love. Kośadâsa said in joy—"May I thus be, O long-eyed one, the object of your favour for the whole of my life?" I smiled and said,—"Friend, do you suppose that this is merely to be hoped for (and not to be realized)? There is a kind of unguent; the prince, when approached by her having her eyes besmeared with that, will see her like a female monkey; and he will in consequence renounce his love and leave her." She replied with a smile—"Your humble servant is greatly favoured by your honour, if in this life she will be converted into an ape, her human form being removed! But let alone this remedy for the present; for we can gain our object even in another way. To-day the princess, having seen you at the ball-festival, is being greatly tormented by the foe of Śambara (*i.e.* Cupid) as if in a rage, as she has been yearning for you who laugh at the form of Cupid. This fact will be communicated by me, who have known her feelings, to my mother, by her to her mother, and by the queen to the king. The king, on knowing the fact, will make you accept his daughter's hand, and the prince will then become your dependant; for such is the course of events ordained by the Goddess. When the kingdom passes into your possession, Bhîmadhanvá will no longer be able to detain me in defiance of you. So he (Kośadása) should therefore wait for three or four days." Having said so, she embraced her lover and went away Night somehow passed away while Kośadása and I held discussion with many misgivings on what she had told. In the morning, after performing my morning devotions, I went to the very region of the grove, charming to me on account of my having seen my beloved there. At the very place the prince approached me; he passed some time (with me), humbly ministering to my pleasure by agreeable talks; and then, taking me to his tent, treated me exactly like himself with such comforts as a bath, food, a bed to sleep on, and so forth. As I lay on my bed enjoying in a dream the pleasure of the embrace of my beloved, the prince got me chained in iron fetters with my stout and long arms pinioned by very sturdy men. When I woke up, the prince at once addressed me—"O wicked man, the speech of that hussy, Chandrasená, escaping through the hole of the lattice, was overheard by this hunch-back, appointed by me to watch her movements. So, indeed, you are the object of love of that wretched Kandukávatî, and it is said that I am to be your servant, and obeying your orders I am to give over Chandrasená to Kośadâsa." Having uttered these words he turned to an attendant and said, "Cast him into the sea." Overjoyed (with the favour of his master) as though he had acquired a kingdom, he did as he was bid. Being quite helpless, I, dashing about here and there with my arms, held to my bosom a piece of timber sent by destiny (to my aid), and floated about till the whole day and night passed away. Early in the morning a ship was sighted; in it there were Yavanas. They picked me up and said to their commander, named Ràmeshu—"Here is found in water a man chained in iron fetters; he is likely to be able to water a thousand vines in an instant." Just at that moment a warship (galley) surrounded by a number of vessels bore down upon us, and the Yavanas were alarmed. In the meantime, ships sailing with very great speed surrounded our ship, like fleet hounds rushing upon a boar; a fight ensued, and the Yavanas were defeated. (Having cheered) them up who had become helpless and were losing courage, I said—"Take off my chains; here I shall destroy all your enemies." They did so; I took a bow, and with it twanging fearfully, poured a shower of huge shafts on them, piercing every inch of their bodies. Jumping into (*i.e.* on the deck of) the ship that had engaged our ship and wherein all the warriors were almost killed or routed, I sprang at the commander, who had not come forth to fight, and captured him alive. He was that Bhîmadhanvá himself. I, having recognized him, addressed him who was overcome with shame—"Well, good sir, did you mark the wilful actions of destiny?" The crew of my ship then tied him very fast with the very chains which I had borne, and uttering sounds of great joy adored me

Our ship, which had now become very difficult to be steered aright, being impelled by a contrary wind, drove to a great distance and came in close contact with an island. There we landed, after letting down the stone-anchor so as to fall heavily on the ground, with a desire to store up the sweet water, fuel, fruits and roots to be found there. There was a lofty mountain on that island. I, who saw it, said to myself—"Oh, beautiful is this skirt of the mountain; lovelier still is this its adjoining ground full of benzoin; cool is this water of the mountain-stream marked by circles spreading owing to the drops of the honey of blue lotuses; charming is the region of the grove of trees attractive by the clusters of flowers of various colours;" and thus observing many a scene with my eyes ever unsatiated, without noticing the distance, I ascended to the top of the mountain without being aware of it; and here I came across a tank which was tinged red by the upward-spreading lustre of the rubies forming the steps leading to its water, and which was dusky with the dust of lotus-filaments. There I performed my ablutions, ate some bits of lotus-stalks as sweet as nectar, and had some white water-lilies hanging on my shoulders, when I was overtaken and menacingly addressed by a Brahmarâkshasa of hideous aspect living on its bank, demanding of me who I was and where I came from. I, undaunted, replied—"Gentle spirit, I am a Bráhmaṇa; having fallen from the hands of enemies into the ocean, and from the ocean into a galley belonging to the Yavanas, I came from that ship of the Yavanas to this lofty mountain full of variegated stones, and by chance lay down for rest (on the bank of) this lake; may you fare well!" He then said:—"If you do not answer my questions, I will devour you." I said—"Very well, ask them." And then the following conversation embodied in an A'ryá ensued between us:—

QUE.—What is cruel (that my be so called)?

ANS.—The heart of a woman.

QUE.—What contributes to the happiness and welfare of a householder?

ANS.—Virtues of a housewife.

QUE.—What is *Kâma* (*i. e.*, attainment of the object desired)?

ANS.—Resoluteness of purpose.

QUE.—What is the means of attaining a difficult object?

ANS.—Ingenuity.

"Of this (these statements) (the accounts of) Dhûminî, Gominî, Nimbavatî, and Nitambavatî are the proof." Thus addressed he said to me—"Tell what sort of women they were." Whereupon I thus began (the story of Dhuminî):—

"There is a country named Trigarta; in it lived three householders who were brothers, having a large property and wealth named Dhanaka, Dhânyaka and Dhanyaka. Once during their life-time there was no rain (*lit.* Indra poured down no rain) for twelve years. The grains were withered; medicinal herbs were rendered futile ; trees bore no fruit ; clouds were empty (*lit.* unimpregnated with water) ; rivers had their currents dried up (*or*, reduced) ; pools had only mud left in them ; streams entirely ceased to flow ; roots and fruits became very rare ; conversations ceased ; the celebrations of religious rites and festivals fell into disuse ; thieves and rogues multiplied ; the people ate one another ; here and there were to be seen wallowing the skulls of men, pale-white like cranes ; swarms of crows suffering from starvation flew about ; and cities, villages, towns, and hamlets were almost depopulated. Now these brothers, having consumed all their store of grain, flocks of sheep and goats, wild buffaloes all the cattle, all their servants, children and even the wives of the eldest and the elder brothers in turn, decided to eat up Dhûminî, the wife of the youngest brother, the following day. Now Dhanyaka, unable to bear the idea of having to eat his own wife, made off with her that very night ; and when she was fatigued by the journey, he bore her on his shoulders and entered a forest. Allaying her hunger and thirst by means of his own flesh and blood, he bore her on, when he saw a man rolling on the ground, having his nose, feet, hands and ears cut off. Dhanyaka, in pity of his sad plight, took him on his back, and carried him on ; and having with great efforts built a hut in the midst of a forest abounding in bulbous roots and deer, he lived there for a long time. And he fed the cripple with meat and vegetables like his own self, after his wounds were healed with Iṅgudî oil and such other things. Once, while Dhanyaka had been out in quest of game for their support, she waited upon the cripple, who had now grown quite fat and had an abundant quantity of vital fluid, with a desire to enjoy herself in his company, and though repulsed by him she compelled him to comply with her desire. When her husband returned and asked for water, she threw before him a bucket with a rope, and desired him to get water from the well himself, alleging that she had been suffering from head-ache ; and as he was drawing up water from the well she came from behind in an instant and pushed him in. Then carrying the cripple on her shoulders and wandering from place to place, she came to be known as a Pativratâ and was worshipped variously. And finally she lived in great affluence by the favour of the king of Avanti. Now that Dhûminî, having discovered her husband, who had been taken out of the well being accidentally seen by some merchants repairing to the well for water, wandering in Avanti in search of food, charged him as the wicked man who had mutilated her husband, and had him sentenced to a torturous death by the king ignorant of the facts of the case. Poor Dhanyaka, who was bound from behind and was being led to the place of execution, as his life-strings were not to be snapped so soon as that, boldly said to the officer in charge—"If the cripple whom I am believed to have mutilated will accuse me of the crime, I shall well merit this punishment." When he was shown to the cripple by being taken to him by the officer with the words—"What harm is there," he, with tears in his eyes, fell at his feet, and being a noble-minded man acknowledged all the obligations he owed him, and revealed all the wickedness of his wife. The king, being highly incensed (on hearing this), ordered that wicked woman to be disfigured and made a cook for the dogs ( *i. e.* disgracefully banished) ; while he made Dhanyaka an object of his favour. Hence I say ( *i. e.* this story proves my assertion), that a woman's heart is very cruel"

Being asked again (to proceed), I began the story of Gominî :—"In the country of Draviḍa is a city called Káñchî. A young merchant of immense fortune ( *lit.* consisting of several crores) named Śaktikumâra resided there. Being in his eighteenth year he once thus mused to himself—"There is no real happiness for those who lead a single life, or for those who have no wives of corresponding virtues. How shall I then obtain an accomplished wife?" Now, not feeling certain of finding the expected degree of excellence in a bride chosen from confidence in others, he adopted the disguise of a fortune-teller and carrying with him a *prastha* of paddy bound up in his cloth, he travelled over the world. Wherever he went, those who had daughters brought them to him, thinking he knew the auspicious marks (on the body) ; and whenever he met with a girl of auspicious marks and of his own class, he asked her this question—"Good girl, can you serve us with good food prepared out of this Prastha of Śâli?" Being laughed at and repulsed, he roamed about, going from house to house. Once, having arrived at a town in the country of the Śibis on the bank of the Káverî, he saw a girl sparingly decorated with ornaments, presented before him by her nurse, who had lost, along with her parents, her great fortune and also the valuable property in her house. His eyes being riveted on her, he pondered—"Indeed, all the limbs of this girl are neither too stout nor too slight, neither too short nor too long, nor are they unduly large, and are bright (*lit.* possessed of cleanness). Her hands have their palms and fingers red, and are marked with a number of auspicious signs, such as Yava, fish, lotus, and a vase; her feet have their ankles well turned and even, and are fleshy and not marked with prominent veins; her thighs are taperingly rounded; her knees are hardly to be seen, oppressed as they are beneath her massive thighs; the region of her hips is evenly divided, symmetrical, beautiful with the well-turned cavities of the loins and round like a wheel. Her deep naval is slender and slightly depressed; her belly is decked with the three folds of skin; her breasts, beautiful on account of their great expanse and with the nipples deep set in, cover her whole bosom; her tender and creeperlike arms have their palms marked with the auspicious signs that ensure abundant wealth, corn and progeny, the jewel-like nails whereof are glossy, prominent and delicate, and the fingers of which are straight, rounded symmetrically and reddish; the region of their shoulders are well-turned; they are delicate, and their joints are depressed. Her neck is slender, round and gracefully curved like a conch; her countenance is lotus-like, where the round lips are tinged red in the middle; its chin is not contracted and is elegant; the orbs of her cheeks are well-developed and firm; the dark glossy eye-brows are beautifully curved and not connected; the nose is like the budding sesamum flower; the eyes, reddish at the corners and bright, are dark, white, rolling unsteadily and beautifully, dull and elongated; her forehead is beautiful like the half-crescent of the moon; her curly ringlets are lovely-looking like the sapphire-stone; her beautiful ear-lobes are gracefully decorated with the now-faded lotus-stalk double-folded round them; and her not very curly mass of hair is luxuriant, not brown even at the tips, and long, wherein the hair grows each by itself and evenly, and is glossy and redolent of sweet scent. Such a lovely figure as this can hardly be inconsistent with good disposition. My heart is attached to her only; so, putting her to test, I will marry her. Surely, successions of (occasions for) regret more than once overtake those who act precipitately." Having reflected thus he asked her with an affectionate look—"Good girl, hast thou the skill to serve me with good food prepared out of this Prastha of Śâli?" At this she looked significantly at her old attendant, and having taken the paddy from him, asked him to sit on a raised seat near the door, which was well-cleaned with cow-dung, after having given him water to wash his feet with. She then pounded the Sâlis, dried them a little in the sun, turned them over and over again on a firm and level ground, and after striking ( rubbing ) them gently with the back of a stalk, separated the husk from them without breaking the grain. She then said to her nurse —" Mother, goldsmiths stand in need of this bran of the rice to clean their jewellery with; sell it to them and purchase with the price ( *lit.* Kákiṇîs obtained ) fuel, neither too dry nor too moist, a cooking utensil of a fixed measure, and two platters." When that was done by her, she brayed the grain in a mortar of Arjuna wood having an upright hole, not very deep and spacious, stirring it up again and again with her fingers, and striking it with a heavy pestle of Khadira with its end covered with iron plate and even-shaped, and with the slenderness of its middle part noticeable, in a manner in which her arms were fatigued by the artistically graceful motions of the pestle, up and down. She removed the grains of dust and the awn from the rice by winnowing it with a winnowing basket, and having repeatedly washed it with water, poured it in five times its quantity of boiling water, worshipping the hearth as she did so. When the grains of the rice became loose, and floated about when they had swollen up properly (*lit.* passed the state of a bud), she lessened the heat of the fire, and passed the scum. She then stirred the rice with a ladle, turned it a little, and when all the grains were equally boiled, placed the boiler with the mouth downwards. She then extinguished the fire-brands, which were not entirely consumed, with cold water, and turning them into black coal sent it (by the old woman) to those who wanted it, telling her to buy, with the *kákiṇîs* obtained by its sale, vegetables, ghee, curds, oil, myrobalans, and tamarind, as far as obtainable. The old woman did so, and the damsel prepared two or three condiments, and cooled the scum of rice-water lying in an earthen vessel placed on moist sand by very gently fanning it with a palm fan, added salt to it, and fumigated it with perfumes evaporated on the charcoals; and having reduced the myrobalans to fine powder she made them lotus-fragrant, and asked him ( Śaktikumâra ), through her nurse, to bathe. She ( the nurse ), who had purified herself by bathing, gave to him oil and myrobalans (to rub his body with); which done, he bathed. When he had performed his ablutions, he sat on a wooden seat placed on the paved floor well swept after being sprinkled over (with cow-dung-water), touching (*i.e.* passing his hand accross) two wet platters that were placed on a third part cut from the vertex of the leaf of a plaintain tree that was grown in the court-yard. She brought him first the rice-gruel she had prepared, which he drank, and being rid of the fatigue of his journey, he sat refreshed, all his limbs having freely perspired. Then she gave him two spoonfuls of the Śâli rice, and also brought him ghee, sauce and condiments ; the rest of the rice she served him with curds spiced with pepper, cinnamon and ginger, and with fragrant and cool butter-milk and sour gruel. His hunger was quite satisfied while part of the food remained, when he asked for water to drink. Thereupon she poured out to him in a stream the water which was contained in a new Bhṛiṅgâra ( a kind of jug ), and which was fumigated with the incense of black aloe-wood, and charged with the smell of fresh Pâṭala flowers mingled with the perfume of full-blown lotuses. He, too, having raised the drinking dish to his mouth, drank the water to his fill, while his eye-brows looked tawny being fringed with cool, snow-like drops of water ; his ears were regaled with the sound of the stream of water, his cheeks looked rough with the horripilation due to the pleasure of touch, his nostrils were filled with thick and diffusing fragrance, and his tongue became quite gratified with the excess of sweetness. Asked to stop pouring water by the simple sign of a nod, the damsel gave him water for *áchamana* from another vase. The old woman then removed the dining-leaf and the fragments ( of his food ), and cleaned the paved ground with fresh cow-dung, whereafter he spread his own garment upon it and went to sleep. Being greatly pleased, he married that damsel according to the proper rites, and took her home After he had taken her there, with (seeming) indifference towards her he attached himself to a courtesan ; her also she nevertheless treated (*or*, served) like a dear friend. She assiduously worshipped her husband as a god, and managed his household affairs without any flaw. Herself a treasure of politeness, she won the love of all her attendants. Subdued by her virtues, her spouse, with his life and body entirely depending on her, left all his domestic concerns to her, and enjoyed the three objects of human existence. Hence I say, that the virtues of his wife are for the happiness and welfare of a householder."

Being then asked by him (to go on), he (thus) narrated the story of Nimbavatî :—"In the country of Sauráshṭra there is a city called Valabhî; in it there dwelt Gṛihagupta, the chief of sea-traders, who possessed immense wealth like Kubera. He had a daughter named Ratnavatî. The son of a merchant-leader, Balabhadra by name, came from Madhumatî and married her. Being thoughtlessly obstructed in private ( *lit.* in his enjoyment of the pleasure of union ), by his new bride, he at once conceived a violent hatred for ( *i. e.* dislike to ) her; ( so much so that ) he did not desire to see her again. Turning a deaf ear to all the importunities of his friends, he even avoided going to her house. Just from that time her relatives as well as others insulted that unfortunate woman by the nickname of Nimbavatî ( *lit.* possessed of the bitternes of the *nimba* tree). After some time had elapsed, she, feeling repentance, and reflecting on her future course of life (*or*, fate), saw some old female recluse, who was like a mother to her, coming to her with flowers taken from an idol. Before her she pitiously shed profuse tears in private. Asked by her, with her face covered with tears and after having consoled her in many ways, the cause of her weeping, she ( Ratnavatî ), though blushing to tell it, somehow addressed her thus, considering the weightiness of the object on hand :—" Mother, what can I say? The state of being hated by one's husband is, as is well known, simply a living death in the case of women (in general ), and more particularly of women of high birth I myself have become a fitting instance of this (such a state of things) ; all my kith and kin, headed by my own mother, regard me with a look of contempt Make me, therefore, one who will be well seen (by all ; *i.e.*, by being taken into his favour by my husband) ; and if it is not possible, here shall I relinquish this hateful life And this my secret should not be revealed until I die ." With these words she fell at her feet. The old woman raised her up and with tears in her eyes said—" Dear girl, do not go in for such a rash act ; here am I ready to do your bidding. I shall be entirely at your service, as long as I can serve you in any way. If at all you are disgusted with this worldly life, practise penance under my guidance to ensure bliss in the next world. This is surely the result of evil deeds done in a previous life, since though endowed with such grace of form, such purity of character and such nobility of birth, you have unaccountably become the object of aversion to your husband. Your intellect is more acute than mine ; if, therefore, you can see a remedy to set right the prejudice of your husband, point it out to me." Thereupon she (Ratnavatî) mused for a moment with her face hung down, and replied—"Revered lady, the husband alone is the idol of women, more especially of those of high birth (*i. e.* respectable station). Hence, something must be done which will be the means of enabling me to serve him. We have a neighbour, a merchant, who by means of his high birth and wealth, as well as being in the confidence of the king, stands pre-eminently above all citizens. His daughter, Kanakavatî, is very like me in person and form; and she is also my very affectionate friend. I will play at ball with her on the terrace of her lofty mansion, doubly decorated as she. Do you somehow contrive to bring my husband to her place, communicating to him in moving terms her mother's desire to that effect. As you approach, I will let down the ball in your direction, as if blundering in the sport. Then, picking it up and placing it in his hand, say to him,—"This is Kanakavatî, the daughter of Nidhipatidatta, the prince of merchants, and a great friend of your wife. She reproaches you very much on account of Ratnavatî, calling you reckless and cruel. You should therefore restore to her this ball, the property of an enemy." Thus addressed, he would certainly look up, and think me to be that same friend of me (Kanakavatî); and when I would beg for it with folded hands, he would, at your request again, return it to me, affected with a longing for me. Taking advantage of this circumstance (*lit.* loop-hole), you should approach him, and having kindled the fire of his passion, you should so contrive it that he would give me an appointment and take me off to another country." Thrilled with joy (at my ingenuous suggestion), she did exactly as she was told. Thereupon Balabhadra, entirely beguiled by that old ascetic that she was none other than Kanakavatî, took her off who had her jewels and choice ornaments with her in the pitchy darkness of the night, and started away. That old ascetic, however, spread this report—"Balabhadra told me the previous day that he, silly that he was, had shown uncalled-for indifference towards Ratnavatî, insulted his parents-in-law, and disregarded the advice of his friends, and that he was, therefore, ashamed to live with her in the same place. Surely he must have taken her away with him; this will soon be clear." On hearing this, Balabhadra's relatives became slack in their efforts to search after him. Now to turn to Ratnavatî; she, on her way, bought a female slave who carried all their baggage, and soon they arrived at a small town ( *or*, a town called Kheṭaka ). Here Balabhadra who was an expert in business. made a large fortune out of a small capital, and in time became the chief of the citizens there and had a large number of servants on account of his wealth. He once beat his first female servant very severely after reproaching her, saying—"You do not attend to your duty, steal whatever you see, and speak disagreable words." The maid, in her rage, disclosed a part of his history, which was communicated to her while she was in favour. When the mayor, who was covetous ( *i. e.* saw his gain in this ), heard this, he reviled Balabhadra before the seniors of the town, saying—"This wicked Balabhadra is living amongst us, having carried away by stealth Kanakavatî, the daughter of Nidhipatidatta. You should not, therefore, come in the way of the confiscation of his whole property." Balabhadra was frightened, when Ratnavatî said to him—"Do not be afraid; say ( to the seniors )—This is not Kanakavatî, the daughter of Nidhipatidatta, but the daughter of Gṛihagupta of the same Valabhî, Ratnavatî by name, who, being given to me by her parents, was married by me with all the due rites; if you do not believe me, send over a messenger to her relatives." Balabhadra said as he was desired, and continued to stay on there under the security of the association of traders, until Gṛihagupta, having learnt everything from the letter sent from the town, came over to the town, and being overjoyed, took back his daughter along with his son-in-law (to his place). When this was seen happening that way, Ratnavatî became greatly endeared to Balabhadra, who had all the while taken her for Kanakavatî. Hence I say that *Káma* is 'resoluteness of purpose'."

Then he asked me to relate the story of Nitambavatî. I then continued—"In Śûrasena is a city called Mathurâ. There dwelt a youth born in a high family, who was exceedingly fond of the fine arts and greatly addicted to courtesans; and who, having fought many a fight merely by the force of his arms for the sake of his friends, was given the significant name of *Kalahakaṇṭaka* by the harsher section of the populace. Once he saw, in the hands of a painter who was a chance visitor, a picture-cloth. A certain youthful damsel painted thereon made the mind of Kalahakaṇṭaka overpowered by love by her mere sight. He then said to the painter—"Dear friend, this appears to me to be inconsistent herein; for here is a form difficult to be obtained by a woman of family, and yet there is a modesty which bespeaks high birth; while the complexion of her face is palish white, her body is graceful, not being very much enjoyed, and her eyes bear the expression of full growth. She cannot be one whose husband is absent from her on a journey; for there is no mark of separation, such as the tying of the hair in a single braid, seen here. And here is this mark (of recognition) visible on her right side. Hence she appears to be the wife, who is in distress for want of enjoyment commensurate with her youth, of some old merchant not having much virility, and painted by you through great skill just as she was seen by you (*i.e.* very faithfully)" The painter commended him for his discernment, and said—"This (*i. e.* what you have said) is true; she is the wife of a merchant of Ujjayinî in Avanti, named Anantakîrti, who bears the significant name of Nitambavatî. She was thus painted by me, being struck with her beauty." Extremely agitated, he (the youth) just then set out for Ujjayinî to obtain a sight of her. Assuming the guise of a fortune-teller, he got access to her house under pretence of soliciting alms, and saw her. His passion being intensified at her sight, he (with a view to effect his project) went and solicited of the chief citizens the care of the cemetery and obtained it. With pieces of cloth used for covering the dead bodies and such other things obtained there, he attached to his interest a female Jaina devotee named Arhantiká. Through her medium he made overtures to Nitambavatî in secret, but she rebuked the woman and sent her way. Learning from the lips of the female Jaina devotee that it was very difficult to make that woman of family fall off from her character, he secretly instructed his messenger (thus)—"Go once more to the merchant's wife and say to her in private—"How can it be expected that a person like me, who by practising penance seeks final beatitude on seeing the evils of this worldly life, would ever endeavour to induce noble women to abandon their virtue of chastity? I simply tried you by doing that in order to find out whether you, too, possessed as you are of very large fortune, superhuman beauty and fresh youth, are affected with that fickleness (infirmity) of character so very common among other (*i. e.* ordinary) women.

I am pleased with the purity (*lit.* the unaffected state) of your character. Now I only wish to see you with a child; your husband, however, has been possessed by a malicious star and enfeebled by jaundice, and has thus become incapable of enjoyment; and, unless the obstacle in his case is removed, it is not possible to have a child from him. Be pleased, therefore, to enter all alone the grove of trees and secretly to place your foot in the hand of a magician brought by me to the spot; and, your foot being charmed with a spell by him, you should strike your husband with it on the chest under the pretence of being lovingly angry. That being done, he will be richly endowed with the best virility that will enable him to obtain a noble son; and he will be devoted to you as to a goddess. You need not at all be afraid in this matter." She will undoubtedly (*lit.* clearly) acceed to that proposal. You should at night take me to the grove and bring her also there. I shall consider myself as favoured by you even by this much (service done to me.)" She did all that according to his instructions. He, too, being exceedingly pleased, went to the grove that same night, and while pretending to touch gently the foot of Nitambavatî, who was with great difficulty brought there by the Śramaṇiká, snatched off one of her gold anklets, scratched a little at the root of her thigh with a knife, and ran off. Being greatly frightened, she reproached herself for her imprudence, and appearing as if ready to kill the Jaina devotee, she washed the wound in the tank attached to her residence, put a bandage on it, and pretending to be ill, took off the other anklet and passed three or four days all alone, confined to bed. That cunning fellow approached Anantakîrti with the anklet, in order to sell it off. Anantakîrti, on seeing it, knew for certain that it was his wife's, and as he kept silence, asked him pressingly to relate to him how he came by it. He remained firm, saying that he would tell it in the presence of the merchants' association Anantakîrti on his part sent a message to his wife to send over her pair of anklets. Ashamed and terrified, she sent him the other anklet with a word that she happened to drop down one of her anklets as its tie was loosened, while she had entered the grove for rest the last night, and that it was not found till then though searched for, the one sent being the other one. With this information

Anantakîrti took him to the merchants' association. There the rogue, when questioned, thus informed them with (all the artful) modesty (of a hypocrite)—"It is, indeed, known to you that I live here maintaining myself by keeping guard over the cemetery by your command. I sleep in the cemetery even at night, lest some miserly people might burn their dead at night, afraid of my sight (*i.e.* unwilling to pay the charges). The other day at night I happened to see a woman of a darkish complexion (*or*, apparently young), forcibly drawing off from the pyre a half-burnt corpse; wishing to make gain out of it, I, dismissing all fear, caught her and made some scratch on her thigh with a knife, and also took off this anklet from her foot. Just as this was done, she ran away with quick steps. This is how the anklet came to be in my possession. Now the decision rests with you." After deliberation, the citizens unanimously came to the conclusion that she was a witch. Abandoned by her husband, she went to the very cemetery at night, and having lamented long, wished to die by hanging herself up with a noose, when she was seized by the cunning youth. He conciliated her, saying—"Beautiful damsel, being maddened by the beauty of your form, I put forth various means to win you through the medium of the female devotee; but they having failed, I employed this extraordinary remedy with a view to enjoy your company for the whole of my life. Favour, therefore, this your slave, who is solely dependent on you." With these words he fell again and again at her feet, used hundreds of conciliatory words to appease her anger, and eventually won her over to him, as she had no other course left to her. Hence it was remarked—"Ingenuity accomplishes what is difficult to attain."

Hearing this (these my narratives), the Brahmarákshasa honoured (*i.e.* expressed a very high opinion of) me. At this very moment, several pearls, as large as half-developed Punnâga buds, fell from the sky along with drops of water. I looked up, wishing to know what it could be, and saw a Râkshasa in the air carrying off a female who was struggling to free herself from his grasp. I felt restless, saying to myself—"How does the wicked Rákshasa carry away the woman against her will," as I had no weapon with me and was also powerless to go up into the sky. My Brahmarákshasa friend, however, reproaching him, saying—"Stop, stop, you miscreant, where can you take her?" rose into the sky and engaged him. Looking up with arms stretched out, I caught her (the female) in my arms falling from the sky like the blossom of a heavenly tree, being cast down through rage (by the ravisher) without any regard for her safety. Having caught her I stood holding her up just as she was trembling, with her eyes closed, and with her hair standing on end at the pleasure of the touch of my body. In the meantime the contending demons dispatched each other by means of mountain-peaks, trees forcibly torn off and by dealing out blows with their fists and feet. I then placed her on the extremely soft, sandy bank of the tank marked with bits of flowers, and eagerly looking at her found her to be none other than the princess Kandukávatî, the sole darling of my life. As I cheered her up, she looked askance at me, and recognizing me piteously moaned (and said)--"Lord, having conceived a strong love for you since I saw you at the Kanduka festival, I was somehow sustained by my friend Chandrasená by means of various talks about you. When I heard that you were drowned in the ocean by my wicked brother Bhîmadhanvá, I eluded (the sight of) my friends and attendants, and went to the garden of sport alone, with intent to put an end to my life. While there, this base demon, capable of assuming any form at will, fell in love with me. His suit being rejected by me, who was frightened, he caught hold of me as I was trembling, and flew off; and he has thus met his end here. While, through good luck, I have fallen into the arms of you, the lord of my life. I wish you every happiness!" Having heard this, I descended with her and got on board the ship. As the ship sailed off, it was driven by contrary winds to that very Dámalipta; and we landed easily. I heard the lamentations of the subjects whose faces were covered with tears, to this effect—"Tuṅgadhanvá, the Lord of the Suhmas, being dejected and pale at the disappearance of his son and daughter, has himself started with his queen to die on the banks of the holy Ganges, abstaining from all food, as he has no other children (to console him); and the old citizens, too, being attached to him and having no other lord, wish to die along with him." Thereupon I related to the king everything as it had happened, and delivered over to him his two children. I was made his son-in-law by the delighted lord of Dámalipta; his son then became my vassal; and he at my bidding resigned Chandrasená, like his own life, who, thereupon, repaired to

Kośadása (*i.e.* became his wife). Thereafter, coming here to the succour of Siṃhavarman, I became the enjoyer of the happiness of the festival of beholding you, my Lord."

On hearing this, Prince Rájaváhana, saying—"Marvellous is the working of destiny; great valour was displayed at the right time,"—again cast his joy-expanded eyes, with a smile playing on his lips, at Mantragupta. He, with his face obscured a little by his lotus-like hand, commenced to narrate his story without the use of any labial letters, his round lower lip being distressed (pained) by the injury caused by the teeth-wounds inflicted by his graceful beloved in passionate sport.

---

## UCHCHHVÂSA VII.

Mighty Prince (*lit.* son of the Imperial Monarch), being desirous of knowing the wherabouts of you who had disappeared in the chasm of the mountain, I (wandering about), happened to arrive at the country of the Kaliṅgas. I sat at the root, having a bed of tender and moist leaves formed about it, of a forest-tree that was close to the public obsequial ground, which was at some distance from the capital of the Kaliṅgas, and lay down with the seal of sleep on my eyes. At the intensely cold dead of night, when darkness was pouring down looking like the thick tressess of the dark night, when the imps of mischief were astir (*i.e.* stalking abroad), when the dew was falling, and when all people were deep in slumber in their respective abodes, I heard the extremely piteous utterance of a goblin and his mate that fell upon my ears resounding through the intervals of the thick branches of the Sála trees, and that removed the sleep that was kissing my eyes, *viz.*—"How has this villain, the wretched magician, who, wishing to give a command at the time of enjoyment, has put an obstacle in our way when we are overpowered by uncontrollable passion! Oh, that some hero of unbounded valour would put a stop to the superhuman power attained by means of spell, of this vile wretch of a magician!" My heart being overpowered by the desire to see who that magician was and what he was ordering this servant of his to do, I went in the direction followed by the goblin to a certain distance, and saw a man, whose body was covered with ornaments made of very bright fragments of human bones, who had besmeared his frame with the ashes of the charcoal of wood completely burnt by fire, and who wore matted hair (bright and tawny) like the flashes of lightning, busily feeding with his left hand a fire, which devoured the darkness over the expanse of the forest and the flames of which glared about as it consumed fuel of various kinds thrown into it every moment, with sesamum and mustard-seed that made a crackling sound (in the fire). The goblin stood before him with folded hands, saying—"What is to be done? Let the order be given." And he was ordered by the extremely mean-minded fellow—"Go and bring here from her palace Kanakalekhâ, the daughter of Kardana, the king of Kaliṅga." The goblin did as he was bid. The magician then seized her by the mass of her hair the tie of which had given way and the garland worn as an ornament in which was scattered about, while she called out to her parents with an anxious heart, being seized with great terror and with her accent choked with tears; and with the desire of striking off her head with a sword sharpened on a whetting stone, he made a movement. I quickly snatched off the weapon from his hand, and with the same struck off his head and deposited it with its mass of matted hair in the hollow of a branch of an old Sála tree that was near. On seeing it the goblin was exceedingly pleased, being rid of all his anxiety. And he said—"Sir, being tormented by this wretch I had never had sleep coming to my eyes; he used to threaten and worry me and order me to do execrable things. You, who are a treasure of goodness, have, therefore, done an excellent thing in dispatching this vile crow of a human being, to taste the agonies of hell, to the city of Yama (*lit.* the son of the sun, the hot-rayed god). I should, therefore, like to execute some order of your honour, a treasure of mercy, and of uncomon lustre. Please order me; away with delay." With these words he made a reverential bow. I said to him—"This is the course of life followed by the good—that a very great respect is observed (in their case) in return for an insignificant act of obligation. If you would not disapprove of it, then take this beautiful princess, who, not deserving of such trouble, has been distressed for nothing by this wicked magician, back to her place; there is nothing else that would be so gratifying to my mind." Now, on hearing this, the princess, casting slantingly her slightly contracted eyes with their pupils tremulous and partaking of the beauty of the blue lotus serving as her ear-ornament, moving with graceful gentleness her creeper-like eye-brows which danced on the stage of her broad forehead and were arched like the bow of the fish-bannered god (*i.e.* Cupid), and with her reddish cheeks bristling with hair, influenced alternately by passion and abashment, drawing idle figures on the ground with her fore-foot with the moonlight of her nails spreading slantingly, while her lotus-like face was turned aside, addressed me these few words, sweet like the notes of a cuckoo, in which the mellow light of her teeth was caused to undulate by the gentle breaths escaping through her mouth, which passed beyond her sprout-like lips, which removed the moisture of the sandal-paste over her ample bosom wetted by the clusters of the drops of the streams of the tears of joy, and which issued with the swiftness of the shafts of Káma (*lit.* Rati's mate) skilled in hitting the target of heart—"Gentle Sir, for what reason do you hurl this your servant (me) into the depths of the ocean of love surging with the waves of yearnings agitated by the blast of passion, after having snatched her off from the grip of death? (Please) regard me just like a particle of the dust of the lotus of your feet. If at all you have some pity for me, I wish to be favoured with the exclusive privilege of serving your feet. If some disaster is apprehended owing to the secret being divulged if you take your residence in the female apartments, that too cannot be. For there my friends and attendants are all exceedingly attached to me; they will endeavour in such a way that no one will know of this." Being very mercilessly struck at heart by Cupid who stretched his bow as far as his ears, and fastened hard with the iron fetters of her side-long looks, I fixed my eyes on the goblin and said—"If I do not act up to what this beautiful damsel (*lit.* of hips as round as a wheel) desires, Cupid will instantly lead her to the state of non-existence; so carry this person (me) to the princess' apartment, along with this fawn-eyed girl." And I was taken by the goblin to the residence of the princess which resembled a mass of autumnal clouds. There I stayed for a short space of time in one part of the attic story at the desire of the moon-faced maiden, having the peace of my mind (moral courage) shaken off at her sight. She, then, by the gentle touch of the palm of her hand, roused from slumber some of her friends who were in sound sleep, and acquainted them with what had happened. Thereupon they came, and placing their heads on my feet, with their eyes roughened with the flowing tears, gently said to me in tones which were confused with the hummings of the bees clinging to the tips of the filaments of the (flowers in the) garlands worn as crest-ornaments—"Sir, our friend was not captured by death as she came to be the mark of the eyes of you, who surpass the sun in lustre. She has now been given over to you by the god-father, Cupid, in the presence of (*lit.* keeping as witness) the fire of love. Let the heart, as firm as a slab of stone on the mountain Meru, of you with eyes like blown lotuses, be set off with this wonderful jewel (in the form of our friend), bright with its twinkling light (whose mind is now agitated with the passion of love). Then will her bosom be blessed with the close embraces of an exceedingly worthy mate." From that time I enjoyed myself in the company of that beauteous princess, my chains of love being made fast by her exceedingly clever (*or*, courteous) friends.

Now once (in the season of Spring)—which torments the minds of travellers (*lit.* persons separated from their wives), when the thick-grown Kesara (=Bakula or Puṃnága) flowers fade under the descent of bees greedy ( of flower-juice ), when Tilaka, the sportive mark on the broad forehead of forest-groves, is all in bloom, when the full-blown Karṇikára flower forms the golden umbrella of the lovely Love-King, when the Malaya breeze produces blossoms on the mango-trees which attract swarms of bees, which eminently prepares women for the field of amorous sports, being inspired with passion by the cooings of the cuckoo, where (all sense of) shame is overridden by the passion of love rising in the minds of modest girls, and wherein all creepers are taught to dance gracefully by the instructor, the breeze, cool owing to its contact with the sandal-trees on the skirts of the Dardura ( mountain ),—the king of Kaliṅga, having got a passion for sport, accompanied by all the ladies of his harem, his daughter and all the citizens, passed 13 days, in the grove by the sea-shore, not to be penetrated by the sun's rays, where the sandy bank was closely touched by the sprouts at the ends of creepers bent down under the weight of the swarms of humming bees, and which was cool on account of its contact with the shower of the sprays of water from the rolling waves. While thus wholly engaged in the pursuit of the pleasures of love, delighted with the emulation in the unrestrained love-sports full of amorous gestures of thousands of beautiful damsels engaged in continuous songs and music, Jayasiṃha, the king of A'ndhra, taking advantage of the weak point, suddenly came upon him with a numerous host conveyed there in boats, and captured him with all his household. My beloved Kanakalekhá, too, her eyes unsteadily rolling through fear, was carried away with all her friends. I became quite dejected (*lit.* with my complexion faded), with all thought of taking food gone, owing to the burning sensation of the heat of passion, and said to myself—" That princess of Kaliṅga has now fallen into the hands of the foe with her father and mother. That king (Jayasiṃha), with the firmness of his mind destroyed by (her charms), will certainly desire to retain her in his possession; and she, resenting that, will at once put an end to her life by means of poison or some such thing. And when such will be her state, Cupid will not allow this person to sustain his life. What is that course which is to be my future lot?"

Just at this time I saw a certain Bráhmaṇa who was coming from the capital of the king of A'ndhra. He told this tale—" Kardana, who was desired to be put to death by Jayasiṃha, exasperated by the various insults offered, was spared, it is said, owing to his passion being roused at the sight of Kanakalekhá; that princess, however, being possessed by a certain Yaksha, does not so much as stand before any man, not even before the king. The king has been essaying to drive him (the Yaksha) away with the help of thousands of magicians, but with no success." This account having inspired me with hope, I repaired to the cemetery, where I pulled off the tufted locks of matted hair from the cavity of an old Sála tree and wore them; then, having obscured all my limbs by means of rags and a patched vestment, I procured a company of disciples whom I kept in good humour with the gifts (of garments, food &c.) which I obtained from the villagers duped by the various wonderful tricks that were performed. In a few days I went to the A'ndhra capital. At some distance from (*lit.* not very near to) it, I took up my abode in a grove on the edge of a lake, vast like an ocean and decked with the flocks of geese and variegated with the bits of filaments dropped from thousands of lotus-petals torn by hosts of royal swans. Clever in the deception of all the citizens drawn to me by my miraculous acts, reported to them by my pupils, I was thus talked of in all the quarters—" That ascetic, who has been lying on an altar on the bank of the lake in the old forest-grove, is said to have (*or*, verily has) all the Vedas, with their secrets, and the six accessory works, on the tip of his tongue. And (the exact meaning of) whatever other Śástras one may not know, one can get that (meaning) settled by him. He has never sullied his tongue with untruth; he is the treasure of mercy incarnate; asceticism has gained its end by his espousal of it; the various diseases of many a man, pronounced incurable by physicians, have vanished, when a few particles of the dust of his feet were scattered on their heads; the influence of terrific stars and planets, that had baffled the power of all magicians and magical diagrams, dies out in an instant, when the heads of men are purified by being sprinkled over with the water used for washing his feet. It is impossible to gauge the extent of his power; he has not even a speck of vanity in him." This report, passing through the mouths of several people, attracted the king whose mind was all the while deeply engaged in exorcizing the Yaksha that had possessed Kanakalekhá. He saw me every day, worshipped me with profound respect, pleased my disciples with gifts, and once seizing an opportunity gently entreated me for the accomplishment of his desired object. I stood in firm meditation, and displaying my knowledge of occult things at the proper time, I surveyed him carefully, and having come to a conclusion said—"Dear Sir, in the right place is this effort (of yours); the acquisition (gaining the hand) of that jewel of a princess, the sole treasure of all auspicious marks, is the very means for the acquisition of the Earth-bride, decorated by the girdle of the milky ocean and ornamented with the necklace formed of the strings of thousands of rivers, the Ganges and others. The Yaksha who possesses her ill bears it that any magician should get the sight of her, whose eyes, beautiful like blue lotuses, are gracefully contracted. You should, therefore, wait for three days, by which time I shall try to achieve this object." Thus advised, the king returned in joy. Thereafter at night, when there was no moonlight and all the quarters were completely swallowed by dense darkness, and when the eyes of all were sealed with (*i. e.* closed fast in) sleep, I issued forth, and formed with great difficulty an excavation in the side of the compact (*lit.* holeless) bank of the lake near the flight of steps, which was to be reached by one diving into the water. Having ascertained that the region of the bank of the lake was not to be suspected by the people (as being tampered with) as the upper mouth of the excavation was covered closely with stones and bricks, I purified my body with a bath in the morning, and having worshipped with handfuls of red lotuses the sun (the thousand-rayed god)—whose spreading rays served as the red paint applied to her body by the Eastern-quarter-lady; who is the witness of all acts, good or bad; the extraordinary crocodile capable of crossing the lines of rolling waves in the form of the clouds of the ocean of the expanse of the sky; the playful actor dancing on the stage of the peak of the mountain of gold (Meru); the one lion that destroys the elephant of the darkness of the night; and who is the central gem attached to the extremity of the necklace of the strings of stars;—and I returned to my abode.

When three days had elapsed, and when the lord of day (sun), whose blaze appeared like the red-mineralled peak of the Western Mountain, was as comely to look at as the one stout breast, smeared over with red sandal, of the beautiful damsel of twilight united with the form of Śaṃkara known as A'káśa (the sky) for the sake of tormenting Párvatî, the king came to me and stood with folded hands, hiding his tiara in the rays of the nails of my feet. And he was thus addressed—"Fortunately, I have seen how to achieve your purpose; in this world, indeed, fortune does not take up her abode with the inactive (*lit.* unambitious); prosperity is always in the hands of the active; for this reason, this reservoir has been sanctified in such a way by this person (me), his mind being drawn by your exceedingly noble conduct which is free from any (*lit.* bears no) stain on it, which is highly esteemed and fraught with great respect, that you will accomplish your object this very day. You should plunge into it at night after it has half worn away (*i e.* at midnight); after entering it you should lie down at the bottom of the water as long as you can, with suppressed breath. On this there will be a splashing sound of the mass of water to be heard in a moment by the people lending their ears to the confused cackle of the royal swans frightened by their bodies being pierced by the ends of the thorns of the lotus-stalks shaken by the beds of the lotuses being covered with the water tossed from the bank; that sound having subsided, you will come forth with a wet body and reddish eyes; and on seeing the form, delightful to the eyes of all people, in which you will appear then, the Yaksha will not be able to stand before you. And the heart of the princess will in an instant be such as will brook no delay in obtaining your sight, being made fast with chains of affection firmly fixed on you.

And the circle of this your bride, the earth, you should look upon as secure ( *lit.* lying on the palm of your hand ), the whole body of your enemies being easily annihilated. There should be no doubt as to that. If you wish to do this, you may take counsel with your officers whose intellect ( judgement ) is matured by the deep study of the various S'ástras, and other well-wishers, and having summoned a hundred fishermen ( *lit.* men with nets ) and caused the inner space of the lake to be carefully examined by them and hundreds of other men in whom you have confidence, have it carefully guarded by your troops stationed at a distance of thirty fathoms. For, who can know what mischief an enemy may mean on getting an opportunity ? " My speech appealed to him. And his officers, who could not see any mischief in it and who knew how firm in his determination the king was owing to his excessive passion for the princess, did not object to the execution of the plan. I then addressed the king, who was ready to carry out my instructions and firmly resolved to secure the maiden,—" O King, we have resided in your country for a long time ; it is not proper for us to remain long in one place. When your purposes are attained, you will not see us any more. A departure from here without doing something to serve you, in whose kingdom we have gained food and other things, would have been condemned by the A'ryas ; this was the reason of our stay here for a long time ; and that is to-day achieved. Go home, bathe in suitable water having an agreeable smell, apply perfumes to your body and put on a white garland and propitiate the Bráhmaṇas, who are no less than gods on this earth, with presents in keeping with your state; and at night, dissipating the mass of darkness with thousands of torch-lights having wicks fed with sesamum oil, advance to the attainment of your desires." The king, expressing his gratitude, said—" This attainment of my object is no attainment if your reverence does not wish to stay here. Woe to this disattachment to worldly objects, which makes you leave your servant without any fault of his ! All the same, the words of the worthy cannot be gainsaid." With these words he went home to bathe. I went forth to the lake in the solitude of midnight, and having entered the hole remained listening through a small aperture to what was going forward. When it was midnight, the king, who had done everything according to my instructions, set guards at different places, and having brought men who cast nets, saw that the interior was free from obstacles, and plunged into the water, without any misgiving at all, with a sportive motion. As he dived in the water, an elephant's height deep, with his hair scattered about and the cavities of his nose and ears filled with water, and lay down there, I approached him in the manner of a crocodile passing very carefully through the water, cast my scarf round his neck, and mercilessly pommelled him with blows of hands and feet as tremendous as the strokes of the rod of Yama, so that he ceased struggling (*i e.* died) in an instant. I then dragged his body, and thrusting it into the hole emerged from the water.

The troops that at once came up were astonished at the surprising change in the king's person. I mounted the royal elephant, and adorned with all the signs of royalty, such as the white umbrella, proceeded along the road, wherein passage was made by the people afraid of being beaten by the staffs of fierce staff-bearers, to the palace, where I passed the night with my eyes stripped of the pleasure of sleep owing to the joy I felt. The next day, when the orb of the sun, the jewelled mirror for the beautiful damsel of the East, looking like the frontal globe of the temple of a quarter-elephant smeared with red lac, became visible to the eyes of the people, I, having performed the customary morning duties, seated myself on a throne glittering with gems variegated with multitude of rays, and addressed my companions, who waited upon me with formalities proper for each, with their limbs contracted through fear—"Observe the power of the saint who was never subdued by objects of sense, by whose purification devoid of the quality of Rajas, I had this transformation of my person lovelier than before, and having the pleasing brightness of the petals of a lotus, in (having plunged into) this pool full of lotuses alive with gladdened bees. Let the heads of heretics be now bowed down in shame! Let all honour be paid by means of sessions of music and dance to the shrines of the gods, such as Śiva, Vishṇu, Brahmadeva and others, and let largesses of money be taken away from here by the poor in order to dissipate all their cares." The ministers, with delighted looks on account of the extreme wonder, exclaimed—"Glory to the lord of the earth! May you, by your conquest, eclipse the fame of all the previous kings, filling the ten quarters with your glory!" With these benedictory words they executed the duties entrusted to them. I then saw one of my wife's most attached servants, Śaśáṅkasená, as she came to me on some mission, when I said to her in private—"Did you ever chance to see this person before?" She looked at me a little, with her heart in the highest transport of joy, moving the creeper of the rays of her teeth in a manner gentle with sport, and hiding her tender sprout-like lips with the fingers of her hand gracefully contracted, folded her hands, while tears of joy flooded her eyes that had no collyrium applied to them, and said with the freedom of affection—"If this is not some fabric of magic of this sort, then I know too well whom I behold. How could this come to pass?" I told her the whole story, and having it imparted through her to Kanakalekhá, thereby filled her heart with ecstatic joy. I was then united with my beloved, who was formally given in marriage to me by the king (Kardana) who was set at liberty and treated with great respect by me. Then coming to be the ruler over both A'ndhra and Kaliṅga, I came with a large army to help the king of the Aṅgas, who was about to be attacked by his enemy, and became overpowered with joy at this accidental meeting here with Your Highness in company of all friends."

Rájavâhana with his friends complimented him on the skill he had shown, with a smile that bathed his lip with its brilliance, and said—"Wonderful is the part played by the great saint! His extremely austere penance bore fruit just in this life! Now, to speak in earnest (*lit.* joking apart), herein we have seen the nature of the union of ingenuity and courage resulting in the highest pitch of joy." Having said this he turned his eye, beautiful like a full-blown lotus, to Viśruta, who was rich in information, saying—"May you now descend (to the path of narration)."

---

## UCHCHHVÂSA VIII.

He, too, said—"Lord, while travelling (in search of you) I came to the Vindhya forest, and there encountered by the side of a well a boy about eight years of age, in great distress, though unworthy of distress, on account of hunger and thirst He said to me, with his voice chocked with fear—"Noble sir, kindly help me, who am in distress. An old man, who was my only support, has fallen into this well as he was drawing water to gratify my exceedingly unbearable thirst. I am not able to rescue him." I immediately approached, and using a certain creeper (as a rope) took out from the well a venerable old man; and knocking down with stones five or six fruits of some Lakucha tree as tall as the ascent of an arrow, and drawing up some water by means of a bamboo pipe, I helped them to refresh their spirits, and then sitting under a tree I asked the old man—"Sir, who is this boy, who are you, and how has this distress come upon you?" With tears choking his throat he said—"Magnanimous one, be pleased to listen. There is a country called Vidarbha whose king was Puṇyavarmá. He was the ornament of the race of Bhoja, a partial incarnation, as it were, of the God of Justice, mighty, truthful, liberal, and well-behaved; he was the educator of his people, and kept his servants well pleased; famous, conspicuous both by his intellect and his imposing form; ambitious of greatness, defender of the faith, and an undertaker of things possible to achieve and benefical in the end. He respected the wise and promoted his dependants; he raised his kinsmen to dignity, but buried his foes in misery; he never lent his ear to nonsensical talk; ever a seeker of merits, he was thoroughly proficient in all the arts; he was fully coversant with sacred lore and political science; he would doubly repay even a slight good turn; he himself looked after his treasury and conveyances, took great pains to supervise (and appreciate) the work of the heads of the various departments, and encouraged with honour and fitting rewards those who well acquitted themselves of the duties entrusted to them. He at once removed calamities human as well as divine; he was an expert in the employment of the six expedients in foreign politics; he himself led (*i.e.* maintained in order) the four classes according to the path laid down by Manu, and his name it was auspicious to repeat. Having lived the full period of human life by the force of meritorious deeds, he came to be numbered among the immortals, owing to the want of religious merit on the part of his subjects. His son Anantavarmá succeeded him; he was graced with every excellence, but unluckily held the science of politics in little esteem. Once an old minister of his, Vasurakshita by name, who was highly respected by his father and was eloquent in speech, said to him in private—"Prince, all the excellences of the soul, beginning with nobility of birth, seem to exist fully (*lit.* do not seem to be wanting) in you. And your intellect, naturally sharp, and developed by its knowledge of the arts of music, dancing, painting, and poetics in all its branches, surpasses that of others. But the same intellect, not being exercised in its proper subject, *viz.* the study of the science of government, does not shine prominently, like gold that has not been refined in fire; and the prince, whose understanding has not been thus cultured, is unable to see, however exalted he may be, how he is overridden by others, nor is he able to act having properly discriminated the objects to be effected and the means by which they are to be attained. Acting injudiciously, and thwarted in his undertakings, he is disregarded by his own servants and by strangers as well; and when a king is despised, his orders fail to give safety to, or ensure the welfare of, his subjects; and when the subjects once learn to transgress the orders of the king, they, talking anything, and doing whatever they like, will upset all order; and demoralized subjects ruin themselves as well as their master, in this world and in the next. When the path of action is seen by the lamp of political science, the course of worldly affairs proceeds smoothly on. The science of politics is but the divine eye, the operation of which is never obstructed in giving insight into things, past, present and future, as well as hidden or far removed from sight. Devoid of that (eye), a man, although having long-stretched and large eyes, is no better than a blind creature, owing to his inability to penetrate into political ends. Abandon, therefore, the attachment to mere external accomplishments, and study the science of government, your family inheritance. Putting into practice its precepts, and with the three royal powers successfully employed, rule long over the sea-girt earth, your authority being unobstructed!"

On hearing (this advice), the king, saying—"Rightly is the advice given by the revered one; it shall be attended to," entered the inner apartment. On hearing the matter mentioned in the course of talk by the king before the ladies of the harem, an associate of the king from his very childhood, Vihárabhadra by name, who was sitting not very far, who was skilled in acting according to the wishes of (*i. e.* in humouring) his master, and who was known to be the royal favourite; who had a good insight into (*i. e.* knew) singing, dancing, and playing; who was libidinous, clever, of licentious tongue, skilled in paronomastic and enigmatical speeches, devoted to finding the weak points of others, and could excite laughter; who took delight in scandal; who was an expert in craft and in the art of receiving bribes even from ministers; and who was a professor of all the wicked acts and a pilot of libertinism;—he smiled and said—"Sire, whenever by the favour of fortune a person is blessed with prosperity, clever rogues, worrying him with various temptations, accomplish their own designss; Thus some, inspiring hopes in him about the supreme felicity to be enjoyed after death, get his head shaved, gird him with a string of holy grass, clothe him in skins, smear his body with butter, send him to sleep without his supper, and manage to appropriate all his property: there are (other) heretics more terrible than these, who persuade him to relinquish children, wives, and even life. If there be a person naturally shrewd enough not to let his property slip out of his hands in exchange for such mirage, then there are others who surround him and say—"We can convert even a single cowrie into a lac of coins, destroy all foes without weapons, or make even a single bodied mortal an Emperor, if only one is ready to follow the path we shall show." And when he asks them what that path is, they reply—"There are four branches of royal knowledge, *viz.*, the three Vedas, the practical arts (such as agriculture, commerce &c.), logic with metaphysics, and the science of government. Of these, the first three are vast and bear fruit slowly; let them alone, therefore; study only the fourth; it has been recently composed by the learned Vishṇugupta in six thousand stanzas for the use of the King, Maurya (Chandragupta), which, when well studied and put into practice, yields the desired fruit." Agreeing to do so, the king reads and hears it, and just grows old while doing so. (For) that Śástra is connected with others; unless all are read, nothing is thoroughly known! Let its principles be grasped after a short or long time (*i. e.* let the question stand apart): When this Śástra is learnt, the first lesson taught is—Not to trust one's wife or child. As regards the filling of one's belly, the precept is—So much rice is needed to make up so much boiled rice, and so much fuel is sufficient for cooking it; hence let them be measured before they are served out.

Now (as regards a king's daily course of life), a king, on rising, when he has scarcely washed his mouth fully, must devote the first watch of the day to the examination of the day's receipts and expenditure, admitting (*i. e.* taking into account) a handful or half a handful* (of anything); and yet even while he hears, the clever superintendents will defraud him of twice as much. By the force of their own ingenuity

* Or, 'admitting a *mushṭi* or half a *mushti* as measures for reckoning.' See Notes for these technical terms.

they multiply a thousandfold the forty modes of defrauding set forth (*i. e.* pointed out) by Chàṇakya. In the second watch, the prince, with his ears painfully assailed by the squabbles of contending subjects, lives a most wretched life. Even therein, the judges and others, disposing of the suits favourably or unfavourably to the litigants as they please, join their sovereign with sin and infamy, and, indeed, themselves with money. In the third watch, he finds leisure to bathe and eat; but, until his food is digested, he lives in dread of poison. In the fourth, he rises to stretch forth his hands to receive gold (presents). In the fifth, he has to suffer great mental strain on account of the consideration of political schemes. In presenting these, too, the counsellors, appearing to be neutral (*i e.* impartial), enter into mutual agreement, and pervert at will merits and defects, misstate the reports of the ambassadors and spies, misrepresent possibilities and impossibilities, confound all distinctions of place and time, and live upon (*i.e.* seek their own ends through) the friends of their own partisans or enemies; and secretly stirring up internal and external factions, and then appearing to allay these openly, they bring their helpless master into their power. In the sixth, the king is to divert himself as he likes or to consult his ministers (of amusements); and the time thus allotted for self-amusement is an hour and a half! In the seventh watch, he has the troublesome task of reviewing his troops. In the eighth he has to worry himself with ambitious projects in the company of his generals (war-ministers). In the evening, in the first watch of the night, after the performance of the evening twilight-duties, he must receive his secret emissaries, and through their medium instruct their extremely cruel-hearted agents entrusted with the work of using the sword or fire or administering poison (where necessary). In the second, after eating, he must begin, like a Bráhmaṇa, to con his portion of study. In the third, with the sounds of the trumpets he is sent to sleep, which he may enjoy in the fourth and fifth; but how possibly can the poor man get any repose, his mind being distracted by constant, anxious thought? In the sixth, he must begin to prepare for the duties prescribed by the Śàstras and the business to be attended to. In the seventh, he must consult with the ministers regarding the dispatch of agents and emissaries; and these fellows, as is well-known, increase the money obtained from both sides by saying sweet things, by trading on the road, being free from the fear of having to pay taxes; and making work even in a slight degree where there is none, they wander about at all times. In the eighth, the Purohita and others, assembling, relate to the king—"Last night we saw a bad dream; the planets are not favourably situated; besides, the omens are evil; so (to avert the threatened misfortune) let propitiatory rites be performed. Let all the sacrificial implements be made of gold; when this is done, the rites are prolific in their effect. Here are these Bráhmaṇas, each like Brahmá himself; the benedictory rites performed by these lead to a blissful result; they are in distressful poverty, have large families, are constantly engaged in devotional rites, are endowed with Brâmhaṇical lustre, and yet have not received any donations (from you); whatever is given to them will be rewarded by long life accompanied by heavenly happiness and good fortune (*lit.* destruction of calamities)." And thus having persuaded the king to confer rich donations upon them, they secretly enrich themselves through these. Thus, leading the day and night in which not the least happiness is to be obtained, which abounds in troubles and is full of constant worry,—let alone the lack of supreme sovereignty on the part of a politic prince, his own principality he will find it difficult to preserve! There is a general mistrust as regards whatever a politic prince (*lit.* guided by politicians) gives, esteems, or lovingly talks of, all that being supposed to be meant for deception: And mistrust is the birthplace of disaster. To what extent the course of worldly existence can proceed without policy, is seen from our usual experience of ordinary life. We need have no recourse to Śâstra in this matter; even a suckling manages to get milk from its mother by various means. Abandon, then, all restraint, and enjoy the pleasures of sense as far as you can. Even those who say—Thus the senses should be subdued; thus the six natural foes should be shunned; expedients of pacification and others should be employed with reference to allies as well as enemies; and all the time should be spent in the discussion of questions of war and peace, and not the slightest room should be allowed to pleasures;—even by these cranes of counsellors, whatever money they manage to pilfer from you, is spent in the houses of harlots. What of these beggarly fellows? Take the case of such stern dictators of policy, as Śukra, A'ṅgirasa, Viśâla, Akshabáhu, Dantiputra, Paráśara and others, who are writers on Śâstras and practical government. Was the troop of the six foes subdued by them, or the precepts of the Śástras put into execution?—They, too, were confronted by success or failure in the undertakings set on foot by them. Again, there are many, who, being well-read, are taken in by those who have never read the S'âstras. Surely, Your Majesty has got all this, *viz.* an exalted pedigree which commands universal homage, unfaded youth, a lovely body, and immeasurable prosperity. Don't you therefore render all these advantages vain by attention to state-craft, which is the source of all mistrust, an impediment in the way of the enjoyment of pleasures, and which is never without uncertainty on account of its having to have recourse to various kinds of tricks You have ten thousand elephants, three lacs of horses, and an innumerable host of foot-soldiers. Besides, your treasury is filled with gold and jewels; and even if all your subjects enjoy them for thousands of years, they cannot exhaust your granaries. Is all this insufficient, that an effort should be made to acquire anything more? The life of mortals lasts but for a short time (*lit.* four or five days); and even out of that, the portion suitable for enjoyment is very small. But fools perish while they go on acquiring money, and do not wish to enjoy even the least of what they have earned. But why expatiate on this? Leave the burden of the kingdom to those who have your confidence, who are able to bear the responsibility, and are loyal, and do you enjoy your corporeal existence sporting with the damsels of the palace that vie with the nymphs of heaven in beauty, holding singing, musical, and drinking parties as would suit the season." So saying, he long prostrated himself on the ground, touching it with the five parts of his body and with his folded hands kissing his forehead, while the youthful denizens of the harem laughed heartily with eyes expanded through joy; the king, too, said with a smile—"Rise! Surely you are my Guru, since you have given me proper advice; why do you then act in a way contrary to the position of a Guru?" So saying, he raised him, and remained there deeply engaged in amusements.

Now the king, being daily urged to his duties, as they arose, by his old and wise counsellor, professed to accept his instructions, but paid no heed to them, as though he did not know his mind (correctly read his thoughts). On seeing this, the wise old man thought—"Oh, my childish action through folly (blind love for this prince)! I have become an eyesore to him and an object of derision, like a beggar, by urging him to attend to matters distasteful to him. Clearly, his behaviour towards me is not as before; for, he has now no affectionate look for me; he does not address me with a courteous smile; does not disclose his secrets to me; does not touch my hand; does not sympathize with me in my misfortunes, and has no favour to bestow upon me during festivities. He no longer sends me any handsome (*lit.* tempting) gifts; takes no notice of (*or*, appreciates no longer) my good deeds; he never asks after my family, nor has a regardful look for my partisans; he never admits me to his inmost secrets, nor ever gives me an access to the harem. But, on the contrary, he appoints me to unworthy (*i. e.* disagreeable) duties, and allows my seat to be occupied by others; he evinces confidence in my opponents, never condescends to reply to my questions, holds up to ridicule those whose offence is similar to mine (*i. e.* who give him wholesome advice), laughs at me so as to prick my vital parts, rejects even his own opinions when set forth by me; does not accept with joy the presents sent by me, howsoever valuable they may be; and makes fools proclaim in my presence the errors of politicians. Truly has Cháṇakya observed—'Counsellors (even though undesirable), if they follow the bent of the king's mind, ingratiate themselves into his favour; while on the other hand, such as are wise and just come to incur his hatred, if they fail to minister to his whims (*or*, if they are ignorant of the fitful tendencies of the king's mind).' Still, what is to be done? This prince, disobedient as he is, is not to be abandoned by men like me who have served his father and grandfather; but, then, what good can I do to him, even though I do not leave him, as he never listens to my counsel? Surely now this kingdom will fall into the hands of Vasantabhânu, the ruler of Aśmaka, who is adept in policy. Would that the calamities that are in store for him would restore him to his natural disposition (bring him to his senses)! But (I feel) that though dislike to certain things may be produced in him when under calamities wherein mishaps easily befall, it will not make him love a life of rectitude. Be it as it may; calamity is sure to occur; I shall anyhow manage to remain at my post, putting a check on my tongue (so) ready to give advice."

While the minister was in this (shaky) state of mind, and the king acting licentiously, (it happened that) Chandrapâlita, the son of Indrapâlita, minister of the king of Aśmaka, under the pretext of being expelled by his father for his profligate conduct, came to Vidarbha with a numerous train of musicians and dancing girls greatly skilled (in their art), and numerous retainers and spies in various disguises, and soon won over Vihârabhadra by means of diverse sports. By such course of conduct he soon acquired a hold upon the king; and on getting an opportunity he eulogized whatever amusement the king diverted himself with, as the proper one. Thus—When hunting was the theme, he would say, "Lord, no other sport can do so much good to the body as hunting. For, being the best kind of exercise, it generates swiftness of foot, which enables a man to traverse a long distance and is thus of great service in times of difficulty; as it removes phlegm, it improves the appetite (*lit.* stirs up the gastric fire), the sole root of health; as it destroys the fat, the limbs become firm, hardy and exceedingly active; by it one gets the power to endure cold and heat, as well as hunger and thirst; and by it one becomes acquainted with the thoughts and actions of various animals in different conditions. By killing the deer and wild Yáks, one can prevent the mischief they do to crops; roads and by-paths are all made safe by the destruction of tigers and wolves; and one comes to have a look into (*lit.* knowledge of) the woods and hilly regions which serve in more than one way; it gains (for the king) the confidence of those that tenant the wilds, and serves to stir their warlike enthusiasm, impressing at the same time intimidation on hostile armies: such, and other virtues, this hunting is calculated to ensure. Even gambling reveals the incomparable largeness (*i. e.* unbounded munificence) of one's mind on account of the abandonment of a heap of wealth as so much straw; it gives power not to yield to joy or sorrow (*i. e.* good or ill luck), owing to the instability of victory or defeat; besides, it kindles to a great extent anger (high-spiritedness), the only main-spring of manliness: it endows one with infinite acuteness of intellect, on account of the marking of subtle tricks, difficult to be observed, used in the handling of dice and moving the pieces in squares. One acquires wonderful power of concentrating the mind, as it has to be fixed on one object, and an extreme love for adventures which depend upon determined perseverance; one becomes unassailable, as one has often to face very rough persons; besides, one knows definitely what self-respect is, and one can maintain the body with a noble dignity. The enjoyment of beautiful damsels is but making the two objects of wealth and virtue yield their fruit; it reveals a great pride in manhood, skill in knowing the inner sentiments, freedom of action not hampered by greed, and cleverness in all the arts; it offers full scope for eloquence and ingenuity, as measures have to be constantly devised for gaining the damsel loved, preserving her when acquired, enjoying her when preserved, pleasing her when enjoyed, and pacifying her when offended; owing to the body being excellently decorated (for her sake), it gives one an imposing look on account of the winsome dress (appearance); it creates affection for friends, a high regard for attendants, sweetness of address (*lit.* speaking with a smile preceding it), an exuberance of spirit (*or*, vitality), and a behaviour marked by courtesy; (but, above all), by the generation of progeny, it becomes the source of felicity both here and in the next world. As regards drinking, it long preserves youth, owing to the use of liquors of various sorts so effective in removing diseases of various kinds, and dissipates anxiety of every kind, as it engenders on overwhelming sense of self-sufficiency; it stimulates one's capacity to enjoy beautiful damsels, as it inflames the passion of love; it removes the darts from (*i. e.* anything rankling in) the mind, as it blots out from memory the crimes committed; it increases a sense of confidence, inspired by the free talks that indicate candour (*lit.* absence of cunning); it creates unmixed joy, as it cuts short all feeling of envy; by it one can have the uninterrupted enjoyment of all the objects of sense, such as sound and others; as it induces the habit of distribution, it enlarges the circle of one's friends, imparts incomparable beauty to the limbs, leads to unsurpassed blandishments, and makes a man fit for the battle-field, as it takes away all sense of fear. Harshness of speech, severe punishment, and imposition of money-penalty, are themselves of service, as occasion arises, to a king; for a king devoted to a life of peace like a saint can neither keep in check his foes nor carry on the administration of his kingdom properly." The king followed his advice like the instructions of a Guru, and the people imitating the king threw off all restraint and became universally licentious. All being equally guilty, nobody tried to poke at the vices of others; the administrators of different departments, acting in imitation of the king and the subjects, devoured the fruits of their offices; then gradually all the channels of revenue were closed, and those of expenditure multiplied, day by day, owing to the subserviency of the king to rogues; the feudatory princes, as well as the chief officers of the state, being fully trusted by the king owing to parity of pursuits and admitted to drinking parties in company with their wives, abandoned their usual observances. The king under various disguises held intercourse with their wives; and these latter, being free from fear, enjoyed various pleasures in the company of the inmates of the royal harem who had abandoned their character. All women of family, taking pleasure in the witty talk (*or*, coaxing words) of the lewd, breaking through all reserve (*lit.* hold on their character), listened to the intrigues of their lovers, in utter defiance of their husbands (*lit.* considering them not worth even a straw); then angry affrays proceeding from such practices became frequent; the weak were assaulted by the strong; the rich were robbed of their money by thieves; all fear of reproof being removed, the paths of sin were freely trodden (*i. e.* all led sinful lives). The people, with their kinsmen killed, deprived of their riches, and distressed by murder and unlawful confinement, piteously cried aloud. Inordinate and unjust punishment gave rise to fear anddis-affection. The families, that were reduced to poverty, grew avaricious; and the spirited, who were disrespected, burned with indignation (*i. e.* smarted under the infliction of insult). Intrigues of the enemy succeeded in bringing to pass foul deeds of every kind. Then the agents of the king of As′maka, employed to administer poison, and others (entrusted with similar duties), reduced Anantavarman's army to sore straits, its principal warriors being killed, by inducing some to enter mountain-valleys full of dry grass and clumps of bamboo-trees and affording no passage out, by giving lively descriptions of hunting dresses and the abundance of game therein and then setting fire to them at the very entrance; by urging some to kill tigers and such other beasts, and then letting them fall into the jaws of the same; by making some go so far off in search of a desirable well to gratify their thirst, that they eventually sank under extreme hunger and thirst; by diverting some tc run along perilous paths that would cause a fall into pits or from precipices covered over with straw and leaves; by extracting thorns from the feet of some, with poisoned lancets; and by killing with ease some when left all alone, their followers being cut off from them, having to run in different directions; by purposely discharging arrows at some under the pretext that they missed to hit the bodies of the deer; having with a wager ascended along with some the peaks of mountains, very difficult to mount, and then by thrusting them down without being noticed by anyone else; by waylaying some who had a spare following, under the guise of mountaineers; and by making some forcibly enter crowds gathered on the occasions of gambling, bird-fights, fairs and festivities, (and getting them) killed by causing injury to others. They secretly caused damage to be done to people, and openly receiving complaints from them, and having communicated the same to witnesses, they made some bolt away as the means of hiding their disgrace; they induced some, who were sensualists, to approach others' wives as their friends, and killed the paramours, the husbands, or both (as was possible), giving out that theirs was that desperate deed; they ignominiously murdered many who were lured to appointed places by means of attractive women, by first lying there concealed and suddenly attacking them; they enticed some to caverns and then worked their destruction, accomplished under the pretext of accidents met with while digging for a treasure, or acquiring some superhuman power by means of incantations; (they destroyed the army) by urging some to ride furious elephants, and then refraining from taking counter-measures (*i. e.* allowing them to be destroyed by the elephants); by rousing to anger a a mad elephant, and then letting him on the bodies of the chief persons as a mark of his vengeance; by secretly killing those who quarrelled over ancestral property, and then casting the ignominy on their opponents; by privately killing many profligates in the towns of the feudatory princes, and then announcing the names of their foes (as the perpetrators of the crime); by causing some to catch consumption by inducing them to indulge day and night in the company of women whose bodies were saturated with poison; by the aggravations of the diseases (of some) under the pretence of treating them, by their skill in saturating with poison clothes, ornaments, garlands and unguents (they were made to wear); and by (many) other means.

Vasantabhánu now incited Bhánuvarman, the king of Vanavási, and made him wage war with Anantavarman. Anantavarman, having the border of his kingdom invaded, mobilized his army to march against him. Vasantabhánu came first of all the feudatory princes, and became a great favourite with the king; other princes, too, soon joined him. Having marched out, they encamped at a short distance on the bank of the Narmadâ. At that time Anantavarmà called Kshmátalorvaśî (Urvaśî-on-earth), a female dancer in the service of the chief feudatory prince, Avantideva, the ruler of Kuntala, whose mastery of the art of dancing was highly praised by Chandrapálita and others, and enjoyed the sight of her dance; and being passionately attached to her, he enjoyed her while she was under the influence of liquor. Vasantabhánu, the ruler of Aśmaka, saw Kuntalapati in private, and said—"This haughty tyrant violates our females; how can we bear such insults? I have one hundred elephants and you have five hundred; let us, therefore, join together and plot with Vîrasena, the chief of Muralà, Ekavîra, the ruler of Ṛishîka, Kumáragupta, the ruler of Konkan, and Nâgapâla, the prince of Nâsikya. They, too, being impatient of insult, will surely follow our counsel. Besides, this Vanavâsî king is my beloved friend. Engaged by him in front, we shall strike this wicked tyrant in the rear. We shall then distribute his treasure and vehicles among ourselves." When he, being delighted, approved of this plan, he won over to his side through confidential agents—sending as presents twenty rich garments and twenty-five saffron-coloured shawls with gold borders—all the other feudatory princes also. The following day Anantavarmà fell a prey to those princes and to the Vânavásya, as he was totally averse to the science of politics. Vasantabhânu, having taken into his possession his dispersed treasure and transport, proposed that it should be divided among all according to their respective power, expressing at the same time his desire of being content with whatever portion they may be pleased to give him; pleasing all with this stratagem, and holding forth that as a bait (bone of contention), he stirred up a quarrel among the princes, brought about the destruction of all, and seized for himself all their wealth. He gave a small portion of it to Vànavâsya, and, marching back, established himself in the kingdom of Anantavarman.

In the meantime, the old minister, Vasurakshita, in conformity with some hereditary servants of the king, managed to escape, taking with him this youth, Bhâskaravarman, and his elder sister Mañjuvâdinî, about thirteen years old, along with the queen Vasuṃdharâ, their mother; but, as it was fated to happen, he died of a burning fever. Friends like me took the queen to Máhishmatî and consigned her with her children to Mitravarman, her husband's brother by another mother, for protection. He, however, wicked that he was, entertained sinister motives regarding the noble queen; and when he was repulsed, he through cruelty wished to put her son to death, saying to himself—"She, of unviolate chastity, means to raise her son to the throne." When the queen knew it, she said to me, "Dear Nâlîjaṅgha, fix upon some (safe) place and dwell with the princ there, while he is alive. If I live, I shall soon follow him; when you will go safely, let me know the news about you." I somehow led him out of the crowded palace and plunged into the Vindhya forest. As he was fatigued by walking on foot, I gave him rest, that he might regain vigour (by staying) in a hamlet of shepherds. But there, too, apprehending an attack by the officers of the king, I travelled to a long distance. In our journey, wishing to give the boy water as he was oppressed by dreadful thirst, I lost my balance and fell into this well, and was thus favoured by you. You yourself should now be the protector of this helpless prince." With these words he folded his hands before me; and when I asked to what family his mother belonged, he replied that she was the daughter of Kusumadhanvan, king of Kosala, by Sâgaradattà, daughter of Vais'ravaṇa, a merchant of Pâṭaliputra. Saying—"If it is so, his mother and my father had the same maternal grandfather," I embraced him very affectionately. The old man asked me which of the sons of Sindhudattá was my father, and he was very pleased when he knew that it was Suśruta. I vowed that I would raise my little kinsman to the throne of his father by removing, by policy alone, the king of Aśmaka, who was very proud of his strategy; and then I began to think of how I should appease his hunger. At this moment, there came up two deer, having outstripped three shafts of some huntsman. I snatched from his hands his bow and the remaining two arrows, and shot them (the two deer). One of them fell with the arrow piercing him to its feathery part, the other with the arrow piercing him through so as to leave its feathers behind. One I gave to the hunter; the other I skinned and cleaned. Then removing the entrails and dissecting it, I removed the thighs, bones, neck &c., and spitting it with a stake roasted it on the embers of a wild fire; and we gratified our hunger with the flesh. I then asked the forester, who was highly pleased with my skill, if he knew of the affairs at Máhishmatî. He replied that he did, since he had just come from the place, having been there to sell tiger-skins and leather-bags; and that the city was astir with a festival, as Prachaṇḍavarman, the brother of Chaṇḍavarman, was to come there for espousing Mañjuvádinî, the daughter of Mitravarman. I then (on hearing this) spoke in the ears of the old man—"By treating the daughter affectionately, clever Mitravarman wishes to gain the confidence of the mother, and through her recover the person of the prince, so that he may put him to death. Go back to the queen, and tell her privately of your safety and my own account; then, in concert with her, give out that the prince has been killed by a tiger. That villain (Mitravarman), pleased at heart, will apparently show himself to be grieved, and will endeavour to pacify the queen. Then the queen should speak to him through you, that the prince for whose sake she had rejected his proposal was dead through her sin; she was therefore, ready that day to do his wish. Thus addressed, he will be pleased and will make advances to her. Then let her dip a necklace in water mixed with this poison named Vatsanâbha, and strike him on the breast with it, saying—'If I am faithful to my lord, may this wreath be as a sword unto thee.' Let her then again wash the garland in water mixed with this drug, and present it to the princess. Finding him (Chaṇḍavarman) dead and her unaffected by it, the subjects will necessarily believe the queen to be a Pativratá, and will abide by her will. She should then send word to Prachaṇḍavarman to accept the princess along with the kingdom, now without a ruler. In the meantime we will arrive in the disguise of Kápâlika mendicants, receive alms from the queen, and take our station in the cemetery outside the city. Let the queen again say in private to the aged citizens, mostly noble-minded, and old ministers who are interested in her—"The goddess Vindhyavàsinî has done a great favour to me in a dream, saying—'Prachaṇḍavarmâ will die on the fourth day from to-day; on the fifth day, from out of my temple on the bank of the Revá, when people will retire home and there will be no one, a Bráhmaṇa youth will issue out in company with your son. He will save this kingdom and will establish your son in sovereignty. I in the form of a tigress had carried off your son, in order to conceal him from his foes. I have also ordained that the princess Mañjudádinî shall be the wife of that Bráhmana youth.' You should keep all this a secret until it comes off to be true." The old man, being highly pleased with my plans, started off, and our purpose was effected fully to our expectations And the people began to talk everywhere, saying—"Oh, the great power of the Pativratás! For, the garland when thrown upon him (the king) proved to be the stroke of a sword; and it cannot be said that there was fraud in it, since the same when given to her daughter became the ornament of her neck. (Therefore), whosoever will trangress the words of this Pativratâ will be reduced to ashes."

Now, on seeing me and her son enter the palace for alms in the disguise of great ascetics, the Queen, with her breasts oozing out milk, rose up in joy and said—"Revered Sir, here I fold my hands before you; be pleased to take this helpless person in your favour, and tell me if what I have seen in a dream would come true or not." I replied that she would see the fruit of it that very day. At this she said—"If it is so, great is the good fortune of this your humble servant! For that dream foretells a protector for this (my daughter) here." With these words she caused Mañjuvádinî, who was confused by the rise of love at my sight, to bow to me, and once more said with suppressed joy—"If the dream proves false, this young ascetic, your follower, will be arrested by me to-morrow." I, too, whose stability of mind was shaken by Mañjuvádinî's glance (*lit.* eye) full of (*lit.* steeped in) love, said smilingly—"So let it be." Having got alms I departed, making a sign to Nâlîjaṅgha to follow us. Then I gently asked him, as he followed me, where the renowned Prachaṇḍavarmá, of short life, was. He replied that he was in the reception hall of the royal palace, amusing himself in the company of the dancers (*or*, singers), now quite sure (*or*, free from fear) that the overeignty was his. "If it be so, wait in the garden;"—so saying to the old courtier, I deposited all our chattels in an empty temple on one side of the wall, and having left the prince to guard them, I put on the gay attire of a dancer, and came to Prachaṇḍavarman and diverted him. When it was sunset, I performed in various styles dancing and singing, and imitated different voices, calculated to add to the knowlege of the multitude, and then displayed different athletic feats, such as jumping on hands, raising my legs up, and whirling my head while my palms rested on the ground, and also raising up one leg and contracting the other (*or*, pressing together the feet) and dancing sideways, as well as moving like a scorpion, or leaping like a crocodile, or darting like a fish. I then borrowed the daggers of the persons near me, and fixing them all round my body, displayed various feats not easy to perform, such as the swoop of a hawk or the flight of an osprey. Whilst thus engaged, I struck Prachaṇḍavarman, although he was at a distance of twenty yards, on the breast with a poniard, exclaiming, 'May Vasantabhánu live a thousand years!' One of the bard-warriors tried to strike me, but I at once jumped on the top of his fat shoulders, making him senseless by that much, and the frightened multitude look up. I then leapt over the wall of the height of two men. I plunged into the (adjacent) garden, and having just said to Nâlîjaṅgha—'This my path can be seen by my pursuers,' I ran in the eastern direction, through a Tamála bower lying along the rampart, while the marks of my foot-steps were levelled by Nálîjaṅgha; and then turning to the south I made off, my track not being noticed owing to the ground being paved with bricks; and at last leaping over the rampart and the encircling ditch, I quickly entered the temple. Then having put on my former (*i. e.* mendicant's) garb, I, in the company of the Prince, repaired to the region of the cemetery, having found my way with difficulty at the royal gate tumultuously crowded owing to my daring deed. In the temple of Durgá, which stood there, I had already dug up a cavity (leading from the outside to) just below the pedestal of the image, with its outer entrance concealed with a large slab of stone, its sides being set loose (*lit.* having their firmness broken).

Then, as midnight was passing, we, having put on the silken dresses, with ornaments of very costly gems, brought to us by a (confidential) eunuch (from the queen), entered that chasm and remained there all still. The queen, having caused the previous day the funeral ceremonies for

Prachaṇḍvarman to be fittingly performed, and sent word to Chanṇḍavarman that his fate was due to the contrivance of the ruler of Aśmaka, came, early in the morning of the next day, as had been previously arranged, to the temple with her ministers, worshipped the goddess, and got it ascertained in the presence of all the people that the surrounding room of the shrine was unoccupied, remained waiting, in company of the people, with her gaze fixed ( on the closed door ), and ordered the drums to be beaten loudly. Receiving the signal at the sound that reached me through a very minute chink, I lifted up with my head the iron pedestal along with the image, and placed it aside, holding one part of it with my two arms although it was too heavy even for a muscular man to be removed with effort, and issued out and also took out the prince. After replacing Durgá as before, I opened the door ( of the sacred closet ), and appearing before all, addressed the subjects, who, filled with astonishment, bowed to me, with their eyes directed to me owing to the realization of the vision, with horripilation clearly visible and folded hands raised up (to their brow) :—"The goddess Vindhyavásinî thus orders you through me—' This prince was in distress; out of pity I, in the form of a tigress, kept him concealed; here I return him to you to-day. Knowing that his maternal party is not weak, as he is considered by me as my son, you should acknowledge him as such.' Besides, you have to consider me as his protector, whose spirit is able to smash the pot in the form of As'maka, cruel by his intrigue now brought to light by the desperate and deep-laid plot that he had cleverly hatched; and, as compensation for the protection extended to him by me, the goddess has allowed me to accept the hand of his sister, this beautiful-browed princess before you." Having heard it, the subjects exclaimed with delight—" Very fortunate, indeed, is the race of Bhoja, that has a guardian like you granted by the goddess ! " As for my mother-in-law, she found herself in a stage of joy impossible to be described in words, and made me accept the very day the sprout-like hand of Mañjuvâdinî. When night fell, I closed the chasm entirely. The people too, who did not detect my trick, dared not transgress my commands, regarding me as a partial divine being on account of my telling what one had lost ( or, what one had in one's clenched hand ), or what one was thinking of and such other things—being employed as other means ( of gaining the object ). The prince, too, came to be believed as the son of the goddess, a belief that was to contribute to his prosperity. On an auspicious day, having got him shaved, I had his thread-ceremony performed by the family-priest; and instructing him in politics, I carried on the work of administration. I thought—"A kingdom, as is well known, is maintained by three kinds of power; these powers are diplomacy, authority (*or*, regal power), and (personal) energy (activity); these, mutually assisting each other, dispatch all affairs. Diplomacy determines objects, authority commences them, and energy effects their attainment. For this reason, the tree of Policy serves an administrator a great deal: it has counsel consisting of five elements for its root; the twofold authority is its stem; the fourfold Utsáha ( personal energy ) forms its main branches; the seventy-two Prakṛitis (subjects) are its leaves, the six qualities of royalty its blossoms, power its flowers and success its fruit; and as it (the tree) is of a nature complex (*lit.* depends upon many supports), it is very hard to make it yield fruit ( *lit.* to turn it to account ) by one who has no one to back him up. It would be very good (*i.e.*, to our advantage ) if we could win over to our side ( secure the services of ) A'ryaketu, the minister of Mitravarman, who was possessed of all the qualifications of a skilful counsellor, and who belonged to the side of the queen, being a native of the same country Kosala, since Mitravarman had come to ruin in consequence of his having disregarded his counsel." So thinking, I privately instructed Nálîjaṅgha thus—" Friend, say to the evered A'ryaketu in private— "Who is this impostor (*or*, a man of marvellous powers) that has appropriated the sovereignty of this state? Moreover, this our prince has been entirely caught in his grip by this serpent. Will he disgorge the prince or swallow him?"—and tell me what he will say on hearing this." He one day brought me his report to this effect—" I waited upon him several times with presents, introduced various topics, shampooed his feet, and in an hour of great confidence asked him the question according to your instructions. A'ryaketu thus replied—" Good man, speak not in this manner. He is evidently descended from a noble (*lit.* pure) family; he has extraordinary acuteness of intellect; he possesses superhuman strength, a boundless nobility of mind, wonderful skill in missiles, not a little knowledge of the arts, and a mind always disposed to favour; while his prowess (lustre) is unbearable and valiant enough to cope with (*i.e.*, quell) all his enemies. He thus combines in himself qualities, which it is very difficult to find in others even singly. He is a poisonous tree to the enemies (of the state), but a sandal tree (that would give its grateful shade) to those who approach him submissively; so regard As'maka, who vainly prides himself upon his being an adept in state-craft, as uprooted, and this prince as firmly and securely placed on the throne of his forefathers You need not entertain doubt (as to his sincerity towards the prince and the state)." Having heard it, and having tested his sincerity by various trials, I admitted him as a colleague in state-craft. With his assistance, I secured the services of devoted and upright ministers and of spies under various disguises. With their help I knew which of the subjects were covetous and rich misers, which very proud, and which mostly refractory; and thinking that I might amass great wealth if I gave proofs of my own want of greed, inspired a sense of duty (among the people), tormented the heretics, cleared out all who stood like thorns in the way of the prosperity of the state, thwarted the secret plans of the foes, and firmly established the four castes in their respective religious spheres and duties—since all undertakings that are based on policy emanate from wealth, and that no sin would be worse than showing weakness in adhering to the principles of policy—I zealously took all the proper measures.

END OF THE DAS'AKUMA'RACHARITA.

---

## UTTARAPI'THIKA'.

I then said to myself—" All the brave servants of the state are so much attached to me that they would forsooth, at my word, count their life as no more than a blade of grass; besides, I am in no way inferior to Vasantabhánu, the king of Aśmaka, having at my command the well-equipped armies of both the kingdoms, and I am also well adept in policy. I am, therefore, powerful enough to reinstate Bháskaravarman, the son of Anantavarman, the king of Vidarbha, in the seat of his ancestors, after having defeated Vasantabhánu. Besides, the report that I am appointed as a guardian to this prince, and that he has been adopted as her son by the goddess Durgâ, has gained ground everywhere. Besides, nobody as yet knows anything of my deceitful deed. The people here have a confirmed hope in this prince Bhâskarvarman that he would, through the favour of Durgá, surely regain the kingdom of his father, Anantavarman. The army of As'maka too, knowing full well the help that the goddess Durgâ accords to the prince, seems to be uncertain in its resolution to fight with us, since it thinks that human power can hardly prevail against divine power. Here also, the hereditary ministers, who were already desirous of the rise of the prince are now particularly zealous in their desire to have the prince, as king, being again received into confidence by me by means of gifts and honours. My most trusted servants, too, at my bidding, have inspired love into the minds of the confidential servants of the prince of Aśmaka, after having made these overtures to them—"You are our friends, and hence we are bound to convey our advice to you calculated to lead to a blissful end. It is this—The goddess Durgâ, having appointed the well-known Vis'ruta as the guardian of the prince, has ordained that through his instrumentality Vasantabhânu, and those who, taking his side, would fight with him, would have to see the abode of Yama. So before he is inclined to take arms against the king of As'maka, you should enrol yourselves as the followers of Bháskaravarman, the son of Anantavarman. He (who will come over to his side) will be out of the reach of danger, and being rewarded with great honour will live in happiness with his servants; or else he will fall beneath the trident of Bhavânî. (He told us also) that Bhavânî had commanded him to inform all once of this; and knowing, therefore, of our friendship with you, she has communicated this message to you through us" Hearing this, the confidential servants of the king of As maka, who were already shaken in their loyalty in consequence of their knowledge of the boon of Bhavânî to the prince, came over to my side all in a body, when they received this message particularly from me. The king of As'maka, when he learnt all this, thought—"All the hereditary subjects desire to have this prince for their master; my servants, private as well as public, seem to be shaken in their attachment to me; so, if I remain apathetic to all this, sitting in my palace, surely I shall not be able to save my own kingdom wherein seeds of dissension have been sown. Therefore, before (the prince) confers (gets an opportunity to confer) with my soldiers who are disaffected, and who would give out my intention, I should arrange to fight with him. If this much can be done, he will stand in front of me but for a moment." With this resolution, he, driv as it were into the jaws of death by the sin of unjustly invading another's kingdom, marched with his army against our force. As soon as the prince knew that he was advancing, he went to meet him; all alone I rode on horseback to the king of As'maka as he was advancing. Then his whole army, deciding that there could be no other extraordinary reason than the boon of Durgá for my going to meet him all alone in the teeth of a numberless host of them, stood stupefied, as if drawn in a picture. I advanced and challenged Vasantabhânu to fight, who closing with me dealt me a hard blow with his sword. On account of my superior swordsmanship, I parried the blow, and having cut off the head of the A'smaka king with one counter-stroke threw it on the ground, and thus addressed his soldiers—"Whoever of you now wish to fight with me, should forthwith come to do so in a body; or you should bow to the feet of the prince, and coming over to his side should enjoy the emoluments of your former offices, and discharging all the duties thereof live here in happiness." On hearing my words, all the servants of the king of As'maka immediately got down from their horses, bent themselves low before the prince, and acknowledged his sovereignty. Having then given the kingdom of As'maka entirely in the possession of the prince, and having appointed faithful officers to protect it, I marched in the company of the army of the king of As'maka, which had now become mine, towards Vidarbha, crowned Bhâskaravarman king in the capital, and seated him on the throne of his ancestors.

On one occassion, I requested the king as he was sitting in company of Vasumatî, his mother, thus—"I wish to achieve a purpose which I have undertaken; and so long as it is not accomplished, it is not possible for me to stay in one place. So let my wife Mañjuvâdinî, your sister, stay with you for some days. I will wander over the earth until I find the person I am in search of, and having found him will join you again here." Upon this the king, with the approval of his mother, said to me—"That we find ourselves in this festivity of the recovery of our kingdom is but due to your extraordinary help. We can hardly bear the yoke of this kingdom even for a moment in your absence We wonder why you should thus propose to us." On hearing this I replied—"You should not entertain even a particle of anxiety on that account. A'ryaketu, whom you have in your palace and who is a minister of rare ability, is capable of bearing the yoke of kingdoms, more than one, like this. I shall appoint him to carry on the administration, and depart."

Although I tried to persuade the king with such and other words, the king, as well as his mother, prevailed upon me after many entreaties to postpone my departure for some days to come. He, moreover, gave to me the kingdom of Prachaṇḍavarman, the king of Utkala. Just as I was making preparations to depart in search of Your Highness after having taken charge of the kingdom and taken leave of the king, I was called by Siṃhavarman, the lord of the Aṅgas, to lend him succour, whom I joined here; and through the fruit of my previous religious merit, I came to be united with Your Highness.'

Then the princes, Apahâravarman, Upahâravarman, Arthapâla, Pramati, Mitragupta, Mantragupta and Vis'ruta, who had now met together, had prince Somadatta brought over to them with his wife by servants from Pâṭaliputra where he was enjoying the heir-apparentship, and who had previously promised to meet them in one place. And while they were enjoying joyful conversation with Râjavâhana, the king's officers came over from Pushpapura, bearing a letter of command from king Râjahaṃsa, and bowing respectfully before Râjavâhana, said—"Lord, here is a letter containing the order of Râjahaṃsa, your father; please take it" Hearing it he got up, again and again respectfully bowed before the assembly, and took up the letter. Touching it with his forehead and then taking it down, Râjavâhana read it aloud while all there listened:—"King Rájahamsa from the capital of Pushpapurî is pleased, after sending his hearty blessings to them, to write this letter to the princes, Rájaváhana and others, now residing in the city of Champá. Having learnt, from some of the soldiers that had returned, that all of you first encamped in a forest-region near the temple of Śiva after your departure from here with our permission, and that the rest of the princes, having been unable to find in the morning prince Râjavâhana, who had remained in the temple of Śiva for adoration the previous night, swore that they would either bow before (me) Rájahaṃsa in company of Râjavâhana or else would give up their lives, sent back the army and started off separately in quest of him,—I myself and your mother were both plunged in the ocean of unbearable sorrow. Having then decided to give up our lives after communicating the news to Vâmadeva, we went to his hermitage. As we stood up, after having bowed to him, the omniscient sage knew both our object and our dreadful resolve, and said—" King, I knew all that you had purposed to do, by my power of prenotion. Now these princes, having experienced some distress for some time on Rájavâhana's account, and then by force of good fortune having secured for themselves various kingdoms after conquering the quarters by means of their uncommon valour, will, at the end of the sixteenth year, return with victorious Rájavâhana, and having bowed down to your and Vasumatî's feet, will act as you will direct. It is, therefore, quite inadvisable to stake anything on their account." Hearing this, we took courage, and supported our lives till this day, fully trusting his words. Then, as the expiry of the period drew near, we went to Vâmadeva's hermitage and preferred our request to him that the period he had previously mentioned had almost been over, and inquired of him whether he knew of your whereabouts. Consequently, the sage replied—" O king, all the princes, Râjavâhana and others, having conquered the quarters after having overcome many powerful foes and having subdued the earth, are living together now in Champâ; dispatch immediately couriers with a written order to convey them here." Accordingly, we have sent our order to bring you over here; and if you now delay even for a moment, you will surely hear us to be mentioned in talks only (*i.e.*, you will not find us living); bearing this in mind, you should forthwith start, even postponing your drink for the road." Having unhesitatingly and reverentially obeyed this order (*lit.* holding it on their heads), the princes resolved to go, and having appointed trusty and capable men with sufficient troops to keep the conquered kingdoms in order, and having guarded their way with a portion of the army, they started in the company of their wives with a limited number of soldiers for the Mâlava king, resolved to conquer Mânasára, their original foe, and to subjugate his kingdom also, and then to bow to the feet of Râjahaṃsa and queen Vasumatî. Having reached Ujjayinî, Râjavâhana, attended by the princes, easily defeated Mânasára, although he was very powerful, and slew him too. Then the princes took over his daughter, Avantisundarî, and having released prince Pushpodbhava, who had been put into prison with his family by Chaṇḍavarman, his minister, took him with themselves, appointed some soldiers to keep the newly-conquered kingdom of Mâlwá in check, arrived at Pushpapura with a limited part of the army that was left, and with Râjavâhana at their head bowed to the feet of Rájahamsa and Vasumatî, the mother of Rájaváhana. These latter too found themselves in greatest joy at the recovery of their son. Then in the presence of the king and the queen, Vâmadeva, knowing the desire of all of the ten princes, addressed them:—"All of you should now go to your respective kingdoms, and rule them with righteousness. You should come to salute the feet of your parents, whenever you would like to see them again." Then the princes bowed to the sage and their parents, and separately narrated their accounts in the presence of the sage in detail The parents, too, having heard their miraculous deeds indicative of their valour, were greatly thrilled with joy. Then the king humbly said to the sage—"Revered Sir, by your favour we have enjoyed the greatest happiness, that is over and above man's desire, and defeats (*i.e.* stands beyond) all thought and expression; now it is proper for us to enter the stage of forest-life in the proximity of the feet of Your Worship, and work for final emancipation. So Your Worship, having installed Râjavâhana on the throne of Pushpapura and of Mànasâra, and having given the remaining kingdoms to the other nine princes, should so arrange it that all of them would be obedient and faithful to Râjavàhana, and acting in perfect accord with him would enjoy the earth engirdled by the four oceans, after having uprooted their foes." When Vâmadeva saw how persistently the princes were opposed to the plan of their parents for entering the life of foresters, he said to them—"Princes, you should not come in the way of your father, who is now by age fit for renunciation; he will remain with me in my hermitage without having to subject himself to any bodily mortification. Stationed here, he will be attached to the service of God; and you, too, will not enjoy happiness in the presence of your parents." Knowing the command of the great sage, they gave up their persistence in their opposition to their father's plan of entering forest-life. Having established Râjavâhana in Pushpapura, all his vassals also well protected their respective kingdoms according to his direction, and saw their parents at intervals whenever they wished. Thus the princes, Râjvâhana and others, entirely acting in one accord while they protected the earth with justice under the suzerainty of Râjavahâna, enjoyed the pleasures of kingdoms, which were even unattainable to Indra and others.

FINIS.

# NOTES.

P. 1. दशकुमारचरितम्—This is to be explained as दश च ते कुमाराश्च दशकुमारं तस्य चरितानि दशकुमारचरितानि । तान्यधिकृत्य कृतं काव्यम् । The Taddhita affix अण्, which would have been added by Páṇ. IV. 3. 87, is elided by a Vârttika of Kátyáyana (लुबाख्यायिकाभ्यो बहुलम्), so that there is no Vṛiddhi of the first vowel. It is also possible to explain the title as (1) दशकुमाराणां चरितं दशकुमारचरितम्, and this word being transferred by Lakshaṇá to the work describing the deeds;—or as (2) दशकुमाराणां चारितानि यस्मिन्काव्ये तद् दशकुमारचरितम्. पूर्वपीठिका—the introductory portion; *cf.* the उत्तरपीठिका which is appended at the end. The original work of Daṇḍin, which begins on p. 54, has neither beginning nor end, which are respectively supplied by the पूर्व० and the उत्तर०. उच्छ्वास—the chapters of an *A'khyáyiká* (like the Daśak.) are technically so called. See Introd. Following the common practice of ancient writers the author (who was a Vaishṇava) pays his tribute of veneration to his favourite deity, at the same time invoking a blessing on his readers. He also pays homage to the name of Daṇḍin, the original writer of the *Charita*, as shown by the conscious use of the word दण्ड in the various epithets occurring in the benedictory stanza.

०च्छत्रदण्डः—The meaning is that Vishṇu is the mainstay of the universe. शतधृति is here a name of Brahmá. *Cf.* महिम्न० Śl. 18. It is also and was originally an epithet of Indra, being the god of 'infinite wisdom;' see our note on शतक्रतु at Ragh. III. 38. अम्भोरुह्—the commoner form of this word is अम्भोरुह. In शतधृति० there is a reference to the mythological story of Brahmá being born from a lotus springing from the navel of Vishṇu, in which he also resides. कूपदण्ड—the main mast. अक्षदण्डः—the pole-staff, axle. ०स्तम्भदण्डः—Vishṇu's foot is the giver of victory to its worshippers. त्रैविक्रमः—त्रयो विक्रमा अस्य त्रिविक्रमस्तस्यायम्; of Trivikrama. Vishṇu in his fifth (Vámana) incarnation was called त्रिविक्रम 'he who took three strides' (with which he covered the three worlds). For the whole story see our note on the word at Ragh. VII. 35. Perhaps in the word त्रैविक्रम 'the result of the exploits of three men,' we have a reference to the present work, the out-come of the literary labours of three workmen. कालदण्डः—the death-dealing, destructive, rod. The stanza indicates the conquest of the world by Rájaváhana, the hero of the work, and his final triumph over all his enemies.

निकषायमाणा--*Lit.* serving as a touchstone, *i. e.* standard to; hence, the perfect model of (a prosperous city). Pres. part. fem. of the denominative formed from निकष a touchstone (निकष इव आचरतीति), according to कर्तुः क्यङ् सलोपश्च Pán. III. 1. 11. शश्वत्—'At all times'—shows that the fortunes of its merchants were not subject to variation, but constant. व्याख्यात--which served as a commentary on, *i. e.* adequately explained, proclaimed. रत्नाकर—*Lit.* the mine of jewels—the ocean, so called being supposed to be the source of all kinds of jewels. It may also mean, 'its jewel-mines.' मगध—The ancient name of Behar, extending as far as Káshmîr or Punjab. पुष्पपुरी--the modern Pátná; also called Kusumapura; see p. 125 *infra*. It is more generally known as Páṭaliputra, the ancient capital of Magadha, situated near the confluence of the Ganges and the Śoṇa. It is said to have been destroyed by a river-inundation about the middle of the eighth century A. D. See our note on पाटलिपुत्र at Mudr. p. 70.

वीर &c.—The enemy's army is compared to the sea—the heroic warriors moving in lines are its heaving waves, the horses and elephants its sharks and alligators—and the king's arm to the mountain Mandâra. The meaning is that the king was able, single-handed, to defeat the whole army of his enemies. The idea is the same as that expressed in Ragh. I. 19.

P. 2. जलनिधिमथन &c.—The reference is to the well-known story of the ocean being churned by the gods and the demons who used the mountain Mandâra as the churning rod. मन्दरायमाण—pres. part. from the denom. from मन्दर; *cf.* निकषायमाणा above. समुद्दण्ड—*Lit.*, 'having a club raised;' hence, fierce, terrible. गीर्वाणगणिका—the heavenly courtesans, the *apsarasas*; गीर्वाण means 'a god'. जेगीयमानया— (qualifying कीर्त्या) Instr. sing. fem. of the pres. part. from जेगीयते which is the Frequentative base of गै 'to sing.' अतिमानया—explains रचितदिगन्तरालपूर्त्या and also why it reached heaven. *Cf.* Ragh. VI. 77. शरदिन्दु &c.—Sanskrit poets compare spotless, untarnished fame to white objects. *Cf.* हंसश्रेणिषु तारासु कुमुद्वत्सु च वारिषु । विभूतयस्तदीयानां पर्यस्ता यशसामिव ॥ Ragh. IV. 19. घनसार—camphor; घनो दृढः सारो यस्य, धनस्य सार इव वा । शीतत्वात्, शीताभ्राकारत्वाच्च Bhân. Dîk. अट्टहास—the loud laugh of Śiva (at the time of his vehement dance ). Laughs and smiles are described by poets as 'white,' probably on account of the brightness of the face and whiteness of the teeth displayed therein. हासादीनां धावल्यं कविसमयसिद्धम् Malli. on Megh.—राशीभूतः प्रतिदिनमिव त्र्यम्बकस्याट्टहासः। I. 60. नीकाश—used only as the latter part of a comp.; this according to Amara is a Nityasamása ( *i. e.* अस्वपदाविग्रहः ). *Cf.* स्युरुत्तरपदे त्वमी । निभसंकाशनीकाशप्रतीकाशोपमादयः । Amara.; अमी उत्तरपदस्था एव सदृशवचना वाच्यलिङ्गाः स्युः । Com.

कीर्त्या सुरभितः—For the idea *cf.* 'सुरभिर्यशोभिः' Ragh. II. 3, where Malli. says सुरभिर्मनोज्ञः amiable. स्वर्लोक०...रुचिर—large and beautiful like those on the peaks of mount Meru (स्वर्लोक). *Cf.* सद्रत्नमुक्ताफलवज्रभाञ्जि...मेरोः शिरांसीव गृहाणि यस्याम् । Bhaṭṭi. I. 7. The word स्वर्लोक, which *lit.* means 'heaven,' is applicable to the mountain Meru because heaven ( the residence of the gods ) is situated on it ; *cf.* मेरुः सुमेरुर्हेमाद्रिः रत्नसानुः सुरालयः Amara. धरणीरमणी—The earth is poetically spoken of as the wife of a king. *Cf.* Ragh. VI. 63, VIII. 83 &c.; Mâlav. I. 15. ०सौभाग्यभोगभाग्यवान्—The addition of the possessive affix वत् here to the preceding comp. which is a Karmadhâraya ( ०सौभाग्यभोगः एव भाग्यम् ) is strictly ungrammatical by the maxim न कर्मधारयान्मत्वर्थीयः बहुव्रीहिश्चेत्तदर्थप्रतिपत्तिकरः, *i. e.* a possessive affix should not be used after a Karm. if its sense could be had by means of a Bahuvrîhi ( *e. g.* ०सौभागभोगभाग्यः in this case ). But the rule is not invariably observed by poets, and Patañjali himself has used similar formations in his Mbh. शिष्ट &c.—The best way of taking the comp. will be शिष्टाः (adept in Vedic studies; see Manu. XII. 109 ; A'pastamba I. 7. 20. 8 ) च ते विशिष्टविद्यासंभारेण ( by the load of the knowledge of the special branches of knowledge ) भासुराश्च. Or विशिष्ट may mean 'eminent' or excellent, and qualify भूसुर. सततुलित &c.—The king *always* shone like the midday-sun. Mark the force of सतत. The brilliancy of the king's प्रताप was constant, not so is that of the sun; thus he was obviously superior to the sun. *Cf.* यस्य च प्रतापानलो दिवानिशं जज्वाल Kâd. p. 12. Note the use of the word हंस in the unusual sense of 'the sun,' solely for the sake of alliteration with the word राजहंस which follows. Similarly the word घनदर्प in the next comp. has no propriety; it is added simply for the sake of the alliteration with कंदर्प. सोदर्य—समाने उदरे शयितः सोदर्यः ( also समानोदर्यः ); a co-uterine brother. Here the sense is that of 'allied to,' 'similar,' since co-uterine brothers resemble each other ; *cf.* सनाभि below. निरवद्य—flawless, without a blemish. अवद्य ( Pot. p. of वद् ) means 'what is not fit to be spoken,' what is censurable. Distinguish this from अनुद्य, another Pot. part. derived from वद् which simply means 'what ought not to be spoken.' अवद्यं पापम् । गर्ह्यं किम् । अनुद्यं गुरुनाम । तद्धि न गर्ह्यं वचनानर्हं च । Sid.-Kau. on अवद्यपण्यवर्या गर्ह्यपणितव्यानिरोधेषु । Pâṇ. III. 1. 101. *Cf.* Kum. III. 57. सुमती—also used for the purpose of alliteration (though defensible). It should rather be सुमतिः. वसुमतीव—*v. l.* 'Like the earth'. But this will be tautological, as the same idea has already occurred in l. 5 above. ०शेखरमणी—Mark the Saṃdhi.

P. 3. भस्मीकृत—Again the poet's fondness for alliteration leads him to use a word which can only be taken with चेतना in its metaphorical sense ( that of 'destroyed'). We shall meet with several instances of the kind hereafter, which the critical student should notice for himself. For the destruction of Kâma see Kum. III. 72. भयेन—Construe this with समभूवन्. अनवद्या—प्रशस्ता ; hence अधृष्या. The idea very beautifully expressed here is that Kâma's रोलम्बावली and other accompaniments clung to her, the best of ladies, believing that womankind enjoyed an exemption from a hostile attack. तस्याः—goes with केशजालं &c. रोलम्बावली—See com. Kâma's bow-string is poetically described as sometimes decked with ( as here), but more often as formed of, black bees. *Cf.* मौर्वीमधुकरपङ्क्ति &c. *infra* p. 44 ; अलिपङ्क्तिरनेकशस्त्वया गुणकृत्ये धनुषो नियोजिता । Kum. IV. 15. Also Ṛit. VI. 1. The sense is that her hair was as deep-dark as bees. प्रेमाकर—brought in simply for *anuprâsa.* विजितार०—Her face combined in itself the beauty of the moon and the lotus. The idea is the same as in चन्द्रं गता पद्मगुणान्न भुङ्क्ते पद्माश्रिता चान्द्रमसीमभिख्याम् । उमामुखं तु प्रतिपद्य लोला द्विसंश्रयां प्रीतिमवाप लक्ष्मीः ॥ Kum. I. 43.

जायायुतः—This is necessary to account for the duality. अङ्गवीर—The principal or chief warrior. Mark the meaning of अङ्ग here. It usually means 'subordinate' (opp. to प्रधान), but here it means 'subordinate to the master alone.' मलयसमीरः—suggests fragrance, gentleness &c. Sanskrit poets describe the breezes from the Malaya mountain, cool and surcharged with the fragrance of sandal, as peculiarly affecting persons in a love-sick condition and inflaming their passion ; *cf.* वहति मलयसमीरे मदनमुपनिधाय । स्फुटति कुसुमनिकरे विरहिहृदयदलनाय ॥ Gît. V. ०करवाल—a saw. The sight of the प्रवाल ( especially that of the mango-tree ) causes anguish in the hearts of people absent on a journey. अधरबिम्बम्—her red lower lip. *Cf.* चूतप्रवालोष्ठमलंचकार Kum. III. 30. जयशङ्खः &c—A conch-shaped neck, *i. e.* one a little tapering above and marked with three lines like a shell, is considered a mark of great beauty and regarded as the sign of good fortune. *Cf.* words like कम्बुकण्ठी, ०ग्रीवा, &c. बन्धुर—may be taken in the sense of 'tapering' ( उन्नतानत ) or 'beautiful' ( सुन्दर ) ; *cf.* Kum. I. 42, Śák. VI. 12, Ragh. XIII. 47, &c. पूर्णकुम्भौ—see note on पूर्णसुवर्णकलश० p. 44 *infra.* ज्यायमान—pres. part. of the denom. ज्यायते from ज्या a bow-string ; ज्या इव आचरति ज्यायते. बाहू—the arms were tender and long. ०सनाभि—*Lit.* connected by the same navel, uterine (समानो नाभिर्यस्य); hence, closely related to, similar or like See note on नीकाश *supra.* A round and deep navel is considered a mark of beauty. *Cf.* नृपं तमावर्तमनोज्ञनाभिः &c. Ragh. VI. 52; दर्शितावर्तनाभेः Megh. I. 28; नाभिमण्डलीमावर्तिनीमुद्वहन्तीं Kâd. p. 281. जैत्ररथ—*i. e.* its wheel. The comparison of buttocks to the round wheels of a chariot is common in Sanskrit ; *cf.* Vikr. I. 11 ( रथोपमश्रोण्याः ). दूरीकृत०—Because the जघन which forms the car of Kâma kindles maddening passion (irresistible to ordinary ascetics ). जयस्तम्भ—a pillar erected in order to commemorate a victory. "The pillars of victory which are found in the Presidency, *e. g.*, at Kapadavanj and Siddhapura and which belong to the times of the Châlukya dynasty of Anhilpur Pátan, consist of two carved columns united by a Toraṇa."—Bühler. The compounds ending in भूत should be noted; dissolve जयस्तम्भः भूतः जय०भूतः, सौन्दर्यं भूतः सौन्दर्यभूतः &c. These are known as सुप्सुपसमासs; *cf.* Malli. on Kum. I. 59, and see our note on पुनरुक्तभूतं Ragh. V. 34. Kaiyaṭa takes the word भूत as equivalent to इव ; according to him the diss. would be जयस्तम्भ इव जयस्तम्भभूतः; but the first way is better. रम्भे च—Thighs tapering and plump like the trunk of the plantain-tree are regarded as a mark of beauty. *Cf* रम्भोरू ( Ragh. VI. 35 ; Śiś. VIII. 19 &c. ). अस्त्रभूतानि प्रसूनानि—For these see com. These are sometimes differently mentioned as:—अरविन्दमशोकं च शिरीषं चूतमुत्पलम्। पञ्चैतानि प्रकीर्यन्ते पञ्च० ॥. This shows that she was in budding youth. *Cf.* कुसुममिव लोभनीयं यौवनमङ्गेषु संनद्धम्। Śâk. I. 19. *Cf.* with the highly poetical description here the passage at pp. 43-45, describing the beauty of Avantisundarî where almost all the ideas and expressions occurring herein recur. अमरपुर—is Amarâvatî, the residence of Indra. अनन्तभोगलालिता—(1) fondled with endless enjoyments; (2) borne on his hoods by Ananta ( Śesha ). See Com. for diss. The reference is to the belief that Śesha the serpent-king supports the earth on his hood; *cf.* आयस्तभुजगराजमस्तक &c. on the next page. अन्वभावि—is the Passive third pers. sing. of the Aorist of भू with अनु; mark our author's fondness for such passive forms, *e. g.* अभाणि (p. 10), समबोधि (p. 11), अगामि (p. 18) अवाचि (p. 31) &c.

परमविधेयाः—Very obedient, *i.e.* always acting in conformity with the wishes of their lord—such as contributed to the wealth and prosperity of the kingdom. *Cf.* सदानुकूलेषु हि कुर्वते रतिं नृपेष्वमात्येषु च सर्वसंपदः। Kir. I. 5. धीरधीषणा०—Who on account of their deep political insight ( *lit.* firm or well-perfected understanding ) disposed of, with little difficulty, matters likely to require the serious attention even of Bṛihaspati.

P. 4. सुमतिसत्यवर्माणौ &c.—The seven sons of the three ministers mentioned here have each a son, as will be discovered as the narrative develops, and thus furnish seven of the *Kumáras* who form the subject of the story. विट—a voluptuary, a person of dissolute habits, a rake. Etymologically विट is described as a procurer or a go-between ( वेश्यानागरिकयोः परस्परं संदेशं विटति कथयति इति विटः ). In Sanskrit dramas he is often introduced as the companion of a prince or of a dissolute young man or a courtesan, and living as a parasite on familiar terms with his associate. वारनारी—wife of the multitude; a harlot. ०अग्रजन्मनोः—the elder brother meant here is Sumitra; see p. 125. पारावार—the sea. पारमावृणोतीति fr. पार + वृ + अण् ( अ ) कर्मणि; or पारावारावस्य स्तः इति। In ancient times Indian merchants carried on an extensive trade by sea. *Cf.* समुद्रव्यवहारी सार्थवाहो धनमित्रो नाम &c. Śâk. VI. p. 167. पुरंदरपुरातिथिषु—is a euphemism for 'when they were dead.'

नानाविध०—See com.; better take रचितानि अगण्यानि जन्यानि (battles) यैः as a Bah. qualifying राजन्य. Such a description of the राजन्यs contributes to the exaltation ( उत्कर्ष ) of the glory of the king. महदायुध—is a faulty comp.; it should be महायुध. This particular comp. may be defended, as Bühler suggests, by explaining it as महदानि (महं ददति तानि) आयुधानि 'weapons giving greatness or glory.' But this will be doubtless far-fetched. The author of the Pūrvapīṭhikâ, though having an excellent command over the language, seems to be at times indifferent to the rules of grammar, as will be seen from his using such compounds as महदाशा p. 30, महदाश्चर्यान्वित p. 53, &c., and the promiscuous use of the two *padas* in a few places; see our note on

परीक्षन् p. 40. राजन्यः—Explain राज्ञः अपत्यं राजन्यः, a prince of the Kshatriya caste or royal blood. See Ragh. III. 48. The affix यत् is added to राजन् in the sense of अपत्य by Pâṇ. IV. 1. 137. Some derive it from राज् to shine and the Uṇâdi affix अन्य. पालि—may mean ( 1 ) top, ridge, or ( 2 ) row: पालिः पङ्क्तिप्रदेशयोः इति शाश्वतः ।.

घस्मर—घसतीति. The aff. मर is added in the sense of ताच्छील्य; *lit.* a voracious eater; here metaphorically 'who habitually committed havoc in battles,' a great warrior. ०मानसारं—whose pride and power were excessive. According to the first way of taking the comp. (see com.) the meaning will be 'whose power simply lay in his excessive pride,' *i. e.* who was a vain boaster, or who derived his strength from his power. सहेल—easily, from हेला meaning 'ease.' न्यक्कृत—( fr. न्यक् derived from न्यञ्च् and कृ ) humbled, put down. *Cf.* न्यग्भावयिता शत्रून् *infra*, p. 187. हठिकाकर्णन—(हठिक sudden and violent + आकर्णन ). The sudden hearing of a loud noise. 'Who were smitten with great terror' &c. Instead of the adj. हठिक some understand the noun हठिका, in which case we must explain the comp. as हठिकया आकर्णन. Neither of these words is found in lexicons, though their derivation from हठ 'violence' is obvious enough. दिग्दन्तावल-The guardian-elephants of the quarters. दन्तावल—'an elephant ;' from दन्त + affix वलच्; दन्तशिखात्संज्ञायाम् । Pâṇ. V. 2. 113. विघूर्णयन्—making them reel, throwing them into agitation. आयस्त—greatly taxing. भुजगराज—is Śesha the serpent-king; see note on अनन्तभोगलालिता above. बलेन—is redundant, having been added simply for alliteration.

P. 5. चतुरङ्ग—Consisting of the four elements, *viz.* elephants, horses ( cavalry ), charriot-warriors, and foot-men ( infantry ). *Cf.* हस्त्यश्वरथपादातं सेनाङ्गं स्याच्चतुष्टयम् । Amara. रोष—seems to be used here in the sense 'of a great passion for,' 'ambition.' *Cf.* the English 'rage' as in 'a rage for writing,' and Latin '*furor*' as in 'furor loquendi.' अनेकप—an elephant, periphrastically used for द्विप for the sake of alliteration. सविग्रहः—embodied, incarnate. साग्रहः—with a determined purpose. भूयः—is without force, being simply added for alliteration. ०मदधाराधौतमूले—This idea is common enough. *Cf.* Mudr. V. 23; Ragh. VII. 43.

नभ्यवलम्ब०—Whenever a fight went on, the nymphs of heaven were supposed to gather in heaven and watch the course of events on the battle-field in order to choose a lover from among the fallen warriors who also were supposed to assume a divine form. *Cf.* Ragh. VII. 53, and our note *ad loc.* The cloud of dust overhanging the battle-field is compared to a nuptial *maṇḍapa* screening the *apsarasas.* जवनिका--( or यवनिका ) a screen. °व्याकुल--thickly spread. दिविषदध्वनि—दिविषद् means 'a god;' दिवि सीदन्तीति. अध्वन् means 'a way,' and the whole expression ( *lit.* 'the path of the celestials' ) signifies 'the sky;' *cf.* the word सुरवर्त्म which is given in Ak. as a synonym of the sky. दिविषदध्वनि must be construed with the word धिक्कृत of the following compound, which is thus a सापेक्ष समास; 'which deafened all space with the roll of its drums that surpassed (*i.e.* drowned ) all other sounds in the aerial region.' शस्त्राशस्त्रि, हस्ताहस्ति--see com. and Gr. § 259. जीवग्राहं--Ṇamul. जीवतीति जीवः; जीवन्तं गृह्णातीत्यर्थः । The ṇamul of ग्रह् is used when it has for its object जीव used as an उपपद; Páṇ. III. 4. 36. See p. 136 *infra,* com.

अनन्यशासनां—not subject to another's rule; *i. e.* who was the supreme monarch. *Cf.* अनन्यशासनामुर्वीं शशासैकपुरीमिव । Ragh. I. 30. नारायण—an epithet of Vishṇu; for its derivation *cf.* आपो नारा इति प्रोक्ता आपो वै नरसूनवः । ता यदस्यायनं पूर्वं तेन नारायणः स्मृतः ॥ Ms. I. 10. देवेन—करणे तृतीया; 'by means of,' through; or सहार्थे तृतीया; 'together with' (देवेन सह ). प्रभातसमये--is significant. There is a widespread belief that dreams visualized towards the close of the night generally prove true; *cf.* अवितथफलाश्च प्रायो निशावसानसमयदृष्टा भवन्ति स्वप्नाः । Kád. p. 65.

P. 6. पुष्पभूतं—is appropriate in connexion with the फल. *Cf.* Ragh. III. 1. संपन्न्यक्कृताखण्डलः—Who despised ( *i. e.* far surpassed ) Indra by reason of his wealth. निजसंपत् &c.—The repetition of the word संपत् again in the same line is inartistic. सीमन्तोत्सव—Also called सीमन्तोन्नयन or 'the parting of the hair' on each side of the head ( which is its essential part ) is one of the twelve ceremonies mentioned by Manu and performed in the sixth or eighth month of a woman's pregnancy. *Cf.* षष्ठेऽष्टमे वा सीमन्तो मासि । Yáj. I. 11.

ललाटतट—broad forehead. विरच्या°—विरच्या to be got ready, *i. e.* with special preparation; विरच्या अर्चना तामर्हतीति. देवेन goes with विरच्या and the whole is a सापेक्ष समास. सम्यग्ज्ञात &c.—having recognized him to be one of his spies in that disguise. For the employment of spies seem Kàm. Nît. XII. 26.

सापदेशं—under disguise; अपदेश *lit.* means 'a pretext;' व्याजोऽपदेशो लक्ष्यं च Ak. *Cf.* केनापदेशेन आश्रमपदं गच्छामः Śák. II. p. 56. शिरसि आज्ञां आदाय—a very common expression, signifying that the command was received with great respect; *cf.* शिरोभिरुह्यते नराधिपैर्माल्यमिवास्य शासनम् Kir. I. 21. उदन्तजात—information of every kind.

P. 7. अन्तराय—An obstacle. संपराय--a battle. वैलक्ष्यलक्ष्यहृदयः—his heart being the target or mark of despair; full of despair; or feeling ashamed. वीतदयः—has no propriety here. It may mean 'full of cruel thoughts,' *i. e.* desirous of taking vengeance. महाकाल—The name of the celebrated temple of Śiva at Ujjain ( one of the twelve ज्योतिर्लिङ्गs ). It is immortalized by Kâlidása in his Meghadûta. काली—the goddess Pârvatî, so called probably because she is the consort of the god Śiva in his form as the Destroyer ( काल ). एकवीर०—एक indicates pre-eminence. 'That would kill an adversary who is a pre-eminent warrior;' or, 'that would kill one warrior opposing him.' अप्रतिभटः—प्रतिभट an antagonistic warrior, or a warrior on the opposite side; न विद्यते प्रति संमुखं भटो यस्य। अभियुज्—to attack. तत्क्रमैः—तत् may refer to the occasion, or better, to the king; 'who determined the steps to be taken at the time ( or, by the king ).' देवसहायेन—देवः एव सहायः तेन। The Instr. is सहार्थे; 'with god Śiva as his ally.' असांप्रतं—improper, inadvisable. For the alliteration *cf.* संपत्स्यसांप्रतं वक्तुं &c. Śiś. II. 70. सहसा—in the sense of 'all at once' may also be taken with the preceding sentence; thus अस्माकं सहसा युद्धं &c. In support of the ministers' argument *cf.* बालिना सह योद्धव्यमिति नास्ति निदर्शनम्। Kâm. Nît. IX. 40. See also Manu. VII. 198-99. अखर्वेण &c.—Conspicuous ( elated ) with great pride. ०शक्तिसारः—Whose strength lay in, or who mainly depended upon, the Śakti given by Śiva. योद्धुमनसां—Bent or resolved on fighting; *cf.* प्रहर्तुमनसः Mud. II. 13. For the dropping of the nasal, see com. p. 130. असाध्य--inaccessible to. अवरोध--the wives of a king ( taken collectively ), the ladies of the harem; *cf.* मूलबलरक्षितावरोधः *infra* p. 14. मूलबल—hereditary force ( whose loyalty was unquestionable ). Kâmandaka enumerates six divisons of the army, and declares that मौल ( hereditary ) is the best of them; *cf.* षड्विधं तु बलं व्यूह्य द्विषतोऽभिमुखं व्रजेत्॥ मौलं भृतं श्रेणि सुहृद् द्विषद् आटविकं बलम्। पूर्वं पूर्वं गरीयस्तु &c. K. N. XIII. 2-3.

P. 8. **प्रशस्त**—Chosen. **वीतदैन्य**—energetic, spirited; or well-equipped. **विविधायुधस्थैर्य०**—who equalled the lord of immortals in battles marked by (*or*, graceful on account of) his steady (unflinching) use of various weapons. **तस्य**—Well known, renowned. **पुरारति**—The enemy of *Tripura* Śiva; so called because he destroyed, at the request of the gods, the three cities of gold, silver and iron built for the demons in the sky, mid-space and on earth by Maya. **पशुपति**—an epithet of Śiva; पशूनां जीवानां पतिः. For other explanations, see our note on the word at Kum. VI. 95. **वीतप्रग्रह**—with reins loosened. **दैवगत्या**—led or inspired by fate. **०शरण्यं**—the resort of the royal ladies. **प्राज्य**—great, prosperous. **समाक्रम्य**—having taken possession of, or occupied. **हेति**—weapons. **दैवगत्या**—fortunately. **आश्वस्य**-having taken courage.

P. 9. **रमणानुगमने**—**रमण** is very appropriately used here. **कल्याणि**—'O fortunate one'; the use of this particular word is significant, indicating that the ministers believed in all turning out well in the future; *cf.* its similar use in तत्कल्याणि त्वमपि नितरां मा गमः कातरत्वम्। Megh. II. 49. **मथितोद्धृतारातिः**—मथित is used in a future sense here; *cf.* भस्मीकृतारयः p. 23. Or भविता may be taken with the epithets, as मथितो० भविता, सार्वभौमः भ० &c. **क्षणहीनया**—Joyless, uneasy. **अर्धरात्रे**—mark the comp. which is *mas.* **उत्तर्तुम्**-is a grammatical inaccuracy, as the correct Inf. would be उत्तरितुं or उत्तरीतुम्. **निःशब्दलेशं**—may also be taken as an *adv.*; 'without the least noise.' **संसक्तया**—being entangled. **मृतिरेखायां**—which was as it were the line of death. "The simile is taken from palmistry. The 'line of death' stands nearly vertically on the line of life, which crosses the hand horizontally." Bühler.

P. 10. **वाङ्माधुरी०**—Who by the sweetness (music) of her voice surpassed (*lit.* made disagreeable the voice of) the cuckoo. **भवानेव** &c.—For a similar idea *cf.* भूयो यथा मे जननान्तरेऽपि त्वमेव भर्ता न च विप्रयोगः। Ragh. XIV. 66. **नीहारकर**—नीहार snow, frost; hence cool;—**०कर** the cool-rayed one, the moon. **अमन्द**—not slow to appear, *i. e.* great, excessive. The word is appropriate, as the joy takes its rise all at once. **संफुल्ल०**—the lotus of whose face was full-blown on account of the great (ecstatic) joy swelling in her heart. **उपोषिताभ्यां** &c.—लोचनाभ्यां or नेत्राभ्यां पा means to look intently at, and with उपोषिताभ्यां it means to look very eagerly or intently at. The idea is common enough; *cf.* पपौ निमेषालसपक्ष्मपङ्क्तिरुपोषिताभ्यामिव

लोचनाभ्याम् । Ragh. II. 19; also 73. विकस्वर—properly means expanding or blowing, as a flower; hence, swelling, loud, audible; *cf.* उदडीयत वैकृतात्करग्रहजादस्य विकस्वरस्वरैः । Nai. II. 5. The word is derived from the root कस् with वि+affix वरच् by Pāṇ. III. 2. 175 ( स्थेशभासपिसकसो वरच् । स्थावरः-ईश्वरः-भास्वरः-पेस्वरः-कस्वरः । ). ०माहात्म्यैः—Because the King was saved, and thereby the Queen also. सैनिकग्राम—ग्राम in the sense of 'a multitude' generally occurs as the second member of a compound. *Cf.* गणयति गुणग्रामं Gît. II.; भूतग्रामः स एवायं Bg. VIII. 19, &c.

P. 11. विरचित०—who did honour to him; or, who exhibited great joy ( मह meaning a festival ). विरचितदैवानुकूल्येन—some take this as adj. to मन्त्रिनिवहेन and interpret as '( the ministers ) who did something to propitiate fate;' but looking to its position, it is better to make it go with कालेन; 'wherein fate acted favourably.' शल्य—points or heads of arrows &c. stuck in the body. सहसा—quickly. विरोपितव्रणः—who had his wounds dressed and healed. पुरुषकार—human effort, manly exertion, as opposed to दैव ( destiny ); *cf.* एवं पुरुषकारेण विना दैवं न सिध्यति Hitop. Pr. 32. सुदुर्भाषिता—p. p. participles are often used abstractively; thus भाषित here is equivalent to भाषण; *cf.* गत used for गमन &c. अधिकाधिः—Whose mental agony grew more intense. अधिकाधिक—*v. l.* The repetition shows excess. मेधाकलिता—who was possessed of wisdom. तेजो०—*i. e.* क्षात्रतेजः । *Cf.* मौर्यस्तेजसि &c. Mud. II. 23. मध्यं निवसति—this should have been मध्ये निवसति, since वस् governs the Acc. case only when preceded by the prepositions उप, अनु, अधि and आ. See A. G. § 32. विराजमाना—shining like, *i. e.* resembling. तडिल्लता—a flash of lightning. हरिश्चन्द्र—A king of the solar race, son of Triśanku and a remote ancestor of Râma. He was known for his liberality, probity and unswerving devotion to duty. दुःखयन्त्रं—crucial or excessive pain. ०दैवसमाधिः—Reconciled to fate, *i. e.* taking consolation from the fact that the present misery is due to the will of providence and not to any personal fault.

P. 12. इति नियमवन्तं &c.—With this thought (or intention) I have come to your reverence devoted to contemplative exercise or asceticism. ०कुलमर्दनः—goes with संभविष्यति; he will be the extirpator of' &c. अवाचि—this is the correct form of the pass. 3rd pers. sing. of वच्. The reading अवोचि found in many

MSS. is ungrammatical. ब्रह्मवर्चसेन—Notice the comp. ending; अ is added to the final of वर्चस् when it is preceded in a compound by ब्रह्मन् or हस्तिन्. See com. जातसंस्कार—The rites attendant on a child's birth. The जातकर्म is a ceremony performed at the birth of a child when the umbilical cord is separated. It consists in touching the infant's tongue three times with ghee with the proper *mantras*. It is the fourth of the 12 Saṃskâras or purificatory rites mentioned by Manu. For a detailed description of it *vide* our note on स जातकर्मण्यखिले &c. Ragh. III. 18. महाभिख्याः—highly lustrous or very handsome. The original reading is महदभिख्याः but we have rejected it as incorrect; see note on महदायुध p. 4.

P. 13. नवोद्यदिन्दु०—Possessing beauty like that of the rising moon; the comparison shows that they were bound to grow in lustre and body. *Cf.* प्रतिपच्चन्द्रनिभोऽयमात्मजः। Ragh. VIII. 65. रसेन—goes with समर्प्य. रस means here 'a feeling of affection or love.' कररुहैः—With the fingers. The reading करसरोरुहैः is bad, since the plural is indefensible; it ought to have been करसरोरुहाभ्याम्. व्यापृतसुधर्माणि—सुधर्मन् (*m. f*) the assembly of the gods; व्यापृत engaged in talk about himself. व्याप्त *v. l.* suggested by the late Prof Taránáth is simpler. व्यापृत, however, might be made to yield the same sense as व्याप्त, if we understand the root पृ in its original sense of 'to fill;' विशेषेण आ समन्तात् पूरिता व्यापृता. असंख्य—bloody; tumultuous (*Lit.* in which countless men fell; अविद्यमाना संख्या यस्मिन्). साति विदेहे—had lost its bodies, *i. e.* was destroyed (*i. e.* for the most part). असाति विधेये *v. l.* ('having fled, not obeying, *i. e.* in defiance of, his order') does not appear to be original, as is shown by the next line. Moreover, विदेहे gives a better alliteration with the next word विदेहेश्वरः. पुण्येन—by virtue of his merit.

P. 14. शबरबल—An army of mountaineers. "The descendants of the *S'abaras* are probably the *Suars* of modern India. Sanskrit poets are not particular about the names of the aboriginal tribes. Below (p. 15. 1. 3) the same people are called *Kirátas* and (p. 16. 1. 10) again *S'abaras*, while (p. 104) the robbers who captured Upahâravarman are named *Bhillas*."—Bühler.

रभसादभिहन्यमानः—Being forcibly attacked or hard pressed. मूलबला०—The ladies of whose harem were protected (safely escorted) by. महानिरोधः—Who encountered a serious calamity. आघ्रातुं—To devour (*lit.*, to smell). मदखिपाणि &c.—*Cf.*

*infra*, Upahâravarman's Charita, p. 102. कपिलाशव—The carcass of a brown cow. क्रोड—cavity under the belly. We should expect क्रोडे ( Loc. ) instead of क्रोडं ( Acc ) अमर्षिण:—furious, raging. बाणासनयन्त्र—A kind of bow with a mechanical contrivance at one of its ends for tightening the string and letting off the arrow. वृष्णिपाल—a shepherd. वृष्णीनां ( rams ) पाल: ( protector, guard ). कुटीर—small hut or cottage ( ह्रस्वा कुटी ); fr. कुटी + र. आविश्य...अभवम्—This sentence is syntactically faulty, since the two actions denoted by these roots ought to have the same agent, which they have not. So it is necessary to supply some such word as स्थापिता after आवेश्य. अनभिज्ञाततया—On account of my being ignorant of her whereabouts or of her fate.

P. 15. तदन्वयाङ्कुर—A scion of his race. चण्डिका—The goddess Durgá in her fierce form ( especially the one she assumed at the time of killing the demon Mahisha ). She was generally worshipped by the fierce forest-tribes engaged in committing robberies &c. Animals ( including human beings) were offered as *Balis* to her. Bâṇa has given a lengthy description of the goddess in his Kádambarî. एवंविध—such as they obtained over the king of Videha. करिष्यन्त:—wishing to offer. किराता:—Mountaineers who lived by hunting and inhabited the borders of forests; किरं पर्यन्तभूमिं अतन्तीति. For the derivation of the word comp. पर्यन्ताश्रयिभिर्निजस्य सदृशं नाम्न: किरातै: कृतम् । Ratn. II. 3. Here they are spoken of as identical with the Śabaras who also form a class of mountaineers. *Cf.* भेदा: किरातशबरपुलिन्दा म्लेच्छजातय: । Amara. असिलता—a poniard. लता in such cases indicates delicacy or slenderness. अनेकचरणै:—This is to be taken with पलायमानं, 'running on all fours' ( as a young boy is expected to do ). Some take it as an adj. of कुक्कुरबालकै:, but the epithet then loses all propriety; what is the point of saying that dogs have more legs than one? दंशयित्वा—*v. l.* दंदशयित्वा is from the Freq. base of दंश्. घोरप्रचारे—Where a journey is perilous or dangerous; प्रचार may also mean 'behaviour,' doings. स्खलितपथ:—Who have missed or lost my way. For the change of पथिन् to पथ, see com. उपचार—appliances, remedies.

P. 16. अभिरक्षतात्—Imperat. third per. sing. The term. तात् is optionally used in the 2nd and 3rd pers. sing. of the Imperat. (instead of हि and तु ) when the sense is that of benediction; see com. अधरीकृत्य—Lessening or softening. पक्कण—

The residence of S'abaras or the mountain-tribes. उपलालितं—fondled, fondly borne in her arms. भामिनी—used as a complimentary term. See com. सराजगुणसंपूर्तिः—Endowed with all princely qualities. पल्ली—The hut of a shepherd. सामदानाभ्यां—by gentle means (*e. g.* verbal pursuasion) and gifts For, force would have been useless and against his कार्यज्ञत्व साम and दान are two of the four political means mentioned by writers on polity, the other two being दण्ड and भेद. रामतीर्थ—is the name of a holy place; it is mentioned in Mah.-Bh. Vanap. 82. 83, but its exact location is uncertain.

P. 17. कालयवन—'By this term probably Zanzibar on the coast of Arabia is meant.' Bühler. व्यवहारी—a merchant. सुवस्तुसंपदा—With an abundance of good things, *i. e.*, a rich dowery and presents. नताङ्गी—The beautiful-limbed lady; *lit* 'with joints low' ( not projecting ). प्रवहण—a ship. कल्लोल—billows. पोत—a boat. कल्पिता—appointed. रत्नोद्भवः—see his recovery mentioned at p. 35. प्रसववेदना—The travails of child-birth. प्रच्छायशीतले—प्रकृष्टा छाया यत्र तत्प्रच्छायं प्रच्छायं च तच्छीतलं च or प्रच्छायेन शीतले; प्रच्छायं means 'a place having thick or dense shade.' The comp. also occurs again on pp. 29, 34.

P. 18. जनपदगामिन्—Leading to the country. विवशा—विगतो वशो यस्याः who had no control over her limbs; hence, lying in an unconscious state. प्राद्रवत्—took to her heels, ran away. गुल्मक—a thicket. परीक्षमाणः—watching the course of events, awaiting the result. कण्ठीरव—a lion; *lit.* 'one whose roar is in his throat' ( कण्ठ्यां रवः यस्य सः). महामहेण—With a terrible or prodigious spring. पक्वफलबुद्ध्या—mistaking it for a ripe fruit. फलेतरतया—that being found to be something other than a fruit. सत्त्वसंपन्नतया—on account of its innate vitality or power of endurance. निवेद्य—having informed. महदाश्चर्यं—may have been used by the author as a comp. ( for महाश्चर्यं ); in the present case, however, this may be taken as two separate words महद् and आश्चर्यं. नामधेय—धेय is added स्वार्थे ( without change of the original sense ) to रूप, नाम and भाग.

P. 19. व्याख्याय—having explained in detail. निद्रामुद्रिता—with my eyes sealed by sleep, under the influence of deep sleep. स्वन्मन्त्रिणः—goes with धर्मपाल, so that धर्मपाल॰ is a सापेक्ष compound. यक्षकान्ता *v. l.*—a woman of the Yaksha class. यक्षेश्वर—Kubera. परिचर्याकरणाय—That he should attend upon. विस्मयविकासित—expanded or dilated through astonishment. स्वक्षी—with fascinating eyes. रञ्जितमित्रं—used for alliteration. भावद्रुच—this compound is grammatically faulty. By Pāṇ. VI.

3. 23, when a word ending in ऋ is compounded with another and there is blood-relationship or some kind of learning, there is non-elision (अलुक्) of the Genitive case; thus in the present instance भ्रातुष्पुत्र would have been the correct form. अन्तेवासी—a disciple; see com. समाराधितदेवकीर्तिम्—who had obtained the glory of the gods; goes with नरपतिं. कीर्ति may mean 'splendour' or 'lustre,' and then समा० may qualify कुमारं; this is more natural. *Cf.* for the idea अमरतेजसि पार्थिवे Ragh. IX. 4.

P. 20. निर्भर्त्सित—put to shame, far surpassed. अवगमय्य—having announced. कावेरी—A river in the south of India; see Ragh. IV. 45. निजशोक०—Able to take out or extricate the dart of sorrow (from her heart). अग्रहार—The royal grant of land to Bráhmaṇas for their maintenance. अग्रं ब्राह्मणभोजनं तदर्थं ह्रियन्ते राजधनात् पृथक् क्रियन्ते ते क्षेत्रादयः। Nílakaṇṭha. Also, a village so granted. तस्यामेकं तनय०—Mark the Sanskrit construction; 'he had a son by her.' प्लवमाना—floating; note that the word प्लव (a boat) is derived from the same root. नदीवेगागत—borne by the current of the river. उद्दीपनता—virulence, malignity. ०ज्वालावलीढावयवा—having her whole body inflamed by the burning poison.

P. 21. विषव्यवस्था—The working or effect of the poison. पावकसंस्कार—Consigning the body to fire. This is the last of the purificatory rites enjoined for a Hindu. अगति—forlorn, helpless. ०स्थितेः—residence. सोमदत्तं नाम—*i. e.* having named him Somadatta. अधिरूढा०—who practised riding. चौल०—चौल is the ceremony of tonsure or cutting off of all the hair on the head of a child except one lock on the crown; it is generally performed in the third year. See Manus. II. 35. उपनयन—investiture with the sacred thread, performed in the eleventh year in the case of Kshatriyas. See A'śv. Gṛi. Sú. 1. 17 and 10 *seqq.* For the deriv. compare गृह्योक्तकर्मणा येन समीपं नीयते गुरोः। बालो वेदाय तद्योगात् बालस्योपनयं विदुः ॥. सकललिपि &c.—A general acquaintance with the different arts and almost every branch of knowledge, as well as a thorough knowledge of the fine arts, formed in ancient days the necessary qualification for the *Yuvarâja* who was being trained to take part in the responsible task of government along with his father. *Cf.* the similar training which Chandrápîḍa is said to have received as described at Kád. p. 175; also Ragh. III. 29,.30. It may be noted that while Daṇḍin includes a knowledge of such arts as चौर्य and दुरोदर in the educational equipment of a prince (that the prince may be able to find out thieves and miscreants by knowing their ways of action), Báṇa omits them. It will be seen that the knowledge was abused by some of the Kumâras, a sign of the degenerate age in which our author wrote.

षडङ्ग—The six subsidiary works ( for their names see com. ), the study of which is indispensably necessary for the proper interpretation and understanding of the Veda. काव्य—is here used in the particular sense of 'metrical compositions.' आख्यानक—A short narrative or episode. आख्यायिका—a continuous narrative or story. कथा—a romance. See Kád. p. 14 and our notes *ad. loc.* See also Introd. पुराणगण—The whole body of the Puràṇas ( *i. e.* the 18 Puràṇas with an equal number of Upapuráṇas ). नैपुण्यं—proficiency in. धर्म—The codes of law, religious and secular. शब्द—grammar. ज्योतिस्—astronomy and astrology. तर्क—logic. मीमांसा—comprises the two systems—पूर्वमी० and उत्तरमी०. The former chiefly concerns itself with the correct interpretation of the Vedic ritual and the settlement of all dubious points in regard to Vedic texts. The latter discusses the nature of Brahman or Supreme Spirit and aims at pointing out the means to salvation. कौटिल्य०—the treatise on politics by Cháṇakya called अर्थशास्त्र. कामन्दकीय—The celebrated Nîtisára of Kámandaki in 19 chapters; it is an epitome of Cháṇakya's great work. नीतिपटल—treatises on political science. शक्यं—skill. संगित—this comprises the three arts of singing, instrumental music, and dancing; गीतं वाद्यं च नृत्यं च त्रयं संगीतमुच्यते ॥.

P. 22. साहित्य—Poetics. हारित्व—ability to attract, *i. e.* perfect knowledge of. मायाप्र०—magic with its branches. माया is said to be derived from मय, the traditional founder of the science ; of magic. This has nothing to do with the Máyâ (illusion) of Śaṃkaráchárya. चञ्चुत्व—skill or proficiency. चञ्चु (also written चुञ्चु) and चण are affixes added in the sense of 'known for or skilled in;' see Páṇ. V. 2. 26. पाटवं—skill to manage. चणत्व—see चञ्चुत्व above. चौर्य &c.—The knowledge of the art of thieving and gambling proves useful to the Kumáras in their future adventures. The work on the art of housebreaking is ascribed to Karṇîsuta; see *infra* p. 76, and notes. कपटकला—The arts based on deceit or fraud. कृत्ये०—prompt in the discharge of their duties.

वामदेव:—subject of अभ्यभाषत ( line 2, p. 23 ). संशयित—Caused to be called in question or confounded with itself.

कल्पित॰—who had formed the tie of fraternity. Mr. Agashe interprets this as '( who were ) formed as if they were the brothers' ( of the God of Love ). It appears that he takes the comp. to mean सोदर्य इव कल्पिताः; this involves unusual twisting, and since the sense obtained is a repetition, to a certain extent, of the preceding epithet कुसुमसायक॰, we have rejected that interpretation. साहसो॰—Who put to shame *Kumâra* ( Kârttikeya, the god of war ) by their exploits or adventurous spirit. सुकुमार—beautifully young, youthful. जयध्वज॰—The linear marks of a flag, an umbrella, and a thunderbolt on the palm of the hand indicate future royalty. *Cf.* अङ्कुशे कुलिशं छत्रं यस्य पाणितले भवेत्। तस्यैश्वर्यं विनिर्दिष्टं अशीत्यायुर्भवेद्ध्रुवम्॥ धनुर्यस्य भवेत्पाणौ पङ्कजं वाऽथ तोरणम्। तस्यैश्वर्यं च राज्यं च अशीत्यायुर्भवेद्ध्रुवम्॥ Sámudrakaśâstra ( as quoted by Mr. Agashe ). See also our notes on Ragh. IV. 88. तां परिचर्यां—'that ( well-known ) worship', *i. e.* such as is usually offered to great sages. काकपक्ष—side-locks of hair. They are so called because in colour as well as in shape they resemble crow's wings; काकस्य पक्षाविव काकपक्षौ. *Cf.* Ragh. XI. 1 and our note thereon. Their locks were like the bees alighting on the two lotuses of his feet. Following the example of the king the Kumâras bowed to the ascetic, touching his feet with their heads so that the former were covered by their long, flowing locks.

P. 23. कुमाराः &c.—Mark the alliterations in this sentence forming what is called शृङ्खलायमक (see Kir. V. 27). भस्मीकृत—though a *past* participle, this is here used in the sense of the immediate future; *cf.* मथितोद्धताराति: above ( p. 9 ). रय—impetuosity; velocity. रणाभियानेन यानेन—by marching out for battle; or, by a march indicative of their ardour or zeal for battle. अभ्युदयाशंसं—hopeful of glory. सहायीकृत्य &c.—having appointed others his helpers. शुभशकुन—Some auspicious omen, such as a favourable sound uttered by a bird &c. *Cf* शुभाशुभज्ञानविनिर्णयार्थो हेतुर्नृणां यः शकुनः स उच्यते। Vasantarâjîya शस्त्रक्षत॰—bearing the marks of the scars of wounds inflicted by weapons. कालायस॰—With a frame of body as hard as iron. कालायस is der. from काल + अयस्, a Karm. comp; कालं च तदयश्च. The अयस् becomes अयस by अनोऽश्मायःसरसां जातिसंज्ञयोः Pâṇ. V. 4. 94. व्यक्तकिरात॰—who clearly possessed the strength of a Kirâta. लोचनपरुष—hideous in appearance, frightful to look at.

P. 24. मृगहिते—Fit for wild beasts, *i. e.* where they can roam without molestation. This is explained by जनसङ्गरहिते. घोरप्रचारे—See p. 15. किरातरीतिः—the life or profession of a Kirâta. शौच—Purity of the mind and body. धर्मव्रात—the various religious observances. व्रात *lit.* means 'a collection;' *cf.* Ragh. XII. 94. पुलिन्दपुरोगमाः—led by the Pulindas. The author, as already remarked, uses the words पुलिन्द, किरात, &c. as synonymous, ignoring the minor differences between them. ब्राह्मणब्रुवाः—Bráhmaṇa-renegades; *lit.* 'Brâhmaṇas in name,' but neglecting the duties of their caste ( see Kullûka on Manu. VIII. 85 ); ब्रुव is used as a depreciatory affix. उद्धत्य—Bearing myself haughtily; fr. उद्+हन्, from which we get उद्धत 'proud.' We have adopted this reading instead of उद्धृत्य which is current in all the editions, but which appears to be a clerical error. उद्धृत्य makes no sense, and Mr. Agashe's attempt to render it by 'having set them free' is an unconvincing makeshift. मदीयसहचरगण—The band of my comrades or associates. जिघांस्यमानं—Prep. p. of the pass. of the Desid. of हन्. निरभर्त्सयत्—A grammatical inaccuracy; भर्त्स् is usually A'tm.; it is, however, oftentimes used in the Paras. in the Purâṇas, the Pañchatantra &c.

P. 25. प्रेतपुरी—The city of Yama ( *lit.* of the dead ). रत्नखचित--set or studded with gems. शमन—an epithet of Yama, the god of death. दण्डप्रणाम—falling prostrate on the ground like a staff ( *i. e.* every part of the body touching the ground) as a mark of extreme humility. चित्रगुप्त—Yama's minister, who records the good or bad deeds of beings. मृत्युसमय—The proper time of death. विगलितकल्मष—who has been absolved from his sins. यातनाविशेषं—particular agonies; torments causing excrutiating pain. For a description of the various kinds of tortures that sinners have to undergo, *vide* Vishṇu-P. II. 6, Bhâg.-P. V. 26, Mârk.-P. 12, &c. जर्जरीकृत—loosened, belaboured. टङ्क—a chisel. परितक्ष्यमाण—being chopped off. पुण्यबुद्धिमुपदिश्य—Advising me so as to create in me a love for meritorious or virtuous acts. वंशबन्धु—agnatic relations. अक्षरशिक्षां विधाय—having taught me the alphabet, *i. e.* reading and writing. आगमतन्त्र—see com. for the comp.; 'the principles or doctrines ( तन्त्र ) of the various Śâstras ( आगम ).' Bühler takes the comp. as a Dvandva, meaning 'Vedas and *Tantras,*' where तन्त्र means a religious text-book dealing with mytsical magic-formulas for the worship of a deity or the attainment of superhuman power ( *Siddhi* ).

P. 26. दूरीकृतकलङ्कः—'With sin far removed,' *i. e.* leading a life of virtue and piety. अतीते निशान्ते—In the last quarter or watch of the last night. दण्डकारण्य—Name of a well-known forest, the scene of many of Râma's exploits, and popularly supposed to be between the Narmadâ and the Godâvarî. It was so named after Daṇḍaka, a son of Ikshváku, who dishonoured Arajâ, a daughter of Śukráchárya, and was cursed by the sage to the effect that his kingdom, which was a hundred *Yojanas* in extent, would be converted into a tenantless forest. See Rám. Uttarakàṇḍa, Adh. 80-81.

सिद्धसाध्य—Classes of demigods. विधेः—of propitious fate. This and शासनं विधातुः ( which means—which is as sure to come off as the order of Providene ) seem to be used simply for the sake of alliteration. आनन—an opening, a door 'As though it were an opening made by Fate;' the meaning is that destiny has here provided a means whereby good luck would accrue. For the idea *cf.* अथ वा भवितव्यानां द्वाराणि भवन्ति सर्वत्र Śâk. I. 15. ताम्रशासनं—properly, a royal grant or edict committed to a copperplate; here, a writing inscribed on a copperplate. विधि—The mode of performing rites and ceremonies for the attainment of an object. तदुपदिष्ट—prescribed thereon. दिष्ट—fate. ०अनुगुणं—In conformity with. तोषिणः—gratified ( now that you have come ).

P. 27. कल्ये—In the morning. साकल्येन—( also used for alliteration ) goes with अनवलोकयन्तः; 'not seeing Râj. in his entirety,' *i. e.* not seeing anywhere even the slightest trace ( कला ) of him. साकल्य is an abstr. noun from सकल, which is explained as कलया सहित. Some take साकल्येन as signifying 'everywhere.' मनीषा—desire; dissolve मनसः ईषा; a word of the शकन्ध्वादि group. चरिष्णवः—wishing to go on a journey. The aff. इष्णु is added to चर with अलं and other roots by Pâṇ. III. 2. 136. अतिसहिष्णु—very hardy. संगमसंकेतस्थान—a rendezvous; 'having appointed their place of meeting.' एकवीर—According to Pàṇ. II. 1. 58, वीर is one of those words which ought always to be placed first in a Karm. comp., so that we should have वीरैकः and not एकवीरः. एकवीर, however, is found used by classical authors, and is to be justified by supposing that the application of the Sútra is not universal (बहुलग्रहणात्—holds good in most cases). विततसारस—with rows of swans spread about. It may also mean 'with beds of full-blown lotuses.' विगत० *v. l.*—has no propriety. ईशशासन०—Collected in accordance with the directions of Ísa. प्रत्यूहपरिहारिणि—who warded off the obstacles (to the sacrifice). पुण्यगेहं—The seat of meritorious actions. Note how the word गेह is brought in here for alliteration. मणिमय—richly set with gems. मण्डल—a collection. सकललोक०—सकललोकेषु &c. 'The ornament of womankind in all the three worlds.' *Cf.* आश्रमललामभूता शकुन्तला Śák. II. p. 51.

P. 28. विनीत—well-trained, of modest deportment. उदञ्जलिः—with joined palms raised up (to the head). निजपराक्रमा०—*i. e.* unable to bear the demon's prowess. दूरीकृतामरे—in which the gods were routed. सिद्धतापस—An ascetic having *Siddhi* or miraculous power. चातकी वर्षागमनमिव—The bird Châtaka is said to depend entirely on clouds for water to drink; *vide* Ragh. V. 17 and our note thereon. मदनकृतसारथ्येन &c.—With a mind led on or impelled (to this act) by the God of love; *cf.* मन्मथाभिसरा *infra* p. 78. The idea is common enough; *cf.* मदनः खलु मां नियोजयति &c. Vik. p. 42. मां तत्सपत्नीं—make me her rival wife, *i. e.* marry me. For the idea comp. note on धरणीरमणी p. 2 and Ragh. VI. 29. हृष्टतर—exceedingly pleased; तर shows excess. उररीकृत्य—having accepted. उररी (occurring also in the form उ-ऊ-री; *cf.* Ragh. XV. 70) is a preposition generally used before the root कृ in the sense of 'acceptance.'

वञ्चयित्वा—Avoiding, *i. e.* 'without the knowledge of.' तदवलोकन०—Anxious to see his friends. क्षुत्पिपासादि—It is a general belief that certain gems possess such a virtue. कंचनाध्वानं—for some distance.

P. 29. विशाला—Ujjain. See Megh. I. 30. उपशल्य—शल्यं (border) उपगतं; borderland, suburb. आक्रीड—a public garden. आन्दोलिका—a swing. पल्लवित०—'with a mind swelling or dilated with;' the metaphor is taken from a tree putting forth sprouts under the genial influence of Spring. अकाण्डे—unexpectedly; suddenly. *Cf.* दर्भाङ्कुरेण चरणः क्षत इत्यकाण्डे तन्वी स्थिता Śák. II. 13. सरभस &c.—According to the Com the meaning is 'who enjoyed the sport of stepping hastily and whose action was full of great joy.' The comp. should rather be taken as सरभसपदविन्यासेषु विलासी appearing forth यः हर्षोत्कर्षस्तेन चरितः (चलितः) 'advancing with hasty steps indicative of ecstatic joy.' गलदुल्लसत्—*i. e.* in the act of bowing. 'The blooming (उल्लसत्) wreath of Malliká flowers on which dropped down.' पुलकित—with the hair standing on end. प्रच्छाय॰—See *supra*, p. 17. व्यतिकर—*lit.* means 'incident'; 'owing to the incident of (*i. e.* by reason of) the sight of his friend.' मुकुलित॰—having folded his lotus-like hands. प्रचारप्रकार—an account of his travels (*lit.* the manner in which he travelled).

P. 30. अम्बरमणि—*lit.* 'the jewel of the sky,' an epithet of the sun. कुशलं—A technical expression for 'asked him questions about his well-being or good condition' &c.; *cf* the precept ब्राह्मणं कुशलं पृच्छेत् &c. महदाशा—See *supra*, note on महदायुध p. 4. It is also possible to explain this as महं ददातीति महदा which gives prosperity; महदा चासौ आशा च. But this was scarcely in the author's mind. अग्रजन्मा—a Brâhmaṇa so called, as he was created first of all the four orders (वर्णानां मध्ये ऽग्रजातत्वात्) or was born from the mouth of God (अग्रात्प्रधानाङ्गात् मुखाज्जातत्वात्). See our Sanskrit foot-note on the word at Ragh. V. 26. महाभाग—*Lit.* 'O fortunate one;' used as a formal title of address. *Cf.* Ragh. V. 14. भैक्ष्यं—food obtained by begging' (भिक्षया संवाद्यम्); fr. भिक्षा + य (ष्यञ्). The other reading भैक्षं *lit.* means 'collection of alms' (भिक्षाणां समूहः) and is derived from भिक्षा by adding अण् (समूहार्थे) by Pāṇ IV. 2. 38. The ultimate meaning is the same in both the readings. कटक—An army encamped. Here we are to suppose that he pointed to an army lying encamped there. लाट—Name of a country said to lie to the west of the Narmadá; it probably included Broach, Baroda and Ahmedabad. Vincent Smith (*Early History of India*, p. 425) identifies it with Southern Gujarat. आवंआवं-The Ṇamulanta is repeated to show frequency. कन्यासारणे—appointed to escort the princess; this is preferable to ॰सारेण *V. l.*—appointed to take charge of the treasure, *scil.* the princess; see com.

P 31. चतुरङ्ग—See *supra*, p. 5, notes. अन्तर्बिभेद—turned treacherous to him; 'secretly plotted treason' (Bühler). निरवेशि—Pass. Aor. of विश् with निर् to enjoy. निगडित-fettered; 'with his arms pinioned.' नैस्त्रिंशिक—निस्त्रिंशः (a sword measuring more than 30 fingers in length) प्रहरणमस्य (aff. ठक्-इक); a swordsman. See Pâṇ. IV. 4. 57. दस्यु—a thief. The word is as old as the Veda, wherein it is applied to the aboriginal and Turanian tribes with whom the Âryans on their occupation of India had often to wage war and whom they conquered. There it is derived from दस् 4th conj to injure, to kill. It acquired the present meaning doubtless from the lawless habits of the mountaineers. भयरहितं—I who was undaunted. Mark the laconic style of the writer. निराश०—निर्गता आशा यस्मात् स निराशः; निराशश्चासौ क्लेशश्च निराशक्लेशः, तस्य अनुभवो यस्य तेन मया—'by me who experienced affliction from which there was no hope of escape, *i. e.* which was irremediable.' निर्विशथ--the root विश् with निर् generally means 'to enjoy' (*cf.* निरवेशि निद्रासुखं above); but here it appears to have been used in the sense of 'to experience' (कारावासदुःख). सुरङ्गा--a subterranean passage; also written as सुरुङ्गा.

P. 32. निकटं—near (*i. e.* into the presence of) the king, Mattakâla. माणिक्या०--To recover the ruby. रत्नरत्न--The most excellent jewel. Or, as the com. takes it; 'who knew about the jewel and the place where it was looked for.' द्वाःस्थगण—The sentinels at the door. पटुपराक्रमलीलया—With the display of sharp prowess. आर्चयत्—received with honour. वराक—poor; or, base, vile. विप्रलाप—insulting words, insolent speech. कुपितोऽपि—although enranged (and therefore he should have brought a larger force with him); the अपि should rather have been placed after लाटपति. संनद्धयोधः—with a force fully enquipped.

P. 33. बहुल—here means 'large.' The meaning 'many' is not so good. तुमुल—Properly means 'the confused noise of warriors engaged in hard fight;' hence, fierce fighting. समुल्लसत्०—with the quick and dexterous movements of the arms. आटोप—pride; hence, skill, the cause of the pride अराति—the context shows that this refers to Mattakâla the hostile King, and we have therefore chosen it in preference to the reading अरातीन्, where the plural cannot be justified. अतिरय—अतिशयेन रयो येषां:, very fleet, swift of foot. शीघ्रलङ्घन—a quick jump. संनत—*lit.* bowed with; hence, filled with. उदन्तजात—The full account. समहोत्सवं—goes with अदात्. आराधित०—gaining the king's favour, ministering to his desires. भवद्वेदना &c.—With his heart tormented with affliction natuarally (*lit.* easily) caused by the dart of the poignant pain of your separation. सिद्धादेशेन—According to the direction of a Siddha. महाकाल—See *supra*, p. 7. आनन्दसंदोह—संदोह *lit.* a flood or mass of; 'ecstatic or great joy.' निरपराधदण्डे—The punishment or suffering inflicted on him without any fault of his.

P. 34. पुरतः पुष्पोद्भवं &c.—This sudden introduction of Pushpodbhava indicates a deficiency of creative power on the part of the author. निटिलतट—his broad forehead. संकुल—overflooded with. करिष्णु—see note on चरिष्णु p. 27. विदितार्थः—If they knew my object. किमिति निश्चित्य—what did they think was the reason of my disappearance?

अशक्नुवानः—This is not the Pres. p. of शक् (which is Paras.), but a verbal derivative formed by affixing आन (चानश् and not शानच्) which is added in the sense of the agent (कर्तरि) to express habit &c. by ताच्छील्यवयोवचनशक्तिषु चानश्। Pāṇ. III. 2. 129. प्रच्छाय०—Mark the comp.; see *supra*, p. 17 (last line). कूर्माकृति—the comparison to a tortoise, all of whose limbs are contracted, is graphic and appropriate, since at mid-day the shadow cast by the body of the falling man would be compressed, all his limbs appearing contracted into very small shape. Compare for a similar idea किरति मिहिरे विश्वद्रीचः करानतिवामनी स्थलकमठवद्देहच्छाया जनस्य विचेष्टते। A.-R. I. 54. अन्तराल—mid-way, before he reached the ground. दयोपनत०—दयया उपनतं (subdued or bent) हृदयं यस्य.

P. 35. निक्षिप्य—Because he could not have entirely arrested his downward descent; he only lessened its rapidity. भृगु—a precipice. Distinguish this from another word भृगु which is the name of a famous sage. Bühler says:—"Etymologically, भृगु means *a broken place.* It is apparently derived from the A'ryan root *bhrag*, which in Latin appears as *fra(n)g-o*, in Gothic as *brik-an*, in English as *break*, and which in Sanskrit appears in the mutilated form *bha(ñ)j*. The Bhṛigupatana or *Bhairavastava* is a favourite mode of religious suicide. A few years ago the Nawab of Junâgadh used still to keep guards on Girnâr who watched the place from which pilgrims frequently attempted to precipitate themselves into the valley. Bāṇa in his Harshacharitra also refers to this practice (Uch. V.). करुरुहैः-see note on the word, *supra* p. 13. वाणिज्यरूपेण—is equivalent to वाणिज्येन 'for trading;' here रूप has no particular force. कालयवनद्वीप—See *supra*, p. 17. प्रवहण—a boat. ०आदरेण—out of regard for. हायन—*m. n.* भावान् जहाति जिहीते वा; a year. नारीकूजित—a cry of pain, uttered with the tenderness of a woman's voice.

वैश्वानर—fire; विश्वे नरा अस्य 'worshipped by all men.' भवते विज्ञापनीयानि—Things to be told or communicated to you. The verb विज्ञापय् is used when one has to say something to one's superior or to a respectable person, as a courteous term. *Cf.* the opposite use of आज्ञापय्. भयंकर &c.—Intent on doing the desperate deed (साहस) of throwing herself into a fire blazing with terrible flames mingling together. अभ्यर्णम्—Irreg p. p. p. of अर्द् to go, with अभि, when the sense is 'near,' 'not very distant,' by अभेश्चाविदूर्ये । Pâṇ. VII. 2. 25; otherwise अभ्यर्दित is the p p. p.

P. 36. तावन्तं—ते (षोडश हायनाः) परिमाणमस्य. साभिज्ञानं—by means of the signs of recognition. विनीतं—Bearing myself humbly towards them. अन्वेषणपरायण:—Soley intent on finding your lordship out; whose chief aim was to search you out. निमित्तं—prime cause. भवदनुग्रहात्—The student will remember that Pushpobdhava was instructed in magic along with Rájávahana. साधकत्व—magic-art. सूचकानां—It was a popular belief that trees under which a treasure lay buried indicated its existence by bending their boughs in a peculiar way. *Cf.* निधिस्तरुविकारेण ... स्पष्टमाख्यायते लोके H.-Ch. IV., where the com Śaṃkara says यत्राधो निधिः तत्र परिणाहोद्गताधोमुखशाखामूलादिभाजः वृक्षा भवन्ति ।. Note that the *existence* of the treasure was indicated by the position of the boughs of the trees, but the exact spot could only be located by the help of the सिद्धाञ्जन. सिद्धाञ्जन—collyrium of magical virtue, enabling the eyes to see through opaque bodies or to see the desired spots.

P. 37. दीनार—a gold coin. *Cf.* Lat. *Denarius* ( which was an ancient Roman silver coin worth about eight annas ). According to Kátyâyana and Bṛihaspati it is equivalent in value to 42 copper *Kárshika Paṇas* (about 2½ Rs.). Dînâras were first coined in India by Kanishka and his successors. गोणी—a bag. Here the double bags used by merchants in conveying grain on bullocks are meant. Mark the *fem.* ending. गोण takes ई in this sense; otherwise गोणा. अन्यद्रव्यमिषेण-Pretending, giving out, that it was some other commodity, such as corn &c. नीयमान—taken *i. e.* introduced by. गूढवसतिम०—Lived under disguise. अपारं—Unlimited. मनोग्लानि—mental disquietude; anxiety of the heart. अवलीढ—a word very aptly used. Youth pervaded all her limbs. *Cf.* कुसुममिवलोभनीयं यौवनमङ्गेषु संनद्धम् । S'ák. I. 19. लतान्तबाण—the god of love. लतान्त—a flower; *lit.* 'growing on the extremities of creepers.' चकित—

frightened. The tremulous glances of young ladies are often compared by Sanskrit writers to the swift-rolling eyes of fawns when frightened. *Cf.* त्रस्तैकहायनकुरङ्गविलोलदृष्टेः। Uttar. III. 28; Mál-Mâdh. VI. 8, &c. कुसुमसायक &c.—acting the part of an arrow of Cupid; *cf.* गाढं निखात इव मे हृदये कटाक्षः Mál.-Mâdh. I. 29; कटाक्षविशिखाः Bh. Śr. Ś. मनसाऽभिमुखैः—मनसा (mentally, silently) अभिमुखैः (directed to me).

P. 38. अपाङ्गवर्तिभिः—(in which the pupils were) directed to the corners of the eyes. The reading साङ्गवर्तिभिः (सा अङ्ग०) makes no satisfactory sense. It may be somehow explained as 'lying (*i. e.* riveted) on my body.' साङ्गभङ्गिभिः *v. l.*—will also do; 'with sportive movements of the limbs.' चतुर०—Cleverly displayed and yet mysterious (or secret) gestures. अन्यदा—On one occasion. प्रेक्षिष्यमाणः—wishing to ascertain (your whereabouts). शकुन्तवचनानि—The sounds of birds are often referred to by poets in this connexion; *cf.* तरुषु चुकुवुरुच्चैः पक्षिणश्चारुकुलाः। Bhaṭṭi. I. 27; Megh. I. 8. उत्कलिका०—seeking to dispel my longing or mental anguish. उत्कलिका is the longing produced by love; उत्कण्ठोत्कलिके समे Amara. *Cf.* क्षुभितमुत्कलिकातरलं मनः Mál.-Mâdh. III. 10. ससंभ्रम-प्रेम०—Charming on account of (the mingled emotions of) flurry, love, bashfulness and curiosity or eagerness. मदनकदन—love-torment. रहस्यसंजात०—On account of the confidence produced in her by privacy. वार्द्धकस्य प्रबलतया &c.—It was the custom of ancient Hindu kings to abdicate the throne in their old age in favour of their sons, and to retire into the forest; *cf.* Ragh. III. 70. Here, however, Mánasára, though he installed his son in his own place, did not retire into the forest, but continued to live in the palace. पैतृष्वस्रीयौ—sons of his paternal aunt. See com. for the derivation. उद्दण्डकर्मन्—despotic, cruel; *cf.* समुद्दण्डभुजदण्डः *supra* p. 2. राजराजगिरि—Kailása, the residence of Kubera. राज्ञां यक्षाणां राजा राजराजः कुबेरः; *cf.* Megh. I. 3.

P. 39. पारदार्य—abstr. noun from परदारा (another's wife); 'having illicit intrigues with others' wives.' भवतः—is connected with लावण्य; so this is a सापेक्ष समास; it should have been भवल्लावण्या०. दूरीकृत्य—Not minding, not caring for. तच्चिन्ता—Anxiety caused by that. रागोद्रेक—intense love. मृदु—clever. अधिष्ठाय—having possessed. आकारसंपद्—her superb charms, exquisite beauty. साहसिकः—a desperado, an adventurer. चक्रवाक०—the simile has occurred before; *cf. supra,* p. 3, line 5. सत्यवाक्य—same as आप्त; 'whose words are always true (or reliable).' क्रीडन्नायुष्मान् &c.—If you sport with her and live. एकान्तनिकेतन—secluded apartment. रभसात्—impetuously; with violence or force. भवतीमनु—Note that अनु is a कर्मप्रवचनीय and governs the Acc. case; see A. G. § 37.

P. 40. वंशसंपत्—noble descent; or, high birth and wealth. किंचिद्वि०—With the lotus of her face a little blown. अर्हति—are able to. मन्मायोपाय०—caught in the nooses of the snares of my deceitful plan. ताटङ्क—an ear-ornament ( called तानवडें in Mar. ) मनोज्ञ—Charming. नगरव्याकुलां—Thickly rumoured in the city; this is rather a strange use of the word व्याकुल परीक्षन्—'ascertaining the truth of.' Mark the Paras. use and *cf.* our note on महदायुध *supra,* p. 4. Bühler, however, says—"This can be defended by the Paribhâshá अनुदात्तेत्व-लक्षणमात्मनेपदमनित्यम्, which though rejected by Nâgojî is admitted by Bhaṭṭoji Dîkshita." ईक्ष् with परि is used in the Paras. in the Mah.-Bhâr. also, but the use is non-Pâṇinian.

P. 41. हंसतूल—The soft feathers or down of a swan. Beds used by kings and rich men were stuffed with the down of swans and were valued for their softness; *cf. infra* p. 97, line 1. चामीकर—gold. सूक्ष्म—thin. निःशङ्कः—fearlessly; or, without scruple. नियुद्ध—निरुध्य नितरां वा युद्धं; pugilistic efforts, close or hand-to-hand fight. विकल—disordered or displaced. उपलालयन्—comforting, coaxing. दिशो बधिरयन्तः—rending or deafening the sky. चटुल—tremulous, unsteady. Tremulous eyes are regarded as a mark of beauty by Sanskrit poets; *cf.* इत्थं चेतश्चटुलनयने &c. Megh. II. 48. सिद्धादेश०—according to the instructions of a *Siddha.*

P. 42. अम्लानमानसः—'With a joyful heart.' अम्लान is the same as उत्फुल्ल. निजकटकं—*i. e.* Vîraketu's territory (see p. 30 ) whence he had come to Ujjain on a visit to the temple of Mahâkâla. भूस्वर्गायमाणं—acting like heaven ( looking like a heavenly city ) on earth. *Cf.* ननु वक्तव्यं स्थानान्तरगतः स्वर्ग इति Vik. II.; शेषैः पुण्यैर्हृतमिव दिवः कान्तिमत्खण्डमेकम् Megh. I. 30. अमुष्य राज्ञः—*i. e.* of Râjavâhana.

अथ &c.—Now follows a description of the Spring season on conventional lines, being much the same as that given by Kâlidâsa and other Sanskrit poets. मीनकेतन &c.—*Cf.*

सकलसैनिकाङ्गवीरः मलयसमीरः *supra*, p. 3. The breeze from the Malaya Mountain is called 'the leader of Káma's force,' because it is a great excitant of passion. मलयगिरिमहीरुह—the sandal trees. It is a popular belief that snakes feed on air; *cf.* such epithets as श्वसनभुक्, पवनाशन &c.; अशनं धात्रा मरुत् कल्पितं व्यालानां &c. Bhar.'s Vair. Śat. This and the next epithet account for the breeze being very gentle ( सुक्ष्मतर less incessant and slow). हरिचन्दन—sandal trees of the best kind. सहकार—( so called because it is a favourite resort of lovers; सह कारयति मेलयाति मिथुनानि ) is a kind of mango-tree known for the fragrance of its blossoms. The throats of cuckoos are supposed to be made tuneful by their tasting the young sprouts of the mango-tree. *Cf.* चूताङ्कुरास्वादकषायकण्ठः पुंस्कोकिलो यन्मधुरं चुकूज । Kum. III. 32. कलकण्ठ—a koil or cuckoo.

P. 43. काकली—a low, indistinct sweet tone. See Ṛit. I. 8. कलकल—a mixed noise. 'Making the quarters ring with (noisy with ) the indistinct and sweet sounds of the bees and the koils whose throats are made tuneful by their tasting the honey and the tender sprouts ( *or*, honey in the blossoms ) of the mango-trees.'

उत्कलिका—See *supra*, p. 38. मदनमहोत्सव—A festival celebrated in honour of the God of love, in Spring. रसिक—Men of taste; here, gay people, flirts. समुल्लासयन्—exhilarating ( so as to lead them to ). चूतपोत०—A young mango-tree, (or sometimes an *As'oka* tree) was generally selected by young ladies for the worship of Madana. गन्ध &c.—Consisting of various kinds such as sandal or saffron, flowers, turmeric-powder, whole grains of rice, fine silk garments and others. चीनाम्बर—China silk, the fine silken cloth imported from China, which was known for its silks from the earliest times. *Vide* our note on चीनांशुक Śák. p. 40. काम इव वसन्तसहायः—The friendship between Cupid and Spring is a constantly recurring idea in Sanskrit poetry; *cf.* क नु ते हृदयंगमः सखा कुसुमायोजितकार्मुको मधुः । Kum. IV. 24. मलय &c.—bright ( majestic ) with fruits, blossoms and tender foliage, grown in thick clusters from the branches gently agitated by the Malaya breeze. श्रावं श्रावं—'hearing repeatedly,' this indicates that he gently paced the region. इन्दीवर—see com. कह्लार—is distinguished from कैरव by its strong sweet odour. चक्रवाल—swarms of. व्याकुल—resounding with. अमन्द-great.

P. 44. पुरुहूत—*Lit.* 'The many-invoked,' is an epithet of Indra. Indra figures prominently in the Ṛigveda and has the greatest number of hymns addresssed to him. **या—** construe with वसन्तसहायेन निर्मिता इव रराज ( p. 45 ), and translate —'Who shone as if created by the God of love, who, wishing, on account of his longing after Rati, to make a sportive image of her, framed an excellent figure of a woman, and formed its feet out of the beauty of the autumnal lotuses growing in his pleasure-lake' &c. वसन्तसहायेन is put in for Madana; वसन्तः सहायः यस्य; see Kum. IV. 24. As to the idea of Madana creating a female form, comp. अस्याः सर्गविधौ प्रजापतिरभूचन्द्रो नु कान्तप्रभः शृङ्गारैकरसः स्वयं नु मदनो &c. Vik. I. 8. **समुत्सुकतया—** may also be taken with रति; a longing on the part of Rati for a companion when Kâma was not with her. **शालभञ्जिका—**a doll. **नारीविशेषं विरच्य—**The writer had undoubtedly Śâk. II. 9 ( चित्रे निवेश्य परिकल्पितसत्त्वयोगा &c. ) before his mind's eye. The present passage is an amplification of the passage at p. 3 which the student should compare with this. The various parts of a woman's body forming the paraphernalia of Cupid are here described by a reverse process as forming those parts. **लीलालस॰—**graceful and stately ( अलस *lit.* slow ) gait due to sportiveness. **लीलामन्दिर—**A sportive bower ( with two plantain-trees placed in front on either side and forming a gateway ). **लालित्य—**Softness and grace. **जैत्ररथ॰—** By means of the skill displayed in fashioning ( the wheels of ) his victorious car. *Cf.* वृत्तानुपूर्वे च न चातिदीर्घे जङ्घे शुभे सृष्टवतस्तदीये । Kum. I. 35. **घन—**Massive. **किंचिद्विकसत्...कोटरानुकृत्या—**By imitating the cavity of the lotus-bud a little blown and forming his sportive ear-ornament. **परिपाट्या—**In the manner of a flight of steps; परिपाटी is a continuous line, a regular succession. *Cf.* मध्येन सा वेदिविलग्नमध्या वलित्रयं चारु बभार बाला । आरोहणार्थं नवयौवनेन कामस्य सोपानमिव प्रयुक्तम् ॥ Kum. I. 39. **पूर्णकलश—** Two gold ( or sometimes silver ) jars are placed at the door of a *Lîlâmandira* as a mark of auspiciousness.

**अभिख्या—**Beauty. *Cf.* Ragh. I. 46. **प्रतिबिम्बीकृतं—**The *bimba* fruit was a standard of comparison before the creation of her lower lip; now it became an imitation. The meaning is that her lip surpassed the *bimba* in redness. **भ्रमदूतिका—** Kâlidása also speaks of the cuckoo as a messenger of *Káma*. *Cf.* त्यजत मानमलं बत विग्रहैर्न पुनरेति गतं चतुरं वयः । परभृताभिरितीव निवेदिते स्मरमते रमते स्म वधूजनः ॥ Ragh. IX. 47. **जयध्वज॰—**With the *makara* proudly displayed on the flag. प्रथमसुहृद्--his dearest friend.

P. 45. लीलामयूर०--बर्हभङ्गि the wave-like arrangement of feathers, *i. e.* the well-arranged plumage. This shows that her treesses were decked with flowers. Poets compare the tresses of a woman, decked with wreaths of flowers of various colours, with the plumage of a peacock. *Cf.* मृदुपवनविभिन्नो मत्प्रियाया विनाशाद्घनरुचिरकलापो निःसपत्नोऽस्य जातः। Vik. IV. 10. संमित-mixed. समस्त०...कर्पूरपरागेण--Her body ( skin ) was first washed with sandal-juice mixed with all kinds of floral juices and musk, and then polished with camphor-dust; *i. e.* her skin emitted a sweet smell and was of a complexion not perfectly white but white mellowed with yellow. स्वेन--by herself. She was then engaged in worshipping मदन. मदनावेशवती--Love having pervaded or thrilled through her body; or, being powerfully affected by love. क्रीडाविश्रम्भात्—stands for विश्रब्धक्रीडायाः; free sport. कानि कानि—Various and indescribable (emotions). *Cf.* दर्पणे च परिभोगदर्शिनी पृष्ठतः प्रणयिनो निषेदुषः। प्रेक्ष्य बिम्बमनुबिम्बमात्मनः कानि कानि न चकार लज्जया॥ Kum. VIII. 11. घुणाक्षरन्यायेन--quite accidentally. *Lit.* 'according to the maxim of the wood-borer tracing out a letter.' The maxim takes its rise from the fact that a certain insect ( *ghuṇa* ) sometimes makes an incision in wood or a leaf of a book which resembles a letter, but which is quite fortuitous. Hence घुणाक्षर means 'any fortuitous or chance occurrence.' *Cf.* Śiś. III. 58. एवंविध०--एवंविधानां, एवंविधं वा निर्माणं तत्र निपुणः. रेचित--Bent, knit. *Cf.* आरेचितभ्रूचतुरैः कटाक्षैः Kum. III. 5. अपाङ्गवीक्षितैः--side-glances. कुरङ्गस्य &c.--whose beauty captivated her as the net captures the deer. आनायमान is a pres. part. from the denom. from आनाय ( a net ); 'acting like a net.' The word आनाय is derived from आ+नी+घञ् by a special Sútra ( III. 3. 124 ) of Pâṇini, जालमानायः। आनीयन्ते मत्स्यादयोऽनेनेत्यानायः। जालमिति किम्। आनयः। Sid.-Kau. उत्पादितभावरसानां--The emotions and feelings of love produced in her. सामग्र्या—समग्रस्य भावः सामग्र्यं, by adding य (ष्यञ्); सामग्री fem., the य being irregularly dropped before ई. The collection of all the necessaries or implements necessary for a purpose. शरव्यायमाण--a denom. from शरव्य (शरवे हितं शरान् व्ययतीति वा); 'serving as a target for.' Love aff cted him also. भाग्यवतीनां—Because they have the opportunities of gazing on his beauty. पुरंध्री --पुरं ( a family ) धरतीति ( a comp. of the पृषोदरादि class ), a woman with husband and sons living. सीमन्तमौक्तिकी० --is made to stand foremost or at the head of; *lit.*, 'is made the pearl on the parting-line of the hair ( सीमन्त )' etc. This is a च्वि-formation; she was not formerly a सीमन्तमौक्तिक, but is made one on the birth of this son.

P. 46. असूययेव—Through envy, as it were; for she was looking at Râja. who laughed with derision at his beauty. सान्वयं—for he is मन्मथ ( मत: of the mind or consciousness, मथ: tormentor or destroyer). See com. भावविवेकैः--by observing their different feelings. वृत्तन्त—an account. लोकसाधारण--conveying a general sense, or sense as generally understood. देवतासांनिध्यकरणः—Who commands the presence of a deity ( देवतासां० करणं यस्य ); or, who causes a goddess to reveal herself to him, *i. e.* who is able to know things beyond the ken of senses through divine agency. अनुवदन्त्या--Mark the force of अनु. She merely recounts what passed in her mind. संकल्पज--Madana so called because love springs from the constant meditation about a person; 'संकल्पः कर्म मानसम् ।' तेन जायते इति। *Cf.* संकल्पयोनि Kum. III. 24. शस्तेन--excellent; goes with ०निचयेन. शापावसानसमये—At the time the curse ( pronounced by the ascetic ) is about to cease. The reference is explained further on; see p. 60. जातिस्मरत्व—power to remember one's species in a previous life ( also the incidents thereof ). The use of this power is a favourite device of our author, utilized for bringing about love-marriages. कालजनित०—suggested by the occasion. विशेषसूचक—indicative of particular circumstances. ज्ञानं—recollection. कदम्ब—a collection. निद्राधीनमानसं—with his mind in the power of ( *i. e.* unconscious on account of ) slumber. मन्दस्मित &c.--the orb of one of his cheeks blooming with a gentle smile.

P. 47. खण्ड—a collection; here, a bed ( of lotuses ); *cf.* कुमुदवनमपाश्रि श्रीमदम्भोजखण्डं Śiś. XI. 64. अनुष्ठानपरायणतया—being totally devoted to my ascetic practices ( *i. e.* lost in contemplation ). नैष्ठिक—निष्ठा मरणं तत्पर्यन्तं ब्रह्मचारी तिष्ठतीति; fr. निष्ठा + ठक्. A perpetual religious student who observes a vow of life-long celibacy and abstinence, while उपकुर्वाण signifies the opposite, *i. e.* a Brâhmaṇa, who, although observing celibacy during the period of his study, wishes to become a गृहस्थ ( married householder ) in due course. करुणाकृष्टचेताः—With his mind touched with pity. अमोघतया—on account of the efficaciousness or infallibility of. रसेन—रस love; *cf.* p. 13 line 3. अभिज्ञात—recollected. रागपल्लवित—*lit.* her mind putting forth the sprouts of love; swayed or affected by love. संदेश—bidding. दाक्षिण्य—over-courtesy, gallantry; see Śâk. VI. 4. अकार्य—an improper act, a sinful or reprehensible deed. वृक्षवाटिका—( *cf.* Marathi वाडी ) a garden; an avenue of trees. ०न्तरितगात्रं—*Cf.* पौरव...आर्या गौतमीत एवागच्छति तद्विटपान्तरितो भव। Śâk. III. p. 82.

P. 48. राजहंस—(1) a royal swan; (2) name of Râjaváhana's father. This is an unconscious reference, on the part of Avantisundarî, to Râj.'s father. At the time of speaking she did not know who Râj. was or to what family he belonged; the fortuitous double-meaning heightens the charm of the speech. Avanti. addresses the following two sentences apparently to a swan (—and her mother understands them as such—), but really to her lover. अकाण्डे—suddenly, unseasonably. समुचितमिति—Because it is proper for me or behoves me to do so. मनोराग—( 1 ) desire of the mind; ( 2 ) love. She means—'I invite you to see me again.' *Cf.* the similar words addressed by Śakuntalâ to Dushyanta—लतावलय संतापहारक आमन्त्रये त्वां भूयोऽपि परिभोगाय Śâk. p. 83. This is called विप्रलम्भशृङ्गार. It is necessary for the development of love. मरालमिव &c.—The author should not have said this himself but left it to the sense of his readers. परिवृत्त०—This is a device followed by love-stricken maidens; *cf.* आसीद्विवृत्तवदना च विमोचयन्ती &c. Śâk. II. 13. बहुलपक्ष—The dark half of a month. क्षामक्षामा—extremely emaciated. रहस्यमन्दिर—the secret chamber. क्षालित—wetted with ( to render them cooler ). तल्प—a bed. हरिचन्दन &c.—Sanskrit poets usually mention these as the proper appliances for the palliation of love-torment. उशीर—A kind of plant ( Mar. वाळा ) the fragrant root of which has cooling properties. कल्पितानि—prepared for. शीतलोपचरणं—application of the cooling remedies. किंकर्तव्यतामूढा—At a loss to know what to do. ग्लपिताधरया—with her lower lip parched by. नताङ्गी—a woman with stooping limbs. The epithet implies beauty in a woman. सगद्गदं—in faltering accents. कुसुमायुधः ( पञ्चबाणः )—used predicatively. To her his shafts are अयोमय ( made of steel ) and असंख्य; *cf.* with this passage Śâk. III. 3.

**वाडवानल**--The submarine fire. It is also called और्व being produced by the sage Ûrva; *cf.* the Śruti ऊर्वेण किल अयोनिजपुत्रार्थिनोरुर्मथितः । तत्र ज्वालामयः पुरुषो जातस्तस्य च समुद्र आधार आसीत् ।. It is represented as a flame with a horse's head, and is also called Kâkadhvaja from carrying a banner with a crow represented on it; तस्य समुद्राद्दुद्गच्छन्त्या ज्वालया जातबाष्पस्य तत्केतनतुल्यत्वात्तथात्वम्. It is supposed to be at the bottom of the sea and to consume a quantity of sea-water every day, thus keeping the sea within bounds; *cf.* ततस्तं क्रोधजं तात और्वोऽग्निं वरुणालये । उत्ससर्ज स चैवाप उपयुङ्क्ते महोदधौ ॥ २१ ॥ महद्धयशिरो भूत्वा यत्तद्वेदविदो विदुः ॥ २२ ॥ Mah.-Bhá. A'di. Adh. 196. For other particulars see our note on और्व Śák. p. 64

P. 49. पारावारः--See p. 4. दोषाकर--The Moon. Mark the pun on and the propriety of the word--(1) the maker of the night (दोषा); (2) the mine (आकर) of crimes (दोष). निजसहोदर्याः--Because both the Moon and Lakshmî arose from the churned ocean. कमलं--*i. e.* पद्मं, the day-lotus which fades away at the rise of the moon. स्वल्पीभवति--is rarefied. निजयष्टि-The trunk of the parent tree. उल्बणगरल--virulent poison. संक्रलित--infected by. अगदंकार--*Lit.* 'curing one of a disease,' a physician. The nasal (in अगदं) is retained by Pâṇ. VI. 3. 70; see com. मनोजज्वरा०...कोमलाङ्गी--mark the contrast. The fever of love raged fiercest and her delicate frame was too weak to bear it. स्मरणीयां गतिं नेष्यति--is a euphemistic way of saying मारयिष्यति (will kill). कुमारयोः--Ekaśesha Dvandva; see com. समं--equally towards both. तूणीरायमानमानसः--so many arrows were shot into his heart by Kâma that it looked like his quiver. Notice our author's fondness for Denom. pres. participles. अन्वेषणीया--To be sought. निटिलतट०--whose folded hands, graceful like the bud of a lotus, decked her spacious forehead. इतो निषीद--is probably suggested by स वासवेनासनसंनिकृष्टमितो निषीदेति विसृष्टभूमिः । &c. Kum. III. 2.

P. 50. वामनेनेव &c.--The student will remember the well-known line of Kálidâsa, 'प्रांशुलभ्ये फले लोभादुद्बाहुरिव वामनः' Ragh. I. 3. सुभग--properly means 'fortunate;' hence, one indebted to fortune for beauty; hence, handsome, lovely. अभिलषति--supply त्वां, so that the following clause becomes an independent sentence. Or, better still, construe the whole clause त्वं चित्तं कुरु तथा मृदुलम् as an object of अभिलषति--'my heart desires that you should make your heart, too, tender like your body.' A third way, but not so good, is to treat अभिलषति as an intransitive root; 'my mind has अभिलाष (desire, *i.e.* love, for you).' तथा मृदुलं—'so tender' (as thy body is delicate). She hereby hints that his heart is hard. अस्यां क्रियायां &c.—*i. e.* your skill has fostered this love. आलवाल—आ समन्तात् लवं जललवं (particles of water) आलाति (takes, draws); a basin at the root of a tree which by holding water in it brings nourishment to the tree. तदनुरूपं—favourable to it. तद् refers to प्रवेश. संगमिष्यामि—We have the Paras. as the root is used transitively; when used intransitively it is A'tm. *Cf.* समो गम्यृच्छिभ्याम् । Pâṇ. I. 3. 29; अकर्मकाभ्यामित्येव । Sid.-Kau. शिरीषकुसुम०—The Śirîsha flower is frequently referred to by Sanskrit poets as a standard of delicacy; *cf.* शिरीषपुष्पाधिक सौकुमार्यौ बाहू Kum. I. 41; Naish. VIII. 24, &c. विरहविनोदाय—To dispel his longing or the pangs of separation. चकोरलोचना०—For ladies' eyes being compared with those of the *chakora* bird, *cf.* Ragh. VI 59, VII. 25 &c.

P. 51. मन्मथसमाराधनस्थानं—The place where she had worshipped the image of the God of love. विलोकनवेला०—'The residues, *i. e.* memories or mementoes, of the occurrences caused at the time' &c. शेष is what is used by one and then abandoned, marked with signs of its having been used. कर्णेजप—Those who whisper something into the ear, informers, the idea being that cuckoos and other birds inform Madana by their cooings &c. as to who are likely to be his victims. कर्णेजप is an *aluk* comp., according to 'स्तम्बकर्णयो रमिजपोः' Pâṇ. III. 2. 13, and has the sense of सूचक (a secret informer), by the Vârt. हस्तिसूचकयोरिति वक्तव्यम् ।. कीर—brought in simply for alliteration; the parrot is not generally mentioned in Sanskrit literature in connexion with love-matters, although the Sârikâ is so mentioned.

सूक्ष्मचित्रनिवसनः—Clad in thin and variegated raiment. चतुरवेष—sumptuous apparel, beautiful or splendid dress. अभ्युल्लसत्—Throbbing, waving. ऐन्द्रजालिकविद्या—magic. इन्द्रजाल (magic) is explained as इन्द्रस्य परमेश्वरस्य जालं मायेव जालं यत्र; ऐन्द्र० is one who practises इन्द्रजाल. कोविद—adept or versed in. लीलावनि—land of pleasure. निजकार्यकरण—able to be serviceable to them. आभाषणपूर्वतया—*Cf.* संबन्धमाभाषणपूर्वमाहुः Ragh. II. 58, which the author had probably before his mind's eye; *cf.* also Pt. II. śl. 47, IV. śl. 101.

P. 52. रागातिरेक—Intense love. सततसंभोगसिद्धि—attainment of constant enjoyment. मोहयत्—confounding, stupefying

अनिमित्त--causeless, disinterested. कृत्रिमक्रिया--artificial acts, *i. e.* jugglery-feats, magic. विप्रलम्भ--deception, trickery. कृत्रिमप्रेम--counterfeit or unreal love. Or the expression might mean 'who knew the tenderness born of love, caused by separation.' This is better, as remarked by Mr. Agashe, as it would show that Vid. could realize the feelings of Râjavâhana. But in this case we have to take कृत्रिम in the somewhat unusual sense of कृत. रसभाव &c.--well-versed in the mode ( way of action ) and progress of sentiments and feelings; *i. e.* who knew how to rouse the emotion and stir the feelings of his spectators. निजवृत्तान्त--his profession. समुत्सुकावरोध--The ladies of the harem eager to behold the spectacle. कक्षान्तर--another apartment. It might also mean 'an inner apartment,' if we explain the comp. as कक्षाया अन्तरम्. वाद्येषु नदत्सु--As the roll of the drums swelled.

P. 53. समधिकराग--Increased curiosity. पिच्छिकाभ्रमणेषु—The whirls of his magic bundle of peacock's feathers which is a stock article in a magician's equipment. It is believed to possess the special effect of creating illusion in the minds of the spectators, when wielded by a conjuror. Bühler adopts the reading पिच्छिका भ्रमणेषु ( two words ) from Táranátha's ed. And he translates—" And while he together with his attendants was violently ( परिवृढं adv. ) whirling brushes of peacock's feathers in circles. " But this reading is not good. पिच्छिका is here Acc. pl.; but a conjuror waves one bundle only, and that too himself. Again, परिवृढं is to be taken as an adverb, and twisted so as to yield the sense of 'violently.' Mr. Agashe quotes the following gloss on the word पिच्छिका occuring in verse 48 of the Mallikâ-Mâruta, which will be found interesting:—अस्याश्चैन्द्रजालिककरे क्षिप्यमाणायाः प्रेक्षकमनःप्रलोभकत्वं मन्त्रशास्त्रे प्रसिद्धम् । यथोक्तं मन्त्रखण्डे इन्द्रजालेषु श्रीनित्यनाथपादैः—सामुद्रतोयमादाय महाभाण्डे विनिक्षिपेत् । खनेत्तद्भूमिमध्ये तु मासमेकं सुरक्षितम् ॥ तदुद्धृत्य विधानेन कज्जलेन तु पेषयेत् । अङ्कोलस्नेहमिश्रं तु उच्चूलिकरजोयुतम् ॥ कृत्वा तु गुलिकां दिव्यां निक्षिपेत्तां नवे जले । बर्हिपिच्छेन संस्पृश्योल्लोलयेत्तु महानिले ॥ महाध्वनि समायुक्तो वडवानलसंयुतः । दृश्यते भुवनं व्याप्य महावारिनिधिः क्षणात् ॥. रत्नराजिनीरा०—lighting or illumining the expanse of the palace with the array of their gems. नीराजन *n.* ( ०ना *fem.* ) *lit.* means 'waving light before an idol by way of worship.' अहिपतीन्--huge serpents. नरसिंहस्य—The gen. is कर्तरि; 'by Narasimha.'

हिरण्यकशिपु—Son of Kaśyapa and Diti, and a celebrated demon-king. By virtue of a boon from Brahmâ he became so powerful that he usurped the sovereignty of Indra and oppressed the three worlds. On account of his subjecting his son, Pralháda to unmerited cruelties for acknowledging Vishṇu as the supreme deity, he was torn to pieces by that deity in the form of a man-lion. See Bhâg. P. VII. अभिनीय--having exhibited. महदाश्चर्य°--Another example of an ungrammatical comp. °संभावन—Prospect of success in. मोहजनक—stupefying. मायामानवा:—men conjured up by magic. यथायथं—in due order, just as they had appeared. °पायचातुर्य—The skilful use of. वाडव--a Bráhmaṇa.

P. 54. सहचरीवर—The best of her friends. चेष्टा--sweet acts of endearment. उपनयन्--creating or producing. रह:—in private. अनुलाप—her response. लोल—eager, earnestly desirous of. चतुर्दशभुवन°—The reference is to the Paurâṇic number of the *Bhuvanas.* Râjaváhana, in order to foster the feeling of love in her, entertained her with stories of heroes and heroines in the fourteen worlds, being mostly taken from the Purâṇas ( the Mah.-Bhâr. especially ). This is according to the precept of Vátsyâyana—वर्धमानानुरागां च चान्वर्थाभि: कथाभिश्चित्तहारिणीभिश्च रञ्जयेत् Kàma-Sûtra III. 3. 17. The fourteen worlds are made up of the seven celestial regions ( भूर्लोक, भुवर्लोक, स्वर्लोक, महर्लोक, जनर्लोक, तपोलोक, सत्यलोक ) and the seven nether regions ( अतल, वितल, सुतल, रसातल, तलातल, महातल, पाताल ).

विस्मय°—With her eyes dilated through wonder. चरितार्था--has its mission fulfilled. श्रोत्रवृत्ति—The function of the ears.

P. 55. तमोपह—Dispelling ignorance. प्रदीप:—a powerful lamp. प्रत्युपकृतवती—What return can I make for your favour? अभवदीयं—not yours; not your property. सरस्वतीमुख°—सरस्वत्या ( Instr. ) यन्मुखग्रहणं तेन &c. Sarasvatî is represented as a rival of Lakshmî and the two rarely as co-wives of a king; see Ragh. VI. 29. उच्छेषणीकृत:—already used by another. चुम्बयितुं—Pass. inf. of the Cau.; 'to cause it to be kissed' ( by me ). अम्बुजासना°--Lakshmî is supposed to wait on a king who is considered a portion of Vishṇu. She thus indirectly praises Râj. for being the common abode of Sarasvatî and Lakshmî. गुरुपयोधरमण्डल--This is paronamastic; ( 1 ) the orbs of her large breasts; ( 2 ) a large train of clouds.

प्रौढकन्दली--Kandalî (Marathi कर्दळ) has small flowers of red colour; it has leaves similar to but very much smaller than those of Kadalí, or the plaintain-tree. Kâlidâsa too compares a woman's large eye to the leaf of the *Kandalî* flower; *cf.* Vik. IV. 5. रूढराग &c.—(1) Adorned *i. e.* beaming with deep love; (2) tinged *i. e* developed with deep colour. बर्हिबर्हावली—The plumage of a peacock. कुसुमचन्द्रक--in which the flowers interwoven looked like the eyes in a pea-cock's tail. शार--variegated. मधुकर &c.—Thickly beset with a cluster of bees; or 'hanging disorderly like a row of bees', *i. e.* dishevelled and dark (मधुकरकुलवद् व्याकुलेन), if it be objected that as she was in a secluded room bees could not have been actually attracted by the flowers in her braid स्फुरदरुण०—(1) augmented with the stream of its spreading reddish lustre; (2) rough with its filaments resembling the throbbing rays of the morning sun. अधरमणि—his ruby-like lower-lip. अधीरं—impatiently, passionately. स्फुरित—enkindled, excited. चित्रोपचार०--highly pleasing or graceful (शीफर) on account of the various means at hand (or, modes of enjoyment).

P. 56. बिसगुण—A string of lotus-fibres. जालपाद—a swan, so called because it possesses webbed feet. कमलमूढ &c. —as if seized (embraced) by the moon with the strings of rays, mistaking them (his feet) for lotuses. उपगूढ—bound or tied together. उपलभ्य—on perceiving it. विह्वला—agitated; or, beside herself with excessive fear or fright. अग्निपरीतमिव— *i. e.* their fright was as great as when a house is on fire उपहत—possessed by. अनिरूप्यमाण &c.—Not knowing how to act then and in the future. *Cf.* तदात्वायतिसंशुद्धमातिष्ठन्नैति वाच्यताम्। साधु लोकद्वयग्राहि विद्वान्कर्म समाचरेत् ॥ Kam. N. X. 25. अगण्यमान०— not caring for or forgetting the condition to keep the secret intact. विप्रविध्यमान—Throwing or dashing against. आकुलीबभूव —became excited, was thrown into commotion. तुमुले समये— At this time of confusion. अन्तर्वंशिकाः पुरुषाः—The guards of the female apartments; अन्तर्वंशः अभ्यन्तरगृहं तत्र नियुक्ताः पुरुषाः. अनुभाव—majesty, effulgence; see Ragh. I. 37. निशाम्योत्पन्न०— having closely eyed him and recognized him. Distinguish निशाम्य from निशम्य which means 'having heard;' *cf.* न्यशामयं *infra*, p. 65. अत्यभिनिविष्ट—greatly puffed up or inflated with.

P. 57. आवर्जित—won over. आरोपित०—To whom is vainly attributed the prowess of a deity, which is, however, futile, by the silly citizens won over by his skill in the various means of deceiving them. कपटधर्मकञ्चुकः—a religious hypocrite (*lit.* wearing a cloak of false religiousness). *Cf.* क इदानीमन्यो धर्मकञ्चुकप्रवेशिनः तृणच्छन्नकूपोपमस्य तवानुकृतिं प्रतिपत्स्यते । Śâk. V. p. 132. चपलः—A mischief-monger. ब्राह्मणब्रुवः—the despicable Bráhmaṇa. Although Ráj. was really a Kshatriya, Chaṇḍavarmâ knew him to be a Brâh. only as he lived under that designation in Avanti. एनमनुरक्ता—For the Acc. case with the derivatives from अनु+रञ्ज्, see A. G. § 94; and *cf.* Śâk. VI. 19. शूलावतंसित—'exalted to the dignity of the sharp-pointed stake' (*lit.* placed like an अवतंस on the stake, impaled). कुलपांसनी—disgracing or defiling the family. निर्भर्त्सयन्—used for निर्भर्त्सयमानः (A'tm.). दूषित—disfigured, fierce. रेखाम्बुज॰—a Madhyamapad. Comp. See Com. सर्वपौरुषातिभूमिः—'The culminating point of,' *i. e.* who possessed in the highest degree all the manly virtues. सहिष्णुतैकप्रतिक्रिया—for which submission was the only remedy. स्मर तस्या &c.—स्मृ governs the Gen. case. See com., and Páṇ. II. 3. 52. बाला—a young woman; *cf.* Mṛich. I. 18, 41. विदित॰—Separate विदितवार्ता+आर्ता; 'pained or distressed on hearing the account.' आकारपक्ष॰—who were attracted solely by his handsome form. आत्मपरित्यागो॰—Threatening to put an end to their lives. As they were in the palace they at once knew of Chaṇḍ.'s evil intention and thus prevented him from carrying it out immediately. अप्रभुत्वात्—They not being the governing bodies. संदिश्य—informing him by a messenger. सर्वस्वहरण॰—having confiscated all his effects or property. कृत्वा दारुपञ्जरनिबद्धं—Chaṇḍ. should rather have selected an iron cage; perhaps the author makes him select a wooden one in his anxiety that the prince should find it easy to break through it after his feet were unfettered.

P. 58. विलीन—Concealed. चूडामणि—as to the jewel dispelling hunger and thirst, see *supra* p. 28, l. 17. अङ्ग—Name of a country situated on the right bank of the Ganges. Its capital was Champâ, also called Aṅgapurî. This town stood on the Ganges about 24 miles west of a rocky island, and is therefore considered the same as, or situated very near to, the modern Bhâgalpur. भेदयित्वा—having caused a passage to be made in. व्रात—a number of. आपतन्तो—Coming from all sides (आ). अदत्तापेक्षः—Not caring to wait for. साक्षात्, वपुष्मान्—Note that one of these words is pleonastic;

'appearing visibly like pride in a bodily form ( incarnate ).' अक्षमापरीत:—full of impatience or exasperation. प्रहरण—a blow or stroke. वर्मन्—armour. भिन्नमर्मा *v. l.*—is not good, as in that case he could not have been long alive. अतिमानुष०—transcending that of a mortal, superhuman. प्राणबल—vital force, innate strength. ०समाख्यातायां—also named *Abaláratna*, 'the jewel among women.' अकल्यसंध:—whose intentions were not to be divined or comprehended. For this sense of कल् ('to understand') *cf.* अकलितमहिमान: केतनं मङ्गलानां Mál.-Mádh. II. 9; अकलितमहिमानं क्षत्रियैरात्तचापै: Veṇî. V. 40. The reading अकल्प्यसंध: would also mean the same. अजीगणत्—computed. कृतकौतुकमङ्गले—when he had performed the ceremony of fastening the auspicious marriage-string. For the meaning of कौतुक see Ragh. VIII. 1, and Malli. thereon. एकपिङ्गाचल—Kailása. एकपिङ्ग is an epithet of Kubera, who is so called because one of his eyes is yellow. The story is given in Râm. Uttara. 13. Kubera, when once on a visit to Śiva, gazed on Párvatî with his left eye, owing to which it was burnt outright and the right one was turned yellow.

एणजङ्घ—*Lit.* deer-footed; swift-footed. जङ्घाकरिक—a runner, a courier. जङ्घसाध्यत्वादुपचाराद्गतिर्जङ्घा सैव कर: राजदेयो भाग: आकर: श्रेष्ठो वा। जङ्घाकर अस्यास्तीति जङ्घाकरिक:। ठन् ( इक ); जङ्घाकरी हस्ती यस्य इति वा। प्रभवत—The ruling monarch. प्रतिसंदेश—a reply to the message. कन्यान्त:पुरदूषक—The violator of the secret apartment.

P. 59. जराविलुप्त—A double Bahuvrîhi. 'Whose sense of self-respect or insult to one's self is rendered blunt by old age.' चित्रवध—Death with peculiar tortures, such as causing a man to be trampled under an elephant's feet, taking out his eyes &c. *Cf.* तदा स चाणक्यहतकेन विचित्रवधेन व्यापादित: Mudrà. II. p. 63. चारक—a prison. मातङ्गपति—The lordly elephant. उचितकल्पना—proper decorations ( ornaments and dress ). क्रीडनक—a play-thing, *i. e.* allowing the elephant to treat him as a toy and so to crush him down. राजन्यक—a multitude of warriors. क्षरितगण्ड:—with ichor flowing from its temples. तदङ्घ्रि०—तत् refers to Râjaváhana. अनुमहार्द्र—full of, disposed to, favour. सोमरश्मि०—*Cf.* Kád. p. 217, where it is mentioned that the Apsarasas had fourteen families, one of which was born from the rays of the moon.

P. 60. **मुग्ध—Foolish.** The swan mistook her mouth for a lotus and so pursued it; *cf.* the similar pursuit of Śakuntalá by a bee, at Śâk. p. 25. **मन्दोदक**—the name of the lake. **०पलितं**—making his head doubly hoary by &c. **कोऽपि**—अपि is used आक्रोशे; 'he pronounced upon me an unjust curse.' **लोहजाति**—a metallic condition. **अजातचैतन्या**—consciousness being suspended. **अपरिक्षीण०**—my senses retaining their powers.

**वेगवत्, मानसवेग**—Two names probably taken from the **Kathâs.** (no such names being found in the list of the kings of the Ikshváku race). **पितृप्रयुक्तवैरे प्रवर्तमाने**—when the hostilities commenced by his father (Mânasavega) were still proceeding. (Loc. Abs. constr.). Bühler, who explains पितृ० and प्रव० both as adjectives of नरवाहनदत्ते, is not correct, since we know from the Kathás. that it was Mánasavega, and not Nara., who had begun the वैर. *Cf.* अस्त्याषाढपुरं नाम विद्याधरपुरं गिरिः । तत्र वेगवतो राज्ञः पुत्रो विद्याधराधिपः । अस्ति मानसवेगाख्यो राजा भुजबलोद्धतः ॥ मायया-ऽपहृता तेन भ्रात्रा मे दयिता तव । &c. Kathás. XIV. 1. **नरवाहनदत्ते**—Naravâhanadatta, son of King Vatsa, is the hero of the Kathásaritsâgara (and also of the Bṛihatkathâ of Guṇáḍhya) wherein his adventures and his elevation to the throne of the Vidyádharas are related. **समसृज्यत**—entered into an alliance with. संसृज् *lit.* means 'to unite;' *cf.* संसृज्यते सरसिजैररुणांशुभिन्नैः Ragh. V. 69. **व्यवदायमानचन्द्रिके**—As the moon shone brightly. व्यवदायमान is the *prep. p.* of the pass. of दै I. Paras., to purify or to brighten. **मनोरथप्रियतमा**—The beloved of his heart (for he had not actually seen her). **अवशेन्द्रियः**—not having control over his senses. **तिरस्करिणी**—The art with which all the denizens of heaven are endowed and by which they can make themselves invisible to others.

P. 61. **त्वदङ्कापाश्रयां**—with her head reclined on your lap. Or अपाश्रय may have the usual meaning of 'support;' 'resting on your lap.' **०सुप्तगात्रीं**—With her body drooping on account of &c. The reading क्लान्त (for सुप्त) should have been preferred. **यात्रा**—continuity, maintenance. **संबद्धाभिः**—connected with (the creation, maintenance and destruction of the world). **प्रत्यानीयमान &c.**—'In whom the tide of passion was caused to swell again.' What is meant is this—When the prince found Avan. reclined helplessly on his lap, he tried to infuse new life into her and to stir up her passion by telling her tales about &c. This has nothing to do with the **चतुर्दशभुवनवृत्तान्त** mentioned at the close of the last Uchchh., as that was narrated to her on their first meeting in order to gain her confidence and love. ०निग्रहा-न्तरा०—his mental resolve to seize you being precluded by your prowess. दैवदत्तोत्साहः—shows that he was quite cowed down in the prince's presence. पाण्डुलोह—silver, लोह being used in the general sense of 'a metal.' दुष्करकर्मणा—दुष्कराणि (difficult to be performed by others) कर्माणि (deeds of valour) यस्य; '(by a thief) of extraordinary prowess.' नख—nail-shaped scimitar. उद्देश—The precincts or environs of. अचकित०—moving fearlessly or undauntedly. उदस्ताधोरणः—having knocked off the driver. रंहसा उत्तमेन—with utmost speed. स्तम्बेरम—an elephant. This is an *Aluk* comp.; see com. अदभ्र—adj., meaning 'large;' अदभ्राणि अभ्राणि तेषां निर्घोषः तद्वद्गम्भीरेण.

P. 62. असक्तं—(आक्रम्य) without touching it or being entangled; *i. e.* nimbly, dexterously. तत्क्षणोद्व०—having disengaged himself from the clasp or fold of the embrace the very instant. कणप–an iron club. कर्पण–a kind of instrument forked at the end. प्रास–a dart, a barbed missile. पट्टिश—a long double-edged sword (Mar. पट्टा). तोमर–a javelin. परिक्षिपतः—surrounding them. बलनिकाय—a collection or body of armies. कर्णिकार—The *Karṇikára* flower has a rich colour but no smell. *Cf.* वर्णप्रकर्षे सति कर्णिकारं दुनोति निर्गन्धतया स्म चेतः। Kum. III. 28. कुरुविन्द—a sapphire. The Bhûshaṇâ explains कुरुविन्द as a kind of grass (dark-green in colour). कर्णचुम्बि—such an eye is supposed to be a mark of beauty. *Cf.* कामं कर्णान्तविश्रान्ते विशाले तस्य लोचने। Ragh. IV. 13.

P. 63. रत्ननखः—A poniard with its hilt set with jewels. पट्ट—a silk-garment. कृतहस्ततया—being well practised in the use of weapons. The root कृ has frequently the meaning of 'to study,' 'to learn' in older language. पादाङ्गुष्ठ &c.—This bespeaks extraordinary physical power on the part of the rider, as he could guide the animal by using the big toes of his feet as spurs. पूर्वोपदेश०—through his knowledge of the description formerly given. स्त्रीबाल &c.—*Cf.* Ragh. VII. 67. आज्ञाकरः—your slave or servant. सोऽयमहमेव &c.—Your Highness should consider him as my own self, only concealed under this form and the designation of Dhanamitra. अपवर्जित—scattered about, left or abandoned by the enemy, spoil. It does not seem to mean 'bestowed or given,' as stated in Apte's Dic. अस्मद्गृह्य—our allies. गृह्यते वशीक्रियते इति गृह्यः, fr. ग्रह्+य (क्यप्); see Páṇ. III. 1. 119. यदि

न दोष:—If your Highness does not find fault with this arrangement, *i. e.* approves of it. रोहिण—The Banian tree. क्षौम—a white silk-garment.

P. 64. उपहारवर्मा......विश्रुते:—These, together with Râj., Somadatta, Pushpodbhava, and Apahâr., make up the list of the ten Kumâras. प्रहारवर्मा—is the father of Apar. and Upahár. कामपाल–son of Dharmapâla, who afterwards became the king of Kâśî. See p. 137. हर्षाविद्धं–transported with joy. कृतयथोचिता०–who were received with proper civilities. सुहृन्निवेदितान्—introduced by his friends. अपश्यत—looked upon, treated. हर्षक०—पलित properly means 'the greyness of hair brought on by old age;' here, the grey hair. 'With their grey hair bristling through joy.'

असुरविवर—Pàtála; the word occurs in Báṇa's H.-Ch. and also in the Kád. ( p. 227, लग्नासुरविवरप्रवेशापिशाचेन ). प्रसृते—dispersed. दिव्यचक्षु:—divine sight, *i. e.* power to know things beyond the perception of the senses.

P. 65. बुभुत्सु:—wishing to ascertain. Desid. noun in उ from बुध्. न्यशामयम्—शामयति is the Cau. of शम् in the sense of 'to see;' otherwise शमयति. *Cf.* निशाम्य *supra* p. 56. चूतपोतक—a young mango-tree. उद्विग्नवर्ण—with a wild look; or, apparently looking dejected. अतिथिवत्—like a guest. अतिथि is properly one who always travels; fr. अत् to go ( अतति ) and the Unádi aff. इथिन् ; then it means one who does not stay at a place for more than a day; *cf.* एकरात्रं तु निवसन्नातिथिर्ब्राह्मण: स्मृत: । अनित्यं हि स्थितो यस्मात्तस्मादतिथिरुच्यते ॥ Manu. III. 102. Or न विद्यते द्वितीया तिथिर्यस्य. उपलिप्सु: &c.—wishing to learn your honour's whereabouts. वतंसस्थानीया—*Lit.* she who held the place of the ornament of the Anga-capital. The अ of the prepositions अव and अपि may optionally be dropped. See com. स्थानाय हिता स्थानीया, fr. स्थान+ईय ( छ ). वारयुवति—*Lit.* a woman of the multitude ( वार ); or वारलभ्या युवति: a woman that can be had for a day; a harlot. तारकित—तारका: अस्य संजाता: studded with stars; hence, chequered with. कीर्णशिखण्डा०—her long dishevelled tresses sweeping the ground. सानुक्रोशं—अनुक्रोशेन सहितं यथा स्यात्तथा।. This may mean ( 1 ) with feelings of pity; or ( 2 ) full of cries of censure or abuses. अविच्छिन्नपातं—close upon her heels. आर्ति—distress. अभाजन—not destined to enjoy. श्वोवसीय—happiness. श्व आगामि वसीयोऽत्र; fr. श्व: + वसीयस्, compar. of वसु, अ being added at the end of the comp. by श्वसो वसीय:श्रेयस: । Pâṇ. V. 4. 80.

वसुशब्दः प्रशस्तवाची तत ईयसुनि वसीयः । श्वःशब्द उत्तरपदार्थप्रशंसामाशीर्विषयतामाह । मयूरव्यंसकादित्वात्समासः । Sid.-Kau. आर्ताभ्यु०—renowned for their being the asylum of the afflicted. अभ्युपपत्ति properly means अनुग्रह, favouring a person; *cf.* अर्हस्यभ्युपपत्त्या जीवितमस्या अवलम्बितुम् Śâk. III. p. 78. वित्त—famous or known for. For this sense *cf.* तेन वित्तश्चुञ्चुप्चणपौ Pâṇ. V. 2. 26. पलितशार०—First touching the ground with her braided hair interspersed ( *lit.* variegated ) with grey, and then rising up.

P. 66. अस्या मे दोषं &c.—The Com. seems to interpret the line as—'Revered Sir, this ( my daughter ) here, your slave, informs you of my fault.' But it seems better to take दासी as referring to the speaker herself. 'This your slave ( the mother, and not the daughter ) will tell you the fault she ( my daughter ) attributes to me.' In this case it will be better to read अस्यां for अस्याः. स्वाधिकारा०—making her perform the duties of her legitimate profession. स्वाधिकार appears naturally to refer to the speaker ( the mother ), but then we should expect अनुष्ठानं instead of the causal form अनुष्ठापनम्. अधिकार—the sole privilege or proper office of. अङ्गक्रिया—cultivation ( improvement of the colour &c. ) of the body by besmearing it with fragrant cosmetics or rubbing it with oil boiled with turmeric powder. ०संवर्धनेन—'helping the development of;' this qualifies आहारेण. दोषाग्नि—maintaining an equilibrium between the ( three ) humours, ( see Com. ), the gastric fire and the vital fluids. The seven Dhátus are वसासृङ्मांसमेदोऽस्थिमज्जाशुक्राणि धातवः । सप्तैव &c. मितेनाहारेण—with proper viands ( *lit.* with measured food ). उत्सवोत्तरः—characterized by, mostly consisting of; hence, attended with. *Cf.* उत्सवोत्तरा पुरी *infra,* p. 203. अध्यापनं &c.—training her in the erotic science in all its branches. नाट्य—pantomimic art, acting. चित्र—painting. आस्वाद्य—confectionery, culinary art. गन्ध—preparing perfumes. पुष्प—bouquets and garlands. वचनकौशल—Skill in expression. सम्यग्विनयन—training them thoroughly in. शब्द—Grammar. हेतु—logic. समय—astrology. वार्ता०—a general acquaintance with. आजीवज्ञान—The art of earning a livelihood. क्रीडाकौशल—excelling in sportive graces or frolic. सजीवनिर्जीवासु—in games of chance and strife ( such as cock-fights, playing with dice &c. ); see Com. अभ्यन्तरीकरण—giving a proper insight into. अभ्यन्तरकला—See com. वैश्वासिक—friendly. प्रयोगग्रहण—practical knowledge. आदरप्रसाधिता—decorated with great care. स्फीत०—attended by servants gorgeously dressed. प्रसङ्गवती—to be required on an occasion. ग्राह्यवाच:—experts ( *lit.* whose instructions must be followed ).

P. 67. दिङ्मुखेषु—This simply means 'in different places.' शिल्पवित्तकै:—professors of the different arts. कार्तान्तिक—palmists, astrologers. 'Loudly proclaiming her possession of auspicious signs by means of' &c. ( to attract people ). पीठमर्द, विट—parasites, gay companions. विदूषक—the jester. भिक्षुकी—Buddhist or Jain nuns, who are frequently represented in Sanskrit dramas as assisting in love-affairs. *Cf. infra*, p. 85, ll. 16, 17; and the part played in this connexion by Kauśikî in the Mâlav. and by Kámandakî in the Mâl.-Mâdh. समवाय—company, society. माधुर्य—affability or amiableness. प्रभूततमेन शुल्केन—receiving a heavy price. तद्भाव—her blandishments or coquetry. वय:—prime of youth. अर्थशक्ति—His power of wealth, *i. e.* to give money; or, wealth and strength. शौच—honesty (*i. e.* one who would keep his word ). अधिकगुणाय—possessing superior qualities. बहुव्ययपदेशेन—giving out that he has given much. गान्धर्वसमागमेन—Here गान्धर्व means गान्धर्वविवाह, which is one of the eight forms of marriage mentioned by Manu, depending upon the mutual love of the two parties. *Cf.* इच्छयाऽन्योन्यसंयोग: कन्यायाश्च वरस्य च । गान्धर्व: स तु विज्ञेय: । Manu. III. 32. 'By means of, *i. e.* under the pretence that, a *Gândharva* marriage was contracted.' अलाभे &c.—When the desired money is not obtained ( by the means suggested in the last sentence ). कामस्वीकृते—won over by friendship. अधिकरण—the court ( the local Pancháyat ). *Cf.* Bhûshaná quoted in the com. साधनम्—gaining one's object. दुहित्रा एकचारिणीव्रत &c.—making the daughter remain faithful to him. नित्यनैमित्तिक &c.—getting by various artifices what remains of the wealth of lovers (गम्य—loved persons), after it has been expended by daily, occasional, and love-gifts. लुब्धप्रायेण—may also mean 'almost a miser.' But लुब्ध in the next clause does not mean avaricious, as such a man can have no दानशक्ति. विगृह्यासनं—to reject him ( असनं ) after picking a quarrel with him; if we separate विगृह्य आसनं, then the meaning is 'waiting, patiently remaining aloof from him till he comes to terms.' प्रतिहस्तिन्—according to the Com. this means 'the lover of a neighbouring courtesan.' It may, however, mean 'a deputy.' संधुक्षणम्—inciting, *i. e.* stirring or calling into activity the liberality &c. वाक्संतक्षण—sarcastic remarks. लोकोपक्रोशन—taunting in the hearing of others, circulating evil reports among the people. निरोधन—withholding. अन्याभियोग—by accepting another lover. This may also mean 'by getting him accused by others.'

P. 68. अपवाहन—discarding. अनिन्द्य—unobjectionable. इभ्य—wealthy people. इभ्यैः—*v. l.* अन्यैः would perhaps be a better reading. As the reading stands, however, take अनुबद्धार्थानर्थ० as one word. 'Give due consideration to all doubts about the gain or loss to follow.' सज्जता—attendance upon. सङ्ग—irrevocable or permanent attachment. She means that a harlot must show that she loves her lover, but must not be solely attached to him. मातृका—maternal grandmother. विहित—prescribed by. स्वेनैव &c.—indulging her passion at her own expense. अर्थयोग्य—capable of giving wealth. प्रत्याचक्षाणया—repulsing. अहार्यनिश्चया—If she proves firm of resolve; if her resolution cannot be shaken. *Cf.* Kum. V. 8. अनशनेन संस्थास्यते—will starve themselves to death. दुःखाकरः—दुःखाकरोतीति; see com. Or दुःखस्याकरः the mine of, full of. अपवर्ग—final beatitude. प्रकृष्टज्ञान—knowledge of the highest, *i. e.* Brahman; or knowledge of the superior order, *i. e.* Brahmavidyà. कुलधर्मानुष्ठायिन्—one who, while remaining in the house, discharges the duties proper for the family. हिरण्यरेतस्—fire. उदमनायत—Impef. of the Denom. from उन्मनस् ( उन्मनायते becomes agitated or uneasy at heart ). व्यसन०—hardships of.

P. 69. धौतोद्गमनीय—A couple of freshly-washed garments. उद्गमनीय itself means 'a pair of washed garments;' but, as the word धौत is used, here it should be taken to mean 'a pair of garments,' by the Paribhâshá विशिष्टवाचकानां पदानां सति पृथग्विशेषणे विशेष्यमात्रपरत्वम्. शरीरसंस्कार—her toilet, personal decoration. कुसुमो०—gathering flowers and collecting them into a heap. उच्चय–plucking flowers from the trees; अवचय—gathering those dropped on the ground; this is according to Bhûshaṇá. According to Páṇini ( हस्तादाने चेरस्तेये ), when flowers are plucked by the hand, *i. e.* are within reach, °चाय is the form used except when theft is meant. So अवचय ought to mean 'the collection of flowers out of reach knocked down by means of a stick' or so; हस्तादाने इत्यनेन प्रत्यासत्तिरादेयस्य लक्ष्यते । पुष्पप्रचायः । हस्तादाने किम् । वृक्षाग्रस्थितानां पुष्पाणां यष्ट्या प्रचयं करोति । Sid.-Kau. But writers do not seem to observe such rigid distinctions. नैक०—न एके विकल्पा येषां, of different sorts, or differently arranged. कामशासन—

Śiva. त्रिवर्ग—The three objects of human pursuit, *viz.* Dharma, Atrha and Kâma. अनुरूपैः—carried on in accordance with her ability. रक्त—affected by passion. गणयति-matches with. Dharma ought to be regarded as of supreme importance; Artha and Káma must be subordinate to it; *i. e.*, the latter two must be secured in such a way as not to violate the principles of the first. केनांशेन—in what degree. लज्जा०—लज्जया मन्थरं यथा स्यात्तथा in a manner slow on account of bashfulness. इतः जनात् —'from a person like myself.' This must be read with a *Káku* (a change or modulation of voice so as to indicate a question)· बलाबल—their respective strength or weakness, *i. e.* superiority or inferiority; their being of greater or less importance. अनुत्पत्तिरेव-for धर्म is the root of all. Unless founded on Dharma, Artha and Káma cannot have lasting existence. *Cf.* त्रिवर्गोऽयं धर्ममूलो नरेन्द्र राज्यं चेदं धर्ममूलं वदन्ति। Mah.-Bhár. तदनपेक्षः—अविद्यमाना अपेक्षा यस्यासौ अनपेक्षः, तयोः अनपेक्षस्तदनपेक्षः, irrespective of the other two; not standing in need of the support of the other two. धर्मः—here धर्म is used in the sense of निवृत्तिलक्षण or that which leads to the attainment of Moksha, and for which contemplation is necessary. आत्मसमाधान०--आत्मसमाधानं concentration of the mind एव आत्मसमाधानमात्रं तेन साध्यः. आत्मसमाधान may also mean a 'a composed or serene state of the soul.' नात्यायतते--does not much depend on (external agents). तत्त्वदर्शन--knowledge of the reality, which according to the Vedânta consists in realizing the identity of the universal and the individual souls. उपबृंहित--supported.

P. 70. बाध्यते--is affected by or interfered with. प्रतिसमाहितः--counteracted, recovered. निर्हृत्य--eradicating. तथा हि--Now she shows how Dharma, though a little affected by Kâma, finally gained its ascendancy over the other two.

पितामहस्य तिलो०—पितामह is Brahmà. It is difficult to see to what account Daṇḍin refers here. The story of Tilottamá is given in Mahá. A'dip. 231. The gods, oppressed by the demons Sunda and Upasunda, approached Brahmá for redress. He commanded Viśvakarman to create a matchless beauty that would bring about the destruction of the demons. This was तिलोत्तमा. As she started on her mission, she went round the gods, when she appeared so fascinating that all the hosts of gods, Śiva and Indra included, and sages, remained gazing upon her, except Brahmà. *Cf.* तिलं तिलं समानीय रत्नानां यद्विनिर्मिता। तिलोत्तमेति तत्तस्या नाम चक्रे पितामहः।......कुर्वत्यां तु तदा तत्र मण्डलं तत्प्रदक्षिणम्। इन्द्रः

स्थाणुश्च भगवान् धैर्येण तु परिच्युतौ ॥ &c. So this could not have been the story referredt o by our author. भवानीपतेः—"It is said that S'iva once visited a forest in the form of a religious mendicant, and the wives of the Ṛishis residing there fell in love with his great beauty, which the Ṛishis, perceiving, resented; in order, therefore, to overpower him, they first dug a pit, and by magical arts caused a tiger to rush out of it, whom he slew, and taking his skin wore it as a garment."—Dowson.

पद्मनाभस्य—*i. e.* Kṛishṇa, the son of Vasudeva and Devakî, and considered as the eighth incarnation of Vishṇu. He had sixteen thousand wives. See Bhâg.-P. X. 59. 33; 69. 8, 44.

प्रजापतेः स्वदुहितरि—*i. e.* सरस्वत्यां; she is identical with संध्या; *cf.* गायत्री नाम पूर्वाह्णे सावित्री मध्यमे दिने । सरस्वती च सायाह्ने सैव संध्या त्रिधा स्मृता ॥. The story is thus related—Brahmá saw his daughter, Samdhyá, of exquisite beauty, and being incestuously disposed towards her, tried to approach her, Ashamed of her father's conduct she became a doe; upon this Brahmá also became a male deer and followed her. Śiva, seeing this, shot an arrow at him, whereupon Brahmá, shorn of his head, stood in the sky in the form of the constellation Mṛigaśiras or Orion, while the arrow of S'iva remained as the constellation A'rdrâ. *Cf.* Mahimnastotra śl. 22; *cf.* also Káliká-P.—ब्रह्माऽपि तनयां संध्यां दृष्ट्वा पूर्वमथात्मनः । कामायाशु मनश्चक्रे त्यक्त्वा बुद्धिं सुतेति वै ॥ तस्याश्च चलितं चित्तं कामबाणविलोडितम् । ऋषीणां पश्यतां तेषां मानसानां महात्मनाम् ॥ &c. See our note on Kum. IV. 41. Samdhyá or evening twilight is the daughter of Brahmá. Kumárila-bhaṭṭa explains away the fable by saying that Brahmâ is the Sun, while संध्या is his daughter Aruṇa ( the Dawn). प्रजापतिस्तावत्प्रजापालनाधिकारादादित्य एव उच्यते । स चारुणोदयवेलायामुषस्युदयन्नभ्येति । सा तदागमनादेवोपजायते इति तद्दुहितृत्वेन व्यपदिश्यते । तस्यां चारुणकिरणाख्यबीजनिक्षेपात्स्त्रीपुरुषसंभोगवदुपचारः इति ।

अहल्याजारता—According to the Purâṇas Indra seduced Ahalyâ, the wife of Gautama. One version of the Râmâyaṇa represents that she knew the god, but being flattered by his condscension yielded to his desire; but another version states that the god assumed the form of her husband and entered the dwelling while Gautama had gone out for ablution, and so deceived her. According to another story Indra secured the help of the Moon who assumed the form of a crow and crowed at midnight. This roused Gautama to his morning devotions, when Indra went in and took his place. Gautama, when he knew of her seduction, cursed her to be a stone and remain invisible until she should be touched by the feet of Ráma the son of Daśaratha and be restored to her former shape. The Vedic version of the story, however, represents Indra as the sun and Ahalyâ as the personification of the early morning. Kumârilabhaṭṭa explains the seduction by Indra's ( the Sun's) gradually carrying away the shades of the night ( अहल्या ) एवं समस्ततेजाः परमेश्वरत्वनिमित्त इन्द्रशब्दवाच्यः सविता एवाहनि लीयमानाया रात्रेरहल्याशब्दवाच्यायाः क्षयात्मकजरणहेतुत्वात् जीर्यत्यस्मादनेन वोदितेनेति अहल्याजारः, न परस्त्रीव्यवहारात् । Tantravárttika.

**शशाङ्कस्य**—The Moon or Soma performed the Râjasûya sacrifice, and became in consequence so arrogant and licentious that he carried off Târâ, the wife of Bṛihaspati, and refused to give her up either at the entreaties of her husband or at the command of Brahmá. A fight ensued, in which Soma had his body cut into two by Śiva's trident. At length Brahmâ interposed, stopped the fight and compelled Soma to restore Târâ to her husband. The result of the intrigue was the birth of Budha, the progenitor of the lunar race. See Vishṇu-P. IV. 6.

**वडवालङ्घनम्**—Saṃjñá ( संज्ञा ) the daughter of Viśvakarman and wife of Sûrya ( the Sun ), not being able to bear her husband's effulgence, gave him Chháyâ (shade) for a handmaid and herself retired to the forest to devote herself to religion. While thus engaged and in the form of a mare, the Sun saw her and approached her in the form of a horse, the result of their union being the two Aśvins. According to another account, Saṃjñâ, not getting permission from her husband to go to her father's house, created, by her superhuman power, a woman exactly like herself ( who was as it were her shadow and therefore called छाया ), and putting her in her own place went away. Chhâyá bore to the Sun three children and lived quite happily with him, so that when Saṃjñâ returned he refused to take her back. Thus repudiated and disappointed, she assumed the form of a mare and roamed over the earth. The Sun, however, on knowing the real state of things, sought his real wife whom he found in the form of a mare. He accordingly assumed the form of a horse and was united with her who bore him two sons, the Aśvinîkumáras.

अनिल—Váyu. केसरिकलत्र—This was Añjaná, the mother of Hanûmat. She was the heavenly nymph Puñjikasthalî born on earth owing to a curse. Once, as she was sitting on the summit of a mountain, assuming a human form of exquisite beauty, her garment was slightly displaced, and the god of wind, being enamoured of her, appeared before her in a visible form and expressed his desire for her. She accepted his suit on condition that her chastity sould remain inviolate. This the god granted and blessed her with a son who was his equal in power, and who came to be called 'Mâruti' after him. उतथ्य—Son of Añgiras and elder brother of Bṛihaspati and Saṃvarta. Bṛihaspati was father of Bharadvâja, by Mamatâ, the wife of Utathya. While Mamatâ was pregnant, Bṛihaspati approached her with a carnal desire. She protested, telling him that she was pregnant, but Bṛihaspati violated her. Even the child in the womb protested against such unnatural conduct, but Bṛihaspati getting angry cursed the child to enter permanent darkness. The child was therefore born blind and was called Dîrghatamas.

दाशकन्या—Satyavatî. The sage Parâśara saw her as she was plying her father's boat across the river Yamuná when she was quite a girl, and became enamoured of her. She yielded to his wishes on condition that her virginity should not be violated and thus became the mother of Vyâsa. See Mahâbh. A'dip. 64.

पाराशर्यस्य—Of Vyâsa. भ्रातृदाराः—The wives of Vichitravîrya, Ambikâ and Ambáliká. As Vichitravîrya died childless, Satyavatî called on Vyâsa to raise up issue to his half-brother; Dhṛitaráshṭra, Páṇḍu and Vidura were born as the result of the request. अत्रेः—Atri was a celebrated sage and author of many Vedic hymns. In the Svâyambhava Manvantara, he appears as one of the ten Prajâpatis. At the beginning of the present Manvantara he was born from the flames of Agni. Anasûyâ was his wife in both the lives. In the first she bore him three sons, Datta, Durvâsas and Soma. See Apte's Dic. सुरा०—We do not know to what incident in Atri's life the author refers here.

आसुरविप्रलम्भनानि—*Lit*. deceitful or evil practices worthy of demons; hence, unworthy acts. Or it may mean 'the deceivings of or deceits practised on the Asuras,' such as Vishṇu's deceiving Bali in his Vâmanâvatâra or depriving the gods by a trick of their share of Amṛita. धर्मपीडा &c.—do not affect or constrain. रजः—( 1 ) the quality of that name; ( 2 ) dust. उदीर्ण०—With his passion inflamed or augmented. *Cf.* उदीर्णरागप्रतिरोधकं जनैः &c. Śiś. I. 31. न धर्म उपरुध्यते—Their piety is not affected or impaired. किंरूपौ &c.—what are their natures, their attending circumstances or concomitants &c. He thus indirectly asks her to explain these to him.

P. 71. पाशुपाल्य—Tending cattle. तीर्थ—worthy objects; *cf.* वित्तस्य पात्रे व्ययः ।. कामस्तु—By Kâma she means शृङ्गार which has रति or love for its स्थायिभाव, man and woman for its substratum ( आलम्बन ), and favourable place, time, &c. (अभिमतदेशकालादि) for its उद्दीपन or excitants. स्त्रीपुंसौ—Note the comp.; see com. यावद्—All that. परस्परविमर्द—close contact with each other; hence, mutual satisfaction. स्मर्यमाणमधुरं—of delightful recollection. अनुत्तम—supreme. उदीरिताभिमानं—By अभिमान the Bhûshaṇá understands सार्थक्यबुद्धि, in which one feels that one has obtained the object of existence. But it seems better to take अभिमान to mean 'jealous anger,' उदीरितः ejected, cast aside अभिमानः यस्मिन्. *Cf.* the meaning of उद्धृत्य *infra* p. 72; also त्यजत मानमलं बत विग्रहैर्न पुनरेति गतं चतुरं वयः। परभृताभिरितीव निवेदिते स्मरमते रमते स्म वधूजनः ॥ Ragh. IX. 47. विशिष्टस्थान—*i. e.* holy places. नियतिबलात्—It may be, through the power of fate. बुद्धिमान्द्य—mental infirmity. सुदूरं—To a great degree, very much. मञ्जु—beautiful. दूयमानं—feeling uneasy or uncomfortable.

P. 72. उदजिहीत—'rose up'. Imperf. 3rd pers. sing. of हा to go. परिबर्ह—retinue स्वार्थः &c.—You should mind (return to) your holy task. उद्भ्राम्य—being greatly agitated or bewildered. संघर्ष—a conflict or contest ( for superiority ). आवर्जितवतीव—as if you have won the affection of or subdued. दास्य०—on condition that the vanquished should be the servant of the other. कृतानुशयः—mortified, full of repentance. शून्यवत्—like one vacant-minded. स्वशक्ति०—generated or excited by her power.

P. 73. स्वस्वार्थ०—*scil.* Apahâravarman's object. तमस्तम०—The darkness of ignorance which once more fell off from (*i. e.* left) his mind. The style here approaches Bâṇa's. राग—mark the pun on राग which means (1) passion ; (2) redness. तत्कथा—*i. e.* the Muni's ( Marîchi's ) tale. वैराग्याणि—वैराग्य also has a double meaning—( 1 ) the loss of राग or bright colour ( विगतो रागः येषां तानि विरागाणि तेषां भावः वैराग्यं ); and

(2) passionless state or disgust for worldly pleasures. अनुशय्य—having slept after he had gone to bed. दावकल्पे—The reddish orb of the morning sun is compared to a wild fire on the summit of the rising mountain. अवधीरिणि—*i. e.* surpassing in redness. अरुणार्चिषि—अरुणाः अर्चिषः यस्य of red rays; *i. e.* the morning red sun. उदचलम्—The root चर् with उद् is Âtm. when used transitively, not otherwise; see Pâṇ. I. 3. 53. क्षपणकविहारः—a convent of Jaina mendicants. The Com. says सौगतावासस्य, but further on it is said to be a जैनायतन (p. 75, l. 2). अस्पृष्टसमाधि—who had not yet taken to asceticism; for this sense of *Samádhi*, *cf.* अस्त्येतदन्यसमाधिभीरुत्वं देवानां Śák. I. p. 31; Kum. V. 45. Or समाधि may mean 'abstract contemplation,' which is the last of the eight stages in the practice of Yoga. आधिक्षीण—reduced by mental worry or anxiety. अनभिरूप—ugly. कृपणवर्ण—miserable-looking. शिथिलित०—'with the dirt of the body loosened;' this shows that he was very dirty. क्व...क्व—shows the great disparity between the two.

P. 74. प्रसिद्धि०—I came to be known by the nickname of. कलागुणैः समृद्धः—accomplished, highly skilled in the different arts. पौरधूर्त—the rogues among the citizens. ०व्यतिकर—bandying reproachful words, mutual abusing. पुंस्त्वमूलं—The test of manliness. सुभगपताका—The banner of being fortunate (as being declared the more handsome of the two). Or सुभग may be taken in the sense of सौभाग्य ( भावप्रधानो निर्देशः ), which means 'the state of being loved by women.' व्यवास्थापयन्—settled, determined. स्मरोन्मादहेतु—The cause of inflaming her passion. अपाङ्गदाम—*lit.* a string, *i. e.* a succession of side-glances. The comparison of glances, cast by ladies having dark-blue eyes, to a garland of blue lotuses is by no means rare. *Cf.* अविरलमिव दाम्ना पौण्डरीकेण नद्धः Mál.-Mádh. III. 16 ; मदयन्तिकामकरन्दयोः दलितनीलोत्पलदामसदृक्षाः कटाक्षविक्षेपाः । *Ibid.* IV. p. 86 &c. सुभगंमन्येन—see com.; 'I who considered myself blessed.' By आत्ममाने खश्च । Páṇ. III. 2. 83, मन् takes खश् or णिनि in the sense of 'one considering oneself as' ( स्वकर्मके मनने वर्तमानान्मन्यतेः सुपि खश् चात् णिनिः । पण्डितमात्मानं मन्यते पण्डितंमन्यः पण्डितमानी । Sid.-Kau. ). मल्लकशेषः—With a strip of cloth only remaining to me for covering the privities ; *i.e.*, reduced to utter penury.

P. 75. अपवाहितः—driven off, discarded. प्रपद्य ०लक्ष्यतां—having reached the state of being the target of; having become the laughing-stock of the people or the butt of public ridicule. जैनायतने—A convent of the Jainas proper (and not Buddhistic mendicants who are also sometimes called Jainas, from जिन a name of Buddha). The Jainas are mainly divided into two classes, the Śvetámbaras and the Digambaras ('who have the directions for their clothing,' *i. e.* who move about in a state of nudity). प्रकीर्ण०—Because the Buddhist and Jaina mendicants are forbidden to attend to bodily comforts and so they do not much care to cleanse their bodies. प्रबल &c.—प्रबला केशलुञ्चनव्यथा यस्य. This *kes'aluñchana* (pulling out the hair) forms a part of the initiatory ceremony when a man becomes a Jaina Bhikshu. It is common to both the sects; *cf.* लुञ्चिताः पिच्छिकाहस्ताः पाणिपात्रा दिगम्बराः । ऊर्ध्वाशिनो गृहे दातुर्द्वितीयाः स्युर्जिनर्षयः ॥. See सर्वदर्शनसंग्रह, आर्हतदर्शन. नवग्रहः—Newly caught (and not broken in yet). यन्त्रणा—restraint. द्विजातिः—here, a Vais'ya. पाखण्ड०—The Jainas (as not recognizing the authority of the Vedas) are called पाखण्डs or heretics. विहित—established, laid down. अपवाद-blasphemy. प्रेत्य—after death. निरयः—निर्गतः अयात् (अयः शुभावहो विधिः) इति निरयः ; hell. प्रत्याकलित—having realized to myself. दुर्नयः—deviation from the proper path. पिण्डी—the Aśoka tree. पर्यस्तं &c.—I give free vent to my tears.

P. 76. लुब्धसमृद्धपूर्ण—Abounding in misers and wealthy people, the miserly wealthy ; construe पुरं लुब्धस०प्रायमिति उपलभ्य. अर्थानां &c.—Wishing to restore them to their primitive natures by proving to them the transitoriness of property (which he would do by robbing the one class of what they had earned by unjust means and the other of what they coveted so fondly). अमून्—this is faulty grammar; अमून् stands for लुब्धसमृद्धान्, but it does not directly refer to them. कर्णीसुत०—*Lit.* the track first beaten by Karṇîsuta ; *i. e.* I resolved to take to the life of a robber. कर्णीसुत is Mûladeva, also known as कलाङ्कुर (*cf.* कलाङ्कुरा इव विदितनगरमण्डनाः—Vâsavadattâ of Subandhu) and मूलभद्र ; he is regarded as the founder of the art of thieving. He is referred to by Śúdraka in his Mṛich. and by Bâṇa in his Kâd.—कर्णीसुतकथेव संनिहितविपुलाचला; see our note on this. He is thus described by Kshemendra in his Kalâvilâsa-तत्राभूदभिभूतप्रभूतमायानिकायशतधूर्तः । सकलकलानिलयानां धुर्यः श्रीमूलदेवाख्यः ॥. अक्षधूर्त—अक्षेषु धूर्ताः अक्षधूर्ताः; those skilled at dice-throw. अक्षभूमि—is the chequered cloth on which the wooden pieces are placed. हस्त—skill (in using the hand) got by practice; skill in cogging dice and shifting a piece. कूटकर्माणि—tricks (to secure a favourable throw). संरम्भविचेष्टितानि—desperate acts. सभिक—सभा द्यूतमाश्रयत्वेनास्यास्तीति; fr. सभा + इक (ठन्) which is added to words of the व्रीह्यादि group. सभिक means 'the president of gamesters,' or the keeper of a gambling house. Transactions done with his knowledge or sanction were held to be legal. See Mṛich p. 46 and our note on the word. ०प्रत्यय-व्यवहारान्—transactions begun with the knowledge of. न्यायबल &c.—'Consisting chiefly in the employment of reasoning, force and boldness.' (Bühler). अङ्गीकृतार्थ०—In which the wagers or stakes could be enforced. बलिषु सान्त्वनानि &c.—To wheedle the strong and bully the weak. पक्षरचना—creation of partisans. उच्चावचानि &c.—proffering or holding forth all sorts of tempting advantages. उदक् च अवाक् च उच्चावचं, *lit.* great and small, high and low. ग्लह—a stake or bet. प्रभेद—may mean 'different ways of,' or 'the breaking of.' द्रव्यसंविभाग—distributing the spoil किंचित्प्रमाद०—Who was somewhat careless in casting the dice; or, who made a blunder in moving a piece. अशिक्षितः—not well-trained; *i. e.* a novice in the art. व्यत्यषजत्—began to play with me. व्यतिषञ्ज् means 'to be mutually connected;' *cf.* for this sense व्यतिषजति पदार्थानान्तरः कोऽपि हेतुः Uttar. VI. 12.

P. 77. तदर्धं—According to law the Sabhika was entitled to 5 p. c. of the money won at gambling when the amount exceeded one hundred; when below that he was to get 10 p. c.; see Yâj. II 199. Apahâr. gave the Sabhika half the amount to please him, and to impress his mind with his nobility of heart. प्रार्थयमान &c.—is a faulty comp. अत्युदारमभ्यवहारविधिं—a splendid feast. यन्मूलः—on whose account. दुरोदर—दुष्टमासमन्तादुदरं यस्य; gambling. सारतः—As regards their wealth. अर्धोरुक—a garment reaching half down to the thighs; an upper-garment, a veil. कौक्षेयकः—कुक्षौ भवः, a sword hanging by the arm. फणिमुख—a scoop, an instrument for digging. काकली—According to the Com.—'scissors;' according to the Bhûshaṇâ—'a whistle,' a musical instrument with a low tone used by thieves to ascertain whether persons are asleep or not. संदंशक—tongs. पुरुषशीर्षक—a sham head (to be inserted into the hole made in a wall). योगचूर्ण—magic powder; the same as the योगरोचना used by शर्विलक in the Mṛich.; for its properties *cf.* अनया हि समालब्धं न मां द्रक्ष्यन्ति रक्षिणः। शस्त्रं च पतितं गात्रे रुजं नोत्पादयिष्यति॥ Mṛich. III. 15.

योगवर्तिका—a magic wick. See com. मानसूत्र—a measuring thread. कर्कटक—a wrench; a crab-shaped instrument. Wilson takes it to mean 'a hook (shaped like a crab)' and connects it with रज्जु; 'a rope with a hook at the end by which to climb up.' भ्रमरकरण्डक—a box containing a beetle or bee to put out a light. उपकरण--implement. लुब्धेश्वर—a great miser, or लुब्धश्चासौ ईश्वरश्च an avaricious, rich man. संधिं छित्वा--removing the bricks, *i. e.* making an opening in the wall. पटभास—the interstices in a lattice-window. This may mean—'he saw through the hole of a lattice-window.' Or rather, 'making at first a hole in the wall of the size of &c.' According to the Bhúshaṇá (which reads पटभाक्ष), this means 'an optical instrument.' ०प्रवृत्ति—the state of things inside. नीवी—The money-box. It appears from the succeeding events that it was not a big box, but a purse containing costly jewels or ornaments. शतह्रदा—lightning; शतं ह्रदाः rays यस्यां or शतं ह्रदाः अव्यक्तशब्दाः यस्याः; a comp. of the पृषोदरादि class. नगरमोष--The theft committed in the city. निःसंबाधवेला—a time when the streets were not crowded. उन्मिषत्—glittering in the darkness.

P. 78. त्रासगद्गदं—in faltering accents through fear. अर्यवर्यः—The prince of merchants. अर्यः is fr. ऋ 1 P. to go, + य (यत्); ऋ takes यत् in the sense of 'a master or Vaiśya;' otherwise it will take ण्यत्; as आर्यः ब्राह्मणः. अन्वजानात्—consented to give in marriage, betrothed. स पुनः—सः goes with मे पिता. दरिद्राति—Loc. Abs. श्लाघ्यनामन्—The praiseworthy epithet. वरयत्येव तस्मिन्—When he was quite willing to marry me. सार्थवाह—the leader of merchants trading with foreign countries. ०दत्तसंकेता—See com.; also, प्रियतमाय दत्तः संकेतो यया, 'having given an intimation to.' मन्मथाभिसरा-guided by Cupid. अभिसरामि—simply means 'go to;' it has not got here its technical sense of 'going for enjoyment.' *Cf.* Bhûshaṇâ—नेयमभिसारिका। तादृशरतिसुखेच्छयाऽभिसरणाभावात्। 'रतार्थिनी तु संकेतं याति या साऽभिसारिका' इति रसरत्नहारः।. भाण्डं—a collection of ornaments. नागरिकबल—a party of policemen, the city watch. मृदुः—gentle, happy. वयमिमां—Here वयं stands for आवां; see com. which quotes Pâṇ. I. 2. 59. एकत्वे द्वित्वे च विवक्षिते अस्मदो बहुवचनं वा स्यात्। वयं ब्रूमः। पक्षे अहं ब्रवीमि, आवां ब्रूवः, इति वा। Sid.-Kau. भावित०—affected with the pangs of venom spreading through my body. दर्वीकर—a snake. दर्वी दर्व्याकारः फणा एव करो यस्य प्रहारसाधनत्वात्। दर्वीं फणां करोति इति वा।

P. 79. बाष्पदुर्दिनाक्षी—Her eyes shedding a profusion of tears. नरेन्द्राभिमानी— Proud of his being an adept in poison-treatment. मुद्रा—a particular shape given to the forehand by intertwining the fingers, at the time of worshipping, or propitiating a deity, &c.; *cf.* योजनात्सर्वदेवानां द्रावणात्पापसंहतेः। तस्मान्मुद्रेति सा ख्याता सर्वकामार्थसाधनी ॥ इति तन्त्रसारः. This had the same effect as the magnetic passes of modern hypnotism have. तन्त्र—magical and mysterious formularies for the propitia tion of deities or the attainment of superhuman power (as opposed to the repetition of spells). उपक्रम्य—having treated me. अकृतार्थ—being unsuccessful. कालदष्ट—bitten by Death or by a deadly snake. स्तब्धश्याव—stiff and darkened. स्तब्ध—fixed, glazed. अतिवर्तते—goes beyond, opposes.

॰पाटितध्वान्त॰—which pierced the darkness by the stream of its splendour. वाक्पुनः &c.—Mark the play on the words दत्ता and अपहृता. 'You have given me my beloved, but deprived me of the power of speech;' *i. e.* I am so much overwhelmed with satisfaction and wonder at this your conduct that I can find no words to express myself. According to the Bhushaṇâ the rhetorical figure is परिवृत्ति here. स्वस्कर्म &c.—There seems to be some confusion here in the text. The न after इदं found in many editions and adopted by Bühler* does not yield a good sense. The Bhûshaṇâ also seems to read the same. We adopt the reading ननु for न, reading—वक्तुम् ।...अद्भुतमिति । इदं ननु ते &c. Now Udâraka explains how he is unable to express himself; he proposes one explanation which ends with इति; but the next clause shows the impropriety of this. This constitutes the rhetorical figure आक्षेप. Thus he says—'(If I were to say) this your act (*viz.* your escorting this damsel to me and restoring the ornaments) is wonderful (then it might be urged) that your character, indeed, appears to be marvellous; and so there is nothing extraordinary in this; it is a thing that can be naturally expected from such a person.' प्रतिनियतैव वस्तु॰—He means that each individual is made of different stuff, and therefore exhibits only those qualities which are peculiar to

* "For, I do not know how to describe this wonderful deed of yours. (If I were to say, 'This deed ) is not in keeping with your character, it appears marvellous, no other (thief) has acted thus before you,' (it might be objected) that the power of things &c." (Bühler's tr.). Here the आक्षेप is not properly brought out.

or inherent in its nature. So others in whom covetousness and such other vices are found may not do it. But in you, they are absent; so there is no point in saying that no one else has done so.

P. 80. त्वयाऽद्य &c.—(If I were to say)—'To-day you have shown what saintly character is, that would not do; since most your previous acts must have been of such nature (and so I might offend you).' Bühler translates—"If I were to say-'You have shown yourself to-day a saint', (that description would be wrong because) it does not agree with your acts performed in former births, *i.e.* your generosity shows that in former births you must have performed many meritorious acts; because you could not act so generously if you had not done so; hence you cannot be said to have begun a course of saintliness *to-day.*" But this is far-fetched.

त्वदाशयं &c.—'It will not be reasonable to arrive at such a decision without having correctly estimated (or, formed a proper notion about) your noble nature (for you might have done nobler acts previously).' आशय may also mean 'opinion.' असारं—something worthless or unsubstantial, *i. e.* his own self. अतिगरीयसा—by a heavy price (obligation). इति स ते प्रज्ञा०—It will be an insult to your high mental powers (for it would mean you do not know how to make a purchase). तदलाभे—had I not obtained my beloved (this body should have perished). So त्वयैव दत्तं—my body is virtually a gift from you. प्राप्तरूपं—excellent for the occasion; fit for me to say. See com. प्रतिपत्तिः—course, way of action; 'what course of conduct do you mean to adopt now?' जिहासामि—I wish to leave स्वदेश: &c.—*Cf.* को वीरस्य मनस्विनः स्वविषयः को वा विदेशस्तथा। Hit. I प्रत्यवायभूयिष्ठ—beset with dangers. शैथिल्य—deficiency. Such an abandonment of the native place bespeaks something like want of talent and spirit (mental calibre), on one's part. अविचारानुमतेन = अविचारकृतमनुमतं यस्य तेन ; an awkward comp., if not positively wrong; 'who assented without any more thought,' *i. e.* readily. अपसर्पभूतया—Who served as our spy or guide. मृद्भाण्डावशेषं—Leaving (*i.e.* everything except) the earthen vessels. नागरिकसंपाते—as we encountered a party of the town-police.

P. 81. ग्रैवेय—ग्रीवायां भवं ग्रैवेयं by adding ढञ् (एय) to ग्रीवा; the neck-chain. पातित०—Who stooped to strike a slanting blow with his tusk on the broad chest of the driver that was thrown down. For परिणत see com.; and *cf* वप्रक्रीडापरिणतगजप्रेक्षणीयं ददर्श

Megh. I. 2; also Śiś. IV. 29, Kir. VI. 7. पुरीतत्—An intestine near the heart. 'With his tusk encircled with his entrails.' अक्षिणोत्—destroyed (the city-guard). शाखामाहिक्रया—by catching hold of the branches of a tree (and holding to them till the animal passed on).

पद्मरागशृङ्ग—A peak formed of rubies. Dissolve उदयाचलेन्द्रस्य पद्मराग॰. आपीड—a cluster. पतङ्ग—the sun. प्रगेतन—to be performed in the morning. तन is added to adverbs of time such as सायं (*cf.* सायंतने सवनकर्मणि Śak. III. 24), चिरं, प्रगे &c. in the sense of 'of that time;' see Pâṇ. IV. 3. 23. अस्मत्कर्मतुमुलं—astir on account of our deeds. ॰वधूगृहेषु—The pl. may be accounted for by supposing that the word used here is गृह *m.* and *pl.* (the house with its environs). कुलपालिका—name of Kuberadatta's daughter. उपह्वरे—in secret. चर्मरत्न॰—This bag of excellent leather; or, handsome leather-bag; or, a leather-bag for holding gems. मूलहरत्वमेत्य—come to be deprived of my paternal wealth or my principal stock of wealth. The other sense given by the Bhûshaṇâ does not seem to be good. अर्थिवर्गात्—to be construed with एत्य.

P. 82. उपनगर॰—उपनगरं भवं उपनगरभवम्; सुप्सुपेति समासः। कण्ठन्यस्त॰—when about to place the weapon on my neck; here the p. p. has the sense of 'immediate futurity' by the Vârttika आदिकर्मणि निष्ठा वक्तव्या. अवज्ञासोदर्यं—The sister of contempt; *i e.* which exposes one to constant humiliation. आत्मत्याग—suicide. आत्मना—by personal efforts; construe this with उद्धरन्ति. *Cf.* उद्धरेदात्मनाऽऽत्मानम् Bg. VI. 5. प्रतिसंधान—rejoining. मन्त्रसिद्धः—possessing the power of spells, rendered efficacious. मन्त्रेषु सिद्धः, or मन्त्राः सिद्धाः यस्य, the comp. being taken as one of the आहिताग्न्यादि class. साधिता—endowed with magical power or properties. लक्षग्राहिणी—holding or granting lacs of coins by being operated upon by *mantras.* कामरूप—Name of a country which extended from the banks of the Karatoyá or Sadánírá to the extremities of Assam. The ancient capital of the kingdom was Prâgjyotisha. See our note on Ragh. IV. 81. मत्सरिणी—exposed to jealousy. मदन्यत्र—excepting me. दुग्धे—yields treasure, fulfils desires. किं तु &c.—But on this condition, that one must first restore whatever one might have dishonestly got from others, &c. अथ—And after that. स एष कल्पः—This is the prescribed way of making it grant one's object. ग्रावच्छिद्रं—a cave (*lit.* a cavity in rocks or a mountain).

P. 83. यथोक्तं--As said before (to the king). वरिवस्यमाना-Prep. p. of the pass. of वरिवस्यति, a Denom. verb from वरिवस्, a word meaning 'worship, service,' formed by adding क्यच् (य) by नमोवरिवश्चित्रङः क्यच् । Pán. III. 1. 19; *lit.*, being waited upon or worshipped for money; hence, being emptied by daily demands. व्यवहर्तुम—To seek redress by legal means; to proceed legally against him. मन्नियोगात—At my command; this may also be construed with वैरमवर्धयत्. विमर्दक:—The gambler whom Apahár. assisted; see p. 77. उदारके—The student will remember that उदारक is another name of Dhanamitra. प्रत्यवध्नात—came in the way; opposed the match.

पञ्चवीरगोष्ठ—The public hall or concert-hall. पञ्चवीर probably means the chief people of the four classes and the Nishádas &c. forming the fifth class; hence, all classes of people. सान्द्रादर:—Full of eager curiosity. तद्दृष्टि &c.—The reading current in most editions is सत्रा० (instead of सचापा०); it is not easy of explanation. One Com. explains it as 'having no other refuge (अपगत: आश्रय:—*i.e.* अन्य आश्रय:—यस्य) than the covering (सत्र=shield) of the lotus-bed of her amorous or coquettish glances;' for the comparison of glances to lotuses comp. note on अपाङ्गदाम p. 74, and लीलाकटाक्षमाला further on. Or the comp may be taken as made up of two Bah.s; ०वनमेव सत्रं यस्य स ०वनसत्र:; अपगत आश्रयो यस्य स: अपाश्रय:; and then ०वनसत्र: चासौ अपाश्रयश्च; 'one who shielded himself with, had no other support than,' &c. The ultimate sense in either case is that her glances were maddening. A third way is to take the comp. as सत्रमेव अपाश्रयो यस्य; अपाश्रय itself is often used in the sense of आश्रय; *cf.* कर्णे कृतापाश्रय: Veṇ. V. 1. It is pretty certain that the reading सत्रा० is a mislection for the original सचा०, which is found in the Calcutta editions, and which means "supported by his excellent bow in the form of the lotus-bed of her sportive glances &c." This yields a readily-understood sense and is free from awkward compounds.

P. 84. भावा:—feelings. रसा:—sentiments; or the Bhávas intensified; see com. सामग्र्य—full display. समुत्थितबल—having gained force. नगरदेवतेव &c.—has occurred before; see p. 77. Here it is out of place. लीलाकटाक्ष०—लीलायुक्ता कटाक्षा लीलाकटाक्षास्तेषां माला एव शृङ्खलास्ताभि: । कटाक्ष:—कटौ अतिशयितौ अक्षिणी यत्र; अक्षि being changed to अक्ष by बहुव्रीहौ सक्थ्यक्ष्णो: &c. Pâṇ. V. 4. 113; or कटं गण्डं अक्षति इति, अण् (अ) being added कर्मणि, to अक्ष्. नृत्य—is a dance accompanied by a pantomimic display of feelings (अन्यद्भावाश्रयं नृत्यम् Daśarúpaka) and is different from नृत्त, which is a dance to the accompaniment of music and the beatings of hands ( ताल ) but without gesticulations. सिद्धिलाभशोभिनी—appearing more graceful, or with her beauty heightened, by the ( flush of ) success. किं विलासात्—whether through coquetry ( natural to her ). सविभ्रमारेचित०—with her bushy eye-brows sportively or gracefully bent. For आरेचित *cf.* Kum. III. 5. सापदेशं—under some pretext. सोऽहं—I thus conditioned, *i. e.* who was thus lovingly looked at by her. दुर्निवारयोत्कण्ठया—with a longing that I could not check. दूरीकृता०—not feeling disposed to take food. ग्लानैरवयवैः—with drooping limbs. निष्णातः—*Lit.* one who dives to the bottom; hence, secondarily, one who knows fully everything about a thing. The स् of स्ना is changed to ष् by Pâṇ. VIII. 3. 89 ( see com. ) when the sense is 'skill in.' भाववृत्तिः—The love-affected state of her mind. शरशयने—On a bed of arrows; *i.e.* he will discharge so many arrows at her, piercing her body, that when she will lie down she will sleep on a bed of them as it were. स्थानाभिनिवेशिनोः—who have fixed your affections each on the proper person.

P. 85. गणिकास्वधर्म०—contrary to the proper duty of courtesans. भद्रोदारेणाशयेन—with good and noble intentions. गुणशुल्का न धनशुल्का—I am to be won by merit, not by wealth (*lit.* the price for my hand is merits and not wealth). प्रतिषिध्याकृतार्था—not having succeeded in dissuading her from her purpose. मूलच्छिन्न—nipped in the bud. अच्युतं—unbranded or blameless, chaste, virtuous. It may also be taken as an adv. 'so as not to fall off from it,' rigidly. अनाश्रवा—*fem.* 'disobedient'. आशृणोतीति आश्रवः one who obeys; fr. श्रु with आ + अ ( अच् ) by पचाद्यच्। Pâṇ. III. 1. 134. आवर्ज्य—having won her or secured her affections. प्रधानदूती—chief agent, principal messenger. शाक्यभिक्षुकी—A Buddhist female mendicant or nun. चीवर—old garments. पिण्ड—food. बन्धकी—( that ) harlot ( Kâmamañjarî ). अजिनरत्न—The gem of, *i. e.* the wonderful bag.

P. 86. संप्रतिपन्नायां—when she agreed to my proposal. करकिसलय—her sprout-like *i. e.* tender hand. *Cf.* Uttar. III. 39; Ṛit. VI. 30. चर्मरत्नस्तेयवादः &c.—The mention of the theft of the wonderful bag was to be made, *i. e.* on which the theft was to be announced as having taken place. मत्प्रणिधिः—my secret emissary. अर्थपतिगृह्यः—a partisan or friend of Arthapati. नाम—is here used अलीके; 'to all appearances,' 'outwardly;' *cf.* परिश्रमं नाम विनीय च क्षणम्।

Kum. V. 32. उल्लङ्घ्य--having insulted. बह्वतर्जयत्--spoke many an angry word; used threatening language. आक्रुश्—to revile. स एष धनगर्वो नाम—It is your well-known pride of wealth. परस्य भार्यां &c.—This refers to Kulapálikâ whom her father Kuberadatta first proposed to give in marriage to Arthapati, but afterwards wished to bestow on Dhanamitra. प्रतीत--well-known. बहिश्चराः प्राणाः--*i. e.* his second self. ब्रह्महत्यामपि &c.--I will make no scruple to kill even a Bráhmaṇa (if there be need). एकरात्रजागर &c.--It needs only one night's wakefulness on my part to remove this burning fever of your pride &c. He means that by keeping awake one night he would be able to steal his bag and so humble his pride. सामर्षम्--Angrily. कृत्रिमार्तिना—who feigned to be uneasy; who wore a look of painfulness. वेशवाट--the street lined with the residences of courtesans. निपुणम्--carefully.

P. 87. उपलभ्येत—उपलभ्यते *v.l.* is not good; for in this case स must be taken as referring to Vimardaka, which does not follow syntactically. स वराकः—The poor fellow, *i.e.* (Arthapati). त्वदभिज्ञान०--त्वत् refers to Râjaváhana to whom Apahâra is narrating his story. प्रत्याख्याय—having denied the charge; supply स्थितः after this to make the context clear. विभाविते--the matter being proved or made clear (to the king). कल्पोक्तेन--according to the prescribed mode of using it. सप्रश्रयं--humbly. निर्ग्रन्थिकग्रह—The dogmas of Jainism, the Jaina cult (com.). ग्रह rather means 'the grip' (power), or clutches of the Jainas. निर्ग्रन्थिक properly signifies 'one having no knots' (of the crest, garments &c.); hence, a Jaina mendicant of the Digambara class. अश्मन्तक--the hearth, *i. e.* she gave away every valuable in her house. अश्मन्तक is derived as अश्मनोऽप्यन्तोऽत्र, where even a stone is destroyed; a word of the शकन्ध्वादि group (the Saṃdhi being पररूप). अभ्युदय--prosperity. मिथः--secretly. लोकोत्पक्रोशपात्रं--the object of the derision of, *i. e.* who has earned from the people the nickname of. निरपेक्षं--with indifference. चर्मरत्नलाभहेतुः—It must be due to her acquisition of the magical purse. कल्प—see p. 82. व्यथितवर्णेनेव—with apparent fear or concern; looking as if agitated.

P. 88. अतिप्रकाशात्—which has been widely known. तदनुयोगाय—to question you about that. निर्बन्धात्—when pressed.

तदागतित्वेन—(तस्य आगतिस्तस्य भावस्तेन) as the source of its acquisition. अहमपदेश्यः—you will certainly point to me, *i e.* disclose my name. चित्रवधः--death with tortures. अनर्थानुबन्धिनी—has in its train, would be followed by, a series of calamities. तदपयशः—the infamy about the purse being stolen. कीनाश—the niggardly fellow or cheat. अभ्युपगमय्य—having thus communicated with me. नैष न्यायः—It is not a proper course of conduct for, it does not behove. अतिप्रणुद्य—having urged this with great force. The Com. says, 'having concealed,' *i. e.* refused to give out the name. उपक्षेप—the mention or suggestion of. दग्धबन्धकीभ्यां—by those dastardly girls.

P. 89. आर्य—is rather a strange term of address for a king. Some propose to read आर्यमौर्यदत्त as one word. There is also a suggestion to take आर्य in this comp. as referring to Chânakya, and मौर्य to Chandragupta. But, as remarked by Mr. Agashe, आर्य though usually prefixed to the name of Chânakya can hardly be used alone to stand for it. It is better to read देव for आर्य which is found in a Southern MS. मौर्यदत्तः—Granted by Maurya (or the Maurya kings); Maurya is probably Chandragupta (see p. 191 *infra*) whose reign begins in 315 B. C. and for whose guidance a code of law was drawn up by Chânakya. वर—a boon, a special privilege. But Chandragupta is not known to have exempted the merchant-class from capital punishment for such offences; nor is there anything to this effect in Chânakya's code. Mr. Agashe, however, says—" The only authority that can be found in the Kautilîya for immunity from capital punishment of the Vaiśyas as a class in contained in the following couplet:—एवं चोरानचोराख्यान् वणिक्कारुकुशीलवान्। भिक्षुकान्कुहकांश्चान्यान्वारयेद्देशपीडनात्॥ p 202, Mysore Series." भर्ता—The king. पटच्चर—a rag. अर्थमत्त- vain of his wealth. अपविद्ध–given away. अभिनोदितेन &c.—*i. e.* at Dhanamitra's instance. शुभिनि--auspicious. सिद्धसंकल्पः--whose plans succeeded or bore their fruit. लुब्ध०--The wealthy misers, the miserly sons of the wealthy. कपालपाणिः--with broken platters in their hands. नियतिलिखिता लेखा-*Lit.* the line drawn by Destiny; what is fated. प्रणयकोप--Love-anger. प्रणयसमर्पित--*i. e* by Rágam.; *cf.* for the idea ददौ रसात्पङ्कजरेणुगन्धि गजाय गण्डूषजलं करेणुः। Kum. III. 37. मदेनास्पृश्ये-I got intoxicated or tipsy. मदोन्मादयोः—of drunkenness and over-excitement (or delirium). For this distinction between मद and उन्माद, *cf.* आचार्येण वृकोदरस्य हलिनोन्मत्तेन मत्तेन वा। Ven VI. 27.

P. 90. प्रव्यथित—Alarmed. ०अतिवर्ती—Turning a deaf ear to, disregarding. नातिपरिकर:--not well-equipped. अवसन्न--enfeebled by. आर्तरव--cries of distress. बोधित:--brought back to my senses. प्रतिभा--ready wit; it is defined in poetics as 'talent shining with ever-new ideas or flashes of imagination;' see com.; this sense, however, is not intended here. व्यचीचरम्--mused, pondered within myself. प्रोर्णुता--P. p. p. of ऊर्णु with प्र; *lit.* 'covered with;' hence, involved in. प्रतिपत्ति--the course or plan to be adopted. The word occurs again at p. 98. जरतिका-- an old hag. तां--The notorious one.

P. 91. साराभरण—precious ornaments. नि:शल्य--free from a dart, easy (for I have accomplished what I had purposed to do for taking vengeance on you). उद्घटितज्ञा—who knew what was meant to be suggested, *i. e.* how to take a hint. सामपूर्वम्—having first addressed them in conciliatory tones. भद्रका:—Good sirs. एकमपरार्धं—her bringing about the union of Rágamañjarí with Dhanamitra. कलत्राभिमर्शी—the violator or ravisher of (your) wife. आकल्पसार: &c.—Courtesans entirely depend upon their decorations (dress and ornaments), *i. e.* by their means alone they can attract others. रूपाजीवा—*Lit.* 'one who gains her living by her beauty;' रूपं आजीवो यस्या:. वैरानुबन्ध—inveterate enmity. प्रतिपन्नार्थेव—seeming to have understood or grasped my meaning. भद्रमुख:—a good fellow; *lit.* having a beautiful or auspicious countenance. It is used as an honorific title of address like प्रियदर्शन, but in the case of ordinary men alone. In dramas a prince is to be so addressed by the low characters; see Sáh.-D. VI. 154. आरक्षिकनायक—The chief of the city-guards; head constable. चारक—a prison.

P. 92. उत्तरेद्यु:—उत्तरस्मिन् अहनि; अहन् is changed to एद्युस् when preceded by पूर्व, अन्य, अपर, उत्तर &c.; see Páṇ. V. 3. 22. दृप्ततर:—highly conceited. सुभगमानी—who considered himself very fortunate. सुन्दरंमन्य:—Kántaka thought that he was loved by women (सुभग) and so considered himself beautiful. see *supra*, notes on सुभगपताका, and सुभगंमन्य; p. 74. अत्यय—death. अनतिपक्व—not much grown wiser by experience. नागरिक—has occurred before in the sense of 'policemen' or city guards; see p. 78, 80 &c.; here it means 'the chief of policemen,' or magistrate, who it seems had to look after jails or to act as a jailor also; *cf.* for this sense तत: प्रविशति नागरिक: श्याल: &c. Śák. VI, p. 138, Vik. V. p. 117. Further on it means 'citizens.' कारणा—crucial or agonizing pain, tortures. मित्रमुख—having the face of, *i. e.* an outward (false) friend. प्रत्याशा--hope to regain. साधीयसी संधा—firm resolve. तर्जन—threatening. वर्तमाने अनुयोगव्यतिकरे-While I was being continually asked all manner of questions. अनुगुण-proper, wholesome. विरोपितव्रण:-with my wounds healed. अच्युताम्बर—the garment of Vishṇu. हृष्टवर्णा—appearing pleased; *cf.* व्यथितवर्णेन p. 87. सुनीतिः—a wise plot, judicious plan.

P. 93. आपन्नः—In distress. सुलभापानदोषात्—on account of the vice of drunkenness, so common &c. लोकवार्ता—common talk, public rumour. निकृष्टाशयः—base-hearted, mean-spirited. समुद्गक—a box. प्रणयानुवर्तिन्—Acting in accordance with the love he bore to her (Râga.). उपायोपक्रान्तः—dealt with, treated with proper remedies. असुभिर्मा &c.—मां refers to Apahâra., whose words, the student should remember, the nurse is quoting as addressed to Dhanamitra. उपच्छन्दन—coaxing, persuasive means. अनतित्रस्नु—not much alarmed at your misfortune. त्वदभिज्ञानप्रत्या०--whose confidence was gained by showing the token of recognition from you. अन्वरञ्जयम्—I pleased her (secured her favour). संक्रमीकृत्य—using her as a means, through her medium.

P. 94. प्राभृत—a present. समादधती—adjusting, putting back in its proper place. प्रच्याव्य—letting it fall, dropping it. उपकन्यापुरं--close to the princess' apartment. भवनाङ्गणं—the courtyard of the palace. अपदेशात्—pretending to frighten &c. प्रहसन्ती प्राहार्षम्—It was Śrigáliká's plan to lead Kântaka into the false belief that the princess was in love with him. This was the first step to entrap him. As Kántaka happened to come to the courtyard of the palace adjoining the princess' apartment, she threw the lotus on him under the pretext of scaring away the pigeons; of course the princess knew nothing about this. स्मयमानः—Smiling. विलासप्रायमाकारं—her amorous-looking features. संज्ञया &c.—In an indescribably clever manner by gesticulation. दिग्धफलेन--with venomed point. अतिमुग्ध—quite beside himself. मुद्रिता--sealed. पट्टांशुक, भूषणावयव—silk garments and a few ornaments. वङ्गेरिका—a cane casket. अवस्थान्तराणि--The different stages of her love-affected condition. These are mentioned as ten नयनप्रीतिः प्रथमं चित्तासङ्गस्ततोऽथ संकल्पः । निद्राच्छेदस्तनुता विषयनिवृत्तिस्त्रपानाशः । उन्मादो मूर्छा मृतिरित्येताः स्मरदशा दशैव स्युः ॥ Ratirahasya.

P. 95. सुदूरमुन्माद्यत—Was made to go exceedingly mad with love; his passion was carried too far. निर्माल्य—garlands worn by her the day before. अपोढानि—taken somewhere else. प्राक्षिपम् *v. l.*—I threw them away. अपाविध्यं *v. l.* means the same thing—'threw or cast them away;' *cf.* अपविद्धसर्वस्वा *supra* p. 89. उपमन्त्रित:—addressed. लक्षणानि &c.—The auspicious marks ( of future elevation ) you bear are not to be in vain or falsified. प्रातिवेश्य:—a neighbour. तदनुरूपं—in conformity with his words. समागत—united with. अयमर्थो &c.—This good fortune will be followed by another, *viz.* your acquisition of the kingdom. न आरभ्यते—The subject to this is अयमर्थ:; why is not this object pursued; *i. e.* why don't you adopt measures to secure the hand of the princess? व्याम—the length of space between the tips of the fingers of both the hands when the arms are extended ( Mar. वांव). आरामप्राकार—the rampart surrounding the pleasure-garden. हस्तवत्-skilful, dexterous; here हस्त means 'skill of the hand.' ऐकागारिक—एकमसहायं अगारं प्रयोजनमस्य ; 'he who seeks to live in a lonely or unprotected house'; hence, a thief or robber. See Pâṇ. V. 1. 113. उपरिष्टात्—after that. सगरसुतानां—The sons of Sagara ( a king of the solar race ), who were appointed the guardians of the sacrificial horse by their father, and who dug the earth down to the nether world in search of the horse when it was carried away by Indra in an invisible form. Here their power of digging is referred to. For their story see Rám. Bála-K. chaps. 38-44; see also our note on सगर at Ragh. III. 50.

P. 96. अभिसंधाय—Having come to an understanding or formed an agreement with him. धाष्टर्यभूमि: -most intrepid. चित्रं—the same as चित्रवधेन ; by subjecting him to peculiar tortures. अर्थ: सिध्यति—the desired object would be gained. प्रतिपद्य—following my counsel. प्राप्तमित: परं—what is necessary to be done hereafter. त्वन्नय:—your plan or stratagem. भूयान्—'of greater importance;' this is meant as a compliment to Śrigâlikâ. विनिगडीकृत:-being liberated, set free. नित्यान्धकारात्—perpetually shrouded in darkness. असत्यवाग्दोषेण—the calumny of being false to my promise. निष्पतत:—as I issued from the passage. असिधेन्वा—with his dagger. असिर्धेनुरिव यस्या: असिधेनु:, to which the sword stands as a cow, it being as it were its calf; *i. e.* a small sword; वा कप् असिधेनुका; this like पुत्री has a diminutive force; असिपुत्री.

संनिवेशैः—situation, position of the different rooms. मणिप्रदीपेषु—मणय एव प्रदीपाः the jewels serving as powerful lamps, *i. e.* wherein gems glowed emiting light. *Cf.* ज्वलन्मणिशिखाश्चैनं वासुकिप्रमुखा निशि । स्थिरप्रदीपतामेत्य भुजङ्गाः पर्युपासते ॥ Kum II. 38. महितमहार्घ &c.—the ivory feet of the shape of a recumbent lion of which were set with flawless and precious jewels. महित according to the Com. means 'big.' मह् properly means 'to be praised or admired,' the महितत्व lying in their size or flawlessness.

P. 97. हंसतूलगर्भ—stuffed with the downy feathers of swans. Diss. हंसतूलः गर्भे यस्यास्ताद्दशी शय्या उपधानं च ताभ्यां शालते इति तथा तस्मिन्. कुसुमलव०—the sides of which were decked with petals of flowers actual or engraved therein. दक्षिणपाद०—This and the following compounds are all adverbial, modifying विश्रब्धप्रसुप्तां. अनुवलित—covered. ईषद्विवृत्त—a little turned to the side. Wilson reads विवृत—'bare or exposed to view', which is a better reading. गुल्फ—The ankle. Diss. ईषद्विवृत्तौ (०तौ वा) मधुरौ गुल्फयोः संधी यथा स्यातां तथा. आश्लिष्ट—in close contact. जङ्घा—The fleshy part between the ankle and the knee. ०काण्ड—*i. e.* stout and long. वेल्लित—bent ( drawn in ). अधिनितम्ब०—नितम्बे इति अधिनितम्बं स्रस्तं मुक्तं च यदेकभुजलताग्रं तेन पेशलं यथा स्यात्तथा; beautiful on account of the extremity (palm) of one arm loosely thrown over the hips. अपाश्रयान्तनिमित०—in which the other arm was contracted and thrown under the crown of the head, the palm of the tender ( sproutlike ) hand lying upstretched. ०न्तनिमित्त *v. l.*—that the extremity of the head might rest on it. अतिश्लिष्ट०—in which her fine undergarment of China silk lay closely adhering to her person. Fine China-silk cloth seems to have been imported into India from the earliest times, and there are numerous references to it in Sanskrit literature; *vide* Śák. I. 33, Kum. VII. 3, Kir. IV. 59, Mál-Mádh. VI. 5, Amaru.—Ś. 75, &c. It is also mentioned in Kauṭilīya Bk. III. अनतिवलित—not much pressed down. अतनुतरनिःश्वासारम्भ—as she began to breathe perceptibly. अतिशयेन तनुः तनुतरः तथा न भवतीत्यतनुतरः (forcible) यः निःश्वासारम्भस्तेन कम्पमानौ कुचौ कुड्मलाविव कुचकुड्मलौ यस्मिन्कर्मणि तद्यथा तथा. आतिरश्चीन०—in a manner in which the neck-ornament made of rubies and woven in the middle of her necklace of burnished gold was to be seen lying near her beautiful neck resting slantingly. अर्धलक्ष्य०—अर्धलक्ष्यमधरकर्णपाशे निभृतं कुण्डलं यस्मिन्कर्मणि तद्यथा

तथा; in which the ear-ornament lay hidden or motionless under her down-turned beautiful ear which was partly (*lit.* half) visible. अधरकर्ण may also mean 'the lower part of the ear,' but the first sense is better (—see com.—) as shown by उपरिपरावृत्त in the next comp. पाश when added to कर्ण or its synonyms signifies 'beauty' (प्रशस्तः कर्णः कर्णपाशः). For its different meanings *cf.* Haima Kośa—पाशस्तु मृगपक्ष्यादिबन्धने । कर्णान्ते शोभनार्थः स्यात्कचार्थे निकरार्थकः । छत्राद्यन्ते च निन्दार्थः । Kshîrasvâmî quotes a śl. bringing these meanings together—अग्रतो बाहुपाशेन केशपाशेन पृष्ठतः । पार्श्वयोः कर्णपाशेन सर्वतो बन्धनं प्रिये ॥. उपरिपरावृत्त—The other beautiful ear which was turned up.

P. 98. पिञ्जरित—tinged red. विषम०—her loosened (व्याविद्ध) braid of hair lying unevenly. उत्तराधरविवर—The interval of the upper lip (from the lower lip), *i. e.* the space between the two lips, was not to be seen, *i. e.* was covered up with the lustre of the lips. Though अधर is used for the lower lip, उत्तर is rarely used in literature for the upper lip; it is, however, so used by Kâlidâsa; *cf.* निवार्यतामालि किमप्ययं बटुः पुनर्विवक्षुः स्फुरितोत्तराधरः । Kum. V. 83. ०कर्णावतंसकृत्यं—her stretched hand placed under the broad cheek served the purpose of the ear-ornament consisting of a sprout. उपरिकपोल &c.—In which the purpose of the ornamental paintings (such as ladies are described to have on the particular parts of their bodies) was served by the chequered (*or,* embroidered) canopy mirrored into her transparent cheek that was turned upwards. विशेषक is an ornamental painting on the face of a woman variegated with dots in the middle, and drawn with such fragrant substances as rubbed sandal, musk, saffron &c.; *cf.* अभिनवा इव पत्रविशेषकाः Ragh. IX. 29; मृष्टचन्दनविशेषकभक्तिः &c. Śiś. X. 84; see also Málav. III. 5. The reflection of the embroidered canopy into her cheek looked like a Viśeshaka.

अविभ्रान्त०—her large and bushy eyebrows were still. श्रमजलपुलक—the drops of perspiration. अलकलता—her long and curly hair. शरदम्भोधर—suggests largeness and whiteness. सौदामनी—the simile bespeaks brightness of colour and slenderness of frame on the part of the princess.

चोरयितव्यनिःस्पृहः—with my desire to steal totally gone. असंकेतित०—touched without previous intimation (without being previously acquainted with my motive). अतिचाला—

quite young (inexperienced in love-matters) व्यक्तं—undoubtedly. अहमेवाघ्नीय—I shall myself be killed, it will be all over with me. This is the meaning required by the context here. आघ्नीय is the Pot. 3rd pers. sing. of हन् with आ which is A tm. when used intransitively and with reference to one's own body. But this restriction is not always observed by the poets; *cf.* आजघ्ने विषमविलोचनस्य वक्षः Kir. XVII 63; or आहस्वं मा रघूत्तमं Bhatti (though grammarians treat these as oversights on the part of the poets; प्रमादाः). So we may supply आत्मानं; I shall ruin myself.

P. 99. निर्यास॰—Coloured or dyed with the viscous exudation or gum (of some tree). कल्कः—a viscous preparation obtained from substances or drugs ground or pounded. वर्णवर्तिका—a drawing brush. तां तथा शयानां &c.—I sketched her sleeping in that posture and myself kneeling at her feet, &c. तस्याश्च—तस्याः goes with चरणलग्न; so this is a सापेक्षसमास, चरण being connected with तस्याः (तच्चरण). वासताम्बूलवीटिका—a roll of betel-nut leaves. ॰स्फुटिका—a bit or piece of. पारिजातक—scented catechu अलक्तकपाटल—red like *alaktaka*. निरष्ठीवम्—spat out a pair of Chakravākas on the white (chunam-plastered) wall, *i. e.* produced the likeness of a pair of Chakravāka birds by skilfully spitting on the wall. The Chakravâka birds are represented in Sanskrit literature as emblems of constancy in love; *cf.* Ragh. III. 24. Apahára.'s object in drawing a pair of these birds was to show that like the male Chakra. he too would be firm and faithful to the princess in case she chose him for her husband. Now, the Chakravâka is a bird of a reddish colour; and Apahâra. produced a reddish liquid in his mouth by chewing a tâmbûla, and by gently ejecting it on the wall through his mouth, he traced on the wall a couple of the Chakravâka birds. This he did, according to Mr. Agashe, in conformity with a diction of Vátsyáyana. The following is quoted from his note. "Vàtsyâyana in his Kâmasútra says-यत्र संपातोऽस्यास्तत्र चित्रकर्मणस्तद्युक्तस्य द्वार्थानां गीतवस्तुकानां क्रीडनकानां छताचिह्नानामापीनकानामङ्गुलीयकस्य च निधानम्। प्रत्युत्तरं तथा दत्तं प्रपश्येत्। Thus, according to Vâtsyâyana, a lover courting a girl is recommended four devices of communicating his wish to his beloved—(1) To paint his own likeness on a board or wall (सानुरागमात्मानं फलके भित्तौ वा विलिख्य निदर्शयात्, says यशोधर the commentator of कामसूत्र). This Apahár. has done. He has also addressed (2) an amorous ditty to her (गीत). The third is क्रीडनकानां पुत्रिकाकन्दुकादीनां कृतचिह्नानां निधानम् । This...seems to suggest the presentation of something suggestive of love, and hence it appears to us that Apahára. fulfilled (3) this third condition by spitting the reddish saliva on the chunam-plastered wall in such a way as to produce the likeness of a pair of Chakraváka birds...Immediately after this...comes the exchange of rings, which according to Vátsyá. is the fourth device indicative of love." नागरिकवर—one of the leading or principal citizens. उपचरित—treated as. तपस्वी—poor, miserable. रहस्यं—*scil.*, that he had set his heart on the princess and attempted to break into the private apartments. लब्धव्यो मोक्षः—you should procure your release. अगृह्ये—came within the reach of. अनामृष्ट—untouched.

P. 100. स्वपृष्ठ०—Placing my elbows on my back (and thus assuming an attitude of submission). वर्षीयसी—old hag. उन्नीत०—having guessed what I had at heart or having divined my intention. वायुग्रस्तः—affected by hysteria or lunacy. पूर्वेद्युः—see note on उत्तरेद्युः p. 92. प्रसन्नकल्पः—almost cured or freed from his malady. निष्प्रवाणि—new unbleached garments; निर्गता प्रवाणी तन्तुवायशलाका अस्मात्. औशीरे कामचारः &c.—he was allowed freely to sit or lie down, *i. e.* he was allowed liberty of action. मातरिश्वा—मातरि आकाशे श्वयति इति; the wind. शौक्रेयः—a hawk. शान्तं पापं—*lit.* 'let the evil be averted', is used to indicate one's disapproval of what is said or heard. कदर्थिता—reproached, despised. वेशकृच्छ्रादुत्थाय—after he had escaped from the calamity brought on by the harlot. This must be connected with प्रत्यापन्न in the next comp., so that both the actions will have the same agent.

P. 101. एवंभूतं त्वद्दर्शनं—That I should thus obtain your sight. अपचार—misconduct, crime. निर्भिद्य—having given out or proclaimed; this should be taken with राज्ञा (निर्भिद्य प्रतिष्ठापितः), so that the use of the gerund would be correct. अभियुज्य—having attacked. अमर्षण—impatient (of the outrage). पारिग्रामिकं विधिं—hostile measures to be adopted on besieging (परि) an enemy's town. Explain ग्रामस्य परि इति परिग्रामं Avya.; परिग्रामं (परिग्रामे वा) भवं पारिग्रामिकं by adding ठञ् (इक); see com. The hostile acts meant are such as harassing the enemy's kingdom by cutting the supplies of food, fodder, &c., breaking of tanks, &c.; these are mentioned by Manu as उपरुध्यारिमासीत राष्ट्रं चास्योपपीडयेत्। दूषयेच्चास्य सततं यवसान्नोदकेन्धनम् ॥ (quoted in the Bhú. as from the Mitákshará further on; see p. 134) भिन्द्याच्चैव तडागानि प्राकारपरिखास्तथा। समवस्कन्दयेच्चैनं रात्रौ वित्रासयेत्तथा ॥ Manu. VII. 195, 196. See also Kâm. Nît. XVI. 3, 4. हठात्—forcibly. प्रतिसर--the auspicious marriage-string (the same as कौतुक; see Ragh. VIII. 1). अङ्गराजाभिसरं—coming to the aid of the King of Aṅga. संभूय—having joined. गतायुषः—the time of whose death had arrived. Here the त indicates near futurity; see *supra*, note on कण्ठन्यस्तशस्त्रिकः, p. 82. उपसमाधीयमान—being collected or arranged.

P. 102. लोकसंबाध—a throng of men coming out and going in. आथर्वणेन--by the domestic priest. A priest versed in the A'tharvaṇa lore was generally selected by the ancient kings that he might perform by means of the spells given therein rites for them that would give them peculiar powers, avert calamity, put down their enemies and so on. *Cf.* Ragh. I. 59, Malli. thereon and Kâm. Nît. IV. 32. The Atharva-Veda contains many charms and imprecations leading to good or evil results (such as bringing about the death of an enemy &c.). For its succint description *cf.* पुण्योऽपि भीमकर्मा निधिर्व्रतानां चकास्त्यमितशक्तिः। मूर्तिमभिरामघोरां बिभ्रद्विवाथर्वणां निगमः ॥ Mv.-Ch. II. 24. आलिप्समान—As he wished (*i. e.* was about) to seize. स्फुरतः—striving (to seize me). अनुविचरन्—moving from one room to another. अभिनिशाम्य—seeing her before me. स्तनितगम्भीरेण--*Cf.* Uttar. VI. 17. A voice deep like the rumbling of clouds is considered as one of the signs (लक्षणs) of a great man; नाभी स्वरः सत्त्वमिति प्रशस्तं गम्भीरमेतत्त्रितयं नराणाम्। उरो ललाटं वदनं च पुंसां विस्तीर्णमेतत्त्रितयं प्रशस्तम् ॥ Var. Brih.-Sam. 67. 25.

विदेहेषु—The country of Videha lay to the north-east of Magadha. Its capital Mithilâ is the same as Janakapura in Nepâl, north of Madhuvâṇî. Videha must have covered, in ancient times, besides a portion of Nepâl, the northern part of the old district of Tirhut and the north-western portion of Champaran.

P. 103. अलिन्द—A raised place oblong in shape near a door. जैवातृकः—'O you of long life!' From जीव् and the Uṇádi aff. आतृक (I. 79); see com. ननु श्रूयते—you must have heard. बलशम्बल (०र)--Names of two demons. प्रथम-

गर्भि०--when blessed with a fœtus for the first time. लेशतोऽपि &c.—what fate overtook the king of Magadha was utterly unknown. मालवेन्द्रप्रयत्न०--who lived by the effort of the Mâlava king. This shows that Mânasâra was noble-hearted. ज्येष्ठस्य--of his eldest brother. व्यासं--occupied, usurped. स्वस्रीय--his sister's son;=स्वसुः अपत्यं, by adding छ ( ईय ) to स्वसृ; see com. सुह्म—A country which lay to the west of Vanga or eastern Bengal. It was so called after Suhma, the fourth son of Bali. Its capital, Támralipta, also called Dâmalipta (see *infra* p. 149), has been identified with the modern Tumlook on the right bank of the Cossya, the Kapiśá of Kâlidâsa. For other particulars see our note on Suhma, Ragh. IV. 35. दण्डावयव—the portion of an army; for दण्ड meaning an army *cf.* तस्य दण्डवतो दण्डः स्वदेहान्न व्यशिष्यत । Ragh. XVII. 62; प्रभवः खलु कोपदण्डयोः Kir. II. 12; see also Manu. VII. 65. लुब्धक—the wild marauders, Bhils. शार्दूल &c.—As I fell beneath the paw of a tiger. कपिला—a brown cow. क्रोड—the cavity under the bosom. इष्वसनयन्त्र—A bow.

P. 104. मोहसुप्ता--lying in a swoon. वृष्णिपाल—a shepherd. कुटीर—a hut, a hovel. उपक्रान्तव्रणा--whose wounds were dressed and tended. यावद्व्याकुलीभवामि--just as I was uneasy at heart. *Cf.* the account given here with that at pp. 13, 14. सार्थघाते--when the body of merchants and soldiers accompanying them were routed. उपयन्तुं--to marry. वैक्लव्य—disgust or horror for. प्रत्याख्यानपारुष्यं—the harshness *i. e.* insult of a refusal. जातः—turned out to be. विधिदोषात्—through adverseness of fate. पुनरसहिष्णुतया--and again finding his position unbearable. दग्धा—unfortunate, cursed. हतजीविताकृष्टा—out of love for her accursed life.

P. 105. तयोश्च सतोः—The two living. प्रसह्यकारिणः—laying violent hands on, dealing harshly with. प्रमन्युः--with her grief intensified. निगूढं--very secretly. कश्चिन्मुनिः--see p. 13. अभ्युपपादनार्थं—For deliverance from distress or for protecting; according to the Bhûshaná 'for rearing up' ( अभ्युपपादनं संवर्धनं ); but this does not appear to be correct. याचितः—This is Upa.'s guess; for no request was actully made to the sage by the woman either to find out the boy or to protect him when found. उपश्लिष्य—having approached or pressed him hard. तैरपि घटन्ते &c.—Present in the sense of the Future; 'and the citizens might make common cause with (or join) them.'

**इदृक्तया**—*Lit.* being such and such; as to my real parentage and rank. **प्रहारवर्मण्यधि**—subject to his rule, under his sway. अधि is a कर्मप्रवचनीय when used in the sense of a Lord (*i. e.* being the lord of or having as lord); *e. g.* अधि भुवि रामः or अधि रामे भूः; so here अधि विदेहेषु प्रहारवर्मा also; for the Loc. see Páṇ. यस्मादधिकं &c. (II. 3. 9) quoted in the com. **प्रलम्बमान**—long (of more than ordinary length). **भागधेय**—धेय is added स्वार्थे to रूप, नाम and भाग. **उपधि**—a fraudulent scheme, a stratagem.

P. 106. **जालमाचरेयम्**—I shall formulate a scheme for working out his destruction. **मार्तण्डः**—the sun; मृते अण्डे भवः। शकन्ध्वादिः; sometimes मार्तण्ड also. **०श्वासरया०**—blown away by the force of the breath. **त्रियामा**—त्रयो यामा यस्याः सा, having three watches or *praharas* (the first and last half-*prahara* being discounted as being spent like a part of the day in business—आद्यन्तयोरर्धयामयोश्चेष्टाकालत्वेन दिनप्रायत्वात्); यद्वा त्रीन् धर्मादीन् यापयति निरवकाशीकरोति (fr. या + मन् Uṇádi) कामप्रधानत्वात्। Bhánujî Dîk. **कच्चित्**—asks a question to which the expected answer is 'Yes'. 'I hope you know.' **कामरूपेश्वरस्य**—for Káma. see *supra* p. 82. **पतिमभिभूय वर्तते**—excels her husband (in accomplishments); *or*, she has not (*or*, acts not having) much regard for her husband, despises her husband. **तदेकवल्लभः**—solely devoted or attached to her. **असमान०**—by finding fault with and condemning the connexion of two unequal persons. **वासवदत्ता**—the heroine of Subandhu's work, named after her, who was betrothed by her father to Pushpaketu but who was carried off by Kandarpaketu. Also name of the daughter of Chaṇḍamahâsena of Ujjayinî (of Pradyota according to Śrî-Harshadeva; see Ratn. I. 10) who was carried off by Udayana, king of the Vatsa country. She has been referred to by Bhavabhúti in Mâl.-Mádh. II. wherein he says she was betrothed by her father to king Saṃjaya, and wherein Kâmandakî also makes use of a similar device to create love for Mâdhava and hatred for every other person in Málatî's mind; *cf.* वरेऽन्यस्मिन्द्वेषः पितरि विचिकित्सा च जनिता &c. II. 13. Here Daṇḍin makes Uphár. follow Vâtsyâyana's suggestions; *cf.* परस्त्रियस्तु सूक्ष्मभावा दूतीसाध्या न तथात्मनेत्याचार्याः। Kâmasû. V. 2. 1; and सैनां शीलतोऽनुप्रविश्याख्यानकपटैः सुभगंकरणयोगैर्लोकवृत्तान्तैः कविकथाभिश्च तस्याश्च रूपविज्ञानदाक्षिण्यशीलानुप्रशंसाभिश्च तां रञ्जयेत्। कथमेवंविधायास्तवायमित्थंभूतः पतिरिति चानुशयं ग्राहयेत्। &c. V. 4. 2, 3; गुणवत्यां चाहल्या-(Gautama's wife)-शाकुन्तलादीन्यन्यान्यपि लौकिकानि च कथयेत्तद्युक्तानि। V. 4. 14; विद्वेषं

ग्राहयेत्पश्यौ रमणीयानि वर्णयेत् ।......नायकस्यानुरागं च पुनश्च रतिकौशलम् । वर्णयेत् । *Ibid*, 63, 64.

P. 107. अनुशय—Regret, resentment. अवरोधान्तरेषु—with the other ladies of the harem. मान—jealous anger ( caused by the husband's attention to a co-wife &c. ); see Sáh.-Dar. III. 199, 200. अम्बा—the old woman, his foster-mother. अनन्यव्यापारया—leaving every other business. उदर्कस्वादु—having an agreeable or welcome end. अनपायिनी—never separated from her. माधवी—is the spring creeper ( मधौ in the spring पुष्यति इति; from मधु + अण् + ई fem. ); also called अतिमुक्त. It is generally described as twining itself round the mango-tree ( sometimes round the Nîpa or मधूक ), but never round such trees as the Nimba even the bark of which is bitter. It becomes शोच्या if it is made to cling to a Nimba tree; hence the appropriateness of the simile. पिचुमन्द—the *nimba* tree. This is derived as पिशुं कुष्ठविशेषं मन्दयति ( destroys ) इति ; पिचुमर्द *v. l.* is also found in Amara as a variant ( पिचुं मर्दयतीति ). मत्तकाशिनी—a belle, a beautiful woman. मत्ता इव काशते looks like one intoxicated, *i. e.* having the flush of wine on her cheeks; hence, beautiful. चित्रीयमाणा—wondering, full of astonishment; pres. p. of the denom. from चित्र by adding य ( क्यच् ) आश्चर्ये; चित्रीयते विस्मयते इत्यर्थः । by Páṇ. III. 1. 19, quoted in the com. सनाथीकृतं—*Lit.* is made to have a master, is graced with the handsome person of.

P. 108. संनिधत्ते—is present, exists in. आदृतवती—received it with respect, or eagerly. आज्ञापयसि—you say. अर्णवनेमिः—अर्णवः नेमिर्यस्याः सा the one encircled by the ocean; the earth, *cf.* उदधिनेमि Ragh. X. 10, उदधिमालामेखला Kád. p. 8 &c.; for the idea comp. कालो ह्ययं निरवधिर्विपुला च पृथ्वी; Mál.-Mádh. I. 8. रूपानुरूप—रूपस्यानुरूपाणि शिल्पं च &c. यस्य. स किं लप्स्यते—is a question; 'what will he get ?' सर्वमिदं &c.-All this is but too little and quite unworthy of him. ( And although I give him all this, he will have obtained nothing ). विप्रलम्भ—fraud, deceit. दर्शनाद्युद्भवेन—by his actual sight. निगूढं चरन्—living *incognito*. अन्ववर्तिष्ट—conciliated me for help in the matter. कुसुमशेखर &c.—कुसुमानां शेखरः a chaplet worn on the crown of the head स्रक् ( a garland ) च अनुलेपनानि च आद्यौ येषां तैः. This is in accordance with the precept of Vatsyá.—तासां मनोहराण्युपायनानि ताम्बूलमनुलेपनं स्रजमङ्गुलीयकं वासो वा तेन प्रहितं दर्शयेत् । V. 4. 35.

गुणातिशय—excellent virtues. त्वत्समाधिगाढत्व—The depth of his devotion to you; ( according to the Bhúshaṇá, to see the depth of your attachment to him ).

P. 109. एष चेदर्थो &c.—If this matter be determined upon, *i. e.* if you are really willing to deliver yourself up to him. प्राण—vital power, strength; सत्त्व mental calibre. By this she indirectly hints that in case she delivered himself up to him, he would be able to rid her of her undesirable husband. संकेत—appointment, engagement or place of meeting, rendezvous. दुहिता देया इति—This is in conformity with Vátsyáyana's precept भवतेऽहमादौ दातुं संकल्पितेत्यभिदधीत। V. 4. 30. दैवात्—such being the will of providence. नात्युपपन्न-संस्थानः—with a body not symmetrically built, not handsome in features. For this meaning of संस्थान *cf.* Śák स्त्रीसंस्थानं चाप्सरस्तीर्थमारात् &c. V. 30. कामोपचार—manner of enjoyment, love-affairs. मन्दाभिनिवेशः—not much fond of. शौर्योन्मादिन्—vain of his valour. अस्थानवर्षी—bestowing gifts on unworthy recipients; reckless in bestowing his favours. मदन्तरङ्गभूता—my confidante, confidential maid. अनात्मज्ञा—who does not know her proper position or state. नाटकीया—The dancing maid. मत्संवर्धितायाः—The selection of a particular tree and a creeper by kings and queens as their particular favourite seems to be a favourite idea with Sanskrit poets.

P. 110. गर्भवेदिका—A dais in a cave of the pleasure-mountain. रत्नतल्प—a bedstead set with gems. अयोग्यश्च &c.—In the first place, the man is unworthy of me and now he has commenced insulting me. अनङ्गशर॰—*Cf.* ॰बाणतूणीरायमाणमानसः *supra*, p. 49. अनिष्टजन॰—The misery arising from their being compelled to associate with a man they hate. अस्ति चायं &c.—I have this treasure in my possession. By its means I will establish him in his ( Vikas.'s ) place and live, having devoted myself entirely to him. अतः परं &c.—what is to be done next rests with you to decide. अन्तर्वंशिक॰—See p. 56 ॰स्थानानि—their particular stations. विभागेन—as regards their different portions or subdivisions. अस्तगिरि॰—As the sun has to fall from the sky he is supposed first to jump on the peak of the setting mountain and then into the sea. क्षुभित—stirred up ( and rushing to the surface ). निर्वापित—extinguished. पतङ्गाङ्गार—The burning charcoal in the form of the sun. Take the comp. as a Tatp. ( अङ्गारः तस्य धूमसंचयः ) and not as a Bah. as the Com. does.

P. 111. परामर्श—Violation, having connexion with. आचार्यकं कर्तुं—to instruct me in. आचार्यस्य कर्म आचार्यकं by affixing अक (वुञ्) which is added to words having a penultimate य preceded by a long syllable in the sense of भाव or कर्मन्; see Páṇ. V. 1. 132. *Cf.* आचार्यकं विजायि मान्मथमाविरासीत्। Mâl.-Mádh. I. 26. गुरुपरिग्रह°—the admirer (coveter) of the wife of Brihaspati; see *supra* p. 70 and note. अतिराग—eager desire. स्मयमान—smiling; shining brightly. संधुक्षमाण°—whose valour was accelerated. विजिगीषा—desire for the conquest of. धर्मपीडा-(*lit.* 'the being constrained'), violation of religious law or righteousness. °संधिना—laying to my heart, having in view. निर्हृत्य—having extenuated or removed. समग्रयेत्—would endow me with; Pot. 3rd pers. sing. of the nominal verb from समग्र (अग्रेण सहितं समग्रं full). निद्रया परामृश्ये—I was seized or overpowered by sleep. दुर्विकल्प—a misgiving, a wrong conception. असौ—*i. e.* Kalpasundarî. वरवर्णिनी—having an excellent complexion; a beautiful woman. विलोडन—sport in; wading through.

P. 112. बहुभोग्या—*Cf.* तद्युक्तं बहुमार्गगां मम पुरो निर्लज्ज वोढुं तव Ratn. I. śl. between 2 and 3 [ Footnote No. 2:—In the *v.l.* ततस्तेन &c. तेन refers to Gajânana and मां to Bharga or Śiva (readings 8 and 10, last page). In this passage it is Śiva who speaks. विलक्षा इव—as if discomfited or abashed. वरिवस्या—service, attendance on; also, worship; fem. noun from वरिवस्यति a denom. from वरिवस्; see p. 83. अनेहस्—time. ]. भव्यः-Destined to happen, pre-ordained. प्रियासंकेत°—प्रियायाः संकेतः the promise to meet, तस्य व्यतिकरः incident स आदौ येषां तेषां स्मर° by thinking of such things or incidents as, &c.; for व्यतिकर *cf. supra*, pp. 29, 74. अनन्यथावृत्तिः—engaged in no other pursuit. कार्दमिकः—dyed with black paint; from कर्दम and aff. ठक् (इक); see com. Lovers are described by poets as dressing in dark in order to escape observation when proceeding on their nightly expeditions. दृढतर°—with my loins tightly girded. प्रकृतोपस्कर—implements necessary for my purpose. By उपात्प्रतियत्नवैकृतवाक्याध्याहारेषु Páṇ. VI. 1. 139, a स् comes before कृ after the prep. उप in the sense of प्रतियत्न (=गुणाधान, adding a new quality to a thing in order to enhance its value, &c.) or वैकृत(=what is prepared or altered), or वाक्याध्याहार (=supplying a sentence); *e. g.* उपस्कृता कन्या an adorned girl, उपस्कृता ब्राह्मणाः the Bráhmaṇas assembled, उपस्कृतमधीते वाक्याध्याहारेण ब्रूते इत्यर्थः। Sid.-Kau. In other cases we have उपकरोति. Some explain the स् here by the Sūtra समवाये च Pāṇ. VI. 1. 138, *i. e.* in the sense of aggregation or collection. मातृ—his foster-mother. उदम्भसं—filled up with water. उपखातं-near the ditch. शायितया—placed athwart the ditch (*i.e.* horizontally). स्थापिता—placed erect or vertically.

P. 113. पक्वेष्टका०—The आ of इष्टका, इषीका and माला, and of words ending in these, is shortened when followed respectively by चित, तूल and भारिन्; as इष्टकचित, पक्वेष्टकचित; इषिकतूलम्; मालभारि, उत्पलमालभारि. गोपुर—A city-gate with the towers attached to it. चम्पकावलि—The avenue of the Champakas. उत्तराहि—in a northerly direction. पाटलिपथ—a row of Pāṭali trees. स्पर्शलभ्य०—where the bulging wall of the spacious palace could be felt. शरक्षेपमिव—nearly a bowshot's distance. उभयपार्श्वं०—Both the sides of which were decked with the thickets of red *as'okas* and jasmines. सैकतपथ—a gravel path. अवाचीं—lying to the south. समुद्रक—a (cylindrical) box; a lantern may have been used. निरन्तर—growing thickly. कुरण्ट—The yellow amaranth. अभिनव०—marked with fresh buds rising up like hair standing on end. ०वस्तुगर्भाः—Containing or having articles in their interiors. संपुटाः—caskets.

P. 114. व्यवहित—hidden. अशुषीमकामा—whose passion was not cold, *i. e.* inflamed or intensified. कण्ठराग०—in faltering accents, charming and impassioned. अध्यवस्य—having deliberately undertaken to do. भामिनि—O passionate (*or* irascible) one; भामिनी-one so delicate and sensitive to injury as to get excited at once; hence, a charminy woman also; hence used sometimes as a complimentary term; see p. 16 कदर्थिता—put to shame. He means that she was as beautiful as Rati, her eyebrows curved like Kāma's bow-staff &c. Similar descriptions have already occurred. *Cf.* pp. 2, 3 and 44. महारजन—रज्यते अनेनेति रजनं a dye महच्च तद्रजनं च; safflower. परिमलपटीयस्—having an excellent smell.

P. 115. मञ्जुल—sweet. प्रलापैः—spontaneous utterances पूर्णकुम्भ—is considered auspicious; see *supra* p. 44. संनाह्य—equipped (for gaining victory); *cf.* जैत्ररथ pp. 3, 44. लीलाकर्ण०—कर्णे कृतं किसलयं कर्ण०, लीलार्थं कर्णकिसलयम्. जीवन—tending to bring back to life. पेशल—bewitching, charming; see com. अवसितार्थां—when she reached her acme of pleasure. आरक्तवलित—reddish and rolling. जर्जरित—covered.

अनर्गल—free or unrestrained. कल—indistinctly. कलकल v. l. is not appropriate. ०अर्पणव्यतिकराम्—bearing the red wounds of. धारणा—fixity of. अतिगूढ—deep-seated; अतिरूढ is a better reading.

P. 116. नातिविशदं—slightly, a faint kiss. असौ दासजन: &c.—'This thy slave feels life to be without purpose.' अवतंसतां &c.—Gracefully placed her folded hands on her forehead. अभिकामयमाना—herself seeking the love of. *Cf.* for a similar thought श्रिया दुराप: कथमीप्सितो भवेत् Śāk. III. 13. अभिसंधि—fixed purpose of the heart, intention. अविचारं—without troubling about (*i. e.* asking) the reason. पारं—the climax or highest perfection of. प्रागल्भ्य—proficiency, skill. आलेख्यरूप—an excellent portrait; प्रशस्तमालेख्यम्; रूप is added प्राशस्त्ये. तादृश—having that virtue. पर्वणि—Here पर्वन् means the new-moon day. विविक्ता—see com.; the first meaning is preferable. हुतभुक्ते—after the priest has worshipped the fire with offerings and retired. अगुरु—aloe-wood.

P. 117. विसंवाद:—disagreement; 'you should not fail to carry out my instructions'. कार्य:—शङ्कय: *V. l.* Then the meaning will be—'Don't you think that the rite will fail to produce the desired end.' संप्रधार्य—having decided upon the matter; taking counsel with. अनुमते—when they approve of it. प्रमदवनवाटी—a part of the female garden. शृङ्गाटिका—a place where four roads meet. आथर्वणिक—prescribed by the Atharva-Veda. संज्ञपित—killed. तद्धूमशमनेन—The disappearance of the smoke was to serve him as a sign. प्रगाढ—far advanced. वेतालोत्थापनं &c.—I will not raise a goblin for my own destruction. शास्त्रोपदेश—injunction of the Veda (which is not to be gainsaid). अद्भुतायमाना—coming as a wonder; prse. p. of the denom. from अद्भुत (अद्भुतायते).

P. 118. एष विप्रलम्भो न—This cannot be a deception but अति०. केव कथा—Whence can there be any possibility of fraud. अभ्यूह्य—Having given due thought or consideration to the matter. प्रौढ—pitchy or dense. गौरसर्षप—white mustard; it is one of the ingredients used in securing the efficacy of charms, etc. वसा—marrow. प्रावात्सीत्—Aor. of वस् with प्र; 'went forth in,' 'spread out'; this use of प्रवस् is rather rare; *cf.* प्रावसत् p. 129, where it is rightly used. निशान्तोद्यान—The garden attached to the palace. अवसित—

has a double meaning.—(1) The fool ) has made up his mind or taken his resolve; ( 2 ) he is doomed; see note on न्यस्त-शस्त्रिक p. 82. त्वदादिष्टया दिशा—according to your instructions ( *lit.* by the way pointed out by you ).

P. 119. रम्भोरु—Voc. of रम्भोरू ; रम्भे इव ऊरू यस्याः सा; ऊ is added in the fem. by ऊरूत्तरपदादौपम्ये Pán. IV. 1. 69. रागाग्नि—रागः love एव अग्निः. गुरु—The father or the elderly person authorized to give away a girl in marriage. प्रपदेन—The forepart of the foot, the tiptoe. इतरेतरव्यतिषक्त—intertwined. विभ्रान्त—sportively turned.

P. 120. चित्रभानु—Fire ( चित्रा भानवो यस्य ). उपधि—उपधीयते आरोप्यते अनेन; उपधा+इ (कि) fraud, trick, imposition. स्वस्वरूपभ्रंशः—you will lose your own form and gain this; you will be transformed. अजीर्णदोषं ख्यापयेयं—I would give out that he suffered from indigestion ( which led to his death ). अध्यवसितं—It has been settled or determined upon. दण्डचक्रं—a portion of an army. पुण्ड्रदेश—a district of eastern Bengal. पाञ्चालिक, परित्रात—two proper names. खनतिनाम्ना यवनात्—Khanati may be a Persian or an Arabic trader. The name, however, sounds somewhat strange. वज्र—a diamond. गृहपतिः—The Bhûshaná says ग्रामाध्यक्षः ; but this does not seem to be the meaning here; for he is also said to be जनपदमहत्तर ; the sense of गृहपति given in the Amarakosha is—a householder who helps the poor by giving them food, money-gifts &c. (सदान्नादिदानकर्ता). This sense will do here. Or it may be taken in the sense of the 'steward or the manager of the king's household;' and hence he was अन्तरङ्गभूतः ( his confidant). जनपदमहत्तर—The principal man of the country; the sheriff. शतहलिः—A proper name; the man was so named probably because he was a great landlord; (शतं हलाः ploughs) यस्य. दुष्टग्रामणीः—the wicked village-leader. His wickedness lay in his being on the side of Prahâravarman; see 1. 3, p. 122. जनपदकोपेन—by exciting the people of the country against him; by stirring factions against him.

P. 121. दण्डधर—A general; or, a judge or a magistrate. उद्धारकर्मन्—the act of uprooting (destroying) him. अचिरप्रस्तुत—lately planned or set on foot. प्रवृत्त०—into which a great quantity of clarified butter was poured. सेवां दत्तवान्—I admitted them to my presence, *i. e.* received their homage संहतोरू—having very stout (*lit.* coming close to each other ) thighs. ऊ is added to ऊरु in the fem. after संहित, शफ &c.

by Pán. IV. 1. 70. ऊरूपपीडं &c.—ऊरूभ्यां भुजाभ्यां चोपपीडं; for the Namuls see com.; the Ṇamulantas of पीड्, रुध् and कृष् preceded by उप are used when there is a noun in the Loc. or Instr. case used as an *Upapada.* राजकुलस्य शीलम्—the customary practices of the royal house. शुश्रूषयैव—only being devoted to his service (and not hostilely disposed towards him). दुःखमोहोपहताः—overpowered by distress and (consequent) despair. त्यक्तात्मानः—being desperate; regardless of their safety. He means—If we give them the least offence, they will seize the opportunity to attack our country and fight desperately, so it will not be a wise step on our part for the present; but if we attack them when they will have a rich harvest, we shall find them unprepared for battle, throw them into confusion by destroying their crops and gain supplies for ourselves. मुष्टिवध, सस्यवध—spoiling their seed-corn or ripe harvest. See Kám. Nít. XVI. 4.

P. 122. यात्रा—a hostile march. धर्मरक्षायै—That there should be no transgression or violation of justice or righteousness. अनुगुणेन—proper or suitable. राष्ट्रमुख्य—The sheriff of the country. निनाशयिषितः—desired to be destroyed. प्रकृतिस्थे—when restored to his own dignity or position. संरम्भः—adopting hostile measures; *lit.* proceeding impetuously against. उद्घोषयन्तः—loudly expressing. प्रहर्षकाष्ठा॰—who had reached the highest point of ecstatic joy. अभङ्ये च &c.—I was at once (च) installed the Yuvarája (crown-prince) at the command of my parents. प्रसाधितात्मा—*lit.* with my elevation secured; whose object was accomplished; or, according to the Com., 'with my intellect closely applied (to my work)'. देवपाद—*i. e.* of course Rája-váhana. दुर्भगान्—unpalatable, insipid, disagreeable. निर्विशन्—enjoying. अभियोग—an attack. लघुसमुत्थान—swift of foot, quickly marching. भूमि—the object of. पारतल्पिक—adultery; from परतल्प; तल्प properly means 'the bed,' hence, figuratively, the wife of; and aff. ठक् (इक). ॰हेतुतया—This is according to the principle 'The end justifies the means.' दुष्टामित्र॰—दुष्टाश्च ते अमित्राश्च; mark that the word अमित्र is *masc.* Note for the gender स्यातामामित्रौ मित्रे च सहजप्राकृतावपि Śiś. II. 36. प्रमापण—destruction; noun from the Cau. of मी 9 P. A'. with प्र to destroy. अर्थधर्मौ—the comp. may also be धर्मार्थौ (which is also the one more generally used) by the Várt. धर्मादिष्वनियमः *i. e.* either of the words may precede. अरीरधत—accomplished.

P. 123. स्निग्धदीर्घा—स्निग्धा च दीर्घा च; 'fixing upon him an affectionate and long gaze.'

सोऽहं--I who am thus commanded. एककर्मा—having the same mission to perform. ऊर्मिमालि०--sea-girt, bounded by the ocean. ऊर्मीणां माला अस्यास्तीति ऊर्मिभिर्मालते इति वा ऊर्मिमाली the sea. नेमि may also be taken separately. काशिपुरी-काशते शिवत्रिशूलोपरि अथ वा काशयति सर्वमिदम् इति काशी–इति शब्दकल्पद्रुमः. वाराणसीं—*Cf.* वरणासी च नद्यौ द्वे पुण्ये पापहरे उभे। तयोरन्तर्गता या तु सैषा वाराणसी श्रुता ॥. उपस्पृश्य--having bathed. मणिकर्णिका—Name of a sacred pool (तीर्थ) at Kâśî and the ghâṭa ( landing-place ) about it. The name is thus explained-विष्णोस्तपस्यापचयदर्शनाद्विस्मिततया शिवस्य मणिमयकुण्डलपतनादस्यास्तथात्वम्. अविमुक्तेश्वर—the lord of (अविमुक्त) Benares or Kâśî. The name Avimukta is thus accounted for—न विमुक्तं शिवाभ्यां यदविमुक्तं ततो विदुः. अन्धकमथन--Śiva, the destroyer of the demon Andhaka; Andhaka was the son of Kâśyapa and Ditî. He is represented as a demon with two arms and heads. He was called Andhaka, as he walked like a blind man though having good sight. He was slain by Śiva when he attempted to carry off the Pârijâta tree from heaven. According to the Matsya-P. he was about to be slain by Śiva for having attempted to carry off Pârvatî, but was admitted to the class of Gaṇas at his humble supplication. आयामवन्तं—very tall. आयसपरिघ—a large iron bar or rod used for locking or shutting a gate. ०परिकरं—who was girding his loins. उच्छून—swollen. कार्पण्य०—misery. क्षीण०—क्षीण worn away, *i. e.* with its animation gone, dull. साहसानुवादी—indicative of some desperate act. कृच्छ्रं—a deed of daring such as suicide. प्रपित्सते—Pres. 3rd pers. sing. of the Desid. of पद् with प्र; wishes to do, *i. e.* is about to undertake. प्रतिपत्स्यते—*V. l.* will also do, though the first is preferable. ०अवकाशः—room or occasion for me to render him help. संनाहः—preparation.

P. 124. निर्वर्ण्य—Having closely observed. पूर्वेषु—in the Western countries. कामचरः—wandering at will. The Bhûshaṇâ takes इषुकाम as the name of a province, but there is no authority for it. In Vámana's Káśiká and in the Sid.-Kau. as well, on Páṇ. II. 1. 50 and on दिक्पूर्वपदादसंज्ञायां ञः and प्राचां ग्रामनगराणाम् ( IV. 2. 107, VII. 3. 14 ) we have a town mentioned, but of the name of पूर्वेषुकामशमी

or इषुकामशमी; इषुकाम is not mentioned separately as the name of a province. गृहपति— may here mean 'the chief man in a village.' प्रयत्न०—Though brought up with care. दैवच्छन्दा०—in obedience to the will of destiny; as was fated. अर्य—a merchant. The word originally signified 'a cultivator of land, a peasant.' रूपाभिग्राहित:—caught with the (stolen) money on me; caught red-handed. वध्य—sentenced to death. हिंसाविहारी—delighting in killing. राजगोपुर:—The turret at the gate of the palace. उत्तम—principal. जनकण्ठरव—The sounds from the throats of, *i. e.* the clamour of; कण्ठरव is used to match with घण्टारव. मण्डलित०—curling his huge trunk ( काण्ड ) परिणमन्—when bending down to strike. दारुखण्ड—a log of wood used as a sort of stocks for the hands ( of a culprit ). सुषिर—holes. चण्डघट्टित—violently struck. प्रतिमान—the part between the two tusks. नेतृ—a driver. जातसंरम्भ:—exasperated, enraged. निवृत्य—turned tail. आक्रुष्ट:—censured, reproached.

P. 125. वारण—the goad. निर्याणभाग—The outer corner of the eye ( as being very sensitive to pain ). द्विपकीट—This vermin or pig of an elephant. निष्ठुर—peremptory. तद्विरम्य &c.—Can you therefore make up your mind to desist from this unworthy act and to follow an honourable course of life by accepting service under me? जातविश्रम्भेण—who had secured his confidence; qualifying मया; or separately, as जातश्वासो विश्रम्भश्च तेन—owing to the confidence he had in me रिपुंजयस्य—conqueror of the enemies ( Rájahamsa ). विश्रुतधी:—reputed for his intellect or ability. श्रुतर्षि:—adept in the Veda; or, a sage distinguished for his Vedic knowledge. Seven classes of Ṛishis are mentioned. *viz.* ऋषि, महर्षि, देवर्षि, ब्रह्मर्षि, परमर्षि, काण्डर्षि and श्रुतर्षि. द्वैमातुर:—born of his second or step-mother. By मातुरुत्संख्यासंभद्र पूर्वायाः Páṇ. IV. 1. 115, मातृ, preceded by a numeral, सं and भद्र takes the aff. अण् and changes its ऋ to उद्; so द्वैमातुर:, षाण्मातुर: &c. वेश—The habitation of harlots. दुर्नय—profligacy, dissolute conduct. मदनदमन—Śiva.

P. 126. चक्रमे—The use of the Perfect in the 1st pers. is a grammatical inaccuracy. छन्नं—secretly. आपन्नसत्त्वा—pregnant. अपविद्ध:—cast off. आरक्षिकपुरुष—the city-watch. दण्डपारुष्य—the severity of punishment. राजाज्ञया—this goes with बद्ध: प्राजिहीर्ष्ये. आक्रीडनगिरि—the pleasure-mountain in the garden. यथोपपन्न—that were ready at hand or could be got at the time. प्राजिहीर्ष्ये—was about to be killed;

Imperf. Pass. of the Desid. of हृ with प्र. लूनबन्धः--The blow did not kill him, but only cut off the cords that bound him. सपरिचारा—having with her the means of service. ०त्तंसितेन--decked with her sprout-like hands. अञ्जलिरेव किसलयः a bunch of sprouts; उत्तंसः अस्य संजातः सः उत्तंसितः; अञ्जलिकिसलयेनोत्तंसितः. मुख०--her curly hair waving about her face. अस्य मे—me in this plight or state. आभाषिता--familiarly addressed. वाङ्मय—in the form of words. परेतावास—the residence of the dead, a cemetery.

P. 127. आस्थानी—The royal court. हरसख—Kubera. वराकी—the poor girl. एतावत् &c.—the sum and substance of the whole I gathered. अभिन्न--the same in different lives. या किल &c.—Târâvalî was Kâmapâla's wife in more lives than one. In a previous birth she had been his wife named Aryadâsî, he being born as Śûdraka, and the mother of the boy whose re-birth from Kàntimatî had involved Kámapâla in his present trouble. This boy finally turns out to be Arthapála who is relating his account to Rájavâhana. For the easy understanding of the relationship here referred to and on the next page, l. 12, we give it clearly below. Kâmapâla was previously born as शौनक, and शूद्रक, so the relations stand thus—

| Name | Wives |
|---|---|
| शौनक | बन्धुमती, वेदिमती, हंसावली, नन्दिनी, गोपकन्या |
| शूद्रक | विनयवती, आर्यदासी, शूरसेना, रङ्गपताका, अर्यदासी |
| कामपाल | कान्तिमती, सोमदेवी, सुलोचना, इन्द्रसेना, तारावली. |

The wives are also said to be the same individuals in different lives. We get no information about Śaunaka and Śûdraka from the text. The relationship of Somadevî, Sulochanâ and Indrasená is also not directly mentioned. Perhaps they were Kântimatî's companions in the harem. It is difficult to see what purpose is served by the mention of the different individuals here. What the context requires is that Kàntimatî's son was also Târâvalî's son, being born of her as आर्यदासी in a previous life and nursed by Vinayavatî. अवस्थेत &c.—It appears that she was separated from the boy soon after his birth, who was therefore brought up by Vinayavatî. देव्यै वसुमत्यै &c.—See p. 19. कृतान्त--Destiny, providence, whose laws are fixed. The second कृतान्त means Yama. ०दर्शित--called into existence, created.

P. 128. प्रत्यपकृत्य--having returned the injury. निर्यातन--retaliation. प्रस्फुरन्तं—trembling. कन्याभिमर्षी—seeking union with your daughter; see p. 91. अनुवृत्त्या--The Com. takes this to mean सेवया; in this case the clause must be taken as ironical. 'I on a previous occasion violated your daughter without your अनुमति; now I have come to wipe off that offence by अनुवृत्ति, त+त, acting according to your wishes.' But it may better be taken to mean 'by repetition of the same act of daring'; *i. e.* 'to wreak my vengeance on you,' as is clear from his words प्रिये प्रत्यपकृत्य &c. above. दुहित॰--who conferred upon me the favour or honour of accepting my daughter's hand. उत्क्रान्तसीमा—transgressing the bounds of propriety. मन्त्रिपदापदेशं—under the guise of the ministerial post; *i. e.* I am a *mantrî* in name but really a *Yuvarája.* स—refers to Kâmapâla. तादृशे जन्तौ—refers to Pûrṇabhadra who is relating the account to Arthapàla. परिचर्यानुबन्धी--showing the favour of receiving service from me. परिचर्या सेवा तस्या अनुबन्धोऽस्यास्तीति. अलसक--consumption.

P. 129. विधिना--properly, duly. यौवनोन्मादिन्--flushed with the pride of youth. पैशुन्यवादिनः--Insinuating something wicked. इत्थमग्राह्यत--he was persuaded to take this view of things. भुजङ्ग--a dissolute fellow, a gallant. देवज्येष्ठं—the elder brother of Your Highness. प्रकृतिवि॰—To gain the confidence of the subjects. क्षिणोति पुरा—पुरा gives the Present the sense of the Future. दूषितः—set against him, made to be inimically disposed towards him. यक्षिणी—Táràvalî. अयथापूर्वं--a change. देवि...भद्रे—It is strange that the Queen should address कान्ति॰ as देवि and be addressed by her as भद्रे. These two should rather be interchanged. अयथातथ्येन—by telling a lie. सत्यमनतिक्रम्य यथातथम्। तथा तथशब्दो वा सत्यार्थः। तस्य भावः यथातथ्यम्. केन—on what account. किमपि कलुषिताशया--who was offended or displeased for some reason or other. मद्गोत्रापदिष्टा-addressed by my name. This misnaming is alluded to by Sanskrit poets as a constant source of trouble and offence to ladies. *Cf.* तस्याः स्त्रिया नामधेयेन &c. Vik. p. 29; गोत्रेषु स्खलितस्तदा भवति च व्रीडाविलक्षश्चिरम्। Sâk. VI. 5; see also Kum. IV. 8. प्रणयं &c.--disregarding entreaty or supplication. उपोढमत्सरा—her jealousy increased all the more. प्रावसत्—left us. अवसीदति—is wasting away. दौर्मनस्य--दुःस्थितं मनोऽस्य दुर्मनास्तस्य भावः दौर्मनस्यं mental distress or grief. प्रायेण—fully; or, with exaggeration (प्राय meaning plenty, abundance).

P. 130. अथ—After that, being thus told. असौ—Simhaghosha. अनतिपेशलाभिः—Not very pleasing or agreeable; or not cleverly uttered; indifferent words. अबन्धयत्–threw into confinement. स्थाने स्थाने—at every station or public centre. तथोद्धरणीये &c.—His eyes are to be put out in such a way that death must ensue. पुरः—before ( he dies ). व्यसन—peril, danger. किं तव &c.—Why should I hide it from you ? संकुले—in the crowd or tumult. भस्मनि हुतमिव &c.—*i. e.* will prove fruitless. *Cf.* 'All my efforts will end in smoke.' आशीविष—आशिषि in the jaw विषमस्य. A comp. of the पृषोदरादि class, स् being dropped and इ lengthened irregularly ; or आस्यां विषमस्य according to some. अभिगृह्य—having caught or secured him यदृच्छया—accidentally. नाम—'as if;' this has here the sense of अलीक (a feigned or pretended action). तथा विषं &c.—I will so restrain or check the poison ( from having a fatal effect ) that he will be cast off or left with indifference, as being dead. बोधयितव्या—should be apprised or informed. अनुप्राप्त—arrived just after these events. त्वया—refers to his mother. प्रेषणीयं—a message should be sent to.

P. 131. निरपेक्षं—Without any consideration of or regard to ( his connexions &c. ). गतिर्गन्तव्या—His course should be followed, *i. e.* should be accompanied in death. *Cf.* प्रमदाः पतिवर्त्मगा इति प्रतिपन्नं हि विचेतनैरपि । Kum. IV. 33. अनुकूल—worthy of, proper for. पश्चिमो विधिः—the last rite, *viz.* dying with their husband. काण्डपटी—canvas screen or curtain. संस्तरण—a bed. कृतानुमरणमण्डना—The woman about to immolate herself on the funeral pyre of her dead husband had to put on the dress of a *Suvásiní*; she had to wear a saffron-coloured garment and a similar bodice, with her hair untied, to put on her ornaments including the *Mangalasútra* or the auspicious neck-ornament, and to besmear her forehead with rubbed turmeric, the symbol of her married life. बाह्यकक्षा—the outer compound. प्रवेशयिष्ये—2nd Fut. pass.

घोषणास्थान—the place of proclamation ( where his eyes were to be taken out ). गूढतनुः &c.—secreted myself. यथायथं—as they were available. उच्चावच—of various sorts, all manner of talk ( about the culprit ). उद्धुरध्वनि—*adv.*; 'accompanied by loud shoutings.' It may also be an adj. qualifying महाजन, the whole being one comp. word. महाजन—a great conclave of people, the mob; *cf.* for this meaning महाजनः स्मेरमुखो भविष्यति Kum. V. 70. It may also mean—'the principal citizens;' महाजन

further on, however, means 'the mob.' मदभ्यासे—just below me. उपांशु—secretly. स्थूण, अङ्गारवर्ष—Two proper names. उपजप्य—having secretly instructed or prompted. उपजप्—means to make secret overtures to, to enter into a plot with. *Cf.* उपजापः कृतस्तेन तानाकोपवतस्त्वयि । Śiś. II. 99. The word occurs again at pp. 199 and 201 below. अन्धतमस—total loss of sight or blindness. Mark the ending; a final अ is added to तमस् after अव &c.; see com. न्याय्यः—*i. e.* is the proper punishment. प्राड्विवाक—a judge or magistrate. प्राट् च विवाकश्च प्राड्विवाकौ प्रश्नविवेकौ अस्य स्तः इति । 'विवादानुगतं पृष्ट्वा पूर्ववाक्यं प्रयत्नतः । विचारयति येनासौ प्राड्विवाकस्ततः स्मृतः ॥'

P. 132. भीतो नाम—See com.; 'as if I was terrified;' or, pretending to be frightened. *Cf.* पतितेन नाम p 130. त्रिहित०—ensuring the preservation of his life. विनाचिकीर्षितः—was desired (condemned) to be deprived of. दर्वीकरः—दर्वी (the expanded hood) एव करः यस्य a snake. रूढत्रास०—fled away, being seized or overpowered by fear. The comp. may also be taken as रूढत्रासो यस्य स चासौ द्रुतश्च. ०अर्थ—अर्थ the real state of things. धीरम्—steadily. कलङ्कयेयम्—I shall bring disgrace to. उत्सवोत्तरम्—उत्तर in such cases means 'conspicuous or distinguished by,' attended with, full of, &c. *Cf.* राज्ञां तु चरितार्थता दुःखोत्तरैव S'ák. V. p. 118; and *infra* उत्सवोत्तरा पुरी p. 203. मत्प्रति-षिद्ध—the effect being counteracted by me. संस्थित—dead; *cf.* Ragh. VIII. 40.

P. 133. मरणमण्डनं—Such ornaments and dress as a *Sati* usually wears. See above, note on कृतानुमरणमण्डनया p. 131. वैनतेयतां गतेन—acting the part of Garuda, *i. e.* in subduing the effect of the poison. Garuda is the principal deity invoked in the charm that nullifies the effect of serpent-poison. प्रस्नुतस्तनी—Such an effect on a mother at the sudden sight of her son is often described by Sanskrit poets. क्रूरा खलु तारावली—For she knew from Kubera that the foundling was then Kântimatî's, but once her own son; and the student has seen how, instead of bringing him to Kântimatî, she took him to Vasumatî; see pp. 19 and 127. परित्यक्तः—see p. 126. उपलभ्यापि &c.—The construction is कुबेरात् तत्त्वतस्तामुपलभ्य. सैव वा—Mark the force of वा introducing an alternative supposition correcting a previous statement. तादृशात—*i., e.* Vasumatî. भाग्यराशेः &c.—भाग्य is the result of a good store of religious merit. She means that she was not destined to enjoy the pleasure of hearing his sweet lispings, being poor in merit;

but Vasumatî was, and hence Táravalî did the right thing in taking the boy to her (Vasumatî). अन्यादृशी—अन्या इव पश्यति looking like another, as if changed, so much frantic with joy she was. तथाभूतम॰—*i. e.* his regaining his life and son. भाग्यवन्तं—is equivalent to भाग्यवत्तरं, the sense of the comparative being expressed by the Abl. मघवतः. मनाक्—a little. प्रतिपत्तिः—What measures are we to adopt, what line of action do you mean to follow? प्राब्रवीत्—Spoke with determination or decision.

P. 134. प्राकार (*v. l.* शाल) वलय—begirt (*i. e.* protected) by a rampart. अक्षय्य॰—the store-house of an inexhaustible number of weapons. अलङ्घ्यतमा—impregnable. गुप्तिः—defence. अनुरुध्यन्ते—approve of, like. बाह्याभ्यन्तर॰—बाह्यs are the people not immediately connected with a king, such as people of the border-kingdoms, foresters &c.; अभ्यन्तरs are the men immediately connected with the king, such as his family-priest, the ministers, commanders of his army, &c. See Kám. Nît. XVI. 19-21. कोप—disturbance, disaffection, rebellion. प्रकृत्यमित्र—ordinary foes. अमति इति अमित्रः; fr. अम् 1 P. to go against or अम् 10 P. to afflict with sickness, + इ + त्र by अमेर्द्विषति चित् (Unâdi IV. 174). सहजान्—natural (*i.e.* born) enemies. Enemies, like friends, are of three classes, *viz.* सहज or those by birth, as a paternal uncle and his sons; प्रकृतिशत्रु or प्रकृत्यरि is one whose property or territory lies close to one's own; and कृत्रिमशत्रु is one so by act, *i. e.* who has done some great harm. See Malli. on Śiś. II. 36. The following verses from Kàm. Nît. XXVII. will throw light on this:—अलब्धवेतनो लुब्धो मानी चाप्यवमानितः। क्रुद्धश्च कोपितोऽकस्मात्तथा भीतश्च भीषितः॥ यथाभिलषितैः कामैर्भिन्द्यादितांश्चतुर्विधान्। परपक्षे स्वपक्षे च यथावत्प्रशमं नयेत्। भेदं कुर्वीत यत्नेन मन्त्र्यमात्यपुरोधसाम्॥ पौराञ्जानपदांश्चैव दण्डमुख्यांश्च दण्डवित्। साधयेद्दानभेदाभ्यां यथायोगेन चापरान्॥ दुर्दान्त—proud, insolent; or, not easily to be quelled or put down. प्रतिविधाय—having taken counter-(defensive) measures; secure against. विज्ञापितोदन्तः—informed of the affair. पारग्रामिक—*Cf. supra*, p. 101. Although Kâmapála was not king, yet he was treated as a hostile person besieged in his residence, and hostile measures were adopted against him, such as that of cutting off supplies, &c. प्रत्यहन्यन्त—were counteracted. उदवसितं—a house. उदूर्ध्वम् अवसीयते; fr. सो 4 P. to finish, complete or सि 5 P. or 9 P. to bind, to fasten; + क्तः. गता च सा—she reached that subterranean passage. इन्दुकला—expresses loveliness, slenderness of the body &c. निर्धुनाना—entirely dispelling. विश्वंभरा-

the presiding goddess of the earth. The simile expresses lofty dignity, brilliance of complexion, &c. *Cf.* Ragh. XV. 82, 83. हरगृहिणीव—Not a happy simile, as भवानी, in her character as दुर्गा (the destroyer of demons), is fierce-looking and not gentle-looking. राजलक्ष्मीरिव &c.—*Cf.* for a similar idea अतिक्रान्तकुनृपतिसहस्र &c. Kád. p. 11.

P. 135. काशयष्टि:—The kâs'a plant. The kâs'a plant is chosen because it has a rich growth of white flowers, and can, therefore, fitly bear comparison with the woman having a hoary head. "This (kás'a) grass grows from ten to fifteen feet high, and the base of the flowers is surrounded with an immense quantity of bright silver-coloured wool which whitens all the fields."—Wilson. त्रासदीनं-piteously through fear. आज्ञापय-Tell us. सुदत्य:—He addresses his speech to all the women there, as he found them frightened and confused. Mark the fem. form; शोभना दन्ता यस्या: सा सुदती a young woman. दन्त becomes दत् at the end of a Bah. when the comp. implies age, or when the whole is a fem. name. See com. सत्यर्थे-there being an occasion for it. अनघ—free from any mishap or danger. सुरालय—the abode of the gods, heaven. अन्तर्वत्नी-big which child. A न् is added to the त् of the words अन्तर्वत् and पतिवत् before the fem. aff ई; see com. उपह्वरे—in secret. विधिवत्—in lawful wedlock; goes with दिशामि. प्रकाशावस्थापन—rearing (*lit.* placing) them openly. अरातिव्यसनाय—to meet calamity arising from, *i. e.* as a safe asylum against an enemy. It does not mean 'for the incarceration of an enemy,' as there is no reason why a subterranean house was needed for that purpose; again, why were the halls comfortably built there? भूमिगृह—an underground mansion. कृत्रिम &c.—कृत्रिमश्वासौ शैलश्च तस्य गर्भे उत्कीर्णा नाना मण्डपा यत्र तादृक् प्रेक्षागृहम्. प्रेक्षागृह—A dancing and music hall. परिबर्ह—retinue or train of attendants.

P. 136. भोग्यवस्तु—articles of luxury, stores. द्व्यङ्गुलभित्तौ —about two inches (fingers) deep in the wall. द्वे अङ्गुली परिमाणमस्या द्व्यङ्गुला भित्ति:. अर्धपाद—a stone-covering (forming a trapdoor). किष्कुविष्कम्भकं—a hand (or a span) in measure (square hand). समा:-years; the word is used generally in the pl. कामं—granted that. स्वमात्रा—her mother. प्राप्तरूपं—Here रूप is added in the sense of excellence (प्रशंसा); see *supra*, p. 80 com.; *cf.* also सुचरूपा Sâ'k. II. 16, and Rághav. on it. प्रत्युद्धृत्य —lifting it up from the opposite side वासगृह—the bed-chamber. स्त्रैण–a multitude of women. The aff. न has the sense of 'a collection of.' संदित–bound; p. p. of दो 4. P. with सम्. मलिन—sullen, gloomy. बिलकथा—the adventure about the subterranean cavern. निकृष्टाशय—base-hearted, vile in purpose. यथार्हेण कर्मणा—with the proper ceremonies. प्रकृति &c.—this explains why he was not set at liberty; it may also be taken with मुमुक्षितः.

P. 137. कृतकर्मा—कृतानि कर्माणि (services) येन; who had been serviceable before. अभियुक्त—attacked. बहूपयुक्ता—made to serve a manifold purpose. ते श्वशुरः—Siṃhaghosha is Arthapála's father-in-law on account of his marriage with Maṇikarṇiká, the posthumous daughter of Chaṇḍaghosha, Siṃhaghosha's elder brother. प्रीतिस्मेरः—smiling joyfully. स्मेर is fr. स्मि + र by नमिकम्पिस्म्यजसकमहिंसदीपो रः Páṇ. III. 2. 167. र is added कर्तरि (in the sense of the agent) to these roots; so we get नम्र, कम्प्र, स्मेर, अजस्र, कम्र, हिंस्र and दीप्र.

अभ्रंकष—touching or scraping the clouds. कष् takes the aff. खच् after सर्व, कूल &c. (Páṇ. III. 2. 42); see com. Before the aff. खच् and खश् the words अरुस्, द्विषत्, and those ending in अ, forming the object of the verb with which they are used prepositionally, take the augment मु. वनस्पति—वनस्य पतिः; a tree. The सु comes in, as the word belongs to the पारस्करादि class; *cf.* Páṇ. VI. 1. 157; see also p. 157. परिणतपतङ्ग &c.—परिणत ripened, about to set; पतङ्ग the evening sun; स एव बालपल्लवः सोऽवतंसः संजातोऽस्य, wearing the head ornament of tender sprouts in the form of the evening sun. उपास्य संध्यां—having performed the evening twilight rites. समीकृत—were levelled (being covered up by darkness). निम्नोन्नत—the high and the low places, irregularities. शरारु—शृणाति इति (fr. शॄ + आरु); ferocious animals. शर्व—Śiva. शार्वर–nocturnal, nightly. आध्मात—covered, screened. "In which the deep caverns were filled up (covered) with the mass (flood) of nocturnal darkness, dark like" &c. Mark the recurrence the letter श in these three lines.

P. 138. एकक—एक एव एकाकी or एककः (aff. कन्); Páṇ. V. 3. 52. उपधाय—using it as a pillow. असुखायिषत किमपि—felt an indescribable pleasure. अभ्यमनायिष्ट—felt cheered or delighted. असुखायिषत and अभ्यमनायिष्ट are Aor. forms of सुखायते (सुखं वेदयते) and अभिमनायते denom. verbs fr. सुख (when the agent experiences the pleasure; see com.) and मनस् with अभि by adding क्यङ् (य). आह्लादयिषत Aor. 3rd pers. pl. of ह्लाद् I. A'. to feel pleasure. हृषिताः—thrilled, bristled.

p. p. p. of हृष् 4 P. to stand on end, as hair; the form is also हृष्ट, इ b ing optionally prefixed to त in this sense by हृषेर्लोमसु Pâṇ. VII. 2. 29. हृष्टं, हृषितं लोम ; see Sid.-Kau. for further particulars. पर्यस्फुरत् &c.—the throbbing of the right arm in the case of males indicates some impending good fortune; *cf.* स्फुरति च बाहु: कुत: फलमिहास्य Sâk. I. 15 and our notes *ad loc* ; see also Ragh. VI. 68. वितान—a canopy. समया—near. चित्रास्तरणं—a bed of diverse colours; चित्रास्तरण may also probably mean 'carpets of various colours.' आगलित—a little displaced. अमृत &c.—अमृत water; ॰फेनपटलवत्, पटलमेव च यद् &c. आदिवराह—The primeval Boar (Vishṇu's 3rd incarnation) that lifted the Earth out of the waters in which she was sinking. See our note on रसातलादादिभवेन पुंसा &c. Ragh. XIII. 8; and *cf.* Vishṇu-P. तत: समुत्क्षिप्य धरां स्वदंष्ट्रया महावराह: स्फुटपद्मलोचन: । रसातलादुत्पलपत्रसंनिभ: समुत्थितो नील इवाचलो महान् ॥ अंसस्रस्त &c.-This corresponds to आगलितस्तनांशुका ; as the earth emerged from the sea the oceanic waters rolled back from her head, and so she looked like the princess with her upper garment slipped off from her bosom

भयसाध्वस—The meaning assigned to भय by the Com. is far-fetched and inappropriate, as it cannot be taken with the princess. The princess was in deep sleep and the earth was also motionless on account of the trance. The tremor was due to the stroke of the snout of the Boar; *cf.* येन प्रलयवराहघोणाभिघातभीता भूतधात्री &c. Kâd. Hence the two are compared here. साध्वस—agitation, perturbation. लास्य—dancing, throbbing. As her breath passed along the lower lip, the rays issuing from it seemed to throb. The poet compares her lower lip, which excited passion, to a spark of the burnt body of Cupid, and she was blowing it up as it were into a flame. षट्चरण—a bee. जातनिद्रं—(1) closed; (2) closed in sleep. लोचनेन्दीवर—The blue-lotus-like eye takes the place of the bee confined in the closed lotus. *Cf.* Bhaṭṭi. IV. 19; Ragh. V. 68. ऐरावत &c. —first plucked off and then cast away (lying disorderly) by वल्लरी—a branch.

P. 139. ऊर्ध्वाण्डकपाल—the upper half of the universal egg, *i. e.* the vault of the sky. उदर—the convex cavity of. शक्तिध्वज-Kârttikeya. शिखर-the dome of his temple. शूल-the trident on its summit. ॰उत्सेधं—lofty like. According to Laghudîpikâ (a short com. on the D.-K.; see the quotation n the com.) it means 'a palace having the god Kârttikeya set on the ground floor and the trident on the dome or top, and technically called Nandyávarta.' This sense seems to be preferable to that given by the Bhúshaṇâ, *viz.* 'as lofty as the temple of Kârttikeya with the trident on its dome.' सौध—a mansion with white-washed walls. कुतस्त्यं—whence comes this. हंसतूल०—a silken bed stuffed with downy feathers; see p. 97. शीतरश्मि०—the nymphs are supposed to be borne along the ropes formed of the lunar rays. देवीव &c.—like the goddess Lakshmî. शारदशशाङ्क—is peculiarly white, and is often referred to by Sanskrit poets; *cf.* Śâk. कः शारदीं ज्योत्स्नां पटान्तेन वारयति III. p. 74.

संवाह्यमाना—(1) being acted upon; (2) gently pressed or shampooed. संकुचति-(1) is closed; (2) closes her eyes in sleep; this is one of the signs which distinguish her from the immortals. निद्राति *v. l.*—sleeps. शबलित—variegated, decked. उद्भिन्न—on which there appear. निर्भर—*v. l.* दुर्लच makes no sense. The Com.'s. meaning असह्य is far-fetched. वैवर्ण्य—change of colour, it being dried up. वर्णक—the paint or unguent. परिभोगा०—according as they are used or worn. धूसरिमन्—duskiness (which does not appear in the case of heavenly beings). These are the accidents from which the denizens of heaven are exempt. Three of the signs here mentioned are among the six by which Damayantî recognized Nala; *cf.* सुरेषु नापश्यदवेक्षताक्ष्णोर्निमेषमुर्वीभृति संमुखी सा। इह त्वमागत्य नले मिलेति संज्ञानदानादिव भाषमाणम् ॥ नाबुद्ध बाला विबुधेषु तेषु क्षोदं क्षितेरैक्षत नैषधे तु। पत्ये सृजन्त्याः परिरम्भमुर्व्याः संभूतसंभेदमसंशयं सा ॥ स्वेदः स्वदेहस्य वियोगतापं निर्वापयिष्यन्निव संसिसृक्षोः। हीराङ्कुरश्वाराणि हेमनीव नले तयाऽऽलोकि न देवतेषु ॥ Nai. XIV. 19-21. तद्देषा &c.—By observing these signs he determines that she is a mortal, and not a superhuman being. सौकुमार्य—loveliness. संहताः—joined together, stout and firm (and not loosened like those of married ladies). पाण्डुता०—mingled with paleness (brought on by her longing, and indicating that she was unmarried yet). Dissolve पाण्डुतया अनुविद्धा. अधरमणि—her ruby-like lower lip. अनत्यापूर्ण—not much rounded, not very fleshy. कठोर—developed, expanded; hence, blooming.

P. 140. अनङ्गबाण०—Because she had not yet been subject to the influence of love. विभ्रमधुरं—gracefully or charmingly on account of innocence or ease of mind (freedom from any misgiving). निर्दय०—cruel, *i.e.* hard-pressing. अनतिक्रान्त०—०मर्यादं चेतो यस्य whose mind has never entertained or harboured a thought unworthy of an honourable man. The intended sense is well brought out in the Com. आसक्त्यनुरूपं—*Lit.* in a manner becoming the love I feel for her; hence, in obedience to the inspiration of love. स्पष्टं—undoubtedly. *Cf* p 98, l 11. अथाहं—and yet. स्पृष्टास्पृष्टं—just touching her body (neither in close contact with, nor separate from, her person). आविद्ध°—in a manner filled with love and fear blended together; overpowered by the joint influence of. लक्ष्यसुप्तः—feigning sleep; outwardly asleep but observing what passed around. लक्ष्य pretence, shame; *cf.* इदानीं परीक्षे किं लक्ष्यसुप्तमुत परमार्थसुप्तमिदं द्वंद्वं Mṛich. III. p. 78; also दीर्घं चापि न मर्षयेदभिमुखं स्याल्लक्ष्यसुप्तं यदि *Ibid.* III. 18. रोमोद्भेद—horripilation caused by the touch is one of the *S'áttvika* bhávas; जृम्भा is a Vibhâva or external sign of a feeling; मन्थर may better be taken to mean 'dull;' see Bhúshaṇâ. स्खलित—moving, trembling. तान्त—wearied, languid; p. p. p. of तम्. अनतिपक्व—incomplete, broken. अपाङ्गपरभाग &c.—with the beautiful corners of her eyes reddened. त्रास°—see com. विलास—particular posture of the body in the presence of a lover; विलासोऽङ्गविशेषो यः प्रियाप्रावासनादिषु. विभ्रम—particular sportive actions of the body under the influence of love; amorous gesticulations. See com. व्यवहितानि—*Lit.* screened or mixed with; hence, full of. व्रीडान्तराणि—controlled by modesty (*i. e.* not freely displayed). कामावेग°—under the sway of vehement love. साध्वसायास—साध्वसजनित आयासः (Madhy. Comp.); languor or exhaustion. स्वेदपुलक—clusters of the drops of perspiration.

P. 141. मधुर°— charmingly contracted at the corner. त्रिभाग-*lit.* means 'the third part.' तृतीयो भागस्त्रिभागः। संख्याशब्दस्य वृत्तिविषये पूरणार्थत्वमिष्यते। यथा शतांशः सहस्रांशः इति। Malli. on Kum. V. 57. आविष्ट—possessed by. किमपि—under the influence of some unknown power; I do not know how. As to the unknown power, see p. 143. l. 11. अननुकूल—unpleasant, disagreeable. विप्रलम्भ—an illusion. माया—magic power by which such illusions are wrought or unreal scenes presented to view. प्रतिशयिता भवामि-I shall lie down without food till I gain my object. *Cf.* अनया च किलास्मै प्रतिशयिताय स्वप्ने समादिष्टम् p. 149; कुरङ्गैरपि प्रतिशयितैरिव Kàd. p. 335. प्रतिशयन means lying down without food, with an intention even to die, before a deity, and keeping there until one secures the desired end.

तान्त—withered; see above. क्लिष्ट—worn out. निवसनो°—Dissolve क्लिष्टं निवसनमुत्तरीयं च यस्याः; because the same garments were used; according to a line quoted by Mr. Agashe, a woman in separation wears—वासस्तदेव वपुषो वलयं तदेव हस्तस्य सैव जघनस्य च रत्नकाञ्ची. निरलक्तक &c.—drily red, being destitute of the red lac-paint. जर्जरित—parched. धूम्र—dusky. रुधिरावशेषं—the animation and glow being gone, only blood remains behind. लोहिततर—excessively red. कुलचारित्र—virtuous conduct worthy of a noble family; चरित्रमेव चारित्रम्. विभ्रमेण—which had the grace of, which looked like. एकवेणी०—The mass of hair collected into a single braid and allowed to hang on the back reaching down the hips. Ladies in separation are often described by poets as wearing this एकवेणी; *cf.* नीलभागामया वेण्या जघनं गतयैकया । नीलया नीरदापाये वनराज्या महीमिव ॥ Rám. Sund. Ká. 15. 25; etc.; Ayodh. K. X. 9 Śák. VII. ततः प्रविशति एकवेणीधरा शकुन्तला p. 194; and Śl. 21; गण्डाभोगात्कठिनविषमामेकवेणीं करेण Megh. II. 32. चूडिका—a sort of bodice, a covering. The technical meaning (a bracelet made of the horn of a rhinoceros or the like, *i.e.* of ivory &c.) given by the Bhú. does not seem to be intended, as is shown by the word परिवृता. पतिव्रतापताका—the banner, *i. e.* the best of. The preceding signs showed that she was like a dutiful wife, in separation, pining for her husband. क्षामक्षामा-greatly emaciated. The repetition shows excess; *cf.* क्षामक्षामकपोलमाननं S'âk. III. 8. अनुभाव—superhuman power. वर्णावकाश-complexion. वात्सल्य-maternal affection.

P. 142. मणिभद्रस्येति—see p. 19. राजराजप्रवर्तितां—See *supra*, p. 127. वो जननी—Being the mother of Arthapála, she bore maternal relation to the other *Kuma'ras* also, as they were bound together by a sort of artificial fraternity.

*Cf.* Wilson's remark on this—"The fifth section relates the adventures of Pramati, who is here represented as the son of Kâmapâla by the Yakshiṇî Tárávalî, and not, as in the Introduction, the son of Sumati. Arthapála is there also called the son of Târa'valî, while, as we have seen in the preceding narrative, he is described as the son of Kántimatî. Either the author has been nodding, or the Introduction is the work of a different writer, who has been heedless or forgetful of the narrative of his predecessor." Such is Wilson's remark; and the sentence further on, कथं मत्सुत एवाय वत्सस्य अर्थपालस्य प्राणभूतः सखा &c. on p. 143, at first sight seems to support it. But it is due to Wilson's ignorance of the fact that Indian ladies regard the friend of their son as a son and address him as such. In the above sentence she calls Pra. her son but calls Artha. वत्स. Even in Nârâyaṇabhaṭṭa's पूर्वपीठिका of the Das. published by Mr. Agashe, he along with प्रमति is called the son of Sumati.

पितुः—*i. e.* his uncle. ०कलुषिताशया—my mind or reason being clouded; see p. 129, ll. 13, 14. अनुशयविधुर—अनुशय is fr. शी

with अनु and means 'what sticks to the mind after ( अनु ) and causes pain,' hence repentance, remorse. विधुर—विगता धूः कार्यभारो यस्मात् (with अच् added at the end); which cannot bear a burden or responsibility; hence, unnerved, helpless; hence, here, distressed; afflicted with repentance. *Cf.* मयि च विधुर भावः कान्ताप्रवृत्तिपराङ्मुखः Vik. IV. 20. रक्षोरूप—in the form of a demon. चण्डिका—a passionate or irascible woman, a virago. प्रवासदुःखाय—that you should experience the pangs of separation. आविष्टा—possessed. श्रावस्ती—name of a town, the modern Sahet-mahal, on the southern bank of the river Irávatî. It was the capital of the Uttar-Kosalas, 58 miles north of Ayodhyá, where Lava is said to have reigned and which is called Śarávatî in Ragh. XV. 97.' "It was the Savatthipura of the Buddhists. Buddha resided here for 25 years." Agashe. न तत्त्वतः परिच्छिन्नः—I did not know you properly or as to your real character. अविरल०—beset with many, abounding in, dangers. सुभग—pleasant or delightful in summer; *cf.* सुभगसलिलावगाहाः S'ák. I. 3. विमानहर्म्य—a very lofty palace ( with seven stories ); विमान may be a name, or a building like a balloon in form; *cf.* विमान-प्रतिच्छन्द. Vik. II.

P. 143. आत्मालीकप्रत्याकलन०—Adv. comp.; with trepidation seizing me at (the consciousness of my crime) the offence I had offered to my husband. She was afraid because Gaurî might know her crime and reprove her for the same. प्रणत—bowed down with, overpowered. It may mean 'favourably inclined,' if the reading be ०हृदयाम्. प्रत्यापन्न०—I regained my superhuman power भाव—heart. आत्मानं &c.—do not disclose or communicate to each other their love. आघ्राता—overpowered or subdued (enslaved by). लब्धलक्षः—on finding an opportunity or leisure. Perhaps the reading is ०लक्ष्यः—on definitely knowing the object of his love ( *lit.* his mark ). प्राञ्जलि—प्रबद्धः अञ्जलिर्येन तम्. अभ्यवर्तिषि—set out for. निगम—a residence of merchants; a market—place. नैगम—a merchant, a citizen. The word occurs in Vik. V. 4. ताम्रचूड—a cock. वृद्धविटः—an old cunning Brâhmaṇa. नारिकेलजातिः—of the cocoanut breed; a large and strong cock. बलाकाजातिः—one of the Balâkâ kind. It is described as long-necked, white, and of great strength. प्रतिविसृष्ट—set up or matched against.

P. 144. व्युत्पादित—enlightened, made acquainted with, the real nature of things. उपहस्तिका—A small purse or box

( see com. ) अतिसंरब्ध—very furious, greatly excited. अनुप्रहार—as each struck the other. स्वपक्ष—the partisans or each. कण्ठीरवरव—*lit.* the lion's roar, the war-cry, the cry or shout of encouragement. स्ववाट०—his own part of the country or party; for the Bráh. belonged to the eastern part of the country. यथोविरुद्धं—Because यथारेव समं वित्तं &c. सत्यर्थे—If there be an occasion for it; see *supra,* p 135. l 6. हंसक—an anklet (ornament for the feet); *cf.* सरित इव सविभ्रमप्रपातप्रणादितहंसकभूषणा विरेजुः। Śiś. VII. 23 पर्यायेण—alternately. निर्वर्णयन्ती—closely marking or observing. सवितर्कम—वितर्केण सहितं यथा तथा (Avya); surmisingly. अनाकस्मिक –not accidental, not surely a matter of chance; *i. e.* occasioned by some motive. चिरस्थिति—standing for a long time. The Com. needlessly takes स्थिति in the sense of स्थैर्य. कथासंश्रिता—engaged in conversation. देशातिथि—one coming from a different country (and not merely a different village), a foreigner. गुणः—favour.

P. 145. संबाध—a crowd. तद् हर्म्यतलं—that (*i. e.* that was seen by me) surface of the mansion. प्रकामवि०—very extensive. प्रतिकृति—a portrait. तावतीं भूमिं—that stage in the progress of love, or that intensity of love. व्यथितोन्मादिता—tormented and driven to insanity. उन्माद is one of the ten stages of love; see *supra* p. 95, note on उन्मादयन. निर्बन्धपृष्ट—asked with importunity, or insistingly. समर्थ—adequate; *lit* capable of explaining the whole. संशयाना—suspecting; pres. p. of शी with सम्. व्याजसुप्ता—feigning sleep. उल्लसन्—swelling, rising. किमेष स्वप्नः—could this be a dream? गमय—allow to pass. निराशङ्क०—which might enable me to reside in the princess' apartment without any apprehension of danger. अभ्युपगमय्य—having somehow made her to agree to it, having persuaded her. खर्वट—a village at the foot of a mountain. See, however, note on नगरग्राम etc. p. 157. विश्रमय्य—having asked me to take rest. *Cf.* शकटदास विश्रामय करभकम्। Mud. p. 70.

P. 146. प्रत्यादेश—*Lit.* ordering back; setting aside; hence, an exceller, a rival. *Cf.* प्रत्यादेशो रूपगर्वितायाः श्रियः Vik I.; प्रत्यादेशो मनुष्मतां Kád. p. 5. It also means 'rejection;' *cf* Śák. VI. 9. नवमालिका—is noted for its softness. *Cf.* येन नवमालिकाकुसुमपेलवा त्वं &c Śák. p. 19. समापत्तिदृष्टा—seen accidentally. *Cf.* समापत्तिदृष्टेन केशिना Vik. p. 10. नाराच—steel-pointed arrows. ०शल्योद्धरणक्षमः—The Com. reads ०णाक्षमः,—evidently taking it with the speaker. धन्वन्तरि—The physician of the gods, and one of the 14 jewels produced at the churning of the ocean, with a cup of nectar in his hand. परिवर्तित०—having changed my dress for a woman's; having disguised myself in female apparel. नाम—अलीके, assuming the character of, giving out that. The author only knows how a strong and well-built young man with muscular arms like Pramati ( all the Kumâras were such ) could assume the disguise of a young girl and pass for such. The device, however, is ingeniously planned. Perhaps this part of the story was suggested by the 15th story of Vetála, wherein mention is made of a boy disguised as a girl and his introduction as such in the royal household and his intrigue with the princess; the following extract from the Kathásaritságara, XII. 22, will make the similarity clear—तद्रूपं तं समादाय गत्वा धूर्ताधिपोऽथ सः । तत्प्रिया-जनकं भूपमास्थाने तं व्यजिज्ञपत् ॥ राजन्नेकोऽस्ति मे पुत्रः कन्या दूराच्च तत्कृते । मयैषा याचिताऽऽनीता स च क्वापि गतोऽधुना ॥ तमन्वेष्टुमहं यामि तदेषा रक्ष्यतां त्वया । आनयामि सुतं यावत्त्वं हि विश्वस्य रक्षिता ॥ तच्छ्रुत्वा शापभीत्या च प्रतिपद्य स भूपतिः । सुतामानाययामास यशःकेतुः शशिप्रभाम् ॥ जगाद चैतां पुत्रीमां कन्यां रक्षेः स्वमन्दिरे । स्वपार्श्वे एव चाहारशय्यां चास्याः प्रकल्पयेः ॥ ślokas 27-31 ; अथ तत्र तया साकं स मन्त्रिसुतभार्यया । तस्थौ द्विजो दिवा नारी रात्रौ च पुरुषोऽभवत् ॥ ९८ ॥ शशिनाऽनुगतः सख्या तरुणद्विजरूपिणा । आगत्य तं यशः—केतुं प्रह्वो राजानमब्रवीत् ॥ आनीतोऽयं मया पुत्रो देहि मे तां स्नुषामिति ॥ * * * * * ब्रह्मन्न जाने क्व गता सा स्नुषा ते क्षमस्व तत् । अपराधात्सुतस्यार्थे ददामि स्वसुतां तव ॥ १०२ ॥ &c. धर्मासन—judgement-seat, throne of justice, *i. e.* sitting on which a king dispenses judgement. विद्यामयं &c.—The only price charged was learning. वैवाह्य—fit for a marriage-connexion. अनुमता दातुं—betrothed. संन्यसिष्ये—संन्यासं ग्रहीष्यामि ( *i. e.* enter upon the fourth stage of life ). दुरभिरक्षतया—the care of ( grown-up ) daughters being an arduous or difficult task. आपन्नशरण—the protector or succour of the distressed. अधीतिन—अधीतमनेन proficient in sacred lore. See com. at p. 147. अगति—helpless, having no other course left. आदिराज—his predecessors ( आदिराजानां &c.); Or sing. आदिराजः, which may refer to Vaivasvata Manu; *cf.* वैवस्वतो मनुर्नाम, माननीयो मनीषिणाम् । आसीन्महीक्षितामाद्यः प्रणवश्छन्दसामिव ॥ Ragh. I. 11 'The chief of those whose careers were as noble and exalted as that of Manu, the first king.' आदिराजो मनुरिव प्रजानाम् । Rámá. According to some आदिराज is पृथु. The Mah.-Bhâr mentions आदिराज as one of the sons of अविक्षित्:—अविक्षितः परिक्षित्तु शबलाश्वश्च वीर्यवान् । आदिराजो विराजश्च शाल्मलिश्च महाबलः ॥ A'śr. V.P. 101. 40. But this king could not have been meant. Daṇḍin probably refers by आदिराज to the preceding kings, as in his

Kâvyâdarśa:-आदिराजयशोबिम्बमादर्शं प्राप्य वाङ्मयम्। तेषामसंनिधानेऽपि न स्वयं पश्य नश्यति ॥-where the Com. says आदिकालीना इक्ष्वाकुप्रभृतयो राजानः as is also clear from the author's word तेषाम् in the third line. धुर्यः—धुरं वहतीति; also धौरेय by adding ढक् (एय); see com.; *lit.* 'one who bears a yoke;' hence, the chief of.

P. 147. भवद्भुज०—gives the हेतु. Her chastity remaining inviolate under the shadow of your arm. अभिमन्यमानः—approving of it. *Cf. supra*, अभ्यमनायिष्ट चान्तरात्मा p. 138. फल्गुनीषु उत्तरासु—The twelfth lunar mansion consisting of two stars having the figure of a bed. Here the full-moon-day is meant, as this is the asterism of that day and gives the name to the month. गोरुतान्तरं—A distance covered by the lowing of a cow. वानीर—a sort of cane. विहारव्याकुले—being deeply engaged in sport. मग्नाप्लुतः—diving and swimming off (under water). जामाता नाम—here नाम is used to indicate a feigned or pretended action (अलीके); *cf. supra* भीतो नामावप्लुत्य p. 132; and *infra* कार्तान्तिको नाम भूत्वा p. 159. उन्मङ्क्ष्यामि—I shall emerge. आस्थानी—the royal assembly. श्रीभुजा०—he is fit to serve you, the enjoyer of wealth, *i. e.* the wealthy king. गृहीतिन्—one who has mastered. Words like अधीतिन्, गृहीतिन् &c., govern the loc. of their object, by the Vârt. 'क्तस्येन्विषयस्य कर्मण्युपसंख्यानम्.' The six *angas* or minor works necessary for the proper understanding of the Vedas and the ritual are:—शिक्षा कल्पो व्याकरणं निरुक्तं ज्योतिषां गतिः। छन्दोविचितिरित्येष षडङ्गो वेद उच्यते॥. आन्वीक्षिकी—logic; it also means metaphysics or आत्मविद्या. *Cf.* Kâmandaka आन्वीक्षिक्यात्मविद्या स्यादीक्षणात्सुखदुःखयोः। ईक्षमाणस्तया तत्त्वं हर्षशोकौ व्युदस्यति ॥.

चतुःषष्टिकला &.—For the sake of the curious reader the sixty-four arts mentioned by Hindu writers are given below in a foot-note from Vâtsyâyana's Kâma.—Sút. III. 16.* आगम—theory. प्रयोग—Practice. तन्त्र—a treatise on a particular art.

---

* गीतं, वाद्यं, नृत्यं, आलेख्यं, विशेषकच्छेद्यं, तण्डुलकुसुमबलिविकाराः, पुष्पास्तरणं, दशनवसनाङ्गरागः, मणिभूमिकाकर्म, शयनरचनं, उदकवाद्यं, उदकाघातः, चित्राश्चयोगाः, माल्यग्रथनविकल्पाः, शेखरकापीडयोजनं, नेपथ्यप्रयोगाः, कर्णपत्रभङ्गाः, गन्धयुक्तिः, भूषणयोजनं, ऐन्द्रजालाः, कौचुमाराश्च योगाः, हस्तलाघवं, विचित्रशाकयूष (०कापूप०) भक्ष्यविकारक्रिया, पानकरसरागासवयोजनं, सूचीवानकर्माणि, सूत्रक्रीडा, वीणाडमरुकवाद्यानि, प्रहेलिका, प्रतिमाला, दुर्वाचकयोगाः, पुस्तकवाचनं, नाटकाख्यायिकादर्शनं, काव्यसमस्यापूरणं, पट्टिकावेत्रवानविकल्पाः, तक्षकर्माणि, तक्षणं, वास्तुविद्या, रूप्यरत्नपरीक्षा, धातुवादः, मणिरागाकरज्ञानं, वृक्षायुर्वेदयोगाः, मेषकुक्कुटलावयुद्ध-

पुराण—A Purâṇa treats of five topics—सर्गश्च प्रतिसर्गश्च वंशो मन्वन्तराणि च । वंशानुचरितं चैव पुराणं पञ्चलक्षणम् ॥. इतिहास—fr. इतिह a particle expressing past occurrences orally handed down; तदास्ते अस्मिन्; properly means the philosophy of history; historical facts so arranged as to teach moral lessons &c. It is defined as धर्मार्थकाममोक्षाणामुपदेशसमन्वितम् । पूर्ववृत्तं कथायुक्तमितिहासं प्रचक्षते ॥. आख्यायिका—see *supra*, p. 21. उपनिषद:—portions of the Veda (forming the उत्तरमीमांसा or वेदान्त) the main object of which is to explain the true relation of the world, as also of the individual soul, to Brahma, and to point out thereby the true means of salvation. अर्थशास्त्र—or the Pûrvamímâmsâ, which explains the Vedic Mantras applicable to the ritual. Or अर्थशास्त्र may have its usual meaning of 'The science of wealth or political economy.' निर्मत्सर: &c.—an appreciator of the merits of others without being jealous.

P. 148. वल्गुवाक्य:—of agreeable or sweet address. संविभाग०—munificient. श्रुतधर:—श्रुतस्य धर:, धरतीति धर:; श्रुत sound knowledge of the Śâstras; *cf.* श्रुतमप्यधिगम्य ये रिपून् &c. Kir. II. 41. न च गुणेषु &c.—Nor do I see any virtue which he does not possess. वैलक्ष्य—embarrassment, perplexity, confusion. अनित्यता०—by mentioning the fact that worldly things are after all transitory. उपक्रमिष्यसे—proceed to, be prepared for. अनर्घै:—of great value. उपच्छन्द्य—having coaxed or gratified. कपटप्रपञ्च—the laying out or formulating a fraudulent plan or scheme. पाञ्चालशर्मा—This somewhat abrupt introduction of the name of the Brâhmaṇa at the close of the episode is probably for the sort of alliteration it gives with पञ्च in प्रपञ्च. निपुणं-cleverly, skilfully. अहीनकाल—immediate, without loss of time. नवमालिका—The princess of that name; also, the creeper of that name. स्मितमुकुलित—blooming with a smile. ऊर्जितं—high spirit, nobility of mind. This may also be taken as an adj. meaning 'lofty', noble, qualifying चेष्टितम्.

---

विधि:, शुकशारिकाप्रलापनं, उत्सादने संवाहने केशमर्दने च कौशलम्, अक्षरमुष्टिकाकथनं, म्लेच्छितविकल्पा:, देशभाषाविज्ञानं, पुष्पशकटिका, निमित्तज्ञानं, यन्त्रमातृका, धारणमातृका, संपाठ्य मानसी. काव्यक्रिया, अभिधानकोश:, छन्दोज्ञानं, क्रियाकल्प:, छलितकयोगा:, वस्त्रगोपनानि, द्यूतविशेषा:, आकर्षक्रीडा, बालक्रीडनकानि, वैनायिकीनां वैजयिकीनां व्यायामिकीनां च विद्यानां ज्ञानम्, इति चतु:षष्टिरङ्गविद्या:। शास्त्रान्तरे चतु:षष्टिमूलकला उक्तास्तासां कर्माश्रयाश्चतुर्विंशति:, द्यूताश्रया विंशति:, शयनोपचारिका: षोडश, चतस्र उत्तरकला:। For these see the com. on the Káma-Sûtras.

P. 149. सुह्मेषु—The Suhma country lay to the west of Vanga (Eastern Bengal). Its capital ताम्रलिप्त (also called दामलिप्त तामलिप्त &c.) is identified with the modern Tumlook on the right bank of the Cossye (the Kapiśá of Kálidása). In ancient times the town was situated nearer the sea and was a place of considerable maritime trade. परिवादिनी—a seven stringed instrument, a guitar. विस्मृत०—adv.; in a manner forgetting her passion for her residence on Vindhya. विन्ध्यवासिनी—the goddess Durgá (as the goddess of the Vindhya Mountain), called further on Somápídá. "A celebrated temple to her under this appellation is in the neighbourhood of Mirzapur."-Wilson. प्रतिशायितव्य—see *supra*, p. 141. l. 8. अनुजीविष्यति—will be the vassal of, will depend on. कन्दुकनृत्य—playing at ball, moving the ball dexterously; see p. 151.ll 9-16. The commentator's कन्दुकवन्नृत्यं तेन does not seem to be right. कन्दुकावती—the final vowel of a word is lengthened before मत् or वत् when it contains many vowels and is not a word of the अजिरादि class and the whole forms a name; see Páṇ. VI. 3. 119 quoted in the com.; thus अमरावती; but वलयवती (which is not a name). धात्रेयिका—her foster-sister; see com. The aff. is ढक् (एय), धात्रेयः m., धात्रेयिका (also धात्रेयी) fem.

P. 150. बलवत्—forcibly; often used an adv. नूपुरक्वणितं—the tinkling of anklets. मे जीवितं—*i.e.* his beloved. निरुष्मता—(1) coldness; (2) want of animation, spiritlessness. सुदृष्टं कारयित्वा—making her take a full view of me. निष्प्रतिक्रियान् -powerless to retaliate, which find no means of retaliation. वेशदास—slave of a harlot. वेशः—the courtesan-class. समर्थयेयं—I shall be upholding or confirming. अध्वदर्शी—I will myself lead the way. उदैरत—Imperfect 3rd pers. pl. of ईर् 2 A'. to go, with उद्. अनिषिद्धदर्शना—a sight of her is freely allowed to all. This shows that in Daṇḍin's time also, princesses and high-class ladies did not expose themselves to public eyes except on occasions.

P. 151. सकाशवर्तिनी—I will stand at her elbow. रङ्गपीठ—any seat for beginning any exhibition. अतिष्ठत्—she at once stood in (*i.e.* occupied, took possession of) my heart. अन्तराले-in her passage from where she stood to my heart. चित्रीया—admiration. A noun from the denom. verb चित्रीयते derived from चित्र by affixing क्यच् (य). The verbs thus formed are A'tm. न हि न हि &c.—He means that she is superior even to Lakshmí in beauty, excellence &c. अनवद्य—a double negative; वद्य is what is fit to be spoken; अवद्य is what is fit to be condemned, or blameable; and न अवद्यमनवद्यं what is faultless, praiseworthy, excellent. Lakshmi is वद्या because she submits to the embraces of many. अयातयाम—यातो यामः उपभोगकालो यस्य; fresh, not previously enjoyed by any one. For यातयाम comp. Bg. XVII. 10. अनघ—unblemished, blameless, excellent, faultless; without blemish or deformity. व्यस्यस्त—thrown crosswise; or, with the palms turned downwards. अमन्दराग°—the spots on which were of a deep-red paint. अक्षि in the case of the ball means 'eye-like spots.' In the other case अमन्दराग means 'excessive or intense passion.' लीलाशिथिलं—gently (*lit.* loosely, not with great force) through sportiveness. समाहत्य—striking it down. हस्तपृष्ठेन &c.—Throwing it up after having caught it on the back of her hand. चटुलदृष्टिलाञ्छित—marked with her quickly-moving glances. A series of glances is often compared, on account of the dark pupil being prominent therein, to a garland of blue lotuses by Sanskrit poets. भ्रमरमाला°—The row of bees corresponds to the series of her glances. मध्यविलम्बित &c.—Striking it with greater or less force; keeping the time of its rapid, slow or ordinary motion. चूर्णपद—has a technical meaning; it means—stepping backwards with a degree of rapidity proportionate to the motion of the ball and impelling it with proportionate force. पक्षं &c.—She kept it fluttering in space like a bird, hitting it alternately with her right or left hand as it approached her obliquely or in a straight line. दूरोत्थितं &c.—When it rose to a great height, she struck it in its rapid descent and took the musical leap, *i. e.* sprang forward ten steps to catch it.

P. 152. प्रत्यागमयत्—brought it back to its original or starting point. अनेककरणमधुरं—gracefully on account of the several feats of dexterity. उच्चावचाः—loud and gentle, manifold. प्रशंसावाचः—exclamations of applause. तत्क्षणा°—In whom I came to confide the very moment. The Com. reads प्रतिक्षणारूढविश्रम्भं—whose admiration grew every moment. If this be the original reading, it must be taken as an adv. along with कण्टकितगण्डं &c.; or it will be better to read प्रतिक्षणारूढविश्रम्भे qualifying मयि. But the reading in the text is better. उत्फुल्लेक्षणं—with my eyes dilated. मयि—The constr. is तस्या अभिमुखीभूय तिष्ठति मयि. तत्प्रथमावतीर्ण &c.—under the influence of love felt then for the first time. तदनुमार्ग—following the motion of the ball. मद्दर्शनलज्जया-abashed by my gaze पुष्पमयं &c.—a flowery cage was as it were formed by the red-spottted ball whirled about her in rapid rotations. पञ्चबिन्दुप्रसृत—giving five strokes to the ball rapidly so as to make it appear like five specks. गोमूत्रिकाप्रचार—a movement like the undulating line of forked lightning ( Wilson). रागविभ्रम—(1) motion of the different colours; (2) the flashing of its colour. भूषणमणि &c.—in which the jewels in her ornaments jingled in correspondence with the fallings of her foot-steps. अपदेशस्मित—smiles under some pretext. प्रतिसमाहित—re-adjusted. शिखण्डभार-mass of her hair, abundant tresses. समाघट्टित—struck together. अश्चितोत्थित—beautifully rising. वेल्लित—waved. आवर्जित०—in which her long arms were converged. त्रिक—the distance between the shoulder-blades. अवगलित &c.—in which the golden sockets of her displaced ear-ornaments were put back with such quickness that her ball-sport was not interrupted. असकृदुत्क्षिप्यमाण०—in which the ball was whirled in circles round and within ( the space of ) the hands and feet lifted up.

P. 153. ०मध्ययष्टिकम्—In which the very thin ( *lit.* stick-like ) middle part of her body was now seen and now lost to view. विपर्यस्त—tossed about. अङ्कुरित—appearing as drops. दूषित—wetted. पत्रभङ्ग—The ornamental paintings on. श्रवणपल्लव—The tender leaf worn on the ear as an ornament. नियमन—restraining, adjusting or keeping in position. निमील्य-bending, shrinking. उन्मील्य—unbending, stretching forth. एकैनैवानेकेनेव-*Cf.* for the idea एकोऽपि त्रय इव भाति कन्दुकोऽयं &c. quoted in the Introduction. सानुराग—(1) full of love; (2) affectionate. कुवलय०—The blue lotus or नीलोत्पल is one of the five arrows of Cupid. सापदेशं—under some pretext; one of the ways in which Sanskrit poets make maidens betray their love. *Cf.* दर्भाङ्कुरेण चरण: क्षत इत्यकाण्डे &c. S'ák. II. 13; and यदियं पुनरप्यपाङ्गनेत्रा परिवृत्तार्धमुखी मयाऽद्य दृष्टा Vik. I. 16. यत्नवत्—with care. अत्युदारं—splendid, liberal. प्रणयपेशलं—gracefully through love. आशास्यं—merely to be wished for (*i. e.* not to be realized). विरक्त:—disgusted with or ceasing to love her,

P. 154. रोषादिव—Because she had fixed her affection on one who had excelled him ( Káma ) in beauty. शम्बरद्विषा—By Káma. Śambara was a demon killed by Pradyumna, son of Krishṇa, and supposed to be Káma re-born as such; hence

शम्बर॰ means Káma. विदितभा॰--By whom the state of her mind (*i. e.* that she was affected by love) was known. विधिः—a thing ordained, or course of events. बहु विकल्पयतोः—who discussed the matter, expressing many misgivings. नियम—morning devotions. अनुकूल—calculated to please, agreeable. उपकार्या—a tent. उपरुद्ध॰—held fast or bound by. हतायाः &c. —that hussy, Chandrasená. जालरन्ध्र—the lattice-holes. तच्चेष्टा॰—appointed to watch her actions. वराकी—the wretch. किल—as is said; or, as I hear. This shows that he treated the prophecy with scorn.

P. 155. स्पन्दमानः—swimming. प्रत्युषसि—the next morning. वहित्रं—A boat or ship; *cf.* प्रलयपयोधिजले धृतवानसि वेदं विहितवहित्रचरित्रमखेदम्। Gíta. I. यवनाः—Wilson says—"By Yavanas we are here probably to understand Arabs, who, we know, were at this period the chief traders and navigators in the Indian and China seas." रामेषुनाम्ने—The name Rámeshu seems to be an Indian name; the Yavanas, therefore, were under the command of an Indian navigator. So it appears the Yavanas mentioned here were some settlers from Arabia on the sea-coast near the Suhma country and mixed up with the Indian fishermen there. नाविकनायक—the captain. अपि—it is possible that. द्राक्षाणां &c.—It seems it was their trade to capture men and sell them as slaves to work in large fields of grape-plants or vineyards. मद्गु—a galley or war-ship. संप्रहार—a hand-to-hand fight. पराजायिषत—Pass. Aor., 3rd pers. pl. of जि with परा. अगतीन्—helpless. अवसीदतः—giving way, whose courage failed them. अवसादय्—to rout, to destroy. भल्ल—a large arrow with a crescent-shaped blade at the end. अनभिसर—who was unattended or without servants; it may also mean, who had not come forth to fight. सांयात्रिकाः—my comrades in the fight. The word properly means a 'merchant trading by sea;' समुदितानां गमनं द्वीपान्तरगमनं वा संयात्रा। सा प्रयोजनमस्य; संयात्रा+ठञ् (इक). कृतान्तविल॰—The evil pastimes of fortune or fate; for this meaning of कृतान्त *cf. supra* p. 127, l. 14. हर्षकिलकिला॰—peculiar shouts of rejoicings. किलकिला is an onomatopoetic word. *Cf.* संसक्ताकुलकेलयः किलकिलाकोलाहलैः संमदात् &c. Mál.-Mádh. V. 11.

P. 156. दुर्वारा—Difficult to be managed or properly steered. दुर्वहा *v. l.*—difficult to be controlled or guided. अननुकूल—contrary, not favourable. गाढपातित॰—having dropped the stone-anchor so that it should stick fast to the ground. This is an adverbial comp. नितम्बभाग—the middle region or the skirts. गन्धपाषाण—minerals, such as red arsenic and others; or, benzoin (शैलेय). उपत्यका—adjoining ground. We should rather expect अधित्यका (table-land) here, first because he is referring to the land above the नितम्ब of the mountain, and also because such minerals are found on the tops of mountains. *Cf.* अधित्यकायामिव धातुमय्यां Ragh. II. 29 चन्द्रकोत्तरं—marked by the spreading circles caused by the drops of &c. गोत्रवारि—water of a mountain-stream. मञ्जुलतर—exceedingly lovely or beautiful, engaging. आभोग—expanse, avenue. अतृप्ततरया—that never got satisfied; that was the more thirsty. पश्यन्—enjoying the sight of; attracted by. शोणीभूत—made red. नालीक—a lotus. भीमरूप—of hideous aspect. निर्भर्त्सयता—menacingly; the root, which is A'tm., is often used in the Paras. by our poet. चित्रग्रावाणं—having, or covered with, (mineral) stones of variegated colours. प्रियहिताय—for happiness and benefit. संकल्प—determination, resolute purpose.

P. 157. प्रमाण—Proofs. त्रिगर्त:—A most arid country in ancient times. It stood for the desert on the east of the S'atadru and included the tract between the Satlej and the Sarasvatî, containing Ludhiana and Patiala on the north and some portion of the desert on the south. स्फीत—large. सार—property, estate. दशशताक्ष:—Indra (the god with a thousand eyes), the dispenser of rain. न ववर्ष दश० is idiomatic for 'there was no rain.' ओषध्य:—ओष: पाक: धीयते आसु इति; annual plants or herbs that die after bearing fruit. See com., and Manu. I. 46. वनस्पतय:—large trees that bear fruit without apparent blossoms; see note on the word at p. 137. क्लीबा:—without watery substance, empty. स्रवन्ती—a river. निस्यन्द—the current. उत्स—a stream. The word occurs in the Veda in the same sense. कथा—jovial talks, merry conversations. शुष्क—lean, starving. नगरग्राम०—नगर is the principal town of a province where a king resides; *cf.* Ragh. IX. 2. खर्वट is a small town having a market-place, and graded between a town and a village. यत्रैकतो भवेद् ग्रामो नगरं चैकतः स्मृतम्। मिश्रं तु खर्वटं नाम नदीगिरिसमाश्रयम् ॥ quoted by Bhânujî Dîkshita in his com. on Amara. III. 5. 33. Kshîrasvâmî says खर्वटश्चतुःशतग्रामाणां संग्रहस्थानं, but there seems to be some inaccuracy here; for, from Daṇḍin's use of it, it does not appear to be such a big thing (*cf.* Marâthi खेडें which is derived from it). पुटभेदन—a town; it is given in Amara. as a synonym of नगरी; it is variously derived as—पुटानि भाण्डानि भिद्यन्तेऽस्मिन्: पुटा भाण्डवासनानि

भिद्यन्ते अस्मिन्; or पुटैः अश्वखुरैर्भिद्यते इति, according to some. Mr. A'gáshe observes, "These terms are found in Kauṭilîya II. 1. 19, and they are explained there in a foot-note as under— नगरं राजधानी, क्षुल्लकप्राकारवेष्टितं खर्वटम्। पट्टनं शकटैर्गम्यं घाटिकैर्नौभिरेव च। नौभिरेव तु यद्गम्यं पट्टणं तत्प्रचक्षते। द्रोणमुखं जलनिर्गमप्रवेशं ( where exit or entrance is by means of boats ) पट्टणमित्यर्थः। इति रायसपेणीसूत्रव्याख्याने। प. २०६. नगराणि करवार्जितानि निगमवणिजां स्थानानि...... खर्वटानि कुनगराणि ( small towns )। पत्तनानि जलस्थलपथयोरन्यतरयुक्तानि। इति प्रश्नव्याकरणसूत्रव्याख्याने। प. ३०६.

अजाविक—flocks of sheep and goats; अजाश्च अविकाश्च तेषां समाहारः. क is added स्वार्थे to अवि; see also com. अजाविकटं v. l.—here कट is the affix in the sense of संघात; see com. ( Várt. on संप्रोदश्च कटच्। Páṇ. V. 2. 29 ). गवल—a wild buffalo. उद्वहन्—bearing her on his back. स्वमांसासृगपनीत etc.—Daṇḍin seems to have taken the principal part of this story from Guṇáḍhya's Brihatkathá; cf. with this the story of a merchant's son related by Gomukha to Naraváhanadatta in Kathás. Lambaka X. विचेष्टमान—rolling, struggling. आर्द्राशयः—with his heart melted with pity. गहनोद्देश—a region in the depth of the forest. रोपित—healed. इङ्गुदीतैल॰—The oil of Iṅgudî is said to have this virtue. Cf. व्रणविरोपणमिङ्गुदीनां तैलं न्यषिच्यत मुखे &c. Śák. IV. 14.

P. 158. उद्रिक्तधातुम्—when there was an abundance of vital fluids in his body. उपातिष्ठत—should rather be A'tm. उदकाभ्यर्थिनं—as he asked for water to drink. उदञ्चन—a bucket, a pot for drawing water out of a well. प्रणुनोद—pushed him in. विकल—the cripple, the mutilated man. स्कन्धेनोदुह्य—Cf. तद्भार्या...बभ्रामेतस्ततो जारं रुण्डं पृष्ठेऽधिरोप्य तम्। Kathás. X. 9. 28 प्रतीति—fame; for a different meaning, see p. 82, l. 11. अवन्तिराजा॰—in the Kathás. the son of the merchant himself becomes the king, himself recognizes her, and punishes her. भूति—riches, wealth. चित्रवध—See supra, p. 59 l. 3. विकलीकृतोऽभिमतः—accepted or set down as maimed by me. पापमाचक्षीत—will accuse me of the crime. अदीनम्—boldly. दर्शितेऽमुष्मिन्स—is not so idiomatic as दर्शितः स विकलः. आर्यबुद्धिः—having noble thoughts, noble-minded. श्वभ्यः पाचिका—a cook for dogs; i.e. degraded her.

P. 159. अनुयुक्तः—questioned. द्रविडेषु—Draviḍa lay to the south of the wild tract between the Krishṇá and the Polar. In its wider sense it included the whole of the Coromandel coast to the south of the Godávarî. In its stricter sense it must not have extended beyond the Kâverî. Its capital was

Káñchî, the same as Conjeeveram, situated on the Vegavati river, 42 miles south-west of Madras. अननुगुण—*lit.* having no corresponding merits, unworthy. यादृच्छिकी संपत्ति—the wealth of virtues, excellence, accidently found ( *i.e.* which may or may not be found). अनभिसमीक्ष्य—without approving of, disregarding. कार्तान्तिको नाम भूत्वा—assuming the character of an astrologer; feigning to be a fortune-teller. लक्षणवती—endowed with auspicious marks. सवर्णा—of his own class. गुणवत्—excellent, well-prepared. शिबिषु—The region on the southern bank of the Káverî; see com. It has nothing to do with the country of S'ibi, the famous king of that name, situated near Gândhára in the north. सह पितृभ्याम्—She had lost her parents as well as her great fortune. भवनसार—the valuables in the house. संसक्त—riveted. विकट—deformed; hideous ; from वि + कट (च्). मृजावन्त:—possessed of purity, *i.e.* fair-complexioned, clean-skinned. रक्त°—This is an auspicious sign indicative of great good fortune; see the quotation from Bṛihatsam. 70, given on the next page. यव—a linear mark on the fingers of the hand resembling a barley-corn and indicating, according to its position, wealth, progeny, good fortune &c. सम—even, fleshy, covered with flesh. अशिरालौ—prominent veins are supposed to be a mark of ugliness. अनुपूर्ववृत्त—tapering. *Cf.* वृत्तानुपूर्वे च न चातिदीर्घे जङ्घे &c. Kum. I. 35. ऊरुपलक्ष्ये—Because they came in close contact with the plump thighs. सकृद्विभक्त:—evenly divided. चतुरस्र—symmetrical; mark the comp.; चतस्र: अस्रयो यस्य. The final इ is replaced by अ by the rule सुप्रात...चतुरस्र &c. Páṇ. V. 4. 120. *Cf.* बभूव तस्याश्चतुरस्रशोभि वपुर्विभक्तं नवयौवनेन । Kum I. 32.

P. 160. ककुन्दर—the cavities of the loins. रथाङ्गाकार—of the form of a wheel; *cf.* रथाङ्गश्रोणिबिम्बया Vik. IV. 18. ईषन्निम्न—A little depressed. वलित्रयेण—the वलित्रय is generally described in connexion with beautiful ladies; *cf. supra*, p. 44, l. 9. उरोभागव्यापिनौ—large enough to cover the whole bosom. विशालारम्भ—their great expanse. स्निग्ध—glossy. उन्नम—prominent. नखमणि—jewel-like, red nails. संनत—well-turned. कम्बु &c.—कम्बुवद्वृत्ता बन्धुरा ( curved ) च. वृत्त—pouting. असंक्षिप्त—not contracted or small ( with the chin, elegant and not small ). असंगत—not joined. अनुवक्र—beautifully curved. अनातिप्रौढ°—not much developed (*i.e.* the bud of the *tila* flower). असित—dark. मधुराधीरसंचार—beautifully and swiftly rolling. मन्थर—dull; or, large इन्दुशकल—*i. e.*

the half-moon on the eighth day of a *paksha*; *cf.* अष्टमीचन्द्रशकलाकारं ललाटदेशम् &c. Kád. p. 31. श्रवणपाशः—beautiful ears; here पाश signifies beauty or admiration; see *supra*, p. 97 l. 9. अनतिभङ्गुर—not much curling. एकैकनिसर्गसम—each growing by itself and evenly ( *i. e.* there was no branching of the hair ). सेयमाकृतिः &c.—Her character must be in keeping with the grace or outward beauty of her form. *Cf.* न ह्याकृतिः सुसदृशं विजहाति वृत्तम् । Mrich. IX. 16; न तादृशा आकृतिविशेषा गुणविरोधिनो भवन्ति । Śák. IV. p. 86; यत्राकृतिस्तत्र गुणा वसन्ति। Varáh. Brihatsam. 70. 23; यत्राकारस्ततो गुणाः । Agnip. 244. 6; आकृतिमनुगृह्णन्ति गुणाः Viddhaśálabh.

P. 161. अविमृश्य०—acting thoughtlessly or precipitately. *cf.* विवेकभ्रष्टानां भवति विनिपातः शतमुखः Bh. Nît. 10; and अतिरभसकृतानां कर्मणामाविपत्तेर्भवति हृदयदाही शल्यतुल्यो विपाकः । Nît. 105. अनुशय--repentance, regret साकूतं—meaningly, inquiringly. अलिन्द—a dais or raised place near a door. पादशौच—water for the feet. गन्धशाली—गन्धविशिष्टा शालयः; fragrant rice. संक्षुद्य—having gently or carefully pounded. मात्रया—a little. स्थिर—firm. नाली—a kind of pestle. अखण्डैः—not bruised or broken. अर्थिनः—stand in need of. मृजा—cleaning, polishing. शराव—an earthen platter. उत्तान—expanded or spread out. ककुभोलूखल—a mortar of the Arjuna tree. ०मध्यतानवेन—Because a pestle is usually grasped by the middle, which part is therefore worn out. तानव—slenderness.

P. 162. चतुरललित०—raising it up gracefully and cleverly &c. शूर्पशोधित &c.—she removed the grains of dust and the awn by winnowing them with a basket. क्वथितपञ्चगुणे—heated to the boiling point and five times in quantity. दत्तचुल्लीपूजा—a custom still observed in many places. The cooking woman throws a few grains into the fire before pouring the rice into the boiling water or placing the vessel containing rice on the hearth. " So Jewish bakers put a little of the dough into the oven. " Prof. Peterson. मुकुलावस्था &c.—When the rice was passing the state of a bud, *i. e.* was moderately swollen. अन्नमण्ड—the scum. दर्वी—a ladle. अवघट्ट्य—having struck. परिवर्त्य—having turned them up and down. आमलक—myrobalans. चिञ्चा—tamarind. उपदंश—condiments. दत्ताङ्गारधूप०—having scented it with perfumes evaporated on the charcoals. श्लक्ष्ण०—finely pulverized ०तैलामलकः—Rubbing the body with oil and powdered myrobalans gives a glossy appearance to the skin. त्रिभाग०—the third part from the upper end of which was cut off; तृतीयो भागः त्रिभागः शेषः तत्र लूनस्य. अभिमृशन्—touching. पेया—water-gruel mixed with some boiled rice; see Vágbhaṭa quated in the Com. प्रक्लिन्न०—his whole body sweating. सर्पिर्मात्रा—a little ghee. सूप—sauce.

P. 163. त्रिजातक—cinnamon oil; or rather, dry ginger, black pepper and long pepper. कालशेय—curds churned with a handle without water. अन्धस्—food भृङ्गार—a kind of jug or vase (झारी in Marathi). अगुरु—agallochum. ग्रथितसौरभं—whose fragrance was mixed with. हिमशिशिर—cool like snow. The śl. कान्तकान्त etc. quoted in the com. from the Śiśupálavadha (X. 3) is meant simply to illustrate how one drink can gratify all the organs of senses. It is the wine that gratifies all the sense there, while in our passage it is the cool fragrant water served out to the merchant that gratifies all his senses. The author himself describes how it did that. करालित—fringed with. कर्कश—rough or rugged. परिमलप्रवाहोत्पीड—strong current or flow of the fragrance. परिमलप्रवाल *v. l.*—परिमलस्य प्रवालाः offshoots of, *i. e.* the spreading fragrance. माधुर्यप्रकर्ष०—his tongue being quite gratified with the excessive sweetness. अच्छ—clear. करक—a small water-pot. आचमनं—Âchamana is the drinking of a little water taken into the hollowed palm of the hand, three times, as a religious rite. It is enjoined at the beginning and at the end of any religious rite; it is also necessary after a bath, drinking, sneezing, sleep, meals, walking through a street, and changing clothes; *cf.* Yáj. Sm. I. 196 quoted in the com., and Manu. V. 145—सुप्त्वा क्षुत्वा च भुक्त्वा च निष्ठीव्योक्त्वाऽनृतानि च। पीत्वाऽपोऽध्येष्यमाणश्च आचामेत्प्रयतोऽपि सन्॥. कुट्टिम—a pavement. उत्तरीयकर्पट—his upper garment. एतदनपेक्षः—regardless of her; growing cold towards her; (this he did, of course, in order to put her virtues to test; he did not really want to be attached to the harlot). अवरोधमकरोत्—introduced her into the harem. सामपि—The force of अपि is this—As a wife with any sense of self-respect, she should have resented this act of her husband and treated the courtesan with jealousy; but as a true *Pativratâ* she felt it her duty to subordinate personal happiness to that of her husband (यद्भर्तुरेव हितमिच्छति तत्कलत्रं) and acted friendly towards her. This is also Kálidása's view of the duties of a co-wife; *cf.* प्रतिपक्षेणापि पतिं सेवन्ते भर्तृ-

वत्सला: साध्व्य: । Málav. V. 19. अहीनं—with assiduous care; *lit.* without any omission ( of duty ). परिजनं च &c.—*Cf.* सुयिष्ठं भव दक्षिणा परिजने Śák. IV. 18. दाक्षिण्यनिधि:—explains how she won the affection of her servants. कुटुम्ब—*i. e.* domestic concerns. त्रिवर्ग—*viz. Dharma, Artha and Káma,* for securing which a wife is to be married.

P. 164. सौराष्ट्र—also called आनर्त, is the modern peninsula of Kathiawar. The ancient Dváraká was its original capital. Valabhî appears to be its next capital, the ruins of which were discovered at Bilbi, 10 miles north-west of Bhavanagar. According to the Bombay Gazetteer (as quoted by Mr. A'gáshe) it was a town in the east of Kathiawar about 25 miles west of Bhavanagar and about 25 miles north of Śatruñjaya. The modern name of the town is Valeh. गुह्यकेन्द्र—Kubera. नाविकपति—a ship-owner. मधुमती—name of a town. It may probably be Mathurá, which was called मधुपुरी in ancient times, being the residence of the demon Madhu, whose son Lavaṇa was killed by Śatrughna; see Ragh. XV. 28, and our note *ad loc.* रभसविघ्नित—obstructed through rashness. तद्गृहागमनं—तद् refers to her; *i.e.* her father's house. From this it seems that Balabhadra lived in the same town after his marriage with रत्नवती, instead of going to his native town. ०अतिवर्ती not listening to. दुर्भगा—an unfortunate woman, one hated by her husband. See note on दौर्भाग्य below. निम्बवती—*Nimba* is a tree known for its bitterness; hence this means 'sour-tempered.' परिबभूव—insulted her by the nickname of. का मे गति: —' what is to be my fate;' or, what course of life should I pursue? देवशेष०—flowers previously offered to deities ( who brought to her flowers from an idol ). अनुनीय—addressing her words of consolation. दौर्भाग्यं—has a technical meaning here-the state of not being loved or favourably looked upon by the husband ; opp. is सौभाग्य, for which see *supra,* note on सुभगमानी p. 92 तस्य—refers to दौर्भाग्य. सुदृष्टा—well or favourably seen by them, and my relatives (—said in contrast with अवज्ञया पश्यति in the last sentence); a favourite of my husband; *cf.* सुदृष्ट p. 150, l. 8. आ विरामात्—until I die. आख्यातव्यम्—should be disclosed. त्वन्निदेशवर्तिनी—ready to act according to your advice. मदधिष्ठिता—led or guided by me. उदर्क—result. आकार-such grace of form. ईदृशेन—such. so amiable ( a disposition ).

P. 165. पतिद्रोह—hatred shown by a husband. प्रातिवेश्य—a neighbour. राजान्तरङ्गभावेन—By his being in the confidence of the king. ०रूपावयवा—in form and body. विमानहर्म्य—विशेषेण मान्त्यस्मिन्निति; fr. मा with वि and affix अन (ल्युट्); a mansion having seven stories; *cf.* नेत्रा नीताः सततगतिना यद्विमानाग्रभूमीः Megh. II. तन्मातृप्रार्थनं—*i. e.* the entreaty of Kanakavatí's mother. क्रीडामत्ता नाम—as if blundering in my sport भ्रंशयेयम्—I shall drop down. अनवस्थः—of loose or irregular conduct, unsteady. विपक्षधन—the property of an enemy. बद्धाञ्जलि—*adv.* 'with folded hands.' साभिलाषं—inspired with love for me. रन्ध्र—an opening; a loop-hole; 'taking advantage of this circumstance.' The construction is तेन रन्ध्रेण तमुपश्लिष्योपेत्य...यथा असौ मामादाय &c. उज्ज्वलीकृत्य—having fanned the fire of his love or inflamed his passion. नीरन्ध्र—thick, pitchy.

P. 166. वार्तामापादयत्—spread or circulated a report. मन्देन—a fool that I was, being a dunce. उपेक्षिता—neglected. अतिवर्तिताः—disregarded. संसृष्टः—united with, living in her company. व्यक्तिः—clearance of; *i. e.* the matter will be clear. पण्यदासी—a female slave she purchased. उपस्कर—provisions. मूल—capital; *lit.* the original sum. प्रसारकालोपा०—The reading in the foot-note is perhaps better, being simpler; in the reading as we have it, the word वृत्तान्त is without propriety. निर्भिन्न—promulgated, disclosed दण्डवाहिन्—the mayor, the magistrate. मोषेणापहृत्य—having kidnapped her. न्यायोढा—law-fully married. प्रणिधि—an emissary. श्रेणीप्रातिभाव्येन—by the security of the association of traders. प्रातिभाव्य is an abstract noun from प्रतिभू 'a security.' भावयतः—who looked upon or believed.

P. 167. शूरसेन—Name of the country about Mathurá. Kálidása has referred to this country in Ragh. VI. 45. कुलपुत्र—a youth of family; or Śúdra, as the Com. takes it. स्वभुजमात्र०—who had successfully fought many a duel with his own arms for the sake of his friends. निर्व्यूढ—successfully carried out; *cf.* निर्व्यूढदुर्वह (दुर्धर) प्रतिज्ञाभारस्य वृकोदरस्य Veṇí. VI. p. 139; निर्वाहः प्रतिपन्नवस्तुषु सतामेतद्धि गोत्रव्रतम्। Bhar. Nít. Misc. Ślokas, Sl. 13. कर्कश—hard-hearted, cruel men. पाण्डुरा—indicating uneasiness of mind, anxiety. अनति०—अनतिपरिभुक्ता अत एव सुभगा. प्रौढता—full growth; her eyes indicate her having passed the age of timidity and bashfulness. एकवेणयादिः—It is usual with ladies whose husbands are absent not to dress or decorate their hair, &c.; see *supra*, note on एकवेणीभूतेन p. 141. लक्ष्म चैतत—It is difficult to know what लक्ष्म is meant here; according to the Bhúshaná it means 'a nail-mark;' it may also be the mark of a mole. ०नामा—The *fem.* is ०नामा or नाम्नी. उन्मनायमानः—being greatly agitated at heart. परिवव्राज—went; परिव्रज् has not got its usual sense here. भार्गव—a fortune-teller. भिक्षा-निभेन—under the pretext of begging alms.

P. 168. श्रमणिका—A Buddhist or Jain female mendicant. A female follower of Śramaṇa or Jina; see Vaijayantî as quoted in the com. on निर्ग्रन्थिक p. 87. It is strange that these nuns should be found employed in the settlement of love-matters. शीलभ्रंश—her falling off, or deviation from, virtuous conduct. उपह्वरे—in secret; or, in a private place. समाधिमास्थाय—having recourse to contemplation or penance; the phrase occurs in Kum. V. 2. घटते—endeavours. क घटते—how can it stand to reason? उदारा—excessive. अदुष्टभावता—inviolate chastity, incorruptibility of character. अप्रतिकृत्य—unless the evil influence exerted by it is counteracted; unless the obstacle interposed by it is removed. छन्नं—secretly. प्रणयकुपिता &c.—pretending to be lovingly angry. उपरि—after this is done; in this sense it occurs in Marathi as उपर. ऊर्जित—noble, strong and good-looking. तावतैव—by doing me that much service. सा तथैव &c.—consenting to do so, she favoured him accordingly. निर्ग्रन्थिका—a female mendicant. See *supra*, note on निर्ग्रन्थिक at p. 87.

P. 169. परामृशन्निव—pretending to rub it gently. आलिख्य-having made a scratch or cut. सान्द्रत्रासा—in great dismay. दुर्नय—folly, ill-advised step. दत्त्वा पटबन्धनं—having put on a bandage or ligature. सामयापदेशात्—pretending to be ill. अनुवाणं—when he refused to tell. निर्बन्धेन—pressingly, imperatively. वणिग्ग्राम—The merchant-guild, the committee of merchants. विश्रामप्रविष्टायां—as I entered for the purpose of repose. अद्यापि—goes with न इष्टः. लुब्धाः—misers, covetous people who do not want to pay the fees. दग्धावदग्ध—partially burnt. यदृच्छया—accidentally. विमर्शे—after deliberation, when the matter was thought over.

P. 170. शाकिनी—A witch, a female seeking the favour of devils. तस्याः शाकिनीत्वम्—This device of proving Nitambavatî a Śâkinî and getting her expelled from her house, used here by the young merchant to gain his object, seems to have been taken from the Vetâlapañchaviṁśikâ, occurring in the Brihatkathâ. Therein one Buddhiśarîra, the minister and companion of Prince Vajramukuṭa, adopts this kind of device to secure to his friend Padmâvatî, a damsel of that name. See Kathâs. Lambaka XII., Taranga 8; *cf.* तदागमनहृष्टोऽथ मन्त्रिपुत्रो नृपात्मजम् । जगाद हन्त गच्छाद्य पद्मावत्या गृहं निशि ॥ ततस्तस्याः सनिद्रायाः शूलेनाङ्कं कटीतटे । दत्त्वाऽग्निस्तेनादाय तदाभरणसंचयम् ॥ प्रातर्गत्वा श्मशानं च सोऽभूत्तापसवेषभृत् । स्वैरं राजसुतं तं च विदधे शुद्धरूपिणम् ॥ अब्रवीत्तं च गच्छैकमितोऽलंकरणादिमाम् । मुक्तावलीं समादाय त्वं विक्रेतुमिवापणे ॥ ** श्रुत्वैतद्विजनं कृत्वा स धूर्तस्तमभाषत । अहं तपस्वी भ्राम्यामि सदाऽरण्येष्वितस्ततः ॥ सोऽहं दैवादिह प्राप्तः श्मशानेऽत्र स्थितो निशि । अपश्यं योगिनीचक्रं समागतमितस्ततः ॥ तन्मध्ये चैकयाऽऽनीय योगिन्या राजपुत्रकः । उद्घाटितहृदम्भोजो भैरवाय निवेदितः ॥ अतिप्रवृत्ता च मया क्रुद्धेन जघनस्थले । अङ्किता सा त्रिशूलेन मन्त्रप्रज्वालिताग्निणा ॥ हृता मुक्तावली चेयं तस्याः कण्ठान्मया तदा । सैषाऽद्य तापसानर्हा विक्रेया मम वर्तते ॥ ग्रस्तः सुतो मे डाकिन्या तयेत्युत्पन्ननिश्चयः । पितृभ्यां शोच्यमानायाः पुरान्निर्वासनं व्यधात् ॥ त्वद्भावर्जने—to win your affection. असाधारणीकृत्य—as an extraordinary ( and therefore never-failing ) remedy. अकामा—*i. e.* against her will. नैर्ऋत-a Râkshasa. मत्संबन्धी—my friend. समसृज्यत—joined in a duel. अनपेक्षापविद्धा—cast down without any regard for her safety. शैलशृङ्गभङ्ग—pieces of the peaks of mountains. अक्षपयेतां—dispatched, destroyed.

P. 171. मत्प्राणैकवल्लभा—The darling of my heart. तिर्यक्—squintingly, obliquely. कामरूप—assuming any form at will. स्फुरन्ती—trembling or struggling for release. अवरूढाः—landed. निष्कल—discomfited, dejected and pale. निष्कलङ्क—free from the contamination of sin. प्राणवत्—goes with चन्द्र०, who was regarded by him as his very life. अवसरेषु—as at the time when he helped the Yavanas against Bhîmadhanvan. स्मिताभिषिक्त—bathed or steeped in smile.

P. 172. ललितवल्लभा०—In the following chapter the poet has accomplished a literary *tour de force* by making Mantragupta tell his tale without the use of any of the labial letters ( including the vowels उ and ऊ). The author here poetically accounts for his hero's inability to use the labial letters. Such literary feats are not rare in Sanskrit literature. Śrirâma's Kamsanidhâna is a longer instance of this kind of feat

कलिङ्गः—The country lay to the south of Odra or Orissa, and extended to the mouth of the Godâvarî. It is identified with the Northern Circars. संस्थितजन०—the ground for burning the dead, a cemetery. धरणिज—a tree. Mark how the author is forced to go in search of such words as संस्थित, धरणिज, &c. for the ordinary words मृत, वृक्ष or पादप, owing to his self-imposed restriction of avoiding all labials. सरसकिसलय—tender (*lit.* juicy) leaves. कालरात्रि &c.—

The night is compared to a lady, and the mass of darkness to the locks of her hair. चलितरक्षसि—Because it is the fit time for goblins and *rákshasas* for stalking abroad. नीहार—dew. निशीथ—midnight. साल—a tree. निर्ह्रादि—qualifies रटितं further on; 'sounding through the branches of the thickly-growing trees.' If the reading be निर्ह्रादिनि, it must be taken as an *adj.* qualifying निशीथे. नेत्रनिर्निरसिनीं etc.—keeping off (preventing ) the sleep that was kissing my eyes. अनेन दग्ध०—this accursed magician. रिरंसा—noun in आ from the Desid. base of रम्. दिरसता—pre. p. of the Desid. of दा. रागेण &c.—overpowered by unbounded passion. खिलीकृत:—*Lit.* nailed down to one spot, made unable to carry out one's object; hence, prevented from enjoying pleasure. अणकनरेन्द्र:—कुत्सितो नरेन्द्र: अणक०; a cursed practiser of charms, a wicked magician; mark the meaning of अणक. See Pâṇ. II. 1. 54 quoted in the com. सिद्ध्यन्तराय:—an obstacle in his attainment of the desired superhuman powers.

P. 173. तरलतर—very bright ( polished ). निष्टप्ताङ्गाररज:—the dust of charcoal reduced to ashes by complete combustion. तडिल्लताकार०—bright and tawny like the flashes of lightning. अरण्यचक्र—the circuit or expanse of the forest. चञ्चत्—waving, flickering. सिद्धार्थक—white mustard seeds. See *supra*, p. 118, note on गौरसर्षप. चटचटायित—crackling; *lit.*, 'which made a *chaṭ chaṭ* sound;' p. p. p. of the verb चटचटायते formed by affixing य ( क्यष् ) to the onomatopoetic word चटचट; see Pâṇ. III. 1. 13. निकृष्टाशय—debased in mind. अश्रुजर्जर—broken or choked with tears. रणरणिकागृहीतेन—overpowered by anxiety. म्लान—withered. शीर्णनहने—the tie of which was broken. शिलाशितेन—whetted on a stone-slab; ०सितेन—'white like'—is not a good reading; it will also not do to take it as शिलावद्सितेन, as the idea of brightness will be left out. चिकर्तिषया—with an intention to cut off.

P. 174. स्कन्धरन्ध्र—a hollow in the trunk. *Cf.* the similar scene in Mâl.-Mâdh. V., where Aghoraghaṇṭa tries to kill Málatí while Mâdhava rescues her. निध्याय—having watched or observed. क्षीणाधि:—freed from his mental worry or anxiety. कदर्थन—torture, teasing. अकृत्य—improper acts, abominable deeds; see com. नरकाक:—wretched or cursed man. कारणा—agony; this word has occurred before; see p. 92, l. 5. इतितर—From इतितर hot and दीधिति rays; the hot-rayed one, the sun;—०देहज: is Yama, son of the sun, and god of death. See com. अणीयस्— trifling. He is underrating his own act. न चेदिदं ने०— If it is not that you do not approve of this ; if you have no objection to do so. अक्लेशार्हा—who ill deserves harsh treatment; who ought to be gently treated. कर्णशेखर— the tip of the ear. The eye looked like a blue lotus placed on the tip of her ear; for she was आयतेक्षणा. अञ्चित--gracefully bent. सलिलचर--A device to avoid the use of मीन or मकर, which contains a labial letter. आनत—curved. चिल्लिकालता- her long and bushy eye-brows. The word चि० or चुल्लिका which can somehow be made to have the meaning of 'an eyebrow' ( fr. चिल्ल् or चुल्ल् I. P. to make amorous gestures ) is purposely used for भ्रू to get rid of a labial letter. लीला- लसं—gently through sportiveness. रागलज्जा०—acting under the influence of love and bashfulness.

P. 175. तिरश्चीन &c.—with the moon-shine of her nails spreading slantingly. साचीकृत—turned aside. साचि is a prep meaning 'sidelong,' 'aside.' साची...सरसिजं—*adv.*; *cf.* Ragh. VI. 14 ; Mâlav. IV. 15. लिखन्ती—drawing figures on. लङ्घिना-- passing across. हृदयलक्ष्य—the target of the heart. रति सहचर—a periphrasis for *Madana,* which cannot be used स्यदायितेन—( going ) with the swiftness of. स्यदायित is the p.p.p. of the denom. verb स्यदायते fr. स्यद speed, a word irregularly formed from स्यन्द्; see Pâṇ. VI. 4. 28, quoted in the com.; स्यन्देर्घञि नलोपो वृद्ध्यभावश्च निपात्यते । स्यदो वेगः । अन्यत्र स्यन्दः । Sid.-Kau. The Com. seems to have read दक्षिण for वक्ष which makes no sense. Dissolve—हृदयमेव लक्ष्यं तस्य दलने दक्षः रतिसहचरशरस्तस्य स्यदस्तद्वदाचरतीति तेन ।. ०सहचरस्य दयितेन *v. l.*—beloved of, *i. e.* friend of, Madana. रागानिल०—with the waves of the heart's yearnings set in motion by the wind of passion. कन्यागारा०—your taking a residence in the secret apartment. देहज—stands for मनसिज *i. e.* Madana. कालायस- निगड--iron fetters. रथचरण--a wheel.

P. 176. नयेत अकीर्त० दशां—*i. e.* will kill me. निकेतनं— Throughout this section the final म् is printed in the form of an Anusvára, as the author has taken care to avoid its labial sound by beginning the following sentence with a letter other than a labial, as then the म् is to be pronounced like the nasal of the class to which that following letter belongs. चन्द्रशाला—a room on the top of a mansion. करतला०—by gently shaking them with the palm of the hand. निजचेलाञ्चल०—clinging to the tips of the filaments of the flowers forming the garlands worn on their heads. **संवलित**—confounded with, mixed. **ततः कृतान्तेन** &c.—and so she escaped death. **इत्था धैर्यं** &c.—*Cf. supra* p. 119, प्रागपि रागाग्निसाक्षिकं &c. **आश्चर्यरत्न**—the gem in the form of this wonderful beauty. **रत्नशैल**—The mountain Meru. **स्थिर**—firm. **रागतरल**—(1) sparkling with its colour (lustre); (2) agitated by passion. **स्नेहनिगल**—the chains of love; ल is often substituted for ड in Sanskrit. **जायारहित**—those separated from their wives. *Cf.* **वियोगिहृदयस्थं मन्मथानल-पुञ्ज्वलयन्** *supra* p. 42. **लालस**—eager to drink the honey. **लग्न**—close contact. **ग्लान**—withered, faded. **घन**—thickly grown.

P. 177. **राजत्**—shining, gay in summer. **लीलायितसतिलक**—making the *tilaka* flowers serve as sportive marks on the forehead of the forest-sites smiling with flowers. **निनिद्र** &c.—the gold-coloured umbrella in the form of the full-blown Karṇikára flower. **दक्षिण०**—stands for the southern (Malaya) breeze. **सहकार०**—सहकारेषु चञ्चरीकाः bees कलिकाश्च. **कालाण्डज**—the cuckoo bird. **रक्तरक्ताधरा**—**रक्ताः** stirred up with passion, amorous **रक्ताधराः** beautiful ladies. **संनाह**—preparation for; **०शालिनि**—standing out as the first preparer for the battle of sport. **लङ्घितलज्जे**—in which the modesty of bashful maidens was overcome by the love which then took possession of their heart. **दर्दुर**—name of a mountain in the south, connected with Malaya. It is that portion of the Ghâts which forms the southern boundary of Mysore. *Cf.* Ragh. IV. 51 (शैलौ मलयदर्दुरौ). The commentator, not remembering this, has given a fanciful explanation. **अनिलाचार्य**—अनिल एवाचार्यः the dancing-master. The wind is often referred to by Sanskrit poets as giving instructions in dancing. **अलङ्घनीय**—impervious to sun-light. **लङ्घित**—leapt over, seated upon. **आलीढ**—touched. **तरलतरङ्ग**—the heaving waves. **क्रीडारस** &c.—was deeply engaged in sport. **संगत**—engaged in. **शृङ्गारहेला**—amorous sports. **अनङ्गसंघर्ष**—emulation in love-matters. **एकतन्त्र**—solely under the power of his passion for pleasures. **तत्र रन्ध्रे**—taking advantage of that weak point. **आन्ध्र**—Name of a country, the same as modern Tailangana. The mouths of the Godávarî were in the possession of the A'ndhras.

P. 178. **गलित**—faded, vanished. **गात्रकान्ति**—the youthful bloom of (the body). **निरस्तधैर्य**—*scil.*, by the charms of the princess. **गररस**—a poisonous potion or drink. **संस्थित**—will die. अनन्यज—Káma. सा का &c.—What will be my future state? How shall I fare? अग्रज—a Bráhmaṇa. किल—As the report goes. निकार—insult, humiliation, offence. दत्तसंघर्ष—having provocation given to him. एधित—enkindled, generated. नरेन्द्रसार्थ—a number of magicians. तन्निराकरिष्यन्—wishing to expel that. शंकरनृत्तदेश—the place where Śaṃkara dances, i. e. a cemetery. जरत्साल—i. e. an old sarja tree. कन्थाचीरसंचय—a collection of rags and patched garments. अतिसंहित—deceived. आकृष्ट—obtained. चेल—a garment. सलिलराशि—the sea. किञ्जल्क०—variegated with bits of filaments. ०शेखरस्य—decked with the lines of.

P. 179. अभिसंधानदक्ष—clever in deceiving or taking advantage of the credulity of. सरहस्य—with their mystical teachings. सषडङ्गानि—for the six aṅgas see supra, note on षडङ्ग p. 21; it will be seen from that passage that the Kumáras had learnt the Vedas with their aṅgas. एतत्संग्रहेण—by his espousal or adoption of. आतङ्क—disease, affliction. ०सेकैर्निष्कलङ्क०—whose heads are washed with, i. e. hallowed by. यन्त्र—mystical or astronomical diagrams used as amulets. ग्रहाः—evil spirits supposed to seize upon children &c. कनकलेखाधिष्ठान०—कनकलेखा अधिष्ठानं यस्य. धनराजाकर—a Yaksha. क्षत्रियस्य—i. e. of Jayasiṃha. अधिगतक्षणः—finding an opportunity or time of leisure. संगृह्णन्—securing in his interest, winning over to his side. ध्यानधीरः—patiently remaining in abstract meditation. स्थानदर्शित०—showing my knowledge of (lit. possession of) occult things at the proper time. निचाय्य—having found out or ascertained (what was in his mind).

P. 180. ०लक्षणैकराशेः—The asylum of all auspicious marks. रशना—waist-zone. राजित—decorated. लीलाञ्चित०—with her dark lotus-like eyes sportively bent, or graceful with their sportive movements. दर्शन is used for नेत्र for alliteration with दर्शन. सहते—allows, bears. सह्यतां—wait for; for this sense cf. द्वित्राण्यहान्यर्हसि सोढुमर्हन् Ragh. V. 25. निर्निशाकरारश्मिषि—void of moon-light, i. e. on a dark night; or, when the moon-light had passed away. नीरन्ध्र—not broken through, i.e. dense or thick. निगीर्ण—swallowed up, shrouded in. निगडित—sealed. जलतल०—to be entered by diving under the surface of water. नीरन्ध्रं—having no opening towards water. छिद्रीकृतान्तरालं—excavated from within. एकतः—in one part (as the Bhûshaṇá has it). The sense of 'near' or 'close to' assigned to एकतः by the commentator is far-fetched. Besides, if सरस्तटं be taken as governed by एकतः, no object is left to अकार्षम्. तीर्थसंनिकृष्टं—close to the landing-stairs. घन—compactly arranged. छन्नच्छिद्राननं—with the opening of the cavity ( or the pit he dug out reaching the bottom of the lake ) covered with. निर्णिक्त--well washed; *p p.* of निज् with निर् 3 P. A'. संतान—a belt or multitude of stars. अमध्यमणि--*i e.* the big gem in the middle. The belt of stars is here compared to a necklace of pearls, and the sun to its central gem. संतानहारिहार० *v. l.*--seems to be better; 'fastened at the end of the necklace in the form of the streaming morning light eclipsing the stars.' क्षणदा--*Lit.* 'the giver of rest;' hence, night. गन्धहस्तिन्--गन्धप्रधानो हस्ती an elephant of the best class, the strong smell of whose ichor is unbearable to other elephants and makes them turn tail at his sight. See com. *Cf.* Ragh V. 47, VI. 7. कनकशैल:--The mountain Meru. The peak of the mountain Meru is compared to a stage and the rising sun to an actor exhibiting the play of light ( the gleaming solar rays being reflected back from the gems on the mountain ).

P. 181. घनतरङ्ग—The clouds are the rolling waves in the ocean of the sky. कार्याकार्य--The sun is one of those who keep watch over a man's actions. *Cf.* आदित्यचन्द्रावनिलोऽनलश्च &c. सहस्राक्षदिक्--the east. रागायित--serving as a red dye or paint; p. p. p. of the denom. from राग. गैरिकतट--the skirt covered with red chalk ; गिरौ भव: गैरिक:, fr. गिरि+ इक ( ठन् ). साधारणच्छाय—with its appearance like, *i. e.* appearing like. कदर्थनया--with a desire to harass or torment. अन्तरिक्षाख्येन--आकाश or the sky is considered as one of the eight forms of Śiva; *cf.* श्रुतिविषयगुणा या &c Śák. I. 1. संध्याङ्गनाया:--Here संध्या is represented as a rival wife. Pârvatî would be pained to see the body of her lord in another form half-shared by another woman, as indicated by एकस्तन. दिनाधिनाथे-*i. e.* when it was about sunset. जनस्यास्य—is used to avoid the use of माम्. धरणिन्यस्त--*i. e.* he bowed to his very feet. आदिष्ट—he was addressed by me. निरीह--unambitious, not aspiring. *Cf.* साहसे श्री: प्रतिवसति ; उद्योगिनं पुरुषसिंहमुपैति लक्ष्मी:; and निवसन्ति पराक्रमाश्रया न विषादेन समं समृद्धय: । Kir. II. 15. अनाकलित--free from. अर्चितेन—held in high esteem, honoured. अत्यादरनिचितेन--filled with great respect, qualifies जनेन. सततगतैः०--the vital airs, *i. e*, प्राण and others. This is used to avoid the word प्राण. स्खलित-'rolled back from;' to be construed with सत्व. स्थगित--covered.

As the water rolled over the lotus-plants, it shook their stalks, and frightened the swans as their bodies were pricked by the points of their thorns. Dissolve— तटाास्खलितं यज्जलं तेन स्थगितं यज्जलजखण्डं तस्य चलितदण्डानां ये कण्टकास्तैषामग्रैर्दलिता देहा येषां ते; now see Bhûshaṇâ quoted in the com. त्रासजर्जर—broken through fear.

P. 182. निचाय्य—having definitely known or observed; *cf. supra*, p. 179. स्थिरतर॰—firmly fixed or fastened by the chains of deep love. असहनीय &c.—She will not brook any delay in obtaining your sight, *i. e.* she will be longing for your company. नात्यादर॰—without much concern, easily. धीर—cultured, developed. आकलय्य—having considered the matter. जालिकशतं च &c.—This precaution was necessary to see that there were no crocodiles &c. there; *cf.* Ragh. आनायिभिस्तां (=सरयूं) अपकृष्टनक्रां XVI. 55. अन्तरङ्गनर—people in whom you can confide. त्रिंशद्दण्डा॰—for a space of thirty *daṇḍas* ( a measure of length equal to 4 *hastas*, or, according to the Com., 16 *hastas* ). रन्ध्रदर्शनासहैः—who could not see any mischief in it. तथास्थित: &c.—being ready to carry out my instructions and firmly resolved to secure the maiden. भवान्त—region, a secluded place. अनाचर्य—without having accomplished. यथार्ह—as may be agreeable to you.

P. 183. धरणितलवैबिलगण—The gods on earth, *i. e.* the Brâhmaṇas. वर्तिका—a wick, a piece of cloth wrapped round the end of a stick ( and used as a torch ). ग्रस्त—swallowed up, dispelled. निःसंगता—indifference, the state of not being attached to the world. निरागस—innocent. जालिक—fishermen, men with nets. संहतकर्णनासं—with the holes of his ears and nostrils stopped. हास्तिनं—the depth of which was an elephant's stature. The constr. is हास्तिनं सरस्तलं गतं सं नक्रलीलया नीरातिनिलीनयायी अहं &c. Some read गत: for गतं; in this case the sentence will close at हास्तिनं; 'he dived into the water and reached the bottom of the lake the depth of which was an elephant's height.' नक्रलीलया—with the ease ( and caution ) of a crocodile. अतिनिलीन॰—&c.—moving forth, having dived deep into water. कालदण्ड-चट्टना॰—tremendous ( killing ) like the strokes of the rod of Yama. निर्दयदत्तनिग्रह:—mercilessly pommelled. This incident of the story, *viz.* the supposed transformation of the person of the king into a superior form, is a repetition of Upahârvarman's personating himself as Vikaṭavarman after he had murdered him in his narration of his account. Perhaps in writing out this part of the story Daṇḍin got his inspiration from the story of Taruṇachandra, a physician, related in the Bṛihatkathá The physician, having promised to cure विनयशील, king of Vilâsapura, of the deformity brought on by old age, in eight months, asked him to dwell in an underground cellar. But, as the king under his treatment instead of becoming young wasted away, the physician secretly murdered him, threw his body into a well with its mouth closed, and having introduced a young man of similar features into the cave, kept him there for some days. He afterwards brought him out and presented him before the subjects as the king brought back to youth again by his medication. *Cf.* अभूच्छ्रीकण्ठनिलये विलासपुरनामनि। पुरे विनयशालाख्यो नाम्नाऽन्वर्थेन भूपतिः ॥...... इत्यादि चिन्तयन्सोऽथ सदस्याहूय भूपतिः। वैद्यं तरुणचन्द्राख्यं मिजगाद कृतादरः॥ अप्यस्ति काचिद्युक्तिः सा ययेयं वार्यते जरा।......एकस्त्वं भूगृहे मासानष्टौ यदिदमौषधम्। उपयुङ्क्षे ततो देव जरामपनयामि ते॥......आजहार कमप्येकं पुरुषं तादृशाकृतिम्। राजानं त्वां करोमीति युवानं कृतसंविदम्॥ ततः सुरङ्गां भूगेहे दूराद्दत्त्वाऽथ तं नृपम्। सुप्तं हत्वा तया नीत्वा सोऽन्धकूपेऽक्षिपन्निशि॥ तयैव पुरुषं तं च तरुणं तत्र भूगृहे। प्रवेश्य स्थापयामास सुरङ्गां पिदधे च ताम्॥ ततः स सर्वाः प्रकृतीर्वैद्योऽन्येद्युरभाषत। अजरोऽयं कृतस्तावत्षड्भिर्मासैर्मया नृपः॥ &c. Kathàs. VII. 6. 60–64.

P. 184. अत्यचित्रीयत—seemed a great wonder. See *supra*, note on चित्रीया p. 151. चण्डतरदण्डि॰—the very fierce staff-bearers. रसनयन॰–with my eyes stripped of the pleasure of sleep owing to the joy ( रस आनन्दजनितभावविशेषः ) I felt then. नयन—getting; stands for प्राप्ति, which could not be used. नयनरस॰ *v. l.*—in this case the comp. becomes clumsy; we have to take it as नयनाभ्यां रसेन निरस्ता &c. दिग्गजशिरः—the frontal globe &c. यथासदृशा॰—who waited upon me with the proper formalities. अजेय—not to be controlled or overpowered by (to be construed with इन्द्रियाणां). नीरजसा—free from all foulness. सरसिज &c.—सरसिजदलेन सदृशी ॰दलसंनिकाशा छाया यस्य; the complexion of which resembles that of lotus-petals. नि–or नी-काश expresses resemblance when at the end of a comp.; see Amara. II 10. 38. नरकशासन—the killer of Naraka (a demon, king of Pràgjyotisha), Kṛishṇa; hence, Vishṇu. सरसिजासना॰—This shows that Brahmá-worship was in vogue in Daṇḍin's time. क्लेशनिरसन—sufficient to dissipate their troubles. सातिशयं—with supreme power. आदिराज—may be Manu; see, however, note on the same at p. 146, last line.

P. 185. हर्षकाष्ठा--The highest pitch of joy. लासयन्ती—causing to dance or glitter. ललिताञ्चित--gracefully bent. दन्तच्छदकिसलया-her sprout-like (red and tender) lip. हर्षजल०-Her eyes, void of collyrium, were filled with the moisture of the tears of joy. जालं—a trick meant to entrap. स्नेहनिर्यन्त्रणं-freely through affection. सहचर्या:—his beloved Kanakalekhâ. निरर्गलीकृता०—निर्गता अर्गला यस्य तथा कृतः (set at liberty) च अतिसत्कृतश्च &c.

P. 186. अतिकष्टं तपः—This is said to please him. प्रज्ञासत्त्वयोः—ingenuity, and courage or mental calibre.

क्लिश्यत्—suffering from. क्लिष्ट—in distress. उदञ्चत्—drawing up. निष्कल---an old man; this word has occurred before on p. 171. वंशनाली०—drawn up in the hollow piece of a long bamboo. पाषाण०—knocked down with stones.

P. 187. विदर्भो नाम &c.—The great kingdom of Vidarbha extended from the banks of the Krishṇá to near the banks of the Narmadá. On account of its great size it was also called Mahárásḥṭra. Its capital, Kuṇḍinapura, is probably the modern Beder. According to the Nalachampú, Kuṇḍinapura was situated on the river Varadá (=Wardhá). The famous race of the Bhojas was a branch of the Yádavas. अंशावतारः—A righteous king is often described as a partial manifestation of Dharma; *cf.* अपवर्गमहोदयार्थयोर्भुवमंशाविव धर्मयोर्गतौ । Ragh. VIII. 16. अतिसत्त्व—of extraordinary prowess or courage. Mark the author's command of language, in how many ways he expresses the same idea. उदग्र—distinguished or ennobled by. उत्थानशील—ambitious of greatness. शास्त्रप्रमाणः—following the authority of, guided by, the *s'ástras*; defender of the faith. शक्यभव्य०—an undertaker of things possible to accomplish, of public utility and beneficial in the end. See com. Daṇḍin seems to have taken this phraseology from Kauṭilya, as remarked by Mr. Agashe; *cf.* शक्यकल्यभव्यारम्भिस्थिरकर्मानुरक्तप्रकृतिभ्यो विशेषः । शक्यारम्भी विषह्यं कर्मारभेत । कल्यारम्भी निर्दोषम् । भव्यारम्भी कल्याणोदयम् । Kau. Nît. Adhi. VII., Ch. 8, 114, 115. प्रभावयिता—who advanced or promoted. उद्भावयिता—raising to dignity. अवितृष्णः—never apathetic, ever eager for. नदीष्ण—proficient in. नेदिष्ठ—*lit.* nearest to; hence, conversant or well acquainted with. धर्मार्थसंहिता—sacred lore and political science. सुकृत—favour obligation. प्रत्यवेक्षित—A superintendent of, who himself carefully looked after. सर्वाध्यक्ष—superintendents of different de partments. कृतकर्मण:—those rendering signal services. *Cf* क्रियापवर्गेष्वनुजीविसात्कृताः कृतज्ञतामस्य वदन्ति संपदः। Kir. I. 14.

P. 188. दैवमानुषीणामा०—The calamities coming from deities are such as fire, water, disease, famine, death, &c.; and from men are such as (corrupt) royal officers, thieves, enemies, favourites of the king, and the greed of the king himself. हुताशनो जलं व्याधिर्दुर्भिक्षं मरणं तथा। इति पञ्चविधं दैवं व्यसनं मानुषं ततः॥ आयुक्तकेभ्यश्चौरेभ्यः परेभ्यो राजवल्लभात्। पृथिवीपतिलोभाच्च नराणां पञ्चधा मतम् (*i. e.* भयम्)॥ Kám. N. XIII. 20; V. 82. See Ragh. I. 60. षाड्गुण्य—The six expedients to be employed in foreign politics; these are (see com.)—(1) संधि or peace or alliance; (2) विग्रह or making of war (when other remedies fail); (3) यान or marching against the enemy when one is in a position to do so and one's own kingdom is well protected; (4) आसन or halting (waiting for opportunity &c.); (5) द्वैध or द्वैधीभाव duplicity, sowing seeds of discord among the ranks of the enemy; and (6) आश्रय or seeking shelter (the help of a powerful king &c.). मनुमार्गेण—According to the line of conduct chalked out by Manu. Here Manu may refer to the great law-giver or to the king of that name. *Cf.* Ragh. I. 17; cf. also Yàjñavalkya—कुलानि जातीः श्रेणीश्च गणाञ्जानपदानपि। स्वधर्माच्चलितान्राजा विनीय स्थापयेत्पथि॥. पुण्यश्लोकः—one whose name it is auspicious to repeat; one of holy fame. पुरुषायुषं—the full period of human life, one hundred years. A final अ is added to आयुस् when preceded by पुरुष &c., by अचतुर विचतुर......निःश्रेयसपुरुषायुषद्व्यायुषत्र्यायुष...। Pàṇ. V. 4. 77.

तदायति—who owed his prosperity or power to him (his father); *i. e.* who succeeded to his prosperous kingdom. Or it may mean 'equal to him in prowess' (तस्य इव आयतिर्यस्य). दैवात्—as fate would have it. दण्डनीति—the science of politics. दण्ड—government; fr. दम् 4 P. to control, to subdue; दम्यते अनेन, ड being added by ञमन्ताड्डः। Uṇádi. I. 114. It is thus praised by Kámandaka—एकैव दण्डनीतिस्तु विद्येत्यौशनसाः स्थिताः। तस्यां तु सर्वविद्यानामारम्भाः समुदाहृताः॥ II. 5. नात्यादृतः—did not much devote himself to, did not at all take interest in. प्रगल्भवाक्—eloquent in speech; whose words could make an impression. The following is a sound piece of advice which can be given only by a consummate politician and a veteran statesman. आत्मसंपत्—qualities of the soul, personal accomplishments. These are शार्य, प्रज्ञा &c.; see the quotation from Kám-

(line 7 of the Com.) विस्तरेषु—Mark the derivation; 'with reference to speech or words;' the word is विस्तर; स च शब्दस्य विस्तरः। Amara. it is formed by adding अ ( अप् ) to स्तृ; the affix घञ् ( अ ) is added to it with the prep. वि ( which gives विस्तार ) in the sense of extension or magnitude. We have a third word विष्टर from the same root in the sense of 'a seat', by वृक्षासनयोर्विष्टरः। Páṇ. VIII. 3. 93. विस्तार—development, culture; see above, note on विस्तर. आत्मसं°—refining, polishing, necessary for it. *Cf.* चतसृष्वपि ते विवेकिनी नृप विद्यासु निरूढिमागता ( मतिः )। &c. Kir. II. 6; and आत्मा प्रयत्नादर्थेभ्यो मनः समधितिष्ठति। संयोगादात्ममनसोः प्रवृत्तिरुपजायते ॥ विज्ञानं हृदयं चित्तं मनो बुद्धिश्च तत्समम्। अनेनात्मा करोतीह प्रवर्तननिवर्तने ॥ प्रयत्नज्ञानसंस्कारा आत्मलिङ्गमुदाहृतम् ॥ Kám.-Nít. I. 28, 30, 31. अर्थशास्त्रेषु—see *supra*, p. 147. अग्निसंशोधिता—the simile shows that proficiency in the science of government is of vital importance to a king. बुद्धिशून्यः—Here बुद्धि means diplomatic talent, statesmanship.

P. 189. अत्युच्छ्रितः—very mighty, supreme. अभ्यारुह्यमाणं—surpassed in diplomacy; brought under their power. विभज्य—assigning their proper province to them. अयथावृत्त—not acting with a right perception of objects to be effected and their means. कर्मसु प्रतिहन्यमानः—defeated or thwarted in his objects ( undertakings ). योगक्षेम—the acquisition of things not obtained and their preservation. See com. अतिक्रान्त°—when contempt is shown to authority. सर्वाः स्थितीः &c.—will upset all order. निर्मर्यादः—when people transgress the bounds of duty, *i e.* are demoralized. आगमदीप &c.—आगम means here नीतिशास्त्र or the science of the conduct of human affairs. लोकयात्रा—the conduct of worldly affairs, the course of worldly life. व्यवहित—hidden from view, secret; or, impeded by obstacles. विप्रकृष्ट—beyond the reach or ken of senses. तेन हीनः &c.—*Cf.* अनेकसंशयोच्छेदि परोक्षार्थस्य दर्शकम्। सर्वस्य लोचनं शास्त्रं यस्य नास्त्यन्ध एव सः ॥. अप्रतिहतवृत्ति—the operation of which is never obstructed. अर्थदर्शन—discernment of political and other ends or objects. आगमय—obtain an insight into, gain proficiency in. तदर्थानु°—by carrying out or acting up to its precepts. आवर्जितशक्ति°—having at command the three regal powers. For the Śaktis, see *infra*, p. 208.

P. 190. प्रसादवित्तः—who enjoyed special royal favour; *lit.* who was known to be a royal favourite. वाद्य—is of four kinds, *viz.* ततं वीणादिकं वाद्यं ( such as playing on lutes, violins and other stringed instuments ) आनद्धं मुरजा ( tabors &c. )—दिकम् । वंशादिकं (playing on harps and other wind-instruments) तु सुषिरं कांस्यतालादिकं ( beating of cymbals and other instruments struck together in pairs ) घनम् ॥ Amar. I. 7. 4. अबाह्य—not out, *i. e.* well-acquainted with. अयन्त्रितमुखः—garrulous, of licentious tongue. बहुभाङ्गि०—clever in periphrastical and enigmatical speeches. परमर्म०—habitually seeking another's weak or vulnerable points. परिवाद०—delighting in circulating scandal. पैशुन्यपण्डितः—adept in craft. उत्कोच—bribes. सकल०—a professor of all wicked acts, of every kind of inequity. कामतन्त्र०—a pilot of libertinism or licentiousness. कामतन्त्र—the science or ways of sexual enjoyment. कुमारसेवकः—one who had served the king from the time he was a boy or crown prince. "The arguments which are urged by one of his (Anantavarman's) favourites," remarks Prof. Wilson, "in behalf of idle pleasures and in detraction of grave advisers and ministers, while they speak the language of the profligate in all ages, afford some curious insight into the abuses of official authority which prevailed in Indian Government at the time of the composition." With the introductory part of this admonition may be compared Nai.-Ch. XVII. Ślokas 37-96, as pointed by Mr. Agashe. उच्चावचैः—of all sorts ; *lit.* high and low; उदक् च अवाक् च उच्चावचम्; irregularly formed. See *supra*, p. 131. कदर्थयन्तः—teasing, harassing. प्रेत्य–after death. *Cf.* मृतः स्मरति जन्मानि मृते कर्मफलोर्मयः । अन्यभुक्तैर्मृते तृप्तिरित्यलं धूर्तवार्तया ॥ Nai. XVII. 53. अभ्युदया०—fortune or prosperity of the highest kind or exalted nature. मुण्डयित्वा etc.—This refers to the initiatory rite at the Agnishṭoma sacrifice, in which the head of the Yajamána is first shaven, then tied with the *kus'a* grass &c. as stated here. पाषण्डिनः—religious hypocrites, heretics. This refers to the Jaina Bhikshus who advocate renunciation of worldly ties, such as wife, sons, &c. पटुजातीय—a clever or shrewd fellow. अस्यै मृगतृष्णिकायै—in pursuit of this mirage. हस्तगतं—what he has in his possession. काकिणी—an inferior coin equal to twenty cowries. कार्षापण—a copper coin of a particular value. See Bhúshaṇá.

P. 191. चतस्रः राज०—See Kám. N. II. 2. त्रयी—the three Vedas. वार्ता—practical arts such as agriculture, commerce &c. The Devî-Puráṇa thus accounts for the name—पश्वादिपालनाद्देवि कृषिकर्मादिकारणात् । वर्तनाद्दारणाद्वापि वार्ता सा पर गीयते ॥ •आन्वीक्षिकी—

logic and metaphysics दण्डनीति—The science of government. *Cf.* Kâm.-Nît. II. quoted in the com., and एकैव दण्डनीतिस्तु विद्येत्यौशनसाः स्थिताः । तस्यां तु सर्वविद्यानामारम्भाः संप्रतिष्ठिताः ॥ Kám. Nît. II. 5. विष्णुगुप्त—better known as Chânakya, a celebrated statesman and diplomatist who flourished in the latter part of the 4th century B. C. He is the author of a work on political science and state-craft called Chánakyanîti after him. मौर्यार्थे—Maurya is Chandragupta, king of Pâṭaliputra, and the hero of the Mudrârákshasa. According to Indian authorities, Chânakya was his principal adviser and minister, he having got the throne of the Nandas chiefly through his help. शास्त्रान्तरानुबन्धि—is connected with other Śâstras (and depends upon them for its thorough understanding). Here begins a satirical description of the study and effects of *Daṇḍanîti* or political science. पुत्रदारमपि &c.—For the Nitîśástra lays down stringent rules for the daily course of action of a king. He is not to trust too much his queen or sons, must eat a measured quantity of food and of a particular kind, well examined by experts and so on. See Kâm.-Nît. VII. आत्मकुक्षेः &c.—for their own belly, *i. e.* meals.

उत्थितेन &c.—Now the author tells us, closely following the authority of Chánakya, how the regal day of 24 hours was apportioned into eight parts, particular duties being assigned to each. मुष्टि—has a technical meaning, according to the Bhûshaṇâ (which see); for a different sense see *supra*, p. 121 (मुष्टिवधः); here मुष्टि means a measure used in checking the account of the income from and expenditure on account of the country, while अर्धमुष्टि is to be used in connexion with a village. See also the Laghudîpikâ. अभ्यवहृत्य—having admitted for reckoning; or taking into account. It may here mean 'having eaten a morsel' also. आयव्ययजातं—all the receipts and expenditure. आहरणोपायान्—modes or ways of defrauding. *Cf.* तेषां हरणोपायाश्चत्वारिंशत् । Chán. II. 8. विकल्पयितारः—adopt as alternatives; hence, multiply into. The precepts are द्वितीये पौरजानपदानां कार्याणि पश्येत् । तृतीये स्नानभोजनं सेवेत स्वाध्यायं च कुर्वीत । चतुर्थे हिरण्यप्रतिग्रहमध्यक्षांश्च कुर्वीत । पञ्चमे मन्त्रिपरिषदं पत्रसंप्रेषणेन मन्त्रयेत । चारगुप्तबोधनानि च बुध्येत । I. 19. जयपराजयौ—decision in favour of or otherwise. For प्राड्विवाक see p. 131, last line. अर्थैः—by securing their own objects or consulting their own advantage. पापेन......योजयन्ति—*Cf.* ईदृशे व्यवहाराग्नौ मन्त्रिभिः परिपातिताः । स्थाने खलु महीपाला गच्छन्ति कृपणां दशाम् ॥ Mrich. IX. 41; see also the next śl.

यावदन्नःपरिणामः—until the food eaten is digested. विषभयं—A king runs the danger of having his food poisoned. *Cf.* याने शय्यासने पाने भोज्ये वस्त्रे विभूषणे । सर्वत्रैवाप्रमत्तः स्याद्वर्जेत विषदूषितम् ॥ Kám. N. VI. 9 (and the succeeding ślokas wherein several modes for detecting poison are given).

P. 192. हिरण्य०—The king is to receive and make presents in the fourth division of the day. प्रसारयन्नेव—*i. e.* he has scarcely time to do that. मन्त्रचिन्ता—deliberation or consideration of political schemes with the ministers and councillors. मध्यस्था इव—outwardly appearing to be neutral (indifferent and impartial). Or, after the Bhúshaṇá, 'like pleaders.' मिथः संभूय—forming a league with one another. दोषगुणौ—merits and defects (of a political scheme). दूताः—ambassadors, envoys. स्वेच्छया—according to their will (as would suit their purpose). विपरिवर्तयन्तः—perverting, misrepresenting and confounding. उपजीवन्ति—live upon, *i. e.* they enrich themselves by getting money and the other objects they seek from the members of their own party, the party of enemy and of the allies or friends. बाह्या०—see *supra*, p. 134. प्रशमयन्त इव—They do not really want to suppress insurrections, but want war; *cf.* मन्त्रिणः स्वार्थतात्पर्याद्दीर्घमिच्छन्ति विग्रहम् । तेषां च भोग्यतामेति दीर्घकार्याकुलो नृपः ॥ Kám. N. XII. 41. अवशमवगृह्णन्ति—hold him helpless in their power. सोऽस्यैता०—स दह्यतां स्वैर० *v. l.* is not so good, as the speaker nowhere condemns a thing directly, but leaves it to be so understood from his words which have an ironical force. तिस्रस्त्रि०—$3\frac{3}{4}$ Nádikás, *i. e.* ghaṭikás (a घटिका = 24 minutes), or an hour and a half. What a long interval of time! चतुरङ्ग०—In the Kauṭ. we have हस्त्यश्वरथायुधीयान्पश्येत्. प्रत्यवेक्षण—reviewing of. सेनापति०—सेनापतेः सखा सेनापतिसखः तस्य; the comp. must be so dissolved, and not as a Bah. विक्रमचिन्ता—projects of victory, *i. e.* how to make the army efficient. गूढपुरुषाः—men in disguise, secret emissaries. In the first portion of the night the king is to receive the reports of his spies and envoys. शस्त्राग्नि &c.—Persons appointed to employ weapons or fire or to administer poison (to compass particular ends). These were the ways of getting an unwelcome person or enemy out of the way. Châṇakya himself takes precautions to thwart the efforts of Rákshasa in this direction, in the Mudrárákshasa. अनुष्ठेय—to be set to work or appointed. तूर्यघोषेण—seated, enjoys rest, listening to the play of trumpets; or तृतीये may be taken with the preceding sentence ; thus द्वितीये...आरभते तृतीये; 'in the second watch he takes his food, and attends to his daily course of studies in the third.' The next sentence would then begin with तूर्यघोषेण &c.—going to bed on hearing the sound of the trumpet, he enjoys sleep &c. किल—as they say, *i. e.* he is not likely to get sleep. अजस्र—constant ; fr. जस् 4 Conj. P. with र added by नमिकम्पिस्म्यजसकमहिंसदीपो रः। Pāṇ. III. 2. 167 ; जसिः ( *i. e.* the root जस् ) नञ्पूर्वः क्रियासातत्ये वर्तते। नम्रः, कम्प्रः, स्मेरः, अजस्रः &c. ॰मनसः—with his mind labouring under the torture of; or, tormented by being on the stretch of constant anxiety. मन्त्रग्रहः—listening to the counsels of the ministers; सप्तमे मन्त्रमध्यासीत गूढपुरुषांश्च प्रेषयेत्। Kauṭ. N. नाम—as is well-known. वीतशुल्कबाध—free from the fear of being subject to taxes. वणिज्यया—by disposing of or selling. वणिजः कर्म वणिज्या formed by affixing य by दूतवणिग्भ्यां च quoted in the Kâs'ikâ. This is not found in the Bháshya, says the Sid.-Kau.—माधवस्तु वणिज्याशब्दः स्वभावात्स्त्रीलिङ्गः भावे एव प्रत्ययः न तु कर्मणि इत्याह। भाष्ये तु दूतवणिग्भ्यां च इति नास्त्येव। So this should be dissolved as वणिजि साधुः, by affixing यत् ( य ) by तत्र साधुः । Páṇ. IV. 4. 98. The word वाणिज्यं is formed by affixing ष्यञ् ( य ) by Páṇ. V. 1. 124. लेशेन—*lit.* in some part; making some occasion for it. क्लेशेन *v. l.*—with difficulty, taking pains to create an occasion.

P. 193. The eighth portion is appropriated to the priest and religious ceremonies, after which the business of the day is resumed. गुणवत्—prolific of fruit, efficacious. ब्रह्मकल्पाः—almost equal to Brahman. This is ironical. स्वस्त्ययन—स्वस्ति ईयते अनेन a rite averting evil and leading to a blissful end. Mr. Agashe quotes the following from the Śabdakalpadruma—माङ्गल्यकर्मारम्भकालविवक्ष्यमाणमन्त्रोच्चारणपूर्वकतण्डुलविकिरणम्। तन्मन्त्रो यथा—अमुककर्मणि पुण्याहं भवन्तो ब्रुवन्तु। इत्युक्ते पुण्याहमिति ब्राह्मणैस्त्रिरुक्ते अमुककर्मणि ऋद्धिं भवन्तो ब्रुवन्तु। तत ऋध्यतामिति ब्राह्मणास्त्रिर्ब्रूयुः। ततः स्वस्ति न इन्द्रो वृद्धश्रवाः स्वस्ति नः पूषा विश्ववेदाः । स्वस्ति नस्तार्क्ष्योऽरिष्टनेमिः स्वस्ति नो बृहस्पतिर्दधातु। इति पठित्वा तण्डुलान् विकिरेत्। अप्राप्तप्राप्त॰—who have not as yet received any donations. स्वर्ग्य—leading to heaven, conferring heavenly happiness. आयुष्यं—conferring long life; आयुः प्रयोजनमस्य ; fr. आयुस्+य ( त् ). तन्मुखेन—through their medium. अविहित॰—This and the following adj. compounds qualify अहर्निशं used as a noun. अविरल॰—full of torments. नयत:—passing. स्वमण्डल—his own territory. अविश्वास:—mistrust. People see a motive in all his acts as they don't seem to be natural, and so do not trust him. यावता च &c.—To what extent the course of worldly existence can proceed without policy, is seen from the experience of ordinary life; *i. e.* it is quite clear from our experience of daily life that the course of the world can go on unimpeded without policy. Some read न याति लोक० ; this means—to what extent does not proceed without &c.; *i. e.* worldly experience itself teaches what policy to follow in this world. नात्र शास्त्रेणार्थ:—We need have no recourse to Śa'stra in this matter. अतियन्त्रणा—too great or absurd restraint. सामादिरुपाय०—see com. मन्त्रिबक—hypocritical or cunning counsellors; a Tatp. Comp. of the Nitya class; see com. मन्त्रकर्कश—advocates of a stern enforcement of counsel or policy. शुक्र—Śukráchârya, the preceptor of the demons and the author of a Smṛiti, named after him. आङ्गिरस—a great sage, one of the inspired law-givers (an author of one of the chief Smṛitis) and a writer on astronomy. विशालाक्ष—name of Śiva, as the author of a Śâstra. बाहुदन्तिपुत्र:—Son of Indra (बाहुदन्तिन् ), name of Jayadatta, author of a Tantra. The two are referred to as writers on Nîti by Kauṭilya; see Prak. IV. p. 13, Mysore Ed. पराशर is well known; his Smṛiti is considered as the chief authority in the Kali age.

P. 194. पठन्तश्च &c.—Those who are well-read are taken in by those who have never read Śástra. ननु इदमुपपन्न &c.—Does not Your Majesty possess all this, *viz.* सर्वलोकस्य &c. अयातयाम—यातयाम (see com.) means 'the time for the enjoyment of which is gone;' exhausted, stale ; hence अया०—what is fresh, youthful. बहुमार्गवि०—On account of its pointing out diverse ways and therefore not leading to one definite end. अमुक्तसंशयेन—never giving up its misgivings (*i. e.* not arriving at a definite conclusion as to the adoption of one way). तन्त्रावाप—giving attention to internal as well as to foreign matters (see com.); cares of state-matters. पादातं—fr. पदाति + अण् (अ) by Páṇ. IV. 2. 38; see com. पादाभ्यामतति इति पदातिः. अन्यार्जित—another's property. अल्पाल्पं—very small. वयःखण्डम्—a portion of life. अर्जयन्त एव &c.—perish while they are acquiring money ; *i. e.* they never curb their desires. आस्वादयितुं—Inf. of the cau. of स्वद् 1 A'.; or read आस्वादितुं. अन्तरङ्गेषु—men enjoying your confidence, trusted men. अप्सर:प्रति०—counterparts . equal to the nymphs of heaven in beauty.

पानगोष्ठी—drinking parties. यथार्हे—यो यो अर्हः यथार्हः suited to i. e. capable of enjoying, every object; *cf.* तं तमाचरतानन्दं स्वच्छन्दं यं यमिच्छथ। Nai. XVII. 50. पञ्चाङ्ग—see com. अञ्जलिचुम्बितचूडः—with his folded hands closely placed across his brow. क्रीडा०—क्रीडानिर्भरमतिः *v. l.* his mind deeply set on sport.

P. 195. एषु दिनेषु—In the days that followed. प्रस्तुतेऽर्थे—the business in hand or for consideration. अचित्तज्ञ इति—Because he did not correctly read his (the king's) thoughts. अरुचितेऽर्थे—In matters distasteful or disagreeable to him. अक्षिगतः—a thorn in the eye; an eye-sore; an object of hatred. विलोभनवस्तूनि—choice gifts, *lit.* things that are tempting or attractive. प्रत्यवेक्षते—has regard for, cares for. आसन्नकार्येषु—things that immediately concern him; his private matters. अवष्टभ्यमान—encroached upon, occupied by. मत्समान०—the faults of those holding equal rank with me; or, मत्समानदोषान् may mean 'whose faults are similar to mine,' *i. e.* who have the courage to advise him like me. विगर्हयति—'censures more particularly' (वि). मर्मणि &c.—so as to touch my vitals, so as to cause intense pain. प्रतिक्षिपति—disapproves, rejects. स्खलित-blunders. मूर्खैः &c.—which is an insult to them. सत्यमाह चा०—the reference is to Chânakya's अनर्थ्याश्च प्रिया दृष्टा चित्तज्ञानानुवर्तिनः। and अप्रिया अपि दक्षाः स्युस्तद्भावाद्ये बहिष्कृताः। Prak. 92. चित्तज्ञानानुवर्तिनः—following the bents of mind of the king, ministering to the desires of the king. अनर्थ्याः—undesirable, *i. e.* wicked or bad counsellors. अनर्थाः *v. l.*—अविद्यमानोऽर्थो येभ्यः from whom no object can be gained; hence, bad. तद्भावबहिष्कृताः—out of, *i. e.* not knowing, his intentions. पितृपैतामहैः—servants of his father and grandfather. अश्रूयमाणवाचः—when our counsels are not listened to. अश्मक—An old name of Travancore. The Aśmakas were also inhabitants of Northern India according to Varáhamihira (Bṛih. Saṃ. XIV. 34) who also speaks of them along with the A'ndhras (XVI. 11). *Cf.* "A tribe of Aśmakas, or Assakas, was settled, at the time when the Sutta-Nipâta was composed, on the banks of the Godávarî. This is, no doubt, the same tribe whose name appears in inscriptions at Ajanta of about the sixth century A. D., and they therefore probably occupied land near the sources of this river in the Western Deccan, south of Berar." (Mark Collins).

प्रकृतिस्थमापादयेयुः—will restore him to his natural disposition, reclaim him. अनर्थेषु—undesirable pursuits. सुलभव्यलीक—easily leading to or bringing on misery or pain. द्वेष—disgust for. स्तम्भितपिशुनजिह्वः—putting a curb over my tongue, and so not allowing it to move in giving advice, refraining from counselling. Or it may mean—'putting (or exercising) a check on the tongues of wicked (or, designing) men.'

P. 196. एवं गते—When the minister had taken this resolve and held himself aloof from state-affairs. असद्वृत्तः &c.—being avowedly expelled by his father for his licentious conduct. Mark the meaning of नाम 'under the pretence of,' 'giving out that;' *cf. supra*, कार्तान्तिको नाम भूत्वा p. 159. शिल्पकारिणी—a dancing girl. छन्न—in disguise (numerous servants in different disguises). विहारभद्र—the king's favourite; see *supra*, p. 190. संक्रम—course of conduct; or, by this 'channel.' राजन्यास्पदमलभत—obtained a hold upon the king. लब्धरन्ध्र—*Lit.* when he found a loop-hole for him to enter, *i.e.* got into the king's confidence or getting an opportunity—refers to Chandrapálita. स refers to राजन्. औपकारिकी—conferring benefits. The author now points out ten beneficial results of chase. व्यायामोत्कर्ष—best kind of exercise. जङ्घाजव—fleetness or swiftness of foot. आशयाग्निदीप्ति—*Lit.* kindling of the gastric fire; quickening or improving the appetite. आशय—the stomach. मेद—fat. स्थैर्य—firmness, power of endurance; see com. अतिलाघव—great agility. अवस्थान्तरेषु—different states of the mind as affected by fright. चित्तचेष्टित—thoughts and actions. हरिण०......... प्रतिक्रिया—This (preventing injury to crops) was the chief object which the Śástrakâras had in view in allowing kings the right of मृगया. स्थलपथ०—clearing the roads of the pestilence of tigers and others. *Cf.* with the ideas expressed here Śâk. II. 4, 5 quoted in the com., and Ragh. IX. 49. Daṇḍin must have had these before his mind's eye when he wrote this passage. विविधकर्म०—fit for undertakings of various kinds. आटविकवर्गविश्रम्भण—gaining the confidence of the people that tenant the wilds. संधुक्षण—quickening, stirring up. प्रत्यनीकवित्रासन—intimidation of hostile parties. आशय—the mind (generosity of heart). अनवस्थान—*Lit.* unsettled state; uncertainty, or instability. अविधेयत्व—the state of not being subject to, power to control the feelings of. अमर्ष—high-spiritedness (which does not allow one to bear the rise of another or to bear insults tamely); *cf.* अमर्षशून्येन जनस्य जन्तुना न जातहार्देन न विद्विषादरः। Kir. I. 33.

P. 197. अक्षहस्तभूम्यादि०—With regard to the handling of dice and moving the pieces in the squares &c. अत्यन्तदुरूप०—too subtle to be marked or noticed. कूटकर्मणा—clever tricks. उपल०—by marking or observing them. एकविषयो०—since the whole is focused or concentrated (*lit.* made to converage to the fulfilment of) one object (*viz.* success in the game). अध्यवसाय०—the concomitant of, *i. e.* to be gained by, determined perseverance. प्रतिसंसर्ग—opposition to. शरीरयापन—passing of life. अर्थधर्मौ—by the Vârttika धर्मादिष्वनियम: the comp. may be धर्मार्थौ or अर्थधर्मौ. पुष्कल—praiseworthy, noble. पुरुषाभिमान:—the pride of one's being a male, *i. e.* gifted with manly (virile) power (पौरुष). अलोभक्लिष्ट—not hampered by greed, as one has to be necessarily generous. अलब्धोपलब्धि—for, as such a man has constant need of money, he must try to obtain what he has not yet obtained. The adjectives अलब्ध &c. may also similary refer to females (अलब्धाया उपलब्धि:, लब्धाया अनुरक्षणं &c.). भुक्तानुसंधान--keeping an eye on what is spent (so that there should be no waste); or, भुक्ताया अनु०—keeping well-pleased (a woman) after enjoyment. शरीरसंस्का०--संस्कार means bodily cleanliness and decoration. A man wishing to win the hearts of ladies must pay special attention to his bodily decoration and dress. सुभग०—charming, attractive. संभावनीयता-imposing appearance, impressiveness; *lit.* capacity to win public esteem. व्यपेक्षा—regard or consideration for, being kind to servants. उद्रिक्तस०—great nobility of mind; or, rather, excessive virility or vitality. स्पृहणीयवयो०—preservation or keeping up of enviable youth (by the flush wine imparts to the face). अहंकारप्रकर्ष—extreme sense of self-respect; an overwhelming sense of self (due to the influence of wine). अङ्गज०—its exciting or inflaming passion. संधुक्षणम्—the stimulation of. अपराधप्रमार्जन—blotting out from memory crimes committed. मन:शल्य—anything rankling in the mind. अशाठ्यशंसिन्—declaring or indicating absence of deceit or guile, *i. e.* straightforwardness. अश्राव्य० *v. l.*—disclosing secrets. उपबृंहण—increasing. अननुबन्ध—break, cessation. आनन्दैकतानता—complete absorption in joy; or, the continuous enjoyment of unmixed joy. संविभाग—the habit of distributing or allotting shares to others.

P. 198. अनुत्तराणि—unsurpassed, excellent beyond comparison. विलसितानि—sportings, dalliances. भयातिहरणाद् &c.—It is useful in war, since it makes one insensible to fear and pain.

वाक्पारुष्यं &c.—These are set forth as qualifications necessary for a king. The Bhú. does not seem to be right in connecting these with पान, as the इति after सांग्रामिकत्वं closes the subject. दूषणानि अर्थानां—*Lit.* misappropriation of money, imposing money-penalty, extravagance, &c. अर्थदूषण is mentioned by writers on polity as one of the faults of kings due to anger; see Ka'm. quoted further on. It is of four kinds—अदानमादानं विनाशः परित्यागश्चार्थस्येत्यर्थदूषणम्। Ka'u. Artha. VIII. 3. 129. औपकारिकाणि—Here it will be seen that Chandra. speaks approvingly (of course with a sinister motive) of the very things which are condemned by writers on polity as grave faults in a king; *cf.* वाग्दण्डयोश्च पारुष्यमर्थदूषणमेव च। स्मृतं व्यसनतत्त्वज्ञैः क्रोधजं व्यसनत्रयम्॥ कामजं मृगया द्यूतं स्त्रियः पानं तथैव च। व्यसनं व्यसनार्थज्ञैश्चतुर्विधमुदाहृतम्॥ Kám. N. XV. 7, 8 ; *cf.* also Hit. II. 103-105. लोकतन्त्र—administration of a kingdom. तच्छीला०—तत् refers to the king. प्रकृतयः—The subjects. समानभर्तृ०—of a like disposition with the king, *i. e.* equally abandoned to vice. तन्त्राध्यक्षाः—*Lit.* the heads of different departments ; the principal officers of state. स्वानि कर्मफलानि—The fruits of their own duties, *i. e.* the income of their offices. आयद्वाराणि—The sources of revenue. विटविधेयतया—The king being in the power of, *i. e.* following the counsels of, his parasites or companions in sensuality. विटवैधेय० *v. l.*—on account of the follies of his parasites. उपारूढ०—for the king did not fear adverse criticism from them. पानगो०...कृताः—admitted to the drinking parties. अपाचरत्—had intercourse with. भिन्नवृत्त—who abandoned their character, deviated from the path of virtue. मन्दत्रासाः—free from fear. पांसुलजन—licentious people. भङ्गिभाषण—crooked (cleverly expressed) speeches, *i. e.* in which there is a hidden meaning in addition to the plain grammatical meaning conveying the real intention of the speaker. भग्नचारित्र०—breaking through the restraint (shackles) of good conduct or character. धातृगण—paramours. सामर्षाः—enthusiasts, exasperated parties. अपहृतपरिभूतयः—freed from the fear of reproof. अपहृतपरिहृतयः *v. l.*—the avoiding of them being removed, *i. e.* there being no necessity to avoid them. प्रहताः &c.—The ways of sin became trodden, *i e.* frequented. वधबन्धातुराः—distressed by slaughter and imprisonment, or confinement for being put to death (वधार्थं बन्धः वधबन्धस्तेनातुराः).

P. 199. अयथाप्रणीतः—unjustly inflicted, or inflicted on the wrong party. क्रोध—disaffection, discontent. कृश—reduced to poverty. तेजस्विनो &c.—*Cf.* तत्तेजस्वी पुरुषः परकृतनिकृतिं कथं सहते

Bhar. N. 37. अकृत्येषु--evil acts, plots against the king. Here अ has the sense of अप्राशस्त्य. प्रासरन्—found scope to act, proved effective. परोपजापाः—intrigues of the enemy; secret overtures or instigating to rebellion. तदा च &c.—The constr. is तदा च अश्मकेन्द्रयुक्ताः तीक्ष्णरसदादयः मृगयु०...अग्निविसर्गैः &c. अनन्तवर्मकटकं जर्जरमकुर्वन्. From here are described the various sinister means employed by the secret agents of Aśmakendra to weaken the army of Anantavarman by the destruction of the eminent warriors in it. अद्रिद्रोणीः—mountain-valleys. अनपसारमार्गाः—having no passage for egress, having but one entrance. शुष्क &c.—Bah. qualifying द्रोणीः. द्वारतोऽग्निवि०—setting fire to them at the entrance causing it to spread inward, which prevented all chance of escape. इष्टकूप—a desirable well, i. e. one the water of which was represented to be excellent and desirable for drinking. तट—a precipice. प्रदर—a crevice, a pit. विश्वग्विसर—moving in different directions. ०भनुयात्तया—as their servants were cut off from them. ०अपराद्धैर्नाम—under pretext that they failed (missed their aim) to hit the deer. सपणबन्धं—with a wager or stipulation (यदि भवानिदं कुर्यात् तर्हीदमहं भवते दास्यामि इति समयकरणं पणबन्धः। Manoramâ). प्रतिरोधन—waylaying, attacking and making prisoners; for this sense of प्रतिरोधन, *cf.* कोदण्डपाणि निनदत्प्रतिरोधकानामापातदुष्प्रसहमाविरदभूनीकम् Málav. V. 10. संकुल—a crowd. इतरेषां हिंसोत्पा०—By causing others to be killed by forcing them to enter crowds of people gathered on such occasions as &c., so as to get them inculpated. गूढोत्पादित०—to whom injuries were secretly caused to be done. पराक्रमैः—by asking them to run away (पराक्रमणैः) secretly. सुहृत्त्वेनाभि०—having asked paramours to approach them as their friends. साहसोपन्यासैः—by mentioning these as their desperate deeds; with the reading भर्तृभयमपहृत्य 'by mentioning their daring deeds' (to their husbands). योग०—a beautiful woman who lures a man into danger, and destroys him; further on, it means a woman with a body fed on particular things, contact with whom leads to consumption. योग in such cases seems to mean—'what leads to the attainment of the desired object by means of the employment of spells, drugs and the like;' योगप्रधाना योगयुक्ता वा नारी; *cf.* words like योगचूर्ण, योगवर्तिका &c. संकेत—appointed places. प्राग्गुप्त०—first lying concealed near; the Com. needlessly takes this in the sense of लीनतां प्राप्य. अकीर्तनीय—secret. प्रमापण—killing. उपप्रलोभ्य—having enticed them.

P. 200. विघ्नव्याज०—to be procured or encompassed under colour of their meeting with obstacles. प्रत्यपाय-निवर्तन—प्रतिगतोऽपायं प्रत्यपाय: a remedy against injury; तस्मान्निवर्तनै: refraining from taking steps to prevent injury, *i. e.* allowing the elephants to kill or wound them. व्यालहस्तिन्—a vicious elephant. अवक्रमण—directing it to; letting it off against. दायाद्यर्थो—for such things as a share of the ancestral property or patrimony. अयथावृत्तान्—those not behaving virtuously, profligates. योगाङ्गना—Some read योग्याङ्गना, and take योग्या to mean a young woman, but here अङ्गना has no propriety. रसविधान—impregnating or saturating with poison. चिकित्सामुखेन—by way of, or under the pretence of, treating. आमयोपबृंहणै:—by fostering diseases, or making the diseases reach a more serious stage, making the cases worse. तीक्ष्णरसदा०—such men as were entrusted with the work of striking in the vital parts ( secret assasins ) by administering poison and the like. Or तीक्ष्णरस may mean ' virulent poison. ' प्रवीर—choicest warriors. वानवास्य—" The king of Vanavâsî, a city in the South of India, the remains of which in the Sunda district were discovered by Colonel Colin Mackenzie. " P. Peterson. " Vanavâsî was one of the seats of the Kadamba kings in the sixth and seventh centuries and is the modern Vanavâsî in North Canara. The Mahàbhârata mentions वनवासिका:, and from the context these appear to be the inhabitants of Vanvâsî. The passage names all the people of the south as under—अथापरे जनपदा दक्षिणा भरतर्षभ । द्रविडा: केरला: प्राच्या मूषिका वनवासिका: । कर्णाटका महिषका: &c. Bhîshma-P. IX. 58-59." Mr. Agashe. प्रोत्साह्य—having fomented or incited against. तत्परामृष्ट &c.—The borders of his kingdom being invaded by him. बलसमुत्थान—the mobilization of his forces. अश्मकेन्द्र:-see p. 195. कुन्तलपते:-Kuntala was the name of the country to the north of Chola. Its capital was Kalyân or Kallian-Doorg. According to Mr. Vincent Smith, Kuntala was the country between the Bhîmâ and the Vedavatî, bounded on the West by the Ghats including Simoga, Chitaldroog, Bellary, Dharwar, and Bijapur, and the adjacent parts. *Early History,* p. 148. आत्मनाटकीया-a dancing girl in his service. परामृशति—violates.

P. 201. मुरलेश—The lord of the Kerala country. Muralá 's the principal river of Kerala ( mentioned by Kálidása,

Ragh. IV. 55 ). Hence the people of Kerala were sometimes called Muralas. Kerala was the strip of land between the Western Ghats and the sea, north of the Kâverî. It corresponds to the modern Canara, and probably included Malabar also. ऋषीक—and नासिक्य, were countries of the South which, together with the others mentioned, form the whole of Southern India. The reading ऋषीक is adopted from Mr. Agashe's ed. in preference to the old reading ऋचीक as it is found in the Rámáyaṇa (विदर्भानृषिकांश्चैव रम्यान्माहिषिकानपि IV. 41) and in the Mahâbhârata Bhîshma-P. IX. 5. 64, and also in the Bṛihatsaṃhitá XIV. 15 (°तापसाश्रमा ऋषिकाः). Násikya is mentioned among the southern countries in the Brih. Saṃ. in the verse कर्णाटमहाटविचित्रकूटनासिक्यकोल्लगिरिचोलाः। &c. XIV. 13. According to some Nâsikya is the present Nâsik on the Godâvarî. उपजपाव—make secret overtures to win over to our side; instigate to rebellion. अग्रतो व्यतिषक्तं—engaged or encountered in front. काञ्चन°—shawls of a saffron hue with lace-borders. प्राभृतीकृत्य—offering as presents, presenting. आमिषत्वमगमत्—fell a victim to them; *i. e.* was overpowered by them and lost his kingdom. अवशीर्ण—*lit.* routed; hence, got as spoil. °आत्माधिष्ठितं—keeping it in his custody. यथाबलं—according to your respective powers. सर्वानुवर्ती—pleasing all. अग्रसत—appropriated to himself.

मौलैः—hereditary ministers. शोकज्वर—a burning fever brought on by grief. माहिष्मती—It was the capital of the Haihayas or Kalachuris (the great Kàrtavîrya and his son Arjuna), whose kingdom lay to the North of the Narmadá. It was situated between the Vindhya and the Ṛiksha mountains, about Beraghar, below Jabalpur. See Ragh. VI. 43. °द्वैमातुराय भ्रात्रे—her husband's brother by another mother. अन्यथाऽभ्यमन्यत—thought otherwise of her; *i. e.* thought that she would yield to his desires if he made the proposal. अवधाय—making sure that it would be a place of safety.

P. 202. क्षेमप्रवृत्त—gone in safety. घोष—a station or residence of cowherds. आश्वासयितुं—to invigorate or refresh. संपात—a sudden attack. किमीया जात्या—what is her family? सस्वजे—Another instance of the author's inadvertence (Perf. in the 1st pers.). सिन्धुदत्तापुत्राणां—Sindhudattâ seems to be the name of Sus'ruta's mother, his father being Pushpodbhava. नयावलिप्त—proud of his state-craft. अविभ्यम्—I shot the arrows at. एकः &c.—One of the deer fell with the arrow piercing him to its feathery part, the other with t e arrow piercing him through, so as to leave its feathers behind. सपत्रनिष्पत्रादतिव्यथने Páṇ. V. 4. 61 ; डाच् (aff. आ) स्यात्. सपत्राकरोति मृगम्। सपुङ्खशरप्रवेशनेन सपत्रं करोतीत्यर्थः। निष्पत्राकरोति सपुङ्खस्य शरस्यापरपार्श्वेन निर्गमनात् निष्पत्रं करोतीत्यर्थः। Sid.-Kau. मृगयु—मृगान् वधार्थं यातीति; a huntsman. अपलोमत्वचः—which was skinned and cleaned. क्लोम—the lungs, or entrails. निष्कुलाकृत्य—having dissected or separated the body into different parts. निर्गतं कुलमन्तरवयवानां समूहो यस्मादिति बहुव्रीहेर्डाच्। निष्कुलाकरोति दाडिमम्। Sid-Kau. on Pa'ṇ. V. 4. 62 (see com.). शूलाकृत्य—spitting it with a rod and roasting it. आ is added to निष्कुल and शूल in the senses given (see com). The author seems to have used these words here purposely, to display his knowledge of Sanskrit grammar.

P. 203. अत्यतार्षम्—अतार्षम् seems to be a mistaken form for अतारिषं which is the proper form. अतक्षिषं *v. l.* must be taken in the sense of 'satisfied.' दृति—a leather-bag. सम्यक्प्रतिपत्त्या—by (treating or acting towards) her well. प्रत्याकृष्य—having attracted him back. आक्रोशन—a report. अभिपत्स्यति—The Paras. is irregular; or read ०पत्स्यते; 'will approach her (with carnal desire);' *cf.* रावणावरजा तत्र राघवं मदनातुरा। अभिपेदे निदाघार्ता व्यालीव मलयद्रुमम्॥ Ragh. XII. 32. संनीय—having mixed. पतिव्रता इति—supply उक्त्वा after this (इति उक्त्वा हन्तव्यः). कापालिक—a mendicant of a particular Śaiva sect, moving with a skull in his hand for collecting alms, &c.

P. 204. रेवा—or 'the roaring one,' was another name for the Narmadá. परीक्ष्य वैजन्यं जनेषु निर्गतेषु—when people will have left it after assuring themselves that there was no one in. प्रतिष्ठापयिष्यति—will re-establish him in his sovereignty. उपपत्स्यते—all this will come to pass. उपधियुक्तं—based on, or proceeding from, fraud. सानाथ्यशंसी &c.—The vision declared that she (Mañjuvádinî) had a protector (was no longer destitute), referring to her espousal by Viśruta.

P. 205. मद्दर्शनराग०—who was agitated on account of the passion she felt for me at my sight. मञ्जुवादिनी०—whose courage was drunk up by the loveful glances of Mañjuvádinî. आकार्य—having made a sign to him to follow us. प्रथितः—much talked of. कुशीलव—musicians, bards. मात्राः—chattels, property; here, his equipments. ०वेषलीलः—having put on the gay dress of. अनुरञ्जित॰ समये—at a time when the sun-light had turned red, i. e. when it was about sunset. समाजज्ञानोप॰ —the reading समाजोपयोगीनि is better, as ज्ञान has no particular propriety here. नानारुतानि—imitations of different voices. ॰रुदितानि v. l. is bad, as रुदित is not applied to the notes of birds. हस्तचंक्रमण—moving on hands with the legs raised up. ऊर्ध्वपाद &c.—movements with different postures of the body, for which see com. करणानि—gymnastic feats.

P. 206. उपाहितवर्मा—with these fixed about my body. उत्क्रोशपात—jumping like an osprey. प्रत्युरसं—अ is added generally to उरस् at the end of an Avyayîbháva. वसन्तभानुः—The king of Aśmaka. His object was to inculpate Vasantabhánu as the instigator of the murder. उत्कर्तुं—अरूकर्तुं v. l. is the reading of both the Bhúshaṇá and the Laghudîpiká. It means 'to wound,' being der. from अरुस्. The final स् of this, as also of चेतस् and चक्षुस्, is dropped before the aff. च्वि ; see com. चारभटः —a valorous man, a warrior ; or, it may mean here one of the bard-warriors; see com. आक्रम्य—having jumped upon. विचेतीकुर्वन्—stunning him, making him senseless. आकुलं—frightened, confused. एष पन्थाः—this line of my foot-marks. ॰अस्पष्ट &c.—my foot-prints being effaced from the sand levelled by. पुनरवाचा—then turning to the west. In this case वप्र will mean the mound that supports a rampart. उच्चितेष्टक &c.—the bricks being unevenly piled up. खात—a ditch. प्रतिमुक्त—having put on. मत्कर्मतुमुल—crowded with people full of talk about my deed. प्रतिमाधिष्ठान—the place or pedestal of the image. भग्नपार्श्व॰—the outer opening of which was concealed with a large stone-slab the sides of which were loosened.

P. 207. वर्षधर—a eunuch. देवी तु—i. e. the queen Vasuṃdhará. अश्मकेन्द्रो॰—sent him word that the unhappy event had been cotrived by the king of As'maka. ॰कुक्षिवैजन्य—carefully ascertained that the interior was quite unoccupied. पटीयांसं—very loud. अणुतर—very minute. लोहपादपीठ—the iron pedestal. अंसलपुरुष॰—not to be shaken even by a strong man after effort. The possessive aff. ल after अंस signifies strength; see com. यथापूर्वमर्पयित्वा—after having replaced Durgá. प्रत्यय-realization, confidence. This and the following are adverbs, to be construed with प्रणिपतन्तीः. रूढविस्मयं—overpowered by astonishment. आपन्नः—in distress, plunged into misery. अमन्दमातृपक्षः—one whose mother's side is strong; i. e. having a protecting mother. The reading मन्द॰ makes no sense. ॰घट्टमात्मानं—whose son

( energy, spirit ) is able to remove ( break off ) the pot in the shape of As'maka, cruel by his intrigue well brought to light &c. निर्वेश—compensation, recompense. आर्यया—by the goddess. वाचामगोचरा—not to be expressed by words, beyond the power of expression.

P. 208. अलब्धरन्ध्रः—who could find no weak point, who could find no trace of our contrivance or secret plot. नष्टमुष्टि &c.–By telling what a man has lost, or what he has in his clenched hand ( or whether the things in his clenched hand are of even or odd number ), or what one is thinking of and such other things—proofs which a man having any pretence to divine knowledge must give. समर्थयमानः—upholding; believing in. आर्यपुत्रः—son of the venerable goddess. प्रभावहेतुः—due to the divine power of the goddess; it may also be a Gen. Tatp. भद्राकृतं—shaved (for an auspicious purpose). मन्त्र—the power arising from good counsel. प्रभाव—the power arising from the majesty or pre-eminent position of the king. उत्साह—the personal energy of the king. परस्परा०—mutually assisted by their right employment. क्रमन्ते—have effect, have power to accomplish. The next sentence explains their respective spheres of action. विनिश्चयः &c.—the determination of objects or political measures. निर्वहणं—the realization of the object. पञ्चाङ्ग—the five elements of statesmanship are:—allies, the means to the end, a proper division of time or space, adopting counter-measures ( to meet an emergency ), and attainment of the desired object. पञ्च अङ्गानि यस्यासौ पञ्चाङ्गो मन्त्रः मूलं यस्य । See Kâm. Nîtis. XII. 26 quoted in the com. Policy or state-craft is here compared to a tree composed of the different parts mentioned here. द्विरूपप्रभावः—The supremacy of the king's position is due to two things, *viz.* greatness of wealth and abundance of men. उत्साह—has four divisions, *viz.* the well-known four *Upáyas* ( साम &c. ); or exertion of mind, speech, body and action. द्विसप्ततिप्रकृति०—द्विसप्ततिः प्रकृतयो यथा–( 1 ) मध्यमः ( 2 ) विजिगीषुः ( 3 ) उदासीनः शत्रुः; एता मूलप्रकृतयः। ( 1 ) मित्रं ( 2 ) अरिमित्रं ( 3 ) मित्रमित्रम् ( 4 ) अरिमित्रमित्रम्; एता विजिगीषोः पुरोवर्तिन्यः शाखाप्रकृतयः। अथ चतस्रः शाखाप्रकृतयः पृष्ठगाः यथा–( 1 ) पार्ष्णिग्राहः ( 2 ) आक्रन्दः ( 3 ) पार्ष्णिग्राहासारः ( 4 ) आक्रन्दासारः। एवमष्टौ शाखाप्रकृतयः। पञ्चद्रव्य-प्रकृतयो यथा—( 1 ) अमात्यः ( 2 ) राष्ट्रं ( 3 ) दुर्गं ( 4 ) कोषः ( 5 ) दण्डः। एताः पूर्वोक्तद्वादशप्रकृतीनामेकैकस्याः भवन्ति। अत एताः ( 12 × 5 ) षष्टिः संपद्यन्ते।

ताश्च द्वादशभिर्मूलप्रकृतिभिर्मिलिता द्विसप्ततिर्भवन्ति। (T. Kaviratna). *Cf.* also मौला द्वादश चैवैता अमात्याद्यास्तथा च याः। सप्ततिर्द्व्यधिकाद्येषा सर्वं प्रकृतिमण्डलम् ॥ Kâm. N. XII. 25. शक्तिसिद्धि०—power and success are the flowers and fruits respectively. नेतुः—The man at the head of political affairs; the king or the prime minister. For a similar fig. comp. Mudr. V. 1; and सखे त्वन्नीतिपादपस्य पुष्पमुद्भिन्नम्। Málav. I.; and for a similar description *cf.* अष्टशाखं चतुर्मूलं षष्टिपत्रं द्वये स्थितम्। षट्पुष्पं त्रिफलं वृक्षं यो जानाति स नीतिवित् ॥ Kám. N. VIII. 42. अनेकाधिकरण०—on account of its dependence on various parts or elements. दुरुपजीव्यः—difficult to be turned to advantage, hard to be made to yield fruit. कोसला०—being a native of Kosala. अवमत्य—because he (Mitravarmâ) despised his counsel.

P. 209. रहस्यशिक्षयम्—The instruction given here is in close conformity with Chânakya's precepts in Kauti. Prak. VI. under the heading उपधाभिः शौचाशौचज्ञानममात्यानाम्. मायापुरुषः—a deceitful person, a rogue. भुजङ्ग—a snake, a gallant; both the senses are here intended. प्राभृत—presents, bribes. अतिविस्रम्भ०—When he was in a pleased mood; or, when I got an opportunity owing to the confidence engendered or gained. त्वदुपदिष्टेन नयेन—according to your direction or instruction. शुद्धिदर्शनं—giving evidence of the nobility or purity of. अनुग्रहार्द्र—tender with, disposed to favour. अभ्यमित्रीण—valliant enough to overpower his enemies. The affixes छ, यत् or ख (ईन as here) are added to अमित्र with अभि in the sense of 'boldly facing an enemy,' by Pâṇ. V. 2. 17; see com.; so अभ्यमित्रीय and अभ्यमित्र्य also. संनिपातिनः—collected together. चिरबिल्वद्रुम—a poisonous tree; *i. e.* a destroyer of. प्रह्व—submissive. नीतिज्ञंमन्य—आत्मानं नीतिज्ञं मन्यतेऽसौ. उपधाभिर्विशोध्य—having tested his sincerity by various special trials. उपधीयते शुद्धिज्ञानमत्र इत्युपधा; from धा + अ (अङ्) by आतश्चोपसर्गे Pâṇ. III. 3. 106. It means a trial by making a man swerve from Dharma, Káma, and Artha. It is said to be of four kinds, *viz.* (1) loyalty, (2) disinterestedness, (3) continence, and (4) courage. Brâhmaṇas and ministers should be so tested. *Cf.* धर्मोपधाभिर्विप्रांश्च सर्वाभिः सचिवान्पुनः। (शोधयेत्) Kálikâ.-P. It is different from उपधि and उपाधि, also derived from धा. मतिसहाय—an accomplice in counsel or statecraft. शौच—uprightness, honesty. विविधव्यञ्जनान्—moving about under various disguises. गूढपुरुष—a spy, a secret agent. लुब्धसमृद्ध—covetous misers. अत्युत्सिक्त—very proud. अविधेयप्राय—mostly turbulent. अभिख्यापयन्—proclaiming as commendable.

P. 210. उद्भावयन्—creating a taste or liking for. उपधि—a wily trick, a stratagem. अभिसमाहरमर्थान्—I collected the revenue. अर्थमूल—proceeding from wealth. दण्ड—stands for दण्डनीति; 'the commencement of all undertakings based on policy.' तत्र दौर्बल्यात—weakness in that, *i. e.* अर्थ (having a good treasury ). योग—stratagems, political measures ( to gain one's ends ).

आज्ञया—when I give the command. राज्यद्वितय०—see com. नीत्याविष्ट—guided by policy, always acting in accordance with the rules of policy. च—in addition to that.

P. 211. चलाचित्त—vacillating, uncertain. मौला: प्रकृतय:—hereditary subjects, *i. e.* the people of the Vidarbha country. आवर्जन—bestowal, conferring. उपजप्ता:—overtures were thus made to them. वाच्यमेव—we are bound to express it. विश्रुत—renowned. जन्यवृत्ति:—engaged in actual warfare; *i. e.* does not take arms against. स वीतभय: &c.—The sense is somewhat obscure. He who comes over to his side stands out of the reach of danger and obtaining great fortune &c. सर्वेभ्यो वार्तम्—the message has been communicated to you all. भिन्नमना इव &c.—appear to have their hearts estranged from me ( *i. e.* their affection alienated from me ). क्षमामवलम्ब्य—remaining passive or apathetic. उत्पन्नोपजापं—in whom seeds of dissension have been sown. मदवबोधकं—my purpose or resolution to fight.

P. 212. क्षणं—only for a moment; *i. e.* cannot long hold out. अन्यायेन—goes with परराज्यक्रमण. परराज्य०—an unjust or unprovoked expedition is condemned by Hindu writers on politics. पुरोऽभवत्—faced the army. आलेख्यलिखितेव—like painted figures. संगर—a duel. शिक्षाविशेष—superior skill. अतः परं—after this, *i. e.* the fall of the king. स्वस्ववृत्ति—their respective incomes. तद्वशवर्तिन: समभवन्—*Lit.* delivered themselves into his power; acknowledged him as their sovereign. राजसूनुसात्—entirely into his possession. अनेहस्—time.

P. 213. ०लक्षण—marked by. राज्यधु:—This ought to be राज्यधुरा; see Pāṇ. V. 4. 74. सचिवरत्न—excellent minister.

आग्रह—importunity. उत्कलाधि०—Utkala, the modern Orissa lay to the South of Támralipta and extended to the river Kapiśá. यावत्प्रयाणोपक्रमं &c.—As soon as I proposed to go आकारित—called. पाटलिपुरे यौवराज्यं &c.—The reader will remember that Somadatta was asked by Râjavâhana to convey his wife to his capital (*i e.* Páṭalî, see p. 30, where we should have read पाटलीं नाम्ना तस्य &c.), the town of Vîraketu, where he was reiging as Yuvarája. See p. 42. सप्रमोदसंवलिताः—सप्रमोदाश्च ताः संवलिताश्च mixed, and full of joy. उत्कील्य—having opened. आशास्य--after expressing his blessings.

P. 214. स्कन्धावार—army; *lit.* what consists of divisions. उदन्वत्--the sea. निश्चयं—our resolution to die. विज्ञान—superhuman knowledge. भाग्योदयात्—their fortune smiling upon them. षोडशाब्दान्ते—This, if the correct reading, must be taken to mean 'at the close of their sixteenth year.' In this case we shall have to suppose that the princes started on their tour of conquest at the beginning of their sixteenth year. It is clear, however, from some statements in the preceding narratives, that the princes started on their mission after their attainment of youth, *i. e.* at the close of the 16th year. So it will be better to read अब्दान्ते, as we cannot reasonably suppose the Kumârás to have been for sixteen years in search of Rájaváhana. अवधि—The limit of time fixed by the ascetic, *viz.* 16 years. सप्रवृत्ति—the doings of the princes. आकारणाय—to call you.

P. 215. पानीयमपि &c.—*Cf.* the similar message of Tárápîḍa to Chandrâpîḍa at Kàd. p 328. समर्थतर—very able. मानसार:—There seems to be some confusion here. Not Mánasára, but Darpasára was the reigning monarch then. But, as he was away, Mánasára might be supposed to have taken up the reins of the government of Ujjayinî after the assasination at Champá of Chaṇḍavarman, Darpasára's regent. निहतश्च—This seems to be strange; for it was Mânasára who had prevented Chaṇḍavarmā from putting Rája. to immediate death; so this ought to be omitted. प्रत्यागमनान्तं-upto their return from their starting on that expedition. अतिदुर्घट—extremely marvellous.

P. 216. अवाङ्मनस०-notice the comp. ending; a final अ is added to वाङ्मनस् by Pâṇ. V. 4. 77. वानप्रस्थाश्रमं—The third stage of life in which a Dvija ought to stay in a forest living as a hermit; see Ya'jñavalkya quoted in the com.; cf. also Manu.

VI. 3. आत्मसाधन—final emancipation by contemplation. यथोदितं—According to the success or rise ( उद् + इत ) attained by each. *Or*—according to your direction ( उदित p. p. p. of वद् ). कायक्लेशं विना—without having to suffer bodily hardships or mortification. परिजनः—his vassals, the other Kumâras.

---

## No. II.

### INDEX OF IMPORTANT WORDS.